The Oxford Handbook of Deaf Studies, Language, and Education

Volume 2

OXFORD LIBRARY OF PSYCHOLOGY

Editor-in-Chief **PETER E. NATHAN**

The Oxford Handbook of Deaf Studies, Language, and Education

Volume 2

Edited by

Marc Marschark

Patricia Elizabeth Spencer

OXFORD
UNIVERSITY PRESS

2010

OXFORD
UNIVERSITY PRESS

Oxford University Press, Inc., publishes works that further Oxford University's
objective of excellence in research, scholarship, and education.

Oxford   New York
Auckland   Cape Town   Dar es Salaam   Hong Kong   Karachi
Kuala Lumpur   Madrid   Melbourne   Mexico City   Nairobi
New Delhi   Shanghai   Taipei   Toronto

With offices in
Argentina   Austria   Brazil   Chile   Czech Republic   France   Greece
Guatemala   Hungary   Italy   Japan   Poland   Portugal   Singapore
South Korea   Switzerland   Thailand   Turkey   Ukraine   Vietnam

Published by Oxford University Press, Inc.
198 Madison Avenue, New York, New York 10016
www.oup.com

Library of Congress Cataloging-in-Publication Data
Oxford handbook of deaf studies, language, and education/
Edited by Marc Marschark and Patricia Elizabeth Spencer.
p. cm.
Includes bibliographic references and index.
ISBN 978-0-19-539003-2
1. Deaf—Social conditions. 2. Deaf—Education. 3. Deaf—Means of communication
4. Sign language. I. Marschark, Marc. II. Spencer, Patricia Elizabeth.
HV2380.O88 2003
362.4'2—dc21
2002010496

9 8 7 6 5 4 3 2 1

Printed in the United States of America on acid-free paper

SHORT CONTENTS

Oxford Library of Psychology   vii

About the Editors   ix

Contributors   xi

Table of Contents   xv

Chapters   1–478

Index   479

OXFORD LIBRARY OF PSYCHOLOGY

The *Oxford Library of Psychology*, a landmark series of handbooks, is published by Oxford University Press, one of the world's oldest and most highly respected publishers, with a tradition of publishing significant books in psychology. The ambitious goal of the *Oxford Library of Psychology* is nothing less than to span a vibrant, wide-ranging field and, in so doing, to fill a clear market need.

Encompassing a comprehensive set of handbooks, organized hierarchically, the *Library* incorporates volumes at different levels, each designed to meet a distinct need. At one level are a set of handbooks designed broadly to survey the major subfields of psychology; at another are numerous handbooks that cover important current focal research and scholarly areas of psychology in depth and detail. Planned as a reflection of the dynamism of psychology, the *Library* will grow and expand as psychology itself develops, thereby highlighting significant new research that will have an impact on the field. Adding to its accessibility and ease of use, the *Library* will be published in print and, later, electronically.

The *Library* surveys psychology's principal subfields with a set of handbooks that capture the current status and future prospects of those major subdisciplines. This initial set includes handbooks of social and personality psychology, clinical psychology, counseling psychology, school psychology, educational psychology, industrial and organizational psychology, cognitive psychology, cognitive neuroscience, methods and measurements, history, neuropsychology, personality assessment, developmental psychology, and more. Each handbook undertakes to review one of psychology's major subdisciplines with breadth, comprehensiveness, and exemplary scholarship. In addition to these broadly conceived volumes, the *Library* also includes a large number of handbooks designed to explore in depth more specialized areas of scholarship and research, such as stress, health and coping, anxiety and related disorders, cognitive development, or child and adolescent assessment. In contrast to the broad coverage of the subfield handbooks, each of these latter volumes focuses on an especially productive, more highly focused line of scholarship and research. Whether at the broadest or most specific level, however, all of the *Library* handbooks offer synthetic coverage that reviews and evaluates the relevant past and present research and anticipates research in the future. Each handbook in the *Library* includes introductory and concluding chapters written by its editor to provide a roadmap to the handbook's table of contents and to offer informed anticipations of significant future developments in that field.

An undertaking of this scope calls for handbook editors and chapter authors who are established scholars in the areas about which they write. Many of the nation's and world's most productive and best-respected psychologists have agreed to edit *Library* handbooks or write authoritative chapters in their areas of expertise.

For whom has the *Oxford Library of Psychology* been written? Because of its breadth, depth, and accessibility, the *Library* serves a diverse audience, including graduate students in psychology and their faculty mentors, scholars, researchers, and practitioners in psychology and related fields. Each will find in the *Library* the information they seek on the subfield or focal area of psychology in which they work or are interested.

Befitting its commitment to accessibility, each handbook includes a comprehensive index, as well as extensive references to help guide research. And because the *Library* was designed from its inception as an online, as well as a print resource, its structure and contents will be readily and rationally searchable online. Further, once the *Library* is released online, the handbooks will be regularly and thoroughly updated.

In summary, the *Oxford Library of Psychology* will grow organically to provide a thoroughly informed perspective on the field of psychology, one that reflects both psychology's dynamism and its increasing interdisciplinarity. Once published electronically, the *Library* is also destined to become a uniquely valuable interactive tool, with extended search and browsing capabilities. As you begin to consult this handbook, we sincerely hope you will share our enthusiasm for the more than 500-year tradition of Oxford University Press for excellence, innovation, and quality, as exemplified by the *Oxford Library of Psychology*.

Peter E. Nathan
Editor-in-Chief
Oxford Library of Psychology

ABOUT THE EDITORS

Marc Marschark

Marc Marschark, Ph.D., directs the Center for Education Research Partnerships at the National Technical Institute for the Deaf, a college of Rochester Institute of Technology, where he founded and edits the *Journal of Deaf Studies and Deaf Education*. He has joint appointments at the Moray School of Education at the University of Edinburgh and the School of Psychology at the University of Aberdeen.

Patricia Elizabeth Spencer

Patricia Elizabeth Spencer, Ph.D., was a public school teacher and science textbook editor before joining Gallaudet University and serving as a diagnostic–prescriptive classroom teacher, assessment center administrator, research scientist, and professor in the Department of Social Work. After retiring from Gallaudet, she has taught at Texas A&M-Corpus Christi, worked with an after-school program for children at-risk for academic difficulties, and remains active as a writer and speaker in the field of education and development of deaf and hard-of-hearing children.

CONTRIBUTORS

Esperanza Anaya
Speech Research Laboratory
Department of Psychological and
Brain Sciences
Indiana University
Bloomington, Indiana, USA

Shirin D. Antia
Department of Disability and
Psychoeducational Studies
University of Arizona
Tucson, AZ

Sue Archbold
The Ear Foundation
Nottingham, UK

Mark Aronoff
Department of Linguistics
SUNY Stony Brook
Stony Brook, NY

H-Dirksen L. Bauman
Department of ASL and Deaf
Studies
Gallaudet University
Washington, DC

Daphne Bavelier
Brain and Cognitive Sciences
Department
University of Rochester
Rochester, NY

Christopher M. Conway
Department of Psychology
Saint Louis University
St. Louis, Missouri, USA

Shani Dettman
Cochlear Implant Clinic
Royal Victorian Eye and Ear Hospital
East Melbourne, Australia

Richard Dowell
Cochlear Implant Clinic
Royal Victorian Eye and Ear Hospital
East Melbourne, Australia

Camille C. Dunn
Department of Otolaryngology
University of Iowa
Iowa City, IA

Susan R. Easterbrooks
Department of Educational Psychology
and Special Education
Georgia State University
Atlanta, GA

Lindsey Edwards
Cochlear Implant Programme
Great Ormond Street Hospital for
Children
London, UK

David J. Ertmer
Speech, Language, and Hearing Sciences
Purdue University
West Lafayette, IN

Matthew L. Hall
Department of Psychology
University of California, San Diego
La Jolla, CA

Margaret Harris
Department of Psychology
Oxford Brookes University
Oxford, UK

Shirley Henning
DeVault Otologic Research Laboratory
Department of Otolaryngology, Head and
Neck Surgery
Indiana University School of Medicine
Indianapolis, Indiana, USA

Daan Hermans
Royal Dutch Kentalis, PonteM R&D
Sint-Michielsgestel, The Netherlands

Suneeti Nathani Iyer
Communication Sciences and Special
Education
The University of Georgia
Athens, GA

Janet R. Jamieson
Department of Educational
& Counselling Psychology,
and Special Education
University of British Columbia
Vancouver, BC

Harry Knoors
Behavioral Science Institute
Radboud University Nijmegen
Royal Dutch Kentalis
Sint-Michielsgestel, The Netherlands

Monika Kordus
Department of Otolaryngology
University of Iowa
Iowa City, IA

Kathryn H. Kreimeyer
Department of Disability and
Psychoeducational Studies
University of Arizona
Tucson, AZ

William Kronenberger
Department of Psychiatry
Child and Adolescent Psychiatry
Services
Indiana University School of Medicine
Indianapolis, Indiana, USA

Greg Leigh
Royal Institute for Deaf and Blind
Children
The University of Newcastle
Newcastle, Australia

Irene W. Leigh
Department of Psychology
Gallaudet University
Washington, DC

John Luckner
School of Special Education
University of Northern Colorado
Greeley, CO

Beth Macpherson
Department of Otolaryngology
University of Iowa
Iowa City, IA

Kenneth Marciniak
Department of Otolaryngology
University of Iowa
Iowa City, IA

Marc Marschark
National Technical Institute for
the Deaf
Rochester Institute of Technology (NY)
University of Edinburgh
Edinburgh, UK

Rachel I. Mayberry
Department of Linguistics & Center for
Research in Language
University of California, San Diego
La Jolla, CA

Connie Mayer
Faculty of Education
York University
Toronto, ON

Irit Meir
Department of Hebrew Language
Department of Communication Sciences
and Disorders
The University of Haifa
Haifa, Israel

Donald F. Moores
Department of Exceptional Student and
Deaf Education
University of North Florida
Jacksonville, FL

Tova Most
School of Education and the Department
of Communication Disorders
Tel-Aviv University

Joseph J. Murray
Department of ASL and Deaf Studies
Gallaudet University
Washington, DC

Catherine Nelson
Department of Special Education
University of Utah
Salt Lake City, UT

Anthony T. Newall
University of New South Wales
Randwick, Australia

John P. Newall
Sydney Children's Hospital
Randwick
Department of Linguistics
Macquarie University
Sydney, Australia

Carol Padden
Department of Communication
University of California, San Diego
La Jolla, CA

Claudia M. Pagliaro
Department of Counseling,
Educational Psychology &
Special Education
Michigan State University
East Lansing, MI

Ann Perreau
Department of Otolaryngology
University of Iowa
Iowa City, IA

David B. Pisoni
Speech Research Laboratory
Department of Psychological and Brain
Sciences
Bloomington, Indiana
DeVault Otologic Research Laboratory
Department of Otolaryngology, Head and
Neck Surgery
Indiana University School of Medicine
Indianapolis, Indiana, USA

Albert Postma
Helmholtz Institute, Experimental
Psychology
Utrecht University
Utrecht, The Netherlands

Barbara Raimondo
Attorney
Washington Grove, MD

Susanne Reed
Department of Disability and
Psychoeducational Studies
University of Arizona
Tucson, AZ

Cathy Rhoten
Western Pennsylvania School
for the Deaf
Pittsburgh, PA

Wendy Sandler
Department of English Language
and Literature
The University of Haifa
Haifa, Israel

Thomastine Sarchet
National Technical Institute
for the Deaf
Rochester Institute of Technology
Rochester, NY

Patricia Elizabeth Spencer
PSpencer Consulting, LLC
Rockport, TX

Michael Stinson
Department of Research and Teacher
Education
National Technical Institute for the Deaf
Rochester Institute of Technology
Rochester, NY

Arlene Stredler-Brown
Department of Speech-Language-Hearing
Sciences
University of Colorado
Boulder, CO

Richard S. Tyler
Department of Otolaryngology
University of Iowa
Iowa City, IA

Jan van Dijk
Radboud University Nijmegen
Haaren, The Netherlands

Rick van Dijk
University of Applied Sciences
Institute for Sign Language and Deaf
Studies
Hemoltz Institute, Experimental
Psychology
Utrecht University
Utrecht, The Netherlands

Alexandra Wheeler
The Ear Foundation
Nottingham, UK

Alys Young
School of Nursing, Midwifery,
and Social Work
University of Manchester
Manchester, UK

Megan Zupan
New York School for the Deaf
White Plains, NY

CONTENTS

1. The Promises (?) of Deaf Education: From Research to
   Practice and Back Again   1
   Marc Marschark and Patricia Elizabeth Spencer

Part One · Educational Issues

2. The History of Language and Communication Issues in
   Deaf Education   17
   Donald F. Moores
3. Legal Advocacy for Deaf and Hard-of-Hearing
   Children in Education   31
   Barbara Raimondo
4. Preparing Teachers of Students Who Are Deaf or Hard of Hearing   41
   John Luckner
5. Effective Instruction for Deaf and Hard-of-Hearing Students: Teaching
   Strategies, School Settings, and Student Characteristics   57
   Harry Knoors and Daan Hermans
6. Supporting Students in General Education Classrooms   72
   Shirin D. Antia, Kathryn H. Kreimeyer, and Susanne Reed
7. Current and Future Technologies in the Education of
   Deaf Students   93
   Michael Stinson

Part Two · Literacy and Curriculum Issues

8. Evidence-based Curricula and Practices That Support Development of
   Reading Skills   111
   Susan R. Easterbrooks
9. Will Cochlear Implants Close the Reading Achievement Gap
   for Deaf Students?   127
   Marc Marschark, Thomastine Sarchet, Cathy Rhoten, and Megan Zupan
10. The Demands of Writing and the Deaf Writer   144
    Connie Mayer
11. Mathematics Instruction and Learning of Deaf and Hard-of-Hearing
    Students: What Do We Know? Where Do We Go?   156
    Claudia M. Pagliaro
12. Deaf Children with Severe Multiple Disabilities: Etiologies,
    Intervention, and Assessment   172
    Rick van Dijk, Catherine Nelson, Albert Postma, and Jan van Dijk

Part Three · Cultural, Social, and Psychological Issues

13. Reflections on Identity   195
    Irene W. Leigh
14. Deaf Studies in the 21st Century: "Deaf-gain" and the Future
    of Human Diversity   210
    H-Dirksen L. Bauman and Joseph J. Murray
15. Cochlear Implants: Family and Young People's Perspectives   226
    Sue Archbold and Alexandra Wheeler
16. The Impact of Early Identification of Deafness on
    Hearing Parents   241
    Alys Young
17. How Does Speech Intelligibility Affect Self and Others'
    Perceptions of Deaf and Hard-of-Hearing People?   251
    Tova Most

Part Four · Language and Language Development

18. Emerging Sign Languages   267
    Irit Meir, Wendy Sandler, Carol Padden, and Mark Aronoff
19. Early Language Acquisition and Adult Language Ability: What Sign
    Language Reveals About the Critical Period for Language   281
    Rachel I. Mayberry
20. Communication Choices and Outcomes During the Early Years:
    An Assessment and Evidence-based Approach   292
    Arlene Stredler-Brown
21. Early Communication in Sign and Speech   316
    Margaret Harris
22. Language Acquisition and Critical Periods for Children
    Using Cochlear Implants   331
    Shani Dettman and Richard Dowell

Part Five · Hearing and Speech Perception

23. Newborn Screening and Earlier Intervention with
    Deaf Children: Issues for the Developing World   345
    Greg Leigh, John P. Newall, and Anthony T. Newall
24. Prelinguistic Vocalizations in Infants and Toddlers with
    Hearing Loss: Identifying and Stimulating
    Auditory-guided Speech Development   360
    David J. Ertmer and Suneeti Nathani Iyer
25. Children and Youth Who Are Hard of Hearing: Hearing Accessibility,
    Acoustical Context, and Development   376
    Janet R. Jamieson
26. Performance Outcomes for Adult Cochlear Implant Users   390
    *Camille C. Dunn, Ann Perreau, Kenneth Marciniak, Beth Macpherson,
    Richard S. Tyler, and Monika Kordus*

Part Six • Cognitive Issues and Correlates of Deafness

27. Play and Theory of Mind: Indicators and Engines of Early
    Cognitive Growth   407
    Patricia Elizabeth Spencer
28. Learning Disabilities in Deaf and Hard-of-Hearing Children   425
    Lindsey Edwards
29. Executive Function, Cognitive Control, and Sequence Learning
    in Deaf Children with Cochlear Implants   439
    David B. Pisoni, Christopher M. Conway, William Kronenberger,
    Shirley Henning, and Esperanza Anaya
30. Working Memory, Deafness, and Sign Language   458
    Matthew L. Hall and Daphne Bavelier
31. Paradigm Shifts, Difficult Truths, and an Increasing
    Knowledge Base in Deaf Education   473
    Patricia Elizabeth Spencer and Marc Marschark

Author Index   479
Subject Index   499

The Promises (?) of Deaf Education: From Research to Practice and Back Again

Marc Marschark *and* Patricia Elizabeth Spencer

Abstract

This chapter considers the promise of research in areas relevant to deaf children and adults—and a variety of promises that too often have been broken. Its twin goals are (1) an attempt to gauge current relations among research, theory, and educational practice and (2) to make explicit some of what we know, what we don't know, and what we only think we know about raising and educating deaf children. Four primary domains of investigation are considered: early identification and intervention, language, educational models, and basic research into cognitive processes. Much has been learned in each of these domains, but there has been surprisingly little measurable impact on practice or academic outcomes. In some areas, the research is not as definitive as is generally believed, and in others, results are not as generalizable as they might appear. This situation, in part, derives from methodological limitations in some of the relevant research, but some intuitively appealing claims in the field appear to be totally lacking in empirical support. The chapter suggests that this field is at a threshold, thanks to recent advances in technology, basic research, and educational innovation. Unless we can do a better job of bridging the gap between research and practice, however, opportunities and possibilities will be lost.

Keywords: early identification, intervention, language development, educational placement, evidence-based practice, learning

As far as we can tell, no one has ever written an article or chapter entitled anything like "The Promises of Deaf Education." We have found similar titles on works that have at least passing reference to deaf studies, language, and education, including "The Promise of Accessible Textbooks," "The Promise of Grants from Private Foundations," "The Promise of Culture," and even "The Promise of Warmth and Life to Come." But why nothing about the promise of deaf education? Is it because people are reluctant, perhaps appropriately so, to make promises they fear they cannot keep? Is it because so many implicit promises in this field have been broken? With all that we have learned from basic research concerning language, learning, and cognition among deaf adults and children, there has been surprisingly little impact on practice in essentially any domain. Yet, clear implications emerge from that work, or at least

testable hypotheses, which have the potential to change people's lives. Similarly, with perhaps the exception of deaf students' mathematics difficulties (see Kelly, 2008; Nunes, Bryant, Burman, Bell, Evans, Hallett, & Montgomery, 2008; Chapter 11, this volume), it is rare when specific issues that arise in practice are taken up by investigators in order to explore their roots through basic research.

The preceding observations notwithstanding, this book is not an education volume. It is a series of chapters describing the state-of-the-art in several disciplines related to deaf individuals, Deaf Studies, language, and yes, education. Yet, a subtext runs throughout most of the chapters, and throughout much of the work in this diverse field, in which research is more than just a means to theoretical ends. For most investigators, anyway, there is hope that their basic as well as applied research ultimately will contribute to improving the lives of individuals who have long faced barriers and challenges that directly or indirectly are related to academic achievement (see Chapter 2, this volume). Whether these are implicit barriers to education resulting from relatively poor literacy skills (see Chapter 8, this volume) or explicit discrimination against individuals who cannot hear or do not speak, it is only by understanding the sources of those challenges that we can overcome them (Detterman & Thompson, 1997).

Surely, significant advances have been made in areas relating to deaf individuals and their education, although it is hard to think of many before the revolution created by Stokoe's (1960/2005) putting American Sign Language (ASL) into the realm of language rather than gesture or manual English. McCay Vernon, one of the pioneering heroes of this field for his work on intelligence and in clinical psychology with regard to deaf individuals, once remarked that deaf people and deaf education owed much to the psycholinguists who brought Stokoe's work from linguistics into psychology and education. Add the contributions of Kathryn Meadow-Orlans, who was the first to tie together sign language, child development, and education, and two pictures emerge. One is the centrality of language to the growth and progress in all facets of this multidisciplinary field. The second is the fact that most of these significant advances have been made by people considered "outsiders," because they are neither deaf themselves nor have deaf parents. From one perspective, the presence of these outsiders is unavoidable, given the barriers confronted by "insiders" (Ladd, 2003). From another perspective, these people made breakthroughs precisely because they used research as an objective tool to better understand phenomena, in the hopes that it would contribute to better lives for other people. This is not charity, but leadership. And perhaps more importantly, they did not make promises they could not keep.

Despite first appearances, this chapter is intended neither as a criticism of research in the field nor as a eulogy for any particular area of investigation. Rather, it has two interrelated goals: First is a desire to honestly gauge the current relations among research, theory (including informal theory), and educational practice—or at least to begin that process. Without some periodic assessment of whether claims are being validated by well-conducted research and assessment, it is impossible to know whether we are making any progress in either basic science or in the academic attainment of deaf children—that is, whether we are looking for answers in the right places and

recognizing them when we find them. The continual failure to objectively evaluate the promises inherent in such claims, while accepting or rejecting them based on philosophy or preference, is one of the continuing embarrassments of our field.

The second but not unrelated goal of this chapter is to begin to make explicit some of what we know, what we don't know, and what we think we know (rightly or wrongly) about raising and educating deaf children. For decades at least, parents and educators have looked to research to inform them about best practice in these domains, yet the field is filled with conflicting claims and beliefs, some of which are without empirical merit. We are not so naïve as to believe that we always can avoid such situations, nor do we think that any panacea exists that will eliminate barriers facing deaf individuals in educational and other settings. We do, however, believe that barriers exist and that better understanding of the cognitive, social, and linguistic correlates of being deaf can help to eliminate those barriers, as well as being interesting in their own right. Perhaps shedding a bit of light on several of these issues will help to indicate areas in which more research is needed and others in which such investment may not be warranted.

For the present purposes, it will suffice to consider four domains of investigation. The domains we have selected relate to many of the chapters in this volume and, not coincidentally, to ongoing debate within the field. These four—early identification and intervention, language, educational models, and cognitive processes—are not intended to be either comprehensive or mutually exclusive, but they are sufficient to make the case we wish to articulate in the limited space available.

The Promise of Early Identification and Intervention

No single aspect of raising and educating deaf children has as much positive evidence and international support as the importance of implementing universal newborn hearing screening (UNHS) and early intervention (see Calderon & Greenberg, 1997; Chapter 23, this volume). Early intervention can greatly ameliorate some of the barriers to learning faced by deaf and hard-of-hearing (DHH) children—at least during the early years of life. Moreover, because UNHS can be conducted while newborns are still in the birthing hospital, it can be done efficiently, effectively, and at low cost. So, who could complain?

As late as 1990, the average age for identification of congenital hearing loss in the United States was around 24 months (Culpepper, 2003). At that time, identification efforts were primarily based on registries or hospital-administered questionnaires designed to identify infants who were at high risk for hearing loss based on family history or events during pregnancy or birth. Families were asked to bring their children back for hearing tests after having left the birthing center or hospital. However, many infants who were deemed at birth to be at high risk for hearing loss were lost to the system when parents failed to return for scheduled appointments for follow-up testing (Mahoney & Eichwald, 1987). This approach is estimated to have identified at most half of the infants who actually had a congenital hearing loss (Mauk, White, Mortensen, & Behrens, 1991). In the United Kingdom and Australia during that time, hearing screening was usually conducted at a well-baby check several months after birth, when a health visitor watched for the infant's reaction to sounds from an unseen source (Ching, Dillon, Day, & Crowe, 2008). This "distraction test" did not prove to be sufficiently reliable in identifying infants with significant hearing loss, despite its long, popular history.

More recently, technology for assessing hearing has advanced sufficiently to allow definitive identification of hearing loss during the neonatal period, and where neonatal hearing screening is conducted, the average age of identification has dropped to the early months of life—from 2 years to 2 months in some countries. Gaps remain in identification because parents still sometimes do not return for follow-up testing and because some infants have progressive hearing losses that were not evident at birth. The promise of universal identification remains, even while the promise of its impact remains uncertain.

Some practitioners initially questioned whether identification of hearing loss at such an early age might interfere with development of positive parent–infant emotional bonding (e.g., Gregory, 1999, 2001) or whether potential advantages in development would justify the effort required (Bess & Paradise, 1994). Both Pipp-Siegel et al. (2002) and Meadow-Orlans and colleagues (2004), however, reported finding no evidence that early identification created any difficulty in early parent–child attachment, and we know of no one who has. Grandori and Lutman (1999) concluded that the risks of anxiety due to early screening were acceptable, given evidence of benefits to developmental outcomes, and parents tend to agree (see Chapter 16, this volume; Young & Tattersall, 2005). Yet, even with the feared negatives out of the way, it remains unclear whether early

identification has a significant positive impact in this area.

One goal of early intervention is to ensure that parents have positive expectations for their children's progress, but Young et al. (2005) and Stredler-Brown (Chapter 20, this volume) have noted that professionals' advice to parents also needs to be realistic. Progress is being made in developing more effective support for the development of young DHH children, but the heterogeneity of this population makes it difficult to predict individual needs and strengths. Nevertheless, research generally has found significant developmental advantages for children following earlier compared to later diagnosis and intervention services. Yoshinaga-Itano and her colleagues (e.g., Mayne, Yoshinaga-Itano, Sedey, & Carey, 2000; Yoshinaga-Itano, Coulter, & Thompson, 2001; Yoshinaga-Itano, Snyder, & Day, 1998), for example, have reported several studies comparing a growing sample of children whose hearing losses were identified early with other children who were identified later. After accounting for variables such as degree of hearing loss, socioeconomic status, communication mode, and cognitive development, they found that younger ages of identification resulted in higher levels of functioning. Identification and the start of intervention by 6 months of age, in particular, were associated with beneficial effects on social-emotional development and language development.

On the basis of the Yoshinaga-Itano and related studies, it is now frequently reported that early identification and intervention prior to 6 months of age lead to "normal" levels of language development by the time deaf children enter school. Yet, the average language level for children in the Yoshinaga-Itano sample was still in the "low-average" range for hearing children (around the 25th percentile; Yoshinaga-Itano, 2006), despite the fact that they were involved in one of the most advanced early intervention programs in the world (the Colorado Home Intervention Program or CHIP). Clearly, other issues are involved and need to be identified. Moeller (2000), for example, assessed language development of a large sample of children with significant hearing losses and found that those who began receiving intervention by 11 months of age acquired language significantly better than those who started later. At 5 years of age, those children were functioning in the low-average range compared to norms for hearing children; again, still better than deaf children who did not receive early intervention. Moeller also found that a measure of parental involvement with the child and with the child's educational programming significantly predicted language development levels (see also DesJardin, 2006), and Calderon and Naidu (1999) found that age of first intervention services predicted deaf children's receptive and expressive language, as well as the frequency of mother–child interaction.

Most investigators, if queried now anyway, recognize that early identification and intervention are important, but neither necessary nor sufficient to guarantee deaf children developmental and educational outcomes commensurate with hearing peers. To date, however, most investigations in this area, out of necessity, have examined only relatively short-term effects of early identification and intervention. As children in the early cohorts progress through school, other studies will examine longer-term outcomes and outcomes in other domains. We can offer one caveat in that regard, based on an unpublished study conducted in collaboration with a school for the deaf in the eastern United States. That investigation initially looked at relationships among whether a child had received early intervention services or not, which of several intervention programs they had participated in, and academic outcomes. Surprisingly, initial analyses indicated that children who had received fewer intervention services performed better on early standardized testing. More detailed analysis, however, revealed that the results were better interpreted as indicating that children who were more in need of intervention support due to individual and family factors did not score as well as children in less complicated situations. Reminder to field: Our interpretations of experimental results must be done carefully, considering the entire context and its participants.

At present, what little research there is comparing development of children enrolled in different intervention programs tends not to focus on evaluating specific aspects of child or parental interventions, even though it is generally agreed that successful early intervention needs to substantially include parents and not involve only individual therapy sessions with the child (Bodner-Johnson & Sass-Lehrer, 2003; Sass-Lehrer & Bodner-Johnson, 2003). Rather, in keeping with the traditional obsession of the field, most researchers have focused on identifying the effects of the specific approach to communication and language that is used—that is, whether strictly oral (auditory-spoken language), or visual (sign language), or a combination of the two approaches is followed (see Chapter 20, this volume). For the current purposes, we will make only two observations in that regard.

First, regardless of language orientation, experiences that increase parents' confidence and feelings of competence in communicating with their deaf child have positive effects on their interactions and the child's language development (DesJardin, 2006; Meadow-Orlans et al., 2004). However, longer-term consequences of these factors apparently have not been explored, even though such findings began to emerge over 25 years ago (see Marschark, 1993, Chapters 3 and 4). Second, a review by Calderon and Greenberg (1997) indicated that, when early intervention programming included exposure to sign language, children tended to show better language, social, and academic outcomes through the early school years. In part, that result likely is a consequence of sign language offering earlier effective communication between adults and deaf children, and there does not appear to have been any research in the ensuing years showing anything different. Nevertheless, as will be described in the next section, "the promise of language" is one that appears not to have been kept, as neither deaf children of deaf parents nor deaf children with hearing parents who grow up with either a sign language orientation or a spoken language orientation typically demonstrate academic achievement comparable to hearing peers (for a review, see Marschark, 1993; Chapter 4, this volume). And, again, until comprehensive, longer-term studies on the outcomes of early intervention are conducted, it is uncertain whether the early advantages documented by Calderon and Greenberg are maintained.

Returning to the promise of early identification and intervention, we currently know that some is better than none, but it is difficult to know whether some approaches and methods are better than others without further information. Due to ethical and practical issues, research into this issue is unlikely to involve randomly assigning children to various programs or different programs using the same outcome measures. As a result, it appears that, for the present, we have to be satisfied with the conclusion that deaf children and their families generally benefit from early intervention, even if we have not identified specifically which aspects are important for which individuals. We also cannot conclude that early identification and intervention are sufficient to provide most deaf children with full equality in later educational opportunities. Language at the 25th percentile of "normal" is a vast improvement compared to findings from earlier studies (Yoshinaga-Itano, 2006), but if research involving children with cochlear implants is any indication (see following section), early benefits observed during the early school years may not be maintained in the later school years (see Chapter 9, this volume).

At the very least, parents and practitioners need to be reminded that early identification and intervention are only the beginning of the process of educating deaf children, not the end (see Chapter 25, this volume). Just as the positive effects of early identification appear to accrue only when they are accompanied by early intervention (Hogan, Stokes, White, Tyszkiewicz, & Woolgar, 2008), early intervention undoubtedly will need to be supplemented by ongoing interventions in various domains. Leigh and colleagues (Chapter 23, this volume) point out, "The notion that children will develop their language and communication, cognitive, and social skills more effectively if intervention is commenced very early is grounded in the premise that there is an optimal period for the development of certain cognitive and linguistic abilities…" (see also Chapter 19, this volume). We suggest that it might be more accurate to say, in the plural, that there are optimal periods for the development of certain cognitive, linguistic, and academic abilities; not all of them occur during the first years of life.

The Promise of Language

Whether the focus is on development, education, or culture, the issue of language modality—sign or speech—always rears its head in both theoretical and practical discussions within this field. This chapter is not the place to try review the literature on language modality, nor do we believe that it would be fruitful (but see Chapters 2 and 21, this volume). Our point is quite simple: Despite all claims to the contrary, neither sign language nor spoken language has lived up to the promises of its proponents when it comes to raising and educating deaf children. There are, of course, many deaf children who thrive in one language setting or another, even if neither sign nor speech alone has proven to provide a sufficient basis to assure most deaf children of academic success. "Success" here refers to performing academically at the level of hearing children, and some observers claim that this criterion is not appropriate (Ladd, 2003; Lane 1992). Nevertheless, it is through academic achievements in the public education system that children in most countries acquire the knowledge and skills necessary to succeed by various metrics relevant to them within their own societies. One could argue that schools intended primarily for hearing children are rife with barriers for those who are deaf, but it has not yet

been demonstrated that schools or special programs for deaf children, in general or any one in particular, obtain significantly better results. But that is a matter for the following section.

It is not necessary to look far to find evidence that the requirement of spoken language for all deaf children is inappropriate. Alexander Graham Bell (1898/2005) articulated that conclusion when he argued for oral education for "the semi-deaf" and the "the semi-mute," presumably those with lesser hearing losses. With regard to oral education for deaf children, he wrote "I am not so sure" (2005, p. 121) and acknowledged the use and utility of sign language. Indeed, in terms of academic outcomes, there simply is no evidence that deaf children who utilize spoken language consistently achieve more than those who utilize sign language. In the case of children with cochlear implants, Marschark and colleagues (Chapter 9, this volume) point out that their academic achievement, on average, does exceed that of deaf children without cochlear implants. The use of spoken language (which still typically falls below that of hearing children) as opposed to sign, however, has not yet been indicated as a critical factor in this relative success. Archbold and colleagues (2000), for example, found that 3 years after cochlear implantation, children's spoken language skills were independent of whether they used sign or speech prior to receiving their implant. Similarly, both Moeller (2000) and Yoshinaga-Itano (2003) reported that benefits to language development from early intervention were independent of the modality emphasized by the program in which children were enrolled.

With regard to older children, there does not appear to be any evidence to indicate that, when other factors are held constant, spoken language has any advantage in facilitating either academic achievement or social-emotional development. Intuitively, one might expect such outcomes, but it is difficult to come up with any convincing explanation of why this would be the case. In the absence of any demonstrated advantage for one kind of school setting or another (see next section), one could not argue that a child who acquires sufficient spoken language to function in a regular school setting with hearing peers necessarily has an academic advantage, and several studies have indicated that those children are at some social-emotional disadvantage (e.g., Kluwin & Stinson, 1993; Chapter 13, this volume). Further, at least one recent study has explicitly demonstrated that spoken language production and receptive skills fail to predict DHH students' college readiness or learning in university classrooms when other factors are controlled (Convertino, Marschark, Sapere, Sarchet, & Zupan, 2009).

For all of our talk about language, it is interesting that few studies have examined the relationships between language and learning among deaf students beyond the extent to which spoken and sign language influence print literacy. Despite the evidence amassed by Calderon and Greenberg (1997) indicating that exposure to sign language during early intervention provides significant benefit to young deaf children, the case for sign skills providing solutions to deaf children's academic challenges remains tenuous. Several studies conducted during the 1960s and 1970s demonstrated that deaf children of deaf parents surpassed deaf children of hearing parents in academic achievement (Meadow, 1968; Stuckless & Birch, 1966; Vernon & Koh, 1970), including literacy, and early access to fluent language has always been an appealing locus of those results. Those results apparently have not been replicated, however, and more recent studies involving deaf children of deaf parents have been more limited. While these studies have shown significant correlations between early ASL skills and reading comprehension, this same research generally has failed to consider contributions from other factors such as residual hearing, spoken language skills, or intelligence (e.g., Chamberlain & Mayberry, 2000; Padden & Ramsey, 2000).

If solid evidence for long-term benefits of early sign language is still lacking, the situation is no different than that for spoken language. Perhaps most obvious are the promises offered by the proponents of auditory-verbal therapy (AVT; e.g., Estabrooks, 1994, 1998). Only recently have measures of its effects been available, and Eriks-Brophy (2004) and Rhoades (2006)—both AVT advocates—concluded that, although descriptive evidence exists to support the approach, no existing studies have employed designs rigorous enough to produce currently acceptable evidence-based judgments of effectiveness. More generally, much of the evidence for the advantages of spoken language, for children with and without cochlear implants, appears to have had an inherent confound. Although most investigators on both sides of the language issue (which really has more than two sides) cringe at the suggestion, an ongoing bias toward spoken language in society and in some quarters of this field (see Chapter 14, this volume) means that children who are "oral failures" frequently have to acquire sign language later than is natural (Chapter 19, this volume). With unnecessary language delays already in place, those children

experience a variety of related cognitive, social, and academic challenges—all of which contribute to some mythical "average" performance level among children who sign (e.g., in schools for the deaf) being lower than for children who speak. Although the extent of this impact is unclear, its locus lies in the unsuitability of spoken language for some children, and possibly other differences between the populations of primarily signing versus primarily speaking deaf children, not in some consequence of using sign language.

Traditional "oral" methods that combine speechreading with aided residual hearing to process spoken language, on average, do not support age-appropriate language development for deaf children, although the number of children who can learn spoken language through this method is clearly increased by the use of cochlear implants and advanced hearing aids. Marschark and Spencer (2006) suggested that, with the advent of cochlear implants and other technologies, we stand at a threshold with regard to spoken language development among deaf children. That may be true, but it appears that some of the early (expected) promises of cochlear implants have not yet been fulfilled.

Research into the benefits of cochlear implants beyond hearing, speech, and language is just now emerging, indicating that academic achievement among children with cochlear implants generally exceeds that of deaf children without cochlear implants, although generally not reaching the level of hearing children (e.g., Thoutenhoofd, 2006; see Marschark, Rhoten, & Fabich, 2007, for a review). Even when early, age-appropriate reading achievement has been demonstrated (e.g., Geers, 2002, 2003), longitudinal data suggest that those gains may not be maintained (Geers, Tobey, Moog, & Brenner, 2008; see Chapter 9, this volume). In the present context, however, it may be more important to note that, thus far, no one has demonstrated that it is the greater use of spoken language that is responsible for achievement gains. Indeed, it appears that the only study that has demonstrated equivalent secondary school performance of hearing students and deaf students with cochlear implants is that of L. Spencer and colleagues (2004) involving a group of implant users who had access to sign language and sign language interpreters throughout their academic careers. The fact that many of those children received their implants relatively late (range 2.4 to 12.7 years, mean = 6.4 years) makes the result all the more impressive, suggesting that this is a potentially important area of investigation, even if it goes against the prevailing attitude of cochlear implants promising spoken language and (therefore) academic success.

Cued speech is another spoken language methodology that has offered promises that have not all been kept. Both phonological and morphological knowledge appear to be enhanced by consistent and early use of cued speech in a child's environment, disambiguating mouth movements through a set of handshapes and places of articulation, and providing visually accessible experience with the grammatical elements of the spoken language. Although cued speech has strong supporters, its use remains relatively uncommon in English-speaking countries, perhaps with good cause. Despite over 40 years of trying, cued speech has never been shown to provide significant support for literacy skills in English, even while its benefits for reading French and Spanish have been documented (e.g., Leybaert & Alegria, 2003). This difference, rarely noted, may be the result of the lesser transparency of sound-to-spelling correspondence in English compared to French and Spanish (Alegria & Lechat, 2005). The traveling conference display for the (US) National Cued Speech Association, for example, touts the benefit of cued speech for deaf children's learning to read, and it is only the fine print at the bottom of the display which notes that the quotation offering that conclusion was translated from the original French, with no explanation given for why that is relevant (see the implied claim at the top of the organization's website, www.cuedspeech.org, retrieved 15 March 2009).

On the basis of the available evidence base concerning communication and language options for young deaf children, we are left with four general conclusions: (1) The acquisition of communication and language skills at age-appropriate or close to age-appropriate times is a necessary requisite for continued development, and *preventing delays is more important than the specific method or modality used.* (2) Parent involvement and support of a communication approach is a critical factor in the child's success, as is the quality of educational support provided to family and child. (3) Advances in technology, including early identification and intervention, use of improved hearing aids based on more specific testing, and use of cochlear implants by children with the most severe hearing loss have increased the amount and quality of auditory information available to children with hearing losses and, as a consequence, their potential for use of spoken language. Specific predictors of language development and literacy achievements for individual children with implants continue to be unreliable, however, and much more research is needed that focuses on the effects of methods related to specific child and family factors. (4) At present, there is no evidence that either sign language or spoken language provides greater opportunities for academic success among deaf children. To evaluate either of these claims, we next consider the promises of alternative educational models for deaf children, keeping in mind that placement models are frequently confounded by associations with language modality.

The Promise of Education

It was noted earlier that research involving the random assignment of deaf students to alternative educational placements in order to obtain objective, unconfounded data is unlikely. Yet any comprehensive, objective evaluation of the benefits of alternative educational placements for deaf students would have to consider whether the students in those placements are comparable to begin with; would have to take into account the qualifications of the teachers and parent involvement, as well as the educational philosophy; and would have to include similar if not identical assessments of outcomes. In the absence of those conditions being met, we are left to muddle through existing data and put stock in the few review articles that have considered this issue (see Spencer & Marschark, in press).

Some researchers have concluded that academic achievement is higher on average for students attending general education classrooms in local schools compared to those in special classrooms or special, separate schools (Holt, 1994; Kluwin, 1993; Kluwin & Stinson, 1993). Kluwin and Moores (1985), for example, found that deaf students in regular education classrooms made more progress in mathematics than those in special classes (see Chapter 11, this volume). What appeared to be an effect of placement, however, has since been recognized as reflecting other variables, primarily those student characteristics that led to the placement choice (Powers, 1999). More academically successful students, for example, are more likely to be placed in general education classrooms, and deaf or hearing students who begin with higher skill levels tend to also make faster progress over a given amount of time. Over a series of studies of DHH students, after accounting for initial student and family characteristics, type of school placement has been found to account for only about 1%–5% of the variance in academic outcome (Allen & Osbourne, 1984; Kluwin & Moores, 1985, 1989;

Powers, 1999). At the college level, Convertino and colleagues (2009) found that enrollment in mainstream university classes (i.e., with hearing students) versus in all-deaf classes was not significantly associated with measures of classroom learning when other factors were controlled.

A stronger and more significant predictor of academic achievement has been the presence or absence of additional disabilities (Chapter 12, this volume), but, overall, an average of 75% of the variance in academic outcome has remained unexplained. Finally, even when DHH students in mainstream settings do show academic achievement somewhat higher than that of their peers in special classrooms or special schools overall (see Chapter 6, this volume), their performance still lags behind that of hearing peers (Antia, Jones, Reed, Kreimeyer, Luckner, & Johnson, 2008; Blair, Peterson, & Viehweg, 1985; Most, 2006). The promise of mainstream education thus persists, but has not yet been delivered.

The situation is not very different with regard to the promise of special education for deaf students. Interestingly, research that has focused on the potential benefits of separate educational placements for deaf students has almost exclusively equated "separate" with "sign language-based." "Oral" programs for deaf children tout their emphases on speech and hearing, but research concerning academic outcomes seems to be lacking. They are not alone in this lack of outcome data. Focusing on more general needs of deaf students, Simms and Thumann (2007) reported on the components of a Gallaudet University program that trains teachers to work within sign/bilingual programs—the Center for ASL/English Bilingual Education and Research (CAEBER). That program stresses the fluent use of natural sign language and understanding its role in a sign/bilingual approach, appreciation of the culture and history of deaf persons, high expectations for the achievements that can be attained by deaf students, and the ability for collaboration between deaf and hearing education professionals. Simms and Thumann posited that deaf learners typically have strengths in visual processing and that a deaf-centered approach to teaching may stress some different aspects of development and skill development than programs that are based on models of hearing students' learning styles. Although intuitively appealing, such programming appears to remain without empirical support.

CAEBER is known for its work with more than a dozen schools for the deaf in the United States, particularly in New Mexico. According to its website, the program "envisions high academic achievement for deaf and hard-of-hearing students by facilitating proficiency in both American Sign Language and English…" Apparently the only outcome information available from the program, however, is its 2002 5-year report to the US Department of Education, which funds the project (http://caeber.gallaudet.edu/assets/PDFs/resources/year5.pdf; retrieved 20 November 2008). According to the data presented in that report, reading comprehension scores[1] on the Stanford Achievement Test, 9th edition for 8- to 18-year-olds enrolled in the program were no higher than those reported by Traxler (2000) for all DHH children in the SAT-9 normative sample. This finding is particularly noteworthy given that 33% of the students in the CAEBER sample had deaf parents, and thus represents a group that is frequently claimed to have higher literacy skills than deaf children with hearing parents. This is not to say that signed/bilingual educational programming has been shown not to be effective, of course, only that positive evidence is lacking despite the promise of the theoretical perspective.

The Promise of Basic Research

It may seem odd to include "basic research" together with the three other areas already considered, yet research into the cognitive processes of individuals who are deaf has been popular for over 70 years. Early on, when many deaf individuals were seen as lacking language (e.g., Furth, 1966), many of those investigations were aimed at understanding the role of language in cognition and learning (see Marschark & Spencer, 2006). From some perspectives (e.g., Lane, 1992), earlier researchers also explicitly or implicitly placed deaf individuals into a category of "deficient." A number of those studies, as well as many today, however, have sought to understand either how the lack of hearing influences cognition or, perhaps more cogently, how those who depend primarily on vision for language differ from those who depend primarily on audition. As various chapters in this volume attest, there is no longer any debate that such differences exist (Chapters 27, 29, and 30), although the actual sources of such differences remain in question. More importantly, the conclusion that those differences need not imply deficiencies is still gaining ground. Yet, for all of the experimental, mostly psychological, research that has been conducted involving deaf adults and children, relatively little of it has been utilized in improving the education of deaf children. The tragedy of this omission is all the more distressing when one considers how research into early parent–child interactions with regard to attention-getting, communication, and social-emotional functioning has, in contrast, had such positive influences on early intervention programming (e.g., Meadow-Orlans et al., 2004).

As an example, perhaps the most popular area of cognitive research involving deaf individuals is memory. For over 100 years, researchers have looked at short- and long-term memory for verbal and nonverbal materials for a variety of theoretical reasons (see Marschark, 1993, Chapters 8 and 9 for reviews), likely making it the most thoroughly investigated area in the field aside from language and literacy (e.g., Luckner, Sebald, Cooney, Young, & Muir, 2005/2006). Many of the early memory studies focused on sequential memory, an area in which deaf adults and children routinely perform below the levels of same-aged hearing peers. Studies involving hearing individuals have suggested that, rather than short-term or working memory capacity being limited to an amodal "magic number of 7±2," memory capacity actually reflects sensory modality effects and is tied to an *articulatory loop* that contains approximately the amount of information that can be articulated in 2 seconds (Baddeley & Hitch, 1974). This conclusion is supported by observations of Hall and Bavelier (Chapter 30, this volume) that the frequently observed relation between articulation rate and sequential memory, a finding consistent with the articulatory loop, does not hold for native deaf signers. This finding suggests that previous studies demonstrating such a relationship in groups of deaf participants with more varied language orientations reflect either use of speech-based coding on the part of some of the individuals and/or use of such coding some of the time.

Of importance to the current discussion, however, it is still to be determined from studies of both shorter- and longer-term memory how the memory mechanisms that have been revealed affect learning by deaf students and how we can put that knowledge about effects to use in removing instructional barriers. Despite frequent reports by teachers of deaf students of apparent memory challenges on the part of their students, research in this area has not led to educational tools for dealing with the issue. Building such a bridge from research to practice might involve ways to modify instruction so as to accommodate deaf students' preferred, individual memory strategies or perhaps even train them to use different strategies in different situations. Whether it would be useful or even possible to teach sequential memory strategies such as verbal rehearsal remains unclear,

but studies by Bebko (1984; Bebko & McKinnon, 1990) provided support for this possibility in groups of deaf children of either deaf or hearing parents.

Another difference observed in cognitive strategies utilized by deaf and hearing students lies in the automatic deployment of associative or relational processing strategies. A review by Ottem (1980) found that when various memory and problem-solving tasks involved only a single dimension, deaf and hearing individuals (children and adults) performed similarly most of the time. When more than one dimension was involved, in contrast, hearing individuals consistently outperformed their deaf age-mates, suggesting that the latter did not spontaneously integrate or balance multiple characteristics. Despite more recent demonstrations that tendencies to treat stimuli in isolation rather than as members of various, perhaps overlapping categories, negatively affect deaf children's mathematics performance (Ansell & Pagliaro, 2006; Blatto-Vallee, Kelly, Gaustad, Porter, & Fonzi, 2007), reading (Strassman, 1997), and memory (Liben, 1979; Marschark, Convertino, McEvoy, & Masteller, 2004), few investigators have either demonstrated alternative strategies that can support improved performance or, apparently, sought ways to promote relational processing in appropriate task situations.

Visuospatial processing is another area in which apparent promises of basic research have failed to materialize despite researchers and educators reporting curriculum approaches based on the emphasis of visuospatial presentation of information (see Chapters 4 and 8, this volume; Nunes & Moreno, 1997, 2002). Investigators over the past 20 years have sought to demonstrate that deaf individuals have visuospatial skills superior to those of hearing individuals, a consequence of growing up in a visuospatial world, frequently with a visuospatial language (see Dye, Hauser, & Bavelier, 2008). One example is the indication from behavioral and event-related potential (ERP) studies that deaf individuals, or in some cases native signers regardless of hearing status, held an inherent advantage in perceiving stimuli presented to the visual periphery (e.g., Corina, Kritchevsky, & Bellugi, 1992; Neville & Lawson, 1987; Parasnis & Samar, 1985).

Yet, no one apparently has utilized such information to improve classroom learning by deaf children, nor even investigated how greater peripheral vision might affect development—both important topics given the visually distracting environment typical in classrooms. This omission is particularly interesting because, at the same time, investigators of mother–child interactions were demonstrating that most deaf mothers recognize the need to gain their deaf child's visual attention before initiating communication. Although individual patterns have been noted in which some deaf mothers sign in what they perceive to be their young children's peripheral visual field (see, for example, Swisher, 2000), deaf mothers usually do not sign to their young children until direct eye contact is obtained—either by waiting or by using methods to direct the children's attention to the signed communication. Accordingly, more recent research has indicated that even if deaf individuals are more sensitive to movement or flashing stimuli in the periphery, neither deaf students at-large nor those who have been signing all their lives have any significant advantage in obtaining information from peripheral vision (at least none that affects learning in the classroom) relative to either each other or to hearing students (Pelz, Marschark, & Convertino, 2008).

Other studies have indicated that deaf individuals do have visuospatial skills that can exceed those of hearing peers. Emmorey and Kosslyn (1996), for example, found that both deaf and hearing individuals who were fluent users of ASL were faster in generating mental images than were nonsigning peers. Emmorey and colleagues (1993) showed that deaf and hearing signers were faster at responding in a mental rotation task, relative to non-signers, even if they did not show an advantage in rotation speed. Talbot and Haude (1993) showed that level, rather than age of acquisition of sign language expertise, was the important factor in the mental rotation task, and Chamberlain and Mayberry (1994) demonstrated that deaf individuals who utilize spoken language rather than sign language do not demonstrate an advantage. Again, the educational implications of this apparent advantage for fluent signers have not been exploited.

Similar findings have been obtained with regard to face recognition. Bettger and colleagues (1997) found that 6- to 9-year-old deaf children with deaf parents (early signers) scored higher on a face discrimination task than did either deaf children with hearing parents (late signers) or hearing age-mates. Enhanced performance appeared to be limited to faces that differ on dimensions of *linguistic* relevance among users of ASL, a finding consistent with the fact that as adults, deaf individuals with hearing parents join deaf children of deaf parents and hearing children of deaf parents in showing face discrimination performance superior to that of hearing individuals with hearing parents (i.e., the only group

without skills in sign language). Although it is unclear what utility face discrimination skill might have in facilitating the academic achievement of deaf children, it seems likely that such abilities influence social-emotional development and, potentially, social functioning at-large (Remmel & Peters, 2009). Yet the link between these domains apparently has not been explored.

More significantly, given the demonstrated challenges in mathematics faced by deaf schoolchildren (see Chapter 11, this volume), it is surprising that no one has sought to, or perhaps been able to (Pelz et al., 2008), develop methods to utilize the visuospatial strengths of deaf students to their educational advantage (but see Nunes & Moreno, 1998, 2000). Dye et al. (2008) suggested the importance of reducing visual distractions for deaf children in the classroom and the benefits of small class sizes and semicircular seating arrangements, but one would think that all of the intellectual power and government funding that went into basic research might lead to some carryover into enhancing academic achievement. Promises, promises…

Where Do We Go From Here?

As noted earlier, the purpose of this chapter is not to criticize research as an enterprise or to index any particular group as impeding or failing to foster the education and development of deaf individuals. As the chapters of this volume will indicate, the amount of research being conducted with regard to deaf individuals, their language, and their education has been increasing steadily, as has its quality. Marschark and Bebko (1997, pp. 119–120) suggested that studies involving deaf adults and children "have been driven by the need to understand the complex learning processes necessary for educational, social, and personal success of deaf individuals. Recent studies of teaching and learning processes among deaf students have pulled these areas closer together, but the gap stubbornly remains." The point of this chapter is that more than 10 years later, we still are not "minding the gap" as well as we should. But perhaps, rather than proscribing, we should be asking why this situation persists and what we can do to change it.

It is common in gatherings of both academic investigators and professionals working with deaf children and their families to lament that many people (at least those in the "other" group) continue to look for simple answers to complex questions. Most of those involved in academic research will readily admit (at least in private) that to many observers, their work appears narrow, if not removed from practice. In part, this perception arises from the frequent methodological necessity of reducing complex questions to simpler ones, approaching them step by step—or perhaps by sneaking around the back way. This approach can give the appearance of naïveté or of living in a simplistic ivory tower, when the reality of the research situation is that most questions pertaining to the language, learning, sociocultural, and emotional functioning of deaf individuals are too complex to lend themselves to simple, straightforward questions and answers. Similarly, a focus on groups rather than individuals can appear to the parent or professional as unlikely to capture the essence of what one individual needs or what is happening in a particular situation. Averages derived from a group that is acknowledged to be so variable are essentially fictitious, and believing them to have too much reality can result in research findings being of little practical use to teachers or other professionals who live with that variability. At the same time, however, because of the heterogeneity inherent in the deaf population, investigations involving one or two individuals, or even small groups, run the risk of obtaining results that do not generalize beyond a limited range of individual differences.

Researchers worth their graduate degrees, of course, will be able to counter such accusations and limitations. They will be able to describe the theoretical importance of their efforts, usually with appropriate descriptions of the *potential* implications for education, society, or the greater good. They can acknowledge individual differences and cogently describe the potential range of applicability for their findings. Even those investigators who limit their work to relatively homogeneous subpopulations (e.g., native signers, deaf university students, children in oral settings who received their cochlear implants prior to 1 year of age) should be able to justify their methodologies and put their findings in larger contexts. Nevertheless, they may not see evaluating ecological validity or practicality of those findings as their concern.

Those who are involved with deaf individuals every day outside of the university research environment—teachers, speech-language therapists and pathologists, sign language interpreters and others—are in situations different from but perhaps parallel to those of researchers. It is frequently suggested that teachers teach the way they were taught rather than the way they were taught to teach (see Chapter 4, this volume), and one can see the same tendency among practicing professionals in this field. Methodologies learned in the classroom frequently determine the nature of one's interaction with clients and students, and strict adherence to them often results in missed opportunities for finding out what is really going on, determining exactly what it is that this child has or that one needs. The appropriateness of one protocol, paradigm, or approach, however, may have been determined more by intuition than by experimental validation (e.g., methods of sign language interpreting that have been developed largely in the absence of demonstration that deaf people actually understand interpreters' productions). Encountering clinicians who seek to understand the whole child rather than a portion of their anatomy or their repertoire is every bit as inspiring as chatting with investigators who seek to share their work with practitioners and find ways to implement it in "the real world," even (and in rare cases especially) when such application could demonstrate that their conclusions or generalizations are incorrect. In some sense, these latter two categories of professionals are exactly what the field needs; the challenge is how to support and encourage them. Job descriptions and funding agencies typically channel us into one stream or another, and even when we are pushed to cross over, habit and security in what we know frequently lead to our staying with what is familiar, not venturing too far from home.

The good news is that the chapters of this volume, like papers presented at some smaller conferences and the occasional enlightened monograph, have the potential to change the way this field does business. Virtually all of the authors in this volume are involved in research to some extent, and the majority also have a role in educating deaf students (that is, in some sense, fostering their cognitive development or supporting their linguistic, social, or emotional growth). At a time when the field seems to be poised at the threshold of change thanks to technology (Chapter 7), research on the foundations of learning (Chapters 9 and 27), and demands for improved outcomes and accountability (Chapters 3 and 20), parents, teachers, and other consumers of research are ready and waiting.

There is no doubt that there are people out there who could take the results of cognitive studies and help to design better early intervention programming, better reading instruction methods, or better college-level support services. There are clinicians, teachers, and other professionals who, if they had the time and resources, could contribute to and benefit from time in research laboratories sharing both expertise and curiosity. Finally, one would like to think that there are funding opportunities that can make such things happen. In times of plenty, there is enough funding to go around, so that individuals are busy with their primary responsibilities and do not get out much. In times of scarcity, the same people feel that they need to stay close to home and focus on necessities, so they still do not get out much. Ultimately, however, using what we know and questioning what we do not know will make what we do more effective and efficient. Ultimately, if we are to make a difference, we have to step out of our comfort zones and cross the threshold of possibility. Ultimately, we have to recognize the promises, make some, and keep them.

[1] The CAEBER report refers to "English" subscores, but the SAT-9 does not have an English subtest, and the Reading Comprehension subscore is apparently what was reported.

References

Alegria, J., & Lechat, J. (2005). Phonological processing in deaf children: When lipreading and cues are incongruent. *Journal of Deaf Studies and Deaf Education, 10*, 122–133.

Allen, T., & Osbourne, T. (1984). Academic integration of hearing-impaired students: Demographic, handicapping, and achievement factors. *American Annals of the Deaf, 129*, 100–113.

Ansell, E., & Pagliaro, C. (2006). The relative difficulty of signed arithmetic story problems for primary level deaf and hard-of-hearing students. *Journal of Deaf Studies and Deaf Education, 11*, 153–170.

Antia, S., Jones, P., Reed, S., Kreimeyer, K., Luckner, H., & Johnson, C. (2008). *Longitudinal study of deaf and hard of hearing students attending general education classrooms in public schools*. Final report submitted to Office of Special Education Programs for grant H324C010142. Tucson: University of Arizona.

Archbold, S.M., Nikolopoulos, T. P., Tait, M., O'Donoghue, G. M., Lutman, M. E., & Gregory, S. (2000). Approach to communication, speech perception and intelligibility after paediatric cochlear implantation.*British Journal of Audiology 34*, 257–264.

Baddeley, A., & Hitch, G. J. (1974). Working memory. In G. H. Bower (Ed.), *The psychology of learning and motivation*, Volume 8 (pp. 742–775). New York: Academic Press.

Bebko, J.M. (1984). Memory and rehearsal characteristics of profoundly deaf children. *Journal of Experimental Child Psychology, 38*, 415–428.

Bebko, J. M., & McKinnon, E. E. (1990). The language experience of deaf children: Its relation to spontaneous rehearsal in a memory task. *Child Development, 61*, 1744–1752.

Bell, A. G. (1898/2005). *The question of sign-language and the utility of signs in the instruction of the deaf*. Washington, DC: Sanders Printing Office. Reprinted in *Journal of Deaf Studies and Deaf Education, 10*, 111–122.

Bess, F., & Paradise, J. (1994). Universal screening for infant hearing impairment: Not simple, not risk-free, not necessarily beneficial, and not presently justified. *Pediatrics, 98*, 330–334.

Bettger, J.G., Emmorey, K., McCullough, S.H., & Bellugi, U. (1997). Enhanced facial discrimination: Effects of experience with American Sign Language. *Journal of Deaf Studies and Deaf Education, 2*, 223–233.

Blair, H, Peterson, M., & Viehweg, S. (1985). The effects of mild sensorineural hearing loss on academic performance of young school-age children. *The Volta Review, 96*, 207–236.

Blatto-Vallee, Kelly, R., Gaustad, M., Porter, J., & Fonzi, J. (2007). Visual-spatial representation in mathematical problem solving by deaf and hearing students. *Journal of Deaf Studies and Deaf Education, 12*, 432–448.

Bodner-Johnson, B., & Sass-Lehrer, M. (Eds.) (2003). *The young deaf or hard of hearing child. A family-centered approach to early education*. Baltimore, MD: Paul H. Brookes Publishing.

Calderon, R., & Greenberg, M. (1997). The effectiveness of early intervention for deaf children and children with hearing loss. In M.J. Guralnik (Ed.), *The effectiveness of early intervention* (pp. 455–482). Baltimore, MD: Paul H. Brookes.

Calderon, R., & Naidu, S. (1999). Further support of the benefits of early identification and intervention with children with hearing loss. *The Volta Review, 100*, 53–84.

Chamberlain, C., & Mayberry, R. I. (1994). Do the deaf "see" better? Effects of deafness on visuospatial skills. Poster presented at TENNET V meetings, Montreal, May.

Chamberlain, C., & Mayberry, R. I. (2000). Theorizing about the relationship between ASL and reading. In C. Chamberlain, J. Morford, & R. I. Mayberry, (Eds.), *Language acquisition by eye* (pp. 221–260). Mahwah, NJ: LEA.

Ching, T., Dillon, H., Day, J., & Crowe, K. (2008). The NAL study on longitudinal outcomes of hearing-impaired children: Interim findings on language of early and later-identified children at 6 months after hearing aid fitting. In R. Seewald & J. Bamford (Eds.), *A sound foundation through early amplification: Proceedings of the Fourth International Conference*. Stafa Switzerland: PhonakAG.

Convertino, C.M., Marschark, M., Sapere, P., Sarchet, T., & Zupan, M. (2009). Predicting academic success among deaf college students. *Journal of Deaf Studies and Deaf Education, Education 14*, 324–343.

Corina, D.P., Kritchevsky, M., & Bellugi, U. (1992). Linguistic permeability of unilateral neglect: Evidence from American Sign Language. In *Proceedings of the Cognitive Science Conference* (pp. 384–389). Hillsdale, NY: Erlbaum.

Culpepper, B. (2003). Identification of permanent childhood hearing loss through universal newborn hearing screening programs. In B. Bodner-Johnson & M. Sass-Lehrer (Eds.), *The young deaf or hard of hearing child* (pp. 99–126). Baltimore MD: Paul H. Brookes Publishing Co.

DesJardin, J. (2006). Family empowerment: Supporting language development in young children who are deaf or hard of hearing. *The Volta Review, 106*, 275–298.

Detterman, D.K., & Thompson, L. A. (1997). What is so special about special education? *American Psychologist, 52*, 1082–1090.

Dye, P., Hauser, P., & Bavelier, D. (2008). Visual attention in deaf children and adults: Implications for learning environments. In M. Marschark & P. Hauser, *Deaf cognition* (pp. 250–263). New York: Oxford University Press.

Emmorey, K., Kosslyn, S., & Bellugi, U. (1993). Visual imagery and visual-spatial language: Enhanced imagery abilities in deaf and hearing ASL signers. *Cognition, 46*, 139–181.

Emmorey, K., & Kosslyn, S. (1996). Enhanced image generation abilities in deaf signers: A right hemisphere effect. *Brain and Cognition, 32,* 28–44.

Eriks-Brophy, A. (2004). Outcomes of Auditory-Verbal Therapy: A review of the evidence and a call for action. *The Volta Review, 104,* 21–35.

Estabrooks, W. (1994). *Auditory-verbal therapy.* Washington DC: A. G. Bell Association.

Estabrooks, W. (1998). *Cochlear implants for kids.* Washington DC: A. G. Bell Association.

Furth, H. G. (1966). *Thinking without language.* New York: Free Press.

Geers, A. (2002). Factors affecting the development of speech, language, and literacy in children with early cochlear implantation. *Language, Speech, and Hearing Services in Schools, 33,* 172–183.

Geers, A. (2003). Predictors of reading skill development in children with early cochlear implantation. *Ear & Hearing, 24* (Supplement), 59S–68S.

Geers, A., Tobey, E., Moog, J., & Brenner, C. (2008). Long-term outcomes of cochlear implantation in the preschool years: From elementary grades to high school. *International Journal of Audiology, 47* (Supplement 2), S21–S30.

Grandori, F., & Lutman, M. (1999). The European Consensus Development Conference on neonatal Hearing Screening (Milan, May 15–16, 1998). *American Journal of Audiology, 8,* 19–20.

Gregory, S. (1999). Cochlear implantation and the under 2's: Psychological and social implications. Paper presented to the Nottingham Paediatric Implant Programme International Conference, Cochlear implantation in the under 2's: Research into Clinical Practice. Nottingham, U.K.

Gregory, S. (2001, September). Consensus on auditory implants. Paper presented to the Ethical Aspects and Counseling Conference, Padova, Italy.

Hogan, A., Stokes, J., White, C., Tyszkiewicz, E., & Woolgar, A. (2008). An evaluation of Auditory Verbal Therapy using the rate of early language development as an outcome measure. *Deafness & Education International, 10,* 143–167.

Holt, J. (1994). Classroom attributes and achievement test scores for deaf and hard of hearing students. *American Annals of the Deaf, 139,* 430–437.

Kelly, R.R. (2008). Deaf learners and mathematical problem solving. In M. Marschark & P. C. Hauser (Eds.), *Deaf cognition: Foundations and outcomes* (pp. 226–249). New York: Oxford University Press.

Kluwin, T. (1993). Cumulative effects of mainstreaming on the achievement of deaf adolescents. *Exceptional Children, 60,* 73–81.

Kluwin, T., & Moores, D. (1985). The effect of integration on the achievement of hearing-impaired adolescents. *Exceptional Children, 52,* 153–160.

Kluwin, T., & Moores, D. (1989). Mathematics achievement of hearing impaired adolescents in different placements. *Exceptional Children, 55,* 327–335.

Kluwin, T., & Stinson, M. (1993). *Deaf students in local public high schools: Backgrounds, experiences, and outcomes.* Springfield: Charles C. Thomas.

Ladd, P. (2003). *Understanding deaf culture: In search of deafhood.* Clevedon, UK: Multicultural Matters.

Lane, H. (1992). *The mask of benevolence: Disabling the deaf community.* New York: Alfred A. Knopf.

Leybaert, J., & Alegria, J. (2003). The role of cued speech in language development of deaf children In M. Marschark & P.E. Spencer (Eds.), *Oxford handbook of deaf studies, language, and education* (pp. 262–274). New York: Oxford University Press.

Liben, L.S. (1979). Free recall by deaf and hearing children: Semantic clustering and recall in trained and untrained groups. *Journal of Experimental Child Psychology, 27,* 105–119.

Luckner, J.L., Sebald, A.M., Cooney, J., Young III, J., & Muir S.G. (2005/2006). An examination of the evidence-based literacy research in deaf education. *American Annals of the Deaf, 150,* 443–456.

Mahoney, T., & Eichwald, J. (1987). The ups and "downs" of high-risk hearing screening: The Utah statewide program. *Seminars in Hearing, 8,* 155–163.

Marschark, M. (1993). *Psychological development of deaf children.* New York: Oxford University Press.

Marschark, M., & Bebko, J. (1997). Memory and information processing: A bridge from basic research to educational application. *Journal of Deaf Studies and Deaf Education 2,* 119–120.

Marschark, M., Convertino, C., McEvoy, C., & Masteller, A. (2004). Organization and use of the mental lexicon by deaf and hearing individuals. *American Annals of the Deaf, 149,* 51–61.

Marschark, M., Rhoten, C., & Fabich, M. (2007). Effects of cochlear implants on children's reading and academic achievement. *Journal of Deaf Studies and Deaf Education, 12,* 269–282.

Marschark, M., & Spencer, P. E. (2006). Spoken language development of deaf and hard-of-hearing children: Historical and theoretical perspectives. In P. E. Spencer & M. Marschark (Eds.), *Advances in the spoken language development of deaf and hard-of-hearing children* (pp. 3–21). New York: Oxford University Press.

Mauk, G., White, K., Mortensen, L., & Behrens, T. (1991). The effectiveness of screening programs based on high-risk characteristics in early identification of hearing impairment. *Ear & Hearing, 12,* 312–319.

Mayne, A., Yoshinaga-Itano, C., Sedey, A., & Carey, A. (2000). Expressive vocabulary development of infants and toddlers who are deaf or hard of hearing. *The Volta Review, 100,* 1–28.

Meadow, K. (1968). Early manual communication in relation to the deaf child's intellectual, social, and communicative functioning. *American Annals of the Deaf, 113,* 29–41.

Meadow-Orlans, K., Spencer, P., & Koester, L. (2004). *The world of deaf infants: A longitudinal study.* New York: Oxford University Press.

Moeller, M. P. (2000). Intervention and language development in children who are deaf and hard of hearing. *Pediatrics, 106,* E43.

Most, T. (2006). Assessment of school functioning among Israeli Arab children with hearing loss in the primary grades. *American Annals of the Deaf, 151,* 327–335.

Neville, H. J., & Lawson, D. (1987). Attention to central and peripheral visual space in a movement detection task: An event-related potential and behavioral study: III. Separate effects of auditory deprivation and acquisition of a visual language. *Brain Research, 405,* 284–294.

Nunes, T., Bryant, P., Burman, D., Bell, D., Evans, D., Hallett, D., & Montgomery, L. (2008). Deaf children's understanding of inverse relations. In M. Marschark & P. C. Hauser (Eds.), *Deaf cognition: Foundations and outcomes (pp. 201–225). New York: Oxford University Press.

Nunes, T., & Moreno, C. (1997). Solving word problems with different ways of representing the task. *Mathematics and Special Educational Needs, 3,* 15–17.

Nunes, T., & Moreno, C. (2002). A intervention program for promoting deaf pupils' achievement in mathematics. *Journal of Deaf Studies and Deaf Education, 7,* 120–133.

Ottem, E. (1980). An analysis of cognitive studies with deaf subjects. *American Annals of the Deaf, 125,* 564–575.

Padden, C.A., & Ramsey, C. (2000). American Sign Language and reading ability in deaf children. In C. Chamberlain, J.P. Morford, & R.I. Mayberry (Eds.), *Language acquisition by eye* (pp. 165–190). Mahwah, NJ: Lawrence Erlbaum Associates.

Parasnis, I., & Samar, V.J. (1985). Parafoveal attention in congenitally deaf and hearing young adults. *Brain and Cognition, 4,* 313–327.

Pelz, J., Marschark, M., & Convertino, C. (2008). Visual gaze as a marker of deaf students' attention during mediated instruction. In M. Marschark & P. C. Hauser (Eds.), *Deaf cognition: Foundations and outcomes* (pp. 264–285). New York: Oxford University Press.

Pipp-Siegel, S., Sedey, A., & Yoshinaga-Itano, C. (2002). Predictors of parental stress in mothers of young children with hearing loss. *Journal of Deaf Studies and Deaf Education, 7,* 1–17.

Powers, S. (1999). The educational attainments of deaf students in mainstream programs in England: Examination results and influencing factors. *American Annals of the Deaf, 144,* 261–269.

Remmel, E., & Peters, K. (2009). Theory of mind and language in children with cochlear implants. *Journal of Deaf Studies and Deaf Education, 14,* 218–236.

Rhoades, E. (2006). Research outcomes of Auditory-Verbal intervention: Is the approach justified? *Deafness & Education International, 8,* 125–143.

Sass-Lehrer, M., & Bodner-Johnson, B. (2003). Early intervention: Current approaches to family-centered programming. In M. Marschark & P. Spencer (Eds.), *Oxford handbook of deaf studies, language, and education* (pp. 65–81). New York: Oxford University Press.

Simms, L., & Thumann, H. (2007). In search of a new, linguistically and culturally sensitive paradigm in deaf education. *American Annals of the Deaf, 152,* 302–311.

Spencer, L.J., Gantz, B.J., & Knutson, J.F. (2004). Outcomes and achievement of students who grew up with access to cochlear implants. *Laryngoscope 114,* 1576–1581.

Spencer, P.E., & Marschark, M. (in press). *Evidence-based practice in educating deaf and hard-of-hearing students.* New York: Oxford University Press.

Stokoe, W. C. (1960/2005). *Sign language structure: An outline of the visual communication system of the American deaf.* Studies in Linguistics, Occasional Papers 8. Buffalo, NY: Department of Anthropology and Linguistics, University of Buffalo. Reprinted in *Journal of Deaf Studies and Deaf Education, 10,* 3–37.

Strassman, B. (1997). Metacognition and reading in children who are deaf: A review of the research. *Journal of Deaf Studies and Deaf Education, 2,* 140–149.

Stuckless, E. R., & Birch, J. W. (1966). The influence of early manual communication on the linguistic development of deaf children. *American Annals of the Deaf, 111,* 452–460, 499–504.

Swisher, M. V. (2000). Learning to converse: How deaf mothers support the development of attention and conversational skills in their young deaf children. In P. Spencer, C. Erting, & M. Marschark (Eds.), *Development in context: The deaf children in the family and at school* (pp. 21–39). Mahwah, NJ: Lawrence Erlbaum Associates.

Talbot, K.F., & Haude, R.H. (1993). The relationship between sign language skill and spatial visualizations ability: Mental rotation of three-dimensional objects. *Perceptual and Motor Skills, 77,* 1387–1391.

Thoutenhoofd, E. (2006). Cochlear implanted pupils in Scottish schools: 4-year school attainment data (2000–2004). *Journal of Deaf Studies and Deaf Education, 11,* 171–188.

Traxler, C.B. (2000). Measuring up to performance standards in reading and mathematics: Achievement of selected deaf and hard-of-hearing students in the national norming of the 9th Edition Stanford Achievement Test. *Journal of Deaf Studies and Deaf Education, 5,* 337–348.

Vernon, M., & Koh, S.D. (1970). Effects of early manual communication on achievement of deaf children. *American Annals of the Deaf, 115,* 527–536.

Yoshinaga-Itano, C. (2003). From screening to early identification and intervention: Discovering predictors to successful outcomes for children with significant hearing loss. *Journal of Deaf Studies and Deaf Education, 8,* 11–30.

Yoshinaga-Itano, C. (2003). Early identification, communication modality, and the development of speech and spoken language skills: Patterns and considerations. In P. E. Spencer & M. Marschark(Eds.), *Advances in the spoken language development of deaf and hard-of-hearing children* (pp. 298–327). NewYork: Oxford University Press.

Yoshinaga-Itano, C., Coulter, D., & Thompson, V. (2001). Developmental outcomes of children born in Colorado hospitals with universal newborn hearing screening programs. *Seminars in Neonatology, 6,* 521–529.

Yoshinaga-Itano, C., Snyder, L., & Day, D. (1998). The relationship of language and symbolic play in children with hearing loss. *The Volta Review, 100,* 135–164.

Young, A., & Tattersall, H. (2005). Parents' of deaf children evaluative accounts of the process and practice of universal newborn hearing screening. *Journal of Deaf Studies and Deaf Education, 10,* 134–145.

PART 1

Educational Issues

The History of Language and Communication Issues in Deaf Education

Donald F. Moores

Abstract

The oral/manual "methods" controversy arose more than 200 years ago. Although many variations exist, there have been three basic approaches. An "oral" approach concentrates on the development of the spoken language of a community. What is now known as a bilingual-bicultural (Bi-Bi) approach emphasizes the development of the natural sign language of a community as the first language, then teaches the majority language through reading. A third approach supports the development of a sign system based on the syntax of a spoken language and modifications of a sign language in instruction. This system can be used either alone or in coordination with speech, known as simultaneous communication (Sim Com), or alone. A fourth approach, known as total communication (TC), encourages the use of all forms of communication, dependent on individual needs. These longstanding debates have not been resolved after two centuries, and represent different perceptions of deafness, the requirements for leading a full, rich life, and resultant educational and social goals.

The oral method was dominant from 1880 to 1960. Since then, constant change has occurred, with sign languages and sign systems receiving significant support. Recent global developments in neonatal screening, early intervention programs, cochlear implants, and the growth of an "inclusion" model in education have major implications for instruction and for the development of language and communication skills in deaf individuals.

Keywords: oral, Bilingual-Bicultural, simultaneous communication, total communication, natural sign language, sign system

Since the formal beginnings in Europe of the education of deaf people in the mid 18th century, the field has faced three complex, highly interrelated questions: What should deaf students be taught? Where should deaf students be taught? How should deaf students be taught? The first question deals with the extent to which the school curriculum for deaf students should follow that of a general education curriculum. In the past, most deaf children would begin school without mastery of the language of their society. Much of the curriculum was devoted to providing them with the linguistic skills that hearing children brought to the educational experience. Significant amounts of the school day concentrated on the development of articulation and grammar at the expense of content areas such as math, literacy, science, and social studies (Moores & Martin, 2006). With the increasing frequency of placing deaf students in classrooms with hearing peers, and with the use of standardized testing, there has been a trend to adopting regular education curricula. The second question addresses academic placement, ranging from complete separation of deaf learners from hearing learners to complete inclusion with hearing students. The third, most intractable and most controversial question is that of the mode of communication and the language of instruction. Several options exist in programs used around the world. One option proposes a complete reliance on a spoken language as the language of instruction, with concentration on the use of residual hearing and training in speech production. Another option uses a sign language as the language of instruction and as a base to acquire a written version of a spoken language.

Because there is a consensus on the importance of written language and the development of print literacy for deaf children, the language issue revolves around through-the-air communication. The primary choices come down to spoken communication and manual communication. If spoken communication is chosen, no language option exists; it is the spoken language of the larger community.

If manual communication is chosen, two language options exist. The first is to use the sign language of the local deaf community. This would be a full *verbal* but not a *vocal* language that has all the elements of a full language. The second option is the development of a manual code for a spoken language. This code, or system, would not be a fully developed language, but rather a mechanism for representing an existing spoken language.

Language and communication choices depend to a great extent on what one perceives to be the goals of education, in this case the education of deaf learners. It has been argued by some that the goal of education of the deaf is to prepare deaf individuals to integrate into the larger hearing world, and that deafness is a condition to be prevented or cured. Lacking this, concentration should be devoted to acquiring fluency in expressive and receptive spoken language as a means of normalization (Ling, 1988). This perspective is opposed by others, who characterize it as a medical or pathological view of deafness held by those who see deaf individuals as broken or deficient. From this opposing perspective, deafness is a normal, or at least not uncommon part of the human condition, and we should support the use of sign languages and embrace the concept of deaf communities. Spoken language may or may not be considered important (Bauman, 2008).

Thus, between the two poles of auditory–vocal communication in a spoken language and visual–motor communication in a natural sign language lay several variations. Typically, these incorporate elements of a spoken language and an invented sign system—not a language—that follows the word order of the spoken language. The base for an invented sign system may come partly from a sign language but, in addition to a changed word order, the invented system will have differences in morphology and syntax.

Complexities in the History of Deaf Education

This chapter examines the history of the "Methods" controversy from the beginnings of education of the deaf to the present, with a concentration on the complexity of the issues and the difficulties inherent in resolving longstanding conflicts.

Although technological advances have altered the situation to some degree, the field of deaf education continues to be riven by bitter controversies over language and communication, a 250–year controversy that appears unlikely to be resolved soon. As might be expected, differences of such a longstanding nature reflect quite complex realities, and the position of any individual or group of individuals is influenced by any number of factors. Chief among these are developmental and educational goals. If the overarching aim is to prepare the deaf student to participate fully—and perhaps completely—in a hearing society, then decisions about language use and mode of communication will tend one way. If the aim is to prepare the deaf student to be a fully functioning member of a deaf community, different decisions will be made. Alternately, if the aim is to help the individual to function comfortably in both deaf and hearing communities, a third set of decisions may be made.

It is important at the outset that a distinction is made between the terms "language" and "communication mode," as used in this chapter. A language can be either signed (Swedish Sign Language, American Sign Language, Greek Sign Language) or spoken (Swedish, English, Greek). In each case, the *sign language* is a full, natural language developed by members of a deaf community, independently of the spoken language of the majority community, with its own vocabulary, morphology, syntax, and pragmatics. One could choose to utilize a sign language, a spoken language, or both in different settings. As discussed in this chapter, *communication* refers to the modality in which a language is conducted. Basically, this could be either through auditory–vocal or visual–motor channels. Print, of course, is assumed to be part of any of the aforementioned alternatives.

At first glance, it may appear that a clear distinction exists between a visual–motor sign language and an auditory–vocal spoken language, implying that a similar distinction exists between communication modes. In reality, complicating factors are present. For example, although numerous sign systems have been developed to reflect spoken languages, there is no spoken corollary to any sign language.

Most classroom instruction through manual communication involves sign systems based on spoken languages. In fact, the first school for the deaf, located in Paris, took a sign language used by deaf Parisians and modified it to develop a system of "methodical" signs to reflect French (Quartararo, 2008; Stedt & Moores, 1990) akin to the signed English popular during the last part of the 20th century and up to the present. In addition to the oral/manual controversy, there are also differences of opinion over the form of manual communication to be used in instruction.

The organization of this chapter will be diachronic to some degree. The reason for this is that history does not always flow smoothly, and events in the education of deaf people are no exception. The seeds of this field were planted in Spain in the 16th and 17th century, but the efforts were restricted to children of the aristocracy, in whom recessive deafness was common. For a period of time, educators in Western Europe taught deaf children from wealthy families, and they kept their methods secret. It was not until around 1750, in Paris, that the Abbé Charles Michel de l'Épée began to teach deaf children from a broader stratum of society. Heavily influenced by the Enlightenment, the French "manual" philosophy of teaching deaf students was adopted in many European countries and, later, in the 19th century, in countries as diverse as Brazil, Russia, and the United States. Oral methods that developed in Germany and Great Britain were adopted to a lesser degree, with particular impact made by British techniques in the British Commonwealth. It was not until the 20th century that the education of deaf people spread across the world and, even today, it is still not universal. There are hundreds of thousands of deaf children who have not spent a day in school.

The education of deaf people, then, began in Europe and expanded throughout the world in fits and starts. In each country, the story has been different. Space limitations restrict the scope of the examination of language and communication issues in the various countries; this chapter, therefore, will address broad multinational developments to the greatest extent possible and will use individual countries during particular periods as illustrative examples when feasible.

Definition of Terms

This section presents basic definitions for some of the related vocabulary used in the chapter. The reader should remember that terminology changes over time and varies from one country to another. The terminology presented here, therefore, is not exhaustive, but rather is designed to provide a common frame of reference.

Sign Languages

A sign language is a language developed by members of a deaf community. It can meet all of the needs of person-to-person communication. In terms of scope, sign languages may range from a local community to one shared on a multinational basis (see Chapter 18, this volume). Sign languages may or may not be coterminous with spoken languages. For example, although English dialects are spoken in Great Britain and the United States, American Sign Language (ASL) and British Sign Language (BSL) are distinct languages. In Canada, ASL is used in English-speaking provinces and La Langue des Signes de Quebecois (LSQ) is used in Francophone areas (Mayer, Akamatsu, Bibby, Jamieson, & LeBlanc, 2009). Spanish is spoken in almost all of the countries of South America, with the notable exception of Brazil (where Portuguese is the vernacular), but each country has a separate sign language.

There are examples of sign languages or systems developed for use in communities with large numbers of deaf members. One occurred in Martha's Vineyard, an island off the coast of Massachusetts (Groce, 1985). The white settlers on the island, who lived separately from their Native American predecessors, came primarily from one area of England and shared a recessive gene for deafness. Through intermarriage of a relatively homogeneous population, the percentages of deaf members of the community increased from the 17th to the 19th century, but then declined as islanders moved to the American mainland and were replaced by a more diverse gene pool. By the time of Groce's research, no deaf individuals remained on the Vineyard, but she was able to interview elderly hearing people who recalled that signing was an integral part of the community and was used in all aspects of daily life. It is possible that Vineyard signs influenced the development of what came to be known as ASL. There were some students from the Vineyard at the American School for the Deaf, in Hartford, Connecticut shortly after its opening in 1817, but an examination of the early annual reports of the school by this author found no mention of signs indigenous to the island. Unfortunately, Groce was not able to find any description of the signs used on the island.

Manual Alphabets

Although sign languages may be independent of their spoken vernaculars, there still may be influences on sign from the much larger hearing/speaking populations. This is most noticeable in countries that use a written Roman or Cyrillic alphabet to represent spoken language and in which manual alphabets are used in conjunction with signs. To some extent, alphabet-based written language is an imperfect attempt to represent spoken language. In order to compensate for some of the inadequacies of transition from voice to print, there is recourse to such devices as uppercase and lowercase letters, commas, periods, colons, semicolons, and other punctuation. In turn, a manual alphabet is an imperfect attempt to represent *written* language. It possesses all of the letters of a written alphabet, but does not differentiate between upper- and lowercase and does not incorporate markers such as commas and periods.

The first documented use of a manual alphabet to teach deaf students also produced the first extant work in education of the deaf, *Reducion de las letres y arte para ensenar a hablar los mudos (The reduction of letters and the art of teaching the mute to speak)* (Bonet, 1620). Bonet advocated that a one-handed manual alphabet be employed to begin instruction and to support the teaching of speech and writing. He insisted that everyone living with a deaf family member should use the manual alphabet. Bonet's manual alphabet, only slightly modified, is the basis for the one-handed alphabets used today in countries such as France, Brazil, and the United States, and it forms the core of the Russian Manual Alphabet, which was modified to represent Russian Cyrillic Print (Moores, 2001).

Again, differences in manual alphabets exist. In Great Britain and some parts of the British Commonwealth, a two-handed alphabet is used that has no connection to one-handed alphabets. Manual alphabets can also be integral parts of sign languages. For example, in France and the United States, some signs for colors are made with the same motion but different hand shapes to represent the first letter of the color. In French sign language *verte* is made with a *v* handshape on the right hand, palm facing left, with small back and forth movements in front of the right shoulder. In ASL, the same position and motion are used, but with the handshape *g* for *green.*

The first teacher of the deaf in the United States was a deaf Frenchman, Laurent Clerc, who introduced the French system, including the manual alphabet. His work greatly influenced the development of ASL. In addition to some initialized colors and other vocabulary items, he developed signs for days of the week from Monday through Saturday by changing hand configurations to represent the first letters of the word: *m* for *Monday, t* for *Tuesday,* with *h* used for *Thursday.* The signs are still used in ASL two centuries later.

Sign Systems

Sign systems are differentiated from sign languages in that they were developed for educational purposes to represent spoken and written languages. They are not full languages in themselves. Sign systems may rely heavily on sign languages for their vocabulary, but not for morphology and syntax, which consciously reflect their spoken vernaculars to varying degrees. Vocabulary items may also be modified through initialization. It is common for sign languages and sign systems to coexist in many countries. For example, ASL plus several English-based sign systems are used in the United States (Moores, Miller, & Corbett, 2009), Swedish Sign Language and Signed Swedish are used in Sweden (Preisler, 2009), and Brazilian Sign Language (LIBRAS) and Signed Portuguese are used in Brazil (Guarinello, Santana, Berberian, & Massi, 2009). It should be noted that a Brazilian Signed Portuguese and a Portuguese Signed Portuguese would be different, just as signed English in the United States differs from sign-supported speech in Great Britain. There have been disagreements over the proper role, if any, of invented sign systems in education and of the proper role, if any, of sign languages in education. This issue will be examined later in the chapter.

Simultaneous Communication

Sim Com entails the coordinated use of spoken language and a spoken language–based sign system. It is designed to provide a spoken language through simultaneous presentation and reception of voice, sign, and whatever residual hearing the individual might possess. This system enjoyed some popularity in the 19th century, but really came into favor in the 1970s. Because it combined speech and sign, it did not include any use of sign language. By definition, because a sign language is independent of any spoken language, it cannot be presented simultaneously with speech.

Total Communication

Total Communication was promulgated by R. Holcomb (1970), the first deaf director of a public school program for deaf students in the United States. Holcomb's position was that all elements of communication should be used, depending on the needs of an individual child at a particular point in development. He included in the TC approach speech, fingerspelling (the American manual alphabet), auditory training, print, gesture, and ASL. Holcomb was one of a group of innovative deaf leaders, centered in California, that had a profound influence on deaf education in the United States (T. Holcomb, 2009). Over time, the meaning of TC became distorted and lost its all-inclusive nature. Essentially the term came to refer to a Sim Com method, without inclusion of ASL.

Bilingual-Bicultural (Bi-Bi)

Bilingual-bicultural education was first established at the Learning Center for Deaf Children in Framingham, Massachusetts, in 1990, and was quickly followed by a similar program at the California School for the Deaf, Fremont (Walworth, Moores, & O'Rourke, 1992). Major components and assumptions include:

1. American Sign Language (or another sign language) will be the first language and the language of instruction for deaf students throughout their entire education.

2. Speech should not be the primary vehicle for learning spoken language. ASL should be used to teach English through reading and writing.

3. Spoken language–based signing should not be used.

4. Sign language and spoken language must be separate.

5. American Sign Language (or another sign language) should be used to establish English competence through reading and writing.

Bi-Bi instruction currently is used with approximately 11% of deaf children in the United States. Numbers in other countries are not available, but there are indications that Bi-Bi instruction is in decline even in countries that officially recognize the national sign languages of their deaf communities. For example, Power (2009) reported that early identification, cochlear implantation, and intervention in Australia are leading to placement in regular schools and lack of access to signing, and Preisler (2009) reported that in Sweden a more medical view of deafness has returned with the introduction of cochlear implants, thus changing habilitation focus from sign language communication to vocal communication.

Cued Speech

Developed by Cornett (1966) at Gallaudet University in Washington, DC, cued speech is designed to present a manual system of cues in combination with speech and speechreading of lip movements. Consonants are presented via eight hand shapes and vowels through four positions near the mouth within a phonemic/syllabic context. The manual clues are not understandable by themselves but must be disambiguated by speechreading. There was considerable interest in cued speech in the United States in the 1970s, but currently less than 1% of American deaf students are taught by the system (Gallaudet Research Institute, 2006). It seems to be more commonly used in those parts of Europe where Romance languages (French, Spanish) are used, rather than in those with Germanic (English, Dutch) or Slavic (Polish, Czech) languages. Alegria and Lechart (2005), in their research on cued speech in French speaking communities, point out that there is more correspondence in French spelling to sound than in English spelling to sound, perhaps explaining why cued French has been found to support literacy development in Belgium, whereas cued English has not been similarly effective in the United States.

Oral–Aural

Oral–aural instruction, or the *oral method* or *pure oral method*, concentrates on the development of speech, speechreading, and use of residual hearing. It does not include any sign language, sign system, or manual alphabet. As with Bi-Bi and Sim Com instructions, there is variability in oral–aural instruction (Beattie, 2006). In one form or another, the oral method has been in existence for more than 200 years; it gained ascendancy in 1880, at the Conference of Milan, which asserted the supremacy of oral methods over both native sign languages and sign systems used in coordination with speech. It remained dominant for a period of 80–100 years, until the spread of Sim Com and TC instruction. It has recently grown in popularity due to improvements in digital hearing aids, miniaturization, and the growing sophistication of cochlear implants, as well as a worldwide trend of inclusion of deaf children in regular education classrooms.

Auditory Verbal

Auditory verbal instruction, as opposed to oral–aural instruction, is a primarily unisensory system that concentrates on the development and use of residual hearing. The roots may be traced to the work of early childhood educators in Great Britain, with a spread first to North America and Australia, and later to other countries. The approach at different times has been labeled the *aural method*, the *acoustic method*, or the *auditory method*. Pollack (1964) popularized the term *acoupedics*, which recently has been replaced by auditory verbal therapy (AVT). Auditory verbal therapy varies from an oral–aural approach in that there is more reliance on residual hearing and a de-emphasis on speeechreading. Much of the auditory training occurs with the teacher or therapist standing behind the child or facing the child with the lips covered (Beattie, 2006). As with oral–aural instruction, the AVT approach has experienced an increase due to advances in hearing aids and cochlear implants. Despite the enthusiasm of its advocates, there is a lack of evidence supporting this approach in children with severe and profound hearing losses.

The Beginnings of the "Methods War" in Deaf Education

Although there are references to deaf individuals in ancient times, the honor of being the first documented teacher of the deaf goes to Pedro Ponce de Leon, a 16th-century Benedictine monk who tutored approximately 16 deaf children, most of whom were members of the Spanish aristocracy (Werner, 1932). Four of his students, two brothers and two sisters, were members of the Velasco family. The eldest brother learned to read and write, and thus gained his inheritance (Peet, 1851). The other brother studied history, Spanish, and Latin and received a papal dispensation allowing him to be ordained a priest (Chaves & Solar, 1974). Unfortunately, no record exists of the techniques used by Ponce de Leon. As previously mentioned, Bonet published the first book on educating deaf students in 1620. Bonet was a soldier of fortune who also entered into the service of the same Velasco family. He began to tutor a deaf child, Luis Velasco, two generations removed from the deaf students taught by Ponce de Leon. It is not clear if Bonet knew of the techniques developed by Ponce de Leon, but Bonet's book was to have an impact in later years.

For more than a century after the publication of Bonet's work, there were tutors and teachers of deaf individuals in several European countries, but little is known of them or their methods of instruction. Most guarded their methods closely. This changed with the work of the Abbé de l'Épée in Paris. He undertook the religious instruction of two deaf sisters, developing a system of instruction that was based on two major sources. The first of these was a sign language employed by deaf Parisians. He believed that sign language was the natural language of the deaf and was their only real vehicle for thought and communication (McClure, 1969). The second major influence came from the donation by a stranger of a copy of Bonet's original book on the education of the deaf (Deland, 1931). De l'Épée used the Spanish manual alphabet to modify and expand the Parisian natural sign language. As previously noted, he developed what he called "methodical" signs to represent French vocabulary, word order, and syntax. Initialization was provided by the manual alphabet, new signs were developed to indicate elements of French morphology that were not present in the existing natural sign language, and sign communication followed spoken French word order. Writing was favored over speech. Conceptually, the system was similar to the spoken language–based sign systems in use today.

De l'Épée's relatively formal system relied heavily on drill and practice, as well as on memorization, and did not reflect everyday use. The inclusion of signs to indicate mood, tense, number, gender, and so on tended to slow down communication. Almost from the beginning, a tension existed between those who favored a more flexible natural sign language and those who had more of a French language orientation.

In 1755, de l'Épée opened the first school for the deaf in Paris and widely disseminated his methods. Reaction was mixed. In countries such as the Netherlands, influenced by the French enlightenment, de l'Épée had a significant influence on the education of deaf students. His major detractors were Jacob Rodriguez Periere and Samuel Heinicke. Periere had immigrated to France from Spain and Portugal and preceded de l'Épée as a teacher of deaf French students. Heinicke is considered the originator of the German, or oral, method and established a school in Leipzig in 1778. It was the first government-funded school for the deaf in the world (Gunther, Hennies, & Hintermair, 2009). Both Pereire and Heinicke were upset when, in 1789, Austria's first school for the deaf was established in Vienna by a protégé of de l'Épée. Heinicke was especially concerned and stated, "The Parisian method of tuition is not simply of no use, but an absolute detriment to the advancement of the pupils" (Garnett, 1968, p. 27). De l'Épée invited both Pereire and Heinicke to visit his school, but both refused. Heinicke refused to publish his methods, but he believed that the teaching of letters before speech went against the natural order of learning. He argued that pure thought was possible only through speech, on which everything else depends. One might argue that the oral versus manual conflict can be traced to correspondence between de l'Épée and Heinicke in the last decade or so of the 18th century.

By the end of the 18th century, major advances with regard to educating deaf children were made in several other European countries. However, there were countries in Europe in which the education of the deaf had not been established by 1800, most notably Spain, where pioneering efforts had begun. Prior to 1800, there is no documentation of any concerted effort to teach deaf students outside of Europe for the 250 years between Ponce de Leon to de l'Épée in France and Heinicke in Saxony; progress was limited to western and central Europe.

The 19th century presents a different and more complex picture. Significant social and cultural advances, as well as fundamental societal changes occurred in Europe. In addition, the education of the deaf was established first in the United States and Canada and later in other parts of North and South America, usually under the influence of French educators and advocates of manual instruction. In parts of the British Empire, the emphasis was more on oral education, although in colonies such as Australia and South Africa, there was an Irish influence that reflected the French method. In Australia, a significant part of the population was of Irish origins. In South Africa, Irish missionaries were active. One of the first schools in Australia was established by Sister Mary Gabriel, a deaf nun from Ireland (Power, 2009). The first school for the deaf in South Africa was established by Irish Dominican nuns, who used Irish signs as the mode of instruction. Incredibly, they allowed to enroll all races (Storbeck, Magangwa, & Parkin, 2009). They were followed by German Dominican nuns, who introduced German signs, but who also introduced oral education (Storbeck et al., 2009). Thus, the establishment of schools for the deaf outside of Europe in the 19th century was led by European religious organization, both Protestant and Catholic, and often had a missionary component. In the 20th century, religious missions in the United States played a similar role.

By the end of the 19th century, education of the deaf had been transformed. The oral/manual conflict had been declared resolved, with the "final" triumph of oral-only education over both natural sign languages and methodical spoken language–based sign systems. The "final" triumph proved not to be final, but oralism was dominant from the last part of the 19th century through the major part of the 20th century.

Europe in the 19th Century

The 19th century in Europe was a turbulent time, even more so than usual for a continent known for its turbulence. At the beginning of the century, countries such as Germany, Italy, and Belgium did not exist, and borders were continually drawn and redrawn, usually as a result of warfare. Education of the deaf at times appeared to be chaotic and subject to constant change. No one constant philosophy of education of deaf learners existed in any country throughout the century. By the end of the period, the whole continent was in accord, in support of oral education and in the belief that deaf teachers should not be employed. The trend over time was a move away from manual instruction to oral instruction.

Germany

As the influence of France began to decline in the 19th century, an upsurge of nationalism swept across Europe. This was particularly strong in German lands as the century unfolded. The country known as Germany was not unified as a nation state until 1871. From the early 1800s, it moved from a patchwork of states of varying size, many of which were under the influence of France in the early part of the century, to an increasingly strong German identification, culminating in 1871 with the German victory in the Franco-Prussian War. In the case of education in general and education of deaf learners in particular, French influence declined in Germany during the period of nationalization.

Thus, for a time, there was a strong French influence in teaching deaf students in Germany. Although there is a misperception that only the oral method was practiced in German schools, it is probable that not even Heinicke taught his students purely orally. His son-in-law, Ernst Eschke, the founder of the Royal Deaf-Mute Institute at Berlin, was influenced by the work of de l'Épée and his followers, and used a combination of oral and manual methods (Gunther, et al., 2009). Deaf teachers were employed in German schools throughout most of the 19th century, although by the end of the century, there were no deaf teachers in the new Germany.

John Baptist Glaser opposed the French method in Germany, maintaining that the two greatest deficiencies in the education of the deaf were the use of manual communication and the isolation of deaf students in residential schools (Gordon, 1885). Under Glaser's influence, deaf children were integrated into regular public school programs in several German states. This adumbration of the modern "inclusion" movement was abandoned within a few years because the children encountered academic difficulty (Bender, 1970; Gordon, 1885).

Most influential of all the German educators was Frederick Hill, who argued that deaf children should learn language the same way that hearing children do—through everyday use as part of the activities of everyday life. He opposed the structured language drill in correct grammatical use advocated by de l'Épée and his followers. Hill believed that speech should be the basis for all teaching and learning, and should involve natural interactions between the child and people in the environment (Moores, 2001). Hill did not allow the use of the manual alphabet or signs. His German, or oral method, then, differed from the French, or manual, method in two fundamental ways. First was the use of speech as opposed to signs and fingerspelling. Second was a concentration on a whole-language approach, rather than the bottom-up building block drill and practice philosophy that was advocated both by de l'Épée and Heinicke. Hill actively trained teachers of the deaf, and his influence spread throughout Europe and eventually to the United States and Canada.

The Netherlands

The establishment of schools for the deaf in the Netherlands over a 100–year period from 1790 to 1888 provides graphic evidence of the evolution of views about deafness and the goals of education (Tellings & Tijsseling, 2005; Tijsseling & Tellings, 2009). In 1790, H.G. Guyot, a Protestant minister, founded the Guyot Institute for the deaf in Groningen, in the northern Netherlands. At that time, French influence predominated. In the early part of the 19th century, the Netherlands was incorporated into France under Napoleon, and it did not achieve independence until 1813. Guyot was influenced by the liberal ideas of the Enlightenment. He went to Paris, studied at de l'Épée's school, returned to the Netherlands, and established a public school for deaf students. He introduced the French method, along with some training in speech. Guyot believed in the separation of church and state and accepted Protestant, Catholic, and Jewish students. Students were boarded in homes, and special arrangements were made for providing kosher food for Jewish students. Religious instruction was provided outside of school, according to parental wishes.

The Guyot Institute remained the only school for deaf students for 50 years. In 1830, the southern part of the Netherlands was partitioned to become Belgium, effectively reducing the number of Catholics in the Netherlands. Although significant portions of the remaining southern part of the Netherlands remained Catholic, they constituted a minority in the country and there was a Catholic emancipation movement against what was perceived as an anti-Catholic atmosphere. An inventory in 1829 reported that fewer than one-quarter of deaf individuals in the south had received any education, and there were concerns that those who had been educated at the Guyot Institute had not received sufficient Catholic education to enable them to receive Holy Communion. In 1840, a Catholic Institute for the Deaf was founded by a Catholic priest, M. Von Beck, in Sint-Michielsgestel. Education and teaching in religion and morals were exclusively Catholic. Von Beck did not visit the Guyot Institute or Paris, but read books about de l'Épée's system and developed his own system of manual signs (Tijsseling & Tellings, 2009).

The establishment of the third Dutch school for the deaf, the Effatha Christian Institute for the Deaf, in 1888, reflected an orthodox Calvinistic consensus that public education in the Netherlands was misguided and that the Guyot Institute did not provide appropriate religious instruction. In essence, the rationale for the establishment of the Protestant Effatha Institute was similar to that for the establishment of the Catholic school in Sint-Michielsgestel, which was that deaf children needed religious instruction in their particular religion as part of their education.

In summary, the Guyot Institute was established in 1790, when the Netherlands was beginning to develop into a united nation. The Sint-Michielsgetel Institute was established in 1840, when much of the Catholic south branched off to become a separate nation, and the remaining segment was energized by a Catholic emancipation movement. Effatha was founded during the development of the uniquely Dutch period of religious segregation—long since passed—in which Protestants went to Protestant schools, read Protestant papers, belonged to Protestant sports clubs, and bought their bread from Protestant bakers only, whereas Catholics bought their bread from Catholic bakers (Tijsseling & Tellings, 2009).

The International Convention of Milan

In all countries of Europe throughout the nineteenth century, there occurred a movement away from instruction using either sign languages (natural signs) or spoken language–based signs (methodical signs). Methodical signs sometimes were used in coordination with speech, much like the Sim Com employed today. The high point for oral education came in 1880, at The International Convention of Milan, which represented an overwhelming victory for the oral method. Among the resolutions passed were two declarations, which in English translation read: (1) given the incontestable superiority of speech over signs in restoring deaf-mutes to society, and in giving them a more perfect knowledge of language that the oral method ought to be preferred to signs; and (2) considering that the simultaneous use of speech and signs has the disadvantage of injuring speech, lipreading, and precision of ideas, that the pure oral method ought to be preferred. Countries such as Germany, Italy, and Great Britain were already oral, and the rest were soon to follow. (It should be noted that the International Congress continues today as the International Convention on Education of the Deaf, which meets every 5 years.) The declarations against signing have long been abandoned, and presentations may be given in sign language, simultaneous use of speech and signs, or spoken language, along with interpreting.

Deaf Teachers

Throughout the 19th century, the position of deaf teachers declined not only in Germany but across Europe, along with the decline of manual instruction and the rise of the oral method. In some countries, such as Sweden, deaf teachers were employed to work with students who had limited intellectual capabilities. The situation was especially stark in France, the home of the manual method and the source of trained deaf teachers of the deaf at the beginning of the century. As early as 1831, in the Paris National Institute for the Deaf, all teachers were required to conduct oral training in class. Deaf professors were demoted in rank, listed as auxiliary professors, and were given "untrained" students who had difficulty with oral instruction (Quartararo, 2008). The Convention of Milan provided the final chapter for deaf teachers in France. After 1884, deaf teachers were officially excluded from teaching in all schools in the country (Quartararo, 2008).

The United States of America

By chance, the first schools for the deaf in the United States followed a manual instead of oral philosophy. Thomas Hopkins Gallaudet, a minister, was sent to Europe in 1815 to study techniques for teaching

deaf students. His goal was to study oral methods at a school established by the Braidwood family in Great Britain, and then travel to France to study the manual system. Braidwood demanded that Gallaudet remain at the school for 4 years in order to be adequately trained, whereupon he instead left for France. At the Paris school, he recruited the deaf teacher, Laurent Clerc, to return to the United States with him. In 1817, the American School for the Deaf, in Hartford, Connecticut, opened its doors with Gallaudet as principal and Clerc as head teacher. Clerc developed an English-based methodical sign system based on the same techniques that were used in the French-based methodical signs. Using the manual alphabet, he used initialization to represent English spelling. For some reason, the change was not complete. Clerc's methodical signs, and those of ASL today, use a "b" handshape (*bon*) instead of a "g" handshape for *good*, a "c" handshape (*checher*) instead of an "s" handshape for *search*, and an "m" handshape (*mil*) instead of a "t" handshape for *thousand*.

Clerc's system of instruction contained four modes of communication: (1) the natural language of signs of the deaf, (2) a methodical sign system, (3) the manual alphabet, and (4) writing. Clerc developed the curriculum for the school with a concentration on the development of written language. A subject might be introduced in natural signs, followed by a presentation in methodical signs, and the lesson ended with the manual alphabet and drill and practice in writing. He trained the teachers, both hearing and deaf, at the school and was also responsible for the training of many of the first superintendents of schools for the deaf across the country. As a result, the system of instruction developed at the American School extended throughout the country by 1828 (T. Gallaudet, 1828).

In 1818, a second school for the deaf, The New York Institution for the Instruction of the Deaf and Dumb, was established in New York City (Moores, 2001). By 1834, the New York Institution had moved away from reliance on methodical signs (Peet, 1834). Peet justified this by arguing that deaf students did not use methodical signs outside of class on a daily basis, the system involved meaningless rote repetition, and the emphasis was on English structure, not content. There was some agreement with this by Thomas Hopkins Gallaudet who, in the first issue of the *American Annals of the Deaf*, in 1847, published an article "On the natural language of signs; and its value and uses in the instruction of the deaf and dumb." Debate raged for 50 years in the United States over the best method for educating deaf students. Natural sign languages were criticized because they did not follow English. Methodical signs were discouraged because they were stilted and artificial. Neither approach appeared to gain favor. Burnet (1854, pp. 1–2) reported that, in the United States, methodical signs were once universal, only to be discarded wholly in some schools and partly in others, and, in some cases, after being denounced were reinstituted.

The debate became moot with the ascendancy of oral education in the United States. The situation can be summed up in the titles of three articles by Edward Minor Gallaudet, the son of Thomas Hopkins Gallaudet, written over the last three decades of the 19th century. In chronological order they were, "Is the sign language used to excess in teaching deaf-mutes?" (E. Gallaudet, 1871), "The value of the sign language to the deaf" (E. Gallaudet, 1887), and "Must the sign language go?" (E. Gallaudet, 1899).

The Growth of Oral Education in the United States

Oral education in the United States began in 1867, much later than in western and northern Europe, with the establishment of the New York Institution for the Impaired (now the Lexington School for the Deaf) and the Clarke School for the Deaf in Northampton, Massachusetts. Both schools were influential in the spread of oral education. The Clarke School had the benefit of support from Alexander G. Bell, the inventor of the telephone and a strong advocate of oral education and an opponent of the use of signs. His father, Alexander Melville Bell, had invented a system to teach articulation called Visible Speech, with which A. G. Bell used to tutor deaf students (Moores, 2001). The younger Bell founded the Alexander Graham Bell Association to further the goals of oral education and established the *Volta Review*, the official organ of the Bell Association. Bell's position was influenced partly by his interest in eugenics and his concerns that, in 1883, around one-third of teachers in residential schools were deaf themselves (Bell, 1884). Bell believed that a move away from residential schooling, combined with hiring only hearing teachers and repressing the use of sign language, would reduce intermarriages of deaf individuals and reduce the incidence of deafness.

The spread of oral education was particularly rapid in the day schools for deaf students that were established in most large cities in the United States during the last decades of the 19th and first decades of the 20th centuries. Almost without exception,

teachers in these schools were hearing, and instruction was through oral-only means. By the beginning of the 20th century, all schools, both day and residential, offered oral-only instruction through the elementary grades or until children were around 12 years of age. After that, some residential schools continued with oral instruction, and others would separate children into oral and manual programs. The children were not segregated outside of class time, and typically communicated through sign. In this reduced form, sign instruction continued in many residential schools with deaf children. Bender (1970) noted that the oral method was adopted by every country in the world except the United States, which remained the only real stronghold for the "silent" method (p. 168), albeit only in the upper school grades.

Deaf American Teachers

Edward Minor Gallaudet, the President of Gallaudet College, now Gallaudet University, was a major force in preserving sign communication in educational settings and was an able antagonist for A. G. Bell. Deaf teachers and dormitory personnel were mainly responsible for the continuation of sign language in the schools, and they still constituted an important presence in many residential schools, although their numbers declined. Continuity was provided by graduates of Gallaudet College, which had been established in 1864 by the federal government as a college for deaf students and remains today the only liberal arts college for deaf students in the world. Deaf students would come to Gallaudet from residential schools in the United States and Canada, marry deaf students who had attended other residential schools, and, frequently, go to work in other residential schools as teachers and dormitory supervisors. Although they were restricted to teaching in "manual departments" at junior and senior high levels and in vocational training, they functioned as role models and spread the Gallaudet sign dialect throughout the United States and English-speaking Canada.

The positive influence of deaf professionals in America continued through the 80–year ascendancy of oral education. Bernard Tervoort, who was affiliated with the Sint-Michielsgestel Institute in the Netherlands, studied extensively the development of communication patterns of deaf children in Belgium, the Netherlands, and the United States (Tervoort, 1961; Tervoort & Verbeck, 1967). Tervoort and Verbeck (1967) found that all children tended to use signs as their preferred means of communication, even those young children who were taught orally. Having no access to deaf adult signers, the children would invent their own exotic in-group sign systems. After age 14, the communication skills of the American students continued to improve, whereas those of the European children leveled off. The authors attributed the superiority of the American children in part to the influence of the educated deaf adults with whom they came into contact. They stated (p. 148), "The sign language of the American deaf adult is a source from above, strongly influencing the interchange of the deaf teenager, on campus too, and on the contrary, the fact that no such source from above is available for their mates from across the ocean with whom they are matched." Their conclusion was that American deaf children benefited from exposure to a true sign language, ASL, and from interaction with deaf adults, but that European deaf children, without comparable interaction with signing deaf adults, continued to be restricted to limited sign systems.

1900 to 1960

During the first six decades of the 20th century, education of the deaf primarily concentrated on speech and spoken language. Elementary school teachers of the deaf, all of whom were hearing, were considered to be primarily speech teachers and "language" teachers with "language" assumed to mean English. Although other systems existed, speech was developed most commonly through the Northampton Charts, consisting of drill and practice on English vowels and consonants that were later combined into words (Moores, 2001). English grammar was similarly taught through an elemental building block system. The most popular system was the Fitzgerald Key (1929), developed by Edith Fitzgerald, a deaf teacher. The Key was developed to provide children with rules by which they could generate correct English sentences. It used visual symbols and began instruction with practice combining words in correct word order and gradually increasing complexity. The complete Key was often presented on blackboards along walls in classrooms for practice, and children would also work with Key paper for seat exercises.

Education of the deaf settled into a pattern from 1900 to 1960. Advances were made in hearing aid technology, and language and communication instruction did not stray far from the oral method. One notable exception was the Israelite Institute of Deaf Mutes in Berlin, which used signing for instruction. One of its students, Wladislaus Zeitlin, was the first deaf graduate of a German university (Gunther et al., 2009). When the Nazis took power in Germany, they passed a law to "prevent genetically diseased offspring." People identified as genetically deaf were either sterilized or sent to hard labor camps and worked to death (Biesold, 1999). The hearing director of the Israelite School was sent to a concentration camp. Upon his release, he was able to immigrate to England with ten children from his school. Zeitlin was murdered by the Gestapo in Paris.

The first move away from a pure oral method with young children occurred after World War II, with pioneering work in Russian in the Soviet Union. Researchers at the Moscow Institute of Defectology concluded that restriction of language to articulation made the entire education process too inefficient. They developed a system labeled *neo-oralism* that included fingerspelling and oral communication with very young children. A curriculum was developed based on the theory of Lev Vygotsky, who was a researcher at the Institute. Morozova (1954) reported that 3– and 4–year-old children taught under neo-oralism could learn in 2 years that which would have taken 3 years under the pure oral method. There was little or no knowledge of the Soviet work outside of the Soviet Union until the American educator Boris Morkovin published his observations of neo-oralism in 1960.

From 1960 to the Present

The education of the deaf has been in a state of constant change since 1960. During that decade and into the 1970s, unprecedented changes occurred in the education of the deaf, especially regarding mode (auditory–vocal, visual–motor, or a combination) but not necessarily language, (spoken or signed) of instruction. Since then, the rate of change has slowed, but is still rapid.

Morkovin's (1960) article caused great interest in the United States, especially in view of reports that followed, which questioned the value of oral-only preschool programs. In separate studies, Craig (1964) and Phillips (1963) compared deaf children who had received preschool training from age 3 to children with no preschool training, and found no differences on language arts, arithmetic, socialization, speechreading, or poor reading skills. McCroskey (1968) also compared children with preschool experience to children with no preschool experience. The few differences found between the groups tended to favor those with no preschool experience. The results raised questions about the benefits of oral-only instruction. Some schools in the United States were already moving toward the use of manual communication, either the Rochester method or Sim Com. The Rochester Method was similar to Russian neo-oralism, in that it combined speech with fingerspelling the manual alphabet but without any use of signs. Quigley (1969) compared children taught through the Rochester method to children taught on an oral-only preschool and reported that the Rochester method students were superior in speechreading, five of seven measures of reading, and three of five measures of written language; oral-only students were superior in one of five measures of written language.

During the same period, several studies were conducted on the academic achievement and social development of deaf children of deaf parents who signed in the home, compared to deaf children of hearing parents who did not. Stuckless and Birch (1966) found that children of deaf parents were superior in reading, speechreading, and written language, with no differences in speech or psychosocial development. Meadow (1968) reported that deaf children of deaf parents were superior in reading, math, written language, maturity, and sociability, with no differences in speech or speechreading. Quigley and Frisina (1961) reported that deaf children of deaf parents were superior in vocabulary, with no differences in speechreading and achievement, whereas children of hearing parents were superior in speech. Vernon and Koh (1970) found that deaf children of deaf parents were superior on academic achievement, reading, written language, and vocabulary, with no differences in speech and speechreading.

Dissatisfaction with the results of the oral-only programs, reports of success in the Soviet Union, and the apparent academic and communicative superiority of signing deaf children of deaf parents called into question assumptions that manual communication was detrimental to the academic and social development of deaf children. Change away from oral-only instruction in the United States was dramatic. Jordan, Gustason, and Rosen (1976) reported that, by 1975, approximately two-thirds of all deaf children in the United States were taught through TC and one-third through oral means. Concurrent with the growth of signing in classroom was the further development of English-based sign systems. The two best-known systems were developed by deaf professionals. The first, *Seeing Essential English (SEE I)*, was developed under the leadership of David Anthony (Washburn, 1971) in the United States, and *Signing Exact English (SEE II)* was developed by

Gustason Pfetzinger and Zowolkow (1972). Both Anthony and Gustason had worked together on SEE I, and similarities are apparent. As with all invented sign systems, they follow a spoken language word order, in this case English. They also have invented signs for pronouns, prefixes, and suffixes for verb tense, number, adverbial markers, and the like. The reader is referred to the sources for full treatments.

Similar systems using simultaneous speech and sign were developed in Scandinavia (Preisler, 2009) and Australia (Power, 2009) and, to a lesser degree, in other parts of the world. The use of sign languages themselves in education came later.

As previously noted, although data are not generally available, the numbers of deaf children being taught either through a national sign language or a manual code on a spoken language declined, beginning around 1990, even in countries that officially recognize sign languages. There are several reasons for this. Perhaps the greatest impact has come from increasing sophistication of digital hearing aids and from a tremendous increase—beginning in the last decade of the 20th century—in the numbers of children worldwide receiving cochlear implants, with concomitant expectations by many that the procedure will result in normal hearing. Related to this, there is a growing worldwide trend toward educational inclusion of deaf children in regular education classrooms (Hyde, 2009), which often leads to an emphasis on oral communication. A third factor has been the introduction of neonatal screening for hearing loss and early intervention programs (Chapter 16, this volume), which is often related to a resurgence of interest in auditory verbal training for deaf children, especially those with cochlear implants. This unisensory concentration on hearing ties in with the expectations and hopes of many parents and professionals. To some extent, it also represents a return to a medical pathological view of deafness.

Some data in the United States document a trend toward oral-only instruction. The Gallaudet Research Institute (2006) reported that a little more than 50% of children were taught through speech alone, approximately 40% through sign and speech, and 10% through sign alone. This contrasts with the report of Jordan et al. (1976) from 30 years earlier, that one-third of children were taught orally.

Summary and Conclusions

After more than 200 years, the methods controversy is nowhere near resolution. The intractable nature of the conflict may be due in part to differing opinions about deafness, the goals of education, and the requirements for leading a full and rich life. Given these differences, research will not answer the issues completely, because different people ask different questions. It is clear that the highly acclaimed final triumph of oralism in 1880 was not so final. Natural sign languages probably have existed for millennia, and spoken language–based sign systems have existed for more than 250 years. At present, increased emphasis is placed on oral–aural instruction, as compared to the situation in the 1970s and 1980s, and this trend may continue as early identification techniques improve and cochlear implants and hearing aids grow more effective. Still, implants do not completely restore hearing. For the foreseeable future, language and communication ideally will depend on the needs of an individual deaf child and will include options from spoken language to spoken language–based sign to natural sign language, and sometimes all of the above.

Acknowledgments

The author would like to acknowledge the input of the members of the graduate class in Language and Instruction for the Deaf and Hard of Hearing at the University of North Florida.

References

Alegria, J., & Lechart, J. (2005). Phonological processing in deaf children: When lipreading and cues are in congruence. *Journal of Deaf Studies and Deaf Education, 11*, 122–133.

Bauman, H. (2008). Introduction: Listening to deaf studies. In H. Bauman (Ed.), *Open your eyes: Deaf studies talking* (pp. 1–34). Minneapolis: University of Minnesota Press.

Beattie, R. (2006). The oral methods and spoken language acquisition. In P. Spencer, & M. Marschark (Eds.), *Advances in the spoken language development of deaf and hard of hearing children* (pp. 103–135). New York: Oxford University Press.

Bell, A. G. (1884). Fallacies concerning the deaf. *American Annals of the Deaf, 28*(2), 124–139.

Bender, R. (1970). *The conquest of deafness*. Cleveland: Case Western Reserve.

Biesold, H. (1999). *Crying hands: Eugenics and deaf people in Nazi Germany*. Washington, DC: Gallaudet University Press.

Bonet, J. (1620). Reducion de las letras y arte para ensenar a hablar los mudos. Madrid: Par Francisco Arbaco de Angelo.

Burnet, J. (1854) The necessity of methodical signs considered. *American Annals of the Deaf, 8*, 1–15.

Chaves, T., & Solar, J. (1974). Pedro Ponce de Leon: First teacher of the deaf. *Sign Language Studies, 5*(1), 48–63.

Cornett, O. (1966). Cued speech. *American Annals of the Deaf, 112*, 3–13.

Craig, W. (1964). Effects of preschool training on the development of reading and lipreading skills of deaf children. *American Annals of the Deaf, 64*, 109, 280–296.

Deland, F. (1931). *The story of lipreading*. Washington, DC: Volta Bureau.

Fitzgerald, E. (1929). *Straight language for the deaf*. Staunton, VA: McClure Company.

Gallaudet Research Institute (2006). *Regional and national summary report of data from the 2006–2007 Annual Survey of Deaf and Hard of Hearing Children and Youth*. Washington, DC: GRI; Gallaudet University.

Gallaudet, E. (1871) Is the sign language used to excess in teaching deaf-mutes? *American Annals of the Deaf, 16*(1), 26–33.

Gallaudet, E. (1887) The value of the sign language to the deaf. *American Annals of the Deaf, 32*(3), 141–147.

Gallaudet, E. (1899). Must the sign language go? *American Annals of the Deaf, 44*(3) 221–239.

Gallaudet, T. (1828). *Twelfth annual report of the Asylum at Hartford for the Education of the Deaf and Dumb*. Hartford, Connecticut.

Gallaudet, T. (1847). On the natural language of signs; and its value and uses in the instruction of the deaf and dumb. *American Annals of the Deaf. 1*(1), 55–66.

Garnett, C. (1968). *The exchange of letters between Samuel Heinicks and the Abbe Charles Michel de l'Épée*. New York: Vantage.

Gordon, J. (1885). Deaf-mutes and the public schools from 1815 to the present day. *American Annals of the Deaf, 30*(3), 121–143.

Groce, N. (1985). *Everyone here spoke sign language*. Cambridge, MA: Harvard University Press.

Guarinello, A., Santana, A., Berberian, A., & Massi, G. (2009). Educational and developmental aspects of the lives of deaf Brazilians. In D. Moores & M. Miller (Eds.), *Deaf people around the world: Educational, developmental, and social perspectives* (pp. 277–283). Washington, DC: Gallaudet University Press.

Gundler, K., Hennies, J., & Hintermair, M. (2009). Trends and developments in deaf education in Germany. In D. Moores & M. Miller (Eds.), *Deaf people around the world: Educational, developmental, and social perspectives* (pp. 178–193). Washington, DC: Gallaudet University Press.

Gustason, G., Pfetzinger, D., & Zowolkow, E. *Signing Exact English*. Rossmoor, CA: Modern Signs Press.

Holcomb, R. (1970). The total approach. *Proceedings of International Conference on Education of the Deaf*. Stockholm, 104–107.

Holcomb, T. (in press). The deaf way of knowing. *American Annals of the Deaf*. Hyde, M. (2009). Inclusion in an international context. In D. Moores & M. Miller (Eds.), *Deaf people around the world: Educational and social perspectives* (pp. 352-357). Washington, DC: Gallaudet University Press.

Hyde, M. (2009). Inclusion in an international context. In D. Moores & M. Miller (Eds.), *Deaf people around the world: Educational and social perspectives* (pp. 352–367). Washington, DC: Gallaudet University Press.

Jordan, I., Gustason, J., & Rosen, R. (1976). Current communication trends at programs for the deaf. *American Annals of the Deaf, 121*(5), 527–531.

Ling, D. (1988). *Foundations of spoken language for hearing impaired children*. Washington, DC: Alexander Graham Bell Press.

Mayer, C., Akamatsu, T., Bibby, M., Jamieson, J., & Le Blanc, R. (2009). Education of deaf and hard of hearing learners in Canada. In D. Moores & M. Miller (Eds.), *Deaf people around the world: Educational, developmental, and social perspectives* (pp. 281–301). Washington, DC: Gallaudet University Press.

McCroskey, R. (1968). Final report of a four-year home training program. Paper presented at A. G. Bell National Convention. San Francisco, June.

Meadow, K. (1968). Early manual communication in relation to the child's intellectual, social, and communicative functioning. *American Annals of the Deaf, 113*, 29–41.

McClure, W. (1969). Historical perspectives in the education of the deaf. In G. Griffith (Ed.). *Persons with hearing loss* (pp. 3-30). Springfield, IL: Charles C. Thomas.

Moores, D. (2001). *Educating the deaf: Psychology, principles, and practices*, 5th edition. Boston: Houghton Mifflin.

Moores, D., & Martin, D. (2006). Overview: Curriculum and Instruction. In D. Moores & D. Martin (Eds.), *Deaf learners: Developments in curriculum and instruction* (pp. 3–14). Washington, DC: Gallaudet University Press.

Moores, D., Miller, M., & Corbett, E. (2009). The United States of America: Deaf people in a multi-cultural society. In D. Moores & M. Miller (Eds.), *Deaf people around the world: Educational, and social perspectives* (pp. 322–345). Washington, DC: Gallaudet University Press.

Morkovin, B. (1960). Experiment in teaching preschool children in the Soviet Union. *Volta Review, 32*, 160–160.

Morozova, N. (1954). *Development of the theory of preschool education of the deaf and dumb*. Moscow: Institute of Defectology.

Peet, H. (1834). *Sixteenth annual Report of the New York Institution for the Instruction of the Deaf and Dumb*. New York.

Peet, H. (1851). Memoir of the origin and early history of the art of educating the deaf and dumb. *American Annals of the Deaf, 4*(2), 129–161.

Phillips, W. (1963). *Influence of preschool training on language arts, arithmetic subjects, and socialization of young deaf children*. Unpublished doctoral dissertation, Columbia University.

Pollack, D. (1964). Acoupedics: a unisensory approach to auditory training. *Volta Review, 66*,(7), 400–409.

Power, D. (2009). Education of the deaf in Australia. In D. Moores & M. Miller (Eds.), *Deaf people around the world: Educational, and social perspectives* (pp. 3–16). Washington, DC: Gallaudet University Press.

Preisler, G. (2009). The situation for the deaf in Sweden. In D. Moores & M. Miller (Eds.), *Deaf people around the world: Educational, developmental, and social perspectives*. Washington, DC: Gallaudet University Press.

Quartararo, A. (2008). *Deaf identity and social images in nineteenth-century France*. Washington, DC: Gallaudet University Press

Quigley, S. (1969). *The influence of fingerspelling on the development of language, communication and educational achievement of deaf children*. Urbana: University of Illinois.

Qquqigley, S., & Frisina, D. (1961). *Institutionalization and psycho-educational development of deaf children*. Washington, DC: Council for Exceptional Children.

Stedt, J., & Moores, D. (1990). Manual codes on English and American Sign Language: Historical perspectives and current realities. In H. Bornstein (Ed.), *Manual communication: Implications for education* (pp. 1–20). Washington, DC: Gallaudet University Press.

Storbeck, C., Magondwa, L., & Parkin, I. (2009). Education of the deaf in South Africa. In D. Moores & M. Miller (Eds.), *Deaf people around the world: Educational and social perspectives* (pp.133–144). Washington, DC: Gallaudet University Press.

Stuckless, E., & Birch, J. (1966). The influence of early manual communication on the linguistic development of deaf children. *American Annals of the Deaf, 111*, 452–460 499–504.

Tellings, A., & Tijssling, C. (2005). An unhappy and utterly pitiful creature? Life and self-images of deaf people in the Netherlands at the time of the founding fathers of deaf education. *Journal of Deaf Studies and Deaf Education, 10*, 193–202.

Tervoort, B. (1961). Esoteric symbolism in the communicative structure behavior of young deaf children. *American Annals of the Deaf, 106*, 436–480.

Tervoort, B., & Verbeck, A. (1967). *Analysis of communicative structure patterns in deaf children* (pp. 583–615). Groningen, the Netherlands: A.W.O. Onderzoek, N.R.

Tijsseling, C., & Tellings, A. (2009). The Christian's duty towards the deaf: Christian views on deaf schooling and education in Dutch nineteenth century society. *American Annals of the Deaf, 153*(1).

Vernon, M., & Koh, S. (1970). Effects of manual communication on deaf children's educational achievement, linguistic competence, oral skills, and psychological development. *American Annals of the Deaf, 115*, 7527–7536.

Walworth, M., Moores, D., & O'Rourke, T. (Eds.). (1992). *A free hand: Enfranchising the education of deaf children*. Silver Spring, MD: T.J. Publishers.

Washburn, A. (1972). *Seeing essential English*. Denver: Community College of Denver

Werner, H. (1932). *History of the problems of deaf-mutes until the 17th century*. (Translated from German by C. K. Bonning). Jena, Germany: Verlag Von Gustav Fisher.

Legal Advocacy for Deaf and Hard-of-Hearing Children in Education

Barbara Raimondo

Abstract

This chapter outlines several laws that are key to the education and lives of deaf and hard-of-hearing (DHH) children and their families: the Individuals with Disabilities Education Act (IDEA), Elementary and Secondary Education Act/No Child Left Behind (ESEA/NCLB) Act, Americans with Disabilities Act (ADA), and Section 504 of the Rehabilitation Act. It discusses the requirements of each law, those places where the laws intersect, and possible directions these laws could take in the future. It describes the evolution of the IDEA from a law that required that students with disabilities be educated, to one that brings their education in line with that of nondisabled children. It outlines the accountability provisions of ESEA/NCLB and the efforts being made to ensure that this law achieves its goal; that is, to bring the achievement of students from disadvantaged groups, including those with disabilities, up to par with that attained by non-disadvantaged students. It addresses the ADA and Section 504 of the Rehabilitation Act, laws that also have application outside of the education setting.

Keywords: education, legal rights, achievement

Federal laws in the United States and similar legislation in other countries help shape the model of educational access and services for DHH children. This chapter summarizes several laws that are key to this model.

Early Hearing Detection and Intervention

As in many countries, today all 50 states in the United States plus the District of Columbia and American territories have instituted early hearing detection and intervention (EHDI) programs to measure babies' hearing levels and offer the opportunity for early intervention for those babies who are deaf or hard of hearing and their families. EHDI systems follow a "one-three-six" plan, in which the goals are screening by age 1 month, identification of DHH babies by age 3 months, and enrollment of the family in appropriate early intervention programs by age 6 months (Joint Committee on Infant Hearing [JCIH], 2007).

Many of these early intervention services are provided through Part C, the Infants and Toddlers with Disabilities section of the federal IDEA legislation. IDEA is described in more detail later. Part C provides developmentally appropriate services to children birth to 3 years, and their families, based on an Individualized Family Service Plan (IFSP). Services include family training, counseling, and home visits; special instruction; speech-language pathology and audiology; sign language and cued language services; service coordination services; diagnostic medical services; vision services; assistive technology devices and assistive technology services; and other appropriate services. Services must be designed to meet the developmental needs of the infant or toddler in one or more of the domains of physical development, cognitive development, communication development, social or emotional development, and adaptive development.

Prior to the establishment of EHDI systems, the average age of identification of DHH children in the United States was age 2.5 years (Mehl & Thomson, 1998). It is believed that many of the language delays commonly experienced by DHH children are the result of late identification and implementation of services. With EHDI, more children are being identified earlier, but barriers to successful EHDI implementation remain.

The National Center on Hearing Assessment and Management states that 12,000 babies who cannot hear well are born each year (National Center for Hearing Assessment and Management, n.d.). Data collected by the Centers for Disease Control and Prevention for 2007 (Centers for Disease Control and Prevention, 2007), the most recent year surveyed, show the following:

- 94% of newborn babies (3,775,361) were screened before age 1 month.
- 1.8% (63,269) of the babies screened did not pass, and should have received a confirmatory hearing assessment.
- Of the babies referred for confirmatory assessment, only 43% (27,445) received it. Nearly 45% of the babies referred were lost to follow-up at this stage.
- 6% (approximately 4,000) of the babies who did not pass the screen were found to have a hearing loss.
- Only 64% of babies (2,541) identified with hearing loss in 2007 were enrolled in early intervention programs.

So, of the 12,000 babies who cannot hear well born in 2007, only 2,541 made it into early intervention.

Experts point out that "qualified personnel with specialized preparation are essential for providing appropriate services..." to infants and young children (Sass-Lehrer, 2002, p. 16). The Joint Committee on Infant Hearing states that "Infants with confirmed hearing loss should receive appropriate intervention at no later than 6 months of age from health care and education professionals with expertise in hearing loss and deafness in infants and young children" (JCIH, 2007, p. 1). However, such personnel often are lacking. One study showed that, out of 388 early intervention sites in 19 states, only 48% had service providers on site who had degrees in deaf education (Stredler-Brown & Arehart, 2000). Lacking sufficient qualified personnel, early intervention sites cannot be expected to help children reach their age-appropriate levels of language and communication ability.

Clearly, EHDI systems need to make vast improvements if they are going to identify and provide appropriate services for DHH babies and their families. Recommendations to improve these systems include improving data systems to support surveillance and follow-up activities, building capacity beyond identified key providers, developing family-to-family support services, and promoting understanding of the importance of early detection (Mathematica Policy Research, 2007). Marge and Marge (2005) further suggest using family-centered approaches and facilitating collaboration between parents and specifically trained professionals.

Individuals with Disabilities Education Act

Since 1975, the IDEA (Government Printing Office, 2004), originally known as P.L. 94–142, the Education for All Handicapped Children Act (EAHCA), has guided and protected the civil right to special education and related services to eligible students with disabilities. IDEA was passed as the Congressional response to two United States federal district court decisions regarding the exclusion of students with disabilities from education: *Pennsylvania Association for Retarded Children (PARC) vs. Commonwealth of Pennsylvania* (334 F.Supp. 1247; E.D. Pa. 1971) and *Mills vs. Board of Education* (348 F.Supp. 866; D.D.C. 1972). The *PARC* and *Mills* courts found such exclusions to be unacceptable and, in each case, ordered the public agency to provide appropriate educational services to students with disabilities and to establish procedural safeguards to protect their rights.

Soon after *Mills*, and building on the principles established in *PARC* and *Mills*, Congress passed the EAHCA, which later became IDEA. At that time, the law applied to children aged 6 through 21 years. Throughout several reauthorizations, it has expanded to also include children aged 3 to 5 years (preschool programs) and (in Part C) children who are newborn to 3 years of age.

IDEA requires states to develop and maintain a system to educate children with disabilities. In return, the federal government provides some funding for these educational systems. Under IDEA, a "child with a disability" is a child whose disability falls into a specific category defined by IDEA, such as "hearing impairment," and, because of this disability, requires special education and related services. State systems for supporting these children must be based on six principles:

- States will locate and identify children with disabilities.
- Children with disabilities will be evaluated to determine their educational needs.

- Schools will provide eligible children with a Free Appropriate Public Education (FAPE).
- Education and placement will be based on an Individualized Education Program (IEP).
- Children with disabilities will be placed in the Least Restrictive Environment (LRE) based on their needs; that is, they will be placed with nondisabled children to the "maximum extent appropriate."
- They and their parents will have access to procedural safeguards to protect their rights.

At the time it was passed, IDEA focused mainly on *access* to education. Over the years, it has become more specific about the *kind* of education that must be offered and how high the expectations for achievement should be. For example, for a child who is deaf or hard of hearing, the law requires the IEP team to consider the child's language and communication needs, opportunities for direct communications with peers and professional personnel in the child's language and communication mode, academic level, and full range of needs, including opportunities for direct instruction in the child's language and communication mode. For children who are blind, Braille must be provided unless the IEP team, after considering specific factors, agrees that instruction in Braille is not appropriate for a child. The IEP team also must consider the use of assistive technologies for each child.

For over a decade, IDEA has required states to ensure that students with disabilities have access to and make progress in the general education curriculum; that is, the same curriculum used by nondisabled children. IDEA also requires states to include students with disabilities in state and local assessments. It requires states to provide appropriate accommodations for students taking those assessments, and to develop alternate assessments for those students for whom the regular assessment is not appropriate. IDEA thus requires individualized planning and programming for each child, yet the purpose of the planning and programming is to help the child learn the same material as nondisabled children, to the extent possible.

Part C, the Infant and Toddler Program of IDEA, was described in the EHDI section earlier. Part B serves children ages 3 through 21 years. The key to determining services for children with disabilities served by Part B is the IEP. Today, over 6 million children in the United States are served by IDEA (United States Department of Education, 2007), including over 72,000 children who are deaf or hard

of hearing (United States Department of Education, 2007). In considering the detailed directives contained in the statute and associated regulations, the varying needs of all these children, and the standard of FAPE by which IDEA services are measured, it is no surprise that parents and other members of the IEP team sometimes have difficulty determining exactly what elements should be included in an IEP for a specific child. However, the steps outlined in the law can be summarized as *evaluation, goals, services needed to achieve goals*, and *placement*. The following sections consider each of these in turn.

Evaluation

Evaluation under Part B of IDEA requires that children be assessed in all areas related to the suspected disability, including, if appropriate, health, vision, hearing, social and emotional status, general intelligence, academic performance, communicative status, and motor abilities.

The evaluation should be sufficiently comprehensive to identify all of a child's special education and related services needs. The public agency must use a variety of assessment tools and strategies to evaluate the child, gathering relevant functional,[1] developmental, and academic information. It must draw upon information from a variety of sources, including aptitude and achievement tests, parent input, and teacher recommendations. It also must consider the child's physical condition, social or cultural background, and adaptive behavior, and ensure that information obtained from all sources is documented and carefully evaluated. Conduct of the evaluation will result in a statement of present levels of performance, which will be documented on the IEP.

Goals

Under Part B, the IEP team must determine measurable goals for the child, including academic and functional goals. Note the use of the word "measurable." If a goal is not measurable, the IEP team cannot know whether the child has achieved it. Goals like "Jenna will improve her vocabulary" or "John will gain additional reading skills" are not measurable without additional specificity. Building upon present levels of performance, IEP teams can determine goals appropriate for a specific child during the time period of the IEP. These goals must relate to a child's needs, based on the particular disability or disabilities identified. They must enable the child to be involved in and make progress in the general education curriculum, regardless of the educational setting in which the child is placed. These measurable goals, set annually, also must meet each of the child's other educational needs that result from the child's disability. Identification of the present levels of performance and goals is necessary to determine which services are appropriate for the child.

Services

The IEP team must determine, and document on the IEP, the special education and related services and supplementary aids and services to be provided to a child under Part B of IDEA. Supplementary aids and services are those that allow the child to participate in the educational setting with nondisabled peers. For example, a DHH child could receive services from a teacher of the deaf, an audiologist, speech-language pathologist, American Sign Language (ASL) instructor, sign language interpreter, and/or other personnel. Provision of services should be based on peer-reviewed research, to the extent practicable. The IEP team also must develop a statement of the program modifications or supports needed for school personnel, such as training for personnel to be able to meet the child's needs. For example, a regular education teacher could receive training to better enable her to teach the child who is deaf.

Placement

By the time of a child's placement in a program, the IEP team will have reviewed the results of relevant evaluations, determined goals for the child, and agreed upon services. The decision about where the child should be placed to receive those services should grow out of these activities. The child should be placed in the setting most likely to meet his needs and requirements for services, as documented by the evaluations, goals, and services listed on the IEP. States are required to ensure that a continuum of alternative placements is available to meet the needs of children with disabilities for special education and related services. The continuum must include instruction in regular classes, special classes, special schools, and home instruction, as well as options for instruction in hospitals and institutions.

Real challenges exist to serving DHH students under IDEA. Eighty-six percent of these students are served in mainstream settings (United States Department of Education, 2007, Vol. II, p. 192), and some people question whether the emphasis on placement in the regular education setting is conducive to DHH students' optimal achievement (Marschark,

Lang, & Albertini, 2002; National Association of the Deaf, 2002; see also Chapter 6, this volume). Further, there is a severe shortage of teachers of the deaf to serve these students. Although there has been a significant increase in the number of DHH students in US schools—an increase of 12,461 between the 1990–91 school year and the 1999–2000 school year—the number of teachers being prepared to teach these students has remained virtually the same. There were 791 deaf education teacher graduates during the 1990–91 school year and 788 during the 2001–02 school year (Johnson, 2004). Meanwhile, a significant number of practicing teachers of the deaf leave the field each year. Given the academic risk experienced by deaf students, the lack of qualified deaf education teachers is problematic both practically and legally.

In the absence of teachers of the deaf, or when a regular class placement is deemed appropriate part- or full-time, DHH children may be provided with sign language interpreting services. Students who use the services of sign language interpreters in school often are deprived of access to communication due to inadequate interpreter skills. A recent study showed that approximately 60% of the educational interpreters evaluated had inadequate skills to provide full access. "In general, the study suggests that many deaf and hard-of-hearing students receive interpreting services that will seriously hinder reasonable access to the classroom curriculum and social interaction" (Schick, Williams, & Kupermintz, 2006, p. 3). Parents also report that schools are reluctant to provide assistive listening systems and that, when there is a problem with such systems, such as a dead battery or a malfunction, schools do not have backup systems children can use. All of these barriers can prevent DHH children from reaching their IEP goals and can prevent IDEA from fulfilling its promise.

Remedies are available when a parent believes a child is being denied FAPE or when other IDEA violations are alleged. IDEA sets out procedures to resolve complaints, including procedures related to mediation, due-process hearings, state complaints, and the filing of lawsuits. However, because of the lack of knowledge about IDEA rights, lack of resources to bring complaints, and discomfort about challenging school authority, parents often are reluctant to bring complaints about their child's educational program.

It is likely that future reauthorizations of and regulations for IDEA will continue its movement to support students with disabilities with access and progress in the general curriculum and other features of general education. These also are tenets of ESEA/NCLB.

Elementary and Secondary Education Act/ No Child Left Behind Act

The NCLB is the current authorization of a statute originally passed in 1965, the Elementary and Secondary Education Act (ESEA) (Government Printing Office 2002). ESEA was part of a series of laws passed in the 1960s to assist impoverished families and individuals. Like IDEA, this law has been reauthorized several times, and its scope expanded. For example, in the 1980s and 1990s, school accountability provisions were added. At the time, these provisions applied only to schools that received ESEA funding. The ESEA/NCLB bill that President George W. Bush signed in 2002 went further, and holds all public schools in the country accountable to meet certain standards, regardless of whether a specific school receives ESEA funds.[2] The expanded law was intended to change the culture of education in the United States. At the time of its signing, then Secretary of Education Rod Paige remarked:

> [No Child Left Behind] offers a plan of attack against the persistent and insidious achievement gap between our disadvantaged students and their more affluent peers by linking federal support for education to strong accountability for results. For too long, the federal government has funded programs without even looking at or asking about the results for our children. The time for change has come, and bold legislation such as [No Child Left Behind] that incorporates high standards, annual measurement and accountability, including expanded parental choice, with increased support and flexibility for our state and local governments will help us usher in that change. (Paige, 2002)

The ESEA/NCLB requires states to determine their own performance standards for *Adequate Yearly Progress* (AYP) based on ESEA/NCLB-mandated criteria. Further, ESEA/NCLB requires State Education Agencies (SEAs), Local Education Agencies (LEAs), and schools to ensure that:

- All three entities make AYP based on students achieving specified "proficiency" levels on regular student assessments.
- Classroom teachers in core academic subjects such as reading, math, and science are "highly qualified"; that is, they meet certain criteria regarding licensure, academic degree, and successful completion of a state exam.

- "Scientifically based research" is used to make educational decisions.
- Parents of children in Title I-funded[3] schools that do not make AYP have the choice to transfer their child to another school and, if the school continues not to make AYP, to have their child receive supplemental educational services.
- Reading or language arts and math assessments are administered annually in grades 3 through 8 and at least once in grades 10 through 12.
- Science assessments are administered at least once during grades 3 through 5, 6 through 9, and 10 through 12.

The ESEA/NCLB requires schools, districts, and states to administer assessments that measure what students have been taught. Results of these assessments must be reported as a whole, but also disaggregated and reported by several subgroups: students who are economically disadvantaged, those who are from major racial and ethnic groups, those who have disabilities, and those with limited English proficiency.

The purpose of reporting data in this way is to provide school personnel, parents, and members of the public with information on the performance of all student groups. Under this arrangement, the high performance of students in one category cannot mask low performance of students in another category, as can happen when all results are aggregated. (However, while disaggregating scores in this matter is desirable, it does not shed light on the achievement of DHH students, or any specific category of students within the category of students with disabilities.) Based on these assessments, states, districts, and schools are responsible for ensuring that all student groups make adequate yearly progress.

When ESEA/NCLB was passed, all children were expected to meet the same benchmarks. At that time, there were three ways of taking the state assessments: (1) regular assessment with no accommodations (such as a sign language interpreter, extra time to take the test, assistive technology, and/or other state-approved testing accommodations); (2) regular assessment with accommodations; and (3) alternate assessments for those children for whom the regular assessment, with or without accommodations, was not appropriate. All of these were aligned with grade-level achievement standards and did not permit the use of standards less than those of the grade level of the student being assessed.

In recent years, the United States Department of Education has provided more flexibility in the implementation of ESEA/NCLB. For example, it has issued rules regarding the provision of alternate assessments aligned with alternate achievement standards, which apply to students with severe cognitive disabilities (Government Printing Office, 2003a). These rules require that states, school districts, and schools include children with severe cognitive disabilities in accountability systems, while acknowledging that a different type of assessment may be appropriate for individuals within this population. The rules limit the number of student scores that can be counted as *proficient* using this assessment. Up to 1% of the scores of those students taking these alternate assessments, based on alternate achievement standards, can be counted as proficient. This rule is mindful that some students are appropriately held to a different standard, while ensuring that schools are held accountable for their academic progress.

The Department issued further rules regarding alternate assessments aligned with "modified" achievement standards (Government Printing Office, 2007). Under the 2007 rules, states may use these assessments for those students whose disabilities have precluded them from achieving grade-level proficiency and whose progress is such that, even if significant growth occurs, the IEP team believes a student will not achieve grade-level proficiency within the year covered by the IEP. The student's IEP must include goals that are based on grade-level academic content standards. The rules thus require that modified achievement standards provide access to grade-level curriculum, be aligned with the state's academic content standards for the grade in which the student is enrolled (although the modified achievement standards may reflect reduced breadth or depth of grade-level content), and do not preclude a student from earning a regular high school diploma. This brings the number of ways students can take assessments to five:

1. Regular assessment with no accommodations
2. Regular assessment with accommodations
3. Alternate assessments based on grade level achievement standards
4. Alternate assessments aligned with alternate achievement standards
5. Alternate assessments aligned with modified achievement standards

In 2005, the Department of Education implemented a "growth-based accountability model" pilot program. Growth models give schools credit for student improvement over time by tracking individual student achievement year to year. The purpose of using a growth model is to allow another avenue for states to demonstrate accountability. In this pilot program, states proposed to the Department how they would use growth measures to demonstrate accountability. This program allowed up to 10 states to use this type of accountability measure. The selected states were required to ensure that all students are proficient by 2014, and to set annual goals to ensure that the achievement gap is closing for all groups of students; to set expectations for annual achievement based on meeting grade-level proficiency and not on student background or school characteristics; and to hold schools accountable for student achievement in reading/language arts and mathematics. They also had to ensure that all students in tested grades were included in the assessment and accountability system, holding schools and districts accountable for the performance of each student subgroup. The selected states were required to include all schools and districts and to administer assessments in each of grades 3–8 and in high school for both reading/language arts and mathematics. In addition, they had to ensure that assessments had been operational for more than 1 year, and proposals had to have received approval through the ESEA/NCLB peer review process for the 2005–06 school year.

This assessment system also was required to produce comparable results from grade to grade and year to year, tracking student progress as part of the state data system, and include student participation rates and student achievement on a separate academic indicator in the state accountability system (United States Department of Education, 2005). Growth models allowed states greater flexibility in meeting the goal of proficiency for all students by 2014. In 2008, the Department of Education began allowing all states to use growth models (United States Department of Education, 2008a).

In March 2008, the Department initiated a "Differentiated Accountability" pilot program for situations in which states had not met AYP. This program allows states to vary the intensity and type of educational interventions to match the academic reasons that led to a school's identification as being in need of improvement. Differentiated accountability is designed to assist those states by targeting resources and interventions to those schools most in need of intensive interventions and significant reform. In other words, it allows states to treat schools differently based on whether they missed AYP by a small or a large margin, and it allows states to focus first on the schools most in need.

Differentiated accountability allows states greater autonomy to tailor actions to their specific challenges. To be eligible to participate in this program, states must build their capacity for school reform; take the most significant actions for the lowest-performing schools, including addressing the issue of teacher effectiveness; and use data to determine the method of differentiation and categories of intervention (United States Department of Education, 2008b).

The Department has introduced more flexibility in other aspects of ESEA/NCLB, such as in the areas of students with limited English proficiency and requirements for highly qualified teachers. These changes acknowledge the variation in how and what students learn, the ways they can show what they have learned, and the avenues schools can use to improve, while ensuring that states, districts, and schools support the academic achievement of all of those students. IDEA and ESEA/NCLB work together by ensuring that students with disabilities who require special education and related services receive them and by ensuring that states, districts, and schools provide these children with an opportunity to meet grade-appropriate benchmarks.

Parent advocacy under ESEA/NCLB is somewhat different than it is under IDEA. Children benefit from having involved parents (Luckner & Muir, 2001; Moeller, 2000), and there are many avenues for parents to advocate for their child under both laws. NCLB allows parents to remove their children from Title I schools that do not make AYP and place them in schools that are making AYP. It also allows parents to request supplemental educational services for children in Title I schools that continue to not make AYP. ESEA/NCLB focuses on the performance of individual students, to the extent that those students' performance impacts the scores of the group. Unlike IDEA, however, ESEA/NCLB does not provide parents the right to be involved in the planning of their child's specific educational program. Further, ESEA/NCLB has not established a complaint process similar to that found in IDEA.

When ESEA/NCLB was written, it was designed to combat the "soft bigotry of low expectations" (Bush, 2006) that was said to plague certain subgroups, such as children in poverty and those who are members of racial or ethnic minorities. The purpose of having the same proficiency standards for all groups was to ensure that they all achieved high levels, and that none was disadvantaged by lower expectations on the part of school systems. Although there is some evidence that test scores have risen since 2002 (e.g., Kober, Chudowsky, & Chudowsky,

2008), it has not been proven that the higher scores are a direct result of ESEA/NCLB (p. 2).

ESEA/NCLB was scheduled to be reauthorized in 2008, and both the House of Representatives and the Senate held hearings, received comments, and held meetings and discussions about the law. However, agreement was not achieved on the finer points of the law. Unresolved questions included: Is the goal of proficiency for all students attainable? If not, which students should be held to lower standards? Or, should all students be held to lower standards? Would that not miss the point of ESEA/NCLB? How much testing is enough? Is testing the only way to demonstrate subject matter proficiency? "This is like a jigsaw the size of a football field," Alice Johnson Cain, a key House advisor on educational policy, said. "The edges are done, and we're still filling out the inside" (Hoff, 2008, p. 21).

Section 504 of the Rehabilitation Act

Two other civil rights laws in the United States can provide protection to students with disabilities in the educational setting: Section 504 of the Rehabilitation Act of 1973, and the ADA. Section 504 is intended to eliminate discrimination on the basis of disability in any program or activity receiving federal financial assistance. Public schools are among the entities covered by this law. Section 504 states: "No qualified handicapped person shall, on the basis of handicap, be excluded from participation in, be denied the benefits of, or otherwise be subjected to discrimination under any program or activity which receives Federal financial assistance" (34 C.F.R. § 104.4 (a); Government Printing Office, 2009).

Under Section 504, a person with a disability is defined as someone who has a physical or mental impairment that substantially limits one or more major life activities, has a record of such an impairment, or is regarded as having such an impairment. "Hearing" and "speaking" are considered major life activities for purposes of Section 504 eligibility. Note that this definition differs from the definition of "child with a disability" under IDEA, in which one of the prongs of the definition is a need for special education and related services. In fact, a child with Section 504 rights may not necessarily be eligible for IDEA services. To be eligible for IDEA, a child must have a disability and, because of that disability, require special education and related services. Lacking the need for special education and related services, a child with a disability is not eligible to be served under IDEA. However, a DHH child who does not require special education services, and therefore is not eligible for IDEA services, is likely to be eligible for 504 modifications and accommodations. Typically, children served under this law have a "504 Plan" that outlines the modifications and accommodations that are necessary to allow them nondiscriminatory access to the educational program. Such modifications and accommodations could include sign language interpreters, assistive listening systems, preferential seating, and other means of communication access. These accommodations also could be offered to individuals in the higher education setting, as both private and public colleges and universities receive federal financial assistance.

Like IDEA, Section 504 requires educational entities that receive federal financial assistance to provide a FAPE to students with disabilities who are in elementary and secondary education. Although an IEP is not required, the implementation of an IEP as outlined by IDEA is one way of meeting the FAPE standard. Section 504 outlines the evaluation and placement procedures entities must follow. It includes provisions related to any recipient of federal financial assistance, including employers, health care providers, housing providers, state and local governments, and other entities. However, Section 504 does not provide any funds with which to carry out its requirements. The Office for Civil Rights in the United States Department of Education is responsible for resolving complaints about Section 504 implementation for recipients of financial assistance from that department.

Americans with Disabilities Act

The ADA, passed in 1990, built upon the nondiscrimination provisions of Section 504. Whereas Section 504 applies only to entities that receive federal financial assistance, the ADA also applies to entities that do not receive such funds. The ADA covers employment, state and local government, places of public accommodation, and the establishment of telecommunications relay services (TRS), which facilitate communication between hearing callers who use a traditional voice telephone and deaf callers who use text or video technology.[4] Many entities, including public schools, are covered by both Section 504 and the ADA. Public schools generally receive federal funds, bringing them within the purview of Section 504. Even if they did not receive federal funds, public schools would be covered by the ADA, as they are a function of local government. Similar to Section 504, the state and

local government provision of the ADA, Title II, states "No qualified individual with a disability shall, on the basis of disability, be excluded from participation in or be denied the benefits of the services, programs, or activities of a public entity, or be subjected to discrimination by any public entity" (34 U.S.C. § 35.130).

The ADA definition of disability is in line with that in the Rehabilitation Act: "Disability means, with respect to an individual, a physical or mental impairment that substantially limits one or more of the major life activities of such individual; a record of such an impairment; or being regarded as having such an impairment."[5] The ADA requires entities to provide "effective communication," such as through the use of qualified interpreters or captioning, unless doing so would create an "undue burden" on the entity or "fundamentally alter" the program, service, or activity (Government Printing Office, 1990). The ADA and 504 also cover situations in which a member of the child's family, such as a parent, needs auxiliary aids and services, such as interpreters or captioning, in order to gain access to school programs, such as an IEP meeting or a school-sponsored event.

Students who are eligible for IDEA services normally are covered by the ADA. However, as with Section 504, it is not the case that eligibility for ADA coverage creates eligibility for IDEA. And, unlike Section 504 and IDEA, the ADA does not require entities to provide students with a FAPE.

The federal government does not provide funding for entities to comply with the ADA. Persons who believe an educational institution has discriminated against a person with a disability may file a complaint with the Office for Civil Rights, US Department of Education, or with the United States Department of Justice.

International Progress

Progress is being made internationally to protect the rights of persons with disabilities. The Convention on the Rights of Persons with Disabilities (CRPD) was adopted by the General Assembly of the United Nations on December 13, 2006, and was opened for signature and ratification on March 30, 2007. By November 2008, 130 countries had signed and 34 countries had ratified the Convention (United Nations, 2008). Countries that have ratified the Convention are obligated to enact domestic laws and policies that are in line with the Convention, while at the same time working to overcome customs and practices that discriminate against persons with disabilities.

Some sections of the CRPD apply specifically to children, and others apply specifically to education rights. For example, the CRPD requires signatories to take appropriate measures in support of people with disabilities. Several sections require signatories to take steps specifically for DHH persons. For example, they are to facilitate the learning of sign language and the promotion of the linguistic identity of the deaf community, and to ensure that the education of persons, (in particular children) who are blind, deaf, or deaf-blind is delivered in the most appropriate languages and modes and means of communication for the individual, and in environments that maximize academic and social development. Signatory nations further agree to take appropriate measures to employ teachers who are qualified in sign language, including teachers with disabilities, to train professionals and staff who work at all levels of education. The training must incorporate disability awareness and the use of appropriate modes, means, and formats of communication, educational techniques, and materials (United Nations, 2008).

The recognition of the rights of persons with disabilities by international bodies is not new. In 1993, the General Assembly adopted the Standard Rules on the Equalization of Opportunities for Persons with Disabilities (United Nations General Assembly, 1993). Although not a legally binding document, the Standard Rules represent a strong moral and political commitment of governments to take action to attain equalization of opportunities for persons with disabilities. The rules serve as an instrument for policy making and as a basis for technical and economic cooperation.

In 2006, the Council of Europe Committee of Ministers adopted the Council of Europe Disability Action Plan (Council of Europe, 2006), which recommended that the governments of member states take steps to promote the rights and full participation in society of persons with disabilities. This document serves as a road map for member states to follow when developing and implementing disability policy. Among other things, this plan encourages member states to recognize that people with disabilities may use sign languages, Braille, and alternative means and modes of communication (including advocacy services), and to seek to accommodate these as far as possible in official interaction.

Individual countries have their own laws and policies regarding the rights of persons with disabilities. For example, Central and Eastern Europe/Commonwealth of Independent States and Baltic States have laws in place that protect and advance the rights of people with disabilities (United Nations Children's Fund, 2005). Further, many countries, including Greece (International Disability Rights Monitor, 2007), Germany (International Disability Rights Monitor, 2007), Spain (Spain, 2007), Finland (Constitution of Finland, 731/1999), and New Zealand (New Zealand Sign Language Act, 2006) officially recognize the sign language of the deaf community in their country.

Summary and Conclusions

Despite the social and educational advances resulting from the laws, there is still far to go before DHH children achieve parity with hearing children. Others have written extensively about the academic and societal deficits experienced by many DHH children. Better enforcement of civil rights laws for persons with disabilities would help improve outcomes for these children. For example, when schools do not provide a FAPE to eligible children, as required by IDEA, parents should file complaints with the proper agency. Also, when schools do not provide communication access, as required by Section 504 and the ADA, parents should file complaints. As long as there is no consequence for failure to observe these laws, schools will not have an incentive to do so. Parents, researchers, educators, and advocates must continue to work together to implement and enforce these laws.

Although unanswered questions remain about the best ways to educate DHH children and to help them succeed commensurate with their potential, much is known about what does work. Schools, school districts, and states must put into place research-based systems and approaches that have been shown to be successful. These entities must ensure that proper resources are being allocated to ensure that DHH children receive the education and services they need. We must continue to expect and demand that our schools support higher achievement for our DHH students. For the well-being and future of these children, we cannot accept anything less.

Notes
[1] Although neither the statute nor the regulations define "functional," the United States Department of Education stated that the term generally refers to "skills or activities that are not considered academic or related to a child's academic achievement …'[F]unctional' is often used in the context of routine activities of everyday living" (United States Department of Education, 2006).
[2] While not all schools receive ESEA funds, all states receive ESEA funds.
[3] Title I funding goes to eligible schools serving a high number of students living in poverty.

[4] Employment and TRS issues are not addressed in this chapter.

[5] The ADA Amendments Act of 2008 amends the ADA and the Rehabilitation Act for several purposes. Among other things, it clarifies the definition of "regarded as" to include the case in which the "individual establishes that he or she has been subjected to an action prohibited under the ADA because of an actual or perceived physical or mental impairment whether or not the impairment limits or is perceived to limit a major life activity" (42 U.S.C. § 12102, 29 U.S.C. § 705). It also clarifies that the "determination of whether an impairment substantially limits a major life activity shall be made without regard to the ameliorative effects of mitigating measures, such as… hearing aids and cochlear implants…" (42 U.S.C. § 12102, 29 U.S.C. § 705). These changes are meant to broaden the scope of coverage of the ADA and the Rehabilitation Act.

References

Bush, G.W. (2006, July 20). Speech before the NAACP annual convention. Washington Convention Center, Washington, DC.

Centers for Disease Control and Prevention. (2007). Annual EHDI data. Retrieved September 21, 2009, from http://www.cdc.gov/ncbddd/EHDI/data.htm. Constitution of Finland, 731/1999.

Council of Europe (2006). Council of Europe disability action plan.

Government Printing Office. (1990). Americans with Disabilities Act, 42 U.S.C. §12101*et seq.* Washington, DC.

Government Printing Office. (2002). No Child Left Behind Act, 20 U.S.C. § 6301*et seq.* Washington, DC.

Government Printing Office. (December 9, 2003). *Federal Register*, Vol. 68, pp. 68697–68708.

Government Printing Office. (2009). Nondiscrimination on the Basis of Handicap in Programs or Activities. 34 C.F.R. § 104 *et seq.* Washington, DC.

Government Printing Office. (2004). Individuals with Disabilities Education Act, 20 U.S.C. § 1401*et seq.* Washington, DC.

Government Printing Office. (April 9, 2007). *Federal Register*, Vol. *72*, pp. 17747–17781.

Hoff, D.J. (2008). Key democrats join president in seeking to revive NCLB renewal. *Education Week*, *27*(22), 20–21.

International Disability Rights Monitor (2007). IDRM regional report of Europe, 2007. Chicago.

Johnson, H. (2004). U.S. deaf education teacher preparation programs: A look at the present and a vision for the future. *American Annals of the Deaf*, 149(2), 75–91.

Joint Committee on Infant Hearing. (2007). Year 2007 position statement: Principles and guidelines for early hearing detection and intervention programs. *Pediatrics*, *120*, 898–921.

Kober, N., Chudowsky, N., & Chudowsky, V. (2008). Has student achievement increased since 2002? State test score trends through 2006–07. Washington, DC: Center for Education Policy.

Luckner, J., & Muir, S. (2001). Successful students who are deaf in general education settings. *American Annals of the Deaf*, *146*(5), 435–445.

Marge, D.K., & Marge, M. (Eds.) (2005). *Beyond newborn hearing screening: Meeting the educational and health care needs of infants and young children with hearing loss in America.* Unpublished manuscript. Syracuse, NY: SUNY Upstate Medical University.

Marschark, M., Lang, H.G., & Albertini, J.A. (2002). *Educating deaf students: From research to practice.* New York: Oxford University Press.

Mathematica Policy Research, Inc. (2007). *Evaluation of universal newborn hearing screening and intervention program.* Washington, DC: United States Department of Health and Human Services.

Mehl, A., & Thomson, V. (1998). Newborn hearing screening: The great omission. *Pediatrics*, *101*(1), e4.

Moeller, M.P. (2000). Early Intervention and Language Development in Children Who Are Deaf and Hard of Hearing. *Pediatrics*, *106*(3), e43.

National Association of the Deaf (2002). Position statement: Inclusion. Silver Spring, MD: Author.

National Center for Hearing Assessment and Management. (n.d.). *Universal newborn hearing screening fact sheet.* Logan, UT: Author.

National Center for Hearing Assessment and Management. (n.d.b). *Implementing universal newborn hearing screening programs.* Logan, UT: Author.

New Zealand. (April 10, 2006). Sign Language Act 2006, No. 18.

Paige, R. (2002). *Statement on the signing of H.R. 1, the No Child Left Behind Act.* Washington, DC: United States Department of Education.

Sass-Lehrer, M. (2002). Early beginnings for families with deaf and hard of hearing children: myths and facts of early intervention and guidelines for effective services. Retrieved August 27, 2008 from http://clerccenter.gallaudet.edu/KidsWorld DeafNet/e-docs/EI/intro.html#how

Schick, B., Williams, K., & Kupermintz, H. (2006). Look who's being left behind: Educational interpreters and access to education for deaf and hard-of-hearing students. *Journal of Deaf Studies and Deaf Education*, *11*(1), 3–20.

Spain. Law 27/2007. (October 23–24, 2007). Official State Bulletin no. 255 from October 24, 2007.

Stredler-Brown, A., & Arehart, K. (2000). Universal newborn hearing screening: Impact on early intervention services. *The Volta Review*, *100*(5), 85–117.

United Nations. (2008). Rights and dignity of persons with disabilities. Retrieved August 20, 2008, from http://www.un.org/disabilities/countries.asp?navid=17& pid=166

United Nations Children's Fund. (2005). Children and disability in transition in central and eastern Europe/Commonwealth of Independent States and Baltic States. Retrieved August 20, 2008, from http://www.unicef-irc.org/publications/pdf/ii12_dr_eng.pdf.

United Nations General Assembly. (1993). Standard rules on the equalization of opportunities for persons with disabilities, A/RES/48/96, 85th plenary meeting, 20 December 1993. Retrieved August 22, 2008, from http://www.un.org/documents/ga/res/48/a48r096.htm.

United States Department of Education. (2005). *Growth models: Flexibility and accountability.* Washington, DC: Author.

United States Department of Education. (2006). *Assistance to states for the education of children with disabilities and preschool grants for children with disabilities; final rule.* 71 Fed. Reg. 46540-46845, Vol. 71, No. 156 (August 14, 2006). Washington DC: Author.

United States Department of Education. (2007). *Twenty-seventh annual report to congress on the implementation of the Individuals with Disabilities Education Act, 2005.* Washington, DC: Author.

United States Department of Education. (2008a). *Growth models: ensuring grade-level proficiency for all students by 2014.* Washington, DC: Author.

United States Department of Education. (2008b). *Differentiated accountability: a more nuanced system to better target resources.* Washington, DC: Author.

chapter 4

Preparing Teachers of Students
Who Are Deaf or Hard of Hearing

John Luckner

Abstract

Well-qualified teachers are critical to the success of students who are deaf or hard of hearing. This chapter focuses on the joys of teaching, as well as on the challenges of preparing teacher candidates to provide appropriate services to the heterogeneous population of students currently in our schools. In addition, recommendations are presented including the need to look beyond the issues of communication and placement, the increased use of formative and standardized data, and a greater attention to developing programs of study that help students leaving high school develop the ability to reach their maximum potential and lead fulfilling adult lives.

Keywords: teaching, teacher preparation, teacher training, preservice teachers, teacher qualifications

Education is considered a fundamental human right and an indispensable means of realizing other human rights (Office of the United Nations High Commissioner for Human Rights, 1966). Education also shapes the personal growth and life chances of individuals. Educational attainment has proven to be one of the most important determiners of individuals' employment, income, health status, and housing, as well as a means to bring greater prosperity to the community and nation (Graham, 2005; Levin, Belfield, Muenning, & Rouse, 2007).

An important condition for the provision of a good education is the availability of well-qualified teachers. Research in general education (e.g., Darling-Hammond, 2000; Sanders & Rivers, 1996; Stronge & Tucker, 2000; Wayne & Youngs, 2003) indicates that teacher effectiveness is a strong determinant of student achievement. This point is illustrated by Kozleski, Mainzer, and Deshler (2000), who wrote, "Whether in special or general education, there is growing evidence that the single most important school influence in a student's education is a well-prepared, caring, and qualified teacher" (p. 1).

Teaching is considered by many (e.g., Darling-Hammond, 1997; Dozier, 1997; Sanders & Rivers, 1996) to be one of society's most important occupations, because of the potential cumulative and enduring effects it has on students, and because it is dedicated to making the world a better place for future generations. It is also a very rewarding profession for a variety of reasons. Luckner and Rudolph (2009) highlighted four often-reported satisfying aspects of the job. First, teachers regularly have opportunities to interact with students who exhibit liveliness, curiosity, freshness, openness, spirit, and independence. Second, they have multiple avenues for being creative through the lessons they develop, the discussions they facilitate, and the projects they often co-create with students. Third, in order to be effective, they are expected to participate in ongoing professional development and to share that knowledge with students. And fourth, they experience the satisfaction of being a part of a team that works together to provide services for students and families.

Yet, like all professions, teaching presents challenges as well as a unique set of pressures. Research (e.g.,

Billingsley, 2005; Greenberg, 1984) as well as anecdotal reports have consistently documented general educators' and general special educators' concerns about discipline, large class or caseload sizes, excessive paperwork, diminishing resources, and unmotivated students. In addition, teachers are currently expected to compensate for the shifts in society and families that affect children (Senge, Cambron-McCabe, Lucas, Smith, Dutton, & Kleiner, 2000). Teachers are also required to comply with legal mandates, respond to public demands and criticism, and teach complex content to a high level of mastery (Reeves, 2000). At the same time, the student population is becoming more diverse across a host of variables such as linguistic, cultural, and socio-economic factors (US Bureau of Census, 2007).

Teaching students who are deaf or hard of hearing, as in the larger fields of general education and special education, is essential, satisfying, and demanding. Research reported by Luckner and Hanks (2003) involving 610 teachers of students who are deaf or hard of hearing from across the United States indicated that they felt extremely positive about their job—expressing satisfaction in 51 out of a possible 59 areas. In addition, on the item asking about their opinion of the "Job as a whole," almost 91% reported that they were pleased with their job. The aspects of the job they enjoyed the most were related to the colleagues they worked with, the importance of the work they did, developing and delivering lessons, explaining vocabulary and concepts, and the sense of job security they felt. The aspects of the job they were least satisfied with were the amount of paperwork, state assessment tests, the lack of family involvement, and the shortage of time for nonteaching responsibilities.

Teacher Preparation

An important condition for the provision of well-qualified teachers is graduation from a quality teacher preparation program. The goal of teacher preparation programs is to facilitate the development of the appropriate attitudes, knowledge, and skills needed by teachers to successfully educate a diverse population of students, as well as to collaborate with professionals, families, and community members. Research in general education (e.g., Darling-Hammond, Holtzman, Gatlin, & Heilig, 2005; Goldhaber & Brewer, 2000; Wilson, Floden, & Ferrini-Mundy, 2001) and special education (e.g., Nougaret, Scruggs, & Mastropieri, 2005) has consistently demonstrated that teachers who attend teacher education preparation programs and become

licensed teachers are more successful at promoting student achievement than individuals who do not attend teacher preparation programs. Similar research in the field of deaf education has yet to be undertaken.

Although disagreements exist about what it means for teachers to be well qualified and what it takes to prepare teachers appropriately, over the course of the past two decades, the general education teaching profession in the United States has begun to organize the knowledge base for professional practice and standards for practitioners. The National Academy of Education (2005) suggests that the common practices of effective teachers draw on three general areas of knowledge that beginning teachers must acquire in order to be successful with students. They include:

1. *Knowledge of learners and their development:* Learning, human development, and language.

2. *Knowledge of subject matter and curriculum goals:* educational goals and purposes for skills, content, and subject matter.

3. *Knowledge of teaching:* Teaching subject matter, teaching diverse learners, assessment, and classroom management.

The importance of these areas of knowledge and skill and their application to teaching students who are deaf or hard of hearing is discussed in greater detail subsequently in this chapter.

Preparation of Teachers of Students Who Are Deaf or Hard of Hearing

Teaching students who are deaf or hard of hearing, as well as preparing teachers of students who are deaf or hard of hearing are challenging undertakings for a variety of reasons. First, hearing loss is a low-incidence disability. In the United States, the student population comprises only .13% (1.3 in 1,000) of the estimated school-age population of students (US Department of Education, 2007). Because of this, most parents, general educators, administrators, or hearing students have never come into contact with a person who is deaf or hard of hearing. Given this general lack of awareness of the needs of persons with hearing loss, many children are not provided accessible language models during their early years and, as a result, they begin formal schooling with impoverished language and communication skills, as well as restricted conceptual knowledge (Marschark & Wauters, 2008; Mayberry, Locke, & Kazmi, 2002).

The lack of language skills and vocabulary and a limited knowledge base hinders students' academic progress. Concomitantly, research on early literacy with hearing children indicates that language skills are central to early and long-term literacy success (e.g., Biemiller, 1999). Yet, many children who are deaf or hard of hearing begin formal schooling with little fluency in either a spoken or signed language or an awareness of print and literacy concepts (Marschark & Harris, 1996). Reading and writing are considered secondary forms of expression, highly dependent on a primary language system, such as speech or sign as a foundation for development. Unlike their hearing peers who learn to read and write in a language they already know, many students who are deaf or hard of hearing learn to read and write while simultaneously learning their first language.

Educational difficulties are compounded by the fact that many students also have an educationally significant disability in addition to a hearing loss (i.e., 25%–33% of the school-age population) (Holden-Pitt & Diaz, 1998). The two most frequently reported additional disabilities are attention-deficit hyperactivity disorder (ADHD) and learning disabilities (Blackorby & Knokey, 2006). The presence of a disability in addition to a hearing loss does not merely add to the complexity of providing appropriate educational services; it compounds them exponentially, making their special needs qualitatively different. This interaction can and often does result in varying degrees of impairment across several domains (e.g., communication, cognition, affective, social, behavioral, and physical) in which optimal levels of functioning are required for adequate adaptation and independent living (Jones, Jones, & Ewing, 2006; Luckner & Carter, 2001).

Another complication results from the variability of degree of hearing loss within the population. Although the field is often referred to as "deaf education," only a small percentage of the population is actually deaf as a result of audiometric assessment. Approximately 9% of the students receiving special education services for a hearing loss in the United States have a severe or profound loss (i.e., greater than 71 decibels) (Blanchfield, Feldman, & Dunbar, 2001). The remainder of the students served have moderate, mild, mixed, fluctuating, or unilateral hearing losses.

The multiple modes of communication used and the utilization of diverse forms of technology add an additional layer of complexity. Although most hearing students rely on speech to communicate with others, students who are deaf or hard of hearing use a range of communication modes (i.e., spoken English, American Sign Language, contact signing/Pidgin Sign English, Signing Exact English, cued speech) and assistive technologies, such as hearing aids, cochlear implants, frequency modulation (FM) systems, or communication boards when communicating with others (Blackorby & Knokey, 2006). It is difficult for teachers to be knowledgeable and skilled in using each of these communication modes and comfortable with the diverse forms of technology.

Determining and establishing the most appropriate educational setting or environment for each student who is deaf or hard of hearing presents another series of difficult decisions that must be made. Students with a hearing loss receive educational services in a variety of educational settings and through several different service delivery models. Examples include a general education classroom with pull-out services from a teacher of the deaf, a general education classroom with interpreter and/or note-taker services, a general education classroom with part of the day in a resource room, or a self-contained classroom for students who are deaf or hard of hearing in a general education school. Additional options include a general education classroom that is co-taught by a general education teacher and a teacher of students who are deaf or hard of hearing, and a special day or residential school program for students who are deaf or hard of hearing.

The process of licensing teachers of students who are deaf or hard of hearing and the diverse roles they are expected to undertake also adds to the challenges of properly preparing teachers. In many places, teachers of students who are deaf or hard of hearing receive a teaching license and/or certification that allows them to work with children and youth ranging in ages from 0 to 21 years. Consequently, in the same day, a teacher may work with a preschool student on counting and a high school student getting ready to transition to the world of work. In addition, many teachers become home interventionists, in which their primary responsibility is to work with the families of children who have a hearing loss, in order to help family members make appropriate adjustments in their routines, so that babies feel loved and have access to the communication of the home. Still other teachers consult with general education teachers and administrators, so that suitable accommodations and modifications in the curriculum and the social ecology of the school and classroom are available for students with a hearing loss.

Additional responsibilities that often become part of the job for teachers of students who are deaf or hard of hearing include conducting assessments, tutoring, providing in-service training, supervising and evaluating paraprofessionals and interpreters, monitoring and repairing auditory training equipment, adapting general education materials, teaching sign language, organizing parent–teacher conferences, working with community agencies, and attending multidisciplinary team meetings. In addition, they are often required to teach a wide variety of content, some of which they did not receive specific training for during their teacher preparation program. Examples include sign language, speech and spoken language, reading, auditory training, content subjects, social/emotional skills, daily living skills, occupational skills, deaf studies, and self-advocacy.

Cultural identity is another topic that teachers of students who are deaf or hard of hearing need to understand. Although the ethnic distribution of the population of students who are deaf or hard of hearing mirrors that of the general school-aged population (Blackorby & Knokey, 2006), the cultural identity of individuals with a hearing loss often includes an additional layer with regard to how individuals perceive themselves. That is, the student population varies across a host of factors such as whether they consider themselves deaf, hearing, or hard of hearing, and how those perceptions interact with other aspects such as race, ethnicity, linguistics, and religion.

Finally, in this era of increased educational standards and accountability, an expectation exists that education policies and practices should be guided by scientifically based research or what has come to be referred to as *evidence-based practices* (EBP). The EBP orientation seeks to improve the quality of services provided to students by shifting to a culture in which judgments guided by data that can be inspected by a broad audience are valued over the opinions of individual experts (Carnine, 2000). Unfortunately, the field of deaf education has a lack of research to establish EBP and to provide guidance to teachers and teacher trainers (Easterbrooks & Stephenson, 2006; Luckner, 2006a; Schirmer & McGough, 2005). As a result, practices in the field of deaf education are often based on research that has been demonstrated to be effective in general special education and general education, or is based on opinion or tradition.

Clearly, the preparation of teachers who are able to establish appropriate educational programs for students who are deaf or hard of hearing is a complex task, requiring the sorting out of multiple factors and collaboration across a variety of stakeholders and service providers. To help guide teacher preparation programs, many countries have developed a set of professional standards for preservice teachers of students who are deaf or hard of hearing. For example, in the United States, the Council for Exceptional Children and the Council on Education of the Deaf developed a set of 46 competency statements, which were divided across 10 standards (Easterbrooks, 2008). Australia established 73 competency statements, divided into four categories (http://www.aatd.org.au). The United Kingdom identified 116 competency statements, divided into three categories, which were then subdivided into 24 subcategories (http://www.tda.gov.uk/upload/resources/pdf/m/mq_hearing_impairment.pdf). Canada divided the standards into 12 core components, and two supportive components, which were further broken down into 47 topical areas (M.A. Bibby, personal communication, September 12, 2008). An examination of the competencies of the four countries indicates many similarities. Although the formats used to present the knowledge and skill statements vary, and the specific wording used differs, each country includes competencies related to language and communication, audiology, speech, sign, curriculum and instruction, assessment, and consultation.

Additional Issues Affecting the Preparation of Teachers of Students Who Are Deaf or Hard of Hearing

SHORTAGE OF TEACHERS

In the United States, there has been a persistent nationwide shortage of teachers of students who are deaf or hard of hearing. The American Association for Employment in Education (AAEE) publishes an annual report on the supply and demand for new teachers. They reported a "considerable teacher shortage" (the highest category of demand) at the national level, and also identified the western, Rocky Mountain, southeast, and middle Atlantic states as having the most pronounced shortages (American Association for Employment in Education [AAEE], 2007). An examination of data reported by AAEE (2000), Moody and Christoff (1993), and Piercy and Bowen (1993) indicates that the field of deaf education has made limited inroads over the course of the past 15 years in recruiting a sufficient number of preservice teachers who complete teacher preparation programs and go on to educate the student population.

As noted earlier, research in general education and special education has consistently demonstrated that individuals who enroll in formal preservice preparation programs are more likely to be effective than those who do not have such training. Unlicensed teachers frequently report that they lack knowledge of the curriculum, teaching strategies, and behavior management. They often experience difficulty working with licensed veteran teachers because they are perceived as not adequately meeting the needs of the students they teach (Darling-Hammond, 2006). Although there are no data on the number of unlicensed teachers working with students who are deaf or hard of hearing and no research examining the effectiveness of unlicensed teachers in deaf education, it may be appropriate to assume that receiving services from an unlicensed professional in any occupation is undesirable.

SHORTAGE OF TEACHER
PREPARATION PROGRAMS

One of the possible reasons for the shortage of teachers of students who are deaf or hard of hearing is the lack of teacher preparation programs. In the United States, currently 66 institutions of higher education prepare teachers of students who are deaf or hard of hearing ("Programs for Training Teachers," 2008). The programs are not geographically evenly distributed. They are located in 34 states and one in the District of Columbia, which indicates that 16 states have no program for preparing the teachers to work with the students who are deaf or hard of hearing in that state. Adding to the problem is the fact that each state has different licensing procedures and requirements, and formal agreements of reciprocity about teacher licensing from state-to-state do not exist. It appears that similar issues may exist in Canada, which has only three deaf education teacher preparation programs for the entire country (Mayer, Akamatsu, Jamieson, Leblanc, & Bibby, 2009); Australia, which also has only three deaf education teacher preparation programs (Winn, 2007); and the United Kingdom, which has seven deaf education teacher preparation programs (http://www. batod.org.uk/index.php?id=%2Farticles%2Fteach ing%2Fteachingde).

Recommendations for Teacher Preparation Programs
Teacher Education Programs Need to Reconceptualize the Field of Deaf Education

The field of deaf education is undergoing significant changes. The factors discussed earlier—the success of newborn hearing screening and early intervention (Moeller, 2000; Yoshinaga-Itano, 2003), the increasing numbers of children receiving cochlear implants (Leigh, 2008), the improvement in hearing aid technology (Bess & Humes, 2008), and the realization that "most deaf and hard of hearing students have the same learning potential as their hearing peers, spend part or all of their school day in general education classes, and will have to compete with their hearing peers for employment opportunities" (Johnson, 2004, p. 85)—are examples of the types of transformations that are occurring. As a result of these changes, Luckner (2008) recently conceptualized the field of deaf education as needing to be a composite of general education, special education, and communication adaptations and curriculum additions.

From this perspective, teachers of students who are deaf or hard of hearing need to be well-versed in general education, which includes the educational standards, the content that needs to be taught, diverse models of pedagogy, and the assessment of learning. Specific special education knowledge and skills needed include an understanding of laws, legislation, differentiated instruction, and specialized curriculum, as well as knowing how to collaborate and consult. In addition, teachers must be able to make accommodations and modifications to the general education program, so that students have access to academic and social learning experiences, strategy instruction, self-advocacy instruction, community-based instruction, supported employment, or life skills training (e.g., money management, community awareness, job-related interpersonal skills, health-related skills).

Hearing loss–related issues include communication as well as the specialized content and services that may be needed by students who are deaf or hard of hearing. Communication adaptations (e.g., FM system, American Sign Language, sign systems, cued speech, interpreter, note-taker, and captioning) need to be implemented, so that students have access to the learning and social environment. Curriculum additions will vary depending on the student's academic, social, and emotional needs, as well as on the preferred method of communication (e.g., language development, deaf studies, speech training, auditory training, counseling, tutoring, and transition planning). Of equal importance is teachers' ability to problem solve, collaborate, and consult with other professionals and families, and to advocate for appropriate services for students who are deaf or hard of hearing and their families.

Positions Offered to Graduates After Completing Their Preparation Program

Currently, in many countries, the majority of students who are deaf are being educated in general education settings alongside their hearing peers. As a result, it has been reported that most students with a hearing loss receive special education services from an itinerant teacher of students who are deaf or hard of hearing in the United States (Miller, 2000), Canada (Akamatsu, Mayer, & Hardy-Braz, 2008), Australia (Leigh, 2008), and the United Kingdom (Powers, 2008). Yet, as placement trends for students who are deaf or hard of hearing and the job responsibilities of teachers have changed, an examination of the professional competencies for teachers noted earlier indicates that only minor modifications in the professional standards for licensed teachers of students who are deaf or hard of hearing have occurred in the past 25 years. Unfortunately, most teacher preparation programs continue to train preservice teachers to work in self-contained classrooms, even though the majority of their graduates will be offered positions as an itinerant teacher.

Many writers and researchers (e.g., Bullard, 2003; Hyde & Power, 2004; Luckner & Miller, 1994; Power & Hyde, 2003; Reed, 2003; Yarger & Luckner, 1999) have reported that itinerant teaching is very different from working as a self-contained classroom teacher. Briefly, the differences include: (a) the percentage of time spent collaborating and consulting with professionals and family members; (b) the amount of time spent directly serving students; (c) the range of ages and the variety of communication modes used by students; (d) the content, procedures and strategies they teach students; (e) the locations where they teach; (f) the required scheduling and organizational skills; and (g) the degree of supervision, independence, and isolation that exists.

Luckner and Howell (2002) surveyed 25 itinerant teachers to identify the specialized knowledge and skills that preservice teachers should acquire during their preparation program related to itinerant teaching. All of the respondents were licensed to teach students who are deaf or hard of hearing, and they had an average of 19 years teaching experience, with an average of almost 14 years experience as an itinerant teacher. The most important coursework and experiences needed to prepare future itinerant teachers, as identified by the sample of veteran itinerant teachers, are provided in Table 4.1.

Although the itinerant approach has been used for decades, a paucity of research about this service delivery model still exists. Future research should be

Table 4.1   Most important coursework and experiences needed to prepare future itinerant teachers

1. Interpersonal skills training
2. Student teaching experience as an itinerant
3. Working with students who are deaf with additional disabilities
4. Troubleshooting hearing aids and FM systems
5. Consultation models and methods
6. Organizational skills including scheduling and time management
7. Reading and language instruction
8. The general education curriculum and educational standards
9. Working with students who are hard of hearing
10. Promoting social-emotional development
11. Working with non-English-speaking students and families
12. The law and the IEP process
13. Cochlear implants
14. Helping students to understand their hearing loss and develop self-advocacy skills

undertaken that examines (a) the optimum size of case loads, (b) how to determine the number of hours of direct service to provide students, (c) where direct services should be provided—in the general education classroom or in a pull-out setting, (d) how best to work with families, (e) the use of technology and/or paralegal services to expedite paperwork, and (f) how best to provide administrative and peer support for itinerant teachers (Hyde & Power, 2004; Luckner & Howell, 2002).

Positive adult-to-adult relationships (e.g., a teacher of students who are deaf or hard of hearing and a general education teacher) are critical for being a successful itinerant teacher. Similarly, the ability to collaborate adult-to-adult with families of children who are deaf or hard of hearing while providing early childhood services is also extremely important. Professional and family collaboration is essential because families are the most important constant in the child's life. The home is also the richest environment for social, emotional, cognitive, and physical development. Furthermore, a high correlation exists between family involvement and school success (Esler, Godber, & Christenson, 2002; Hallau, 2002; Henderson & Berla, 1994). In addition, it is through these partnerships that family members learn to communicate with the child with a hearing loss in a manner that is responsive to the child's verbal and nonverbal behavior (Calderon, 2000; Moeller, 2000; Spencer, 2001). They also learn how to build conversations, use play, develop concepts, manage behavior, and read stories (Moeller, Schick & Williams, 1992).

An expanding body of research indicates that a child with a hearing loss has the best chances of achieving proficiency in communication, language, and literacy as a result of early identification and enrollment in an early education program (e.g., Yoshinaga-Itano & Apuzzo, 1998). Consequently, it is necessary that preservice teachers acquire the essential interpersonal skills needed to communicate with families, so that they are able to enhance families' strengths and support their priorities while providing developmentally appropriate practices (Sass-Lehrer & Bodner- Johnson, 2003). Concomitantly, teachers should develop the knowledge and skills to work with newborn babies and with children up to 3 years of age. Through a collaborative process with national experts, practicing professionals, family members, and training professionals, Compton, Niemeyer, and Shroyer (2006) developed a set of standards for professionals serving families with infants and toddlers who are deaf or hard of hearing. The topical areas are relationships with families, infant development, communication, teaming and service, assessment, technology, legislation, and ethics/professionalism. Each topical area includes a list of specific standards.

Preservice teachers should also acquire adult-to-adult consultation and collaboration skills to allow them to work as members of multidisciplinary teams to effectively develop and implement educational programs for students who are deaf or hard of hearing and have additional disabilities (Jones, Jones, & Ewing, 2006). As previously noted, it has been consistently reported that approximately one-third of the students whom teachers work with have at least one additional educationally significant disability (e.g., Holden-Pitt & Diaz, 1998; Karchmer & Allen, 1999). Luckner and Carter (2001) identified 67 specific competencies needed for working with this diverse population of students. The highest rated competencies focused on modifying instructional materials and methods, strategy instruction, multisensory authentic experiences, behavior management, and collaboration with other professionals and families.

Reconceptualize Service Delivery Options
The many options that are now available in programming for students who are deaf or hard of hearing require that their teachers be knowledgeable about each alternative. For far too long, the field of

deaf education has focused on the search for the best communication system and the most appropriate placement, with limited emphasis on curriculum issues or establishing effective learning environments (Johnson, 2004). Unfortunately, these actions have resulted in far too many students leaving school not adequately prepared for postsecondary training or the world of work (Bullis, Bull, Johnson, & Peters, 1995; Luckner, 2002; Macleod-Gallinger, 1992).

As noted by Stewart (2006), "There is more to good teaching than just the way a teacher communicates" (p. 207). Yet, ongoing disagreements about the optimum way to communicate with students who are deaf or hard of hearing have diverted attention from the important matters of what is taught—content, and how it is taught—methods. In addition, as explained by Hauser and Marschark (2008) "Our convenient division between individuals who use spoken language and those who use sign language is largely a fiction. Regardless of the hearing status of their parents, their hearing thresholds, and their educational placements, most deaf students are exposed to both language modalities. Hard-of-hearing students are in a similar situation" (p. 450).

Placement, where students receive educational services, has also been an issue that has generated continuing debate. Many professionals have expressed concern that the language, communication, and social needs of students who are deaf or hard of hearing cannot be met in a public school environment (e.g., Cohen, 1994; Hawkins, Harvey, & Cohen, 1994; Innes, 1994). However, to date, there has been no research to support the assertion that placement in and of itself is an important factor. In contrast, in a study comparing the educational consequences of different placements, Stinson and Kluwin (2003) reported, "placement per se accounts for less than 5% of the differences in achievement" (p. 57). Rather, it can be argued that effective teaching—curriculum, instruction, assessment, classroom organization, and management—are the key components of the educational process for all students.

Recent research reported by Howell (2008) highlights this point specifically for students who are deaf or hard of hearing. Howell observed 31 teachers of students who are deaf or hard of hearing and followed 154 students with hearing losses being served in different educational settings for a period of 3 years to examine the relationship between teacher qualifications, teacher behaviors, and students' achievement. At the end of the 3-year period she reported (a) no difference in student achievement based on student demographics, (b) no difference in student achievement based on teacher demographics, but (c) teacher activity level and teacher time on task explained 68% of the variance in students' gains. That is, teachers' ability to establish learning environments in which students were actively, successfully, and productively engaged in learning was the best predictor of educational success. Comparable results regarding the importance of effective teaching were reported by Marschark, Sapere, Convertino, and Pelz (2008) who noted that students learned the material best from excellent teachers, independent of the communication mode used (e.g., teachers signed for themselves, used an interpreter, used simultaneous communication, or used ASL without voice accompaniment) and independent of whether the teacher was deaf or hearing.

Hauser and Marschark (2008) summarized the limitations of current practices and suggested a change in how educators conduct their work when they stated, "Rather than presuming that language in one modality or another or schooling in one kind of program or another is a panacea, it is time to fully understand the cognitive, social, and linguistic functioning of deaf children and adjust our educational placements and practices so as to accommodate their strengths and needs" (p. 450). Consequently, it may be an appropriate time for the field of deaf education to embrace a *response to intervention* (RTI) perspective, which is being implemented in many school districts in the United States. As described by the National Center on Response to Intervention (n.d.), RTI is an assessment and intervention process for systematically monitoring student progress and making decisions about the need of instructional modifications or increasing the intensity of services using progress monitoring data. Within the RTI model, school personnel conduct formative assessments—measurement of student learning that provides information used to adapt teaching and learning to meet student needs while they are happening. Formative assessments take into consideration students' learning rate and level of performance and compare them to expected performances (either criterion- or norm-referenced) that inform both teachers and students about student understanding at a point when timely adjustments can be made, rather than waiting for the end of the unit test or the annual standardized tests. These adjustments help to ensure that students achieve targeted standards-based learning goals within a set time frame and allow teams of professionals to establish a comprehensive

continuum of supports and services, and to adjust the intensity and nature of the interventions depending on the students' responsiveness. In essence, an RTI approach encourages professionals to make ongoing adjustments to what, how, and where students are taught, rather than using a wait-to-fail model, which allows too much time to pass while students make minimal gains and develop negative attitudes about education and about their abilities as learners. And, most importantly, when students are not making appropriate progress, changes in the educational program are made.

To determine if students who are deaf or hard of hearing are benefiting from the educational program that is being provided for them, preservice teachers need instruction in monitoring students' performance, conducting and analyzing formative assessments, and collaboratively developing educational programs that help students become productive citizens. The National Center on Student Progress Monitoring (n.d.) reports that when educators conduct frequent and ongoing measurement of student knowledge and skills, and examine the data to evaluate instruction that students receive more appropriate instruction, more efficient communication with families and other professionals occurs, and teachers have higher expectations for students.

Because placement is not synonymous with appropriate services, teachers in training need to become skilled at examining the learning environments of students who are deaf or hard of hearing across a variety of factors. Table 4.2 is an example of a questionnaire that can be used to guide the structured observations of students who are deaf or hard of hearing who receive services in general education settings (Luckner, 2006b). Additional instruments such as the *Classroom Participation Questionnaire* (Antia, Sabers, & Stinson, 2007) and the *Functional Assessment of Students Who Are Deaf or Hard of Hearing* (Karchmer & Allen, 1999) should be introduced to help professionals in training learn to examine the interplay between communication and academic and social functioning in the classroom. The most frequently reported standardized tests used by teachers of students who are deaf or hard of hearing should also be introduced to preservice teachers during their preparation program. Luckner and Bowen (2006) identified those tests in the United States as including the *Stanford Achievement Test Series* (Harcourt Assessment, 2004), the *Woodcock-Johnson III Test of Achievement* (Woodcock, McGrew, & Mather, 2000), and the *Brigance Comprehensive Inventory of Basic Skills – Revised* (Brigance, 1999).

Table 4.2 Questions to guide observation of students who are deaf or hard of hearing in general education settings

A. Student behavior and participation.
1. Does the student attend to classroom instruction?
2. What percentage of time is the student on-task?
3. Is the student able to understand and follow directions?
4. Does the student ask questions when he or she does not understand?
5. Does the student seek assistance appropriately?
6. Is the student able to follow the speaker(s) during classroom discussions?
7. Does the student raise his or her hand to answer questions, volunteer additional information, or volunteer for classroom activities and responsibilities?
8. Can the student work independently?
9. Does the student know how to use an educational interpreter?
10. Would/does the student benefit from the services of a note-taker?

B. The teacher's classroom style.
1. Is the student encouraged to participate in discussions or answer questions?
2. Does the teacher periodically check for student comprehension?
3. Does the teacher use visual teaching strategies and visual aids?
4. Does the teacher modify his or her teaching to help students comprehend important concepts and vocabulary?
5. Are the questions and responses of other students being repeating by the teacher or interpreter?
6. Do the classroom teacher and educational interpreter work well together?
7. Does the teacher provide appropriate wait time for student responses?

C. Student and teacher interactions.
1. Is the student treated like he or she is a member of the class?
2. Are there interactions between the student and the teacher?
3. Are the expectations of the teacher appropriate?
4. Is the teacher patient?

D. Student and peer interactions.
1. How do the student and his or her peers communicate with each other?
2. Does the student have friends?
3. Are efforts made to help the student follow social conversations?
4. Is there an effort on the part of the teacher to help the student become accepted by his or her peers?

E. Level, location, and source of speech and noise sources.
1. What are the major noise sources in the room? Can some of them be eliminated?
2. Is the student sitting next to a fan, air conditioner, overhead projector, film projector, heater, an open window or the door (hallway noise), which could cause distractions?
3. What type of acoustics does the classroom have? Do they reflect or absorb sound?

F. The use of an FM auditory trainer.
1. Does the student benefit from an FM auditory trainer?
2. Does the teacher and the student know how to use the unit properly?
3. Does the student inform the teacher when something is wrong or if the teacher is using the unit incorrectly?
4. Is the unit being checked daily to make sure that it is in working order?

From Luckner, J. L. (2006). Providing itinerant services. In D.F. Moores & D.S. Martin (Eds.), *Deaf learners: Developments in curriculum and instruction* (pp. 93–111). Washington, DC: Gallaudet University Press. Reprinted with permission of the publisher.

The use of multiple assessment instruments can help professionals identify the demands and expectations placed upon students, as well as the supports and accommodations that need to be provided for students to succeed. In addition, they can help identify those students who need changes in their program, such as more direct service, less direct service, or an alternate curriculum, as discussed in greater detail subsequently.

Additionally, preservice teachers should become skilled in person-centered planning (Jones, Jones, & Ewing, 2006; O'Brien & Lovett, 1992) and backward planning (Bonds, 2006; Flexer, McMahan, & Baer, 2001; Luckner, 2002). *Person-centered planning* involves conducting a series of meetings with a student, his or her family and friends, and other professionals working with the student to share information about the student and to collaboratively identify positive outcomes for the student, based on the preferences and strengths of the individual student. Input from everyone involved leads to the development of specific goals and objectives, and to the development of strategies for achieving those goals and objectives. Person-centered planning can be structured to focus on one academic year, several years, or on life after completing school.

Backward planning is similar to person-centered planning in that it also involves bringing together the student, family members, friends, and professionals. However, the primary objective with backward planning is to specifically focus on what the student wants to do when he or she completes school. Backward planning begins with the end in mind (i.e., the goal), then asks the student as well as members of the team to identify the actions that must be accomplished between the current date and the date that the goal will be achieved. The identified actions can then be integrated in a timely manner into the Individualized Education Plan (IEP), and each team member's responsibility can be delineated in the IEP. The backward planning process can be used to focus on a variety of postschool goals such as daily living, health, relationships, employment/further education, transportation, finances, leisure, and community participation. The types of questions that can be used for backward planning that draw from the work of Morningstar (1995) and Flexer and Luft (2001) are provided in Table 4.3. Responses from the student to these types of questions and discussion among the individuals who know and care about the student will facilitate the identification of goals for the student. This will allow the team to collectively work backward to

Table 4.3 Questions for backward planning

What age do you want to graduate from school?
What kind of work or education do you hope to see yourself doing after you graduate from high school?
Where do you want to live?
What do you want to do with your free time?
How will you get to work/school and around town?
Who will be your friends?
Are there postsecondary education or specific learning experiences that you want to have?

identify and implement the actions that need to be taken each year prior to graduation for the student to be ready to leave school and to pursue his or her aspirations.

A framework for determining the focus of the curriculum using the results of the formative assessments and standardized assessments, such as those described earlier, and the aspirations of students and their family members, is provided in Figure 4.1. The purpose of this model, which draws from the work of Cessna and Adams (1993), is to make adjustments, if needed, in what is taught, how it is taught, and sometimes where it is taught, based on the current functioning of the student and how that compares to other students. Specifically, the model can be used as a catalyst for discussions about how students are currently functioning, how they compare with same-age peers, and what the focus of their program of study should be.

Using, Integrating, and Sharing Technology

Technology is changing the world. Different forms of communication, information, instructional, assistive, medical, and translation technologies are used daily by many people. Researchers (e.g., CEO Forum on Education and Technology, 2001; Cradler, McNabb, Freeman, & Burchett, 2002; Heafner, 2004) suggest that the effective use of technology does increase K–12 students' motivation, time on task, amount of work completed, self-confidence, interest in content, and skills for critical thinking, research, and organization.

On a fundamental level, preservice teachers should become skilled at using technology to save themselves time and energy (e.g., to develop and store documents such as practice activities, quizzes, tests, lesson plans, and educational goals and objectives), to reinforce skills that have previously been introduced, and to adapt learning activities to meet the needs of specific students. In addition, they should learn how to develop and use graphic organizers to teach content, as well as to promote reading comprehension (Nover & Andrews, 1998). Graphic organizers allow teachers to omit extraneous information while emphasizing important concepts and demonstrating their connection to each other. In addition, the visual representation of information is easier for students to remember than extended text (Bromley, Irwin-DeVitis, & Modlo, 1995; Dye, 2000). Luckner, Bowen, and Carter (2001) reported that graphic organizers could be used to provide an advanced organizer for content, provide assistance for difficult reading passages or concepts, highlight

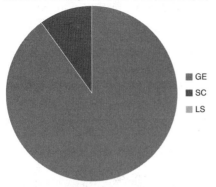

Student Level of Functioning Normal to Mild Disability - Curriculum Focus (age appropriate to 1.5 years delayed)

- GE
- SC
- LS

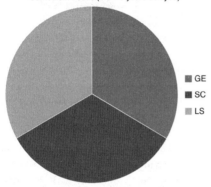

Student Level of Functioning Mild to Severe Disability - Curriculum Focus (1.5 – 3 years delayed)

- GE
- SC
- LS

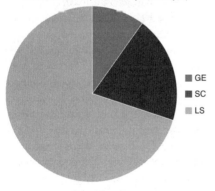

Student Level of Functioning Severe Disability - Curriculum Focus (3 and more years delayed)

- GE
- SC
- LS

Fig. 4.1 A framework for determining individual needs and curriculum focus. Individual needs and curriculum focus: student level of functioning, normal to mild disability – curriculum focus (age appropriate to 1.5 Years delayed) student level of functioning, mild to severe disability – curriculum focus (1.5–3 Years delayed) student level of functioning, severe disability – curriculum focus (3 or more years delayed) GE, General Education Curriculum (e.g., reading, writing, mathematics, science, social studies) with appropriate accommodations and modifications; SC, Specialized Curriculum – Deaf Education and Special Education content, strategies, and curriculum (e.g., language, speech, auditory training, study strategies, self-advocacy, Deaf studies, social skills); LS, Life Skills Curriculum (e.g., self-care, budgeting, planning meals, travel, community safety, using medications, community-based instruction, recreation and leisure, supported employment).

key points, preview reading material, assess prior knowledge, review, and assess. Figure 4.2 is an example of a general graphic organizer of this chapter. More specific detail can be integrated into each section.

As explained by the National Research Council (2000), "All learning involves transfer from previous experiences" (p. 68). Consequently, how quickly students grasp concepts, strategies, and procedures depends largely on their prior direct or vicarious experiences with the topic. Background knowledge builds connections between new and known information (Ormrod, 2008). Preservice teachers should be taught how to use technology to develop background knowledge, because many students who are deaf or hard of hearing demonstrate experiential deficits (Marschark & Wauters, 2008; Stewart & Kluwin, 2001) and impoverished vocabularies (Lederberg & Spencer, 2001) that negatively impact their ability to understand information, concepts, and procedures. As a result of these gaps in their experiential background and vocabulary, some students may lack the schemata and/or language skills needed to follow abstract conversations, comprehend what is happening in a story, understand current events, or access information about the unit of study. Consequently, it is important for educators to incorporate techniques that clarify concepts and makes lessons relevant.

Although the best way to acquire background knowledge is through authentic mediated experiences, technology can be used to help students increase their background knowledge and to develop schema and vocabulary related to content subjects, narrative, and expository texts, as well as for learning strategies and procedures. Technology in the form of visual aids, such as movies, CD-ROMs, and websites with videos, photos, and graphics related to the subject matter can be used to preteach, reteach, or provide multiple examples of concepts or routines (Rose, Meyer, Strangman, & Rappolt, 2002). Interactive experiences that offer opportunities for experimentation and practice can also be set up. Similarly, technology can be used to create hyperlinks to help explain difficult vocabulary, produce glossaries, or to access multiple distributed exercises for morphology, semantics, or syntax practice. Also, given the large percentage of the student population that has an educationally significant additional disability, preservice teachers should become familiar with the principles of Universal Design for Learning (UDL) (US Department of Education, n. d.). The UDL philosophy encourages

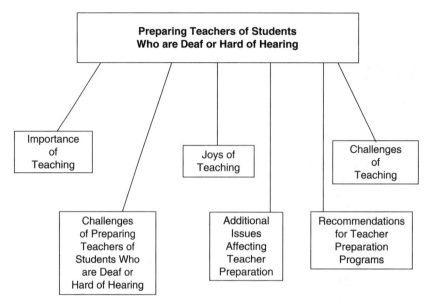

Fig. 4.2 A general graphic organizer of this chapter

educators to use multiple and flexible methods of (a) presenting content, such as using digital books, specialized software, websites, and highlighted handouts; (b) having students demonstrate what they know, such as using online concept mapping software, and graphing to a computer, which collects data regarding students' learning progress; and (c) tapping into students' interests, challenging them appropriately, and motivating them to learn, such as using interactive software, recorded readings or books, and visual graphics.

Preservice teachers also need to be knowledgeable about using technology as an avenue for reducing the isolation of students who are deaf or hard of hearing, for accessing advanced coursework, and for conducting independent studies that build on students' strengths and interests. Educators need to introduce those students who are deaf or hard of hearing they work with to services such as videophones, video relay services, and video remote interpreting, so that they can reach out to communities beyond their homes, schools, and hometowns. Similarly, accessing specialized courses that are not available at the school students attend can occur via technology. In addition, teachers in training will want to become knowledgeable about using WebQuests with the students they teach. WebQuests are inquiry-based activities in which some or all of the information comes from resources on the Internet. Students can undertake WebQuests related to course content to address (a) contemporary problems, such

as issues concerning population, energy, and poverty; (b) use of imagination, such as journeys to distant places like Mars, or inaccessible places like the digestive system; (3) common activities, such as applying for a job or visiting a city; and (4) evaluating history, such as exploring important inventions and discoveries, as well as elections, wars, and laws (Thorsen, 2003).

Finally, increased use of technology and sharing of expertise needs to occur across faculty and researchers working in various deaf education teacher preparation programs and/or research institutes focusing on issues related to the field of deaf education. Most of the teacher preparation programs in the United States have one full-time faculty member in the area of deaf education and hire adjunct professors to teach additional courses (Moores, 2003). To augment their experiential and knowledge base, university faculty will want to draw on the expertise of their colleagues from across the globe. Sharing PowerPoint presentations, recorded lectures, course syllabi, and research summaries are examples of activities that can occur as a result of the World Wide Web. Expanding on projects such as the Deaf Education Virtual Library (http://www.deafed.net/PageText.asp?hdn PageID=189) and the Journal of Deaf Studies and Deaf Education: Author's Corner (http://jdsde-author-corner.wiki.educ.msu.edu/), as well as developing other avenues for sharing would be highly beneficial for deaf education teacher preparation programs.

Summary and Conclusions

Teacher quality is widely recognized by policy-makers, practitioners, and researchers alike to be the most powerful school-related influence on students' academic performance. According to the National Council for the Accreditation of Teacher Education (NCATE) (2005), enrolling in a high-quality teacher preparation programs is advantageous for three reasons. First, teacher preparation works. It helps candidates acquire essential knowledge and develop teaching skills. Second, teacher preparation makes a positive difference in student achievement. And third, teacher preparation increases beginning teacher retention because, while enrolled in the training program, preservice teachers have a wide variety of supervised field experiences that foster the three-stage learning loop of planning, doing, and evaluating before they are required to undertake the daily challenges of the job.

Learning to teach, like acquiring the knowledge and skills to practice any profession, is a complex undertaking. Darling-Hammond (2006) noted three specific challenges. First, new teachers need to understand that teaching is very different from their experience as students. Second, new teachers need to think like a teacher as well as act like a teacher. Third, new teachers need to understand, as well as to respond to, the intense and multifaceted nature of educational settings, juggling multiple academic and social goals, and often being forced to make decisions about moment-to-moment and day-to-day trade-offs.

Learning to teach students who are deaf or hard of hearing includes all of the same challenges as teaching hearing students along with a variety of additional factors, such as those described earlier in the chapter. As a result, Stewart and Kluwin (2001) reported that,

> Deaf students arguably present the most complex challenge for teachers of any group of students in both the general and special education populations. Every corner of their educational process is multidimensional and each dimension has the potential to significantly impact their academic achievement (p. 14).

Yet, like in many aspects of life, greater challenges often yield more satisfying rewards.

This chapter has contended that teacher preparation programs must focus on developing effective teachers; that is, professionals who (a) engage students in active learning, (b) articulate their expectations for high-quality work, (c) provide models of student work that meets those standards, (d) provide constant feedback that helps students improve, (e) design and manage learning environments, (f) work with families to create strong connections between the school and home, and (g) and collaborate with their professional colleagues (National Academy of Education, 2005). It has also been suggested that teacher preparation programs must look beyond the issues of communication and placement. A framework of providing services based on gathering formative and standardized data, obtaining input from the significant individuals in a student's life, and developing a program of study that provides a match between the services and the specific needs of the student was recommended. Finally, the use of technology to bring together students, teachers, and information has been advocated. Given the low-incidence nature of the field of deaf education, it is critical to identify ways to share resources and expertise.

References

Akamatsu, C. T., Mayer, C., Hardy-Braz, S. (2008). Why considerations of verbal aptitude are important in educating deaf and hard-of-hearing students. In M. Marschark & P.C. Hauser (Eds.), *Deaf cognition: Foundations and outcomes* (pp. 131–169). New York: Oxford University Press.

American Association for Employment in Education (2000). *2000 Job search handbook for educators*. Evanston, IL: Author.

American Association for Employment in Education (2007). *2008 Job search handbook for educators*. Evanston, IL: Author.

Antia, S. D., Sabers, D., & Stinson, M. S. (2007). Validity and reliability of the Classroom Participation Questionnaire with deaf and hard of hearing students in public schools. *Journal of Deaf Studies and Deaf Education, 12*, 158–171.

Bess, F. H., & Humes, L. E. (2008). *Audiology: The fundamentals*, 4th edition. Philadelphia: Lippincott Williams & Wilkins.

Biemiller, A. (1999). *Language and reading success*. Cambridge, MA: Brookline Books.

Billingsley, B. S. (2005). *Cultivating and keeping committed special education teachers: What principals and district leaders can do*. Thousand Oaks, CA: Corwin Press.

Blackorby, J., & Knokey, A. M. (2006). *A national profile of students with hearing impairments in elementary and middle school: A special topic report from the Special Education Elementary Longitudinal Study*. Menlo Park, CA: SRI International.

Blanchfield, B., Feldman, J., & Dunbar, J. (2001). The severely to profoundly hearing-impaired population in the United States: Prevalence estimates and demographics. *Journal of American Academy of Audiology, 12*, 183–189.

Bonds, B. G. (2006). School-to-work transitions. In D. F. Moores & D. S. Martin (Eds.), *Deaf learners: Developments in curriculum and instruction* (pp. 145–158). Washington, DC: Gallaudet University Press.

Brigance, A. H. (1999). *Brigance Comprehensive Inventory of Basic Skills – Revised*. North Billerica, MA: Curriculum Associates, Inc.

Bromley, K., Irwin-De Vitis, L., & Modlo, M. (1995). *Graphic organizers: Visual strategies for active learning*. New York: Scholastic Professional Books.

Bullard, C. (2003). *The itinerant teacher's handbook*. Hillsboro, OR: Butte Publications, Inc.

Bullis, M. B., Bull, B., Johnson, B., & Peters, D. (1995). The school-to-community transition experiences of hearing impaired young adults and young adults who are deaf. *The Journal of Special Education, 28*(4), 405–423.

Calderon, R. (2000). Parent involvement in deaf children's education programs as a predictor of child's language, early reading, and social-emotional development. *Journal of Deaf Studies and Deaf Education, 5,* 140 – 155.

Carnine, D. (2000, April). *Why education experts resist effective practices.* Washington, DC: Thomas B. Fordham Foundation.

CEO Forum on Education and Technology. (June, 2001). The CEO Forum school technology and readiness report: Key building blocks for student achievement in the 21st century. Retrieved November 11, 2007, from http://www.ceoforum.org/downloads/report4.pdf.

Cessna, K. K., & Adams, L. (1993). Implications of a needs-based philosophy. In K. K. Cessna (Ed.), *Instructionally differentiated programming: A needs-based approach for students with behavioral disorders* (pp. 7–18). Denver, CO: Colorado Department of Education.

Cohen, O. P. (1994). An administrator's view on inclusion for deaf children. *American Annals of the Deaf, 139*(2), 159–161.

Compton, M. V., Niemeyer, J. A., & Shroyer, E. (2006). *Standards for professionals serving families with infants and toddlers who are deaf/hard of hearing.* Retrieved October 2, 2008 from http://center.uncg.edu/

Cradler, J., McNabb, M., Freeman, M., & Burchett, R. (2002). How does technology influence student learning? *Learning & Leading with Technology, 29*(8), 46–49, 56.

Darling-Hammond, L. (1997). *Doing what matters most: Investing in quality teachers.* New York: National Commission on Teaching & America's Future.

Darling-Hammond, L. (2000). Teacher quality and student achievement: A review of state policy evidence. *Education Policy Analysis Archives, 8*(1). Retrieved September 27, 2007, from http://epaa.asu.edu/epaa/v8n1/

Darling-Hammond, L. (2006). *Powerful teacher education: Lessons from exemplary programs.* San Francisco: Jossey-Bass.

Darling-Hammond, L., Holtzman, D., Gatlin, S., & Helig, J. V. (2005). Does teacher preparation matter? Evidence about teacher certification, teach for America, and teacher effectiveness. *Education Policy Analysis Archives, 13*(42). Retrieved July 15, 2008, from http://epaa.asu.edu/epaa/v13n42/

Dozier, T. (1997). *Statement by Terry Dozier, Special Advisor to the Secretary, U.S. Department of Education before the House Committee on Education and the Workforce Subcommittee on Postsecondary Education, Training, and Lifelong Learning.* Washington, DC: Author.

Dye, G.A., (2000). Graphic organizers to the rescue: Helping students link-and remember-information. *Teaching Exceptional Children, 32*(3), 72–76.

Easterbrooks, S. R. (2008). Knowledge and skills for teachers of individuals who are deaf of hard of hearing: Initial set revalidation. *Communication Disorders Quarterly, 30*(1), 12–36.

Easterbrooks, S. R., & Stephenson, B. (2006). An examination of twenty literacy, science, and mathematics practices used to educate students who are deaf or hard of hearing. *American Annals of the Deaf, 151*(4), 385–397.

Esler, A. N., Godber, Y., & Christenson, S. L. (2002). Best practices in supporting home-school collaboration. In A. Thomas & J. Grimes (Eds.), *Best practices in school psychology: Volume 1* (pp. 389–411). Bethesda, MD: The National Association of School Psychologists.

Flexer, R. W., & Luft, P. (2001). Transition assessment and post-school outcomes. In R. W. Flexer, T. J. Simmons, P. Luft, & R. M. Baer (Eds.), *Transition planning for secondary students with disabilities* (pp. 197–226). Upper Saddle River, NJ: Prentice Hall.

Flexer, R. W., McMahon, R. K., & Baer, R. (2001). Transition models and best practices. In R. W. Flexer, T. J. Simmons, P. Luft, & R. M. Baer (Eds.), *Transition planning for secondary students with disabilities* (pp. 38–69). Upper Saddle River, NJ: Prentice Hall.

Goldhaber, D. D., & Brewer, D. J. (2000). Does teacher certification matter? High school certification status and student achievement. *Educational Evaluation and Policy Analysis, 22*(2), 129–145.

Graham, P.A. (2005). *Schooling America: How the public schools meet the nation's changing needs.* New York: Oxford University Press.

Greenberg, S. F. (1984). *Stress and the teaching profession.* Baltimore: Paul H. Brookes Publishing Co.

Hallau, M. (Ed.). (2002). *We are equal partners: Recommended practices for involving families in their child's educational program.* Washington, D.C. Laurent Clerc National Deaf Education Center Gallaudet University.

Harcourt Assessments, Inc. (2004). *Stanford Achievement Test series,* 10th edition. San Antonio, TX: Author.

Hauser, P. C., & Marschark, M. (2008). What we know and what we don't know about cognition and deaf learners. In M. Marschark & P. C. Hauser (Eds.), *Deaf cognition: Foundations and outcomes* (pp. 439–457). New York: Oxford University Press.

Hawkins, L., Harvey, S., & Cohen, J., M. (1994). Parents' position on full inclusion for deaf children. *American Annals of the Deaf, 139*(2), 165–167.

Heafner, T. (2004). Using technology to motivate students to learn social studies. *Contemporary Issues in Technology and Teacher Education* (CITE). Retrieved November 11, 2007, from http://www.citejournal.org/vol4/iss1/socialstudies/article1.cfm

Henderson, A. T., & Berla, N. (1994). *A new generation of evidence: The family is critical to student achievement.* Washington, DC: National Committee for Citizens in Education.

Holden-Pitt, L., & Diaz, J.A. (1998). Thirty years of the annual survey of deaf and hard-of-hearing children and youth: A glance over the decades. *American Annals of the Deaf 142,* 72–76.

Howell, J. J. (2008, April). *Teacher qualities impacting achievement of students who are deaf/hard of hearing.* Paper presented at the Council for Exceptional Children Annual Convention and Expo, Boston, Massachusetts.

Hyde, M., & Power, D. (2004). The personal and professional characteristics and work of itinerant teachers of the deaf and hard of hearing in Australia. *The Volta Review, 104*(2), 51–67.

Innes, J., J. (1994). Full inclusion and the deaf student: A consumer's review of the issue. *American Annals of the Deaf, 139*(2), 152–156.

Johnson, H. A. (2004). U.S. deaf education teacher preparation programs: A look at the present and a vision of for the future. *American Annals of the Deaf, 149*(2), 75–91.

Jones, T. W., Jones, J. K., & Ewing, K. M. (2006). Students with multiple disabilities. In D.F. Moores & D.S. Martin (Eds.), *Deaf learners: Developments in curriculum and instruction.* (pp. 127–143). Washington, DC: Gallaudet University Press.

Karchmer, M.A., & Allen, T.E. (1999). The functional assessment of deaf and hard of hearing students. *American Annals of the Deaf, 144*(2), 68–77.

Kozleski, E., Mainzer, R., & Deshler, D. (2000). *Bright futures for exceptional learners: An agenda to achieve quality conditions for teaching & learning.* ERIC Document Reproduction Service No. ED451668.

Lederberg, A. R., & Spencer, P. E. (2001). Vocabulary development of deaf and hard of hearing children. In M. D. Clark, M. Marschark, & M. Karchmer (Eds.), *Context, cognition, and deafness* (pp. 88–112). Washington, DC: Gallaudet University Press.

Leigh, G. (2008). Changing parameters in deafness and deaf education. In M. Marschark & P.C. Hauser (Eds.), *Deaf cognition: Foundations and outcomes* (pp. 24–51). New York: Oxford University Press.

Levin, H., Belfield, C., Muenning, P., & Rouse, C. (January, 2007). The costs and benefits of an excellent education for all of America's children. Retrieved July 14, 2007, from www.cbcse.org/media/download_gallery/Leeds_Report_Final_Jan2007.pdf

Luckner, J.L. (2002). *Facilitating the transition of students who are deaf or hard of hearing.* Austin, TX: PRO-Ed.

Luckner, J. L. (2006a). Evidence-based practices and students who are deaf. *Communication Disorders Quarterly, 28*(1), 49–52.

Luckner, J.L. (2006b). Providing itinerant services. In D.F. Moores & D.S. Martin (Eds.), *Deaf learners: Developments in curriculum and instruction* (pp. 93–111). Washington, DC: Gallaudet University Press.

Luckner, J. L. (2008). *Communication considerations A- Z: Deaf education.* Retrieved July 14, 2008, from http://www.handsandvoices.org/comcon/articles/deafEd.htm

Luckner, J. L., & Bowen, S. (2006). Assessment practices of professionals serving students who are deaf or hard of hearing: An initial investigation. *American Annals of the Deaf, 151*(4), 410–417.

Luckner, J. L., Bowen, S., & Carter, K. (2001). Visual teaching strategies for students who are deaf or hard of hearing. *Teaching Exceptional Children, 33*(3), 38–44.

Luckner, J. L., & Carter, K. (2001). Essential competencies for teaching students with hearing loss and additional disabilities. *American Annals of the Deaf, 146*(1), 7–15.

Luckner, J. L., & Hanks, J. A. (2003). Job satisfaction: Perceptions of a national sample of teachers of students who are deaf or hard of hearing. *American Annals of the Deaf, 148*(1), 5–17.

Luckner, J. L., & Howell, J. (2002). Suggestions for preparing itinerant teachers: A qualitative analysis. *American Annals of the Deaf, 147*(3), 54–61.

Luckner, J.L., & Miller, K. J. (1994). Itinerant teachers: Responsibilities, perceptions, preparation, and students served. *American Annals of the Deaf, 139*(2), 111–118.

Luckner, J. L., & Rudolph, S. M. (2009). *Teach well, live well: Strategies for success.* Thousand Oaks, CA: Corwin Press.

Macleod-Gallinger, J. (1992). Employment attainments of deaf adults one and ten years after graduation from high school. *Journal of the American Deafness and Rehabilitation Association, 25*(4), 1–10.

Marschark, M., & Harris, M. (1996). Success and failure in learning to read: The special case (?) of deaf children. In C. Cornoldi & J. Oakhill (Eds.), *Reading comprehension difficulties: Processes and intervention* (pp. 279–300). Mahwah, NJ: Lawrence Erlbaum Associates.

Marschark, M., Sapere, P., Convertino, C. M., & Pelz, J. (2008). Learning via direct and mediated instruction by deaf students. *Journal of Deaf Studies and Deaf Education, 13*(4), 546–559.

Marschark, M., & Wauters, L. (2008). Language comprehension and learning by deaf students. In M. Marschark & P.C. Hauser (Eds.), *Deaf cognition: Foundations and outcomes* (pp. 309–350). New York: Oxford University Press.

Mayer, C., Akamatsu, C.T., Jamieson, J., Leblanc, R., & Bibby, M. (2009). Educating deaf and hard of hearing students in Canada. In D. Moores & M. Miller (Eds.), *Deafness around the world: Educational, developmental and social perspectives.* (pp. 284–301). Washington, DC: Gallaudet University Press.

Mayberry, R. I., Locke, E., & Kazmi, H. (2002). Linguistic ability and early language exposure. *Nature, 417*, 38.

Miller, K. (2000). Welcome to the real world: Reflections on teaching and administration. *American Annals of the Deaf, 145*, 404–410.

Moeller, M. P. (2000). Early intervention and language development in children who are deaf and hard of hearing. [Electronic version]. *Pediatrics, 106*(3), e43.

Moeller, M. P., Schick, B., & Williams, K. T. (1992). Sign with me: A family sign program. In B. Schick & M.P. Moeller (Eds.), *The use of sign language in instructional settings: Current concepts and controversies* (pp. 127–142). Omaha, NE: Boys Town National Research Hospital.

Moody, A., & Christoff, D. (1993). *A study of U.S. teacher supply and demand.* Evanston, IL: Association of School, College, and University Staffing.

Moores, D. F. (2003). Teacher preparation. *American Annals of the Deaf, 148*(3), 211–212.

Morningstar, M.E. (1995). *Planning for the future: A workbook to help young adults with disabilities, their families, and professionals to plan for living, working, and participating in the community.* Topeka: Department of Special Education, University of Kansas.

National Academy of Education. (2005). *A good teacher in every classroom: Preparing the highly qualified teachers our children deserve.* San Francisco: Jossey-Bass.

National Center on Response to Intervention. (n.d.). What is RTI? Retrieved August 13, 2008, from http://www.rti4success.org/

National Center on Student Progress Monitoring. (n.d.). What are the benefits of progress monitoring? Retrieved February 1, 2007, from http://www.studentprogress.org/

National Council for the Accreditation of Teacher Education. (August, 2005). *Research supporting the effectiveness of teacher preparation.* Retrieved July 14, 2008, from http://www.ncate.org/public/summaryData.asp?ch=48

National Research Council (2000). *How people learn: Brain, mind experience, and school.* Washington DC: National Academy Press.

Nougaret, A. A., Scruggs, T. E., & Mastropieri, M. A. (2005). Does teacher education produce better special education teachers? *Exceptional Children, 71*(3), 217–229.

Nover, S. M., & Andrews, J. F. (1998). *Critical pedagogy in deaf education: Bilingual methodology and staff development.* Santa Fe: New Mexico School for the Deaf.

O'Brien, J., & Lovett, H. (1992). *Finding a way toward everyday lives: The contribution of person centered planning.* Harrisburg, PA: Pennsylvania Office of Mental Retardation.

Office of the United Nations High Commissioner for Human Rights. (December 16, 1966). International Covenant on

Economic, Social and Cultural Rights (ICESCR). Retrieved July 12, 2008, from http://www.unhchr.ch/html/menu3/b/a_cescr.htm

Ormrod, J. E. (2008). *Human learning*, 5thedition. Upper Saddle River, NJ: Pearson Education, Inc.

Piercy, S., & Bowen, M. (1993). *Current and projected practices for certification and monitoring of personnel needs in special education*. Normal, IL: Department of Specialized Educational Development, Illinois State University.

Power, D., & Hyde, M. (2003). Itinerant teachers of the deaf and hard of hearing and their students in Australia: Some state comparisons. *International Journal of Disability, Development and Education, 50*(4), 385–401.

Powers, S. (March, 2008). Vital statistics. *British Association of Teachers of the Deaf Magazine*, 44–45.

Programs for Training Teachers. (2008). *American Annals of the Deaf, 153*(2), 203–210.

Reed, S. (2003). Beliefs and practices of itinerant teachers of deaf and hard of hearing children concerning literacy development. *American Annals of the Deaf, 148*(4), 33–343.

Reeves, D.B. (2000). *Accountability in action: A blueprint for learning organizations*. Denver, CO: Center for Performance Assessment.

Rose, D.H., Meyer, A., Strangman, N., & Rappolt, G. (2002). *Teaching every student in the digital age: Universal design for learning*. Alexandria, VA: Association for Supervision and Curriculum Development.

Sanders, W. L., & Rivers, J. C. (1996). *Cumulative and residual effects of teachers on future student academic achievement*. Knoxville: University of Tennessee Value-Added Research and Assessment Center.

Sass-Lehrer, M., & Bodner-Johnson, B. (2003). Early intervention: Current approaches to family-centered programming. In M. Marschark & P. E. Spencer (Eds.), *Oxford handbook of deaf studies, language, and education* (pp. 65–81). New York: Oxford University Press.

Schirmer, B. R., & McGough, S. M. (2005). Teaching reading to children who are deaf: Do the conclusions of the National Reading Panel apply? *Review of Educational Research, 75*(1), 83–117.

Senge, P., Cambron-McCabe, N., Lucas, T., Smith, B., Dutton, J., & Kleiner, A. (2000). *Schools that learn: A fifth discipline fieldbook for educators, parents, and everyone who cares about education*. New York: Doubleday.

Spencer, P.E. (January, 2001). *A good start: Suggestions for visual conversations with deaf and hard of hearing babies and toddlers*. Retrieved June 4, 2003, from http://clerccenter2.gallaudet.edu/KidsWorldDeafNet/e-docs/visual-conversations/

Stewart, D. (2006). Instructional and practical communication: ASL and English-based signing in the classroom. In D. F. Moores & D. S. Martin (Eds.), *Deaf learners: Developments in curriculum and instruction* (pp. 207–220). Washington, DC: Gallaudet University Press.

Stewart, D. A., & Kluwin, T. N. (2001). *Teaching deaf and hard of hearing students: Content, strategies, and curriculum*. Boston: Allyn and Bacon.

Stinson, M. S., & Kluwin, T. (2003). Educational consequences of alternative placements. In M. Marschark & P. E. Spencer (Eds.), *Oxford handbook of deaf studies, language, and education* (pp. 52–64). New York: Oxford University Press.

Stronge, J. H., & Tucker, P. D. (2000). *Teacher evaluation and student achievement*. Washington, DC: National Education Association.

Thorsen, C. (2003). *TechTactics: Instructional models for educational computing*. Boston: Allyn and Bacon.

US Bureau of Census. (2007). *Minority population tops 100 million*. Retrieved October 3, 2007 from http://www.census.gov/Pressrelease/www/releases/archives/population/010048.html

US Department of Education. (n.d.). Tool kit on universal design for learning. Retrieved August 28, 2008, from http://www.osepideasthatwork.org/UDL/index.asp

US Department of Education, Office of Special Education and Rehabilitative Services, Office of Special Education Programs. (2007). *27th annual report to Congress on the implementation of the Individuals with Disabilities Education Act*. Washington, DC: Author.

Wayne, A. J., & Youngs, P. (2003). Teacher characteristics and student achievement gains: A review. *Review of Educational Research, 73*(1), 89–122.

Wilson, S. M., Floden, R. E., & Ferrini-Mundy, J. (2001). *Teacher preparation research: Current knowledge, gaps, and recommendations: A research report prepared for the U.S. Department of Education. Seattle*: Center for the Study of Teaching and Policy.

Winn, S. (2007). Preservice preparation of teachers of the deaf in the twenty-first century: A case study of Griffith University, Australia. *American Annals of the Deaf, 152*(3), 312–319.

Woodcock, R., McGrew, K., & Mather, N. (2000). *Woodcock-Johnson 3: Tests of Achievement*. Chicago: Riverside Press.

Yarger, C.C., & Luckner, J.L. (1999). Itinerant teaching: The inside story. *American Annals of the Deaf, 144*(4), 309–314.

Yoshinago-Itano, C. (2003). Early intervention after universal neonatal hearing screening: Impact on outcomes. *Mental Retardation and Developmental Disabilities Research Reviews, 9*(4), 252–266.

Yoshinago-Itano, C., & Apuzzo, M. (1998). Identification of hearing loss after 18 months of age is not early enough. *American Annals of the Deaf, 143*(5), 380–387.

Effective Instruction for Deaf and Hard-of-Hearing Students: Teaching Strategies, School Settings, and Student Characteristics

Harry Knoors *and* Daan Hermans

Abstract

Answering the question of what constitutes qualitatively good instruction for deaf students entails an analysis of what actually defines quality of instruction in education in general; what, in addition, is needed for effective instruction for deaf students; and, finally, to what extent special and regular schools are able to provide quality instruction to deaf students. This chapter explores these issues: What emerges from this exploration is a picture that is, at best, fragmented. Under specific conditions, it seems possible for deaf students to learn as much as their hearing peers, at least in postsecondary education. Whether these conditions are met frequently and in different educational settings is simply unknown. What we do know is that regular and special schools face different challenges in educating deaf students. Teaching mixed-ability groups (with respect to communication, language, literacy, and cognition) certainly is a challenge to teachers in these settings, and this challenge deserves much more attention in teacher training and coaching, since adaptive instruction seems problematic both in regular and in special education. To increase our knowledge about effective instruction for deaf students in different settings and at different education levels, we need more research and more focused research. Preliminary efforts in this direction are discussed in this chapter.

Keywords: deaf-instruction, special education, mainstream education, mixed ability

Since the 1980s, the education of deaf students has changed considerably. Bilingual programs have been established, incorporating both signed and spoken language (or, in some cases, signed and written language) in the curriculum, in instruction, and in interaction. There has also been a considerable increase in the variety of settings for the education of deaf students, not only in secondary and postsecondary education but also in preschool and primary education. The educational spectrum has been broadened from predominantly residential schools for the deaf (in the 1940s and 1950s) to day-school programs, units attached to regular schools, co-enrollment classes, and individual placement of deaf and hard-of-hearing (DHH) students in regular classes. Improved access to spoken language, introduction of sign language interpreting, and changes in educational policies have all contributed to this growing variation in school settings available for deaf students.

Educational settings and programs may differ with respect to policy, curriculum, and instruction. The question is how characteristics of educational programs and school settings are related to achievement of deaf students. In an overview of the research literature available on this topic, Karchmer and Mitchell (2003) concluded that the connection between program characteristics and academic achievement of deaf students remains largely unclear.

An often-encountered expectation is that the actual school setting, regular or special education, directly influences the achievement of deaf students. However, this is not supported by the available research data. According to Stinson and Kluwin (2003), the unexplained variance in studies into the efficacy of placements of deaf students (in terms of academic achievement) typically ranges from 65% to 80%, with the norm probably being 75%. The impact of placement—the actual school setting—on achievement is limited to approximately 1% of the total variance. Of the total variance, 20% to 25% is accounted for by differences between students, already in existence before they enter school.

The limited influence of school setting on the attainment of deaf students is surprising. One would expect deaf students to progress faster in specialized schools for the deaf, since the idea that deaf students need specialized instruction is one of the core constituting elements of special education. The results reported by Stinson and Kluwin (2003) question to what extent regular and special schools are able to provide conditions for optimal learning of deaf students. Stinson and Kluwin suggest that the quality of instruction should be looked into as an essential part of these conditions: "although it is easy on a theoretical and experiential basis to describe significant process differences among the placement types, seldom have instructional factors (much less quality of instruction) entered into the analysis of between-placement differences. One could easily speculate that much of the 75% of unexplained variance lies there" (p. 58).

Given the fact that only limited empirical research is available into the effectiveness of instruction for deaf students (Easterbrooks & Stephenson, 2006), this chapter raises more questions than it answers; these questions will, however, provide directions for future research.

Effective Education

Schools differ considerably in the extent to which they succeed in creating conditions that enable their pupils to achieve maximum school results. This discovery fueled the effective school movement in the 1970s. The aim of this movement was to study factors in education that influence achievement of students and to encourage schools to (re)structure their educational processes in ways that lead to effective and successful learning. Much research since then has been carried out, leading to various, often overlapping models of educational effectiveness by scholars such as Walberg (1984), Creemers (1994), and Scheerens and Bosker (1997). All models address various factors that influence attainment. These factors are typically grouped at three levels: the level of society (e.g., educational policy, resources, and educational system), school (e.g., educational leadership and pupil grouping principles), and classroom (e.g., teacher factors, student characteristics, and emotional climate).

Models of educational effectiveness are typically static. Teaching and learning, however, are dynamic processes (Creemers & Kyriakides, 2006). Many of the factors listed in empirically based models of educational effectiveness interact in often complex ways. This interaction especially takes place at the level of the classroom. For example, teacher factors, such as instruction style, interact to a considerable extent with student characteristics, such as learning style. Furthermore, the way in which each factor may influence achievement may not be linear, but curvilinear. One widely held belief is that teacher subject knowledge influences the attainment of students. Yet, in most studies only very moderate correlations between these two factors have been found. A possible explanation might be that subject knowledge is necessary to a certain extent to achieve effectiveness of education, but after a certain threshold, it negatively influences student attainment. A similar curvilinear relationship has been established for emotional climate in the classroom and for classroom management.

Models of effective education are almost entirely built upon research in regular education schools. Research into the educational effectiveness of special education is very limited. A noticeable exception is a Dutch study by Van Ambt et al. (2000). Van Ambt's group argued that the lack of research into the effectiveness of special education stems from a lack of *output thinking*. In many cases, the outcomes of special education are defined in terms of the individually attained level of each pupil in terms of cognitive and social emotional attainment. In most cases, common goals that all pupils have to attain are not present. Often, lack of consensus also exists about the content of the curriculum in special education. In many countries, accountability and cost effectiveness also are important aspects of educational policy with respect to special education. This changing context has increased the call for clear and accessible information about the effectiveness of special education. Van Ambt et al., therefore, studied the effectiveness of education in more than 100 schools for special education addressing the needs of children with learning difficulties and cognitive disabilities. They concluded that the differences in educational effectiveness among schools for special education were at least as large as they are in general primary education. These differences among schools were not limited to academic achievement, but also linked to achievement in the social and emotional domains. Unfortunately, no specific variables were identified in this study that were causally related to more or less effective special education.

Effective Instruction in General Education Settings

Learning by students is facilitated through instruction. This instruction may be classroom-based or computer- or web-based. For some educational content, web-based instruction may be at least as effective if not somewhat more effective as classroom-based instruction, for example, for the teaching of declarative knowledge in postsecondary education (Sitzmann, Kraiger, Stewart, & Wisher, 2006). Computer- or web-based instruction also seems promising in teaching deaf students (Lang & Steely, 2003; Long, Vignare, Rappold, & Mallory, 2007). In this chapter, however, we restrict ourselves to classroom instruction.

Instruction in classrooms is first and foremost provided by teachers. To study the effectiveness of instruction is, therefore, also to study the effectiveness of teachers. Marzano (2003) pointed out that instruction by teachers is extremely important in accomplishing successful learning by students. The most effective teachers can establish a growth in learning by their pupils that is almost four times that of pupils taught by the least effective teachers.

The importance of adequate instruction for students' learning is already apparent in preschool, both for children in regular and in special education. Pianta et al. (2005) studied 238 classrooms in the United States, providing education for 3- and 4-year-olds. Process quality of education was globally assessed by observing learning experiences, sensitive social interaction, and academic stimulation. Attributes of programs and teachers turned out to be statistically significant predictors of observed quality in these classrooms. If classrooms entailed many children from poor families, were taught by teachers without proper qualifications or by teachers who acted from an adult-centered perspective, then global educational quality turned out to be lower. Teacher attributes—especially teacher experience, level of education, and credentialing—and teacher attitudes, also accounted for quality.

Effective instructional techniques are especially important in dual, or bilingual, language education programs using spoken languages (Lindholm-Leary, 2005). In these programs, instruction is complicated because students need to reach competency in two or more languages. These competencies not only include language production and language comprehension but also literacy. Instructional techniques must be adapted to respond to different learning styles and language proficiency levels. Research summarized by Lindholm-Leary indicates further that positive interactions between students and teachers and among students are important in these complex linguistic programs. A reciprocal interaction model of teaching including genuine dialogues seems effective, as does cooperative learning in group situations that are characterized by intensive interactions between students to promote bilingual proficiency, by social equity in groups and classrooms, and by interdependent work of groups of students on tasks with common objectives. It seems that the application of these effective instruction principles is even more important in bilingual deaf education, using sign language and spoken/written language. This type of education is far more complex than bilingual education using two spoken languages, because students in bilingual deaf education have restricted access to spoken language and often experience delayed exposure to sign language.

As stated earlier, instruction facilitates learning. The relation between instructional factors and student achievement is therefore frequently studied. Many variables have been identified that contribute to the effectiveness of teachers, at least those in regular education schools. Weinert, Schrader, and Helmke (1989) gave a research-based overview of instructional variables related to achievement. Factors that most influence achievement are the quantity and pacing of instruction, pupil grouping principles (whole class versus small group versus individual instruction), the process of information delivery, posing questions to students, giving them appropriate feedback, homework assignments, and classroom management.

Creemers and Kyriakides (2006) mentioned eight factors related to the effectiveness of teacher instruction. *Orientation* is the explanation of the objectives of a task or specific lesson to students. The way information and materials are presented is called *structuring*. Since effective teachers succeed in involving students in class discussions by asking many questions of them, question techniques are also an important instructional variable. To develop higher-order thinking skills, and especially problem-solving skills, it is helpful if teachers support students in the development of problem-solving strategies.

Grouping students in ways that contribute to effective teaching and learning is called *application*. Teachers have an important contribution in promoting a healthy classroom climate. Positive relations among pupils and between pupils and the teachers, and the application of techniques that lead to a focus to educational content while reducing disturbing student behavior are all part of creating a stimulating classroom climate. *Management of time* relates to aspects such as opportunity to learn, student engagement, and time on task. An efficient learning environment is one in which there is plenty of opportunity to learn, in which students are very engaged in learning, and in which most of the available time is devoted to learning tasks. Evaluation of students' progress in learning is very important, too, not only to establish individual needs of students, but also to assess the effectiveness of instructional techniques.

In an attempt to establish synergy between various models of educational effectiveness and to make research information about effective education and instruction accessible for teachers, Marzano and colleagues conducted extensive meta-analyses of what constitutes qualitatively good education and instruction (Marzano, 2003; Marzano, Pickering, & Pollock, 2001). Eleven factors are presented that enhance the learning of students. These factors are grouped at the level of the school, the student, and the teacher. School factors include a guaranteed and viable curriculum, challenging goals, parent and community involvement, a safe and ordered environment, and collegiality and professionalism of the staff. Student factors include learned intelligence and background knowledge, motivation, and home environment. Teacher variables entail three closely related categories: instructional strategies, classroom management, and classroom curriculum design.

Instructional strategies are the basic ingredients for the enhancement of transmission of information in the classroom. Marzano, Pickering, and Pollock (2001) identified nine effective instructional strategies. These strategies include identifying similarities and differences, summarizing and note-taking, reinforcing effort and providing recognition, homework and practice, nonlinguistic representation, cooperative learning, setting objectives and providing feedback, generating and testing hypothesis and cues, and questions and advance organizers. Classroom management includes establishing good relationships between teacher and students and among students, handling disruptions, and supervising rules and procedures.

Classroom curriculum design is the application of instructional strategies and classroom management techniques in ways that are adapted to the individual needs and characteristics of students. This individualized instruction in regular classrooms is what is labelled by other educational researchers as *adaptive instruction*. According to Houtveen, Booij, De Jong, and Van de Grift (1999), adaptive instruction requires good diagnostic and instructional skills on the part of the teacher, adequate pedagogical functioning, and adequate organization of the learning process. Adaptive instruction directly contributes to the academic achievement of students, including reading achievement.

Instruction in Special Education

One would expect schools for special education to excel in adaptive instruction. The question is whether instructional techniques in special education differ from those applied in regular education. As far as Detterman and Thompson (1997) are concerned, there is nothing special about special education. In their opinion, too often, the goals special education tries to achieve are only vaguely described. Evidence for effects of specific programs on achievement is largely lacking. The most serious problem, according to Detterman and Thompson, is that individual differences in cognitive ability among students are only poorly understood. Differences in student characteristics are problematic to interpret, and this limits real improvement of education in general and special education in particular. Detterman and Thompson state that a thorough understanding of individual differences in cognitive abilities is needed. This understanding may be used as a base for rational, well-designed educational intervention programs.

Norwich and Lewis (2001) support the view that empirical evidence for instructional practices specific to certain types of disability is largely lacking. Their review of existing evidence indicates that many general teaching principles and strategies are relevant to children with disabilities, because, conversely, there also exist nondisabled children with difficulties in learning who need more intensive and explicit teaching. Instead of conceptualizing instructional techniques as either fit for regular or for special education, Norwich and Lewis argue that it would be better to speak of a continua of teaching approaches. The application of teaching approaches differs in degree: various strategies and procedures in teaching should be used to a greater or lesser extent in the teaching of students with differing characteristics. Thus, a mix of instruction strategies and procedures needs to be used in actual practice, depending on the educational needs of the children involved, a suggestion also emphasized by Knoors (2007) with respect to education of deaf students. Knoors stressed the importance of using tricky mixes (Nelson, Loncke, & Camarata, 1993) in selecting languages for instruction and in curriculum design. He introduced three principles: The "no exclusion principle" states that parents should be encouraged to incorporate both sign and spoken language in early language environments of their deaf child. The "language mixing principle" states that mixing of spoken and sign language in forms of English-based signing (where "English" refers to any spoken/written language) deserves encouragement if it adds to the effectiveness and richness of communication between hearing parents and teachers and deaf children. The "flexibility principle" advocates the differentiation of the amount and type of language input in bilingual deaf education, depending on the linguistic and educational needs of deaf children.

The need for the application of a mix of instructional strategies is confirmed by a review of evidence-based teaching strategies used in special and inclusive education for children with disabilities (Mitchell, 2008). The core philosophy of inclusive education is the creation of classroom environments that enable all pupils, those with and without disabilities, to profit equally from education. On the basis of an extensive meta-analysis, Mitchell described 24 strategies used with learners who have special educational needs. These strategies range from cognitive strategy instruction to *reciprocal teaching*—that is, the construction of dialogues between teacher and students to enable learning. They also include aspects of parental involvement, peer tutoring, and collaborative group teaching. According to Mitchell, there is no single strategy that all teachers should use when teaching children with disabilities: one size will not fit all. Rather, it is most effective to incorporate a variety of effective teaching strategies. As an exception, some students with disabilities do need distinct teaching strategies, specifically deaf students. They may require sign language and FM listening devices, and need systems for maintaining hearing aids or cochlear implants. In general, however, students with disabilities simply require good teaching. In Mitchell's words, "There is little evidence to support the notion of disability-specific teaching strategies, but rather that all learners benefit from a common set of strategies, even if they have to be adapted to take account of varying cognitive, emotional, and social capabilities" (Mitchell, 2008, p. 8).

Classroom Instruction for Deaf Students

Those who teach deaf students, whether in special or regular education classrooms, ideally have to adhere to all the general principles (instructional strategies and classroom management techniques) known to enhance the quality of instruction in general or regular education, in order to establish the best possible conditions for learning. Teachers of deaf students, however, need to do more. They have to adapt instruction to the highly diverse individual characteristics of deaf students in their classes.

The question is whether application of general principles and of adapted instruction really takes place, and if so, to what extent and whether in a similar or different fashion in regular compared to special education. In fact, we hardly have any information about this issue. It might be that the adaptations required for maximum achievement of deaf students pose different challenges for regular and special education schools, since regular and special schools and their deaf pupils differ in certain aspects. In general, regular schools are closer to deaf children's homes than are special schools, and distance may influence parental involvement. A review by Van Weerdenburg, Slofstra-Bremer, van Balkom, and Bonder (2008) on the quality of education in special schools for children with specific language impairments in the Netherlands revealed that teachers in these schools found parental involvement very important, but at the same time, because of distance, very difficult to achieve.

The characteristics of deaf students play a central role in placement decisions concerning mainstream versus special education. Mainstreaming depends on degree of hearing loss, proficiency in spoken and written language, cognitive abilities, socioeconomic position of the parents, and ethnicity, among other variables. Deaf students in special schools tend to have greater hearing losses, and more often experience additional disabilities (Ramsey, 1997). It seems not implausible to assume that the heterogeneity of deaf students in special education exceeds that of those in mainstream education. Differences in skills and learning styles among deaf children in special education thus may require a more "individualized" approach to teaching. In these circumstances, one of the big challenges seems to be how teachers can organize their lessons most effectively, for instance, in terms of the quantity of instruction.

On the other hand, regular education schools will have to deal with (possible) differences between the learning styles of hearing and deaf children, and they will have to adjust their instructional system in such a way that suits both hearing and deaf children. For instance, how will different learning styles affect collaborative learning for hearing and deaf children? Regular schools also have to deal with the question of how instruction can be made accessible for deaf children (e.g., through sign language interpreters) without making too many concessions on the quality of the instruction.

Is it possible for teachers of deaf students to create a learning environment that enables optimal achievement for their students? Again, the answer is that we do not really know. Experimental research is fairly scarce. Marschark, Sapere, Convertino, and Seewagen (2005) studied the amount of learning through either sign language interpreting or sign language transliteration by deaf college students, compared to learning gains by hearing college students following the same lesson. The sign language interpreters in this study differed considerably in interpreting experience at the college level. Experience ranged from less than 3 years to more than 10 years. The study revealed that deaf students with deaf parents did not learn more than deaf students with hearing parents, and both groups of deaf students learned significantly less than their hearing peers. Marschark et al.(2005) hypothesized that either interpreter-mediated instruction creates a problem for deaf students, that deaf students at college level are insufficiently equipped for the full comprehension of classroom instruction, or that instructional strategies used by hearing, mainstream instructors are less effective for deaf students.

However, recent evidence seems to indicate that it is possible for deaf students to learn as much as hearing students learn in lessons, at least in postsecondary education and under specific conditions. Marschark, Sapere, Convertino, and Pelz (2008) studied the effect of direct and mediated instruction (instruction via sign language interpreting) on classroom learning by deaf students in postsecondary education by carrying out four related experiments. The study took place at Rochester Institute of Technology/National Technical Institute for the Deaf (RIT/NTID). Only the very best teachers (with respect to experience and sign language proficiency) and sign language interpreters participated in the experiments. In an experimental setting, the learning gains of deaf and hearing classmates were examined by comparing prior content knowledge, scores on assessment after the lectures, and gain scores. It turned out that direct and mediated instruction were equally effective for deaf college students, provided that the signing skills of both teachers and interpreters are excellent. Second, although deaf students started learning with less prior content knowledge than their hearing classmates, the learning gains of both groups turned out to be generally equal. Marschark's group explained these

remarkable results by pointing at the outstanding sign language skills of the instructors and interpreters involved in their study. Accessible communication, and in this particular case, excellent sign language skills, are simply a precondition for efficient instruction—necessary, but not sufficient. Even more important is the quality of instruction. Apparently, teachers and interpreters succeeded in adapting their instruction language to the linguistic and cognitive characteristics of the deaf students involved. The teachers and interpreters involved in the experiments were not only highly skilled in ASL and simultaneous communication, but also had exceptional teaching skills. In addition, they obviously were familiar with differences in learning styles and cognitive and linguistic abilities of deaf students, because they had prolonged experience with these students.

Marschark et al.(2008) summed up the key elements that seem to be required to create the optimal learning environment for deaf students in postsecondary education: (a) good didactic skills, (b) excellent sign language skills, and (c) ability to adapt those skills to the learning styles and cognitive abilities of deaf students. In other words, the study by Marschark et al. (2008) demonstrates that it is possible to create an optimal learning environment for deaf students, at least in an experimental setting in college education. One needs to keep in mind, however, that colleges such as RIT/NTID are exceptional in a number of ways. Teaching staff are trained extensively in teaching in signed and spoken language, instruction may frequently be whole-group instruction, and the students are a relatively homogeneous group, at least according to intellectual abilities. It is improbable that the conditions present at NTID, and certainly those in the experimental setting, can be met easily in many other educational programs, and certainly not in many mainstream classes where, for example, many sign language interpreters lack appropriate training (see e.g., Schick, Williams, & Kupermintz, 2006).

In the remainder of this section, we will focus on adaptations in relation to the specific linguistic (language of instruction) and cognitive needs of deaf students, on the application of general and specific instruction strategies, on the teacher–student relationship (including hearing status), and on providing opportunities to learn. We conclude this section by focusing on ongoing Dutch research in which instruction processes in the education of deaf students in regular and special education are compared.

Language of Instruction

Classroom instruction provided by teachers can only be accessible if students can perceive and comprehend the language being used. In the case of deaf students, this obviously is a crucial issue. Instruction using spoken language is often inaccessible because of restricted auditory perception and limitations in the possibilities for speechreading. Written instructions are difficult to understand for the many deaf students who have limited reading comprehension. And, sign language instruction may be hampered by limited proficiency on the part of the (often hearing) teachers (Singleton & Morgan, 2006), by sign language interpreters lacking competency (Schick, 2008), and by variations in the sign language proficiency of the deaf students (Marschark & Wauters, 2008).

The point made by Marschark et al. (2008), that excellent sign language skills are a necessary but insufficient prerequisite for effective teaching of many deaf students, was also made by Akamatsu, Stewart, and Mayer (2002) and Lang, McKee, and Conner (1993). Akamatsu and colleagues stated that both the instructional method and the style of teaching are crucial elements of effective teaching. An optimal learning environment for deaf students requires that teachers' good communication skills and sound teaching practices go hand in hand.

Manual communication in deaf education may either refer to simultaneous communication or to the use of indigenous, natural sign languages such as American Sign Language, British Sign Language, or Sign Language of the Netherlands. In simultaneous communication, spoken language is combined with manual signs. In fact, these signs constitute a manual code for spoken language. Akamatsu and colleagues examined research about ways teachers sign in the classroom. They conclude that there is actually not much information about the effect of the type of signing (simultaneous sign/speech or natural sign language) on classroom instruction. What is clear is that spoken language–based sign systems may play a role in classroom instruction as well as sign language. Spoken language–based sign systems can be accessible and learnable, especially with respect to the lexicon and the word order. The ability to learn is enhanced if these systems are sign driven, so that they contain sign elements (e.g., spatially modified verbs) that adhere to the constraints of communication in a visual–manual mode. Although certain aspects of the morphology of spoken language–based signing are not easily accessed and learned,

Akamatsu's group (2002) assert that the actual language or mode of communication used by teachers matters less than the way this language or mode is used in classroom instruction. It is therefore essential that we find out what factors, apart from accessible communication, constitute effective and responsive teaching.

Lang, McKee, and Conner (1993) examined the perceptions of effective teacher characteristics among staff and deaf students in a postsecondary educational program. Teacher effectiveness was defined in terms of enhanced student learning and achievement. Staff and students agreed on characteristics such as competency in sign language communication, mastery of subject matter, understanding of deafness as an educational condition, and establishment of clear expectations. Compared to staff members, deaf students attached less importance to classroom management characteristics like active learning, the pace of presentation, and emphasizing important information. With respect to the importance of communication, Lang and his colleagues noted: "Effective communication as a crucial component of effective teaching was emphasized repeatedly. Ability to communicate effectively goes beyond formal sign and spoken English skills…" (p. 258).

In a study into sign language–based literacy practices provided by a deaf teacher in a residential school for the deaf, Ramsey and Padden (1998) explored the issue of effective communication somewhat further (see also Mather, 1987; and Smith & Ramsey, 2004, for similar observations). Their study is based on videotaped observations during 20 school days with third graders. The class had 12 deaf students, a fairly big class for most schools for the deaf. The school followed a bilingual and bicultural education policy. Participating in classroom activities meant not only perceiving and comprehending instruction by the teacher, but also attending group discussions in sign language. This required deaf children not simply to pay attention. Making and keeping eye contact with other signers, whether the teacher or peers, was essential and helped in maintaining and directing the attention of the pupils. Therefore, the teacher needed to cue the duration and direction of eye gaze by the pupils, a skill that is also needed in deaf pupils themselves. To produce fluent classroom discourse, students had to adhere to what Ramsey and Padden called the "etiquette" of standing and moving to the front of the room to take the floor.

In actual practice, language of instruction often seems less accessible than in the experimental study by Marschark et al. (2008). In a study into the teaching strategies of two teachers in primary education classrooms with a mix of deaf and hearing students, Cawthon (2001) noted that the deaf students received only limited language input from their teachers. This was remarkable because both teachers had ample experience with the education of deaf children. One was fairly proficient in sign language, the other one very proficient. The frequency of questions posed to deaf students also was much lower than to hearing students. Cawthon concluded that "Opportunities for linguistic expression and interaction in these classrooms were perhaps fewer than one would find in a special education classroom with only deaf students" (p. 218).

Focusing on special education for deaf students, Matthews and Reich (1993) studied constraints on communication in classrooms. The study involved teachers and students in two high school classes in special education (a school for the deaf). Teachers were very experienced, and used multimodal communication. Each class consisted of 4 to 6 students. Lessons were videotaped and analyzed for the percentage of teacher signing that was seen by the students. This percentage turned out to be an overall average of 44%. Students were often distracted by each other or were looking at materials or the blackboard. It seemed that information loss was limited, however, because of the fact that teachers repeated instructional content frequently. Of course, this is at the expense of the total amount of information transmitted. Matthews and Reich (1993) recommended that if teachers want to instruct their students, student-to-student communication should be limited and the tendency to sign to a particular student, as opposed to visually scanning to include all students, should be resisted.

In a longitudinal study into reading instruction in primary education for deaf children in New Zealand, considerable variation in the use of simultaneous communication among teachers was noted (Limbrick, McNaughton, & Clay, 1992). Some teachers supported their speech 75% of the time with signs, but others virtually used no sign at all.

Classroom Participation

If instruction is relatively inaccessible, this may lead to restrictions in the level of classroom participation by deaf students. Classroom participation is related to academic achievement. More, and more active, participation leads to enhanced achievement (Lang, Stinson, Basile, Kavanagh, & Liu, 1998). Teachers who succeed in increasing the participation of their

deaf students are clearly the more effective ones (Marschark, Lang, & Albertini, 2002). Teachers, administrators, and teacher educators agree, at least in the United States, that teachers of deaf students should have strong communication skills, be up-to-date in their teaching, employ cognitive strategies, have a passion for teaching, and support students in becoming independent learners (Scheetz & Martin, 2008).

Instruction Strategies

Access to instruction goes beyond access to the language being used. The rapid rate of discussion, the pace of topic change, the number of speakers involved in classroom discussions, the number of people talking at the same time, all may present barriers to classroom participation by deaf students (Stinson & Antia, 1999). The use of interpreters in the classroom may lead to time lags between spoken and signed messages. The pace of communication also may slow down in interpreter-mediated instruction, the content of the lecture may sometimes be altered, and interpreters can be so helpful to deaf students that, in the end, they isolate them from their hearing peers.

Factors that promote participation of deaf students in mainstreamed classrooms were described by Stinson and Liu (1999). Data from a focus group and observational study indicated that participation of deaf students in regular classes in primary and secondary education can be increased by the application of specific strategies. Classroom teachers should allow time for students to read information before starting to discuss it. Controlling of the pace of discussion in mixed groups of students is important, too. Information processing and interaction should be structured by classroom teachers to accommodate the requirements of visual information processing by deaf students, allowing them time to look from speaker to speaker or from speaker to text or visual display. For effective cooperative learning situations in small groups, teachers need to select group members, arrange seating, and monitor the collaboration process.

The application of instructional strategies proven effective in general education by teachers of deaf students is less straightforward than one would expect. The use of many strategies seems hampered to some extent by a lack of training, time pressure, and challenges resulting from teaching mixed-ability groups. From research concerning mathematics instruction in primary special education, involving both deaf and hearing teachers, we know that teachers of the deaf often are insufficiently prepared to teach mathematics (Kelly, Lang, & Pagliaro, 2003). Teachers' expectations of deaf students' capability to solve math problems were generally low. As a consequence, deaf students were provided only limited exposure to challenging problem-solving situations. The problems of communication in English with their deaf students caused many teachers to change math lessons into language comprehension lessons. In general, instructional practices thus were not in line with those recommended for either regular or deaf education (Pagliaro & Ansell, 2002).

Based on an extensive examination of the literature, Easterbrooks and Stephenson (2006) identified 20 practices with at least some research support, relating to literacy, science, and math education. Examples of practices in the domain of literacy are independent reading, phonemic awareness and phonics, metacognitive strategies, and fluency. Skilled teacher communication, adequate content knowledge, visual organizers (graphs, charts, and visual maps), and critical thinking are among the practices identified in the domain of science and mathematics. Easterbrooks and Stephenson (2006) concluded from their inventory that "the body of evidence regarding best practices in deaf education leaves much to be desired" (p. 395).

In a subsequent survey by Easterbrooks, Stephenson, and Mertens (2006), master teachers active in the field of deaf education were asked to indicate the value they attach to each of the 20 identified practices and to indicate the frequency with which they use these practices. There was substantial agreement about the benefits of the practices identified. Teachers expressed major concern, however, about the application of these practices because they were perceived as increasing time pressure for teachers and because of the challenge of applying these practices in mixed-ability classrooms.

Instruction Adapted to Learning Style and Cognitive Profile

A proven effective practice is the adaptation of the instruction process to the individual needs of learners, including deaf students. An important first step needs to be the recognition and acceptance of those differences among deaf students and between deaf and hearing students that are important for academic learning. It is clear that deaf students differ in language proficiency both in spoken and in sign language proficiency. There is also increasing evidence that clear individual differences exist in other domains, including the cognitive domain.

Many deaf students have a learning style that may be labelled "dependent." They need teachers who present curricular content in a structured and well-organized way (Lang et al., 1998). Marschark, Convertino, and LaRock (2006) suggested that deaf students may be less prepared compared to hearing peers with respect to learning strategies, prior content knowledge, and world knowledge. This difference might even be more important than the difference in communication proficiency. Marschark and colleagues stated: "At its heart, however, the problem is that deaf students often receive instruction that is inconsistent with their prior knowledge, learning strategies, and language comprehension skills" (Marschark, Convertino, & LaRock, 2006, p. 184). They pointed out that the differences in visual processing, long-term memory, working memory, and metacognition between deaf and hearing students need to be addressed in classroom instruction. Consequently, educators need to develop instruction techniques that address these differences and that may enhance students' knowledge.

The nature of these instruction strategies is still unknown, and empirical research available about their application is lacking. What we do know is that there are limits to adaptive instruction. Sometimes the differences in learner characteristics are so huge that typical group instruction becomes impossible (Bosker, 2005). Instruction in small, more homogeneous groups may then become necessary. Sometimes, splitting the class into two or more smaller ones is the only solution. Teachers for the deaf indicate that instructing mixed-ability groups is difficult, and it may prevent them from applying effective instructing strategies (Easterbrooks et al., 2006).

Teacher–Student Relationship and Hearing Status

Effective teaching is enhanced if teachers succeed in establishing good teacher–student relationships (Lang et al., 1993). This might be interpreted to mean deaf rather than hearing teachers. Marschark et al. (2008) suggested that, in theory, deaf teachers might be more sensitive to differences among deaf students and more able to adapt their teaching toward their students' varied strengths and needs. Alternatively, deaf teachers might prompt higher levels of motivation in deaf students because the students can identify more easily with them than with hearing teachers. Finally, instruction from deaf teachers may be more communicatively accessible to deaf students than instruction from hearing teachers. However, the experiments by Marschark's group (2008) obtained the same results for deaf and hearing teachers, as well as for direct and mediated (interpreted) instruction. The finding of equivalent gains for deaf and hearing students led them to hypothesize that skill in instructing deaf students is more important than either of the other factors.

The Marschark group's (2008) findings notwithstanding, it is known that deaf signing students in college prefer being taught by deaf teachers (Lang et al., 1993; Lang, Dowaliby, & Anderson, 1994), and they associate deaf teachers more often with effective teaching. Roberson and Serwatka (2000) studied whether deaf students in primary and secondary school also perceived deaf teachers as being more effective in instruction. The answer was affirmative. However, consistent with Marschark et al. (2008) findings, the hearing status of the teacher in their study was not associated with differences of achievement among the pupils. So far, the empirical support for a conclusion that hearing status defines the effectiveness of teachers seems at best equivocal.

Opportunity to Learn

Effective teachers provide their students with ample opportunities to learn in the classroom. They do so by using a sensitive and responsive interaction style, thus allowing students plenty of opportunities to initiate interactions and to participate in classroom discourse. In addition, students need to have enough time for their learning tasks. Disruptions that are handled ineffectively by teachers may lead to a reduction of education time.

From several studies carried out in the United Kingdom by Wood and colleagues, we know that hearing teachers of deaf students tend to dominate classroom interactions. Hearing teachers, at least those who do not have native-like sign language fluency, may find it hard to give students the opportunity to initiate interactions, probably because contributions to classroom discourse by students are often not or not adequately understood by the teachers (Wood, Wood, Griffiths, & Howarth, 1986). In such a situation, teacher–student interactions are characterized by dominance of teacher contributions, relatively few student initiations, and infrequent open-ended questions posed to students.

An important variable in predicting learning success of students is the level of engagement of deaf students and the amount of time they are engaged in a task. The level of engagement of deaf students may be as high as that of hearing peers, at least in primary education (Knoors & Renting, 2000). The actual time young deaf students may display their engagement, however, may be limited. The results of an observational study of deaf students from two schools for the deaf in England showed that deaf students spend less time reading than hearing peers (Howarth, Wood, Griffiths, & Howarth, 1981).

Limbrick et al. (1992) studied the amount of time spent on reading and the types of teacher interactions during reading instruction in a school for the deaf and in special units attached to a local regular education school in New Zealand. Forty-five severely and profoundly deaf students, aged 5–10 years, participated. Time engaged in reading varied markedly among deaf students and was significantly less compared to the time hearing students spend reading in a general education classroom. There was also considerable variation across classrooms. More proficient deaf readers spent considerably more time reading than less proficient readers. Teachers of young deaf children spent more time at reading instruction than did teachers of older deaf children. Most teachers did not actually instruct children to read for meaning, although they stated that was one of the goals of reading instruction. Instead, much of the instruction time was devoted to language modeling and correction. Again, there was considerable variation across teachers and classrooms.

Time on task in reading lessons was also studied by Donne and Zigmond (2008). They examined reading lessons in grades 1–4 in general education, in resource classrooms, and in self-contained classrooms. Participants were DHH students and their teachers. Results indicated that grade level and instructional setting were significantly associated with the time engaged in reading, but that the degree of hearing loss and the presence or absence of additional disabilities were not. Deaf students who read at grade level spent more time on reading than deaf students with severe delays in reading proficiency. Also, DHH students in general education or in a combination of general education and resource rooms spent more time on reading than deaf students in self-contained classrooms. However, this finding does not necessarily reflect a difference between educational settings. The differences in time spend on reading also may have existed prior to placement in one or the other type of educational setting.

Instruction in Regular and Special Education Compared: Ongoing Dutch Research

In 2004, one of the schools for special education for deaf children in the Netherlands started a co-enrollment program in collaboration with a mainstream primary school. This co-enrollment program, the "Twinschool," is situated at the mainstream school located near the special school. A first group of three deaf pupils and one hard-of-hearing pupil enrolled in this program in 2004 in grade 2. A second group of seven deaf children started in K–1 in the co-enrollment program 2 years later. In a longitudinal evaluation of this co-enrollment program, various aspects of the quality of instruction for (deaf) children in the two co-enrollment classes in mainstream education and in several classes in schools for the deaf are being studied.

The co-enrollment class in preschool (K–1) consisted of a mixed group of 19 hearing and seven deaf children. The deaf children all used cochlear implants and were implanted before the age of two. Two classroom teachers, one of whom had considerable experience in teaching deaf children in special schools, taught the children in a co-teaching system. A hard-of-hearing teacher assistant supported the teachers. The two kindergarten classes in the special school consisted of, respectively, nine and ten deaf children. Among them, 18 had cochlear implants. Each class was taught by an experienced hearing classroom teacher who was supported by a deaf teacher assistant. Instruction by teachers in the co enrollment classroom and in the two classrooms in special education for deaf children was compared using several scales from the Preschool Instructional Rating Scale (PIRS) developed by Wheeden and Mahoney (2000). This scale measures cognitive problem solving (instructional techniques), developmental match (adaptive instruction), and strategies for reward and punishment (classroom management). Another category, "communicative adaptations," was added to the PIRS to investigate to what extent teachers made communicative adaptations (e.g., using signs and visualization) that were vital for (especially) the deaf children in the classroom.

The K–1 class in the co-enrollment program differed significantly from the two classes in the special school on each of the aforementioned scales. The class in the co-enrollment program scored lower on the scales related to the adaptation of instruction (developmental match and communicative adaptations) in comparison to the two classes in the special school. This finding is hardly surprising, as teachers in schools for the deaf are trained to adapt their instruction to the individual needs of their pupils. In addition, smaller group sizes in special schools make adaptations easier to implement than in the co-enrollment classroom. The co-enrollment classroom,

however, scored significantly higher on the scale related to instructional techniques (cognitive problem solving). In other words, the teacher(s) in the co-enrollment class more extensively stimulated the cognitive problem-solving skills of the deaf and hearing children than did the teachers in the special school. The co-enrollment classroom also scored higher on the scale related to classroom management (strategies for reward and punishment), indicating that the teachers in the co-enrollment class rewarded (the deaf and the hearing) children's positive behavior and punished children's negative behavior to a larger degree than did the teachers in the special school.

The quality of instruction was also investigated in the upper grades of the co-enrollment school (grade 4) and in several special schools for deaf children (grades 4 and 5). The co-enrollment class consisted of a mixed group of 25 hearing and DHH children. The DHH children started co-enrollment education in grade 2; the study took place when they were in grade 4. As in the co-enrollment preschool class, two teachers taught the children in a co-teaching system. One of the teachers had several years of experience in teaching deaf children in special education. The group size in the special schools varied between five and nine children. In the co-enrollment class and in the special school classes, the distribution of instructional activities and the engagement of pupils were studied in a series of lessons. A time sampling observation instrument was used, based on a model of direct instruction. During a very brief period of 7 seconds, the (instructional) activity of the teacher and the engagement of one of the pupils in this activity were observed. The activity of the teacher was subsequently classified in one of the following three major categories: (a) group instruction activities (i.e., looking back at the previous lesson, explaining the content, doing exercises with the whole class, giving pupils feedback); (b) individual activities (i.e., explaining the content, individual help with exercises); and (c) management activities (i.e., changing lessons, preparing lessons). In addition, the engagement of the pupil during this activity was scored on a binary scale. In the next interval, the activity of the teacher and the engagement of another pupil in this activity were observed. In general, in the special school for the deaf, the amount of classical instructional activities was much less than in the co-enrollment program. Teachers in the special school tended to give deaf students more individual help. The small number of children in the groups in special schools and the large variation in skills in math and reading may be the cause for this difference. The time that deaf and hearing pupils were engaged during the lessons in the co-enrollment program was high, a mean 77% of the time, when compared to the time engaged during the lessons for hearing children in mainstream education observed by Veenman, Lem, Roelofs, and Nijssen (1992). As a group, deaf pupils in the co-enrollment program turned out to be slightly less engaged in learning, in comparison to their hearing classmates. The time the deaf pupils in the co-enrollment program were engaged in the instructional activities, however, was higher when compared to the deaf pupils in the special school, where children were pulled out for activities such as speech therapy more often. When pull-out time was neglected, the engagement rates of both groups of deaf children did not differ. In other words, pull-out causes deaf pupils to miss a considerable proportion of instructional activities in the special schools.

A questionnaire concerning the pupils' perception of the quality of instruction was given to hearing and deaf pupils in the co-enrollment class and to deaf children from the special education schools. The ZEBO (Hendriks & Bosker, 2003) consists of 70 questions, comprising seven scales: achievement pressure, teacher–pupil relationship, teaching strategies, relation with peers, adaptive instruction, amount of learning time, and classroom climate. The instrument has norms for primary education in the Netherlands. The pupils in the co-enrollment program were, in general, satisfied with their education. The classroom climate was perceived as good, and deaf and hearing children experienced their relationships with their deaf and hearing classmates as good. Compared to hearing classmates, deaf pupils in the co-enrollment program indicated that they experienced somewhat more achievement pressure, but they were generally satisfied about their teachers' instruction, the classroom climate, the difficulty level of the educational content, and the pace of instruction. However, these deaf students judged their relationship with teachers as somewhat less positive than their hearing classmates did.

In the special schools, deaf pupils were also, in general, quite satisfied with their education. As in the co-enrollment program, deaf children perceive their teachers' instruction, the classroom climate, and the difficulty of the educational content as being good. Quite interestingly, they were also less positive about their relationships with their teacher.

Our ongoing research on the quality of instruction in the co-enrollment program and in special education up to now suggests that, in preschool, the co-enrollment program and the special school have different strengths in providing children qualitatively good education. The special school excelled in adapting their education to the communicative and individual needs of their pupils, whereas the co-enrollment program scored significantly higher on scales related to classroom management and instructional techniques. These findings suggest that special schools and mainstream schools face different challenges in providing deaf children with qualitatively good education.

In the upper grades, the differences between the schools were less apparent. Pull-out in special schools tends to cause deaf pupils to miss a considerable proportion of instructional activities. But the perceptions of the pupils themselves on the quality of instruction were comparable in the special schools and the co-enrollment program. What seems troublesome is that older deaf children in both programs seem to experience slightly negative relationships with their teachers. As teachers are the primary mechanism through which learning takes place in the classroom, a positive student's relationship with the teacher is vital. We are currently looking into the teacher–pupil relationship in both educational settings in more detail.

Summary and Conclusions

The picture of the quality of instruction for deaf students that emerges from the research literature available is at best fragmented. Under specific conditions, it seems possible for deaf students to learn as much as their hearing peers, at least in postsecondary education. Conditions that must be met include excellent communication skills, on the part of signing deaf students, and outstanding sign language skills, on the part of teachers and interpreters. In addition, for effective instruction, teachers need to go beyond fluent language. The application of effective general and specific instructional strategies and of classroom management techniques is as important.

The extent to which these conditions are met in daily practice and the identification of possibilities to improve existing educational practices are key issues for further research. Evaluating the quality of instruction for deaf students requires additional comprehensive research into instructional strategies, classroom management, and accessibility of instruction at all educational levels (from preschool to postsecondary education) and in all educational settings (mainstream, co-enrollment, unit, and special school). Current research lacks this comprehensive character, thus contributing to a lack of a definitive state of the art. Taking the long tradition of specialized education for deaf students into account, it is surprising to find so few thorough empirical investigations of factors that contribute to effective instruction for deaf students. No doubt the continuing debates about issues such as the preferred mode of communication, the language of instruction, and the application of rehabilitation devices such as cochlear implants have distracted researchers and practitioners from studying what constitutes the core of education—instruction.

As Marschark et al. (2002) rightfully state, no one type of school setting is ideally suited for all deaf students. Arguing about whether regular or special education is more adequate for deaf students is missing the central point. The diversity of individual linguistic and cognitive abilities among deaf students and between deaf and hearing students is great, and these differences must be addressed.

What we do know illustrates, to a certain extent, the different challenges regular and special schools face in educating deaf students. Instruction does not always seem to be clear to deaf students, either in regular or in special education. In regular education, it clearly seems a challenge to attain the excellent communication conditions that existed in the study by Marschark et al. (2008), not for a limited amount of time, but for all the time that deaf students attend a regular class. In addition, even if interpreting is excellent, time lags in information processing seem unavoidable, and the isolation of deaf students in mixed-group discussions is almost inevitable. Pacing of group discussions to allow for the visual turn-taking necessary for deaf students is thus of crucial importance in regular classes. In special education settings, variation in quality of communication by teachers seems an important issue. Although many deaf students prefer deaf teachers, empirical support for the added value of these teachers with respect to effectiveness of instruction is equivocal. This is not to say that hearing teachers cannot learn much from their deaf colleagues. Handling group discussions and attracting and maintaining visual attention are clearly skills in which deaf teachers seem to be more proficient than their hearing counterparts. For example, the intentional use of eye gaze seems to be an essential ingredient in these skills that is not typically developed spontaneously by hearing teachers.

Challenges associated with teaching mixed-ability groups deserve more attention in teacher training and coaching, since this seems problematic not only in regular education, but also in special schools. Engagement of deaf students does not seem to be a major cause for concern. Deaf pupils seem to have fewer opportunities to learn than their hearing counterparts, especially in special education. Providing enough time for a task is problematic in special schools, partly due to the pull-out of students for activities such as therapy sessions. Teacher–student relationships do not appear to be a reason for major concern, although sometimes hearing students are more slightly positive about this relationship than deaf peers. Teaching of subject matter (e.g., mathematics) in special schools needs to be improved, both by realizing more content training for teachers of the deaf and by coaching them to have higher expectations for their deaf students' achievements.

Finally, to increase our knowledge about the elements of effective instruction for deaf students in different settings and at different education levels, we clearly need more research. Research into the exact nature of the individual differences in linguistic and cognitive abilities of deaf students is needed, as is more intervention-focused research. Theoretically sound, practice-based instructional strategies and classroom management techniques need to be designed and/or implemented, and their effects on the learning gains of deaf students need to be studied in carefully designed intervention studies, in both regular and special education settings.

References

Akamatsu, C. T., Stewart, D. A., & Mayer, C. (2002). Is it time to look beyond teachers' signing behavior? *Sign Language Studies 2*(3), 230–254.

Bosker, R. J. (2005). *De grenzen van gedifferentieerd onderwijs.* [The limits of adaptive education]. Groningen: Inaugurele rede. Rijksuniversiteit Groningen.

Cawthon, S. (2001). Teaching strategies in inclusive classrooms with deaf students. *Journal of Deaf Studies and Deaf Education, 6*(3), 212–225.

Creemers, B. P. M. (1994). *The effective classroom.* London: Cassell.

Creemers, B. P. M., & Kyriakides, L. (2006). Critical analysis of the current approaches to modelling educational effectiveness: the importance of establishing a dynamic model. *School Effectiveness and School Improvement, 17*(3), 347–366.

Detterman, D. K., & Thompson, L. A. (1997). IQ, schooling, and developmental disabilities: What's so special about special education? *American Psychologist, 52*, 1082–1091.

Donne, V., & Zigmond, N. (2008). Engagement during reading instruction for students who are deaf or hard of hearing in public schools. *American Annals of the Deaf, 153*(3), 294–303.

Easterbrooks, S. R., & Stephenson, B. (2006). An examination of twenty literacy, science, and mathematics practices used to educate students who are deaf or hard of hearing. *American Annals of the Deaf, 151*(4), 385–397.

Easterbrooks, S. R., Stephenson, B., & Mertens, D. (2006). Master teacher responses to twenty literacy and science/math practices in deaf education. *American Annals of the Deaf*, *151*(4), 398–409.

Hendriks, M. A., & Bosker, R. (2003). *ZEBO instrument voor zelf-evaluatie in het basisonderwijs. Handleiding bij een geautomatiseerd hulpmiddel voor kwaliteitszorg in basisscholen.* [ZEBO, instrumentation for self-evaluation in primary education. Manual to the computerized instrumentation for quality care in primary education]. Enschede: Twente University Press.

Houtveen, A. A. M., Booij, N., De Jong, R. A., & Van de Grift, W. J. C. M. (1999). Adaptive instruction and pupil results. *School Effectiveness and School Improvement*, *10*(2), 172–193.

Howarth, S. P., Wood, D. J., Griffiths, A. J., & Howarth, C. I. (1981). A comparative study of the reading lessons of deaf and hearing primary-school children. *British Journal of Educational Psychology*, *74*, 429–437.

Karchmer, M., & Mitchell, R. (2003). Demographic and achievement characteristics of deaf and hard-of-hearing students. In, M. Marschark & P. Spencer (Eds.), *Oxford handbook of deaf studies, language and education* (pp. 21–37). New York: Oxford University Press.

Kelly R. R., Lang, H. G., & Pagliaro, C. M. (2003). Mathematics word problem solving for deaf students: A survey of perceptions and practices. *Journal of Deaf Studies and Deaf Education*, *8*(2), 104–119.

Knoors, H. (2007). Educational responses to varying objectives of parents of deaf children: A Dutch perspective. *Journal of Deaf Studies and Deaf Education*, *12*(2), 243–253.

Knoors, H., & Renting, B. (2000). Measuring quality of education: the involvement of bilingually educated deaf children. *American Annals of the Deaf*, *145*(3), 268–274.

Lang, H. G., McKee, B. G., & Conner, K. N. (1993). Characteristics of effective teachers: A descriptive study of perceptions of faculty and deaf college students. *American Annals of the Deaf*, *138*(3), 252–259.

Lang, H. G., Dowaliby, F. J., & Anderson, H. (1994). Critical teaching incidents: Recollections of deaf college students. *American Annals of the Deaf*, *139*(2), 119–127.

Lang, H. G., Stinson, M. S., Basile, M., Kavanagh, F., & Liu, Y. (1998). Learning styles of deaf college students and teaching behaviors of their instructors. *Journal of Deaf Studies and Deaf Education*, *4*(1), 16–27.

Lang, H., & Steely, D. (2003). Web-based science instruction for deaf students: What research says to a teacher. *Instructional Science*, *31*(4–5), 277–298.

Limbrick, E. A., McNaughton, S., & Clay, M. M. (1992). Time engaged in reading. A critical factor in reading achievement. *American Annals of the Deaf*, *137*(4), 309–314.

Lindholm-Leary, K. (2005). *Review of research and best practices on effective features of dual language education programs.* Washington DC: Center for Applied Linguistics.

Long, G. L., Vignare, K., Rappold, R. P., & Mallory, J. (2007). Access to communication for deaf, hard-of-hearing and ESL students in blended learning courses. *International Review of Research in Open and Distance Learning*, *8*(3), 1–13.

Marschark, M., Lang, H., & Albertini, J. (2002). *Educating deaf students: From research to practice.* Oxford-New York: Oxford University Press.

Marschark, M., Sapere, P., Convertino, C., & Seewagen, R. (2005). Access to postsecondary education through sign language interpreting. *Journal of Deaf Studies and Deaf Education* *10*(1), 38–50.

Marschark, M., Convertino, C., & LaRock, D. (2006). Optimizing academic performance of deaf students: Access, opportunities, and outcomes. In D. F. Moores & D. S. Martin (Eds.), *Deaf learners: New developments in curriculum and instruction* (pp. 179–200). Washington, DC: Gallaudet University Press.

Marschark, M., Sapere, P., Convertino, C., & Pelz, J. (2008). Learning via direct and mediated instruction by deaf students. *Journal of Deaf Studies and Deaf Education 13*(4), 546–561.

Marschark, M., & Wauters, L. (2008). Language comprehension and learning by deaf students. In, M. Marschark & P. C. Hauser (Eds.), *Deaf cognition. Foundations and outcomes* (pp. 309–350). New York: Oxford University Press.

Marzano, R. (2003). *What works in schools: translating research into action.* Alexandria, VA: Association for Supervision and Curriculum Development.

Marzano, R., Pickering, D., & Pollock, J. E. (2001). *Classroom instruction that works.* Alexandria VA: Association for Supervision and Curriculum Development.

Mather, S. (1987). Eye gaze and communication in a deaf classroom. *Sign Language Studies*, *54*, 11–30.

Matthews, T. J., & Reich, C. F. (1993). Constraints on communication in classrooms for the deaf. *American Annals of the Deaf*, *138*(1), 14–18.

Mitchell, D. R. (2008). *What really works in special and inclusive education: using evidence-based teaching strategies.* London-New York: Routledge.

Nelson, K. E., Loncke, F., & Camarata, S. (1993). Implications of research on deaf and hearing children's language learning. In, M. Marschark & M. D. Clark (Eds.), *Psychological perspectives on deafness* (pp. 123–152). Hillsdale, NJ: Lawrence Erlbaum Associates.

Norwich, B., & Lewis, A. (2001). *Mapping a pedagogy for special educational needs.* British Educational Research Journal, *27*(3), 313–329.

Pagliaro, C., & Ansell, E. (2002). Story problems in the deaf education classroom: Frequency and mode of presentation. *Journal of Deaf Studies and Deaf Education*, *7*(2), 107–119.

Pianta, R. C., Howes, C., Burchinal, M., Byrant, D., Clifford, R., Early, C., & Barbarin, O. (2005). Features of pre-kindergarten programs, classrooms, and teachers: Do they predict observed classroom quality and child-teacher interactions? *Applied Developmental Science*, *9*(3), 144–159.

Ramsey, C. L. (1997). *Deaf children in public schools. Placement, context, and consequences.* Washington DC: Gallaudet University Press.

Ramsey, C., & Padden, C. (1998). Natives and newcomers: Gaining access to literacy in a classroom for deaf children. *Anthropology and Education Quarterly*, *29*, 5–24.

Roberson, J. L., & Serwatka, T. S. (2000). Student perceptions and instructional effectiveness of deaf and hearing teachers. *American Annals of the Deaf*, *145*(3), 257–263.

Scheetz, N. A., & Martin, D. S. (2008). National study of master teachers in deaf education: Implications for teacher education. *American Annals of the Deaf*, *153*(3), 328–343.

Scheerens, J., & Bosker, R. J. (1997). *The foundations of educational effectiveness.* Oxford: Pergamon.

Schick, B. (2008). A model of learning within an interpreted K-12 educational setting. In, M. Marschark & P. C. Hauser (Eds.), *Deaf cognition: Foundations and outcomes* (pp. 351–386). New York: Oxford University Press.

Schick, B., Williams, K., & Kupermintz, H. (2006). Look who's being left behind: Educational interpreters and access to education for deaf and hard of hearing students. *Journal of Deaf Studies and Deaf Education, 11*(1), 3–20.

Singleton, J. L., & Morgan, D. D. (2006). Natural signed language acquisition within the social context of the classroom. In, B. Schick, M. Marschark & P. E. Spencer (Eds.), *Advances in the sign language development of deaf children* (pp. 344–375). New York: Oxford University Press.

Sitzmann, T., Kraiger, K., Stewart, D., & Wisher, R. (2006). The comparative effectiveness of web-based and classroom instruction: A meta-analysis. *Personnel Psychology, 59*, 623–664.

Smith, D. H., & Ramsey, C. L. (2004). Classroom discourse practices of a deaf teacher using American Sign Language. *Sign Language Studies, 5*(1), 39–62.

Stinson, M., & Liu, Y. (1999). Participation of deaf and hard-of-hearing students in classes with hearing students. *Journal of Deaf Studies and Deaf Education 4*(3), 191–202.

Stinson, M., & Antia, S. (1999). Considerations in educating deaf and hard-of-hearing students in inclusive settings. *Journal of Deaf Studies and Deaf Education 4*(3), 163–175.

Stinson, M. S., & Kluwin, T. (2003). Educational consequences of alternative school placements. In, M. Marschark & P. E. Spencer (Eds.), *Oxford handbook of deaf studies, language, and education* (pp. 52–64). New York: Oxford University Press.

Van Ampt, C. M., Artist, M. A. H., Borgers, N., Busman, L., Deken, C., Donmez, B., Dronkers, J., Hoogvink, T., & Meijnen, G. W. (2000). *De effectiviteitsverschillen tussen scholen voor speciaal onderwijs.* [Differences in effectiveness between schools for special education]. Amsterdam: Publications of the University of Amsterdam.

Van Weerdenburg, M., Slofstra-Bremer, C., Van Balkom, H., & Bonder, F. (2008). *Veelzeggend! Een onderzoek naar de speciale en onderscheidende expertise van het cluster-2-onderwijs aan kinderen met ESM.* [Outspoken! A study in to the special and specific knowledge in special schools for children with specific language impairment]. Nijmegen: Pontem.

Veenman, S., Lem, P., Roelofs, E., & Nijssen, F. (1992). *Effectieve instructie en doelmatig klassemanagement: Een schoolverbeteringsprogramma voor enkelvoudige en combinatieklassen.* [Effective instruction and classroom management: a school improvement program for single and combined classes]. Amsterdam: Swets & Zeitlinger, 3rd edition.

Walberg, H. J. (1984). Improving the productivity of America's schools. *Educational Leadership, 41*(8), 19–27.

Weinert, F., Schrader, F. -W., & Helmke, A. (1989). Quality of instruction and achievement outcomes. *International Journal of Educational Research, 13*, 895–932.

Wheeden, C. A., & Mahoney, G. (2000). *Preschool Instructional Rating Scale.* Tallmadge, OH: Family Child Learning Center.

Wood, D. J., Wood, H. A., Griffiths, A. J., & Howarth, C. I. (1986). *Teaching and talking with deaf children.* London: Wiley and Sons Ltd.

Supporting Students in General Education Classrooms

Shirin D. Antia, Kathryn H. Kreimeyer, *and* Susanne Reed

Abstract

A high percentage of children and youth who are deaf or hard of hearing (DHH) currently receive much of their instruction in general education classrooms with support from itinerant teachers. With the widespread use of early newborn hearing screening and access to early intervention, increasing numbers of DHH children are expected to be educated in general education classrooms, integrated with their hearing peers. The purpose of this chapter is to review the academic and social status of DHH students in general education classrooms, examine the factors that contribute to their success, and develop a framework for the kinds of support that they need from itinerant teachers. A review of the academic status and progress of DHH students in general education classrooms reveals that they achieve at a higher level and make more academic progress than that reported for the general population of DHH students. However, they may not perform academically as well as hearing students. The data on social behavior are scarce and the results are mixed. Nevertheless, recent research indicates that these students are not lacking in social competence, and may be as liked as their hearing peers. Based on the research on factors contributing to the success of these DHH students, we describe a framework for the kinds of support that itinerant teachers should provide in the areas of communication and literacy, learning strategies, self-advocacy, classroom participation, and social skills.

Keywords: deaf and hard-of-hearing students, general education classrooms, public schools, academic progress, academic achievement, social behavior, social integration, itinerant teachers, support services

A large percentage of deaf or hard-of-hearing (DHH) students are educated in general education classrooms in local public schools, either full- or part-time. In the United States, data collected by the Gallaudet Research Institute (GRI) indicated that, in 2006–07, 44% of DHH students attended general education classrooms for 16 or more hours per week (Gallaudet Research Institute, 2006). This percentage likely underestimates the numbers of US students who attend general education classrooms because of the difficulty in obtaining accurate data from states and school districts about this low-incidence and widely scattered population (Mitchell, 2004). However, the percentage of US students receiving most or part of their instruction in general

education classrooms has increased in the past decades, whereas the percent of students in separate facilities or classrooms has declined (Mitchell & Karchmer, 2006). Data from other countries indicate that the majority of DHH students are receiving instruction in general education settings. In Israel, 75% of DHH students are educated in general education classrooms (Most, 2004), whereas in Australia 85% of students are reported to be placed in regular schools and attending some general education classrooms (Power & Hyde, 2003).

There are several reasons for the high numbers of DHH students served in local schools and receiving instruction in general education classrooms. In the US, one reason is legislation promoting education of all students in the least restrictive environment (with "least restrictive" usually defined as the general education classroom), and the concomitant movement toward educational inclusion and integration (Stinson & Antia, 1999). Another reason may be the increasing awareness of the problems encountered, and support services needed, by hard-of-hearing students who have mild and moderate hearing loss (Centers for Disease Control and Prevention: Early Hearing Detection and Intervention Program, July 2005). The GRI reports that, in 2006–07, 46% of students receiving services had hearing losses of less than 55 dB. Most of these students are likely to be placed in general education classrooms, with support from teachers of DHH children.

In the next few decades, increasing numbers of DHH children are likely to enter general education. In 2006, 96% of all children born in the United States were screened for hearing loss (National Center for Hearing Assessment and Management, 2008), thus a majority of these children are likely to be identified early and receive early intervention. These children potentially will have language and communication skills within the range of their hearing peers (Yoshinaga-Itano, Sedey, Coulter, & Mehl, 1998), as will children who are early recipients of cochlear implants (Geers, Nicholas, & Sedey, 2003). Because of access to early intervention and auditory information, increased numbers of children with severe to profound hearing loss, who have been educated in separate classrooms and taught primarily by a teacher of DHH children, are instead expected to be educated in their local schools in general education classrooms. In the near future, it is possible that the primary role of teachers of DHH children will be to provide support services in local public schools. This chapter examines the characteristics of DHH students in general education classrooms, their academic achievement and needs, their social status and needs, and the support that is, and should be, provided to them by teachers of DHH students.

Characteristics of Deaf and Hard-of-Hearing Students in General Education Classrooms

Students placed in general education classrooms have less severe hearing loss, are more likely to prefer spoken communication, and are more likely to belong to the majority ethnic group than are students in self-contained classrooms (either in local or special schools). Survey data from the United States from 2000–01 showed that 78% of DHH students educated in general education settings had severe or less-than-severe hearing loss, whereas only 12% had profound hearing loss (Karchmer & Mitchell, 2003). Similar data were reported from Australia, where 68% of students in general education had severe or less-than-severe losses (Power & Hyde, 2002). A recent US study of students in grades 2–8 in local schools indicated that 17% of students receiving services had a unilateral hearing loss (Antia, Jones, Reed, Kreimeyer, Luckner, & Johnson, 2008). Because of their lesser degree of hearing loss, these students are more likely to use spoken than sign language. However, as noted earlier, more children with profound losses are likely to enter general education in the next few years, many of whom are likely to need sign language support.

In the United States, DHH students in general education classrooms are more likely to belong to the majority ethnic group than are those in self-contained classrooms. Karchmer and Mitchell (2003) reported that 64% of students in general education classrooms were white, compared to 41% of students in self-contained classrooms, and 49% of students in special schools. Ethnicity is sometimes a proxy for socioeconomic status (SES), which, in turn, impacts students' educational opportunities and outcomes (Jensema, 1975; Kluwin, 1994). It is possible that, as early intervention improves, children entering general education will also be more diverse in ethnicity and SES.

Academic Outcomes

Deaf and hard-of-hearing students who receive instruction in general education classrooms have better academic achievement than those who receive instruction in self-contained classrooms (Holt, 1994; Kluwin, 1993; Kluwin & Moores, 1985; Kluwin & Stinson, 1993). However, it is not always possible to identify a cause and effect relationship between placement and academic achievement because higher achieving students are likely to be placed in general education classrooms for academic subjects; thus, exposure to the general education curriculum coupled with their own motivation and academic ability are likely to lead to continued high achievement (Kluwin & Stinson, 1993).

Nevertheless, there are some indications that exposure to the general education curriculum may contribute to academic achievement. Holt (1994) compared reading and math achievement scores for 58,000 DHH students who participated in the norming of the Stanford Achievement Test during 1989–90 and found that program type was related to achievement, even when accounting for other demographic factors (degree of hearing loss, number of additional handicaps, presence of a cognitive handicap, age cohort, ethnicity, and gender). Students in local schools who attended general education classrooms for more than 16 hours a week scored higher than those who attended general education classrooms for 6–10 hours a week. Students who attended general education classrooms scored higher than students who attended self-contained classrooms. Kluwin and Moores (1985) compared students who were similar on initial math achievement, reading ability, hearing loss, and social maturity, but who received math instruction either in a general education math class or a math class taught by a teacher of DHH students. They found that students receiving instruction from the general educators made greater annual progress in math than did the students in the class taught by teachers of DHH students.

Kluwin (1993) and Kluwin and Stinson (1993) suggest that, although the achievement of students receiving instruction in general education classrooms is higher than that of students receiving instruction in special classrooms, their achievement is influenced primarily by demographic characteristics such as family resources, ethnicity, and degree of hearing loss. Kluwin and Stinson (1993) completed a 5-year longitudinal study of 451 adolescents in public high schools and found that adolescents who were mainstreamed into several general education classrooms had higher reading comprehension scores in twelfth grade than those who were mainstreamed into fewer classes; mainstreamed students, in turn, scored higher than those who received instruction in self-contained classrooms. The authors also reported that ninth grade achievement was a significant predictor of twelfth grade achievement; ninth grade achievement, in turn, was predicted by elementary class placement, which was influenced by family resources, ethnicity, and degree of hearing loss. Kluwin (1993), reporting on these same students, found that those students who regularly received their instruction in general education classes made more positive academic change than students who did not receive such instruction. However, he also reported that 29% of the variance in twelfth grade achievement was attributable to demographic variables, whereas placement variables accounted for only 1.3% of the variance. Clearly, disentangling the separate influence of demographic and placement variables is difficult, and may not, in fact, be possible.

Even though DHH students receiving instruction in general education classrooms have higher academic achievement than those receiving instruction in self-contained classrooms, they often lag behind their hearing peers at similar ages and grade levels. An early study of students with mild hearing loss in grades 1–4 found that these students, although performing at grade level, received scores that were lower than matched hearing peers at all grades, with the gap widening as students got older (Blair, Peterson, & Viehweg, 1985). Antia et al. (2008) recently completed a 5-year longitudinal study of 197 DHH students, grades 2–8, in general education classrooms. The students' hearing levels ranged from mild to profound, and 85% spent 3 or more hours per day in the general education classroom at the beginning of the study. Data were obtained annually on students' academic scores on national and state standardized tests, teacher ratings of academic competence, and social skills. Students' academic scores were interpreted using norms for hearing students. The results on academic achievement showed that, on the average, these students were functioning in the low-average range for math, reading, and language. Over the 5-year period, the DHH students achieved, on average, at the 36th percentile for math, the 25th percentile for reading, and the 26th percentile for language/writing when compared to the test norms for hearing peers. Approximately two-thirds of the students achieved within the average range (within 1 standard deviation [SD] above and 1 SD below the test mean; i.e. within the 23rd and 76th percentiles). However, one-third of the students scored more than 1 SD below the test mean, higher than the 16% that would be expected in a normal distribution.

Scores on standardized tests are not the only way to assess the academic status of DHH students in general education classes. Deaf and hard-of-hearing students may be achieving poorly compared to the national norms on standardized academic achievement tests, but be performing as well (or as poorly) as their hearing classmates. The opposite might also be true, as reported by Blair et al. (1985) whose study showed that DHH students were performing on grade level compared to national norms, but falling academically behind their hearing classmates. Academic status, therefore, should also be measured using teacher ratings that compare the academic performance of the DHH students to grade level and curricular expectations, or to their hearing classmates. Several studies have obtained such data on teacher perceptions of student academic performance (Antia et al., 2008; Most, 2006; Power & Hyde, 2002) with mixed results.

Power and Hyde (2002) used a questionnaire that asked itinerant teachers to rate the academic performance of 151 Australian DHH students in general education classrooms. Teachers reported that 66% of their students were academically competitive with their hearing peers, whereas an additional 17% met minimal academic standards. Most (2006) compared the academic performance of 33 DHH Arab–Israeli students in general education classrooms with 60 hearing classmates. General education teachers completed the Screening Instrument for Targeting Educational Risk (SIFTER; Andersen, 1989). The SIFTER includes 15 items (including items on academic performance) on which the teacher rates the DHH student in comparison to the average hearing student in the class. The students with hearing loss were perceived by their teachers as performing significantly less well academically than their hearing peers at all grade levels. Antia and her colleagues (Antia et al., 2008), as part of their longitudinal study of DHH students in general education classrooms, asked classroom teachers to rate students' academic competence on a standardized questionnaire, the Social Skills Rating System (SSRS) (Gresham & Elliott, 1990). Teacher ratings were obtained annually for 5 years. The SSRS provides an Academic Competence score based on nine items rated on a 5-point scale. These items include reading and math performance compared to hearing classmates, reading and math performance compared to expected grade-level performance, motivation, intellectual functioning, classroom behavior, and parental encouragement. Over the 5-year period, between 67% and 77% of DHH students received ratings for Academic Competence in the average range when compared to hearing peers in their classrooms; between 20% and 31% of students received below-average ratings, and only 3%–7% were rated above-average. Compared to a normal distribution, the expected number of students fell into the average range, but the number of students in the below-average range was higher than expected, whereas the number in the above-average range was lower than expected. The mean standard score on teacher-rated Academic Competence was between 92 and 96, compared to the average standard score of 100, indicating that the students were performing slightly below the norm group but well within the average range. Teacher reports of student performance on both the SIFTER and the SSRS have been found to be reliable and valid for both DHH and hearing students (Andersen, 1989; Antia et al., 2008; Gresham & Elliott, 1990). However, correlations of the teacher ratings with standardized achievement scores of DHH students are not yet available.

The next issue is the academic progress that students in general education classrooms make over time, and whether their progress is sufficient to keep up with their hearing classmates. Blair et al. (1985) reported that DHH students made about one grade's progress in 1 year's time, but also found that the gap between DHH students and their matched hearing classmates was wider at fourth grade than at first grade. Kluwin and Stinson (1993) examined DHH students' achievement in high school from ninth to twelfth grade and reported that ninth grade achievement was the best predictor of twelfth grade achievement, indicating that students who do well early in their school careers continue to do well. Antia et al. (2008) obtained standardized achievement data on math, reading, and writing/language over a 5-year period. They conducted individual regressions on the scores for each DHH student over 5 years and found that approximately 77% of students made gains of 1 year or more in 1 year's time. The average gain in the area of language/writing was significantly greater than that expected for same-grade hearing students in the norming sample.

To summarize, the research indicates that DHH students attending general education classrooms outperform their DHH peers in self-contained classrooms in academic achievement, and are making 1 year's progress over 1 year's time. As a group, however, they are not performing as well as their hearing peers when academic achievement is measured through standardized achievement tests. In contrast, teachers report that most DHH students in general education classrooms are performing academically, based on daily work, in a manner similar to hearing classmates. It should be remembered that academic progress refers to positive change over time. Students who start the academic year achieving at a lower level than their classmates would need to make more than a year's progress in a year's time if they are to "catch up" and show achievement commensurate with hearing classmates. However, the positive news is that at least one study (Antia et al., 2008) has shown that such progress is possible.

When interpreting the data on academic achievement it is worth noting that most DHH students in general education classrooms have severe or less-than-severe hearing loss and would be categorized as hard of hearing rather than deaf. Because hard-of-hearing students use spoken English as their preferred mode of communication, they are often perceived as having more in common with hearing than with deaf students. There is a belief that students who are hard of hearing, and who can function in oral environments, need less explicit intervention and have less need for intervention than students who are deaf (Marschark, Lang, & Albertini, 2002).

It is true that students with a greater degree of hearing loss are likely to have lower achievement (particularly in reading) than students with a lesser degree of hearing loss (Allen, 1986; Davis, Shepard, Stelmachowicz, & Gorga, 1981). Davis et al. found that while students with unilateral and mild bilateral hearing loss achieved at about the 50th percentile in reading and math, students who had moderate to severe hearing loss achieved lower, between the 25th and 40th percentiles. Allen (1986), drawing from data collected from the GRI's annual survey, reported that students with a profound hearing loss performed significantly less well in reading comprehension than students who had less-than-profound hearing loss. However, although a greater degree of hearing loss may depress academic achievement, any degree of hearing loss can create problems for classroom functioning. Poor acoustic and communication environments are likely to make it difficult for hard-of-hearing students to function appropriately in the classroom (Ross, Brackett, & Maxon, 1982, 1991) or to interact with their teachers and classmates (see Chapter 25, this volume). Thus, professionals should not ignore the potential negative consequences of mild or moderate hearing loss on achievement.

Factors Contributing to Academic Outcomes

Studies of factors relating to the success of DHH students can inform the field about best practices to support students. Much research has focused on unchangeable demographic factors, such as degree of hearing loss, presence of additional handicapping conditions, ethnicity, or family resources (Karchmer & Mitchell, 2003; Powers, 2003). The focus here is on factors that provide information about the kinds of conditions and support that will be effective for students.

Professionals and parents have an impact on the success of DHH students. High academic expectations on the part of teachers, schools, and parents is a key variable that influences success (Jimenez-Sanchez & Antia, 1999; Kluwin & Moores, 1985; Luckner & Muir, 2001; Reed, Antia, & Kreimeyer, 2008). Kluwin and Moores (1985) interviewed general education math teachers and asked about their expectations for the DHH students who attended their classes; the unanimous response was that teachers expected DHH students to learn the same content as their hearing peers. Jimenez-Sanchez and Antia (1999) interviewed teachers in co-enrolled programs, while Luckner and Muir (2001) interviewed parents and teachers of successful DHH students. Again, high expectations on the part of the teachers, and a belief that DHH students were capable of mastering the regular curriculum were perceived as contributing to student success. Finally, Reed et al. (2008) interviewed teachers, parents, and school administrators of 25 DHH students in general education classrooms. The two factors most frequently perceived as facilitating achievement were the expectations that the DHH students would achieve in a manner commensurate with their hearing classmates, and high academic expectations for all students within the school.

Unfortunately, teachers of DHH students may underestimate their students' capabilities (Gaustad, 1999; Jimenez-Sanchez & Antia, 1999). Gaustad required general educators and teachers of DHH students to collaboratively develop and teach a unit of instruction to combined classes of DHH and hearing students. The teachers of DHH students noted that their classes were more capable than they had anticipated, and that they needed to hold higher expectations of their academic performance.

Good communication and teamwork, both between parents and professionals and among professionals, is important to the academic success of DHH students. Parents who are unable to communicate with professionals because of language or other barriers may not know the capabilities of their children, and therefore may not have appropriate expectations for their success. Luckner and Muir (2001) reported that teamwork among professionals was an important facilitator of student success. Reed et al. (2008) found that DHH students achieving at high academic levels had good communication networks in place; there was ongoing communication between parents and professionals, and among the professionals themselves (e.g., the general educator, teacher of DHH students, interpreter, and audiologist). Deaf and hard-of-hearing students who were achieving at below-average levels had at least one ineffective communication network; either poor communication existed between the professionals and parents, or among the professionals themselves.

Several student variables are associated with academic success. Students' communication skills are an obvious and important variable. Kluwin and

Moores (1985) identified the following communication factors as crucial to the success of DHH students in general education classrooms: oral and/or sign production and reception, knowledge of English, and literacy. These factors, although necessary, may not be sufficient to ensure successful communication. Successful communication includes not only syntactically and semantically accurate production and reception of language, but also pragmatic skills such as the ability to interact appropriately within different classroom contexts and to tailor the message and mode of communication for communication partners. A good communicator perseveres to correct miscommunication, can take the listener's perspective to clarify and repair conversations, and finds alternate modes of communication when necessary. Antia et al. (2008) found that global teacher ratings of student expressive and receptive communication were significantly related to reading and writing outcomes, accounting for between 18% and 23% of the variability in reading and writing achievement. These teacher ratings were based on students' communication skills and fluency using the mode of communication customary for the student. High ratings indicated that the student communicated with teachers and peers fluently and easily, whereas low ratings indicated that the student was severely limited, even when using accommodations such as amplification systems and/or interpreters.

An important variable contributing to academic success is students' ability to participate in the classroom (e.g., the ability to communicate with teachers and classmates during instruction, to understand and express ideas in the classroom, and to engage in classroom discussions). Several studies have found a strong relationship between student self-rated classroom participation, academic engagement, and academic achievement (Antia, Sabers, & Stinson, 2007; Braeges, Stinson, & Long, 1993; Long, Stinson, & Braeges, 1991). Braeges et al. (1993) reported that DHH high school students' academic engagement in the classroom, as rated by their teachers, was a significant predictor of academic achievement. Antia et al. (2007) found that, for school-age students in general education classrooms, self-rated classroom participation was a significant predictor of academic outcomes.

Classroom participation may be a more influential factor than degree of hearing loss, as profoundly deaf students who can make use of good educational interpreters may be able to participate as well as students who use oral communication, and better than students with mild or unilateral hearing loss who struggle to communicate in poor acoustic environments without amplification. For hard-of-hearing or oral students, classroom participation may be related to consistent use of amplification (Reed et al., 2008). Classroom participation may also be related to students' expressive and receptive communication skill, regardless of the mode of communication (Antia et al., 2008). However, classroom participation is also influenced by hearing students' communication skills, as well as classroom instructional practices, such as general educators' willingness to make accommodations and to work with interpreters (Reed et al., 2008; Stinson & Liu, 1999).

Students' ability to advocate for themselves contributes to their academic success (Luckner & Muir, 2001; Reed et al., 2008). Such self-advocacy might include the student taking the initiative to sit in classroom locations that maximize access to communication, or learning how to request clarification of teachers and classmates. Self-advocacy skills may be related to metacognitive skills. Metacognition is broadly defined as an awareness of how one learns, and the awareness of when one does or does not comprehend (Flavell, 1979). It is therefore, an important skill for monitoring and improving learning (Gourgey, 1998). Students who have good metacognitive skills are likely to be better at understanding what they read, and also at monitoring their understanding of classroom content and discourse, thus leading to better academic achievement, especially in general education classrooms in which the communication and teaching may not be adapted to students' with hearing loss (Marschark, Convertino, Macias, Monikowski, Sapere, & Seewagen, 2007; Strassman, 1997).

Social Outcomes

In addition to academic learning, schools provide opportunities for social learning. Students learn the social skills necessary to interact with other students and adults, initiate and exchange conversations, develop friendships, and take others' perspectives and understand their feelings. Mastery of social skills may be as important as mastery of academic skills, as these are necessary to negotiate the challenges of interpersonal relationships within school and future employment situations (Calderon & Greenberg, 2003; Stinson & Whitmire, 2000). Additionally, research with hearing students indicates that social behavior and skills can predict later academic achievement, in some cases with better accuracy than early academic performance scores (Caprara, Barbaranelli, Pastorelli, Bandura, & Zimbardo, 2000;

Malecki & Elliott, 2002). Social relationships require mutually comprehensible communication, thus prompting concern as to whether the general education setting provides opportunities for positive social outcomes for DHH students.

Positive social outcomes are more difficult to define than academic outcomes. A socially integrated student is one who has developed the social skills and social competence to interact with peers, be socially accepted by them, and have emotionally secure friendships (Stinson & Antia, 1999). For DHH students in general education classrooms, social relationships will, out of necessity, involve hearing peers. The following sections describes some of the findings on social interaction and competence, social acceptance, and friendships.

Social Interaction and Social Competence

Early observation studies of the interactions between elementary-age DHH and hearing students within public school settings found that DHH students interacted less frequently and with fewer peers (DHH or hearing) than same-age hearing students (Antia, 1982, 1985; Antia & Dittillo, 1998; Levine & Antia, 1997; McCauley, Bruininks, & Kennedy, 1976; Vandell & George, 1981), thus prompting concerns about the level of social integration of these students. However, most of these studies were conducted with students who attended the same school, but did not necessarily attend general education classes with their hearing peers, and the results are thus not necessarily relevant or generalizable to DHH students in general education classrooms.

Several studies of the peer interaction of high school students attending varying numbers of general education classes have been conducted using student self-reports of interaction and social participation (Musselman, Mootilal, & MacKay, 1996; Stinson & Whitmire, 1991, 1992; Stinson, Whitmire, & Kluwin, 1996). Stinson and Whitmire (1991) obtained student self-ratings on the frequency of involvement in both in-school and out-of-school social activities using the Social Activity Scale (Stinson & Whitmire, 1992). The authors studied 84 DHH adolescents in secondary schools and further education programs in England. The mean age of these students was 14.7 years. Time in general education classes ranged from 9% to 43% of classes for the group spending the least time in general education, to 85%–100% of classes for the group spending the most time in general education. Results indicated that the DHH students rated themselves as interacting more frequently with hearing than

with DHH peers during in-classroom and out-of-school social activities, and equally frequently with DHH and hearing peers for in-school social activities (e.g., eating lunch with friends). As the number of general education classes increased, a corresponding increase in the amount of time interacting with hearing peers was reported. Students who spent the least amount of time in general education classrooms reported significantly less interaction with hearing peers in class and in school than those who spent the most amount of time in general education classes.

Stinson, Whitmire, and Kluwin (1996) used the Social Activity Scale in a larger study of 220 DHH high school students in the United States and Canada who spent varied amounts of time in general education classes, reported as the number of classes completed with hearing students during the current and previous year. Although it is not possible to directly compare the amount of time these students spent in general education classes with the British students in the previous study, it appears that it was substantially less. In the British study, the group spending the most time in the general education setting completed 85%–100% of their classes with hearing students. In this study, the group spending the most time in general education classes completed 10–23 classes with hearing students over a 2-year period. In contrast to the results obtained with British students, United States and Canadian students reported more frequent in-school interaction with DHH than with hearing peers. A progressive increase in in-school interaction with hearing peers occurred as the number of general education classes attended increased. Out-of-school social participation for the DHH students was influenced both by grade level and number of general education classes attended. Students in tenth and eleventh grades reported similar levels of out-of-school participation with hearing peers, regardless of the number of general education classes attended. However, by twelfth grade, DHH students who attended the most general education classes reported less out-of-school participation with hearing peers than did DHH students who attended the fewest general education classes. There is no obvious reason to explain this change in pattern.

Musselman et al. (1996) administered the Social Activity Scale to 72 DHH and 88 hearing high-school students in Canada. Both groups of students were comparable in age, with the mean age of DHH students 16.4 years and that of hearing students 16.1 years. This study included three groups of

DHH students: those who attended no general education classes, those who attended one to four general education classes, and those who attended five or more general education classes. The group of students who attended the most general education classes appeared to spend a higher percentage of their time in this setting than the comparable group of students in the Stinson et al. study. The researchers found that both in-class and out-of-school social participation with hearing peers increased for DHH girls with increased time in general education classrooms. No differences in in-class participation were found between DHH girls who attended five or more general education classes and hearing girls. However, this was not true for DHH boys, who demonstrated comparable levels of in-class and out-of-school social participation regardless of the amount of time in general education classes.

Another picture of students' social behavior can be obtained by teacher ratings of social competence. Antia et al. (2008), as part of their longitudinal study, obtained teacher ratings of social skills and problem behaviors of DHH students annually for 5 years using the SSRS (Gresham & Elliott, 1990). The Social Skills scale of the SSRS requires teachers to rate students' cooperation, assertion, responsibility, empathy, and self-control. The Problem Behaviors scale requires teachers to rate behaviors such as inappropriate aggression, anxiety, sadness, loneliness, and hyperactivity. Antia and her colleagues found that, over the 5-year period, between 79% and 86% of students were rated as displaying average or above-average social skills, a percentage comparable to that of the typical hearing normative group. In addition, 86% to 94% of students were rated as displaying average or below-average problem behaviors, which was better than expected of the normative group. Teacher ratings of social skills remained constant as students moved into middle and high school, whereas ratings for problem behaviors significantly declined as students became older.

The data on students' social participation and social competence are generally positive. Student self-reports of participation (Musselman et al., 1996; Stinson & Whitmire, 1991; Stinson et al., 1996) indicate that participation in school and in social activities with hearing peers increases as time in general education classes increases. One exception was noted in the Stinson et al. study, as twelfth grade students who spent the most time in general education reported lower levels of social participation than same-grade students who spent less time in general education. Teachers report that DHH students have social skills comparable to hearing peers, and fewer problem behaviors (Antia et al., 2008).

Social Acceptance

Socially accepted students are known and liked by their classmates, thus not rejected or neglected by peers. Studies of social acceptance have been conducted primarily with elementary-age students and yield varying results across studies and locations (Cappelli, Daniels, Durieux-Smith, McGrath, & Neuss, 1995; Nunes & Pretzlik, 2001; Wauters & Knoors, 2008).

Social acceptance is typically measured through the use of peer nomination and peer rating scales (Cappelli et al., 1995; Wauters & Knoors, 2008). Peer nomination scales measure peer group functioning in individual students and require students to select most-liked and least-liked classmates. Nominations across classmates provide information on social status (popular, neglected, rejected, controversial, or average). *Popular* students have a high mean "like" score and a low mean "dislike" score. *Neglected* students receive low scores on both "like" and "dislike" ratings. *Rejected* students receive a high "dislike" score and a low "like" score. *Controversial* students receive high "like" and "dislike" scores, and *average* students are those who do not fall into one of the previously described categories. Mutual nominations identify friendships and antipathies. Peer rating or likability rating scales provide a measure of overall social acceptance or likability. Students indicate how much they like to spend time with each classmate using a scale that varies from "don't like to" to "like to a lot." The positive (like) and negative (dislike) nominations are used to generate a social preference score (how much a student is liked by classmates), and a social impact score (how well a student is known by classmates).

Cappelli et al. (1995) studied 23 first through sixth grade oral DHH students and 23 hearing classmates matched for gender. All students completed peer rating and peer nomination measures. Results indicated that the DHH students received significantly lower likability and social preference ratings than their hearing classmates. To examine potential developmental differences, the researchers separated the DHH students into younger (first to third) and older (fourth to sixth) grade levels, and found that seven of the 12 younger students were classified as having low social status, compared to two of the 11 older students, a significant difference. All seven of the younger students fell into the category of being "rejected" by their hearing classmates.

One of the older students was classified as "neglected" and the other as "controversial" ("liked" by some classmates and "disliked" by others). A self-perception profile completed by all students indicated that DHH students perceived themselves to be less socially accepted than the hearing students.

In a more recent study, Nunes and Pretzlik (2001) examined the social status of nine oral fourth and fifth grade DHH students and 62 hearing classmates attending two schools in London. Results indicated that the DHH students were no more likely than their hearing peers to be disliked. No significant differences were found between DHH and hearing students on the proportion identified as *popular* or *rejected*. However, the proportion of DHH students identified as *neglected* was significantly higher than that of hearing classmates.

Finally, in a study conducted in the Netherlands, Wauters and Knoors (2008) gave a sociometric assessment to 18 elementary DHH students who attended general education classrooms, and 344 hearing classmates. These researchers found no differences between the social status (popular, rejected, neglected, controversial, or average) of DHH and hearing students, or how much students were liked or known within the classroom. Moreover, data collected over a 2-year period showed that these outcomes remained stable over time.

The research on peer acceptance appears to indicate that some DHH students may be as liked as their hearing peers and are not actively disliked or rejected by peers, although they may be neglected. However, the small number of studies with small samples of DHH students indicates the need for further research in this area.

Friendship

Although social interaction and participation with peers, and acceptance by peers, is important, the most critical social outcome for students is having and maintaining friendships. Because DHH students in general education classes may not have regular contact with DHH peers of their age, friendship with hearing peers is significant. Students who have friends have fewer adjustment problems, higher self-esteem, less loneliness, wider peer acceptance, better school adjustment, more positive attitudes toward school, and higher achievement than those who do not (Gifford-Smith & Brownell, 2003). Friendships between DHH and hearing students have been investigated by obtaining student perceptions on sociometric measures, student self-report using the Emotional Security subscale of the Social

Activity Scale, and parent perceptions through interviews.

Sociometric measures require individual students to select classmates whom they like most and least. Mutual "like" nominations define friends and mutual "dislike" nominations define antipathies. Two studies of elementary students described earlier (Nunes & Pretzlik, 2001; Wauters & Knoors, 2008) provided contradictory results on friendships. Nunes and Pretzlik (2001) reported that the DHH students were significantly less likely than their hearing classmates to have a friend in their classroom, while Wauters and Knoors (2008) found no differences between DHH and hearing students in the number of mutual friendships or antipathies.

Students' perception of positive stability in relationships has been obtained using the Emotional Security subscale of the Social Activity Scale (Stinson & Whitmire, 1992). Students rate statements such as, "When I'm with hearing students my age, I feel nervous," or, "I wish I had more friends who were hearing/DHH," using a 4-point scale varying from "almost never" to "always." Results from the previously described research with adolescent students in England (Stinson & Whitmire, 1991) indicated that mean ratings of emotional security with both hearing and DHH peers increased as time in general education classes increased. Students felt more emotionally secure with DHH peers than with hearing peers, perhaps reflecting easier communication and a shared perception of "likeness."

Analysis of Emotional Security ratings of American students (Stinson et al., 1996) revealed a more complex pattern, with significant interaction between grade level, number of general education classes, and peer group (DHH or hearing). Matching their report (discussed earlier) of decreased out-of-school social participation with hearing peers as time in class with them increased, twelfth grade DHH students who spent the most time in general education classes felt significantly lower emotional security with hearing peers than did those who spent the least time in general education classes. These twelfth grade students also reported lower emotional security with hearing peers than tenth grade DHH students who spent a comparable amount of time in general education classes. Thus, in this study, it appeared that as students got older they felt less emotionally secure with hearing peers (and, presumably, had fewer close friendships) despite the amount of time they spent with these peers. It is possible that these DHH students experienced unmet needs for belonging to a peer group that became more pronounced as they grew older.

Musselman et al. (1996) found that DHH girls who attended five general education classes felt as emotionally secure with hearing peers as did hearing girls. In contrast with findings of Stinson et al. (1996), Musselman et al. (1996) found that DHH girls who attended fewer general education classes felt less secure with hearing peers than did the DHH girls who attended more general education classes. These findings were not true of DHH boys, who maintained the same feeling of emotional security with hearing peers, regardless of the number of general education classes attended. Research on emotional closeness within the friendships of hearing adolescents has found significant differences between male and female friendships; girls reported spending significantly more time with their friends, and had more cohesive relationships and more closeness in their friendships than did boys (Johnson, 2004). Thus, for DHH girls (but not for DHH boys) additional time in general education classes may positively influence feelings of friendship.

Another perspective on friendships between DHH and hearing students is that provided by parents (Martin & Bat-Chava, 2003). Interviews were conducted with the parents of 35 DHH children between 5 and 11 years of age, most of whom were in general education classrooms full- or part-time, indicated that about half the children were described as confident when interacting with hearing peers. Parents reported that most of the children established satisfactory relations with their hearing peers, with 34% having good relationships, 51% having fair relationships, and 14% having poor relationships. Although not significant, there was a trend for children's relationships to improve with age.

Although the research on friendships between DHH and hearing students is limited, it appears that, whereas elementary students may have mutual friendships with hearing peers, such friendships may be more challenging as students move into the adolescent years. During adolescence, peer relationships assume higher priority in the social life of students than during the elementary years. Adolescents also make finer distinctions between acquaintances and true friendships within their social relationships (Stinson & Whitmire, 2000). Gender may influence friendship, with girls developing increasing friendships as time in general education increases.

Factors Contributing to Social Outcomes

As with academic outcomes, multiple factors contribute to social outcomes. One factor is the spoken language competence of DHH students. Students with intelligible speech and strong aural skills are more successful interacting with hearing peers than those with poor oral skills or students who prefer to use sign language (Bat-Chava & Deignan, 2001; Musselman et al., 1996; Stinson & Kluwin, 1996; Stinson & Whitmire, 1992; Tvingstedt, 1993; Wauters & Knoors, 2008). Stinson and Whitmire (1992) investigated the relationship between communication preference and social participation of 64 DHH high school students attending a summer camp. Students stated their preferred mode of communication: oral, American Sign Language (ASL), or simultaneous communication. They also completed the Social Activity Scale. Students who preferred oral communication reported more frequent social participation with hearing peers than with DHH peers, whereas those who used ASL or simultaneous communication reported more social participation with DHH peers. Musselman et al. (1996) examined the relationship between communicative competence in spoken English, simultaneous communication, and ASL, and social adjustment with hearing peers. These authors reported that competence in spoken English made a significant contribution to both in-class participation and emotional security with hearing peers.

Newborn hearing screening, improved amplification options that include cochlear implants, digital hearing aids, and assistive listening devices, all increase the potential for students with any degree of hearing loss to develop intelligible spoken language. However, students who are not comfortable communicating receptively or expressively in oral language will need to have access to hearing and DHH peers who communicate in sign.

The amount of time within the general education setting is another variable that has positive and negative impact on relationships with hearing peers. Generally, DHH adolescents reported increased frequency of interaction with hearing peers in school with increased time spent in general education classrooms (Musselman et al., 1996; Stinson & Whitmire, 1991; Stinson et al., 1996). However, this pattern did not occur for out-of-school social participation with hearing peers. Stinson et al. (1996) reported that, for tenth and eleventh graders, increased time in the classroom had no impact on out-of-school participation, but by twelfth grade, students who attended the most general education classes reported less out-of-school participation with hearing peers than students who attended the least general education classes. For these students, increased time in general education also negatively impacted emotional security with hearing peers.

Although increased time in general education classes might provide more opportunities for peer socialization, it is also possible that such socialization does not necessarily lead to close friendships or feelings of emotional security.

Age appears to affect social relationships and behaviors. Elementary-age DHH students appear to have more positive relationships with hearing peers than do DHH adolescents (Nunes & Pretzlik, 2001; Stinson et al., 1996; Wauters & Knoors, 2008). Although acquaintance may suffice for some period of time, as students reach the final years of high school, they may become increasingly aware of a lack of intimate peer relationships. However, teachers appear to rate DHH students in general education classrooms as having positive social behaviors over time, indicating that older students are not perceived to have more problems than younger students (Antia et al., 2008).

Gender also influences social outcomes. Musselman et al. (1996) reported that DHH boys and girls showed different patterns of participation with hearing peers with increased time in general education. For girls, increased time resulted in increased participation with hearing peers, whereas boys reported similar participation with hearing peers regardless of the amount of time in general education classrooms. Martin and Bat-Chava (2003), using parental interviews to examine friendships, found that although there were no differences between elementary-age boys' and girls' success in relationships with hearing peers, they used different social strategies to establish these relationships. An effective strategy for girls was the ability to assert their needs, whereas for boys the single most effective strategy was to excel in sports.

How Teachers Support Deaf and Hard-of-Hearing Students in General Education Classrooms

Many professionals support DHH students in general education classrooms. Interpreters, captioners, and audiologists help with access to classroom communication. Speech pathologists and other specialists may also provide a variety of direct services. The purpose of this section is to highlight the support that should be offered specifically by teachers of DHH, rather than providing a list of all the kinds of support that students may need.

Responsibilities of Itinerant Teachers of Deaf and Hard-of-Hearing Students

Typically, teachers of DHH students are prepared to teach in self-contained settings and to deliver curriculum content. To effectively support DHH students in general education classrooms, the role of these teachers needs to be distinctly different from that of a teacher in a self-contained classroom. The model most often used is an itinerant teaching model. Currently, no data are available on numbers of itinerant teachers, but, given the number of DHH students in general education, it is likely that there are at least as many itinerant teachers as there are teachers of self-contained classrooms. Also, the numbers of itinerant teachers are likely to increase in the future (Teller & Harney, 2005/2006). Through surveys and interviews, some information about the role of the itinerant teacher is available. However, there has been little conceptualization, discussion, or research on the effectiveness of the support services provided by these teachers. Thus, at this time, only descriptive research is available on the responsibilities of these teachers. Given what is known about the factors contributing to the success of DHH students in general education, it is possible to begin to conceptualize and evaluate the effectiveness of support that teachers should be able to provide.

Itinerant teachers travel to different schools and have a caseload of DHH students who vary considerably in age, grade level, hearing loss, and presence of additional disabilities. A survey of 319 itinerant teachers in the United States (Luckner & Miller, 1994) found that the typical student served by these teachers spent 80% of the time in the general education classroom and worked with the itinerant teacher 2.5 hours per week. The degree of support provided varied; some students received direct services, whereas others received indirect services or monitoring to ensure that difficulties did not occur. The teachers reported an average caseload of 11 direct service students and seven students whom they monitored. A summary of competencies needed by teachers for direct and indirect service to DHH students (Bullard, 2003; Smith, 1997) is provided in Table 6.1.

Several surveys of and interviews with itinerant teachers have provided information on the kind of instruction provided, the amount of time these teachers spend in direct contact with DHH students, and where the teachers learned about itinerant teaching (Foster & Cue, 2007; Power & Hyde, 2003; Yarger & Luckner, 1999). Itinerant teachers surveyed provided instruction to their students in communication, academic, and nonacademic skills. Communication skills included oral and sign language, speech, speechreading, listening skills, and use of interpreters. Academic areas included reading,

Table 6.1 Competencies Needed by Itinerant Teachers of Deaf and Hard-of-Hearing Students

Competencies needed to provide direct service:	Competencies needed to provide indirect service:

1. Ability to provide direct instruction to DHH student in
  a. academics
  b. language
  c. speech
  d. hearing
2. Ability to assess
  a. academics
  b. language
  c. speech
  d. hearing
3. Ability to write IEP goals and objectives
4. Ability to adapt and rewrite materials for use by general education teachers
5. Ability to find visual materials
6. Ability to teach small groups within general education classroom
7. Ability to teach sign language in individual and group settings
8. Ability to conduct hearing evaluations
9. Ability to assist with hearing aid maintenance
10. Ability to teach students and teachers how to appropriately use amplification devices and other materials (e.g., closed captioning)
	1. Ability to develop working relationship with general education teachers
	2. Ability to coordinate instructional planning with general education teachers
	3. Ability to coordinate support services with other specialists
	4. Ability to coordinate community resources
	5. Ability to serve as student's case manager
	6. Ability to maintain records of student performance
	7. Ability to communicate with parents
	8. Ability to supervise aids and interpreters
	9. Ability to instruct community and other professionals about hearing loss
	10. Ability to be an advocate for DHH students

Adapted from Bullard, C. (2003). *The itinerant teachers' handbook*; and Smith, M. D. (1997). *The art of itinerant teaching*. Hillsboro, OR: Butte Publications, with permission of the publisher.

writing, and math. Nonacademic areas included social skills, study skills, living skills, and deaf awareness (Foster & Cue, 2007; Power & Hyde, 2003). Itinerant teachers considered direct teaching of students to be the most important part of their job. Teachers surveyed by Power and Hyde (2003) reported that they spent 56% of their time directly teaching individual students, primarily by pulling the student out of the classroom. However, some itinerant teachers reported working directly with students in the general education classroom. Time spent working with students varied from less than 1 hour per week per student, to more than 4 hours per week per student. Most students (43%) received 2 to 3 hours per week of direct instruction from the itinerant teacher.

Indirect services primarily involved consulting with general education teachers. In Australia, 70% of itinerant teachers surveyed by Power and Hyde (2003) reported spending 10–30 minutes per week consulting with general education teachers. In contrast, teachers interviewed by Yarger and Luckner (1999) in the United States reported that they spent an average of 2 hours a day in consultation. Teacher

preparation programs, at least in the United States, typically prepare teachers to directly deliver curriculum to DHH students. The teachers in Foster and Cue's (2007) study reported learning to be an itinerant teacher while on the job and through in-service education.

Teacher surveys provide a global picture of the services provided to all DHH students on a teacher's caseload. Antia et al. (2008), in their longitudinal study, obtained information on the services provided to each student by the teachers of DHH learners. The difference between these data and the survey data described by Luckner and Miller (1994) or Foster and Cue (2007), is that Antia's group (2008) provide student-level data, rather than teacher-level data. The data on services received were obtained on each student annually for 4 years. (Although the academic and social data were collected for 5 years, data on services were only obtained for 4 years; no data on services were obtained the first year of the study.) Table 6.2 shows the percentage of students receiving specific direct services from teachers of DHH learners, averaged over the 4-year period. The students received instruction from teachers of DHH learners in (a) communication skills that included auditory skills, language, and speech; (b) literacy skills that included reading and writing; (c) academic subjects that included math, science, and social studies; (d) academic skills that cut across subject matter, such as learning strategies and study skills; (e) nonacademic skills that included use of assistive technology (e.g., amplification devices, or captioning), career development, and self-advocacy; and (f) social skills. In the area of communication, more than one-third of students received instruction from the teacher in language, fewer received help in developing auditory skills, and very few students received speech services from teachers of DHH learners. Speech services may be offered by other professionals (for example, speech pathologists), or reflect a lack of perceived need, priority, or teacher skill. Almost half the students received support from their teacher in reading and writing. Less than one-quarter of the students received instruction in academic subjects from their teacher of DHH learners, reflecting the fact that curricular instruction is primarily provided by general educators. Some students received instruction in learning strategies (strategies designed to make them independent learners), but over one-third of students received instruction in study skills, which could be considered a subset of learning strategies. Among nonacademic skills, most emphasis appeared to be placed on self-advocacy, with over half the students receiving instruction in this area. Despite the concerns expressed in the literature about students' social outcomes, only 15% of the students received support in the area of social skills. However, it should be remembered that a high percentage of this sample of students were rated as having average social skills by their general education teachers, so it is quite possible that social skills instruction was not a priority for them.

Clearly, not all students receive all possible services. How do teachers decide which services to provide? Antia's group (2008) completed in-depth case studies on 25 students. For each case study student, the researchers interviewed a general education teacher, the teacher of DHH students, support staff (interpreters or notetakers), parents, and the students themselves. From these interviews, which included questions about services provided to each student, the researchers were able to examine the relationship between intensity of support and specific kinds of services offered by the teacher of DHH students. Figure 6.1 shows the continuum of support services, arranged with services for students needing

Table 6.2 Percentage of Deaf and Hard-of-Hearing Students Receiving Specific Services from Itinerant Teachers

Instructional area	Percentage of students in grades 3–12 receiving service (averaged over 4 years)
Communication Skills	
Auditory Skills	24
Language	37
Speech	6
Literacy Instruction	
Reading	46
Writing	43
Academic Subjects	
Math	22
Science	11
Social Studies	15
Academic Skills	
Learning Strategies	18
Study Skills	38
Non-Academic Skills	
Assistive Technology	27
Career Development	16
Self Advocacy	59
Social Skills	15

the least amount of support at the top, to those needing the most support at the bottom. All students received indirect services; these included communication with general education teachers, support in developing self-advocacy skills, and using amplification (when appropriate). When students needed additional support, teachers first typically provided support that cut across specific content, such as instruction in organization, help with homework, and study skills. Students needing the most support received instruction in academic subjects, typically math and language arts.

Support Needed by Deaf and Hard-of-Hearing Students to Succeed in General Education Classrooms

Based on the research, it is possible to begin conceptualizing the kind of support needed by DHH students. Five general areas are identified: communication and literacy, learning strategies, self-advocacy, classroom participation, and social skills, with content areas infused as appropriate. In each of these areas the teacher of DHH students can provide direct instruction and also communicate and collaborate with

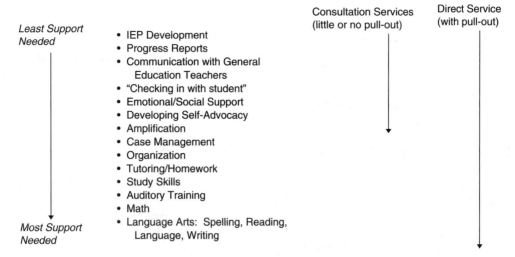

Fig. 6.1 Continuum of support services

general educators and family members to support the DHH student.

Although itinerant teachers have reported that direct instruction of DHH students is an essential part of the support they provide, it is important to remember that the student is (or should be) primarily a member of the general education classroom (Antia, Stinson, & Gaustad, 2002). If general educators are to make accommodations or adaptations, they must feel ownership of the DHH student. Bullard (2003) writes that teachers of DHH students often feel that they are the only persons who understand DHH students' learning needs and are therefore tempted to schedule as much direct service as possible. However, frequent pull-outs, even for needed direct service, can impact students' access to the general education curriculum and affect their social relationships. Additionally, frequent pull-outs can communicate to the general educators that the DHH students' learning and welfare is primarily the responsibility of the itinerant teachers, leading to a reluctance to make changes that might benefit students. Thus, an important part of supporting DHH students is the empowerment of general educators.

Several researchers have discussed the importance of collaboration between the teacher of DHH students and the general educator (Antia, 1999; Antia & Stinson, 1999; Foster & Cue, 2007; Luckner & Miller, 1994). Certain aspects of collaboration are worth mentioning here. Collaboration is easier if the teacher of DHH students is felt to "belong" to the school. To develop this feeling of belonging, the teacher of DHH students needs to have (or find)

opportunities to interact with general education teachers, principals, and other staff at the schools being served. In the absence of such interaction, the teacher of DHH students is an invisible person with an unknown role. Such a teacher cannot be effective.

Second, collaboration occurs among equals (Antia & Stinson, 1999). If the teacher of DHH students is seen as the expert with knowledge only about students with hearing loss, or as an aide providing secondary support services, true collaboration cannot occur. Collaboration occurs when teachers respect each other's knowledge and skills, recognize their skills as necessary and complementary, and are focused on using their complementary skills to benefit all the students in the classroom. Thus, it is important for the teacher of DHH students to have a flexible schedule that allows time to observe and collaborate with the general education teacher, in order to become familiar with the culture of the classroom, the general educator's preferred teaching practices, and the needs of the other students in the classroom. Administrators need to consider collaboration time when planning teacher schedules and assigning caseloads.

Communication between school and family is related to the academic success of DHH students. Teachers of DHH students need to collaborate with students' families in multiple ways. Such collaboration might involve communicating with families, not only during parent–teacher meetings, but also through weekly phone calls, e-mails, or home visits to exchange information about student successes and needs. Teachers and parents can exchange journals to keep both parties informed of school and home experiences that impact the student. In some cases, it might be appropriate for teachers to visit the student's home to facilitate communication with parents.

COMMUNICATION AND LITERACY

Communication and literacy are basic to the success of DHH students in any setting, and include a wide range of skills. Although a complete description of skills to be learned (or taught) and how to develop them is beyond the scope of this chapter, some areas are highlighted.

Language proficiency is important to access content, and is therefore necessary (although not sufficient) for academic learning. Teachers of DHH students will likely need to support the development of all aspects of language (pragmatics, semantics, and syntax) in the mode that is preferred, or needed, by the student. Direct teaching of vocabulary probably needs particular attention because it may be difficult for DHH students to learn new vocabulary from classroom discourse. For hard-of-hearing students, poor classroom acoustics may obscure classroom talk, while for deaf students, interpreters may have difficulty accurately conveying all the necessary vocabulary (Schick, Williams, & Bolster, 1999). Itinerant teachers should also advocate for improved communication access for their DHH students within the general education classroom.

Fluency and ease in receptive and expressive communication are related to academic success. For many students, this requires specific attention to auditory and speech skills. Some teachers of DHH students may not be comfortable addressing these areas, or they may believe that instruction in these skills falls within the domain of a speech-language pathologist. For DHH students, however, auditory and speech skills are essential not only for communication, but also for literacy learning. These skills are best addressed in the context of the classroom curriculum during in-class or pull-out sessions. When auditory and speech skills are taught within a skill sequence disconnected from classroom content, there is little opportunity, or incentive, for generalization to the classroom. Teachers of DHH students may be in the best position to promote transfer of auditory and speech skills into classroom curriculum, but only if they have the time and skills needed for collaboration.

Literacy is fundamental to academic learning; thus, teachers of DHH students may find that they need to provide supplemental, remedial, or complementary instruction in this area. In one of the few studies of the literacy practices of itinerant teachers, Reed (2003) found that these teachers used a wide repertoire of literacy teaching strategies and spent much of their pull-out sessions with students developing literacy skills. Teachers of DHH students should provide direct instruction in English vocabulary or syntax that are likely to create problems for the student in upcoming content (often known as pre-teaching); remedy misperceptions of content caused by the lack of vocabulary knowledge or background information; and provide additional learning experiences to develop a deeper understanding of concepts. In some cases, the teacher may have to find complementary strategies to teach aspects of literacy that are not accessible to DHH students. Thus, when hearing students in a classroom learn to decode using letter–sound relationships, the teacher of DHH students might provide direct instruction in the same area using visual strategies. Reed (2003) also found that itinerant teachers who perceived themselves as the primary teacher for literacy development seemed to express more frustration (and possibly experienced less success) than those who perceived their role as supplementary to that of the general educator.

LEARNING STRATEGIES

The goal of the teacher of DHH students should be to help each student develop strategies to become an independent learner and problem solver in the general education classroom. Communication and literacy, although important, are not sufficient to create independent learners. Learning strategies instruction is essential, especially as some research indicates that DHH students may not develop these metacognitive strategies spontaneously (Marschark, Sapere, Convertino, & Seewagen, 2005; Strassman, 1992). It is also important that the teacher not create dependence on the part of the DHH student. Frequently, teachers of DHH students, like teachers of other students with learning needs, may contribute to dependence by providing tutoring that "rescues" the student (Eisenberger et al., 2000). Providing direct instruction in learning strategies prevents the teacher of DHH students from being an expensive tutor.

Strategy instruction helps students develop the techniques and routines to solve problems and tackle learning tasks independently and effectively (Snyder & Pressley, 1995). Students, therefore, need to acquire procedural knowledge (specific learning strategies), as well as metacognitive knowledge

(knowledge to monitor their effective use of strategies). Although some students develop effective learning strategies independently, others need explicit and structured teaching. Guidelines and materials for teachers to assist in strategy instruction are available through many sources (Eisenberger, Conti-D'Antonio, & Bertrando, 2000; Tierney & Readence, 2005). Examples of often-used strategies for reading comprehension include summarization, activating prior knowledge, or re-reading sections of text. (A good source for reading comprehension strategies is http://www.k8accesscenter.org.) Examples of study strategies might include notetaking, or creating graphic organizers (see Chapter 8, this volume). These strategies are probably familiar to teachers of DHH students. However, it is not sufficient merely to teach the students a strategy, or to have the students engage in using the strategy under the teacher's direction. Students should understand the value of the strategy, learn to monitor their performance while using the strategy, and know when and where to use specific strategies. Snyder and Pressley (1995) state that students need to be "aware that competent functioning is often a result of using appropriate strategies rather than superior ability or just trying hard" (p. 9).

Strategies are taught through modeling and explanation by the teacher, followed by rehearsal and practice. Students might start by using the strategy with teacher guidance, but should be taught to use the strategy steps independently. They should be explicitly taught to monitor their strategy use, and to generalize strategies to similar learning content. Eventually, students should be taught how to select those strategies that are most efficacious for learning specific content or for tackling a specific learning task. Strategy instruction can be adapted to student grade and needs. Elementary school children can learn the strategy steps for studying spelling words, whereas middle and high school students can learn the strategies for organization and study skills.

Strategy instruction is preferable to tutoring the student. Tutoring may be sometimes necessary, but direct teaching time is probably better spent teaching students learning strategies, while using the content material they encounter in the general education classroom. Tutoring should be seen as an occasional rescue, rather than a daily routine. For example, instead of tutoring students on the content for a test, the teacher should work with students on a plan for studying for the test, teach test-taking strategies, and then have students reflect on the success of the strategies being used by examining their own test results.

SELF-ADVOCACY

One of the findings about successful DHH students is that they are able to advocate for themselves (Luckner & Muir, 2001; Reed et al., 2008). Although much of the literature on self-advocacy has focused on teaching college-age students to advocate for their own needs, or on high school students transitioning to postsecondary settings (English, 1997; Test, Fowler, Brewer, & Wood, 2005), self-advocacy is a necessary skill for students receiving instruction in general education classrooms at all levels. Self-advocacy includes having knowledge of oneself and of one's rights, and the ability to express these rights (Fiedler & Danneker, 2007; Test et al., 2005). Knowledge of oneself includes knowing one's interests, learning abilities and styles, strengths and limitations, and, in the case of DHH students, the attributes of one's own hearing loss and how it might influence communication in different situations. Knowledge of rights includes the knowledge of legal rights and services. To self-advocate, students need communication skills such as negotiating, persuading, and listening. They also need to learn how to be assertive and effective.

One important area for self-advocacy is students' participation in their own Individual Education Plan (IEP). Students who are taught how to participate in their own IEP meetings learn about their rights and accommodations and the resources available to them. They also assume more responsibility for their own learning (Mason, McGahee-Kovac, & Johnson, 2004). Steps for teaching students to be involved in their own IEPs include: (a) providing them with the knowledge of the purpose and importance of the IEP; (b) having students understand and describe the results of their own assessments, including strengths and needs; and (c) assisting students in identifying and modifying learning and social goals (Mason et al., 2004).

Several self-advocacy curricula for special-education students can be adapted for DHH students. Many of these curricula focus on self-awareness, goal setting, communication and partnership skills, and problem-solving and decision-making skills (Fiedler & Danneker, 2007; Test, Karvonen, Wood, Browder, & Algozzine, 2000). Two resources for teachers of DHH students include the Knowledge Is Power (KIP) curriculum (Mississippi Bend Area Education Agency, 2008) and Self-advocacy for Students Who Are Deaf or Hard of Hearing (English, 1997).

Students who use interpreters should understand their interpreter's role. The difficulty is that this role is not well defined, especially in elementary grades.

Debate continues as to whether interpreters primarily convey information or whether they should have additional responsibilities, such as modeling language, communicating with the teacher, and tutoring DHH students (Antia & Kreimeyer, 2001; Seal, 1998). Young students may not realize that the interpreter is conveying the teacher's words or when it is appropriate to communicate with the interpreter. If interpreters assume the responsibility of communicating DHH students' comprehension of class content to general educators, the DHH students may not learn that it is their responsibility to communicate directly with classroom teachers. In addition, students using interpreters or amplification should learn about the visual and acoustic conditions that facilitate their functioning and how to self-advocate for these conditions.

It should be noted that the issue of learning content through mediated communication (e.g., through interpreting or captioning) is one of considerable controversy. It is beyond the scope of this chapter to address these issues. However, DHH students who use interpreters or captioners in the classroom should learn about the problems that they might encounter. The itinerant teacher will need to work collaboratively with interpreters, captioners, and general education teachers to facilitate access to classroom content for the DHH student.

CLASSROOM PARTICIPATION

There is body of research indicating that classroom participation is related to academic outcomes (Antia et al., 2007; Braeges et al., 1993). A reliable and valid instrument to measure classroom participation is the Classroom Participation Questionnaire (CPQ). Although the CPQ was originally developed for college and high school students (Garrison, Long, & Stinson, 1994; Long et al., 1991) a shortened version has been shown to be reliable and valid with elementary and middle school students (Antia et al., 2007). The CPQ yields four subscale scores: Understanding Teacher, Understanding Students, Positive Affect, and Negative Affect (see Chapter 4, this volume). Teachers can use the subscales and individual items as a diagnostic tool.

Teachers and interpreters can explain the benefit of, and model effective strategies for promoting classroom participation (Stinson & Liu, 1999). Examples include: (a) listening to each speaker without interruption; (b) raising hands to request a turn to speak, and then pausing briefly to provide all students an opportunity to locate the speaker; (c) obtaining the visual attention of students prior

to presenting information; (d) rephrasing comments or directions that are unclear; (e) speaking at a pace that allows an interpreter to effectively convey what is being said; and (f) moving close to students before speaking or using an FM microphone to mitigate noise distractions. Most of these suggestions will benefit all students within the classroom. Many excellent strategies to address this area are available through the Classact website (http://www.rit.edu/~classact) developed at the National Technical Institute for the Deaf specifically to promote participation of DHH students in general education settings.

Teachers can use numerous cooperative learning structures to encourage all students to participate in classroom learning activities (Slavin, 1990). It is not sufficient to simply place students in learning groups, however: the teacher needs to establish the group goals and hold each member of the team, including the DHH student, accountable for his or her own learning and for the learning of the group (Marr, 1997). The teacher should select the group members carefully, arrange seating to encourage involvement, and monitor and mediate hearing and DHH students' participation (Stinson & Liu, 1999). As is apparent, classroom participation cannot be taught in a one-to-one pull-out instructional context, and will require considerable collaboration between the general educator and the teacher of DHH students.

SOCIAL SUPPORT

Social supports should be provided at both the program and classroom level. A key factor that facilitates social relationships is the ability of DHH and hearing students to meaningfully communicate with one another. Even though students may have adequate social skills, they may not be able to successfully negotiate some of the difficult social situations that occur in school settings. Teaching all students strategies to initiate conversation and repair conversational breakdowns can be of benefit both within and outside the instructional setting (Stinson & Liu, 1999). If DHH students utilize sign language, it is important to teach hearing classmates to sign and to prompt them to use sign within their conversations. Providing easily accessible opportunities for general educators and other support personnel to develop sign skills conveys to all students the value of this additional language.

Familiarity occurs when students come to know one another, and is a first step toward building social relationships. However, it is important to realize that merely putting students together in a class does not necessarily result in meaningful interactions and friendships (Antia, 1985; Lee & Antia, 1992). Small-group cooperative learning activities and paired assignments create opportunities for sustained interaction between DHH and hearing students. Such sustained interaction in the classroom can be a precursor to friendship formation.

It may be beneficial to implement interventions that improve or expand all students' (DHH and hearing) social skills. Teaching specific social interaction skills within common classroom activities, pairing appropriate language with these skills, and teaching approaches to interpersonal problem solving have improved the social skills of DHH students (Antia & Kreimeyer, 1996; Antia, Kreimeyer, & Eldredge, 1994; Suarez, 2000). Modeling and prompting these skills within varied situations will help DHH and hearing students interact across settings. Several commercially available curricula can be used to develop social skills (Elliott & Gresham, 2007, 2008) including cooperation, empathy, assertion, self-control, and responsibility. Promoting Social Success (Siperstein & Rickards, 2004) is a curriculum developed to improve the social skills of elementary students with mild to moderate disabilities and their peers, by focusing on the cognitive skills needed for appropriate social behavior. Topics include understanding feelings and actions, noticing and interpreting social clues, problem solving, and making and keeping friends.

Program considerations should address the placement of students in classes, as well as in lunch and recess schedules, and the appropriate support necessary to participate in extracurricular activities. During the elementary years, keeping cohorts of classmates or small groups of friends together for several years can increase the probability of students building and maintaining friendships. One program (Kreimeyer, Crooke, Drye, Egbert, & Klein, 2000) maintained a cohort of students for three years by making use of multigrade grouping. Lunchtime and recess should be scheduled to allow DHH students to interact with familiar peers.

Extracurricular activities become significant at middle and high school because nonacademic activities often provide opportunities for students to learn about one another's common interests in a way that may encourage friendships. Relationships between DHH and hearing students can be positively impacted by joint participation in athletic activities (Martin & Bat-Chava, 2003; Stewart & Stinson, 1992). Other extracurricular activities, such as clubs or school newspapers, can provide interaction opportunities around a range of interests. The school program can facilitate full access to extracurricular activities by providing after-school interpreters, assistive listening devices, and transportation.

Summary and Conclusions

Increasingly, DHH students are receiving much of their instruction in the general education classroom with support from teachers of DHH learners. Academically, DHH students in general education classrooms achieve better than DHH students in self-contained settings, and they appear to be making a year's progress in a year's time. As a group, however, they continue to achieve below their hearing peers.

Comparatively little information is available on the academic outcomes of students with mild or moderate hearing loss. These students appear to be at some risk for academic achievement, yet may not be receiving support services, nor may they be perceived as needing support. These students are difficult to locate and difficult to study. However, they constitute a large proportion of the total population of DHH students and deserve attention from researchers and teachers.

Regarding social outcomes, the literature is difficult to interpret, and the picture is more complex. Teachers report that DHH students have social skills comparable to hearing peers. Younger DHH students appear to be socially accepted by peers, but DHH adolescents may have some difficulty feeling emotionally secure and making close friends with hearing peers. Because DHH students in a general education classroom may have only hearing peers, social isolation may be a problem. However, it should be noted that the studies on adolescents were completed over 15 years ago, and these students may not be representative of those who will be in general education classrooms in the next few decades. Nevertheless, it is important that researchers continue to examine the social integration of DHH students in general education classrooms using as informants teachers, parents, hearing peers, and the students themselves. Social behavior is highly dependent on context, so it is important to investigate the kinds of family and school environments that support positive social outcomes.

Teachers who support DHH students in general education classrooms must be prepared to be collaborators and to provide support to general education teachers, as well as to the DHH students. Little is known about how effective services can be provided, what kinds of services are effective, and why they might be effective. The data currently available primarily describe itinerant teacher responsibilities, but there remains remarkably little information about how these teachers determine the intensity and manner of support services provided to students on their caseload. In this chapter, the authors have outlined important support areas, but further research is needed to indicate the circumstances under which services promote academic and social success.

There is a need to follow DHH students in general education classrooms beyond high school graduation to determine whether academic success translates into college and career success. This is a challenging task, as many students enter mainstream universities and are difficult to locate. Those DHH students who are easiest to locate are also those most likely to use services. Students functioning independently are likely to be lost to follow-up.

Finally, changes in the field, such as widespread cochlear implantation, early identification, and early intervention are likely to change the characteristics of DHH children entering school, making data collected today outdated. The field must continue to focus research on students in general education classrooms, examining not only the support provided by teachers of DHH students, but also the characteristics of effective instruction within this setting.

References

Allen, T. (1986). Patterns of academic achievement among hearing impaired students: 1974 and 1983. In A. Schildroth & M. Karchmer (Eds.), *Deaf children in America* (pp. 161–206). Boston: Little, Brown & Co.

Andersen, K. (1989). *SIFTER: Screening Instrument for Targeting Educational Risk*. Danville, IL: Interstate Printers and Publishers.

Antia, S. D. (1982). Social interaction of partially mainstreamed hearing-impaired children. *American Annals of the Deaf, 127*, 18–25.

Antia, S. D. (1985). Social integration of hearing-impaired children: fact of fiction? *The Volta Review, 87*, 279–289.

Antia, S. D. (1999). The roles of special educators and classroom teachers in an inclusive school. *Journal of Deaf Studies and Deaf Education, 4*, 203–214.

Antia, S. D., & Dittillo, D. A. (1998). A comparison of the peer social behavior of children who are deaf/hard of hearing and hearing. *Journal of Children's Communication Development, 19*, 1–10.

Antia, S. D., Jones, P., Reed, S., Kreimeyer, K., H., Luckner, J., & Johnson, C. (2008). Longitudinal study of deaf and hard of hearing students attending general education classrooms in public schools. Final report submitted to Office of Special Education Programs for grant H324C010142. University of Arizona.

Antia, S. D., & Kreimeyer, K., H. (1996). Social interaction and acceptance of D/HH children and their peers. *The Volta Review, 98*, 157–180.

Antia, S. D., & Kreimeyer, K., H. (2001). The role of interpreters in inclusive classrooms. *American Annals of the Deaf, 146*, 355–365.

Antia, S. D., Kreimeyer, K., H., & Eldredge, N. (1994). Promoting social interaction between young children with hearing impairments and their peers. *Exceptional Children, 60*, 262–275.

Antia, S. D., Sabers, D., & Stinson, M. S. (2007). Validity and reliability of the Classroom Participation Questionnaire with deaf and hard of hearing students in public schools. *Journal of Deaf Studies and Deaf Education, 12*, 158–171.

Antia, S. D., & Stinson, M. S. (1999). Some conclusions on the education of deaf and hard-of-hearing students in inclusive settings. *Journal of Deaf Studies and Deaf Education, 4*, 246–248.

Antia, S. D., Stinson, M. S., & Gaustad, M. G. (2002). Developing membership in the education of deaf and hard of hearing students in inclusive settings. *Journal of Deaf Studies and Deaf Education, 7*, 214–229.

Bat-Chava, Y., & Deignan, E. (2001). Peer relationships of children with cochlear implants. *Journal of Deaf Studies and Deaf Education, 6*, 186–199.

Blair, J. C., Peterson, M. E., & Viehweg, S. H. (1985). The effects of mild sensorineural hearing loss on academic performance of young school-age children. *The Volta Review, 96*, 207–236.

Braeges, J., Stinson, M. S., & Long, G. (1993). Teachers' and deaf student's perceptions of communication ease and engagement. *Rehabilitation Psychology, 38*, 235–247.

Bullard, C. (2003). *The itinerant teachers' handbook*. Hillsboro, OR: Butte Publications.

Calderon, R., & Greenberg, M. T. (2003). Social and emotional development of deaf children: Family, school and program effects. In M. Marschark & P. Spencer (Eds.), *Oxford Handbook of Deaf Studies, Language, and Education* (pp. 177–189). New York: Oxford University Press.

Cappelli, M., Daniels, T., Durieux-Smith, A., McGrath, P. J., & Neuss, D. (1995). Social development of children with hearing impairments who are integrated into general education classrooms. *The Volta Review, 97*, 197–208.

Caprara, G., Barbaranelli, C., Pastorelli, C., Bandura, A., & Zimbardo, P. (2000). Prosocial foundations of children's academic achievement. *Psychological Science, 11*, 302–306.

Centers for Disease Control and Prevention Early Hearing Detection and Intervention Program. (July 2005). *Workshop proceedings*. Paper presented at the National Workshop on mild and unilateral hearing loss. Breckinridge, Colorado.

Davis, J. M., Shepard, N. T., Stelmachowicz, P. G., & Gorga, M. P. (1981). Characteristics of hearing-impaired children in the public schools: Psycho-educational data. *Journal of Speech and Hearing Disorders, 46*, 130–137.

Eisenberger, J., Conti-D'Antonio, M., & Bertrando, R. (2000). *Self efficacy: Raising the bar for students with learning needs*. Larchmont, NY: Eye on Education.

Elliott, S., & Gresham, F. M. (2007). *Social skills improvement system: Classwide intervention program*. Circle Pines, MN: American Guidance Service.

Elliott, S., & Gresham, F. M. (2008). *Social skills intervention guide*. Circle Pines, MN: Pearson.

English, K. (1997). *Self-advocacy for students who are deaf or hard of hearing*. Austin, TX: Pro-ed.

Fiedler, C. R., & Danneker, J. E. (2007). Self-advocacy instruction: Bridging the research-to-practice gap. *Focus on Exceptional Children, 39*(8), 1–20.

Flavell, J. H. (1979). Metacognition and cognitive monitoring: A new area of cognitive-developmental inquiry. *American Psychologist, 34*, 906–911.

Foster, S., & Cue, K. (2007). *Roles and responsibilities of itinerant specialist teachers of deaf and hard of hearing students.* National Technical Institute for the Deaf.

Gallaudet Research Institute. (2006). *Regional and national summary report of data from the 2006–2007 Annual Survey of Deaf and Hard of Hearing Children and Youth.* Washington DC: GRI Gallaudet University.

Garrison, W., Long, G., & Stinson, M. S. (1994). The classroom communication ease scale. *American Annals of the Deaf, 139*, 132–140.

Gaustad, M. G. (1999). Including the kids across the hall: collaborative instruction of hearing, deaf, and hard of hearing students. *Journal of Deaf Studies and Deaf Education, 4*, 176–190.

Geers, A., Nicholas, J. G., & Sedey, A. (2003). Language skills of children with early cochlear implantation. *Ear and Hearing, 24*, 46S–58S.

Gifford-Smith, M., & Brownell, C. (2003). Childhood peer relationships: Social acceptance, friendships and peer networks. *Journal of School Psychology, 41*, 235–284.

Gourgey, A. F. (1998). Metacognition in basic skills instruction. *Instructional Science, 26*, 81–96.

Gresham, F. M., & Elliott, S. N. (1990). *Social Skills Rating System.* Circle Pines, MN: American Guidance Service.

Holt, J. (1994). Classroom attributes and achievement test scores for deaf and hard of hearing students. *American Annals of the Deaf, 139*, 430–437.

Jensema, C. (1975). *The relationship between academic achievement and the demographic characteristics of hearing-impaired children and youth.* Washington DC: Gallaudet College, Office of Demographic Studies.

Jimenez-Sanchez, C., & Antia, S. D. (1999). Team teaching in an integrated classroom: Perceptions of deaf and hearing teachers. *Journal of Deaf Studies and Deaf Education, 4*, 215–224.

Johnson, H. D. (2004). Gender, grade, and relationship differences in emotional closeness within adolescent friendships. *Adolescence, 39*, 243–255.

Karchmer, M., & Mitchell, R. E. (2003). Demographic and achievement characteristics of deaf and hard-of-hearing students. In M. Marschark & P. E. Spencer (Eds.), *Oxford handbook of deaf studies, language and education* (pp. 21–37). New York: Oxford University Press.

Kluwin, T. N. (1993). Cumulative effects of mainstreaming on the achievement of deaf adolescents. *Exceptional Children, 60*, 73–81.

Kluwin, T. N. (1994). The interaction of race, gender and social class effects in the education of deaf students. *American Annals of the Deaf, 139*, 465–471.

Kluwin, T. N., & Moores, D. (1985). The effects of integration on the mathematics achievement of hearing impaired adolescents. *Exceptional Children, 52*, 153–160.

Kluwin, T. N., & Stinson, M. S. (1993). *Deaf students in local public high schools: Backgrounds, experiences, and outcomes.* Springfield: Charles C. Thomas.

Kreimeyer, K., H., Crooke, P., Drye, C., Egbert, V., & Klein, B. (2000). Academic and social benefits of a coenrollment model of inclusive education for deaf and hard-of-hearing children. *Journal of Deaf Studies and Deaf Education, 5*, 174–185.

Lee, C., & Antia, S. D. (1992). A sociological approach to the social integration of hearing-impaired and normally hearing students. *The Volta Review, 94*, 425–434.

Levine, L. M., & Antia, S. D. (1997). The effect of partner hearing status on social and cognitive play. *Journal of Early Intervention, 21*, 21–35.

Long, G., Stinson, M. S., & Braeges, J. (1991). Students' perception of communication ease and engagement: how they relate to academic success. *American Annals of the Deaf, 136*, 414–421.

Luckner, J. L., & Miller, K. J. (1994). Itinerant teachers: Responsibilities, perceptions, preparation and students served. *American Annals of the Deaf, 139*, 111–118.

Luckner, J. L., & Muir, S. (2001). Successful students who are deaf in general education settings. *American Annals of the Deaf, 146*, 435–445.

Malecki, C., & Elliott, S. (2002). Children's social behaviors as predictors of academic achievement: A longitudinal analysis. *School Psychology Quarterly, 17*, 1–23.

Marr, M.: (1997). Cooperative learning: A brief review. *Reading and Writing Quarterly, 13*(1), 7–14.

Marschark, M., Convertino, C., Macias, G., Monikowski, C. M., Sapere, P., & Seewagen, R. (2007). Understanding communication among deaf students who sign and speak: A trivial pursuit? *American Annals of the Deaf, 152*, 415–424.

Marschark, M., Lang, H. G., & Albertini, J. A. (2002). *Educating deaf students: From research to practice.* New York: Oxford University Press.

Marschark, M., Sapere, P., Convertino, C., & Seewagen, R. (2005). Educational interpreting: Access and outcomes. In M. Marschark, R. Peterson, & E. A. Winston (Eds.), *Sign language interpreting and interpreter education* (pp. 57–83). New York: Oxford University Press.

Martin, D., & Bat-Chava, Y. (2003). Negotiating deaf-hearing friendships: coping strategies of deaf boys and girls in mainstream schools. *Child Care, Health and Development, 29*, 522–521.

Mason, C. Y., McGahee-Kovac, M., & Johnson, L. (2004). How to help students lead their IEP meetings. *Teaching Exceptional Children, 36*(3), 18–24.

McCauley, R. W., Bruininks, R. H., & Kennedy, P. (1976). Behavioral interactions of hearing impaired children in regular classrooms. *Journal of Special Education, 10*, 277–284.

Mississippi Bend Area Education Agency. (2008). Knowledge Is Power: A program to help students learn about their hearing loss. Westminister Co: Education Audiology Association.

Mitchell, R. E. (2004). National Profile of Deaf and Hard of Hearing Students in special Education from Weighted Survey Results. *American Annals of the Deaf, 149*, 336–349.

Mitchell, R. E., & Karchmer, M. A. (2006). Demographics of deaf education: More students in more places. *American Annals of the Deaf, 151*, 95–104.

Most, T. (2004). The effects of degree and type of hearing loss on children's performance in class. *Deafness and Education International, 6*, 154–166.

Most, T. (2006). Assessment of school functioning among Israeli Arab children with hearing loss in the primary grades. *American Annals of the Deaf, 151*, 327–335.

Musselman, C., Mootilal, A., & MacKay, S. (1996). The social adjustment of deaf adolescents in segregated, partially integrated and mainstreamed settings. *Journal of Deaf Studies and Deaf Education, 1*, 52–63.

National Center for Hearing Assessment and Management. (2008). State summary statistics: Universal Newborn Hearing Screening. Publication. Retrieved June 4, 2008 from http://www.infanthearing.org/status/unhsstate.html

Nunes, T., & Pretzlik, U. (2001). Deaf children's social relationships in mainstream schools. *Deafness and Education International, 3,* 123–136.

Power, D., & Hyde, M. (2002). The characteristics and extent of participation of deaf and hard-of-hearing students in regular classes in Australian schools. *Journal of Deaf Studies and Deaf Education, 7,* 302–311.

Power, D., & Hyde, M. (2003). Itinerant teachers of the deaf and hard of hearing and their students in Australia: some state comparisons. *International Journal of Disability Development and Education, 4,* 385–401.

Powers, S. (2003). Influences of student and family factors on academic outcomes of mainstream secondary school deaf students. *Journal of Deaf Studies and Deaf Education, 8,* 57–78.

Reed, S. (2003). Beliefs and practices of itinerant teachers of deaf and hard of hearing children concerning literacy development. *American Annals of the Deaf, 148,* 333–343.

Reed, S., Antia, S. D., & Kreimeyer, K., H. (2008). Academic status of deaf and hard-of-hearing students in public schools: Student, home, and service facilitators and detractors. *Journal of Deaf Studies and Deaf Education, 13,* 485–502.

Ross, M., Brackett, D., & Maxon, A. B. (1982). *Hard of hearing children in regular schools.* Englewood Cliffs, NJ: Prentice-Hall.

Ross, M., Brackett, D., & Maxon, A. B. (1991). *Assessment and management of mainstreamed hearing-impaired children: Principles and practices.* Austin, TX: Pro-ed Inc.

Schick, B., Williams, K., & Bolster, L. (1999). Skill levels of educational interpreters working in public schools. *Journal of Deaf Studies and Deaf Education, 4,* 144–155.

Seal, B. C. (1998). *Best practices in educational interpreting.* Needham Heights, MA: Allyn & Bacon.

Siperstein, G. N., & Rickards, E. P. (2004). *Promoting social success: A curriculum for children with special needs.* Baltimore: Paul. H. Brookes.

Slavin, R. E. (1990). *Cooperative learning: Theory, research and practice.* Englewood Cliffs, NJ: Prentice Hall.

Smith, M. D. (1997). *The art of itinerant teaching.* Hillsboro, OR: Butte Publications.

Snyder, B., & Pressley, M. (1995). Introduction to cognitive strategy instruction. In M. Pressley & V. Woloshyn (Eds.), *Cognitive strategy instruction that really improves children's academic performance.* (pp. 1–18). Cambridge, MA: Brookline Books.

Stewart, D. A., & Stinson, M. S. (1992). The role of sport and extracurricular activities in shaping socialization patterns. In T. Kluwin, D. F. Moores, & M. Gonter Gaustad (Eds.), *Toward effective public school programs for deaf students.* New York: Teachers College Press.

Stinson, M. S., & Antia, S. D. (1999). Considerations in educating deaf and hard-of-hearing students in inclusive settings. *Journal of Deaf Studies and Deaf Education, 4,* 163–175.

Stinson, M. S., & Kluwin, T. N. (1996). Social orientations toward deaf and hearing peers among deaf adolescents in local public high schools. In P. C. Higgins & J. E. Nash (Eds.), *Understanding deafness socially* (pp. 113–134). Springfield: Charles C. Thomas.

Stinson, M. S., & Liu, Y. (1999). Participation of deaf and hard of hearing students in classes with hearing students. *Journal of Deaf Studies and Deaf Education, 4,* 191–202.

Stinson, M. S., & Whitmire, K. (1991). Self-perceptions of social relationships among hearing-impaired adolescents in England. *Journal of the British Association Teachers of the Deaf, 15,* 104–114.

Stinson, M. S., & Whitmire, K. (1992). Students' views of their social relationships. In T. N. Kluwin, D. F. Moores, & M. G. Gaustad (Eds.), *Towards effective public school programs for deaf students: context process and outcomes* (pp. 149–174). New York: Teachers College Press.

Stinson, M. S., & Whitmire, K. (2000). Adolescents who are deaf or hard of hearing: a communication perspective on educational placement. *Topics in Language Disorders, 20,* 58–72.

Stinson, M. S., Whitmire, K., & Kluwin, T. N. (1996). Self perceptions of social relationship in hearing-impaired adolescents. *Journal of Educational Psychology, 88,* 132–143.

Strassman, B. (1992). Deaf adolescents' metacognitive knowledge about school-related reading. *American Annals of the Deaf, 137,* 326–330.

Strassman, B. (1997). Metacognition and reading in children who are deaf: A review of the research. *Journal of Deaf Studies and Deaf Education, 2,* 140–149.

Suarez, M. (2000). Promoting social competence in deaf students: The effect of an intervention program. *Journal of Deaf Studies and Deaf Education, 5,* 323–336.

Teller, H., & Harney, J. (2005/2006). Views from the field: Program directors' perceptions of teacher education and the education of students who are deaf or hard of hearing. *American Annals of the Deaf, 150,* 470–479.

Test, D. W., Fowler, C. H., Brewer, D. M., & Wood, W. M. (2005). A content and methodological review of self-advocacy intervention studies. *Exceptional Children, 72*(1), 101–125.

Test, D. W., Karvonen, M., Wood, W. M., Browder, D., & Algozzine, B. (2000). Choosing a self-determination curriculum. *Teaching Exceptional Children, 33*(2), 48–54.

Tierney, R. J., & Readence, J. E. (2005). *Reading strategies and practices: A compendium.* Boston: Pearson Education Inc.

Tvingstedt, A. (1993). *Social conditions of hearing-impaired pupils in regular classrooms.* (Monograph No. 773). Malmo, Sweden: University of Lund, Department of Educational and Psychological Research.

Vandell, D. L., & George, L. (1981). Social interaction in hearing and deaf preschoolers: Successes and failures in initiations. *Child Development, 52,* 627–635.

Wauters, L., & Knoors, H. (2008). Social integration of deaf children in inclusive settings. *Journal of Deaf Studies and Deaf Education, 13,* 21–36.

Yarger, C. C., & Luckner, J. (1999). Itinerant teaching: The inside story. *American Annals of the Deaf, 144,* 309–314.

Yoshinaga-Itano, C., Sedey, A., Coulter, D., & Mehl, A. (1998). Language of early-and later-identified children with hearing loss. *Pediatrics, 102*(5), 1161–1171.

Current and Future Technologies in the Education of Deaf Students

Michael Stinson

Abstract

This chapter considers six key educational technologies that are used with deaf and hard-of-hearing (DHH) students: (1) television and in-class captioning, (2) interactive whiteboards, (3) tablet PCs, (4) World Wide Web, (5) sign language and bilingual media, and (6) handheld technologies. In regard to television captioning, neither a slower rate of displaying captions nor less linguistic complexity consistently enhances performance. In addition, classroom-captioning services appear to produce either equal or increased student performance compared to interpreting services. Although interactive whiteboards appear to have considerable education potential, reports of the use of these whiteboards with DHH students have been descriptions of experiences instead of empirical research. Tablet PCs appear to have potential in educating DHH students, however, studies that include more than a few students and thorough objective measurement are needed to provide reliable findings. Web-based instruction can promote the learning of content by DHH students when the material engages them, and web-based instruction through online learning provides a means for direct, asynchronous, text-based communication between DHH and hearing students. Many, if not most, DHH people usually carry with them a handheld technology, primarily for communication purposes.

Keywords: Captioning, interactive whiteboard, tablet PC, World Wide Web, sign language and bilingual media, handheld technologies

Recent years have seen dramatic advances in technology, such as the World Wide Web, that people around the world use everyday. Educators, including those in the education of deaf and hard-of-hearing (DHH) students, have hailed technology's potential for improving the quality of education (e.g., Andrews, Leigh, & Weiner, 2004; Porter & Clymer, 2001). This chapter considers the extent to which six key educational technologies are benefiting DHH students: (a) television and in-class captioning, (b) interactive whiteboards, (c) tablet PCs, (d) the World Wide Web, (e) sign language and bilingual media, and (f) handheld technologies.

The following discussion of these six topics includes an assessment of the extent of research support for these practices, which is important because educational technology is a field largely driven by the marketplace and

development cycle, as opposed to research that informs design and utilization (Gersten & Edyburn, 2007). Thus, literature that includes reliable findings regarding the extent of educational benefit receives greatest attention here. Reports of the extent of use of technology receive some attention, and descriptions of technology use that do not include data receive least attention.

This chapter does not discuss cochlear implants, hearing aids, assistive listening devices, or related technologies. Readers may consult Dunn, Tyler, Kordus, and Marciniak (Chapter 26, this volume) and Harkins and Bakke (2003) for information on this topic.

Captioning
Television Captioning
Television exerts a substantial influence upon children's learning and socialization. Of the more than

50 million children in the United States, 85% watch television every day (National Captioning Institute, 1983). Deaf and hard-of-hearing children watch television as often as do hearing children (Lewis & Jackson, 2001; Liss & Prince, 1981). Today, as mandated by law, virtually all television programs may be viewed with captions. These captions are a text display of the audio component of the television program, generally displayed at the bottom of the television screen (Lewis & Jackson, 2001). To see these captions, which are generally transmitted in closed format, the viewer must set the captioned decoder, which is contained in virtually all television sets, so that it displays captions. A major reason for the production of captions is to provide DHH people access to the audio component of the program.

Research by Jensema, McCann, and Ramsey (1996) collected caption data for 205 television programs, which provided descriptive information regarding captions on everyday programming. They found that the average caption speed for programs was 141 words per minute. They analyzed the words included in these captions. The captions contained 834,726 words, of which 16,102 were unique. Just 250 words accounted for more than two-thirds of all words contained in the captions. The authors concluded that understanding only 500 words will enable viewers to understand most of the vocabulary in television programs.

A concern of the producers of captions and of educators has been whether DHH individuals are able to understand captions that are presented at relatively fast speeds (e.g., 141 words per minute or greater) and that sometimes contain complex grammatical forms. This concern is based upon the limited reading proficiency of many DHH persons (Ward, Yang, Paul, & Loeterman, 2007).

Some research on the effects of captions on comprehension has focused upon whether the captions have been edited to delete information considered nonessential and to simplify grammatical structure. Additional research has examined the speed at which captions are presented, and the association of reading proficiency with comprehension. Studies on the effects of editing of captions to reduce linguistic complexity have obtained mixed results. Braverman and Hertzog (1980) found with college students and Baker (1985) found with children that reduction of language complexity increased comprehension of a television program. In the Baker (1985) study, the editing of captions was accompanied by a reduction in the caption presentation rate, so that it was not clear whether rate or language complexity

was the primary factor that accounted for the results. In contrast, Ward et al. (2007) did not find with children and Burnham et al. (2008) did not find with adults that a reduction in linguistic complexity increased (or decreased) comprehension of captions.

Although matching of caption language complexity to the language proficiency of a DHH audience would appear to increase comprehension, various factors could affect the extent of comprehension, in addition to language complexity. For example, Schilperoord, de Groot, and van Son (2005) determined that reduction of linguistic text in captions, relative to verbatim captions, was associated with a reduction in coherence relations in the material, such as causal relations among concepts, which may affect comprehension.

Two studies examined effects of caption rate upon comprehension. These studies indicate that rate either has no effect upon comprehension or that variation in rate only affects selected readers. Braverman and Hertzog (1980) found that rates of 60, 90, and 120 words per minute did not differentially affect comprehension by students. Burnham et al. (2008), in contrast, found that rates of 130, 180, and 230 words per minute selectively affected participants' comprehension, depending upon the reading proficiency of the participants. Slower caption rates tended to assist comprehension of more proficient readers, but this was not the case for less proficient readers.

Jensema (1998) presented captions at different speeds to viewers and surveyed their reactions. Participants stated that they were most comfortable with captions presented at a speed of about 145 words per minute. This speed is similar to the captioning speed of a typical television program (average of 141 words per minute), and the finding could have been influenced by viewers' familiarity with that particular captioning rate (Jensema et al., 1996). However, comprehension was not assessed.

An additional factor that affects the comprehension of captions is the viewer's reading proficiency. Burnham et al. (2008) and Lewis and Jackson (2001) found that higher performance on a paper-and-pencil reading comprehension test was associated with better comprehension and retention of captioned information presented on a video.

Captioned Web Media and Videos
Currently, only a small portion of the extensive Web media (e.g., You-Tube) are captioned. This limitation in accessibility for DHH people is being addressed two ways: first, an Internet Captioning Forum has been established to overcome the challenges of

producing captions for large video aggregation websites (Stein, 2008). The National Center for Accessible Media is managing this forum, which includes AOL, Google, Microsoft, and Yahoo. The challenges of creating captions for Web media are substantial because of the varied content of each site and the varied media players at the host site and in the individual computers that access these host sites. A second way that this limitation in captioned web media is being addressed, at least in the United States, is through legislation being developed by the U.S. Congress to ensure access to video programming on the Web by individuals with disabilities. A Coalition of Organizations for Accessible Technology (COAT), which includes organizations such as the National Association of the Deaf, is promoting this legislation (Hamlin, 2008).

Another form of captions pertinent to education is that of videos that are shown in classrooms. The Captioned Media Program, which is managed by the National Association of the Deaf, supports captioning of videos and provides a free lending service to schools (Kelly, 2008).

Classroom Captioning

Captions are used in classrooms as well as on television programs. Captioning is often provided for DHH students who attend general education or mainstream classes with hearing students. With this type of captioning, which is also called a *real-time speech-to-text service*, a service provider, who is often in the classroom with the DHH student, produces text as it is being spoken by a teacher or classmate and displays it, usually on a laptop computer, so that the student can understand what is happening in class (Stinson, Eisenberg, Horn, Larson, Levitt, & Stuckless, 1999).

The two more common speech-to-text approaches that support DHH students in mainstream classes are those in which a service produces the text display with either a standard typing QWERTY keyboard or a stenographic machine. A little used, newer option is *automatic speech recognition* (Aylesworth, 2006). The three approaches vary in the extent to which they provide a verbatim display, and in the accuracy of the display. Stenographic machine-based services, also called Communication Access Real-time Translation (CART), and some speech recognition–based services more often produce a verbatim text display. Speech recognition services are less accurate than the other two (Preminger & Levitt, 1998 Steinfield, 1998; Stinson, Elliot, McKee, & Francis, 2001; Stuckless, 1999; Viable Technologies, 2002). Standard

keyboard approaches are not verbatim, but with the assistance of computerized word abbreviations, capture all the meaning of a lecture. In the United States today, there is a general expectation that a postsecondary program will provide a speech-to-text service if a DHH student requests it. Elementary and secondary education programs may provide speech-to-text services as part of a student's Individual Education Plan under the Individuals with Disabilities Act (IDEA; see Chapter 3, this volume).

With a CART system, the provider produces special code using combinations of keystrokes on a special keyboard. Special software converts this code into words (Graves, 2003). Davis, Francis, and Harlan (2000) noted that the normal accuracy rate for CART services in a mainstream classroom ranges from 80% to 100%. Accuracy may depend on the number of words included in a lecture that are not in the steno-system's computer dictionary, as well as the skill of the provider. With standard keyboard approaches (C-Print, Typewell), the provider types abbreviated versions of words (e.g., "stdt" for "student") for full words (CodeWell, 2007; National Technical Institute for the Deaf, 2008). With the conversion software, the computer displays the abbreviations as full words.

According to a survey of postsecondary programs that provide services for DHH students in the United States, word abbreviation systems are used more often in educational programs (49% of the programs surveyed) than CART (35%). Automatic speech recognition was used by fewer than 5% of the programs (Aylesworth, 2006).

Two studies investigated the benefit of CART services for students. Steinfield (1998) presented six DHH and six hearing students sets of 60 sentences that students were asked to recall. All participants viewed a video and audio playback of a speaker. In the caption condition, the captions were superimposed on the video. The main findings were that (a) deaf students recalled substantially more words from sentences with captions than words from sentences without captions (80% versus 25%); (b) hearing students recalled more words than did DHH students, and (c) students recalled more words when four lines of captions were displayed than when two were displayed. The dramatic difference between DHH persons' recall of words in sentences with and without captions is particularly noteworthy and indicates how important a support service can be for DHH students' comprehension of spoken material. This is the only known study that compared DHH students' comprehension with a support service to comprehension without the services. In contrast, a number of studies have compared students' performance with different support services (e.g., Stinson, Elliot, Kelly, & Liu, 2009).

Stinson, Stuckless, Henderson, and Miller (1988) surveyed mainstreamed DHH students who viewed both interpreting and CART services during sessions in classes. Students assigned significantly higher ratings of teacher comprehension for CART services than for interpreting services. In addition, printouts of the CART transcripts and notes taken by a paid student notetaker were distributed to students after each class session. Students assigned significantly higher ratings of helpfulness to printouts than to the notes.

Research has compared the benefits of C-Print support services, which uses a standard keyboard and computerized word abbreviations, with those of interpreting support services. In five questionnaire studies with DHH mainstreamed secondary or postsecondary students, students who had used C-Print services and/or who had used interpreting in classes were asked to rate, as a percentage, the amount of information that they understood in class. In two studies, postsecondary school students assigned higher ratings of understanding for C-Print than for interpreting, and the difference between the mean ratings for these two services was statistically significant in each study (Elliot, Stinson, McKee, Everhart, & Francis, 2001; Stinson, Stinson, Elliot, & Kelly, 2004). In one postsecondary and two secondary school studies, students assigned ratings of understanding for C-Print and for interpreting that were not significantly different from each other (Stinson, Stinson, Elliot, & Kelly, 2006; Elliot, Stinson, & Coyne, 2006; Elliot, Stinson, Easton, & Bourgeois, 2008).

In five experiments with DHH secondary or postsecondary school students, retention of lecture information, as measured by objective recognition and recall tests, was compared for video displays of C-Print and interpreted presentations: In one experiment with secondary school students and in one with postsecondary school students, participants retained significantly more information from the C-Print presentation than the interpreted one (Marschark, et al., 2006; Stinson et al., 2009). In one experiment with secondary school students and two experiments with postsecondary school students, significant differences were not observed between retention of information from the C-Print presentation and retention from the interpreted one (Marschark et al., 2006; Stinson et al., 2009). The locus of these contradictory findings (even within studies) remains to be determined.

In one study with secondary school students, classroom teachers were asked to rate student performance when students were using C-Print, as well as when students were not using C-Print. Teachers rated students' academic performance, learning vocabulary, and classroom participation higher when students were using C-Print than when they were not using C-Print (Elliot et al., 2006).

After the C-Print provider completes producing the real-time display for a class, this saved text is available for further study by students. In one questionnaire study with secondary mainstreamed students and three studies with postsecondary students, respondents who have used C-Print and notetakers' notes were asked to rate the helpfulness of the two sets of materials. In each study, students reported that they used the saved C-Print text for study significantly more than they used notes from notetakers (Elliot et al., 2001; Elliot et al., 2008; Stinson et al., 2004; Stinson, et al., 2006). In addition, students used more study strategies, such as highlighting and outlining, with the C-Print text than with notetaker notes (Elliot et al., 2008; Stinson et al., 2004; Stinson, et al., 2006).

One experiment has directly compared student retention of a lecture with CART, C-Print, and interpreting services. In this experiment, there were no significant differences between retention of information from a C-Print presentation, from a CART presentation, and from an interpreted one by DHH postsecondary students (Marschark et al., 2006).

Summary

The key findings related to captioning are that proficiency in reading appears to be positively related to DHH people's comprehension and retention of televised captions, but neither a slower rate of caption display nor less linguistic complexity consistently enhance performance. In addition, classroom captions appear to dramatically increase DHH students' comprehension and performance compared to no support services, but captioning services do not consistently increase performance compared to interpreting services. Furthermore, there is no difference between student performance with word abbreviation-based or CART-based captioning services. Students report using the saved text of captions to study after class more often than handwritten notes from notetakers.

Interactive Whiteboards

Another technology that is growing in its use with DHH student is interactive whiteboards, such as the SMART Board and ActivBoard. These are combinations of a standard whiteboard and a computer with a screen that responds to touch and/or stylus input. A teacher can write or draw on the interactive whiteboard in the same manner as with a marker; however, annotation tools provide additional capability, such as the ability to straighten out lines in a geometric figure. An electronic highlighter, an eraser, and a keyboard (Gage, 2002) are also available. In addition, the interactive whiteboard is a computer and can display, save, or format anything that can appear on a computer screen (Excel, PowerPoint, specialized mathematics, educational game software, etc.; Florida School for the Deaf and Blind, 2008; Gage, 2002). For some of these technologies, such as the SMART Board, a touch of the board functions as a computer mouse. This can be helpful to teachers when alternating between signing and using the board.

The computer capability of the interactive whiteboard allows it to function in the same manner as a liquid crystal display (LCD) projector, because the board can provide large displays of materials prepared ahead of time in the same manner as an LCD projector. In addition, because the display screen enables touch and/or an electronic stylus to function as the mouse, the teacher can quickly alter the display, such as moving from one software application to another (Edmonds, Hartnell, & Martin, 2002; Richardson, 2002). Additional functions of interactive whiteboards include a spotlight that permits selection of a particular part of a large display and a magnifier that expands the spotlighted selection.

Interactive whiteboards appeal to many educators because the technology allows teachers to bring a wide variety of materials (such as websites) to the classroom, and the teacher and students can use the board in a variety of ways, from viewing research data in a website to working on a lesson that requires students to match pictures with words and that provides immediate feedback (Edwards et al., 2002). Materials presented on the board may be saved and distributed to students after class as notes (Elvers, 2000). The technology appears to engage many students because they can easily go to the board and interact with it, such as to mark a correct answer or highlight a sentence. The application on the interactive whiteboard often provides an immediate response; for example, figures that represent climbers advance up a mountain with the solution of each puzzle in the computerized display of the educational game Avalanche (Klawe, 2000). Whiteboards are currently used in approximately 12% of classrooms in

the United States and more extensively in other countries, such as the United Kingdom, in which 60% of classrooms have whiteboards (Davis, 2007).

Limitations of interactive whiteboards include high cost, the requirement for extensive teacher preparation and training, especially at beginning of use, and the fact that certain computer learning activities may work more effectively when small groups or individual students use standard computers (Kennewell & Morgan, 2003; Klawe, 2000).

USE IN INSTRUCTION OF DEAF AND HARD-OF-HEARING STUDENTS

Liles (2005) and Mackall (2004) have described the use of interactive whiteboards in the instruction of DHH students. Liles (2005) suggests that use of a whiteboard gives students a visual break from constantly focusing on the teacher's signing hands, which can be fatiguing. Another benefit of the whiteboard is the teacher's ability to control the technology from the front of the classroom, where one needs to stand in order to be seen by all students. If a standard computer and projector are used, the teacher may need to go to the back of the room to operate the device. An example of use of the whiteboard in the instruction of DHH students is to make English more visual. In one English class, the teacher color-codes words and sentences, and this procedures seems to help students understand how words function in sentences. The teacher or a student can quickly vary the color of words and sentences, and students can see how the change affects sentence structure (SMART, 2005). These reports are descriptions of experience, and they do not provide any data.

Summary

With an interactive whiteboard, teachers can bring a variety of materials to classrooms, and teachers and students can interact with these boards in a variety of ways. Unfortunately, reports of the use of these whiteboards with DHH students have been descriptions of experiences and not empirical research.

Tablet PCs

As with interactive whiteboards, tablet PCs support student interaction with instructional materials. Tablet PCs are slate-shaped mobile computers with a screen that can be activated by an electronic stylus, and by touch for some models. This technology has the same computer capability as a standard laptop computer, and the tablets accept keyboard as well as graphical input (Jackson, 2004; Wikipedia, 2008).

Tablet PCs, along with handheld computing devices, are a set of technologies that has been growing in educational settings (Jackson, 2004). Increasingly, wireless tablets PCs are being created that have full computer performance, coupled with the mobility that approaches that of a handheld device (Hiner, 2008; Jackson, 2004).

Tablet PCs are useful in education because they are responsive, portable, and function collaboratively. Tablets are responsive because they accept stylus or touch input, which enables students to quickly highlight or mark material such as teacher handouts that have been inserted on the tablet. Tablets are more portable than standard laptop computers because they can lie flat on a student's desk and be used with a stylus, rather than a keyboard, and because increasingly smaller versions are being produced (Hiner, 2008; Jackson, 2005). Tablets support collaborative activities by being able to connect to a computer network in which participants can share their notes, other work that has been added to previously inserted documents or graphics, and other materials (Kam et al., 2005). The tablet's capability to record diagrams, formulas, equations, and the like make tablets particularly suitable for science and mathematics courses (Barton & Coltura, 2003; Borja, 2003). Use of tablet PCs appears to be slowly increasing. Major manufacturers of computers, such as Dell, continue to add tablets to their line of products, and tablet PC manufacturers are expanding into the same market niche as handheld computers (Dell, 2008; Hiner, 2008).

Use with Deaf Students

Tablet PCs have been used to teach academic content to DHH students, to support communication access and learning in classes that DHH students attend with hearing students, and to facilitate collaboration among DHH and hearing students in work groups. Liu, Chou, Liu, and Yang (2006) used wireless networked tablet PCs in a junior high school class with seven hard-of-hearing students to teach mathematics. Each student and the teacher had a tablet, and software permitted a display of the teacher's or any of the student's tablet screen on a shared whiteboard at the front of the class. The software also included a scaffold tool that supported the display of and work on mathematics problems in a step-by-step manner and an assessment tool that enabled the teacher to present students' problems, receive responses, and quickly provide feedback. To evaluate the effect of the technology, the investigators compared student responses to teacher questions

and number of errors on worksheets for two class sessions in which the technology was used, with responses and errors for two sessions in which it was not used. Students responded in 90% of the opportunities to answer questions in sessions with the tablet PC in contrast to responding in 55% of the opportunities in sessions without the technology. In addition, students made 60% fewer errors on worksheets when the tablets were used than when they were not used. Thus, the tablet technology appeared to benefit student engagement and learning.

Even and Peterson (2005) reported on teachers' use of tablet PCs connected to an LCD projector that displayed information at the front of classes of DHH high school students. The teacher saved the displayed material after class and distributed it to the students as notes, but educational benefits were not evaluated.

Francis, Stinson, and Elliot (2008) adapted the C-Print classroom captioning system to work with the tablet to create two options for supporting DHH students in mainstream classes. One option provides students and notetakers with wirelessly networked tablets and supports handwritten, real-time notetaking, which allows students access to these notes as they are being created. The second option enables a C-Print service provider to incorporate graphical information written on the tablet with a real-time display of text for the spoken dialogue. To evaluate these options, the investigators asked regular classroom teachers to rate 15 DHH middle and high school students' performance on academic achievement, learning of new vocabulary in the course, and class participation during the trial, in comparison to their previous performance. Teachers' ratings of student performance suggested that most students performed better when they used one of the tablet PC–based options.

The Rochester Institute of Technology has used tablet PCs for notetaking; in this program, students did not have a tablet, and thus the notes were not transmitted wirelessly in real-time during the class to the DHH students, but were available for students after class (Microsoft, 2004). Notetakers commented that the tablet was particularly effective when there were preloaded materials, such as PowerPoint slides that the teacher had made available before class, to which the notetakers could add their own notes.

Beaton (2006) distributed tablet PCs to teams of DHH and hearing students in a postsecondary class. Teams with DHH students were instructed to communicate by messaging each other, in addition to using the tablets for team assignments. Examination of the transcripts for team discussions indicated that students were able to steadily progress toward completion of assignments. Observation of group work showed that the pace of communication and of group progress slowed for students who used messaging to communicate, but it is unclear how this factor would affect learning and retention. Students commented on surveys that they felt that the tablet assisted teams that included students with a disability.

Summary
A few studies with small samples and limited objective measurement indicate that tablet PCs have the potential to teach DHH students directly, to support their access and learning in mainstream classes, and to facilitate collaboration between DHH and hearing students in workgroups; however, larger studies that include more thorough objective measurements are needed to provide reliable findings regarding the usefulness of tablet PCs.

Web-based Instruction
The World Wide Web is another rapidly evolving technology used for the direct instruction of DHH students. Three uses of this technology are the delivery of instructional content, support for participation in out-of-class learning, and provision of databases for research. These uses of the Web for educational purposes, however, are only three of a number of ways in which this technology is being used for education, and additional ways of using the Web continue to emerge.

Content Instruction
The limited research with Web materials that were created for instruction of DHH students indicate that they can promote learning of content if they are appropriately designed (e.g., Dowaliby & Lang, 1999; Lang & Steely, 2003). A particularly important principle appears to be presentation of the instructional material in a manner that encourages student interaction. Additional important principles may be that the language of the material appropriately matches the reading proficiency of the students and that the materials include graphic organizers that provide schematics of key concepts (Lang & Steely, 2003). Only a few educational materials created for instruction through the Web have been created with consideration of the needs of DHH students.

Lang and Steely (2003) describe three studies that examined the effect of media appropriate for Web-based learning. Today, all three studies would generally be presented via the Web, and are, therefore, included in this section. In actuality, two of the studies used instructional units (Earth and physical sciences) with videodisc technology, and the third unit (chemistry) was delivered via the Web to DHH students in grades 6–11. The instructional programs included: (a) carefully sequenced lessons; (b) text that matched the language proficiency of the students; (c) graphic organizers of key concepts; (d) animation of key concepts; (e) frequent questions interspersed through the text and at the end of units; and (f) separate presentation of text, an ASL version of this material, and an animated version of important concepts in each unit. In each study, students were randomly assigned to either the treatment or control condition (study n was 37–49). For each study, those students who viewed the videodisc or Web media learned significantly more material, as assessed by objective pre- and posttests, than did students who were taught a normal curriculum. Each of these studies examined the effect of the aggregated instructional approach (e.g., sequenced lessons, appropriate level of text, etc.) and did not disentangle these several instructional factors that could have contributed to the increased learning with the media.

Dowaliby and Lang (1999) conducted a study that permitted independent assessment of the contributions of a text version of the material, an American Sign Language (ASL) version, an animated version of important concepts, and insertion of questions about content for each of several segments of a lesson. They presented various combinations of materials to 671 postsecondary students using computerized displays. They found that use of adjunct questions led to increased learning, but that the animated or ASL display did not. The authors concluded that their findings were consistent with the principle that learner engagement with instructional materials is critical for learning.

Studies by Barman and Stockton (2002) and Daniele et al. (2001) also demonstrated learning of content presented on the Web; however, neither of these studies included a "practice as usual" control group. The SOAR-High Distance Learning Program, which provided a 1-year course in Earth sciences to three schools for the deaf, was assessed by Barman and Stockton (2002; Lang & Steely, 2003). The program provided instructional units on the Web and also included video conferencing. Students made significant gains in science process and independent learning skills. Daniele et al. (2001) taught a five-session mathematics course to five DHH high school students using lecture demonstrations that were presented by video conferencing and providing homework on a website. The five students made a pre- to posttest average gain of 72%.

Other reports have described websites or materials suitable for delivery of instruction or educational information to DHH students via the Web. Andrews and Jordan (1998) created multimedia stories geared to DHH students with a Hispanic background, in order to increase these students' literacy. The materials included videos of Hispanic American role models and versions in English, Spanish, and ASL. PROJECT SOLVE is a website that provides a large practice bank of mathematic word problems for students to solve (Kelly, 2008). The website is designed for middle school to postsecondary-level DHH students, and includes provision of cues to help students learn to solve word problems. The COMETS website provides extensive resources pertaining to science learning for teachers of DHH students and for their students (Lang, 2004). With respect to the students, the website provides information on college programs that may lead to a science career and on student survival strategies for college.

Participation in Out-of-Class Learning

Two common forms of out-of-class learning that are supported by Web technology are *online learning* and *blended learning*. The Web may also be used to enable students who are out of class to communicate with peers in classes. In online learning, all course material, as well as opportunities for student interaction with the course delivery system, occurs through a Web-based course management system. In blended learning, between 25% and 50% of course time occurs online and the other 75%–50% occurs in a regular classroom (Long, Vignare, Rappold, & Mallory, 2007). For DHH students, the online format may provide certain advantages, such as the asynchronous and largely text-based features of this environment. The common use of text in this environment provides the DHH student direct communication with the course material, instead of communication being mediated through an interpreter, which often occurs when the DHH student is enrolled in a course with primarily hearing students. In addition, in the online course, there are usually no time constraints that require the DHH person to respond immediately to ask a question or make a comment, as there are in a class with hearing students.

Long, Vignare, Rappold, and Mallory (2007) surveyed 908 postsecondary students attending the Rochester Institute of Technology who were enrolled in blended learning courses to determine their perceptions of communication and of the blended learning experience. Students consisted of four groups: hearing, deaf, hard of hearing, and English as a second language (ESL) learners. The deaf and hard-of-hearing groups reported greater increases in the quality of communication and interaction with peers as a result of blended learning than did the hearing and ESL groups. All groups of students stated that they were satisfied with the online learning component of the course, with the level of satisfaction being higher for deaf and hard-of-hearing groups. In short, the deaf and hard-of-hearing groups reported the greatest benefit from the online learning, although learning was not objectively assessed.

Richardson, Long, and Foster (2004) compared the perceptions of learning in an environment that included online learning, but also other forms, such a group tutoring, for an entire course in the Open University in the United Kingdom. Participants were 267 students who indicated they were DHH and 178 students who indicated that they did not have a disability (i.e., were hearing). The modal (most frequent) response for the DHH students regarding their hearing loss was a moderate impairment, with 22% of respondents in this group stating that the impairment was severe or profound. The DHH students assigned significantly lower ratings to questionnaire items that measured perceived effectiveness of communication with other students than did the hearing students. Thus, Richardson et al. (2004) found that their participants reported less positive perceptions of class communication than did those of the Long group (2007). One reason for this difference in perceptions may have been variation in support for communication access in the two classroom environments. In non-online parts of the course, the DHH participants in the study by Long et al. (2007) had interpreter support, but this support was generally not available in the study by Richardson et al. (2004). In addition, the populations in the two studies were different. In the Long group's (2007) investigation, the DHH students were generally young individuals who had their hearing loss since birth, who knew sign language, and who were familiar with dealing with communication issues due to hearing difficulties. In contrast, the DHH students in the Richardson group's (2007) study tended to be older individuals who did not know sign language and who had acquired their hearing loss later in life. It should be noted, however, that according to qualitative analyses of responses to open-ended questions, many of the DHH students felt that the text nature of the material and other aspects of the online format made communication in this setting easier than in a class with hearing students. Mean ratings in each of the two groups on questions that measured general engagement with the course were not significantly different from each other.

The Classroom of the Seas project (Babb et al., 2003) provides an example of how Web technology can be used by students in and out of class to communicate with each other. This project included the establishment of real-time webcasts between an ocean-going research vessel and a classroom at the American School for the Deaf. With this technology, shipboard students and teachers were able to sign and share information with their counterparts at the school and vice versa.

Use of the Web for Student Research

Use of researched information in Web databases by students is widely practiced in education. The previously mentioned COMETS is one of many such websites of particular interest to deaf students (Lang, 2004). Gallaudet University and The National Technical Institute for the Deaf websites contain large databases with lists of other websites related to deafness. The Gallaudet Digital Archive Video for Education, which preserves, indexes, and makes available archival video material, such as the oldest known film in ASL of Edward Miner Gallaudet, is a notable example of this type of educational website (King, Dellon, & Parks, 2005).

Media for Development of Proficiency in Sign Language/Bilingualism

A variety of computer-based materials support the acquisition of ASL and other sign languages, particularly the development of vocabulary. These media support the development of general proficiency in sign language and also the development of sign and printed vocabulary for technical areas, such as science. Additional media have been developed to display signs and provide students opportunities to translate the signs into English captions. The reviewed literature in this area has quite limited data on the educational use of these media by students or on the media's educational impact, and hence it receives limited attention here.

Media for Development of General Proficiency in American Sign Language and Other Sign Languages

The American Sign Language Video Dictionary and Inflection Guide is a general resource that supports the development of vocabulary and inflection of signs in sentence context (Kelly, 2008; Poor, 2003). This Web-based resource was created for users from elementary to postsecondary level and includes 2,700 signs. Of these signs 2,000 are linked to 650 sentences, which show how sentence context influences selection and use of these signs and also how sentence context can influence the meaning of signs. One thousand of these signs are grouped into general categories, such as careers, clothing, and food.

Other examples of sign language instruction and informational materials are downloads and DVDs that are available from companies such as Burton Vision, which publishes media such as six ASL dictionaries (e.g., *First Words, General Dictionary 1*) and Dawn Sign Press, which has lists of various media, including the *Signing Naturally* series DVDs. Some of these materials are interactive and provide feedback, such as a student being able to view a signed sentence, type the English equivalent on a computer, and receive feedback as to whether the response was correct (Burton, 2003).

Media That Support Acquisition of Technical Signs

A major issue with respect to the learning of academic content by DHH students, particularly in science and technical courses, is that these students need to acquire an extensive vocabulary of specialized terms and symbols. Students are exposed to up to about 3,000 new terms in a typical science course, and few signs are available for these terms (Babb et al., 2003). The *Signing Science* dictionary (Vesel, 2006) and course- specific media for teaching vocabulary are examples of materials that have been developed to address the limited availability of technical signs.

The *Signing Science* dictionary is being developed to include 1,500 key terms that are used in elementary and middle school science courses (Vesel, 2006). This dictionary used the SigningAvatar software to present signed explanations of science terms. A study with 15 elementary or middle school students at two schools for the deaf found that students learned a significant amount of content from pre- to posttest for the instructional unit, "What's the Weather." Students had access to the Signing Science dictionary while learning the material for the unit on weather. However, the study did not include a control group that studied the unit without the Signing Science dictionary. Thus, it was not clear what the exact contribution of the dictionary was to the learning of the content.

Egelston-Dodd and Ting (2005) reported on the development of online video tutorials that taught vocabulary for a college-level astronomy course. Students view units that include an instructor who signs specific vocabulary items (e.g., azimuth, altitude) as well as definitions or explanatory information.

Student Production of Captions

To help students further understand how ASL translates into English, CDs have been developed that provide segments of ASL and space on the display interface for students to create captions by inserting an English translation of the signing. In one application of this type, students watch one or two sentences of ASL on a video display and then type their translation into a text box. Next, the program automatically displays and synchronizes the student translation as captions with the signing on the video. Chastel (2003) noted that when a variety of deaf students used the program, those with at least a fourth grade reading level appeared able to use the technology independently, but those with less proficiency in reading appeared to need teacher assistance. Students who were more proficient readers expressed greater enthusiasm for the system than did those who were less proficient.

Summary

Web-based instruction can promote the learning of content by DHH students when the material engages them, such as by providing pre- or post-questions about the content. These findings are consistent with research with printed materials (e.g., Mayer & Wittrock, 2006). However, use of Web media may provide greater flexibility when the display format includes animation and video and easier and faster provision of feedback to students, compared to still pictures and print.

Web-based instruction through online learning provides a means for direct, asynchronous, text-based communication between DHH and hearing students, in contrast to communication that is mediated through an interpreter, as often occurs in classes in which DHH students are educated alongside hearing students. In some of these circumstances, DHH students appear to appreciate the online learning environment.

Research has not determined whether the extensive media regarding the production and use of sign, such as sign dictionaries, actually enhance learning of sign, learning of academic content, or acquisition of vocabulary.

Handheld Technologies

Portable, handheld technologies include pagers, such as the PageWriter; personal digital assistants (PDAs) without capability to access a cellular phone network, such as the I-Pod Touch; and Smartphones that combine computing capability with a cell phone, such as the Sidekick. The rapid development of these devices continues and includes increasing computing power and ability to interact with websites via wireless networks and/or cell services (Gray, 2008). Deaf and hard-of-hearing people have primarily used pagers and Smartphones, mainly for communication. The rapid adoption of these technologies has greatly diminished the use of telephone typewriters (TTYs, minicoms) that were popular only 10 years ago.

With respect to the educational capability of these devices, educators and technology innovators have suggested numerous uses in addition to communication. Ray (2005) and others (e.g., Vath et al., 2005) have noted that software is now available so that students can use handhelds to read electronic texts, use reference materials, produce documents, and collaborate by sharing files with each other. In addition, teachers may use these devices to assess student progress, maintain databases, and perform other actions. Advantages of handhelds relative to standard desktop/laptop computers are their greater portability and substantially lower cost (Norris & Soloway, 2004; Vath et al., 2005). Widespread use of handhelds in classrooms with either hearing or DHH students has not yet occurred, due to limitations in available software, costs, electronic networking difficulties, and challenges to integrating the technology with teaching and learning (Penuel, Tatar, & Roschelle, 2004; Vath et al., 2005).

Consistent with the extensive use of handhelds by DHH people for communication, the two known studies of use of handhelds in an educational intervention with DHH students focused on the communication aspect, as discussed later (Akamatsu, Mayer, & Farrelly, 2005; Liu & Hong, 2007). A handheld technology that DHH students do not have access to and that is being used increasingly in education is the delivery of instruction via podcasts of audio recordings.

Use by Deaf and Hard-of-Hearing People for Communication

Several survey investigations have documented the recent and growing use of handheld technologies by DHH people to send and receive text messages.

In general, these studies show widespread use of the technologies for text communication, a growing predominance in the use of short message services (SMS) as the means for communication, significant use of e-mail on mobile devices, and decreasing use of TTYs. Power and Power (2004) discussed the increasing international availability of text messaging services for use by hearing as well as deaf persons and the growth in popularity of the services among DHH people. They reported that 80% of the deaf people in the province of Victoria, Australia, between the ages of 15 and 50 used text messaging. Power, Power, and Horstmanshof (2007) surveyed 172 members of the Australian Association of the Deaf and found that 90% of the respondents reported access to handheld devices, and that they sent an average of 171 messages per month. Respondents reported using the device for browsing the Web, and playing games, in addition to sending/receiving text messages. Respondents who had completed college used the devices more than those who had received less education. Pilling (2004) surveyed British deaf people and found that 65% preferred SMS, 35% preferred e-mail, and 12% preferred TTYs. Pilling and Barrett (2008) surveyed 381 British deaf people who were recruited through national organizations. The study's findings were similar to those of the Power, Power, and Horstmanshof (2007) survey of Australians. Almost all respondents (96%) who were prelingually deaf sign language users reported communicating via SMS on handheld technology. Use of SMS was increasing more than any other form of communication, and was particularly favored by respondents under 30 years of age.

Power, Power, and Rehling (2007) conducted an online survey of German deaf people in which 102 participants completed questionnaires about handheld technology use. Results were similar to those in previous surveys, with 96% of the respondents reporting that they had SMS available for communication. In comparison, 69% of respondents indicated that they had computers available for communication. Respondents used SMS primarily for social communication.

In regard to DHH people's use of handheld technology for communication, two technology trends deserve comment. First, new technologies such as Sidekick Smartphones offer more features, such as the capability to send longer messages and to use the Internet, than do simpler devices, such as pagers. Deaf and hard-of-hearing persons are increasingly using these devices, but at a slower rate than might be expected, given the advantages of the newer technologies (Power, Power, & Rehling, 2007). Power et al. (2007) suggest that DHH persons are not moving more quickly to the new technologies because these technologies do not add significant enough benefits for them—both the old and new technologies involve texting messages. The second trend has been the increasingly wide use of video phone/messenger services via the Internet (e.g., Sorenson) by deaf people to communicate directly with each other through sign. In the United States, these services are currently only available on desktop or laptop computers; however, in certain countries, such as Japan and Sweden, that have 3G high-bandwidth cell phone technology, deaf people are already using sign language to communicate with each other over the phone (Cavender, 2008).

Educational Interventions with Deaf and Hard-of-Hearing Students

In one of two studies that examined the use of handheld technologies in educational interventions with deaf students, Akamatsu, Mayer, and Farrelly (2005) distributed pagers to provide students with a means for communication that might increase their independence and decision-making skills. In addition, the investigators were interested in reducing parental concern regarding the safety of their DHH children as they traveled about a large city. Pagers were distributed to 48 DHH students 13–19 years of age, staff of the deaf education departments for these students, and the students' parents. At the beginning and end of the trial, the investigators distributed surveys with open and fixed-alternative questions to the students, staff, and parents. Virtually all participants were enthusiastic about use of the pagers. Students and staff noted how pager communication enabled students to report directly to classes at a different school rather than first detouring to check in at the local deaf education program. Parents reported less concern regarding the whereabouts of the children because of the SMS communication. The investigators also noted considerable student variability in extent of use of the devices.

Liu and Hong (2007) investigated use of Smartphones to support the after-class learning of mathematics by six Taiwanese DHH middle school students. The Smartphones had access to the Internet, text messaging, and software that provided shortcuts for the teacher and student to use in sending frequent phrases, such as, "Did you do your homework?" Over the 5-week trial period, the teacher and students communicated approximately 350 times. Completion of homework increased from 70% for the semester prior to initiation of the trials to 90% for the trial period. Nevertheless, teacher praise provided through a Smartphone did not appear to elicit a favorable response from students. The parents of the children reported that they felt that the Smartphone-based support system had helped the students learn mathematics, but the study did not measure the effect of the intervention upon the students' mathematics test performance.

Focused application of handheld technologies to improve education of DHH students has just begun. There appear to be many as yet unexplored ways in which these technologies might be used with DHH students, such as the use of reference tools that include communication in sign.

Summary

Many, if not most DHH people, usually carry with them a handheld technology, primarily for communication purposes. These technologies, however, may also be used for other purposes, including educational ones. Although there is much potential regarding educational uses, data are not yet sufficient to draw conclusions regarding the educational impact of this technology.

Summary and Conclusions

From this review, it is clear that few reliable findings are available regarding the educational benefits of various technologies used to educate DHH students. As has been the case for the past 25 years, there continues to be a dire need for evidence that informs the field of whether a technology actually helps DHH students learn (Kelly, 1982). A few studies have shown that Web materials that engage DHH students do promote learning (e.g., Lang & Steely, 2003). In addition, several studies indicate that it is not clear whether altering the presentation of captions affects learning, and a number of studies indicate that, for many DHH students, classroom captions can facilitate comprehension of lectures as well as an interpreter. With respect to other uses of educational technology with DHH students, however, research appears to be lacking that tells the field with any kind of reliability whether these uses are educationally beneficial.

Currently, more and more technologies, such as interactive whiteboards, are emerging with the potential to improve communication and learning of DHH students. Some of these technologies include data collection mechanisms (e.g., a record of student responses to test questions during a lesson). This availability is important, as evidence-based practice continues to increase in the field (Odom et al., 2005). Thus, there is a critical need for new resources and a new level attention by workers to obtain the reliable data that will tell the field what uses of technology work with which DHH students.

References

Akamatsu, C., Mayer, C., & Farrelly, S. (2005). An investigation of two-way text messaging use with deaf students at the secondary level. *Journal of Deaf Studies and Deaf Education, 10,* 120–131.

Andrews, J.F., & Jordan, D.L. (1998). Multimedia stories. *Teaching Exceptional Children, 30,* 28–33.

Andrews, J.F., Leigh, I.W., & Weiner, M.T. (2004). *Deaf people: Evolving perspectives from psychology, education, and sociology.* Boston: Pearson Education.

Aylesworth, S. (2006). *2006 Survey of postsecondary speech-*to-text *services salary and program demographics.* St. Paul, MN: Midwest Center for Postsecondary Outreach, St. Paul Technical College. Retrieved August 2, 2006 from http://www.mcpo.org/speechtotext_survey.asp

Babb, I.G., Lang, H., Brown, S., Scheifele, P., LaPorta-Hupper, M., Monte, D., et al. (2003, June). *The classroom of the sea: Developing technologies to bring the sea to the classroom.* Paper presented at the Instructional Technology and Education of the Deaf Symposium, National Technical Institute for the Deaf, Rochester, New York. Retrieved August 17, 2008 from http://www.rit.edu/ntid/vp/techsym

Baker, R. (1985). Subtitling television for deaf children. *Media in Education Research Series, 3,* 1–46.

Barman, C.R., & Stockton, J.D. (2002). An evaluation of Project SOAR-High: A web-based science program for deaf students. *American Annals of the Deaf, 147,* 5–10.

Barton, C., & Collura, K. (2003). Catalyst for change. *The Journal, 31*(4), 39.

Beaton, C. (2006). Work in progress: Tablet PC's as a leveling device! *Proceedings Frontiers in Education,* 15–16, 36th Annual Conference.

Borja, R.R. (2003). Classroom notetaking goes digital with tablet devices. *Educational Week, 23*(12), 8.

Braverman, B.B., & Hertzog, M. (1980). The effects of caption rate and language level on comprehension of a captioned video presentation. *American Annals of the Deaf, 125*(7), 943–948.

Burnham, D., Leigh, G., Noble, W., Jones, C., Tyler, M., Grebennikov, L., & Varley, A. (2008, March). Parameters in television captioning for deaf and hard-of-hearing adults: Effects of caption rate versus text reduction on comprehension. *Journal of Deaf Studies and Deaf Education* doi: 10.1093/deafed/enn003. Retrieved July 28, 2008 from http://jdsde.oxfordjournals.org

Burton, M.J. (2003). *Technology positively impact deaf students? You betcha!.* Paper presented at the Instructional Technology and Education of the Deaf Symposium, National Technical Institute for the Deaf. Retrieved November 8, 2008 from http://www.rit.edu/ntid/vp/techsym

Cavender, A. (2008). MobileASL. Retrieved August 8, 2008 from http://mobileasl.cs.washington.edu

Chastel, M. (2003). *Student generated captions: A multimedia bridge between ASL and English.* Paper presented at the

Instructional Technology and Education of the Deaf Symposium, National Technical Institute for the Deaf. Retrieved August 15, 2008 from http://www.rit.edu/ntid/vp/techsym

CodeWell. (2007). *Typewell*. Retrieved July 28, 2007 from http://www.typewell.com

Daniele, V.A., Aidala, C., Parrish, R., Robinson, V., Carr, J., & Spiecker, P. (2001). *Distance learning pilot: Physics and mathematics*. Paper presented at the Instructional Technology and Education of the Deaf Symposium. National Technical Institute for the Deaf, Rochester, NY.

Davis, C., Francis, P., & Harlan, D. (2000). *Providing real-time captioning, C-print speech to print transcription and assistive listening devices: Questions and answers*. St. Paul, MN: Midwest Center for Postsecondary Outreach and the Postsecondary Education Programs Network.

Davis, M.R. (2007). Whiteboards Inc.: Interactive features fuel demand for modern chalkboards. *Education Week*. Retrieved August 20, 2008 from http://www.edweek.org/dd/articles/2007/09/12/02board.h01.html

Dell. (2008). Latitude *XT* tablet PC. Retrieved November 20, 2008 from http://www.dell.com/content/productdetails.aspx/latit_

Dowaliby, F.J., & Lang, H.G. (1999). Adjunct aids in instructional prose: A multimedia study with deaf college students. *Journal of Deaf Studies and Deaf Education, 4*, 270–282.

Edwards, J.A., Hartnell, M., & Martin, R. (2002). Interactive whiteboards: Some lessons from the classroom. *Micromath, 18*(2), 30–33.

Egelston-Dodd, J., & Ting, S. (2005). *Video-tutorials for tech sign vocabulary in astronomy*. Paper presented at the Instructional Technology and Education of the Deaf: Supporting Learners, Preschool-College, National Technical Institute for the Deaf. Retrieved July 10, 2008 from http://www.rit.edu/ntid/vp/techsym

Elliot, L., Stinson, M., & Coyne, G. (2006, April) *Student learning with C-Print's educational software and automatic speech recognition*. Paper presented at the Annual Meeting of the American Educational Association, San Francisco, CA.

Elliot, L., Stinson, M., Easton, D., & Bourgeois, J. (2008, March) *College students' learning with C-Print's educational software and automatic speech recognition*. Paper presented at the Annual Meeting of the American Educational Association, New York City.

Elliot, L., Stinson, M., McKee, B., Everhart, V., & Francis, P. (2001). College students' perceptions of the C-Print speech-to-text transcription system. *Journal of Deaf Studies and Deaf Education, 6*, 285–298.

Elvers, G.C. (2000). The digital whiteboard as a notes-taking aid. *Smarter Kids Foundation*. Retrieved September 19, 2005 from http://www.smarterkids.org/research/paper1.asp

Even, P., & Peterson, K. (2005). *Toward a boundless learning environment*- TABLET. Paper presented at the Instructional Technology and Education of the Deaf International Symposium, National Technical Institute for the Deaf. Retrieved August 7, 2008 from http://www.rit.edu/ntid/vp/techsym

Florida School for the Deaf and Blind. (2008). *Interactive whiteboards in the classroom*. Retrieved August 20, 2008 from http://www.fsdb.k12.fl.us/rmc/tutorials/whiteboards.html

Francis, P., Stinson, M., & Elliot, L. (2008, April). *Using Tablet PCs to integrate graphics with text to support students who are deaf and hard of hearing*. Paper presented at the PEPNet Biennial Conference, Columbus, OH.

Gage, J. (2002). So what is an electronic whiteboard? Should you want one? *Micromath, 18*(2), 5–7.

Gersten, R., & Edyburn, D. (2007). Defining quality indicators for special education technology research. *Journal of Special Education Technology, 22*(3), 3–18.

Graves, P. (2003). CART in the classroom: *Meeting the communication access needs of students requires an individual approach*. Paper presented at the Instructional Technology and Education of the Deaf Symposium, National Technical Institute for the Deaf. Retrieved August 17, 2008 from http://www.rit.edu/ntid/vp/techsym

Gray, T. (2008). *Trends and challenges in 2008*. Paper presented at the Office of Special Education Programs Project Directors Meeting: Washington, DC.

Hamlin, L. (2008). National update. *Hearing Loss, 29*(4), 24.

Harkins, J.E., & Bakke, M. (2003). Technologies for communication: Status and trends. In M. Marschark & P.E. Spencer (Eds.), *Oxford handbook of deaf studies, language, and education* (pp. 406–419). New York: Oxford University Press.

Hiner, J. (2008). Will your plumber and repair technician soon be carrying tablet PCs? *Techrepublic*. Retrieved August 20, 2008 from http://blogs.techrepublic.com/hiner/?p=606

Jackson, L. (2004). One-to-one computing: Is your school ready? *Education World*. Retrieved March 22, 2005 from http://www.educationworld.com/a_tech/tech/tech202.shtml

Jackson, L. (2005). Computers in high school classrooms. *Education World*. Retrieved March 22, 2005 from http://www.educationworld.com/a_tech/tech/tech211.shtml

Jensema, C. (1998). Viewer reaction to different television captioning speeds. *American Annals of the Deaf, 143*(4), 318–324.

Jensema, C., McCann, R., & Ramsey, S. (1996). Closed-captioned television presentation speed and vocabulary. *American Annals of the Deaf, 141*, 284–292.

Kam, M., Wang, J., Iles, A., Tse, E., Chiu, J., Glaser, D., et al. (2005). Livenotes: A system for cooperative and augmented note-taking in lectures. *CHI 2005*, 531–540.

Kelly, R.R. (1982). Microcomputers in education: Age of romance, or age of reason?. *American Annals of the Deaf, 127*(5), 693–697.

Kelly, R.R. (2008). Technology for individuals with vision or hearing challenges. In J.D. Lindsey (Ed.), *Technology and exceptional students*, 4th edition (pp. 445–479). Austin, TX: Pro-ed.

Kennewell, S., & Morgan, A. (2003). Student teachers' experiences and attitudes towards using interactive whiteboards in the teaching and learning of young children. *Computer Education, 106*, 12–15.

King, C.M., Dellon, J., & Parks, E. (2005). *Gallaudet digital archive video for education (DAVe)*. Paper presented at the Instructional Technology and Education of the Deaf Symposium, National Technical Institute for the Deaf, Rochester, NY. Retrieved from http://www.rit.edu/~techsym/detail.html#T2D

Klawe, M. (2000). Best screen play: A comparison of paired team play using SMART board interactive whiteboards versus paired individual play using computers. *Smarter Kids Foundation*. Retrieved September 20, 2005 from http://www.smarterkids.org/research/paper4.asp

Lang, H. (2004). *Clearinghouse on mathematics, engineering, technology and science (COMETS): A comprehensive resource in the education of deaf students*. Retrieved November 10, 2008 from http://www.rit.edu/ntid/msse/aboutpage.htm

Lang, H.G., & Steely, D. (2003). Web-based science education: What research says to the teacher. *Instructional Science, 31*, 277–298.

Lewis, M.S.J., & Jackson, D.W. (2001). Television literacy: Comprehension of program content using closed captions for the deaf. *Journal of Deaf Studies and Deaf Education, 6*(1), 43–53.

Liles, M. (2005). Interactive whiteboard system drives increased achievement at Texas School for the Deaf. *THE Journal, 32*(10), 49–50, Academic Search Elite.

Liss, M.B., & Price, D. (1981). What, when & why deaf children watch television. *American Annals of the Deaf, 126*, 493–498.

Liu, C., & Hong, Y. (2007). Providing hearing-impaired students with learning care after classes through smart phones and the GPRS network. *British Journal of Educational Technology, 38*(4), 727–741.

Liu, C., Chou, C., Liu, B., & Yang, J. (2006). Improving mathematics teaching and learning experiences for hard of hearing students with wireless technology-enhanced classrooms. *American Annals of the Deaf, 151*(3), 345–355.

Long, G.L., Vignare, K., Rappold, R.P., & Mallory, J. (2007). Access to communication for deaf, hard-of-hearing and ESL students in blended learning courses. *The International Review of Research in Open and Distance Learning, 8*(3), ISSN: 1492–3831. Retrieved August 6, 2008 from http://www.irrodl.org/index.php/irrodl/article/view/423/933

Mackall, P. (2004). Interactive whiteboards enhance the learning experience for deaf, hard-of-hearing students. *THE Journal, 31*(10), 64–66.

Marschark, M., Leigh, G., Sapere, P., Burnham, D., Convertino, C., Stinson, M., et al. (2006). Benefits of sign language interpreting and text alternatives for deaf students' classroom learning. *Journal of Deaf Studies and Deaf Education, 11*(4), 421–437.

Mayer, R.E. & Wittrock, M.C. (2006). Problem solving. In P. Alexander and P. Winne (Eds.) *Handbook of educational psychology* (pp. 287-304). Mahwah, NJ: Lawrence Earlbaum Associates.

Microsoft (2004). *RIT delivers notes to students who are deaf, better and faster, at lower cost*. Retrieved March 31, 2005 from http://www.microsoft.com/resources/casestudies/CaseStudy.asp?CaseStudyID=15482

National Captioning Institute (1983). *Hearing impaired children's comprehension of closed captioned television programs*. Falls Church, VA: National Captioning Institute, Research Report 85–3.

National Technical Institute for the Deaf. (2008). *C-Print speech-to-text system*. Retrieved November 11, 2008 from http://www.ntid.rit.edu/cprint

Norris, C., & Soloway, E. (2004). Envisioning the handheld-centric classroom. *Journal of Educational Computing Research, 30*(4), 281–294.

Penuel, W.R., Tatar, D.G., & Roschelle, J. (2004). The role of research on contexts of teaching practice in informing the design of handheld learning technologies. *Journal of Educational Computing Research, 30*(4), 353–370.

Pilling, D. (2004). *Text communication survey*. London: City University. Retrieved January 20, 2005 from www.city.ac.uk/sonm/dps/news/07_09_04.pdf

Pilling, D., & Barrett, P. (2008). Text communication preferences of deaf people in the United Kingdom. *Journal of Deaf Studies and Deaf Education, 13*(1), 82–103.

Poor, G.S. (2003). *American Sign Language video dictionary and inflection guide (A FIPSE Project)*. Rochester, NY: National Technical Institute for the Deaf, Rochester Institute of Technology.

Porter, J.E., & Clymer, E.W. (2001). *Recommendations report*. Paper presented at the Instructional Technology and Education of the Deaf Symposium, National Technical Institute for the Deaf. Retrieved May 23, 2002 from http://www.rit.edu/~techsym

Power, D., Power, M.R., & Rehling, B. (2007). German deaf people using text communication: Short message service, TTY, relay services, fax, and e-mail. *American Annals of the Deaf, 152*(3), 291–301.

Power, M.R., & Power, D. (2004). Everyone here speaks TXT: Deaf people using SMS in Australia and the rest of the world. *Journal of Deaf Studies and Deaf Education, 9*, 343.

Power, M.R., Power, D., & Horstmanshof, L. (2007). Deaf people communicating via SMS, TTY, relay service, fax and computers. *Journal of Deaf Studies and Deaf Education, 12*, 80–92.

Preminger, J.E., & Levitt, H. (1998). Computer-assisted remote transcription (CART): A tool to aid people who are deaf or hard of hearing in the workplace. *Volta Review, 99*(4), 219–230.

Ray, B.B. (2005). Mining what we know about handheld computers: A review of the [anecdotal] evidence. *The Turkish Online Journal of Educational Technology, 4*(2), 3–6.

Richardson, A. (2002). Effective questioning in teaching mathematics using an interactive whiteboard. *Micromath, 18*(2), 8–12.

Richardson, J.T.E., Long, G.L., & Foster, S.B. (2004). Academic engagement in students with a hearing loss in distance education. *Journal of Deaf Studies and Deaf Education, 9*, 68–85, doi: 10.1093/deafed/enh009.

Schilperoord, J., de Groot, V., & van Son, N. (2005). Nonverbatim captioning in Dutch television programs: A text linguistic approach. *Journal of Deaf Studies and Deaf Education, 10*(4), 402–416.

SMART. (2005). A schoolwide installation of whiteboards. *Media and Methods*. Retrieved July 12, 2008 from www.media-methods.com

Stein, M.S. (2008). Captioning the internet. *NADmag, 8*(1), 18–21.

Steinfield, A. (1998). The benefit of real-time captioning in a mainstream classroom as measured by working memory. *Volta Review, 100*(1), 29–44.

Stinson, M., Elliot, L., Kelly, R., Liu, Y., & Stinson, S. (2009). Deaf and hard-of-hearing students' memory of lectures with speech-to-text and interpreting/notetaking services. *Journal of Special Education, 43*(1), 52-64.

Stinson, M., Elliot, L., McKee, B., &Francis, P. (2001). The C-Print real-time speech-to-text support service. *Volta Voices, 8*, 16–22.

Stinson, M., Stinson, S., Elliot, L., & Kelly, R. (2004, April). *Relationships between use of the C-Print speech-to-text service, perceptions of courses, and course performance*. Paper presented at the Annual Meeting of the American Educational Research Association, San Diego, CA.

Stinson, M., Stinson, S., Elliot, L., & Kelly, R. (2006). [Relationships between use of the C-Print speech-to-text service, perceptions of courses, and course performance in high school students]. Unpublished data.

Stinson, M., Stuckless, E., Henderson, J., & Miller, L. (1989). Perceptions of hearing-impaired college students toward real-time speech to print: RTGD and other support services. *Volta Review, 90,* 336–348.

Stinson, M.S., Eisenberg, S., Horn, C., Larson, J., Levitt, H., & Stuckless, R. (1999). Real-time speech-to-text services. In R. Stuckless (Ed.), *Reports of the National Task Force on Quality Services in Postsecondary Education of Deaf and Hard of Hearing Students.* Rochester, NY: Northeast Technical Assistance Center, Rochester Institute of Technology.

Stuckless, E.R. (1999). Recognition means more than just getting the words right. *Speech Technology, 4,* 30–38.

Vath, R., Bobrowsky, W., Soloway, E., Blumenfield, P., Krajcik, J., Meriweather, A., et al. (2005). *Supporting teachers using palm computers: Examining classroom practice over time.* Paper presented at the National Education Computing Conference, Philadelphia, PA.

Vesel, J. (2006). *The signing science dictionary research study report of findings.* Retrieved November 11, 2008 from http://www.nationaltechcenter.org/index.php/2006/03/29

Viable Technologies, Inc. (2005). *Viable realtime translation.* Retrieved January 7, 2005 from http://www.viabletechnologies.com

Ward, P., Wang, Y., Paul, P., & Loeterman, M. (2007). Near-verbatim captioning versus edited captioning for students who are deaf or hard of hearing: A preliminary investigation of effects on comprehension. *American Annals of the Deaf, 152*(1), 20–28.

Wikipedia (2010) Tablet PC. Retrieved January 8, 2010 from http://en.wikipedia.org/wiki/Tablet_PC.

PART 2

Literacy and
Curriculum Issues

Evidence-based Curricula and Practices That Support Development of Reading Skills

Susan R. Easterbrooks

Abstract

The Individuals with Disabilities Education Improvement Act (2004) and No Child Left Behind Act (2001, 2002) require teachers to use evidence-based practices (EBPs) in instruction. This is not an easy task as the evidence base in deaf education tends to be woefully lacking. This chapter begins with a discussion of the challenges that deaf or hard-of-hearing (DHH) children face in acquiring reading skills, focusing especially on the apparent bifurcation in the population between those with access to sound and those without. Next, it provides a review of the relations between early skills and later reading acquisition, examining those factors that are related to positive literacy outcomes. The field of literacy instruction is changing rapidly, and teachers need guidelines for reviewing the existing knowledge base. The chapter presents a discussion of levels of research effort through which educators may examine the knowledge base. In the absence of clear evidence, educators may choose to investigate practices from the perspective of their relation to correlates of language acquisition. Finally, it identifies curricula accepted for use with hearing children by the What Works Clearinghouse (WWC) and relates these to our evidence of their use with DHH children. In no other area of deaf education is the challenge to educators more important and complex. We must make the effort to keep abreast of newly identified EBPs as research becomes available.

Keywords: alphabetic knowledge, comprehension, evidence-based practice, literacy, literacy curriculum, phonics, phonological awareness

Existing mandates require that all teachers engage in evidence-based practices (EBPs) with their students (Individuals with Disabilities Education Improvement Act, 2004; No Child Left Behind Act of 2001, 2002). This is a challenge for teachers of children who are deaf or hard of hearing because in the past, many in the field have maintained a belief-driven focus rather than an evidence-driven focus. The first part of this chapter describes the challenges posed by diversity within the population of students who are deaf and hard of hearing and reviews the relationship between early skills and later reading acquisition. This is followed by a discussion of what constitutes appropriate evidence in the area of reading. Next, the chapter explores curricula for which an evidence base is available. Some of these curricula have empirical evidence

in their support from the literature on both hearing and deaf students; others have a developing evidence base primarily of teacher reports and case study—emerging, albeit insufficient, empirical support.

Challenges to Reading Development in the School Years

A hearing loss imposes a serious risk to language and reading development (Carney & Moeller, 1998). Reports on reading outcomes for high school graduates suggest a median of fourth to fifth grade in achievement (Allen, 1986; Traxler, 2000). Perspectives on reading outcomes for deaf or hard-of-hearing (DHH) students vary depending on the subset of the population on whom researchers report their data. Reports on large, national samples, which tend to include older students, provide a bleak outlook (Marschark, Lang, & Albertini, 2002), whereas reports on smaller samples of subsets of the population appear more hopeful (Connor & Zwolan, 2004; Geers, 2002; Kaderavek & Pakulski, 2007).

Factors contributing to reading failure in DHH children include limited access to a phonological code, starting school without a language or literacy base, inadequate literacy experience prior to school, and delayed vocabularies, (Luckner, Sebald, Cooney, Young, & Muir, 2005/2006). Other variables contributing to the overall picture of literacy among students with hearing loss include (a) the use of amplification and cochlear implants (James, Rajput, Brinton, & Goswami, 2007; Marschark, Rhoten, & Fabich, 2007); (b) early intervention (Moeller, 2000); (c) linguistic ability (Chamberlain & Mayberry, 2008); (d) a home language consistent with the majority language of the school (Geeslin, 2008); (e) consistent access to signed or spoken language (Kaderavek & Pakulski, 2007); and (f) parental involvement in literacy (Aram, Most, & Simon, 2008; Stobbart & Alant, 2008).

Because of the variations in the aforementioned conditions, the population of individuals who are deaf or hard of hearing is very diverse. Hearing losses range from mild to profound, and hearing level relates to differences in potential for learning and using auditory–oral versus visual–manual languages. Reading comprehension outcomes are also influenced by the severity of hearing loss (Karchmer, Malone, & Wolk, 1979). Age at which hearing loss occurs adds to the diversity of the population in regard to language modality. Many individuals are born with a hearing loss, but at least 7% of the population with hearing loss acquires the loss after the age of 2 years.

In the population of children with hearing loss as a whole, approximately 51% use speech and residual hearing as their primary mode of communication, 35.5% use speech and sign, and about 11.2% use sign only (Gallaudet Research Institute [GRI], 2006). Differences in language modality may affect the emergence of literacy skills, although there is no universal agreement on this (cf., Padden & Ramsey, 1998, 2000; Rayner, Foorman, Perfetti, Pesetsky, & Seidenberg, 2001; Svirsky, Stallings, Lento, Ying, & Leonard, 2002). These differences almost certainly affect individual educator's perspectives on approaches that may be most effective to build literacy.

The presence of a disability that is not necessarily related to a child's hearing loss may have significant effects on the path to literacy skills, and almost half (48.6%) of children with hearing loss are reported to have a disability such as low vision, deafblindness, developmental delays, learning disabilities, orthopedic impairments, attention deficit disorders, speech and language disorders, traumatic brain injury, mental retardation, emotional disturbance, autism, or other health impairments (GRI, 2006). The presence of one or more of these disabilities adds a unique character to reading acquisition problems and may require varied intensity and approaches to support literacy.

In addition, there are differences in the types of schools that children with hearing loss attend. The majority of students attend regular schools, whereas about 20%–25% attend special schools. Placement in the general education environment may result in the use of the general education curriculum objectives and materials rather than the use of specialized objectives and materials. The racial/ethnic backgrounds of individuals who are deaf or hard of hearing also vary, with 47.4% on the GRI's Annual Survey reporting as non-white. Considering all of these differences, it is apparent that the population is widely heterogeneous. If one were to ask any classroom teacher of five DHH students, he or she might respond that this necessitates conducting five individual programs simultaneously. This being the case, educators can no longer engage in the age-old battle of which way is *the* right way to teach reading or the language base upon which it is built. Educators need multiple options, serving multiple needs from multiple perspectives, all of which should undergo rigorous validation.

Are There Two Segments of the Populations with Distinctly Different Needs?

Without a doubt, the demographic landscape is changing among the population that teachers of DHH students are serving. For example, etiologies from 25 years ago (Holt, Hotto, & Cole, 1994) form a different pattern among the population today, in part because gestational rubella has almost disappeared in industrialized countries and hearing loss due to prematurity has increased. Early detection of hearing loss (American Academy of Pediatrics, 1999), changes in the availability of technology that make access to audition a reality for more children than ever before (Easterbrooks, Lederberg, Miller, Bergeron, & Connor, 2009; Yoshinaga-Itano, 2006), and the influx of children from other countries, where early support was not available (Gerner de Garcia, 1995; GRI, 2006; Holt et al., 1994) contribute to the formation of two segments of the population: those with sufficient early access to sound to support an auditorily based phonological code and those without.

To the extent that children have access to early intervention and advanced technologies, they have increased opportunities to develop language on time and thus to have a better base for building literacy skills than was the case in the past. For many, but not all, of these children, their potential for developing auditory skills is significantly higher than has previously been assumed or expected (Easterbrooks et al., 2009). This segment of the population, then, needs to be recognized, and curriculum approaches that support auditory skills are both necessary and important. For another segment of the population, and for a variety of reasons, auditorily based learning continues to be inaccessible. For example, of the children identified through early intervention, only slightly more than half participate in early intervention programs (Centers for Disease Control [CDC], 2008). Therefore, some children may have sufficient access to audition to acquire literacy through the auditory pathway; some will have sufficient access to audition but, for reasons still not well understood, will not develop an auditory base for literacy; and others still will always be candidates for visual pathways to literacy. No matter the case, many will need more visually oriented programs, thus necessitating the development of reading curricula and materials oriented toward a visual learning style. Assuming that all children with hearing loss will be primarily visual learners—or all will be primarily auditory learners—is not appropriate, and curriculum efforts need to recognize both possibilities.

In short, the time has come to recognize two distinctly different segments of the population for which the field of deaf education is responsible: those who acquire literacy through an auditory path, and those who acquire it through a visual path. Future efforts to develop curricula and pedagogy must account for these distinctions and must address the needs of both groups with equal rigor and research.

Early Skills and Their Relation to Later Reading Development

Emergent reading skills provide the foundation for later literacy and academic development in children with typical levels of hearing (Whitehurst & Lonigan, 1998). The same holds true for DHH children; the factors that contribute to reading success in hearing preschoolers also contribute to reading success in DHH preschoolers. Language ability, vocabulary knowledge, alphabetic knowledge, phoneme–grapheme correspondence, and fluency are significant contributors to reading comprehension in all children (National Reading Panel [NRP], 2000). In addition, the type and amount of skills acquired at the emergent literacy stage set a trajectory for development that continues well into the school years, both for hearing children (Foster & Miller, 2007; Mann, 1993; Stanovich, 1992) and for DHH children (Colin, Magnan, Ecalle, & Leybaert, 2007). Thus, early reading instruction is a critical factor in establishing the foundation for later literacy outcomes.

Research with DHH children repeatedly documents a strong relation between vocabulary and reading skills (Geers & Moog, 1989; LaSasso & Davey, 1987; Paul, 1996), in particular, vocabulary production (Kyle & Harris, 2006). Although some DHH children achieve age-typical levels of vocabulary, most show severe delays in vocabulary knowledge. However, vocabulary instruction alone is not sufficient to raise reading scores. Unless deaf children achieve a certain level of syntactic ability, they will not be able to use their lexicon maximally in comprehending information written in higher-order grammatical forms (Kelly, 1996). A focus on early language acquisition is essential because intensive instruction is required to teach the grammar of the language they will confront in print to students who do not learn it early (Calvert, 1981), and, in fact, DHH children identified and served early are usually able to make progress in language at rates that exceed those of their later-identified peers (Moeller, Tomblin, Yoshinaga-Itano, Connor, & Jerger, 2007). When hearing preschoolers have teachers who use complex syntax, they in turn develop more complex syntax than those whose teachers use simpler syntax (Huttenlocher, Vasilyeva, Cymerman, & Levine, 2002). This indicates the importance of providing complete models of linguistic syntax to young children with hearing loss, and the modality or modalities of that model will necessarily differ depending upon the child's available processing abilities. Any early reading program for DHH children should focus rigorously on children's development of higher-order grammatical abilities.

Phonological awareness (PA) refers to a "broad class of skills that involve attending to, thinking about, and intentionally manipulating the phonological aspects of spoken language, especially the internal phonological structure of words" (Scarborough & Brady, 2002, p. 312). Phonological skills include blending, segmenting, elision, and rhyming, and (at least for hearing children) are relatively stable from the late-preschool period forward (Burgess & Lonigan, 1998; Lonigan, Burgess, & Anthony, 2000; Wagner et al., 1997). These skills are strong independent predictors of beginning reading and spelling in children with typical levels of hearing (Lonigan et al., 2000; MacLean, Bryant, & Bradley, 1987). Recall the earlier discussion of two segments of students, those with and those without early access to sound. If PA is a critical element in emergent literacy, then educators must address this need in both segments of the populations. For DHH children with limited access to sound, alternatives to PA, or alternative methods for its development, are necessary (Mayer, 2007). For children whose families are non-English speakers, teachers must make special effort to help clarify the sound systems of the two languages, as the sound system of one language plays a unique role in the mastery of phoneme–grapheme correspondence in the other (Durunoglu, Nagy, & Hancin-Bhatt, 1993; Gottardo, Siegel, Yan, & Wade-Woolley, 2001). Gottardo et al. studied 65 hearing Chinese children whose first language (L1) was Cantonese and second language (L2) was English and found that phonological skills in L1 and L2 contributed to the variance of L2 reading, even though written Cantonese does not use an alphabetic orthography. Both cued speech and visual phonics researchers (LaSasso & Metzger, 1998; Trezek & Malmgren, 2005) have indicated that DHH children can acquire PA even when auditory skills are severely limited. Thus, both of the groups discussed earlier—those with some audition and those who remain overwhelmingly dependent upon visual input—may have the potential to develop PA, a necessary precursor to the phoneme–grapheme correspondence that undergirds phonics instruction. The methods for acquiring this knowledge will differ.

Whereas PA is necessary for the development of graphophonemic correspondence, it is distinctly different from phonics per se, in that PA is a skill and phonics is an instructional strategy for teaching children to master graphophonemic correspondence (Scarborough & Brady, 2002). A second skill necessary for graphophonemic correspondence is knowledge of alphabetics, a significant contributor to early literacy. Children who begin school knowing their letters are more likely to become successful readers (Adams, 1990; Stevenson & Newman, 1986) than those who do not. Once thought to be outside the DHH child's range of ability, the production of letter sounds in addition to letter names is not only often an accessible skill but also thought to be related to improvements in children's word identification

skills (Aghababian, Nazir, Lancon, & Tardy, 2001; Trezek & Malmgren, 2005). Further, deaf children's letter-sound knowledge appears to correlate strongly with PA and other literacy skills, both concurrently and across time (Easterbrooks et al., 2009). Williams (2004) noted that "deaf children's emergent reading reflected the developmental sequence of hearing children described in the research literature" (p. 356). However, Mayer (2007) clarified that the sequence differs from that of hearing children later in the emergent literacy stage when the graphophonemic relationship becomes increasingly important. Alphabetic knowledge and phonological awareness, then, are separate but equally important underlying skills that support graphophonemic correspondence, which is often taught through the instructional strategy of phonics.

All of the abilities described earlier—vocabulary, syntax, PA—are reflected in a child's reading fluency. Reading fluency as defined by the National Reading Panel (2000) is the ability "to read orally with speed, accuracy, and proper expression." The first component of the definition of fluency, speed, is generally defined as words per minute or words correct per minute (Carnine, Silbert, Kame'enui, & Tarver, 2004) and correlates positively with reading comprehension in hearing children (Jenkins, Fuchs, van den Broek, Epsin, & Deno, 2003; Swanson & Howell, 2001). Poorer readers have demonstrated improvements in their reading comprehension skills upon direct instruction in fluency (Mercer, Campbell, Miller, Mercer, & Lane, 2000). When children do not read orally, fluent signed renderings of text can provide teachers with information regarding their students' reading comprehension. Easterbrooks and Huston (2007) found a relationship similar to that of Mercer et al.'s study (2000), between reading comprehension outcomes and fluent, signed renderings of text in deaf, middle school-aged students. The second component of the definition of fluency, accuracy, involves accurate decoding and comprehension at word, phrase, and discourse levels. Accuracy is generally evaluated using miscue analysis or tallies of decoding error types (Johns, 2004), and although rapid, automatic word recognition is a necessary precondition of fluency, it is not in itself sufficient (Carnine, et al., 2004). Fluency is also dependent upon comprehension at the discourse level, and such comprehension is displayed via the third component of the definition of fluency, which is proper expression. Proper expression refers to the prosodic characteristics of reading (e.g., use of pitch, stress): "When readers embed appropriate volume, tone, emphasis, phrasing, and other elements in oral expression, they are giving evidence of actively interpreting or constructing meaning from the passage" (Rasinski, 2004, p.3). Children who do not use proper expression but instead read word for word overburden their memory capacities and struggle to make sense of what they have read (LaBerge & Samuels, 1974). Grouping words into phrases is important because the meaning of English is often based on phrase and clause units.

Although the "fluency" of hearing children is measured by their oral reading, and their prosodic patterns are those learned and used in their spoken language, fluency can also be noted and assessed in children using signs (Easterbrooks & Huston, 2007). Reading fluency in DHH students who use sign language involves the automatic rendering of print into signed form (Chrosniak, 1993). This process is similar to the process hearing students apply when they see text, form a mental image, and present it through spoken language. Students must do more than simply read words at an appropriate rate; they must form a mental visualization of the printed English text and then render it expressively either through spoken English, English-like signing, or American Sign Language (ASL). The ability of middle grade DHH students to render English text through sign correlates highly with reading comprehension (Easterbrooks & Huston).

Although research with hearing children has firmly established alphabetic knowledge, PA, vocabulary, and fluency as key skills integral to successful reading comprehension among hearing children (National Reading Panel, 2000), research with deaf children is much less extensive. Clearly, it is important to begin reading instruction with DHH children at very young ages, because the rates and trajectories established in the preschool years remain strongly contributing factors well into the school years. However, not all children have equal access to the level of intensity of instruction required. For example, some children may have been placed in generic preschool special education classes with teachers who were unaware of necessary instructional strategies, others may have lived their early years in countries that did not provide comprehensive special education services, and still others may have additional learning challenges that complicated the learning process.

Another factor of significance in vocabulary acquisition is access to incidental language experiences (DeConde-Johnson, Benson, & Seaton, 1997; Easterbrooks & Baker, 2002; Rose, McAnally, & Quigley, 2004), which plays a major role in the child's developing lexicon (Calderon & Greenberg, 2003; Hart & Risley, 1995). Because of their hearing loss, many DHH children do not have opportunities to learn information by overhearing it; likewise, they may not have learned how to track conversations visually at home (Hauser, Lukomski, & Hillman, 2008). Thus, children whose parents are actively involved in their early language acquisition, including the provision of incidental language experiences, perform better on literacy skills than do children without this level of access (Marschark, Convertino, & Larock, 2006).

For these and other reasons, many DHH students do not begin the language learning process or the early reading process until they enter the elementary school years. These students will need special, intensive services to make adequate progress in literacy. All of the "early skills" described up to this point in the chapter are important regardless of the primary communication modality used by a DHH child and regardless of his or her access to sound. Children in both of the previously described populations (i.e., with and without access to sound) need support regardless of modality, and educators need to understand and be able to apply appropriate interventions based on each individual child's learning needs and communication mode. It is important that teachers use EBPs as the basis for instruction of DHH children in these and related reading skills. Not only must teachers use existing EBPs, they must also stay abreast of changes in the field, as the evidence base is still emerging and, in some cases, is not yet available.

Levels of Evidence in Instructional Practice and Their Relation to Reading

The term "evidence" in the phrase "evidence-based practice" means different things to different people but generally reflects varying levels of scientific rigor and quality. In fact, there may be dozens of schema one could apply in an attempt to place rigor and quality into hierarchical order (Robey, 2004). One common way of looking at the evidence base is to set up a system for classifying the type of evidence gathered; another is to rate the evidence holistically, usually also involving a prior system of classifying evidence type. Table 8.1 provides two examples of classification systems. The first looks at type of research, the second at quality. Of course, the gold standard for research is the randomized controlled trial (RCT), in which researchers choose a sample of students matched closely to the demographics of the population, pair them with equally randomly chosen and carefully matched participants, and then implement a treatment or intervention to one group but not the other. Few studies in deaf education meet this level of rigor. When gold-standard studies are not available in support of a practice, it is necessary to turn to the second type of hierarchy, which rates practices holistically. A practice may have a single, high-quality study in its support or a large number of lesser-quality studies all of which come to the same conclusion. Both might be considered to meet a high standard.

In real terms, research in deaf education tends to be fraught with inherent problems that make outcomes questionable. For example, the variability in the relative degree of hearing loss, language skills, mode of communication, school placement, and the presence or absence of additional disorders, among other factors, makes it difficult to stratify and match subjects to controls. The low incidence of the population makes it difficult to acquire a sufficient number of participants to do RCTs at all. Divisiveness among professionals leads to fractioning of research funds rather than pooling of effort to solve problems of concern to all. Clearly, practical issues surrounding research contribute to the problems with the evidence base. Nevertheless, educators must still grapple with legal mandates requiring instructional choices to be evidence based.

Although there is much evidence supporting all sides of the communication mode issue, and additional evidence demonstrating positive influences on literacy from early intervention and early cochlear implantation, the available evidence on commonly

Table 8.1 Types and levels of evidence related to research rigor and/or quality

Source	Type of Evidence	Description
Robey, 2004	Meta-analysis of multiple well-designed controlled studies	Looks at the effect size of multiple randomized controlled trials (RCTs) to determine overall effect of a treatment, intervention or product.
	Well-designed RCTs	Requires the highest level of empirical rigor involving randomized choice of a sample matching stratification of a population, matched controls, pre- and post-testing of a treatment, intervention or product.
	Well-designed non-RCTs (quasi-experiments)	Requires high level of empirical rigor, but samples tend to be based on convenience or availability rather than a randomized, stratified sample.
	Observational studies with controls (retrospective studies, interrupted time-series studies, case-control studies, cohort studies with controls)	Involves investigation of a phenomenon by quantifying its nature by such means as correlation, t-tests, baseline and intervention data points, and holistic designations in comparison with a control group.
	Observational studies without controls (cohort studies without controls and case series)	Involves investigation of a phenomenon by quantifying its nature without comparison to a control group.
What Works Clearinghouse, 2008	Meets Evidence Standards	Refers to support from well-conducted RCT studies that do not have problems with regression discontinuity or attrition
	Meets Evidence Standards with Reservations	Refers to support from strong quasi-experimental studies that have equivalent comparison groups. May have problems in randomization, attrition or regression discontinuity.
	Does Not Meet Evidence Standards	Refers to support from studies that provide insufficient evidence of causal validity.

From Robey, R. (2004, April 13). Levels of evidence. *The ASHA Leader*, p. 5; and What Works Clearinghouse. U.S. Department of Education, Institute for Education Sciences. Retrieved November 15, 2008, from http://ies.ed.gov/ncee/wwc/references/standards, by permission of the publishers.

known and widely used instructional practices is meager. Reviews of the knowledge base in specific areas (Easterbrooks & Stephenson, 2006), and reviews of four decades of the knowledge base in literacy (Luckner et al., 2005/2006), point out the dearth of available data in the extant literature.

In Luckner et al.'s (2005/2006) review of 964 articles, only 22 met their criteria for inclusion in the review. Their primary findings were that no two studies examined the same dimension of literacy, well-designed group studies were seriously lacking, few replications of studies had been conducted, and there are simply not enough data in support of most practices. Since that time, additional research has been conducted to address these issues. Easterbrooks and Stephenson (2006) reviewed ten literacy strategies (i.e., independent reading, use of technology, phonemic awareness and phonics, metacognitive reading strategies, writing to promote reading, reading in the content areas, shared reading and writing, semantic approaches to vocabulary acquisition, morphographemic approaches to vocabulary acquisition, and instruction in fluency) and found a range from no evidence to developing evidence. In addition, Easterbrooks, Stephenson, and Mertens (2006) questioned master teachers regarding their use of the ten aforementioned literacy strategies. All were in agreement that they were maximally likely to use nine of the ten strategies, and that these strategies were maximally beneficial to students. The tenth strategy, phonemic awareness and phonics, received mixed reviews, with those who did not favor the practice indicating either they did not believe that deaf students could learn phonemics and phonics, or that they themselves did not know how to provide sufficient instruction.

Luckner and Handley (2008) examined 52 studies of reading comprehension in DHH students, most of which were descriptive or quasi-experimental, with over half including an intervention. Although not identifying overwhelming support, these authors presented findings in a usable table format that identified tentative support for five teaching strategies: explicit instruction in comprehension strategies, teaching students to understand story grammar elements, use of a modified Directed-Reading Thinking Activity approach (Stauffer, 1969), activation of prior knowledge, and the use of well-written, high-interest texts. However, much still needs to be done. Ferreting out the evidence base on any instructional issue in deaf education is a challenge.

An Approach to the Problem

What is a reasonable way to address the present challenge of providing EBPs in the face of limited evidence? It is highly unlikely that one will find RCTs conducted on many interventions, yet this kind of evidence could be forthcoming if multischool, multistate research efforts were to take place to overcome the problems of low participant numbers. In the interim, educators and researchers alike should start building bases of evidence starting from the ground up.

Easterbrooks (2005) outlined three levels of effort to identify the evidence base, presented here in reverse order with recommendations given for the use of each level (Table 8.2). *Level 1 Efforts* (from the field) include narrative information regarding case studies, overall program outcomes from schools using a practice, classroom action research, single subject studies, and consensus documents from expert and practitioner groups. There should be a

Table 8.2   Levels of effort to develop the evidence base in deaf education

Level of Effort	Description
Level 1 (from the field)	Narratives, case studies, program outcomes, action research, single subject studies, practitioner and expert consensus. Requires hypothesis testing and documentation in the classroom.
Level 2 (research with flaws and discrepancies)	Quasi-experimental, qualitative, or quantitative; correlational or causal with intervention; may not meet all standards of rigor. Requires hypothesis testing and documentation in the classroom.
Level 3 (RCT)	Empirical research of the highest quality; replication studies; based on RCTs Few are available.

Adapted from Easterbrooks, S. (2005, January). Review of literature in literacy development and instruction in students who are deaf or hard of hearing. Retrieved March 24, 2008, from htpp://www.deafed.net/DeafedForums/ShowPost/aspx?PostID=1964

large body of Level 1 evidence in support of a practice when implementing it with deaf children. This evidence should be used to establish a hypothesis regarding how the practice might work with a child, a group, or a school. This hypothesis should then be tested on the target child, group, or school. Level 1 evidence should always lead to Level 2 efforts.

Level 2 Efforts (research with flaws and discrepancies) include quasi-experimental research in which qualitative or quantitative methods are used to provide correlational or, occasionally, causal evidence of intervention outcomes with or without a comparison group, single subject studies, and pre- and post-test data. There should be a sufficient and growing body of Level 2 evidence and consensus of outcomes across the body of evidence provided. This begs the question: How much evidence at this level is enough? While the answers will vary from practice to practice, there should be at least enough evidence to demonstrate clear weighting toward more positive outcomes than lack of positive outcomes. Level 2 efforts should always lead researchers and practitioners to seek the funding and engage in the collaboration necessary to bring about Level 3 efforts.

Most *Level 3 Efforts* (RCT) will not occur without sufficient and extensive funding. Level 3 efforts include true experimental research of the highest level of quality and rigor, containing RCTs with matched groups, on an actual treatment or intervention evaluated with the most appropriate statistical methodology and replicated. To date, no practice in reading in deaf education has gone through all three levels of investigation.

Reading Curricula and Instructional Practices

With the advent of early intervention and better access to sound for more DHH children, some researchers are suggesting that the field revisit the literature on what works for hearing students. Schirmer and McGough (2005) reviewed literacy instruction for DHH students relative to the National Reading Panel's findings and concluded that "in light of the research that shows greater similarities than differences between the reading processes of deaf and hearing readers, we suggest that future research with deaf readers should investigate the instructional practices found to be effective with normally achieving and disabled readers" (p. 111). With this in mind, this review of reading instruction begins by looking at what curricula have been found to have positive effects for hearing students as well as deaf students.

Curricula with Evidence for Both Hearing and Deaf and Hard-of-Hearing Students

The What Works Clearinghouse (WWC) (http://ies.ed.gov/ncee/wwc) reviews the evidence base in support of various intervention programs. The WWC identified several programs that demonstrated success with hearing children (e.g., Stepping Stones to Literacy, DaisyQuest, Earobics, Kaplan SpellRead, and Fast ForWord, DLM Express plus Open Court Pre-K program). Most of these programs have a strong focus on PA and phonics as a primary objective. Some are computer-based packages that either involve practice after instruction from a teacher or are self-paced and directed. Although a strong focus on PA and phonics may be appropriate for a larger segment of the preschool DHH population than ever before (see previous discussion), they may not meet the needs of children who rely on visual information or processing. Additionally, the programs that were computer-based may be sufficient for a child with typical hearing, but most children with hearing loss will still need support from a teacher to understand the directions and to make maximum use of the program (Cannon, Easterbrooks, & Fredrick, 2009).

Of the aforementioned curricula, evidence of effectiveness for DHH students was uncovered for only one in the knowledge base. A search of the literature pertaining to DHH students over six comprehensive library search engines revealed no empirical studies that demonstrated the effectiveness of any of the other programs. That is not to say that they are ineffective, only that there was no evidence for their use with DHH children at this point in time. Researchers in deaf education might start by identifying those students for whom and conditions under which these curricula might be effective. The strong evidence in support of their effectiveness with hearing children should spur researchers to consider investigating their use with DHH children.

The curriculum for which evidence was found on use with DHH students was Reading Recovery® (Charlesworth, Charlesworth, Raban, & Rickards, 2006; Heenan, 2007; Needham, 1997). Based on the theories of Marie Clay (Clay, 2005a, 2005b, 2006), Reading Recovery is a one-to-one tutorial program for struggling first graders, who receive a half-hour lesson daily for up to 20 weeks with a specially trained Reading Recovery teacher (http://www.readingrecovery.org/reading_recovery/facts/index.asp). It is a therapeutic program focusing on letter–sound correspondence, phonemic awareness, and phonics and incorporating spelling, comprehension, and fluency work.

Two of the studies on Reading Recovery with deaf students are in the form of case studies (Heenan, 2007; Needham, 1997). Both of these authors adapted the Reading Recovery program for use with two deaf students in qualitative case studies of efficacy. Both indicated that their participants made gains in literacy, but since adaptations were made, such as incorporation of conceptually accurate signing into the lessons, it is difficult to draw conclusions on the meaning of their outcomes.

Charlesworth, Charlesworth, Raban, & Rickards (2006) compared the progress of 12 deaf first graders with that of 12 hearing first graders using the Reading Recovery curriculum, all of whom were considered to be at risk for reading failure. Eight of the deaf students attended a school for the deaf; four were mainstreamed with support from a teacher of the deaf. Ranging in age from 5.9 to 7.9 years, all but one child used either simultaneous communication or Australian Sign Language (Auslan). Four were cochlear implant recipients; seven wore hearing aids. One child had normal hearing but was severely dyspraxic and used sign for expressive communication. One had a severe loss, the rest were reported to have profound losses. One was mildly intellectually disabled; one had vision impairment in addition to hearing loss. Six trained Reading Recovery specialists worked with the children; three had experience with hearing children and three were teachers of deaf children.

Clay's (2006) Observation Survey of Literacy Achievement formed the primary source for data collection. The observation collected information in seven areas: text level reading, word reading, writing vocabulary, letter identification, print concepts, "ready to read" word test, and hearing and recording sounds in words. Children were assessed four times over the course of the year unless they completed the program successfully, at which point they no longer participated. Intervention for the hearing children was conducted for 30 minutes daily; the deaf children received intervention for 45 minutes daily. There were no significant differences between hearing and DHH at the beginning or end of the study, indicating that the deaf students made gains similar to the hearing children, with one exception: text level reading as measured by a running record. Although they improved in many areas of underlying literacy skill commensurate with their hearing peers, their growth lagged behind that of their peers when measured by spoken expression of print. Perhaps best described as a cohort study with comparisons, this study has many weaknesses, including a small number of participants, no assessments external to the program's own survey, and no evidence of its effectiveness in transferring to the participants' reading skills in general. However, it is the only study available on any of the curricula deemed to have met standards of rigor for hearing children. Certainly Reading Recovery warrants further investigation regarding its usefulness with DHH children.

Curricula with Growing Evidence for Deaf and Hard-of-Hearing Children

Although the literature is meager in support of programs with evidence for both hearing and DHH children, the evidence is slowly developing regarding curricula developed specifically for the DHH population. These curricula tend to be language based, controlling carefully for the introduction of new vocabulary and grammar skills.

In the 1970s and 1980s, many states had their own language and/or literacy curricula for deaf children, and many state schools for the deaf had the same (e.g., Schuch & Jones, 1976). Today, most state schools' curriculum guides sit on shelves, having been pushed aside by the standards movement. This is unfortunate because, in many instances, a product or process contains at least some part that is of benefit to some teachers trying to teach DHH students to read. For example, the Clarke School for the Deaf built a reading curriculum for school-aged students around different genres of writing, including descriptive, expository, narrative, and persuasive genres (Clarke School for the Deaf, 1978). Unknown in many schools supporting sign language, this curriculum was a casualty of the modality bifurcation in the field. Unfortunately, those in support of spoken language miss out on rich resources from the signed language camp, and those in the signed language camp miss out on rich resources from the spoken language camp.

Over a decade ago, LaSasso and Mobley (1997) conducted an extensive investigation of 267 instructional programs serving 13,500 DHH students to identify the most commonly used instructional materials and programs. Strikingly, 72% indicated that they used basal readers for instruction, and of that group, 67% used Reading Milestones (1981–85), a syntactically based reading series developed specifically for DHH students. The most commonly cited reason for using Reading Milestones was that it was developed for DHH students, not because responders had experienced success or because there was an evidence base for its use. Since that time, the Reading Bridge (Quigley, McAnally, Rose, & Payne,

2003) series for middle school-aged students has been added to the revised version of Reading Milestones (Quigley, McAnally, Rose, & King, 2001), thus increasing the applicability of the series.

In a recent study at the Research Institute for Progress Monitoring (Rose, McAnally, Barkmeier, Vernig, and Long, 2006), 101 DHH students were given the Measures of Academic Progress (MAP; Northwest Evaluation Association, 2003) and the Silent Reading Fluency Test (SRFT), which was comprised of passages from Reading Milestones and Reading Bridge in the spring, winter, and fall. Although not directly measuring Reading Milestones and Reading Bridges as treatment interventions, this study did demonstrate: (1) improvements on the SRFT (based on Milestones and Bridges) over the three measurements in the middle and high school students; (2) improvement from fall to spring in the elementary students; and (3) a moderate to strong correlation with the MAP within and across times. Since the purpose of this study was to assess the technical adequacy of the SRFT, considerable research is still needed to determine treatment efficacy of Reading Milestones and Reading Bridges.

The Edmark Reading Program: Levels 1 & 2 (Edmark, n.d.) is a highly structured program emphasizing word, then phrase, then sentence reading that has been used successfully by practitioner report with school-aged DHH students who have additional learning disorders or who come to the literacy process with little to no language. The publishers offer two case studies on their website as evidence of its effectiveness with the special-needs segment of the DHH population The Fairview Learning Network's (n.d.) Fairview Reading Program is a reading system developed for students who are deaf or hard of hearing. This program has five components: adapted Dolch words, Bridge lists, phonemic awareness activities, ASL/English as second language (ESL) writing activities, and structured reading comprehension activities to develop decoding and contextual cues. Although research to date is descriptive (Schimmel & Edwards, 2003; Schimmel, Edwards, & Prickett, 1999), instruction in correlates of the components has strong support in the deaf education literature. For example, phonemic awareness (James, et al., 2007), decoding (Transler, Gombert, & Leybaert, 2001), contextual cues (McKnight, 1989), and figurative language (Iran-Nejad, Ortony, & Rittenhouse, 1980) all play an important role in literacy acquisition. Quasi-experimental data are presently being gathered on treatment efficacy

(Schimmel, 2008, personal communication) of the Fairview program.

Promoting Alternative Thinking Strategies (PATHS) curriculum (Greenberg & Kusche, 1998; Greenberg, Kusche, Cook, & Quamma, 1995) is a social skills curriculum. Although not a reading curriculum, PATHS has an evidence base to support its effectiveness as a social skills curriculum. This is relevant to reading because pragmatic language is distinctly social in nature, and pragmatic skills predict language and literacy success in DHH students (Thagard, 2007). Thagard studied the relationship between socio-linguistic/pragmatic language and the success of 81 DHH children in grades K–8 on her state's general education criterion-referenced tests. She found a significant relationship between socio-linguistic/pragmatic language and performance on the criterion-referenced test of reading. She found a significant relationship no matter whether the students' language was ASL or English, and no matter whether their degree of loss was moderate or profound. In other words, it did not matter which language the participants used or how deaf they were; what did matter was the level of their pragmatic language ability. This being the case, it could be useful to refocus efforts on pragmatic language development. Lessons in PATHS curriculum address various skills surrounding feelings and behaviors, as well as using self-talk, reading and interpreting social cues, understanding the perspectives of others (now called Theory of Mind), using steps for problem-solving and decision-making, having a positive attitude toward life, nonverbal communication skills, and verbal communication skills.

Correlates of Good Reading Instruction

In a longitudinal study of 2,296 hearing first graders, Chatterji (2006) found that reading level at kindergarten entry, class size, level of preparation of the teacher, attendance, and reading time at home were all significant contributors to first grade literacy outcomes. Underlying contributors to reading in DHH children also include the level of productive vocabulary (Kyle & Harris, 2006), early use of cochlear implants (James et al., 2007), linguistic ability (Chamberlain & Mayberry, 2008), home language (Geeslin, 2008), consistent access to language (Kaderavek & Pakulski, 2007), and parental involvement (Aram et al., 2008; Stobbart & Alant, 2008). Additionally there are theoretical correlates of good instruction that may add support to the use of a practice or strategy when the evidence base is weak.

Instructional Correlate 1

The first correlate of good instruction is that teachers should be skilled in using the language of their students. This is such a well-known prerequisite as to be one of the ten standards of knowledge and skill required of all beginning teachers across the board (Council for Exceptional Children, 2003). Whether the teacher works with oral children, children who understand simultaneous communication, or children who use ASL, no excuse is acceptable for a teacher to communicate poorly with students.

Instructional Correlate 2

A second correlate of good instruction is explicit instruction versus implicit instruction. For example, deaf children of deaf parents may acquire vocabulary in ASL incidentally (Brackenbury, Ryan, & Messenheimer, 2006; Hauser et al., 2008), but most require explicit instruction to improve their vocabulary performance (Paatsch, Blamey, Sarant, & Bow, 2006). Explicit instruction is more than just a clear set of objectives to differentiate itself from whole language or literature-based instruction. Explicit instruction involves a set of procedures whereby teachers set the stage for learning, present a clear goal to the student, demonstrate the goal, guide the student in implementing and practicing the goal, and then provide sufficient support for mastery of the goal (Hall, 2002). The evidence increasingly points to the importance of explicit instruction of language and literacy skills, rather than implicit instruction of such. This is true for children with typical levels of hearing (Adams, 1990; National Reading Panel, 2000; Snow, Burns, & Griffin, 1998). There is also ample evidence that for most DHH children, in the absence of a sufficiently developed first language, proficient literacy will not develop without explicit instruction. Such evidence is available in the areas of vocabulary instruction (MacGregor & Thomas, 1988), the development of inferential reading skills and reading comprehension (Banks, Gray, & Fyfe, 1990; Walker, Munro, & Rickards, 1998a, 1998b), and the use of morphologic, keyword, and context clues (Calvert, 1981).

Instructional Correlate 3

A third correlate of good instruction is that it promotes higher-order language use and critical thinking, including the ability to think inferentially. A substantial amount of text cannot be understood literally; instead, the reader must infer the meaning. Deaf or hard-of-hearing students have difficulty calling up prior knowledge that contributes to drawing inferences (Strassman, 1997) as well integrating information from previous parts of the text (Richardson, MacLeod-Gallinger, McKee, & Long, 2000). Drawing inferences is a difficult skill for all students struggling to read, but it is a skill that can be taught and learned (Fritschmann, Deshler, & Schumaker, 2007).

Instructional Correlate 4

A fourth correlate of good instruction is the availability of a teacher who can help the student see beyond the information given (Bruner, 1973). Vygotsky (1978) demonstrated that teachers could provide instructional scaffolding to students to help them increase their skills within their zone of proximal development (ZPD). In the ZPD, the child is ready to grow cognitively but needs guidance or support. During cognitive growth, students master intellectual skills progressively. Students who are just learning a skill make many mistakes and rely a great deal on help and feedback from their teachers (Byrnes, 2001, p. 37). Skills below the ZPD are in the learner's *frustration* level. Skills within the ZPD are in the learner's *instructional* level, and skills above the ZPD are in the learner's *independent* level. Scaffolding involves a careful de-escalation of support from modeling to imitating, to careful removal of the scaffold, and then to independent mastery (Byrnes, 2001).

Along the continuum of high to low teacher involvement are modeling of desired behaviors, explaining information, providing a tool (such as an organizer) for the child to use in order to participate, verifying and clarifying student understandings, reminding students of the scaffold and how to use it, and providing hints and cues. Associated with this correlate is what Vygotsky referred to as the *more knowledgeable other*, or MKO, who mediates learning. This is not the same as current definitions of mediated learning, such as learning through signed mediation or real-time text mediation (Marschark & Wauters, 2008). The role of the MKO is to provide multiple perspectives on meaning for the learner. Through practice and corrective feedback from an MKO, children progress to higher and higher levels of understanding until they can perform a skill or task independently.

But mediated learning is far more than merely propping up or releasing props to instruction. In a mediated learning experience (Feuerstein, Hoffman, & Miller, 1980; Kozulin & Presseisen, 1995) the "mediator" has the intentional purpose of selecting, monitoring, intensifying, and directing a child's experiences with the world for the purpose of heightening the child's awareness, helping him to observe and understand relationships among concepts and to see the situation from multiple perspectives. Because DHH students tend to have difficulties coordinating ideas across material (Marschark & Hauser, 2008), mediation strategies are needed to help them see relationships across content and to develop strategies for retention and recall of information. For example, DHH students remember individual words better than they do relations among words and concepts (Marschark, De Beni, Polazzo, & Cornoldi, 1993). Mediated instruction allows the teacher to expand beyond the given to help students see the possibilities. Mediated learning is not the opposite of explicit instruction; it is its expansion.

Instructional Correlate 5

One final correlate of good instruction for DHH students is that it should involve visual supports. The use of visual supports is a time-honored strategy for assisting students with intact hearing (Clarke, 1991), and it supports learning in students with hearing challenges (Stoner & Easterbrooks, 2006). Paivio (2008) demonstrated that imagery is one of two types of cognitive code, and children with typical levels of hearing benefit from the use of visual representations of information even though they have an intact auditory system (Clarke, 1991). Many if not most DHH students are visually oriented and may have special strengths in visuospatial abilities (Hauser et al., 2008). Instructional strategies that support visualization or use of visuospatial strategies for comprehension, retention, and memory should receive primacy in the teacher's instructional arsenal. However, this must be done carefully so as not to usurp visual attention from one source of information to another, as is the case when DHH students must take notes and watch an interpreter simultaneously.

Summary and Conclusions

In no other area of deaf education is the challenge to educators more important and complex. One cannot survive optimally in an industrialized and computerized society without being literate. Teachers of DHH students serve a heterogeneous population with multiple languages, communication modes, and learning needs. Two distinct segments of the population appear to be evident in most classes: those who learn primarily through the auditory pathway

and those who learn primarily through the visual pathway. However, successful acquisition of literacy skills is within the grasp of many as long as teachers engage in EBPs. In fact, teachers are required to utilize EBPs, yet those practices are neither extensive nor transparent. Educators and researchers alike must intensify efforts to identify EBPs and the specific children for whom each is effective. Funding agencies must provide the resources necessary to support the highest and the best research efforts, which should include multisite and multistate research to overcome the problems associated with low numbers of participants. The effectiveness of newer research designs such as growth modeling, which uses children as their own controls, must be investigated as means to address the problem that deaf education researchers have with control groups. Administrators must provide support so that teachers can learn about EBPs and can engage in classroom research that will help elucidate EBPs. Teachers must make the effort to keep abreast of newly identified EBPs as research becomes available. Teachers, parents, researchers, administrators, and politicians must take up the challenge to collaborate so that the next generation of DHH students, no matter their pathway to acquiring literacy skills, will leave school armed with the literacy tools necessary to meet today's and tomorrow's challenges.

References

Adams, M. J. (1990). *Learning to Read: Thinking and Learning about Print*. Cambridge, MA: The MIT Press.

Aghababian, V., Nazir, T. A., Lancon, C., & Tardy, M. (2001). From "logographic" to normal reading: The case of a deaf beginning reader. *Brain and Language*, 78, 212–223.

Allen, T. (1986). Patterns of academic achievement among hearing impaired students: 1974 and 1983. In A. Schildroth and M. Karchmer (Eds.), *Deaf children in America* (pp. 161–206). Boston, MA: College-Hill Press.

American Academy of Pediatrics (1999). Newborn and infant hearing loss: Detection and intervention. *Pediatrics*, *103*(2), 527–530.

Aram, D., Most, T., & Simon, A. (2008). Early literacy of kindergartners with hearing impairment: The role of mother-child collaborative writing. *Topics in Early Childhood Special Education*, *28*(1), 31–41.

Banks, J., Gray, C., & Fyfe, R. (1990). The written recall of printed stories by severely deaf children. *British Journal of Educational Psychology*, *60*(2), 192–206.

Brackenbury, T., Ryan, T., & Messenheimer, T. (2006). Incidental word learning in a hearing child of deaf adults. *Journal of Deaf Studies and Deaf Education*, *11*, 76–93.

Bruner, J. (1973). *Going Beyond the Information Given*. New York: Norton.

Burgess, S. R., & Lonigan, C. J. (1998). Bidirectional relations of phonological sensitivity and prereading abilities: Evidence from a preschool sample. *Journal of Experimental Child Psychology*, *70*, 117–141.

Byrnes, B. (2001). *Cognitive development and learning in instructional contexts*, 2nd edition. Needham Heights, MA: Allyn and Bacon.

Calderon, R., & Greenberg, M. (2003). Social and emotional development of deaf children. In M. Marshark & P. E. Spencer (Eds.), *Oxford handbook of deaf studies, language, and education* (pp. 177–189). New York: Oxford University Press.

Calvert, D. R. (1981). EPIC (Experimental project in instructional concentration): Report of a study of the influence on intensifying instruction for elementary-school age deaf children. *American Annals of the Deaf, 126*(8), 865–984.

Cannon, J., Easterbrooks, S., & Fredrick, L. (2009). Vocabulary instruction through books read in ASL in English language learners with hearing loss. *Communication Disorders Quarterly*, 0: 1525740109332832v1.

Carney, A. E., & Moeller, M. P. (1998). Treatment efficacy: Hearing loss in children. *Journal of Speech, Language, and Hearing Research, 41*, S61–S84.

Carnine, D., Silbert, J., Kame'enui, E., & Tarver, S. (2004). *Direct instruction reading*, 4th edition. Upper Saddle River, NJ: Pearson.

Centers for Disease Control (2008). *Summary of 2006 EDHI Data. 2006 CDC EHDI Hearing Screening and Follow-up Survey (HSFS)*. Retrieved August 31, 2008 from http://www.cdc.gov/ncbddd/ehdi/documents/EHDI_Summ_2006_Web.pdf.

Chamberlain, C., & Mayberry, R. (2008). American Sign Language syntactic and narrative comprehension in skilled and less skilled readers: Bilingual and bimodal evidence for the linguistic basis of reading. *Applied Psycholinguistics, 29*(3), 367–388.

Charlesworth, A., Charlesworth, R., Raban, B., & Rickards, F. (2006). Reading recovery for children with hearing loss. *Volta Review, 106*(1), 29–51.

Chatterji, M. (2006). Reading achievement gaps, correlates, and moderators of early reading achievement: Evidence from the Early Childhood Longitudinal Study (ECLS) kindergarten to first grade sample. *Journal of Educational Psychology, 98*(3), 489–507.

Chrosniak, P. N. (1993). Reading in English as a translation task: Fluent deaf young adult bilinguals. In D. J. Leu & C. K. Kinser (eds.), *Examining central issues in literacy research, theory, and practice. Forty-second yearbook of the National Reading Conference*. Chicago, IL: National Reading Conference.

Clarke, J. (1991). Using visual organizers to focus on thinking. *Journal of Reading, 34*(7), 536–34.

Clarke School for the Deaf (1978). *Language and literacy curriculum*. Northampton, MA: Author.

Clay, M. M. (2005a). *Literacy lessons designed for individuals part one: Why? when? and how?* Portsmouth, NH: Heinemann.

Clay, M. M. (2005b). *Literacy lessons designed for individuals part two: Teaching procedures*. Portsmouth, NH: Heinemann.

Clay, M. M. (2006). *An observation survey of early literacy achievement*. Portsmouth, NH: Heinemann.

Colin, S., Magnan, A., Ecalle, J. & Leybaert, J. (2007). Relation between deaf children's phonological skills in kindergarten and word recognition performance in first grade. *Journal of Child Psychology and Psychiatry, 48*(2), 139–146.

Connor, C. M., & Zwolan, T. A. (2004). Examining multiple sources of influence on the Reading comprehension skills of children who use cochlear implants. *Journal of Speech, Language, and Hearing Research, 47*(3), 509–526.

Council for Exceptional Children (2003). *What every special educator must know: Ethics, standards, and guidelines for special educators*, 5th edition. Alexandria, VA: Author.

DeConde-Johnson, C., Benson, P. V., & Seaton, J. B. (1997). *Educational audiology handbook*. San Diego: Singular Publishing Group.

Durunoglu, A. Y., Nagy, W. E., & Hancin-Bhatt, B. J. (1993). Cross-language transfer of phonological awareness. *Journal of Educational Psychology, 85*(3), 453–465.

Easterbrooks, S. (2005, January). Review of literature in literacy development and instruction in students who are deaf or hard of hearing. Retrieved March 24, 2008, from htpp://www.deafed.net/DeafedForums/ShowPost/aspx?PostID=1964.

Easterbrooks, S., & Baker, S. (2002). *Language learning in children who are deaf and hard of hearing: Multiple pathways*. Boston: Allen and Bacon.

Easterbrooks, S., & Huston, S. (2007). Visual reading fluency in signing deaf children. *Journal of Deaf Studies and Deaf Education, 13*(1), 37–54.

Easterbrooks, S., and Stephenson, B. (2006). An examination of twenty literacy, science, and mathematics practices used to educate students who are deaf or hard of hearing. *American Annals of the Deaf, 151*(4), 385–397.

Easterbrooks, S., Lederberg, A., Miller, E., Bergeron., & Connor, C. (2008/2009). Emergent literacy skills during early childhood in children with hearing loss: Strengths and weaknesses. *The Volta Review, 108*(4), 91–114.

Edmark Company. (n. d.) EnableMart Case Study: Edmark Reading Program Improves Reading Achievement. Retrieved August 5, 2008, from http://www.enablemart.com/Catalog/Books-Guides/Edmark-Reading-Program-Print-Edition;jsessionid=0a0101421f4356208eadae47435c8122e49effbe21fe.e3eSc3iSaN0Le34Pa38Ta38Nb310

Fairview Learning Network (n. d.) *Fairview reading program*. Retrieved August 21, 2008 from http://www.fairviewlearning.net/deaf-components.php.

Foster, W. A., Miller, M. (2007). Development of the literacy achievement gap: A longitudinal study of kindergarten through third grade. *Language, Speech, & Hearing Services in Schools, 38*(3), 173–181.

Feuerstein, R, Hoffman, M., & Miller, R. (1980). *Instrumental enrichment: An intervention program for cognitive modifiability*. Baltimore, MD: University Park Press.

Fritschmann, N. S., Deshler, D. D., & Schumaker, J. B. (2007). The effects of instruction in an inference strategy on the reading comprehension skills of adolescents with disabilities. *Learning Disability Quarterly, 30*(4), 245–262.

Gallaudet Research Institute. (December 2006). *Regional and National Summary Report of Data from the 2006–2007 Annual Survey of Deaf and Hard of Hearing Children and Youth*. Washington, DC: GRI, Gallaudet University. Retrieved August 31, 2008, from http://gri.gallaudet.edu/Demographics/2006_National_Summary.pdf

Gallaudet Research Institute. (January 2001). *Regional and National Summary Report of Data from the 1999–2000 Annual Survey of Deaf and Hard of Hearing Children and Youth*. Washington, DC: GRI, Gallaudet University. Retrieved August 31, 2008, from http://gri.gallaudet.edu/Demographics/2000_National_Summary.pdf

Geeslin, J. D. (2008). Deaf bilingual education: A comparison of the academic performance of deaf children of deaf parents and deaf children of hearing parents. *Dissertation Abstracts International Section A: Humanities and Social Sciences, 68*(11–A), 4582.

Geers, A. (2002). Factors affecting the development of speech, language, and literacy in children with early cochlear implantation.

Language, Speech, and Hearing Services in Schools, 33(3), 172–183.

Geers, A., & Moog, J. (1989). Factors predictive of the development of literacy in profoundly hearing-impaired adolescents. *Volta Review, 91*, 69–86.

Gerner de Garcia, B. A. (1995). ESL applications for Hispanic deaf students. *The Bilingual Research Journal, 19*, 453–467.

Gottardo, A., Siegel, L. S., Yan, B., & Wade-Woolley, L. (2001). Factors related to English reading performance in children with Chinese as a first language: More evidence of cross-language transfer of phonological processing. *Journal of Educational Psychology, 93*(3), 530–542.

Greenberg, M. T., & Kusche, C. A. (1998). Preventive intervention for school-aged deaf children: The PATHS curriculum. *Journal of Deaf Studies and Deaf Education, 3*, 49–63.

Greenberg, M. T., Kusche, C. A., Cook, E. T., & Quamma, J. P. (1995). Promoting emotional competence in school-aged children: The effects of the PATHS curriculum. *Development and Psychopathology, 7*, 17–36.

Hall, T. (2002). *Explicit instruction*. Wakefield, MA: National Center on Accessing the General Curriculum. Retrieved September 7, 2008, from http://www.cast.org/publications/ncac/ncac_explicit.html

Hart, B., & Risley, T. R. (1995). *Meaningful differences in the everyday experiences of young American children*. Baltimore, MD: Paul H. Books Publishing.

Hauser, P., Lukomski, J., & Hillman, T. (2008). Development of deaf and hard-of-hearing students' executive function. In M. Marschark & P. Hauser (Eds.), Deaf cognition: Foundations and outcomes (pp. 286–309). Cary, NC: Oxford University Press.

Heenan, R. A. (2007). Literacy and deafness: A qualitative analysis into the efficacy of an adapted reading recovery program. *Dissertation Abstracts International Section A: Humanities and Social Sciences, 67*(10–A), 3711.

Holt, J., Hotto, S., & Cole, K. (1994). Demographic aspects of hearing impairment: Questions and answers. 3rd edition. Washington, DC: Center for Assessment and Demographic Studies, Gallaudet University. Retrieved August 31, 2008, from http://gri.gallaudet.edu/Demographics/factsheet.html#Q14

Huttenlocher, J., Vasilyeva, M., Cymerman, E., & Levine, S. (2002). Language input and child syntax. *Cognitive Psychology, 45*, 337–374.

Individuals with Disabilities Education Improvement Act of 2004, 20 U. S. C. 33 § 1400 et seq. (2004). Reauthorization of the Individuals with Disabilities Education Act of 1990.

Iran-Nejad, A., Ortony, A., & Rittenhouse, R. (1980). The comprehension of metaphorical uses of English by deaf children. Technical report # 184. Center for the Study of Reading. Illinois University, Urbana.

James, D., Rajput, K., Brinton, J., & Goswami, U. (2007). Phonological awareness, vocabulary, and word reading in children with cochlear implants: Does age of implantation explain individual variability in performance outcomes and growth? *Journal of Deaf Studies and Deaf Education, 13*, 117–137.

Jenkins, J., Fuchs, L., van den Broek, P., Espin, C., & Deno, S. (2003). Accuracy and fluency in list and context reading of skilled and RD groups: Absolute and relative performance levels. *Learning Disabilities Research & Practice, 18*(4), 237–245.

Johns, J. (2004). *Basic reading inventory: Pre-primer through grade 12- Revised*. New York: Kendall Hunt.

Kaderavek, J., & Pakulski, L. (2007). Facilitating literacy development in young children with hearing loss. *Seminars in Speech & Language, 28*(1), 69–78.

Karchmer, M. A., Malone, M. N., & Wolk, S. (1979). Educational significance of hearing loss at 3 levels of severity. *American Annals of the Deaf, 124*, 97–109.

Kelly, L. (1996). Vocabulary during reading by deaf students. *Journal of Deaf Studies and Deaf Education, 1*(1), 75–90.

Kozulin, A., & Presseisen, B. Z. (1995). Mediated learning experience and psychological tools: Vygotsky's and Feuerstein's perspectives in a study of student learning. *Educational Psychologist, 30*(2), 67–75.

Kyle, F., & Harris, M. (2006). Concurrent correlates and predictors of reading and spelling achievement in deaf and hearing school children. *Journal of Deaf Studies and Deaf Education, 11*(3), 273–288.

LaBerge, D., & Samuels, S. J. (1974). Toward a theory of automatic information processing in reading. *Cognitive Psychology, 6*, 293–323.

LaSasso, C., & Davey, B. (1987). The relationship between lexical knowledge and reading comprehension for prelingually, profoundly hearing impaired students, *The Volta Review, 89*(4), 211–220.

LaSasso, C., & Metzger, M. (1998). An alternate route for preparing deaf children for BiBi programs: The home language as L1 and cued speech for conveying traditionally-spoken languages. *Journal of Deaf Studies and Deaf Education, 3*, 265–289.

LaSasso, C. & Mobley, R. (1997). National survey of reading instruction for deaf and hard of hearing students in the U. S. *The Volta Review, 99*(1), 31–60.

Lonigan, C. J., Burgess, S. R., & Anthony, J. L. (2000). Development of emergent literacy and early reading skills in preschool children: Evidence from a latent-variable longitudinal study. *Developmental Psychology, 36*(5), 596–613.

Luckner, J., & Handley, M. (2008). A summary of the reading comprehension research undertaken with students who are deaf or hard of hearing. *American Annals of the Deaf, 153*(1), 6–136.

Luckner, J., Sebald, A., Cooney, J., Young, J., & Muir, S. (2005/2006). An examination of the evidence-based literacy research in deaf education. *American Annals of the Deaf, 150*(5), 443–454.

MacGregor, L., & Thomas, S. (1988). A computer-mediated text system to develop communication for hearing-impaired students. *American Annals of the Deaf, 133*(4), 28–284.

MacLean, M., Bryant, P., & Bradley, L. (1987). Rhymes, nursery rhymes, and reading in early childhood. *Merrill-Palmer Quarterly, 33*, 255–282.

Mann, V. A. (1993). Phoneme awareness and future reading ability. *Journal of Learning Disabilities, 26*, 259–269.

Marschark, M., & Hauser, P. (2008). Cognitive underpinnings of learning by deaf and hard-of-hearing students. In M. Marschark & P. Hauser (Eds.), *Deaf cognition: Foundations and outcomes* (pp. 3–23). Cary, NC: Oxford University Press.

Marschark, M., & Wauters, L. (2008). Language comprehension and learning by deaf students. In M. Marschark & P. Hauser (Eds.), *Deaf cognition:Foundations and outcomes* (pp. 309–350). Cary, NC: Oxford University Press.

Marschark, M., Convertino, C., & Larock, D. (2006). Optimizing academic performance of deaf students: Access, opportunity, and outcomes. In D. F. Moores & D. S. Martin

(Eds.), *Deaf learners: Development in curriculum and instruction* (pp. 179–200). Washington DC: Gallaudet University Press.

Marschark, M., De Beni, R., Polazzo, M. G., & Cornoldi, C. (1993). Deaf and hearing-impaired adolescents' memory for concrete and abstract prose: Effects of relational and distinctive information. *American Annals of the Deaf, 138*, 31–39.

Marschark, M., Lang, H., & Albertini, J. (2002). *Educating deaf students: From research to practice.* New York: Oxford University Press.

Marschark, M., Rhoten, C., Fabich, M. (2007). Effects of cochlear implants on children's reading and academic achievement. *Journal of Deaf Studies and Deaf Education, 12*, 269–282.

Mayer, C. (2007). What really matters in the early literacy development of deaf children. *Journal of Deaf Studies and Deaf Education, 12*(4), 411–431.

McKnight, T. K. (1989). The use of cumulative cloze to investigate contextual build-up in deaf and hearing readers. *American Annals of the Deaf, 134*(4), 268–s72.

Mercer, C. D., Campbell, K. U., Miller, M. D., Mercer, K. D., & Lane, H. B. (2000). Effects of a reading fluency intervention for middle schoolers with specific learning disabilities. *Learning Disabilities Research, 15*(4), 177–187.

Moeller, M. P. (2000). Early intervention and language development in children who are deaf and hard of hearing. *Pediatrics, 106*(3), p. e43. Retrieved December 14, 2007, from http://pediatrics.aappublications.org/cgi/content/abstract/106/3/e43

Moeller, M. P., Tomblin, J. B., Yoshinaga-Itano, C., Connor, C. M., & Jerger, S. (2007). Current state of knowledge: Language and literacy of children with hearing impairment. *Ear and Hearing, 28*(6), 740–753.

National Reading Panel. (2000). *Teaching children to read: An evidence-based assessment of the scientific research literature on reading and its implications for reading instruction* (No. NIH Pub. No. 00-4769). Washington DC: U. S. Department of Health and Human Services, Public Health Service, National Institutes of Health, National Institute of Child Health and Human Development.

Needham, E. (1997). The relevance of a Reading Recovery program for hearing impaired children. *Proceedings, Australia and New Zealand Conference on Education of the Deaf* (pp. 239-242). Adelaide, Australia: ANZCED.

No Child Let Behind Act of 2001, 20 U. S. C. 70 § 6301 et seq. (2002).

Northwest Evaluation Association. (2003). *Technical manual for the NWEA Measures of Academic Progress and Achievement Level Tests.* Portland, OR: Northwest Evaluation Association.

Paatsch, L., Blamey, P., Sarant, J., & Bow, C. (2006). The effect of speech production and vocabulary training on different components of spoken language performance. *Journal of Deaf Studies and Deaf Education, 11*(1), 39–55.

Padden, C., & Ramsey, C. (1998). Reading ability in signing deaf children. *Topics in Language Disorders, 18*(4), 30–46.

Padden, C., & Ramsey, C. (2000). *Language acquisition by eye.* Mahway, NJ: Erlbaum.

Paivio, A. (2008). How children learn and retain information: The dual coding theory. In S. B. Newman (Ed.), *Literacy achievement for young children in poverty.* Baltimore: Paul H. Brookes.

Paul, P. (1996). Reading vocabulary and deafness. *Journal of Deaf Studies & Deaf Education, 1*(1), 3–15.

Quigley, S. P., McAnally, P., Rose, S., & King, C. (2001). *Reading milestones.* Austin, TX: Pro-ed.

Quigley, S. P., McAnally, P., Rose, S., & Payne, J. (2003). *Reading bridge.* Austin, TX: Pro-ed.

Rasinski, T. V. (2004). *Assessing reading fluency.* Honolulu, HI: Pacific Resources for Education and Learning.

Rayner, K., Foorman, B. R., Perfetti, C. A., Peretsky, D., & Seidenberg, M. S. (2001). How psychological science informs the teaching of reading. *Psychological Science in the Public Interest, 2*(2), 31–74.

Richardson, J., MacLeod-Gallinger, J., McKee, B. G., & Long, G. I. (2000). Approaches to studying in deaf and hearing students in higher education. *Journal of Deaf Studies and Deaf Education, 5*, 156–173.

Robey, R. (2004, April 13). Levels of evidence. *The ASHA Leader,* p. 5.

Rose, S., McAnally, P., & Quigley, S. (2004). *Language learning practices with deaf children.* Austin: TX: Pro-ed.

Rose, S., McAnally, P., Barkmeier, L., Virnig, S., & Long, J. (2006). *Technical Report #9: Silent Reading Fluency Test: Reliability, validity, and sensitivity to growth for students who are deaf and hard of hearing at the elementary, middle school, and high school levels.* Research Institute on Progress Monitoring (RIPM), University of Minnesota. Retrieved September 8, 2008, from http://www.progressmonitoring.org/Techreports/TR9dhhsrftTR. doc

Scarborough, H. S., & Brady, S. A. (2002). Toward a common terminology for talking about speech and reading: A glossary of the 'phon' words and some related terms. *Journal of Literacy Research, 34*, 299–334.

Schimmel, C., & Edwards, S. (2003). Literacy strategies for the classroom, Putting Bi-Bi theory into practice. *Odyssey, 5*(1), 58–63.

Schimmel, C., Edwards, S., & Prickett, H. (1999). Reading?… Pah! (I Got It!). *American Annals of the Deaf, 144*(4), 298–308.

Schirmer, B., & McGough, S. (2005). Teaching reading to children who are deaf: Do the conclusions of the National Reading Panel apply? *Review of Educational Research, 75*(1), 83–117.

Schuch. A. & Jones, G. (1976). *Language curriculum: Atlanta Area School for the Deaf.* Atlanta, GA: Author.

Snow, C.E., Burns, M.S., & Griffin, P. (Eds.) (1998). *Preventing reading difficulties in young children.* Washington, DC: National Academy Press.

Stanovich, K. E. (1992). Speculation on the causes and consequences of individual differences in early reading acquisition. In P. B. Gough, L. C. Ehri, & R. Treiman (Eds.), *Reading acquisition* (pp. 307–342). Hillsdale, NJ: Erlbaum.

Stauffer, R. G. (1969). *Teaching reading as a thinking process.* New York: Harper & Row.

Stevenson, H. W., & Newman, R. S. (1986). Long-term prediction of achievement and attitudes in mathematics and reading. *Child Development, 57*, 646–659.

Stobbart, C., & Alant, E. (2008). Home-based literacy experiences of severely to profoundly deaf preschoolers and their hearing parents. *Journal of Developmental and Physical Disabilities, 20*(2), 139–153.

Strassman, B. (1997). Metacognition and reading in children who are deaf: A review of the research. *Journal of Deaf Studies and Deaf Education, 2*, 140–149.

Stoner, M., & Easterbrooks, S. (2006). Using a visual tool to increase adjectives in the written language of students who are deaf or hard of hearing. *Communication Disorders Quarterly*, *27*(2), 95–109.

Svirsky, M. A., Stallings, L. M., Lento, C. L., Ying, E., & Leonard, L. B. (2002).Grammatical morphologic development in pediatric cochlear implant uses may be affected by the perceptual prominence of the relevance markers. *Annals of Otology, Rhinology & Laryngology*, *189*(Supplement), 109–112.

Swanson, H. L., & Howell, M. (2001). Working memory, short-term memory, and speech rate as predictors of children's reading. *Journal of Educational Psychology*, *93*(4), 720–734.

Thagard, E. (2007). *Pragmatic language in students who are deaf and hard of hearing: A search for correlation with success in general education*. Unpublished doctoral dissertation. Birmingham, AL: Stamford University.

Traxler, C. (2000). The Stanford achievement test, 9th edition: National norming and performance standards for deaf and hard of hearing students. *Journal of Deaf Studies and Deaf Education*, *5*, 337–348.

Transler, C., Gombert, J. E., & Leybaert, J. (2001). Phonological decoding in severely and profoundly deaf children: Similarity judgment between written pseudowords. *Applied Linguistics*, *22*(1), 61–82.

Trezek, B. J., & Malmgren, K. W. (2005). The efficacy of utilizing a phonics treatment package with middle school deaf and hard-of-hearing students. *Journal of Deaf Studies and Deaf Education*, *10*(3), 256–171.

Vygotsky, L. S. (1978). *Mind in society*. Cambridge, MA: Harvard University Press.

Wagner, R. K., Torgesen, J. K., Raschotte, C. A., Hecht, S. A., Barker, T. A., Burgess, S. R., et al. (1997). Changing relations between phonological processing abilities and word-level reading as children develop from beginning to skilled readers: A 5-year longitudinal study. *Developmental Psychology*, *33*, 468–479.

Walker, L., Munro, J., & Rickards, F. (1989a). Teaching inferential reading strategies through pictures. *The Volta Review*, *100*(2), 105–120.

Walker, L., Munro, J., & Rickards, F. (1998b). Literal and inferential reading comprehension of students who are deaf or hard of hearing. *The Volta Review*, *100*(2), 87–103.

What Works Clearinghouse. U. S. Department of Education, Institute for Education Sciences. Retrieved November 15, 2008, from http://ies.ed.gov/ncee/wwc/references/standards

Whitehurst, G. J., & Lonigan, C. J. (1998). Child development and emergent literacy. *Child Development*, *68*, 848–872.

Williams, C. (2004). Emergent literacy development of deaf children. *Journal of Deaf Studies and Deaf Education*, *9*, 352–365.

Yoshinaga-Itano, C. (2006). Early identification, communication modality, and the development of speech and spoken language skills: Patterns and considerations. In P.E. Spencer & M. Marschark (Eds.), *Advances in the spoken language development of deaf and hard-of-hearing children*. (pp. 298–327). New York, NY: Oxford University Press.

Will Cochlear Implants Close the Reading Achievement Gap for Deaf Students?

Marc Marschark, Thomastine Sarchet, Cathy Rhoten, *and* Megan Zupan

Abstract

This chapter provides an overview and critical analysis of studies examining reading achievement among children with cochlear implants. A variety of recent studies have demonstrated benefits to hearing, language, and speech from implants, leading to assumptions that early implantation and longer periods of implant should be associated with higher reading achievement. Yet, reading achievement has not been found to be related to hearing thresholds in deaf and hard-of-hearing (DHH) children without implants, so hearing is not the only factor that has to be considered. Indeed, while there are clear benefits of cochlear implantation to reading achievement in young deaf children, empirical results and practical outcomes have been somewhat variable. Examination of the literature is made with an eye toward possible implications of confounding variables, such as cognitive abilities, age of implantation, and language skills prior to implantation. Evidence suggesting that early advantages to reading from cochlear implantation may not be maintained implies that we do not yet know how best to educate children with implants. A similar situation exists with regard to hard-of-hearing children, and insofar as most children with cochlear implants are functionally (at least) hard of hearing, we may be able to learn much from comparative studies of reading abilities within the two populations. The chapter discusses methodological shortcomings in existing research, as well as theoretical and practical questions to be addressed in future research.

Keywords: cochlear implants, reading achievement, hard-of-hearing children, cognitive development, deaf children

Most research involving children with cochlear implants has focused on hearing, speech, and language development. As pediatric cochlear implantation becomes more common, however, and as earlier cohorts of children with implants reach secondary and postsecondary educational settings, there is increasing interest in academic, cognitive, and social outcomes. Possible interactions of the earlier and more recent areas of interest also are now beginning to receive empirical attention. Although a full understanding of the pedagogical implications of cochlear implantation lies in the future, the broadening of research questions, together with the increasing sample sizes and experimental controls that are now possible, provide a body of literature from which some robust conclusions can be drawn. The considerable variability observed among children with implants warns against overly broad generalizations, but we believe that even the limited progress thus far can contribute to improved methods for supporting their language and academic achievement (Archbold, 2005).

This chapter addresses a particular intersection of language growth and academic achievement that has long been challenging for deaf children: reading. A variety of previous studies has examined the reading abilities of deaf children who have received cochlear implants, but it remains unclear exactly why cochlear implantation usually improves reading outcomes, and why those outcomes vary so widely. Improved reading following cochlear implantation cannot simply be a function of better hearing, because some studies have shown hearing thresholds to be unrelated to reading in deaf students (e.g., Convertino, Marschark, Sapere, Sarchet, & Zupan, 2009) and others have found skilled readers among deaf students without cochlear implants (DeLana, Gentry, & Andrews, 2007). Improved reading following implantation cannot be a function solely of using spoken language, because studies like that of Connor et al. (2000) have found the language orientation among students with implants to be unrelated to reading ability, while Padden and Ramsey (2000) and others have found good readers among deaf signing children without implants. Similarly, as will be discussed later, the issue also cannot be simply a matter of better phonological processing or phonemic awareness among children with implants, because of findings from some studies indicating that these are unrelated to reading among children with implants (e.g., Johnson & Goswami, 2005), and because of evidence indicating that children without implants can develop mental representation that is functionally equivalent to auditorily based representation through the integration of information derived from speechreading, orthography, fingerspelling, and limited hearing (Leybaert, 1993).

The variable attracting perhaps most current attention in predicting reading abilities in children with cochlear implants is age of implantation. Even there, however, results are inconsistent, as a variety of studies have indicated both negative (Archbold, Harris, O'Donoghue, Nikolopoulos, White, & Richmond, 2008) and positive (Geers, 2004) correlations between age of implantation and reading ability. So, why does cochlear implantation frequently improve reading outcomes, when, and for whom?

Beyond contradictory research evidence specifically relating to postimplantation reading abilities, these questions have been complicated by methodological confounds, a paucity of longitudinal data, and emerging findings concerning other developmental outcomes in children with and without implants. At the same time, findings from several domains suggest that the improved hearing provided by cochlear implants is not sufficient either to fully support or to explain reading abilities of deaf children following implantation. This chapter, therefore, will argue for consideration of cognitive and other abilities beyond language in order to provide a more complete understanding of reading outcomes among those children, better reading-related educational and support services for them, and greater reading achievement for all deaf children (Archbold, 2005).

The proposal we will describe is so straightforward that we hesitate to refer to it as a model or present the obvious diagram. In related terms, however, those interested in reading following cochlear implantation often appear to adopt either a two-box or three-box model. The two-box model, often embraced by practitioners and parents of deaf children, represents the simple just-mentioned notion that a cochlear implant and better hearing (Box #1) leads to enhanced language skills and academic outcomes (Box #2), including reading. Audiologists and implant specialists typically see the world as somewhat more complex, including in their thinking a Box #3 containing what are often called "implant characteristics," even though these pertain to both the child (e.g., preimplant hearing thresholds and age at implantation) and the implant (e.g., speech processor and number of active electrodes).

Still, something seems to be missing from both the two- and three-box models, perhaps explaining why neither is a very good predictor of postimplant achievement (Pisoni, Cleary, Geers, & Tobey, 1999). What appears to be needed is another, fairly large box (Box #4) containing many of the elements that developmental psychologists recognize as being essential to normal growth. Included there would be various cognitive processes, dynamic social and physical interactions with individuals and objects in the environment, and related incidental learning, all of which feed into developmental and academic achievements. Unfortunately, even this more complex model is lacking, requiring something that resides outside of the four boxes. As we describe later, there is a cumulative interaction of language, learning, and experience in development that both reflects and determines how these boxes (and their contents) influence each other (Marschark & Everhart, 1997). To the extent that the contents of Box #4 are assumed to be the same for deaf and hearing children, one would expect that improved hearing (in Box #1) would provide deaf children with all of the opportunities, knowledge, and skills necessary for Box #2 success. Yet, deaf children with cochlear implants are still deaf children, with differences in hearing, language, social, and cognitive relative to hearing children (Hauser, Lukomski, & Hillman, 2008; Marschark, 2003). As a result, the contents of Boxes #1–4 are likely to be somewhat different for deaf than hearing children and influence each other in different ways. Ignoring these differences, we believe, will doom deaf children with (and without) cochlear implants to academic mediocrity.

Deaf Students Are Not Hearing Students Who Cannot Hear

Both the existing literature and our own experiences as educators indicate that we do not yet know how to optimize academic opportunities and success for children with implants. In mainstream classrooms, those students typically are taught as though they are hearing students, and in separate (all deaf) classrooms they usually are taught as though they are deaf students. There is abundant evidence, however, that deaf students with implants are not quite the same as other deaf students nor quite the same as hearing students (see Chapters 22 and 29, this volume; Spencer & Marschark, 2003). Where any particular student's characteristics fall within that range will depend on a variety of factors and, at least at present, are not easily predicted. As we shall see, however, the available evidence suggests that both the large variability in postimplant outcomes and the accrual of only limited gains in reading achievement may have some origins in common.

The present proposal is based on three tenets that we believe would help to explain some of that variability in implant outcomes and could help to guide future investigation and instructional development in the field. First, it is essential that educators and investigators explicitly consider in their work the well-documented but infrequently acknowledged fact that most children with cochlear implants are functionally hard of hearing (Boothroyd & Boothroyd-Turner, 2002; see also Marschark, 2001; Spencer & Marschark, 2003). This is not to minimize the linguistic, educational, and personal benefits of cochlear implantation. The goal is to draw on existing research involving hard-of-hearing children, as limited as it is, and demonstrate that research and practice involving children from either population can inform the other. Indeed, we believe that the longstanding poor state of knowledge concerning literacy and other academic skills among hard-of-hearing children (Marschark, 2001) places them and their peers with cochlear implants at risk, both developmentally and educationally. Reviews by Goldberg and Richburg (2004) and Moeller et al. (2007), for example, have documented the fact that even minimal hearing losses are sufficient to disrupt language development and the acquisition of reading abilities (Box #2)—presumably the result of something having to do with the interaction with Boxes #1 and #4. Insofar as most children with cochlear implants maintain hearing thresholds significantly above hearing peers (Boothroyd & Boothroyd-Turner, 2002), there is no reason to believe that they will be immune to the same challenges as other hard-of-hearing children.

Second, as alluded to earlier, research on the cognitive abilities of children with cochlear implants is under way (e.g., Chapter 29, this volume), but we are only beginning to recognize the importance of interactions among their cognitive, language, and reading abilities. Earlier investigators demonstrated that language skills, whether spoken or signed, are positively associated with higher levels of cognitive functioning in DHH children (for a review, see Marschark, 2007, Chapters 7, 8), and the dependence of reading on language skills in deaf children is well established, regardless of whether they utilize a spoken or signed language (Mayer & Akamatsu, 2003). Yet, empirical consideration of the influences on reading of preimplant hearing (Nicholas & Geers, 2007), language (Marschark, Rhoten, & Fabich, 2007), and cognitive abilities have yet to be explored.

In the following sections, we review available research concerning reading achievement and cognitive abilities in children with cochlear implants, suggesting that further research in this area would enhance our understanding of their functioning in other domains, as well as in reading achievement for deaf children at large. At the heart of this approach is a description of language, cognition, and experience after cochlear implantation offered by P. Spencer (2001):

> Asking a child to make sense of, and be able to reproduce, spoken language received only through a cochlear implant is somewhat like asking the child to recognize and draw a picture of an exotic animal they have never seen before that is standing behind a tall picket fence. Only parts of the strange animal are visible through the spaces between the wooden slats of the fence. The child must complete the image in his or her mind, imagining the shape of the parts of the animal that are not directly visible.

In short, we need to consider whether any particular deaf child has the cognitive and linguistic scaffolding necessary to be able to accommodate new knowledge and language that might be acquired through his implant. Practical issues also are involved here as, for example, younger children often are not the best reporters during mapping and may not fully understand and use appropriate (optimal) processor programs in the classroom. Previous studies have examined children's language, cognition, or learning following implantation, but Spencer's description clearly indicates that the three are inextricably entwined and significantly dependent on preimplant functioning in these domains. Reading is simply a particularly powerful example of this interaction and one of continuing concern to the parents and educators of deaf children.

The third assumption underlying our view of reading achievement following cochlear implantation was mentioned earlier: that learning and language are cumulative as well as interactive (Marschark & Everhart, 1997). Mayberry and Lock (2003) described some of the long-term implications for learning a second language when deaf children lack fluency in a first language from an early age. Mayberry (Chapter 19, this volume) makes it clear that, even if critical periods for language development do not have boundaries as rigid as we once thought, their implications are very real for children with implants, as well as for those without. Here we are suggesting parallel consideration of deaf children's cognitive development, assuming that critical periods exist for developing the foundations of learning that will be used for language development, as well as for reading and other aspects of academic learning (Hauser et al., 2008; Marschark & Wauters, 2008). As Marschark and Everhart (1997) argued, however, the issue is not just one of more or less, because qualitative as well as quantitative dimensions of language and cognition will influence the character of subsequent learning and problem-solving skills, including reading.

Are Students with Cochlear Implants So Different from Those Who Are Hard of Hearing?

Spencer and Marschark (2003) described several ways in which children with cochlear implants differ from both deaf children without implants and hearing children. Children with cochlear implants do appear similar to hard-of-hearing children, however, not only in their well-documented audiological characteristics, but apparently also in their cognitive development, academic achievement, and reading abilities (Moeller et al., 2007). If we cannot make the case unequivocally for the latter three domains, it is only because so little is documented with regard to hard-of-hearing children in these areas.

Marschark (2007, p. 29) estimated that there might be more than 100,000 children in the United States with some degree of hearing loss, and noted that more than 70,000 have losses of sufficient severity to have received related special education services. Goldberg and Richburg (2004, p. 152), however, reported that over 6 million American school-aged children "have some degree of hearing loss that could potentially affect communication, learning, social development, and academic achievement," whether or not they are eligible to receive such services (see Chapter 3, this volume). Their interest was primarily in children with minimal hearing losses (*minimal hearing impairment* or MHI). Children with MHI have hearing thresholds of 16–25 dB and frequently are not identified in early hearing screenings. Relative to hearing peers, however, even children with such minor hearing losses frequently demonstrate academic and social-emotional difficulties, especially during the earlier grades. These challenges, at least in part, stem from straightforward communication issues. Antia et al. (2002) noted that children with mild to moderate hearing losses, like those with cochlear implants, frequently have less than optimal access to communication, particularly in noisy environments such as classrooms. Both groups, for example, are particularly vulnerable to missing finer nuances of language, such as intonation, stress, and other suprasegmental information (Goldberg & Richburg, 2004; Most & Peled, 2007). Reduced access to ongoing teacher and peer communication, in turn, is likely to have cumulative effects on the development of learning strategies, metacognition, social functioning, and language, all of which underlie reading achievement.

Language, Cognition, and Reading of Children Who Are Functionally Hard of Hearing

Research involving individuals who are hard of hearing, with or without cochlear implants, has only recently begun to consider the complexity of potential factors affecting language and learning (e.g., James, Rajput, Brinton, & Goswami, 2008; Marschark et al., 2007; Stacey, Fortnum, Barton, & Summerfield, 2006). In the case of students traditionally considered hard of hearing (with hearing thresholds between 25 and 40 dB), relatively little is known about their cognitive and academic functioning (Marschark, 2001; Moeller et al., 2007). So why not draw on the somewhat larger literature involving hard-of-hearing students with cochlear implants?

With the gains in hearing, language, and speech that frequently accompany pediatric cochlear implantation, there has been an expectation that enhanced phonemic awareness and phonological processing skills will result in better reading abilities among those children, relative to peers without implants (e.g., Geers, 2002; James et al., 2008; Johnson & Goswami, 2005; Nicholas & Geers, 2006).

Moeller et al. (2007) warned, however, that "degree of hearing impairment rarely acts alone in contributing to development" (pp. 740–741). One indicator of the complexity of the situation is the enormous variability observed in the vocabulary development of children with mild to moderate hearing losses. Some studies indicate significant delays and the need for intervention for that population, whereas others find that those children generally perform at levels comparable to hearing peers (p. 741).

Such variability derives from both limitations on access to phonological information and on opportunities for linguistic interaction and incidental learning. Gilbertson and Kamhi (1995), for example, demonstrated a link between auditorily based phonological processing skills and novel word learning in hard-of-hearing children, whereas James et al. (2008) made a similar observation regarding children with cochlear implants. Gilbertson and Kamhi suggested a locus of *specific language impairment* for their finding of relatively poor performance, whereas James et al. emphasized intelligence and preimplant language skills as helping children to decipher the degraded auditory input from cochlear implants. Underlying both studies is the assumption that phonological skills are intimately involved in the acquisition of reading ability, but neither examined reading directly. Johnson and Goswami (2005), however, compared phonological awareness skills in reading abilities of deaf children who had received cochlear implants prior to age 3.2 years, children who received implants after age 3.8 years, and a group who used hearing aids. The three groups did not differ significantly on either the reading or phonological awareness tasks.

Boothroyd and Boothroyd-Turner (2002) followed language and educational progress of eight children with cochlear implants over a 4-year period. All of the children had congenital hearing losses, but age of implantation varied (mean = 5.8 years), as did length of experience with their implants (mean = 4.9 years). Preimplant testing indicated that seven of the eight children had nonverbal IQ scores of between 96 and 126, with the eighth scoring 72 on the Wechsler Intelligence Scale for Children (WISC-III). At the end of the 4-year period, Boothroyd and Boothroyd-Turner reported that the children showed auditory speech perception levels and language skills comparable to those of severely deaf children without hearing aids (consistent with their earlier studies). With regard to reading, the children's scores on the Canadian Test of Basic Skills indicated that on reading and vocabulary tests "the

grade lag was marked and increased over time" (p. 82), reaching a lag of almost 3 years by grade 8. Relations among intelligence, language, literacy, and educational attainment were not reported, however, beyond the observation that "the disparity between performance and [grade] placement increased with increasing language demand of the test. This performance disparity between nonverbal and verbal tasks parallels that described… for the WISC-III [nonverbal and verbal IQ] scores" (p. 82).

Perhaps most prominent in the literature on reading abilities following cochlear implantation is a series of reports by Geers (2002, 2003, 2004, 2005) and Geers et al. (2002, 2008) involving various subgroups from a sample of 181 8- to 9-year-old children. The children, all of whom had received their implants by age 5, had attended a summer camp at which they had been tested extensively. Geers (2002) reported data on 136 children, tested 4–6 years after cochlear implantation, and Geers (2003) reported data on all 181 children. The Reading Recognition and Reading Comprehension subtests from the Peabody Individual Achievement Test provided assessments of reading skills (responses were spoken and/or signed), and the Word Attack subtest from the Woodcock Reading Mastery Test provided grade-equivalent scores for phonic and structural analysis skills (responses were spoken). Phonological coding skills were assessed by two tasks. The RHYME recognition task requires children to sort cards into pairs that "sound alike" and "don't sound alike." In the lexical decision task (deciding whether a letter string is a word or not), half of the nonwords were homophonic to a corresponding real word (e.g., word, werd) and half were nonhomophonic.

Geers (2002) reported that nonverbal IQ was the only independent, significant predictor of speech perception, speech production, and spoken language scores. When implant and family characteristics were controlled, mode of classroom communication was the one consistently significant variable associated with performance on speech perception, speech production, spoken language, and reading scores. The RHYME and lexical decision scores were reported to load on a reading factor (the lowest of five factor loadings), but no information is provided with regard to whether these tests of phonological processing were independent predictors of reading performance.

Geers (2002, 2003) reported that later rather than earlier implantation was associated with better reading and spoken language scores, contrasting with other studies (e.g., Archbold et al., 2008; Connor et al., 2000). Marschark et al. (2007) noted that positive relations between age of implantation and various outcome measures might reflect benefits of preimplant language skills associated with later hearing loss onsets, a suggestion consistent with Geers's finding of better reading skills among children who became deaf later (see Stacey et al., 2006). This advantage contrasts with the oft-described costs of longer periods of auditory deprivation associated with later implantation. Alternatively, a discontinuity in outcomes may occur between children who receive their implants prior to age 2 or 3 years and those who receive them later (Archbold et al., 2008; Nicholas & Geers, 2007). In Geers's sample, age of implantation ranged from 1 to 5 years, and comparisons of younger and older subgroups were not reported.

Geers (2002) also reported that time spent speaking and listening were positively correlated with better speech and language skills, and that children who used spoken language in mainstream programs were better readers. Although the causal connections in these findings are unclear, she concluded that an emphasis on spoken language is an important educational choice for children who receive their cochlear implants early. Moog (2002) also concluded that a spoken language orientation contributes to reading achievement for children with cochlear implants, following a study involving 17 children who had been implanted between 2.4 and 7.7 years (mean = 4.2 years). Moog, however, did not report statistical analyses, comparison groups, or direct relations between language and reading. Her findings thus do not allow assessment of whether it was children's postimplantation language orientations, their preimplant language skills, and/or aspects of the cognitive functioning that were responsible for their reading success.

Geers (2004) reported data from children in her sample of 8- to 9-year-olds who had congenital hearing losses and performance IQ scores of 80 or greater (assessed several years after implantation). More than half of the children scored in the average range in word reading and sentence comprehension, but neither age of implantation nor duration of implant use was found to be related to reading comprehension. IQ scores prior to implantation were not reported, so it is unknown whether cognitive abilities were affected by receiving an implant. Nevertheless, the elimination of children who demonstrated lower nonverbal intelligence is an interesting aspect of Geers's study and similar ones in the literature. Beyond creating a bias toward better

performance (Beadle, McKinley, Nikolopoulos, Brough, O'Donoghue, & Archbold, 2005; James et al., 2008), such findings create the impression that implants are generally effective, when in fact little is known about implant outcomes among children with lesser cognitive abilities.

Geers (2005) reported a follow-up to her earlier studies involving data from 24 of the original 181 children in her study. Although that group had been reading at grade level when they were 8 to 9 years old, Geers found that they were close to 2 years behind grade level by the time they were 15 to 16 years old. Geers et al. (2008) reported on a larger follow-up, involving 85 of the original children. Retesting when the students were 15 to 18 years old involved speech perception, language, and reading assessments. Results indicated that speech and language scores improved for a majority of the students. Progress in reading, in contrast, declined significantly from the earlier testing. Only 44% of the students obtained standard reading scores within the average range for hearing age mates, compared to 56% in the younger sample. Importantly, beyond reading scores being predicted best ($r = .82$) by a weighted performance score from the original testing, the best predictor of reading performance ($r = .35$) was nonverbal IQ. There were also smaller but significant correlations of reading with age at implantation ($r = -.24$) and age of hearing loss onset ($r = .23$), so that both receiving an implant earlier and having more exposure to language prior to becoming deaf (and receiving an implant later) were associated with higher reading scores in high school. The correlation between the latter two variables ($r = -.16$) was not significant, however, thus indicating that their contributions were at least partially independent.

Geers et al. (2008) did not offer any hypotheses about the increasing lags in reading achievement as the children got older. They suggested only that reading ability "was expected to decrease over time, since it has been frequently documented that students with profound deafness experience a gap in reading achievement relative to typical hearing children that increases as they get older" (p. S27), a prediction that runs counter to the tenor of most cochlear implant literature. At the same time, the increasing lags in reading ability and the corresponding association with nonverbal IQ are consistent with findings indicating that students with and without implants lag behind hearing peers in the development of those cognitive processes involved in reading (see Burkholder & Pisoni, 2006; Conway, Pisoni, Anaya, Karpicke, & Henning, 2009;

Marschark & Wauters, 2008; Pisoni, Conway, Kronenberger, Horn, Karpicke, & Henning, 2008). The Geers et al. results also converge with those of El-Hakim et al. (2001), who conducted a retrospective review of the progress of 72 children over a 4-year period following cochlear implantation. They found increased vocabulary growth and a greater frequency of age-appropriate scores following implantation, but the rate of growth soon declined, especially among children who had received their implants later. It is possible that some of the initial growth in this study was the consequence of intensive speech therapy immediately following implantation, with the decline corresponding to children moving into mainstream classrooms where they are expected to be "just like the other kids." More fine-grained longitudinal analyses are needed to evaluate changes in reading-related language skills as a function of the quantity and quality of speech therapy and other postimplantation interventions.

Reports of specific reading-related cognitive skills among children following cochlear implantation are rare. Pisoni et al. (Chapter 29, this volume) report that children with implants generally do not use sentence context as a *top-down* strategy in reading, as do their hearing peers. This relative lack of automatic top-down processing has been observed in several other studies of reading by deaf children without cochlear implants (e.g., Banks, Gray, & Fyfe, 1990; Marschark, De Beni, Polazzo, & Cornoldi, 1993). A similar tendency also is commonly found among DHH children in problem solving, memory, and language comprehension at large (see Marschark, 2003; Ottem, 1980, for reviews). However, although Marschark and his colleagues have suggested that an orientation toward an individual-item processing rather than relational processing is a relatively stable cognitive *difference* between deaf and hearing individuals, Pisoni et al. concluded that their findings reflected basic neurocognitive dysfunctions or delays in information processing among deaf children with cochlear implants. They suggest that such comorbidity is a result of periods of auditory deprivation during critical periods of development, and that subsequent neural and behavioral reorganization likely contributes to the large variability observed in language outcomes in children with implants (see also Chapter 30, this volume). Yet, because the Pisoni studies have not included comparison groups of deaf children without cochlear implants or with deaf parents, their data do not necessarily indicate general cognitive *disabilities* in deaf children as a function of auditory deprivation.

Why Does Age of Implantation Affect Reading Ability?

Although results have been inconsistent and the age at which implantation is considered "early" has steadily decreased, it is generally assumed that earlier cochlear implantation leads to better academic outcomes, as well as to better spoken language skills. Results indicating that longer periods of auditory deprivation affect specific cognitive processes underlying reading and language (e.g., Chapter 30, this volume; Pisoni et al., 1999; Proksch & Bavelier, 2002) point to one potential explanation for such findings. Nicholas and Geers (2007) suggested that "special opportunities may exist for preservation or restoration of the auditory system of deaf infants in preschool-age children that may not be available to children who are just a few years older at the time of implant surgery" (p. 1049). That is, earlier stimulation of the auditory nerve and related centers in the brain may preserve underlying neural mechanisms that might otherwise atrophy. Accordingly, Spencer and Marschark (2003) had argued that hearing aids should be used by deaf infants and toddlers, even if they were not very effective, just in case cochlear implantation becomes desirable later. The only other explanation Nicholas and Geers offered for why early implantation should be associated with better outcomes was the fact that previous studies had found such a relation (p. 1049).

Inconsistency in the relations among reading, age at implantation, and phonological skills suggest that their associations are mediated by factors other than or in addition to spoken language per se. Connor and Zwolan (2004) examined the possibility of an indirect link between language and reading abilities in a study involving 91 children using cochlear implants, most of whom received their implants after 5 years of age. They found that earlier implantation was associated with higher reading comprehension scores. The use of spoken versus sign language was unrelated to those scores, and length of implant use was negatively rather than positively related to reading comprehension when other variables were controlled. The latter finding is consistent with the reports of Geers (2005) and Geers et al. (2008), and is becoming increasingly common (Archbold et al., 2008; Ibertsson, Vass, Arnason, Sahlén, & Lyxell 2006; Johnson & Goswami, 2005; Thoutenhoofd, 2006).

Thoutenhoofd (2006), for example, conducted a study involving 152 school-aged deaf students with cochlear implants drawn from the population of 1,752 deaf students in Scotland. Children ranged in age from 5 years to 12 years (mean = 8 years), were an average age of 3 years old when they received their cochlear implants, and had an average of 4 years experience with their implants. Thoutenhoofd examined National (UK) Test scores and found that older students with implants were further behind in their reading skills (for their chronological age) compared to younger students, a finding similar to that reported by Geers et al. (2008). Students aged 11–13 years lagged behind their hearing peers in reading scores by approximately 3 years, whereas students aged 15–17 lagged by 4 to 5 years. Analyses controlling for age of implantation were not conducted, so it is unclear whether such results reflect a real widening gap in literacy skills for implanted children over the school years or a confound due to the fact that older children may have received their implants after a longer period of auditory deprivation.

Vermeulen et al., (2007) examined reading comprehension and word recognition as separate indicators of reading ability for children in the Netherlands. The study involved a comparison of 50 students with implants (aged 7–22 years) with data collected from 504 deaf students with hearing aids and a group of hearing students. The mean age of hearing loss onset was 1.1 years (standard deviation [SD] = 1.6 years) and the mean age of implantation was 6.2 years (SD = 2.3 years). All of the children with implants had a minimum of 3 years implant experience, but there was a mean duration of auditory deprivation prior to implantation of 5.1 years (SD = 2.8 years). Vermeulen et al. found that reading comprehension among the children with implants significantly exceeded that of children with hearing aids, but still lagged significantly behind hearing peers. Implants were associated with an advantage in word recognition relative to having hearing aids among secondary school students, but not among primary school students. Vermeulen et al. noted, however, that the participants in their study had been implanted relatively late (between 2 and 12 years, with a mean of 6.2 years).

Archbold et al. (2008) examined the reading abilities of 105 children who received cochlear implants between the ages of 1.3 years and 6.9 years (mean = 4.1 years). These children had achieved reading levels ranging from 4.3 years below grade level to 2.6 years above grade level (mean = 0.9 year delay) 5 years after implantation. The mean reading delay was over twice as large at 7 years after implantation. Importantly, however, there also were significant effects of age of implantation. After 7 years, 100% of the children who had been implanted

between 6 and 7 years of age were reading more than 1 year below grade level. Among those children implanted between 1 and 3 years, only 44% were reading more than 1 year below grade level, whereas 46% were reading within 1 year of grade level. Another 10% were reading more than 1 year ahead of grade level. These results led Archbold et al. to conclude that early implantation leads to better and longer-lasting outcomes in reading achievement. However, at the time of testing, the earliest implanted children were still only 8–9 years old, the age at which Geers's children were reading at grade level. The relatively poorer reading outcomes of the later-implanted children, therefore, could be taken as a replication of findings indicating an apparent attenuation of implant-related reading gains with age, leaving the loci of both gains and losses undetermined.

Two other findings from the study by Archbold et al. (2008) are noteworthy in the present context. First, they reported that, 5 years after implantation, nonverbal IQ (measured using Raven's Progressive Matrices) accounted for only 18% of the variance, whereas adding age at implantation brought the total variance accounted for to 77%. At 7 years postimplantation, nonverbal IQ accounted for 5% of the variance, and adding age at implantation accounted for a total of 57%, clearly "showing that age at implantation was a powerful and independent predictor of reading outcomes 7 years postimplant" (p. 1474). Those results, however, derived from multiple regression analyses in which nonverbal IQ was entered first and age at implantation second. Had the analyses been fully stepwise (in which variables accounting for greater independent proportions of the variance are entered first), the results might have been different. Second, because only five children in the study had been implanted by 24 months, Archbold et al. were not able to treat them as a separate group. Nevertheless, the finding that their net reading scores (chronological age minus reading age) ranged from –0.12 to +1.6 years suggests either that the benefits of early implantation will increase as "early" becomes earlier, or that there might be a discontinuity age of implantation effects, of the sort suggested earlier, related to critical periods in development.

Relations of Language and Reading in Children with Cochlear Implants

If age of implantation, prior auditory experience, and cognitive ability represent potentially confounding variables in efforts to understand the effects of cochlear implants on reading, children's preferred modes of communication add yet another layer of complexity, one that is controversial and frequently ignored. Clinicians usually emphasize the importance of spoken language skills for children with cochlear implants, and there are many anecdotal reports in the United States of centers refusing to implant children unless their parents agree to provide oral-only educational placements. The *raison d'être* of cochlear implants is the improvement of hearing, and it is not surprising that children benefit from placements that emphasize audition and spoken language. At the same time, prohibitions against the use of sign language, which frequently can be acquired earlier than spoken language, appear misplaced.

A series of studies by Tomblin, L. Spencer, and their associates have evaluated the literacy skills of children who were exposed to both sign language and spoken language after receiving their cochlear implants. Most also received support from sign language interpreters during their school years and used both sign and speech (not necessarily together) in various contexts. L. Spencer et al. (1997), for example, investigated the reading skills of 40 children with prelingual, profound hearing losses. They had received their implants between 2 and 13 years of age and had an average of 5.3 years implant experience. Spencer et al. found that approximately 25% of the children were reading at or above their grade levels, and almost 20% were below but within 8 months of their grade levels. Another 25% were reading at a level 30 months or more below grade level, but relations among age of implantation, duration of implant use, and reading ability were not reported.

L. Spencer et al. (2003) examined a similar sample of 16 children with an average age of 9.8 years. They had received their implants at an average age of 3.9 years and had an average length of experience with their implants of 5.9 years. Reading comprehension scores of the children with implants were significantly below those of an age-matched comparison group of hearing children, but only by about 10%. Grade-equivalent scores indicated that the children with cochlear implants were reading at an average grade level of 3.3 years and the hearing children at 3.8 years. L. Spencer et al. (2004) obtained similar results in a study involving 27 children who had received their implants between 2.4 and 12.7 years of age (mean = 6.4 years) and had an average of 9.9 years experience with their implants. Follow-up testing was conducted when the students

were in the tenth grade or at least 16 years of age. At that point, the 17 consistent users (8 or more hours per day) were reading at grade level, and the group as a whole was well within normal range. This sample appears similar to that of Geers (2002, 2003), although the children received their implants somewhat later on average. Adolescent reading outcomes, in contrast, were clearly better in the L. Spencer et al. study (2004), appearing to support the value of the availability of both signed and spoken language.

Crosson and Geers (2001) examined the reading and oral narrative abilities of 87 8- to 9-year-olds who had used their implants for at least 4 years. The reading data revealed wide variability, as scores for these children in grades 3–4 ranged from grade level 0.1 to 8.3, with a mean of 2.5. With an SD of only 0.15, most of the children apparently were reading below grade level. In the oral narrative task involving stories prompted by an eight-picture sequence, children's performance was significantly correlated with reading ability ($r = .63$) and speech reception skills ($r = .57$), but not nonverbal IQ ($r = .30$). Narration skills lagged significantly behind those of a hearing comparison group. The latter result contrasts with findings from a study of sign narrative abilities among deaf 7- to 15-year-olds without cochlear implants conducted by Marschark et al, (1994). These researchers had children create stories on supplied themes and narrate them in sign language or write them, rather than narrating in spoken language. Even without picture prompts, both signed and written stories were of comparable complexity to those of an age-matched hearing comparison group, according to story grammar analyses focusing on goals, actions, and outcomes. Crosson and Geers, in contrast, utilized a discourse scoring system that was linguistically rather than conceptually based, emphasizing the use of conjunctions and particular referents. These results suggest that Crosson and Geers's results may reflect the fact that the deaf children with implants did not have language skills fully comparable to their hearing peers (Yoshinaga-Itano, 2006), rather than saying anything about their narration and reading skills per se.

As suggested earlier, language skills prior to implantation are particularly relevant in considering the effects on subsequent language and reading abilities, but they are rarely reported in the literature. The review by Marschark et al. (2007) suggested that later implantation may be associated with progressive or later-onset acute hearing losses that provide children with opportunities to establish a foundation in a sign language—at least in the case of a progressive loss—or a spoken language (e.g., Blamey, Sarant, Paatsch, Barry, Bow, Wales, Wright et al., 2001). The modality of early (preimplant) language may be largely irrelevant, with the important point being that children acquire socially based symbolization and vocabulary acquisition strategies, as well as some understanding of grammar. Alternatively, later implantation might reflect delayed parental decision-making or lesser access to implant services, situations that would adversely affect language and other reading-related development. Complicating this issue, however, at least in deciphering the available literature, are the later ages of onset (Stacey et al., 2006), greater degrees of hearing loss (Nicholas & Geers, 2007), and variability and exposure to spoken language and sign language among children with implants than those without implants. The literature also is confounded by the fact that implantation for children with congenital hearing losses began more recently than for those with acquired losses, so that data from different populations have been reported at different points in time.

In the case of spoken language, Nikolopoulos et al. (1999) found that improvements in speech perception continued at least through 6 years postimplantation, and the potential impact on the acquisition of literacy and other academic skills might be expected to follow a similar course. Alternatively, some threshold or asymptote may exist as a function of variables such as chronological age, age of implantation, language skills prior to implantation, and cognitive ability (Chapter 19, this volume). Some language skills may not be fully acquired simply because of the lower fidelity of auditory information received through a cochlear implant. Most and Peled (2007), for example, found that children with implants did not differ from peers with hearing aids in the perception of stress and intonation. These suprasegmental features do not change the meaning of lexical items, but they do affect the meaning of larger units, such as indicating the difference between a statement, a question, and a command. The extent to which such higher-level language skills affect reading and other academic outcomes remains unclear.

Watson (2002, p. 85) suggested that the auditory benefits offered by cochlear implants provide information that benefits bottom-up reading skills, those relating to grammar, morphology, and vocabulary. Top-down skills, such as making inferences and metacognition, were seen to require more complex cognitive and social interactions with others

language users. Marschark and Wauters (2008) argued that this perspective should not be limited to print materials, but applies equally to through-the-air communication, either signed or spoken. Watson examined inferencing and phonological strategies in reading among ten children aged 7 years and older, all of whom apparently had at least 5 years experience with their cochlear implants. Data were drawn from the children's scores on the National Curriculum assessments in England. Watson reported that seven out of ten children demonstrated reading skills at the "expected" level for their (unspecified) age groups, although complete information apparently was available for only five children. Children's abilities to draw inferences from text were of particular interest, as they demonstrate children's ability to "go beyond simple retrieval of information and infer meaning from the text" (p. 92). Only one child reached a score of 50% (five of nine) on inference questions, however.

Torres et al., (2008) also examined inferencing during reading. A group of four 12- to 13-year-olds who received their implants between age 3 and 7 and used cued speech was compared to groups of hearing children matched on chronological age or reading age. Relative to hearing norms, the deaf students' spoken language skills were at or above what would be expected for their chronological ages. Torres et al. reported that the deaf students also performed at least as well as the hearing controls on a reading task. The latter conclusion, however, was based solely on students' reading times for congruent and incongruent sentences in the context of "emotional" stories, in which larger difference scores were interpreted to mean that the incongruence was recognized. Comprehension was not assessed directly.

Small sample sizes and other limitations in the studies mentioned earlier make it difficult to assess their generality, but all of them suggest that better language skills before and after cochlear implantation facilitate the acquisition of reading abilities. Although most investigations have explored children's spoken language skills, it appears that there are other routes to reading for children with cochlear implants, including sign language (L. Spencer, Gantz, & Knutson, 2004), speechreading (Johnson & Goswami, 2005), and cued speech for languages with more regular sound–spelling correspondences than English (Alegria & Lechat, 2005; Leybaert & Alegria, 2003). To date, however, evidence has come only from studies in which these "alternate routes" accompany spoken language, and we are unlikely to see samples of children who have cochlear implants and rely solely on natural sign languages, mouth movements, or mouth movements and cues without audition. Therefore, it is unclear to what extent these alternatives support spoken language in providing redundant or disambiguating information versus having additive effects, providing information not easily obtained through implant-aided hearing.

Relations of Cognition and Reading in Children with Cochlear Implants

James et al. (2008) and Stacey et al. (2006) have argued that, because of the important role of cognitive abilities and family factors in acquiring spoken language and reading abilities (or not) following implantation, intelligence and other possible confounds must be controlled in studies involving children with cochlear implants. Geers (2002) and Geers et al. (2002), for example, found that nonverbal intelligence accounted for a significant proportion of the variance in children's reading scores, as well as their spoken language skills, when age at implantation and other factors were controlled (presumably leading Geers to restrict the range of cognitive abilities in her 2004 study). Still to be determined is whether spoken language skills account for a significant proportion of variance in children's cognitive abilities and reading scores after implantation.

Deaf children with and without implants, however, have been found comparable on several cognitive dimensions on which both groups fall below hearing peers. Figueras et al. (2008), for example, found that 8- to 12-year-old children with and without cochlear implants did not differ on tests of executive function, but generally performed below the level of hearing peers (Hauser et al., 2008). Fagan et al. (2007) cautioned that even when deaf children with cochlear implants demonstrate language and literacy skills at a level comparable to that of hearing children, those scores may not be measuring the same skills (Marschark & Everhart, 1997). They noted, for example, that for some children with implants, tests of vocabulary comprehension may tap speechreading rather than auditory language skills (p. 470), an argument also made by Johnson and Goswami (2005). Similarly, we know that the mental lexicon is organized somewhat differently for deaf and hearing students (Marschark, Convertino, McEvoy, & Masteller, 2004; McEvoy, Marschark, & Nelson, 1999), a finding consistent with Borovsky and Elman's (2006) finding that the amount of language input and the size of early vocabulary influences the organization of semantic categories. Categories, concepts, and their labels thus likely have subtly different meanings, depending on the mix of spoken language and sign language to which a child has been exposed.

James et al. (2008) explored the cognitive underpinnings of reading ability in 19 children with cochlear implants, nine of whom had received them between the ages of 2 and 3.6 years, and ten who had received them later. Both nonverbal intelligence and, unusually, preimplant spoken language abilities were included. The children were matched to hearing peers on the basis of reading levels and evaluated using tests of phonological awareness, vocabulary, and word reading. Phonological awareness was evaluated using similarity judgment tasks in which children had to decide which of three line drawings (1) had the same number of syllables as a cue picture, (2) a label that rhymed with the cue picture, or (3) started with the same sound. Those children who had received their implants early performed at or near the level of reading-matched hearing peers on all measures, whereas the children who had received their implants later lagged behind. Despite considerable variability, children who demonstrated the most progress over time had higher nonverbal IQs and greater spoken language receptive skills prior to implantation. Overall, results indicated that even when children receive their implants relatively early, they tend to fall toward the lower end of the distribution of hearing children with regard to phonological awareness, just as they do on other measures of language and reading ability (Yoshinaga-Itano, 2006).

Similarly to James et al. (2008), Fagan et al. (2007) noted that age of implantation is insufficient to account for the wide variability observed in spoken language and academic outcomes among children with cochlear implants. They utilized several measures including neuropsychological, sensorimotor, visuospatial, memory, and literacy tasks in a study of 26 children, aged 6 to 14 years, who received their implants between the ages of 1 and 6 years. Although most of the children scored within the normal range on the neuropsychological and reading tasks, they lagged behind hearing norms on the visuospatial task and vocabulary comprehension. Most notable, perhaps, was the finding that, although forward digit-span scores were better than backward digit-span scores (as is usually the case), most of the children were more than one SD below the mean for hearing children on forward spans (as is typically found in deaf children without implants;

see Chapter 30, this volume). This finding is important because digit spans were significantly correlated with all measures of reading. Pisoni and Geers (2000) also had found digit-span scores significantly related to reading, as well as to various language measures (Watson, Titterington, Henry, & Toner, 2007).

Although Fagan et al. found that children with implants generally did not demonstrate any sensorimotor deficits, Pyman et al. (2000) found that speech perception skills in children with implants developed more slowly among those who had motor or cognitive delays. P. Spencer (2002) similarly found a positive relation between nonverbal cognitive skills and postimplant language outcomes. Pisoni et al. (1999) found that implanted children who had achieved higher levels of spoken language made greater use of phonologically based working memory and were faster in global information processing.

Utilizing a continuous visual attention task, Quittner et al. (1994) found that deaf children with and without cochlear implants had more difficulty than hearing children, overall, but there was an interaction of age and implant use. Younger deaf children (6–8 years of age) performed similarly, significantly below hearing peers, regardless of whether they had implants. Among older children (9–13 years of age), performance of those with implants was more similar to that of hearing children, whereas that of children without implants did not even reach the level of the younger hearing children. Performance on the task was unrelated to length of implant use and whether children with implants used spoken language only or both spoken and sign language. Interestingly, Tharpe et al. (2002) failed to replicate the differences between children with and without implants using the same visual attention task, when they controlled age and nonverbal intelligence, both of which were significantly related to performance on the primary task.

Khan et al. (2005) compared the cognitive abilities of 25 children, aged 2.8 to 6.75 years (mean = 4.22), who had cochlear implants (for 12 months) to those of 13 hearing children and 18 children with moderate to severe hearing losses who used hearing aids. All of the children with hearing losses attended schools that utilized both spoken language and sign language. Khan's group found that children in the implant group scored significantly higher on several cognitive dimensions, including IQ and sequential processing, relative to children who used hearing aids. Children with implants scored much the same as children in the hearing comparison group on all cognitive dimensions except sustained attention, with hearing children scoring higher (Quittner et al., 1994). Although Khan's group concluded that "after 12 months of cochlear implant use, hearing-impaired children with cochlear implants are cognitively more comparable with hearing children than with hearing impaired children without implants" (p. 123), the limited experience children had with their implants suggests that at least some of these difference must have existed a priori (Stacey et al., 2006).

Taken together, these studies suggest that children's cognitive abilities may have discernible effects on cochlear implant outcomes—and perhaps vice versa—clearly affecting language and also reading abilities in the few studies in which they have been examined. With the exception of the work by Pisoni and his colleagues, however, there do not appear to be any programmatic attempts to explore cognitive abilities and their potential impact on reading (and other outcomes) among implant users.

Summary and Conclusions

The present chapter suggests the need for a broader perspective on cochlear implantation and reading. Rather than considering only the effects of better hearing and language skills (phonology, speech perception, etc.), we have argued that cochlear implants affect cognitive, social, and other aspects of development which, in turn, influence learning and academic performance. Reading has always represented a challenge for deaf children (e.g., Traxler, 2000), presumably due to their limited access to phonology and the lack of clear relations between printed text and either low-fidelity spoken language or sign language. Deaf children with cochlear implants, deaf children with only minimal hearing losses, and deaf children of deaf parents frequently display reading achievement higher than peers without any of those benefits, but none of those groups typically reaches the level of hearing peers. Such findings suggest that neither access to spoken language nor language fluency per se can fully account for the levels of reading achievement observed among deaf children. What frequently seems to be missing is consideration of the various cognitive abilities underlying reading and the ways in which they interact with hearing loss, language modality, and language fluency.

Pisoni and his colleagues (e.g., Pisoni et al., 2008) have argued that the acquisition of spoken language skills following cochlear implantation supports the acquisition of various cognitive abilities that, in turn, support reading. An alternative perspective is suggested by the arguments of Hauser et al. (2008) and Marschark and Wauters et al. (2008) that deaf and hearing children have cognitive abilities that differ qualitatively as well as quantitatively. From this view, audition (and its social and linguistic correlates) may provide for the acquisition of various cognitive skills that support both spoken language and reading, rather than the other way around. In the process of "figuring out" the novel auditory input provided by a cochlear implant, children thus may acquire problem-solving skills that are more generally useful. A third possibility is that because language, cognitive growth, and experience/environment are cumulative and interactive (Marschark & Everhart, 1997), the preceding two alternatives both may be true to perhaps differing extents for different children at different developmental stages. In short, this situation represents the "tricky mix" of environmental and individual factors that undergirds the development and education of deaf children (Nelson, Loncke, & Camarata, 1993), and is one confronted by teachers and researchers seeking to understand growth in these domains. Considerably more research must be done to discern their mutual influences among these domains, but efforts in this regard have at least begun.

Evidence for a link between age of implantation and length of implant use has been inconsistent, likely reflecting the considerable heterogeneity of deaf children relative to hearing children, as well as the variable benefits of cochlear implantation. Also at play are preimplant language and cognitive abilities and children's exposure to signed and spoken language. Various studies have demonstrated a positive link between early expressive language skills and later language-related achievements by children with and without cochlear implants, whatever the modality of their preimplant communication (see P. Spencer & Marschark, 2003; Yoshinaga-Itano, 2006, for reviews). Findings indicating positive and negative links between age of implantation and literacy scores thus may have different loci. Earlier implantation provides access to phonological information and other aspects of spoken language during the most sensitive period of language development (see Chapters 19 and 22, this volume), but it also offers the availability of auditory signals in the environment to alert children to significant events. Later implantation may be associated with better preimplant receptive and productive language skills, early acquisition of sign language, and better-developed cognitive abilities (i.e., in these older children) that can support the acquisition of literacy skills. It also

frequently reflects later or progressive hearing losses, so that studies that do not disentangle these variables are likely to miss identifying true causal connections.

Complicating assessment of the link between age at implantation and the acquisition of language and literacy skills, children who receive cochlear implants earlier versus later are likely to differ from other children terms of etiologies of their hearing losses, the diversity of their social experiences, and the involvement of their parents in various support functions (Moeller, 2000; Toscano, McKee, & Lepoutre, 2002). The limited findings indicating that children with implants who have access to both spoken and sign language also have higher levels of reading achievement are similarly confounded. Most of the latter studies have involved samples that were quite variable with regard to age and age of implantation, and it remains unclear whether the findings reflect a contribution simply of early access to language or of enhanced comprehension in the classroom through the availability of both speech and sign (including simultaneous communication). Convertino et al. (2009) found that simultaneous communication and English-based signing skills (but not American Sign Language skills) were positive predictors of academic achievement and classroom learning among deaf college students, but a similar result was not obtained in the subgroup that had cochlear implants.

Children with cochlear implants, as well as those with minimal, mild, or moderate hearing losses, frequently may appear to hearing teachers as having little or no hearing-related difficulties, and thus may seem not to require any support services in the classroom. All of those children, however, typically encounter communication difficulties in noisy classrooms, when more than one speaker is involved, and when unfamiliar speakers are involved. It appears a tacit assumption in the field—and certainly one taken home by many parents of deaf children—that the enhanced language skills typical of most deaf children who receive cochlear implants will allow them to function at the level of hearing peers in regular school classrooms. This frequently is not the case, but children who have better social, language, and cognitive skills are likely to have an easier time than those who do not.

The literature review pursued here indicates that even if children with cochlear implants frequently surpass deaf age-mates who have hearing aids and similar hearing losses, implants do not guarantee literacy skills comparable to hearing age-mates. Although young deaf children in some studies have been reported to be reading at age-appropriate grade levels, several studies have indicated that a later divergence occurs, as those advantages are not maintained by all children, even among those who received their implants relatively early (e.g., Geers, 2005; Geers et al., 2008; Ibertsson et al., 2006; Johnson & Goswami, 2005). In most of those studies, however, "early" referred to ages up to 5 years of age. Recent reports like those of Archbold et al. (2008) suggest even greater benefits from implantation in the first year or two of life provided by opportunities for incidental learning and social interaction, as well as from improved hearing and language per se. Nevertheless, given the findings thus far, it seems doubtful that differences between deaf children and their hearing peers will disappear even with earlier implantation. Certainly, there will continue to be attenuation in differences directly linked to speech and hearing, but there likely will remain qualitative differences that arise from social, language, and cognitive factors.

These conclusions in no way dismiss the benefits of cochlear implants for most children. Rather, they follow from the observation of both audiological and cognitive differences between deaf children with implants and hearing age-mates, and are intended to motivate more inclusive research concerning their academic achievement. Children with implants do not have hearing, speech, or language skills equivalent to those of hearing peers. They therefore will miss some amount of information in the classroom and experience somewhat different social and academic dynamics. Similar subtle and not-so-subtle differences are likely to be observed in informal learning situations prior to the school years, as well as during them. Earlier access to language through sign language and/or more advanced cognitive development might help children offset some of those potentially delaying challenges. Given the evidence obtained thus far, research is clearly needed into possible interactions among reading ability, language skills (and modalities) prior to hearing loss, age at implantation, and postimplant fluencies in signed and spoken language.

Pediatric cochlear implantation clearly provides many deaf children with significant advantages in language, reading, and other academic domains. For those children, as well as others with minimal or mild hearing losses, it is still unclear to what extent such advantages stem directly from better auditory reception as opposed to factors such as greater engagement in face-to-face language and other "educational" interactions, more opportunities for incidental learning, and the automatization of lower-level language and cognitive skills (Bebko & Metcalfe-Haggert, 1997). Rather than assuming a simple, linear relation of enhanced hearing and spoken language skills with literacy and other academic abilities (i.e., a two-box model), it is essential that we start to disentangle the various factors that will support development for children with different auditory, linguistic, cognitive, and personality characteristics, in different academic placements and family settings. We cannot assume that simply because children with cochlear implants or with mild hearing losses are in mainstream classrooms, they learn just like hearing children. Nor can we assume that when children with implants are in separate classrooms, they learn just like other deaf children.

We suggested earlier that inconsistent results pertaining to age at implantation and reading achievement are due in part to the heterogeneity of deaf children and variability in the benefits of cochlear implantation. But wait, there's more! A significant body of literature now indicates that children with cochlear implants, like other deaf children, are cognitively somewhat different from their hearing age-mates. Unfortunately, most of the relevant research has failed to include matched deaf children without cochlear implants, who would allow for a better understanding of the role of audition in cognitive development and in the acquisition of literacy and other academic skills. Meanwhile, we are lacking evidence with regard to the cognitive skills underlying the academic achievement of hard-of-hearing children without cochlear implants, and it appears that they, like children with implants, are typically taught like hearing children in regular education classrooms. With the continuing insistence that children in both populations function "almost" like hearing children, we have failed to seek out the information necessary to fully accommodate their needs and take advantage of their strengths.

As the population of children who are functionally hard of hearing becomes more diverse, both language and academic outcomes also will show increasing variability. Previously, when contradictory findings were obtained in outcome studies of children with implants, they usually were dismissed or ignored. The fact that many of those results also characterize hard-of-hearing children is rarely acknowledged. As such findings have become more frequent and the limitations of earlier studies that utilized carefully selected samples are recognized, researchers must expand the scope of their investigations, not narrow them. Observing similarities and differences between these two populations, as well as among them and their deaf and hearing peers, will benefit both theoretical and practical domains. More importantly, it will provide us with a better understanding of the foundations of learning by all children with hearing loss, thus enabling us to develop and modify instructional methods so as to be more effective. To do otherwise would be a terrible waste of time, money, and human potential.

Acknowledgments

Preparation of this chapter was supported by grant REC-0633928 from the National Science Foundation. Any opinions, findings and conclusions, or recommendations expressed in this material are those of the authors and do not necessarily reflect the views of the National Science Foundation. Portions of this chapter were drawn from Marschark, M., Rhoten, C., Fabich [Zupan], M. (2007). Effects of cochlear implants on children's reading and academic achievement. *Journal of Deaf Studies and Deaf Education, 12*, 269–282. Reprinted by permission.

References

Alegria, J., & Lechat, J. (2005). Phonological processing in deaf children: When lipreading and cues are incongruent. *Journal of Deaf Studies and Deaf Education, 10* 122–133.

Antia, S. D., Stinson, M. S., & Gaustad, M. G. (2002). Developing membership in the education of deaf and hard of hearing students in inclusive settings. *Journal of Deaf and Deaf Education, 7*, 214–229.

Archbold, S. M. (2005). Paediatric cochlear implantation: Has cochlear implantation changed the face of deaf education? *ENT News, 14* (5), 52–54.

Archbold, S. M., Harris, M., O'Donoghue, G. M., Nikolopoulos, T. P., White, A., & Richmond, H. L. (2008). Reading abilities after cochlear implantation: The effect of age at implantation on outcomes at five on seven years after implantation. *International Journal of Pediatric Otorhinolaryngology, 72*, 1471–1478.

Banks, J., Gray, C., & Fyfe, R. (1990). The written recall of printed stories by severely deaf children. *British Journal of Educational Psychology, 60*, 192–206.

Beadle, E. A. R., McKinley, D. J., Nikolopoulos, T. P., Brough, J., O'Donoghue, G. M., & Archbold, S. M. (2005). Long-term functional outcomes and academic-occupational status in implanted children after 10 to 14 years of cochlear implant use. *Otology & Neurotology, 26*, 1152–1160.

Bebko, J. M., & Metcalfe-Haggert, A. (1997). Deafness, language skills, and rehearsal: A model for the development of a memory strategy. *Journal of Deaf Studies and Deaf Education, 2*, 131–139.

Blamey, P., Sarant, J., Paatsch, L., Barry, J., Bow, C., Wales, R., Wright, M., Psarros, C., Rattigan, K., & Tooher, R. (2001). Relationships among speech perception, production, language, hearing loss, and age in children with impaired hearing. *Journal of Speech, Language and Hearing Research, 44*, 264–285.

Boothroyd, A. & Boothroyd-Turner, D. (2002). Postimplantation audition and educational attainment in children with prelingually acquired profound deafness. *Annals of Otology, Rhinology, and Laryngology, Supplement, 189*, 79–84.

Borovsky, A., & Elman, J. (2006). Language input and semantic categories: A relation between cognition and early word learning. *Journal of Child Language, 36*, 759–790.

Burkholder, R. A., & Pisoni, D. B. (2006). Working memory capacity, verbal rehearsal speed, and scanning in deaf children with cochlear implants. In P. E. Spencer & M. Marschark (Eds.), *Advances in the Spoken Language Development of Deaf and Hard-of-Hearing Children* (pp. 328–357). New York: Oxford University Press.

Connor, C., Hieber, S., Arts, H., & Zwolan, T. (2000). Speech, vocabulary and the education of children using cochlear implants: Oral or total communication? *Journal of Speech, Language, and Hearing Research, 43*, 1185–1204.

Connor, C. M. & Zwolan, T. (2004). Examining multiple sources of influence on the reading comprehension skills of children who use cochlear implants. *Journal of Speech, Language, and Hearing Research, 47*, 509–526.

Convertino, C. M., Marschark, M. Sapere, P., Sarchet, T. & Zupan, M. (2009). Predicting academic success among deaf college students. *Journal of Deaf Studies and Deaf Education 14*, 324–343.

Conway, C. M., Pisoni, D. B., Anaya, E. M., Karpicke, J., & Henning, S. C. (in press). Implicit sequence learning and deaf children with cochlear implants. *Development Science*.

Crosson, J., & Geers, A. (2001). Analysis of narrative ability in children with cochlear implants. *Ear & Hearing, 22*, 381–394.

DeLana, M., Gentry, M. A., & Andrews, J. (2007). The efficacy of ASL/English bilingual education: Considering public schools. *American Annals of the Deaf, 151*, 73–87.

El-Hakim, H., Papsin, B., Mount, R. J., Levasseur, J., Panesar, J., Stevens, D., & Harrison, R. V. (2001). Vocabulary acquisition rate after pediatric cochlear implantation and the impact of age of implantation. *International Journal of Pediatric Otorhinolaryngology, 59*, 187–194.

Fagan, M. K., Pisoni, D. B., Horn, D. L., & Dillon, C. M. (2007). Neuropsychological correlates of vocabulary, reading, and working memory in deaf children with cochlear implants. *Journal of Deaf Studies and Deaf Education, 12*, 461–471.

Figueras, B., Edwards, L., & Langdon, D. (2008). Executive function and language in deaf children. *Journal of Deaf Studies and Deaf Education, 13*, 362–377.

Geers, A. (2002). Factors affecting the development of speech, language, and literacy in children with early cochlear implantation. *Language, Speech, and Hearing Services in Schools, 33*, 172–183.

Geers, A. (2003). Predictors of reading skill development in children with early cochlear implantation. *Ear & Hearing, 24* (Supplement), 59S–68S.

Geers, A. (2004). Speech, language, and reading skills after early cochlear implantation. *Archives of Otolaryngology Head and Neck Surgery, 130*, 634–638.

Geers, A. (2005). Factors associated with academic achievement by children who received a cochlear implant by 5 years of age. Presentation at preconference workshop on Development of Children with Cochlear Implants at biennial meetings of the Society for Research in Child Development. Atlanta, Georgia, April 7–10.

Geers, A., Brenner, C., Nicholas, J., Uchanski, R., Tye-Murray, N., & Tobey, E. (2002). Rehabilitation factors contributing to implant benefit in children. *Annals of Otology, Rhinology, and Laryngology, 111*, 127–130.

Geers, A., Tobey, E., Moog, J., & Brenner, C. (2008). Long-term outcomes of cochlear implantation in the preschool years: From elementary grades to high school. *International Journal of Audiology, 47* (Supplement 2), S21–S30.

Gilbertson, M., & Kamhi, A. G. (1995). Novel word learning in children with hearing impairment. *Journal of Speech and Hearing Research, 38*, 630–642.

Goldberg, L. R. & Richburg, C. M. (2004). Minimal hearing impairment: Major myths with more than minimal implications. *Communication Disorders Quarterly, 25*, 152–160.

Hauser, P. C., Lukomski, J. & Hillman, T. (2008). Development of deaf and hard-of-hearing students' executive function. In M. Marschark & P. C. Hauser (Eds.), *Deaf cognition: Foundations and outcomes* (pp. 286–308). New York: Oxford University Press.

Ibertsson, T., Vass, M., Árnason, L. A., Sahlén, B., & Lyxell, B. (2006). The relationship between language, working memory and reading in Swedish prelingually deaf children with CI. Paper presentation at meetings of the European Society for Pediatric Cochlear Implantation (ESPCI), Venice, March 25–28.

James, D., Rajput, K., Brinton, J., & Goswami, U. (2008). Phonological awareness, vocabulary, and word reading in children who use cochlear implants: Does age of implantation explain individual variability in performance outcomes and growth? *Journal of Deaf Studies and Deaf Education, 13*, 117–137.

Johnson, C. A., & Goswami, U. C. (2005). Phonological skills, vocabulary development, and reading development in children with cochlear implants. Presentation at the 20th International Congress on the Education of the Deaf, Maastricht, Netherlands, July 17–20.

Khan, S., Edwards, L., & Langdon, D. (2005). The cognition and behaviour of children with cochlear implants, children with hearing aids and their hearing peers: *A comparison. Audiology and Neuro-otology, 10*, 117–126.

Leybaert, J. (1993). Reading in the deaf: The roles of phonological codes. In M. Marschark & M. D. Clark (Eds.), *Psychological perspectives on deafness* (pp. 269–310). Mahwah, N. J.: Lawrence Erlbaum Associates.

Leybaert, J. & Alegria, J. (2003). The role of cued speech in language development of deaf children In M. Marschark & P. E. Spencer (Eds.), *Oxford Handbook of Deaf Studies, Language, and Education* (pp. 262–274). New York: Oxford University Press.

Marschark, M. (2001). *Language development in children who are deaf: A research synthesis.* Alexandria, VA: National Association of State Directors of Special Education.

Marschark, M. (2003). Cognitive functioning in deaf adults and children. In M. Marschark & P. E. Spencer (Eds.), *Oxford handbook of deaf studies, language, and education* (pp. 464–477). New York: Oxford University Press.

Marschark, M. (2007). *Raising and educating a deaf child*, 2nd edition. New York: Oxford University Press.

Marschark, M., Convertino, C., McEvoy, C., & Masteller, A. (2004). Organization and use of the mental lexicon by deaf and hearing individuals. *American Annals of the Deaf, 149*, 51–61.

Marschark, M., De Beni, R., Polazzo, M. G., & Cornoldi, C. (1993). Deaf and hearing-impaired adolescents' memory for concrete and abstract prose: Effects of relational and distinctive information. *American Annals of the Deaf, 138*, 31–39.

Marschark, M. & Everhart, V. S. (1997). Relations of language and cognition: What do deaf children tell us? In M. Marschark, P. Siple, D. Lillo-Martin, R. Campbell, & V. S. Everhart, *Relations of language and thought: The view from sign language and deaf children* (pp. 3–23). New York: Oxford University Press.

Marschark, M., Mouradian, V., & Halas, M. (1994). Discourse rules in the language productions of deaf and hearing children. *Journal of Experimental Child Psychology, 57*, 89–107.

Marschark, M., Rhoten, C., & Fabich, M. (2007). Effects of cochlear implants on children's reading and academic achievement. *Journal of Deaf Studies and Deaf Education, 12*, 269–282.

Marschark, M., & Wauters, L. (2008). Language comprehension and learning by deaf students. In M. Marschark & P. C. Hauser (Eds.), *Deaf cognition: Foundations and outcomes* (pp. 309–350). New York: Oxford University Press.

Mayberry, R. I., & Lock, E. (2003). Age constraints on first versus second language acquisition: Evidence for linguistic plasticity and epigenesis. *Brain and Language, 87*, 369–383.

Mayer, C., & Akamatsu, C. T. (2003). Bilingualism and literacy. In M. Marschark & P. E. Spencer (Eds.), *Oxford handbook of deaf studies, language, and education* (pp. 136–147). New York: Oxford University Press.

McEvoy, C., Marschark, M., & Nelson, D. L. (1999). Comparing the mental lexicons of deaf and hearing individuals. *Journal of Educational Psychology, 91*, 1–9.

Moeller, M. P. (2000). Early intervention and language development in children who are deaf and hard of hearing. *Pediatrics, 106*, E43.

Moeller, M. P., Tomblin, J. B., Yoshinaga-Itano, C., Connor, C. M., & Jerger, S. (2007). Current state of knowledge: Language and literacy of children with hearing impairment. *Ear & Hearing, 28*, 740–753.

Moog, J. S. (2002). Changing expectations for children with cochlear and plants. *Annals of Oncology, Rhinology, and Laryngology, 189* (Supplement), 138–142.

Most, T., & Peled, M. (2007). Perception of suprasegmental features of speech by children with cochlear implants and children with hearing aids. *Journal of Deaf Studies and Deaf Education, 12*, 350–361.

Nelson, K. E., Loncke, F., & Camarata, S. (1993). Implications of research on deaf and hearing children's language learning. In M. Marschark & M. D. Clark (Eds.), *Psychological perspectives on deafness* (pp. 123–152). Hillsdale, NJ: Lawrence Erlbaum Associates.

Nicholas, J. G., & Geers, A. E. (2006). The process and early outcomes of cochlear implantation by three years of age. In P. E. Spencer & M. Marschark (Eds.), *Advances in the spoken language development of deaf and hard-of-hearing children* (pp. 271–297). New York: Oxford University Press.

Nicholas, J. G., & Geers, A. E. (2007). Will they catch up? The role of age of cochlear implantation in the spoken language development of children with severe to profound hearing loss. *Journal of Speech, Language, and Hearing Research, 50*, 1048–1062.

Nikolopoulos, T., O'Donoghue, G. M., & Archbold, S. (1999). Age at implantation: Its importance in paediatric cochlear implantation. *Laryngoscope, 109*, 595–599.

Ottem, E. (1980). An analysis of cognitive studies with deaf subjects. *American Annals of the Deaf, 125*, 564–575.

Padden, C., & Ramsey, C. (2000). American Sign Language and reading ability in deaf children. In C. Chamberlain, J. Morford, & R. Mayberry (Eds.), *Language acquisition by eye* (pp. 165–189). Mahwah NJ: Lawrence Erlbaum.

Pisoni, D., Cleary, M., Geers, A., & Tobey, E. (1999). Individual differences in effectiveness of cochlear implants in children who are prelingually deaf: New process measures of performance. *Volta Review, 101,* 111–164.

Pisoni, D. B., Conway, C. M., Kronenberger, W., Horn, D. L., Karpicke, J., & Henning, S. (2008). Efficacy and effectiveness of cochlear implants in deaf children. In M. Marschark & P. C. Hauser (Eds.), *Deaf cognition: Foundations and outcomes* (pp. 52–101). New York: Oxford University Press.

Pisoni, D. B., & Geers, A. (2000). Working memory in deaf children with cochlear implants: Correlations between digit span and measures of spoken language processing. *Annals of Otology, Rhinology, and Laryngology, 185* (Supplement), 92–93.

Proksch, J., & Bavelier, D. (2002). Changes in the spatial distribution of visual attention after early deafness. *Journal of Cognitive Neuroscience, 14,* 687–701.

Pyman, B., Blamey, P. J., Lacy, P., Clark, G. M., & Dowell, R. C. (2000). The development of speech production in children using cochlear implants: effects of etiologic factors and delayed milestones. *American Journal of Otology, 21,* 57–61.

Quittner, A. L., Smith L. B., Osberger, M. J., Mitchell, T. V., & Katz, D. B. (1994). The impact of audition on the development of visual attention. *Psychological Science, 5,* 347–353.

Spencer, P. E. (2002). Language development of children with cochlear implants. In J. Christiansen & I. Leigh, *Cochlear implants in children: Ethics and choices* (pp. 222–249). Washington DC: Gallaudet University Press.

Spencer, L. J., Barker, B. A., & Tomblin, J. B. (2003). Exploring the language and literacy outcomes of pediatric cochlear Implant users. *Ear & Hearing, 24,* 236–247.

Spencer, L. J., Gantz, B. J., & Knutson, J. F. (2004). Outcomes and achievement of students who grew up with access to cochlear implants. *Laryngoscope, 114,* 1576–1581.

Spencer, L. J., Tomblin, J. B., & Gantz, B. J. (1997). Reading skills in children with multichannel cochlear-implant experience. *Volta Review, 99,* 193–202.

Spencer, P. (2001). Language performance of children with early cochlear implantation: Child and family factors. 8th Symposium on Cochlear Implants in Children. Los Angeles, California, March.

Spencer, P. E., & Marschark, M. (2003). Cochlear implants: Issues and implications. In M. Marschark & P. E. Spencer (Eds.), *Oxford handbook of deaf studies, language, and education* (pp. 434–448). New York: Oxford University Press.

Stacey, P. C., Fortnum, H. M., Barton, G. R., & Summerfield, A. Q. (2006). Hearing-impaired children in the United Kingdom, I: Auditory performance, communication skills, educational achievements, quality of life, and cochlear implantation. *Ear & Hearing, 27,* 161–186.

Stinson, M. S., & Kluwin, T. N. (2003). Educational consequences of alternative school placements. In M. Marschark & P. E. Spencer (Eds.), *Oxford handbook of deaf studies, language, and education* (pp. 52–64). New York: Oxford University Press.

Tharpe, A., Ashmead, D., & Rothpletz, A (2002). Visual attention in children with normal hearing, children with hearing aids, and children with cochlear implants. *Journal of Speech, Hearing and Language Research, 45,* 403–413.

Thoutenhoofd, E. (2006). Cochlear implanted pupils in Scottish schools: 4-year school attainment data (2000–2004). *Journal of Deaf Studies and Deaf Education, 11,* 171–188.

Torres, S., Rodriguez, J. -M., Garcia-Orza, J., & Calleja, M. (2008). Reading comprehension of an inferential text by deaf students with cochlear implants using cued speech. *Volta Review, 108,* 37–58.

Toscano, R. M., McKee, B. G., & Lepoutre, D. (2002). Success with academic English: Reflections of deaf college students. *American Annals of the Deaf, 147,* 5–23.

Traxler, C. B. (2000). Measuring up to performance standards in reading and mathematics: Achievement of selected deaf and hard-of-hearing students in the national norming of the 9th Edition Stanford Achievement Test. *Journal of Deaf Studies and Deaf Education, 5,* 337–348.

Vermeulen, A., van Bon, W., Schreuder, R., Knoors, H., & Snik, A. (2007). Reading comprehension of deaf children with cochlear implants. *Journal of Deaf Studies and Deaf Education, 12,* 283–302.

Watson, D. R., Titterington, J., Henry, A., & Toner, J. G. (2007). Auditory sensory memory and working memory processes in children with normal hearing and cochlear implants. *Audiology and Neurotology, 12,* 65–76.

Watson, L. (2002). The literacy development of children with cochlear implants at age seven. *Deafness and Education International, 4,* 84–98.

Yoshinaga-Itano, C. (2006). Early identification, communication modality, and the development of speech and spoken language skills: Patterns and considerations. In P. E. Spencer & M. Marschark (Eds.), *Advances in the spoken language development of deaf and hard-of-hearing children* (pp. 298–327). New York: Oxford University Press.

The Demands of Writing and the Deaf Writer

Connie Mayer

Abstract

Writing is a complex cognitive activity requiring the coordination of graphomotor and cognitive-linguistic abilities, as well as knowledge of social, rhetorical, and text production conventions (Singer & Bashir, 2004). All of these must be managed in the process of learning to write, and ultimately, writing to learn—whether the process is viewed from a cognitive or a sociocultural perspective (Nystrand, 2006). To consider these demands in relation to the deaf writer, a summary and analysis of studies examining written language development and achievement in the deaf population is presented in this chapter. Relationships among spoken and signed language, and reading and writing are identified, and shifts in pedagogical approach are discussed. Issues and shortcomings related to effectively assessing and reporting the quality of written language for purposes of both research and pedagogy are also addressed. The chapter concludes by considering areas for future research including the potential impact of cochlear implantation on written language development.

Keywords: Deafness, pedagogy, writing, writing process, composing processes, pedagogy, bilingualism

The demands made on any writer are staggering, requiring the coordination of graphomotor and cognitive-linguistic abilities, as well as knowledge of social, rhetorical, and text production conventions (Singer & Bashir, 2004). Whether the process is viewed from a cognitive or a sociocultural perspective (Nystrand, 2006), all of these demands must be managed in the process of learning to write, and ultimately, writing to learn not only stagger, they can overwhelm. Writing becomes a laborious process that is neither effective nor efficient in producing texts that convey intended meanings, or in using text as a tool to mediate thinking and learning. Many deaf writers are among this group who find writing and learning to write especially challenging. Although advances in writing technologies have ameliorated some of these challenges, it remains the case that writing is a complex and cognitively demanding activity for this group.

The production of spoken or written language calls upon the same set of cognitive processes (e.g., encoding, organizing, storing, and reconstructing information) (Cook, Chapman, & Gamino, 2007), with patterns of performance being similar for both modalities (Bracewell, Frederickson, & Frederickson, 1982). To expand on this point, it has been argued that the production of signed language involves essentially the same set of linguistic processes that operates in a spoken language (Lillo-Martin, 1997). That said, even though written discourse builds on these abilities in spoken and/or signed discourse, writing requires more cognitive control than speaking or signing, as incomplete utterances, false starts, and the like are less well-tolerated in print than in a face-to-face modality.

Written language lacks the auditory features and visual–gestural aspects of face-to-face discourse, and in the composing process all writers struggle to capture both the propositional content and illocutionary force of the spoken (or signed) word in the written text (Olson, 1977, 1993). Written discourse occurs in the absence of a physically present interlocutor, demanding a sense of audience, a precision of expression, and an expansion and elaboration of thought not necessary in face-to-face communication (Halliday, 1989). "Considering how painlessly children learn to talk [and sign], the difficulties they face in learning to write are quite pronounced. Indeed, some children never learn to write at all, and many fall far short of full proficiency in the task" (Kress, 1982, p. ix). In many ways, the demands of writing and learning to write are more onerous than those encountered in learning to read, and it could be argued that this is particularly true for learners who are deaf (Mayer, 1999; Moores, 1987).

Yet, with respect to researching the literacy development of deaf learners, reading has typically been afforded more attention than writing (Marschark, Lang, & Albertini, 2002). It would be difficult to find an article or paper focusing on literacy development in the population with hearing loss that did not make some reference to Grade 4 reading levels and the fact that no movement has occurred in this disappointing outcome over time. In contrast, references made to achievement in writing are much less frequent. This focus on reading over writing is typical of literacy research in general, with writing being the most neglected of the "three Rs." Instructional, systematic research in the area is not as mature as the research in reading and has not engendered the same level of concern, distinction, and attention (Troia, 2007).

This chapter provides a summary and analysis of the research examining written language development and achievement in the deaf population, and considers this research in terms of the demands that writing makes on the deaf writer. Relationships among spoken and signed language, and reading and writing will be identified. Issues and shortcomings related to effectively assessing and reporting the quality of written language for purposes of both research and pedagogy will also be addressed. The chapter will conclude by considering areas for future research, including the potential impact of cochlear implantation on written language development.

Theoretical Landscapes

Before considering the research on deaf writers, it would be instructive to situate this discussion within the context of the shifts that have taken place in the broader field of literacy research, and writing research in particular. One of the most fundamental

shifts of the past 40 years has been the conceptualization of writing as process, in contrast to the focus on product that typified the discourse in the field prior to 1970 (Nystrand, 2006).

Flower and Hayes (1980, 1981) were among the first to describe the cognitive juggling inherent in the process of text production, and this was followed by the work of Bereiter and Scardamalia (1987), Berninger and Swanson (1994), and Hayes (2000), among others. It is beyond the scope of this chapter to give a comprehensive account of this body of work, but its defining feature is the notion that writing is a recursive rather than a linear process, involving planning, generating, organizing, and revising. The process is viewed as a messy one that involves managing the tensions between meaning and form, in which writers must convert a set of ideas with many internal mental connections into a linear sequence that satisfies certain grammatical rules (Collins & Gentner, 1980).

Although most researchers and educators would be in general agreement with this conceptualization of writing as process, interpretations and applications of the model differ. This is a consequence of framing the process in terms of one of the two broad perspectives that relate to conceptualizations of language and literacy development—cognitive science and sociocultural effects (Stone, 2004). As Stone explains it, each of these perspectives represents an attempt to provide a coherent account of what it means to know and come to know something, how to conceptualize this knowing, and how this knowing can be taught. Whether explicitly or implicitly, researchers operate within one of these traditions, and although the demarcation between the two is not absolute, there are features that mark each perspective as distinct.

"For the cognitive scientist, language is a knowledge system that must be acquired, perhaps by means of a dedicated processing system. For the socioculturalist, language is a system of cultural practices into which the child is gradually socialized" (Stone, 2004, p.13). While acknowledging variations in emphasis, the focus in a cognitive science tradition is on the individual learner and the processes by which he or she learns. In a sociocultural perspective, much more emphasis is put on context, with a view that writing is an interactive, dialogic process situated in and shaped by particular discourse communities (Prior, 2006). Research is conceived, conducted, and interpreted in terms of one of these frameworks, thus shaping the ways in which writing and the writing process are viewed with respect to the individual writer, the demands of the activity, and how these demands are met.

At the risk of oversimplifying a complex issue, the tension between these views plays out most pointedly in thinking about the role of the individual in the writing process. In the cognitive science tradition, the emphasis is on writing processes as they are manifested in the mind of the individual writer, with a focus on how writers make linguistic decisions in order to generate texts that make semantic and pragmatic sense. If the writer is unable to meet the demands of the writing process, it could be argued that the "problem" rests in the individual. From a sociocultural view, it is seen as impossible to separate the individual from the context, putting paid to any notion that the individual writer should constitute the unit of analysis.

From either perspective, the text creation process can be viewed as a communicative enterprise, with the difference lying in the relative emphasis placed on the cognitive resources the individual brings to the process versus the resources that the context affords. In a recent iteration of the model, Singer and Bashir (2004) propose that the composing process involves the interaction between two components—writing foundations (i.e., executive and self-regulatory skills) and writing processes. They suggest that the foundational variables encompassed in a notion of writing foundations (e.g., cognitive-linguistic abilities) can differentially influence the act of writing, as mild delays or deficits in one skill or process can have significant effects on the rapid and precise coordination required to manage the process. These issues have played out in the research on writing and deaf writers, in considerations of process and product, and particularly in the extent to which (and how) hearing loss is implicated in the process of writing and learning to write.

Deaf Writers—Product and Process

By its very nature, writing produces a tangible product, readily accessible for examination and analysis. Typically, these analyses have been descriptive accounts, both qualitative and quantitative, of the texts that deaf writers produce. A review of these studies dating from the early 20th century to the present day reveals a consistent finding—that deaf writers do not write as well as their hearing age peers. In line with the Grade 4 levels documented for reading, it is reported that the typical 17- to 18-year-old deaf student writes at a level comparable to that of an 8- to 10-year-old hearing child (Marschark et al., 2002; Paul, 1998, 2001), "failing to master elements

of English morphology, grammar structures, and transformational grammar rules, even by age 21" (Yoshinaga-Itano, Snyder,& Mayberry, 1996a, p. 10).

Most early studies focused on the lexical and grammatical quality of the written product (Cohen, 1967; Cooper, 1967; Heider & Heider, 1941; Kretschmer & Kretschmer, 1978; Myklebust, 1964; Wilbur, 1977). It was found that deaf writers tended to use a greater number of nouns, verbs, and determiners, but demonstrated less frequent use of adverbs, auxiliaries, and conjunctions. They relied on shorter, simpler sentences often employing subject-verb-complement sentence patterns. Word order was found to be less flexible, and the writing featured numerous grammatical errors and non-standard usages of English (for a detailed overview see Yoshinaga-Itano, 1986).

During the 1980s and 1990s, the focus of these analyses was expanded to consider the organization of written discourse, with concentration placed on conceptual coherence, and text and discourse structures. The prevailing view was that deaf writers also experienced difficulties in these areas (Banks, Gray, & Fyfe, 1990; deVilliers, 1991; Klecan-Aker & Blondeau, 1990; Maxwell & Falick, 1992; Webster, 1986; Weiss & Johnson, 1993; Yoshinaga-Itano, 1986; Yoshinaga-Itano et al., 1996a; Yoshinaga & Downey, 1992; Yoshinaga & Snyder, 1985; Yoshinaga-Itano, C., Snyder, L.S. & Mayberry, R., 1996b). In contrast to hearing children who produced stories with adult structures by age 6, the vast majority of deaf students by age 18 still did not use minimal components of a story in spontaneously generated written narratives (Yoshinaga-Itano & Downey, 1996). In an opposing view, Marschark, Mouradian, and Halas (1994) suggested that deaf writers could make appropriate use of discourse rules in the production of narratives, but that these were "obscured by disfluencies in writing" (p. 89).

Examinations of product during this period continued to indicate that deaf writers had problems with the lexicon and syntax of the written form (Berent, 1996; Conte, Rampelli, & Volterra, 1996; Fabbretti, Volterra, & Pontecorvo, 1998; Musselman & Szanto, 1998; Powers & Wigus, 1983; Quigley & King, 1980; Taeschner, 1988), raising questions as to the extent to which the problems deaf writers have with syntax impact on the ability to organize content and make meaning in a written text. In a recent look at this question, Arfe and Boscolo (2006) found that although the deaf writers in their study did make use of causal coherence in narrative writing, it was less coherent than the writing of their hearing peers and relatively immature, with syntax skills being only partially correlated with these difficulties.

That said, it has been reported that, even though deaf writers encounter problems with most aspects of form, they are able to successfully convey content, often as well as their hearing peers (Marschark, Mouradian, & Halas, 1994; Svartholm, 2008; Yoshinaga et al., 1996a). Although this strikes a positive note, it should be pointed out that these studies were limited to the production of narrative discourse, leaving the question open as to whether deaf writers would be as effective in conveying content in an expository text. Given that "expository writing requires students to employ skills that can be particularly challenging for students with language disorders" (Calfee & Wilson, 2004, p. 585), it would seem reasonable to suggest that deaf writers might also find this type of writing difficult. This issue has significant educational implications, as expository writing is the genre of schooling, especially in the later grades and in subject areas where students are required to write texts such as science reports, book summaries, and essay answers on tests.

One aspect of learning to write that has received particular attention is that of spelling, with an early claim that this area is relatively less problematic, and the suggestion that deaf writers experience less delay in this domain (Gates & Chase, 1926; Hoemann, Andrews, Florian, Hoemann, & Jensema, 1976; Templin, 1948). The rationale behind this view rests on the notion that spelling, unlike reading, is open to orthographic analysis, in which the visual mode can serve as well as the auditory one to mediate the encoding/decoding process.

More recently it has been argued that deaf writers do make more frequent and qualitatively different spelling errors than their hearing counterparts (Leybaert & Alegria, 1995) as a consequence of their inability to hear acoustically based languages and thus develop the phonological capacity required for accurate encoding (for a detailed discussion see Alamargot, Lambert, Thebault & Dansac, 2007). Taking a different view, Padden (1993) suggested that, whereas studies of hearing children reveal the ways in which print is amenable to phonemic analysis, investigations of deaf spellers demonstrate that the same system is amenable to a positional-graphemic analysis.

With respect to the development of early literacy, investigations have been done on the use of invented spelling by deaf writers who use predominantly manual (Mayer, 1994, 1998; Schleper, 1992) or oral modes (Johnson, Padak, & Barton, 1994) as their primary means of communication. Although both groups were found to invent spellings, the children in the manual group made relationships between sign and print that are unique to learners with hearing loss (i.e., relationships between handshape and print), while the oral group made grapheme-phoneme connections that are developmentally similar to those of hearing children. It has been suggested that these early attempts at spelling provide insights into whether deaf children are developing the relationships between face-to-face language and print that are necessary for ultimately learning to read and write (Mayer, 2007).

Although the texts produced have probably been studied more than any other aspect of written language development in individuals with hearing loss (Webster, 1986), there is far less research of the individual composing processes of the deaf writer in order to develop a clearer picture of how the texts of these writers "come to be." This generative process of text production is concerned with how it is that an individual writer makes linguistic decisions to create texts that will make semantic and pragmatic sense. Examples of studies in this area include investigations of grammatical decision making while writing (Kelly, 1987, 1988), strategies reported while encoding (Albertini, Meath-Lang, & Harris, 1994; Mayer, 1999), and working memory capacities (Alamargot et al., 2007).

An area that remains particularly understudied, but which could provide insights into the composing process, is that of revising. *Revising* is that aspect of the writing process that requires making modifications to a text so that it communicates intended meanings, while still following accepted linguistic and discourse conventions. In addition, it requires "reading like a writer"—reading the text as if its meaning were unknown (to the writers themselves), in order to assess its effect on an unknown reader. In one of the early studies that looked at this issue, Livingston (1989) investigated the differences between first and second drafts in the writing of 22 high school-aged deaf students, finding that most of the edits involved substitutions and deletions. In a recent study, Hermsen and Franklin (2008), using keystroke analysis, examined revisions made by a college-aged deaf student to investigate how writing functioned as a tool for learning discipline-specific content in physics.

Overall, it is apparent that deaf writers struggle with the process of text generation, producing texts that are not at the level of their hearing age peers—a situation that has not changed substantially over time. However, during this period, shifts also occurred in the focus of writing instruction, meant to address the concerns with the quality of the writing that deaf writers produce.

Pedagogical Shifts

In the first half of the 20th century, a structured approach to language teaching was the norm in programs for both hearing and deaf learners. "Through processes of direct imitation, memorization and drill, usually in the framework of a strictly sequenced curriculum, the deaf child was expected to acquire a grammatically correct version of the general language of society" (McAnally, Rose, & Quigley, 1987, p. 78). Influenced by the work of Groht (1958), there was some tempering of this approach to a more natural, holistic model in which learners were expected to acquire English via constant exposure to appropriate language patterns.

That said, the prevalent philosophy continued to be one in which it was assumed that deaf students could not acquire English solely via interaction, instead requiring some controlled activities and teaching (Streng, 1972), and prompting the development of structured intervention programs (e.g., Anderson, Boren, Caniglia, Howard, & Krohn, 1980; Blackwell, Engen, Fischgrund, & Zarcadoolas, 1978; Costello & Watkins, 1975). But, as is evident from the overview of written products presented in the previous section, deaf writers were still not developing age-appropriate written English abilities. Wilbur (1977) blamed this lack of improvement on a flawed instructional system, asserting that the prevalence of grammar drills had led to a set of nonstandard but well-learned grammatical generalizations that were applied with a minimal draw on attention.

In step with what was happening in language and literacy education for hearing learners, the early 1980s saw the advent of whole-language programming in the education of learners with hearing loss. These approaches to language instruction "have underlined the fact that language learning can best be promoted when language is used purposefully and communicatively, when language is viewed as a means for true expression, when language accuracy serves linguistic fluency and is subordinate to it" (Zamel, 1983, p. 184). With respect to writing instruction in particular, this signaled a move to process writing approaches (Graves, 1983) and the use of strategies such as dialogue journals (Livingston, 1997).

Just as it was for hearing learners, this pedagogical shift was seen as a way to improve the generally poor written language performance of children in the education system. This had particular resonance for the field of deaf education, given that most students were not reading and writing at age-appropriate levels. Numerous studies followed across a range of age and educational settings and philosophies, employing a variety of approaches for data collection (Albertini & Meath-Lang, 1986; Cambra, 1994; Conway, 1985; Ewoldt, 1985; Harrison, Simpson, & Stuart, 1991; Kluwin & Kelly, 1992; Mayer, 1994; Neuroth-Gimbrone & Logiodice, 1992; Truax, 1985; Williams, 1993).

In summing up the findings of these studies, it would be fair to say that, overall, students developed a more positive attitude to writing, learning that writing could serve as a powerful communication tool. Students were actively engaged in the writing process, seeing it as purposeful and meaningful. But, while their texts did show improvements in terms of the content and idea space, there were no real improvements with most aspects of structure and linguistic form. In terms of composing and revising, deaf writers continued to make liberal and indiscriminate use of derivational morphemes and functors, more to signal that "this is English" than to carry semantic or grammatical information (Maxwell, 1990).

This move to whole language was closely followed by the advent of bilingual education for deaf learners in the late 1980s and early 1990s, with the establishment of programs in which natural signed languages were used as the primary languages of instruction. Most studies of literacy development in these programs focused on reading, with only a few studies specifically addressing writing performance. Overall, these studies did not show significant improvements in the quality of the writing relative to hearing age-matched peers (or even with those deaf learners educated in other settings), although claims were made for a positive relationship between proficiency in a natural signed language (American Sign Language; ASL) and text-based literacy (Strong & Prinz, 2000), and between ASL proficiency and the use of low-frequency vocabulary and less formulaic constructions (Singleton, Morgan, DiGello, Wiles, & Rivers, 2004).

Using data collected in two previous studies conducted in 1983 and 1996, Svartholm (2008) describes the written language of 10 deaf children educated in a bilingual program in Sweden, suggesting that "deviations from the target language norm are typical of the early stages of L2 learning in general" (p. 235). This seems to imply that these deaf children are on a similar trajectory as that of hearing second-language learners, who typically gain control of the target language given adequate time, exposure, and opportunities for interaction. It would be interesting to see later samples from these writers to determine whether this turned out to be the case.

In sum, despite pedagogical shifts to more meaning-based, process approaches, improvements in the quality of the texts produced by deaf writers have not been as significant as anticipated, with no particular communication approach or philosophy proving to be more effective than any other in developing written language abilities.

Summary and Conclusions

Writing is a linguistically and cognitively demanding activity that places the same set of demands on writers whether they are hearing or deaf. The variables lie, not in the activity, but in the relative strengths the writer brings to the activity and the context in which the activity occurs. This consideration of the literature, particularly as it pertains to the quality of the texts produced, has underscored the fact that, at least to date, it appears that significant hearing loss serves to make the process of writing and learning to write more difficult. And given that the text is a product of the process, it could be argued that deaf writers are not engaging as effectively in the writing process as they need to in order to become skilled writers and to use writing as a tool for thinking and learning. Depending on whether a cognitive-science or sociocultural world view predominates, these challenges can be viewed primarily as a matter of the constraints inherent as a consequence of deafness, or of those imposed by the context in which writing has been traditionally taught. To consider these challenges in light of this review of the literature, Singer and Bashir's (2004) model will be used as a framework to discuss the demands writing makes on the deaf writer, and to consider the extent to which pedagogical interventions can support these writers as they work to manage these demands.

Focus on the Deaf Writer

According to Singer and Bashir (2004) "for texts to be built, writers must recruit and coordinate a set of cognitive and linguistic processes" (p. 561), comprised of two components—processes and foundations. In encoding a text, writers employ the processes of planning, organizing, generating, and revising. These processes are under the direction of executive functions and self-regulatory processes that are constrained by foundational variables in four domains—cognitive-linguistic, social-rhetorical, text production, and beliefs and attitudes. When these "executive and self-regulatory processes are impaired or poorly developed, the coordination of the composing processes is not managed efficiently or effectively. This affects the writer's process and product, as well as the extent to which the writer is able to compensate for variables constraining those processes" (p. 562).

A prevailing theme of this review is that the texts produced by deaf writers are lacking in many respects, with performance in the area falling far short of that of hearing age-matched peers. These descriptions of the writing performance of deaf individuals appear to have much in common with those of learners with language-learning disabilities. Writers with language-learning disabilities also "struggle with planning, organizing, and revising their writing. Their texts are short and poorly structured. Their use of language is problematic in terms of syntax, vocabulary diversity, and cohesion, and they make frequent errors in spelling and writing mechanics" (Singer & Bashir, 2004, p. 559). The similarity in description between the two groups raises questions as to the extent to which hearing loss, like language-learning disabilities, puts individuals at biological risk for writing difficulty—a view that would resonate for those with a cognitive science perspective, but be concerning for those who adopt a more sociocultural view.

To address this question, it would be important to better understand which of the four foundational variables are most heavily implicated in compromising the efficient and effective engagement of deaf writers in the writing process. However, to date, very little research affords insights into how these variables are impacted by deafness, especially with respect to learners who are operating in both a spoken and a signed language. One aspect of the challenge is to sort out how different modalities, phonologies, representational systems, and languages come together (or not) to mediate the writing process (see Grushkin, 1998 for the view on ASL).

It may be the case that the skills measured in written language reflect the semantic skills already acquired in face-to-face communication, as is the case with hearing children (Yoshinaga et al., 1996a), leading to the conclusion that it is primarily cognitive-linguistic variables that explain the challenges deaf writers face. These cognitive-linguistic constraints include processing speed, working memory, meta-abilities, conceptual knowledge, content knowledge, and linguistic knowledge (Singer & Bashir, 2004), and it seems reasonable to suggest that the weaknesses evidenced in the texts of deaf writers are a consequence of weaknesses in these areas, with the most obvious being that of linguistic knowledge. That said, the relationships between the development of face-to-face language and print for the deaf writer remain unclear and represent an area in need of further study.

As discussed earlier, it has been suggested that, despite challenges at the linguistic level, deaf writers are able to effectively convey content in narrative discourse, implying that meaning does not need to be intimately tied to form. However, issues of meaning and form are not so easily separated. Expository writing in particular requires facility in the use of complex rhetorical structures and technical and topic-specific vocabulary, to say nothing of the application of grammatical rules in complex sentence structures. Most studies, even of older writers (e.g., Arfe & Boscolo, 2006), have focused on the more familiar narrative forms. Therefore, it would be important to design studies that investigate the writing of expository texts to get a better sense of whether meaning can still be made in more complex writing tasks where control of linguistic form becomes a greater issue.

One explanation for the lack of research in these areas is that investigations of composing processes typically rely on data collection techniques such as think-aloud protocols, clinical experimental interviews, retrospective accounts, and taped recordings (Ericsson & Simon, 1993) that tend to be time consuming, labor intensive, and relatively difficult to conduct, especially when the writers communicate in a signed language, as it is not possible to "think aloud" in sign and write at the same time.

A promising development in the field is the application of new technologies that allow for investigations of the composing/revising process in natural writing settings in unobtrusive ways. One such example is key-capture software. This technology allows a researcher to track every keystroke a writer makes within a writing session, thus providing a record of the composing process in real time in almost any context without requiring the writer to "think (sign) aloud" (Hermsen & Franklin, 2008). It reveals "all the typological differences not only between the first and second drafts, but within a single writing episode or session" (p. 422), thus painting a picture of what the writer did and the order in which it was done. Greater use of such tools should make it possible for increasing numbers of researchers to investigate the composing processes of deaf writers in more depth, to provide a fuller picture of how texts gets written and which foundational variables support or constrain the process.

Focus on the Pedagogical Context

Few in the field would argue for a return to traditional approaches to writing instruction, with their singular focus on form, privileging language over meaning. There is no denying that moves to process-oriented approaches have had a positive impact in terms of the content and ideas that deaf writers convey in their texts, with students displaying more positive beliefs and attitudes about writing and learning to write. However, even with respect to hearing writers, "critics of the process approach argue that attention to the processes of creating texts has made writing products into by-products" (Pritchard & Honeycutt, 2006, p. 285) in which focusing on the procedural strategies involved in text creation writing has trumped concerns related to the quality of the texts produced and the cognitive strategies and subprocesses that underpin the process. Pritchard and Honeycutt (2006) suggest that this may be because process models of writing instruction evolved more quickly in practice than did the research and theories that support them.

With respect to the situation of deaf writers, significant improvements in text quality have not been realized as a consequence of the move to a process-focused pedagogy—if these improvements are framed in terms of age-appropriate performance. Given this lack of improvement, it could be argued that a research shift is called for, in which as much attention is paid to the cognitive strategies underpinning text production (and the subsequent quality of the texts produced), as to accounts of the pedagogical processes involved in producing them. This concern is not unique to the field of deaf education, as the majority of reports on the writing process approach tend to pedagogical description, with few citations of empirical studies and targeted interventions (Nystrand, 2006).

"It appears that the written medium is acquired not in implicit, automatic fashion, but carefully, explicitly, and attentively. It has, in the first place to be taught. Unlike spoken [or signed] language for hearing [or deaf] speakers [or signers], written language for most users demands metalinguistic skills: awareness of the components of the language and the ability to muster them appropriately" (Campbell,

1997, p. 128). This should not be taken as a call for the abandonment of process approaches, but rather an underscoring of the need to attend to the foundational variables that support the writing process in a balanced approach to literacy instruction. Research indicates that the majority of literacy learners with normal hearing, whether adults or children, need some form of intentional instruction to become skilled at decoding and encoding print (Purcell-Gates, Jacobson, & Degener, 2004), indicating that learners with hearing loss are not unique in this regard. Studies of targeted interventions (Berent, Kelly, Schmitz, & Kenney, 2009; Wolbers, 2008), particularly if they are carried out over time, are one avenue for investigating the efficacy of such intentional instruction.

One of the ongoing research challenges in measuring the relative efficacy of various programs and pedagogical interventions is how to assess the writing that is produced. It is ironic that, although the texts themselves are readily available, reporting on their quality in ways that allow for comparisons within and to other populations and in terms of typical development are problematic. Recognizing the ongoing issues as to the reliability and applicability of most measures to assess language and literacy in the population with hearing loss, challenges are amplified when considering the assessment of written language. In contrast to reading, where it is possible to access a relatively broad range of both formative and summative assessment tools, far fewer measures are available to assess written texts, even in the hearing population. Standardized writing assessments are limited not only in their number but in their diagnostic breadth, usually focusing only on the familiar narrative genre when requiring writing of an extended text (Calfee & Wilson, 2004).

Despite these concerns, standardized measures can be used to describe written language performance in powerful ways. Antia and Reed (2005) used the Test of Written Language (TOWL-3; Hammill & Larsen, 1996) to assess the writing of 110 deaf and hard-of-hearing public school students between third and twelfth grade. They found that although the average written quotient for the sample was in the below-average range, it was within 1 standard deviation of the test mean, with 49% of the sample within or above the average range. These are compelling data in that a significant number of writers with hearing loss are scoring at age-appropriate levels, although the authors do caution that there is still the need to attend to the writing abilities and instruction of these students.

What makes the evaluation of the texts of deaf writers particularly challenging is that they feature idiosyncratic uses of language that are not accounted for in typical assessments of written language, or are simply subsumed under the category of "conventions" in many of the rubrics that are popular as assessment tools in the field for both hearing (Spandel & Stiggins, 1997) and deaf learners (Heefner & Shaw, 1996; Schirmer, Bailey, & Fitzgerald, 1999). Because problems with English grammar, syntax, spelling, and punctuation are all conflated under the heading "conventions," a poor score is not very informative as to the exact nature of the concerns related to language form and sentence structure. These holistic approaches to assessment, although informative for planning and pedagogical purposes, are not precise enough in their scoring criteria to identify the specific problems that deaf writers have with text production, or to allow for making meaningful comparisons among groups. One way to address this concern would be to regularly include written language samples in reports of research on writing, as this would allow the reader direct access to the data.

FOCUS ON THE FUTURE

As with reading, changes in pedagogical approach and communication philosophy have not effected significant improvements in the writing performance of deaf learners over the better part of the past 80 years. Among the explanations Marschark and Hauser (2008) put forward to account for this relatively slow pace of improvement in academic achievement is the suggestion that we are only beginning to take advantage of recently gained insights into the cognitive underpinnings of language and learning.

On this point, this review of the literature indicates that, although there is a substantial body of research investigating the written products of deaf writers and the consequences of implementing various pedagogical practices in writing instruction (see also Albertini & Schley, 2003), there is only a scant research literature on the cognitive processes that underpin and drive text generation. As Singer and Bashir (2004) have suggested, these are the critical foundational variables upon which the writing process depends, and identifying deficits in these variables can go a long way toward explaining the challenges particular writers have with text creation. Akamatsu, Mayer, and Hardy-Braz (2008) frame these challenges for deaf writers in terms of the Catell-Horn-Carroll (CHC) theory—"a three-stratum hierarchical framework of cognitive abilities that postulates a general factor (g) and 10 broad factors (e.g., crystallized intelligence)" which subsume 70 narrow-stratum abilities (e.g., language development) (p. 146). They report that in the hearing population writing is associated with crystallized intelligence (Gc)—knowledge of the language to be written; processing speed (Gs)—automaticity of executing mechanics such as spelling; auditory processing (Ga)—phonological analysis and synthesis, and acquisition of spoken language; and fluid intelligence (Gf)—planning what to say and how to make an argument (for a detailed discussion see McGrew & Knopik, 1993). They argue that these are the foundational variables necessary for the development of all writers, and as such must be accounted for in both research and practice when working with the deaf population—even though these are the areas that are typically viewed as problematic.

Such a view is in line with a cognitive science perspective, shifting the focus of the research, and ultimately the teaching, to the individual writer as the unit of analysis. In shifting the emphasis in this way, it must be stressed that this is not a rationale for a return to a conceptualization of deaf writer as deficient, placing the blame for poor writing on the individual. Rather it should be seen as an opportunity to illuminate the constraints deaf writers face, as a consequence of their hearing loss, so that these constraints can be more fully investigated in research and addressed in practice.

With the advent of newborn hearing screening and advances in amplification technologies, including cochlear implantation, there has probably never been a time in the history of the field when it is more important to look at these issues in depth. There are expectations that earlier identification of hearing loss, with earlier intervention, will result in improved literacy outcomes for many deaf learners. But research work in this area is still in its infancy, especially as it relates to learners with cochlear implants.

Although numerous studies have investigated auditory and spoken language development in the population with cochlear implants (Geers, 2006; Spencer, 2002), there are still few studies that focus on literacy development, and these have tended to focus on reading rather than writing (Connor & Zwolan, 2004; Spencer, Barker, & Tomblin, 2003; Vermeulen, van Bon, Schreuder, & Knoors, 2007; for a review see Marschark, Rhoten, & Fabich, 2007, and Chapter 9, this volume). This presents a unique opportunity to carefully track the writing

development of these learners from the outset, particularly as it pertains to how they manage the cognitive demands of the writing process (see Fagan, Pisoni, Horn, & Dillon, 2007, and Chapter 29, this volume, for a consideration of cognitive process underlying reading). It may be the case that the enhanced access to spoken language via a cochlear implant will have a positive impact on the quality of engagement in the composing process and the written language produced—in ways that no shifts in pedagogy or communication approach have yet accomplished. The challenge will be to sort out how this information can have relevance and impact pedagogy, intervention, and educational practice.

These are exciting research and teaching times. Possibilities for gaining new insights into the processes of writing and learning to write are on the horizon. As more is learned, it may become possible to identify the ways in which deaf writers can be better supported as they engage in the process of text creation, allowing it to become a more meaningful and effective tool for communicating, thinking, and learning. Deaf writers, as all writers, will continue to be staggered by the demands of the writing process. The hope is that less often will they be overwhelmed.

References

Akamatsu, C. T., Mayer, C., & Hardy-Braz (2008). Why considerations of verbal aptitude are important in educating deaf and hard of hearing students. In M. Marschark & P. Hauser (Eds.), *Deaf cognition: Foundations and outcomes* (pp. 131–169). New York: Oxford University Press.

Albertini, J. A., & Meath-Lang, B. (1986). An analysis of student-teacher exchanges in dialogue journal writing. *Journal of Curriculum Theorizing, 7,* 153–201.

Albertini, J. A., Meath-Lang, B., & Harris, D. P. (1994). Voice as muse, message and medium: The views of deaf college students. In K. Yancy (Ed.), *Voices on voice: Perspectives, definitions, inquiry* (pp. 172–190). Urbana, IL: National Council of Teachers of English.

Albertini, J., & Schley, S. (2003). Writing: Characteristics, instruction, and assessment. In M. Marschark & P. Spencer (Eds.), *Oxford handbook of deaf studies, language and education* (pp. 123–135). New York: Oxford University Press.

Alamargot, D., Lambert, E., Thebault, C., & Dansac, C. (2007). Text composition by deaf and hearing middle-school students: The role of working memory. *Reading and Writing, 20,* 333–360.

Anderson, M., Boren, N., Caniglia, J., Howard, W., & Krohn, E. (1980). *Apple tree.* Beaverton, OR: Dormac.

Antia, S. D., & Reed, S. (2005). Written language of deaf and hard of hearing students in public schools. *Journal of Deaf Studies and Deaf Education, 10,* 244–255.

Arfe, B., & Boscolo, P. (2006). Causal coherence in deaf and hearing students' narratives. *Discourse Processes, 42,* 271–300.

Banks, J., Gray, C. Fyfe, R. (1990). The written recall of printed stories by severely deaf children. *British Journal of Educational Psychology, 60,* 192–216.

Bereiter, C., & Scardamalia, M. (1987). *The psychology of written composition*. Mahwah, NJ: Erlbaum.

Berent, G. P. (1996). The acquisition of English syntax. In W. Ritchie & T. Bhatia (Eds.), *Handbook of second language acquisition (pp. 469–506)*. San Diego, CA: Academic Press.

Berent, G. P., Kelly, R. R., Schmitz, K. L., & Kenney, P. (2009). Visual input enhancement via essay coding results in deaf learners' long term retention of improved English grammatical knowledge. *Journal of Deaf Studies and Deaf Education, 14*, 190–204.

Berninger, V. W., & Swanson, H. L. (1994). Modifying Hayes and Flower's model of skilled writing to explain beginning and developing writing. In E. C. Butterfield (Ed.), *Children's writing: Toward a process theory of the development of skilled writing* (pp. 57–81). Greenwich, CT: JAI Press.

Blackwell, P. M., Engen, E., Fischgrund, J. E., & Zarcadoolas, C. (1978). *Sentences and other systems: A language learning curriculum for hearing impaired children*. Washington, DC: A. G. Bell Association for the Deaf.

Bracewell, R., Frederickson, C., & Frederickson, J. D. (1982). Cognitive processes in composing and comprehending discourse. *Educational Psychologist, 17*, 146–164.

Calfee, R. C., & Wilson, K. M. (2004). A classroom-based writing assessment framework. In C. Stone, E. Silliman, B. J. Ehren, & K. Apel (Eds.), *Handbook of language and literacy: Development and Disorders* (pp. 583–599). New York: The Guilford Press.

Cambra, C. (1994). An instructional program approach to improve hearing impaired adolescents' narratives: A pilot study. *The Volta Review, 96*, 237–245.

Campbell, R. (1997). Read the lips: Speculations on the nature and role of lipreading in cognitive development of deaf children. In M. Marschark, P. Siple, D. Lillo-Martin, R. Campbell, & V. Everhart, *Relations of language and thought: The view from sign language and deaf children* (pp. 110–146). New York: Oxford University Press.

Cohen, (1967). Predictability of deaf and hearing story paraphrasing. *Journal of Verbal Learning and Verbal Behavior, 6*, 916–921.

Collins, A. M., & Gentner, D. (1980). A framework for a cognitive theory of writing. In L. W. Gregg & E. R. Steinberg (Eds.), *Cognitive processes in writing* (pp. 51–72). Mahwah, NJ: Lawrence Erlbaum.

Conte, M. P., Rampelli, L. P., & Volterra, V. (1996). Deaf children and the construction of written texts. In C. Pontecorvo & M. Orsolini (Eds.), *Children's early text construction* (pp. 303–319). Hillsdale, NJ: Lawrence Erlbaum Associates.

Connor, C. M., & Zwolan, T. A. (2004). Examining multiple sources of influence on the reading comprehension skills of children who use cochlear implants. *Journal of Speech, Language and Hearing Research, 47*, 509–526.

Conway, D. (1985). Children (re)creating writing: A preliminary look at the purpose of free choice writing of hearing impaired kindergartners. *The Volta Review, 87*, 91–126.

Cook, L. G., Chapman, S. R., & Gamino, J. F. (2007). Impaired discourse gist in pediatric brain injury: Missing the forest for the trees. In K. Cain & J. Oakhill (Eds.), *Children's comprehension problems in oral and written language: A cognitive perspective* (pp. 218–243). New York: The Guilford Press.

Cooper, R. (1967). The ability of deaf and hearing children to apply morphological rules. *Journal of Speech and Hearing, 10*, 77–86.

Costello, E., & Watkins, T. (1975). *Structured tasks for English practice*. Washington, DC: Gallaudet College Press.

deVilliers, P. A. (1991). English literacy development in deaf children: Directions for research and intervention. In J. F. Miller (Ed.), *Research on child language disorders: A decade of progress* (pp. 349–378). Austin, TX: ProEd.

Ericsson, K. A., & Simon, H. A. (1993). *Protocol analysis: Verbal reports as data*. Cambridge, MA: MIT Press.

Ewoldt, C. (1985). A descriptive study of the developing literacy of young hearing impaired children. *The Volta Review, 87*, 109–126.

Fabbretti, D., Volterra, V., & Pontecorvo, C. (1998). Written language abilities in deaf Italians. *Journal of Deaf Studies and Deaf Education, 3*, 231–244.

Fagan, M. K., Pisoni, D. B., Horn, D. L., & Dillon, C. M. (2007). Neuropsychological correlates of vocabulary, reading, and working memory in deaf children with cochlear implants. *Journal of Deaf Studies and Deaf Education, 12*, 461–471.

Flower, L., & Hayes, J. R. (1980). The dynamics of composing: Making plans and juggling constraints. In L. W. Gregg & E. R. Steinberg (Eds.), *Cognitive processes in writing* (pp. 31–50). Mahwah, NJ: Lawrence Erlbaum.

Flower, L., & Hayes, J. R. (1981). A cognitive process theory of writing. *College Composition and Communication, 32*, 365–387.

Gates, A. I., & Chase, E. H. (1926). Methods and theories of learning to spell tested by studies of deaf children. *Journal of Educational Psychology, 17*, 289–300.

Geers, A. (2006). Spoken language in children with cochlear implants. In P. Spencer & M. Marschark (Eds.), *Advances in the spoken language development of deaf and hard of hearing children* (pp. 244–270). New York: Oxford University Press.

Graves, D. (1983). *Writing: Teachers and children at work*. Boston: Heinemann.

Groht, M. (1958). *Natural language for deaf children*. Washington, DC: The Volta Bureau.

Grushkin, D. A. (1998). Why shouldn't Sam read? Toward a new paradigm for literacy and the deaf. *Journal of Deaf Studies and Deaf Education, 3*, 179–204.

Halliday, M. A. K. (1989). *Spoken and written language*. Oxford: Oxford University Press.

Hammill, D. D., & Larsen, S. C. (1996). *Test of written language*, 3rd edition. Austin, TX: Pro-Ed.

Harrison, D. R., Simpson, P. A., & Stuart, A. (1991). The development of written language in a population of hearing impaired children. *The Journal of British Association of Teachers of the Deaf, 15*, 76–85.

Hayes, J. R. (2000). A new framework for understanding cognition and affect in writing. In R. Indrisano & J. R. Squire (Eds.), *Perspectives on writing: Research, theory and practice* (pp. 6–44). Newark, DE: International Reading Association.

Heefner, D. L., & Shaw, P. C. (1996). Assessing the written narratives of deaf students using the six-trait analytical scale. *The Volta Review, 98*, 147–168.

Heider, F., & Heider, G. M. (1941). Comparison of sentence structure of deaf and hearing children. *Volta Review, 43*, 357–360, 536–540, 599–604.

Hermsen, L. M., & Franklin, S. V. (2008). A new research agenda for writing to learn: Embedding cognition in discipline. In M. Marschark & P. Hauser (Eds.), *Deaf cognition: Foundations and outcomes* (pp. 411–438). New York: Oxford University Press.

Hoemann, H. W., Andrews, C. E., Florian, V. A., Hoemann, S. A., & Jensema, C. J. (1976). The spelling proficiency of deaf children. *American Annals of the Deaf, 121*, 489–493.

Johnson, H. A., Padak, N. D., & Barton, L. E. (1994). Developmental strategies of hearing impaired children. *Reading and Writing Quarterly, 10*, 359–367.

Kelly, L. P. (1987). The influence of syntactic anomalies on the writing processes of a deaf college student. In A. Matsuhashi (Ed.), *Writing in real time: Modeling production processes* (pp. 161–196). Norwood, NJ: Ablex Publishing Company.

Kelly, L. P. (1988). Relative automaticity without mastery: The grammatical decision making of deaf students. *Written Communication, 5*, 325–351.

Klecan-Aker, J., & Blondeau, R. (1990). An examination of the written stories of hearing impaired school-age children. *The Volta Review, 92*, 275–282.

Kluwin, T., & Kelly, A. B. (1992). Implementing a successful writing program in public schools for children who are deaf. *Exceptional Children, 59*, 41–53.

Kress, G. (1982). *Learning to write*. London: Routledge and Kegan Paul.

Kretschmer, R. R., & Kretschmer, L. W. (1978). Language development and intervention with the hearing impaired. *Topics in Language Disorders, 9*, 17–32.

Leybaert, J., & Alegria, J. (1995). Spelling development in deaf and hearing children: Evidence from the use of morpho-phonological regularities in French. *Reading and Writing, 7*, 89–109.

Lillo-Martin, D. (1997). The modular effects of sign language acquisition. In M. Marschark, P. Siple, D. Lillo-Martin, R. Campbell, & V. Everhart, *Relations of language and thought: The view from sign language and deaf children* (pp. 62–109). New York: Oxford University Press.

Livingston, S. (1989). Revision strategies of deaf student writers. *American Annals of the Deaf, 134*, 21–26.

Livingston, S. (1997). *Rethinking the education of deaf students*. Portsmouth, NH: Heinemann.

Marschark, M., & Hauser, P. (2008). Cognitive underpinnings of learning by deaf and hard-of-hearing students. In M. Marschark & P. Hauser (Eds.), *Deaf cognition: Foundations and outcomes* (pp. 3–23). New York: Oxford University Press.

Marschark, M., Lang, H., & Albertini, J. (2002). *Educating deaf students: From research to practice*. New York: Oxford University Press.

Marschark, M., Mouradian, V., & Halas, M, (1994). Discourse rules in the language productions of deaf and hearing children. *Journal of Experimental Psychology, 57*, 89–107.

Marschark, M., Rhoten, C., & Fabich, M. (2007). Effects of cochlear implantation on children's reading and academic achievement. *Journal of Deaf Studies and Deaf Education, 12*, 269–302.

Maxwell, M. (1990). Simultaneous communication: The state of the art and proposals for change. *Sign Language Studies, 69*, 333–390.

Maxwell, M. M., & Falick, T. G. (1992). Cohesion and quality in deaf and hearing children's written English. *Sign Language Studies, 77*, 345–371.

Mayer, C. (1994). Action research: The story of a partnership. In G. Wells (Ed.), *Changing schools from within: Creating communities of inquiry* (pp. 151–170). Portsmouth, NH: Heinemann.

Mayer, C. (1998). Deaf children learning to spell. *Research in the Teaching of English, 33*, 158–180.

Mayer, C. (1999). Shaping at the point of utterance: An investigation of the composing processes of the deaf student writer. *Journal of Deaf Studies and Deaf Education 4*, 37–49.

Mayer, C. (2007). What really matters in the early literacy development of deaf children. *Journal of Deaf Studies and Deaf Education, 12*, (411–431).

McAnally, P. L., Rose, S., & Quigley, S. P. (1987). *Language learning practices with deaf children*. Boston: College Hill Press.

McGrew, K., & Knopik, S. N. (1993). The relationship between WJ-R Gf-Gc cognitive clusters and writing achievement across the life span. *School Psychology Review, 22*, 687–695.

Moores, D. (1987). *Educating the deaf: Psychology, principles and practices*. Boston: Houghton Mifflin.

Musselman, C., & Szanto, G. (1998). The written language of deaf adolescents: Patterns of performance. *Journal of Deaf Studies and Deaf Education, 3*, 245–257.

Myklebust, H. R. (1964). *The psychology of deafness*. New York: Grune & Stratton.

Neuroth-Gimbrone, C., & Logiodice, C. (1992). A co-operative bilingual language for deaf adolescents. *Sign Language Studies, 74*, 79–91.

Nystrand, M. (2006). The social and historical context of writing research. In C. A. MacArthur, S. Graham, & J. Fitzgerald (Eds.), *Handbook of writing research* (pp. 11–27). New York: The Guilford Press.

Olson, D. (1977). From utterance to text: The bias of language in speech and writing. *Harvard Educational Review, 47*, 257–281.

Olson, D. (1993). Thinking about thinking: Learning how to take statements and hold beliefs. *Educational Psychologist, 28*, 7–23.

Padden, C. A. (1993). Lessons to be learned from the young deaf orthographer. *Linguistics and Education, 5*, 71–86.

Paul, P. (1998). *Literacy and deafness*. Boston: Allyn and Bacon.

Paul, P. (2001). *Language and deafness*, 3rd edition. San Diego, CA: Singular.

Powers, A. R., & Wigus, S. (1983). Linguistic complexity in the written language of hearing impaired children. *The Volta Review, 85*, 201–210.

Prior, P. (2006). A sociocultural theory of writing. In C. A. MacArthur, S. Graham & J. Fitzgerald (Eds.), *Handbook of writing research* (pp. 54–66). New York: The Guilford Press.

Pritchard, R. J., & Honeycutt, R. L. (2006). The process approach to writing instruction: Examining its effectiveness. In C. A. MacArthur, S. Graham, & J. Fitzgerald (Eds.), *Handbook of writing research* (pp. 275–290). New York: The Guilford Press.

Purcell-Gates, V., Jacobson, E., & Degener, S. (2004). *Print literacy development: Uniting cognitive and social practice theories*. Cambridge, MA: Harvard University Press.

Quigley, S., & King, C. (1980). Syntactic performance of hearing impaired and normal hearing individuals. *Applied Psycholinguistics, 1*, 329–356.

Schirmer, B., Bailey, J., & Fitzgerald, S. M. (1999). Using a writing assessment rubric for writing development of children who are deaf. *Exceptional Children, 65*, 383–397.

Schleper, D. (1992). When "F" spells "Cat: Spelling in a whole language program. *Perspectives in Deaf Education, 11*, 11–14.

Singer, B. D., & Bashir, A. S. (2004). Developmental variation in writing composition skills. In C. Stone, E. Silliman, B. J. Ehren, & K. Apel (Eds.), *Handbook of language and literacy: Development and disorders* (pp. 559–582). New York: The Guilford Press.

Singleton, J. L., Morgan, D., DiGello. E., Wiles, J., & Rivers, R. (2004). Vocabulary use by low. Moderate, and high

ASL-proficient writers compared to hearing ESL and monolingual speakers. Journal of Deaf Studies and Deaf Education, 9, 86–103.

Spandel, V., & Stiggins, R. J. (1997). *Creating writers: Linking writing assessment and instruction*, 2nd edition. New York: Longman.

Spencer, L. J., Barker, B. A., & Tomblin, J. B. (2003). Exploring the language and literacy outcomes of pediatric cochlear implants users. *Ear and Hearing*, 24, 236–247.

Spencer, P. (2002). Language development of children with cochlear implants. In J. B. Christensen & I. Leigh (Eds.), *Cochlear implants in children: Ethics and choices* (pp. 232–249). Washington, DC: Gallaudet University Press.

Stone, C. A. (2004). Contemporary approaches to the study of language and literacy development: An integration of perspectives. In C. Stone, E. Silliman, B. J. Ehren, & K. Apel (Eds.), *Handbook of language and literacy: Development and disorders* (pp. 3–24). New York: The Guilford Press.

Streng, A. H. (1972). *Syntax, speech, and hearing: Applied linguistics for teachers of children with hearing loss and language disabilities*. New York: Grune and Stratton.

Strong, M., & Prinz, P. (2000). Is American Sign Language skill related to English literacy? In C. Chamberlain, J. Morford, & R. Mayberry (Eds.), *Language acquisition by eye* (pp. 131–141). Mahwah, NJ: Lawrence Erlbaum Associates.

Svartholm, K. (2008). The written Swedish of deaf children: A foundation for EFL. In C. J. Kellet Bidoli & E. Ochse (Eds.), *English in international deaf communication* (pp. 211–249). Bern: Peter Lang.

Taeschner, T. (1988). Affixes and function words in the written language of deaf children. *Applied Psycholinguistics*, 9, 385–401.

Templin, M. (1948). A comparison of the spelling achievement of normal and defective hearing subjects. *Journal of Educational Psychology*, 39, 337–346.

Troia, G. (2007). Research in writing instruction: What we know and what we need to know. In M. Pressley, A. K. Billman, K. H. Perry, K. E. Reffitt, & J. Moorehead-Reynolds (Eds.), *Shaping literacy achievement: Research we have, research we need* (pp. 129–156). New York: The Guilford Press.

Truax, R. (1985). Linking research to teaching to facilitate reading-writing communication connections. *The Volta Review*, 87, 155–169.

Vermeulen, A., van Bon, W., Schreuder, R., & Knoors, H. (2007). Reading comprehension of deaf children with cochlear implants. *Journal of Deaf Studies and Deaf Education*, 12, 283–302.

Webster, A. (1986). *Deafness, development and literacy*. London: Methuen.

Weiss, A., & Johnson, C. (1993). Relationships between narrative and syntactic competencies in school-aged, hearing impaired children. *Applied Psycholinguistics*, 14, 35–59.

Wilbur, R. B. (1977). An explanation of deaf children's difficulty with certain syntactic structures. *Volta Review*, 79, 85–92.

Williams, C. L. (1993). Learning to write: Social interaction among preschool auditory/oral and total communication children. *Sign Language Studies*, 80, 267–284.

Wolbers, K. A. (2008). Using balanced and interactive writing instruction to improve the higher order and lower order writing skills of deaf students. *Journal of Deaf Studies and Deaf Education*, 13, 257–277.

Yoshinaga-Itano, C. (1986). Beyond the sentence level: What's in a hearing-impaired child's story? *Topics in Language Disorders*, 6, 71–83.

Yoshinaga-Itano, C., & Downey, D. M. (1992). When a story is not a story: A process analysis of the written language of hearing impaired children. *The Volta Review*, 95, 131–158.

Yoshinaga-Itano, C., & Downey, D. M. (1996). The effect of hearing loss in the development of metacognitive strategies in written language. *The Volta Review*, 98, 97–143.

Yoshinaga-Itano, C., & Snyder, L. S. (1985). Form and meaning in the written language of hearing impaired children. *The Volta Review*, 87, 75–90.

Yoshinaga-Itano, C., Snyder, L. S., & Mayberry, R. (1996a). How deaf and normally hearing students convey meaning within and between sentences. *The Volta Review*, 98, 9–38.

Yoshinaga-Itano, C., Snyder, L. S., & Mayberry, R. (1996b). Can lexical/semantic skills differentiate deaf or hard of hearing readers and nonreaders? *The Volta Review*, 98, 39–61.

Zamel, V. (1983). The composing process of advanced ESL students: Six case histories. *TESOL Quarterly*, 17, 165–187.

Mathematics Instruction and Learning of Deaf and Hard-of-Hearing Students: What Do We Know? Where Do We Go?

Claudia M. Pagliaro

Abstract

In 1994, a group of professionals involved in mathematics education convened at Gallaudet University to discuss the state of mathematics education for deaf and hard-of-hearing (DHH) students. The result was the National Action Plan for Mathematics Education Reform for the Deaf (NAPMERD) (Dietz, 1995), which proposed recommendations for changes in curriculum, pedagogy, teacher preparation, assessment, and research. Since that time, however, student performance in mathematics computation and problem solving, as measured by standardized assessments, has not significantly improved (Allen, 1995; Broadbent & Daniele, 1982; Traxler, 2000). Deaf and hard-of-hearing students continue to perform well below grade level in mathematics, graduating on average with less than a sixth grade achievement level. In light of the NAPMERD report, this chapter provides an overview of research regarding the mathematics instruction and learning of DHH students over the past 25 years (encompassing the 11 years leading up to the NAPMERD report—and coinciding with the beginnings of the National Council of Teachers of Mathematics education reform movement—and the 14 years since). Specifically, this review summarizes what is known regarding the deaf learner's understanding of mathematics and performance with related concepts and the mathematics instruction received by the deaf learner, as well as possible factors surrounding these topics. The chapter highlights gaps in the knowledge base pertaining to mathematics instruction and learning with this population and suggests areas for future research.

Keywords: achievement, deaf, education, hard of hearing, instruction, language, mathematics, number, performance, problem solving, teacher preparation, research

In 1994, a group of professionals involved in mathematics education convened at Gallaudet University to discuss the state of mathematics education for deaf and hard-of-hearing (DHH) students. The result was the *National Action Plan for Mathematics Education Reform for the Deaf* (NAPMERD) (Dietz, 1995), a document recommending alignment of mathematics education for DHH students with the vision of reform put forth by the National Council of Teachers of Mathematics (NCTM) in their historic *Standards* documents (NCTM, 1989, 1991, 1995).

Arguably the NCTM Standards (most recently revised in *Principles & Standards for School Mathematics* [NCTM, 2000]) address the kind of

mathematics education—knowledge and skills— necessary for preparing students to meet the challenges of a technologically advanced, global society. It describes a course of instruction that establishes a foundation in mathematics education for all students while also recognizing the individual learner. There are six principles and ten standards (five content standards and five process standards) that form the basis for this vision. The six principles are Equity ("high expectations and strong support for all"), Curriculum ("coherent, focused on important mathematics, and well articulated across the grades"), Teaching ("understanding what students need to know and need to learn and then challenging and supporting them to learn it well"), Learning ("understanding, actively building new knowledge from experience and prior knowledge"), Assessment ("support[ing] the learning of important mathematics and furnish useful information to both teachers and students), and Technology ("influences the mathematics that is taught and enhances students' learning) (NCTM, 2000, p. 11). The content standards include Number and Operations, Algebra, Geometry, Measurement, and Data Analysis and Probability, while the process standards include Problem Solving, Reasoning and Proof, Communication, Connections, and Representation (NCTM, 2000). The standards are interconnected and apply to all grade levels K–12 (as do the principles), but with varying emphases. In accordance with this vision, the NAPMERD outlines recommendations in the areas of curriculum and pedagogy, assessment, teacher preparation, and research (see Appendix for NAPMERD recommendations).

This chapter is intended to serve as a review of the research related to mathematics education with DHH students over the past 25 years, leading up to and since the NAPMERD report, highlighting themes, and answering the questions: What do we know? And, where do we go?

Where Have We Come From?

In reviewing the empirical research in deaf education related to mathematics instruction and learning over the past 25 years, two broad categories emerge: those studies indicating achievement/performance and those studies seeking to explain that performance.

Achievement and Performance

Studies on achievement and performance over the past two and a half decades have painted a perpetually bleak picture of DHH students' academic progress in mathematics. The most recent data from the Gallaudet Research Institute's norming study on the Stanford Achievement Test, 9th Edition (Traxler, 2000) shows DHH students significantly behind grade level in mathematics procedures (computation) and problem solving (application) throughout their school years. Upon graduation, 50% of DHH students perform below a sixth grade level in procedures and below a fifth grade level in problem solving (Traxler, 2000). This means that, at the age when DHH students are leaving their mandatory K–12 education and heading out to college or into the workforce, half are at best doing so equipped with about a junior high school mathematics education and functioning at a "partial" to "less than partial mastery"—a substandard understanding—of mathematics concepts (Traxler, 2000, p. 341).

Although there is no clear indication as to when this delay in achievement begins, studies show evidence of poor performance in middle, elementary, and even preschool. The Traxler study (2000) revealed that more than 80% of DHH students in both grades four and eight scored at a "basic" or "below basic" level in both procedural performance and problem solving, with half of the fourth graders falling below a third grade level in procedures and at a second grade level in problem solving, and eighth graders scoring at a fourth grade level in both areas. Further, studies on young DHH children by Leybaert and Van Cutsem (2002) in Belgium and Nunes and Moreno (1998a) and Stanwick, Oddy, and Roper (2005) in the United Kingdom found similar results, with DHH children starting their formal academic instruction already behind hearing counterparts by as much as two grade levels.

More recently in the United States, Kritzer (2007a) measured the understanding of foundational mathematics concepts of 29 preschool DHH children (ages 4–6; mean age 4.8 years) on the Test of Early Mathematics Ability (TEMA-3), a norm-referenced assessment and diagnostic tool of foundational mathematics concepts such as number, numeral literacy, simple calculations, and categorization in children ages 3–9 years old. In her study, none of the children except one (an outlier) performed above average according to the normed scores of the test, with half scoring "below average" to "very poor." A pilot study done earlier by Kritzer (2007b) with older children (5–11 years old) found similar results in sorting and classifying objects, critical pre-mathematics skills.

Unfortunately, this poor performance and low achievement in mathematics by DHH students is nothing new. Data from previous norming samples of the 1974, 1982, and 1990 (Allen, 1995) Stanford Achievement Tests show that DHH students have made little progress in mathematics achievement over the past three decades, consistently falling behind their hearing peers by up to 65 points (Allen, 1995; Marschark & Everhart, 1999; Nunes & Moreno, 1998a).

In addition to the picture of overall mathematics performance, several studies in the past 25 years have shown DHH students to be behind in their mathematical understanding of more specific concepts such as fractions, geometry, and problem solving. For example, Titus (1992) conducted a study comparing two groups of DHH and hearing students, ages 10–12 and 13–15, on their understanding of fractions. Measuring their abilities to identify and order equivalent fractions, she found that both age groups of DHH students presented a low level of understanding of fractional numbers. Older deaf students often used similar strategies and made similar errors as younger hearing students, including choosing the greater fraction as the one having the "larger counting numbers" within it—an error typically made by those with beginning or weak conceptual understanding of fractions. Titus concluded that deaf students are delayed in their understanding of fractions by up to 3 years.

Likewise, research has shown a significant weakness in DHH students' level of understanding of geometry concepts. Mason (1995) found knowledge of geometry among a group of DHH students ages 7–11 years (and sadly that of their teacher as well) to be at a beginning level of understanding (visualization). Shockingly, Kemp (1990, 2004) found similar results among 173 DHH college students, where more than 70% tested at just the first level of the van Hiele scales of geometry knowledge (two levels below that which is expected of students to understand *high school* geometry). Even after some intervention, no student in the Mason study and only 17% of the students in the Kemp study reached a van Hiele level two.

PROBLEM SOLVING

Problem solving is a predominant area in the research on mathematics performance of DHH students over the past 25 years, perhaps due to its emphasis in the NCTM *Principles & Standards* (2000) and in most curricula and textbooks today. These studies have primarily focused on student success and strategy use in solving problems presented in various forms, including written language (Hyde, Zevenbergen, & Power, 2003; Kelly & Mousley, 2001; Serrano Pau, 1995), graphics or animation (Frostad & Ahlberg, 1999), numerics (i.e., computation equations) (Chien, 1993; Frostad, 1999; Secada, 1984), and sign language (Ansell & Pagliaro, 2006). Results are fairly consistent across presentation modes and age ranges, showing some areas in which DHH students perform similarly to hearing students and other areas in which they differ.

Relative Difficulty

Several studies from across the globe, including Ansell and Pagliaro (2006) and Kelly and Mousley (2001) (United States); Frostad and Ahlberg (1999) (Norway), Hyde, Zevenbergen, and Power (2003) (Australia); and Serrano Pau (1995) (Spain) investigated the relative difficulty of problems for DHH

students as indicated by student success rates. Although each study presented the problems differently (Ansell & Pagliaro [ASL]; Frostad & Ahlberg [animation without words/signs]; Kelly & Mousley and Hyde et al. [English], and Serrano Pau [Spanish]), the results were similar. The easier problems tended to be those having the least amount of inference; that is, where the story and/or presentation of numbers matched an equation such as a + b = ?. Problems in which the unknown was either in the "middle"—i.e., the change position (e.g., a + ? = c)—or in the beginning or start position (e.g., ? + b = c) were of increased difficulty, respectively. Thus, a problem with the result unknown (e.g., John has nine cars. He gives Sarah four cars. How many cars does John have now?) would most likely be easier to solve than a problem having the change unknown (e.g., John has nine cars. He gives Sara some cars. Now John has five cars. How many cars did he give to Sarah?), and much easier than problems in which the start is unknown (e.g. John has some cars. He gives Sarah four cars. Now John has five cars left. How many cars did John have to start?). Problems that were considered to be the most difficult were compare problems; that is, those problems in which two sets are compared (e.g., John is 5 ft tall. Sarah is 4 ft tall. How much taller is John than Sarah?).

Although some researchers claim that the relative difficulty of the given problems are the result of the reading difficulties experienced by DHH students (see Language section), the fact that similar results have been noted regardless of the way in which the problems are presented points to something beyond simply reading or language proficiency (see Chapter 9, this volume). In fact, the aforementioned findings are typical for hearing students as well, although with some major differences. For example, whereas young (primary level) hearing students may also find a problem with a missing result or end quantity easier than one in which the beginning quantity or middle quantity is missing (Carpenter & Moser, 1984), the critical dimension in problem difficulty for these children seems to be the presence or absence of explicit action in the problem situation. Carpenter and Moser (1984) found that problems were easier for primary-level hearing children to solve when the story or problem context involved an explicit action (either joining or separating) versus when no action was included (e.g., part–whole and comparisons). In studies with DHH students, however, that critical dimension in problem difficulty seems to be based on the canonical operation typically used to solve the problem, not the story within the problem. That is, findings show a division in problem difficulty whereby easier problems required the quantities to be put together (finding a sum) and more difficult problems required a quantity to be divided or separated (finding a difference) (Ansell & Pagliaro, 2006; Serrano Pau, 1995).

Still another distinction between DHH and hearing students that may impact problem solving is their understanding of time factors present in problem contexts. Nunes and Moreno (1997, 2002) found that, although DHH students and hearing students were similar in their processing of sequential information that was strictly chronological, their processing of information for which an inference about the time sequence was needed differed. After observing teachers and students in mathematics more broadly, Nunes (2004) concluded that processing of time factors was just one example of the way in which DHH and hearing students differ in how they encode and remember information, with these differences affecting their learning.

Differences in the relative difficulty of the problems, by age, in studies that included participants from a wide age range suggest a "delay" in DHH students' success. However, because of the distinct differences in problem difficulty just outlined, a "difference" may be a more appropriate conclusion, perhaps resulting from different learning styles and/or cognitive organization.

Solution Strategies

Another difference, or perhaps delay depending on your perspective, in problem solving comes in relation to strategy use. Studies on problem solving show no difference in the kinds of strategy types used by DHH students and hearing students, regardless of the way in which those problems are presented. Both groups make use of modeling strategies in which each quantity in the problem is physically represented and acted upon, counting strategies in which one quantity is used as a starting point to a number string while the other is used as a marker, and fact-based strategies in which solvers use a known fact to determine the answer. The pattern of development, however, and the use of those strategies seem to differ between DHH and hearing students. Young hearing children tend to primarily make use of modeling strategies first, then counting, then fact-based strategies, progressing in general from the more concrete to the more abstract (Briars & Larkin, 1984; Carpenter, Fennema, Franke, Levi, & Empson, 1999; Riley, Greeno, & Heller, 1983). However, although studies do show that there is a

tendency for successful DHH problem solvers to move to more concrete strategies for more difficult problems (Ansell & Pagliaro, 2006), and for older DHH students to make more use of abstract strategies than younger students (Frostad, 1999; Kelly & Mousley, 2001), overall, DHH students tend to make primary use of counting strategies with little use of modeling strategies (Ansell & Pagliaro; 2006; Kelly & Mousley, 2001). Ansell and Pagliaro's (2006) study of 59 K–3 DHH children from across the United States showed an overwhelming use of counting strategies at all grade levels regardless of the success that the children had with the problems. (Very few fact-based strategies were used across all students.) As with the pattern of problem difficulty, this dissimilarity in pattern of strategy use is thought by some researchers to be a "delay" in DHH students' problem-solving and by others as a "difference" influenced by the unique experiential, linguistic, and educational experiences of these students.

Other researchers who investigated problem solving, but in a more general way, also found delays or differences in the problem-solving strategies and success of DHH and hearing students. Luckner and McNeill (1994) matched 43 DHH students with an equal number of hearing students and compared their performances on the Tower of Hanoi. The Tower of Hanoi is a puzzle whereby the solver must move five discs of different sizes from the first peg on a board to the third peg in the least number of moves possible. Discs must be moved one at a time and no larger disc can ever sit atop a smaller disc. Luckner and McNeill found significant differences across age levels between DHH and hearing participants, although there was in both groups an increase in ability with age, with DHH participants "closing the gap" (p. 375). Marschark and Everhart (1999) also looked at general problem-solving strategies. They studied patterns of response in the game "20 Questions" among two age groups of DHH and hearing students (7- to 14-year-olds; college students). Across both groups, DHH students employed different strategies that the authors judged to be "less efficient" and "less sophisticated" than those of the hearing students. In addition, 7- to 14-year-old DHH students were less successful than hearing peers; however, no difference was found in success between the older groups. Once again, because of the difference in results between age groups, the researchers in both of these studies also judge the performance of the DHH participants to represent a delay in problem solving as compared to hearing students.

Delay or difference, the studies outlined earlier in this chapter provide evidence that DHH students may consider and respond to mathematics differently than their hearing peers, perhaps affecting their performance and ultimately their achievement. In summary, while there is no denying that a disparity in performance and achievement exists in mathematics between DHH students and their hearing counterparts, questions remain as to the reasons for the disparity. Although limited, researchers over the past 25 years have sought to answer this question, focusing attention to such possible contributing factors as fundamental mathematics understanding, language, and instruction.

Possible Factors in Mathematics Performance by Deaf and Hard-of-Hearing Students

NUMBER KNOWLEDGE AND PROCESSING

Although the cognitive capacity and capability of DHH persons are comparable to those of hearing persons (Barham & Bishop, 1991; Moores, 2001), the encoding of information (in memory) and resulting cognitive organization of concepts may be different (Marschark, Lang, & Albertini, 2002). The linguistic and experiential differences DHH children have, compared to their hearing peers, determine how they explore what is around them and can provide a different foundation for later, more formal, learning of concepts. Further, the extent to which these experiences are used and are discussed and/or mediated can have a profound impact on what is learned and how it is recalled. Although no study was found that specifically tested the effect of early experiences on mathematics, evidence suggests limited incidental learning opportunities and informal learning experiences are possible factors in the poor mathematics performance of DHH students (Kritzer, 2009; Nunes & Moreno, 1998a, 2002). Along these lines, several studies have investigated the fundamental mathematics understanding of DHH persons as a possible contributing factor for DHH students' low mathematics achievement. These studies have focused almost exclusively on early number knowledge and number processing.

Several studies focused on early number knowledge and processing as exhibited in adults (Bull, Marschark, & Blatto-Vallee, 2005; Bull, Blatto-Vallee, & Fabich, 2006; Epstein, Hillegeist, & Grafman, 1994; Korvorst, Nuerk, & Willems, 2007). These studies presented the numbers to the participants in sign and/or Arabic numerals, with no significant difference in the results. Two such studies by Bull

and colleagues (2005, 2006) used visual enumeration and magnitude processing as an indication of numerical understanding in deaf and hearing adults ages 18–28 years. Three tasks were used in these studies: subitizing, that is, identifying the number of elements in small sets (1–4 elements) without having to count; the Spatial Numerical Association of Response Codes (SNARC), in which the magnitude of a number is thought of spatially as on a number line, with lesser quantities represented to the left and greater quantities represented to the right; and Stroop-like tasks in which the identification of number and magnitude are interfered with in various ways. For example, in Bull and colleagues' 2006 study, subjects were asked to indicate spatially (by pressing specific computer keys to the left or right) which number was greater in the following pair: 3 1. This represents a Stroop task, as the numeral "3" is presented smaller in relation to the numeral "1," although the magnitude of the number 3 is greater than the number 1. It is a SNARC task in that the numeral "1" is presented to the right of the numeral "3," incongruent with a number line. In both studies, results showed that DHH adults were similar to hearing adults in their processing of basic numerical information.

In another study of adult understanding of number, Korvorst, Nuerk, and Willmes (2007) presented DHH adults in Germany with a task in which they were shown a specific set of three numbers (triplets) and asked to respond whether the middle number was "the exact numerical middle" (p. 366); that is, representing an equal difference from each of the other two numbers. The numbers were presented in both Arabic and signed form. As in Bull and colleagues' (2005, 2006) studies, the DHH subjects here performed similarly to the hearing subjects, although somewhat slower when the stimuli were presented in Arabic form.

An early study by Epstein and colleagues (1994) also showed no difference in number processing—here determined by three tasks including "magnitude comparison, calculation verification, and short-term memory span" (p. 336)—between DHH and hearing subjects, although DHH subjects were consistently slower in responding. This time difference increased with an increase in problem difficulty, the inclusion of greater numbers, and an increased tax on working memory.

Only one study was found that focused on understanding of number in children. Zarfaty, Nunes, and Bryant (2004) compared 3- and 4-year-old DHH children's ability to represent number with that of hearing peers. They found that the DHH children performed as well (temporal presentation) or better (spatial presentation) in their ability to remember and reproduce a specific set given nonlinguistically.

Although the implication of these studies seems to indicate that number knowledge and number processing are not factors in the mathematics difficulties exhibited by DHH students, one must note that the ways in which number sense was measured in these studies reflects only a portion of what would constitute "number sense." Further studies should continue to address these measures, as well as others including the use of benchmarks and flexible manipulations of numbers (e.g., decomposition/recomposition, relative operational effects, and estimation).

LANGUAGE

Language was a second area targeted as a contributing factor to the poor performance and achievement of DHH students in mathematics, including difficulties with spoken, written, and signed systems. The link between language and cognitive development is strong (Marschark et al., 2002; Mayberry, 2002; Schick, deVilliers, deVilliers, & Hoffmeister, 2002). Deaf and hard-of-hearing children who have early and complete access to a true language perform better academically than those for whom language acquisition has been delayed or is not fully accessible. This, however, is not the case for most DHH students. Over 90% of children who are deaf or hard of hearing, who obviously have limited access to an oral language, have hearing parents (Moores, 2001; Mitchell & Karchmer, 2002), the majority of whom do not sign or have limited proficiency in some form of sign language (Moores, 2001). Thus, the interaction between hearing parents and their DHH child is often limited to directive, surface-level communication (Charleson, Bird, & Strong, 1999; Evans, 1995, 1998; Jamieson, 1994; Spencer, Bodner-Johnson, & Gutfreund, 1992; Wedell-Monnig & Lumley, 1980), which does not allow for positive, rich, mediating experiences (Kritzer, 2008). Studies of parent–child interactions reveal that the nature of parental feedback, guidance, emphasis on use of language, and overall responsiveness when children are toddlers was predictive of their achievement later in school (Hart & Risely, 2003). Such learning is well-documented in mathematics (Saxe, Guberman, & Gearhart, 1987; Walkerdine, 1988). A recent study that related mathematics achievement with DHH children and their experiences at home (Kritzer, 2008) showed that those who scored higher on a standardized early mathematics ability test tended to have clear communication and more meaningful mediated interactions with adult figures in the home. These parents were able to take advantage of everyday activities asking higher-quality questions that helped the child build understanding by enhancing and making connections between concepts.

In school, language is likewise critical for building the knowledge of individual students. In mathematics, it is the vehicle for discussing and learning abstract concepts. The research over the past 25 years has shown the impact of this important relationship, highlighting issues related to a DHH child's language abilities, whether oral, written, or signed.

Specific structures and features of language have also been shown to impact DHH students' mathematics performance. For example, in studies of English (whether spoken or written), researchers (Hyde et al., 2003; Kelly & Mousley, 2001; Kelly, Lang, Mousley, & Davis, 2003; Kidd & Lamb, 1993; Kidd, Madsen, & Lamb, 1993) have reported all of the following to cause some level of hindrance to DHH students' learning of mathematical concepts and/or performance in problem solving:

- Use of conditionals (i.e., if/then statements), comparatives (e.g., greater than), negatives, and inferentials (e.g., knowing boys and girls are children)
- Words with different meanings within and outside mathematics (e.g., interest or square [which has multiple meanings both in and out of mathematics])
- Multiple ways to express a single idea (e.g., active vs. passive voice)
- Varied forms that have related but specific and importantly distinct meanings (e.g., "multiply, multiplicand, multiplier, multiplication"; year vs. yearly; hundred vs. hundreds vs. hundredth)
- Abbreviations (e.g., lb.) and symbols ("/" meaning a fraction bar or "per" as in "per year"; "x" as a algebraic variable vs. as a symbol for multiplication)
- Technical vocabulary exclusive to mathematics (such as annual rate)

In addition, it is well documented that DHH students experience difficulty with the reading and comprehension of written text (Allen, 1995; Traxler, 2000). This difficulty—related to overall reading performance, word/phrase comprehension, and syntactic-semantic comprehension—has been shown to have a direct impact on the performance and understanding of mathematics. Results from every study that investigated mathematics and reading over the past 25 years have shown reading proficiency to be significantly correlated with mathematics success and performance, regardless of the mathematics investigated (Kelly & Gaustad, 2007; Kelly et al., 2003; Kelly & Mousley, 1999) Kelly and Mousley (2001) compared the effect of reading level among college students on success with computation problems versus word or story problems. They concluded that reading skill not only impacted success, but also may have played a role in the errors that students made, including not answering a problem and/or having difficulty with understanding relationships between computation and word problems. Reading level was also shown to be positively correlated with mental calculations (Davis & Kelly, 2003) among DHH college students. Here, the researchers conclude that poor reading ability may (a) limit a student's experiences with mathematics and mathematics learning, and (b) overburden working memory during problem solving because reading skills that would typically easily transfer to mathematics must now be part of problem solving (see Chapter 30, this volume).

It is hypothesized that the unfamiliar and often esoteric nature of oral/written languages like English may cause confusion for DHH students when learning mathematics and add strain on working memory when solving problems (Kelly et al., 2003). Supportive of this theory, a study by Lang and Pagliaro (2007) found that the DHH students had more success in recalling those mathematical (geometry) terms with which they were familiar and which had a high level of imagery associated with them; that is, when the word conjured a picture in the minds of the students, although not necessarily representing a concrete object. (Concreteness and signability were not found to predict recall, however.) Familiar words that invoke strong images, therefore, would not tax working memory—thus allowing the solver to focus attention on meaningful aspects in solving the problem.

Signed Languages and Mathematics
Other studies have looked at mathematics presented to DHH students in sign language. Findings from these investigations suggest that select features of sign language may also influence mathematics learning—either positively or negatively (Ansell & Pagliaro, 2001; Bryant, 1995; Frostad, 1999; Frostad & Ahlberg, 1996; Mason, 1995; Nunes & Moreno, 1998b; Pagliaro & Ansell, 2007; Secada, 1984). For example, factors related to the representation of

number and counting in signed languages are said to be either a hindrance and/or assistance to problem solving and mathematics understanding.

Leybaert and Van Cutsem (2002) studied the development of counting in signing DHH children in Belgium. The counting system in Belgian French Sign Language (BFSL) has a base-5 structure, similar to ASL, although different in actual sign (for example, "three" in BFSL is shown by extending the index, middle, and ring fingers with palm facing the signer, whereas in ASL, "three" is represented with the extension of the thumb, index, and middle finger with palm facing the signer). A base-5 signing structure means that number signs follow a progression of related movements and/or handshapes until the fifth term in the sequence, after which there is a distinct change in sign formation. For example, in ASL number signs for 1–5 are made by extending an additional finger (showing the number of elements in the set), a shift in base formation then takes place for 6, with 6–9 represented by simply moving the thumb to the next finger (pinkie to index). At 10, there is another shift in base form of the sign. Leybaert and Van Cutsem hypothesized a link between the linguistic counting system of BFSL and Belgian DHH children's learning of the number sequence/counting. They analyzed the performance of 17 DHH children between the ages of 3 and 7 years on three tasks: abstract counting ability (i.e., rote counting as high as they could), object counting, and creating a given number of objects. Results showed that the DHH children were delayed by 2 years in their signed number production, making errors that reflect the base-5 counting system (e.g., breaks or errors in form at the signs for 6 and 16 where base-form changes occur). The DHH children were more accurate, however, in their performance of object counting and in creating sets, performing beyond what would be expected of a child with their rote counting performance, and indicating a better overall understanding and labeling of quantities than that of the hearing students.

In his early study, Secada (1984) reasoned that the ease and transparency of the counting system in ASL caused DHH children's counting to be rote-like, meaning the children could "count" by simply moving to the next finger without really understanding the concept of number and its representation. He reasoned that errors in counting exhibited by DHH children were possibly due then to a misunderstanding of the production rules or the difficulties in forming some numbers, particularly at major points of change in handshape or base form (moving from 5 to 6 for example).

Nunes and Moreno (1998b) also claimed that young DHH children's ability to compute successfully was influenced by the signed counting system, as indicated by errors found in their counting production after being taught a signed algorithm. They claimed that the errors show a negative influence on computation processes in signing young DHH children. Although an influence of signing on the process of computation is probable, the authors failed to take into account the mathematical understanding necessary to successfully use the algorithm, such as the commutative property and cardinality; therefore, the level of impact that signed numbers truly have remains unknown.

Although these studies point to possible negative effects of sign counting on mathematics understanding and problem solving, others over the years have suggested potential assets to mathematics learning. Much like the situation in other cultures whose languages hold meaningful indications to mathematics concepts like place value (e.g., in Japanese, the word for 12 is literally "ten two"; Fuson, 1992; Fuson & Kwan, 1992), some believe that there may be benefit in creating opportunities to build on the counting systems in signed languages (Frostad, 1999; Frostad & Ahlberg, 1996; Pagliaro & Ansell, 2007). For example, in ASL (and many other signed languages), there is a denotation of cardinality inherent in the signs for the numbers 1 through 5 (i.e., the number of fingers shown in the sign match the value the sign represents) that may affect understanding of number.

In addition, DHH solvers of story problems who use sign as their primary mode of communication have been shown to make use of this cardinality aspect, easily "toggling" between the sign as the label for the set and the sign as either a manipulative representation of the elements within the set and/or as a way to keep track of their counting, positively affecting success and strategy choice (Ansell & Pagliaro, 2006; Pagliaro & Ansell, 2007). For example, signing, primary-level DHH children in the Pagliaro and Ansell study were presented a story problem (in ASL) in which the sum of the two quantities (8 and 3) was unknown; most children put out the sign EIGHT on one hand and the sign THREE on the other. They then made use of the three raised fingers on the THREE sign as markers to keep track of the number of counts needed to increment the sequence on the other hand (9, 10, 11). The use of this aspect was seen across problems. For problems that had both quantities greater than 5, some children "separated" one of the quantities into two smaller quantities (addends) to facilitate the use of

toggling. For example, splitting the number 7 by first putting out the sign FOUR and counting back from 11 on each finger (toggling) (10, 9, 8, 7), then putting out the sign THREE and continuing to count back, marking the count on each finger (6, 5, 4). Use of the cardinality of the number signs allowed the child a more efficient procedure with less chance of error or miscount. Use of the raised fingers, while also having the number sign present, assured the children of the correct number of markers to use.

Frostad (1999) and Pagliaro and Ansell (2007) conclude that the cardinality in the counting system in sign language—the sign's close relationship to the concept—may thus act as an "aid" to DHH students' solution strategies. They also warn, however, that if not properly supported with appropriate, conceptually-based instruction, students may develop a procedural understanding and apply the principle of cardinality to number signs for which it is not appropriate (e.g., number signs above 5 in ASL).

In the understanding of geometric figures, too, researchers point to the close sign–concept relationship as having an effect on learning. Studies by Mason (1995) and Bryant (1995) postulate that many of the signs used for geometric forms (e.g., "triangle") caused misconceptions regarding the properties of the figures and the position in space that they may take. For example, in Mason's study of geometrical knowledge of a class of five deaf students, the students were asked to categorize and label various triangles (right triangles, scalene triangles, equilateral triangles, etc.). All but one of the students in the study grouped the figures into two groups—triangles and "not triangles"—with those identified as triangles being only the equilateral or isosceles triangles. Mason hypothesizes that the students were focusing on the iconicity of the sign they used for triangle (an outline of an equilateral triangle with one side at the bottom) and thus grouped only those figures as "triangles." Thus, the sign for "triangle" was not perceived to be the linguistic symbol representing conceptual properties, but rather a true picture and definition of a triangle. Both Bryant (1995) and Mason (1995), while conceding that this could be because of the overall low level of geometric knowledge displayed by the students, hypothesized that the iconic nature of the sign could have been a negative influence, interfering with a student's "ability to consider inclusion relationships" and perhaps limiting the learner's ability to fully understand the concept.

Research on the signed presentation of story problems indicates that teachers of DHH students must also consider issues of language, particularly regarding translations of story problems into sign (Ansell & Pagliaro, 2001). In an effort to bypass linguistic obstacles, teachers of DHH students may choose to translate problems from oral or written modes to sign language; however, no standardized signs exist for many mathematics concepts (and there is debate as to whether they should). This circumstance creates great variety in the ways in which mathematics concepts are signed by teachers, which in turn may cause confusion for students as they build their knowledge and move from teacher to teacher. In a study by Ansell and Pagliaro (2001), teachers were asked to sign basic arithmetic story problems given to them in written English as they would for their DHH students. Results showed that in doing so, they unknowingly changed the semantic structure of the problem, resulting in substantially different mathematical situations. In an instructional situation, then, students would not be solving the same problem in sign as was originally presented to them in a textbook, for example. These results indicate that deaf education teachers are not fully considering (and most likely do not have the knowledge needed to do so) the relationship between language and mathematics for their students, a practice supported by the NCTM Standards (NCTM, 2000).

Further evidence can be found in the results of an earlier study by Pagliaro and Ansell (2000) on teachers' knowledge and beliefs of their students' success with story problems. Remarks of primary-level deaf education teachers revealed an overwhelming, but superficial, awareness of linguistic issues. Surface-level language characteristics were more prevalent than features associated with the linguistic-related, mathematical structure of the problem. For example, teachers focused on the presence or absence of keywords/signs, word order, problem length, or contextual features such as names and places used in the problem. The degree to which the teachers' discussion was permeated by ideas about language is indicative of the importance language has in the education of the DHH child. Whether spoken, written, or signed, expressive or receptive, language seemed to underlie teachers' thought processes; however, there is little evidence that teachers are aware of the profound impact that language has on their students' mathematics learning. Thus, while the link between language and cognitive development is strong (Marschark et al., 2002; Mayberry, 2002; Schick et al., 2002), the question remains as to how teachers can take advantage of the positive aspects of language and diminish its negative effects on mathematics understanding.

INSTRUCTION

Instruction is a final area of research that has been looked at as a contributing factor in the poor performance of DHH students in mathematics. Despite several studies showing the benefits of reform-based interventions and strategies (Martin 1987; Martin, Craft, & Sheng, 2001; Mousley & Kelly, 1998; Nunes & Moreno, 2002), and nonempirical articles that urge mathematics reform (Daniele, 1993; Dietz, 1994; Fridriksson & Stewart, 1988) and provide suggestions and clear examples of curricula, units, and lessons (Dietz, 1991a,b; Dublmeier & Fields, 1996; Hartman, 1994; Horten & Katz-Kaseff,1991; Robinson & Cash, 1996), survey research studies show mathematics instruction for DHH students to be far from the recommended practices of NAPMERD and the NCTM *Principles and Standards*. These studies show a continued emphasis on memorization, drilling, and practice exercises/worksheets, rarely allowing students to investigate open-ended problems or include/integrate other disciplines or writing. Less than half of the teachers surveyed in several studies included any kind of group work or cooperative learning (Kelly et al., 2003; Pagliaro, 1998b; Pagliaro & Ansell, 2002; Pagliaro & Kritzer, 2005), and there is reportedly limited use of technology (Allen, 1995; Pagliaro, 1998b; Pagliaro & Kritzer, 2005) despite several studies throughout the past 25 years that support its use in mathematics education of DHH students—particularly as a tool to enhance or promote true problem solving and to increase active participation and success (Campbell, Neill, & Dudley, 1989; Innes, 1985; Liu, Chou, Liu, & Yang, 2006; Wilson, 1989),

Although "problem solving" does seem to be a part of the current mathematics curriculum (Kelly et al., 2003b; Pagliaro & Kritzer, 2005; Pagliaro, 1998b), the quality of problem-solving opportunities is questionable. Investigations show a very traditional approach to mathematics instruction, in which problem solving is left for the application of previously taught concepts and procedures (Pagliaro & Ansell, 2002). Kelly et al. (2003) investigated problem solving among teachers at the middle school and high school levels from across instructional settings (68 center schools; 64 mainstream programs). A total of 133 sixth to twelfth grade teachers of DHH students from across the United States responded to a survey about their classroom practices in regard to problem solving. Results showed that teachers more often give their students familiar, one-step "practice exercises" than they do "true problem solving," in which students must synthesize information and think critically in order to solve the problem.

Overall, the present state of mathematics instruction within deaf education makes it unlikely that DHH students have opportunities for challenging problem solving in which they would use higher-order cognitive functions and thinking skills, such as analyzing, synthesizing, and evaluating information. In addition, the often-used direct instruction of strategies in problem solving may result in students not developing the metacognitive skills that are critical to their success in mathematics (Marschark et al., 2002). The reasons most often given for teachers' continued use of a traditional approach to mathematics instruction include a disbelief that DHH students are able to perform under a reform-based curriculum, time constraints, and teachers' own lack of preparation and knowledge about mathematics and mathematics education (Easterbrooks,. Stephenson, & Mertens, 2006; Pagliaro & Kritzer, 2005).

Teacher Preparation

The importance of teachers' knowledge to successful instruction has been the focus of much research among the general education population (Fennema & Franke, 1992; Ma, 1999; Mewborn, 2003; Shulman, 1986). Teachers' knowledge includes subject-matter knowledge, general pedagogical knowledge, and pedagogical content knowledge (teachers' knowledge of students' thinking within a specific domain, as well as knowledge of ways to make that content understandable to others). Within deaf education as well, studies have found a positive relationship between content-area preparation and instructional practices/knowledge (Kelly et al., 2003b; Lang & Pagliaro, 2007; Pagliaro and Ansell, 2002). For example, Pagliaro and Ansell (2002) found a positive correlation between the number of mathematics education courses taken by primary-level deaf education teachers and the frequency of their use of problem solving (via story problems) in their instruction, a practice that is supported in the reform documents in both general education (NCTM, 1989, 1991, 1995, 2000) and deaf education (Dietz, 1995). Thus, teachers' preparation may have a direct link to student achievement. Further, the preparation of teachers is particularly important given the unique circumstances of the deaf learner.

Despite the strong and obvious need for, and indications of the positive effect of, preparation on

teachers' knowledge and beliefs and instructional change—as well as suggestions given over the past 25 years by professionals in the field—study upon study in the field of deaf education has shown insufficient preparation of teachers in mathematics (Dietz, 1995; Kelly et al., 2003b; Kluwin & Moores, 1985; Pagliaro, 1998a; Pagliaro & Kritzer, 2005). In three national studies that involved teachers across grades K–12, no more than 41% and as little as 14% of teachers in any one of the studies (sample sizes ranging from 133–290 (mean = 188) had a mathematics-related degree and/or certificate.

Surveys of teacher education programs for preservice teachers of DHH students reveal a program of preparation that focuses on language and communication to the virtual exclusion of content-area disciplines (Jones & Ewing, 2002; Moores & Martin, 2006). Thus, while preservice preparation allows deaf education teachers to bring to their instruction abundant knowledge in the communication needs of their students, it leaves them generally unprepared in the content-specific knowledge required for effective instructional decisions in the mathematics classroom.

Although the relatively recent legislation of No Child Left Behind and its mandate for "highly qualified" teachers may now force the issue of having at least some preparatory coursework in mathematics education, research reviewed here has shown that taking a course in general mathematics education is *not* adequate and *not* the same as taking a course in teaching mathematics to DHH students. Deaf education professionals must make sure that the preparation of future teachers for DHH students includes knowledge and experience in mathematics instruction and learning appropriate to the DHH learner.

Summary and Conclusions

In reviewing the studies of the past 25 years, with a particular eye to the NCTM Standards and to the NAPMERD recommendations, it is clear that, although researchers and educators have made some progress, there is still a very long way to go. We have barely begun to address what is needed to improve DHH students' performance and achievement in mathematics. So, where do we go from here? The reviewed studies offer the following suggestions for research, practice, and teacher preparation.

Research

A variety of studies have demonstrated that DHH students, on average, struggle with mathematics. However, it is also known that some DHH students are successful in mathematics and specifically in problem solving. What is not known is why these students are successful while so many others are not. The research also tells us that although language proficiency plays a big part in this success, it is not the only factor in it. Thus, future studies are needed in defining how the DHH learner, in general, approaches and organizes mathematics concepts and problem solving given specific and often unique circumstances regarding language, experience, and prior knowledge. A focus is needed not only on the deficits that DHH students experience in mathematics learning, but also specifically and in particular on what successful problem solvers and students of mathematics who are deaf or hard of hearing do—how they think, what strategies they use, and in general how the successful deaf learner organizes concepts. Investigations are also needed on the impact of language—oral, written, and signed—on their success and conceptual organization. It is important to identify not just whether language has an impact, but the specific ways in which language plays a part or can play a part in mathematics learning and successful problem solving for DHH students. Finally, research is needed to identify those instructional methods, techniques, and/or materials that support DHH students' success in mathematics learning and problem solving, and to identify those concepts and strategies from general education that need to be adapted or modified, given the unique linguistic and experiential makeup of DHH learners.

Practice

Despite all the indications and the explicit suggestions for including reform-based strategies, practices, and curricula into mathematics instruction, the research shows that current practice with DHH students does not reflect those standards put forth by the NCTM documents and supported by the NAPMERD. Experts in the field continue to call for more work and specific attention to troublesome areas, particularly true problem solving and conceptually based learning. Specifically, researchers stress that more experience is needed in the following learning activities: (a) solving and constructing story/word problems of various kinds, presented in various forms as the basis for mathematical thinking, communication, and higher-order concepts; (b) more, and more explicit, use and teaching of technical mathematics vocabulary, including discussing mathematical versus generic meanings, incorporating reading and language arts strategies into mathematics instruction, and using conceptually

accurate signs and fingerspelling with visual reinforcement when appropriate; and (c) integrating mathematics concepts and thinking skills throughout the curriculum to promote minds-on, authentic problem solving and encourage analysis and explanation across disciplines.

Teacher Preparation

Obviously, nothing can happen in the classroom unless teachers are fully prepared to execute the recommendations put forth in the literature. Teachers need knowledge of mathematics content, of proposed pedagogy, and of their own students as learners (see Chapter 4, this volume). The literature supports the need for reform-based professional development programs to work with in-service teachers to improve their instruction in mathematics. In addition, specific coursework focusing on adaptations and modifications in mathematics instruction that meet the unique learning needs of DHH students should be required of preservice teachers. Teacher preparation programs, state licensure boards, and hiring officials (particularly administrators) should follow what they know and what the research shows to be true— that simple "workshops" or superficial "credit for time" programs, in which preservice and in-service teachers are given credit for attendance, are insufficient to truly address the needs of DHH students. A commitment must be made to ongoing instruction and mentorship of teachers in mathematics education that includes explicit attention to diverse student needs, planning and time management, conceptual development, and higher-order thinking skills.

Of course, none of the aforementioned by itself is sufficient or can stand alone—all are interdependent. A teacher cannot appropriately instruct a deaf or hard-of-hearing learner when what is truly *appropriate* instruction for a DHH learner, and how a DHH learner organizes information and mathematical concepts is unknown. Teacher preparation programs cannot properly educate teachers of DHH learners if *proper* instructional practices are not empirically defined. Furthermore, the true potential of a DHH learner cannot be understood nor effectively achieved if that learner has received *ineffective* instruction. Yet, in essence, this is what needs to be done if there is to be a change in mathematics achievement in the next 25 years. The world continues to evolve into a more interactive, technologically advanced society, where problem solving and mathematical concepts are not simply used for personal expediency, but are critical to global economic and social progress. If DHH persons are to have a productive place in that society, we can no longer afford to ignore their mathematics education. And so one last question to close this chapter: What are we waiting for?

(The author wishes to thank Dr. Ellen Ansell (University of Pittsburgh) for her contributions to this chapter.)

References

Allen, T. (1995). Demographics and national achievement levels for deaf and hard of hearing students: Implications for mathematics reform. In C.H. Dietz (Ed.), *Moving toward the Standards: A national action plan for mathematics education reform for the deaf* (pp. 41–49). Washington DC: Pre-College Programs, Gallaudet University.

Ansell, E., & Pagliaro, C. (2001). Effects of a signed translation on the type and difficulty of arithmetic story problems. *Focus on Learning Problems in Mathematics, 23*(2 & 3), 41–69.

Ansell, E., & Pagliaro, C. (2006). The relative difficulty of signed arithmetic story problems for primary level deaf and hard-of-hearing students. *Journal of Deaf Studies and Deaf Education, 11*, 153–170.

Barham, J., & Bishop, A. (1991). Mathematics and the deaf child. In K. Durkin & B. Shire (Eds.), *Language in mathematical education: Research and practice.* Philadelphia: Open University Press.

Briars, D., & Larkin, J. H. (1984). An integrated model of skill in solving elementary word problems. *Cognition & Instruction, 1*, 245–296.

Broadbent, F. W. & Daniele, V. A. (1982). A review of research on mathematics and deafness. *Directions, 3*(1), 27–36. Washington DC: Gallaudet College.

Bryant, J. (1995). Language and concepts in geometry: Implications for sign language research. *FOCUS on Learning Problems in Mathematics, 17*(3), 41–56.

Bull, R., Blatto-Vallee, G., & Fabich, M. (2006). Subitizing, magnitude representation, and magnitude retrieval in deaf and hearing adults. *Journal of Deaf Studies and Deaf Education, 11*(3), 289–302.

Bull, R., Marschark, M., & Blatto-Vallee, G. (2005), SNARC hunting: Examining number representation in deaf students. *Learning and Individual Differences, 15*, 223–236.

Campbell, D., Neill, J., & Dudley, P. (1989). Computer-aided self-instruction training with hearing-impaired impulsive students. *American Annals of the Deaf, 134*(3), 227–231.

Carpenter, T.P., Fennema, E., Franke, M., Levi, L., & Empson, S. (1999). *Children's mathematics: Cognitively guided instruction.* Portsmouth, NH: Heinemann.

Carpenter, T.P., & Moser, J. (1984). The acquisition of addition and subtraction concepts in grades one through three. *Journal for Research in Mathematics Education, 15*, 179–202.

Charleson, E., Bird, R., & Strong, M. (1999). Resilience and success among deaf high school students: Three case studies. *American Annals of the Deaf, 144*(3), 226–235.

Chien, S. (1993). Cognitive addition: Strategy choice in young children with normal hearing and children with hearing impairment (Doctoral dissertation, The Ohio State University, 1993). *Dissertation Abstracts International, 54*, 2930.

Daniele, V.A. (1993). Quantitative literacy. *American Annals of the Deaf, 138*, 76–81.

Davis, S., & Kelly, R. (2003). Comparing deaf and hearing college students' mental arithmetic calculation under two interference conditions. *American Annals of the Deaf, 148*(3), 213–221.

Dietz, C. H. (1995). *Moving toward the Standards: A national action plan for mathematics education reform for the deaf.* Washington, DC: Pre-College Programs, Gallaudet University.

Dietz, C. (1991a). Communicating mathematics: Meeting new challenges. *Perspectives in Education and Deafness, 9*(3), 22–23.

Dietz, C. (1991b). Problem solving: Getting to the heart of math. *Perspectives in Education and Deafness, 9*(4), 22–23.

Dietz, C. (1994). Math reform: One step closer. *Perspectives in Education and Deafness, 13*(2), 20–21.

Dublmeier, J., & Fields, B. (1996). Science, mathematics, and the Mimi. *Perspectives in Education and Deafness, 14*(4), 12–16.

Easterbrooks, S., Stephenson, B., & Mertens, D. (2006). Master teachers' responses to twenty literacy and science/mathematics practices in deaf education. *American Annals of the Deaf, 151*(4), 398–409.

Epstein, K., Hillegeist, E., & Grafman, J. (1994). Number processing in deaf college students. *American Annals of the Deaf, 139*(3), 336–347.

Evans, J. (1995). Conversation at home. *American Annals of the Deaf, 140*(4), 324–332.

Evans, J. (1998). Changing the lens. *American Annals of the Deaf, 143*(3), 246–254.

Fennema, E., & Franke, M. (1992). Teachers' knowledge and its impact. In D. Grouws (Ed.), *Handbook of research in mathematics teaching and learning* (pp. 147–164). New York: MacMillan.

Fridriksson, T., & Stewart, D. (1988). From the concrete to the abstract: Mathematics for deaf children. *American Annals of the Deaf, 133*(1), 51–55.

Frostad, P. (1999). Deaf children's use of cognitive strategies in simple arithmetic problems. *Educational Studies in Mathematics, 40*, 129–153.

Frostad, P., & Ahlberg, A. (1996). *Conceptions of numbers: The perspectives of hearing impaired Norwegian school children.* Trondheim: Papir Publishers. Det Kongelige Norske Videnskabers-Selskap. Skrifter 2/1996.

Frostad, P., & Ahlberg, A. (1999). Solving story-based arithmetic problems: Achievement of children with hearing impairment and their interpretation of meaning. *Journal of Deaf Studies and Deaf Education, 4*(4), 283–293.

Fuson, K. (1992). Research on whole number addition and subtraction. In D. Grouws (Ed.), *Handbook of research on mathematics teaching and learning* (pp. 243–275). New York: Macmillan.

Fuson, K., & Kwan, Y. (1992). Korean children's single-digit addition and subtraction: numbers structured by ten. *Journal for Research in Mathematics Education, 23*(2), 148–165.

Hart, B., & Risely, T. (2003). The early catastrophe. The 30 million word gap. *American Educator, 27*(1), 4–9.

Hartman, M. (1994). Making sense of math through writing. *Perspectives in Education and Deafness, 12*(3), 6–9.

Horten, L., & Katz-Kaseff, M. (1991). Super signing circus. *Perspectives in Education and Deafness, 10*(1), 16–18.

Hyde, M., Zevenbergen, R., & Power, D. (2003). Deaf and hard of hearing students' performance on arithmetic word problems. *American Annals of the Deaf, 148*(1), pp. 56–64.

Innes, J. (1985). Graphing and percentage applications using the personal computer. *American Annals of the Deaf, 130*(5), 424–430.

Jamieson, J. (1994). Teaching as translation: Vygotskian perspectives on deafness and mother-child interaction. *Exceptional Children, 60*(5), 434–450.

Jones, T., & Ewing, K. (2002). An analysis of teacher preparation in deaf education programs approved by the Council of Education of the Deaf. *American Annals of the Deaf, 147*(5), 71–78.

Kelly, R., & Gaustad, M. (2007). Deaf college students' mathematical skills relative to morphological knowledge, reading level, and language proficiency. *Journal of Deaf Studies and Deaf Education, 12*, 25–37.

Kelly, R., Lang, H., Mousley, K., & Davis, S. (2003a). Deaf college students' comprehension of relational language in arithmetic compare problems. *Journal of Deaf Studies and Deaf Education, 8*(2), 120–132.

Kelly, R. R., Lang, H. G., & Pagliaro, C. M. (2003b). Mathematics word problem solving for deaf students: A survey of perceptions and practices in grades 6–12. *Journal of Deaf Studies and Deaf Education, 8*(2), 104–119.

Kelly, R., & Mousley, K. (1999). *Deaf and hearing students' transfer and application of skill in math problem solving.* Paper presented at the 25th Annual Conference of the Association of College Educators for the Deaf and Hard of Hearing, Rochester, NY. (ERIC Document Reproduction Service No. ED440501.)

Kelly, R., & Mousley, K. (2001). Solving word problems: More than reading issues for deaf students. *American Annals of the Deaf, 146*(3), 251–262.

Kemp, V. (1990). The van Hiele levels of geometric thought and achievement in Euclidean geometry among deaf undergraduate students. (Doctoral dissertation, George Mason University 1990). *Dissertation Abstracts International, 51*, 1148A.

Kemp, V. (2004). The van Hiele levels of geometric though and achievement among deaf undergraduate students. In D. Martin (Ed.), *Advances in cognition, education, and deafness.* Washington, DC: Gallaudet University Press.

Kidd, D., & Lamb, C. (1993). Mathematics vocabulary and the hearing-impaired student: An anecdotal study. *Focus on Learning Problems in Mathematics, 15*(4), 44–52.

Kidd, D., Madsen, A., & Lamb, C. (1993). Mathematics vocabulary: Performance of residential deaf students. *School Science and Mathematics, 93*(8), 418–421.

Kluwin, T., & Moores, D. (1985). The effects of integration on the mathematics achievement of hearing impaired adolescents. *Exceptional Children, 52*(2), 153–160.

Korvorst, M., Nuerk, H., & Willmes, K. (2007). The hands have it: Number representations in adult deaf signers. *Journal of Deaf Studies and Deaf Education, 12*(3), 362–372.

Kritzer, K. (2007a) *Factors associated with mathematical ability in young deaf children: Building foundations, from networks to numbers.* Unpublished doctoral dissertation, University of Pittsburgh. Retrieved August 2, 2008, from http://etd.library.pitt.edu/ETD/available/etd-04012007-195017/unrestricted/ KritzerKL_etdPitt2007.pdf

Kritzer, K. (2007b). The construction of a classification schema as a foundation for mathematical understanding in young deaf children. *FOCUS on Learning Problems in Mathematics, 29*(3), 15–29.

Kritzer, K. (2008). Family mediation of mathematically based concepts while engaged in a problem-solving activity with their young deaf children. *Journal of Deaf Studies and Deaf Education, 13*(4), 503–517.

Kritzer, K. (2009). Barely started and already left behind: An analysis of the mathematics ability demonstrated by young deaf children. *Journal of Deaf Studies and Deaf Education, 14*, 409–421.

Lang, H., & Pagliaro, C. (2007). Factors predicting recall of mathematics terms by deaf students: Implications for teaching. *Journal of Deaf Studies and Deaf Education, 12*(4), 449–460.

Leybaert, J., & Van Cutsem, M. (2002). Counting in sign language. *Journal of Experimental Child Psychology, 81*(4), 482–501.

Liu, C., Chou, C., Liu, B, & Yang, J. (2006). Improving mathematics teaching and learning experiences for hard of hearing students with wireless technology-enhanced classrooms. *American Annals of the Deaf, 151*(3), 345–355.

Luckner, J., & McNeill, J. (1994). Performance of a group of deaf and hard-of-hearing students and a comparison group of hearing students on a series of problem-solving tasks. *American Annals of the Deaf, 139*(3), 371–377.

Ma, L. (1999). *Knowing and teaching elementary mathematics: Teachers' understanding of fundamental mathematics in China and the United States.* Mahwah, NJ: Erlbaum.

Marschark, M., & Everhart, V. (1999). Problem-solving by deaf and hearing students: Twenty questions. *Deafness and Education International, 1*(2), 65–82.

Marschark, M., Lang, H.G., & Albertini, J.A. (2002). *Educating deaf students: From research to practice.* New York: Oxford University Press.

Mason, M. (1995). Geometric knowledge in a deaf classroom: An exploratory study. *FOCUS on Learning Problems in Mathematics, 17*(3), 57–69.

Martin, D. (1987). *Improving cognitive skills of hearing impaired college students.* (Final Report, U.S. Department of Education) Washington, DC: Gallaudet University. (ERIC Document Reproduction Service No. ED302993.)

Martin, D., Craft, A., & Sheng, Z. (2001). The impact of cognitive strategy instruction on deaf learners: An international comparative study. *American Annals of the Deaf, 146*(4), 366–374.

Mayberry, R. (2002). Cognitive development in deaf children: The interface of language and perception in neuropsychology. In S. J. Segalowitz & I. Rapin (Eds.), *Handbook of neuropsychology*, 2nd edition, 8(part 2) (pp. 71–107). Netherlands: Elsevier.

Mewborn, D. (2003). Teaching teachers' knowledge, and their professional development. In J. Kilpatrick, W.G. Martin, & D. Schifter (Eds.), *A research companion to principles and standards for school mathematics* (pp. 45–52). Reston, VA: NCTM.

Mitchell, R, & Karchmer, M. (2002). Chasing the mythical ten percent: Parental hearing status of deaf and hard of hearing students in the United States. *Sign Language Studies, 4*(4), 138–163.

Moores, D. (2001). Educating the deaf: Psychology, principles, and practices. Boston: Houghton Mifflin.

Moores, D., & Martin, D. (2006). Preface. In D. Moores and D. Martin (Eds.), *Deaf learners: Developments in curriculum and instruction* (pp. ix–xiii). Washington, DC: Gallaudet University Press.

Mousley, K. & Kelly, R. (1998). Problem-solving strategies for teaching mathematics to deaf students. *American Annals of the Deaf, 143*(4), 325–336.

National Council of Teachers of Mathematics. (1989). *Curriculum and evaluation standards for school mathematics*. Reston, VA: Author.

National Council of Teachers of Mathematics. (1991). *Professional standards for teaching mathematics*. Reston, VA: Author.

National Council of Teachers of Mathematics. (1995). *Assessment standards for school mathematics*. Reston, VA: Author.

National Council of Teachers of Mathematics. (2000). *Principles and standards for school mathematics*. Reston, VA: Author.

Nunes, T. (2004). *Teaching mathematics to deaf children*. London: Whurr Publishers.

Nunes, T., & Moreno, C. (1998a). Is hearing impairment a cause of difficulties in learning mathematics? In C. Donlan (Ed.), *The development of mathematical skills: Studies in developmental psychology*. Hove, UK: Psychology Press Ltd.

Nunes, T., & Moreno, C. (1998b). The signed algorithm and its bugs. *Educational Studies in Mathematics, 35*(1), 85–92.

Nunes, T., & Moreno, C. (1997). Solving word problems with different ways of representing the task: How do deaf children perform?. *Mathematics and Special Educational Needs, 3*, 15–17.

Nunes T., & Moreno, C. (2002). An intervention program for promoting deaf pupils' achievement in mathematics. *Journal of Deaf Studies and Deaf Education, 7*(2), 120–133.

Pagliaro, C. (1998a). Mathematics reform in the education of deaf and hard of hearing students. *American Annals of the Deaf, 143*, 22–28.

Pagliaro, C. (1998b). Mathematics reform in the education of deaf and hard of hearing students. *American Annals of the Deaf, 143*(1), 22–28.

Pagliaro, C., & Ansell, E. (2000). *Primary-level deaf education teachers' pedagogical content knowledge related to arithmetic story problems*. Paper presented at the meeting of the American Educational Research Association, New Orleans, LA.

Pagliaro, C., & Ansell, E. (2002). Story problems in the deaf education classroom: Frequency and mode of presentation. *Journal of Deaf Studies and Deaf Education, 7*, 107–119.

Pagliaro, C., & Ansell, E. (2007). *Aspects of American Sign Language that facilitate deaf children's arithmetic problem solving: A qualitative analysis*. Paper presented at the ASL Roundtable Conference, Washington, DC.

Pagliaro, C. M., & Kritzer, K. (2005). Discrete mathematics in deaf education: A survey of teachers' knowledge and use. *American Annals of the Deaf, 150*(3), 251–259.

Riley, M., Greeno, J., & Heller, J. (1983). Development of children's problem-solving ability in arithmetic. In R. Lesh & M. Landau (Eds.), *The development of mathematical thinking* (pp. 153–196). New York: Academic Press.

Robinson, M., & Cash, P. (1996). Students discover the value of bartering. *Perspectives in Education and Deafness, 14*(4), 11, 16–18.

Saxe, G., Guberman, S., & Gearhart, M. (1987). Social processes in early number development. *Monographs of the Society for Research in Child Development, 52*(2).

Schick, B., deVilliers, J., deVilliers, P., & Hoffmeister, R. (2002). Theory of mind: Language and cognition in deaf children. *ASHA Leader Online*. Retrieved November 10, 2006, from http://www.asha.org/about/publications/leader-online/archives/2002/q4/f021203.htm

Secada, W. (1984). Counting in sign: The number string, accuracy and use. Doctoral dissertation, Northwestern University, 1984. *Dissertation Abstracts International, 45*, 3571.

Serrano Pau, C. (1995). The deaf child and solving problems of arithmetic: The importance of comprehensive reading. *American Annals of the Deaf, 140*, 287–294.

Shulman, L. (1986). Those who understand: Knowledge growth in teaching. *Educational Researcher, 15*(2), 4–14.

Spencer, P., Bodner-Johnson, B., & Gutfreund, M. (1992). Interacting with infants with a hearing loss: What can we learn from mothers who are deaf?. *Journal of Early Intervention, 16*(1), 64–78.

Stanwick, R., Oddy, A., & Roper, T. (2005). Mathematics and deaf children: An exploration of barriers to success. *Deafness and Education International, 7*(1), 1–21.

Titus, J. (1992). *The concept of fractional number among hearing-impaired students*. Paper presented at the Annual Conference of the American Educational Research Association, San Francisco, CA, April 20–24.

Traxler, C. B. (2000). The Stanford Achievement Test, 9th edition: National norming and performance standards for deaf and hard-of-hearing students. *Journal of Deaf Studies and Deaf Education, 5*, 337–348.

Walkerdine, V. (1988). *The mastery of reason*. London: Routledge.

Wedell-Monnig, J., & Lumley, J. (1980). Child deafness and mother-child interaction. *Child Development, 51*, 766–774.

Wilson, L. (1989). *Application of technology to cognitive development*. Duluth: University of Minnesota. (ERIC Document Reproduction Service No. ED313850.)

Zarfaty, Y., Nunes, T., & Bryant, P. (2004). The performance of young deaf children in spatial and temporal number tasks. *Journal of Deaf Studies and Deaf Education, 9*(3), 315–326.

Appendix
NAPMERD Recommendations
CURRICULUM AND PEDAGOGY

• The mathematics content of the curriculum be changed in the ways expressed in the Standards at all levels, preschool–12;

• [The] change in emphasis in curriculum content be consistent, preschool–12;

• Textbooks should serve programs, teachers, and students as resources only and not as definitive curriculum guides;

• Instructional approaches must facilitate students' construction of their own complex knowledge structures;

• Instruction must build on students' prior knowledge and experience, recognizing that the knowledge and experience base of deaf students may be different from that of hearing students of the same age;

• Instructional tasks and materials must be appropriate to the age of the student;

• Instruction must require students to actively make use of a variety of tools to construct knowledge, solve problems, and communicate ideas. These include manipulative materials, calculators, video tapes, computers and related technologies, and visual aids;

- Instruction must include a variety of techniques to encourage students to construct knowledge, solve problems, and communicate ideas. These include writing, longer projects, and cooperative learning;
- Remedial instruction, when required, should provide a broader range of experiences upon which students can base appropriate conceptual understandings rather than on repetition of previous instructional tasks or on drill and practice;
- The classroom environment needs to be organized to encourage clear communication and peer interaction;
- Classroom communication in mathematics content should not be limited by communication policies. [Dietz, 1995, pp. 14–21]

TEACHER PREPARATION AND PROFESSIONAL DEVELOPMENT

- All programs preparing teachers of deaf students include courses and experiences that:

  - Will enable the teacher to design and effectively implement, with deaf students, the teaching strategies described in the Standards;
  - Provide the teacher with a working knowledge of a broad range of mathematics content required to include appropriate, relevant mathematics in the instruction they design;
  - Will enable the teacher to communicate clearly and accurately about mathematical ideas to a wide variety of deaf students;
  - Provide the teacher with a knowledge of how children learn mathematics including theories of concept development, theories of intellectual development, implications of these theories for students who are deaf and hard of hearing

- Teachers implementing mathematics reform in their classrooms be given time and opportunity for discussion and planning with other teachers both within the school unit and across programs;
- In-service development activities in mathematics be made a major priority of any education program serving deaf students;
- In-service activities include education and training in the language aspects of mathematics for all faculty and staff: teachers, aides, and interpreters. Such education and training should include: technical sign vocabulary; ways of communicating mathematical meaning;
- Part of the role of Gallaudet University Pre-College Programs be to emphasize mathematics education in its federally mandated

national mission activities as a model/demonstration/dissemination agency. Other organizations with responsibilities in guiding the field such as the National Technical Institute for the Deaf need to also support this effort;
- In mainstream settings where interpreters are required, only certified, qualified interpreters familiar with mathematics content be used. Training for interpreters should include the accurate communication of mathematics concepts;
- Elementary teachers of deaf and hard-of-hearing students hold dual certification in elementary education and the education of the deaf. The mathematical requirements for certification should follow the NCTM and Mathematics Association of America (MAA) guidelines;
- Secondary teachers of deaf and hard-of-hearing students hold dual certification in mathematics education and the education of the deaf. The mathematical requirements for certification should follow the NCTM and MAA guidelines;
- Teachers must demonstrate proficiency in communicating mathematical ideas to deaf students. [Dietz, 1995, pp. 22–27]

ASSESSMENT

- Existing national tests that are more consistent with the content of mathematics reform curriculum…should be explored as alternative when standardized testing is required;
- Deaf educators need to become more proactive with organizations and companies involved in revising and developing assessment tools;
- Deaf students should be included in pilot programs of new assessment instruments in mathematics;
- In deaf education, it should be emphasized that the curriculum must drive assessment and not assessment drive the curriculum;
- Evaluation instruments and techniques that are consistent with the Standards and that will appropriately assess the knowledge and performance of deaf students are critically needed. Their development must be a priority;
- Work on assessment and evaluation instruments should be done in cooperation with the NCTM. [Dietz, 1995, pp. 29–30]

RESEARCH

- The role in which language and communication systems are related to the learning of mathematics, including the areas of appropriate signs, context, consistency, and communication of generalizations and abstractions;

• The use and effectiveness of assessment tasks, narratives, activities, and methodologies in evaluating deaf students' understandings of mathematics;

• The description of deaf students' cognition and metacognition during problem-solving activities;

• The nature and influence of deaf students' prior experience related to mathematics learning;

• The impact of various teacher characteristics...on students' learning of mathematics;

• Identification of program characteristics that are associated with successful mathematics programs for deaf students;

• The growth of deaf students' understandings of mathematical concepts as they progress through the grades;

• The current status of mathematics education programs serving deaf students so that a baseline exists against which to mark progress. [Dietz, 1995, p. 14–31]

Deaf Children with Severe Multiple Disabilities: Etiologies, Intervention, and Assessment

Rick van Dijk, Catherine Nelson, Albert Postma, *and* Jan van Dijk

Abstract

The population of individuals who are deaf or hard of hearing (DHH) and have additional disabilities is a large and diverse one. The additional disabilities may be relatively mild (e.g., learning disability), but others are more severe. The emphasis of this chapter is on the latter group. Individuals who are deaf or hard-of-hearing may also have intellectual disabilities (ID), autism, or they may be deafblind. Their disabilities can be due to many factors including genetic syndromes; problems that occur before, during, or slightly after birth; or infections such as meningitis or injuries such as traumatic brain injury that are acquired later in life. The purposes of this chapter are to (a) delineate and describe several of the major causative factors, and (b) present important evidence-based practices that have the potential to enhance the communication, education, and quality of life of individuals who are deaf or hard of hearing and have additional severe disabilities.

Keywords: intellectual disabilities, multiple disabilities, augmentative communication, rehabilitation, autism, CHARGE syndrome, Usher syndrome

The focus of this chapter is on children who are deaf and have severe multiple disabilities, such as autism, intellectual disabilities (ID), or a combination of hearing and vision loss. Due to the interaction of the disabilities, these children typically cannot be adequately served by programming designed for children with a single disability or programming designed for deaf children whose academic development is complicated by less severe problems, such as learning disabilities or behavioral issues. For example, children who are deafblind will not be able to fully benefit from programs for children with visual impairments alone because of their hearing loss. By the same token, children who are deafblind will likely not profit from educational programs for children with hearing loss only because their lack of vision precludes taking advantage of the visually based programming that is often employed in classrooms for children who are deaf or hard of hearing. The same type of problem arises for children who are deaf or hard of hearing and also have autism spectrum disorders (ASD), as well as for children who are deaf or hard of hearing and have concomitant ID. In each case, the presence of the second disability reduces the potential for compensation for the first (Knoors & Vervloed, 2003). Highly specialized programming thus is required for children who have a hearing loss and one or more additional disabilities. Such curricula have been developed for children with deafblindness and, to a more limited extent, for children who are deaf with ID and children who are deaf and have ASD. These programs do not necessarily require specialized placements, but may be delivered in various settings including general education classrooms and classrooms for children who are deaf or hard of hearing.

This chapter begins with a discussion of etiologies that are commonly identified for multiple disabilities that include hearing loss. This is followed by more specific information about characteristics of and programming for children who have ID and deafness, children who have ASD and deafness, and children who are deafblind. Evidence-based intervention techniques and programs will be presented for each group.

Etiologies of Deafness and Multiple Disabilities

It is important to consider the etiologies of deafness and concurrent disabilities because in some instances the cause of the concurrent disability provides information that is necessary for appropriate intervention that promotes the person's physical and mental health. Included in the etiologies described here are those that are of a genetic origin and those that occur as a result of maternal or child infection.

A number of etiologies are known to result in hearing loss associated with additional disabilities, including prematurity and other pregnancy-related complications, cytomegalovirus (CMV), meningitis, and deafness associated with genetic syndromes (e.g., Down syndrome, Treacher-Collins syndrome, Usher syndrome, CHARGE syndrome) (Berke, 2007). In many of these etiologies, problems originate before, during, or shortly after birth, when vital organs are still in the developmental stage. The U. S. National Institute of Child Health and Human Development (Shriver, 2006) defines prematurity as childbirth occurring earlier than 37 completed weeks of gestation. Low birth weight, which is likely present in infants with prematurity, also occurs in full-term infants, and is further delineated as "low" (between 1,500 and 2,500 g) or "very low" (>1,500 g). Both infants who are born preterm and those who have low birth weight despite full gestation are at increased risk of developing a visual and/or auditory impairment. Often, motor impairments may also be present, and if the infant's immature central nervous system is unable to regulate the attention process, attention disorders can result.

If a child is prenatally infected with CMV virus (congenital CMV), health problems such as hearing and vision loss may not occur until months or years after birth (Berke, 2007). Although CMV does not always lead to disabilities, intellectual impairments can result from the virus. In addition, autism is frequently linked to CMV (Sweeten, Posey, & McDougle, 2004), as well as calcification of white matter of the brain, which is associated with learning difficulties (Malinger et al., 2003). Other pre- and perinatal viral etiologies are associated with multiple disabilities including hearing loss. For example, although diseases such as rubella have been largely controlled in industrialized countries, there are still children in the educational system whose academic/cognitive difficulties result from this infection, and it continues to be a significant cause of multiple disabilities in nonindustrialized areas of the world.

Many genetically based syndromes are associated with deafness and multiple disabilities. In some instances, a gene defect causes deafness and possibly other symptoms. For instance, in Usher syndrome, one gene causes both visual and auditory impairment. In Pendred syndrome, the mutation of a specific gene results in a disorder typically associated with hearing loss and the thyroid condition called goiter. In Waardenburg syndrome, six genes are mutated, which can cause facial and pigmentation abnormalities as well as deafness. These syndromes may require medical attention throughout life, but learning abilities and behavior are generally not affected. In contrast, a chromosome defect such as a deletion or the presence of an extra set of genes will lead to over- or underexpression of the involved genes and, as a consequence, to increased production of certain biochemical products, as is seen in trisomy 21 (Down syndrome). There are several other syndromes in which one of the chromosomes is broken (deletion). This often leads to severe involvement of total body systems, including the central nervous system. An example is Wolf-Hirschhorn syndrome, in which a part of chromosome 4 is missing. When a minor breakage occurs in chromosome 8, a very complex syndrome called CHARGE syndrome (which is discussed in more detail later in this chapter) can result.

As this brief review indicates, there is a significant group of children who are deaf or hard of hearing and who have concurrent intellectual or related disabilities that affect their development. It is reported that more than one-quarter of children with mild cognitive impairment have a sensory loss, and more than half of the children with severe cognitive impairment have a concurrent sensory loss, either of vision or hearing (Batshaw & Shapiro, 2002; Westling & Fox, 2008). Unfortunately, there is a scarcity of documentation regarding the education of these children.

Students Who Are Deaf and Have Intellectual Disabilities

The Center for Assessment and Demographic Studies of the Gallaudet Research Institute reported that of 37,352 children who were identified in their U. S. survey as being deaf or hard of hearing, 8% also have mental retardation (Gallaudet Research Institute, 2006).

According to the American Association of Intellectual and Developmental Disabilities (AAIDD), intellectual disability is characterized by significant limitations both in intellectual functioning and in adaptive behavior as expressed in conceptual, social, and practical adaptive skills. This disability originates before age 18 (Schalock et al., 2007). The population of persons with ID can be classified based on the amount and kind of support that is needed (Luckasson et al., 2002; Wehmeyer, 2003). Some persons with ID only need *intermittent support*. Others require limited but consistent support throughout life, with the intensity of that support differing across individuals and over time. Persons who function in this range typically acquire communication skills in childhood. Specialized programs have been developed for students who are deaf or hard of hearing who meet this criterion. Persons with ID who need *extensive* or *pervasive* support are often served in group homes or supported apartments and have a personal job coach. These services are longstanding. Deaf or hard-of-hearing persons who need this intensive support may be able to communicate through signals that indicate their needs, while others may use pictures, drawings, pictograms, or more high-tech alternative and augmentative communication (AAC) aids. They may profit from a curriculum designed for deafblind children even if vision is not affected. However, there is much variation in their functioning.

Intervention, Communication, and Sign Development in Persons with Deafness and Intellectual Disabilities

Communication and language may utilize several forms and represent varied symbolic levels. Such forms include personalized gestures, iconic gestures, pictures, iconic signs or speech, and abstract signs or speech. All of these forms should be considered when deciding upon a communication approach for an individual who is deaf and also has an ID. However, it is also important to consider the ability of the individual to develop a natural language that allows for communication with others in his or her environment.

The research examples given here illustrate different ways of looking at the use of signs, sign systems, and sign language in persons with ID and deafness. A basic element that applies to almost all systems used is *iconicity* or the ability to recognize the meaning of a sign by its appearance. This is in contrast to signs that are arbitrarily associated with their referent. It is frequently assumed that the understanding of iconic signs is a cognitively less complex task than understanding abstract or arbitrary signs. This assumption was questioned by Tolar, Lederberg, Gokhale, and Tomasello (2008), who examined the development of the ability to interpret iconic signs and hypothesized that this ability would develop somewhere between 2.5 and 3.5 years of age. The outcome of their research demonstrated that "the ability to interpret iconic symbols is fragile before 3 years of age, even for such transparent representations as pictures and physical replicas" (Tolar et al., 2008, p. 227). This ability is relatively established by 3.5–4.5 years of age, and approximates adult-like understanding by 4.5–5.0 years of age. From this study, we can conclude that the understanding of iconic signs is based on cognitive maturity and, therefore, iconic representations are only transparent to older children with advanced cognitive skills.

It is generally accepted that the use of signs can be of great importance for deaf persons with ID or with autism (Mirenda, 2001). However, the extent to which the use of signs or sign language is going to be successful depends on a variety of variables, such as the degree of ID, short-term memory constraints, physical effort required in sign production, and the extent to which the signs are understood by others in the environment. To determine what type of communication system is most advisable, an assessment should always be carried out by specialized professionals, such as an expert on AAC, an occupational and/or physical therapist, and the child's teacher. Adaptation of signs (if necessary) should be based on the individual person's motor and intellectual abilities and his or her environment. It should be noted that various levels of communication sophistication need to be available to persons with hearing loss and ID. Data collection and ongoing assessments of progress need to be important components of communication programming.

An intervention study that was carried out in the Netherlands provides an example of the effects of an adapted sign system that was designed to enhance the development of communication of individuals who are deaf and have moderate ID (Stoep, Van Balkom, Luiken, Snieders, & van der Schuit, 2008). It was demonstrated in the study that the persons were able to profit from devices that support and augment communication (e.g., the Vocaflex that emits a request when a button is pushed) and adapted signs from Sign Language of the Netherlands (SLN). The adapted signs required less motor skill when compared with actual SLN signs and were highly iconic.

A descriptive pilot study that was carried out in the Netherlands by R. Van Dijk, Van Helvoort, Aan den Toorn, and Bos (1998) indicated more potential for use of a natural sign language by persons with moderate ID than had been previously expected. The communication of five deaf adults with moderate ID was analyzed through the use of video recordings that were produced under both elicited and spontaneous communication conditions. The participating individuals had lived together for over 20 years in a residential setting without any contact with the Deaf community—and at the time of the research, no deaf staff members were employed. During their school time, the participants had learned sign-supported Dutch, a system based on the grammar of spoken Dutch that utilizes signs derived from an old Dutch sign system called the Van Beek system. The Van Beek system was used in the southern part of the Netherlands during the beginning of the last century to educate students who were deaf and hard of hearing.

The primary research question pursued in this study was whether the five participating deaf adults utilized specific aspects of SLN (e.g., nonmanual grammatical markers, classifiers, and the use of space and verb agreement) despite their lack of formal exposure to them. This research project was initiated because communication therapists observed that when deaf adults were communicating among themselves within daily routines, the method of communication was different from that used when they were communicating with their hearing caregivers. In the latter case, the communication was less fluent and there was less variation in the signs used. This difference was investigated in spontaneous communicative situations, as well as in testing situations that utilized elicited communication through the means of stimulus pictures developed by Volterra, Laudanna, Coranzza, Radutzky, and Natale (1984) and those developed by Coerts (1994).

Although the individuals had never been exposed to SLN, specific sign language elements could be observed in their productions (R. Van Dijk et al., 1998). For example, the linguistic analysis of the material revealed that *classifiers* such as a "B-flat hand" (palm down, fingers closed) referring to a car were used in the elicited communication situations, even though this structure is not used in the sign-supported Dutch to which the participants had been exposed at school. It was also frequently observed that the classifiers used by the participants were incorporated in the verb (e.g., a flat hand with the palm down making horizontal movement refers

to driving a car). There was also a strong tendency to put the verb in final position of the utterance and put the subject before the verb, as is typical in SLN and some, but not all, other sign languages (Pfau & Bos, 2008). A typical grammatical structure that was also observed was the use of pronoun copy structures (e.g., "I sleep I"). Again, this structure does not occur in spoken Dutch or sign-supported Dutch, but occurs in SLN.

The researchers drew the conclusion that there was a strong tendency for these individuals to develop a communication system that incorporates sign language elements beyond those they had been specifically taught. This indicates more possibilities than previously were thought for learning a productive, generative language system that incorporates structural rules consistent with the modality of expression. The development of a more complete and flexible sign language by these individuals might occur if adequate instruction and support, including high-quality accessible language input, are provided. It is therefore important that the caregivers and other professionals who work with these individuals be fluent in sign language or, minimally, possess a large sign lexicon. It should be noted that not all deaf persons with ID will have the cognitive ability to learn sign language, and supporting persons should also be able to adapt communication to the specific needs of the clients or children. These adaptations can involve the use of photographs, pictures, drawings, or pictograms depending on the specific needs of the individual.

In addition to signs that originate from the various national sign languages, sign systems have been developed that focus on simplifying expression and perception of a sign. Based on this premise, the Makaton system developed in 1976 by Walker, Johnston, and Cornforth (Makaton Charity, 2008) has been used in Europe and Australia. Originally, Makaton consisted of 350 signs derived from British Sign Language (BSL). The signs used were divided into eight different categories, with each stage representing increased complexity: Stage 1 (language level 1;0–1;5 years) presents a basic lexicon upon which the other stages are built. Examples of Stage 1 are *come, sit, toilet*, and *drink*. In stage 2 (language level 2;0–2;5 years), more basic lexical items are taught. In stage 3 (language level 3;0 years), stage 4 (language level 3;5–4 years), and stages 5 and 6 (4;0-4;5 years) the focus is on increasing the growth of vocabulary in a structured manner and gradually introducing syntactic concepts. Stages 7 and 8 are slightly different and focus on more complex language concepts and the vocabulary needed to expand the previous stages. The ninth stage focuses on the lexicon that is needed in a specific environment that is not included in Makaton (Makaton Charity, 2008). Worldwide clinical practice has demonstrated the effectiveness of this system.

To enhance communication for deaf persons, cochlear implants are becoming widely used. It is a point of debate whether this aid should be recommended for persons who are deaf and have ID (Stacey, Fortnum, Barton, & Summerfield, 2006; see Chapter 9, this volume). In a large survey in the United Kingdom (Stacey et al., 2006) that included questionnaires for parents and teachers (n = 5,099), it was concluded that, across all domains, the reported outcomes were better for children with fewer disabilities occurring in addition to hearing impairment. Schlumberger, Narbona, and Maurique (2004) argue, however, that early cochlear implantation enhances the improvement of nonverbal capacities and that having access to auditory stimulation plays a role in "building the brain" (p. 605; see Chapter 29, this volume). This presents an interesting issue for discussion regarding DHH children with ID, but one beyond the scope of this chapter.

Students Who Are Deaf and Have Autism Spectrum Disorders

Traditionally, it was assumed that because of their hearing losses, children who are deaf or hard of hearing would withdraw from their social world as children with autism often do (Bailly, De Chouly de Lenclave, & Lauwerier, 2003). Researchers have concluded that this is not the case, however, and hearing loss is not considered to be a cause of autistic-like behaviors. For example, Juré, Rapin, and Tuchman (1991) reviewed information from a sample of 46 children who were deaf or hard of hearing and had autism. In this study, the diagnostic criteria for autism were those of the *Diagnostic and Statistical Manual of Mental Disorders*, 3rd Edition, Revised (DSM-III-R) criteria (American Psychiatric Association, 1987). The core symptoms are impaired and atypical socialization, impoverished play, a language disorder (affecting comprehension, expression, and nonverbal communication), inadequately modulated affect, stereotypic behaviors, and a narrow range of interest (Juré et al., 1991, p. 1063). The authors of the study, however, failed to obtain any evidence to support the hypothesis that "sensory deprivation is responsible for autistic symptomatology" (Juré et al., 1991, p. 1068).

In a review article on this subject, Bailly et al. (2003) concluded that hearing loss should not be considered as an etiological factor for autism. It was suggested that, rather, hearing impairment and autism sometimes share an underlying pathology. A clear example occurs in children with congenital rubella syndrome (CRS). As early as 1971, Chess, Korn, and Fernandez demonstrated a high prevalence of autism in children who were deaf as a result of rubella. This relationship has been confirmed in other subsequent studies (Gordon, 1993; J. Van Dijk, 1982, 1991).

The question arises as to what the consequences are for the educational management of students who are deaf or hard of hearing and also have ASD. It is important that a teacher or a caregiver be knowledgeable about programs for children with autism, such as Treatment and Education of Autistic and Related Communication Handicapped Children (TEACCH; Mesibov, Shea, & Schopler, 2004). This program is an intervention for the treatment and support of persons with autism and also seems to be useful for children with autism in combination with hearing loss (Koppers & Joyeux, 2004). Demonstrated strengths of the TEACCH program are that it (a) includes a clear daily schedule, (b) consists of a highly visual and predictable teaching method (e.g., the use of signs, pictures, icons, or drawings), (c) has a clear environmental structure, and (d) parents are actively involved in the program.

The idea of using visual supports is also emphasized in the work of Denteneer-van der Pasch and Verpoorten (2007). They stress the fact that concept formation in children with ASD is quite different from that of typically developing children. For example, after a visit to a castle, a child with ASD was asked to draw the building; he drew only a number of very detailed hinges, because he focused solely on these details. It is important to consider this possible focus on extraneous minutia when using AAC and visual supports with children with ASD. Therefore, teaching should occur in concrete or actual situations if the visual supports are to assist in accurate concept development. The AAC and/or visual support should then be faded out if possible (Denteneer-van der Pasch & Verpoorten). The TEACCH Program and the ideas from Denteneer-van der Pasch and Verpoorten have many similarities to the curriculum designed by Jan van Dijk (MacFarland, 1995; J. Van Dijk, 1986) for children who are deafblind, which is discussed in the next section of this chapter. As in the education of children with ID, signs also play an important role in communication intervention and development in the education of children with ASD (Bonvillian, Nelson, & Rhyne, 1981).

Persons Who Are Deafblind

There has been much discussion regarding the definition of deafblindness. It was Salvatore Lagati (S. Lagati, personal correspondence, 1991) who first advocated dropping the hyphen between the words deaf and blind (deaf-blind) (see also Lagati, 1995). It was Lagati's opinion that the concurrent impairment of the loss of hearing and sight results in a unique disability that encompasses more than the additive affects of each of the sensory deficits. This can be understood best through an example: A person with an average hearing loss of 60 decibels will have difficulties understanding a person speaking to him in a noisy environment. The person will try to compensate for his hearing impairment by watching the speaker's face. in order to receive additional information. It can be assumed that this person will be able to receive most of the exchanged information. However, if this person has a vision loss of 70% in addition to the hearing loss, it is very likely that the speaker's facial expressions and the shape of his mouth will be difficult to discern. In this instance, the person will miss almost all of the conversation. The person can thus be considered to be deafblind. By the same token, a person who has a vision acuity loss of 10% and a mild hearing loss of 35 decibels will likely not understand all spoken information in a noisy environment.

After a long-term international debate, the following statement was issued by the European Parliament on January 12, 2004:

> Deafblindness is a distinct disability that is a
> combination of both sight and hearing
> impairments, which results in difficulties
> having access to information, communication,
> and mobility.

The Declaration states further that it should be recognized that there is a wide range in the degree of combined sensory losses. There is a vast difference between a person who is nearly or completely blind and has a profound/severe hearing impairment and a person whose distance senses are moderately impaired. Nevertheless, the Parliament agreed that persons with combined sensory losses ranging from mild to profound should be identified as being "deafblind" in order to emphasize their unique living circumstances. On the basis of the Declaration, the European Parliament estimates that there are 150,000 individuals who are deafblind in the countries of the European Union (a union of approximately 400 million people). This figure includes differing groups of individuals who are deafblind, including the largest group by far—individuals who are elderly and deafblind.

The number of children with congenital or early acquired deafblindness is unknown in many European countries. The latest census of children and youth in the United States reports nearly 10,000 children classified as being deafblind (Killoran, 2007). In addition to degree of loss, the developmental stage at which the loss occurred has an impact on functioning. The effects of a concurrent impairment of vision and hearing are significantly different between persons with congenital and early-acquisition deafblindness and those with late-acquisition deafblindness. Persons with late-acquisition deafblindness will have already developed a wide range of competencies, typically including spoken or signed language. In congenital or early-acquisition deafblindness, the disability occurs before these competencies are developed and interferes significantly with their development. Development of communication and other competencies is thus a challenging process, and particularly so for persons with ID. It is estimated that two-thirds of children with congenital deafblindness also have ID (Killoran, 2007), and a customized educational program is highly recommended for these children.

Deafblindness and Intellectual Disability

A deafblind person's intellectual ability is an important factor for consideration when designing an educational program. For example, a person with an extensive knowledge base of concepts and rich language experiences needs only relatively minor sensory clues in order to access information and conceptualize his environment. This is much more difficult for a person with ID, who may have limited language skills and few completely developed concepts, or for a child who has never had full vision or auditory experience to use as a basis for developing communication skills and learning about the environment.

To delineate support needs, several studies have been carried out in the Netherlands to differentiate among the populations of people with sensory impairment (Evenhuis, Theunissen, Denkers, Verschuure, & Kemme, 2001; Van den Broek, Janssen, Van Ramshorst, & Deen, 2006; Van Splunder, 2003). These researchers report an underreferral of persons with a concurrent visual and auditory impairment in organizations that serve persons with moderate to severe intellectual disability. As a consequence, adequate services are often denied to a group of vulnerable citizens.

Syndromic Deafblindness

About 80 syndromes are associated with deafblindness (Regenbogen & Coscas, 1985). Many of these syndromes are rare, and specialized knowledge is required for their diagnosis. The classification system used in Online Mendelian Inheritance in Man (OMIM), a database of human genes and genetic disorders developed by staff at Johns Hopkins University and hosted on the Web by the National Center for Biotechnology Information (United States), provides diagnosticians with an important body of information (www.ncbi.nlm.nih.gov/omim/). Several syndromes are of a hereditary origin, whereas in other syndromes, the sensory loss is caused by a spontaneous mutation of a gene. Sometimes, a part of a chromosome is "broken" or deleted. This means that some of the genes that are located on a particular chromosome are unable to program a particular enzyme that serves as a fundamental building block of the body's DNA. In the following paragraphs we will discuss three major syndromes of deafblindness: CHARGE syndrome, Usher syndrome, and congenital rubella syndrome.

CHARGE SYNDROME

In the most recent deafblind census count of persons between 0 and 21 years in the United States (Killoran, 2007), CHARGE syndrome is listed as the most frequent genetic syndromic cause of deafblindness. This name is an acronym for the six characteristics that are often present in this syndrome: Coloboma (keyhole-type opening in iris and retina), Heart defect, Atresia of the choanae (blockage of the passages between the nasal cavity and the nasopharynx), Retarded growth and/or development, Genital hypoplasia, and Ear anomalies/deafness. Since the first description of the syndrome, several other characteristics have been added, including balance problems (Admiraal, Joosten, & Huygen, 1998). A working party of international experts on CHARGE syndrome has agreed that any neonate or child can be diagnosed with this syndrome when the following classic symptoms are present: coloboma, choanal atresia, and asymmetric facial palsy or short, wide ear with little or no lobe, in combination with other specific congenital anomalies (Blake & Prasad, 2006). From the first description of the syndrome by Hall (1979) until 2004, there was uncertainty concerning the genetic origin of the syndrome. In 2004, a group of Dutch researchers (Jongmans et al., 2006) found that a gene called CHD 7hd located on chromosome 8 was defective and caused the multiple organ dysfunction in these persons. In

a small percentage, this defect is hereditary, but in by far the majority of the cases it results from a spontaneous mutation of the gene (Jongmans et al., 2006).

The degree of physical and mental impairments varies considerably among individuals with CHARGE syndrome. In some persons, the retina is almost completely closed (minor colobomas in the periphery of the retina), whereas in others there is a large keyhole involving the macula area. The macula is the highly sensitive area of the retina that allows people to see fine details, thus the syndrome results in vision loss ranging from mild to severe visual impairment. Variations in hearing also occur; some individuals with CHARGE are profoundly deaf, whereas others have useful residual hearing. The child's muscle strength can also vary, from so low (hypotonia) that the child will not learn to walk independently until quite late in life, to more normal tone that supports walking at around age 2 years. In a further complication, the majority of children with CHARGE syndrome lack the organ of balance. This has repercussions for walking, as well as for developing the skills necessary for learning (Brown, 2005).

It has been shown by brain imaging techniques (magnetic resonance imaging and computed tomography) that there is an array of structural cerebral anomalies in persons with CHARGE syndrome that correlate with deficits of impulse control, sleeping problems, and aggressive behavior (Johansson et al., 2006). Poorly modulated sensory systems are very common in this population (Brown, 2005). Not providing a person with CHARGE syndrome sufficient time to integrate sensory information may lead to severe outburst of anger (J. Van Dijk & De Kort, 2004; J. Van Dijk, Nelson, & De Kort, 2007). This is further documented by a neuropsychiatric investigation including 31 persons with CHARGE syndrome (Johannson et al., 2006). It was found that one-third of the participants in the sample had forebrain abnormalities that could explain difficulties in emotional control. Sensory integration problems and ASD can co-occur in CHARGE syndrome (Brown, 2005; Hartshorne, Grialou, & Parker, 2005). Very often the bones of the middle ear are malformed in these children, causing a significant degree of conductive hearing loss (Brown, 2005; Thelin, Hartshorne, & Hartshorne, 1999). However, the majority of children with CHARGE syndrome have a sensorineural hearing loss due to a malformed cochlea (Thelin et al., 1999).

The medical and health conditions of persons with CHARGE syndrome are quite fragile and often require continuous attention. This is particularly true for children with feeding problems. A number of children with CHARGE need surgery early in life to allow food to reach the stomach. This is often a traumatic experience that can cause refusal of solid food for many years and may result in feeding via a stomach tube. Much skill and patience on the part of therapists and parents is necessary if the child is to learn to receive adequate nutrition by mouth (J. Van Dijk et al., 2007). It can therefore be understood that the early years of life are particularly difficult for both parents and child. The physical care, which often requires frequent hospitalization, demands much energy from parents during the first years and leaves little time for the fostering of harmonious interactions and education.

The diagnosis of CHARGE syndrome is rather new, and there have been few studies conducted regarding the educational outcomes of persons with this syndrome. It was reported by Blake (2005) that a group of 30 individuals with CHARGE syndrome who were in their teens and adolescence manifested behavioral concerns, including aggressiveness, self-harm, and sleep problems. It was quite alarming that 62% of the persons needed psychotropic drugs for behavior control.

USHER SYNDROME

Usher syndrome involves the co-occurrence of retinitis pigmentosa (RP) and hearing impairment, and is one of the leading causes of deafblindness in the United States (Killoran, 2007). Usher syndrome is classified into three types: Usher type I, II, and III. Usher type I is characterized by severe to profound congenital sensorineural deafness, constant vestibular dysfunction (balance deficiency), and prepuberal onset of retinitis pigmentosa and night blindness. Persons with Usher type II have a congenital mild to moderate hearing loss, normal vestibular responses, and RP during the second decade of life. Persons with Usher type III have a progressive hearing loss, variable vestibular problems, and variable RP (Kumar, Babu, Kimberling, & Venkatesh, 2004). The percentage of persons with Usher syndrome varies between 4% and 6% of the deaf population. Most of the individuals considered in these percentages are individuals with Usher type I, who are more often known to service providers of children with hearing loss.

It is only in countries with a high standard of medical services that children's retinal anomalies can be detected at an early age. Before the age of 4–5 years, the rod cells function normally. These are photoreceptor cells that are responsible for peripheral and night vision. Therefore, the child's visual field is not restricted, nor does the child suffer from night blindness. The eyes are still able to adapt to darkness or dimly lit environments. However, the complete absence of balance function in Usher type I can be observed at a young age when children normally begin walking. After attempts to stand and take the first steps are unsuccessful, the children may cease their efforts and begin creeping on their legs and arms until they feel that their muscles are strong enough to compensate for the lack of balance. Most of the children with Usher syndrome type I do not learn to walk independently before the age of 18 months (Möller et al., 1989).

As a general rule, night vision loss in Usher syndrome begins first and then blind spots develop in the periphery of the retina. These spots enlarge and merge into a doughnut shape, producing tunnel vision. Central vision is reduced and blurred, but in some cases, the field of vision might be very limited yet remain sharp for many years. The speed of the degenerative process differs from person to person. Even in sisters or brothers with the syndrome, the process can develop quite differently. To obtain an understanding of the visual function of persons with Usher syndrome, it is important to note that even when "tunnel vision" occurs, there may be living cells left in the periphery of the retina that signal movements. This explains why a person with Usher syndrome and a very restricted field of 20 degrees may still pick up moving signals, such as may be seen when a person sitting at his side begins signing. At middle age, about half of the individuals in the Usher type I population are completely or nearly blind. Others may retain central vision until very late in life. As mentioned previously, it is difficult to predict the rate of deterioration.

The transition process from a visual communication mode to touch-based communication in a person with deterioration of vision was studied by Lahtinen (2008). She described and analyzed the process by following two highly educated individuals over a period of 14 years, describing 24 stages that showed the transition from visual to tactile communication. An increasing number of body parts play a role in this process (e.g., head movements, tapping on the leg, drawing on the palm of the hand).

The life of a person with Usher type II is quite different from that of an individual who has Usher type I. The diagnosis of Usher type II often comes in early adulthood after formal education has been completed. In some instances, an individual with

Usher syndrome type II might have already selected a profession that is not in accordance with future visual deterioration. As opposed to individuals with type I, individuals with type II do not generally consider themselves to be members of the Deaf community.

Persons with Usher type III have intact hearing and sight at birth. Hearing deteriorates with time, as does vision. Most of the hearing problems are noticed by the teenage years, and individuals with the disorder become deaf by mid- to late adulthood. Night blindness begins around puberty. Blind spots appear in the retina in their late teens or early 20s and by middle age, these individuals are usually blind.

Medical Considerations and Therapies for Usher Syndrome

Usher syndrome is inherited according to Mendelian law and is autosomal recessive. This means that both parents must be carriers of a defective gene. This gene may occur on more than one chromosome, and the chromosomal location varies depending on specific syndrome type (e.g., Usher type I is located on five different chromosomes). Sometimes the location on different chromosomes affects the clinical manifestation of the syndrome (Davenport, 2008). Since both parents are carriers of the defective gene that causes Usher syndrome, the chance that their offspring will have the syndrome is 1:4. If one of the parents actually has the syndrome, the chance will be 50% that one of their children will inherit the syndrome. If both parents have the syndrome, the odds increase to nearly 100% (Online Mendelian Inheritance in Man [OMIM], 2008). It therefore is very important to explain the genetic nature of the syndrome to the family and the individual with Usher syndrome. Many times over the years, Jan van Dijk, one author of this chapter, has found that there is a misunderstanding about the origin of the syndrome, particularly in the Deaf community (e.g., it is rumored that Usher syndrome is associated with alcohol misuse). Such misconceptions contribute an extra psychological burden to all persons involved.

During the last decade, a great deal of research has been carried out on treatments to inhibit degeneration or improve RP, the major eye disease seen in the syndrome. Some of the therapies were misleading or lacked scientific evidence of their efficacy. Recently, ten patients with RP were implanted with a capsule in the vitreous body of the eye that contained a substance called *ciliary neurotropic factor*, which might stop the progression of retinal deterioration. The results were not unambiguously positive, but were, on the whole, promising (Sieving, Caruso, Tao, Coleman, Thomson, Fullmer, & Bush, 2006).

Cochlear implants have proven to be very valuable for persons with all three types of Usher syndrome. Such individuals are considered to be good candidates for this intervention because of the accessibility of the electrodes in the cochlea and the general emotional stability of individuals with Usher syndrome (Damen, Pennings, Snik, & Mylanus, 2006; Pennings, Damen, Snik, Hoefsloot, Cremers, & Mylanus, 2006).

Emotional Stability and Usher Syndrome

During his career, J. van Dijk has assessed over 300 clients with differing types of Usher syndrome. Consistently, informing the young client and his or her parents and other family members about the outcome of the medical diagnosis was a tremendous shock to all parties. Surprisingly enough, this rarely led to prolonged periods of depression on the part of the client with Usher syndrome, nor did it lead to posttraumatic stress disorders. We have attempted to back up this clinical experience, which is shared by many colleagues, with some research. The sample of participants in the resulting study (Vermeulen & Van Dijk, 1994) was a group of 16 adolescents (mean age 13;6 years) who were diagnosed with Usher syndrome type I. Persons who knew the youngsters very well were asked to fill out the California Q test (Block, 1978). Using this test, questions were answered concerning several dimensions of the youngsters' personalities. The conclusion of this pilot study was that the clients were judged to have a very strong ego-resilience, a high level of pro-social competence (which is advantageous for social contacts), and high self-esteem, but lacked assertiveness, perhaps because of overprotection. These characteristics enabled the youth to be good candidates for successful rehabilitation. Similar findings were reported in a research study carried out in six European Union countries (Damen, Krabbe, Kilsby, & Milanus, 2005). The sample consisted of 26 persons with Usher syndrome type I, 27 with type II, four with type III, and ten with an unknown type. The main findings were that these individuals worked very hard to remain independent and keep a positive outlook about their lives. The interviews revealed that the individuals with Usher syndrome wanted to be well-informed about adaptive hearing and sight equipment, as well as about new methods that might help them keep in contact with their environments.

CONGENITAL RUBELLA SYNDROME

Persons who are deafblind due to maternal contraction of rubella during the first trimester of pregnancy display a triad of symptoms including cataracts, hearing loss, and a systolic heart murmur. The early gestational period is when important organs are developing, including the eyes, ears, and heart. In this period, the rubella virus also inhibits the growth of brain cells, which has a detrimental effect on the person's behavior and ability to learn. During 1963–64, a pandemic of rubella spread throughout the world and caused the birth of thousands of children with impairments of vision and/or hearing, as well as other mental and physical symptoms. Medical authorities were able to isolate the virus and, in 1969, developed a vaccine to protect future mothers and their children. Vaccination campaigns were launched in various countries and diminished the outbreak of the disease significantly (Hinman, 2007). According to the data of the World Health Organization (2008), 127 countries include a rubella vaccination in their health systems. Therefore, about 40% of the birth cohort in the year 2008 (http://www.who.int/immunization) received the immunization. However, it is estimated that 110,000 new cases of CRS still occur each year.

In response to the rubella outbreak of the 1960s, educational authorities developed large-scale programs for children who were deafblind from rubella. Until that time, few children with deafblindness had been identified and educated, and parents and teachers who were confronted with the rubella pandemic found it inspirational to learn from the experiences of other parents and professionals. When children with CRS began to enter educational programs, it became obvious that they had many disabilities in addition to hearing and vision impairments. Virtually all the children with rubella-related cataracts showed patterns of repetitive, stereotypical behaviors (e.g., waving their hands in front of their eyes, jumping, or whirling) that were hard to control (J. Van Dijk, 1982, 1991). When attempts were made to eliminate these repetitive behaviors, the children went on to develop other challenging behaviors. Many of the children with CRS displayed autistic tendencies or were diagnosed as having autism (Chess, Korn, & Fernandez, 1971). Despite these overwhelming difficulties, many individuals with CRS manage to overcome their problems and reach a satisfying level of independent living. Others need life-long support or care (J. Dijk, 1991).

A question that has been raised concerning the CRS population is whether there are late manifestations of the disease. It is known that, because of high eye pressure (leading to glaucoma), some individuals with CRS lose their sight later in life. Others develop diabetes and/or experience a deterioration of hearing (Munroe, 1999; O'Donnell, 1991; J. Van Dijk, 1991). In the framework of the Health Watch Program, a research project was undertaken in the Netherlands (Kingma, Schoenmaker, Damen, & Nunen, 1997). The study included 69 participants with CRS etiology (average age 32 years), all of whom were receiving custodial care and were considered to have severe to profound ID. The research clearly demonstrated the vulnerability of the eyes in this population. One-fourth of the participants had developed glaucoma, and in 13% the retina had become detached (ablatio retinae). In CRS, the increasing visual impairment that often leads to total blindness occurs so slowly that the person and individuals in his or her environment are scarcely aware of its worsening. Even when totally blind, the person may still exhibit visually oriented behaviors, such as staring at the hands. Not surprisingly, early research showed that increasing visual impairment had a negative effect on the person's level of functioning (J. Van Dijk, 1991).

The Kingma et al. study (1997) also looked at hearing losses in their sample population and found that the hearing loss increased over time in 30% of the individuals. In addition, the behavior of 70% of the sample was considered to be "difficult," with reported high levels of aggression, social withdrawal, and obsessive behaviors. Results of follow-up studies in Canada yielded similar findings. It was reported that, in the Canadian sample, 15.3% of the participants had a mild to moderate hearing loss and 83.7% had a severe to profound hearing loss. Change in hearing acuity was experienced by 30.1% (Munroe, 1999). Individuals with CRS often experience increasing physical problems (e.g., diabetes mellitus) with age, and this appears to lead to increased difficulties coping with the demands of ordinary life. It has been shown that synaptic growth is delayed in children with CRS, which offers an explanation for the general intellectual and emotional arrest of these persons (Brown, Cohen, Greenwald, & Susser, 2000). Further investigations of the underlying causes of physical and mental problems in this population are urgently needed (Nicholas, 2000).

Intervention and Educational Curricula for Children Who Are Deafblind

The rubella outbreak of the mid-1960s and the subsequent exponential increase in the number of children with deafblindness necessitated the urgent development of effective teaching methods appropriate to their needs. Until the outbreak, reports had appeared pertaining to the successful but challenging efforts of educators to teach individual students who were deafblind, but who apparently did not have the cognitive and behavioral sequelae of many children with CRS. The detailed writings of Samuel Gridley Howe (1801–1876) are, to this day, interesting to read. They describe how Howe worked to teach language to his deafblind student, Laura Bridgman. Howe tried to teach Laura to associate a wooden letter with an object (e.g., the wooden letters K-E-Y presented with an actual key). However, no matter the object, Laura did not seem to understand the meaning of the exercise until she wanted to get her favorite doll, which had been locked away. When the letters of the word "key" were put in front of her, she put them in the correct order and immediately the door was unlocked by the key. Despite her obvious intelligence, Laura had great difficulty learning to understand that words have meaning.

A similar process was described by Helen Keller's teacher, Ann Sullivan Macy. Sullivan Macy worked tirelessly to teach Helen, via fingerspelling in the hand, that objects have names (Herrmann, 1998). In their landmark study on symbolization, Werner and Kaplan (1963) illustrated the idea of symbolization in a child's mind by using Helen Keller as an example. They theorized that in the symbolic development of a child, there is a stage in which the child discovers the similarity between the vehicle (the onomatopoeic utterance or iconic gestures) and its referent. In Helen's case, it occurred when Ms. Sullivan fingerspelled w-a-t-e-r at the same time water from a pump was running over her hand into Helen's hand. The discovery of the similarity between the "running" of the water over one hand and running of the finger spelled word w-a-t-e-r in the other hand enabled a breakthrough in Helen's symbolic understanding of language. The examples of Laura Bridgman and Helen Keller demonstrate how difficult it is for a child with congenital deafblindness, even in the presence of at least normal levels of cognitive potential, to understand that arbitrary, symbolic vehicles can refer to ideas that exist in the minds of other people.

The descriptions of these two children were useful in the development of curricula for children born after the rubella pandemic, because they made educators aware of the many steps a typically developing child has to take before he or she reaches the level of symbolic use of a language. J. van Dijk and his colleagues at the Sint-Michielsgestel deafblind school, Rafael, in the Netherlands analyzed these steps and used them in the development of a curriculum. The curriculum was first published in a short article entitled, *The first steps of a deafblind child towards language* (J. Van Dijk, 1966). The Dutch approach received a great deal of attention because it provided teachers with concrete ideas on how to teach their students who were deafblind with CRS. The original ideas were expanded over the years into a comprehensive curriculum (MacFarland, 1993, 1995). This curriculum is now known as "The van Dijk curriculum." However, it should be noted that the original author collaborated with a team at the deafblind school and that all team members contributed to these curricular methods.

PRINCIPLES OF THE VAN DIJK CURRICULUM

In the van Dijk approach, the interpersonal *relationship* between the child and his or her educator is crucial. It is felt that the majority of children with congenital deafblindness are at risk of failing to develop a warm relationship with their principal caregiver, and healthy attachment is considered fundamental for emotional, social, and cognitive development (J. Van Dijk & Janssen, 1993; Janssen, Riksen-Walraven, & Van Dijk, 2002). With this in mind, the approach is "child guided." This means that the educator follows the children in their interests and from there develops a relationship with them by responding to their initiatives. For example, if a child is obsessed by a certain sensory stimulation, toy, or activity, the educator does not try to stop these behaviors, but rather tries to engage *with* the child in these activities. In this manner, interaction between the educator and child is established. The formation of attachment bonds are an integral part of the child-guided approach, and this leads to a pleasant and positive climate surrounding the child. This does not preclude the use of other approaches such as Social-Learning theory (Janssen et al., 2002) or Positive Behavior Support (Bambara, Dunlap, & Schwartz, 2004) if the needs of individual children dictate a need for additional supports (Sterkenburg, Schuengel, & Janssen, 2008).

It is generally agreed that about two-thirds of children with congenital deafblindness have cognitive impairment (Killoran, 2007). This is partly due to *sensory deprivation* that results in the lack of rewarding sensory input. It is therefore essential to pursue the possibilities of including the systematic use of prosthetic devices in the educational program (e.g., low-vision aids, hearing aids, and cochlear implants).

BUILDING BLOCKS OF THE VAN DIJK CURRICULUM

The following building blocks are used throughout the van Dijk curriculum. It must be noted however, that while these building blocks appear hierarchical in nature, the methods do not necessarily occur in any sequence and some might, in fact, occur concurrently.

Resonance

This method is used to establish a relationship with a child who has congenital deafblindness and is responding at an emotional level to stimuli. When using resonance, the educator tries to engage within the emotional status of the child and becomes, in essence, an extension of the child's emotions. He mirrors the child's laugh, hand flapping of excitement, pushing away of an undesired toy, or the stroking of his or her own body. Through the use of this approach, the child is met on his or her own grounds, and they share the world of emotions. Pleasurable situations are repeated over and over again, so they become "engraved" in those structures of the hippocampus that are involved in memory.

When the child's nervous system is deprived of adequate stimulation, he or she will compensate by producing self-stimulatory behaviors. Some external stimuli (e.g., smell or touch) might trigger strong reactions in the individuals, as situations in which the child previously found homeostasis between the status of the brain and the external stimuli are remembered (e.g., a person who has a unique scent and is comforting to the child). This behavior can only be understood by considering the function of the limbic system. The limbic system (from the Latin "limbus" or arch) consists of those brain structures that are involved in emotion, motivation, and pleasure. It is also involved in the memory of emotions. In the evolution of mankind, the limbic system developed quite early. It can be considered to belong to the "ancient" brain, but also contains a few newer structures. Sensory input that enters our brain is strongly interwoven with emotions, and in particular, feelings of approach (appetite) and withdrawal (aversion). This process plays an important role in the development of *attachment*. Individuals

to whom the child becomes attached leave traces in important nuclei of the limbic system, particularly the amygdala and the hippocampus, as the child experiences the touch, odor, facial expressions, and voice intonations of these individuals. In normal development, a connection develops between the limbic brain structures and higher cortical areas. For example, the child not only senses our presence at an emotional level, but also *knows* that we are there through use of cortical processes (Beatty, 1995; Rocha do Amaral & Martins de Olieveira, 2008).

At the end of the last century, the role of a unique neural system (*the mirror neuron*) was described (Rizolatti, Gallese, Fadiga, & Fogassi, 1996). The mirror neurons function as a matching system between persons. When the motor actions or emotions of a person are perceived, neuronal activity corresponding to similar actions are triggered in the observer. It is believed that these mirror neurons play a critical role in processes such as empathy, imitation, and language. There is evidence that a dysfunction of the mirror neurons in children with ASD, at least in part, explains the social and language deficits that are often seen in these children (Oberman, Pineda, & Ramachandran, 2007). By the same token, it helps to explain why symptoms of ASD are so prominent in children who are completely blind (Cass, 1996; Dale & Sonksen, 2002). It is likely that mirror neurons also play a role in the sense of touch. Intensive physical contact between the child who is deafblind and his caregiver, in combination with the use of other senses, might well lead to better personal relationships and interactions (Nafstad & Rødbroe, 1999).

Co-active Movement

Jan Van Dijk introduced the term "co-active movement" to describe a method that is a bridge between "joining in" with the child's emotional behavior at a preconscious, limbic level and behavior that occurs at a more conscious, cortical level. The term *co-active movement* is used when the caregiver or educator is in direct physical contact with the child. The two move and act together, and when the child shows intentional behavior (e.g., waiting, approach, withdrawal), the partner (caregiver or educator) senses the intention through the changes of the child's body. He or she responds by either following the child's initiative or beginning a new initiative. In this way, a subtle kind of *interaction* develops and the beginning of a dialogue can be seen (Enerstvedt, 1996; MacFarland, 1995; J. Van Dijk, 1986; Wheeler & Griffin, 1997; Writer, 1987).

There is evidence that even educators who have a great deal of experience with children who are deafblind miss most of the signals sent by a child who is deafblind and is functionally in an early developmental stage. This is often caused by the very idiosyncratic nature of the child's communications (Janssen et al., 2002; Nelson, Van Dijk, McDonnell, & Thompson, 2002; Vervloed, R. Van Dijk, Knoors, & J. Van Dijk, 2006). In a microanalysis of the effects of the interaction between a deafblind child and his or her teacher, Vervloed et al. (2006) revealed that both teacher and child missed the initiatives of each other frequently (59% and 67%, respectively). On the basis of this study, it could be concluded that the effective interaction time between teacher and child was limited. It is thus acceptable, when beginning the co-active stage, that the educator or caregiver makes the majority of the initiatives, but gradually, he or she should carefully follow the child's movements and allow the child to take the lead.

Imitation

Co-active movement leads the child directly to *imitation*. In co-active movement, the educator or partner copies the child's movements, but later, the child is encouraged to copy the movements of the partner (e.g., tapping, clapping, touching the face, opening and closing the mouth, etc.). Initially, the imitation activities will be simultaneous, but later, the activities can be deferred. It seems that specific mirror neurons are activated during the imitation process. Due to external conditions such as sensory impairments, endogenous causes, or an interaction between the two, there might be a failure or distortion in the development of these neurons. The consequence of this might be an impaired representation of self and relationship to others, or even a lack of understanding of the emotions of others.

Symbols

As the child moves toward symbolism, the exercises of mutual copying become less strict and more independent of the original. Materials can then be used in a more flexible way by both partners because there is a growing "distance" from the original model (Bruce, 2005). The child's hands may point or touch the partner to make him or her aware of a shared experience, and from this it becomes obvious that the body has become a medium for representation. In some instances, this leads to the child initiating gestures or incorporating the signs that are offered by the educator in playful conversation.

A subcommittee within the organization Deafblind International (DbI) has expanded upon this theory of the enhancement of the development of symbolism. They speak about co-creating a situation with the child who is deafblind and that this co-creation is possible only when there is an intimate knowledge of the child's life (Rødbroe & Souriau, 1999). In a vein similar to Van Dijk's co-active movement, the subcommittee speaks of situations in which the child and his or her partner share the world of "intimate knowledge" (Souriau, 2007, p.13). This togetherness is then the source for the creation of gestures by the child. The communication partner engages in negotiation with the child about what is really in his or her mind. For example, the partner might repeat the child's gesture and ask through bodily signs, "Is this what you mean?" Through such negotiation, a shared meaning is created. The sign or symbol is what is negotiated, and the shared meaning is what emerges from the sequences of negotiations (Nafstad & Rødbroe, 1999). When this successfully occurs, the child has reached the level of *symbolic behavior.* To put it in the words of Cassirer, a famous philosopher on symbolization, the child has entered "the world of contemplation" (Cassirer, 1944). The developed signs or symbols can be very personal, but gradually can be incorporated into a more formal system and combined with other signs. "This marks the beginning of linguistic understanding and expression" (Bruce, 2005, p. 234).

An important stage in the development of symbolization is "joint attention." In situations in which there is mutual involvement of the deafblind child and his conversational partner, an attempt is made to direct the partner's attention to other persons, situations, or objects that are of interest. Joint attention is often a difficult juncture in the deafblind child's path to symbol processing. Failure of this development might inhibit the child's social development and even lead to autistic-like behaviors (Ramachandran, 2000; Williams, Whiten, Suddendor, & Perrett, 2001). This provides at least one explanation for why children who are deafblind sometimes also have features of autism.

It is worthwhile when considering communication in the child who is deafblind to look closely at the tactile modality (Bruce, 2005; Nafstad & Rødbroe, 1999). Miles (1998) advocates having mutual tactile experiences by using the *hand under hand approach.* This provides both partners with information concerning the emotional status of the other in much the way co-active movement does. In these shared experiences, there is a need for both partners to reflect upon the situation. For this reason, two important building blocks, objects of reference and calendars, are introduced into van Dijk's curriculum. These building blocks contribute to the enhancement of the child's gradual transition from natural gestures and other nonsymbolic communication to knowledge of concrete, iconic representation, and finally, to more abstract symbolism. Bruce (2005) emphasizes that *symbolic play* will facilitate the (deafblind) child's symbolic development.

Objects of Reference

Communication with a deafblind child is facilitated when concrete objects are used to represent activities. Initially, the selected objects are ones that have the most meaning to an individual child's activities (e.g., chain on a swing, soap for taking a bath, buckle for a seat belt when going in the car). The selected objects should be small (e.g., one link of the swing chain or a small piece of therapy mat to represent physical therapy), so they can go into a calendar or sequence box or system and be reasonably portable. An important step in the development of symbolization occurs when the actual object used in the activity is replaced with one that represents or symbolizes the "real" object. The transition to higher symbolism can then evolve as more symbolic, but still iconic pictures are used, and finally, more abstract icons or pictures come to represent the activities or objects. Objects of reference that stand for activities or objects are now widely used with persons who have significant difficulties in communication. It has been shown that so-called *tangible symbols* (three- or two-dimensional objects of reference) are effective in enhancing receptive and expressive communication (Rowland & Schweigert, 2004).

Calendar Systems

The use of the calendar system is an essential part of the van Dijk curriculum (J. Van Dijk, 1986). Originally, calendar systems were designed as a means of sharing joint experiences with the deafblind child. But because they were understood by both communication partners, they also evolved to serve as topics of *conversation* (Blaha, 2001; Tellefson, 2007). A calendar book or box helps to store and organize concepts in the mind of the deafblind child and facilitates the development of cohesive structures of knowledge. In discovering that a certain sequence exists in events (*routines*), the possibility arises that the child will *anticipate* the next step in a sequence. Anticipation has always played an important role in the curriculum. In anticipatory events, the brain is focused on a certain target, and this focus will enhance memory, storage, and subsequent retrieval of the target. There is some neurobiological evidence that anticipation contributes to growth of synaptic density (Quartz & Sejnowski, 1997), and synaptic density is crucial for learning.

VALIDITY OF THE VAN DIJK CURRICULUM

During the period 1965 through 1985 in which pre- and perinatal rubella was a leading cause of childhood deafblindness, many programs were funded worldwide. The "Dutch approach" was, for many of these programs, a beacon. Because of the subsequent widespread use of the rubella vaccination, rubella has decreased but there has been an increase in the number of children born with very low birth weight, thus resulting in a continued, significant population of children who are deafblind. However, the behavioral and ability profiles of the population have changed over the years and, accordingly, the original curriculum has been adapted many times. Many elements have become integral components in diverse programs for children with multiple sensory impairment and children with autism. For example, the calendar system was extended to become a detailed teaching instrument and has been used for children with severe ID and for children with multiple disabilities (Alsop, 2002; Blaha & Moss, 1997; Miles & Riggio, 1999; Park, 1997). The same can be said of routines, anticipation, and co-active movements that are interwoven within the van Dijk curriculum. This supports the conclusion that the positive effects of the curriculum can be generalized from unique and idiosyncratic settings, procedures, and participants to other populations and conditions.

An example of such an adaptation of the curriculum methods of the van Dijk approach is seen in the Promoting Learning through Active Integration curriculum (PLAI) (Chen, Klein, & Haney, 2007) (Note: this is not the same as the PLAI language test.) In this curriculum, interventionists are taught to promote early communication in infants and toddlers who are deafblind. To realize this objective, a curriculum was designed that consists of five modules. These modules contain activities drawn from the van Dijk approach, such as using routines and anticipatory cues, imitation, interrupting familiar routines (stop and go), and object cues or objects of reference. Field testing with 25 infants and toddlers and their interventionists demonstrated that 35% of the interventionists in the study said that cues helped them to communicate better, and 74% of the children anticipated and participated more in activities. On the whole, the curriculum increased communication between the interventionist and child.

Another curriculum of note is based on the van Dijk approach and the ideas developed by Nafstad and Rødbroe (1999) of "co-creating communication." This curriculum is called *Contact* and is available on CD-ROM (Van den Tillaart & Janssen, 2006). The *Contact* curriculum came into being through the analysis completed by Janssen, Riksen-Walraven, and Van Dijk (2003) that examined the reasons why high-quality interactions between children with disabilities and their caregivers are so often at risk. The first risk factor identified was the complexity of the children. Such children need an assessment that is customized to their needs, and this is often not accomplished. Therefore, there is a lack of certainty on the part of the caregiver as to how to approach the child. A second factor identified was self-stimulating behavior. Such behavior makes it difficult to contact and interact with the child. The third factor was that the caregiver did not respond in an appropriate manner to the child who is deafblind. A final factor was the high degree of arousal often observed in this population. Small, unexpected changes on the part of the caregiver can trigger strong negative reactions (Janssen et al., 2003).

Janssen et al. (2003) developed intervention strategies to improve child–caregiver and child–educator interactions. The strategies proved to be appropriate for students who are deafblind and have severe impediments of interaction and communication. A multiple baseline design across participants (four children and 14 educators) was used to evaluate the functional relationship between the intervention and changes in the frequencies of target behaviors. The results indicated that positive effects of the intervention on children's interactive competence were brought about by improved educator responses. In subsequent research studies, adaptations of the interactive context (e.g., communicative aids such as calendar boxes or object cues) were included (Janssen et al., 2003). Teachers and care staff were trained to elicit as many appropriate interactions as possible from the child and to appropriately respond to these behaviors. These events were video recorded and discussed during group supervision sessions. It was demonstrated that the now-adapted curriculum led to higher-quality interactions by teachers in a relatively short period of time. When appropriate interactive teacher behaviors increased, the number of inappropriate behaviors on the part

of children decreased (Janssen et al., 2003). A similar intervention program has been produced on DVD by Axelrod, Conlin, and Smith (2008).

Assessment of Students with Congenital Deafblindness

School professionals who are asked to assess students with congenital deafblindness face many challenges due to the unique nature of the disability and its low incidence of occurrence (Silberman, Bruce, & Nelson, 2004). Such challenges are magnified when the student also has additional disabilities such as cognitive, motor, and/or health impairments. Perhaps the most problematic of available assessment instruments are standardized evaluations that purport to measure IQ or provide mental age levels (Mar, 1996). It is important to remember that very few standardized instruments have been developed specifically for the population of children and youth who are deafblind, and those few only measure accomplishments that do not require language (Geenens, 1999). Such instruments are sometimes adapted in an attempt to accommodate for deafblindness. However, once such accommodations are implemented, results must be very cautiously interpreted because the standard procedures have been altered and thus, the scores may not be valid (Mar, 1996). When such "adapted" instruments are used with children with multiple disabilities and sensory impairments, resulting information is often inaccurate and may underestimate true potential (Linder, 2008; Mar, 1996; Nelson et al., 2002).

Standardized testing instruments often do not take into account the impact the combined sensory impairments, motor disabilities, communication impairments, and health problems seen in this population of children has on every area of development (Greenspan & Meisels, 1994; McCune, Kalmanson, Fleck, Glazenwski, & Sillari, 1990; Nelson et al., 2002). For example, children who are congenitally deafblind will often have limited understanding of abstract concepts such as the relationship of miniature objects to their larger referents. Therefore, adequate accommodation using standardized prescribed, artificial testing materials would be impossible. In addition, if such children have limited receptive communication, they will be unable to see or hear what is being asked of them (Nelson et al., 2002). In the same vein, children with health impairments may tire easily and be reluctant to perform tasks that demand motor activity (McCune et al., 1990). Finally, children who are congenitally deafblind and/or have other severe multiple disabilities may have difficulty establishing relationships with individuals with whom they are not familiar and have difficulties with unfamiliar settings and materials (Greenspan & Meisels, 1994; Linder, 2008; Mar, 1996; Van Dijk, 1999). Thus, if a child is anxious and has difficulty with expressive language, he or she may choose to communicate through behaviors that are deemed inappropriate and serve to further undermine the assessment process (J. Van Dijk, 1999).

Due to the limitations posed by such assessments, as well as by the need to have assessments that provide information that can serve to enhance educational programming, several different approaches to assessment have emerged. Such instruments include developmental checklists, ecological inventories, and informal interactional and observational tools (Silberman et al., 2004; Westling & Fox, 2008). Because of the complex nature of deafblindness, a complete assessment process will involve a combination of tools and instruments and utilize a collaborative team approach (Silberman et al., 2004).

The Callier-Azusa Scale, Edition G (Stillman, 1978) is a developmental scale that was developed for young children who are deafblind and was strongly influenced by the work of Jan van Dijk. It contains 18 subscales that include the areas of communication and language, motor, perception, daily living skills, cognition, and social development. The scale is lengthy and requires extensive observation of a child in varied contexts. It can be used with children who are 8 years of age and under, but it is most helpful for children with very significant impairments and delays. As with other developmental scales, it is not appropriate for children older than 8 (Silberman et al., 2004).

Other approaches to assessment include ecological inventories that analyze the skills and activities required within a given setting (Brown, Evans, Weed, & Owen, 1987). Often, ecological inventories begin with the assessor first listing those skills that a person without disabilities uses to perform a given task within an activity and then go on to analyze the student's ability to perform the now delineated necessary skills. When a discrepancy is seen between the demands of the task or activity and the student's performance, accommodations and therapeutic interventions can be designed. Ecological inventories should be conducted across environments and learning areas, including home, school, workplace, and recreational settings (Downing, 2002; Westling & Fox, 2008).

The *van Dijk Approach to Assessing Children Who Are Deafblind or Have Multiple Disabilities* (Nelson & Van Dijk, 2002; Nelson et al., 2002) is an example of an informal tool that is child-guided and involves careful observation and interaction with children. After an interview with parents to determine the child's interests and what parents would like to see as a result of the assessment, the process proceeds through the use of playful activities that are guided by the child's interests and successes (Westling & Fox, 2008). The evaluator takes time during the assessment to establish rapport and a trusting relationship with the child through these play activities. Throughout the nonlinear process, the evaluator is looking to determine the underlying developmental abilities or processes the child uses as he or she learns. The areas looked at are (a) biobehavioral state, including the ability to maintain and modulate state; (b) preferred learning channels; (c) stimuli the child approaches or withdraws from; (d) ability to accommodate new experiences within existing schemes; (e) ability to learn, remember, and anticipate routines; (f) approach to problem solving used; (g) social interaction skills, including the ability to form social attachment; and (h) communication modes and skills (Nelson, et al., 2002; Silberman et al., 2004; Westling & Fox, 2008). This approach is further illustrated in the CD-ROM *Child-Guided Strategies for Assessing Children Who Are Deafblind or Have Multiple Disabilities* (Nelson & Van Dijk, 2002).

Another example of a more informal instrument is Dimensions of Communication (Mar & Sall, 1999). The tool was designed specifically for children with multiple disabilities, including deafblindness, who communicate primarily on a nonsymbolic level, but it also assesses the child's ability to use and understand more symbolic communication. Therefore, assessed areas include the communicative areas of symbol use, intent, complexity, social action, vocabulary use, and comprehension. Both the Mar and Sall (1999) and the Nelson and Van Dijk (2002) assessment tools provide guidance and instruction on how to use the obtained assessment information to guide intervention. This is, without doubt, the most important function of assessment.

Summary and Conclusions

The population of individuals who are deaf or hard of hearing and have additional disabilities is a large and diverse one. Of all DHH children at least 20% have one or more additional disabilities (Schirmer, 2001). Although many of these additional disabilities are of a mild nature (e.g., learning disability), approximately 9% have a significant cognitive disability (Heward, 2003). As seen earlier, children who are deaf or hard of hearing may have autism and again, others may be deafblind. Their concurrent disabilities can be due to many factors. Causal factors include genetic syndromes; problems that occur before, during, or slightly after birth; and those that might be acquired later in life through infections or traumatic brain injury. Regardless of the diagnosis or etiology, there is one constant across all the individuals. They deserve to have communication, education, rehabilitation, and adaptive and augmentative equipment that will allow them to maximize their potential and lead lives that are full and rich and high in quality.

As the field of special education has grown and evolved, many promising practices and treatments have emerged from research, but as has been seen, there is still a paucity of evidence-based practices designed to meet the needs of these individuals with multiple disabilities. In addition, as evidence-based practices emerge, we need highly skilled educators and therapists trained and ready to make the transition from research to practice, to ensure that the individuals discussed in this chapter have opportunities that will lead to full and productive lives in every sense.

References

Admiraal, R., Joosten, T., & Huygen, P. (1998). Temporal bone CT findings in the CHARGE association. *International Journal of Pediatric Otorhinolaryngology, 45*, 151–162.

Alsop, L. (2002). *Understanding deafblindness.* Logan, UT: Ski-hi Institute.

American Psychiatric Association (1987). *Diagnostic and statistical manual of mental disorders: DSM-III-R.* Washington DC. Author.

Axelrod, C., Conlin, K., & Smith, T. (2008). *You make the difference: An educator-oriented process for supporting high quality interactions with students who are deafblind* (DVD). Austin, TX: The Texas School for the Blind and Visually Impaired.

Bailly, D., De Chouly de Lenclave, M., & Lauwerier, L. (2003). Déficience auditive et troubles psychopathologiques chez l'enfant et l'adolescent: Revue de la littérature récente [Hearing Impairment and psychopathological disorders in children and adolescents.Review of recent literature]. *L'Encéphale, 29*(1), 329–337 (with a summary in English).

Bambara, L. M., Dunlap, G., & Schwartz, I. S. (2004). *Positive behavior support: Critical articles on improving practice for individuals with severe disabilities.* Pro-ed, Inc. and TASH.

Batshaw, M., & Shapiro, B., (2002). Mental retardation. In M. Batshaw (Ed.), *Children with disabilities,* 5th edition (pp. 287–306). Baltimore, MD: Paul H. Brookes.

Beatty, J. (1995). *Principles of behavioral neuroscience.* Chicago: Brown & Benchmark.

Berke, J. (2007). *Top 10 causes of hearing loss in children.* Retrieved September, 18, 2008 from www.deafness.about.com

Blaha, R. (2001). *Calendars for students with multiple impairments including deafblindness.* Austin, TX: Texas School for the Blind and Visually Impaired.

Blaha, K., & Moss., K. (1997). Let me check my calendar. *See Hear Newsletter,* Winter 97. Retrieved November 9, 2009 from http://www.tsbvi.edu/outreach/seehear/archive

Blake, K.D. (2005). Adolescent and adult issues in CHARGE syndrome. *Clinical Pediatrics, 44*(2), 151–159.

Blake, K.D. & Prasad, C. (2006). Charge syndrome. *Orphanet Journal Rare Diseases, 1,* 34.

Block, J. (1978). *The California Q-Sort method in personality assessment and psychiatric research.* Palo Alto, CA: Consulting Psychologists Press.

Bonvillian, J., Nelson, K., & Rhyne, J. (1981). Sign language and autism. *Journal of Autism and Developmental Disorders, 11*(1), 125–137.

Brown, D. (2005). CHARGE syndrome "behaviors": Challenges or adaptations? *American Journal of Medical Genetics, 133A* (3), 268–272.

Brown, A., Cohen, P., Greenwald, S., & Susser, E. (2000). Nonaffective psychosis after prenatal exposure to rubella. *American Journal of Psychiatry, 157,* 438–443.

Brown, F., Evans, I. M., Weed, K. A., & Owen, V. (1987). Delineating functional competencies: A component model. *Journal of the Association for Persons with Severe Handicaps, 12,* 117–124.

Bruce, S.M. (2005). The application of Werner and Kaplan's "distancing" to children who are deaf-blind. *Journal of Visual Impairment and Blindness, 99*(8), 464–477.

Cass, H. (1996). Visual impairments and autism—What we know about causation and early identification. Autism and Visual Impairment Conference. *Sensory Series, 5,* 2–24.

Cassirer, E. (1944). *An essay on man: An introduction to a philosophy of human culture.* New Haven & London: Yale University Press.

Chen, D., Klein, M., & Haney, M. (2007). Promoting interaction with infants who have complex multiple disabilities. *Infants & Young Children, 20,* 149–162.

Chess, S., Korn, S.J., & Fernandez, P. (1971). *Psychiatric disorders of children with congenital rubella.* New York: Bruner/Mazel.

Coerts, J. (1994). Constituent order in Sign Language of the Netherlands and the functions of orientations. In I. Ahlgren, B. Bergman, & M. Brennan (Eds.), *Perspectives on sign language structure (Vol. 1), Papers from the Fifth International Symposium on Sign Language Research* (pp. 69–88). Durham, UK: ISLA.

Dale, N., & Sonksen, P. (2002). Developmental outcome, including setback, in young children with severe visual impairment. *Developmental Medicine & Child Neurology, 44,* 613–622.

Damen, G.W.J.A., Krabbe, P.F.M., Kilsby, M., & Mylanus, E.A.M. (2005). The Usher lifestyle survey: Maintaining independence: A multi-centre study. *International Journal of Rehabilitation Research, 28*(4), 309–320.

Damen, G., Pennings, R., Snik, A., & Mylanus, E. (2006). Quality of life and cochlear implantation in Usher syndrome type I. *The Laryngoscope, 116,* 723–728.

Davenport, S. (2008). *Gene studies in Usher syndrome* [On-line]. Minnesota DeafBlind technical assistance project. Retrieved May 7, 2008 from www.Dbproject.mn.org

Denteneer-van der Pasch, W., & Verpoorten, R. (2007). *Autisme Spectrumstoornissen.* Sint-Michielsgestel, The Netherlands: Viataal.

Downing, J. (2002). *Including students with severe and multiple disabilities in typical classrooms: Practical strategies for teachers,* 2nd edition. Baltimore, MD: Paul H. Brookes.

Enerstvedt, R.T. (1996). *Legacy of the past, those who are gone but have not left: Some aspects of the history of blind education, deaf education and deafblind education with emphasis on the time before 1900*. Dronninglund, Denmark: Forlaget Nord-Press.

Evenhuis, H., Theunissen, M., Denkers, I.,Verschuure, H., & Kemme, H. (2001). Prevalence of visual and hearing impairment in a Dutch institutionalised population with intellectual disability. *Journal of Intellectual Disability Research, 45,* 457–464.

Gallaudet Research Institute. (2006). *Regional and national summary report of data from the 2006–2007 annual survey of deaf and hard of hearing children and youth.* Washington, DC: GRI, Gallaudet University.

Geenens, D. (1999). Neurobiological development and cognition in the deafblind. In J. McInnes (Ed.), *A guide to planning and support for individuals who are deafblind* (pp. 150–174). Toronto: University of Toronto Press.

Gordon, A.G. (1993). Debate and argument: Interpretation of auditory impairment and markers for brain damage in autism. *Journal of Child Psychology and Psychiatry, 34,* 587–592.

Greenspan, I. S., & Meisels, S. (1994). Toward a new vision for the developmental assessment of infants and young children. *Zero to Three, 14*(6), 1–8.

Hall, B. (1979). Choanal atresia and associated multiple anomalies. *Journal of Pediatrics, 95,* 395–398.

Hartshorne, T. S., Grialou, T. L., & Parker, K. R. (2005). Autistic-like behavior in CHARGE Syndrome. *American Journal of Medical Genetics, 133A*(3), 257–261.

Herrmann, D. (1998). *Helen Keller: A life.* New York: Knopf

Heward, W. (2003). *Exceptional children: An introduction to special education.* Upper Saddle River, NJ: Merrill Prentice Hall.

Hinman, A. (2007). Rubella vaccination strategy. *Jornal de Pediatria, 83*(5), 389–391.

Janssen, M. J., Riksen-Walraven, J. M. A., & Van Dijk, J. (2002). Enhancing the quality of interaction between children and their educators. *Journal of Developmental and Physical Disabilities, 14,* 87–108.

Janssen, M. J., Riksen-Walraven, J. M. A., & Van Dijk, J.(2003). Contact: effects of an intervention program to foster harmonious interactions between deaf-blind children and their educators. *Journal of Visual Impairment and Blindness, 97*(4), 215–229.

Johansson, M., Rastam, M., Billstedt, E., Danielsson, S., Stromland, K., Millar, M., & Gillberg, C. (2006). Autism spectrum disorders and underlying brain pathology in CHARGE association. *Developmental Medicine & Child Neurology, 48,* 40–50.

Jongmans, M. C. J., Admiraal, R. J., Van der Donk, K. P., Vissers, L. E. L. M., Baas, A. F., Kapusta, L., et al. (2006). CHARGE syndrome: the phenotypic spectrum of mutations in the CHD7 gene. *Journal of Medical Genetics, 43,* 306–314.

Juré, R., Rapin, I., & Tuchman, R. R. (1991). Hearing impaired autistic children. *Developmental Medicine and Child Neurology, 33*(12), 1062–1072.

Killoran, J. (2007). *The national deaf-blind child count: 1998–2005 in review.* Monmouth: Teaching Research Institute Western Oregon University.

Kingma, J., Schoenmaker, A., Damen, S., & Nunen, T. (2007). *Late manifestations of congenital rubella.* Retrieved October 21, 1997 from www.nud.dk

Knoors, H., & Vervloed, M. (2003). Educational programming for deaf children with multiple disabilities. In M. Marschark & P. E. Spencer (Eds.), *Oxford handbook of deaf studies,* *language and education* (pp. 82–94). New York: Oxford University Press.

Koppers, E. & Joyeux, D. (2004). Meervoudig gehandicapte dove kleuters [Multiple handicapped deaf infants]. *Logopedie, 17*(3), 47–56.

Kumar, A., Babu, M., Kimberling, W., & Venkatesh, C. (2004). Genetic analyses of a four generations Indian family with Usher syndrome: a novel insertion mutation in MYO7A. *Molecular Vision, 10,* 910–916.

Lagati, S. (1995). "Deaf-blind" or "deafblind"? International perspectives on terminology. *Journal of Visual Impairment and Blindness, Special Issue on Deaf-Blindness, 89*(3), 306.

Lahtinen, R. (2008). *Haptices and haptemens. A case study of developmental process in social haptic communication of acquired deafblind people.* Unpublished doctoral dissertation, University of Helsinki.

Linder, T. W. (2008). *Administration guide for TBPA 2 and TPBI 2.* Baltimore, MD: Paul H. Brookes.

Luckasson, R., Brothwick-Duffy, S., Buntinx, W., Coulter, D., Craig, E., Reeve, A., et al. (2002). *Mental retardation: definition, classification and systems of support,* 10th edition. Washington, DC: American Association on Mental Retardation.

MacFarland, S. (1993). *Teachers' understanding and implementation of van Dijk's learning theory for students who are deafblind.* Unpublished doctoral dissertation University of Arizona, Tucson.

MacFarland, S. (1995). Teaching strategies of the van Dijk Curricular approach. *Journal of Visual Impairment and Blindness, 89,* 22–28.

Makaton Charity, The. (2008). *Makaton: the early years.* Retrieved November 12, 2008 from http://www.makaton.org/about/mvdp_history.htm

Malinger, G., Lev, D., Zahalka, N., Aroia, Z., Watemberg, N., Kidron, D., et al. (2003). Fetal cytomegalovirus infection of the brain. The spectrum of sonographic findings. *American Journal of Neuroradiology, 24,* 28–32.

Mar, H. (1996). *Psychological evaluation of children who are deafblind: An overview with recommendations for practice.* Monmouth, OR: DB-LINK: The National Information Clearinghouse on Children Who Are Deaf-Blind.

Mar, H., & Sall, N. (1999). *Dimension of communication.* Paterson, NJ: Authors.

McCune, L., Kalmanson, B., Fleck, M. B., Glazenwski, B., & Sillari, J. (1990). An interdisciplinary model of infant assessment. In S.J. Meisels & J.P. Shonkoff (Eds.), *Handbook of early childhood intervention.* New York: Cambridge University Press.

Mesibov, G., Shea, V., & Schopler, E. (2004). *The TEACCH approach to autism spectrum disorders.* New York: Plenum Publishing.

Miles, B. (1998). *Talking the language of the hands to the hands.* The National Information Clearing House on Children who are Deaf-Blind, April, 1–7. Retrieved November 9, 2009 from http://www.dblink.org/lib/hands.htm

Miles, B., & Riggio, M. (1999). *Remarkable conversations.* Watertown, MA: Perkins School for the Blind.

Mirenda, P. (2001). Autism, augmentative communication, and assistive technology: What do we really know? *Focus on Autism and other Developmental Disabilities, 16,* 141–151.

Möller, C., Kimberling, W., Davenport, S., Prilluck, I., White, V., Biscone-Halterman, K., et al. (1989). Usher syndrome: An otoneurologic study. *The Laryngoscope, 99,* 73–79.

Munroe, S. (1999). *A summary of late emerging manifestations of congenital rubella in canada.* Ontario: Canadian, Deafblind and Rubella Association.

Nafstad, A., & Rødbroe, I. (1999). *Co-creating communication*. Dronninglund, Denmark: Forlaget Nord-Press.

Nelson, C., & Van Dijk, J. (2002). *Child guided-strategies for assessing children who are deaf-blind or have multiple disabilities* (CD-ROM). The Netherlands: Aapnootmuis.

Nelson, C., Van Dijk, J., McDonnell, A., & Thompson, K. (2002). A framework for understanding young children with severe disabilities: The van Dijk approach to assessment. *Research and Practice for Persons with Severe Disabilities*, *27*(2), 97–111.

Nicholas, J. (2000). *Congenital Rubella Syndrome Neuropsychological Functioning and Implications Illustrated by a Case Study*. Oslo: Nordens Välfärdscenters.

Oberman, L. M., Pineda, J. A., & Ramachandran, V. S. (2007). The human mirror neuron system: A link between action observation and social skills. *Social Cognitive and Affective Neuroscience*, *2*, 62–66.

O'Donnell, N. (1991). *A report on a survey of late emerging manifestations of congenital rubella syndrome*. New York: Helen Keller National Center.

Online Mendelian Inheritance in Man (2008). *Usher Syndrome*. Retrieved September 15, 2008 from www.ncbi.nlm.nih.gov/omim

Park, K. (1997). How do objects become objects of reference? A review of the literature on objects of reference and a proposed model for the use of objects in communication. *British Journal of Special Education*, *24*, 108–114.

Pennings, R., Damen, G., Snik, A., Hoefsloot, L., Cremers, C., & Mylanus, E. (2006). Audiologic performance and benefit of cochlear implantation in Usher syndrome Type I. *The Laryngoscope*, *116*, 717–722.

Pfau, R. & Bos, H. (2008). Enkelvoudige zinnen. In A. Baker, B. van den Bogaerde, R. Pfau, & T. Shermer (Eds.), *Gebarentaalwetenschap een inleiding* (pp. 120–144). Deventer, The Netherlands: Van Tricht.

Quartz, S., & Sejnowski, T. J. (1997). The neural basis of cognitive development: A constructivist manifesto. *Behavioral and Brain Sciences*, *20*(4), 537–596.

Ramachandran, V. S. (2000). Mirror neurons and imitation learning as the driving force behind "The great leap forward in human evolution." *Edge*, *69*, May 29.

Regenbogen, L., & Coscas, G. (1985). *Oculo-auditory syndromes*. New York: Masson Publishing.

Rizolatti, G., Fadiga, L., Fogassi, L., & Rizzoltti, G. (1996). Premotor cortex and the recognition of motor action. *Cognitive Brain Research*, *3*, 131–141.

Rocha do Amaral, J., & Martins de Oliveira, J. (2008). *Limbic system: The center of emotions*. Retrieved November 11, 2008 from http://www.healing-arts.org

R dbroe, I., & Souriau, J. (1999). Communication. In J. McInnes & J. McInnes (Eds.), *Programming intervention and support for persons with congenital and early adventitious deafblindness* (pp. 119–149). Toronto: University of Toronto Press.

Rowland, C., & Schweigert, P. (2004). *First things first: Early communication for the pre-symbolic child with severe disabilities*. Portland, OR: Design to Learn Products.

Schalock, R., Luckasson, R., Shogren, K., Borthwick-Duffy, S., Bradley, V., Buntix, W., et al. (2007). The renaming of mental retardation: Understanding the change to the term intellectual disability. *Intellectual and Developmental Disability*, *45*(2), 116–124.

Schirmer, B. R. (2001). *Deafness: Psychological, social, and educational dimensions of deafness*. Needham Heights, MA: Allyn & Bacon.

Schlumberger, E., Narbona, J., & Maurique, M. (2004). Nonverbal development of deaf children with or without cochlear implants. *Developmental Medicine & Child Neurology*, *46*, 599–606.

Shriver, E. K. (2006). *Research on preterm labor and premature birth*. National Institute of Child Health and Human development. Retrieved September 20, 2008 from www. nichd. nih.gov

Sieving, P., Caruso, R., Tao, W., Coleman, H., Thomson, D., Fullmer, K., & Bush, R. (2006). Ciliary neurotrophic factor (CNTF) for human retinal degeneration: Phase 1. Trail of CNTF delivered by encapsulated cell intraocular implants. *Proceedings of the National Academy of Sciences of the United States of America*, *103*(10), 3896–3901.

Silberman, R. K., Bruce, S. M., & Nelson, C. (2004). Children with sensory impairments. In F. P. Orelove, D. Sobsey, & R. K. Silberman (Eds.), *Educating children with multiple Disabilities: A collaborative approach* (pp. 425–527). Baltimore: Paul H. Brookes.

Souriau, J. (2007). Key note speech: the theoretical framework of the conference. In *Report Course on Communication and Congenital Deafblindness* (pp. 8–18). Dronninglund, Denmark: Nordic Staff Training Centre for Deafblind Services.

Stacey, P., Fortnum, H., Barton, G., & Summerfield, A. (2006). Hearing-impaired children in the United Kingdom, I: Auditory performance, communication skills, educational achievements, quality of life, and cochlear implantation. *Ear & Hearing*, *27*(2), 161–186.

Sterkenburg, P., Schuengel, C., & Jansen, C. (2008). Developing a therapeutic relationship with a blind client with a severe intellectual disability and persistent challenging behaviour. *Disability & Rehabilitation*, *30*(17), 1318–1327.

Stillman, R. (Ed.). (1978). *The Callier-Azusa Scale*. Dallas: The University of Texas.

Stoep, J., Van Balkom, H., Luiken, H., Snieders, J., & Van der Schuit, M. (2008). Het KLINc-Atelier: ruimte voor het beleven en verwerven van communicatie, taal en beginnende geletterdheid [The KLINc-atelier: environment for experiencing and acquiring communication, language, and early literacy]. In H. Van Balkom & J. Knoops (Eds.), *In-Com-Clusie: Inclusie door communicatieontwikkeling en -ondersteuning* [In-Com-Clusie: inclusion through communication development and support] (pp. 111–163). Leuven, Belgium: Acco.

Sweeten, T., Posey, D., & McDougle, C. (2004). Autistic disorder in three children with cytomegalovirus infection. *Journal of Autism and Developmental Disorders*, *34*, 583–586.

Tellefson, M. (2007). *Calendar systems: A developmental approach for young children with sensory impairments*. Retrieved September 24, 2008 from www.wcbvi.k12.wi.us

Thelin, J., Hartshorne, T., & Hartshorne, N. (1999). Audiologic and educational issues in CHARGE syndrome. *Journal of Educational Audiology*, *7*, 34–41.

Tolar, T., Lederberg, R., Gokhale, S., & Tomasello, M. (2008). The development of the ability to recognize the meaning of iconic signs. *Journal of Deaf Studies and Deaf Education*, *13*(2), 225–240.

Van den Broek, E., Janssen, C., Van Ramshorst, T., & Deen, L. (2006). Visual impairments in people with severe and profound multiple disabilities: An inventory of visual functioning. *Journal of Intellectual Disability Research*, *50*, 470–475.

Van den Tillaart, B., & Janssen, M. (2006). *CONTACT*. Sint-Michielsgestel, The Netherlands: Aapnootmuis, Educainment.

Van Dijk, J. (1966). The first steps of the deaf-blind child towards language. *Journal of the Education of the Blind*, *1*, 14–22.

Van Dijk, J. (1982). *Rubella handicapped children*. Lisse, The Netherlands: Swets & Zeitlinger.

Van Dijk, J. (1986). An educational curriculum for deaf-blind multi-handicapped persons. In D. Ellis (Ed.), *Sensory impairments in mentally handicapped people* (pp. 374–382). London: Croom Helm.

Van Dijk, J. (1991). *Persons handicapped by rubella: victors and victims a follow-up study*. Amsterdam: Swets and Zeitlinger.

Van Dijk, J. (1999). *Development through relationships: Entering the social world*. Paper presented at the Development Through Relationships 5th annual World Conference on Deafblindness, Lisbon, Portugal.

Van Dijk, J., & De Kort, A. (2004). Reducing challenging behaviors and fostering efficient learning of children with CHARGE syndrome. *American Journal of Medical Genetics*, *133A*, 273–277.

Van Dijk, J., & Janssen, M. (1993). Doofblinde kinderen [Deafblind Children]. In H. Nakken (Ed.), *Meervoudig gehandicapte kinderen* [Multi-impaired children] (pp. 34–73). Rotterdam, The Netherlands: Lemniscaat.

Van Dijk, J., Nelson, C., & De Kort, A. (2007). *Charge syndrome revisited* (CD-ROM). St.Michielsgestel, The Netherlands: Aapnootmuis.

Van Dijk R., Van Helvoort, M., Aan den Toorn, W., & Bos, H. (1998). *Niet zomaar een gebaar* [Not just a sign]. Sint Michielsgestel, The Netherlands: Instituut voor Doven.

Van Splunder, J. (2003). *Visual Impairment: Prevalence and Causes of Visual Impairment in Adults with Intellectual Disabilities*. Utrecht: University of Utrecht.

Vermeulen, L., & Van Dijk, J. (1994). Social-emotional aspects in a sample of young persons with Usher's syndrome type 1. In A. Kooijman, P. Looijestijn, J. Welling, & J. van der Wildt (Eds.), *Low vision* (pp. 411–414). Amsterdam: IOS Press.

Vervloed, M., Van Dijk, R., Knoors, H., & Van Dijk, J. (2006). Interaction between the teacher and a congenitally deafblind child. *American Annals of the Deaf*, *151*(3), 336–344.

Volterra, V., Laudanna, A., Coranzza, S., Radutzky, E., & Natale, F. (1984). Italian Sign Language: The order of elements in declarative sentence. In F. Loncke, P. Boyes Braem, & Y. Lebrun (Eds.), *Recent research on European sign languages* (pp. 19–48). Lisse, The Netherlands: Swets & Zeitlinger.

Wehmeyer, M. (2003). Defining mental retardation and ensuring access to the general curriculum. *Education and Training in Developmental Disabilities*, *38*(3), 271–282.

Werner, H., & Kaplan, B. (1963). *Symbol formation*. New York: John Wiley & Sons.

Westling, D. L., & Fox, L. (2008). *Teaching students with severe disabilities*, 4th edition. Upper Saddle River, NJ: Pearson.

Wheeler, L., & Griffin, H. C. (1997). A movement based approach to language development in children who are deaf-blind. *American Annals of the Deaf*, *142*(5), 387–390.

Williams, J. H. G., Whiten, A., Suddendorf, T., & Perrett, D. I. (2001). Imitation, mirror neurons, and autism. *Neuroscience Biobehavioral Reviews*, *25*(4), 287–295.

World Health Organization (2008). *Statistics on Rubella*. Retrieved February 19, 2010 from http://www.who.int/immunization

Writer, J. (1987). A movement-based approach to the education of students who are sensory impaired/multihandicapped. In L. Goetz, D. Guess, & K. Stremel-Campbell (Eds.), *Innovative program design for individuals with dual sensory impairments* (pp. 191–224). Baltimore: Paul H. Brookes.

PART 3

Cultural, Social, and Psychological Issues

Reflections on Identity

Irene W. Leigh

Abstract

The importance of identity is highlighted by the explosion of publications on the topic, in view of the cultural and ethnic challenges the United States is facing and the ongoing focus on how individuals assume identities based on group associations. This chapter explores the various theories of identity development relevant to deaf identities, including the disability-based framework, the social paradigm, racial identity development models, and acculturation models. Information is also presented on the relationships between deaf identity classifications (culturally Deaf, culturally hearing, bicultural, and marginal) and psychosocial adjustment. Additional categories that are explored include those covering the hard-of-hearing constellation, as well as the ethnic constellation. Technological influences on identity, including hearing aids, cochlear implants, and genetic technology, are also the subject of scrutiny. Issues pertaining to the complexities of biculturalism as based on the Deaf–hearing paradigm are examined, along with current influences that reinforce the concept of a multicultural identity as opposed to strict biculturalism. Current evidence suggests an increasingly fluid nature of identity, depending on environmental pull and individual characteristics.

Keywords: identity, bicultural, deaf identities, deaf identity theories, technology

The Importance of Identity

For centuries, people have debated the meaning of identity (Hoffman, 1996; Mischel & Morf, 2003). More recently, the relevance of identity has been reinforced by social movements including not only increased immigration, which has greatly increased cultural diversity in many countries, but also a renewed focus on globalization, with its increased information-sharing through technological advances. These social influences have far-reaching implications for how cultures view themselves (Croucher, 2004; Hermans & Dimaggio, 2007). In tandem, there has been an exponential increase of scholarly study on the topic of identity in general (e.g., Côté & Levine, 2002; Leary & Tangney, 2003) and

specifically with reference to those who are deaf, culturally Deaf, and hard of hearing.

Identity is a complex cognitive and social construct incorporating an array of characteristics, self-understanding, and psychological adjustments that typically serve to connect the person to specific social groups (e.g., Erikson, 1968, 1980; Harter, 1999; Leary & Tangney, 2003; Moskowitz, 2005; Waterman, 1992). This construct evolves through a dynamic and ongoing compilation of the meanings of past and present experiences, integrated with one's images of future possibilities (Tatum, 1997). Based on one's understandings of the biological (i.e., race, disability, gender, and age), psychological (drives, intellect, competencies, and self-understandings), social (cultural, social roles, and the resolution of conflict and crisis), and religious-spiritual aspects of our beings, constructions of identity help individuals define who and what they are (Tatum, 1997).

Identities are forged through perceptions of interpersonal similarities and differences, including—among others—those based on gender, ethnicity, educational levels, occupational categories, abilities, sexual orientation, and, most relevant here, hearing status (Corker, 1996). The interface of language, communication, and hearing status with social surroundings and one's temperament wields significant influence on how one internalizes a deaf or hard-of-hearing (DHH) identity. It is critical to maintain the perspective that DHH identities are among a multitude of identities interacting with each other to form the uniqueness of each individual. Exactly what constitutes DHH identities and how these are acquired constitute areas ripe for study.

For centuries, writers have been intrigued by the ways in which deaf people deal with their daily lives, considering that their pathways to language and communication rely on vision alone or along with limited access to audition, thus diverging from the full auditory access available to the large majority of individuals. Those who view themselves as a visual variety of the human race (Bahan, 2008) have coalesced into what is now popularly known as a Deaf cultural community. The focus of this community is on a Deaf center involving the use of a different "normality" based on the use of signed languages and visual ways of relating, such as eye contact, body movements, and facial expressions, not on the "normality" of audition and auditory experiences (Bauman, 2008; Ladd, 2003; Lane, Hoffmeister, & Bahan, 1996; Padden & Humphries, 1988, 2005). The end result has been an evolving standard of cultural and linguistic beliefs and values that focus on identifying as Deaf and reinforcing social relations with Deaf people, whether through school, social groups, or organizations, within families, or on an informal basis. The term "Deafhood," coined by Paddy Ladd (2003), encapsulates this evolving process as reflecting a Deaf consciousness concept involving the ongoing attempts of sign language peoples (Ladd's term) to explore and reconstruct what it means to become and continue to be culturally Deaf.

An estimated less than 5% of deaf children have deaf parents (Mitchell & Karchmer, 2004; Moores, 2001). Although most of these deaf children, as well as a good number of hearing offspring of deaf

parents, will be immersed within a Deaf culture environment, other deaf children may not readily identify as Deaf if their deaf parents use a spoken language at home. As for the roughly 95% of deaf children born to hearing parents, Deaf culture is typically an unfamiliar phenomenon, at least until young adulthood (Moores, 2001). Corker (1996) hypothesizes that the core identity for these children is more likely to be ethnic rather than D/deaf or hard of hearing. Incorporating a deaf identity becomes an additional developmental task, as the child recognizes there is a hearing difference and receives social messages about the meaning of that difference. Entry into a Deaf community takes place, if at all, in a variety of ways based on individual experiences that create interest in the community or socialization opportunities that happen to be available during critical periods in the deaf person's life. In their life journeys, these individuals can assume a large variety of labels that mirror their identities, depending on information provided by the family, the social or educational context, and the language used (Leigh, 1999a). Each label will convey meanings about the individual's identity related to the hearing–deaf dimension. Examples of labels include oral deaf, hard of hearing, cochlear implant user, Deaf, hearing impaired, and late deafened.

What all this means is that identity is not necessarily consolidated only during adolescence. This expectation of adolescent identity consolidation was popularized by Erik Erikson (1968, 1980), who focused on developmental issues within various stages of the life cycle. Erikson's developmental framework rested on the concept that psychosocial issues within each stage had to be resolved in order to enable one to progress to the next stage, thereby implying continuity and stability. However, more recent authors have emphasized the dynamic nature of identity work as a process of restructuring as new information about oneself emerges out of ongoing experiences encompassing specific educational, family/social, and work environment, as well as one's cultural, linguistic, communicative, and skill competencies, and individual proclivities such as temperament (e.g., Hintermair, 2008; Leigh, 1999a, 2009; Nikolaraizi & Hadjikakou, 2006). This process clearly does not happen only during adolescence, but rather evolves over time. In terms of DHH identities, ongoing identity development occurs as people explore how and whether various labels or identity conceptualizations apply to them during different phases of their lives.

Theoretical Conceptualizations

So, how are DHH identities conceptualized? Different theoretical frameworks have been utilized in the attempt to answer this question. One is the disability-based framework that relies on the medical model of a dysfunctional ear in need of remediation (Gonsoulin, 2001). This framework was utilized by Weinberg and Sterritt (1986) to categorize hearing identity as able-bodied, reflecting a self-perception of someone who endeavors to communicate as much like a hearing person as possible; deaf identity as disability-related; and dual identity reflecting identification with both deaf and hearing peers. In their research using a brief questionnaire administered to deaf participants, dual identity was associated with more positive adjustment outcomes.

Stinson and Kluwin (1996) used a social orientation paradigm group to create the following labels for DHH students: deaf-oriented, hearing-oriented, or oriented to both deaf and hearing groups. These identity categories were predicated on whether social peers were deaf, hearing, or both deaf and hearing. The assigned label depended on the perceived quality of social experiences with deaf and hearing peers, with the outcome relying largely on communicative competency and comfort in relation to each group.

In an attempt to further capture the sociolinguistic approach to deaf identities, which encapsulates a shared common language, common attitudes, social relationships, and unique life style, Yael Bat-Chava (2000) selected as the theoretical foundation for her work a social identity paradigm. This focuses on the relationship between individual and group membership identification (Tajfel, 1981; Turner, 1996). How group affiliation is decided depends on how relevant to oneself information about the group is, whether positive or negative, and how others are evaluated. A DHH person who sees a specific Deaf, deaf, or hard-of-hearing group as positive may identify with that particular group, depending on circumstances, even if in the public eye that group is stigmatized. Should the person perceive that specific group negatively due to stigmatization by more dominant or majority groups or societies, connections with that group will be minimized or disavowed in deference to the dominant perspective.

Bat-Chava (2000) derived three identity categories: culturally hearing, culturally Deaf, and bicultural, utilizing an analysis of cluster items based on four criterion variables related to communication and socialization, specifically the perceived importance of signing, the importance of speech, group identity, and attitudes toward deaf people. The focus was not primarily on the hearing disability. Rather, the importance of language and communication, socialization, and social perspectives about what it means to hear or not to hear in forging deaf-related or hearing-related identities were paramount.

The emergence of racial identity development models inspired Glickman (1996) to develop classifications for deaf identities that paralleled the conforming, dissonance, immersion, and introspection/integration stages of racial identity development. He labeled these developmental stages as culturally hearing, culturally marginal, immersion, and bicultural stages, each of which reflected an identity category. The culturally hearing individual is one who emulates hearing ways of being and favors spoken language, ostensibly to align with the majority hearing culture in a conforming manner. From that perspective, hearing loss is a deficit to be overcome, if not through medical means, then through audiological habilitation or rehabilitation. According to Glickman, those who are identified with this category include not only those who are late deafened, but also deaf persons who have grown up using spoken language and prefer to interact primarily with hearing peers. Because of the effort required to follow spoken dialogue in multiple situations ranging from one-on-one to group settings, Glickman assumes that this stage is not psychologically healthy for those early-onset deaf individuals who disavow any essential difference between themselves and hearing peers.

The dissonance stage reflects cultural marginality, as exemplified by individuals who are on the fringe of hearing and deaf environs, without a sense of belonging to either. According to Glickman, deaf children born to hearing parents frequently cannot find affinity within hearing families and are not always provided the wherewithal to connect with deaf peers, particularly if they are placed in mainstream education; they thus become culturally marginalized based on the deaf–hearing dimension.

Considering that psychological health is dependent on one being moored internally, it follows that these individuals searching for a solution to their marginality will potentially find a home when they are exposed to Deaf community events. The excitement generated by such encounters can positively reinforce an uncritical immersion into Deaf culture, which becomes a safe haven from the hearing world. During this stage, hearing values, including one's spoken language, are renounced in favor of the community's signed language. Along this vein, hearing people who encourage conformity into hearing society are perceived with mistrust. Finally, as individuals move into the introspective/integration stage, which Glickman labels as the bicultural stage, they engage in the process of reframing their notions about Deaf and hearing people in the direction of rapprochement, recognizing the importance of coexistence and integrating Deaf and hearing values into their lives. Spoken languages, particularly in written form, and signed languages are both respected. The power of the Internet to bring deaf and hearing people together has facilitated the potential for these individuals to be more fully bicultural.

Although Glickman's model appears to be developmentally linear, he acknowledges that the stages outlined here do not necessarily follow this linearity, considering that people can move forward, backward, or skip stages. Children born into homes where hearing speakers and deaf signers coexist will logically start off as bicultural, and possibly gravitate toward hearing or Deaf cultural identities as the occasion or their lives may demand, whereas those born to hearing parents could start off as culturally Deaf rather than culturally hearing or marginal if their parents become fluent sign language users and send them to schools incorporating a Deaf culture environment. The Deaf Identity Development Scale (DIDS) was developed with the goal of psychometrically determining all four deaf identity categories (Glickman, 1996). In response to the unexpectedly low reliability of the bicultural subscale as demonstrated by Leigh, Marcus, Dobosh, and Allen (1998), the DIDS was revised by Fischer and McWhirter (2001) to strengthen reliability.

Maxwell-McCaw (2001) noted that, although Glickman's deaf identity development theory focused primarily on internal dimensions of identity that facilitate a self-actualization process to overcome exclusion and oppression, behavioral components supporting each of his deaf identity categories were missing. Consequently, she took a different theoretical direction in focusing attention on acculturation models based on immigration experiences involving the fluidity of separate cultural categories, depending on which cultural manifestation or behavior is more prominent at a given moment in time. Maxwell-McCaw wanted to encourage the possibility of identity categories shifting as the occasion demanded, with each identity category becoming more salient depending on the extent and level of interactions between a person and various cultural environments. Her theory is that acculturation patterns vary in terms of the level of psychological identification with Deaf culture and the cultures of the relevant hearing societies with which the individual is in contact, as well as with the degree of behavioral involvement and the level of cultural competence in these cultures.

To evaluate this theory, Maxwell-McCaw (2001; Maxwell-McCaw & Zea, in press) developed the Deaf Acculturation Scale (DAS), which consists of two subscales: Deaf Acculturation and Hearing Acculturation. The overall scale produces four acculturation categories: Hearing acculturated (high scores in hearing acculturation and low scores in deaf acculturation); Marginal (low scores in both hearing and deaf acculturation); Deaf acculturated (high scores in deaf acculturation and low scores in hearing acculturation), and Bicultural (high scores in both acculturations). Reliability and validity were demonstrated to be in the acceptable range.

With the understanding that identity constellations have implications for psychological well-being, the DAS was used to assess the presence of healthy adaptation for each of the four acculturation categories. Psychological well-being was more evident for those who demonstrated bicultural and deaf acculturation than for those who were hearing acculturated, and least for individuals in the marginal group (Maxwell-McCaw, 2001). It seems that those who are hearing acculturated may face more communicative stress, thereby increasing vulnerability to some level of dissatisfaction with their lives. The findings for deaf and bicultural acculturation serve to emphasize the importance of finding social collegiality within the Deaf community and comfort in interacting with both deaf and hearing environments. Supporting evidence for these findings, using the DAS and other measures, has appeared in the literature (e.g., Bat-Chava, 2000; Hintermair, 2008; Jambor & Elliott, 2005). These findings counteract earlier perspectives that monoculturalism led to better psychological adjustment. This proposition was originally critiqued by theorists such as LaFromboise, Coleman, and Gerton (1993), who advocated for alternating between cultures being more conducive to psychological health. It is important to acknowledge, however, that the acculturation process is a complex one, contingent on the level of access to each culture, behavioral competency, the process of internalizing behavioral and cultural components, linguistic mastery, societal perceptions, and a host of other factors (Sam & Berry, 2006).

With reference to the findings on marginality, for example, the standard perception is that marginal individuals are misfits who cannot find a home in any one culture and are doomed to psychological rootlessness. However, Hintermair (2008) cautions that some individuals classified as marginal nonetheless may demonstrate sufficient positive personal resources. They simply refuse to be part of hearing or deaf worlds and prefer to assume what appears to be a hard-of-hearing position. Hintermair also notes the importance of relevant good communication skills (either spoken or signed, depending on surroundings), as well as psychological resources such as optimism and self-efficacy. Emerton (1996) additionally takes the position that marginality can be used interchangeably with biculturalism as the person traverses both cultures, not always fully rooted in either but taking an individualistic approach.

Hard-of-Hearing: Mixed Messages

Despite the fact that the hard-of-hearing population is demographically far greater compared to those who are categorized as deaf (Mitchell, 2006a), this group has received minimal attention in terms of definitions and needs, as well as in terms of theories regarding hard-of-hearing identity development. Not only does this group incorporate those individuals who are audiologically between the mild and severe to profound categories of hearing loss (Ross, 2005), it increasingly includes severe to profoundly deaf individuals who maximize the use of their residual hearing and oral–aural communication methods supplemented by auditory aids (Israelite, Ower, & Goldstein, 2002; Laszlo, 1994; Punch, Creed, & Hyde, 2006; Ross, 2001; Warick, 1994).

On the surface, these individuals can appear to "pass for hearing." They ally with hearing counterparts rather than with a recognizable hard-of-hearing group (Collins, 2005; Harvey, 2003; Laszlo, 1994; Ross, 2005; Sorkin, 2000). This proclivity is supported by a variety of studies or observations that confirm that distancing from similar peers is a means of reinforcing their identification with hearing peers (e.g., Kent & Smith, 2006; Leigh, 1999a; Nakamura, 2003). Some will go so far as to deny their hard-of-hearing identity status (Arnold & MacKenzie, 1998; Kent, 2003; Kent & Smith, 2006, Laszlo, 1994) or even avoid associating with nonsigning/oral deaf peers, whom they perceive as having a distinct deaf identity (Harvey, 2003). One suggested rationale is that such encounters might stir up fears of assuming a "spoiled identity" associated with impairment

(Goffman, 1963; Harvey, 2003). The hard-of-hearing label itself may turn people off because of the lack of positive association and multiple negative experiences that detract from the possibility of involved individuals "coming out" to find a comfort zone labeled "hard of hearing" (Harvey, 2003).

Although most hard-of-hearing adults will tend to perceive signing Deaf adults as comparatively more impaired in communication and therefore avoid any association with them (Harvey, 2003), some will be motivated to call themselves Deaf (Vesey & Wilson, 2003). For such individuals, revealing their "Deaf" self can facilitate far better communication access, based on awareness of situational communication needs and, in turn, a better sense of connection with Deaf peers in addition to interactions with the hearing community. However, the linguistic and communication requirements within the Deaf community, as well as the mere appearance of "hearing" involved in this journey toward rapprochement with the Deaf community, can exacerbate the potential of being rejected, particularly when the hard-of-hearing person may be perceived as too much like a hearing person (Padden & Humphries, 1988). Since "hard-of-hearing" typically implies identification with hearing people and their spoken language, it is not necessarily seen as a positive attribute in Deaf culture (Grushkin, 2003; Padden & Humphries, 1988). Thus, such individuals may land squarely on the fringe, feeling alienated, isolated, and stuck between cultures (Brueggemann, 1999; Harvey, 2003).

These multiple perceptions of "hard of hearing" reinforce the amorphous or invisible nature of this specific identity. Most telling, none of the theories described earlier considers "hard-of-hearing" as an identity per se. Sometimes hard-of-hearing individuals themselves do not even know what hard of hearing means, and appear not to have a clear identity (Laszlo, 1994). This is likely to exacerbate a sense of marginality, being neither hearing nor Deaf. The vagueness in defining hard-of-hearing identity and its distance from Deaf identities is buttressed by the findings of Leigh et al. (1998) in their study of deaf/hearing cultural identity paradigms based on 40 hard-of-hearing respondents with hearing parents and 22 hard-of-hearing respondents with Deaf/hard-of-hearing parents out of a sample of 244 deaf, hard-of-hearing, and hearing respondents. Results indicated that there were no significant differences between deaf and hard-of-hearing respondents with hearing parents. Specifically, these respondents tended to be more hearing and more marginalized than their counterparts with deaf parents and not as immersed in deaf values, similarly to hearing respondents with hearing parents. Essentially, they perceived themselves as relatively more aligned with hearing values. Additionally, hard-of hearing respondents with deaf parents endorsed more hearing values, fewer deaf values, and more marginalization in comparison to deaf respondents with deaf parents. Warick's (2004) study of 14 hard-of-hearing university students in Canada revealed identity constructions that were complex, partly based on these students striving to be part of the hearing world, but simultaneously encountering differences because of their hearing loss that compounded their identity struggle.

Grushkin (2003) recommends dealing with marginalized hard-of-hearing identity issues through immersion in Deaf school programs and bicultural approaches to acculturation. Contrary to expectations, his research on four hard-of-hearing participants attending a Deaf residential school indicated that receptive and expressive spoken language skills were not negatively affected by such immersion. These interviewees demonstrated an amalgam of Deaf/hearing identity components, which led Grushkin to suggest the possibility that these constituted a third culture. However, even among his four participants, this was a debatable concept because of the nebulous nature of the hard-of-hearing label, a label that can reflect various hearing levels and auditory abilities, hearing immersion, marginality and stigmatization, or combined Deaf/hearing components, depending on the individual.

So, what might constitute a hard-of-hearing identity: the "hearing" identity claimed by those immersed in the mainstream, the "stuck in between" state Brueggemann (1999) describes, the marginality that emerged in the Leigh (1999a) study, or the combined Deaf-hearing components described by Vesey and Wilson (2003)? Laszlo (1994) takes a different angle in supporting the notion of a hard-of-hearing identity based on increased self-awareness, acceptance of hearing status, and shared experiences. Affirming "hard of hearing" takes a certain amount of resiliency and comfort with difference. This can be reinforced through proximal association, as demonstrated by a study of seven students ranging from 14 to 17 years of age who were in classrooms specifically for hard-of-hearing students. They were comfortable with their hard-of-hearing identity when it was reinforced by positive connotations based on unique differences between them and hearing as well as Deaf peers (Israelite, Ower, &

Goldstein, 2002). In his autobiography, Paul Jacobs (2007) rejects Lane's assertion that those ostensibly like him or the students in the Israelite, Ower, and Goldstein (2002) study are "culturally homeless" (p. 213). Rather, Jacobs claims to be part of a new social entity, which he labels "neither-nor," neither hearing nor Deaf, but rather an identity that is emerging out of a confluence of technology, environment, and individual temperament components such as willpower.

Paralleling the notion that there are many ways to be deaf or Deaf, it appears that there also are multiple ways to be hard of hearing. To understand this requires not necessarily creating a theory of "hard-of-hearing" identity but rather close scrutiny of how hard-of-hearing individuals and environments interact to create specific meanings of hard-of-hearing identities.

The Ethnic Dimension[1]
Deaf and hard-of-hearing identities are inalienably affected by the ethnic dimension, marked as it is by surrounding social, cultural, linguistic, religious, political, and regional influences (e.g., Corker, 1996; Lane, Hoffmeister, & Bahan, 1996; Leigh, 1999b; 2009). Even as the ascendancy of bicultural possibilities takes place, these inevitably are giving way to multicultural paradigms (Eldredge, in press). This is exemplified by potential participation in at least four communities, depending on availability and accessibility: the ethnic deaf community, the ethnic hearing community, and, if applicable, the majority ethnic community and the larger Deaf community (Corbett, in press; Leigh, 2009). To maintain psychological well-being, deaf people are confronted with the need to develop adaptive abilities as they face the dilemma of somehow integrating these various involvements into their ethnic/cultural identities, rather than limiting themselves to one aspect to the detriment of the others (Wu & Grant, in press).

The ethnic dimension has defied easy definition because of its malleable nature (Trimble, 2005). Typically, ethnic identity is considered to be an affiliative construct indicating membership with a particular ethnic or cultural group (Trimble, 2005). Responses to skin color, as well as other interactive experiences that include identifying physical differences and recognizing their implications in terms of differential treatment based on social inequalities, contribute to ethnic identity formation and feelings of membership (Franklin, Carter, & Grace, 1993). The Deaf community has not been immune to these repercussions, which impact education, socialization, and employment (e.g., Ahmad, Atkin, & Jones, 2002; Anderson & Bowe, 1972/2001; Burch, 2002; Jankowski, 1997; Ladd, 2003; Lane et al., 1996; Moores, Jatho, & Dunn, 2001; Padden & Humphries, 2005).

The question of how ethnic identity emerges has been addressed by racial identity development and acculturation models, both of which were referenced earlier in this chapter. The former relies on a paradigm that assumes that minority individuals move from a passive-acceptance, pre-encounter, or conformity phase that involves internalization of the dominant culture's oppressive views of their minority group, toward an immersion stage in which the majority culture is rejected in favor of one's minority group. Last, there is an integration phase in racial identity development, in which individuals freely select particular cultural behaviors that seem most appropriate for specific situations. In contrast, acculturation models have incorporated an ecocultural framework that encapsulates the process of adaptation to ecological context, including contacts with other cultures, to explain how different cultural groups intersect with each other and change as they coexist (Berry, 2002; Berry & Sam, 1997; Rudmin, 2003; Sam & Berry, 2006). The acculturation process is twofold, consisting of (1) the acculturation process per se, which covers broader cultural changes resulting from cultural encounters facilitating changes in cultural behavior, as well as competence in the relevant cultures being acculturated to, and (2) psychological acculturation, which specifically reflects the psychological changes accompanying acculturation experiences, such as those affecting the sense of well-being relative to the culture being adapted to (Berry, 2002; Berry & Sam, 1997). Both concepts serve to explain how individuals can be at varying points in terms of ethnic identity, depending on individual and context.

Deaf identities and ethnic identities do not necessarily evolve in tandem. There is no set way in which these stages and experiences are sequenced and integrated to create internal ethnic and Deaf identities. Much depends on ecocultural influences, as well as on individual characteristics that impact on one's development trajectories. Ethnic identity tends to be recognized as a core identity that generally precedes other identities (Corker, 1996; Helms, 1994). That identity is more salient in hearing families, with Deaf identity gradually emerging as a response to recognition of differences from hearing family members in the auditory communication arena. The degree to which both identities are internalized depends on circumstance, family communication, environmental influence, and positive or negative associations with the hearing difference and the reactions of others. If the person is exposed to others who are deaf or hard of hearing, the positive or negative nature of that exposure will influence the evolution of that person's Deaf or deaf identity. If the parents are Deaf and white in majority white countries, the Deaf identity will be more immediately salient, with the white identity implicitly internalized. But if, instead, these parents are members of an ethnic minority, both the Deaf and ethnic identities may be identified and reinforced more simultaneously than might have happened otherwise.

Deaf and hard-of-hearing individuals thus may experience their ethnic identities very differently from their hearing ethnic minority counterparts, depending on how they place themselves within or outside of their ethnic minority group because of that additional Deaf, deaf, or hard-of-hearing identity. To complicate matters, Deaf members of an ethnic minority group confront even more multiple identity issues emanating not only out of interactions with their hearing ethnic group members and their Deaf ethnic group contingent, but also the dominant, typically white hearing and Deaf groups, each of which may have different meanings for these individuals and, as such, different pulls for various manifestations of identity (Anderson & Grace, 1991; Andrews, Martin, & Velásquez, 2007; Corbett, in press; Eldredge, in press). Each membership requires dealing with different sets of norms and values, tensions and countertensions, all of which can compound issues of stigmatization and oppression. More so, the specter of double oppression hovers over those who may feel excluded from both their dominant hearing society and from their ethnic group, thereby complicating the process of identity internalization (Corker, 1996; Ladd, 2003).

Individuals who migrate to other countries have that much more to deal with in confronting a new language, as well as the new country's perception toward both their ethnic identity and their Deaf/hearing difference, whether deaf or hard of hearing. How all these aspects interact or compete with each other for a deaf or hard-of-hearing individual, whether an immigrant or born with ethnic minority status, can deeply impact identity development and acculturation (Collins, Devine, & Paris, 2005; Corbett, 2003; Dively, 2001/1999; Hernández, 1999; Steinberg, Davila, Collazo, Lowe, & Fischgrund, 1997).

Much depends on the availability of cultural reinforcement and community support. Whether the deaf or ethnic identity is more salient for any one individual is not as critical for many as is the need to assert each identity depending on environmental context, whether within their ethnic community or their Deaf community. Many will integrate their identities rather than dichotomize them, for example, Asian American and Deaf (Wu & Grant, in press), Black deaf (Anderson & Grace, 1991), or Māori and Deaf (Smiler & McKee, 2007). This reinforces the importance of juxtaposing the two minority identities in ways that maintain the salience of both identities, rather than acceding to the subtle message regarding the dominance of Deaf cultural ways of being (Foster & Kinuthia, 2003). These individuals also do change labels; that is, oral deaf, culturally Deaf, or hard of hearing as components of their identity, depending on social context and communication stress.

Such malleability reinforces a contextual and interactive model of identity that Foster and Kinuthia (2003) have described as consisting of four evolving contributory factors: individual characteristics, situational conditions, social conditions, and societal conditions. The individual characteristics encompass physical, mental, and spiritual attributes such as gender, racial or ethnic heritage, language, age, and hearing level. These are internal, and they reflect core elements of identity. The other three factors reflect interactions between the individual and the environment that are recognized by the individual and factored into ongoing identity construction. Situational conditions include geographic, educational program, and functional (home, school, work, etc.) locations. Social conditions include, for example, feeling accepted, comfortable, rejected, or set apart. Societal conditions represent broad societal trends and patterns, such as racism, socioeconomic status, or popular culture (e.g., the civil rights movement).

All these factors can create internally congruent or dissonant identity components emerging out of context and individual perceptions, with these components changing as perceptions change (Ahmad, Atkin, & Jones, 2002; Foster & Kinuthia, 2003; Parasnis & Fischer, 2005). For example, some may wish to connect with their ethnically similar peers, but gravitate toward identifying with deaf counterparts because of communication ease, particularly when a critical mass of their ethnic deaf peers is lacking (Foster & Kinuthia, 2003). They may connect with the latter group when the opportunity arises.

Those with multiple identities (ethnic hearing, ethnic deaf, and dominant Deaf) may struggle to integrate these aspects due to the lack of a cadre with similar multiple identities. Foster and Kinuthia (2003) found that those with more positive internalized ethnic identity reported more positive reinforcement or ability to positively internalize that identity despite discriminatory experiences. They also noted the relevance of cultural perceptions of gender interweaving with ethnic and deaf identities in ways that are difficult to disentangle. The presence of additional conditions such as limited vision or mobility, or of sexual orientation adds yet another level of complexity in terms of deciphering identity constellations (Leigh, 2009).

In contrast to this integrative and interweaving multiple identity paradigm, some discredit the notion of "in-between" or integrated identities on the basis that identities are more exclusive than inclusive (e.g., Ladd, 2003). For instance, a Deaf Māori in New Zealand might not have an easy time integrating a "hearing white" identity component that is framed as exclusionary. The role of narrative is critical in how these identities are integrated or rejected as the individual journeys through various situational contexts (McAdams, 1993).

Because of the significant changes in US school demographics, the educational setting is now the focal point for dealing with cultural plurality, accepting diversity, and confronting the need to counteract low expectations (Christensen & Delgado, 2000; Lane et al., 1996). Although educational programs have come to recognize that positive valences assigned to ethnic diversity encourage an atmosphere that facilitates overall learning and mutual respect, contradicting this is the sense of privilege that is pervasive in white-dominant societies, as well as societal ambivalence about specific ethnic identities (Davidson, 1996; Parasnis, Samar, & Fischer, 2005). Such ambivalence tends to be reinforced by the ongoing underachievement typically demonstrated by deaf African American, Hispanic/Latino, Native American, and to some extent Asian American students (Karchmer & Mitchell, 2003), as well as the perpetual problem of minimally available ethnic minority role models (Anderson & Grace, 1991; Andrews & Covell, 2007; Andrews, Martin, & Velásquez, 2007; LaSasso & Wilson, 2000), all of which can create difficulties in positive self-perceptions of ethnic identities.

Some authors have argued that Deaf people represent an ethnic group, similarly to those who possess a collective name, shared language, feelings of community and solidarity, behavior norms, distinct values, culture knowledge and customs, social/organization structures, the arts, history, and kinship, and who experience disempowerment within a majority society (e.g., Baker, 1999; Lane, 2005). Davis (2008) takes the position that relying on ethnicity as applicable to Deaf people could be a precursor to racial profiling. Additionally, the state of not hearing does cross ethnic boundaries, thereby weakening the unique ethnic status for deaf people (Johnston, 2005). Baynton (1996) considers the possibility that the ethnic identity concept is weakened by social perceptions of the need for access to language and communication to counteract a sensory disability. Whether the concept of ethnic identity is applicable for Deaf people remains an ongoing debate yet to be resolved in the face of paradoxes not easily reconciled.

Technology, Science, and Identity
Access to technology has profoundly affected how DHH people interact with each other and with hearing counterparts. Formerly insurmountable communication boundaries have been breached by text and video phones, electronic mail, the Internet, wireless text pagers, FM systems, Communication Access Real-Time Translation (CART), cochlear implants, improved hearing aids, and so on (e.g., Akamatsu, Mayer, & Farrelly, 2005; Breivik, 2005; Hendershot, 2001; Kinzie, 2006; Pilling & Barrett, 2008; Power, Power, & Horstmanshof, 2007; Power, Power, & Rehling, 2007; Zazove, Meador, Derry, Gorenflo, Burdick, & Saunders, 2004). Captioned television and the Internet bring news and event information closer to home. Sign language has also entered cyberspace, with broadband and video technologies capable of transmitting clear videos (Bernstein, 2006). Due to the increased use of virtual space (Bernstein, 2006; Murray, 2008), the interactive Deaf eye gaze in face-to-face communication is giving way to the eye gaze of the bent head over the pager or focusing on the computer monitor. The question then becomes that of how this technology affects social identity relative to human connections between deaf, hard-of-hearing, and hearing people.

The ability to increasingly utilize mainstream technology suggests that such technology provides "universal access," meaning that everyone can use it without stigmatization and there is no need for adaptation because of one's unique needs, ability, or disability. Individual identities, whether real or assumed, can now travel through space and evolve based on technical or virtual rather than in-person connections. The possibility of controlling which specific Deaf, deaf, hard-of-hearing, or hearing-based identity is revealed can be seen as liberating in terms of freely communicating with strangers, whether hearing, hard of hearing, or deaf, without concern about whether one will be rejected due to the revelation of a stigmatized identity. How instant communication devices really connect or disconnect members of Deaf communities and how these may radically change these communities, as well as individual identity perceptions, are increasingly becoming topics for study (Brueggemann, 2008; Murray, 2008).

Hearing Aids
Despite progress in auditory enhancement technology, there continues to be ongoing stigmatization related to awkwardness in communication, aging, and having a mechanical appellation on the body (e.g., Arnold & MacKenzie, 1998; Branson & Miller, 2002; Kent & Smith, 2006). The "hearing aid effect," which devalues the process of assuming a DHH identity, continues to pervade societal attitudes, including those of not only older adults, but also parents of dependents with hearing differences who are diffident about getting hearing aids for their children (Hétu, Riverin, Getty, Lalande, & St-Cyr, 1990; Kochkin, Luxford, Northern, Mason, & Tharpe, 2007). Those who can "normalize" hearing aid use tend to be comfortable identifying as having a hearing difference (Kent & Smith, 2006).

Cochlear Implants
Cochlear implants may be less subject to this "hearing aid effect" due to their similarity to handheld computing/communication devices (e.g., i-Pods) and its media portrayal as a miracle cure for hearing loss. In part because of this, appended technology per se has become more mundane and less stigmatizing. Yet, the interface of this technology with identity has become a battlefield. Views portraying the cochlear implant as denying a vibrant community and a normal Deaf way of life have clashed with viewpoints espousing the cochlear implant as a way-station to sound and in turn a means of overcoming exclusion, connecting with hearing counterparts, and potentially disaffirming disability status. Negative opinions about the cochlear implant appear to be a reaction to messages that deaf is defective and reflects a "spoiled identity." For many Deaf community members and their supporters, to get an implant is seen essentially as a representation of the need to

get rid of the deaf person's "spoiled identity" through repairing a so-called defect and gaining some semblance of hearing identity to achieve a more "normalized" stance (Cherney, 1999; Crouch, 1997; Lane et al., 1996; Mitchell, 2006b; Montgomery, 1991; Tellings, 1996). This demonstrates how the power of a technology inserted within the person can affect the perceived value and identity of the person. The ultimate result of this effort to create an "artificial" hearing identity for the deaf child is viewed by many Deaf people and their advocates as reinforcing "outsider" status for cochlear implantees, who ostensibly can never be fully immersed in hearing culture because cochlear implants do not replicate the way hearing people hear sounds and do not guarantee full access to the hearing world (Ladd, 2003, 2007).

In contrast, advocates for cochlear implantation have referred to a multitude of studies and observations in support of the usefulness of cochlear implants in facilitating interaction with hearing peers and improving educational opportunities (e.g., Fagan, Pisoni, Horn, & Dillon, 2007; Geers, 2006; Spencer & Marschark, 2003; Tucker, 1998; Wheeler, Archbold, Gregory, & Skipp, 2007). For a significant majority in developed countries, cochlear implants may typically be framed as a social good. Nonetheless, this perspective must be tempered with caution related to the nature of expectations regarding language, communication, education, happiness, and identity (Spencer & Marschark, 2003). Again, much depends on individual variables and environmental opportunities. Some benefit amazingly, others receive no benefit, and many find themselves left in-between.

The authors of studies investigating the interface of cochlear implants and the Deaf experience (Christiansen & Leigh, 2002/2005; Most, Wiesel, & Blitzer, 2007; Preisler, Tvingstedt, & Ahlström, 2005; Wald & Knutsen, 2000; Wheeler, Archbold, Gregory, & Skipp, 2007) have basically concluded that bicultural types of experiences allow for the potential to benefit from technological advances without feeling threatened with the loss of the Deaf experience, whatever the level of auditory enhancement. They recommend ongoing exposure to both Deaf culture and the auditory advantages of the cochlear implant, in order to avoid creating a body of cochlear-implanted children stuck between the deaf and hearing worlds, lacking a clear identity. This recommendation is geared toward increasing the comfort in shifting identities in conjunction with changing environmental contexts.

Recognizing the efficacy of the cochlear implant while simultaneously recognizing that it is not a panacea can hopefully lead to a reduction in opposition terminology, minimization of the expectations that a hearing/normalized identity will be achieved (Hyde & Power, 2006), and common ground in terms of recognizing the fluidity of identities that a person with a cochlear implant may demonstrate, depending on life circumstances. In fact, the pervasive perception of the "either-or" paradigm—either cochlear implantee or Deaf (Hintermair & Albertini, 2005)—is gradually becoming moot, as witness the changing (albeit grudging and despite pockets of resistance) acceptance of this technology within Deaf communities today, based in part on demographics indicating the significant increase in pediatric implantation (Christiansen & Leigh, 2002/2005). The potential of creating a fusion between the cochlear implant and Deaf identities (Brueggemann, 2008; Padden & Humphries, 2005) is increasingly being entertained. This is particularly salient now that a number of Deaf people are getting cochlear implants for themselves or for their Deaf children. Although they may understand the limitations related to auditory access, they also desire to maximize the ability to ease into hearing environments as the occasion may demand while maintaining Deaf cultural affiliation.

Genetics

The social and psychological implications related to the increasing "power of knowledge" regarding genetic inheritance and choices about human characteristics are profound. These implications are becoming increasingly salient since advances in genetic technology have begun to create actual situations that involve selecting certain genes or genetic mutations, including those that can create deaf or hearing characteristics in babies. A number of social communities will abide by longstanding, culturally centered belief systems and uniquely framed perceptions about how nature works when confronted with these new genetic possibilities (e.g., Kisch, 2004). For individuals in many societies, awareness of the possibilities related to genetic manipulation will force them to acknowledge preferred identity-based perceptions and their level of comfort or discomfort in choosing to go with nature as opposed to making specific reproductive choices based on social preferences. The acceptability of prenatal testing procedures essentially involves a social decision that challenges the oft-endorsed proclamations of many societies that persons with disabilities, including deaf persons and those affiliated with Deaf communities, are entitled to respect and treatment equal to those not in the disability category (Asch, 2001; Burke, 2006; Sandel, 2007). Specifically, the prenatal testing procedure itself at some level does reflect covert views about the unacceptability of disabilities as a typical variation of the human race and as a different way of being, with unique forms of identity.[2]

When reproductive choices are made that counteract prevailing views of "normalcy," repercussions are bound to follow, as witness the example of the lesbian couple whose efforts to ensure the birth of a deaf child resulted in worldwide notoriety and a revisiting of social values concerning "disabled" versus "normal" status (e.g., Bova, 2008; Henderson, 2002; Johnston, 2004, 2005; Middleton, 2004; Mundy, 2002). This controversy is reminiscent of the specter of social control in terms of passing judgment on the value of certain kinds of human lives typical of the Nazi era in Germany as based on arguments that purposefully bringing a deaf child into the world does that child a disservice.

The increasing prevalence and acceptability of genetic testing, together with the real possibility of institutional eradication of genes for deafness based on political decisions as genetic technology evolves (e.g., House of Lords, 2007), may very well result in fewer deaf children being born (Johnston, 2004, 2005). However, from an economic perspective, the current cost of genetic testing and the fact that many families may not be aware of familial inheritance possibilities may limit the scope of this contraction. Additionally, the limited availability of genetic technology in evolving countries where signing Deaf communities exist presages the ongoing existence of individuals who claim a Deaf identity.

Summary and Conclusions

In today's complex environment, the fluidity of identity takes on greater meaning as people are exposed to and learn different ways of being, whether in auditory or signing communities. Additionally, even with the popularization of cochlear implantation and genetic technology, there is no realistic way to eradicate worldwide populations of deaf people. Providing opportunities for interacting with various Deaf and hearing communities through ever-improving interactive technology will allow DHH children and adults to explore identities that fit not only how they perceive themselves but also the situations in which they find themselves.

This chapter has attempted to emphasize that specific deaf identity categories perpetuate the danger of oversimplifying the meanings attributed to, for example, "Deaf," "deaf," "hard of hearing," "hearing impaired," or "hearing." To counteract this limitation, which essentially denies the complexities of integrating diverse components of one's identity constellation, the tendency to rely on a single and primary unifying identity is giving way to the plurality of identities and self-labels (Mishler, 2004). Binary notions of identity (e.g., deaf versus hearing, or Deaf versus hearing) are now giving way to a far more multifaceted notion of identity that encompasses who a person is (Davis, 2008; Skelton & Valentine, 2003), such as, for example, an Asian American hard-of-hearing female parent, a Latino Deaf gay business entrepreneur, a Deaf-blind Australian friend, or multiple other complex interfaces. Some will still center themselves within a clearly delineated identity and cultural home.

Today's globalized environment, increasingly connected by advanced technology encompassing increased visual and auditory communication interchanges among diverse groups, has encouraged the fluidity of deaf identities depending on access to information, circumstances, and desire. This has generated thinking about new conceptualizations of *deaf* such as, for example, the construct of Deafhood or being Deaf with a cochlear implant. These examples reflect evolving expectations that go beyond biology, linguistics, historically adverse oppression, and fixed understandings of shared experiences (Davis, 2007). These new developments have been the focus of Deaf Studies scholars in the interest of understanding the complex identity choices and life adjustments that involve the populations discussed in this chapter (e.g., Brueggemann, 2008). These complexities emphasize the importance of being sensitive to how individuals incorporate their DHH identities as they intermingle with others, whether similar to or different from them. As McAdams (1993) put it, if we want to know these individuals, we need to know them through careful analyses of their life stories. These stories will only serve to reinforce the fascinating complexities of DHH identities.

Notes

[1]The focus on ethnic identities in this chapter does not deny the importance of other identity dimension such as those linked with gender, sexual orientation, religion, age, language, and additional disabilities. All of these must be considered as composites of the deaf and hard-of-hearing identity.

[2]The implications of managing life-threatening medical issues through the use of genetic technology is also a critical area of consideration, one that is beyond the scope of this chapter.

(This chapter is based on Leigh, I. W. (2009). A lens on deaf identities. New York: Oxford University Press.)

References

Ahmad, W., Atkin, K., & Jones, L. (2002). Being deaf and being other things: Young Asian people negotiating identities. *Social Science & Medicine, 55*, 1757–1769.

Akamatsu, C.T., Mayer, C., & Farrelly, S. (2006). An investigation of two-way text messaging use with deaf students at the secondary level. *Journal of Deaf Studies and Deaf Education, 11*(1), 120–131.

Anderson, G., & Bowe, F. (2001/1972). Racism within the deaf community. In L. Bragg (Ed.), *Deaf world* (pp. 305–308). New York: New York University Press.

Anderson, G., & Grace, C. (1991). Black deaf adolescents: A diverse and underserved population. *Volta Review, 93*(5), 73–86.

Andrews, J., & Covell, J. (2006/2007). Preparing future teachers and doctoral-level leaders in deaf education: Meeting the challenge. *American Annals of the Deaf, 51*(5), 464–475.

Andrews, J., Martin, T., & Velásquez, J. (2007, April 23). The need for additional Latino professionals in deaf education. *Hispanic Outlook*, 40–43.

Arnold, P., & MacKenzie, I. (1998). Rejection of hearing aids: A critical review. *Journal of Audiological Medicine, 7*, 173–199.

Asch, A. (2001). Disability, bioethics, and human rights. In G. Albrecht, K. Seelman, & M. Bury (Eds.), *Handbook of disability studies* (pp. 297–326). Thousand Oaks, CA: Sage.

Bahan, B. (2008). Upon the formation of a visual variety of the human race. In H.-D. Bauman (Ed.), *Open your eyes: Deaf Studies talking* (pp. 83–99). Minneapolis, MN: University of Minnesota Press.

Baker, C. (1999). Sign language and the deaf community. In J. Fishman (Ed.), *Handbook of language and ethnic identity* (pp. 122–139). New York: Oxford.

Bat-Chava, Y. (2000). Diversity of deaf identities. *American Annals of the Deaf, 145*, 420–428.

Bauman, H-D. (2008). Introduction: Listening to Deaf Studies. In H-D. Bauman (Ed.), *Open your eyes: Deaf Studies talking* (pp. 1–32). Minneapolis, MN: University of Minnesota Press.

Baynton, D. (1996). *Forbidden signs*. Chicago: University of Chicago Press.

Bernstein, P. (2006, June 4). March of technology opens doors to deaf. Retrieved June 4, 2006 from http://www.baltimoresun.com/technology/bal-id.vision04jun04,0.1476375.story?coll=bal-technology-headlines

Berry, J.W. (2002). Conceptual approaches to acculturation. In K. Chun, P.B. Organista, & G. Marín (Eds.), *Acculturation* (pp. 17–37). Washington, DC: American Psychological Association.

Berry, J.W., & Sam, D.L. (1997). Acculturation and adaptation. In J.W. Berry, P.R. Dasen, & T.S. Saraswathi (Eds.), *Handbook of cross-cultural psychology, Volume 3: Basic processes and human development*, 2nd edition (pp. 291–326). Needham Heights, MA: Allyn & Bacon.

Bova, M. (2008, March 17). Retrieved 3/26/2008 from http://abcnews.go.com/print?id=4464873

Branson, J., & Miller, D. (2002). *Damned for their difference: The cultural construction of deaf people as disabled*. Washington, DC: Gallaudet University Press.

Breivik, J. (2005). *Deaf identities in the making*. Washington, DC: Gallaudet University Press.

Brueggemann, B.J. (1999). *Lend me your ear: Rhetorical constructions of deafness*. Washington, DC: Gallaudet University Press.

Brueggemann, B.J. (2008). Think-between: A Deaf Studies commonplace book. In H-D. Bauman (Ed.), *Open your eyes: Deaf Studies talking* (pp.177–188). Minneapolis, MN: University of Minnesota Press.

Burch, S. (2002). *Signs of resistance; American Deaf cultural history, 1900 to 1942*. New York: New York University Press.

Burke, T.B. (2006). Comments on "W(h)ither the Deaf Community." *Sign Language Studies, 6*(2), 174–180.

Cherney, J.L. (1999). Deaf culture and the cochlear implant debate: Cyborg politics and the identity of people with disabilities. *Argumentation and Advocacy, 36*, 22–34.

Christensen, K., & Delgado, G. (Eds.) (2000). *Deaf plus*. San Diego, CA: DawnSign Press.

Christiansen, J.B., & Leigh, I. W. (2002/2005). *Cochlear implants in children: Ethics and choices*. Washington, DC: Gallaudet University Press. (First published, 2002.)

Collins, R. (2005). *Few HOH people employed by "Deaf and HOH" agencies – One of a series of articles on the awakening oral hearing loss community*. Retrieved March 28, 2006 from http://www.hearinglossweb.com/Issues/Identity/ohl/nat/nat.htm

Collins, S., Devine, D., & Paris, D. (2005, May). *Navigating the path to understanding: The Arizona Native American deaf and hard of hearing task force*. Lecture presented at ADARA Biennial Conference, Orlando, FL.

Corbett, C. (2003). Special issues in psychotherapy with minority Deaf women. In M. Banks & E. Kaschak (Eds.), *Women with visible and invisible disabilities* (pp. 311–329). New York: The Haworth Press.

Corbett, C. (in press). Mental health issues for African American Deaf people. In I. W. Leigh (Ed.), *Psychotherapy with deaf clients from diverse groups*, 2nd ed. Washington, DC: Gallaudet University Press.

Corker, M. (1996). *Deaf transitions*. London: Jessica Kingsley.

Côté, J., & Levine, C. (2002). *Identity formation, agency, and culture: A social psychology synthesis*. Mahwah, NJ: Lawrence Erlbaum.

Crouch, R. (1997). Letting the deaf be Deaf. *Hastings Center Report, 27*(4), 14–21.

Croucher, S. (2004). *Globalization and belonging: The politics of identity in a changing world*. Lanham, MD: Rowman & Littlefield.

Davidson, A. (1996). *Making and molding identity in schools*. Albany, NY: State University of New York Press.

Davis, L.J. (2007, January 12). Deafness and the riddle of identity. *The Chronicle Review, 53*(19), B6.

Davis, L.J. (2008). Postdeafness. In H-D. Bauman (Ed.), *Open your eyes: Deaf Studies talking* (pp. 314–325). Minneapolis, MN: University of Minnesota Press.

Dively, V. (2001/1999). Contemporary Native Deaf experience: Overdue smoke rising. In L. Bragg (Ed.), *Deaf world* (pp. 390–405). New York: New York University Press.

Eldredge, N. (in press). Culturally Responsive Psychotherapy with Ameican Indians Who Are Deaf. In I. W. Leigh (Ed.), *Psychotherapy with deaf clients from diverse groups*, 2nd ed. Washington, DC: Gallaudet University Press.

Emerton, G. (1996). Marginality, biculturalism, and social identity of deaf people. In I. Parasnis (Ed.), *Cultural and language diversity and the deaf experience* (pp. 136–145). New York: Cambridge University Press.

Erikson, E. (1968). *Identity: Youth and crisis*. New York: W.W. Norton.

Erikson, E. (1980). *Identity and the life cycle*. New York: W.W. Norton.

Fagan, M., Pisoni, D. Horn, D., & Dillon, C. (2007). Neuropsychological correlates of vocabulary, reading, and working memory in deaf children with cochlear implants. *Journal of Deaf Studies and Deaf Education, 12*, 461–471.

Fischer, L. C., & McWhirter, J. J. (2001). The Deaf Identity Development Scale: A revision and validation. *Journal of Counseling Psychology, 48*, 355–358.

Franklin, A.J., Carter, R., & Grace, C. (1993). An integrative approach to psychotherapy with Black/African Americans. In G. Stricker & J. Gold (Eds.), *Comprehensive handbook of psychotherapy integration* (pp. 465–479). New York: Plenum.

Foster, S., & Kinuthia, W. (2003). Deaf persons of Asian American, Hispanic American, and African American backgrounds: A study of intraindividual diversity and identity. *Journal of Deaf Studies and Deaf Education, 8*(3), 271–290.

Geers, A. (2006). Spoken language in children with cochlear implants. In P. Spencer & M. Marschark (Eds.), *Advances in the spoken language development of deaf and hard-of-hearing children* (pp. 244–270). New York: Oxford University Press.

Glickman, N. (1996). The development of culturally deaf identities. In N. Glickman & M. Harvey (Eds.), *Culturally affirmative psychotherapy with deaf persons* (pp. 115–153). Mahwah, NJ: Lawrence Erlbaum.

Goffman, E. (1963). *Stigma*. Englewood Cliffs, NJ: Prentice-Hall.

Gonsoulin, T. (2001). Cochlear implant/Deaf World dispute: Different bottom elephants *Otolaryngology-Head and Neck Surgery, 125*, 552–556.

Grushkin, D. (2003). The dilemma of the hard of hearing within the U.S. Deaf community. In L. Monaghan, C. Schmaling, K. Nakamura, & G. Turner (Eds.), *Many ways to be Deaf: International variation in Deaf communities* (pp. 114–140). Washington, DC: Gallaudet University Press.

Harter, S. (1999). *The construction of the self*. New York: Guilford.

Harvey, M. (2003). *Psychotherapy with deaf and hard-of-hearing persons: A systemic model*, 2nd edition. Mahwah, NJ: Lawrence Erlbaum.

Helms, J. (1994). The conceptualization of racial identity and other "racial" constructs. In E. Trickettt, R. Watts, & D. Birman (Eds.), *Human diversity* (pp. 285–311). San Francisco: Jossey Bass.

Hendershot, G. (2001). *Internet use by people with disabilities grows at twice the rate of non-disabled, yet still lags significantly behind*. Retrieved June 8, 2007 from http://www.nod.org/index.cfm?fuseaction=page.viewPage7pageID=1430&nodeID=1&Feat

Henderson, S. (2002, September 25). Our right to be normal. *Melbourne Herald Sun*, p. 19.

Hermans, H., & Dimaggio, G. (2007). Self, identity, and globalization in times of uncertainty: A dialogical analysis. *Review of General Psychology, 11*(1), 31–61.

Hernández, M. (1999). The role of therapeutic groups in working with Latino deaf adolescent immigrants. In I. W. Leigh (Ed.), *Psychotherapy with deaf clients from diverse groups* (pp. 227–249). Washington, DC: Gallaudet University Press.

Hétu, R., Riverin, L., Getty, L., Lalande, N., & St-Cyr, C. (1990). The reluctance to acknowledge hearing difficulties among hearing-impaired workers. *British Journal of Audiology, 28*, 313–325.

Hintermair, M. (2008). Self-esteem and satisfaction with life of deaf and hard-of-hearing People: A resource-oriented approach to identity work. *Journal of Deaf Studies and Deaf Education, 31*(2), 278-300.

Hintermair, M., & Albertini, J. (2005). Ethics, deafness, and new medical technologies. *Journal of Deaf Studies and Deaf Education, 10*(2), 185–192.

Hoffman, K. (1996). *Concepts of identity: Historical and contemporary images and portraits of self and family*. New York: HarperCollins.

House of Lords (2007). *Human fertilization and embryology bill*. Retrieved 3/28/2008 from http://www.publications.parliament.uk/pa/ld200708/ldbills/006/en/08006x–.htm

Hyde, M., & Power, D. (2006). Some ethical dimensions of cochlear implantation for deaf children and their families. *Journal of Deaf Studies and Deaf Education, 11*(1), 103–111.

Israelite, N., Ower, J., & Goldstein, G. (2002). Hard-of-hearing adolescents and identity construction: Influences of school experiences, peers, and teachers. *Journal of Deaf Studies and Deaf Education, 7*, 134–148.

Jacobs, P. (2007). *Neither-nor*. Washington, DC: Gallaudet University Press.

Jambor, E., & Elliott, M. (2005). Self-esteem and coping strategies among deaf students. *Journal of Deaf Studies and Deaf Education, 10*(1), 63–81.

Jankowski, K. (1997). *Deaf empowerment*. Washington, DC: Gallaudet University Press.

Johnston, T. (2004). W(h)ither the Deaf community? Population, genetics, and the future of Australian Sign Language. *American Annals of the Deaf, 148*(5), 358–375.

Johnston, T. (2005). In one's own image: Ethics and the reproduction of deafness. *Journal of Deaf Studies and Deaf Education, 10*(4), 426–441.

Karchmer, M., & Mitchell, R. (2003). Demographic and achievement characteristics of deaf and hard-of-hearing students. In M. Marschark & P. Spencer (Eds.), *Oxford handbook of deaf studies, language, and education* (pp. 21–37). New York: Oxford University Press.

Kent, B. (2003). Identity issues for hard-of-hearing adolescents aged 11, 13, and 15 in mainstream settings. *Journal of Deaf Studies and Deaf Education, 8*, 315–324.

Kent, B., & Smith, S. (2006). "They only see it when the sun shines in my ears": Exploring perceptions of adolescent hearing aid users. *Journal of Deaf Studies and Deaf Education, 11*(4), 461–476.

Kinzie, S. (2006, June 3). Deaf students express dissent along a high-tech grapevine. *The Washington Post*, p. B3.

Kisch, S. (2004). Negotiating (genetic) deafness in a Bedouin community. In J. Van Cleve (Ed.), *Genetics, disability, and deafness* (pp. 148–173). Washington, DC: Gallaudet University Press.

Kochkin, S., Luxford, W., Northern, J., Mason, P., & Tharpe, A.M. (2007, September). Are 1 million dependents with hearing loss in America being left behind? *Hearingreview.com*, 2–12.

Ladd, P. (2003). *Understanding Deaf culture*. Clevedon, UK: Multilingual Matters.

Ladd, P. (2007). Cochlear implantation, colonialism, and Deaf rights. In L. Komesaroff (Ed.), *Surgical consent* (pp. 1–29). Washington, DC: Gallaudet University Press.

LaFromboise, T., Coleman, H., & Gerton, J. (1993). Psychological impact of biculturalism: Evidence and theory. *Psychological Bulletin*, *114*(3), 395–412.

Lane, H. (2005). Ethnicity, ethics, and the Deaf-World. *Journal of Deaf Studies and Deaf Education*, *10*(3), 291–310.

Lane, H., Hoffmeister, R., & Bahan, B. (1996). *A journey into the Deaf-World*. San Diego, CA: DawnSign Press.

LaSasso, C., & Wilson, A. (2000). Results of two national surveys of leadership personnel needs in deaf education. *American Annals of the Deaf*, *145*(5), 429–435.

Laszlo, C. (1994). Is there a hard-of-hearing identity? *Journal of Speech-Language Pathology and Audiology*, *18*, 248–252.

Leary, M., & Tangney, J. (Eds.). (2003). *Handbook of self and identity*. New York: Guilford.

Leigh, I. W. (1999a). Inclusive education and personal development. *Journal of Deaf Studies and Deaf Education*, *4*, 236–245.

Leigh, I. W. (1999b). *Psychotherapy with deaf clients from diverse groups*. Washington, DC: Gallaudet University Press.

Leigh, I. W. (2009). *A lens on deaf identities*. New York: Oxford University Press.

Leigh, I. W., Marcus, A., Dobosh, P., & Allen, T. (1998). Deaf/hearing cultural identity paradigms: Modification of the Deaf Identity Development Scale. *Journal of Deaf Studies and Deaf Education*, *3*, 329–338.

Maxwell-McCaw, D. (2001). *Acculturation and psychological well-being in deaf and hard-*of-hearing *people*. Doctoral dissertation, The George Washington University. *Dissertation Abstracts International*, *61*(11-B), 6141.

Maxwell-McCaw, D., & Zea, M.C. (in press). The Deaf Acculturation Scale (DAS): Development and validation of a 58-item measure. *Journal of Deaf Studies and Deaf Education*.

McAdams, D. (1993). *The stories we live by*. New York: Guilford.

Middleton, A. (2004). Deaf and hearing adults' attitudes toward genetic testing for deafness. In J. Van Cleve (Ed.), *Genetics, disability, and deafness* (pp. 127–147). Washington, DC: Gallaudet University Press.

Mischel, W., & Morf, C. (2003). The self as a psycho-social dynamic processing system: A meta-perspective on a century of the self in psychology. In M. Leary & J. Tangney (Eds.), *Handbook of self and identity* (pp. 15–43). New York: Guilford.

Mishler, E. (2004). Historians of the self: Restorying lives, revising identities. *Research in Human Development*, *1*, 101–121.

Mitchell, R. (2006a). How many deaf people are there in the United States? Estimates from the survey of income and program participation. *Journal of Deaf Studies and Deaf Education*, *11*, 112–119.

Mitchell, R. (2006b). Comments on "W(h)ither the Deaf Community." *Sign Language Studies*, *6*(2), 210–219.

Mitchell, R., & Karchmer, M. (2004). When parents are deaf versus hard of hearing. *Journal of Deaf Studies and Deaf Education*, *9*, 133–152.

Montgomery, G. (1991). Bionic miracle or megabuck acupuncture? The need for a broader context in the evaluation of cochlear implants. In M. Garretson (Ed.), *Perspectives on deafness* (pp. 97–106). Silver Spring, MD: National Association of the Deaf.

Moores, D. (2001). *Educating the deaf: Psychology, principles, and practice*, 5th edition. Boston: Houghton Mifflin.

Moores, D.F., Jatho, J., & Dunn, C. (2001). Families with deaf members: American Annals of the Deaf, 1996–2000. *American Annals of the Deaf*, *146*(3), 245–250.

Moskowitz, G. (2005). *Social cognition: Understanding self and others*. New York: Guilford.

Most, T., Wiesel, A., & Blitzer, T. (2007). Identity and attitudes towards cochlear implant among deaf and hard of hearing adolescents. *Deafness and Education International*, *9*(2), 68–82.

Mundy, L. (2002). A world of their own. Retrieved January 23, 2003 from http:www.washingtonpost.com/ac2/wp-dyn?pagename=article&node=&contented=A231

Murray, J. (2008). Coequality and transnational studies: Understanding Deaf lives. In H-D. Bauman (Ed.), *Open your eyes: Deaf Studies talking* (pp. 100–110). Minneapolis, MN: University of Minnesota Press.

Nakamura, K. (2003). Uturns, Deaf Shock, and the hard of hearing: Japanese deaf identities at the borderlands. In L. Monaghan, C. Schmaling, K. Nakamura, & G. Turner (Eds.), *Many ways to be Deaf: International variation in Deaf communities* (pp. 211–229). Washington, DC: Gallaudet University Press.

Nikolaraizi, M., & Hadjikakou, K. (2006). The role of educational experiences in the development of deaf identity. *Journal of Deaf Studies and Deaf Education*, *11*(4), 477–492.

Padden, C., & Humphries, T. (1988). *Deaf in America: Voices from a culture*. Cambridge, MA: Harvard University Press.

Padden, C., & Humphries, T. (2005). *Inside Deaf culture*. Cambridge, MA: Harvard University Press.

Parasnis, I., & Fischer, S. (2005). Perceptions of diverse educators regarding ethnic-minority deaf college students, role models, and diversity. *American Annals of the Deaf*, *150* (4), 343–349.

Parasnis, I., Samar, V., & Fischer, S. (2005). Deaf college students' attitudes toward racial/ethnic diversity, campus climate, and role models. *American Annals of the Deaf*, *150*(1), 47–58.

Pilling, D., & Barrett, P. (2008). Text communication preferences of deaf people in the United Kingdom. *Journal of Deaf Studies and Deaf Education*, *13*(1), 92–103.

Power, D., Power, M., & Rehling, B. (2007). German deaf people using text communication: Short message service, TTY, relay services, fax, and e-mail. *American Annals of the Deaf*, *152*(3), 291–301.

Power, M., Power, D., & Horstmanshof, L. (2007). Deaf people communicating via SMS, TTY, relay service, fax, and computers in Australia. *Journal of Deaf Studies and Deaf Education*, *12*(1), 80–92.

Preisler, G., Tvingstedt, A., & Ahlström, M. (2005). Interviews with deaf children about their experiences using cochlear implants. *American Annals of the Deaf*, *150*(3), 260–267.

Punch, R., Creed, P., & Hyde, M. (2006). Career barriers perceived by hard of hearing adolescents: Implications for practice from a mixed methods study. *Journal of Deaf Studies and Deaf Education*, *11*(2), 224–237.

Ross, M. (2001). Definitions and descriptions. In J. Davis (Ed.), *Our forgotten children: Hard of hearing pupils in the schools, third edition* (pp.11–37). Bethesda, MD: SHHH Publications.

Ross, M. (2005, Fall). Personal and social identity of hard of hearing people. [Electronic version]. *IFHOH Journal*, 6–9.

Rudmin, F. (2003). Critical history of the acculturation psychology of assimilation, separation, integration, and marginalization. *Review of General Psychology*, *7*, 3–37.

Sam, D., & Berry, J. (Eds.). (2006). *The Cambridge handbook of acculturation psychology*. New York: Cambridge University Press.

Sandel, M. (2007). The case against perfection. Cambridge, MA: Harvard University Press.

Skelton, T., & Valentine, G. (2003). 'It feels like being Deaf is normal': An exploration into the complexities of defining D/deafness and young D/deaf people's identities. *Canadian Geographer, 47*(4), 451–466.

Sorkin, D. (2000). *Developing an identity for people with hearing loss.* Retrieved 9/6/2000 from http://www.ifhoh.org/sorkin.htm

Smiler, K., & McKee, R. (2007). Perceptions of *Maori* deaf identity in New Zealand. *Journal of Deaf Studies and Deaf Education, 12*(1) 93–111.

Spencer, P., & Marschark, M. (2003). Cochlear implants. In M. Marschark & P. Spencer (Eds.), *Oxford handbook of deaf studies, language, and education* (pp. 434–448). New York: Oxford University Press.

Steinberg, A., Davila, J., Collazo, J., Loew, R., & Fischgrund, J. (1997). "A little sign and a lot of love …": Attitudes, perceptions, and beliefs of Hispanic families with deaf children. *Qualitative Health Research, 7*(2), 202–222.

Stinson, M., & Kluwin, T. (1996). Social orientations toward deaf and hearing peers among deaf adolescents in local public high schools. In P. Higgins & J. Nash (Eds.), *Understanding deafness socially* (pp. 113–134). Springfield, IL: Charles C Thomas.

Tajfel, H. (1981). *Human groups and social categories.* Cambridge, England: Cambridge University Press.

Tatum, B. (1997). *Why are all the black kids sitting together in the cafeteria?* New York: Basic Books.

Tellings, A. (1996). Cochlear implants and deaf children. The debate in the United States. *Journal of the British Association of Teachers of the Deaf, 20*(1), 24–31.

Trimble, J. (2005). Ethnic identity. In C.B. Fisher & R. Lerner (Eds.), *Encyclopedia of applied developmental science, Vol. I* (pp. 415–420). Thousand Oaks, CA: Sage.

Tucker, B. (1998). *Cochlear implants: A handbook.* Jefferson, NC: McFarland.

Turner, J. (1996). Henri Tajfel: An introduction. In W.P. Robinson (Ed.), *Social groups and identities: Developing the legacy of Henri Tajfel* (pp. 1–23). Oxford, England: Butterworth-Heinemann.

Vesey, K., & Wilson, B. (2003). Navigating the hearing classroom with a hearing loss. *Odyssey, 4,* 10–13.

Wald, R., & Knutsen, J. (2000). Deaf cultural identity of adolescents with and without cochlear implants. *Annals of Otology, Rhinology & Laryngology* (Supplement 185), *12*(2), 87–89.

Warick, R. (1994). A profile of Canadian hard-of-hearing youth. *Journal of Speech Language Pathology and Audiology, 18,* 253–259.

Warick, R. (2004). Voices unheard: The academic and social experiences of university students who are hard of hearing. (Doctoral dissertation, The University of British Columbia, 2003). *Dissertation Abstracts International, 64*(12), 4390.

Waterman, A. (1992). Identity as an aspect of optimal psychological functioning. In G. R. Adams, T.P. Gullotta, & R. Montemayor (Eds.), *Adolescent identity formation* (pp. 50–72). Newbury Park, CA: Sage.

Weinberg, N., & Sterritt, M. (1986). Disability and identity: A study of identity patterns in adolescents with hearing impairments. *Rehabilitation Psychology, 31,* 95–102.

Wheeler, A., Archbold, S., Gregory, S., & Skipp, A. (2007). Cochlear implants: The young people's perspective. *Journal of Deaf Studies and Deaf Education, 12*(3), 303–316.

Wu, C., & Grant, N (in press). Asian American and Deaf. In I. W. Leigh (Ed.), *Psychotherapy with deaf clients from diverse groups,* 2nd *ed.* Washington, DC: Gallaudet University Press.

Zazove, P., Meador, H., Derry, H., Gorenflo, D., Burdick, S., & Saunders, E. (2004) Deaf persons and computer use. *American Annals of the Deaf. 148*(5), 376–384.

Deaf Studies in the 21st Century: "Deaf-gain" and the Future of Human Diversity

H-Dirksen L. Bauman *and* Joseph J. Murray

Abstract

This article provides an overview of the field of Deaf Studies, as it has emerged in the latter part of the 20th century, and then provides a new rhetorical frame for future directions that this field may take in the 21st century. Historically, Deaf Studies and Deaf communities have been put on the defensive, as they have been constructed within frames of "deafness as lack" and "disability." Within these constructions, attempts to rid society of deafness have been conducted as "progress," whether through 19th- and early 20th-century eugenics, or contemporary medical interventions and denial of signed languages in deaf education. The result has been a precipitous decline in the usage of sign language among deaf children at a time when, ironically, research shows cognitive benefits of sign language for hearing children. A vigorous response to the human right of sign language education for deaf children can best be found in reframing deafness, not as a lack, but as a form of human diversity capable of making vital contributions to the greater good of society. We refer to this notion as the opposite of hearing loss: Deaf-gain. This article explores the cognitive, creative, and cultural aspects of Deaf-gain, with specific examples, from discoveries about the human capacity for language, advances in visual learning, and creative insights into architecture, literature, and collectivist cultural patterns. In the end, deaf people may be seen through a lens of human diversity and, therefore, worth valuing as they are, without recourse to 'normalization.'

Keywords: bioethics, Deaf-gain, Deaf studies, human diversity, language death

What Is Deaf Studies?

The academic field of Deaf Studies is comprised of interdisciplinary approaches to the exploration of Deaf individuals, communities, and cultures as they have evolved within a larger context of power and ideology. Deaf Studies curricula are likely to include perspectives from, among others, anthropology, linguistics, literary theory, bilingual education, and a host of cultural studies practices including gender, disability, and ethnic studies. Although this wide diversity of disciplines offers multiple perspectives, the field's fundamental orientation is derived from the notion that deaf people are not defined by their lack of hearing, but by linguistic, cultural, and sensorial ways of being in the world.

Building on this central precept, the field of Deaf Studies grew from a few courses in the 1970s to offer its first degree-granting programs in the early 1980s at Boston University and California State University at Northridge. Since that time, Gallaudet University established an undergraduate Deaf Studies degree in 1994 and an MA degree in 2002. Bristol University also offers undergraduate and graduate degrees in Deaf Studies. In addition to a growing number of degree-granting programs in Deaf Studies, national and international conferences, peer-reviewed journals, and a growing body of research and publications continue to shed light on the unique linguistic, cultural, and epistemological implications of the formation of a Deaf variety of the human race.

As the field of Deaf Studies matures into the 21st century, it finds itself having to move beyond the initial tasks of explaining Deaf culture and identity to confronting questions about the very reasons Deaf people and their sign languages should continue to exist. This chapter will first provide a brief overview of the formation of Deaf Studies in the late 20th century, then will examine current and future trajectories of Deaf Studies that include a fundamental reframing of the meanings of "deaf" from loss to gain.

Deaf Studies in the Late 20th Century

The emergence of the field of Deaf Studies was brought about by the convergence of two transformative occasions. The first was the revelation of the full linguistic status of sign languages. Once the linguistic nature of sign languages took hold, a very different construction of the users of these languages appeared warranted. In the 1970s, Deaf people began to see themselves as belonging to a linguistic minority rather than a group of people bonded through disability. Soon, a body of work and flurry of cultural productivity emerged that worked toward the rewriting of Deaf identity from pathology to culture. To understand this culture, a body of inquiry soon developed. Deaf culture needed Deaf Studies to explore itself.

Although the validation of signed languages and the formation of Deaf cultural rhetoric are cited as the immediate causes of the formation of Deaf Studies, the remote, but nonetheless, integral cause is the emergence of ethnic and minority studies in the last quarter of the 20th century. These minority studies movements emerged out of a tradition of Cultural Studies that was set in motion within the Birmingham School of Cultural Studies, where a critique of class structures led scholars like Hoggart (1957), Williams (1958, 1961), and Hall (1973) to recognize that traditional curricular offerings were manifestations of the ideologies of the cultural elite. In the wake of the critique of class within Marxist cultural criticism, the hold on the sanctity of the canon was loosened, opening the way for alternative fields of study aligned with the politics of race and gender. Accordingly, the first African American studies programs formed in the late 1960s, and Women's studies programs emerged soon after.

In the vein of other cultural studies disciplines, Deaf Studies has been largely concerned with the recovery of a forgotten history (Lane, 1984; Lane & Fischer, 1993; Van Cleve, 1993; Van Cleve & Crouch, 1989), the celebration of cultural productivity

(Erting, Johnson, Smith, & Snider, 1993), the reconceptualization of identity along an axis of culture rather than pathology (Lane, Hoffmeister, & Bahan, 1996; Padden & Humphries, 1988), and a critique of the dominant ideological structures that have created unequal power relations (Davis, 1995; Lane, 1992). This latter critical activity can be found either implicitly or explicitly throughout Deaf Studies since its inception, and may be considered a defining element of what distinguishes Deaf Studies from other disciplines that have evolved around the audiological condition of deafness. These professions, namely education and medicine, have often been in a contentious battle with Deaf Studies to define the meanings of the overdetermined four letter word: DEAF.

But this reexamination and modification has only gone so far, and at times, academic journals, books, and academic programs have adopted the name of Deaf Studies without incorporating its basic critical orientation. When research on educational or rehabilitation practices involving deaf people do not recognize the pervasive presence of power, they often reinscribe the very ideological constructions called into question by Deaf Studies. Currently, many American Sign Language (ASL) and Deaf Studies programs are housed in Speech, Language, and Hearing Sciences departments across the nation. If one perceives deaf people as being identified with hearing loss, then this would be an appropriate affiliation; yet, there is a fundamental contradiction in the idea of putting the study of a natural human language and social formation within departments that focus on pathological constructions of sign languages and their users. To put this into perspective, it is difficult to imagine placing Native American, Hispanic, or African American Studies in academic journals and departments with a medicalized view of these groups of people. Indeed, although sign language linguists have contributed to a fundamental redefinition of the human capacity for language, the field of Deaf Studies still finds itself facing dominant ideologies of normalcy that pigeonhole the meanings of deaf to medical constructions.

The overall frame of Deaf Studies is becoming increasingly important now as burgeoning numbers of hearing students are taking ASL for academic credit in high schools and postsecondary education. A study of foreign language enrollment indicated an increase of over 430% in students enrolled in ASL classes between 1998 and 2002 (Welles, 2004) and another increase of 29% between 2002 and 2006

(Furman, Goldberg, & Lusin, 2007). Currently, ASL is the second most-taught language in community colleges and the fourth most-taught in 4-year colleges and universities (Furman et al., 2007). This growth of interest in ASL has also brought about an increase in the numbers of Deaf Studies degrees, programs, and courses, given the integral connection of language and culture. With the proliferation of Deaf Studies programs and scholarly output, the field of Deaf Studies is clearly on solid footing and looking forward to continued growth. However, the popularity of ASL and Deaf Studies has been primarily among hearing students, while deaf children are increasingly not educated in bilingual–bicultural academic programs, thus resulting in the cultural paradox that ASL is promoted for hearing individuals but may be discouraged among deaf individuals (Bauman, 2008). In fact, as will be discussed later, the very existence of several sign languages and their communities may be at risk. As a result, the future of Deaf communities and their languages may rest in how well Deaf Studies scholars can articulate the value of maintaining vibrant Deaf communities, so that they are not washed away in the tidal wave of normalizing practices that are gaining momentum in the early 21st century.

In what follows, we examine the position that Deaf Studies scholars now find themselves in—in an existential defense of why deaf people and their languages should continue to exist. To approach this question, it is important to look at past and current discourses of normalcy and how they have affected Deaf lives. We then outline a shift in the field of Deaf Studies from interrogation of deafness to explorations of Deaf ways of being in the world as ways that contribute to the cognitive, creative, and cultural diversity of the human experience.

Deaf Studies in the 21st Century: Lessons from the History of Normalization

Although 21st-century threats to the future vitality of Deaf communities and their languages are very real, they are by no means a recent development. The 19th century saw the development of the concept of *normalcy* emerge from statistical science and its application to human beings and human societies via tests of mental and physical health (Baynton, 2000; Davis, 2006). This concept of a norm replaced an earlier concept of the "classical ideal," the difference being, Davis (2006, p. 6) notes, that "the majority of the population must or should…be a part of the norm." Institutions designated for the education and treatment of deaf people embodied normalcy as a

hearing and speaking subject, with the deaf and signing person relegated to the category of "oral failures." This was a dramatic change from earlier understandings of sign language, which was understood by antebellum educators as a natural language, one that elevated its users by bringing to them the word of God (Baynton, 1996). This change in the status of sign language was paralleled by a reconceptualization of deaf bodies into potential threats to national societies. In the context of evolutionary science and the rise of fears of the infection of national bodies by "hereditary defectives," fears of a "deaf-mute race" were raised (Bell, 1883). The final decades of the 19th century saw a transatlantic debate among scientists, educators, and legislators over the purported menace of deaf people marrying other deaf people (Murray, 2002; Van Cleve & Crouch, 1989).

In both cases, international Deaf leaders responded to forces of normalcy by redefining what it meant to be normal. Nineteenth-century Deaf leaders saw much value in teaching deaf children to speak but maintained that normalcy lay in full citizenship, and this could only come through an education in sign language. At national and international meetings, deaf leaders consistently claimed sign language was the best means to educate deaf children. This was not only an end in itself, but was a means of forming deaf children into productive, tax-paying adult citizens. This argument accepted the premises of larger social debates on citizenship but pointed to an alternate path to achieving the same aims. A similar reinscription of larger social discourses to fit Deaf ways of being can be seen in the opposition to interventions in Deaf people's choice of marriage partners. Their opposition was framed partially as resisting restrictions on the rights of autonomous liberal subjects, especially male subjects. Why, asked Deaf leaders, should deaf people be discouraged from marrying one another when it was precisely Deaf to Deaf marriages that carried the greatest chance of happiness for the couple? If it was in the best interests of society to have stable families, then Deaf people should be allowed to marry one another. In both cases, normalcy was defined as the ability to participate in larger social discourses, but as sign-language-using Deaf people (Murray, 2007).

This is not to say Deaf people were always successful at resisting normalizing pressures. Oral education, if not necessarily the purely oral variant, was the dominant method of education in Western societies for decades. In addition, Finland banned the marriage of certain categories of deaf people for half of the 20th century, with provisions made for sterilization before marriage rights would be granted (Salmi & Lakso, 2005, p. 503; Wallvik, 1997, pp. 284–288). In 1930s Germany, deaf people were also victims of a law that sought to sterilize those seen as hereditarily diseased, carried out with the complicity of teachers and administrators at schools for deaf people and Protestant pastoral workers who worked with deaf people (Biesold, 1999). Even here, however, deaf people adopted the larger rhetoric of eugenicists concerned with promoting healthy national populations. Early 20th-century Deaf Americans put forth images of themselves and their children as healthy and fit (Burch, 2002), adapting eugenic ideologies to their deaf bodies. Deaf people put forth reinterpretations of eugenic imagery that could fit their lives.

What emerges from these histories is the continuous interaction between Deaf ways of living in the world and larger social discourses, some of which seek to redefine or eliminate these ways of living. How society views deaf people may be a bellwether of how it manages difference. Deaf people are part of a small population subgroup in continuous interaction with an existing apparatus of pedagogical and medical professionals. The existence of bodies of authority ready to act upon deaf bodies makes deaf people an early target for policies of normalization. The existence of politically organized, longstanding Deaf communities in Western countries provides a space for counter-discourses to emerge. The lesson from Deaf history may be that we see deaf people as the canary in the coal mine of social engineering.

Deaf Studies in the 21st Century: Existential Threats

Despite the 20th-century advances made by Deaf Studies, the terrain is again shifting. New technologies of normalization are being applied to deaf people. Whereas the first 30 years of Deaf Studies could be summed up by the effort to redefine Deaf identity from pathology to cultural identity, the future of Deaf Studies finds itself facing the very real consequences of bio-power (Foucault, 1990). Whereas the eugenic drive to normalcy dealt with the structural dissolution of the Deaf community, the 21st-century Deaf community faces rapid advances in technologies that stand to reduce the numbers of this community.

The questions, it seems, are even more challenging for Deaf Studies than for other minority studies fields. No one discusses whether or not, for example, if women will continue to exist, or if African

Americans will continue to exist in future generations; however, the key question for Deaf Studies is the fundamental existential question—*why should deaf people and their sign languages continue to exist?*

Indeed, this is a difficult question to have to ask, and some may rightly feel offended, as if anyone had to defend their right to exist, a right that precedes all others. Yet, this question is being asked on an everyday basis, by genetic counselors and prospective parents, in the House of Commons, and on Deaf Studies blogs. For Deaf communities, the implications of technology and biomedical interventions have been taken up in theatrical productions, lectures, community forums, and video blogs globally (Burke, 2007; Frontrunners, 2005; Haualand & Otterstedt, 2007; Murray, 2006). Deaf people are acutely attuned to the shifting social conditions under which they are operating.

Within this long history of normalization, we may now see the current threats to sign language and deaf bodies in context. In following sections, we provide an overview of the current and future threats to signing Deaf communities, which take the form of rapid increase in cochlear implantation coupled with nonsigning educational settings, and advances in genetic options that allow parents to avoid having deaf babies in the first place.

The Threat to Sign Languages

Concern has been raised at the rapid decrease of early exposure to sign language (Snoddon, 2008), which could lead toward a contraction and potential endangerment of these very sign languages. This concern was echoed by science writer Michael Chorost in a recent autobiographical text revolving around the use of cochlear implants: "When twenty-second century historians write the history of cochlear implants and the end of ASL…they will not find malice. Not deliberate genocide. Only thousands of separately made rational decisions gradually accumulating into a computational tidal wave so overwhelming that even the clearest eyed observers could only stand by in helpless wonder and sorrow" (Chorost, 2005, p. 144). Chorost's concern is buttressed by the analysis presented by Trevor Johnston in his article "W(h)ither the Deaf Community" (2004/2006), which has generated considerable attention, given its dire prediction of pending language death for Australian Sign Language (Auslan). Johnston cites declining rates of deafness at birth, increased rates of cochlear implantation, increased educational placements that do not incorporate Auslan, and advances in genetic screening that may allow parents to avoid having deaf children altogether. Johnston alerts readers that cochlear implantation rates of 75% and the systematic implementation of genetic knowledge to avoid deaf births "could effectively bring an end to the community within half a lifetime" (p. 160). While others have predicted a much slower decrease and the ultimate survival of Auslan (Carty, 2006; Hyde, Power, & Lloyd, 2006), there is a general consensus that, due to cochlear implantation and educational approaches that do not use signed languages, the early exposure to a fully developed natural sign language for deaf children is diminishing. As Johnston writes, "The 'negative' impact of the cochlear implant program, on the future growth of the signing Deaf community must be deemed to be significant, irreversible, and well under way" (Johnston 2006; p. 157–158.).

Although Johnston is clearly correct in noting the impact that implants have on the Deaf community, an important distinction must be made in that implants themselves are not the threat, but rather the educational methods that have been designed for children with cochlear implants. The discredited myth that using one language will hinder a child's ability to use another language has proven to be especially tenacious when the languages in question are signed and spoken. This belief is entrenched within certain geographical areas such as Australia, Denmark, and Ontario in Canada.

The President of the Danish Deaf Association reports near 99% infant and childhood cochlear implantation with a corresponding precipitous decline in enrollment in signing deaf schools (Bergmann, personal communication, November 16, 2008). As of 2008, the Skolen på Kastelsvej (Copenhagen Deaf School) does not have enough students for separate classes in grades 1–4, a situation reflected in another center school (Johannsen, personal communication, December 29, 2008). With such a rapid decline in sign language instruction and signing deaf peers, deaf families with deaf children have migrated to Malmo, Sweden, for sign language–based instruction.

Similarly, Ontario, Canada, has witnessed a rapid contraction of early childhood sign language–based education. Snoddon (2008, p. 583) notes that, "In Ontario, public support for learning ASL has not been available for infants and young children with cochlear implants." This significant decrease in exposure to sign language has been attributed partly to the rise of audio-verbal therapy (AVT), which emphasizes spoken language development through intensive speech therapy in conjunction with amplification (Cripps & Small 2004). According to Snoddon, "Ontario's two children's hospitals require deaf children who undergo cochlear implant surgery to enroll in AVT. According to the senior program consultant of the IHP, auditory-verbal therapists refuse to treat children who are learning signed language" (Snoddon, 2008, p. 584). Such systematic denial of signed language to deaf children is devastatingly ironic, given the concurrent explosion of interest in ASL for hearing infants.

Despite overwhelming numbers of deaf children enrolled in nonsigning educational environments early in their lives, they often do not remain there. According to Akamatsu, Musselman, and Zweibel (2000, pp. 264–266), "93% of severely to profoundly deaf children in Ontario had initially been enrolled in auditory–oral intervention programs, and 67% of deaf preschool children had been educated orally; the figures dropped to 58% for children in elementary school and 31% for students in high school." These statistics suggest that deaf individuals may gravitate toward a sign-based education and a signing community later in life. Clearly, this would have an impact on the nature of the language; with so few native users of the language, this could conceivably lead to a phenomenon similar to revitalization programs of Native American languages.

The Threat to Deaf Bodies

Research into the genetic causes of hearing loss has progressed to the point at which more than 100 genes for deafness have been mapped, with one, Connexin 26, identified as the most productive gene for causing deafness (Arnos 2003). Much current research is in the identification stage, studying which genes affect hearing and how. As with any medical technology, the ultimate aims are prevention and cure. Thus, research into genetics has the potential for the ultimate normalization of the deaf body: its elimination. Although this is not yet imminent, researchers in the field have "raised hopes that the first steps towards implementing a cure for [hearing loss] is just around the corner" (Brownstein & Avraham, 2006, p. 199). If this were to happen, it would likely start in developing countries, since access to genetic testing and abortion are less accessible in the countries of the global South. Genetic causes are responsible for an estimated 68% of cases of children born with a hearing loss in the United States (Morton & Nance, 2006), and researchers are exploring strategies to decrease the incidence of genetic hearing loss (Kochhar, Hildebrand, & Smith, 2007), as well as recommending a role for genetic counselors on hearing loss health care teams (Genetic Evaluation of Congenital Hearing Loss Expert Panel, 2002). It has been predicted that the reduced numbers of deaf people will drastically reduce the size of a particular national Deaf community, and along with it, the viability of that community and its sign language (Carty, 2006; Johnston, 2006, p. 165).

A definition of normalcy based on genetic manipulation would preclude deafness from being an acceptable lifestyle choice. In this view, it would not be socially acceptable for a person to choose to have a deaf child. We can see this in strident reactions in the global mediascape and among members of the general public whenever stories appear of deaf people wanting deaf children (Gray, 2008, Mundy, 2002). We can already see this attitude being read into legislation in Clause 14(4) of the United Kingdom's Human Fertilisation and Embryology Act (HFEA). The HFEA can be interpreted to prohibit the selection of a deaf embryo over a non-deaf one. The clause reads

> (9) Persons or embryos that are known to have a gene, chromosome, or mitochondrion abnormality involving a significant risk that a person with the abnormality will have or develop—(a) a serious physical or mental disability, (b) a serious illness, or (c) any other serious medical condition, must not be preferred to those that are not known to have such an abnormality (Office of Public Sector Information, The National Archives, 2008)

When the HFEA was submitted as a bill to Parliament, language in the explanatory notes and a debate in the House of Lords made it clear that the idea of deaf embryos was an important inspiration for the clause. A Lord commented, "I hope that your Lordships will be pleased that the deliberate choice of an embryo that is, for example, likely to be deaf will be prevented by Clause 14" (Bryan, 2007). Academics and community activists in and outside of the United Kingdom mounted an attempt to amend the Bill, but succeeded only in removing a reference to deafness in the explanatory notes. The Act, however, passed with the clause intact. The existential threat is not coming; it is here.

The issues in question reach beyond deaf people. In Australia, a couple seeking in vitro fertilization initially declined to implant embryos that carried the Connexin 26 gene. The embryos in question would have developed into a child with normal hearing (and thus would probably not have fallen under the HFEB) but that person would have carried within himself or herself the potential to have a deaf child. In this case, we see a glimpse of a time when the concept of normalcy is projected into the future: one's potential genetic legacy can determine whether or not one is allowed to exist (Burke, 2006; Noble, 2003). How the case of genetics and deafness plays out in the coming *years* will gives us insight into the coming *decades*, when social policy, popular opinion, and genetic technology will reshape standards of normalcy for all human beings.

In this and other existential debates, Deaf Studies has a role to play that goes beyond those issues immediately confronting deaf people. Science writer Michael Chorost refers to himself as a cyborg, because his cochlear implant mediates between his being and the world, and he suggests his experience will become common as technology supplements the organic functions of the human body (Chorost, 2005). The genetics of deafness will not be determinative of how humanity confronts genetic engineering, but the strategies and discourses used in the contestations of normalcy that are emerging in this case may very well reappear when applied to other instances of genetic diversity.

Deaf-gain: Cognitive, Cultural, and Creative Diversity

Given the threats posed to the signing Deaf community by the medical and educational institutions of normalization, the Deaf community and Deaf Studies scholars find themselves cornered into the fundamental existential question: Why should deaf people continue to exist? Indeed, on what grounds can one argue for the preservation of what most consider a disability? As Burke (2006) notes, such bioethical arguments hinge on the demonstration of the intrinsic and extrinsic value of Deaf communities and their languages. Intrinsic arguments seek to prove the worth of deaf people and sign languages for their own good, whereas extrinsic arguments demonstrate the useful contributions of deaf people and their languages for the greater good of humanity. Although intrinsic arguments have long been made (i.e., Deaf culture and sign languages should be preserved because they are as valid as other cultures and languages), extrinsic arguments have not yet been fully developed or understood. Future directions in the field of Deaf Studies may be thought of as the vigorous exploration and demonstration of the important extrinsic value of Deaf communities and their languages.

While having to argue for the most basic right of all—the right to exist—Deaf Studies is put on the defensive. However, scholars are beginning to recognize that the most vigorous response would be to cease arguing against medical and educational institutions of normalization, and instead, go on the offensive by reframing representations of deafness from sensory lack to a form of sensory and cognitive diversity that offers vital contributions to human diversity. Within the frame of human diversity, Deaf Studies scholars are inquiring into the insights that may be gleaned from deaf people whose highly visual, spatial, and kinetic structures of thought and language may shed light into the blindspots of hearing ways of knowing.

The overarching extrinsic value of Deaf communities and their languages, then, may best be explained by the emerging discipline of biocultural diversity, a field that has arisen as an area of transdisciplinary research concerned with investigating the links between the world's linguistic, cultural, and biological diversity as manifestations of the diversity of life. The impetus for the emergence of this field came from the observation that all three diversities are under threat by some of the same forces, and from the perception that loss of diversity at all levels spells dramatic consequences for humanity and the earth (Maffi, 2005). A body of research has begun to link the decreases in biocultural and linguistic diversity, noting that when an indigenous language dies, the unique knowledge of the local environment, developed over centuries, dies with it (Harmon, 2002; Maffi, 2005; Skutnabb-Kangas, 2000). Most predictions suggest that within the next century, half of the world's 6,000 spoken languages will disappear, which is at the rate of a language death every two weeks (Crystal, 2002). There are currently no statistics about the number of signed languages in the world, and clearly, when a signed language dies, there may not be the same amount of biological and environmental knowledge lost with it. However, in the same vein, Deaf Studies scholars may begin to add to the notions of linguistic and biodiversity new categories of diversity foregrounded by signed languages—namely, cognitive, cultural, and creative diversity.

Once we place Deaf communities and their languages within the framework of biocultural diversity, a new frame emerges. The task of Deaf Studies in the new century is to ask a fundamental question: How does being Deaf reorganize what it means to be human? Indeed, what dramatic consequences would arise from the (neo)eugenic drive toward normalization? Embracing deaf people and their languages will invariably lead toward a deeper understanding of the human proclivity for adaptation. In the face of sensory loss, we may better appreciate the dynamic and pliable nature of the mind and the human will to communicate and to form community. In this light, deafness is not so much defined by a fundamental lack, as in *hearing loss*, but as its opposite, as a means to understand the plenitude of human being, as *Deaf-gain*.[1]

Deaf-gain, as we explore later, is the notion that the unique sensory orientation of Deaf people leads to a sophisticated form of visual-spatial language that provides opportunities for exploration into the human character. In this spirit, the Gallaudet University's Vision Statement commits to promoting "the recognition that deaf people and their sign languages are vast resources with significant contributions to the cognitive, creative, and cultural dimensions of human diversity" (http://www.gallaudet.edu/mission.xml). In what follows, contemporary and future directions for each of these forms of human diversity and "Deaf-gain" will be discussed as emerging and future trajectories of the field of Deaf Studies that collectively demonstrate the value of Deaf Studies to the academy and Deaf communities to humanity.

Cognitive Diversity and Deaf-gain: Redefining the Nature of Language

The prime example of the extrinsic value of deaf people and their languages is the wholesale redefinition of language that has come about as a result of sign language studies. Just as we once thought the flat Earth to be at the center of the universe, we once assumed that language could only take the form of speech. Now that we know the brain may just as easily develop a signed as a spoken language, we must reconfigure our understanding of language, in all its complexities. Four decades of sign language research has now deepened our awareness of the nature of language—from language acquisition, structure, and more. We now know that the fundamental character of the brain is plasticity and flexibility (Petitto, Zatorre, Gauna, Nikelski, Dostie, & Evans, 2000). This redefining would not have come about without the study of signed languages, and may be seen as the initial instance of Deaf-gain. Due to the existence of signing communities, linguists and anthropologists have been able to peer into the development of language, revealing insights into the debates over the innateness or social origins of language acquisition (Sandler, Meir, Padden, & Aronoff, 2005). In addition, sign languages have also provided insight into new and revived theories of the origins of language (Armstrong, 2002;

Armstrong & Wilcox, 2007; Armstrong, Wilcox, & Stokoe, 1995; Corballis, 2003; Stokoe, 2001). The implications of these discoveries extend into the core of what it means to be human, but have yet to be applied to Deaf education. As Stokoe (2001, p. 16) wrote, "the status of deaf people, their education, their opportunities in life, and the utilization of their potential—all these could be much enhanced if we understood the way deaf people still make language may be the way the whole human race became human." As a result of the natural human proclivity to sign, hearing parents are increasingly using sign language, with results that suggest increased linguistic, cognitive, and social development.

Cognitive Diversity and Deaf-Gain: Visual Language/Visual Learning

Another significant area of future research in the area of Deaf-gain is the particular, highly developed visual ways of being in the world brought about by the unique sensory orientation of deaf individuals and communities (Bahan, 2008; Marschark, 2003). The link between enhanced visuospatial abilities and use of sign languages has been documented in studies of speed in generating mental images (Emmorey & Kosslyn, 1996; Emmorey, Kosslyn, & Bellugi, 1993), mental rotation skills (Emmorey, Klima, & Hicock, 1998), increased facial recognition skills (Bettger, Emmorey, McCullough, & Bellugi, 1997), increased peripheral recognition skills (Bavelier, Tomann, Hutton, Mitchell, Corina, Liu, & Neville, 2000), and increased spatial cognition (Bellugi, O'Grady, Lillio-Martin, O'Grady Hynes, Van Hoek, & Corina, 1989; see also Chapter 30, this volume). We may take these indications of increased visual-spatial cognition and develop them into future research into practices of visual learning for all sighted individuals. The benefits may be far reaching, for as Stokoe recognized, "vision may have an advantage, for it is neurologically a richer and more complex physiological system than hearing. Sight makes use of much more of the brain's capacity than does hearing" (p. 20). Given the drive to diversify education along the lines of "multiple intelligences" (Gardner, 1993), it would only makes sense that the most visually oriented of all humans would take the lead toward future experimentation in visual learning.

As testimony to the promises of the field of visual language and visual learning, the National Science Foundation recently funded a Science of Learning Center at Gallandet University to "gain a greater understanding of the biological, cognitive, linguistic, sociocultural, and pedagogical conditions that influence the acquisition of language and knowledge through the visual modality" (VL2, 2008; http://vl2. gallaudet.edu/). Given the immense amount of information processed visually[2] (for sighted people), it is not surprising that learning may be enhanced when pedagogies focus on transmitting visual information (Gardner, 1993; Moore & Dwyer, 1994). This project goes beyond the Deaf education model of addressing alternative (read: remedial) ways of teaching deaf people, to ask how deaf people's visual orientation to the world may be able to offer hearing people new ways of learning, even in fields traditionally dominated by an auditory/phonetic orientation, such as literacy development. Indeed, as textuality in the 21st century is becoming increasingly visual and digital, there is a trend away from traditional print-based texts to video and multimedia texts. Insights from the world's most visually acute people may provide insights on how we may all process information visually.

If this is the case, then future directions of Deaf Studies and Deaf education may have less to do with audiological loss than Deaf-gain—that is, a bilingual, visual learning environment could be so rich in processing information in multiple channels that hearing parents would want their children to go to sign language schools. In this scenario, Deaf education would give way to dual-language education, open to all who desire such a learning environment. Two examples of these types of bilingual sign language schools are P.S. 47: The ASL–English Bilingual School in New York City and The Cassato School, near Torino, Italy. Indeed, before such a paradigm shift were to take root in a systematic way, the status of sign languages as academic languages would have to be reconceived.

Cognitive Diversity and Deaf-gain: Sign Languages and Academic Discourse

Traditionally, signed languages have been seen as essentially "oral" languages as they have no written form.[3] Common wisdom holds that writing is an essential element to the development of literacy, as essential as water is to swimming. The word "literacy," after all, derives from the Greek *littere*, or "written letter." However, as Kuntze (2008) has suggested, just as definitions of language have changed in the wake of the validation of sign languages, so may the definition of literacy. Kuntze shows how one may demonstrate characteristics of literate thought in written, signed, and visual modalities. One such characteristic, notes Kuntze, is inference making. Whether the information that an individual receives "is expressed in written language or in a different language such as ASL or in a different mode like film, the act of inference making will be necessary if one is to achieve a richer interpretation of the content" (p. 150). Clearly, one may exercise inference and other critical thinking strategies using a nonwritten language such as ASL or through watching silent films.

Evolving definitions of literacy are happening in tandem with emerging video technologies that allow greater ease of producing academic texts in ASL. Once video journals such as the *Deaf Studies Digital Journal* (dsdj.gallaudet.edu) mature, standards for academic publishing in signed languages will develop. The significance of academic discourse in ASL may be most prominent if the visual, spatial, and kinetic dimensions of the language are explored for their greatest rhetorical power. For example, imagine how precisely an ASL-fluent biology professor would describe the process of cell mitosis, using ASL's rich classifier system to indicate pairs of chromosomes splitting and cell walls dividing, so that students may witness the linguistic reenactment of a physical process, or the precise description of the French philosopher Michel Foucault's notion of the "microphysics of power," which would be shown as a dispersion of multiple sites of power throughout society, rather than a more traditional top-down model of power. The point here is that sign languages are rich in what Taub (2001) calls "metaphoric iconicity," in which complex ideas are demonstrated through visual-spatial metaphors. Such a language does not lack in abstraction, but gains in clarity of the concrete representation of complex ideas.

This unique advantage of sign languages was originally articulated by the early 19th-century teacher of the deaf, Auguste Bebian, who believed that "sign language has a superior capacity for expressing mental operations" (1984, p. 151). The difference, Bebian explains, is that spoken language is fundamentally arbitrary, but discourse in sign language, would "frequently acquire a self-evident certainty or become a manifest absurdity to all" (p. 151). Indeed, the speaking biology student could say, "the chromosomes split," whereas the signing biology student would reveal the internal mental images of her conception of how the chromosomes split visually and spatially. Similarly, the philosophy student would reveal the degree of precision of his understanding of Foucault's unique conception of "power" through the spatial arrangement of his description. Clearly, the validity of such observations

about the unique qualities of intellectual discourse in sign language now lay before the fields of Deaf education, Deaf Studies, and linguistics to explore this vein of potential Deaf-gain.

Creative Diversity and Deaf-gain: Film Language/Sign Language

Comparisons have often been made between the film language and sign languages (Bahan, 2006; Bauman, 2006; Sacks, 1990). In addition to a traditional linguistic means of describing sign languages through phonology, morphology, and syntax, one may also see fluent signers as everyday filmmakers, a skill that is heightened in the literary and dramatic uses of sign language. Indeed, when seen through lens of film grammar (Arijon, 1991), sign languages present a constant tableau of close-up and distant shots, replete with camera movements and editing techniques. Given such an intimate, cognitive relationship with cinematic grammar, we must wonder what innovations might emerge if we were to invest in the cinematic education of the next generation of deaf children. Again, no research has been conducted to this point about the potential innovations that would emerge from Deaf filmmakers, but such exploration is clearly an important trajectory for Deaf Studies to explore the potential of Deaf-gain in this area. A rigorous educational film program in deaf schools would have the added benefit of inserting a deaf public voice into popular media.

Creative Diversity and Deaf-gain: Deaf Space and the Built Environment

Although Deaf Studies is inherently interdisciplinary, one may not immediately think of architecture as an important area of creative exchange. However, in 2005, Gallaudet University hosted a two-day "Deaf Space" workshop, which resulted in what has grown into a series of Deaf Studies courses, the Gallaudet University Deaf Space Design Guide (H. Bauman, in press), and the incorporation of some key Deaf Space principles in the Sorenson Language and Communication Center at Gallaudet.

The Deaf Space project does not focus on issues of accommodation, but rather on Deaf cultural aesthetics that are embodied in the built environment. In the original workshop in 2005, a common aesthetic emerged that was described as organic, curvilinear, and bathed in light. Since that time, students and faculty have researched core issues, such as the qualities of lighting, proxemics of signers, and the tension between open, visually accessible spaces and privacy. Although the notion of Deaf space generates from designing the optimal environment for Deaf signers, the basic precept is that Deaf space principles would create exceptional buildings for everyone, regardless of audiological status.

Further study of Deaf space and planning in the future of Deaf Studies may also lead toward an understanding of the urgency that Deaf communities may be strengthened by gaining control over the spaces where deaf individuals live. As deaf individuals are born into a dispersion among hearing families, they are subject to a diasporic condition from the onset (Allen, 2007). Indeed, one of the primary differences between the linguistic minority of sign language users and other language groups is that deaf people have never occupied a homeland. They may have congregated at residential schools, but these spaces were designed on 19th-century asylum architecture—hardly the autochthonous creation of a group with deep ties to the land. From schools to Deaf clubs, Deaf spaces have generally reflected the design of hearing architects. On a personal level, however, deaf people have a long tradition of home renovations that bear similarities—such as increasing the visual reach throughout a house—that permit greater visual communication, as well as a sense of connection (Malzkuhn, 2007). The cultural significance of home renovations and the deaf relationship to place cannot be underestimated, for as Findley (2005, p. 5) notes, "not having control of the space one is occupying is in some way demoralizing." For this reason, Deaf people have always felt the need to dream of a homeland, from Jacob Flournoy's 19th-century proposals for a Deaf state (Krentz, 2000) to the recent proposal for Laurent, South Dakota (Willard, n.d.) as just such a homeland. Indeed, as Le Corbousier wrote, "the occupation of space is the first proof of existence" (Findley, 2005, p. 5). As such, Deaf people may find architecture and community planning an integral element to linguistic and cultural revitalization. Such a future exploration would result in diversity of the design and qualities of living spaces.

Deaf-gain and Creative Diversity: Sign Language Literature

Just as the validation of sign language revolutionized the study of language, so too must the nature of literature be reconsidered from the ground up. The unique visual and spatial properties of sign language make it a particularly rich medium for poetic image and metaphor (Bauman, 2008; Bauman, Nelson, & Rose, 2006; Davidson, 2008; Taub, 2001; Wilcox, 2000). For centuries, writers have been seeking to extend both the visual and performative aspects of literature, resulting in various experimental forms, from the unity of painting and poetry in the works of William Blake to concrete poetry, slam, and performance poetry. Sign poetry extends both the performative and visual traditions of literature into new forms. Sign language poetic practice has become increasingly innovative in its use of visual textual forms, as sign language poets have experimented with the interaction of the components of film language—camera movement, editing, visual prosody, *mise en scene*—and sign language. Ella Mae Lentz's collaboration with Lynette Taylor (Lentz, 1996), and Dutch poets Wim Emmerik and Giselle Meyer's collaboration with Anja Hiddinga and Lendeert Pot (Hiddinga et al., 2005) represent the creative potential of a blending cinematic techniques with sign language poetry. In addition to experimentation with visual textuality, sign language poetry extends the embodied, performative tradition, exemplified by the Beat generation's spoken word poetry. Allen Ginsberg, for one, recognized the enormous potential of sign language performance when he participated in a gathering of Deaf and hearing poets in Rochester, New York. When he asked Deaf poets to translate the phrase "hydrogen jukebox" from his poem, "Howl," Patrick Graybill responded with a translation that led Ginsberg to exclaim, "that is exactly it, what I have been trying to convey, the hard clear image of it" (Cohn, 1999; Cook, 2006).

Similarly, the history of theater reveals an enduring human desire for nonverbal, visual spectacle. The history of mime and theatrical tableau, and explorations in experimental visual theater by directors and writers like Antonin Artaud and Robert Wilson, indicate that theater yearns to draw particular attention to the spatial and kinetic modalities. Golden (2009) suggests that Deaf/sign language theater and the practice of visual theater engage in an exchange to the mutual benefit of each practice. Clearly, the highly visual nature of Deaf theater, Golden suggests, may enhance the genre of visual theater.

Cultural Diversity and Deaf-gain: Transnational Deaf Community

The tools of cultural studies that have served Deaf Studies so well in earlier eras have now also changed. Scholars have called into question the old anthropology of culture, with its language of bounded cultural entities, cultural contact, and cross-cultural communication. The dangers of essentialism have gained increasing urgency, especially among scholars of South Asia, who see the results of religious essentialism in the violent clashes on the Indian subcontinent (Appadurai, 2006). Deaf Studies has begun to encompass a cosmopolitan, transnational perspective that moves outside the phase of legitimization of the category of Deaf and into a critical inquiry into the nature of being deaf, how ways of understanding and living as deaf have shaped the material and ideological worlds of Deaf and hearing people. In fact, the very trope of "Deaf worlds" and "hearing worlds" is being understood as a product of a particular set of historical conditions (Murray, 2007).

There is a small, but growing, body of work that explores how deaf people interact across national boundaries (Breivik, Haualand, & Solvang, 2002; Murray, 2007; Nakamura, 2006). Transnational contact between deaf people existed since the early 19th century, emerging at a series of Parisian Deaf-mute banquets, and a transnational Deaf public sphere developed alongside a series of international congresses of Deaf people from 1873 onward (Ladd, 2003; Murray, 2007). This sphere created a shared discursive field in which deaf people could articulate common strategies on living as visual minorities in societies governed by auditory principles. Taking a transnational orientation to deaf people's lives foregrounds the commonality of Deaf ways of being, but paradoxically also heightens our understanding of deaf people as intimately tied to local discursive constructions of nation and society. The physical assemblage of large numbers of deaf people often brings with it a reorganization of physical space according to Deaf norms, as deaf people temporarily colonize portions of a city at large-scale quadrennial events such as World Federation of the Deaf Congresses or Deaflympic sporting competitions. A complete understanding of the spatial reorganization that occurs and its implication in terms of "Deaf-gain" have yet to be realized. However, by viewing deaf peoples' lives in different national contexts, we also understand how integrated deaf people are into their national and social contexts. There are many ways to be Deaf, because deaf people are not isolated from the societies in which they live (Monaghan, Schmaling, Nakamura, & Turner, 2003).

An expanded frame of reference will naturally include the global South, which will have an increasingly prominent role in transnational Deaf communities of the future, especially if current demographic analyses regarding developed countries trend as predicted (Johnston, 2006). Economic disparities between the North and South have resulted in lesser rates of cochlear implantation, less use of genetic testing, and hindrances in the prevention of childhood illnesses, all of which have the result of expanding the population of deaf children and potential native signers. These factors will likely not persist, but what they mean for the present generation of deaf people is that the demographic imbalance between deaf people in developing and developed countries will likely become even more prominent, with the rate of sign language use presumably shifting to developing countries as well. The central loci of Deaf Studies may well shift from Western countries to the global South, from discretely bounded national communities to a more fluid array of affinitive networks of various sizes and forms, existing in both physical and virtual space (Breivik, 2007 Kusters, 2007).

Cultural Diversity and Deaf-Gain: International Sign and Signed Languages

Communication at international meetings of Deaf individuals often occurs in International Sign (IS), a form of cross-national communication that emerges when signers from different signed languages come into contact. Most research on IS to date has studied its linguistic properties. Although this research is still developing, early conclusions indicate that IS has more language-like properties than pidgins, another form of communication that emerges when two or more languages come into contact (Supalla & Webb, 1995). There is evidence of IS being used as far back as the early 19th century (Ladd, 2003), when it was used for political discourse at international meetings, as well as in informal interactions between Deaf travelers (Murray, 2007). The ability of signing deaf people to meet and interact across linguistic boundaries—without sharing a common language beforehand—has existed for at least two centuries. Some of this is no doubt due to the common experience of being Deaf in nondeaf societies. One author attributes this ease of understanding to a shared theory of mind among Deaf people, the term referring to the ability to "inhabit and intuit" another person's consciousness (Fox, 2008, pp. 80–81). Fox notes that semantically related signs for mental processes (think, decide, believe) are located at or near the head in ASL and European signed languages (Fox, 2008, p. 82), thus possibly assisting users of one signed language in understanding another signed language. The study of IS is still in its early stages and questions remain. If international signed communication has existed for two centuries, has there been continuity in lexical or other structural properties of IS in this period? Can we characterize "it" as an "it," or were there many versions of IS throughout the decades? A community of users has existed, but was there generational transmission and if so, what does this tell us about the language-like properties of IS? Beyond a focus on IS as a distinct entity are questions IS raises by its very existence. At the very least, IS calls into question the inevitability of linguistic dissimilarities, with its apparatus of interpretation, and raises larger questions on the histories and modalities of communication between linguistically distinct groups of people.

The study of IS is part of a body of work going beyond the study of sign languages under national markers—ASL, Danish Sign Language—to a realization that signing exists in a diverse array of situations and communities. Scholars have seen a sign language being born in Nicaragua (Senghas, 1995, 2003) and are studying the use of signing among a Bedouin community in Israel (Fox, 2007 Sandler et al., 2005), one of many communities around the world where both hearing and deaf people sign (Groce, 1985; Johnson, 1994; Marsaja, 2008; see Chapter 18, this volume). There are obvious benefits to scholars in seeing linguistic phenomena take place in the field: scholars have never witnessed a spoken language being created, and the study of Nicaraguan sign language allows linguists the opportunity to see if their theories are correct. Think of astrophysicists being able to witness the Big Bang. Beyond this, the existence—and persistence—of sign languages allows us to understand the diversity of human ways of being and communicating, and offers a direct challenge to conceptions of normalcy that would peg all humans into a phonocentric square hole.

Cultural Diversity and Deaf-gain: Deaf Collectivist Culture and the Future of Community

A growing body of research points toward the dissolution of a sense of community and civic engagement. Robert Putnam's *Bowling Alone: The Collapse and Revival of American Community* points to the factors of work, television, computers, suburban life, and family structures as having contributed to this decline. Other studies confirm Putnam's observations, noting that social networks and people's sense of connectedness have taken a precipitous decline in the past three decades (McPherson, Smith-Lovin, & Brashears, 2006). As a culture that exhibits a high degree of collectivism (Mindess, 2006), Deaf cultural relations may offer insights and examples to understand, if not emulate. The circular proxemics of deaf people as they align themselves to be seen are the structural embodiment of nonhierarchical relations. Although Derrida (1973) has highlighted the significance of "hearing oneself speak" as a prime source of deriving a sense of presence, deaf individuals can neither hear themselves speak nor fully see themselves sign (Bauman, January, 2008). Granted that signers may see their own hand movements from their vantage, they will never be able to see their own faces, which are so vital to the linguistic and emotional content of sign language expression. The sense of presence conveyed through the system of hearing oneself speak is radically altered through the self-awareness of one's own signing. The sense of presence for signers, then, is derived through the presence of the *other*. This constant confirmation of presence through the face of the other may partially explain the prevalence of collectivism of Deaf cultures. Although the significance of prolonged face-to-face engagement and eye contact over a lifetime cannot be underestimated, little research has been done to understand the psychological implications of Deaf ways of being together.

One study is currently under way to examine the nature of human contact in the example of the "Deaf walk" as opposed to the hearing walk (Sirvage, forthcoming). As two hearing individuals engage in discussion while walking, they simply need to ensure that they are close enough and speak loudly enough for the other to hear. There is no need for eye contact. Significantly, when deaf people walk, however, they engage in constant eye contact, and more significantly, they must take care of the other person, extending their peripheral vision to ensure that the other person does not walk into any objects. Although this may seem a minor point, there is a larger lesson about the nature of Deaf collectivist relations. Signers take care of each other, whether strangers or intimate friends, when engaged in a peripatetic conversation. Future studies should inquire into expanding the notion of the Deaf walk to larger cultural ways of being that may have lessons for an increasingly isolated society.

Summary and Conclusions: Media Production and the Deaf Public Voice

This brief discussion of human diversity and Deaf-gain has little to do with a critique of audism, or any other defensive posture that has largely characterized late 20th-century and early 21st-century Deaf Studies. The critique of power relations that forms a principal activity of all cultural studies is implicit in pointing out what has been lost in the oversight of sign languages and Deaf communities as having intrinsic and extrinsic value to human diversity. By taking advantage of the unique Deaf ways of being, forms of cultural production may provide new areas of experimentation and insight, left hidden in the phonocentric blindspots within the ways that cultural practices and disciplines have evolved.

Commerson (2008) suggested that such a reframing of human diversity and Deaf Studies would be more likely to take place if there is a strong visual presence in media. If deafness is reframed from lack to gain, then the sense of gain may be embodied through characters in film, television, video, Internet sites, newspapers, and other forms of public discourse. Given the existential threats to Deaf communities and their languages, the 21st-century practice of Deaf Studies must move from a defensive posture to one that actively seeks to redefine public perception—and do so quickly.

As 21st-century Deaf Studies argues for both intrinsic and extrinsic value, it must be careful to make the point that this argument is not simply for the preservation of deaf people and sign languages for the sake of scientific exploration of the human character. Instead, Deaf Studies may want to take the counterintuitive position that all individuals would be enriched by become a bit more Deaf. By that we mean society would do well to become more acutely aware of the nuances of communication, more engaged with eye contact and tactile relations, more fluent in a language rich in embodied metaphor, more aware of the role of being a member of close-knit communities, and if nothing else, more appreciative of human diversity, so that we are constantly reminded that the bedrock of reality may be just as diaphanous as any other social construction. As Sandel (2007) argues in *The Case Against Perfection*, human diversity teaches us the value of moving from an ethic of molding individuals to beholding them in their extraordinarily rich ways of being.

[1]The notion of "Deaf-gain" was originally articulated by the British performance artist, Aaron Williamson, who, when presenting to Dirksen Bauman's graduate class, "Enforcing Normalcy," stated that while all his doctors told him that he was losing his hearing, not one told him that he was gaining his deafness.

[2]As Stokoe (2001) described, "The nerves connecting eyes and brain outnumber by far all the brain connections to the other sensory organs, the ears included. Visual processing involves so much of the brain that a visual field may convey an enormous amount of information simultaneously, whereas language sounds have to reach the ear sequentially, one by one, until the whole message is received and can be interpreted."

[3]Despite no widely accepted written form, there have been many attempts throughout history. One of the earliest is August Bebian's Mimography (Renard, 2004), the most well-known is probably SignWriting (http://www.signwriting.org/), and a promising new form is being developed by Arnold (2007).

References

Akamatsu, C.T., Musselman, C., & Zweibel, A. (2000). Nature versus nurture in the development of cognition in deaf people. In P. Spencer, C. Erting, & M. Marschark (Eds.), *The deaf child in the family and at school*. (pp. 255–274). Mahwah, NJ: Lawrence Erlbaum Associates.

Allen, S. (2007). *A deaf diaspora: Exploring underlying cultural yearnings for a deaf home*. Master's thesis, Gallaudet University, Washington, DC.

Appadurai, A. (2006). *Fear of small numbers: An essay on the geography of anger*. Durham, NC: Duke University Press.

Arijon, D. (1991). *Grammar of the film language*. Los Angeles: Silman-James Press.

Armstrong, D. (2002). *Original signs: Gesture, sign, and the sources of language*. Washington, DC: Gallaudet University Press.

Armstrong, D., & Wilcox, S. (2007). *The gestural origins of language*. Cambridge: Cambridge University Press.

Armstrong, D., Wilcox S., & Stokoe, W. (1995). *Gesture and the nature of language*. Cambridge: Cambridge University Press.

Arnold, R. (2007). *Proposal for a written form of American Sign Language*. Unpublished master's thesis, Gallaudet University, Washington, DC, United States of America.

Arnos, K. (2003). The implications of genetic testing for deafness. *Ear and Hearing, 24*, 324–331.

Bahan, B. (2006). Face-to-face tradition in the American deaf community: Dynamics of the teller, the tale and the audience. In Bauman, H-D., Nelson, J., & Rose, H. (2006). *Signing the body poetic: Essays on American Sign Language literature*. (pp. 21–50). Berkeley: University of California Press.

Bahan, B. (2008). On the formation of a visual variety of the human race. In Bauman, H-D., ed (2008). *Open your eyes: Deaf studies talking*. (pp. 83–99). Minneapolis: University of Minnesota Press.

Bauman, H. (in press). *Gallaudet university deaf and diverse campus design guide*. Washington, DC: Gallaudet University institutional document.

Bauman, H-D. (2006). Getting out of line: Toward a visual and cinematic poetics of ASL. In Bauman, H-D., Nelson, J., & Rose, H. (2006). *Signing the body poetic: Essays on American Sign Language literature*. (pp. 95–117). Berkeley: University of California Press.

Bauman, H-D. (2008). Body/text: Sign language poetics and spatial form in literature. In K. Lindgren, D. DeLuca, & D. J. Napoli (Eds.), *Signs and voices: Deaf culture, language, identity, and arts*. (pp. 163–176). Washington, DC: Gallaudet University Press.

Bauman, H-D. (2008). Listening to phonocentrism with deaf eyes: Derrida's mute philosophy of (sign) language. *Essays in Philosophy, 9*(1). Retrieved October 22, 2009 from http://www.humboldt.edu/~essays/bauman.html

Bauman, H-D., Nelson, J., & Rose, H. (2006). *Signing the body poetic: Essays on American Sign Language literature*. Berkeley: University of California Press.

Bavelier, D., Tomann, A., Hutton, C., Mitchell, T. V., Corina, D. P., Liu, G., & Neville, H. J. (2000). Visual attention to the periphery is enhanced in congenitally deaf individuals. *Journal of Neuroscience, 20*, 1-6.

Baynton, D. C. (1996). *Forbidden signs: American culture and the campaign against sign language.* Chicago: University of Chicago Press.

Baynton, D. C. (2000). Disability and the justification of inequality in American history. In P. Longmore & L. Umansky (Eds.), *The new disability history: American perspectives.* (pp. 33–57). New York: New York University Press.

Bebian, A. (1984). Essay on the deaf and natural language, or introduction to a natural classification of ideas with their proper signs. In H. Lane (Ed.), *The Deaf experience: classics in language and education.* [Trans. Philip, F.] Cambridge, MA: Harvard University Press.

Bell, A. G. (1883). *Memoir upon the formation of a deaf variety of the human race.* Washington, DC: Volta Bureau.

Bellugi, U., O'Grady, L., Lillio-Martin, D., O'Grady Hynes, M., Van Hoek, K., & Corina, D. (1989). In V. Volterra & C. Erting (Eds.), *Enhancement of spatial cognition in deaf children. Gesture to language in hearing children.* (pp. 278-298). New York: Springer-Verlag.

Bettger, J. G., Emmorey, K., McCullough, S. H., & Bellugi U. (1997). Enhanced facial discrimination: Effects of experience with American Sign Language. *Journal of Deaf Studies and Deaf Education, 2*, 223-233.

Biesold, H. (1999). *Crying hands: Eugenics and deaf people in Nazi Germany.* Washington, DC: Gallaudet University Press.

Breivik, J. K. (2007). *Døv identitet i endring–lokale liv–globale bevegelser.* Oslo: Universitetsforlaget.

Breivik, J. K., Haualand, H., & Solvang, P. (2002). *Rome—a temporary deaf city! Deaflympics 2001.* Bergen, Norway: Rokkansentret Working Paper 2-2003.

Brownstein, Z., & Avraham, K. B. (2006). Future trends and potential for treatment of sensorineural hearing loss. *Seminars in Hearing, Genetics and Hearing Loss, 27*(3), 193–204.

Bryan, A. (November 22, 2007). Parliament: Deaf embryo selection to be made illegal. [Blog entry]. Retrieved November 20, 2008, from http://www.grumpyoldeafies.com/2007/11/parliament_deaf_embroyo_select.html

Burch, S. (2002). *Signs of Resistance: American Deaf Cultural History, 1900 to World War II.* New York: New York University Press.

Burke, T. B. (2006). Bioethics and the deaf community. In K. Lindgren, D. DeLuca, & D. J. Napoli (Eds.), *Signs and voices: Deaf culture, identity, language, and arts.* (pp. 63–74). Washington, DC: Gallaudet University Press.

Burke, T. B. (December 5, 2007). British bioethics and the human fertilisation and embryology bill. [Blog entry]. Retrieved November 20, 2008, from http://www.deafdc.com/blog/teresa-blankmeyer-burke/2007-12-05/british-bioethics-and-the-human-fertilisation-and-embryology-bill/

Carty, B. (2006). Comments on "w(h)ither the deaf community?" *Sign Language Studies 6*(2), 181–189.

Chorost, M. (2005). *Rebuilt: How becoming part computer made me more human.* Boston. MA: Houghton Mifflin Harcourt.

Cohn, J. (1999). *Sign mind: Studies in American Sign Language poetics.* Boulder, CO: Museum of American Poetics Publications.

Commerson, R. (2008). *Media, power and ideology: Re-presenting DEAF.* Master's thesis, Gallaudet University, Washington, DC. Retrieved from http://mosinternational.com/

Cook, P. (Author and Signer). (2006). Hydrogen jukebox [ASL story on DVD]. In Bauman, H-D., Nelson, J., & Rose, H. *Signing the body poetic: Essays in American sign language literature.* Berkeley: University of California Press.

Corballis, M. (2003). *From hand to mouth: On the origins of language.* Princeton, NJ: Princeton University Press.

Cripps, J., & Small, A. (2004). *Case report re: Provincial service delivery gaps for deaf children 0–5 years of age.* Mississauga, ON: Ontario Cultural Society of the Deaf.

Crystal, D. (2002). *Language death.* Cambridge: Cambridge University Press.

Davidson, M. (2008). Tree-tangled in tree: Re-siting poetry through ASL. In K. Lindgren, D. DeLuca, & D. J. Napoli (Eds.), *Signs and voices: Deaf culture, identity, language and arts.* (pp. 177-188). Washington, DC: Gallaudet University Press.

Davis, L. (1995). *Enforcing normalcy: Deafness, disability and the body.* London: Verso Press.

Davis, L. (2006). Constructing normalcy: The bell curve, the novel, and the invention of the disabled body in the nineteenth century. In L. Davis (Ed.), *The disability studies reader.* (pp. 3–16). New York: Taylor and Francis.

Derrida, J. (1973). *Of grammatology.* Trans. Spivak, G. Baltimore: Johns Hopkins University Press.

Emmorey, K., Klima, S. L., & Hickok, G. (1998) Mental rotation within linguistic and nonlinguistic domains in users of American Sign Language. *Cognition, 68*, 221–226.

Emmorey, K., & Kosslyn, S. (1996). Enhanced image generation abilities in deaf signers: A right hemisphere effect. *Brain and Cognition, 32*, 28-44.

Emmorey, K., Kosslyn, S., & Bellugi, U. (1993). Visual imagery and visual-spatial language: Enhanced visual imagery abilities in deaf and hearing ASL signers. *Cognition, 46*, 139-181,

Erting, C. J., Johnson, R. C., Smith, D. L., & Snider, B. C. (1993). *The deaf way: Perspectives from the international conference on deaf culture.* Washington DC: Gallaudet University Press.

Findley, L. (2005). *Building change: Architecture, politics and cultural agency.* New York: Routledge.

Foucault, M. (1990). *History of sexuality Vol. 1. The Will to Knowledge.* New York: Vintage Press.

Fox, M. (2008). *Talking hands: What sign language reveals about the mind.* New York: Simon & Schuster.

Frontrunners Weekly Reports. (2005, September 30). Interviews on genocide. *Frontrunners.* Retrieved November 29, 2008, from http://fr1.frontrunners.dk/Weekly%20Reports/weeklyreports.htm

Furman, N., Goldberg, D., & Lusin, N. (November 13, 2007). Foreign language enrollments in united states institutions of higher education, fall 2006. *Modern Language Association.* Retrieved November 23, 2009, from http://www.mla.org/2006_flenrollmentsurvey

Gardner, H. (1993). *Frames of mind: The theory of multiple intelligences.* New York: Basic Books.

Genetic Evaluation of Congenital Hearing Loss Expert Panel. (2002). Genetics evaluation guidelines for the etiologic diagnosis of congenital hearing loss. *Genetics of Medicine, 4*(3), 162–171.

Golden, J. (2009). *Deaf/ASL and visual theatre: Connections and opportunities.* Unpublished master's thesis, Gallaudet University, Washington, DC.

Gray, R. (2008, April 13). Couples could win right to select deaf baby. *Telegraph.co.uk.* Retrieved (November 29, 2008, from http://www.telegraph.co.uk/news/uknews/1584948/Couples-could-win-right-to-select-deaf-baby.html (Reader comments at: http://www.telegraph.co.uk/news/yourview/1584973/How-far-should-embryo-selection-go.html)

Groce, N. (1985). *Everyone here spoke sign language: Hereditary deafness on Martha's Vineyard.* Cambridge, MA: Harvard University Press.

Hall, S. (1973). *Encoding and decoding in television discourse.* Birmingham, AL: Birmingham Centre for Cultural Studies.

Harmon, D. (2002). *In light of our differences: How diversity in nature and culture makes us human.* Washington, DC: Smithsonian Institution Press.

Haualand, H. (Writer), & Otterstedt, L. (Director). (2007). *Arven etter frankenstein.* [Theatrical Production]. Oslo, Norway: Theater Manu.

Hiddinga, A., Pot, L. (Filmmakers); Emmerik, W., & Meyer, G. (Poets). (2005). *Motioning.* Amsterdam, Holland: Geelprodukt Productions.

Hoggart, R. (1957). *The uses of literacy in everyday life.* London: Chatto & Windus.

Hyde, M., Power, D. J., & Lloyd, K. (2006). Comments on "W(h)ither the deaf community?" *Sign Language Studies,* 6(2), 190–201.

Johannsen, K. (2008). Electronic mail communication received December 29, 2008.

Johnson, R. (1994). *Sign language and the concept of deafness in a traditional Yucatec Mayan village.* In C. Erting, R. Johnson, D. Smith, & B. Sniden (Eds.), *The deaf way: Perspectives from the international conference on deaf culture.* (pp. 102–109). Washington, DC: Gallaudet University Press.

Johnston, T. (2004). W(h)ither the deaf community? Population, genetics, and the future of Australian Sign Language. *American Annals of the Deaf, 148(5).* Reprinted in (2006) *Sign Language Studies,* 6(2), 137–173.

Kochhar, A., Hildebrand, M. S., & Smith, R. J. (2007). Clinical aspects of hereditary hearing loss. *Genetics in Medicine,* 9(7), 393–408.

Krentz, C. (2000). *A mighty change: An anthology of deaf American writing, 1816–1864.* Washington DC: Gallaudet University Press.

Kuntze, M. (2008). Turning literacy on its head. In H.-D. Bauman (Ed.), *Open your eyes: Deaf studies talking.* Minneapolis: University of Minnesota Press.

Kusters, A. (2007). *"Reserved for the handicapped?" Deafhood on the lifeline of Mumbai.* Unpublished master's thesis, University of Bristol.

Ladd, P. (2003). *Understanding deaf culture: In search of deafhood.* Clevedon, UK: Multicultural Matters.

Lane, H. (1984). *When the mind hears: A history of the deaf.* New York: Random House.

Lane, H. (1992). *The mask of benevolence: Disabling the deaf community.* New York: Alfred A. Knopf.

Lane, H., & Fischer, R. (1993). Looking back: A reader on the history of deaf communities and their sign languages. *International Studies on Sign Language and Communication of the Deaf, 20.* Hamburg: Signum Verlag.

Lane, H., Hoffmeister, R., & Bahan, B. (1996). *Journey into the deaf world.* San Diego: DawnSign Press.

Lentz, E. (Poet), & Taylor, L. (Filmmaker). (1996). *The treasure* [Signed Poetry]. Berkeley, California: InMotion Press.

Maffi, L. (2005). Linguistic, cultural, and biological diversity. *Annual review of anthropology,* 34, 599–617.

Malzkuhn, M. (2007). *Home customization: Understanding deaf ways of being.* Unpublished master's thesis, Gallaudet University, Washington, DC.

Marsaja, I. G. (2008). *Desa Kolok: A deaf village and its sign language in Bali, Indonesia.* Nijmegen, the Netherlands: Ishara Press.

Marschark, M. (2003). Cognitive functioning in deaf adults and children. in Marschark M. and Spencer, P. Eds. *Oxford handbook of deaf studies, language, and education.* Oxford: Oxford University Press.

McPherson, M., Smith-Lovin, L., & Brashears, M. E. (2006). Social isolation in America: Changes in core discussion networks over two decades. *American Sociological Review,* 71, 353-375.

Mindess, A. (2006). *Reading between the signs. Intercultural communication for sign language interpreters,* 2nd edition. Boston: Intercultural Press.

Monaghan, L., Schmaling, C., Nakamura, K., & Turner, G. H. (2003). *Many ways to be deaf: International variation in deaf communities.* Washington, DC: Gallaudet University Press.

Moore, D., & Dwyer, F. (1994). *Visual literacy: A spectrum of visual learning.* Englewood Cliffs, NJ: Educational Technology Publications.

Morton, C. C., & Nance, W. E. (2006). Newborn hearing screening–a silent revolution. *New England Journal of Medicine,* 354(20), 2151–2164.

Mundy, L. (2002, March 31). A world of their own. *The Washington Post,* pp. W22.

Murray, J. (2002). True love and sympathy: The deaf-deaf marriages debate in transatlantic perspective. In J. V. Van Cleve (Ed.), *Genetics, disability, and deafness.* (pp. 42–71). Washington, DC: Gallaudet University Press.

Murray, J. (2006). Genetics: A future peril facing the global deaf community. In H. Goodstein (Ed.). *The Deaf way II reader: Perspectives from the Second International Conference on Deaf Culture.* (pp. 351–356). Washington, DC: Gallaudet University Press.

Murray, J. (2007). *A touch of nature makes the whole world kin: The transnational lives of deaf Americans.* Unpublished doctoral dissertation, University of Iowa.

Nakamura, K. (2006). *Deaf in Japan: Signing and the politics of identity.* Ithaca, NY: Cornell University Press.

Noble, T. (2003, July 11). Deafness-test embryo fails to take. *The Age.* Retrieved November 23, 2009, from http://www.theage.com.au/articles/2003/07/10/1057783282446.html

Office of Public Sector Information. (2008). *The National Archives.* Retrieved January 2009, from http://www.opsi.gov.uk/acts/acts2008/ukpga_20080022_en_2#pt1-pb5-l1g14

Padden, C., & Humphries, T. (1988). *Deaf In America: Voices from a culture.* Cambridge, MA: Harvard University Press.

Petitto, L. A., Zatorre, R., Gauna, K., Nikelski, E. J., Dostie, D., & Evans, A. (December 5, 2000). Speech-like cerebral activity in profoundly deaf people while processing signed languages: Implications for the neural basis of human language. *Proceedings of the National Academy of Sciences,* 97(25), 13961–13966.

Putnam, R. (2000). *Bowling alone: The collapse and revival of American community.* New York: Simon & Schuster.

Renard, M. (2004). *Écrire les signes. La mimographie d'Auguste Bébian et les notations contemporaines. [Escribir las señas. La Mimografía de Auguste Bébian y las notaciones contemporáneas].* París: Éditions du Fox.

Sacks, O. (1990). *Seeing voices: Journey into the deaf world.* Berkeley: University of California Press.

Salmi, E., & Laakso, M. (2005). *Maahan lämpimäänn: Suomen viittomakielisten historia*. Helsinki: Kuurojen Liittory.

Sandel, M. (2007). *The case against perfection: Ethics in the age of genetic engineering*. Cambridge, MA: Harvard University Press.

Sandler, W., Meir, I., Padden, C., & Aronoff, M. (2005). The emergence of grammar in a new sign language. *Proceedings of the National Academy of Sciences, 102*(7), 2661–2665.

Senghas, A. (1995). Conventionalization in the first generation: a community acquires a language. *USD Journal of Contemporary Legal Issues, 6*, Spring, 1995.

Senghas, A. (2003). Intergenerational influence and ontogenetic development in the emergence of spatial grammar in Nicaraguan Sign Language. *Cognitive Development, 18*, 511–531.

Sirvage, R. (forthcoming). *Walking signers: An investigation on proxemics*. Unpublished master's thesis. Gallaudet University, Washington, DC.

Skutnabb-Kangas, T. (2000). *Linguistic genocide in education— or worldwide diversity and human rights?* Mahwah, NJ: Lawrence Erlbaum Associates.

Snoddon, K. (2008). "American Sign Language and early intervention." *Canadian Modern Language Review". 64*(4). June (pp. 581–604).

Stokoe, W. (2001). *Language in hand: Why sign came before speech*. Washington, DC: Gallaudet University Press.

Supalla, T., & Webb, R. (1995). The grammar of international sign: A new look at pidgin languages. In K. Emmorey & J. S. Reilly (Eds.), *Language, gesture, and space*. (pp. 333–351). Hillsdale, NJ: Lawrence Erlbaum Associates.

Sutton, V. (2008). Retrieved November 20, 2008 from www. signwriting.org

Taub, S. (2001). *Language from the body: Iconicity and metaphor in American sign language*. Cambridge: University of Cambridge Press.

Van Cleve, J. V. (1993). *Deaf history unveiled: Interpretations from the new scholarship*. Washington, DC: Gallaudet University Press.

Van Cleve, J. V., & Crouch, B. A. (1989). *A place of their own: Creating the deaf community in America*. Washington, DC: Gallaudet University Press.

VL2. (2008). Visual language and visual learning website introduction. Retrieved November 20, 2008, from http://vl2. gallaudet.edu/

Wallvik, B. (1997).… *ett folk uten land* … Borgå: Finland: Döva och hörselskadade barns stödforening r.f.

Welles, E. B. (2004). Foreign language enrollments in United States institutions of higher education. *ADFL Bulletin, 35*(2-3).

Wilcox, P. (2000). *Metaphor in American Sign Language*. Washington, DC: Gallaudet University Press.

Willard, T. (n.d.). Special Report: Laurent, SD in Deafweekly. Deafweekly electronic mailing list. Retrieved November 20, 2008, from http://www.deafweekly.com/backissues/laurent. htm

Williams, R. (1958). *Culture and society, 1780–1950*. London and New York: Columbia University Press.

Williams, R. (1961). *The long revolution*. London and New York: Columbia University Press.

Cochlear Implants: Family and Young People's Perspectives

Sue Archbold *and* Alexandra Wheeler

Abstract

Cochlear implants have now become a routine intervention for profoundly deaf children in many countries, providing useful hearing and changing the educational options and communication choices for many. With increasing newborn hearing screening and the introduction of technology earlier than ever into family life, the experiences of families with deaf or hard-of-hearing (DHH) children are changing in many respects, yet in some respects the issues remain the same. For the first time, we have families that must make decisions about their child's future in this technology-driven era. We also have large groups of young people who, for the first time, have grown up with an implant, and other young people who are choosing implants for themselves. There has been great controversy about cochlear implantation over the years, and concerns that young people with implants will have greater socioemotional difficulties than before. This chapter explores the issues surrounding cochlear implantation and families, including what we know of parental perceptions about decision making, and the expectations and outcomes from implantation, particularly educational outcomes. It also explores the current research on young people with implantation and what they themselves are telling us about life after childhood implantation.

Keywords: children, cochlear implants, families, education, young people

Technological advances have revolutionized the management of childhood deafness, transforming the opportunities for deaf children and their families. In particular, the development of cochlear implantation in children from the mid 1980s onward has had a great impact (sometimes in unforeseen ways), and the majority of profoundly deaf children in many countries now have cochlear implants. We now have growing numbers of deaf young people and adults who received implants as children from whom we can learn about the experience of implantation and its outcomes.

Cochlear implantation began initially in adults who had been deafened, allowing surgeons and audiologists to restore lost hearing. Only later, amid much controversy, did implantation become available for children who had been deafened, and later

still for children who had been born deaf. Because deafened adults had already developed the spoken language of their community and their auditory system had been stimulated, the results of implantation in this population were extremely encouraging, leading to a perception that implantation in children was likely to be straightforward, and the outcomes equally predictable.

Deafness from birth, however, has a significant impact on the development of spoken language (Marschark & Spencer, 2006), and those educating deaf children have long been looking for ways to overcome this impact. Whether to use sign language to ameliorate the negative effects of the hearing loss on the development of language, or whether to utilize residual hearing with the most effective technology available and use only oral methods to support language development has long been a subject of debate. At the Milan conference of 1880, oral methods were considered "superior," and this decision fuelled the oral–manual debate (Lang, 2003), which persists today.

For hearing parents caught up in the ongoing controversy, the dilemma about communication choices has often been a difficult one, and one which may add to the challenges of handling the diagnosis of deafness in the child. The vast majority of deaf children are born to hearing parents (Mitchell & Karchmer, 2004) and for hearing parents, the language of the home will be the natural language with which to communicate with their newborn. In a series of interviews with families of deaf children conducted over several years by Gregory, Bishop, and Sheldon (1995), and with the young people themselves as they grew up, the major issue for virtually all families was language and communication. In the midst of continuing controversy about the crucial issue of the most effective way to develop communication and language, the arrival of a new technological advance—cochlear implantation—seemed likely to offer new opportunities for developing spoken language for deaf children and a new option for parents. In addition, the recent developments of newborn hearing screening and digital hearing aids have had a major impact on the development of deaf children, including the development of language and communication (Calderon & Greenberg, 2003).

However, there was a huge amount of controversy about making implants available for children, particularly for those born deaf. The differing perspectives of those coming from a medical standpoint, who see cochlear implants as a "cure" for deafness, and those who came from a Deaf perspective, who view cochlear implants as a violation of the child's right to be Deaf, raged for years (Lane & Bahan, 1998; see Chapter 14, this volume). At one stage, the debate seemed irreconcilable. Many contended that parents should not be able to make this decision for their young child, and the decision to have an implant should be taken only when the child himself was old enough to do so. Others argued that to wait until the child was old enough wasted crucial years in which the auditory system could be stimulated and spoken language developed (see Chapter 22, this volume). In spite of the controversy, parents worldwide chose to move forward with implantation for their children, at ever earlier ages, and as results emerged, the numbers receiving implants grew.

By 2008, about 80,000 children had received implants worldwide (personal communication, Advanced Bionics, Cochlear, MED-EL), and increasingly in the first year of life, following early diagnosis of hearing loss. Those implanted now include deaf children of deaf parents and children with additional complex needs, and increasing numbers of teenagers are choosing implants for themselves. With this vast range of experience, what have we learned about the impact of implantation on those issues important to families, and to the children and young people themselves? Thoutenhoofd, Archbold, Gregory, Lutman, Nikolopoulous, and Sach (2005), in their review of outcomes from cochlear implantation, suggested that in focusing research on speech perception and production, the areas of family perspectives and psychosocial issues had been underresearched and deserved fuller attention. In spite of the comparatively sparse literature, this chapter looks at what we know of the perspectives of parents and young people, at their views on the process, the decision to implant, and on the impact implantation has had on their lives. Since a major issue for parents reflecting on implantation is its effect on the education of their child, we also include a section on the educational implications of cochlear implantation.

Parental Perspectives

"Raising and parenting a deaf child is about having choices and making decisions. When those decisions are informed, and when the differences between the choices are clear, parents and practitioners will be able to optimize developmental and educational opportunities for all deaf children" (Marschark & Spencer, 2006, p. 17).

The advent of newborn hearing screening and the earlier diagnosis of deafness bring a whole range of professionals with a wealth of information into family lives earlier than ever before. This happens even before early parenting routines have been established and baby–caregiver bonding has taken place. The diagnosis of deafness frequently brings with it feelings of confusion and inadequacy and of vulnerability (Clark & English, 2004; Luterman & Ross, 1991). At this fragile time, when it is vital that early communication skills, the precursors of language, are established, the intrusion of clinic appointments and professionals may exacerbate the feelings of inadequacy and confusion (Luterman, 2005). We do have strong evidence that *the earlier implantation is carried out, the more effective it is* (Dettman, Pinder, Briggs, Dowell, & Leigh, 2007; Miyamoto, Houston, & Bergeson, 2005; Nikolopoulos, O'Donoghue, & Archbold, 1999; O'Donoghue, Nikolopoulous, & Archbold, 2000;

Tait, Nikolopoulos, & Lutman, 2007), and the drive to make an early decision can be an added pressure at a time when families may already be vulnerable (Luterman, 2005).

The Decision-making Process

The decision to implant involves considerable personal investment by parents in terms of time (and possibly money), in addition to the emotional investment. Making the decision may be confounded by the range of outcomes, for reasons not largely understood (Thoutenhoofd et al., 2005), and the comparative lack of long-term studies on large numbers of unselected groups. Hyde and Power (2006) explored fully the ethical issues involved in the decision-making process for parents and the dilemma they may face in needing to make the decision quickly while struggling to obtain the unbiased information necessary to make a rational decision. The 30 parents studied by Archbold, Lutman, Gregory, O'Neill, and Nikolopoulos (2002a) were asked what their advice would be to parents thinking about implantation, and over half spontaneously used the phrase "Go for it!" or something similar (see Chapter 16, this volume). However, cautions were also given as to the importance of obtaining as much information as possible in the decision-making process and the need to be patient in expectations.

Archbold et al. (2002a) asked open-ended question of these parents to develop a questionnaire with responses measured on a Likert scale. The development of the questionnaire (Parental Perspectives) was described by O'Neill, Lutman, Archbold, Gregory, and Nikolopoulos (2004); independently validated by Nunes, Pretzlik, and Ilicak (2005); and further evaluated by Damen, Krabbe, Archbold, and Mylanus (2007). The questionnaire covers the areas of decision making, the process of implantation itself, and parental views of outcomes. The study of 101 parents of implanted children by Archbold, Sach, O'Neill, Lutman, and Gregory (2006) using the Parental Perspectives Questionnaire also highlighted the need felt by parents for as much information as possible to be provided before implantation. Just over half of these parents considered that making the decision was the most difficult part of the process. Incesulu, Vural, and Erkam (2003) also found that the 27 parents who responded to their questionnaire at their clinic in Turkey considered the decision to implant very stressful. The group of 103 parents of children with implants studied by Spahn, Richter, Burger, Lohle, and Wirsching (2003) obtained most of their information from the media and from other parents,

rather than from within the medical and audiological professions, highlighting the need for parents to have ready access to up-to-date, reliable information. The 44 families studied by Edwards, McArdle, Doney, and Bellman (2000) felt that they had received sufficient information to make an informed choice.

A number of other studies have considered the decision-making process and have highlighted the influence of personal beliefs and characteristics in the process (Steinberg, Brainsky, Bain, & Montoya, 2000; Li, Bain & Steinberg, 2004). The parental decision reflects their hopes for their children, their previous experiences, information, and the recommendations of professionals (Li et al., 2004). For example, Kluwin and Stewart (2000) interviewed a random sample of 35 parents asking how they learned about implants and how they made the decision to implant their child. They distinguished two different types of decision making. The first is that of parents who have their main contact through a medical practitioner, and want a "normal" pattern of communication with their child. The other type of parents actively seek a range of information sources and are driven by their child's lack of communication skills. In Steinberg et al.'s study (2000), there was little agreement among parents as to the different values placed on differing areas of the child's well-being. The parents in that study disagreed as to the major goal of implantation: whether to attain only spoken language proficiency or proficiency in both spoken language and sign language. In the study by Archbold et al. (2006), although the parents' major goal was spoken language, there was also some support for the value of sign language.

In the large study of Sach and Whynes (2005) involving 216 families of children with implants and carried out through semi-structured interview, parents commented that their expectations were continually revised during the process after implantation. Of the 216 parents, all but one felt they had made the right decision to implant their child. Similarly, 29 out of the 35 parents interviewed by Kluwin and Stewart (2000) said they would make the same decision again without reservation. Three expressed some reservations, two would not do it again, and one was uncertain.

Now that parents often have a choice of implant devices for their child, more complexity may be added to the decision-making process. For the parents surveyed by Archbold et al. (2006), device reliability was the most important factor in making this decision, and all the parents in the Incesulu et al. (2003) study were anxious about possible device failure. How parents ensure that they have accurate and accessible information on this topic may be another matter.

The Process of Implantation

What about parents' experiences of the process of implantation itself, in the long term as well as the short? Implantation is set in a medical and scientific context and involves parents and families in a world of complex, changing information and in a medical/scientific environment. Li et al. (2000) recognized the importance of medical risk, and this may be linked with the heightened stress experienced by the group of parents studied by Spahn et al. (2003) at the time of cochlear implant fitting. Both the group of parents whose children used conventional aids and the group whose children had implants showed comparable levels of stress at the diagnosis of hearing loss. Parents whose children went on to receive implants later experienced heightened distress at fitting, whereas the fitting of hearing aids did not have the same effect. Edwards et al. (2000), in studying 44 families, also found that parents experienced more stress than they had anticipated, although their children experienced less discomfort than expected. Considering parents' experiences after the surgery itself, Anagnostou, Graham, and Crocker (2007) investigated parental emotions following implantation. They found that parents experience grief before and up to 2 years after implantation and are generally less satisfied than the parents of children implanted for longer than 2 years. Kushalnagar et al. (2007) also looked at parental feelings and considered the behavior of children with implants in relation to nonverbal intelligence and parental depression. They found that the child's adaptive behavior showed a strong relationship with intelligence, and moderate, negative correlations were found in the younger group between parental depression and adaptive behavior. They concluded, as did Hintermair (2006), that family-centered interventions are required for promoting early communication and language development.

Mothers' stress and expectations were also investigated by Weisel, Most, and Michael (2007). They found no change in stress levels before and after implantation, and found that expectations for communication and academic attainments decreased as time after implantation increased. Hintermair (2006) examined parental resources and stress, and found that high parental stress was associated with frequent socioemotional problems in children, especially when they had additional disabilities (see Chapter 12, this volume). He emphasized the importance of a resource-oriented consultation and support strategy in early intervention, because parental access to personal and social resources is associated with significantly lower experiences of stress.

When Archbold et al. (2006) asked parents about their experiences of the process of implantation, a majority of the 101 parents agreed that the process had been no more stressful than expected, with 82% reporting that the most difficult time had been waiting for the results of the assessments. However, 3 years after implantation, there was a diversity of opinion as to whether the process remained stressful, with 43% agreeing that this was the case. These parents commented strongly on the need for patience following implantation. The parents interviewed by Perold (2001) also found that their expectations changed after implantation, with a feeling of disappointment being common immediately after the fitting of the external systems. They reported increasing anxiety after the "switch-on" of the implant system when immediate expectations of listening and speaking were not realized. The parents studied by Sach and Whynes (2005) also commented on their changing and revised expectations after implantation; this is in common with the finding reported by Archbold et al. (2006) of parents encouraging others to be patient and to be prepared for the "long haul." It is worth noting that the parents participating in these studies had their children implanted rather early in the development of implantation as a procedure. It will be interesting to continue such studies with parents of children implanted later, after cochlear implantation has become more routine, and to note whether such stress levels persist or diminish.

Whether intensive support after cochlear implantation is necessary has been the subject of much debate. Parents in the study by Archbold, Sach, O'Neill, Lutman, and Gregory (2008a) considered that their children may require less support after implantation, and over 90% agreed that the support the parents gave was more productive than that given prior to implantation.

Outcomes from Implantation

Parents' main goal for proceeding with implantation is to provide their children with access to spoken language (Archbold et al., 2006; Kluwin & Stewart, 2000; Perold, 2001), even when value is also placed on the role of sign support or sign language (Christiansen & Leigh, 2004; Archbold et al. 2006). Parents' goals of environmental sound recognition and communication development from implantation were found to be more than met in the study by Nikolopoulos, Lloyd, Archbold, and O'Donoghue (2001). In the Archbold et al. (2008a) study of parents' views on outcomes, a majority responded that progress after implantation had exceeded their expectations, but 20% disagreed with this statement. Their reasons for dissatisfaction would be worth exploring. It may be that these are children who have additional difficulties that may or may not be identifiable prior to implantation, or they may be those who have experienced difficulties with the technology itself. A third of the parents in that study were still concerned about their child's speech 3 years after cochlear implantation. This corresponds with the reports of Incesulu et al. (2003), Nikolopoulos et al. (2001), and Sach and Whynes (2005). We know that speech intelligibility develops over a longer time scale than speech perception (Beadle, McKinley, Nikolopoulous, Brough, O'Donoghue, & Archbold, 2005), and it may be that reviewing parents' views of outcomes 3 years after implantation is using a time scale that is too short. Lin et al. (2008) considered the use of speech and language measures in relation to parental perceptions of development in those with early implantation and found that all outcome measures were positively associated with parental perceptions of development. The reasons for this would be interesting to explore further. Nicholas and Geers (2003) also found that parents' satisfaction with the implant was linked to improved speech and language attainments.

For families, deafness in one member of the family affects other members (Luterman & Ross, 1991; Clark & English, 2004). Parents in the Archbold et al. (2002a) and Archbold et al. (2006) studies indicated positive changes in relationships within the family, arising from "just easier two-way communication," as parents commented. The everyday language in the home is likely to be a spoken one, and the shift observed by Watson, Archbold, Hardie, and Wheeler (2007) to spoken language after implantation is likely to facilitate communication in the home, with consequent effects on the quality of family life.

Measuring quality of life (QoL) is a complex process, and Lin and Niparko (2006) concluded that most current studies of QoL are flawed and that no well-validated, deafness-specific Health Related Quality of Life (HRQL) instruments currently are available. They recommend that future research should be done with existing, generic HRQL instruments and with strict study inclusion criteria. However, Sach and Barton (2007) suggested that use of QoL assessments based on HRQL is likely to underestimate the benefits of cochlear implantation because generic health-related quality of life measures would not pick up the subtle changes to family QoL that they found in their in-depth interview study and analysis.

The development of the Parental Perspectives instrument and some reports generated from it have already been described; Damen et al. (2007a) explored its use further, finding it to be an important tool in assessing the impact of cochlear implantation on a child as it pertained to the QoL for the family and the child. They suggested that a short form would be useful for prospective follow-up studies.

For parents reviewed by Archbold et al. (2002a), the children's greatest areas of change after implantation were more confidence, easier communication, and speech development. A typical comment was: "Spoken language has developed from almost nonexistent to using words and short phrases he hasn't been taught e.g. *move over!*" The strongest response of all in the study by Archbold et al. (2008a) was that parents reported that they were able to attract their child's attention by calling to them, making communication in the family easier. For the parents in this group, being able to chat with their children when not being able to see each others' face was important. This reflects real-life situations at home, in the car, around the meal table, or in a different room, and this ease of communication may have a real impact on family QoL.

Percy, Jensen, Josvassen, Jonsson, Andersen, and Samar (2006) in their study of 62 families reported satisfactory levels of well-being after implantation, and Beadle, Shores, and Wood (2000) also reported that parents considered their child's overall QoL to be positive after implantation. The children in the Archbold et al. (2008a) report were also considered as independent as children of the same age and able to amuse themselves. Parents in the large Nicholas and Geers (2003) study of 181 school-aged children who had had their implants for at least 4 years reported that the children were socially and emotionally well-adjusted after implantation. Interestingly, that study found that none of the social-emotional adjustment measures were significantly related to speech perception, production, or language measures after implant. However, as described earlier, parents' satisfaction was related to their children's attainments in these domains.

Educational Implications

For parents, a major concern is education and educational attainments—regardless of whether their child is deaf or hearing. For the parents of deaf children, there are major concerns about where their child should go to school (placement decisions), whether their child should be taught by oral language or sign language (communication decisions), and about the level of educational attainment that is likely to be reached. For parents in several studies (for example, Sach & Whynes, 2005; Archbold et al., 2008a), education is one of the most important aspects of implantation, both because of its effect on educational attainments and its role in educational management in the long-term process of support after implantation.

EDUCATIONAL ATTAINMENTS

The concerns over the years about reading attainments of deaf children, for example, have led to the expectation that cochlear implantation early in life may support improved educational attainments and literacy levels, and ameliorate the educational effects of a hearing loss (Spencer & Marschark, 2003). However, the literature in this area remains scant and mixed, and a recent review (Marschark, Rhoten, & Fabich, 2007) of the reading and academic literature continues to show this. Investigations beyond those evaluating reading are few. Marschark et al. commented on the need to control variables such as age at implantation, language and reading skills before implantation, and consistency of implant use. Thouthenhoofd et al. (2005) made similar observations: the variability in outcomes from implantation is huge, and the reasons for this remain largely unknown. Into an already complex area for research, that of the development of deaf children, cochlear implantation has added yet more potentially confounding yet often-ignored variables, including the specific device used and the effectiveness of system programming. The assumptions that early implantation should lead to improved reading and academic outcomes is not yet proven in the long term, although there are some early positive indications. However, the relationship between hearing, language, and literacy attainments is complex, and one has to be careful not to infer cause and effect when the evidence merely indicates an association. Comparing groups is fraught with difficulties and hence in drawing conclusions, as shown by Fortnum, Stacey, and Summerfield (2006) in a large study in the United Kingdom. Compared with nonimplanted profoundly deaf children, implanted children had greater degrees of hearing loss, fewer additional disabilities, and a later age of onset. In addition, they were younger, came from more affluent families, were more likely to use spoken language at home, and were more likely to be taught using spoken language only. These are all variables likely to affect outcome.

Of the few studies looking at academic attainments, Thoutenhoofd (2006) in a study of 152 Scottish deaf children, found that those who were profoundly deaf and used cochlear implants achieved reading and writing levels comparable to children with moderate/severe hearing losses who used hearing aids. In mathematics, students with cochlear implants were comparable to students with moderate losses who used hearing aids. Stacey, Fortnum, Barton, and Summerfield (2006) investigated the same large group in the United Kingdom as Fortnum and colleagues and found that implantation before 5 years of age was associated with reported improvements in spoken communication skills and in some aspects of educational achievements and QoL. However, when compared to hearing peers (e.g., Damen, Langereis, Snik, Chute, & Mylanus, 2007b), children with implants did less well than their hearing peers. Similar findings were reported by Mukari, Ling, and Ghani (2007).

Studies of reading, for example that of Vermeulen, Van, Schreuder, Knoors, and Snik (2007), found that children with implants do better than those without implants, but not as well as their hearing peers. Archbold, Harris, Nikolopoulos, O'Donoghue, White, and Lloyd (2008b), in a study of the reading attainments of 105 children who had been implanted before the age of 7 and tested 5 and 7 years after implantation, found a strong negative correlation between net reading age (the difference between reading age and chronological age) and age at implantation; age at implantation accounted for just over 50% of the variance when nonverbal IQ was taken into account. In addition, for those implanted before the age of 42 months, average reading was in line with chronological age at both assessment points. Similarly, Spencer, Gantz, and Knutson (2004), reported that the academic and reading achievement of 27 secondary students was equivalent to that of hearing peers. Interestingly, this study showed a significant difference in performance between students who were consistent users and those who were not.

The picture of outcomes following cochlear implantation is not clear-cut. Care must be taken when drawing long-term conclusions from short-term studies. Claims of normal language development at an early age may not be maintained at later ages, when language becomes more challenging. For example, Geers, Tobey, Moog, and Brenner (2008) reported reading levels within the normal range when the children were tested during the primary school years. However, when they were retested as teenagers, the variation was considerably larger. Although some young people had reading ages within the normal range, others had made little or no progress in the intervening years. Geers et al. concluded from their large, long-term study of implanted children in United States that "early cochlear implantation had a long-term positive impact on auditory and verbal development, but did not result in age-appropriate reading levels in high school for the majority of students." The challenges of reading in adolescence, with its demands of complex language, the need to make inferences, and the need for more subtle reading skills may be more demanding for these young people who still have a hearing loss, in spite of implantation. Archbold et al. (2008b) found that age at implantation (ranging in their study from 16 to 83 months) was clearly a factor, but researchers need to follow young children with cochlear implants over a longer time scale before further claims can be made about the influence of implantation on long-term reading or other academic attainments.

EDUCATIONAL MANAGEMENT

Why is there such a range of outcome, and why do some children not do as well as expected? Do we know what the influence of educational management is on outcomes for children with implants? The 216 parents interviewed by Sach (Sach & Whynes, 2005) reported that the greatest challenge faced by parents was that of obtaining appropriate education, and that many felt that the effectiveness of cochlear implantation was reduced by ineffectual educational support. Similar findings were found by Sorkin and Zwolan (2004): a significant proportion of parents felt that their child had inappropriate or no support. However, none of these studies defined what was meant by "appropriate" educational support; it may be that the lack of homogeneity in a group of deaf children with implants makes it impossible to define, and more work needs to be done to consider what is appropriate for each child at each stage (see Chapter 12, this volume).

What do we know of the influence of cochlear implantation on the educational decisions of placement and of choice of communication mode? The traditional choices of educational placement have been special schools for the deaf, either residential or day schools; a special class (often called a resource center) in a mainstream school; and a placement within a mainstream school with varying levels of specialist support. These complex variations were illustrated by Francis, Koch, Wyatt, and Niparko (1999) in a useful matrix of educational resource use illustrating the continuum of support; for example, a child in mainstream with full-time support in class may in fact have less educational independence than a child in a class of 10 in a special school.

Following cochlear implantation, there has been a trend toward increased participation in mainstream schooling, in line with the worldwide trend toward inclusion of all children with disabilities (Archbold, Nikolopoulos, O'Donoghue, & Lutman 1998; Nevins & Chute, 1996). Educational placement has often been used in studies of the cost effectiveness of pediatric implantation to show that the health service–related costs could be offset by savings in educational support over time (O'Neill, O'Donoghue, Archbold, & Normand; Francis et al., 1999). However, as indicated earlier, measures of educational support and of its cost are complex, and caution must be taken in drawing such conclusions.

The Archbold, Nikolopoulos, Lutman, and O'Donoghue (2002b) study showed significantly more profoundly deaf children with implants (ages 5–7 years) in mainstream schools in the United Kingdom, and significantly fewer in schools for the deaf, when compared with profoundly deaf peers with hearing aids. Geers and Brenner (2003) also found a trend in the United States toward mainstreamed education, but again this was in children at the primary stage of education. Thoutenhoofd (2006) did not find such a long-term trend toward mainstream placement in his Scottish study. In fact, there is anecdotal evidence that children with implants are finding challenges in managing in the secondary or high school environment. In secondary school, in particular, the situation is more linguistically, cognitively, and acoustically challenging. The Archbold et al. (2002b) study only included children who were aged between 5 and 7; it would be useful to follow them up to observe educational placement at secondary or high school levels.

Difficulties in educational settings were also found by Mukari et al. (2007), who explored the educational performance of children with implants in everyday life using the Screening Instrument for Targeting Educational Risk Teacher Rating (SIFTER; Anderson, 1989), which is a validated scale to target educational risk. They found that children with implants were rated poorly in the SIFTER communication assessments and concluded that children with implants continue to need specialist support in mainstream classes. Young people in the study by Wheeler, Archbold, and Gregory (2007b) indicated that they may do extremely well in terms of speech perception in clinical situations, but life is more challenging in busy classrooms and in group situations. They may not keep up with the fast-moving pace of curriculum delivery or social exchanges, as the reports of the young people themselves will reveal.

Reviews of parents' and professionals' needs after pediatric implantation(Archbold et al. 2002b; Sach & Whynes, 2005) have revealed that ongoing appropriate educational management and close liaison between implant center and school were priorities for parents. Parents studied by Archbold et al. (2002a,b) and Sorkin and Zwolan (2004) indicated that one of their main concerns is liaison between school and implant center, and that they are particularly aware of the demands of managing the technology successfully in the long term. Children with implants may have clinically excellent levels of speech intelligibility that actually mask their difficulties in noisy classrooms and make their true educational needs more difficult to identify. In addition to appropriate communication support, students with cochlear implants also require ongoing daily technical support related to their implants, and local service providers may not be up-to-date or possess the necessary knowledge or skills (Archbold & O'Donoghue, 2007).

The new technology offers exciting new educational opportunities but also some challenges, and as Marschark and Spencer (2003) commented: "there appears to be little emphasis on development of specialist teaching or habilitation strategies to build on the potential provided by cochlear implants and other advances in hearing amplification" (p. 492).

CHOICE OF COMMUNICATION MODE

This chapter began with the importance of effective communication skills. Choice of communication mode, as described earlier, has often been a source of contention and one of the most difficult decisions for parents to make. It is a decision often influenced by political or professional pressures. The choice of sign or spoken language, or of total communication, in which spoken language is supported by sign, remains difficult for parents since the advent of cochlear implantation, even in the face of increasing evidence of effectiveness. For parents choosing cochlear implantation for their child, spoken language is typically the major goal and is likely to be the language of the home and largely of the community. It is the most effective way of attaining the goal that has been the subject of debate. Some researchers have reported that an oral educational setting is most effective (e.g., Geers, Nicholas, & Sedey, 2003; Tobey, Geers, Brenner, Altuna, & Gabbert, 2003), while others have concluded that there is no difference between those in oral environments and those in settings where signed communication is used (e.g., Connor, Hieber, Arts, & Zwolan, 2000; Robbins, Svirsky, & Kirk, 1997).

Geers (2006) provided a useful summary of the research in this area for those interested in further detailed reading. Although there is varying evidence of the influence of oral and signing environments on outcomes from implantation, on the whole, the trend is to support the use of oral input; however, the situation is complex. For parents, this can be a huge challenge, with an apparently major decision to make about communication choice, often while dealing with the diagnosis of deafness. Increasing the pressure on parents, the literature frequently implies that the decision about communication mode is one that is made once and for all, and that children do not change the type of communication they use over time. However, several researchers have shown that the situation is not clear-cut and that approaches to communication mode may be more flexible than was once thought to be the case.

Tait et al. (2007) found that those implanted between the ages of 1 and 2 typically change communication mode toward spoken language within the first 6 months after implantation. Archbold, Nikolopoulous, Tait, O'Donoghue, Lutman, and Gregory (2000) showed that there was no difference in the outcomes in terms of speech perception and production 3 years after implantation in those studied who had used some form of signed input initially and then changed to oral communication, and those who had used oral communication throughout. Further investigation by Watson et al. (2006) showed that children implanted before the age of 3 changed from using signed communication to oral communication over time after implantation. When asked about the reasons for the change of communication mode in this large group of children who came from the complete range of educational settings throughout the United Kingdom, parents responded that they wanted the most useful and effective means of communication for their children. The change to oral communication was driven by the change in hearing following implantation. Common responses included "It was a very natural and child-driven change to spoken language. He prefers spoken language both receptively and productively"(Watson et al. 2007, p. 8).

Interestingly, although spoken language was these parents' goal for their child, they valued sign support (Watson et al., 2007). Interestingly, too, the one point on which these parents were neutral was whether they had followed the advice of the teacher of the deaf in selecting communication approach: they appeared to have made their own decision.

In a follow-up interview study (Wheeler, Archbold, Gregory, & Skipp, 2007a), a few parents mentioned that they had chosen to relocate to find the communication support they felt their child needed because they believed the local service did not meet those needs. They talked about a "communication journey" in which, prior to implantation, communication, regardless of methodology, was the goal—and for hearing parents the method chosen was likely to be spoken language with or without some gesture or sign support. Over time after implantation, spoken language, driven by the use of audition and good oral input, was achieved by a majority of the children, and the use of any gesture or sign support declined. However, in the teenage years, both the young people and their parents in the study expressed an interest in learning sign language as another language or using some sign support. Depending on imperfect hearing can be tiring, particularly in noisy settings, and some signed support can be helpful. Parents appeared rather more pragmatic about communication mode than professionals often are, and parents commented on their difficulties in dealing with strong advice from professionals in one direction or another.

Implantation does seem to be making a difference in the choice of communication mode, it does make acquiring spoken language through hearing a viable choice—but it may not be as straightforward a process as once thought. Most deaf children using cochlear implants can acquire excellent levels of spoken language through use of the implant, given the right opportunities and input. There remains a lack of objective evidence, however, whether some signed input can help or hinder the development of spoken language with this new technology (Marschark & Spencer, 2003), and there is considerable thought currently being given to the use of signed support, rather than sign language with its own grammar and used without voice. It is clear that if children are to develop spoken language they need to be in an educational environment that values it and promotes its use.

Parental Concerns

Despite parents' reports of being mostly satisfied about the outcomes from implantation (e.g., Sach & Whynes, 2005; Archbold et al. 2008a), a number of parental concerns reoccur. The major ones reported are educational support and long-term technological support and management, and how these are best provided. These concerns are not new (Archbold & Robinson, 1997, Geers & Moog, 1995; Hasenstab, VanderArk, & Kastetter, 1997), but we have yet to find ways of making the technology accessible and manageable in the long-term as the numbers of implanted children have increased. Parents realize the long-term nature of the process, the reliance their children place on their implant systems (Archbold et al., 2006, 2008a), and the necessity for the long-term support to be in place in the community rather than in the implant center alone. What then of the views of the young people themselves?

The Views of Young People with Implants

There is a growing group of young people with cochlear implants whose experiences can be explored in order to help inform future practice. Although increasing numbers of young people are choosing to have implants as teenagers, the majority were implanted as young children. Hyde and Power (2006) discussed the issue of informed consent, particularly with reference to elective surgery and Deaf cultural issues. They draw attention to legislation on the rights of children supporting their right to be involved and informed in decision making, relative to their age and maturity.

Wheeler et al. (2007a) found that teenagers in the United Kingdom, some of whom had been implanted many years earlier, were not unduly concerned that their parents had made the decision on their behalf. They appeared to understand that a decision had to be made when they were young in order to obtain the best benefit from cochlear implantation, and many were grateful that their parents had chosen a cochlear implant for them, thus supporting the view of Balkany, Hodges, and Goodman (1996). Those who are implanted at a later age, perhaps as a result of suddenly acquired deafness or gradual progressive loss, were likely to have had more of a say in the decision to have a cochlear implant. However, even for teenagers, weighing up the pros and cons of implantation is not easy. Wheeler et al. (2007a) asked young people whether they would recommend an implant to someone else. Their views differed, depending on whether the person in question was a very young, congenitally deaf child or a teenager of a similar age to themselves. Most felt that the parents of very young children should take up the offer of a cochlear implant, but they did not necessarily reject hearing aids altogether. This was reflected in their more cautious responses to whether they would recommend a cochlear implant to a teenager with suddenly acquired deafness. They sometimes expressed the opinion that hearing aids should be given a proper trial before rushing to implantation.

The decision-making process for a young person gradually going deaf is more finely balanced. At what point should hearing aids be abandoned in favor of a cochlear implant? Young people in the study by Wheeler et al. (2007a) felt that hearing aids should be used for as long as they gave benefit. One young person articulated very clearly the disadvantages of cochlear implantation in terms of the medical intervention and postimplant monitoring required:

> It depends what you think is best for the child. A cochlear implant would be quite good, but there is the side of the operation. The doctors have to be involved, have to look inside you, which might bother some people. And the cochlear implant doesn't always work. There's years of hard work, years of speech therapy, years of going to the hospital and having to overcome the technical problems and having to have another operation sometimes later, whereas with hearing aids you don't have to have an operation to cope with them. (Wheeler et al., 2007a, p. 313)

However, Kent and Smith (2006) have drawn attention to the difficulties experienced by hearing aid users with a moderate to severe hearing loss and their struggles with issues of "normality." Progressive as well as suddenly acquired hearing loss can be accompanied by psychological difficulties, increasing social isolation (Polat, 2003), and particular issues with psychosocial adjustment. Having established one clear identity as a hearing person, these adolescents find themselves moving through a fairly rapid transition to profound deafness followed by cochlear implantation. If deafness has been acquired as a result of meningitis, then the process may be very swift indeed. The adolescents' desire may be to recapture "normality," and their first language will certainly be a spoken one. They may recognize the fact of their deafness but also resent the necessary changes and adaptations in their life. To be the object of special attention is not welcome at an age when most adolescents want to blend in with their peers.

Experience suggests that the period of adjustment following activation of the cochlear implant may be difficult for adolescents, especially if they find themselves dealing with private disappointment that their "new" hearing is not the same as their memory of "normal" hearing or the more natural sound that may be provided by a hearing aid. Wheeler et al. (2007b) reported a comment by a teacher in the United Kingdom working with just such a teenager:

> She was very much thinking she is not deaf, "don't want to wear this thing on my head." She was starting to reject it [the implant] at age 12–13 years, she was not getting on with her support teacher. The adjustment to the implant was too difficult, she needed it to be perfect straight away. The last straw was when someone, a boy, called her an alien. (p. 3)

Careful preoperative counseling and dedicated postoperative support are needed in these cases (Cohen, 2006). Pans, Speel, Gehring, Rozier, Brokz, and Gerrits (2006) reported on the development of a psychosocial support program for teenagers with cochlear implants, having found evidence that they do experience some problems related to social-emotional development.

In addition to struggles with their own identity and adjustment to loss of hearing, adolescents who become deaf and begin to use cochlear implants may face other pressures. For example, Wheeler et al. (2007a) discussed some negative experiences of implanted young people in the United Kingdom, with regard to bullying. This was reported by 17% of the group, together with other accounts of spiteful peer behavior. Bullying may arise from difficulties with interaction with the peer group and can occur both in mainstream schools and special schools for the deaf. Bullying can occur when the young person in question is seen as "different." Although a cochlear implant may facilitate inclusion into a mainstream school, it may not provide access to the sophisticated level of linguistic understanding needed to access the peer group culture.

The greatest test of whether young people feel that they really benefit from their cochlear implant is to ask them if they would have another implant if their present one failed. Wheeler et al. (2007a), looking at a group of young people implanted across all ages, found that all the young people would have another cochlear implant operation if needed, although they might want to control the timing, for example in relation to important events such as exams. In contrast, Todini, Cavicchiolo, Ceriani, Ugazio, and Zaghis (2006) reported that over one-third of prelingually deafened, late-implanted adolescents would not wish to be reimplanted should their system fail. The different results from the two studies may be accounted for by the fact that Todini et al. (2006) are reporting on a group who received their cochlear implant after the optimum age of implantation without the benefit of having established oral language skills through hearing beforehand.

Of the group studied by Wheeler et al. (2007a), 41% reported that they felt bereft if they were unable to use their cochlear implant due to a technical fault with their speech processor. One young person expressed very clearly the distress that she experienced in such situations:

> Sometimes you start to panic, wonder whether it's going wrong on the inside. I'm fine with being deaf it's just the actual breaking down. It's like having some of your organs failing. (Wheeler et al., 2007a, p. 308)

Some even disliked losing sound for the short time taken to change a battery.

Currently, a large proportion of young people have only one implant. It is a further measure of their satisfaction that some of them are now asking for a second (sequential) implant. This may reflect in part the difficulties that they experience both socially and educationally. Using one ear instead of two can result in difficulties in understanding speech in the presence of background noise and in locating the source of sound (Wei, O'Leary, & Dowell, 2007), creating difficulties in social situations and in the classroom. Young people have reported difficulties with following group interaction and taking part in whole-class discussions. Wheeler et al. (2007b) interviewed young people in secondary schools to find out their perspective on this:

> Group work is the biggest pain you could ever possibly imagine. Small group is all right but big group or class discussions they are the worst. I need one person at a time, just one person at a time not all the same time, whoo, over my head, I lose control. It is quite hard to work …. Other people talk too fast, then walk off. (p. 4)

The young people in this study were quite clear about their needs at secondary school, asking for flexibility of approach, with a high standard of both spoken and signed support. Wheeler et al. (2007a) found that two-thirds of the young people, however, felt that their cochlear implant helped them to understand the lessons in the classroom.

Gregory et al. (1995), reporting in a preimplant era, commented on the rigidity of choice, with regard to education and communication, as reported by the young people and their families. In the United Kingdom in the 1970s and 1980s, an oral philosophy predominated, without the opportunity of access to sign language in any formal sense. Results from interviews by Gregory et al. (1995) suggest that for some profoundly deaf young people, this created a sense of not fully "belonging" to the hearing world because limited access to hearing resulted in poor spoken language skills and speech intelligibility—but without the sense of deaf identity that might be associated with the full use of sign language. Many of these young people had subsequently learned sign language once they reached adulthood. Potentially, young people with cochlear implants, growing up in a less rigid educational system, have the option to both learn to speak and to use sign language.

Gregory et al. (1995) reported that some young people struggled with family communication, feeling left out and uninformed. However, the most frequently cited advantage of having a cochlear implant in the study by Wheeler et al. (2007a) was improved interaction with family and friends. Over two-thirds of the group felt they were understood by their family all or most of the time.

> Yes, cochlear implants work because you can hear more, talking to friends, understand everything, go out have a good time … if [you] have a cochlear implant [it's] easier to have a good time. (Wheeler et al., 2007a, p. 310)

Recent studies (Watson et al., 2007; Wheeler, Archbold, Hardie, & Watson, 2008) have demonstrated that cochlear implantation widens the choice for young people, and although many develop spoken language skills, they do not necessarily reject the use of sign language. Some choose to pick it up again, acquiring a natural sign language like British Sign Language as an alternative language. These young people may wish to talk with their family but they may also choose to sign with their deaf peers even if they are also capable of speaking to each other. This flexible attitude toward communication—or "code-switching"—may come as a surprise to those who were concerned that the arrival of cochlear implants would result in the reduction of the use of sign language and the loss of Deaf cultural identity (e.g., Lane & Bahan, 1998).

The teenage years are ones in which issues of selfhood and identity come to the fore, and this may be a particularly difficult time for deaf adolescents (Lukomski, 2007). Gregory et al. (1995) discussed the dawning realization on the part of deaf children as they grow up that their deafness is permanent—a third were reported to believe as children that they would become hearing when they grew up, mainly because of the absence of deaf adult role models. Ohna (2004) suggested that this realization occurs when the deaf individual experiences difficulties in communication with hearing people. Wald and Knutson (2000) questioned adolescents with and without a cochlear implant and concluded that the two groups had many similar views on deaf identity, but that the young people with cochlear implants had a stronger concept of a hearing identity as a positive goal. Some views gathered by Wheeler et al. (2007a) are remarkably similar to those reported by Gregory et al. (1995), in which spoken language skills are associated with a hearing identity, and in some cases with "normality." However, young people also expressed the view that they are intrinsically "deaf" because they cannot hear without their implant. Wheeler et al. (2007a) reported that the majority of the group interviewed saw themselves as either deaf *and* hearing or as deaf, with only 21% of the group expressing a strongly "hearing" identity. Leigh, Maxwell-McCaw, Bat-Chava, and Christianson (2009) have recently reported that adolescents with cochlear implants tend to be more hearing acculturated, whereas those without an implant tended to be more Deaf acculturated. However they found that the two groups did not differ on the psychosocial variables used in the study.

For young people with cochlear implants, having well-established spoken language skills and good speech intelligibility may give rise to incorrect assumptions on the part of those around them. These young people refer to being treated as "hearing" or "normal" (Wheeler et al., 2007a) because they can communicate with hearing people. This concept is also reflected by hearing aid users in the study by Kent and Smith (2006). However, hearing people, and particularly educators, may fail to realize the full reality of profound deafness, even with the advantage of cochlear implantation, and may not appreciate these children's needs, especially in secondary and further education (Preisler, Tvingstedt, & Ahlstrom, 2005; Wheeler et al., 2007b).

With developments in cochlear implant technology, the more precise timing of cochlear implantation, and the increasing trend toward simultaneous bilateral implantation, the benefits young people gain from cochlear implantation are likely to increase. However, current research suggests that many will have a sense of identity, which, like their communication choice, is fluid and flexible.

Summary and Conclusions

The diagnosis of deafness in a child, with its impact on developing communication and spoken language skills, is one which not only changes the opportunities of the child, but has impacts on parents and the wider family and their interactions and relationships. The provision of useful hearing through cochlear implantation over the last 20 years has transformed opportunities for deaf children and hence for their families, particularly in the realm of improved communication and confidence. Cochlear implantation has changed communication options and education management for deaf children. Both are issues that have exercised the minds of parents over the years, and that have impacted on their own lifestyles and the management of their deaf child.

However, while ameliorating some of the effects of profound deafness, cochlear implantation in children does not provide a "cure" for deafness, and implications for the family and child remain. The limited literature to date on psychosocial outcomes from implantation for family, child, and young person indicates that these families and young people are finding a new way forward dealing with deafness, while also having better access to hearing than ever before. For families, expectations have been changed by implantation, and will continue to change as children are implanted earlier, with improved devices, and increasingly with two implants rather than one. As expectations and outcomes change, a challenge remains as to what parenting a deaf child is like today, which issues from a psychosocial perspective remain, and which have changed irrevocably.

We are yet to have sufficient data from long-term studies on those implanted early as they progress into adulthood, and can reflect on their interactions within their families and with their peer group. However, the current indications are that young people with cochlear implants have no greater difficulties with socioemotional functioning than previously, and may be better able to function with a greater range of choices in what is largely a hearing society. They appear to feel positively about their implants and to have a pragmatic view of communication, seeing themselves functioning as hearing in some settings and as deaf in others.

Parenting a deaf child in this technological era is to face different choices, and for many of these choices the long-term outcomes and changes to family dynamics, family interaction, and the psychosocial well-being of the children themselves are still unknown. More long-term studies are required to ensure that those working in this field, particularly in deaf education, listen to the families and young people to ensure that services change to meet their changing needs. The following quote by two leading researchers in the field of deaf education summarizes well the opportunities and challenges faced by those of us supporting deaf children young people and their families in this technological era:

> Spoken language development of deaf children may be more possible today than ever before .... we are now presented with the opportunity to learn from earlier mistakes and misunderstandings and to synthesize the best ideas from the past with the technological, programming, and social advances of today ... we may finally be able to fulfil the promise of effective support for speech and spoken language with hearing loss. (Marschark & Spencer, 2006, p. 17)

References

Anagnostou, F., Graham, J., & Crocker S. (2007). A preliminary study looking at parental emotions following cochlear implantation. *Cochlear implants international*, 8, 68–86.

Anderson, K. (1989). Screening Instrument for Targeting Educational Risk teacher rating scale (SIFTER). Little Rock, AR: Educational Audiology Assessment Product Manager.

Archbold, S., Harris M., Nikolopoulos T. P., O'Donoghue G., White, A., & Lloyd Richmond, H. (2008b). Reading abilities after cochlear implantation: The effect of age at implantation on reading age, five and seven years after implantation. *International Journal of Pediatric Otorhinolaryngology*, 72, 1471–1478.

Archbold, S., Nikolopoulos, T., O'Donoghue, G., & Lutman, M. (1998). Educational placement of children following cochlear implantation. *British Journal of Audiology*, 32, 295–300.

Archbold, S., & O'Donoghue, G. M. (2007). Ensuring the long-term use of cochlear implants in children: the importance of engaging local resources and expertise. *Ear and Hearing, 28*, 3S–6S.

Archbold, S., & Robinson, K. (1997). A European perspective on paediatric cochlear implantation, rehabilitation services and their educational implications. *American Journal of Otology, 18*, 575–578.

Archbold S., Sach T., O'Neill C., Lutman M., & Gregory S. (2008a). Outcomes from cochlear implantation for child and family: parental perspectives. *Deafness and Educational International, 10*(3), 120–142.

Archbold S., Sach T., O'Neill, C., Lutman, M., & Gregory, S. (2006). Deciding to have a cochlear implant and subsequent after-care: parental perspectives *Deafness and Education International, 8*, 190–206.

Archbold, S. M., Lutman, M. E., Gregory, S., O'Neill, C., & Nikolopoulos, T. P. (2002a). Parents and their deaf child: Their perceptions three years after cochlear implantation. *Deafness and Education International, 4*, 12–40.

Archbold, S. M., Nikolopoulos, T. P., Lutman, M. E., & O'Donoghue, G. M. (2002b). The educational settings of profoundly deaf children with cochlear implants compared with age-matched peers with hearing aids: implications for management. *International Journal of Audiology, 41*, 157–161.

Archbold, S. M., Nikolopoulos, T. P., Tait, M., O'Donoghue, G. M., Lutman, M. E., & Gregory, S. (2000). Approach to communication, speech perception and intelligibility after paediatric cochlear implantation. *British Journal of Audiology, 34*, 257–264.

Balkany, T., Hodges, A. V., & Goodman, K. W. (1996). Ethics of cochlear implantation in young children. *Otolaryngology Head Neck Surgery, 114*, 748–55.

Beadle, E. A. R., McKinley, D. J., Nikolopoulos, T. P., Brough, J., O'Donoghue, G. M., & Archbold, S. M. (2005). Long-term functional outcomes and academic-occupational status in implanted children after 10 to 14 years of cochlear implant use. *Otology & Neurotology, 26*, 1152–1160.

Beadle, E. A. R., Shores, A., Wood, E. J. (2000). Parental perceptions of the impact upon the family of cochlear implantation in children. *Annals of Otology, Rhinology and Laryngology, 185*, 111–114S.

Calderon, R., & Greenberg, M. T. (2003). Social and emotional development of deaf children: Family, school and program effects. In M. Marschark & P. E. Spencer (Eds.), *Oxford handbook of deaf studies, education and language* (pp. 177–189). New York: Oxford University Press.

Christianson, J. B., & Leigh, I. W. (2004). Children with cochlear implants: Changing parent and deaf community perspectives. *Archives of Otolaryngology Head and Neck Surgery, 130*(5), 673–677.

Clark, J. F., & English, K. (2004) *Counselling in audiologic practice*. Boston: Pearson Education.

Cohen, N. (2006). *Cochlear implants in the adolescent: selection criteria and expected outcomes*. Paper presented at 8th Symposium Pediatric Cochlear Implantation. Venice, Italy.

Connor, C., Hieber, S., Arts, A., & Zwolan, T. (2000). Speech, vocabulary, and the education of children using cochlear implants: Oral or total communication? *Journal of Speech, Language, and Hearing Research, 43*(5), 1185–1204.

Damen, G., Krabbe, P., Archbold, S., & Mylanus, E. (2007a). Evaluation of the Parental Perspective instrument for pediatric cochlear implantation to arrive at a short version. *International journal of pediatric otorhinolaryngology, 71*, 425–433.

Damen, G. W., Langereis, M. C., Snik, A. F., Chute, P. M., & Mylanus, E. A. (2007b). Classroom performance and language development of CI students placed in mainstream elementary school. *Otology & Neurotology, 28*, 463–472.

Dettman, S. J., Pinder, D., Briggs, R. J., Dowell, R. C., & Leigh, J. R. (2007). Communication development in children who receive the cochlear implant younger than 12 months: Risks versus benefits. *Ear and Hearing, 28*, 11S–18S.

Edwards, L., McArdle, B. M., Doney A., & Bellman, S. (2000). Parental experiences of a paediatric cochlear implant programme. *Cochlear Implants International, 1*, 95–107.

Fortnum, H., Stacey, P., & Summerfield, A. Q. (2006). An exploration of demographic bias in a questionnaire survey of hearing-impaired children: Implications for comparisons of children with and without cochlear implants. *International Journal of Pediatric Otorhinolaryngology, 70*, 2043–2054.

Francis, H. W., Koch, M. E., Wyatt, J. R., & Niparko, J. K. (1999). Trends in educational placement and cost-benefit considerations in children with cochlear implants. *Archives of Otolaryngology Head and Neck Surgery, 125*, 499–505.

Geers, A., & Brenner, C. (2003). Background and educational characteristics of prelingually deaf children implanted by five years of age. *Ear and Hearing, 24*, 2S–14S.

Geers, A., & Moog, J. (1995). Assessing the benefits of cochlear implants in an oral education program. In A. Uziel & M. Mondain (Eds.), *Cochlear implants in children* (pp. 119–124). Basel: Karger.

Geers, A. E. (2006). Spoken language in children with cochlear implants. In P. Spencer & M. Marschark (Eds.), *Advances in spoken language development of deaf and hard-of-hearing children*. (pp. 244–270). New York: Oxford University Press.

Geers, A. E., Nicholas, J. G., & Sedey, A. L. (2003). Language skills of children with early cochlear implantation. *Ear and Hearing, 24*, 46S–58S.

Geers, A., Tobey, E., Moog, J., & Brenner, C. (2008). Long-term outcomes of cochlear implantation in the preschool years: From elementary grades to high school. *International Journal of Audiology, 47* (Supplement 2), S21–S30.

Gregory, S., Bishop, J., & Sheldon, L. (1995). *Deaf young people and their families*. Cambridge UK: Cambridge University Press.

Hasenstab, S., VanderArk, W. D., & Kastetter, S. K. (1997). *Parent report of support services for their children using cochlear implants*. Paper presented at the Vth International Cochlear Implant Conference, New York.

Hintermair, M. (2006). Parental resources, parental stress, and socioemotional development of deaf and hard or hearing children. *Journal of Deaf Studies and Deaf Education, 11*, 493–513.

Hyde, M., & Power, D. (2006). Some ethical dimensions of cochlear implantation for deaf children and their families. *Journal of Deaf Studies and Deaf Education, 11*, 202–111.

Inceselu, A., Vural, M., & Erkam, U. (2003). Children with cochlear Implants: Parental perspectives. *Otology and Neurotology, 24*(4), 605–11.

Kluwin, T. N., & Stewart. D. A. (2000). Cochlear implants for younger children: A preliminary description of the parental decision process and outcomes. *American Annals of the Deaf, 145*(1) 26–32.

Kent, B., & Smith, S. (2006). They only see it when the sun shines in my ears: Exploring perceptions of adolescent hearing aids users. *Journal of Deaf Studies and Deaf Education, 11*, 461–476.

Kushalnagar, P., Krull, K., Hannay, J., Mehta, P., Caudle, S., & Oghalai, J. (2007). Intelligence, parental depression, and behavior adaptability in deaf children being considered for cochlear implantation. *Journal of Deaf Studies and Deaf Education, 12*, 335–349.

Lane, H., & Bahan, B. (1998). Ethics of cochlear implantation in young children: a review and reply from a Deaf-World perspective. *Otolaryngology Head Neck Surgery, 119*(4), 297–313.

Lang, H. G. (2003). Perspectives on the history of deaf education. In M. Marschark & P. E. Spencer (Eds.), *Oxford handbook of deaf studies, language and education* (pp. 9–20). Oxford University Press: New York.

Leigh, I. W., Maxwell-McCaw, D., Bat-Chava, Y., & Christiansen, J. B. (2009). Correlates of psycho-social adjustment in deaf adolescents with and without cochlear implants: A preliminary investigation. *Journal of Deaf Studies and Deaf Education, 14*, 244–259.

Li, Y., Bain, L., & Steinberg, A.G. (2004). Parental decision-making in considering cochlear implant technology for a deaf child. *International Journal of Pediatric Otorhinolaryngology, 68*, 1027–1038.

Lin, F., & Niparko, J. (2006). Measuring health-related quality of life after pediatric cochlear implantation: A systematic review. *International Journal of Pediatric Otorhinolaryngology, 70*, 1695–1706.

Lin F. R., Wang N. Y., Fink N. E., Quittner, A. L., Eisenberg, L. S., Tobey, E. A., & Niparko, J. K. (2008). Assessing the use of speech and language measures in relation to parental perceptions of development after early cochlear implantation. *Otology & Neurotology, 29*(2), 208–213.

Lukomski, J. (2007). Deaf college students' perceptions of their social-emotional adjustment. *Journal of Deaf Studies and Deaf Education, 12*, 486–494.

Luterman, D. (2005). Early childhood deafness—a status report. *ENT News, 14*, 44–45.

Luterman, D., & Ross, M. (1991). *When your child is deaf*. Baltimore: York Press.

Marschark, M., Rhoten, C., & Fabich, M. (2007). Effects of cochlear implants on children's reading and academic achievement. *Journal of Deaf Studies and Deaf Education, 12*, 269–282.

Marschark, M., & Spencer, P. (2006). Historical and theoretical perspectives. In P. Spencer & M. Marschark (Eds.), *Advances in spoken language in deaf and hard of hearing children* (pp. 3–21). New York: Oxford University Press.

Marschark, M., & Spencer, P. (2003). What we know, what we don't know, and what we should know. In M. Marschark & P. Spencer (Eds.), *Oxford handbook of deaf studies, language, and education* (pp. 491–494). New York: Oxford University Press.

Mitchell, R. E., & Karchmer, M. A. (2004). Chasing the mythical ten percent: Parental hearing status of deaf and hard of hearing students in the United States. *Sign Language Studies, 4*(2), 138–163.

Miyamoto, R. T., Houston, D. M., & Bergeson, T. (2005). Cochlear implantation in deaf infants. *Laryngoscope. 115*(8), 1376–1380.

Mukari, S., Ling, L., & Ghani, H. (2007). Educational performance of pediatric cochlear implant recipients in mainstream classes. *International Journal of Pediatric Otorhinolaryngology, 71*, 231–240.

Nevins, M. E., & Chute, P. M. (1996). *Children with cochlear implants in educational settings*. San Diego: Singular.

Nicholas, J. G., & Geers, A. E. (2003). Personal, social and family adjustment in school-aged children with a cochlear implant. *Ear and Hearing, 24*, 69S–81S.

Nikolopoulos, T., Lloyd, H., Archbold, S., & O'Donoghue, G. M. (2001). Paediatric cochlear implantation: The parents' perspective. *Archives of Otolaryngology Head Neck Surgery, 127*, 363–367.

Nikolopoulos, T., O'Donoghue, G. M., & Archbold, S. (1999) Age at implantation: Its importance in paediatric cochlear implantation. *Laryngoscope, 109*, 595–599.

Nunes, T., Pretzlik, S., & Ilicak, S. (2005). Validation of a parent outcome questionnaire from pediatric cochlear implantation. *Journal of Deaf Studies and Deaf Education, 10*(4), 330–356.

Ohna, S. E. (2004). Deaf in my own way. *Deafness and Education International, 6*, 20–38.

O'Donoghue, G. M., Nikolopoulos, T. P., & Archbold, S. M. (2000). Determinants of speech perception in children after cochlear implantation. *The Lancet 356*(9228), 466–468.

O'Neill, C., Lutman M. E., Archbold S. M., Gregory, S., & Nikolopoulos T. P. (2004). Parents and their cochlear implanted child: questionnaire development to assess parental views and experiences. *International Journal of Pediatric Otorhinolaryngology*, *68*(2), 149–160.

O'Neill, C., O'Donoghue, G. M., Archbold, S. M., & Normand, C. (2000). A cost-utility analysis of pediatric cochlear implantation. *The Laryngoscope*, *110*, 156–160.

Pans, D., Speel, M., Gehring, I., Rozier, E., Brokz, J., & Gerrits, E. (2006). *Towards understanding teenagers with CI*. Paper presented at 8th Symposium Pediatric Cochlear Implantation, Venice.

Percy S., Jensen, J. H., Josvassen, J. L., Jonsson, M. H., Andersen, J., & Samar, C. F. (2006). Parents' perceptions of their deaf children's speech, language and social outcome after cochlear implantation. *Ugeskrift for Laeger*, *168*(33), 2659–2664.

Perold, J. L. (2001). An investigation into the expectations of mothers of children with cochlear implants. *Cochlear Implants International*, *2*(1), 39–58.

Preisler, G., Tvingstedt, A. L., & Ahlstrom, M. (2005). Interviews with deaf children about their experiences with cochlear implants. *American Annals of the Deaf*, *150*(3), 260–267.

Polat, F. (2003). Factors affecting the psycho-social adjustment of deaf students. *Journal of Deaf Studies and Deaf Education*, *83*, 325–339.

Robbins, A. M., Svirsky, M., & Kirk, K. I. (1997). Children with implants can speak, but can they communicate? *Otolaryngology-Head and Neck Surgery*, *117*, 115–160.

Sach, T., & Whynes, D. (2005). Paediatric cochlear implantation: the views of parents. *International Journal of Audiology*, *44*, 400–407.

Sach, T. H., & Barton, G. R. (2007). Interpreting parental proxy reports of (health-related) quality of life for children with unilateral cochlear implants. *International Journal Pediatric Otorhinolaryngology*, *71*, 435–445.

Sorkin, D. L., & Zwolan, T. A. (2004). Trends in educational services for children with cochlear implants. *International Congress Series*, *1273*, 417–421.

Spahn, C., Richter, B., Burger, T., Lohle, E., & Wirsching, M. (2003). A comparison between parents of children with cochlear implant and parents of children with hearing aids regarding parental distress and treatment expectations. *International Journal of Pediatric Otorhinolaryngology*, *67*, 947–955.

Spencer, L. J., Gantz, B. J., & Knutson, J. F. (2004). Outcomes and achievements of students who grew up with access to cochlear implants. *Laryngoscope*, *114*, 1576–1581.

Spencer, P. E., & Marschark, M. (2003). Cochlear implants: Issues and implications. In P. E. Spencer & M. Marschark (Eds.), *Oxford handbook of deaf studies, language and education* (pp. 434–450). New York: Oxford University Press.

Stacey, P., Fortnum, H., Barton, G., & Summerfield, A. (2006). Hearing-impaired children in the United Kingdom, I: Auditory performance, communication skills, educational achievements, quality of life, and cochlear implantation. *Ear and Hearing*, *27*, 161–186.

Steinberg, A., Brainsky, L., Bain, L., & Montoya, M. (2000). Parental values in the decision about cochlear implantation. *International Journal of Pediatric Otorhinolaryngology*, *55*, 99–107.

Tait, M. E., Nikolopoulos, T. P., & Lutman, M. E. (2007). Age at implantation and development of vocal and auditory pre-verbal skills in implanted deaf children. *International Journal of Pediatric Otorhinolaryngology*, *71*, 603–610.

Thoutenhoofd, E. (2006). Cochlear implanted pupils in Scottish schools: 4-year school attainment data 2000–2004. *Journal of Deaf Studies and Deaf Education*, *11*, 171–188.

Thoutenhoofd, E., Archbold, S. M., Gregory, S., Lutman, M. E., Nikolopoulos, T. M., & Sach. T. M. (2005). *Paediatric cochlear implantation*. London: Whurr.

Tobey, E. A., Geers, A. E., Brenner, C., Altuna, D., & Gabbert, G. (2003) Factors associated with development of speech production skills in children implanted by the age of five. *Ear and Hearing*, *24*(1), 36S–46S.

Todini, L., Cavicchiolo, S., Ceriani, N., Ugazio, G., & Zaghis, A. (2006). *Cochlear implant failures in prelingually deaf adolescents*. Paper presented at 8th Symposium Pediatric Cochlear Implantation, Venice.

Vermeulen, A. M., Van, B. W., Schreuder, R., Knoors, H., & Snik, A. (2007). Reading comprehension of deaf children with cochlear implants. *Journal of Deaf Studies and Deaf Education*, *12*, 283–302.

Wald, R. L., & Knutson, J. F. (2000). Deaf cultural identity of adolescents with and without cochlear implants. *Annals of Otology, Rhinology and Laryngology*, *185*, 87–89.

Watson, L. M, Archbold, S., Hardie, T., & Wheeler, A. (2007). Parents' views on changing communication after cochlear implantation. *Journal of Deaf Studies and Deaf Education*, *13*, 104–116.

Watson, L. M., Archbold, S., & Nikolopoulos, T. P. (2006). Children's communication mode 5 years after cochlear implantation: changes over time according to age at implantation. *Cochlear implants International*, *7*(2), 77–91.

Wei, B., O'Leary, S., & Dowell, R. (2007). Two cochlear implants: Halving the number of recipients. *The Lancet*, *370*, 1686.

Weisel, A., Most, T., & Michael, R. (2007). Mothers' stress and expectations as a function of time since child's cochlear implantation. *Journal of Deaf Studies and Deaf Education*, *12*, 55–64.

Wheeler, A., Archbold, S., Gregory, S., & Skipp, A. (2007a). Cochlear implants: The young peoples' perspective. *Journal of Deaf Studies and Deaf Education*, *12*, 303–316.

Wheeler, A., Archbold, S., & Gregory, S. (2007b). *Supporting children with cochlear implants in secondary school*. Report to RNID, United Kingdom.

Wheeler, A., Archbold, S. M., Hardie, T. & Watson, L. M. (2008). Children with cochlear implants: The communication journey. *Cochlear Implants International*, *10*, 41–62.

The Impact of Early Identification of Deafness on Hearing Parents

Alys Young

Abstract

The proliferation of national and statewide universal newborn hearing screening (UNHS) programs is ensuring that early identification of deafness (within the first few months of life) is now the norm in many developed counties. In combination with sustained and quality multiprofessional intervention services, early identification holds the promise of enhanced developmental outcomes for deaf children. However, medium- and long-term developmental outcomes remain largely unknown. Following a brief review of this background, this chapter will primarily focus on the impact on the family context of the very early identification of deafness through routine UNHS. It will begin by assessing how much and in what respects it is possible to claim that early identification is changing the basis on which hearing parents engage with the challenges of parenting a deaf child. Three issues in particular are considered: potential changes in grief and loss responses, the impact of the timing of confirmation of childhood deafness, and influences on parental envisioning of the implications of their children's deafness. The evidence review will enable an analysis of the extent to which it is still possible to trust the findings of longstanding studies on how hearing parents adjust to childhood deafness, or whether new questions for research and practice now arise.

Keywords: universal newborn hearing screening; parental adjustment; early intervention; early identification

The routine early identification of childhood deafness following programs of universal newborn hearing screening (UNHS), whether on a state, regional, or national basis, is now the norm in many developed countries worldwide. The age of diagnosis has consequently dramatically changed from averages of around 26 months in the late 1990s (Davis, Bamford, Wilson, Ramkalawan, Forshaw, & Wright, 1997), to a median in some programs of 10 weeks (Uus & Bamford, 2006). However impressive the achievement of such universal and accurate coverage, swift identification is not of itself the end goal. It is only the necessary gateway to a new set of circumstances in which deaf children's optimal development may be supported. Namely, early recognition enables very early intervention, and the infant develops in a context in which the family is aware from the earliest months of life that its new member is deaf.

In the United States, the recent Joint Committee on Infant Hearing 2007 Position Statement (JCIH, 2007) concluded that a considerable body of evidence now exists demonstrating that, when deafness is confirmed and intervention begun before 6 months of age, significantly better outcomes are achieved in a number of domains, in comparison with later-identified children. The domains cited include vocabulary development (Mayne, Yoshinaga-Itano & Sedey, 1998; Mayne, Yoshinaga-Itano, Sedey & Carey, 1998), receptive and expressive language (Pipp-Siegel, Sedey, VanLeeuwen, & Yoshinaga-Itano, 2003), syntax (Yoshinaga-Itano, Coulter, &

Thomson, 2001), speech production (Apuzzo & Yoshinaga-Itano, 1995; Yoshinaga-Itano & Apuzzo, 1998a, 1998b; Yoshinaga-Itano, Coulter, & Thomson, 2001), and socioemotional development (Yoshinaga-Itano, 2001). In some studies, language development has been shown to be within age-appropriate parameters at 3 years, albeit at low-average levels (Yoshinaga-Itano, 2003); however, this evidence of benefit is not without its problems.

Early evidence of the benefits of UNHS was criticized for being derived from convenience samples harboring a selection bias (e.g., participants were drawn from those children enrolled in specific intervention programs), rather than being derived from controlled, population-based studies (Thompson, McPhillips, Davis, Lieu, Homer, & Hefland, 2001; Wake, Poulakis, Hughes, Carey-Sargeant, & Rickards, 2005). However, as research has progressed, overall developmental advantages in comparison with late-identified deaf children are being confirmed (Kennedy et al., 2006; Nelson, Bougatsos & Nygern, 2008), although the picture is becoming more differentiated. For example, a comparison of the vocalizations of early-identified infants with those of age-matched hearing children has demonstrated that at 10–16 months of age, the two groups did not differ significantly on parent-reported measures of receptive vocabulary. However, the deaf child group (with a mean pure tone average measured at 67dB HL) was found to be much slower to develop expressive vocabulary, and larger individual differences were found than in the hearing group (Moeller et al., 2007). A cohort study comparing, at a mean age of 7.9 years, 61 early-identified deaf children (defined as deafness confirmed ≤9 months of age) with 57 whose deafness was confirmed after 9 months of age, found that early identification was associated with higher scores for language, but not for speech (Kennedy et al., 2006). Thus, the claims that early identification will bring in its wake levels of spoken language development equivalent to hearing peers is not as clear as it might first have seemed, although the advantages in comparison with later-identified children are confirmed (Nelson et al., 2008).

However, any evidence of developmental benefits for early-identified deaf children is firmly predicated on the coexistence of quality early intervention to which the child and family has access from the earliest months of life and continuing throughout infancy (JCIH, 2000, 2007). Indeed, in many countries the implementation of UNHS has been a significant catalyst for the improvement of early support services for deaf children and their families.

The 2007 Joint Committee on Infant Hearing Position Statement offers principles and specific guidelines for early hearing detection and intervention (EHDI) programs as an integrated whole. Similarly, in the English context, the quality assurance mechanism for the newborn hearing screening program (NHSP, 2008) extends to include, within its remit, quality assurance of multiprofessional follow-up services, inspected on a national basis.

Many improvements in service provision for children and families have been born out of necessity. The provision of quality pediatric audiology services to very small infants, for example, poses some significant technical challenges in the accurate fitting and regular replacement of ear molds for very small and rapidly developing ears (McCracken, Young, & Tattersall, 2008). Other changes have taken the form of systemic rethinking what a comprehensive and quality multiprofessional system of support for families should look like (Stredler-Brown, 2005), and what additional skills professionals might need in working with very young babies. In this respect, the EHDI movement in the United States has pioneered the greater involvement of parents of deaf children as trained professional counselors supporting new parents, as self-advocates, and in taking lead roles in advisory boards, setting policies and standards with respect to family support (e.g. http://www.handsandvocies.org). Deaf and hard-of-hearing (DHH) professionals and parents in the United States and the United Kingdom are also starting to take a greater role in service provision. The JCIH (2007) statement specifically cites their inclusion as a quality marker for intervention services. Although Deaf mentor (Watkins, Pittman, & Walden, 1998) and Deaf role model (Sutherland, Griggs, & Young, 2003) services for families are nothing new, this is the first time their significance has been structurally acknowledged within national guidelines.

Early Identification: A Changing Context for Parents and Professionals

For hearing parents of deaf children, the circumstances in which and processes by which they will first encounter deafness in their family have also radically altered in the new age of routine early identification. This perspective is of course a professional one—new parents themselves are unlikely to be aware of the changed circumstances that shape their experience in comparison with parents of deaf children from what now appears a bygone age of "late" identification. Nonetheless, those circumstances are radically different in four fundamental respects. First, there is a changed discovery mechanism. It is now a routine and medically driven, "institution-initiated" (Luterman, 2001) process, rather than one that, in the vast majority of earlier cases, had been significantly informed by parental observation and discovery (Beazely & Moore, 1995; Gregory, 1976; Luterman & Kurtzer-White, 1999). Second, there is a highly compressed time scale between birth and identification of deafness. Third, the identification of deafness occurs at a much earlier stage of relationship formation between parent and child; it is integral to the earliest experiences of getting to know the new family member. Fourth, early intervention occurs very quickly in the child's life, intensively and essentially as part of the same process: birth–screening—identification—diagnosis—intervention.

There is also, for those professionals and services that parents of deaf children will encounter, a significant paradigm shift that is challenging practice. Research evidence on the developmental benefits of early identification and intervention frames deaf children within a discourse that emphasizes the graspable reality of normative achievement. This is a far cry from deficit models that expect significant delays and deficiencies in aspects of development. Thus, previous models of intervention that have sought to rescue families and children from the expected outcomes of less than optimal development are supplanted by approaches that emphasize the achievement of full potential and the reinforcement of competency.

However, despite the radical nature of these many changes associated with deaf children's early developmental context and the intensity of research activity, there remains a huge amount that is unknown about the impact and effects of the routine early identification of deafness. One of the areas in which we have least knowledge concerns the impact on the family of what we have characterized as the new circumstances surrounding the discovery of their child's deafness and the consequences for families of the changed basis (at least theoretically) on which professionals approach the job of family support and early intervention. Both concerns are of the highest relevance if one conceptualizes the potential benefits of early identification of deafness in terms of long- term quality of life for child and family, rather than in terms of specific impacts on particular aspects of the child's early developmental profile (Fitzpatrick, Graham, Durieux-Smith, Angus, & Coyle, 2007). In fact, not to think of the potential

benefits of UNHS in this way is to unlearn long-standing knowledge about deaf children's development; namely, the primary significance of the family environment in terms of its attitudinal, communicative, emotional, and social resources (Marschark, 1997). How these are shaped and challenged by very early knowledge of childhood deafness and its accompanying early intervention philosophies and structures thus becomes a critical question.

As Kurtzer-White and Luterman (2003) remark: "The emotional climate of the parent–child relationship is a necessary context for the unfolding of child development .... " (p. 232). A considerable literature exists on adjustment processes variously conceived according to a range of psychological and psychosocial models, including grief and loss (Kampfe, 1989; Luterman, 1999), stress and coping (Calderon & Greenberg, 1993), family systems theory (Harvey, 1985; Henderson & Henershott, 1991) and, more recently, trauma (Hunt, 2008). But, given the changed circumstances of when and how families discover their child's deafness, does our knowledge about processes of family adaptation and adjustment still hold true, or are there new considerations? Evidence is sparse and in some respects contradictory.

Grief, Loss, and Action
As far back as 2000, Siegel (cited by Yoshinaga-Itano & de Uzcategui, 2001) had suggested that earlier identification could lead to a quicker resolution of parental grief processes among hearing parents, based on a small pilot study of parents of early- and later-identified deaf children. However, the rationale and mechanisms whereby this should be the case remained unelaborated. By contrast, Kurtzer-White and Luterman (2003) have argued strongly that early identification does not fundamentally change parental grief processes, but it may engender new features affecting them. This assumption has been supported by two empirical studies of hearing parents of early-identified deaf children. Fitzpatrick et al. (2007) compared and contrasted the experiences of seven parents of early- and ten parents of late-identified deaf children and found no major differences in how they described the impact of the shock of discovery and subsequent emotional responses. Young and Tattersall (2007), in a study of 45 parents of early-identified deaf children also found that none described early identification in terms of having taken away the grief and shock they felt, nor of its having been lessened by knowing so early about their child's deafness. Parents described

the impact more in terms of a trade-off between the advantages of knowing so early about their child's deafness and distressing feelings that were bound to have happened at some point—it was just that they were happening earlier. The advantages were, in part, expressed in terms of time to come to terms with having a deaf child. However, interestingly, for some parents, this meant having more time to do things from an earlier point in the child's life to help their child, whereas for others knowing early created more time to get used to what was happening, but without the expectation of having to take specific actions themselves.

Certainly, a key parent-perceived benefit reported across a range of studies, whether of attitudes and expectations or of actual experience, is the advantage of being able to act early to mitigate likely effects of childhood deafness (Baringer & Mauk, 1997; Luterman & Kurtzer-White, 1999; Watkin, Beckwin, & Baldwin, 1995; Young & Andrews, 2001). This sense of positive action is reported both in terms of actions parents can take themselves to prepare for the road ahead and actions that professionals and service providers can take to ensure the best start for deaf babies, particularly in terms of communication development. However, the perceived advantages of early identification opening the way to early action is not unproblematic.

Young and Tattersall (2007) identified a subsample of parents for whom early identification had created expectations of swift professional action which, when not lived up to, caused considerable additional distress. That is to say, parents equated delays in service provision with actual harm because the advantages of early identification were thought of as being squandered. This is a very different kind of frustration from that previously commonly reported among parents of late-identified deaf children who may have been annoyed or distressed by knowing in retrospect that more could have been done if their child's deafness had been recognized earlier.

Parents of early-identified deaf children in this subsample of the Young and Tattersall (2007) study perceived their infants to be "losing ground," and it was the immediacy of this experience combined with the discourse about the beneficial effects of early identification that led parents to suffer considerable pressure and distress. Compare, for example, the views of two different parents cited in the study, one for whom early knowledge was positively useful in coming to terms with her child's deafness, one for whom early knowledge created the pressure of unfulfilled opportunities:

We just feel so lucky that she has been picked up, and we know that she's going to have as much help as she needs, and she's going to be able to do as much as she can with it being part of her life. [Mother of a 6-month-old]

The whole thing about this newborn hearing is that you tackle it at an early stage and basically get the nerve ending, the auditory nerve to sort of work at an early stage, and we haven't achieved that yet because we've not obtained … that level in the digital ear we should have … at the moment he is not benefiting at all, so we're still 4 months behind, we're still 4 months behind, we haven't benefited from this newborn hearing. [Father of a 4-month-old]

In their discussion of grief and adjustment processes, Young and Tattersall (2007) draw attention to the complex relationship between grief and action that is released in the new circumstances of early identification. Parents describe synchronous emotions of grief and being positive about having obtained the knowledge that led to the grief. The perceived benefits of early identification are manifestly obvious to parents in the opportunities created, *and* they can be emotionally precarious if they entail unrealistic or unfulfilled expectations of early action that engender additional pressure and distress.

Early identification neither eradicates nor necessarily lessens the usual processes of grief and loss experienced by hearing families, but it does provoke new and additional aspects to these processes, the nature of which we are only beginning to glimpse. Further evidence from parents is badly needed, particularly studies that involve parents over a long period of time, rather than in a snapshot manner in the earliest months of their adjustment. As DesGeorges (2003) has remarked, so-called "adjustment" is a life-long process whereby parents may make and unmake a host of decisions concerning their deaf children. She characterizes the end point not as acceptance, but as positive action in the form of advocacy for child and family alike.

Timing of Identification: Can It Be Too Early?

An early question in the development of UNHS was whether parents themselves would perceive any benefit in knowing about their child's deafness within the first few months of life. Studies done of attitudes in the general public and surveys of parents of deaf children in general, as well as those whose children had been identified early through targeted screening, all revealed the same result;

namely, that the overwhelming majority of parents would prefer to know at an early stage (Baringer & Mauk 1997; Luterman & Kurtzer-White, 1999; Watkin, Beckman, & Baldwin, 1995). The few studies that have been carried out with parents whose babies have been identified following UNHS have gone on to confirm these results (Fitzpatrick et al. 2007; Magnuson & Hergils, 1999; Young & Tattersall, 2005; Young & Tattersall, 2007).

In the Young and Tattersall (2007) sample, parents described how knowledge brought reassurance that, in turn, could serve to lessen distress. For some parents, this sense of reassurance was about certainty. They speculated on how guilty they might have felt in retrospect if they had not known their baby was deaf—for example, misconstruing an infant's behavior as naughtiness, or not realizing they needed to do extra things to make sure their baby could understand them. Avoiding the regret of missed opportunities was also a significant theme in the sample of parents of late-identified deaf children in the Fitzpatrick et al. (2007) study, who described the pain of retrospective knowledge, for example:

> And you know, we look back on her first birthday, and we see her and we're singing happy birthday, and realize she was never hearing any of that. I think wow, you know, you look at those videos, I can't watch them really, I have a hard time. (cited in Fitzpatrick et al., 2007, p. 101)

This evidence also serves to justify one of the early arguments for the benefits of UNHS. Namely, that the common experience of prolonged parental anxiety and stress that was often associated with what we would now term late diagnosis would be relieved (Canadian Working Group on Childhood Hearing [CWGCH], 2005). Parents previously have described protracted processes of discovery of their child's deafness that would include professionals disbelieving their observations of their own child, or children routinely "passing" a hearing test that depended on behavioral responses (such as turning to the source of a sound) only for parents to suspect differently (Russ et al., 2004).

However, there has always been an alternative way of thinking about this previously lengthy experience of discovery, in light of UNHS. One of the conditions associated with a protracted period of discovery was that diagnosis came as a confirmation in which parents had played a significant role (Luterman & Kurtzer-White, 1999). Their relationship with their child, over 2 years or (in some cases) more, was an essential element in the pathway to diagnosis; therefore, in some part, they "owned" the diagnosis too. Therefore one of the new questions posed early in the implementation of UNHS programs was what the effect would be of parents not being part of that discovery process, if instead it were overtaken by a routine medical process? A difference Luterman and Kurtzer White (1999) refer to as: "a paradigm shift in the identification process from one that is parent-driven to one that is system-driven" (p. 4). It has also been suggested that knowing early may be too early for some parents (Gregory, 1999; Luterman & Kurtzer-White, 1999) and may actually interfere with the normal processes of early bonding (Yoshinaga-Itano & de Uzcategui, 2003). In effect, parents are unable to enjoy their newborn as their baby before they have to engage with both the knowledge of deafness and the services and professionals that come with that knowledge.

Fitzpatrick et al. (2007) found that parents were equivocal about the impact on bonding of the early detection of their babies' deafness. Some parents in both the early- and late-identified groups would have preferred to have time just to know their baby as a baby and to adjust to being a parent first. Similarly, in the Young and Tattersall sample (2005, 2007), some parents found early knowledge of their child's deafness distressing, and they would have preferred to have had more time before professionals became involved and they had to deal with a host of new considerations on top of being new parents. But in both studies, this point of view was not universal and did not supersede the stronger parental views of the advantages for their children of early detection. However, the variation in parental responses does raise a question of timing: Does early identification of deafness have to mean confirmation by 3 months, or is this too early?

The JCIH (2007) is unequivocal in its support of confirmation by 3 months of age as a primary condition of effective hearing screening, based on the weight of evidence of the language gains for early-identified children and in line with the goals embodied in Healthy People 2010 (US Department of Health and Human Services, 2000). Indeed, one of the revisions between the 2000 and 2007 JCIH statement was to revise the recommendation down from confirmation by 6 months of age to confirmation by 3 months of age. However, one could argue that the primary justification for this position is derived from evidence of outcomes in one sphere only—namely, functional language. The recent systematic review to update the 2001 preventative services task force recommendation on UNHS (Nelson et al., 2008) points out that other functional outcomes may also be of relevance to parents, such as quality of life.

Clearly, initial attention has been paid to outcomes in the domains of language and communication because these serve as an essential gateway to sociodevelopmental and cognitive growth. Yoshinaga-Itano et al. (1998a,b) found, for example, that early-identified deaf children had significantly higher personal social skills development, as measured by the Minnesota Child Development Inventory, in comparison with later-identified (>6 months of age) deaf children. However, as discussed earlier, it is the family context that, in the earliest years, will have an enormous influence on the realization of that developmental potential initiated by early detection and intervention. Therefore, failure to attend comprehensively to questions such as the effect on family adjustment processes and family functioning of early knowledge of childhood deafness obscures our assessment of the benefits and disadvantages of UNHS, including the question of whether identification at 3 months is too early.

That said, the significance of the ongoing effects of childhood deafness on the family (and whether this is different for families of early-identified deaf children) is beginning to be considered. The most recent statement of the implications of routine early detection of childhood deafness for developmental research (Eisenberg, Widen, Yoshinago-Itano, Norton, Thal, Niparko, & Vohr, 2007) includes "Parenting stress and impact of hearing loss on the family" (p. 775) as a key outcome domain in studies across all age spans from birth onward. Also, the impact of intervention on outcome as a function of parental psychosocial factors is clearly flagged as a central question for developmental outcomes research in the future. It may yet take several years of prospective studies with families of early-identified deaf children to answer worries about whether early identification is just too early for some families, and whether, ethically, there could be any justification for a delay when the advantages for children's language development are so evident.

Envisioning Childhood Deafness: The Influence of Early Identification

The first US systematic review of evidence in support of UNHS (Thompson et al., 2001) drew attention to the link between early detection of deafness, theoretical approaches to language development, and the favoring of particular strategies for management. In essence, it pointed out the risk of linking early detection with strategies to support the development of speech, as if the connection between the two were self-evident. Based on the evidence of the time, Thompson et al. concluded that the connection is not axiomatic:

> The argument for early intervention is based on the prevailing theory of language development, which holds that early auditory input is an important precursor of language development. An opposing viewpoint suggests that, during infancy, nonverbal communication, joint attention, shared experiences, and mutual understanding are more important precursors of language development than are hearing speech and forming sounds. Proponents of this view theorize that early intervention could harm infants because it leads parents to focus on "means of communication the child has the least prerequisites for" and on the child's disability instead of his or her competencies. Because there are no randomized trials of different management strategies, it is impossible to assess the merits of these concerns. (p. 2007)

Yet, the recently published list of recommended domains to be taken into consideration when conducting research on early-identified children (Eisenberg et al., 2007) privileges speech production and intelligibility and spoken word recognition, while failing to mention specifically sign language development. This emphasis exists despite the conclusion of the updated systematic review of evidence for UNHS (Nelson et al., 2008) that cautions:

> No studies addressed the potential adverse effects of early treatment using hearing aids, American Sign Language, English instruction, speech and language therapy, or family education and support. (p. e272)

The purpose in drawing attention to these points is not to reopen old arguments about the superiority or inferiority of one approach or another to language development, nor to take an anti-speech, pro-sign position. The purpose is to demonstrate the extent to which the discourse of screening and early detection is closely allied with that of deaf children developing through hearing and speaking. In terms, therefore, of the impact on parents of early identification of deafness, a key question is whether and how it might influence the choices they make about approaches to language development for their child.

For some authors (e.g. Luterman & Kurtzer-White 1999; Kurtzer-White & Luterman, 2003; Young & Tattersall, 2007), this question is bound up with trying to understand whether a diagnosis of deafness occurring as a result of a routine health technology procedure and with the condition of *early* detection, has an influence on parents' understanding of deafness itself. As previous work has pointed out, how parents develop their understanding of what it is to be deaf and how they envision their own particular child's deafness has a profound impact on the choices they make about family support and desired approaches to early intervention (Young, 2002). So, does the knowledge of deafness as a result of a systems-driven process really have a discernible effect on shaping parents' expectations and understandings?

Young and Tattersall (2007) attempted to investigate this issue through an analysis of how hearing parents of early-identified deaf children talked about their children's likely communication development. Parents in the sample were interviewed when their children were on average 25 weeks old, with a range of 8 to 51 weeks. All had been early identified and all were involved in early intervention programs. They found that the majority of parents regarded early detection as enabling normal language development, where normal was defined almost exclusively in terms of speaking and hearing. This trend was found regardless of the degree of deafness of the children concerned. For some of the parents in the sample, there was an obvious connection with the medical framework through which their children's deafness had been detected. Parents used metaphors that likened the early detection of deafness to the early detection of illness. The earlier found, the more likely it is that the problem might be cured or fixed (where "fixed" was taken to mean "make hearing"). For example:

> It was a kind of reassuring thing … they are the ones that told us because we have caught, you know *caught it early* … then you know the chances of her going to a mainstream school and speaking normally are so much better. So they put that positive thought in your head kind of things, which is obviously what you want to hear, but it's not that you just need to hear it, you know it's the truth. [Mother of a 5-month-old profoundly deaf child, emphasis added]

The researchers were also able to document the influence, for some parents, of the discourse of the professionals they encountered. Parents recounted horror stories they had been told of the days before early identification, which demonstrated how poor many deaf children's development had been in the past, and how, by comparison, much better the opportunities their own children would have.

As [the Teacher of the Deaf] says, the children who are picked up when they are 6 or 7 months old, you have to teach them to listen, whereas he's actually just come along with it, he knows how to listen … so it's just like all positive, and she said like because Michael is so young being picked up, we expect him to be even more sort of normal … he's not missed out on 10 months of noise, we haven't got to make up for that. [Mother of a 5-month-old, severely deaf child]

Young and Tattersall (2007) concluded that these responses from hearing parents are entirely understandable. The twin emphases of the earliness of detection and it occurring within a routine medical procedure quite obviously reinforce the notion of deafness as a biophysiological problem (an impairment) to be overcome. The real question is how other parents and professionals may assist in developing new parents' understanding beyond these initial assumptions, to enable their exploration of the complexities of what it is to be deaf and how deafness is understood.

However, Young and Tattersall (2007) regarded as more worrying the long-term consequences of parents' earliest assumptions about normal achievement, where "normal" was almost universally assumed to mean "as if hearing." With one exception, there was no early awareness that deaf children will develop characteristically as deaf children (whether one is referring to spoken or signed language), and may have different learning patterns and cognitive strengths and vulnerabilities in comparison with their hearing peers (Marschark, Convertiono, & LaRock, 2006). In other words, no awareness was expressed that deaf children may reach the same levels of developmental achievement as their hearing peers, but that the pathways to those achievements may be different. Normal as "differently achieved" was not the dominant discourse.

This simultaneous potential and danger of early detection for how hearing parents envision their child's deafness, its consequences, and the basis of their decision making within early intervention, were recognized early on in such pioneering initiatives as the Colorado Home Intervention Program (Stredler-Brown, 2005). This program has emphasized the potential that is unlocked by early identification, in that parents have more time to get used to the diagnosis, to consider their options, and to try out a range of different approaches to language development. The early intervention program includes a period of supportive counseling and information given *before* a parent becomes associated with choosing any specific approach to language development. It offers parents a "taster menu" of the different kinds of language support their child may receive. Deaf adult role models with a wide variety of preferred language(s) interact with families. Parents have the possibility of changing their minds at any point and trying alternative approaches to support and language development. This latter point is particularly emphasized by the parent-led organization Hands and Voices, that originally grew up connected with the Colorado program, but which is now active throughout the United States (http://www.handsandvoices.org), with chapters in other countries, such as Canada. They stress the preeminence of choice based on what works for the child and the family in their specific circumstances, rather than based on any particular orthodoxy. As one of the parent-founders writes:

> We've come to understand that it is not the child who "fails" with a method, but the methods can fail the child and family …. Hands & Voices developed this slogan to articulate our philosophy that "what makes the choice work for your child and family is what makes the choice right." (Seaver, 2004, unpaginated)

Legitimate concerns clearly do exist about the influence of the new medical context in which childhood deafness is identified. The linking of early detection with speech and "development-like-a-hearing child" is a powerful discourse. However, early identification is also proving the catalyst for a new generation of early interventions aimed at supporting parental exploration of a host of developmental support options for deaf children, promoting family-centered decision making (Sass-Lehrer & Bodner-Johnson, 2003), and emphasizing the significance of informed choice (Young, Carr, Hunt, Tattersall, & McCracken, 2008).

Summary and Conclusions

This chapter has looked critically at the impact of early identification of deafness on hearing parents' experience. It has drawn attention to the importance of moving on from evidence of the effectiveness of early identification that is based on functional language and communication outcomes, to evidence that is based more holistically on quality of life in the context of the family environment. It has challenged overly simplistic notions of the positive benefits for grief resolution and negative concerns about

bonding. Although evidence is sparse, parents clearly attest to the new challenges in each of these domains, thus forcing a reexamination of both research knowledge and practice wisdom. Finally, the basic idea that early intervention is needed for the potential gains of early identification to be achieved has been further developed to consider its significance in enabling parents to move on from their first encounter with deafness as a medically derived fact and to explore its complexities for decision making on family terms.

It is quite clear that, from a research perspective, there is still much to be discovered about the impact on hearing families of the early identification of childhood deafness. Prospective longitudinal data are lacking that focus firmly on the family environment and trace the development of the whole family, not just the developmental outcomes of the child. The impact of early identification on how hearing parents adjust to childhood deafness over time is almost completely unknown. The few parent-centered studies that have been carried out have begun to demonstrate the potential for further work of this kind in informing the future development of early intervention and follow-on services for deaf children and their families yet to come.

References

Apuzzo, M.L., &Yoshinaga–Itano, C. (1995). Early identification of infants with significant hearing loss and the Minnesota Child Development Inventory. *Seminars in Hearing, 16,* 124–137.

Baringer, D.G., & Mauk, G.W. (1997). Survey of parents' perception regarding hospital-based newborn hearing screening. *Audiology Today, 9*(1), 18–19.

Beazley, S., & Moore, M. (1995). *Deaf children, their families and other professionals.* London: David Fulton.

Calderon, L., & Greenberg, M. (1993). Considerations in the adaption of families with school-aged deaf children. In M. Marschark & H. Clark (Eds.), *Psychological perspectives on deafness.* Hillsdale, NJ: Laurence Erlbaum Associates.

Canadian Working Group on Childhood Hearing (2005). *Early hearing and communication development: Canadian Working Group on Childhood Hearing (CWGCH) Resource Document.* Ottawa: Minister of Public Works and Government Services Canada.

Davis, A., Bamford, J., Wilson, I. Ramkalawan, T., Forshaw, M., & Wright, S. (1997). A critical review of the role of neonatal hearing screening in the detection of congenital hearing impairment. *Health Technology Assessment, 1*(10).

DesGeorges, J. (2003). Family perceptions of early hearing, detection and intervention systems: Listening to and learning from families. *Mental Retardation Developmental Disability Research Review, 9*(2), 89–93.

Eisenberg, L. Widen, J. E., Yoshinaga-Itano, C., Norton, S. Thal, D., Niparko, J. K., & Vohr, B. (2007). Current state of knowledge: implications for developmental research – key issues. *Ear and Hearing, 28*(6), 773–777.

Fitzpatrick, E., Graham, I. D., Durieux-Smith, A., Angus, D., & Coyle, D. (2007). Parents' perspectives on the impact of the early diagnosis of childhood hearing loss. *International Journal of Audiology*, 46, 97–106.

Gregory, S. (1976). *The deaf child and his family*. London: George Allen and Unwin.

Harvey, M. A. (1985). Toward a dialogue between the paradigms of family therapy and deafness. *American Annals of the Deaf*, 130, 305–314.

Henderson D., & Hendershott, A. (1991). ASL and the family system. *American Annals of the Deaf*, 136, 325–329.

Hunt, R. (2008). The Early Support Monitoring Protocol for deaf children: An evaluation in practice. Unpublished doctoral dissertation, University of Manchester. Joint Committee on Infant Hearing (2000). Year 2000 position statement: Principles and guidelines for early hearing detection and intervention programs. *Pediatrics*, 106, 798–817.

Joint Committee on Infant Hearing. (2007). Year 2007 position statement: Principles and guidelines for early hearing detection and intervention. Retrieved September 15, 2008 from http://www.asha.org/policy

Kampfe, C. M. (1989). Parental reaction to a child's hearing impairment. *American Annals of the Deaf*, 134, 255–259.

Kennedy, C. R., McCann, D. C., Campbell, M. J., Law, C. M., Mullee, M., Petrou, S., et al. (2006). Language ability after early detection of permanent child hearing impairment. *The New England Journal of Medicine*, 354(20), 2131–2141.

Kurtzer-White, E., & Luterman, D. (2003). Families and children with hearing loss: Grief and coping. *Mental Retardation and Developmental Disabilities Research Reviews*, 9, 232–235.

Luterman, D. (1999). Counselling families with a hearing impaired child. *Otolaryngologic Clinics of North America*, 32, 1037–1050.

Luterman, D. (2001). Closing remarks. In E. Kurtzer-White & D. Luterman, (Eds.), *Early childhood deafness* (pp. 149–155). Baltimore: York Press.

Luterman, D., & Kurtzer-White, E. (1999). Identifying hearing loss: Parents' needs. *American Journal of Audiology*, 8, 13–18.

Magnuson, M., & Hergils, L. (1999). The parents' view on hearing screening in newborns: Feelings, thoughts and opinions on otoacoustic emissions screening. *Scandinavian Audiology*, 28(1), 47–56.

Marschark. M. (1997). *Raising and educating a deaf child*. Oxford: Oxford University Press.

Marschark, M., Convertiono, C., & LaRock, D. (2006). Optimizing academic performance of deaf students: Access, opportunities, and outcomes. In D. F. Moores & D. S. Martin (Eds.), *Deaf learners: New developments in curriculum and instruction* (pp. 179–200) Washington, DC: Gallaudet University Press.

Mayne, A. M., Yoshinaga-Itano, C., & Sedey, A. L. (1998). Receptive vocabulary development of infants and toddlers who are deaf and hard of hearing. *The Volta Review*, 100, 29–52.

Mayne, A. M., Yoshinaga-Itano, C., Sedey, A. L., & Carey, A. (1998). Expressive vocabulary development of infants and toddlers who are deaf and hard of hearing. *The Volta Review*, 100, 1–28.

McCracken, W., Young, A. M., & Tattersall, H. (2008). Universal newborn hearing screening: Parental reflections on early audiological management. *Ear and Hearing*, 29(1), 54–64.

Moeller, M. P., Hoover, B., Putman, C., Arbataitis, K., Bohnenkamp, G., Peterson, B., et al. (2007). Vocalizations of infants with hearing loss compares with infants with normal hearing: Transitions to words. *Ear and Hearing*, 28(5), 628–642.

Nelson, H., Bougatsos, B. S., & Nygern, P. (2008). Universal Newborn Hearing Screening: systematic review to update the 2001 US preventative services task force recommendation. *Pediatrics*, 122(1), e266–e276.

NHSP (2008). NHS newborn hearing screening programme quality assurance report 2006–2008. Retrieved October 25, 2008 from http://hearing.screening.nhs.uk/QA_Reports

Pipp-Siegel, S., Sedey, A. L., Van Leeuwen, A. M., & Yoshinaga-Itano, C. (2003). Mastery motivation and expressive language in young children with hearing loss. *Journal of Deaf Studies and Deaf Education*, 8, 133–145.

Russ, S. A., Kuo, A. A., Poulakis, Z., Marker, M., Rickards, F., Saunders, K., et al. (2004). Qualitative analysis of parents' experience with early detection of hearing loss. *Archives of Disease in Childhood*, 89, 353–358.

Sass-Lehrer, M., & Bodner-Johnson, B. (2003). Early intervention: Current approaches to family-centred programming. In M. Marschark & P. E. Spencer (Eds.), *The Oxford Handbook of Deaf Studies, Language and Education* (pp. 65–81). New York: Oxford University Press.

Seaver, L.: (2004). Hands and Voices: supporting families without bias. Retrieved November 9, 2008 from http://www.handsandvoices.org

Siegel, S. (2000). *Resolution of grief of parents with young children and hearing loss*. Unpublished manuscript. Boulder, CO: University of Colorado.

Stredler-Brown, A. (2005). Family-centered intervention: Proven strategies to assure positive outcomes. In R. Seewald & J. Bamford (Eds.), *A sound foundation through early amplification 2004, proceedings of the third international conference*. (pp. 185–196). London: Cambrian Printers Ltd.

Sutherland, H., Griggs, M., & Young, A. M. (2003). Deaf adult role models in family intervention services. In C. Gallaway & A. M. Young (Eds.), *Deafness and education in the UK: Research perspectives*. London: Whurr.

Thompson, D. C., McPhillips, H., Davis, R. L., Lieu, T. L., Homer, C. J., & Hefland, M. (2001). Universal newborn hearing screening: Summary of evidence. *JAMA*, 286, 2000–2010.

US Department of Health and Human Services, Office of Disease Prevention and Health Promotion (2000). *Healthy People 2010. Vol. II: Objectives for improving health*, 2nd edition. Rockville, MD: Author.

Uus, K., & Bamford, J. (2006). Effectiveness of population-based newborn hearing screening in England: Ages of intervention and profile of cases. *Pediatrics*, 117(5), e887–e893.

Wake, M., Poulakis, Z., Hughes, E. K., Carey-Sargeant, C., & Rickards, F. W. (2005). Hearing impairment: A population study of age at diagnosis, severity, and language outcomes at 7–8 years. *Archives of Disease in Childhood*, 90, 238–244.

Watkin, P. M., Beckman, A., & Baldwin, M. (1995). The views of parents of hearing impaired children on the need for neonatal hearing screening. *British Journal of Audiology*, 29(5), 259–262.

Watkins, S., Pittman, P., & Walden, B. (1998). The deaf mentor experimental project for young children who are deaf and their families. *American Annals of the Deaf*, 143(1), 29–34.

Yoshinaga-Itano, C. (2001). The social-emotional ramifications of universal newborn hearing screening. Early identification and intervention of children who are deaf or hard of hearing.

In R. Seewald & J. Bamford (Eds.), *Proceedings of the second international pediatric conference: A sound foundation through early amplification.* Stafa, Switzerland: Phonak. Retrieved September 15, 2008 from http://www.phonak.com/professional/informationpool/proceedings2001.htm

Yoshinaga-Itano, C. (2003). From screening to early identification and intervention: Discovering predictors to successful outcomes for children with significant hearing loss. *Journal of Deaf Studies and Deaf Education, 8*(1) 11–30.

Yoshinaga-Itano, C., & Apuzzo, M. L. (1998a). The development of deaf and hard of hearing children identified though the high-risk registry. *American Annals of the Deaf, 143*, 416–424.

Yoshinaga-Itano, C., & Apuzzo, M. L. (1998b). Identification of hearing loss after age 18 months is not early enough. *American Annals of the Deaf, 143*, 380–387.

Yoshinaga-Itano, C., Sedey, A., Coulter, D., & Mehl, A. L. (1998). Language of early- and later- identified children with hearing loss. *Pediatrics, 102*, 1161–71.

Yoshinaga-Itano, C., & de Uzcategui, C. A. (2001). Early identification and social-emotional factors of children with hearing loss and children screened for hearing loss. In E. Kurtzer-White & D. Luterman, (Eds.), *Early childhood deafness* (pp. 13–28). Baltimore: York Press.

Yoshinaga-Itano, C., Coulter, D., & Thomson, V. (2001). Developmental outcomes of children with hearing loss born in Colorado hospitals with and without universal newborn hearing screening programs. *Seminars in Neonatology, 6*, 521–529.

Young, A. M. (2002) Parents of deaf children: Factors affecting communication choice in the first year of life. *Deafness and Education International, 4*(1), 1–12.

Young, A. M., & Andrews, E. (2001). Parents' experience of universal neonatal hearing screening: A critical review of the literature and its implications for the implementation of new UNHS programs. *Journal of Deaf Studies and Deaf Education, 6*(3), 149–160.

Young, A. M., & Tattersall, H. (2005). Parent of deaf children's evaluative accounts of the process and practice of universal newborn hearing screening. *Journal of Deaf Studies and Deaf Education, 10*(2), 1–12.

Young, A. M., & Tattersall, H. (2007). Universal Newborn Hearing Screening and early identification of deafness: Parents' responses to knowing early and their expectations of child communication development. *Journal of Deaf Studies and Deaf Education, 12*(2), 209–220.

Young, A. M., Carr, G., Hunt, R., Tattersall, H., & McCracken, W. (2008). Informed choice and families with deaf children. In R. Seewold & J. Bamford (Eds.), *A sound foundation through early amplification 2004, proceedings of the fourth international conference* (pp. 107–117). London: Cambrian Printers Ltd.

How Does Speech Intelligibility Affect Self and Others' Perceptions of Deaf and Hard-of-Hearing People?

Tova Most

Abstract

The extent to which a deaf person's spoken language is intelligible to hearing listeners is an essential component of spoken language communication, influencing both the quality and the success of interactions. Beyond affecting the ability to communicate ideas, feelings, and experiences efficiently and successfully, speech intelligibility may also have an impact on interpersonal functioning and on others' perceptions of the speaker.

Many deaf and hard-of-hearing (DHH) persons have voice and speech characteristics that affect their speech intelligibility. As a result of special education laws and recent technological developments with regard to sensory aids and assistive listening devices, DHH children are predominantly included in classes with hearing peers, where spoken language is the primary mode of communication. For DHH children, therefore, analysis of the effects of spoken language intelligibility on social interactions is of special importance. Accordingly, this chapter examines the ability of DHH individuals at different ages and in various educational programs to use spoken language for communication. More generally, it addresses the impact of speech intelligibility on the lives of DHH individuals. It focuses on how speech intelligibility affects others' attitudes toward these individuals, as well as ways in which it affects their own emotional states, social relationships, and perspectives on occupational competencies.

Keywords: speech intelligibility, deaf and hard of hearing, attitudes, emotional and social functioning

As a result of their hearing loss, many deaf and hard-of-hearing (DHH) individuals have specific voice and speech characteristics that differ from those of hearing people. For example, DHH persons tend to omit or substitute consonants and to neutralize vowels, they may have monotonous speech, and their voices may be characterized by inappropriate resonance, pitch, or intensity (Eisenberg, 2007; Monsen, 1983; Most & Frank, 1994; Peng, Tomblin, & Turner, 2008). In recent years, the use of improved sensory aids, such as digital hearing aids, FM systems, and especially cochlear implants has enabled better speech perception, at least in instances of low background noise, among individuals with severe and profound hearing loss. Yet problems remain, and these technological advances still fail to provide

access to complete auditory information like that available through natural hearing. Information is especially degraded in noisy environments (Pisoni, 2000; Spencer & Marschark, 2003; see Chapter 25, this volume). Despite these as-yet unresolved difficulties, use of devices such as cochlear implants have been able to support great improvements in the speech produced by deaf individuals, compared with those with a similar degree of hearing loss who use only hearing aids (e.g., Blamey et al., 2001; Meyer, Svirsky, Kirk, & Miyamoto, 1998; Osberger, Fisher, Zimerman-Phillips, Geiger, & Barker, 1998). However, the aforementioned speech characteristics persist among many individuals with severe and profound hearing loss. For example, Blamey et al. (2001) found that, 4 years after cochlear implantation, the speech production performance of children with profound hearing impairment only improved to the level of children with severe hearing loss who used hearing aids.

The specific characteristics typifying the speech of DHH individuals—including segmental (e.g., phoneme omissions and substitutions), suprasegmental (e.g., monotonous intonation), and voice quality (e.g., breathiness or harshness) characteristics—may affect the ability of others to comprehend them (Bench, 1992; McGarr, 1987; Monsen, 1983). Due to the resulting poor speech intelligibility, it is unsurprising that DHH individuals may therefore encounter difficulties in communicating ideas through spoken language. In addition to impeding communication, difficulties in speech intelligibility may also affect a range of other domains.

The Spread Effect

Since the 1960s, researchers have documented a phenomenon known as "the spread effect," in which people perceive that someone has a certain dominant quality and then base their entire evaluation of that person on that initial perception (Asch, 1964; Wright, 1983). In fact, some personal characteristics such as age, sex, and mood (Raphael, Borden, & Harris, 2007) can realistically be inferred from individuals' voice characteristics. Accordingly, hearing listeners tend to evaluate people based on how they sound (Kappas, Hess, & Sherer, 1991; Markel, Eisler, & Reese, 1967; Sherer & Ekman, 1982). At the same time, listeners tend to overgeneralize (spread) the meaning of the voice to individuals' other qualities like appearance, intelligence, or achievements, based solely on how those individuals sound and speak, despite the lack of an empirical basis for these inferences (Sherer & Ekman, 1982).

As will be shown subsequently, as a result of the fact that DHH individuals' voice and speech characteristics often differ from those of speakers with normal hearing, and because listeners' evaluations of speakers' personalities are influenced by speakers' oral language, speakers with hearing loss are generally evaluated less positively than hearing speakers. These perceptions, in turn, can affect a DHH individual's interpersonal world.

Listener's Extent of Experience

One issue related to the degree to which speech is understood, and thus to its effect on attitudes of listeners toward speakers, is the listener's experience level. Listeners who are more familiar with the speech of DHH people ("experienced listeners")

may be less preoccupied by its atypical characteristics, and more able to focus on and use redundant contextual information to help them understand the speech. Consequently, several researchers have shown that experienced listeners generally show better understanding in comparison to naïve, inexperienced listeners (Boothroyd, 1985; Klimacka, Patterson, & Patterson, 2001; McGarr, 1983; Monsen, 1983). It may be hypothesized that experienced listeners will evaluate DHH individuals more positively because such listeners can understand them better.

It should be noted that previous research on attitudes has demonstrated that familiarity with other populations, for example, people with physical disabilities, positively affects attitudes toward that population (Yuker, 1988). Additional research is needed to unravel the complex question of whether more positive evaluations of speakers' personal qualities among experienced versus inexperienced listeners stem not only from better speech intelligibility but also from a more general attitude change in experienced listeners as they become more familiar with DHH individuals over time.

Regular and Special Education

The effects of listeners' experience level on speech intelligibility ratings, as well as on attitudes, are particularly important regarding children in the educational system. Currently, the majority of DHH children are integrated with hearing children within regular schools. In Israel, for example, 80% of the DHH children (including those with severe and profound hearing loss) are included in regular education classrooms, 15% attend group inclusion programs (special classes located in a regular school and integrated partially with a regular class, either as a group or individually), and only 5% attend special schools (Zandberg, 2005). This movement toward integrating DHH and hearing students is also evident elsewhere (e.g., Karchmer & Mitchell, 2003; Power & Hyde, 2002; see Chapter 6, this volume). The current predominance of individual inclusion results from two trends: recent intensive efforts to implement special education laws that call for maximum inclusion (e.g., Al-Yagon & Margalit, 2001) and recent technological developments in sensory aids and assistive listening devices (hearing aids, cochlear implants, and FM systems), which have substantially improved use of the auditory channel (Anderson & Goldstein, 2004; Bentler, Wu, Kettel, & Hurting, 2008; Moog & Geers, 1999). As a result of these technological developments, many DHH children who previously could not use their residual hearing functionally have become candidates for auditory habilitation or rehabilitation, and therefore may successfully acquire spoken language. Education systems, therefore, are now increasingly including these children in regular classes with hearing peers, where spoken language comprises the mode of communication. Thus, many DHH children are exposed to inexperienced listeners, both adults such as teachers and the hearing children with whom they study.

Effects of Speech Intelligibility on Attitudes Toward Deaf and Hard-of-Hearing Speakers

Several studies have been conducted to examine the effects of speech intelligibility on listeners' evaluations of personal qualities and the effects of listeners' experience on speech intelligibility ratings as well as personal qualities (Most, Weisel, & Lev-Matezky, 1996; Most, Weisel, & Tur-Kaspa, 1999). In one study (Most et al., 1996), the listeners were 60 adults differing in their level of experience with DHH individuals. The 30 inexperienced listeners had no close relationships with DHH people. The 30 experienced listeners were professionals, either speech and language clinicians or teachers of the deaf, who had worked with children with hearing loss for at least 2 years. The listeners were introduced to recorded speech materials, comprising a text that had been read aloud by children who differed in their hearing status and their speech intelligibility. The recorded children were all asked to read the same text aloud in order to prevent language level as a confounding variable in ratings by listeners. None of the children had any reading difficulties.

The listeners were asked to listen to the speech recordings in random order and to rate each speaker's personal qualities using a semantic differential scale of bipolar adjective pairs. Listeners were asked to choose the adjective in each pair that best described the speaker's cognitive competence (e.g., successful-loser; intelligent-stupid) and personality traits (e.g., daring-hesitant; fearless-fearful; independent-dependent). At the end of the listening session, they listened once again to the same recorded passages but in a different random order and were asked to rate each speaker's speech intelligibility on a 6-point rating scale, ranging from very poor intelligibility (1) to very good intelligibility (6).

In a second study using the same procedure (Most et al., 1999), 140 hearing high school students, who differed in their level of exposure to DHH individuals, first listened to the speech recordings, then evaluated each of the recorded children's cognitive competence and personality based on based on those recordings, and finally rated each recording's speech intelligibility along the aforementioned 6-point scale. The 70 experienced listeners in this study were students who attended a comprehensive high school that included DHH students. To ensure that all these students had significant exposure to the speech of the students with hearing loss, only those hearing students who had at least two DHH students as classmates were included in this group. The inexperienced listener group consisted of 70 students in a general education high school, none of whom had previous contact with DHH individuals.

Results of the study with *adult* listeners showed that those classified as "experienced" tended to rate DHH speakers' speech as more intelligible than did those classified as "inexperienced." In contrast, no such difference emerged between the "experienced" and "inexperienced" high school *student* listeners. Students in both groups evaluated the recorded DHH children's speech intelligibility similarly. In a comparison between the high school students' and the adults' ratings of speech intelligibility, it was noted that, *overall, the experienced adults gave higher rating scores than the students*, whereas among the inexperienced listeners, the students gave higher rating scores than the adults.

The researchers attributed this incongruence to the different amounts of experience between the "experienced" listeners in the two studies. The adult "experienced" listeners had worked with and treated DHH individuals on a regular basis as part of their profession (Most et al., 1996) and therefore had extensive experience. This gave them a genuine advantage in comprehending the speech of children with hearing loss. By contrast, the high school students classified as "experienced" typically had contact with DHH speakers only in the classroom environment and thus did not have ongoing and intensive exposure to their DHH classmates' speech. As a result, the experienced high school listeners did not have as big an experiential difference from "inexperienced" high school listeners as was the case between experienced and "inexperienced" adult listeners (Most et al., 1999). These outcomes on speech intelligibility suggest that the mere presence of classmates with hearing loss did not necessarily turn hearing students into more experienced listeners. In other words, the real exposure of the hearing students to the speech of their peers with hearing loss may have been quite limited, in spite of their presence in the same classroom.

These results raise important questions with regard to the nature of everyday school life for DHH students in mainstream programs. Does real, significant social interaction occur between hearing students and DHH students? Other research studies that addressed the social aspect directly have shown that mainstreamed students with hearing loss are often socially isolated, mainly because of difficulties with oral communication (Antia, Kreimeyer, & Eldredge, 1993; Bat-Chava & Deignan, 2001; Markides, 1989; Stinson, Whitmore, & Kluwin, 1996; Strong & Shaver, 1991). For example, Stinson et al. reported that, although mainstreamed DHH adolescents were surrounded by hearing peers, their contact did not appear to promote mutual identification or relational bonds. These authors also claimed that in situations offering an opportunity for joint participation, the quality of the adolescents' relationships was not necessarily positive. Likewise, although hearing college students' perceived their DHH classmates' placement on shared college campuses as successful for education purposes, they reported that full social integration did not occur (Brown & Foster, 1989; Foster & Brown, 1989). The DHH students themselves experienced separation and even isolation. In another study on the socialization experiences of deaf adults who were raised using spoken language, most respondents reported some level of social isolation because of limitations in communicating with hearing peers (Bain, Scott, & Steinberg, 2004). Future studies should further assess the specifics of behavior that increase communication and interaction between these students.

Speech Intelligibility's Links with Perceived Personal Qualities

Results of the two studies showed similar results with regard to the effect of speech intelligibility on the personal evaluations of speakers by the experienced and inexperienced listeners. For inexperienced listeners, both adults and high school students, a linear relationship emerged between speech intelligibility evaluations and personal evaluations (both regarding cognitive competence and personality). Thus, as speech intelligibility decreased, the evaluations of inexperienced listeners became more negative.

Ratings by the experienced listeners did not show this linear trend between perceived intelligibility and personal evaluations. Although experienced listeners, both adults and high school students, differentiated between speech intelligibility of moderate and poor speakers, they made no such differentiation on personal characteristics. Both moderately intelligible and poorly intelligible speakers were characterized similarly—but less positively than the

more intelligible speakers. Thus, experienced listeners did not show the fine gradations in evaluation of personal characteristics within the range of moderate to poor intelligibility that were shown by the inexperienced listeners. With regard to inexperienced listeners, the "spread effect" phenomenon was evident, but this effect was not as linearly related to intelligibility for the experienced listeners. Gradations within the entire range of intelligibility of speech of individuals with hearing loss had a major and consistent effect on inexperienced listeners' stereotyped perceptions and judgments of their personal characteristics. Moderately intelligible speakers were rated somewhat higher personally, and intelligible speakers were given even higher ratings on personal characteristics.

Exposure to DHH individuals did seem to change the way they were perceived, because the experienced listeners did not attribute more negative personal qualities to those speakers whose message could not be understood at all (i.e., those with poor intelligibility) than to speakers whose message was moderately but not completely intelligible. The experienced listeners, nevertheless, viewed the moderately and poorly intelligible speakers more negatively than they did the speakers with good intelligibility. Thus, experience seemed to reduce the spread effect phenomenon and to elicit generally more positive perceptions, but stereotypical negative attitudes continued to be expressed even by experienced hearing listeners when speech was not completely intelligible.

The fact that these differences between experienced and inexperienced listeners held true for the high school students as well suggests that hearing students' exposure to mainstreamed DHH students affected how they evaluated the personalities of their DHH peers, even if it did not improve the ability to understand their communications. This finding offers further support to studies showing that mainstreaming rendered a somewhat but limited positive effect on attitudes toward individuals with hearing loss (Weisel, 1989). Because speakers' speech intelligibility was similarly rated by both groups of high school listeners (experienced and inexperienced), it can be concluded that the difference in attribution of personal qualities reflected differences in listeners' attitudes toward DHH persons, perhaps based on opportunities for personal experiences with them.

In sum, the results of both studies pinpoint the salience of speech intelligibility in hearing people's perceptions of others' personalities and abilities. Obtaining intelligible speech skills is, therefore, essential not only for conveying ideas and communicating with hearing people but also for gaining and maintaining social status in and adjusting to predominantly hearing, speaking environments.

It should be noted that the effect of speech on listeners' attitudes toward speakers has been investigated among other populations, and similar results have emerged. For example, researchers have examined attitudes toward individuals who stutter among adults (parents of stuttering children, teachers, speech and language pathologists; Horsley & Fitzgibbon, 1987; Yeakle & Cooper, 1986), as well as among peers ages 9–11 years (Frank, Jackson, Pimentel, & Greenwood, 2003). These studies reported that, as a whole, respondents judged the stuttering individuals as having more negative personal characteristics, such as dullness.

It would be interesting to determine to what degree spoken language intelligibility relates to hearing listeners' judgments of DHH children's personal characteristics when they are participating in a setting in which sign language is at least an alternative avenue available for communication between deaf and hearing students. This model, in which a number of DHH children are placed in a class with a majority of hearing students and where sign language is taught to all as one means of communication, has been reported to increase social interactions between DHH and hearing students (Kreimeyer, Crooke, Drye, Egbert, & Klein, 2000; see Chapter 6, this volume). It is not clear, however, the degree to which DHH students' ability to communicate fluently with hearing peers, even if using sign language, results in their being accepted as one of the group and perceived as someone with positive characteristics.

Effect of Speech Intelligibility on Social and Emotional Aspects of the Development of Deaf and Hard-of-Hearing Children

Thus far, this chapter has concentrated on the effect of speech intelligibility on how hearing people perceive DHH individuals. The following section addresses the subjective socioemotional experiences of DHH individuals themselves when they are interacting in a primarily hearing environment.

Many studies have documented that DHH children who are mainstreamed in the regular educational systems feel socially isolated (Antia & Kreimeyer, 1992; Coryell, Holcomb, & Scherer, 1992). Moreover, research suggests that these subjective feelings are based on actual difficulties in establishing friendships with hearing peers. Markides (1989), for example, reported a gap between hearing and DHH classmates in how they viewed their relationships. Although 27% of DHH children reported having a hearing

friend, only 3% of hearing children in the same settings reported having a DHH friend. Hearing children explained that they do not have DHH friends because they cannot understand what the DHH children say, indicating that speech intelligibility influences hearing children's ability to interact with a child with hearing loss.

The ability to use spoken language for communication appears to be a central factor affecting the social relationships of children who are deaf or hard of hearing, particularly with hearing individuals. Reciprocal social perceptions and interactions may lay the groundwork for children's socioemotional development, particularly with regard to self-image and attitudes toward the self. Despite the many research studies investigating the speech production abilities of DHH individuals (see, for example, Spencer & Marschark, 2006) and examining social aspects of DHH individuals, studies are lacking regarding the direct relations between speech production skills and social aspects. In the few studies discussed next, these relations were initially explored.

To determine how speech intelligibility is related to the socioemotional perceptions of DHH children themselves, Most (2007) scrutinized the relations between self-reported emotional and social feelings—specifically, children's sense of coherence and loneliness and the children's peer-rated speech intelligibility. To examine the impact of educational setting, these socioemotional perceptions and their interrelations with speech intelligibility were examined in two different school settings: group inclusion (special classes of DHH children integrated partially within regular schools) and individual inclusion (in regular classrooms with only hearing children) among DHH children aged 12–14 years. Nineteen students completed two self-report questionnaires: the Hebrew adaptation of the Loneliness and Social Dissatisfaction Questionnaire (including items like "I have nobody to talk to in my class" or "I am lonely"; Asher, Hymel, & Renshaw, 1984; Margalit, 1991) and the Sense of Coherence Scale (including items like "I feel that I don't understand what to do in class"; Antonovsky, 1987; Margalit & Efrati, 1996). The loneliness scale tapped the child's social and emotional loneliness (with scores of 16–80, where higher scores indicated a higher sense of loneliness). The sense of coherence scale tapped global feelings of optimism about the child's sense of comprehensibility, manageability, and meaningfulness (with scores of 16–64, where higher scores indicated a higher sense of coherence).

The DHH participants' speech intelligibility was evaluated using a procedure based on the one described earlier. All participants were recorded reading the same text aloud, and a group of same-aged children with normal hearing, who had never been exposed to the speech of DHH children, rated the intelligibility of the participants' speech recordings using the aforementioned 6-point scale.

The results revealed no significant differences in socioemotional perceptions between children in the two educational settings for either their sense of loneliness or their sense of coherence. Yet, the quantitative nature of this analysis may have masked qualitative differences. It is possible that the DHH children in the two educational settings scored their feelings similarly, but that the sources of these feelings differed. Perhaps the negative feelings of the children in individual inclusion stemmed from feelings of being ostracized or socially rejected by their hearing peers, whereas the negative feelings among the children in special classrooms within mainstream settings may have resulted from a sense of isolation because they were not studying with the mainstream students for the majority of the school day.

Several other studies on the mixed feelings of DHH individuals in regular educational programs provide support for these assumptions. Stinson and Foster (2000) reported that DHH children felt disappointed when not studying with hearing children, and that those who did were proud of themselves for being able to attend regular programs. Bain et al. (2004), in contrast, studied deaf adults who were raised using spoken language, attended mostly mainstream schools, and later worked in settings where they interacted with hearing co-workers and employers. Those individuals reported difficult childhood and later work experiences. Most of these adults recounted social isolation because of missed information, communication difficulties, and being negatively perceived as "different" by hearing peers. The literature is as yet inconclusive on these issues, calling for future research to obtain a deeper understanding and broader view by collecting more qualitative data on the sources and contents of these children's feelings, as well as by drawing on multiple sources of information beyond children's self-reports, including direct observations of children during school recess, sociometric measures from peers, or teacher evaluations of children's social functioning.

Regarding relations between speech intelligibility and socioemotional measures (loneliness and sense of coherence) in the Most (2007) study, significant correlations emerged for the children who were in individual inclusion: Those who had better speech intelligibility reported less loneliness and a higher sense of coherence. In contrast, no such significant relations emerged among these measures for the children in special classroom settings. Apparently, when children attend a special class within a regular school, their socioemotional self-perceptions do not depend on their speech intelligibility, probably because they have other means of communication available (sign language and mixed speech and signs). Altogether, these results imply that difficulties in establishing and maintaining peer interactions in a full inclusion setting (with only one DHH child among a hearing group) correlate with poor speech intelligibility. Poor speech intelligibility may prevent the child's effective social interaction with others and indeed may lead to feelings such as loneliness, especially with respect to hearing peers.

Interestingly, the aforementioned socioemotional outcomes for DHH children aged 12–14 (higher loneliness and lower sense of coherence) resembled those of hearing children a bit younger (8–11 years) who were at risk for learning disorders (Al-Yagon & Mikulincer, 2004). Moreover, the outcomes of both the DHH and the children at risk for learning disorders differed significantly from those of hearing children who were not at risk for developing learning disorders. Children's sense of loneliness was significantly higher in the DHH group ($M = 34.21$, $SD = 9.97$) and in the at-risk for learning disorders group ($M = 35.37$, $SD = 12.53$) than for the hearing, non-risk group ($M = 26.46$, $SD = 9.20$). Likewise, children's sense of coherence was lower in the DHH group ($M = 48.34$, $SD = 3.61$) and in the at-risk for learning disorders group ($M = 47.38$, $SD = 6.43$) than in the hearing, non-risk group ($M = 52.22$, $SD = 5.68$). The similarity of findings for the DHH children and the hearing children at risk for learning disabilities suggests that the child's status as "different" may lead to unique social and emotional self-perceptions. In other words, children who feel different from the rest of the group (in hearing or learning ability) appear to feel lonelier and less coherent. Again, these results appear to reflect more than speech intelligibility alone.

The effect of speech intelligibility on different social aspects was further examined with younger DHH children. One study explored the relationship between speech intelligibility and social perceptions and functioning among DHH kindergartners who were enrolled in two educational settings: group inclusion (a separate DHH class integrated partially in a general education school) and individual inclusion (Most, 2004). Due to the children's young age, the teachers completed the socioemotional questionnaires, and the children's speech intelligibility was evaluated by speech and language therapists who were experienced in working with DHH children. The teachers completed a questionnaire regarding their impression of the kindergartner's loneliness (an adaptation of the self-report questionnaire that was used in the previous study, with items like "The child is lonely"), as well as a questionnaire developed for teachers to evaluate social adjustment (Amitay Ben-Ami & Binyamini, 1988, with items like "The child is usually calm in school").

Once again, the results showed significant relations between speech intelligibility and the socioemotional questionnaires. However, this time the relations were obtained across all the participants, with no differentiation between the two educational settings. Kindergartners whose speech was rated by professionals as more intelligible were given a higher social adjustment score by their teachers, and were described as less lonely. The speech intelligibility ratings by the experienced, trained listeners (speech/language therapists) may be considered expert and reliable; yet, the teachers' reliability for rating children's loneliness requires a caveat. It should be noted that although previous studies have supported the use of adult ratings for children's externalizing characteristics like social maladjustment, emphasizing higher reliabilities for adult reports than for children's self-reports, the opposite outcomes have been found for internalizing characteristics like loneliness (Ronen, 1997). Future research should attempt to test young children's subjective socioemotional feelings as well as adults' ratings, and to further explore how speech intelligibility may influence DHH children's personal experiences of their own social functioning and well-being.

Despite the similar pattern of association between intelligibility and social-emotional functioning across the two educational settings, differences were found between the settings for both speech intelligibility and also the socioemotional measures. That is, children who were included individually into a general kindergarten classroom were rated to have better speech intelligibility, higher social adjustment, and lower loneliness than their DHH peers in the co-enrollment classroom. It should be remembered, however, that the placement of the children in individual versus co-enrollment settings was a function of their spoken language characteristics, including intelligibility, as well as their overall social and cognitive functioning. Thus, cause–effect relations cannot be assumed between setting and these study measures. On the whole, these outcomes call for further research on the connections between speech intelligibility, socioemotional variables, and educational settings in young children.

The importance of good speech intelligibility for positive social interactions was further explored by Weisel, Most, and Efron (2005) with very young DHH preschoolers aged 2.8–3.0 years. These preschoolers' educational framework enabled a comparison of how they interacted with hearing versus DHH peers. The children were concurrently attending two different preschool programs: a special program with other DHH children three times per week, and a regular program with hearing children three times per week. All the children used spoken language as their main mode of communication (either as the sole mode or in addition to signs). Specifically, this study examined types of interaction initiation strategies (e.g., vocalization, neutral touch, aggression, gesture; based on Vandell and George's categories, 1981), as well as these initiations' rate of success and failure with hearing and with DHH partners. An initiation strategy was considered successful if it elicited a response from the targeted partner within 5 seconds and was considered unsuccessful if it failed to elicit a response within 5 seconds. The children were videotaped during randomly selected free play situations in each educational program. From these recordings, the researchers established an initiation strategy profile for each child based on strategies preferred by the child in social interactions in the two school programs.

Findings with regard to success rate demonstrated that the DHH children were more successful in their interaction initiations in the special program than in the regular program. Regarding the types of strategies, in general, the results showed some similarities and some differences between the two educational programs regarding these preschoolers' choices. For the purposes of this chapter, the vocalization strategy employed is of greatest interest, as it may provide insight into the preschoolers' speech intelligibility. Vocalization, either as a simple strategy or in combination with other strategies (such as gestures), was the most frequent initiation strategy used in both programs, comprising almost 50% of the total strategies in each setting. However, success rates differed in the two programs. Vocalization was used successfully in the special program 52.6% of the time, but only 17% of the time in the regular program.

These results clearly indicate the DHH children's greater difficulty in initiating interactions with hearing children than with deaf children, even though they used vocalization as their preferred strategy in both settings. With respect to the speech intelligibility issues discussed in this chapter, the preschoolers' low rate of success, especially in the regular programs, may be presumed to relate to their vocalization quality. The quality of the vocalizations made by the DHH children may often have been unsuitable for their partners, especially in the regular program. In fact, qualitative inspection of the recordings revealed that the vocalizations made by the DHH preschoolers were mostly preverbal, consisting of single vowels, single syllables, and repeated syllables. A more systematic analysis of the quality of the vocalizations should be conducted in future research to determine whether young hearing children tend to respond more frequently to specifically linguistic-level vocalizations than to prelinguistic-level vocalizations.

All in all, these results indicate, unfortunately, that mutual exposure of DHH and hearing children is insufficient, and that communication difficulties may prevent meaningful intergroup social interactions. Research outcomes thus far raise questions regarding the negative social experiences that even very young DHH children may encounter in regular preschools and thus raise questions about the effectiveness of deaf children's integration (Antia & Kreimeyer, 1988a,b). Preschool educational programs that integrate deaf children together with their hearing peers should be aware that these social difficulties can occur at a very young age, and professionals should consider incorporating early interventions in the area of social interaction, including initiation strategies. Altogether, the studies surveyed here concerning the effect of speech intelligibility on different aspects of socioemotional self-perceptions and behavioral functioning, at various ages and in different educational settings, suggest that speech intelligibility may be viewed as not only essential for basic spoken communication but also as a factor that affects DHH children's social experiences and feelings when they are in a social context with hearing children.

Relations Between Speech Intelligibility and Occupational Competence

Thus far, this chapter has mainly discussed research on children and adolescents, which suggested that speech intelligibility has an influence upon different aspects of development. To continue the investigation into the effects of speech intelligibility on DHH individuals, older adolescents and young adults should also be a focus of study. Beyond the communication

and socioemotional issues described earlier, speech intelligibility may further affect feelings of competence during late adolescence and adulthood. Considering that the major developmental task confronting adults is to seek a sense of competence and satisfaction through productivity in a career (Erikson, 1968), researchers have examined DHH teenagers' and adults' decisions regarding their career plans and especially their evaluation of their occupational competence.

The extent to which DHH individuals believe they will be capable of succeeding in certain jobs is a powerful determinant of career choice and development (Read, 1994). Self-image and attitudes manifest themselves in self-efficacy, which constitutes the belief in one's ability to successfully perform specific tasks in various aspects of life (Bandura, 1986). For adults, self-efficacy focuses significantly on career development variables such as feelings of one's own occupational competence. A review of the literature on individuals with disabilities shows that they generally demonstrate relatively low occupational expectations (Burkauser & Houtenville, 2003) and that their lower aspirational levels have a negative impact on their vocational choices (Saunders, Leahy, & Frank, 2000). Weisel and Cinamon (2005) specifically reported lower self-perceptions of occupational competencies among DHH than hearing individuals.

Based on such previous research, Most, Weisel, and Cinamon (2008) expected that DHH young adults would feel less competent regarding occupations that require communication and that are relatively more prestigious, particularly when they feel that their speech is not sufficiently intelligible. Thus, we assumed that better speech intelligibility would be related to self-reports of higher occupational competence: If respondents felt they were more easily understandable, they would consequently feel more competent regarding a career.

To examine this assumption, 36 young adults aged 18–36 years with moderate to profound hearing loss were each asked to rate their suitability for various occupations that differed in level of prestige and in required level of communication. The sample included 20 participants who communicated through spoken language and 16 participants who used simultaneous communication (speech and signs). All participants had sensory aids (six cochlear implants and 30 hearing aids). Most of the participants (25) were college/university students or graduates, and the remaining 11 were high school graduates. Participants rated their own speech intelligibility as well their suitability for four categories of occupations: high communication-high prestige (HCHP; e.g., lawyer), high communication-low prestige (HCLP; e.g., waiter), low communication-high prestige (LCHP; e.g., computer programmer), and low communication-low prestige (LCLP; e.g., carpenter).

As expected, results indicated that these young adults considered occupations requiring less communication to be more suitable than those requiring more communication. This finding reflected the fact that the participants were aware of their difficulties as a result of their hearing loss. Although most of them used spoken language as their main mode of communication, they confronted many difficulties, such as communication in the presence of background noise, communication in a group (such as in meetings), or communication over the telephone. Surprisingly, however, level of prestige did not have a significant influence upon their choices. This finding contradicted previous research in which both DHH individuals' self-assessments and assessments by hearing persons judged DHH individuals to be most suitable for low-prestige jobs that do not necessarily reflect their ability and skills (DeCaro, Mudgett-DeCaro, & Dowaliby, 2001; Parasnis, Samar, & Mandke, 1996; Weisel & Cinamon, 2005). DeCaro et al. even suggested that the effect of deafness on attitudes was similar in different cultures.

One explanation for these contradictory results may relate to the positive current or past educational experiences of the participants in the Most et al. (2008) study, compared to those of previous samples. In Most et al.'s study, the participants were graduates of regular educational programs and, moreover, many were either college students or college graduates. Personal experiences in coping with the various difficulties in the hearing world may have strengthened beliefs and expectations among the participants in the Most group's study with regard to their occupational capabilities.

Another possible explanation for these results may lie in the rapid, significant advancements characterizing technology in recent years, a fact which could perhaps have had an effect on these young people's self-evaluation of occupational competence. First and foremost, sensory aids such as hearing aids, cochlear implants, and FM systems now provide better audibility, and consequently, better interactions with hearing people. Second, the variety of available technologies such as fax, e-mail communication, instant messaging, and the like, which are common today in many highly prestigious occupations, do not require as much use of hearing in communication as previously required. Another explanation could have been the fact that the participants rated their speech intelligibility as quite high and suggested that they did not view their speech as unintelligible.

These results concerning normative career aspirations for prestigious occupations among DHH individuals, in contrast to prior research that showed them to feel less suitable for such occupations, support recent findings by Punch, Creed, and Hyde (2005) on other aspects of career development. Punch et al. examined hard-of-hearing high school students who attended regular classes and a matched group of normally hearing peers. Thus, their sample resembled that of Most et al. (2008) regarding quality of spoken communication mode and participation in regular educational settings. Punch et al. found similarities between hard-of-hearing students and their normally hearing peers in career maturity, that is, in their extent of thinking and planning about career-related activities or in their willingness and ability to find and use good resources for career planning,

Interestingly, in Most et al.'s study (2008), no significant relations emerged between speech intelligibility and occupational competence. Perhaps the distinction made by the participants between occupations with high and low communication needs suggests that they viewed career barriers as originating in environmental demands rather than internal limitations. In other words, although participants believed they had intelligible speech, they nevertheless expected occupational obstacles from their environment. This last assumption is supported by specific findings on hard-of-hearing students' career barriers. Punch, Creed, and Hyde (2006) found that misunderstanding of the hearing loss by others was perceived as the main potential career barrier to the fulfillment of students' career and educational goals. In another interesting finding, Punch et al. (2005) reported that hard-of-hearing students who believed that their hearing loss imposed many obstacles to their career experiences were less likely to actively explore and plan their career than were students who perceived fewer obstacles. Thus, perception of the impairment's impact on their future career possibly affected their self-efficacy, which, in turn, may have influenced their involvement in career planning activities.

Further research should be conducted to unravel the origins of feelings of occupational incompetence, whether in the individuals' realistic evaluations of their own profile of skills or in the demands, expectations, biases, or discrimination originating in the workplace. Moreover, researchers would do well to study the function of speech intelligibility in career development. Such studies should use more diversified populations with more heterogeneous speech intelligibility levels, as well as objective measures of speech intelligibility, to establish a firmer basis for the current conclusions. Furthermore, based on findings on DHH persons who were raised using spoken language, which reported social isolation in the work environment because of limitations in communication with hearing peers (Bain, Scott, & Steinberg, 2004), the effect of speech intelligibility on socioemotional aspects at work environments should be a focus of investigation as well.

In sum, DHH individuals have tended to choose occupations that require less communication but not less prestigious occupations, thus exhibiting what may be considered an adaptive stance to their hearing status. Self-perceived speech intelligibility did not play a role in occupational competence, but our particular sample of participants (Most et al., 2008), who used spoken language and were highly educated, revealed very high self-ratings.

Educational Implications and Future Research

As documented in the research surveyed in this chapter, attaining intelligible speech holds important implications that reach beyond the efficacy of direct spoken communication. Speech intelligibility affects others' attitudes toward DHH individuals, especially the attitudes of those people who are not ordinarily exposed to this population. Intelligibility also affects the emotional states and social relationships of this population at various ages, especially in the context of predominantly hearing, speaking environments. In addition to effects of speech intelligibility on social experiences during the school years, DHH adolescents and adults who perceived their speech as intelligible showed a higher sense of occupational competency. This provides additional evidence of the importance of supports for speech intelligibility as one of the prime objectives within educational and rehabilitation programs.

One assumption underlying the recent major educational trend toward inclusion of DHH children within regular programs containing primarily hearing peers is that exposure to hearing children will enhance DHH children's communication skills and will better prepare them for future interactions with the hearing world. However, these integration efforts do not always consider the socioemotional impact on the DHH children in terms of how others perceive them. Constant feelings of being different, loneliness, and a lower sense of coherence while in the company of hearing peers can result in DHH students having negative perceptions of self and of their possibilities for later employment.

In selecting a school setting, educators, speech and language therapists, and parents should look beyond academic factors and should not ignore the significant effect of speech intelligibility on the child's well-being in school, and on the child's normal social and emotional development. They cannot assume that once a child is included in the regular class, he or she will become an active and integral member of the group. In other words, mere mutual exposure may be insufficient, and interaction difficulties may prevent effective social interaction between DHH and hearing students (Antia et al., 1993; Bat-Chava & Deignan, 2001; Stinson et al., 1996).

As noted earlier, even preschool educational programs that integrate DHH children together with their hearing peers should be aware of these social difficulties, which already occur at a very young age. Professionals should consider incorporating early interventions into their programs, not only in the area of social interaction but also in spoken language skills, with specific emphasis on socially related vocalizations such as behaviors to initiate play and communicative exchanges.

At the same time, whenever such integration programs are implemented, educators should consider the design of interventions to modify hearing persons' perceptions of DHH individuals based on their speech. Well-planned programs should be directed specifically to diverse target populations at different ages—the general public, who is not familiar with the DHH population; school professionals, such as teachers and other school staff, classmates, and other students; and at older ages, employers and colleagues of DHH employees. A range of school-based peer and faculty interventions, career-focused programs, as well as human resource interventions may be encouraged. Such programs, for example, could enhance awareness of the natural human tendency to attribute negative personality and competency stereotypes to persons with poorly intelligible speech (the spread effect), or with other learning and/or cognitive differences, which could help prevent this phenomenon in children and adults who work and interact with DHH individuals.

Furthermore, the need for children to spend time in the company of other DHH children from a very young age, should not be ignored. Smoother and more comfortable interactions with same-status peers have been shown to allow children to experience successful social interactions that may foster positive social development (Bat-Chava & Deignan, 2001). By learning to effectively communicate and interact with same-status peers, DHH children can gain a sense of social competence and accumulate a repertoire of skills within a safer, easier environment; then they can more confidently generalize such social skills to the more challenging interpersonal interactions characterizing the hearing world of school, work, and leisure.

Summary and Conclusions

On the whole, future studies would do well to continue examining the effect of spoken language skills on the different aspects of DHH individuals' adjustment at various stages of their lives. Studies should maintain empirical focus on the links between socioemotional perceptions among DHH children and their actual social behaviors and peer interactions. Based on such empirically derived connections, interventions could then help teachers initiate activities and opportunities to encourage interactions between children in integrated settings and to foster more personal and intimate familiarity between children with and without hearing loss, in order to improve subjective feelings.

Interdisciplinary research that entails both quantitative and qualitative methodologies is crucial. Collaboration of professionals from the diverse fields involved in the rehabilitation process of DHH individuals—speech and language therapists, educators, medical personnel (involved in cochlear implantation), occupational therapists, and occupational counselors, along with parents—may be enlightening, and may permit a more effective, holistic approach to the well-being of these individuals. Consideration of the relevant issues and difficulties from different points of view will furnish better understanding of the impact of hearing loss not only on the linguistic and academic realms but also on the emotional, social, and occupational aspects of life quality over the lifespan.

Acknowledgments

The author would like to express her appreciation to Dee Ankonina for her editorial contribution.

References

Al-Yagon, M., & Margalit, M. (2001). Special and inclusive education in Israel. *Mediterranean Journal of Educational Studies*, 6(2), 93–112.

Al-Yagon, M., & Mikulincer, M. (2004). Socio-emotional and academic adjustment among children with learning disorders: The mediational role of attachment based factors. *Journal of Special Education*, 38, 11–123.

Amitay Ben-Ami, N. & Binyamini, K. (1988). *SHALGI: An instrument to identify adjustment difficulties and positive resources in kindergarten children.* Jerusalem: Psychological-Educational Services. (Hebrew).

Anderson, K. L., & Goldstein, H. (2004). Speech perception benefits of FM and infrared devices to children with hearing aids in a typical classroom. *Language, Speech and Hearing Services in Schools*, 35(2), 169–184.

Antia, S., & Kreimeyer, K. (1988a). The development and generalization of social interaction skills in preschool hearing-impaired children. *The Volta Review*, 90, 219–230.

Antia, S., & Kreimeyer, K. (1988b). Maintenance of a positive peer interaction in preschool hearing-impaired children. *The Volta Review*, 90, 325–337.

Antia, S. D., & Kreimeyer, K. H. (1992). Social competence intervention for young children with hearing impairment. In S. L. Odom, S. R. McConnel, & M. A. McEvoy (Eds.), *Social competence of young children with disabilities.* (pp. 135–164). Baltimore: Paul H. Brooks.

Antia, S. D., Kreimeyer, K. H., & Eldredge, N. (1993). Promoting social interaction between young children with hearing impairments and their peers. *Exceptional Children*, 60(3), 262–275.

Antonovsky, A. (1987). *Unraveling the mystery of health.* New York: Scribner.

Asch, S. E. (1964). Forming impressions on personality. *Journal of Abnormal and Social Psychology*, 41, 258–290.

Asher, S. R., Hymel, S., & Renshaw, P. D. (1984). Loneliness in children. *Child Development*, 55, 1456–1464.

Bain, L. Scott, S. & Steinberg, A. G. (2004). Socialization experiences and coping strategies of adults raised using spoken language. *Journal of Deaf Studies and Deaf Education*, 9(1), 120–128.

Bandura, A. (1986). *Social foundation of thought and action: A social cognitive theory.* Englewood Cliffs, NJ: Prentice-Hall.

Bat-Chava, Y., & Deignan, E. (2001). Peer relationships of children with cochlear implants. *Journal of Deaf Studies and Deaf Education*, 6(3), 186–199.

Bench, R. J. (1992). *Communication skills in hearing impaired children.* London: Whurr.

Bentler, R., Wu, Y. H., Kettel, J., & Hurting, R. (2008). Digital noise reduction: Outcomes from laboratory and field studies. *International Journal of Audiology*, 47(8), 447–460.

Blamey, P. J., Sarant, J. Z., Paatsch, L. E., Barry, J. G., Bow, C. P., Wales, R. J., et al. (2001). Relationships among speech perception, production, language, hearing loss, and age in children with impaired hearing. *Journal of Speech, Language & Hearing Research*, 44, 264–285.

Boothroyd, A. (1985). Evaluation of speech production of the hearing impaired: Some benefits of forced choice testing. *Journal of Speech and Hearing Research*, 28, 185–193.

Brown, P, & Foster, S. (1989). Integrating hearing and deaf students on a college campus. *American Annals of the Deaf*, 136(1), 21–27.

Burkhauser, R. V., & Houtenville, A. J. (2003). Employment among working-age people with disabilities: What current data can tell us. In E. M. Szymanski & R. M. Parker (Eds.), *Work and disability: Issues and strategies in career development and job placement*, 2nd edition (pp. 53–90). Austin, TX: Pro-Ed.

Coryell, J., Holcomb, T. K., & Scherer, M. (1992). Attitudes towards deafness: A collegiate perspective. *American Annals of the Deaf*, 137, 299–302.

DeCaro, J. J., Mudgett-DeCaro, P. A., & Dowaliby, F. (2001). Attitudes toward occupation for deaf youth in Sweden. *American Annals of the Deaf*, *146*(1), 51–59.

Eisenberg, L. S. (2007). Current state of knowledge: Speech recognition and production with hearing impairment. *Ear and Hearing*, *28*(6), 766–772.

Erikson, E. (1968). *Identity: youth and crisis*. New York: Norton.

Foster, S., & Brown, P. (1989). Factors influencing the academic and social integration of hearing impaired college students. *Journal of Postsecondary Education and Disability*, *7*(3 & 4), 78–96.

Frank, A. L., Jackson, R. A., Pimentel, J., & Greenwood, G. S. (2003). School-age children's perceptions of a person who stutters. *Journal of Fluency Disorders*, *28*, 1–5.

Horsley, I. A., & Fitzgibbon, C. T. (1987). Stuttering children: Investigation of a stereotype. *British Journal of Disorders of Communication*, *22*, 19–35.

Kappas, A., Hess, U., & Sherer, K. R. (1991). Voice and emotion. In R. S. Feldman & B. Rime (Eds.), *Fundamentals of nonverbal behavior* (pp. 200–239). Cambridge, UK: Cambridge University Press.

Karchmer, M.A., & Mitchell, R.E. (2003). Demographic and achievement characteristics of deaf and hard of hearing students. In M. Marschark & P.E Spencer (Eds.), *Oxford handbook of deaf studies, language, and education* (pp. 21–51). New York: Oxford University Press.

Klimacka, L., Patterson, A., & Patterson, R. (2001). Listening to deaf speech: Does experience count? *International Journal of Language and Communication Disorders*, *36*(Supplement), 210–215.

Kreimeyer, K., Crooke, P., Drye, C., Egbert, V., & Klein, B. (2000). Academic benefits of co-enrollment model of inclusive education of deaf and hard-of-hearing children. *Journal of Deaf Studies and Deaf Education*, *5*, 174–185.

Margalit, M. (1991). Loneliness among students with learning disabilities. *Behavior Change*, *8*, 167–173.

Margalit, M., & Efrati, M. (1996). Loneliness, coherence and companionship among children with learning disorders. *Educational Psychology*, *16*, 69–79.

Markel, N., Eisler, M., & Reese, W. (1967). Judging personality from dialect. *Journal of Verbal Learning and Verbal Behavior*, *6*, 33–35.

Markides, A. (1989). Integration: The speech intelligibility, friendship and associations of hearing impaired children in secondary schools. *Journal of the British Association of Teachers of the Deaf*, *13*(3), 63–72.

McGarr, N. S. (1983). The intelligibility of deaf speech to experienced and inexperienced listeners. *Journal of Speech and Hearing Research*, *26*, 451–458.

McGarr, N. S. (1987). Communication skills of hearing impaired children in schools for the deaf. *ASHA Monographs*, *26*, 91–107.

Meyer, T. A., Svirsky, M. A., Kirk, K. I., & Miyamoto, R. T. (1998). Improvement in speech perception by children with profound prelingual hearing loss: Effects of device, communication mode, and chronological age. *Journal of Speech, Language & Hearing Research*, *41*, 846–858.

Monsen, R. B. (1983). The oral speech intelligibility of hearing impaired talkers. *Journal of Speech and Hearing Disorders*, *48*, 286–296.

Moog, J. S., & Geers, A. E. (1999). Speech and language acquisition in young children after cochlear implantation. *Otolaryngologic Clinics of North America*, *32*(6), 1127–1141.

Most, T. (2004). *Speech intelligibility and social aspects among hearing impaired children*. Paper presented at the 50th Anniversary Celebration Conference for the "MICHA" Society for Deaf Children, Tel-Aviv, Israel. (Hebrew).

Most, T. (2007). Speech intelligibility, loneliness and sense of coherence among deaf and hard-of-hearing children in individual inclusion and group inclusion. *Journal of Deaf Studies and Deaf Education*, *12*, 495–503.

Most, T., & Frank, Y. (1994). The effects of age and hearing loss on tasks of perception and production of intonation. *The Volta Review*, *96*, 137–149.

Most, T., Weisel, A., & Cinamon, R. G. (2008). Is speech intelligibility of deaf and hard of hearing people a barrier for occupational competence? *Journal of the American Deafness and Rehabilitation Association*. *42*, 7–23.

Most, T., Weisel, A, & Lev-Matezky, A. (1996). Speech intelligibility and the evaluation of personal qualities by experienced and inexperienced listeners. *The Volta Review*, *98*, 181–190.

Most, T., Weisel, A., & Tur-Kaspa, H. (1999). Contact with students with hearing impairment and the evaluation of speech intelligibility and personal qualities. *Journal of Special Education*, *33*, 103–111.

Osberger, M. J., Fisher, L., Zimerman-Phillips, S., Geiger, L., & Barker, M. J. (1998). Speech recognition performance of older children with cochlear implants. *American Journal of Otology*, *19*, 152–157.

Parasnis, I., Samar, V. J., & Mandke, K. (1996). Deaf adults' attitudes toward career choices for deaf and hearing people in India. *American Annals of the Deaf*, *141*(5), 333–339.

Peng, S. C., Tomblin, J. B., & Turner, C. W. (2008). Production and perception of speech intonation in pediatric cochlear implant recipients and individuals with normal hearing. *Ear and Hearing*, *29*(3), 336–351.

Pisoni, D. (2000). Cognitive factors and cochlear implants: Some thoughts on perception, learning, and memory in speech perception. *Ear & Hearing*, *21*, 70–78.

Power, D., & Hyde, M. (2002).The characteristics and extent of participation of deaf and hard-of-hearing students in regular classes in Australian schools. *Journal of Deaf Studies and Deaf Education*, *7*(4), 302–311.

Punch, R., Creed, P. A., & Hyde, M. (2005). Predicting career development in hard of hearing adolescents in Australia. *Journal of Deaf Studies and Deaf Education*, *10*(2), 148–160.

Punch, R., Creed, P. A., & Hyde, M. (2006). Career barriers perceived by hard of hearing adolescents: Implications for practice from a mixed methods study. *Journal of Deaf Studies and Deaf Education*, *11*(2), 224–237.

Raphael, L. J., Borden, G. J., & Harris, K. S. (2007). *Speech science primer: Physiology, acoustics, and perception of speech*, 5th edition. Baltimore: Lippincott Williams & Wilkins.

Read, B. K. (1994). Motivational factors in technical college women's selection of non-traditional careers. *Journal of Career Development*, *20*(3), 239–258.

Ronen, T. (1997). *Cognitive-developmental therapy with children*. Chichester, UK: John Wiley.

Saunders, J. L., Leahy, M. J., & Frank, K. A. (2000). Improving the employment self-concept of persons with disabilities: A field-based experiment. *Rehabilitation Counseling Bulletin*. *43*, 142–149.

Sherer, K. R., & Ekman, E. (1982). *Handbook of methods in nonverbal behavior research*. Cambridge, UK: Cambridge University Press.

Spencer, P., & Marschark, M. (2003). Cochlear implants: Issues and implications. In M. Marschark & P. Spencer (Eds.), *Oxford handbook of deaf studies, language, and education* (pp. 434–450). New York: Oxford University Press.

Spencer, P., & Marschark, M. (Eds.). (2006). *Advances in the spoken language development of deaf and hard-of-hearing children*. New York: Oxford University Press.

Stinson, M. S., & Foster, S. (2000). Socialization of deaf children and youths in school. In P. E. Spencer, C. J. Erting, & M. Marschark (Eds.), *The deaf child in the family and at school: Essays in honor of Kathryn P. Meadow-Orlans* (pp. 191–209). Hillsdale, NJ: Lawrence Erlbaum.

Stinson, M. S., Whitmore, K., & Kluwin, T. N. (1996). Self-perceptions of social relationships in hearing-impaired adolescents. *Journal of Educational Psychology, 88*, 132–143.

Strong, C. J., & Shaver, J. P. (1991). Modifying attitudes towards persons with hearing impairments: A comprehensive review of the research. *American Annals of the Deaf, 136*, 252–260.

Vandell, D. L., & George, L. B. (1981). Social interaction in hearing and deaf preschoolers: Successes and failures in initiations. *Child Development, 52*(2), 627–635.

Weisel, A. (1989). Educational placement of hearing impaired students as related to family characteristics, students' characteristics and preschool intervention. *Journal of Special Education, 23*(3), 303–312.

Weisel A, & Cinamon, R. G. (2005). Hearing, deaf and hard-of-hearing Israeli adolescents' evaluation of deaf men's and deaf women's occupational competence. *Journal of Deaf Studies and Deaf Education, 10*, 376–389.

Weisel, A., Most, T., & Efron, C. (2005). Initiations of social interactions by young hearing impaired preschoolers. *Journal of Deaf Studies and Deaf Education, 10*, 161–170.

Wright, B. A. (1983). *Physical disability: A psychosocial approach*, 2nd edition. New York: Harper Collins.

Yeakle, M. K., & Cooper, E. B. (1986). Teacher perceptions of stuttering. *Journal of Fluency Disorders, 11*, 345–359.

Yuker, H. E. (1988). The effects of contact on attitudes toward disabled persons: Some empirical generalizations. In H. E. Yuker (Ed.), *Attitudes toward persons with disabilities* (pp. 262–274). New York: Springer.

Zandberg, S. (2005). *Educating children with hearing impairment: Targets and their realization*. [Internal report]. Jerusalem: Israel Ministry of Education. (Hebrew).

PART 4

Language and Language Development

Emerging Sign Languages

Irit Meir, Wendy Sandler, Carol Padden, *and* Mark Aronoff

Abstract

Emerging sign languages may be divided into two types: village sign languages and Deaf community sign languages. Village sign languages develop within small communities or villages where transmission is within and between families. They include languages such as Al-Sayyid Bedouin Sign Language (ABSL, Israel), Martha's Vineyard Sign Language (United States), Ban Khor Sign Language (Thailand), Kata Kolok Sign Language (Bali), and Adamarobe Sign Language (Ghana). Deaf community sign languages arise from bringing together unrelated signers of different backgrounds in locations such as cities or schools. In such cases (e.g., Nicaraguan Sign Language and Israeli Sign Language [ISL]), language learning takes place in large measure between peers. We assume that the social conditions under which a language develops interact with the development of its linguistic structure. Emerging sign languages are crucial for developing and evaluating such assumptions. Because of their young age, much is known about the social conditions and histories of their communities, and their linguistic development is observable from very early stages. These factors make emerging sign languages a natural laboratory for studying the development of linguistic structure and its interaction with the nature of the language community.

Keywords: sign language, village sign language, Deaf community sign language, language emergence

Herodotus tells the story of the Egyptian king Psammetichos's effort to answer the question: Who were the first people in the world? He placed newborn twins in the custody of a shepherd on an uninhabited island, with instructions not to speak to them. After two years, he returned to learn that the children's first recognizable word was "bekos," the Phrygian word for bread, and so concluded that the Phrygians were the first.

The tale of Psammetichos has long been one of the best remembered of Herodotus's stories because it strikes a nerve. Language is the most human of all behaviors, and it is natural to want to know how it all started. But we cannot go back in time, and there is little if any evidence in the fossil record that can tell us about the origin of language. Although this lack of hard evidence has not prevented scholars, especially in the last decade, from speculating about the evolution of language (see e.g., the papers in Knight, Studdert-Kennedy, & Hurford, 2000; Tallerman, 2005; Wray, 2002), others have turned their attention to more concrete pursuits by attempting to study how new languages are born, on the assumption that new languages will shed some light on what the first languages were like and under what conditions they were able to develop and thrive.

Modern students of language are just as eager to discover the "first" language of humans as Psammetichos was, but for somewhat different reasons. Underlying the contemporary interest in new languages are three main theoretical questions: First, we would like to know what must be the most basic ingredients of any language in order for it to function fully as a language. What does a new language look like? This is the quest for the fundamental elements of language. Second is the question of how these basic ingredients of language emerge in a community of humans without a linguistic model, and how long it takes for this to transpire. Is the ability to construct a language so hard-wired that language will arise full-blown in all its complexity in a single generation? Or, do interaction and experience over time play a crucial role in the emergence and development of language as we know it? We may think of this as a question about the contributions of nature and nurture in language birth and development. Last is the question of the relation between language and the characteristics of its community. Do the size and composition of the community make a difference in the scope and structure of the language it creates? Do patterns of interaction within the community influence the course of a language's development?

The only known new spoken languages are the pidgin and creole languages. *Pidgins* come into being when speakers of two or more mutually unintelligible languages need to communicate with one another. Once such languages become the native language of children born into a pidgin-speaking household, they are referred to as *creoles*. Some scholars argue that these languages can reveal much about what is essential to any language, because they are new (McWhorter, 1998). However, pidgins and creoles are rooted in two or more existing spoken languages, and therefore are never free of influence from their source languages. For this reason, they are not entirely new.

Recently, linguists have realized that one type of language can arise in the manner of Psammetichos's experiment. There are circumstances under which a small group of people can form a language apparently out of nothing. We are referring to new sign languages, which are created when deaf people without any prior exposure to either signed or spoken language find themselves together and form a communicative community. Through careful investigation of these languages, we hope to discover some possible answers to the three basic questions we have raised.

The new sign languages that linguists have begun to study fall into two categories, distinguished by the social conditions of their formation (Sandler, 2005; Woll & Ladd, 2003), which we will call *village sign languages* and *Deaf community sign languages*. The major difference between the two is in the social homogeneity of their origins. A village sign language arises in an existing, relatively insular community into which a number of deaf children are born. A Deaf community sign language, on the other hand, arises when a group of deaf individuals, often from different places, are brought together (typically for educational purposes, as in a residential school) and form a community.

Categorizing new sign languages in this way allows us to consider potentially important differences arising from the two types of linguistic environments. In the village sign language setting, from the beginning, people share a common culture and social environment at a very intimate level. Their shared context, expectations, and knowledge make it easier for them to communicate than it is for people with diverse backgrounds. This degree of familiarity may allow them to be less explicit verbally than people who do not have as much in common, yet at the same time to communicate effectively across a range of topics, provided the context is shared. The broad diversity that characterizes the users of new sign languages of the other type, the Deaf community sign languages, may have the effect of increasing the speed at which systematic linguistic structures develop. These are intriguing possibilities, for which some evidence already exists. By discovering and investigating new languages in each of these two categories, linguists are gaining new insight into the three fundamental theoretical issues raised earlier.

In what follows, we assume a distinction between gesture, home sign, and sign language, and focus exclusively on sign languages. Gesture and sign language are distinguished primarily by conventionalization and systematicity. *Home sign* is a basic communication system created within a family with one or a few deaf members (Goldin-Meadow 2003). The obvious difference between such a system, which may be conventionalized for the solitary child who creates it, and sign language is the number of people for whom manual-visual language is primary. In home sign, it is one, whereas in either a village or a Deaf community sign language, it is many, and this difference leads to structural differences between the two kinds of language. However, the distinction is not categorical but gradient. Home sign systems can emerge in a family with more than one deaf child. In such cases, the community numbers several individuals. Whether the emerging communication system looks more like a home sign created by one individual or a sign language is an empirical question that should be studied for each case. In addition, different sign languages can exhibit different degrees of conventionalization, as we describe later. Readers are referred to McNeill (1992) for criteria that distinguish sign language from co-speech gesture, and to Singleton, Morford, and Goldin-Meadow

(1993) for an interesting discussion of gesture, home sign, and sign language form.

Village Sign Languages: Social Characteristics and Examples

Village sign languages develop within small communities or villages with a high incidence of hereditary deafness. The percentage of deaf people in the community may reach as high as 3.5%, more than 40 times the usual incidence elsewhere.[1] Village sign language communities are typically socially separated by reason of ethnicity or geography. The deaf people born into such communities may not attend school, since the local schools, attended by hearing people in the same communities, have no special provisions for deaf students. Consequently, they do not have access to the national deaf educational system or to the major Deaf community, if there is one. Therefore, these deaf individuals are not exposed to any existing sign language in the region. In such contexts, the birth of even a small group of deaf children in the community may give rise to a sign language that develops without contact with other sign languages. These languages emerge from the need to communicate within families, and they are characteristically used by both deaf and hearing members of the community.

The creation of such a system is vividly described by a hearing son of a first-generation deaf person from the Al-Sayyid village, who explained to us how the Al-Sayyid Bedouin Sign Language (ABSL) arose: "The parents needed to communicate with the deaf children born into the family. They wanted to transmit information about everyday activities and interactions, as well as values and traditions important for the community. They used whatever communication system worked. Since the children were deaf, they used gestures. Some of the gestures were already being used in the community, others were invented by the children and still others by their parents".

Since the language is used by both deaf and hearing members of the community, initially there is not a Deaf community per se, but rather a signing community, which is actually much larger than the number of deaf people in the community. The transmission of the language is within and between families, and both deaf and hearing members play a role as linguistic models and as acquirers. In village sign languages, many children, both hearing and deaf, acquire the language from birth, or very early in life.

Using archival records and interviews with the oldest residents of Martha's Vineyard, an island off the coast of Massachusetts, Groce (1985) traced the history of a community that had used a sign language for communication among its hearing and deaf residents for several generations. At one time, the percentage of deaf people on the island was high, especially in two villages, Tisbury (2%) and Chilmark (4%). Even within these villages, deafness was not evenly spread. Groce points out that in one particular neighborhood of Chilmark with about 60 people, the rate of deafness was 25% (1985, p. 42). Use of sign language was frequently noted in written records of the island through the latter half of the 19th century, when the collapse of the whaling industry on the island forced many to relocate to the mainland, and the language was lost in favor of American Sign Language (ASL).

Unlike the situation in Martha's Vineyard, where the number of deaf people in particular villages was very high, the number of deaf people on Providence Island in the Western Caribbean was very small and widely distributed (Washabaugh, 1986). According to Washabaugh's investigation, deafness on the island could be traced back at least three generations. Washabaugh identified 20 deaf individuals out of a population of about 3,000 in the island, distributed in five or six villages. In addition, people from different villages did not interact with each other on a daily basis because of geographic separation and social stratification. For these reasons, many of the interactions of deaf people on the island were with hearing people in their own village.

A similar situation was described by Osugi, Supalla, and Webb (1999) on Amami Island in Japan. Although there is a high percentage of deaf people on the island (between 0.27% and 1.4% of the population), deaf people in one village had little contact with deaf people on the other side of the island because of the difficulty of navigating across the island's mountainous terrain. When Osugi et al. elicited a basic vocabulary list from the Amami signers, they found consistent use of vocabulary among members of the same family in one village, which differed from that used by deaf people elsewhere on the island.

In recent years, several detailed studies of other village sign languages have appeared. In Israel, a sign language emerged and developed in a small, relatively insular and endogamous Bedouin community with a high incidence of nonsyndromic recessive deafness (Scott, Carmi, Elbedour, Duyk, Stone, & Sheffield, 1995). The Al-Sayyid founding family settled in present-day southern Israel about 200 years ago, and five generations later (about 75 years ago), four deaf siblings were born to one family. In the next two generations, deafness appeared in a number of other families, resulting in what today is estimated at about 150 deaf adults, teenagers, and children, in a community of about 4,000 members (or 3.75%). The sign language that arose in the village, ABSL, is different in word order from Israeli Sign Language (ISL), and from the surrounding spoken languages, the local Arabic dialect, and Hebrew (Sandler, Meir, Padden, & Aronoff, 2005). It differs in vocabulary from the other sign languages of the region, Israeli, Palestinian, and Jordanian sign languages (Al-Fityani, 2007).

Vocabulary comparison is considered a strong measure for establishing possible genealogical relationships between languages. Since the vocabulary of ABSL differs significantly from that of other sign languages, a very plausible conclusion is that ABSL developed independently and is not modeled after an already existing sign language. The language is used widely in the community by both deaf and hearing members (Kisch, 2000, 2004), and is seen as another language of the village in addition to spoken Arabic. Deaf people are fully integrated in the social life of the village: they are married into different families, and their social interactions are similar to those of hearing people. The common use of ABSL in the village has led to widespread exposure to the language by deaf signers and many of their hearing siblings, relatives, and neighbors from birth or a very young age.

Another village sign language that has been under recent study is Kata Kolok, literally "deaf language," which developed in Bengkala, an Indonesian village located on the north shore of Bali (Marsaja, 2008; Winata, Arhya, Moeljopawiro, Hinnant, Liang, Friedman, & Asher, 1995). In the village, often referred to as Desa Kolok, literally "deaf village," there are 47 deaf people (out of a population of 2,186), distributed through the major clans in the village. Although the deaf people themselves constitute 2.59% of the village's population, the percentage of hearing people with deaf family members is 4.29%, and most of the people in the village are in close daily contact with deaf people. Marsaja (2008, p. 99) reports that about two-thirds of the people sign to some degree, and about 500 people are fluent signers. Therefore, the entire signing community is about 1,200 people. The deaf people in the village are fully integrated into the secular and religious activities of the community and have some special roles, such as burying the dead. According to Marsaja (2008, p. 70), the people of the village

believe that deaf people are on better terms with both deaf and hearing gods and spirits, and are therefore more suited to this task.

Nonaka (2007, 2009) reported on a sign language that emerged in Ban Khor, a small rice-farming community consisting of a few neighboring villages in northeastern Thailand. The number of deaf people in this community is about 16 out of about 2,700 (0.65%), and deafness is known to have existed there for at least three generations, making the sign language about 60–80 years old.

Nyst (2007) studied the sign language that emerged in Adamorobe, an Akan village in the Eastern region of Ghana. The incidence of hereditary deafness is about 2.5% (35 people in a village of 1,400 inhabitants), and it may have been higher in the past. The village is thought to be 200 years old, with deaf inhabitants present from the beginning (see Nyst, 2007). Deaf people seem fully integrated, but deaf–deaf marriages were banned in the past, and currently are tolerated but not favored. Most deaf men do not marry, whereas deaf women may become second wives in this polygamous community.

A different type of social setting for a village sign language has been discovered among Algerian Jews originating from Ghardaia, a mostly Berber town located in the M'zab (sub-Saharan) region of Algeria. The Jewish community of Ghardaia goes back 700–800 years. Inhabiting a walled-in neighborhood within the town, the Jewish community was socially and genetically isolated. Consanguineous marriage was very common in the community, and it resulted in a high percentage of deafness (2.5% according to Briggs & Guede, 1964). As with the other communities described, a sign language developed, used by both deaf and hearing individuals. By the 1960s, the entire Jewish community had left Ghardaia, and its members emigrated to Israel or to France. Families with deaf members continued to use their sign language in their new countries, but it was kept as a private family language. Most users of this sign language in Israel today are bilingual in ISL and Ghardaia Sign Language, and the language is hardly used by the younger generation, who have adapted entirely to using ISL.

Deaf Community Sign Languages: Social Characteristics

The second type of new sign language, the *Deaf community sign language*, arises when unrelated signers of different backgrounds come together in one place. Typically, the establishment of a school for deaf children draws together deaf people from within a larger region to one location, but other institutions such as Deaf associations and clubs can also provide meeting places for communication among signers. In such cases, language learning takes place in large measure between peers and unrelated adults. The history of major European sign languages and those of North America is directly linked to the building of Deaf schools in the 18th and 19th century, and the clubs that formed in communities around them (Woll, Sutton-Spence, & Elton, 2001).

In situations like these, the deaf people typically have varied language backgrounds. Some may have already learned an existing sign language. Others may have grown up using sign communication only within the family—that is, home sign. This mix of linguistic systems can be compared to that found in the initial stages of pidgin formation. However, unlike spoken pidgins, in the signing situation, some people may come with little or no prior exposure to any language. In some rare cases, none of the members of the new language community know an existing sign language beyond their home signs, and the sign language that emerges can be regarded as new.

The linguistic origins of most established and well-studied Deaf community sign languages are not well documented. We can assume that they arose under the conditions of linguistic interaction just described, yet details about the languages and sign systems that gave rise to modern day sign languages are sparse. For example, it is well known that French Sign Language (LSF) played an instrumental role in the development of ASL in the first school for deaf children founded in 1817 in Hartford, Connecticut. Woodward (1978) compared the lexicons of ASL and LSF and found that between 50% and 60% of the two languages' vocabularies were identical or similar, showing that the two languages were related, as expected. But the fact that there remained a large number of unrelated vocabulary items suggested that ASL must have had other lexical or structural contributions during its history. Based on the evidence of ASL's lexicon, Woodward argued that other sign languages in America, dating from before the arrival of LSF in Hartford, must have played a role in the emergence of ASL. Woodward's claim has been further supported by recent historical descriptions of deaf individuals and sign language communities in colonial New England and Canada before the beginning of the 19th century (Carbin & Smith, 1996; Lane, Pillard, & French, 2000). From these records, we learn that deaf individuals were not confined to their families, but

traveled frequently within the region, and some married each other and formed communities, as in the case of a signing community in Maine and another in New Hampshire. There must have been home signers in addition to village sign languages like that of Martha's Vineyard, yet we have no documentation of these different systems or how they contributed to the development of ASL.

Fortunately, there are new Deaf community sign languages, of which the very early stages are now being documented, thus enabling us to study the course of their development in more detail. A key characteristic of new Deaf community sign languages, as opposed to village sign languages, is that most of the signers are unrelated to one another and may come from different regions or cultural backgrounds. Also, the community of the emerging language consists largely of deaf people who come together because of their common experience of deafness and continue to stay together in the presence of institutions like Deaf schools, clubs, and associations. In other words, these are Deaf communities as well as signing communities; the language emerges simultaneously with the community.

Two New Deaf Community Sign Languages
Nicaraguan Sign Language is a modern-day example of an emerging Deaf community sign language (Kegl, Senghas, & Coppola, 1999; Senghas 1995). The first Deaf school in Nicaragua was opened in Managua in 1977. Deaf children who had previously lived with their hearing families in remote parts of the countryside were brought into the city to attend school. Within two decades, a new common sign language was formed through the intermingling of different sign systems: the home sign systems of individual deaf children, a few cases of deaf siblings sharing a sign language within a family (similar to the Amami case described by Osugi et al., 1999), and possibly, contributions from users of established sign languages in Europe and North America who visited the school.

Israeli Sign Language is another new Deaf community sign language. It evolved along with the Israeli Deaf community beginning about 75 years ago, in a pidgin-like situation (Meir & Sandler, 2008). Deaf Israelis of the first generation came from different backgrounds, both in terms of their country of origin, and in terms of their language. A few were born in Israel, and some went to the school for the deaf in Jerusalem that was founded in 1932, but the majority of deaf people who would form the clubs and attend the new schools were immigrants, first from Europe (Germany, Austria, France, Hungary, and Poland), and later from North Africa and the Middle East (Morocco, Iraq, Iran, Algeria, and Egypt). Some of these immigrants brought with them the sign languages of their respective communities. Others had no signing, or used their own home sign. Today, four generations of signers exist simultaneously within the Deaf community, which numbers about 10,000 members. It includes people from the very first generation, who contributed to the earliest stages of the formation and development of the language, to the present generation, now the fourth, that has acquired and further developed the modern language as a full linguistic system. Israeli Sign Language, then, is an example of a Deaf community sign language that is not entirely new in the Psammetichos sense of "original," since some of its first-generation signers had been exposed to other sign languages before becoming a part of the emerging ISL community. What is special about ISL is its recent origins, making the signing of the first generation still available to us today (Meir, 2010; Padden, Meir, Sandler, & Aronoff, 2010b), unlike older Deaf community languages such as ASL. Since ISL is more or less the same age as ABSL, a village sign language, a comparison between new languages resulting from the two different social settings is made possible.

Variables in Emerging Sign Languages

Emerging sign languages are young by definition; the social conditions and histories of their communities are often traceable and their linguistic development is sometimes observable from a very early point. As we have noted, emerging sign languages develop under two distinct settings: inside small communities or villages where transmission is within and between families, and under circumstances in which unrelated signers of different backgrounds are brought together in locations such as clubs or schools. Yet within each type, languages may differ from one another in various respects. It is precisely this variation within types that makes them so valuable to linguists and sociolinguists. Since all of these languages offer natural situations in which access to social and linguistic factors are restricted in terms of either size of community, exposure to a full language, or exposure to language from a very young age (Senghas, 2005), they provide natural laboratories in which we may examine and pin down with some precision the relative contribution of different factors to the linguistic system that emerges. By

isolating these variables and comparing linguistic systems, we may learn more about the contribution of each variable to the emergence and development of language. We describe here several dimensions along which emerging languages may vary, starting with variation in the social structure of the communities, and then turn to linguistic properties of the languages themselves.

Characteristics of Sign Language Communities
SIZE OF COMMUNITY
In general, Deaf community sign languages have much larger communities than those of village sign languages. Because of their institution-based origin, new members enter the community regularly and remain together over an extended period of time. In Nicaragua, 15–20 deaf children enroll in the school in Managua every year (Senghas, 2005). In 2005, the community numbered 800 deaf members according to Senghas. In Israel, the establishment of the Deaf Association in 1944 drew deaf people from around the country, including new immigrants. The Deaf community grew in about six decades from a few dozen to about 10,000 members. Deaf community sign languages often become national sign languages. American Sign Language, which originated in the first American school for the deaf, quickly spread across North America and into Canada, where it is now the primary language of about a quarter of a million people.

Village sign languages, on the other hand, depend solely on human reproduction and genetic transmission of deafness. The number of deaf people born into the community may be very small. For example, Ferreira-Brito (1984) reports five deaf people in the Urubu-Kaapor tribe in Brazil; Ban Khor has 16 deaf people,[2] and Adamorobe has 35 deaf individuals. Desa Kolok in Bali has 47 deaf people. The largest deaf population in a village community reported so far is that of the Al-Sayyid village (about 150 deaf members). However, the size of the signing community in the village setting depends not only on the number of deaf people, but also on the involvement of hearing villagers in sign communication. In Desa Kolok, almost two-thirds of the village's more than 2,000 inhabitants sign to some degree. Ferreira-Brito (1984) reports on a Brazilian village with only one deaf child, but where all the hearing people in the village communicate with that child in signs. Here, the signing community can be said to consist of the entire village, although signing is the primary language for only one person. Kuschel (1973) describes a similar case. This situation contrasts with the home sign situation in some families, in which the entire language community consists of a single person because other family members do not adopt the gestural system invented by the deaf child, or do so very minimally (Goldin-Meadow, 2003). The total village signing community, then, may be much larger than the number of deaf people in the village, but typically villages grow more slowly than do urban Deaf communities.

Senghas (2005) suggests that the difference in community size and growth rate may have repercussions for language change. She argues that the regular influx of new signers into the NSL community led to more rapid change in that language compared to what might be observed in a village sign language. Washabaugh claims that the limited direct interaction among deaf signers on Providence Island is one factor that accounts for the simplicity of the structure of the language. For spoken languages, Hay and Bauer (2007) have shown that languages with larger populations tend to have a larger phonemic inventory than do those with smaller populations. With respect to sign languages, we do not yet know of such a direct community size effect for any aspect of their structure.

AGE OF LANGUAGE

Some of the languages under discussion are very young. Of the village languages, ABSL is about 75 years old, and the language is currently in its third generation. Other languages may be much older. Adamorobe Sign Language is estimated to be about 200 years old. In some cases, it is very difficult to determine the age of the language, since there are no written or reliable oral records about the time of the appearance of deafness in the community. Kata Kolok, the sign language of Desa Kolok in Bali, is estimated to be as much as 500 years old, according to oral history and local myths. However, geneticists who studied the distribution of the genetic mutation for deafness in the village suggest that the language is much younger. According to their measures, deafness first appeared in the community between 63 and 134 years ago (Winata et al., 1995, p. 342). If this estimate is correct, then Kata Kolok cannot be much older than ABSL. The large discrepancy between the two estimates, a difference of about 400 years, shows that caution must be exercised when clear-cut evidence is lacking. The two new

Deaf community sign languages that we have described (ISL and NSL) are also quite young; ISL was born about the same time as ABSL (in the 1930s), and NSL is the youngest of any of the emerging sign languages documented so far, dating from the founding of the Managua Deaf school in 1977.

DISTRIBUTION OF DEAF PEOPLE IN THE COMMUNITY

As pointed out earlier, the two language types differ with respect to the composition of the signing community. In Deaf community sign languages, many of the signers are deaf. The largest fraction of hearing signers in these communities consists of hearing children of deaf parents. Others include interpreters, teachers, and relatives. Hearing spouses may also be part of the community, but in the large majority of cases, deaf marry deaf in these communities. Marriage between deaf and hearing is generally the exception.

Village sign languages are more varied in terms of the distribution of deaf and hearing members of the signing community. Usually, the number of deaf people is much smaller than that of hearing signers, but the distribution of deaf people differs across communities. Deafness may be restricted to one or two families within the community, as in the case of Amami Sign Language (Osugi et al., 1999), or it may be distributed widely across the community. In the former case, a few families have many deaf members; in the latter, many families have a few deaf members, so that many hearing people have contact with deaf people. Lane et al. (2000) suggest that this difference in distribution might be the result of different types of genetic transmission. If the gene for deafness is dominant, deafness runs in immediate families, and there are likely to be deaf children in every generation. The majority of deaf children will have a deaf parent, and most deaf parents have deaf children. Therefore, fewer hearing people are part of the signing community, and fewer hearing people acquire the sign language as a native language. In recessive transmission, on the other hand, deaf children do not usually have deaf parents, but rather other deaf relatives. Deafness usually results from marriage among relatives, hence deaf people are part of an extended family that includes many hearing members as well. More hearing people are likely to sign, since so many of them have deaf relatives, and many hearing members are native signers. Also, many more mixed marriages between hearing and deaf occur. Most of the village communities reported in the literature show the pattern of recessive transmission, which results in deafness spreading across many families in the community. The distribution of deafness in the community affects the involvement of hearing people in the signing community and vice versa. If many families have deaf members, then more hearing people use the language on a daily basis. The result is a larger and more stable signing community. In Desa Kolok, for example, Marsaja (2008) reports that more than two-thirds of the community use the sign language, although deaf people constitute only 2% of the population. In Adamorobe, with 35 deaf people, about 300 people use sign language.

Nonaka (2007) argues that cultural practices may play a larger role than type of genetic deafness in shaping interaction between deaf and hearing signers. In Ban Khor, most deaf people are descendants of a family in which the condition of deafness is dominant, not recessive. Despite Lane et al.'s prediction, the village sign language is well-distributed across both deaf and hearing people, in large part because of the close proximity of their houses in the village.

SOCIAL STATUS OF DEAF PEOPLE

The communities may vary as to the social status of deaf members. In some communities, deaf people do not differ from hearing members in their social status and rights. In Martha's Vineyard, deaf people were fully integrated in the community, held land and political offices, owned businesses and engaged in trade, so much so that the distinction between hearing and deaf was vague in the mind of the islanders (Groce, 1985, p. 51). Most deaf people married hearing spouses (65%), and took part in all social aspects of life in the community. In Desa Kolok, deaf people participate in all the social and ritual duties and obligations of the community. In other communities, deaf people are quite marginalized. Washabaugh (1981, 1986) reports that in Providence and Grand Cayman islands, hearing people had a paternalistic attitude toward deaf people, who were regarded as simple-minded and were not encouraged to socialize or work outside of the family. Washabaugh suggests that the social position and geographic distribution of deaf people and their language in the community may have restricted the structural development of the sign language. He noticed that hearing people did not share complex information with deaf people, and did not engage in extended or detailed linguistic

exchanges with them. The geographic isolation of small groups of deaf people from one another on the island was another factor that discouraged the expansion of the language.

EXPOSURE TO OTHER SIGN LANGUAGES

Many of the communities in which village sign languages have arisen have become less isolated and closed over the years. Social changes may lead to increased social mobility, and the development of educational institutions for the deaf increases the contact of deaf members of the village with deaf people from outside. As a result, over the years, the deaf members of all of these communities come into contact with other sign languages that have more signers and enjoy greater status in the country. These changes endanger the delicate social networks of the community and its sign language. Therefore, all village sign languages are fragile, and they are often endangered (Nonaka, 2004).

Properties of the Languages

FUNCTIONS OF LANGUAGE

Language may be used for different communicative purposes and functions (Jakobson, 1960): for transmitting information about the world, for making other people perform certain actions, for getting information from others, and for regulating social interactions. Crucially, language also has a meta-linguistic function and an artistic function: it may be used to talk about language itself, and it may be used to create art forms, such as literature and poetry. Most of the literature on emerging sign languages does not directly refer to the different uses of the language in question. Washabaugh's book (1986, pp. 66–69) is an exception. He explicitly mentions that Providence Island Sign Language (PSL) lacks meta-language. Signers do not use the language to talk about their language. He never witnessed anyone correcting another signer for incorrect signing. Interestingly, there are also no name signs. People use descriptive signs to refer to other people, but there is lots of variation in these signs, and, crucially, the people themselves have no idea that a particular sign is used as their name. In contrast, ABSL signers use their language for a wide variety of topics, including meta-linguistic functions. They have no problem participating in linguistic tasks that require some meta-linguistic abilities; they can make comparisons between ABSL and other sign languages, and signers often comment on and criticize other signers' language productions. As for artistic functions, no poetry has been reported in any new sign language, but ISL is commonly used in public story-telling gatherings in recent years.

LANGUAGE INTERFERENCE FROM
THE SPOKEN LANGUAGE

Since the communities of all village sign languages documented to date consist of both deaf and hearing signers, a large percentage of the language users (all hearing signers) are bilingual in the sign language and the spoken language of the hearing community. It might be expected that this language contact would result in interference from the spoken language in the sign language. Nyst (2007) reports that in Adamorobe, hearing signers may be strongly influenced by the structure of Akan, the spoken language of the village, using what she refers to as "Sign-supported Akan." In addition, mouthing of spoken words as well as loan translations are very common in that language. In ABSL, on the other hand, mouthing is very rare in both hearing and deaf signers, especially in the older generation. Also, the sentence structure of hearing people using ABSL does not show more similarity to their spoken Arabic dialect than does the sentence structure of deaf signers.

WORD ORDER

Some village sign languages have been reported to develop a predominant word order. Al-Sayyid Bedouin Sign Language developed a subject-object-verb (SOV) order by its second generation (Sandler et al., 2005). This order differs from the word order found in the Arabic vernacular spoken in the surrounding areas, which is SVO. Literary Arabic is VSO, and Hebrew, also spoken in the region, is SVO. Kata Kolok adheres to SVO order when possible ambiguities may arise (e.g., when both participants in an action can be either the subject or the object, as in *X sees Y*), but uses more flexible word order when the sentence can be disambiguated by its semantics alone (Marsaja, 2008, p. 168–169). Basic word order in the spoken languages of Indonesia is SVO (Dryer, 2005), but it is hard to determine the effect of this on the word order tendencies found in Kata Kolok. In PSL, there is much variation in word order (Washabaugh, 1986, p. 60). Deaf signers in the 1986 study tended to put the verb at the end, but did not use consistent order between agents and patients. Hearing signers were more consistent: they tended to have agents before patients in 99% of their utterances. As for the position of the verb, those hearing signers who had deaf family members placed the verb in final position in 64% of their responses, while those who did not have daily

contact with deaf people had verb-final order only 23% of the time. This may be interpreted as more interference from the spoken vernacular, Providence Island Creole, as creoles in general are characterized by an SVO order (Arends, Muysken, & Smith, 1995).

The two Deaf community sign languages reported here exhibit a variety of word orders. Signers of the first two generations of ISL do not show preference for any specific word order. Third-generation signers use SOV order more than other orders, but SVO and SVOV are also quite common (Meir, 2010). The SVO order thus might reflect interference from Hebrew. Nicaraguan Sign Language shows a rapid change in word order. First-cohort signers used mainly noun-verb (NV) or NNV order (that is, sentences consisting of a noun or two nouns and a verb), whereas second-cohort signers introduced many more orders (Senghas, Coppola, Newport, & Supalla, 1997).

USE OF SPACE

Sign languages may use signing space to represent real-world locations, or to encode more abstract relations, such as transitivity relations. The former is often referred to as *topographical use of space*, and the latter, *grammatical* or *metaphorical use of space*. A few village sign languages have been reported to employ space for topographical use, but not for metaphorical or grammatical use. In ABSL, signers point to the direction of the real-world location of a house, in order to refer to a person who lives in that house. They also attach pointing signs to names of locations such as cities and countries (Aronoff, Meir, Padden, & Sandler, 2008). These pointing signs are consistent with the real-world locations of the cities and countries in relation to the Al-Sayyid village. In Kata Kolok, pointing to real-world locations is very common, as is pointing to real-world locations of referents. However, Kata Kolok does not use space in an abstract or metaphorical way, or to represent transitivity or transfer relations. An interesting use of space in that language is to use pointing for times of the day by pointing to the location of the sun in the sky, which varies little from day to day in a tropical latitude. In contrast to village sign languages, the two new Deaf community sign languages discussed here, ISL and NSL, eventually developed grammatical use of space, but this development was gradual. It took ISL three generations to develop a full verb-agreement system (Meir, 2010; Padden et al. 2010b); a more consistent use of space in NSL developed in signers who entered the community between 1985 and 1990 (referred to as "second-cohort signers" by

Senghas, 2003), but it is unknown as yet whether any signers of NSL have a verb-agreement system. If it turns out that Deaf community sign languages are more likely to have spatial verb-agreement systems, it would be an interesting case in which a specific linguistic structure correlates with the sociolinguistic characteristics of the community.

The Theoretical Significance of Emerging Sign Languages

As pointed out earlier, emerging sign languages provide natural laboratories for the study of some fundamental theoretical issues in language evolution, emergence, and development. We outlined three questions in the introduction: (1) What does a new language look like? (2) How does linguistic complexity arise in language? And, (3) What is the relation between language and the characteristics of the community? Studies of the different emerging sign languages to date provide some answers to these questions, which we turn to next. However, the study of new languages is in its infancy, and researchers use different methods and materials for discovering the nature of the language they investigate. Furthermore, they may come from different academic disciplines—linguistics, psychology, anthropology—leading them to ask different research questions. For these reasons, caution is called for in comparing emerging languages to one another, since the methodologies and research frameworks of these studies differ greatly from one another.

What Does a New Language Look Like?

It might be taken for granted that all languages have words and sentences. But it is still empirical to determine which units are present in the very initial stages of a language. The three youngest languages described here, ABSL, ISL, and NSL, all have recognizable words (both content and function words) and larger syntactic units with internal structure, such as phrases (e.g., ABSL; Aronoff et al., 2008: WOMAN HEBRON FAT "the fat woman from Hebron," GIRL GOOD PEASANT JERUSALEM "a good peasant girl from Jerusalem") and sentences (e.g., ISL: WOMAN BOX TABLE PUT-ON "The woman put the box on the table'").

However, the syntactic structures found in new languages tend to be simple. In the early stages of the three languages under discussion, there is a strong tendency for sentences to contain only one nominal. Some action concepts, such as "fall," "run," and "smile," require only one argument, but many require two or three arguments, for example "push"

(two) or "give" (three). In such cases, signers of the first generation of ISL, ABSL, and NSL tend to break the event into two clauses, with two verb signs, each predicating of a different argument (Meir, 2010; Padden, Meir, Sandler, & Aronoff, 2010a; Senghas et al., 1997). An event in which a girl feeds a woman may be described as: WOMAN SIT; GIRL FEED. An event in which a man throws a ball to a girl can be rendered as: GIRL STAND; MAN BALL THROW; GIRL CATCH. This tendency is especially strong when two animate arguments are involved. Apparently, languages take time to develop grammatical methods of distinguishing between the subject and the object nominals in a clause. Without such marking, it may be hard to indicate "who is doing what to whom." Having only one argument in a clause eliminates the need for such methods.

Little or no inflectional morphology has been found in emerging sign languages. But one morphological process is quite prevalent: compounding. This basic grammatical strategy is available for expanding the vocabulary of languages from very early on, and they make extensive use of it. Washabaugh found that 40% of the elicited signs in PSL were compounds (compared to 11.5% in ASL). Different types of compounds were described for ABSL (Aronoff et al., 2008), ISL (Meir & Sandler, 2008), and Adamorobe Sign Language (Nyst, 2007). In addition to more ordinary compounding, both ABSL and Adamorobe Sign Language have a specific type of compounding, in which one member of the compound is a sign indicating the relative length and width of an object by pointing to various parts of the hand and arm. These "measuring stick signs," which are akin to Size and Shape Specifiers, have not been reported in other sign languages so far. The specifiers pattern somewhat differently in these two languages, revealing grammatical differences within the same type of structure in different emerging sign languages.

Another important component of languages found very early on is prosody. Al-Sayyid Bedouin Sign Language (Aronoff et al., 2008; Sandler et al., 2005) and ISL (Nespor & Sandler, 1999) use systematic prosodic cues for chunking information units and connecting them to one another. As in more established sign languages, these cues consist of rhythmic patterns conveyed by the hands, accompanied by facial expressions and head and body postures. In fact, it is through studying the prosodic chunking of the emerging ABSL that researchers were able to identify constituents for determining word order patterns in otherwise unclear cases.

How Does Linguistic Complexity Arise in Language?

Although emerging sign languages have properties such as communicative depth and the existence of words and sentences that characterize them as languages, they seem to lack complex structures, suggesting that languages accrue complexity over time, and do not arise full-blown in a single generation. For instance, there are no reports of a village sign language with syntactic embedding—that is, the embedding of a clause inside another, as in "He told me *that he is coming*," or "The boy *that you met yesterday* is my son." Similarly, the complex spatial morphology that marks verb agreement in many sign languages has not been attested in any village sign language. The mechanism of verb agreement in sign languages involves associating discourse participants with locations in the signing space, and moving the path of verbs denoting transfer between these locations in a rule-governed manner. This mechanism was generally thought to be a typological mark of sign languages, yet it is absent from village sign languages. Aronoff, Meir, and Sandler (2005) suggest that grammatical use of space in verb agreement and in a system of classifier constructions tend to occur in all established sign languages, even when relatively young, due to the iconically motivated basis of these systems. Yet the evidence so far indicates that emerging sign languages do not have structures of this kind from the beginning. Village sign languages do not seem to have these spatially based grammatical systems (Aronoff, Meir, Padden, & Sandler, 2004; Marsaja, 2008), and research on ISL and NSL has shown that the grammatical use of space in these Deaf community languages develops gradually.

Although some types of grammatical conventionalization have been reported, not all new sign languages share the same types of grammatical structures, showing that there is no single path to development. For example, ISL and ABSL chose different paths when developing grammatical devices for marking of argument structure: ABSL moved toward relying on word order, whereas ISL developed verb agreement (Meir, 2010).

What Is the Relation Between Features of Language and Characteristics of the Community?

Earlier, we described several dimensions along which emerging languages may vary. By comparing languages of communities that differ along well-specified dimensions, it is possible to pin down the relative contribution of these factors to the development of the language.

One such factor is the degree of integration of deaf people in the language community. According to Washabaugh, PSL did not develop into a fully structured system, despite the fact that it is at least three generations old, because of paternalistic attitudes toward deaf people and their isolation from one another. This explanation suggests that language requires more than human individuals and time to develop into a fully structured system; varied and frequent social interactions are also a crucial factor.

Further evidence for the role of the community in language development comes from comparing the two types of emerging sign languages presented in this chapter. Deaf community sign languages appear to be more dynamic than village sign languages, perhaps because of the rapid influx of new signers into the community and the wider range of contact with one another and of informational contexts that are found in institutionally supported communities. Senghas and her colleagues (Senghas, 1995; Senghas et al., 1997) have shown rapid language development and change between cohorts of school children in Nicaragua. Israeli Sign Language and ABSL are more or less of the same age, but they developed under very different circumstances, and show differences in grammatical development. In ISL, the rapid growth of the community resulted in a quicker rate of change than in ABSL. The difference between third-generation versus first- and second-generation signers is larger for ISL than for ABSL with respect to the development of grammatical use of space (Meir, 2010; Padden et al., 2010b).

One observation that recurs in accounts of village sign languages is the extent of lexical variation. A surprising degree of lexical variation is reported to be found in Adamarobe, Providence Island, Amami Island, and ABSL. For example, in ABSL three lexical variants exist for commonly used words such as *cat, lemon, train,* and *morning,* and many signs have two variants, such as *fish, white, red, tree,* and many others. Figure 18.1 shows three variants of the sign *cat* in ABSL, each built on a different image: whiskers, licking the front paws, and the cat's footprints.

Since village sign language communities are quite small, degree of variation in their languages may be more accessible to examine than in larger language communities. Washabaugh (1986, pp. 50–51) conducted a study of lexical variation in PSL: he found that out of 63 signs that five signers signed, only two were perfectly conventionalized (having one unified form), 11 were extremely unconventionalized (five variants), and 70% of the signs had three or more variants. In comparison, the same study was run on

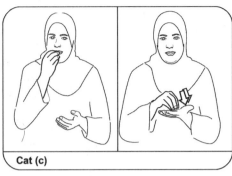

Fig. 18.1 Three variants of the sign *cat* in Al-Sayyid Bedouin Sign Language

five ASL hearing signers from four different places in the United States. The results showed that ASL is much more unified: only 28.6% of the signs had more than three variants. It is possible that the iconicity afforded by languages in the visual modality facilitates the coexistence of variants within the community. Iconic signs tend to be more transparent; that is, their meaning can be deduced from their form, since their form is determined by some aspects of their meaning. But although the auditory modality allows for a much lesser degree of iconicity, this does not mean that the variation described here did not characterize early spoken language as well, as humans are capable of storing a vast number of different lexical items, including synonyms.

In our study of the ABSL vocabulary, we have found that there is far less variation within nuclear families with several deaf members than there is across the community. This observation underscores the centrality of the family as a sociolinguistic unit. It is reasonable to expect that the variants will tend to converge on a single exemplar as the overall vocabulary expands, provided frequent community-wide interaction occurs.

Summary and Conclusions

Roger Shattuck's book, *The Forbidden Experiment* (1980), tells the story of Victor, the Wild Boy of Aveyron, who emerged from the woods near the southern French town of Aveyron at about the age of 12, having apparently grown up alone in the wild. The forbidden experiment of Shattuck's title is the experiment that Psammetichos undertook, that of raising children without human company. Its purpose is to discover human nature, what we are endowed with before culture intervenes. But, as Aristotle so memorably put it (Nicomachean Ethics 9.9), "man is a social being, and designed by nature to live with others." Having a culture is part of

human nature. That is what sets us apart more than anything else from other creatures. The experiment is forbidden because it is inhuman to deprive people of what is natural to them, language and culture. Emerging sign languages come closer than any other circumstance to the forbidden experiment. By comparing the languages created under such circumstances, we can begin to learn something about the nature of language and of people. What they reveal is first and foremost that humans placed together without a cultural model to emulate (in this case, without a language) are so driven to create a community in which they can communicate with each other that they will create their own language.

Because researchers approach their investigations with different questions, different materials, and different analytic tools, it is at present difficult to rigorously compare emerging sign languages. Nevertheless, it is fair to say that such languages all have properties that characterize them as languages, properties such as communicative power and the existence of symbolic units—words—as well as sentences. They also allow their users to participate in the social life of their communities. Yet these new languages also differ from older and more established languages, both spoken and signed. And it is precisely these differences that shed light on what it takes for a language to develop, and how it does so.

Two important points arise from this survey. First, it takes more than a human brain for a language to develop. Interaction is a factor no less crucial. Home sign systems, systems created by an individual or by very few individuals, do not have the expressive capabilities and the structure of even new languages. Therefore, one brain (or two? or three?) is not enough to make a language. But even larger numbers of communicators may not guarantee that a full-fledged language will develop. The lesson to learn from PSL, as Washabaugh (1986, p. 146) argues, is that without varied and frequent social interactions, a communication system will not develop into a complex and context-free system:

> This conclusion to the PSL research reinforces assumptions which run contrary to [those]... behind much current linguistic research ... that human individuals, by reason of being endowed each with a language faculty, are autonomous and independent of one another. But a result of this investigation of PSL is that the operation of each individual's language faculty is not autonomous but very much dependent on appropriate relationships with others.

The specific conditions under which PSL emerged and developed are essential for evaluating the contribution of social interactions to the development of language. The same is true for the other languages surveyed here.

Second, new languages show that linguistic complexity takes time to develop. Languages do not suddenly materialize, complete with syntactic embedding and morphological inflection. Even a clause structure containing two animate arguments (as in "*The girl is feeding her mother*") takes some time to develop in a new language. More complex grammatical systems evolve over time, and the structures they develop will vary. The fact that syntactic embedding is not found in new languages brings into question the hypothesis that recursion, the syntactic mechanism underlying the ability to create an embedded clause, is the hallmark of human capacity for language, as Hauser, Chomsky, and Fitch (2002) argue. The study of new sign languages makes it possible to raise questions such as these, and therein lies its importance for our understanding of human language. As more such languages and communities come under study, and more structured and controlled comparative studies are conducted we will be able to refine our questions, and, we hope, to answer them.

Acknowledgment

This article is supported by grants from the National Institute on Deafness and other Communication Disorders (R01 DC 6473) and the Israel Science Foundation (#553/04).

Notes

[1] For example, in the United States the incidence of congenital deafness is about 0.07% (Marazita et al., 1993).

[2] If not otherwise mentioned, facts about the Ban Khor are from Nonaka (2007), Adamorobe from Nyst (2007), Desa Kolok from Marsaja (2008), and Providence Island from Washabaugh (1986).

References

Al-Fityani, K. (2007). Arab sign languages: A lexical comparison. *Technical Report. Center for Research in Language Newsletter*, *19*(1).

Arends, J, Muysken, P, & Smith, N. (1995). *Pidgins and creoles: An introduction*. Amsterdam/Philadelphia: Benjamins.

Aronoff, M., Meir, I., Padden, C. A, & Sandler, W. (2004). Morphological universals and the sign language type. In G. Booij & J. van Marle (Eds.), *Yearbook of Morphology* (pp. 19–40). Dordrecht: Kluwer Academic Publishers.

Aronoff, M., Meir, I., Padden, C. A., & Sandler, W. (2008). The roots of linguistic organization in a new language. *Interaction Studies: A Special Issue on Holophrasis vs. Compositionality in the Emergence of Protolanguage*, *9*(1), 131–150.

Aronoff, M., Meir, I., & Sandler, W. (2005). The paradox of sign language morphology. *Language*, *81*(2), 301–344.

Briggs, L. C., & Guede, N. L. (1964). *No more for ever: A Saharan Jewish town*. Cambridge, MA: The Peabody Museum.

Carbin, C. F., & Smith, D. L. (1996). *Deaf heritage in Canada: A distinctive, diverse, and enduring culture*. Toronto, New York: McGraw-Hill Ryerson.

Dryer, M. S. (2005). Order of subject, object, and verb. In Haspelmath, M., M. S. Dryer, D. Gil, & B. Comrie (Eds.), *The world atlas of language structures* (pp. 330–334). Oxford: Oxford University Press.

Ferreira-Brito, L. (1984). Similarities and differences in two Brazilian sign languages. *Sign Language Studies*, *42*, 45–56.

Goldin-Meadow, S. (2003). *The resilience of language: What gesture creation in deaf children can tell us about how all children learn language*. New York: Psychology Press.

Groce, N. E. (1985). *Everyone here spoke sign language: Hereditary deafness on Martha's Vineyard*. Cambridge, MA: Harvard University Press.

Hay, J., & Bauer, L. (2007). Phoneme inventory size and population size. *Language*, *83*(2), 388–400.

Hauser, M. D., Chomsky, N., & Fitch, W. T. (2002). The faculty of language: What is it, who has it, and how did it evolve? *Science*, *298*, 1569–1579.

Jakobson, R. (1960). Linguistics and poetics. In T. Sebeok (Ed.), *Style in Language* (pp. 350–377). Cambridge, Mass: MIT Press.

Kegl, J., Senghas, A., & Coppola, M. (1999). Creation through contact: Sign language emergence and sign language change in Nicaragua. In M. DeGraff (Ed.), *Language creation and language change: Creolization, diachrony, and development* (pp. 197–237). Cambridge, MA: MIT Press.

Kisch, S. (2000). Deaf discourse: The social construction of deafness in a Bedouin community. MA Thesis, Tel-Aviv University, Israel (in Hebrew).

Kisch, S. (2004). Negotiating deafness in a Bedouin community. In J. V. Van Cleve (Ed.), *Genetics, disability and deafness* (pp. 148–173). Washington, DC: Gallaudet University Press.

Knight, C., Studdert-Kennedy, M., & Hurford, J. R. (2000). *The evolutionary emergence of language: Social function and the origins of linguistic form*. Cambridge, UK: Cambridge University Press.

Kuschel, R. (1973). The silent inventor: The creation of a sign language by the only deaf-mute on a Polynesian island. *Sign Language Studies*, *3*, 1–27.

Lane, H., Pillard, R. C., & French, M. (2000). Origins of the American deaf-world: Assimilating and differentiating societies and their relation to genetic patterning. *Sign Language Studies*, *1*(1), 17–44.

Marazita, M. L., Ploughman, L. M., Rawlings, B., Rremington, E., Arnos, K. S., & Nance, W. E. (1993). Genetic epidemiological studies of early-onset deafness in the U. S. school-age population. *American Journal of Medical Genetics*, *46*(5), 486–491.

Marsaja, I. G. (2008). *Desa kolok - A deaf village and its sign language in Bali, Indonesia*. Nijmegen: Ishara Press.

McNeill, D. (1992). *Hand and Mind*. Chicago: University of Chicago Press.

McWhorter, J. (1998). Identifying the creole prototype: Vindicating a typological class. *Language*, *74*, 788–818.

Meir, I. (2010). The emergence of argument structure in two new sign languages. In M. Rappaport Hovav, E. Doron & I. Sichel (Eds.), *Syntax, lexical semantics and event structure* (pp. 101–113). Oxford: Oxford University Press.,

Meir, I., & Sandler, W. (2008). *A language in space: The story of Israeli Sign Language*. New York: Lawrence Erlbaum Associates.

Nespor, M., & Sandler, W. (1999). Prosody in Israeli sign language. *Language and Speech*, *42*(2–3), 143–176.

Nonaka, A. M. (2004). The forgotten endangered languages: Lessons on the importance of remembering from Thailand's Ban Khor sign language. *Language in Society*, *33*(5), 737–767.

Nonaka, A. M. (2007). *Emergence of an indigenous sign language and a Speech/Sign community in Ban Khor, Thailand. Unpublished*. Los Angeles: University of California.

Nonaka, A. M. (2009). Estimating, size, scope, and membership of the speech/sign communities of undocumented indigenous/village sign languages: The Ban Kor case study. *Language and Communication 29*, 210–229.

Nyst, V. (2007). *A descriptive analysis of Adamorobe Sign Language (Ghana)*. Utrecht: LOT.

Osugi, Y., Supalla, T., & Webb, R. (1999). The use of word elicitation to identify distinctive gestural systems on Amami island. *Sign Language & Linguistics*, *2*(1), 87–112.

Padden, C. A., Meir, I., Sandler, W. & Aronoff, M. (2010a). Against all expectations: Encoding subjects and objects in a new language. In D. Gerdts, J. Moore, & M. Polinsky (Ed.), *Hypothesis A/Hypothesis B* (pp. 383-400). Cambridge MA: MIT Press

Padden, C. A., Meir, I., Sandler, W., & Aronoff, M. (2010b). The grammar of space in two new sign languages. In D. Brentari (Ed.), *Sign languages: A Cambridge language survey*. Cambridge, UK: Cambridge University Press.

Sandler, W. (2005). An overview of sign language linguistics. In K. Brown (Ed.), *Encyclopedia of language and linguistics*, 2nd edition (pp. 328–338). Oxford, UK: Elsevier.

Sandler, W., Meir, I., Padden, C., & Aronoff, M. (2005). The emergence of grammar: Systematic structure in a new language. *PNAS*, *102*(7), 2661–2665.

Scott, D. A., Carmi, R., Elbedour, K., Duyk, G. M., Stone, E. M., & Sheffield, V. C. (1995). Nonsyndromic autosomal recessive deafness is linked to the DFNB1 locus in a large inbred Bedouin family from Israel. *American Journal of Human. Genetics*, *54*(4), 965–968.

Senghas, A. (1995). Children's contribution to the birth of Nicaraguan Sign Language. Ph.D. Dissertation. Cambridge: Massachusetts Institute of Technology.

Senghas, A. (2003). Intergenerational influence and ontogenetic development in the emergence of spatial grammar in Nicaraguan Sign Language. *Cognitive Development* 18(4), 511–531

Senghas, A. (2005). Language emergence: Clues from a new Bedouin sign. *Current Biology*, *15*(12), 463–465.

Senghas, A., Coppola, M., Newport, E., & Supalla, T. (1997). Argument structure in Nicaraguan Sign Language: The emergence of grammatical devices. In E. Hughes, M. Hughes, & A. Greenhill (Eds.), *The proceedings of the Boston University conference on language development* (pp. 550–561). Boston: Cascadilla Press.

Shattuck, R. (1980). *The Forbidden Experiment*. New York: Farrar Straus Giroux.

Singleton, J. L., Morford, J. P., & Goldin-Meadow, S. (1993). Once is not enough: Standards of well-formedness in manual communication created over three different timespans. *Language*, *69*, 683–715.

Tallerman, M. (2005). *Language origins: Perspectives on evolution*. Oxford: Oxford University Press.

Washabaugh, W. (1981). The deaf of Grand Cayman, British West Indies. *Sign Language Studies*, *10*, 117–34.,

Washabaugh, W. (1986). *Five fingers for survival*. Ann Arbor: Karoma Publishers, Inc.

Woll, B., & Ladd, P. (2003). Deaf communities. In M. Marschark & P. Spencer (Eds.), *Oxford handbook of deaf studies, language, and education* (pp. 151–162). Oxford: Oxford University Press.

Woll, B., Sutton-Spence, R., & Elton, F. (2001). Multilingualism: The global approach to sign language. In C. Lucas (Ed.), *The sociolinguistics of sign languages* (pp. 8–32). Cambridge, UK: Cambridge University Press.

Woodward, J. (1978). All in the family: Kinship lexicalization across sign languages. *Sign Language Studies*, *7*(19), 121–138.

Winata, S., Arhya, I. N., Moeljopawiro, S., Hinnant, J.T., Liang, Y., Friedman, T. B., & Asher, J. H. (1995). Congenital nonsyndromal autosomal recessive deafness in Bengkala, an isolated Balinese village. *Journal of Medical Genetics 32*, 336–343.

Wray, A. (2002). *The transition to language*. Oxford: Oxford University Press. Jakobson, R. (1960). Linguistics and poetics. *Style in Language*, 350–377.

Early Language Acquisition and Adult Language Ability: What Sign Language Reveals About the Critical Period for Language

Rachel I. Mayberry

Abstract

This chapter examines the critical period for language through the prism of deafness. The first topic is the concept of critical periods, followed by a summary of research investigating age of acquisition effects on the outcome of second-language learning (L2). The phenomenon of late first-language (L1) acquisition among deaf children is then described. The focus of this chapter is on a series of studies that compare and contrast the long-range outcome of L1 and L2 acquisition in relation to age of acquisition. The effects of late L1 acquisition are greater than those for L2 learning. The effects include a compromised ability to process and understand all forms of language. Late L1 acquisition has deleterious effects on the ability to learn other languages and on reading development. The findings come from experiments in American Sign Language (ASL) and English using a variety of psycholinguistic paradigms across levels of linguistic structure and include narrative comprehension and shadowing, sentence shadowing and memory, grammatical judgment, and reading comprehension. How these psycholinguistic phenomena illuminate the critical period for language is then discussed.

Keywords: critical period, sign language, ASL, language acquisition, second-language acquisition, reading, development, psycholinguistics, comprehension, phonology, grammar, education, early intervention, Wild Boy of Aveyron, Itard,

In 1806, Jean Itard wrote that adolescence was too late to learn language. He concluded this in a report to the government describing his 2-year attempt to teach the famous Wild Boy of Aveyron to speak French. Itard called the boy Victor because the only sound to which he responded was the French [ɔɪ] (Itard, 1896/1962:29). Eventually Victor could communicate his desires to a limited degree with actions on objects, as in holding his bowl next to the porridge pot when he wanted more, but he never learned French despite intense and structured lessons (Itard, 1896/1962). The idea that language proficiency is linked to the age when the learning begins is known as the *critical period for language* and, as Itard's report demonstrates, is an old idea. Because Itard was the physician for the Institution Nationale de Sourdes-Muets, the world's first school

for deaf children and the birthplace of one of world's largest sign language families (Zeshan, 2006), it is curious that he never tried to teach Victor sign language (Lane, 1976). The school was 40 years old by then, and the historical record shows that French Sign Language was in full bloom (Van Cleve & Crouch, 1989). The idea that sign language is *language* was unheard of in the 1800s, however, and research uncovering its linguistic architecture would not begin for another hundred years (Klima & Bellugi, 1979; Stokoe, Casterline, & Croneberg, 1965).

Could Victor have learned French Sign Language, even though he failed to learn spoken French? The question is whether there is a critical period for language acquisition that encompasses sign language. Because professionals who work with deaf children often appear to implicitly assume that there is a critical period for spoken but not sign language, the question is central to clinical and educational practice. The question is also fundamental to language theory because it requires that we understand the complex relations among language acquisition, brain maturation, and sensory-motor modality. Germane to our discussion is research that investigates age of acquisition effects on the outcome of language acquisition, both spoken language and sign language. The linguistic details of these studies are outside the scope of this chapter, but discussing the research in broad strokes allows us to see the larger picture of how age of acquisition affects the outcome of language acquisition. To foreshadow the conclusion, Victor would not have acquired French Sign Language even though he developed rudimentary, nonvocal communication using objects. The goal of this chapter is to examine the reasons why. We begin by considering what a critical period is with respect to language.

Critical Period Learning

A critical period is a phase during development when learning is most efficient. Critical period phenomena were first observed and documented for animal behavior at a number of levels, for example in chicks' identification and attachment to mother birds (Lorenz, 1965) or in cats' visual perceptual development (Wiesel, 1982). Although critical periods are sometimes characterized as being limits on learning, they represent a unique form of learning in which an interaction between biology and environment produces quick and unconscious learning. Some researchers prefer to replace the term *critical* with adjectives such as *sensitive* or *optimal* to denote the facts that (a) learning can occur after a critical period and (b) that multiple subskills can be involved in a complex skill, each with its own temporal sensitivity in development (Werker & Tees, 2005).

Language acquisition is an example of a complex skill consisting of numerous subskills. Although scientists have observed and documented time-limited sensitivity over development for many types of learning, they disagree as to what the underlying mechanisms might be, both in terms of what causes the heightened sensitivity to a particular type of environmental input and why the sensitivity ends. One class of explanations proposes that environmental complexity directly affects the creation of neural networks (Greenough & Black, 1992), although this neural effect has not yet been found for language. Another type of explanation based on connectionist modeling proposes that early learning itself affects

subsequent learning (Seidenberg & Zevin, 2005), especially with respect to second-language (L2) *vis à vis* first-language (L1) learning, as explained here.

Infants and young children acquire the languages in their environment quickly and effortlessly. By contrast, most adults appear to struggle, and learn new languages only with sustained and conscious effort. The neurosurgeon Wilder Penfield, who first mapped the language areas of the brain during surgeries designed to limit recurrent seizures, observed that the brain has strong biological biases for language in early life. He noted the overwhelming tendency of the anterior left hemisphere to control language—except in cases of injury to the left hemisphere, when homologous regions in the right hemisphere then take control of language, but only if the injury occurs in early childhood (Penfield & Roberts, 1959). This suggests some level of plasticity for language in brain development that is only present in early life.

Age of Acquisition Effects on Spoken Language Outcome

Scientific investigation of the critical period for language requires that we study individuals whose initial exposure to a language varies temporally over the course of human development. One source of information comes from children who experience atypical social isolation during early childhood, including feral children such as Victor, or severely abused children such as the well-known case of Genie who lived without human contact for the first 13 years of her life (Curtiss, 1977). Genie was able to learn some spoken English with intense instruction, but she was unable to maintain her language in adulthood (Garmon, 1994). The multiple complications suffered by these rare cases, such as nutritional and emotional deficiencies, means that we must use caution in interpreting their difficulty with language acquisition because of these confounding factors.

The most common means of investigating age constraints on the outcome of language acquisition has been to measure the language proficiency of people who learn a second language at varying ages. Several studies have found a negative correlation between age of L2 acquisition and eventual L2 proficiency and/or significant differences in language performance between native and non-native learners. These effects have been found across an array of linguistic structures in morphology, syntax, and phonology, while mostly investigating English as the second language, using a number of measurements of spoken and written language, including quality ratings by judges, error counts, memory tasks, and grammaticality judgments (Birdsong & Molis, 2001; Flege, Yeni-Komshian, & Liu, 1999; Johnson & Newport, 1989).

Although these findings confirm the widespread folk belief that learning a second language at a younger age leads to higher L2 proficiency, compared to learning it at older ages, researchers disagree as to how the trend should be interpreted. At issue is whether the decline in L2 proficiency in relation to age provides evidence for a critical period for language. The data suggest that there is no terminal age when a second language can no longer be learned. After the age of 8, the decline in L2 proficiency in relation to age continues throughout the lifespan into senescence (Hakuta, Bialystok, & Wiley, 2003). This finding is interpreted to mean that some factor other than a critical period causes the negative correlation between age of acquisition and L2 proficiency, such as cognitive aging. Moreover, age of acquisition is not the sole predictor of L2 proficiency. Many L2 learners attain near-native proficiency despite older ages of L2 acquisition. Factors such as the amount of education in the second language, and the linguistic relationship of the L1 and L2 also predict L2 outcome (Birdsong & Molis, 2001; Flege, Yeni-Komshian, & Liu, 1999).

When weighing the effects of age of acquisition on L2 proficiency, it is important to bear in mind that L2 learning entails, by definition, acquisition of a first language in early life. If there is a critical period for language acquisition, some researchers argue that it should affect acquisition of the *first* language, rather than the second, based on evidence from rare cases of social isolation in early childhood, in which the outcome of L1 acquisition is severely limited (Eubank & Gregg, 1999). However, these case studies do not provide straightforward evidence for a critical period due to the multiple and severe deprivations suffered by these children, as explained earlier (Mayberry, 1994).

Age of Acquisition Effects on Sign Language Outcome
Variation in Age of Acquisition of Sign Language

A major contribution of sign language research to cognitive science is the discovery that linguistic structure and processing transcend sensory–motor modality (Klima & Bellugi, 1979; Stokoe, Casterline, & Croneberg, 1965). Like spoken languages, sign languages are structured at the sentence (syntax),

word (morphology), subword (phonology), and semantic (word and sentence meaning) levels. Unlike gesture or pantomime, but like spoken language, sign language comprehension requires the unpacking of meaning via the multilayered and hierarchical structure of language. In other words, the meaning of sign language sentences does not come for free by simply looking at signs as if they were pictures. Rather, sign language comprehension requires knowledge of its linguistic structure. Linguistic structure is what young children acquire so readily in early life, leading some researchers to hypothesize that acquisition of linguistic structure is governed by a critical period (Lenneberg, 1967).

That the signer's mind must use the linguistic structure of sign language to understand and produce it has been amply demonstrated in psycholinguistic experiments (for a review see Emmorey, 2002). Neurolinguistic research has further shown that the brain treats sign language like spoken language. Consistent with Penfield's early observations of how the brain represents spoken language (Penfield & Roberts, 1959), researchers have since discovered that anterior regions of the left hemisphere are responsible for sign language processing in deaf and hearing signers, and not regions which process nonlinguistic visual information (for a review see Corina & Knapp, 2006). Damage to these classic language regions cause aphasia in signers comparable to aphasia in speakers (Poizner, Klima, & Bellugi, 1987). Thus, language structure and processing are amodal; the mind and brain treat sign language as language because it is language.

Given what is now known about the nature of sign language, it follows that children's acquisition of it from birth is similar to that of spoken language acquisition with respect to the timing and content of linguistic milestones (Anderson & Reilly, 2002; Mayberry & Squires, 2006; Reilly, 2006). Although sign and spoken language show parallel developmental trajectories when the acquisition begins at birth, most deaf signers are first exposed to sign language at ages well after birth. The crucial question is whether variation in age of acquisition affects sign language proficiency in adulthood. If so, then the question becomes whether such effects are similar to, or different from, those observed for L2 learning of spoken languages described earlier. Before turning to this body of work, it is important to consider why age of sign language exposure is heterogeneous among deaf signers.

A small percentage (less than 10%) of deaf children are born to deaf parents, and this subset of the population is likely to be exposed to sign language from birth. For the remaining 90% of deaf children, sign language acquisition begins at various ages. No single factor underlies this variation, even in cases in which the deaf child lacks functional spoken language. For example, the child may not have been enrolled in school until an older age, especially if the family lived in a rural area. A school that used sign language may not have been in close proximity to the family, and the parents may have been reluctant to send the child away to school or relocate. Alternatively, the family may have insisted that the child remain in an oral program, despite a notable lack of functional language, in the hope that the child would eventually develop spoken language with more time and instruction. Teachers and administrators often share these beliefs. Inaction in exposing a deaf child without functional language to sign language often reflects the assumption that exposing the child to sign language is "giving up" on spoken language, even though this is a mistaken idea. The deaf child's growing maturity and inability to function at school or home without language is often the catalyst for the decision to educate the child in sign language.

These varying circumstances create heterogeneity in the age of sign language exposure within the deaf population. At the same time, these diverse circumstances of sign language acquisition mean that no underlying pathology covaries and/or worsens with age of sign language acquisition, aside from human development with incomplete or sparsely developed language. The cognitive consequences of human development in the face of limited linguistic interaction with the environment have only begun to be investigated (Mayberry, 2002; Schick, de Villiers, de Villiers, & Hoffmeister, 2007).

Another factor in the heterogeneity of sign language acquisition among deaf individuals is whether it is acquired as a first or second language. Some deaf individuals learn sign language as a second language after successful acquisition of spoken language, but for other deaf individuals age of sign language acquisition is more representative of L1 acquisition. This occurs when deaf individuals begin to learn sign language with little or no functional language. Acquiring sign language at older ages with little or no functional language is common among deaf children, although no currently available data describe the frequency of the phenomenon. Some of this L1 language delay is educationally induced, for reasons explained earlier. Indeed, only among deaf signers do we find individuals who are otherwise

intact and were lovingly cared for as children but nonetheless acquired little or no language in early childhood.

Experimental Studies of Age of Acquisition Effects

Similar to the L2 research summarized earlier, several studies have found a negative correlation between age of acquisition and sign language proficiency. Among college-aged students, accuracy of narrative and sentence recall declines as a linear function of American Sign Language (ASL) acquisition between the ages of birth and 15 years (Mayberry & Fischer, 1989). The negative correlation between age of ASL acquisition and sentence recall accuracy persists in adults who have had 20 to 40 years of ASL experience (Mayberry & Eichen, 1991), as shown in Figure 19.1. Similar results have been obtained using a battery of ASL tasks (Newport, 1990) and a sign monitoring task (Emmorey, Bellugi, Friederici, & Horn, 1995). These results show that age of acquisition affects language outcome independently of sensory–motor modality, consistent with what we now understand to be the amodal nature of linguistic structure and processing.

Another question is whether age of acquisition differentially affects the outcome of L1 as compared to L2 proficiency. One study investigated the accuracy of ASL sentence recall in deaf L2 and L1 learners who were matched for years of experience and age of ASL acquisition (Mayberry, 1993). The deaf L2 learners were born with normal hearing, which they lost in late childhood due to viral infections; they learned ASL in immersion settings when they became deaf. By contrast, the deaf L1 learners were first exposed to ASL at the same ages as the L2 learners, but were deaf from birth and had little or no functional spoken language when they began to acquire ASL. The L2 learners recalled the ASL sentences with significantly greater accuracy than the delayed L1 learners, as Figure 19.2 shows (Mayberry, 1993).

These findings demonstrate that age of acquisition has far greater effects on the outcome of the L1 compared to the L2 proficiency, suggesting that the scope of the critical period for language acquisition pertains to the first rather than the second language. A corollary implication is that L1 acquisition in early life facilitates later L2 learning. If early acquisition of spoken language facilitates later acquisition of sign language, the question is whether the reverse situation is true. Does early learning of a sign language facilitate subsequent acquisition of spoken language?

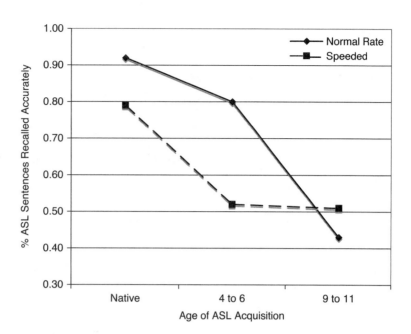

Fig. 19.1 Adjusted mean proportion of recall responses that were grammatical as a function of age of acquisition and sign presentation rate (normal and speeded). Figure 2 from Mayberry, R. I., & Eichen, E. B. (1991). The long-lasting advantage of learning sign language in childhood: Another look at the critical period for language acquisition. *Journal of Memory and Language, 30,* 486–512, with permission of the publisher.

The question was investigated by comparing the English syntactic processing of four groups of adults with contrasting types of L1 experience in early childhood (Mayberry & Lock, 2003). One hearing group served as the control and consisted of native English speakers. The second hearing group consisted of L2 learners of English who were immersed in it in school when they immigrated to Canada in early childhood; their native languages were Urdu, Spanish, German, and French. The third group was born deaf and exposed to ASL from birth; they subsequently learned English as a second language in school at the same ages as the hearing L2 learners. It is important to highlight the fact that two different

types of English L2 learners participated in the study: one hearing group whose early first language was a spoken language other than English, and one deaf group whose early first language was sign language. The fourth group was also deaf but began to learn ASL and English in school at the same age as the other groups. However, their school enrollment marked their first experience with fully perceivable language; that is, they entered school with little or no previously acquired functional language.

Both groups of L2 learners, regardless of whether they were hearing or deaf, or whether their first language was spoken or signed, performed at near-native levels across the English syntactic structures tested,

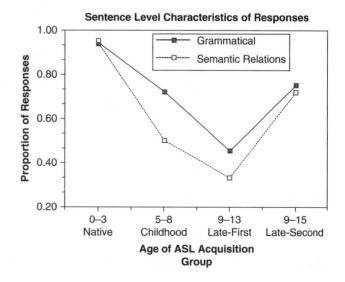

Fig. 19.2 The mean proportion of the subjects' total responses that were grammatically acceptable and semantically parallel to the stimuli for subjects grouped by age of American Sign Language acquisition and first versus second language acquisition. Figure 4 from Mayberry, R. I. (1993). First-language acquisition after childhood differs from second-language acquisition: The case of American Sign Language. *Journal of Speech and Hearing Research, 36,* 1258–1270, with permission of the publisher.

as Figure 19.3 shows (Mayberry & Lock, 2003). These results are consistent with earlier described studies investigating the effects of age of L2 acquisition on spoken language, namely that L2 learners can sometimes attain near-native levels of L2 proficiency. The results show that this is true even when the first language is an early-acquired sign language, as was the case in this study. These results also replicate the previous finding that delayed L1 acquisition impedes language proficiency in adulthood: the deaf delayed L1 learners entered school with little functional language. A dearth of language acquisition in early childhood has deleterious effects on the outcome of all subsequent language learning in later life (sign language and written and read language); neither the first nor the second language is acquired to near-native levels in adulthood.

In another experiment, the English task was changed from grammatical judgment to sentence-to-picture matching. Despite the added nonverbal context of pictures, the delayed L1 learners, all of whom had normal nonverbal IQ, performed at low levels on several English structures including conjoined, passives, and relative clauses. Replicating the results of previous experiments, the two L2 groups, one hearing and one deaf, again performed at near-native levels. Thus, three experiments in two languages (ASL and English) show, first, that age of acquisition effects are robust and persist into adulthood for L1 acquisition. Second, the results show that L1 acquisition in early life supports and facilitates subsequent L2 learning independently of sensory–motor modality (Mayberry, 2007).

When L1 Exposure Is Delayed Until Adolescence: Effects on Language Outcomes

Experimental studies of groups of deaf adults show that the scope of the critical period for language pertains to the first language, and that a lack of language acquisition in early life impedes the ability to learn language throughout life. The few available case studies of deaf individuals' L1 acquisition begun in adolescence corroborate the main findings of these experiments. First, the rate of delayed L1 acquisition is significantly slower than that of timely L1 acquisition. Second, adult language proficiency is significantly limited in comparison to early L1 acquisition or later L2 acquisition.

Two studies longitudinally followed the spoken L1 acquisition of a deaf adolescent and an adult

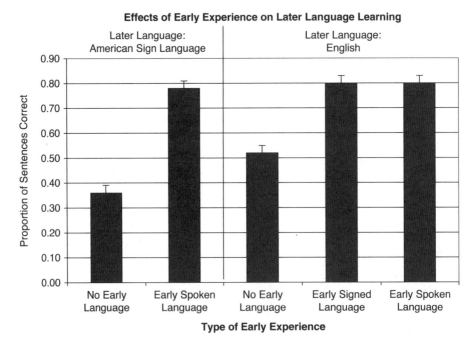

Fig. 19.3 Effects of early experience on later language learning. **a.** American Sign Language (ASL) performance of deaf adults who had experienced no language in early life. Subjects were tested using a task requiring recall of complex ASL sentences. **b.** English performance of deaf adults who had had experienced ASL in infancy, and of hearing adults who had experienced a spoken language other than English in infancy. Subjects were tested using a task requiring judgments of whether complex English sentences given in print were grammatically correct; chance performance is 50%. Figure 1 from Mayberry, R. I., Lock, E., & Kazmi, H. (2002). Linguistic ability and early language exposure. *Nature, 417*, 38, with permission of the publisher.

who had no exposure to sign language. In one study, the spoken Spanish acquisition of an adolescent boy was observed once he obtained hearing aids (Grimshaw, Adelstein, Bryden, & MacKinnon, 1998). After 4 years, he acquired limited vocabulary, could combine single words with gestures, but produced only a single two-word utterance. Another study followed the spoken English acquisition of a woman whose hearing loss was not identified until she was 31 years old. After 10 years of hearing aid use and spoken English instruction, she was reported to have a vocabulary of approximately 2,000 words and a grade 2–3 reading level, but her spoken utterances were described as being ungrammatical (Curtiss, 1988). The slow rate of delayed L1 acquisition observed in this adolescent and adult contrasts sharply with the rate of L1 acquisition in young deaf and hearing children. Early childhood language acquisition is characterized by voracious vocabulary learning (Anderson & Reilly, 2002; Bates & Goodman, 1997). By the age of 6 years, hearing children can comprehend as many as 14,000 words and most grammatical structures of their language (Clark, 2003).

Another study longitudinally observed the L1 acquisition of ASL begun at age 13 by two deaf adolescents who had received no special services in their home countries prior to immigrating with their families to North America (Morford, 2003). After 31 months of ASL exposure, both adolescents had replaced the bulk of their gestures with ASL signs. No vocabulary assessment was made, but comprehension tasks given after 7 years of exposure showed both adolescents to suffer from severe comprehension deficits in ASL (Morford, 2003). These comprehension deficits caused by delayed L1 acquisition corroborate the experimental findings summarized earlier (Mayberry, 1993; Mayberry, Lock, & Kazmi, 2002).

Deaf individuals who are not exposed to language in childhood are not completely devoid of communication with those in their surroundings. Deaf children who acquire little functional, spoken language in early childhood have been observed to gesture for communicative purposes with their families, a phenomenon called *home sign* in ASL. Detailed analyses of home sign show that deaf children combine points with iconic gestures in a rule-governed fashion to name things in their environment, make comments, and make their needs known to some extent (Goldin-Meadow, 2003). This line of research shows that the deaf child creates the gesture system and, although they understand it, hearing parents do not appear to use it with the deaf child

instead of speech. Home sign has been documented to occur cross-culturally among deaf children who have otherwise not acquired a spoken or sign language (Goldin-Meadow, 2003). Home sign was the means of communication used by the two adolescent L1 learners of ASL studied by Morford (2003). Although home sign displays many language-like features, it does not appear to function as early L1 acquisition in the critical period phenomenon. The deaf delayed L1 learners who participated in the experimental and case studies described here did not attain near-native levels of ASL proficiency despite years of using it, even though they had used home sign as young children.

Together the results of these diverse studies indicate the effects of critical period for language to be threefold: (1) early L1 acquisition leads to native-like language proficiency in adulthood; (2) early L1 acquisition supports and facilitates subsequent L2 learning, often leading to near native-like L2 proficiency in adulthood; and (3) a lack of early L1 acquisition impairs the ability to learn language throughout life, that is, L1 acquisition that begins uncommonly late in human development leads to limited language proficiency for any language in adulthood.

The critical period phenomenon described here may explain the frequent clinical anecdotes from several countries, including the United States, Canada, Norway, Denmark, and Sweden, that young deaf children who have acquired sign vocabulary are more successful with cochlear implants than those with no sign vocabulary. Early language acquisition facilitates subsequent language acquisition cross-linguistically (Mayberry, Lock, & Kazmi, 2002). The first stage of language acquisition is vocabulary learning. Computer modelling shows that the amount of language input and size of early vocabulary affects the organization of semantic categories across the early lexicon (Borovsky & Elman, 2006). Vocabulary acquisition in sign may thus help the young child with a cochlear implant identify the meaning of distorted acoustic stimuli and bind it to already acquired word meaning and semantic categories. This is an area where research is needed due to the substantial rise in the number of deaf children receiving cochlear implants (see Chapters 9 and 29, this volume).

Preliminary research suggests that delayed L1 acquisition has significant neural consequences as well. The degree to which the classic language areas of the anterior left hemisphere are activated during sign language processing are negatively correlated to the age at which the first language was acquired in childhood (Mayberry, Klein, Witcher, & Chen, 2006).

Sign Language Skill and Reading Development

Given that early L1 acquisition facilitates subsequent L2 learning to near-native levels, but late L1 acquisition impedes it, the next question is whether this critical period phenomenon relates to reading development in the deaf population. Some, but not all, theories of reading development posit that the reader must be able to speak the language represented in the written text in order to comprehend it. In these models, recognizing word meaning occurs only after written letters have been mentally transformed into the speech sounds they represent. Such theories predict that readers who are deaf and do not speak well will have difficulty reading. Note that this prediction is at odds with the research findings summarized earlier in this chapter, in which early and robust language acquisition supports other kinds of language acquisition independently of sensory–motor modality. Early spoken language acquisition supports later sign language acquisition and vice versa, including written representations of spoken language. This line of research suggests an alternative explanation for low, median literacy levels in the deaf population. If L1 acquisition in early life scaffolds subsequent L2 learning, then it should support L2 reading too, even when the first language is ASL and the second is English. Many deaf individuals have weakly developed language skills in any language, for all the reasons just described. The question is how such weakly developed language skill relate to reading achievement.

To answer the question, adult deaf signers were classified as having either strong or weak ASL skills as measured by grammatical judgment and narrative comprehension tasks (Chamberlain & Mayberry, 2008). The two groups of signers were also given standardized reading tests. The results were striking. There was a bimodal distribution of reading achievement between the two groups with no overlap, as Figure 19.4 shows. Average English reading achievement for the group with strong ASL skill was between the grade 10 to college level, depending upon the particular reading test. By contrast, the average reading achievement of the group with weak ASL skill was between grade 3 and 4 (Chamberlain & Mayberry, 2008). Thus, sign language proficiency is a strong predictor of reading achievement among

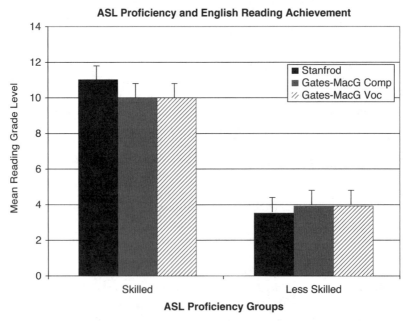

Fig. 19.4 Mean performance of deaf adults grouped by American Sign Language proficiency level, skilled and less skilled, on the reading comprehension subtest of the Stanford Achievement Test and the Gates-MacGinitie passage and vocabulary comprehension subtests of the Gates-MacGinitie. Data from Chamberlain, C., & Mayberry, R. I. (2008). ASL syntactic and narrative comprehension in skilled and less skilled adult readers: Bilingual-bimodal evidence for the linguistic basis of reading. *Applied Psycholinguistics, 28,* 537–549.

deaf signers, just as language proficiency has been found to be a strong predictor of reading achievement in the hearing population (Dickensen, McCabe, Anastasopoulos, Peisner-Feinberg, & Poe, 2003). Note that the average reading level of the signers with weak ASL skill was identical to the median reading achievement reported for the deaf school-aged population in the United States, namely between grades 3 and 4 (Traxler, 2000). This provides preliminary evidence that delayed L1 acquisition may be a significant factor in the attenuated reading achievement in the deaf population (Chamberlain & Mayberry, 2008).

Implications of the Critical Period for Language

This review of research investigating age of acquisition effects on L1 and L2 outcomes allows us to reconsider the question of whether Victor could have become proficient in French Sign Language in the early 1800s had the idea to use it occurred to Itard. Victor was believed to be about 12 years old when Itard began to teach him French (Frith, 2003). Itard described the boy as having no gestures and no language, although eventually, after being socialized, he spontaneously used objects to communicate some of his needs (Itard, 1896/1962). Toddlers use objects to communicate with their caretakers and then begin to use their hands and arms to point at objects and people before they speak their first words (Bates, 1979). This means that Victor achieved a prelinguistic level of communication. The research summarized here completes the picture by suggesting that Victor would not have become proficient in French Sign Language because he had grown into adolescence without having acquired any language. Scholars have suggested that Victor may have been autistic (Lane, 1976). Socially isolated children, including feral children, often develop autistic-like tendencies, but young autistic children can and do acquire sign and spoken language (Frith, 2003).

If the critical period phenomenon for language described here is robust and a key factor in adult sign language proficiency, why are incomplete language acquisition and low sign language proficiency among deaf signers not more often identified and urgently treated by clinical and educational professionals? One reason is a lack of educational or clinical models of normal versus delayed sign language acquisition, such as are in place for spoken language acquisition, including assessment tools and specialists. Educators and clinicians need to be trained to assess language development in sign.

A clinical anecdote illustrates the serious nature of the problem. An adolescent boy who had been educated in total communication in a public school for deaf students was brought to a university clinic for an educational assessment. His ability to read English was limited, as was his ability to comprehend simple sentence structure in ASL or signed English. When asked about his sign language skills, his teachers uniformly replied that they could not understand him and attributed this to his quick signing rate. His parents, who did not sign, were aware of his limited reading ability but assumed him to be a proficient signer, again due to his fast signing rate. In short, neither his teachers nor his family were aware of his aphasic-like symptoms in sign language. Magnetic resonance imaging (MRI) scans revealed numerous and widespread brain lesions due to birth complications. The lesions explained the aphasic-like symptoms in his signing, but they were invisible to professionals unprepared to ascertain the difference between normal and aphasic development in sign language.

In conclusion, research investigating whether a critical period exists for language acquisition has used several kinds of variation in the temporal onset of language acquisition over human development: spoken language, sign language, case studies of childhood social/linguistic isolation, and two types of acquisition, L1 and L2. L2 research with sign and spoken language has found a negative correlation between age of acquisition and L2 attainment. Nonetheless, near-native skills are often achieved by older L2 learners depending upon amount of education undertaken in the second language and the linguistic similarities between the first and second languages. However, unlike the findings for L2 acquisition, delayed L1 acquisition impedes the ultimate proficiency attained in any language, signed or spoken.

Acknowledgments

The research reported here was supported by grants from the National Institutes of Health, the Natural Sciences & Engineering Council of Canada (#171239), and the Social Science and Humanities Research Council of Canada (#410-2004-1775). The author thanks Deaf communities in Chicago, Detroit, Quebec, Ontario, Alberta, and Nova Scotia for their invaluable assistance with this research; Drucilla Ronchen, Patricia Viens, and Pamela Witcher for their ASL insights and testing help; and Amy Lieberman and Carl Vonderau for helpful comments on earlier versions of this chapter.

References

Anderson, D., & Reilly, J. (2002). The MacArthur Communicative Development Inventory: Normative data for American Sign Language. *Journal of Deaf Studies and Deaf Education, 7,* 83–106.

Bates, E. (1979). *The emergence of symbols: Cognition and communication in infancy.* New York: Academic Press.

Bates, E., & Goodman, J. C. (1997). On the inseparability of grammar and the lexicon: Evidence from acquisition, aphasia and real-time processing. *Language and Cognitive Processes, 12,* 507–584.

Birdsong, D., & Molis, M. (2001). On the evidence for maturational constraints in second language acquisition. *Journal of Memory & Language, 44,* 235–249.

Borovsky, A., & Elman, J. (2006). Language input and semantic categories: A relation between cognition and early word learning. *Journal of Child Language, 36,* 759–790.

Chamberlain, C., & Mayberry, R. I. (2008). ASL syntactic and narrative comprehension in skilled and less skilled adult readers: Bilingual-bimodal evidence for the linguistic basis of reading. *Applied Psycholinguistics, 28,* 537–549.

Clark, E. V. (2003). *First language acquisition.* New York: Cambridge University Press.

Corina, D., & Knapp, H. (2006). Sign language processing and the mirror neuron system. *Cortex, 42,* 529–539.

Curtiss, S. (1977). *Genie: A psycholinguistic study of a modern-day "wild child."* New York: Academic Press.

Curtiss, S. (1988). Abnormal language acquisition and the modularity of language. In F. J. Newmeyer (Ed.), *Linguistic theory: Extensions and implications* (Vol. 2, pp. 96–116). New York: Cambridge University Press.

Dickensen, D. K., McCabe, A., Anastasopoulos, L., Peisner-Feinberg, E. S., & Poe, D. M. (2003). Bringing it all together: The multiple origins, skills, and environmental supports of early literacy. *Learning Disabilities Research and Practice, 16,* 186–202.

Emmorey, K. (2002). *Language, cognition and the brain.* Mahwah, NJ: Lawrence Erlbaum Associates.

Emmorey, K., Bellugi, U., Friederici, A. D., & Horn, P. (1995). Effects of age of acquisition on grammatical sensitivity: Evidence from on-line and off-line tasks. *Applied Psycholinguistics, 16,* 1–23.

Eubank, L., & Gregg, K. R. (1999). Critical periods and (second) language acquisition: Divide et impera. In D. Birdsong (Ed.), *Second language acquisition and the critical period hypothesis* (pp. 65–99). Mahwah, NJ: Lawrence Erlbaum Associates.

Flege, J. E., Yeni-Komshian, G. H., & Liu, S. (1999). Age constraints on second-language acquisition. *Journal of Memory and Language, 41,* 78–104.

Frith, U. (2003). *Autism: Explaining the enigma,* 2nd edition. Oxford: Blackwell.

Garmon, L. (Writer) (1994). The secret of the wild child. In L. Garmon (Producer), *Nova.* USA: WGBH Boston.

Goldin-Meadow, S. (2003). *The resilience of language.* New York: Psychology Press.

Greenough, W. T., & Black, J. E. (1992). Induction of brain structure by experience: substrates for cognitive development. In M. R. Gunna & C. A. Nelson (Eds.), *Developmental behavioral neuroscience* (Vol. 24, pp. 155–200). Hillsdale, NJ: Lawrence Erlbaum.

Grimshaw, G. M., Adelstein, A., Bryden, M. P., & MacKinnon, G. E. (1998). First language acquisition in adolescence: Evidence for a critical period for verbal language development. *Brain and Language, 63,* 237–255.

Hakuta, K., Bialystok, E., & Wiley, E. (2003). Critical evidence: A test of the critical-period hypothesis for second-language acquisition. *Psychological Science, 14,* 31–38.

Itard, J. M. G. (1894/1962). *The wild boy of Aveyron (L'enfant sauvage). (Rapports et memoires sur le sauvage de l'Averyron,* G. Humphrey & M. Humphrey, Trans.). New York: Appleton-Century Crofts.

Johnson, J., & Newport, E. L. (1989). Critical period effects in second language learning: The influence of maturational state on the acquisition of English as a second language. *Cognitive Psychology, 21,* 60–69.

Klima, E. S., & Bellugi, U. (1979). *The signs of language.* Cambridge: Harvard University Press.

Lane, H. (1976). *The wild boy of Aveyron.* Cambridge: Harvard University Press.

Lenneberg, E. H. (1967). *Biological foundations of language.* New York: John Wiley & Sons, Inc.

Lorenz, K. (1965). *Evolution and modification of behavior.* Chicago: University of Chicago Press.

Mayberry, R. I. (1993). First-language acquisition after childhood differs from second-language acquisition: The case of American Sign Language. *Journal of Speech and Hearing Research, 36,* 1258–1270.

Mayberry, R. I. (1994). The importance of childhood to language acquisition: Insights from American Sign Language. In J. C. Goodman & H. C. Nusbaum (Eds.), *The development of speech perception: The transition from speech sounds to words* (pp. 57–90). Cambridge: MIT Press.

Mayberry, R. I. (2002). Cognitive development of deaf children: The interface of language and perception in neuropsychology. In S. J. Segalowitz & I. Rapin (Eds.), *Handbook of neuropsychology,* 2nd edition. (Vol. 8, pp. 71–107). Amsterdam: Elsevier.

Mayberry, R. I. (2007). When timing is everything: Age of first-language acquisition effects on second-language learning. *Applied Psycholinguistics, 28,* 537–549.

Mayberry, R. I., & Eichen, E. B. (1991). The long-lasting advantage of learning sign language in childhood: Another look at the critical period for language acquisition. *Journal of Memory and Language, 30,* 486–512.

Mayberry, R. I., & Fischer, S. D. (1989). Looking through phonological shape to lexical meaning: The bottleneck of nonnative sign language processing. *Memory and Cognition, 17,* 740–754.

Mayberry, R. I., Klein, D., Witcher, P., & Chen, J.-K. (2006). *Neural systems underlying early language experience.* Paper presented at the Society for Neuroscience, Atlanta, GA.

Mayberry, R. I., & Lock, E. (2003). Age constraints on first versus second language acquisition: Evidence for linguistic plasticity and epigenesis. *Brain and Language, 87,* 369–383.

Mayberry, R. I., Lock, E., & Kazmi, H. (2002). Linguistic ability and early language exposure. *Nature, 417,* 38.

Mayberry, R. I., & Squires, B. (2006). Sign language acquisition. In K. Brown (Ed.), *Encyclopedia of language & linguistics,* 2nd edition. (Vol. 11, pp. 291–296). Oxford: Elsevier.

Morford, J. (2003). Grammatical development in adolescent first-language learners. *Linguistics, 41*(4), 681–721.

Newport, E. L. (1990). Maturational constraints on language learning. *Cognitive Science, 14,* 11–28.

Penfield, W., & Roberts, L. (1959). *Speech and brain-mechanisms.* Princeton: Princeton University Press.

Poizner, H., Klima, E. S., & Bellugi, U. (1987). *What the hands reveal about the brain.* Cambridge, MA: MIT Press.

Reilly, J. (2006). How face comes to serve grammar: The development of nonmanual morphology in American Sign Language. In B. Schick, M. Marschark, & P. Spencer (Eds.), *Advances in sign language development of deaf children* (pp. 261–290). New York: Oxford University Press.

Schick, B., de Villiers, P., de Villiers, J., & Hoffmeister, R. (2007). Language and theory of mind: A study of deaf children. *Child Development, 78,* 376–396.

Seidenberg, M. S., & Zevin, J. D. (2005). Connectionist models in developmental cognitive neuroscience: Insights about critical periods. In Y. Munakata & M. H. Johnson (Eds.), *Attention and performance XXI: Processes of change in brain and cognitive development.* Oxford: Oxford University Press.

Stokoe, W. C., Casterline, D. C., & Croneberg, C. G. (1965). *A dictionary of American Sign Language on linguistic principles.* Washington DC: Gallaudet University Press.

Traxler, C. B. (2000). The Stanford Achievement Test, 9th Edition: National norming and performance standards for deaf and hard-of-hearing students. *Journal of Deaf Studies and Deaf Education, 5,* 337–348.

Van Cleve, J. V., & Crouch, B. A. (1989). *A place of their own: Creating the deaf community in America.* Washington DC: Gallaudet University Press.

Werker, J., & Tees, R. C. (2005). Speech perception as a window for understanding plasticity and commitment in language systems of the brain. *Developmental Psychobiology, 46,* 233–251.

Wiesel, T. N. (1982). Postnatal development of the visual cortex and the influence of the environment. *Nature, 299,* 583–591.

Zeshan, U. (2006). Sign languages of the world. In R. E. Asher (Ed.), *Encyclopedia of language and linguistics,* 2nd edition. (pp. 335–365). Oxford: Elsevier.

Communication Choices and Outcomes During the Early Years: An Assessment and Evidence-based Approach

Arlene Stredler-Brown

Abstract

A longstanding debate attempts to identify the best approach to language learning for children who are deaf or hard of hearing. Empirical evidence has not provided an answer. Each communication approach has been demonstrated to work with some children; it then becomes the responsibility of an early interventionist or educator to participate in the selection of an approach that supports the development of effective and age-appropriate communication and language for the individual child. This chapter describes the language approaches available to children with hearing loss. Historical approaches and recent adaptations are presented according to the modality or modes that are used. An extensive review of procedures, old and new, dedicated to the use of objective and prescriptive procedures to select an approach is discussed. A recent movement to use evidence-based practices (EBP) to document developmental outcomes of children is described, along with the challenges associated with implementing this practice.

Keywords: early intervention, communication approaches, efficacy of early intervention, evidence-based practice

The capacity to learn language is part of the unique endowment of human beings. Language is fundamental to communication, socialization, and learning, and is used to represent thoughts and feelings. It is a conventional and rule-governed symbolic system. Acquiring language is the foremost challenge for a child who is deaf or hard of hearing, irrespective of the degree of the hearing loss (P. Spencer, 2004). Moeller et al. (2007a; 2007b) studied children with all degrees of hearing loss. These longitudinal studies found the preverbal development of children with hearing loss to be delayed compared to children with normal hearing. The same cohort of children continued to exhibit delays in their development of true words. When speech production was analyzed at 24 months of age, the children with hearing loss made word approximations that were less complex, these word approximations were less complex, these word approximations

contained consonants that were less accurate, and the utterances were recognized less often by their mothers than did children with normal hearing.

There are many ways to understand language and to communicate expressively. Receptively, one understands a message by listening to it, watching someone sign it, or by reading print. Expressively, one can speak, sign, or write the message. The modalities used by people with hearing loss, young or old, have been discussed and debated for centuries (Marschark, 2007; L. Spencer & Tomblin, 2006). Over time, some of the names ascribed to specific approaches or methods have acquired new labels. Some existing methods have been combined and given other designations. All of these approaches, both historical and current, will be organized here according to the receptive and expressive modalities utilized.

Language Approaches Available to Children with Hearing Loss

The primary senses used to communicate are visual and auditory. Although language can be presented using the tactile sense, this approach is less efficient because the skin is significantly less sensitive than the ear (Sherrick, 1985). And although the skin is an effective sense to serve emotional needs (Thayer, 1982), is not as well suited to be an intellectual sense. The Tadoma Method (Hanson, 1930), originally intended for use with individuals with both hearing and vision loss, supported speech reception with only moderate accuracy and only when speech was presented at moderate rates (Reed, Rabinowitz, Durlach, Braida, Conway-Fithian, & Schultz, 1985). Present-day teachers use Tadoma differently from those who used the approach in the past. Rather than using it as a primary means of speech reception, current users of this technique utilize it as a supplementary source of information delivery (Schultz, Norton, Conway-Fithian, & Reed, 1984). Wearable tactile and vibrotactile devices have also been used to facilitate speechreading and to improve vocal production with deaf children who received negligible help from conventional hearing aids (Goldstein & Proctor, 1985). Although the effectiveness of both single-channel and multichannel devices has been explored, these efforts have been replaced with more advanced hearing technology provided by digital hearing aids and cochlear implants.

The various communication options are organized in Figure 20.1 according to the auditory or visual modality or combination of modes that are employed.

Emphasis on Auditory Communication

The goal for the child using an auditory approach is to acquire spoken language through listening. To enhance access to auditory information, auditory approaches capitalize on the use of hearing technology, such as hearing aids and/or cochlear implants, to augment the child's residual hearing and to provide access to sound (Estabrooks, 2006; Flexer, 1999; Ling, 2002; Nicholas & Geers, 2006). Children who are not using amplification—a common situation for children with minimal hearing loss—would benefit from a systematic auditory approach to learning that is included in the two approaches described later (Stredler-Brown, Hulstrom, & Ringwalt, 2008). Historically, auditory methods of communication included the auditory–oral approach and the auditory–verbal approach, which was originally known as Acoupedics (Pollock, 1997). Although both the

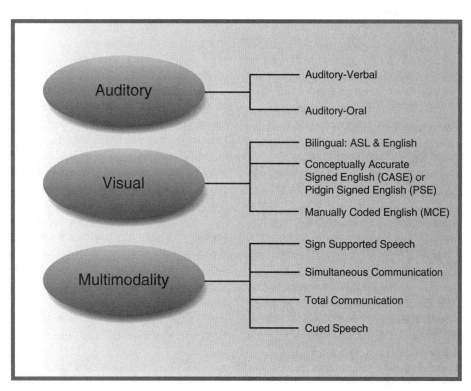

Fig. 20.1 Communication approaches, methods, and systems

auditory–oral and the auditory–verbal approaches focus on auditory access to language, there is an inherent distinction.

AUDITORY–VERBAL APPROACH

The auditory–verbal approach is a unisensory approach to communication and language; the most important sense is audition. The child's attention, both in therapy and in natural settings, is continually directed to listening to environmental sounds and voices. Hearing and listening are incorporated into every aspect of the child's life (Estabrooks, 1994). This refinement of the oral–aural approach described later in this chapter makes a concerted effort to remove visual cues during therapy sessions, so that the child can develop the auditory system through directed listening practice. Estabrooks states that speechreading is not a primary teaching strategy; in fact, access to speechreading cues is reduced or eliminated during therapy by covering most of the face while presenting speech stimuli.

AUDITORY–ORAL APPROACH

This is a multisensory approach. Although access to sound and learning to listen are the foundation of the approach, listening is supplemented with visual cues such as speechreading, gestures, and print, as well as with environmental clues to supplement residual hearing (Bowen, Howell, Juir, Reed, & Yarger, 2004; Stredler-Brown, 2009). Both hearing and vision are used to recognize speech, whereas residual hearing, speechreading, and touch can be used to teach the child to talk (Tye-Murray, 1998). In addition to specialized instruction and individual therapy, parents are relied upon to implement practiced skills in natural communicative settings.

Emphasis on Visual Communication

Sign language affords complete access to language through the visual mode. While American Sign Language (ASL), the example that will be addressed in this chapter, is considered the native language of the Deaf community in the United States, other visual systems are also prevalent. Similarly, many other countries and cultures have naturally developed sign languages that exist along with other visual systems that have been created for pedagogical and communication purposes (Schick, Marschark, & P. Spencer, 2006).

AMERICAN SIGN LANGUAGE

American Sign Language is said to be the fourth most common language in the United States today (National Institute on Deafness and Communication Disorders, 2008). Although the Deaf community is linked by this common language, as with any community, it also has a shared history and cultural norms (Lane, Hoffmeister, & Bahan, 1996). When a child is in an environment with fluent ASL users, the child receives exposure to a complete, structured, and rich language that provides the context to support the natural acquisition of ASL. American Sign Language has unique rules, like any other language. It has phonetic, phonemic, syllabic, morphologic, syntactic, discourse, and pragmatic levels of organization (Newport & Meier, 1985; Petitto, 1994). It also incorporates facial expression and nonmanual signs (e.g., movement of the signer's eyes, face, head, and body), it uses space, and it utilizes specific classifiers (e.g., handshapes to describe shape, size, and quantity).

BILINGUAL COMMUNICATION

In the education of the deaf, bilingual learning expects fluency in both the signed language of the Deaf community (e.g., ASL, Swedish Sign Language, Danish Sign Language, British Sign Language) and the language of the local hearing community (e.g., English, Swedish, and Danish). English may be acquired using a sign system that organizes signs in the same word order as the spoken language or it may be acquired through print, and some programs consider the acquisition of spoken English. One of the goals of bilingual learning is to provide children with skills in both languages in order to support their academic success (Marschark, 2001; Marschark, Lang, & Albertini, 2002; Wilbur, 2000). The bilingual approach has also gained support as a way to develop literacy skills for children who are deaf (DeLana, Gentry, & Andrews, 2007; Grushkin, 1998; Nelson, 1998; Wilbur, 2000). Although there are numerous descriptive accounts of bilingual programs, there has been a lack of longitudinal research to track the efficacy of the approach (Mayer & Akamatsu, 2003).

CONCEPTUALLY ACCURATE SIGNED ENGLISH

Conceptually Accurate Signed English (CASE) is not a language in and of itself. Also known as Pidgin Signed English (PSE) (Woodward, 1972), CASE uses ASL signs and places them in English word order (Valli & Lucas, 1995). In addition to the use of some ASL sign glosses, CASE incorporates other features of ASL, such as the use of facial expressions. It also includes some features of English, although it does not utilize English grammatical morphemes such as the affixes denoting verb tense and plurals.

It is significant to note that CASE is, in point of fact, an incomplete representation of both ASL and English.

MANUALLY CODED ENGLISH

A number of sign systems were constructed by American educators in the 1960s and 1970s with the intent to facilitate the learning of English. Two Manually Coded English (MCE) systems that have withstood the test of time are Signed English (Bornstein, Saulnier, & Hamilton, 1983) and Signing Exact English (Gustason, Zawolkow, & Lopez, 1993). These systems attempt to visually represent English on the hands. They combine sign glosses from ASL, put them in English word order, and add invented signs to represent the grammatical aspects of the English language (e.g., plurals, possessives, and tenses). Every morpheme is signed, and all structure words of English, such as "the" and "to," are signed in these manually coded systems. It is important to note that the research is not conclusive that the learning of English is facilitated when using these manually coded systems (Bornstein, Saulnier, & Hamilton, 1980; Moeller, 2000; Power, Hyde, & Leigh, 2008; Schick & Moeller, 1992). It has been demonstrated in both the United States (Schick & Moeller, 1992) and Australia (Power, Hyde, & Leigh, 2008) that students using an MCE system demonstrated substantial strengths in their expressive English. However, the syntactic rules that were used by students with hearing loss were still not completely equivalent to native English. Although grammatical competence on a test of global language showed the students to be performing well, the use of English morphology (e.g., inflectional morphemes, auxiliaries and copulas, verb processes, complex relative clauses) was weak. Studies by Schick and Moeller (1992) and Luetke-Stahlman (1990) included children from advantageous home environments, who did not have additional disabilities, and who also received strong educational support for the learning of the MCE system. These factors make it difficult to generalize their results to the broad population of young children with hearing loss.

Combining Visual and Auditory Modalities

Some approaches incorporate both spoken language and a form of visual communication. The spoken language component is consistent among all of the combined approaches, which place an equal emphasis on listening and speech. The visual component may be represented in various ways: a signed language, a sign system, or another type of visual code (Watkins, Taylor, & Pittman, 2004). Some professionals use the Building Blocks of Communication (Centers for Disease Control, 2008) to graphically portray the particular components of communication. Each building block represents one element of communication, such as the use of gestures, speechreading, conceptual signs, speech, audition, fingerspelling, and English-based signs. A family is asked to select the specific building blocks that match the way in which they want their child to communicate.

SIGN-SUPPORTED SPEECH AND LANGUAGE

The term sign-supported speech (SSS) was first coined by Johnson, Liddell, and Erting (1989). In recent years, the terminology has been adapted to refer to the use of an auditory approach that is augmented with a few signs in order to support both speech and language development. Part of the current interest in using sign-supported speech and language with children with hearing loss is the recent popularity of using sign language to facilitate early communication with hearing children (Garcia, 2001). This has resulted in sign language gaining recognition with families who have children who are deaf or hard of hearing. Today, when a family elects to use signs to support the development of speech and language, the foremost goal is the child's acquisition of speech. A small number of signs may be used strategically and only in specific situations, as a back-up form of communication. For instance, signs may be used when a hearing device is not in use, when the child is in a noisy environment, or when trying to communicate from a distance (Lane, Bell, & Parson-Tylka, 2006). Signs are used as a bridge to completely oral communication; visual information is used to enhance words that are not heard or are not heard easily. Signs can also be used to emphasize or highlight words that are not articulated correctly. Once the child utilizes auditory information accurately and produces spoken words correctly, the signs are no longer used.

SIMULTANEOUS COMMUNICATION

When Johnson, Liddell, and Erting (1989) defined SSS, it was also referred to as *simultaneous communication*. According to their definition, SSS was the use of a form of MCE, audition, speechreading, and signs at the same time. Although the authors did not support the use of this approach, simultaneous communication has gained popularity. Today, it remains the systematic use of signs and speech at the same time. To provide language in two modes simultaneously, a sign system, such as MCE or CASE, is used to depict the spoken language on the hands. It is important to note that sign language, such as ASL, cannot be used when using simultaneous communication, as the syntactic rules of ASL and English are different and cannot be produced simultaneously (Johnson et al., 1989; Marschark, 1997).

TOTAL COMMUNICATION

Introduced in the 1960s by Roy Holcomb, this philosophy was first adopted by the Maryland School for the Deaf as the official name for their educational philosophy. This philosophy, which is not a method or an approach, aims to make use of different modalities and a number of different strategies, providing whatever is needed to foster communicative success. The choice of modes and the specific strategies used to communicate depend on the particular abilities and needs of the child. Therefore, when reporting that a child uses a total communication approach, it is critical to define the specific strategies that are being used.

CUED SPEECH

Developed in the mid-1960s, this technique was intended to improve the reading abilities of children who are deaf or hard of hearing (Cornett, 1967; Cornett & Daisey, 1992; Cornett & Daisey, 2001). Specific handshapes are strategically placed near the mouth, throat, and chin to provide the child with an accurate visual representation of spoken English by distinguishing phonemes that look alike on the lips. When the cued speech approach is adopted, the goal is for the child to develop spoken English. The cues are used as an accompaniment to enhance understanding. Although cued speech was developed in the United States based on the phonological system of English, it has been modified to represent the phonology of various other languages as well.

Much of the recent research on cued speech has come from countries in which French or Spanish is the primary spoken language (Hage & Leybaert, 2006).

Comparative Description of the Communication Approaches

McConkey Robbins (2001) developed a graphic representation of the modalities used by the various communication approaches. Her terminology describes the characteristics of communication rather than simply naming an approach. There are two continua, one depicting receptive communication and the other describing expressive communication. Figure 20.2 illustrates five points along the receptive language continuum used to describe a child's communication.

Receptively, a child's communication can range from fully visual to fully auditory. A child who relies fully on visual communication depends on a natural sign language or a sign system to understand language. The mostly visual communicator also receives some benefit from auditory information. In the center of Figure 20.2 is the communicator who relies equally on the use of visual information, via signs, and auditory information through access to spoken language. Moving to the right, some children rely primarily on auditory information via spoken language, which is augmented by visual information that is delivered through signs, speechreading, or cues. Last, a child who is fully auditory depends solely on auditory information that is delivered through spoken English.

A companion continuum for expressive communication is depicted in Figure 20.3 illustrating the ways in which a child expresses language. The child may use only sign language. Or, the child may rely predominantly on signs that are accompanied by some oral communication. Some children rely

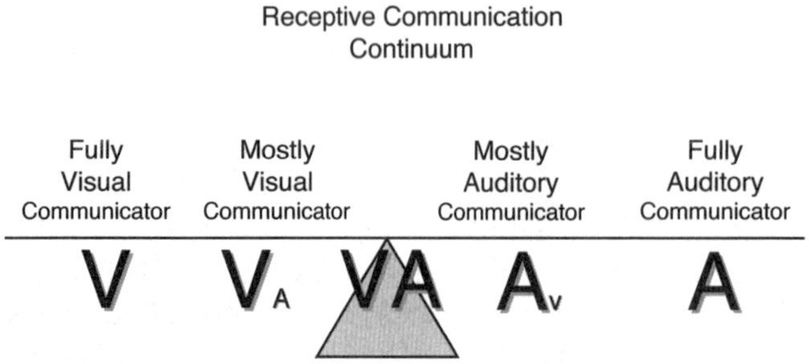

Receptive Communication Continuum

Fully Visual Communicator	Mostly Visual Communicator	Mostly Auditory Communicator	Fully Auditory Communicator

Fig. 20.2 Description of receptive language modes. McConkey Robbins, A. (2001) A sign of the times. *Loud and Clear Newsletter, 4(2)*. Valencia: Advanced Bionics. Reprinted with permission.

Fig. 20.3 Description of expressive language modes. Nussbaum, D., Scott, S., Waddy-Smith, B., & Koch, M. (2006, May). *Spoken language and sign: Optimizing learning for children with cochlear implants.* Paper presented at the Laurent Clerc National Deaf Education Center, Washington, DC. Adapted from McConkey-Robbins, A. (2001). A sign of the times. *Loud and Clear Newsletter, 4(2).* Valencia: Advanced Bionics.

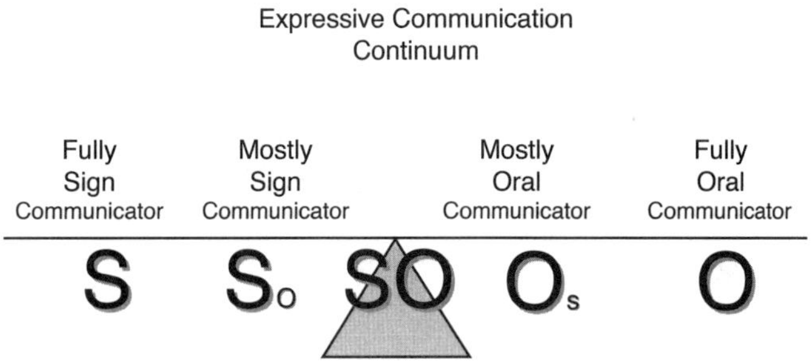

Expressive Communication
Continuum

| Fully Sign Communicator | Mostly Sign Communicator | Mostly Oral Communicator | Fully Oral Communicator |

S S_O S_O O_S O

equally on signs and oral communication, others rely primarily on oral communication and use signs only for clarification. At the right side of the continuum are those children who are fully oral communicators.

Each communication approach, language, and system has been presented in an attempt to provide a clear, unbiased, objective depiction. This objective means of describing the communication approaches is an effort to support a prescriptive and pragmatic approach to the development of communication and language for a child with hearing loss (M. Marschark, personal communication, November 4, 2006). New developments in the 21st century are contributing to the dissolution of age-old debates about the "best" or "right" communication approach for all children with hearing loss (Stredler-Brown, in press). By replacing the historical debates with pragmatic and prescriptive procedures, it may be possible to diminish the polarization that has existed among professionals and parents for far too long. The alternative approach being advocated here is prescriptive, in that choices are based on recommendations that are made with objective information about the child and the child's family that is obtained through assessment procedures. The approach is pragmatic in that sufficient information can be accumulated continually in order to ascertain if the approach is efficacious.

Early Efforts to Use Objective and Prescriptive Procedures to Select a Communication Approach

It can be a challenge for parents to select a communication approach. To do so, they have to understand complex and unfamiliar information (e.g., hearing aids, language development, sign language, and medical diagnoses) (Young, Carr, Hunt, McCracken, Skipp, & Tattersall, 2006; Young &

Tattersall, 2007). Frequently, parents undertake this education while they are in the throes of an emotional reaction to the diagnosis of their child's hearing loss. Furthermore, not all approaches are available in all locales. Far too often, professionals may complicate the decision-making process by advocating for the only approach they have the training and expertise to provide.

Some historical attempts have been made to objectively identify the most suitable approach for individual children who are deaf or hard of hearing. Checklists such as the Spoken Language Predictor (Geers & Moog, 1987) and the Deafness Management Quotient (Downs, 1974) were early attempts to help parents make communication methodology decisions. The questions on both of these checklists made inquiries about the child's audiologic thresholds, the child's cognitive profile, characteristics of the family, and the rate of the child's language development. Developed only a few years later, the SKI*HI curriculum (Watkins, 1993) included a rubric with ten questions similarly intended to help parents select a communication approach to use with their child. The answers to the questions in this rubric were collected repeatedly over time and used to provide insights into the receptive and expressive modes of communication used by the child, the parents' attitudes about the different communication approaches, and the parents' use of specific techniques. All three of these checklists assigned points or percentages in an attempt to quantitatively guide the selection of an approach or to identify the need to modify the method being used.

A more prescriptive tactic for the selection of a communication approach was developed by Brookhouser and Moeller (1986). As children proceeded through their Deafness Early Intervention Program (DEIP), it became apparent that the audiogram was a poor predictor of communication method in more than 65% of their cases (Brookhouser and Moeller, 1986). Their prescriptive methodology recommended using objective criteria to select and monitor the effectiveness of a communication approach. Accordingly, a documented developmental profile of the child was obtained, used as baseline criteria, and updated at regular intervals. This information was then used to determine the components of the intervention program and the frequency and extent of therapy sessions.

Moeller and Condon (1994) refined the DEIP protocol, articulating the following underlying premises:

1. Children with hearing loss represent a heterogeneous group and, therefore, each child requires individualized management.

2. Development is a dynamic process and requires the consideration of multiple developmental domains.

3. Intervention methods are tailored to the individual family.

4. The selection of intervention strategies is supported by objective evidence of their success.

5. Families benefit from opportunities to develop balanced partnerships with professionals as they make their decisions.

6. A comprehensive evaluation of the child's needs and the family's needs is conducted regularly to guide the intervention.

Table 20.1 identifies the type of information collected on each child enrolled in the Diagnostic Early Intervention Program.

The value of the DEIP protocol is the commitment to objectively choose a communication approach that is appropriate for each child and family. Decisions can be made over time as information about the child and the family is gathered and analyzed. Moeller and Condon (1994) state that "early decisions should not be regarded as predictive; rather, decisions should be viewed as short-term management plans, which may require continual modification as objective evidence of the child's problems and progress become available." (p. 54).

These historical approaches to selecting a communication approach for children with significant hearing losses are all based on the same fundamental principle: families participate with professionals who are knowledgeable about hearing loss to select a communication approach that capitalizes on the family's preferences and the child's needs. The specific instruments described earlier in this chapter were early attempts to provide parents with criteria to

Table 20.1 Assessment criteria

Characteristics of the child:
- Cognitive status
- Medical status
- Receptive language learning rates
- Expressive language learning rates
- Functional hearing
- Motor speech control
- Rate of phonologic development
- Behavior

Characteristics describing the family: Family supports

Characteristics describing the communicative dyad: Interpersonal or social interaction between parent and child

From Moeller, M. P., & Condon, M. (1994). D. E. I. P.: A collaborative problem-solving approach to early intervention. In J. Roush & N. D. Matkin (Eds.), *Infants and toddlers with hearing loss: Family centered assessment and intervention* (pp. 163–192). Baltimore: York Press. With permission of the publisher

choose a communication approach, to consider ways to access the selected approach, and to collect and analyze data to monitor the efficacy of the selection.

Current Efforts to Provide an Unbiased Representation of Communication Approaches

Following the diagnosis of hearing loss, parents are quickly introduced to different communication approaches. The information about the approaches may be provided in various forms (e.g., written material, discussion) and through different media (e.g., print, video, Internet websites). It is ideal for parents to engage in an informed decision-making process by discussing the information with a professional who has knowledge about the different approaches (Stredler-Brown, 2005; Stredler-Brown, 2009). Professionals can partner with the parents to help them learn about the various ways children and adults who are deaf or hard of hearing communicate. It is appropriate for the professional to take steps to systematically join the family as they create this partnership (Haley, 1976; Jones, 1993). Haley (1987) suggests that this joining process, which starts during the very first contact, is critical because it allows the professional to obtain information about the family's needs, their hopes, and their dreams for their child. Satir, Stachowiak, and Taschman (1975) further suggest that professional interactions with families depend on trust and that this trust starts to develop during the initial interactions between the professional and the parents.

It is ideal when each approach can be demonstrated by a professional with expertise using that approach. As this is frequently not an option, providing a videotape or DVD explaining and demonstrating the approaches can serve as an acceptable alternative. Additional written information describing the various communication approaches must be provided. Family members may ask to meet others who are using the approach, which is an opportunity afforded by some early intervention programs that have created networks of deaf and hard-of-hearing (DHH) role models. As opportunities exist, parents may elect to visit programs, such as a clinic or a preschool classroom, where the communication approach is used. Since the decision is a course of action that takes some time, families can take the information they receive and review it at a later time with other people who are part of their informal support networks (e.g., extended family members, friends, neighbors, and people in their religious community) (Roush & McWilliam, 1994). The professional's role all the while is to discuss the family's unique circumstances, answer their questions, and support them as they make their decision.

Li, Bain, and Steinberg (2003) surveyed 83 families and reported on several factors that influenced decisions about communication approach, including availability of services close to home, recommendations of friends, and the cost of services. Notably, the most influential factor was the recommendations made by the professionals, audiologists, early interventionists, service coordinators, or physicians. Eleweke and Rodda (2000) conducted a qualitative study that described the factors contributing to parents' selection of a communication approach. Four factors were found to influence parents' decisions: the information that was provided at the time of diagnosis by professionals and other parents, parents' perceptions of the benefits of hearing technology, the availability and quality of support services, and the attitudes of professionals toward a particular communication approach. These studies support the critical need for the professional to routinely inquire about parents' needs and the relative importance of parental attitudes, beliefs, values, and aspirations with regard to the decision-making process. And once a decision is made, the professionals must assure that they can provide parents with the resources they will need to learn the approach.

Some parents benefit from parent-to-parent support that allows them to learn from others who have "walked in their shoes." Social support can be regarded as a cornerstone of early intervention (Dunst, Leet, & Trivette, 1988; Hintermair, 2000), with some families reporting that the support they receive from other families helps them to feel more competent and more at ease raising their DHH child (Bodner-Johnson, 2001; Jackson, Becker, & Schmitendorf, 2002). Toward this end, an ever-growing number of national, state, and local parent organizations provide support by disseminating information and conducting meetings. Well-known organizations include the Alexander Graham Bell Association for the Deaf and Hard of Hearing, the American Society for Deaf Children, Families for Hands and Voices, and the John Tracy Clinic.

Monitoring the Efficacy of the Selection

Professionals, in partnership with parents, should conduct informal and formal observations of the child's development in a variety of domains such as cognition, preverbal communication, language, behavior, social-emotional skills, and motor skills. In addition, the parents' implementation of the approach needs to be monitored to assure a complete language model is provided, so that the child has full access to language (Marge & Marge, 2005). It is critical for the child to have multiple role models using the approach, both within the family and in the community. Even for infants and toddlers, parents must learn to use the communication approach with ease. Professionals working with the family must also have the requisite expertise to teach the selected approach (Stredler-Brown, 2008). Is the selected approach used consistently? Are parents actively seeking strategies to use the approach effectively? Are appropriate communication strategies readily incorporated into daily routines? Does the child understand the parents? Do the parents understand their child? Are the modalities used by the child complemented by the modalities used by the parents, as would be expected?

Observations are made and critically analyzed to give both parents and professionals the opportunity to review the benefits of the selected approach. If satisfactory progress is being made, use of the approach is reinforced. If progress is not satisfactory, the approach can be revised accordingly (Stredler-Brown & Yoshinaga-Itano, 1994). The key is the use of objective and prescriptive procedures to document the success or limitations of the communication approach for each individual child. These procedures may include assessments of the vocabulary, the mean length of utterance (MLU), and the language modalities being used by both the child and the parents. Additional measurements may include the child's phonologic repertoire, the functional listening skills acquired by the child, and the rate of acquisition of these skills. Not to be mistaken for research, assessment is a relevant, indeed integral, aspect of intervention (Kamhi, 2006; Ratner, 2006).

Providing Access to a Complete Language Model

There is consensus on specific characteristics that make an approach successful (Stredler-Brown, 1998). Access to the approach should be made available *early* in the child's life, as children learn language from fluent language models (Kuhl & Meltzoff, 1982; Locke, 1994). Language acquisition has critical periods: periods of time when exposure to language, or lack thereof, will have an effect on the child's language outcomes. If language is not learned during this sensitive time, the impact may not be reversible by subsequent experiences (Bailey, Bruer, Symons, & Lichtman, 2001).

In addition, *full access* to the approach must be provided; this is a challenge specifically for children with hearing loss. A child with hearing loss, even a relatively mild degree of hearing loss, lacks access to the complete auditory signal available to a hearing child (Bess, Dodd-Murphy, & Parker, 1998; Cho Lieu, 2004; Kiese-Himmel & Ohlwein, 2003; Meadow-Orlans, Mertens, & Sass-Lehrer, 2003, P. Spencer, 2004). Babies and toddlers with typical hearing learn language primarily through direct interactions with parents and caregivers in the course of everyday routines and activities. As they get older, children expand their language learning through interactions with their peers and through incidental learning when they overhear conversations around them. The same principles apply to children who are learning a visual language from their parents who are fluent users of sign language. These children learn sign language from natural interactions with adults and with their peers. They too acquire language through incidental learning by "overseeing" conversations.

Similar to limited access to a complete auditory signal, children learning sign language may have limited visual access. This is not a reference to problems with visual acuity, although that may be at issue, but rather to the fact that most hearing parents are not fluent signers at the time of their child's diagnosis and, consequently, must acquire the language at the same time their child is learning it (Swisher, 1991). Another complication to learning appears to be hearing parents' ineffective use of visual attention

strategies (Swisher, 1991; Swisher, 1992). Baker (1977) describes the mutual reliance on visual attention when deaf adults sign with one another. This use of visual attention is considered a learned convention (Swisher, 1991) that hearing parents often do not use when they are first learning sign language. P. Spencer (2000) reports that 18-month-old children who are deaf and have deaf mothers can more easily switch their attention between a communication partner and an event or object in the environment than can deaf children with hearing parents. P. Spencer and Harris (2006) report that children with deaf parents maintain another type of visual attention, known as "onlooking," for longer periods of time than deaf children with hearing parents. It is shown, then, that mothers who are comfortable with and have good skills in sign language communication promote more effective "uptake" (Harris, 1992) than do hearing parents who are in the initial throes of learning to sign.

Parents and professionals can ask straightforward questions to determine if their child is benefiting from full access to language (Lane, Bell, & Parson-Tylka, 1997). One might ask if the child understands most of what is said or signed. Or, can the child communicate easily enough, so that adult and child can share information about what is happening? In addition, does the child have access to the same information as hearing siblings?

An additional challenge to the provision of full access is the ability of the interventionist to teach parents the strategies that they must use to implement the approach early and completely. A professional may have a degree and certification as a teacher of the deaf and hard of hearing, as a speech and language pathologist, an audiologist, an early childhood educator, or an early childhood special educator (Stredler-Brown & Arehart, 2000), but there is no assurance that the professional, irrespective of the discipline that awarded the degree, has experience working with this young population of children with hearing loss. To date, there are no uniformly accepted quality standards for early interventionists. Each preservice training program provides unique curriculums which, to varying degrees, have content related to infants and toddlers with hearing loss. White (2006) conducted a survey of programs training teachers of the deaf and hard of hearing to investigate the communication approaches that were taught in these preservice training programs. A total of 75% of these programs trained professionals to use a visual communication approach. The remaining 25% focused on auditory approaches.

Training programs for speech and language pathologists present different, although no less challenging, circumstances. Until 2005, these graduate training programs were required to include three semester credit hours in auditory rehabilitation and an additional three semester credit hours in audiology assessment. However, the current standards, effective in 2006, have no required coursework in audiologic rehabilitation or audiologic assessment (American Speech-Language Hearing Association [ASHA], 1997–2008). Based on these standards, it is evident that the coursework for teacher preparation programs is limited in scope, whereas the coursework for speech and language pathologists may be restricted in basic content. Stredler-Brown and Arehart (2000) conducted a survey of 188 programs in the United States working with infants and toddlers with hearing loss. In response to a question identifying the educational background of providers, 30% were identified as paraprofessionals who did not have formal preservice training in any of the aforementioned disciplines. These professionals are also restricted in how much they can teach parents of young children with hearing loss.

Evidence-based Practices Are Emerging

Evidence-based practice (EBP) has become increasingly prominent in the fields of psychology and audiology (Johnson & Danhauer, 2006), and it is recently emerging among speech and language pathologists (Tyler, 2006). Assessment, a critical component of EBP, is a means of gathering information about a child to help parents and professionals plan effective and supportive services. A thorough description of a child's profile, including documentation of cognitive skills, communication, and language, can be obtained through the administration of assessment protocols.

There is a growing body of support for the use of assessment. In the United States, Part C of the Individuals with Disabilities Education Act (IDEA) (2004) requires specific services for children with hearing loss, from birth to 36 months of age. Each child is required to have an Individual Family Service Plan (IFSP); this is a written plan documenting the desired developmental outcomes for the infant or toddler and the services that are to be provided to the child and to the child's family. The IFSP requires statements of the child's present level of development. Although specific characteristics of the assessment protocol are not mandated by law, assessment is recognized as the method to document a child's development. Furthermore, in their Position Statement, the Joint Committee on Infant Hearing (JCIH, 2007) explicitly recommends interdisciplinary assessment during the early years. The recommendation is to conduct an evaluation of the child's cognitive skills, language, auditory skills, speech, and/or social-emotional development using assessment tools that have been standardized on children with normal hearing and/or norm-referenced assessment tools that are appropriate to measure progress in vocal and visual language. They further recommend that all children with hearing loss receive this assessment at 6-month intervals during the first 3 years of life.

Evidence-based practice sets a new standard for selecting a communication approach. The basic premise is to assess, on a regular basis, to determine if the communication approach is having the desired results. Assessment provides objective information about the child, the parents, and the dynamics of the interaction between parent and child. This information can be used to determine which elements of an approach are working and what might need to change.

Several researchers ask each interventionist to become a data seeker, a data integrator, and a critical evaluator when working with young children and their families. Ratner (2006) urges one to ask if it is the therapies, the therapist, or both that do the work to achieve the best outcomes. Kamhi (2006) and Sheldon and Rush (2001) support EBP by stating that each clinician is responsible for validating the treatment he or she provides. To validate the treatment protocol, Kamhi suggests the interventionist starts with trial therapy and diagnostic teaching, conducts dynamic assessment, and uses the information gleaned from the assessments to measure treatment outcomes. Tyler proposes that each practitioner select intervention strategies that are based on thorough descriptions of a client's profile and evidence that the treatment is efficacious.

Setting High Expectations

In the past, parents and professionals often set a standard for the developmental progress of a DHH child that did not expect the child to meet the norms for his or her chronological age. When a child had hearing loss identified at 2 or 3 years of age, which was not uncommon in the past, that child usually experienced significant language delays before intervention services were started (P. Spencer, 2004). Statements such as "this child is making good progress for a deaf child" were frequent (Stredler-Brown, 2009). This statement implies that children with hearing loss are making adequate progress, even though they are not meeting the standard set for their typically developing peers. Perhaps it was the parents who accepted this lower standard. Or, perhaps it was the teachers and therapists who believed that the prospects for children with hearing loss were inferior to those of their hearing peers.

In the 21st century, however, a new criterion has been established. First and foremost, newborn hearing screening programs are now commonplace in the United States (Green, Gaffney, Devine, & Grosse, 2007) and in many, if not most, industrialized countries including Austria (Weichbold, 2006), Japan (Iwasaki, 2003), Norway (Barneavdelinge, 2002), Spain (Morales Angulo, 2003), New Zealand (National Foundation for the Deaf, 2004), and the United Kingdom (Davis & Hind, 2003; Davis, Bamford, Wilson, Ramkalawan, Forshaw, & Wright, 1997). Furthermore, the Early Hearing Detection and Intervention (EHDI) initiative supports the 1–3–6 rule (White, 2003). This guideline expects a baby to receive a newborn hearing screening by 1 month of age, to have a confirmed diagnosis by 3 months of age, and for intervention to start by 6 months of age.

When intervention starts early, children are more likely to have communication and language skills that are within normal limits for their chronological (or cognitive) age (Moeller, 2000; Yoshinaga-Itano, Sedey, Coulter, & Mehl, 1998). Although the study by Yoshinaga-Itano, Sedey, Coulter, and Mehl identified a statistical advantage for children who started intervention by 6 months of age, it should be noted that although average functioning for early-identified children was within normal limits, it remained in the low-average range. Moeller's findings correlated early enrollment with stronger vocabulary (it is notable that the definition of "early" in Moeller's study was 11 months of age rather than 6 months). Research has also shown that attainment of early linguistic milestones by deaf children exposed to fluent sign language is a realistic expectation (Morford & Mayberry, 2000; Newport & Meier, 1985; Schick, 2003). Manual babble occurs from 6–14 months of age (Meier & Willerman, 1995; Petitto & Marentette, 1991), first signed words occur at 8–10 months of age (Anderson & Reilly, 2002), communicative pointing emerges at 11 months of age (Folven & Bonvilian, 1991), and the child's ability to understand the intent of the mother's facial expressions starts at 10–12 months (Reilly, McIntire, & Bellugi, 1990).

Based on the opportunities provided by early identification, a new standard needs to be considered.

The "one-for-one rule" (Johnson, 2006) expects a young child with hearing loss to develop communication and language skills at the same rate as a child without hearing loss. In 1 month's time, 1 month's growth is expected. In 6 months' time, 6 months of language growth will be attained. No longer should a DHH child's program be a remedial one. Nor should progress be rated according to a unique standard for the population with hearing loss. The same high standard can be considered for a child learning language through audition, accessing language visually, or using an approach that combines both modalities.

The Position Statement from the Joint Committee on Infant Hearing (JCIH, 2007) further supports the "one-for-one rule" by recommending the use of norm-referenced and standardized assessment tools. For children learning a spoken language, tests would be standardized on children with normal hearing. For children learning a natural sign language, be it ASL, British Sign Language, or the Langue des Signes Française, the signing skills of the child are expected to develop commensurate with the norms of that native language. Only in this way can one precisely monitor that measurable progress is being achieved in language and that the progress is commensurate with peers. Although acknowledging that checklists may provide valuable information for establishing intervention strategies and goals, the JCIH Position Statement does not support use of these checklists alone, in that they are not sufficient to determine if the child's developmental progress is comparable to his or her peers.

Evidence-based Practices Document Developmental Outcomes

Early intervention provides a *habilitative* approach rather than a *rehabilitative* approach. Whereas a rehabilitative program intends to restore or reestablish skills that have been lost, a habilitative approach aims to reduce the potential of developmental delays subsequent to having a hearing loss. A habilitative intervention program encourages and facilitates typical development. The rate at which a child's language skills develop is compared to existing norms for spoken language or sign language.

Children with hearing loss are at an increased risk for additional disabilities (Moores & Martin, 2006) that can include visual impairments, motor disabilities, cognitive delay, attention-deficit disorder, or learning disabilities, among others. One study has shown that up to 38% of children with hearing loss, from birth to 3 years of age, have an additional developmental disability (Schildroth & Hotto, 1993). Therefore, at a minimum, a screening protocol must be used to monitor a child's development in domains other than language, speech, and functional auditory skills. The developmental domains included in a multidisciplinary assessment, listed in Table 20.2, provide sufficient information collectively to quantify the child's skills in the areas of communication, language, audition, speech, cognition, play, social-emotional development, and gross and fine motor development. If problems in any domain are apparent, additional diagnostic testing is recommended. If an additional disability is diagnosed, a child with hearing loss may receive other therapies such as occupational therapy, physical therapy, vision therapy, or mental health services to address these delays.

A comprehensive evaluation of spoken or signed language includes comprehensive measures of semantics, syntax, phonology, and morphology. Studies have shown that valid and reliable documentation of developmental progress in these domains is possible through the use of parent-completed questionnaires, as well as through clinically administered tests (Arehart, Yoshinago-Itano, Thomson, Gabbard, & Brown, 1998; Moeller, 2000; Yoshinaga-Itano, 2003, 2004). Measurements of each of these critical aspects of language should take into consideration normative data that are based on hearing children and native signers.

Measuring Cognitive Development—A Foundation for Language Development

Piaget (1962) postulated that language may not be essential to conceptual development in the very early stages of growth. Slobin (1996) corroborated

---

Table 20.2 Domains included in a multidisciplinary assessment

Communication and Language Skills
- Preverbal communication
- Semantics
- Syntax
- Pragmatics
- Speech
- Auditory skills

Skills in a variety of developmental domains
- Cognitive development
- Fine and gross motor skills
- Behavior
- Social-emotional skills

---

this by proposing that some core cognitive functions are acquired independently of language. Although Vygotsky (1962) concurred that some basic thought processes do not require language, he proposed that higher mental processes do necessitate language. A study by Bornstein, Selmi, Haynes, et al. (1999) supported this theory, finding that language and play were correlated for children younger than 22 months of age, but that language and cognition seemed to develop independently after 22 months of age. This suggests that linguistically coded concepts may be more difficult for children with delayed language (Furth, 1961).

McCune-Nicholich (1981) identifies several benchmarks documenting the relationship between the development of play and language acquisition: the onset of first words correlates with the onset of pretend play, the onset of word combinations coincides with the onset of combinations in symbolic play, and the use of syntactical forms correlates with hierarchical combinations in play. Of interest, it has been shown that children who are deaf and have hearing parents often do not follow these benchmarks (Meadow, 1980; Rodda & Grove, 1987). Although the deaf children in these studies usually demonstrate delayed language, they also demonstrate cognitive development that is not delayed.

Since the acquisition of language is the foremost challenge for a child who is deaf or hard of hearing, how might this information impact the intervention for children with hearing loss? By obtaining a measurement of cognitive skills, the professionals and parents acquire critical information to guide the activities they use; some activities are selected to facilitate the child's language growth and others are chosen to support the development of play. When the child's cognitive potential is within normal limits, it is appropriate, indeed essential, to expect communication and language skills to develop commensurate with the child's chronological age. Meadow-Orlans and Steinberg (1993) have demonstrated that professional support can increase mothers' responsiveness to their children which, in turn, can facilitate higher levels of play. When a child has a cognitive delay, the activities are still designed to facilitate the development of play and language. However, the child's communication and language skills are expected to develop at a rate that corresponds with the child's cognitive age, rather than the chronological age. The findings by Snyder and Yoshinaga-Itano (1998) encourage professionals to examine the play of infants and toddlers with hearing loss first, in order to design activities that link objectives for language development to the level of the child's symbolic play.

Starting in the first year of life, then, it is important to obtain a measure of cognition that is not influenced by the child's hearing loss. A measure of a child's symbolic play behaviors can accomplish this, with the understanding that symbolic play is a representation of cognitive development (Fewell & Rich, 1997; Saracho & Spodek, 1995; Snyder & Yoshinaga-Itano, 1998; Yoshinaga-Itano, Snyder, & Day, 1998). The Play Assessment Scale (Fewell, 1984) and the Play Assessment Questionnaire (Calhoun, 1987), an adaptation of the aforementioned scale, are useful tools to assess symbolic play behaviors in young children starting at 6 months of age.

Semantic Development

Receptively, word learning starts as young as 5 months of age for hearing children, when they selectively respond to certain words such as their own name (Mandel, Jusczyk, & Pisoni, 1995). Great variability in receptive vocabulary exists at 6 months of age, with hearing children having a receptive vocabulary that ranges from 11 to 154 words (Fenson, Dale, Reznick, Bates, Thal, & Pethick, 1994). By 8 months of age, a baby will start to understand the meanings of individual words. This inventory of words continually increases over time, with the average 16-month-old understanding 92 to 321 words (Fenson et al., 1994).

Expressively, the magical milestone of first words is achieved toward the end of a baby's first year. Hearing children acquiring spoken English typically produce their first words at 10–15 months of age (Benedict, 1979; Fenson et al., 1994; Huttonlocher & Smiley, 1987). For children exposed to fluent signers, first signs have been reported to emerge even earlier, at approximately 8–12 months of age (Bonvillian, 1999; Folven & Bonvillian, 1991; Bonvillian, Orlansky & Novack, 1983; Prinz & Prinz, 1979; Schlesinger & Meadow, 1972). It is notable, however, that the age at which children produce their first signs is not yet universally accepted, because some researchers (Petitto, 1988; Voltera, Beronesi, & Massoni, 1994) have suggested that some emerging signs are actually less-specific motor behaviors that are common to deaf and hearing infants and not signs at all. In addition, Folven and Bonvillian raise a question about the definition of a sign versus an early gesture.

By 18 months of age, a hearing toddler is expected to accumulate an average inventory of 50 expressive words (Nelson, 1973). Once the child has acquired approximately 50 expressive words, a "word spurt" or "word explosion" is often reported. At this point, hearing children typically add approximately 22–37 words each month to their expressive vocabulary (Benedict, 1979; Goldfield & Reznick, 1990). Research on the early vocabulary development of children acquiring ASL suggests that, from 12–17 months of age, signs for these children are acquired more rapidly than hearing children learning spoken English (Anderson & Reilly, 2002; Meier & Newport, 1990). However, by 18–23 months of age, the size of the expressive lexicon for children using sign is similar to the size of the expressive vocabulary of hearing children using spoken English (Anderson & Reilly, 2002). Anderson and Reilly found no evidence for a vocabulary burst in the group of deaf children with deaf parents they studied.

IMPACT OF HEARING LOSS

Children with hearing loss demonstrate delays in vocabulary development (Connor, Hieber, Arts, & Zwolen, 2000; Davis, 1974; Osberger, Moeller, Eccarius, Robbins, & Johnson, 1986). This may be the result of less exposure to the rich language heard by hearing children with hearing parents or seen by deaf children with deaf parents. The vocabulary development of children with hearing loss who have hearing parents is slower and more variable (Lederberg & P. Spencer, 2001; Mayne, Yoshinaga-Itano, Sedey, & Carey, 2000; Moeller, 2000). These studies show an effect on the age when children transition from slow to rapid learning of new words and on the size of the child's lexicon. Characteristics that impact vocabulary acquisition may include age of identification (Mayne et al., 2000), the age at which intervention started (Moeller, 2000), parent involvement (Moeller, 2000), and/or the quality of the intervention provided (Lederberg, 2003).

COLLECTING THE EVIDENCE

By obtaining samples of the child's semantic repertoire, the interventionist can be precise and prescriptive about the strategies to be taught. When learning English, either signed or spoken, readily available norms for hearing children can be utilized. In addition, it is important to monitor the development of different types of words, including the easier-to-learn nouns and verbs along with the abstract concepts conveyed by adjectives, prepositions, and adverbs. The MacArthur Communicative Development Inventories (CDI) (Fenson et al., 1993) are constructed as parent-completed questionnaires and provide an estimate of the number of words a child understands, the number of words a child produces, and/or the types of words in the child's lexicon. These inventories are normed on hearing children from 8 to 30 months of age. The MacArthur CDI for American Sign Language (ASL-CDI) (Anderson & Reilly, 2002), based on the English CDI, focuses on measuring the ASL lexicon for deaf children between the ages of 8 and 36 months.

Syntax Development

Starting at approximately 18–24 months of age, typically developing hearing toddlers exhibit productive word combinations (Brown, 1973). Using simple two-word utterances, they generate many syntactic forms. Babies, whether hearing or deaf, who are exposed to fluent signers also start to use multi-sign combinations at approximately 18 months of age (Bellugi, van Hoek, Lillo-Martin, & O'Grady, 1993; Newport & Meier, 1985; Petitto, 2000). During the third year of life, the child learning English, be it spoken English or a manual form of English, uses more and varying sentence forms and increases the MLU. The same is true for children learning ASL when they are exposed to a language-rich environment (Bellugi, et al., 1993; Meier & Newport, 1990; Newport & Meier, 1985; Petitto, 2000).

IMPACT OF HEARING LOSS

To varying degrees, children with hearing loss learning English, whether spoken or in sign, exhibit a shorter MLU, tend to use simpler sentence structures, and are inclined to overuse the subject-verb-object sentence pattern (Culbertson, 2007). Some children learning spoken English use inappropriate syntactic patterns (e.g., "Who a girl give you a candy?" to convey the message, "Which girl gave you some candy?"). Culbertson reports that children may also arrange words in non-English word order.

For children learning ASL from fluently signing adults, lexical word combinations start to occur at 16–18 months (Bonvillian, Orlansky, & Novack, 1983; Folven & Bonvillian, 1991; Pizzuto, 1990). Facial expressions, which have grammatical functions in ASL, are used to convey negation, questions, topic changes, conditionals, and adverbials (Schick, 2003). As early as 12 months of age, babies have been observed to use a head shake to convey negation (Anderson & Reilly, 1997). Facial expressions for adverbials, who, what, where, when (WH) questions; and conditionals appear later (Anderson & Reilly, 1997; Anderson & Reilly, 1999; Lillo-Martin, 2000).

COLLECTING THE EVIDENCE

Syntactic competencies in English can be evaluated by measuring the MLU, the parts of speech used, and the sentence structures employed. The rules governing the development of syntax using ASL are unique, and assessment tools specific to the development of ASL need to be used. Mann and Prinz (2006) report, however, that the number of assessment tools available to evaluate sign language proficiency at various ages remains small, and they explain the need to establish standards for the assessment of ASL so that benchmarks for development can be readily made. Two informal checklists currently available to evaluate the development of sign skills in young children under 3 years of age are the ASL Development Checklist (Evans, Zimmer, & Murray, 2006) and the Kendall Conversational Proficiency P-Levels Scale (French, 1999).

Development of Functional Auditory Skills

The development of auditory skills is an essential ability underlying spoken language. Although hearing infants do not produce intelligible words until about 1 year of age, their ability to recognize and differentiate speech sounds is a critical precursor to the production of those words (Sininger, Doyle, & Moore, 1999). Erber's normative data (1982) associate specific listening skills with precise ages of acquisition for hearing children. For example, even at 1 month of age, a baby demonstrates better behavioral and physiologic responses to low-frequency sounds than to sounds at higher frequencies. From 2 to 3 months of age, a baby is quieted by mother's voice, and at 3 to 4 months of age a baby can recognize mother's voice. Localization to sound starts at approximately 5–6 months of age. Auditory feedback, the interest in listening to one's own voice, starts at 6–7 months of age. Before the first birthday, at 10–11 months of age, words are understood to varying degrees, with object names being understood far more often than action verbs.

Recent research by Ching (2007) tested the auditory skills of 90 children with normal hearing using the Parent's Evaluation of Aural/Oral Performance of Children (PEACH). This protocol includes 13 items that assess listening in both quiet and noise. The items are arranged in two categories: auditory awareness and aural–oral function. Some items measure relatively easy awareness skills such as responding to one's name, recognizing environmental sounds, and distinguishing familiar voices. More difficult items assess the ability of the child to follow verbal instructions, follow a story that is read aloud, and participate in conversations. Long-awaited normative information shows that hearing children start to acquire the auditory skills in this checklist at approximately 6 months of age, and these skills are near-perfect by approximately 3 years of age.

IMPACT OF HEARING LOSS

The acquisition of auditory skills proceeds through the same stages for hearing children and those with hearing loss, albeit at a slower pace for the latter (Ching, 2007). Ching reports that her sample of children with hearing loss, ranging in age from 4 months to 19.75 years, demonstrate a decrease in functional performance with increase in hearing loss. The value of this normative information is the ability to relate the listening performance of a child with hearing loss to age-matched, normally hearing children or to children with similar degrees of hearing loss.

We know that the development of auditory skills is systematic (Laughton and Hasenstab, 2000; Pollock, Goldberg, & Caleffe-Schenck, 1985) and follows an inherent hierarchy of skills (Cole & Flexer, 2008; Erber, 1982; Estabrooks, 1998; Flexer, 1999; Stout & Windle, 1992; Tye-Murray, 1992; Watkins, 1993). A typical hierarchy of skills follows an order from easier to more difficult skills: auditory awareness, assigning meaning to sounds, searching for and localizing to the sound source, auditory discrimination, auditory comprehension, and the ability to utilize auditory information to process language (e.g., sequencing, correct use of syntactic information, understanding spoken language). Children with hearing loss depend on prescriptive teaching to acquire these skills. This is often referred to as auditory training, auditory skill development, or auditory–verbal therapy. Irrespective of the terminology used, the purpose is to facilitate the development of auditory skills given compromised access to the auditory signal.

COLLECTING THE EVIDENCE

The professionals providing instruction on the acquisition of functional auditory skills must have a

Table 20.3   Hierarchy of auditory skills in the Functional Auditory Performance Indicators (FAPI)

Stages of Auditory Development	Definition
Awareness and Meaning of Sounds	The child is aware that an auditory stimulus is present. The child may demonstrate awareness of loud environmental sounds, noisemakers, music, and/or speech. The child further demonstrates that sound is meaningful by associating a variety of auditory stimuli with their sound source. The stimuli include loud environmental sounds or noisemakers, music, vocalizations (non-true words) and speech stimuli.
Auditory Feedback and Integration	The child changes, notices, and monitors his/her own vocal productions. A child may demonstrate this skill by responding to sound when amplification is turned on, by vocalizing to monitor when amplification is working, and/or by noticing his/her own vocalizations. Furthermore, the child uses auditory information to produce an oral spoken utterance that approximates or matches a spoken stimulus.
Localizing Sound Source	The child searches for and/or finds the auditory stimulus.
Auditory Discrimination	The child distinguishes the characteristics of different sounds as being the same or different including environmental sounds, suprasegmental characteristics of speech (e.g., intensity, duration, pitch), non-true words, and true words.
Auditory Comprehension	The child demonstrates understanding of linguistic information that is heard, by identifying what is said, identifying critical elements in the message, and by following directions.
Short-term Auditory Memory	The child can hear, remember, repeat, and recall a sequence of units (e.g., digits, unrelated words, sentences, etc.).
Linguistic Auditory Processing	The child utilizes auditory information to process language. These skills measure the ways in which audition is used to sequence language, to learn and use morphemes, to learn and use syntactic information, and to understand spoken language.

From Stredler-Brown, A., & Johnson, C. D. (2001). Functional auditory performance indicators: An integrated approach to auditory development. Retrieved November 23, 2009 from http://www.arlenestredlerbrown.com

broad base of knowledge about speech acoustics, the hierarchy of auditory skills, and specific techniques. To determine if the treatment program is effective, a progress monitoring tool should be used (Stredler-Brown, 2004). The Functional Auditory Performance Indicators (FAPI) assessment protocol (Stredler-Brown & Johnson, 2001) provides a procedure to establish a profile of a child's auditory skill development, to quantify the level of competency a child acquires with each skill, and to provide accountability. There are seven categories in the entire protocol that are presented in hierarchical order. The skills in each of the seven categories are also presented in hierarchical order. Table 20.3 lists the hierarchy of auditory skills.

A unique feature of the FAPI is the in-depth examination of a child's skill in a variety of listening conditions. Most measurements are created to assess the acquisition or attainment of skills. In these checklists (Kühn-Inacker, Weichbold, Tsiakpini, Coninx, & D'Haese, 2003; Watkins, Taylor, & Pittman, 2004), a skill is identified as "present" or "absent." However, it is important to calculate the child's ability to use a skill in different listening situations. Table 20.4 presents a list of the conditions that impact successful use of auditory skills.

Table 20.4 Listening conditions that affect functional auditory skills

- Auditory stimuli that are paired with *visual cues* contrasted with responses to an *auditory stimulus alone*
- Stimuli that are presented in *close proximity* to the child contrasted with stimuli that are presented *far away*
- Auditory stimuli in a *noisy situation* contrasted with stimuli presented in a *quiet environment*
- Auditory stimuli that are observed when the child is *prompted* to listen contrasted with *spontaneous* responses to auditory stimuli
- Auditory stimuli that are presented as a *closed set* of a limited number of choices contrasted with items that are presented in an unlimited *open set*
- Words that are *familiar* to the child contrasted with *unfamiliar* words
- The use of *words* as the stimulus contrasted with *words in sentences*
- Stimuli are presented when the child is in an *active listening state* contrasted with the presentation of stimuli while the child is engaged in *other activities*

From Stredler-Brown, A., & Johnson, C. D. (2001). Functional auditory performance indicators: An integrated approach to auditory development. Retrieved November 23, 2009 from http://www.arlenestredlerbrown.com

Ideally, assessment is based on a quantitative measure to allow the interventionist to calculate changes over time. The lack of quantitative measurements has been a shortcoming of auditory assessments to date. The FAPI (Stredler-Brown & Johnson, 2001) offers a unique scoring rubric that provides this quantitative documentation of a child's skills. The FAPI is scored by assigning a value to each of the 31 skills that are distributed among each of the seven categories. A summary of acquired skills is generated by calculating the scores on each item of the profile.

Speech Development

An infant's communication starts as a cry, with the addition of other vegetative vocalizations (Hoff, 2008). Cooing is the production of prolonged vowels and starts when an infant approaches 2 months of age (Hoff). Vocal play begins when the baby is approximately 4 months of age (Stark, 1986). Reduplicated babble, also known as canonical babbling, follows at approximately 6–9 months of age (Oller, 1986, 2000; Oller & Lynch, 1992). Nonreduplicated, or variegated, babbling appears next and consists of more varied consonant+vowel (CV) combinations and some consonant + vowel + consonant (CVC) syllables (Hoff, 2008). Jargon emerges at this time, and is characterized by nonreduplicated babble with added intonation contours (Hoff). By 12–18 months, the hearing toddler is practicing the suprasegmental characteristics of speech while imitating the words used by others.

IMPACT OF HEARING LOSS

Babies with hearing loss, even those with profound degrees of hearing loss, produce vocalizations (Yoshinaga-Itano, 2000; Yoshinaga-Itano, 2006). However, there is a direct effect on the quality of early vocalizations, the emerging phonemic repertoire, and speech intelligibility as a result of a child's auditory access to sound. It is notable that infants with profound degrees of hearing loss do not produce canonical babbling—well-formed syllable strings (Oller, 2006)—as early as their hearing peers (Eilers & Oller, 1994; Oller & Eilers, 1988) or their peers with less severe degrees of hearing loss (Nathani, Neal, Olds, Brill, & Oller, 2001). Common errors in the suprasegmental characteristics of intensity, duration, and pitch, all of which can contribute to speech intelligibility, have been documented in very young children with hearing loss (Gold, 1980). Voice quality is affected by changes in the rate (Tye-Murray, 1992), stress, nasality, and the overall rhythm patterns of speech (Formby & Monsen, 1982). Challenges to the accurate articulation of words are demonstrated by errors in vowel and consonant production (Hudgins & Numbers, 1942). Wallace, Menn, and Yoshinaga-Itano (2000) report that children with mild to profound degrees of hearing loss have similar vocal productions in the first 12 months of life and that the vocalizations of their group differ from hearing children. The group with hearing loss generated fewer CV productions in the first year of life. The impact of degree of hearing loss was evident, with less severe degrees of hearing loss correlating with larger phonetic inventories (Obenchain, Menn, & Yoshinaga-Itano, 2000). Once children start to produce spoken words, those with mild to moderately-severe hearing loss continue to misarticulate consonants (Elfenbein, Hardin-Jones, & Davis, 1994) and consonant blends (Cozad, 1974). In general, studies of children who are deaf or hard of hearing show that phoneme acquisition occurs later than in hearing children, and use of the full phonetic repertoire is infrequent (Blamey, 2003).

COLLECTING THE EVIDENCE

Assessments analyze the characteristics of preverbal vocalizations, true words, and speech intelligibility. Monitoring can start very early, when the infant is producing reduplicated and nonreduplicated babble and jargon. Once a transcript is collected, analyses of the total number of vocalizations can be calculated. In addition, a measurement of the mean length of syllables per utterance and a phonetic repertoire of all sounds produced can be gathered (Lund & Duncan, 1993). Once a child is producing true words, an additional analysis of the accuracy of vowel and consonant production can be conducted (Sander, 1972; Shriberg, Austin, Lewis, Sweeny, & Wilson, 1997). The Logical International Phonetics Program (LIPP) (Oller & Delgado, 1999) is one useful tool to conduct these analyses. An accepted procedure to measure speech intelligibility is the use of a rating scale (Levitt, McGarr, & Geffner, 1987; Sedey, 1996; Shriberg & Kwiatkowski, 1982) by which naïve and familiar listeners may appraise their understanding of the child's speech production. Progress in the development of speech is witnessed when there is an increase in the total number of vocalizations made over time, an increase in the mean length of syllables per utterance as a child uses more sophisticated patterns of babble, jargon, and word strings, and an increase in the diversity and accuracy of the phonemic repertoire.

Summary and Conclusions

Building on early identification and the early start of intervention, a proposed model for selecting a communication approach for a very young child follows five steps (Stredler-Brown, 2009). First, parents engage in an informed decision-making process. Then, professionals and parents conduct informal and formal observations of the child's developmental profile. The modalities used by the child during spontaneous communication are observed. Professionals and parents document, analyze, and share their observations. Periodically, parents actively review the approach they are using, maintain it if progress is satisfactory or revise it if they see that appropriate developmental gains have not been made.

Many families change the communication approach they originally selected during the first few years of their child's life (Sedey, 2003). In a study by Brookhouser and Moeller (1986), the parents of 10 of 15 children changed the communication approach they were using based on an analysis of the child's progress. Although these changes may reflect new information the parents obtained, it is more likely that the objective information describing the child's communication and language skills justified an adaptation of the approach being used. This premise supports the usefulness of data collection in the decision-making process.

When parents who are not familiar with hearing loss are presented with all communication approaches, they may find it difficult to commit to one approach. Some parents, believing that "more is better," attempt to use all communication approaches. It is the responsibility of the professionals working with families to discuss the communication approaches, knowing that one should not be recommending families use all communication approaches just because all options are presented. This can only result in parents' dabbling in elements of different approaches. This naïve decision has never been credited with success, nor is it endorsed.

The chosen approach should not be guided solely by the professionals' skills, nor should the professionals' own commitment to an approach unfairly prejudice a parent toward one approach or another. Rather, it is suggested that professionals use empirical evidence to recommend, choose, maintain, or change an approach. Unfortunately, experience has shown that many interventionists choose not to assess. Some rely solely on their experience and do not believe formal assessments will add to their knowledge about the child. Assessment may be seen as intrusive or taking time away from regularly scheduled therapy. However, by using assessment data, a more efficient and effective prescriptive intervention program can be developed for each child. Those interventionists who have experience using assessment data to drive a child's intervention program report that the objective information helps to identify gaps not otherwise noticed. Assessment helps to monitor the rate of progress and, in so doing, supports appropriately high expectations. As well, collecting the evidence teaches the interventionist critical observation skills.

Interventionists may need some amount of encouragement to conduct assessment in order to support high standards, guide the individualized program, and educate parents about the developmental progress their child is making. There are several means by which to encourage interventionists to use assessment procedures. Program administrators can provide an incentive for interventionists to conduct evidence-based programming. Once assessment is required, it is essential to provide training to the interventionists as they learn to administer the tests, interpret the results, and apply the information to appropriately adapt and then guide the treatment program. Some programs are implementing a mentor program (Rall & Brunner, 2006; Tiberius, 2008) to assist interventionists in learning new skills in the context of the session. Most important, assessment must be seen as part of the intervention program, not just an add-on or an incidental occurrence. When assessment is an integral part of the program, it becomes a relevant tool to guide parents' communication choices and ongoing decisions about effective implementation of intervention activities.

References

American Speech-Language-Hearing Association. (1997–2008). *History of ASHA membership and certification requirements.* Retrieved October 27, 2008, from http://www.asha.org/about/publications/leader-online/archives/2007/070529/070529c3.htm

Anderson, D., & Reilly, J. S. (1997). The puzzle of negation: How children move from communicative to grammatical negation in ASL. *Journal of Child Language, 18*(4), 411–429.

Anderson, D., & Reilly, J. S. (1999). PAH! The acquisition of non-manual adverbials in ASL. *Sign Language and Linguistics, 1,* 115–142.

Anderson, D., & Reilly, J. S. (2002). The MacArthur Communicative Development Inventory: Normative data for American Sign Language. *Journal of Deaf Studies and Deaf Education, 7*(2), 83–106.

Arehart, K. H., Yoshinaga-Itano, C., Thomson, V., Gabbard, S. A., & Brown, A. S. (1998). State of the states: The status of universal newborn screening, assessment, and intervention systems in 16 states. *American Journal of Audiology, 7,* 101–114.

Bailey, D., Bruer, J., Symons, F., & Lichtman, J. (2001). *Critical thinking about critical periods.* Baltimore: Paul H. Brookes Publishing Co., Inc.

Baker, C. (1977). Regulators and turn-taking in American Sign Language discourse. In L. Friedman (Ed.), *On the other hand: New perspectives in American Sign Language* (pp. 215–236). New York: Academic Press.

Barneavdelinge, S. H. (2002). Universal neonatal hearing screening of infants with otoacoustic emissions. *Tidsskr Nor Laegeforen, 122*(22), 2187–2189.

Bellugi, U., van Hoek, K., Lillo-Martin, D., & O'Grady, L. (1993). The acquisition of syntax and space in young deaf signers. In D. Bishop & K. Mogford (Eds.), *Language development in exceptional children* (pp. 132–149). Hove, UK: Erlbaum.

Benedict, H. (1979). Early lexical development: Comprehension and production. *Journal of Child Language, 6,* 183–200.

Bess, F., Dodd-Murphy, J., & Parker, R. (1998). Children with minimal sensorineural hearing loss: Prevalence, educational performance, and functional status. *Ear and Hearing, 19*(5), 339–354.

Blamey, P. (2003). Development of spoken language by deaf children. In M. Marschark & P. Spencer (Eds.), *Oxford handbook of deaf studies, language, and education* (pp. 232–246). New York: Oxford University Press.

Bodner-Johnson, B. (2001). Parents as adult learners in family-centered early education. *American Annals of the Deaf, 146*(3), 263–269.

Bonvillian, J. D. (1999). Sign language development. In M. Barrett (Ed.), *The development of language.* East Sussex: Psychology Press.

Bonvillian, J. D., Orlansky, M. D., & Novack, L. L. (1983). Developmental milestones: Sign language acquisition and motor development. *Child Development, 54,* 1435–1445.

Bornstein, H., Saulnier, K., & Hamilton, L. (1980). Signed English: A first evaluation. *American Annals of the Deaf, 125,* 467–481.

Bornstein, H., Saulnier, K. L., & Hamilton, L. B. (1983). *The comprehensive signed English dictionary.* Washington, DC: Gallaudet University Press.

Bornstein, M. H., Selmi, A. M., Haynes, O. M., Painter, K. M., & Marx, E. S. (1999). Representational abilities and the hearing status of child/mother dyads. *Child Development, 70,* 833–852.

Bowen, S., Howell, J. J., Muir, S. G., Reed, S., & Yarger, C. C. (2004). Communication methodologies: Matching communication options to children. In S. Watkins, D. J. Taylor, & P. Pittman (Eds.), *SKI-HI curriculum: Family-centered programming for infants and young children with hearing loss* (pp. 1491–1568). Logan, UT: HOPE, Inc.

Brookhouser, P. E., & Moeller, M. P. (1986). Choosing the appropriate habilitative track for the newly identified hearing-impaired child. *Annals of Otology, Rhinology, & Laryngology, 95,* 51–59.

Brown, R. (1973). *A first language: The early stages.* Cambridge, MA: Harvard University Press.

Calhoun, D. (1987). *A comparison of two methods of evaluating play in toddlers.* Unpublished Master's Thesis, Ft. Collins: Colorado State University.

Centers for Disease Control (CDC). (2008). *A parents' guide to hearing loss.* Retrieved October 29, 2008, from http://www.cdc.gov/ncbddd/ehdi/CDROM/building/index.html

Ching, T. Y. C. (2007). The parents' evaluation of aural/oral performance of children (PEACH) scale: Normative data. *Journal of the American Academy of Audiology, 18*, 220–235.

Cho Lieu, J. E. (2004). Speech-language and educational consequences of unilateral hearing loss in children. *Archives of Otolaryngology & Head and Neck Surgery, 130*, 524–530.

Cole, E. B., & Flexer, C. (2008). *Children with hearing loss: Developing listening and talking birth to six*. San Diego, CA: Plural Publishing, Inc.

Connor, C. M., Hieber, S., Arts, H. A., & Zwolen, T. A. (2000). Speech, vocabulary, and the education of children using cochlear implants: Oral or total communication? *Journal of Speech, Language, and Hearing Research, 43*, 1185–1204.

Cornett, R. O. (1967). Cued speech. *American Annals of the Deaf, 112*(1), 3–13.

Cornett, R. O., & Daisey, M. E. (1992). *The cued speech resource book*. Raleigh, NC: National Cued Speech Association.

Cornett, O. & Daisey, M. E. (2001). *The cued speech resource book for parents of deaf children*, 2nd edition. Cleveland, OH: National Cued Speech Association.

Cozad, R. L. (1974). *The speech clinician and the hearing-impaired child*. Springfield, IL: Charles C. Thomas.

Culbertson, D. S. (2007). Language and speech of the deaf and hard of hearing. In R. L. Schow & M. A. Nerbonne (Eds.), *Introduction to audiologic rehabilitation*. Boston: Pearson Education, Inc.

Davis, J. (1974). Performance of young hearing-impaired children on a test of basic concepts. *Journal of Speech and Hearing Research, 17*, 342–351.

Davis, A., & Hind, S. (2003). The newborn hearing screening programme in England. *International Journal of Pediatric Otorhinolaryngology, 67*, S193–S196.

Davis, A., Bamford, J., Wilson, I., Ramkalawan, T., Forshaw, M., & Wright, S. (1997). A critical review of the role of neonatal hearing screening in the detection of congenital hearing impairment. *Health Technology Assessment, 1*:i-iv, 1–176.

DeLana, M., Gentry, M. A., & Andrews, J. (2007). The efficacy of ASL/English bilingual education: Considering public schools. *American Annals of the Deaf, 152*(1), 73–87.

Downs, M. (1974). *Hearing in children*. Baltimore: Williams & Wilkins.

Dunst, C. J., Leet, H., & Trivette, C. M. (1988). Family resources, personal well-being, and early intervention. *Journal of Special Education, 22*, 108–116.

Eilers, R. E., & Oller, D. K. (1994). Infant vocalizations and the early diagnosis of severe hearing impairment. *Journal of Pediatrics, 124*, 199–203.

Eleweke, C. J., & Rodda, M. (2000). Factors contributing to parents' selection of a communication mode to use with their deaf children. *American Annals of the Deaf, 145*, 375–383.

Elfenbein, J. L., Hardin-Jones, M. A., & Davis, J. M. (1994). Oral communication skills of children who are hard of hearing. *Journal of Speech and Hearing Research, 37*, 216–226.

Erber, N. P. (1982). *Auditory training*. Washington, DC: Alexander Graham Bell Association for the Deaf.

Estabrooks, W. (1994). *Auditory-verbal therapy for parents and professionals*. Washington, DC: Alexander Graham Bell Association for the Deaf.

Estabrooks, W. (1998). Auditory-verbal ages & stages of development. In W. Estabrooks (Ed.), *Cochlear implants for kids*. Washington, DC: Alexander Graham Bell Association for the Deaf, Inc.

Estabrooks, W. (2006). *Auditory-verbal therapy and practice*. Washington, DC: Alexander Graham Bell Association for the Deaf and Hard of Hearing.

Evans, C. J., Zimmer, K., & Murray, D. (2006). ASL development checklist. In C. J. Enns (Ed.), *A language and literacy framework for bilingual deaf education*. Winnipeg, Canada: University of Manitoba.

Fenson, L., Dale, P. S., Reznick, J. S., Thai, D., Bates, E., Hartung, J. P., et al. (1993). *MacArthur communicative development inventories*. San Diego: Singular Publishing Group, Inc.

Fenson, L., Dale, P. S., Reznick, J. S., Bates, E., Thal, D. J., & Pethick, S. J. (1994). Variability in early communicative development. *Monographs of the Society for Research in Child Development, 59* (Serial No. 242).

Fewell, R. (1984). *Play assessment scale*. Seattle, WA: University of Washington.

Fewell, R. R., & Rich, J. S. (1997). Play assessment as a procedure for examining cognitive, communication, and social skills in multihandicapped children. *Journal of Psychoeducational Assessment, 5*(2), 107–118.

Flexer, C. (1999). *Facilitating hearing and listening in young children*, 2nd edition. San Diego, CA: Plural Publishing.

Folven, R. J., & Bonvillian, J. D. (1991). The transition from nonreferential to referential language in children acquiring American Sign Language. *Developmental Psychology, 27*, 806–816.

Formby, C., & Monsen, R. B. (1982). Long-term average speech spectra for normal and hearing-impaired adolescents. *Journal of the Acoustical Society of America, 71*, 196–202.

French, M. M. (1999). *Starting with assessment: A developmental approach to deaf children's literacy*. Washington, DC: Gallaudet University Press.

Furth, H. G. (1961). The influence of language on the development of concept formation in deaf children. *Journal of Abnormal and Social Psychology, 63*, 386–389.

Garcia, J. (2001). *Sign with your baby*. Seattle, WA: Sign2Me.

Geers, A. E., & Moog, J. S. (1987). Predicting spoken language acquisition of deaf children. *Journal of Speech & Hearing Disorders, 52*, 84–94.

Gold, T. (1980). Speech production in hearing-impaired children. *Journal of Communication Disorders, 13*, 397–418.

Goldfield, B. A., & Reznick, J. S. (1990). Early lexical acquisition: Rate, content, and the vocabulary spurt. *Journal of Child Language, 17*, 171–184.

Goldstein, M. H., & Proctor, A. (1985). Tactile aids for profoundly deaf children. *Journal of the Acoustical Society of America, 77*(1), 258–265.

Green, D. R., Gaffney, M., Devine, O., & Grosse, S. D. (2007). Determining the effect of newborn hearing screening: An analysis of state hearing screening rates. *Public Health Reports*, March-April, Vol. 122.

Grushkin, D. (1998). Why shouldn't Sam read? Toward a new paradigm for literacy and the deaf. *Journal of Deaf Studies and Deaf Education, 3*, 149–202.

Gustason, G., Zawolkow, E., & Lopez, L. (1993). *Signing exact English*. Los Alamitos, CA: Modern Signs Press.

Hage, C., & Leybaert, J. (2006). The effect of cued speech on the development of spoken language. In P. Spencer & M. Marschark (Eds.), *Advances in the spoken language development of deaf and hard-of-hearing children* (pp. 193–211). New York: Oxford University Press.

Haley, J. (1976). *Problem solving therapy*. New York: Harper Colopmon Books.

Haley, J. (1987). *Problem solving therapy*, 2nd edition. San Francisco: Jossey-Bass.

Hanson, A. (1930). The first case in the world: Miss Petra Heiberg's report. *Volta Review, 32*, 223.

Harris, M. (1992). *Language experience and early language development: From input to uptake*. Hove, UK: Lawrence Erlbaum.

Hintermair, M. (2000). Hearing impairment, social networks, and coping: The need for families with hearing impaired children to relate to other parents and to hearing impaired adults. *American Annals of the Deaf, 145*(1), 41–53.

Hoff, E. (2008). *Language development*, 4th edition. Belmont, CA: Wadsworth, Cengage Learning.

Hudgins, C. V., & Numbers, F. C. (1942). An investigation of the intelligibility of the speech of the deaf. *Genetic Psychology Monograph, 25*, 289–392.

Huttonlocher, J., & Smiley, P. (1987). Early word meanings: The case of object names. *Cognitive Psychology, 19*, 63–89.

Individuals with Disabilities Education Improvement Act of 2004. (2004). 20 U. S. C. § 1400 et seq.

Iwasaki, S. (2003). A model of two-stage newborn hearing screening with automated auditory brainstem response. *International Journal of Pediatric Otorhinolaryngology, 67*(10), 1099–104.

Jackson, C. W., Becker, S., & Schmitendorf, K. (2002, September). *Survey of speech-language services for children that are deaf or hard of hearing in Kansas*. Poster session at the Kansas Speech-Language-Hearing Association (KSHA). Overland Park, KS.

Johnson, C. D. (2006, Spring). One year's growth in one year, expect no less. *Hands & Voices Communicator, 9*(3), 1.

Johnson, C. D., & Dauhauer, J. L. (2006, November–December). Evidence-based practice in audiology: A tutorial. *Audiology Today, 81*(6), 16–20.

Johnson, R. E., Liddell, S. K., & Erting, C. J. (1989). *Unlocking the curriculum: Principles for achieving access in deaf education* (Gallaudet Research Institute Working Paper 89–3). Washington, DC: Gallaudet University.

Joint Committee on Infant Hearing. (2007). Year 2007 position statement: Principles and guidelines for early hearing detection and intervention programs. *Pediatrics, 102*(4), 893–921.

Jones, E. A. (1993). *Partnering with families: A clinical training manual*. Unpublished manuscript, University of Colorado at Boulder.

Kamhi, A. G. (2006). Some final thoughts on EBP. *Language Speech and Hearing Services in Schools, 37*, 320–322.

Kiese-Himmel, C., & Ohlwein, S. (2003). Characteristics of children with permanent mild hearing impairment. *Folia Phoniatrica et Logopaedica, 55*(2), 70–79.

Kuhl, P. K., & Meltzoff, A. N. (1982). The bimodal perception of speech in infancy. *Science, 218*, 1138–1141.

Kühn-Inacker, H., Weichbold, V., Tsiakpini, L., Coninx, S., & D'Haese, P. (2003). *Little ears: Auditory questionnaire*. Innsbruck: MED-EL Medical Electronics.

Lane, H., Hoffmeister, R., & Bahan, B. (1996). *A journey into the deaf-world*. San Diego, CA: Dawn Sign Press.

Lane, S., Bell, L., & Parson-Tylka, T. (1997). *My turn to learn: A communication guide for parents of deaf and hard of hearing children*. British Columbia, Canada: Elks Family Resource Centre.

Lane, S., Bell, L., & Parson-Tylka, T. (2006). *My turn to learn: A communication guide for parents of deaf or hard of hearing children*. British Columbia, Canada: Bauhinea Press.

Laughton, J., & Hasenstab, S. M. (2000). Auditory learning, assessment, and intervention with school-age students who are deaf or hard-of-hearing. In J. Alpiner & P. McCarthy (Eds.), *Rehabilitative audiology: Children and adults*. Baltimore: Lippincott, Williams, and Wilkins, Inc.

Lederberg, A. R. (2003). Expressing meaning: From communicative intent to building a lexicon. In M. Marschark & P. E. Spencer (Eds.), *Oxford handbook of deaf studies, language, and education* (pp. 247–260). New York: Oxford University Press, Inc.

Lederberg, A. R., & Spencer, P. E. (2001). Vocabulary development of deaf and hard of hearing children. In M. D. Clark, M. Marschark, & M. Karchmer (Eds.), *Context, cognition and deafness* (pp. 88–112). Washington, DC: Gallaudet University Press.

Levitt, H., McGarr, N. S., & Geffner, D. (1987). Development of language and communication skills in hearing-impaired children. *ASHA Monographs 26*.

Li, Y., Bain, L., & Steinberg, A. G. (2003). Parental decision making and the choice of communication modality for the child who is deaf. *Archives of Pediatric Adolescent Medicine, 157*, 162–168.

Lillo-Martin, D. (2000). Early and late language acquisition: Aspects of the syntax and acquisition of WH questions in American Sign Language. In K. Emmorey & H. Lane (Eds.), *The signs of language revisited: An anthology to honor Ursula Bellugi and Edward Kilma* (pp. 401–414). Mahwah, NJ: Lawrence Erlbaum Associates.

Ling, D. (2002). *Speech and the hearing impaired child*, 2nd edition. Washington, DC: Alexander Graham Bell Association of the Deaf and Hard of Hearing.

Locke, J. L. (1994). Gradual emergence of developmental language disorders. *Journal of Speech and Hearing Research, 37*, 608–616.

Luetke-Stahlman, B. (1990). Types of instructional input as predictors of reading achievement for hearing-impaired students. In C. Lucas (Ed.), *Sign language research: Theoretical issues* (pp. 325–336). Washington, DC: Gallaudet University Press.

Lund, N. J., & Duncan, J. F. (1993). *Assessing children's language in naturalistic contexts*, 3rd edition. Englewood Cliffs, NJ: Prentice Hall.

Mandel, D. R., Jusczyk, P. W., & Pisoni, D. B. (1995). Infants' recognition of the sound patterns of their own names. *Psychologoical Science, 6*, 314–317.

Mann, W., & Prinz, P. M. (2006). An investigation of the need for sign language assessment in deaf education. *American Annals of the Deaf, 151*(3), 356–370.

Marge, D. K., & Marge, M. (2005). *Beyond newborn hearing screening: Meeting the educational and health care needs of infants and young children with hearing loss in America*. Report of the National Consensus Conference on Effective Educational and Health Care Interventions for Infants and Young Children with Hearing Loss, September 10–12, 2004. Syracuse, New York: Department of Physical Medicine and Rehabilitation, SUNY Upstate Medical University.

Marschark, M. (1997). *Raising and educating a deaf child: A comprehensive guide to the choices, controversies, and decisions faced by parents and educators*. New York: Oxford University Press.

Marschark, M. (2001). *Language development in children who are deaf and hard of hearing: A research synthesis*. Washington, DC: National Association of State Directors of Special Education.

Marschark, M. (2007). *Raising and educating a deaf child*, 2nd edition. New York: Oxford University Press.

Marchark, M., Lang, H. G., & Albertini, J. A. (2002). *Educating deaf students: From research to practice*. New York: Oxford University Press.

Mayer, C., & Akamatsu, D. T. (2003). Bilingualism and literacy. In M. Marschark & P. E. Spencer (Eds.), *Oxford handbook of deaf studies, language, and education* (pp. 136–147). New York: Oxford University Press.

Mayne, A. M., Yoshinaga-Itano, C., Sedey, A. L., & Carey, A. (2000). Expressive vocabulary development of infants and toddlers who are deaf or hard of hearing. *Volta Review*, *100*(5), 1–28.

McConkey Robbins, A. (2001) A sign of the times. *Loud and Clear Newsletter*, *4*(2). Valencia: Advanced Bionics. Reprinted with permission.

McCune-Nicholich, L. A. (1981). Toward symbolic functioning: Structure of early pretend games and potential parallels with language, *Child Development*, *52*, 785–797.

Meadow, K.P. (1980). *Deafness and child development*. Berkeley: University of California Press.

Meadow-Orlans, K., & Steinberg, A. (1993). Effects of infant hearing loss and maternal support on mother-infant interactions at 18 months. *Journal of Applied Developmental Psychology*, *14*, 407–426.

Meadow-Orlans, K., Mertens, D., & Sass-Lehrer, M. (2003). *Parents and their deaf children: The early years*. Washington, DC: Gallaudet University Press.

Meier, R. P., & Newport, E. L. (1990). Out of the hands of babes: On a possible sign advantage in language acquisition. *Language*, *66*(1), 1–23.

Meier, R. P., & Willerman, R. (1995). Prelinguistic gesture in deaf and hearing infants. In K. Emmorey & J. Reilly (Eds.), *Language, gesture, and space* (pp. 391–409). Hillsdale, NJ: Lawrence Erlbaum Associates.

Moeller, M. P. (2000). Early intervention and language development in children who are deaf and hard of hearing. *Pediatrics*, *106*(3), 1–9.

Moeller, M. P., & Condon, M. (1994). D. E. I. P.: A collaborative problem-solving approach to early intervention. In J. Roush & N. D. Matkin (Eds.), *Infants and toddlers with hearing loss: Family centered assessment and intervention* (pp. 163–192). Baltimore: York Press.

Moeller, M. P., Hoover, B., Putman, C., Arbataitis, K., Bohnenkamp, G., Peterson, B., et al. (2007a). Vocalizations of infants with hearing loss compared with infants with normal hearing: Part I – Phonetic development. *Ear & Hearing*, *28*(5), 605–627.

Moeller, M. P., Hoover, B., Putman, C., Arbataitis, K., Bohnenkamp, G., Peterson, B., et al. (2007b). Vocalizations of infants with hearing loss compared with infants with normal hearing: Part II – Transition to words. *Ear & Hearing*, *28*(5), 628–642.

Moores, D. F., & Martin, D. S. (2006). Overview: Curriculum and instruction in general education and in education of deaf learners. In D. F. Moores & D. S. Martin (Eds.), *Deaf learners: Developments in curriculum and instruction*. Washington, DC: Gallaudet University Press.

Morales Angulo, C. (2003). Program of hearing loss early detection in newborn infants in Cantabria: Results of the first year of activities. *Acta Otorrinolaringológica Española*, *54*(7), 475–482.

Morford, J., & Mayberry, R. (2000). A reexamination of 'early exposure' and its implications for language acquisition by eye. In C. Chamberlain, J. Morford, & R. Mayberry (Eds.), *Language acquisition by eye* (pp. 111–127). Mahwah, NJ: Lawrence Erlbaum.

Nathani, S., Neal, A. R., Olds, H., Brill, H. J., & Oller, D. K. (2001, April). *Canonical babbling and volubility in infants with moderate to severe hearing impairment*. Paper presented at the meeting of the International Child Phonology Conference, Boston, MA.

National Foundation for the Deaf (NFD). (2004). Project HIEDI (Hearing Impairment Early Detection and Intervention): Improving outcomes for children with permanent congenital hearing impairment. Retrieved November 13, 2008, from http://www.nfd.org.nz/ site_resources/library/ OrganisationFiles/HIEDI_Evidence_Based_Case.pdf

National Institute on Deafness and Other Communication Disorders (NIDCD) (2008). *American Sign Language*. Retrieved September 25, 2008 from http://www.nidcd.nih. gov/health/hearing/asl.asp

Nelson, K. (1973). Structure and strategy in learning to talk. *Monographs of the Society for Research in Child Development*, *38* (1 and 2, Serial No. 149).

Nelson, K. (1998). Toward a differentiated account of facilitators of literacy development and ASL in deaf children. *Topics in Language Disorders*, *18*, 73–88.

Newport, E., & Meier, R. (1985). The acquisition of American Sign Language. In D. Slobin (Ed.), *The cross-linguistic study of language acquisition* (pp. 881–938). Hillsdale, NJ: Lawrence Erlbaum.

Nicholas, J. G., & Geers, A. E. (2006). Effects of early auditory experience on the spoken language of deaf children at 3 years of age. *Ear and Hearing*, *27*, 286–298.

Nussbaum, D., Scott, S., Waddy-Smith, B., & Koch, M. (2006, May). *Spoken language and sign: Optimizing learning for children with cochlear implants*. Paper presented at the Laurent Clerc National Deaf Education Center, Washington, DC. Adapted from McConkey-Robbins, A. (2001). A sign of the times. *Loud and Clear Newsletter, 4(2)*. Valencia: Advanced Bionics.

Obenchain, P., Menn, L., & Yoshinaga-Itano, C. (2000). Can speech development at thirty-six months in children with hearing loss be predicted from information available in the second year of life? *Volta Review*, *100*(5), 149–180.

Oller, D. K. (1986). Metaphonology and infant vocalizations. In B. Lindbloom & R. Zetterstrom (Eds.), *Precursors of early speech*. New York: Stockton Press.

Oller, D. K. (2000). *The emergence of the speech capacity*. Mahwah, NJ: Erlbaum.

Oller, D. K. (2006). Vocal language development in deaf infants: New challenges. In P. E. Spencer & M. Marschark (Eds.), *Advances in the spoken language development of deaf and hard-of-hearing children* (pp. 22–41). New York: Oxford University Press.

Oller, D. K., & Delgado, R. E. (1999). *Logical International Phonetics Program*. Miami, FL: Intelligent Hearing Systems Corporation.

Oller, D. K., & Eilers, R. E. (1988). The role of audition in infant babbling. *Child Development*, *59*, 441–449.

Oller, D. K., & Lynch, M. P. (1992). Infant vocalizations and innovations in infraphonology: Toward a broader theory of development and disorders. In C. A. Ferguson, L. Menn, & C. Stoel-Gammon (Eds.), *Phonological development: Models, research, implications.* Timonium, MD: York Press.

Osberger, M. J., Moeller, M. P., Eccarius, M., Robbins, A. M., & Johnson, D. (1986). Language and learning skills of hearing-impaired students: Expressive language skills. *ASHA Monographs, 23,* 54–65.

Petitto, L. (1988). "Language" in the prelinguistic child. In F. S. Kessel (Ed.), *The development of language and language researchers: Essays in honor of Roger Brown* (pp. 187–221). Hillsdale, NH: Lawrence Erlbaum.

Petitto, L. (1994). Are signed languages "real" languages?: Evidence from American Sign Language and Langue des signes quebecoise. *Signpost, 7*(3), 1–10.

Petitto, L. A. (2000). The acquisition of natural signed languages: Lessons in the nature of human language and its biological foundations. In C. Chamberlain & J. P. Morford (Eds.), *Language acquisition by eye.* Mahwah, NJ: Erlbaum.

Petitto, L. A., & Marentette, P. F. (1991). Babbling in the manual mode: Evidence for the ontogeny of language. *Science, 251,* 1493–1496.

Piaget, J. (1962). *Play, dreams, and imitation in childhood.* New York: Norton.

Pizzuto, E. (1990). The early development of deixis in American Sign Language: What is the point? In V. Volterra & C. J. Erting (Eds.), *From gesture to language in hearing and deaf children* (pp. 142–161). New York: Springer-Verlag.

Pollock, D. (1997). *Educational audiology for the limited hearing infant and preschooler: An auditory-verbal program.* Springfield, IL: Charles C. Thomas.

Pollock, D., Goldberg, D. M., & Caleffe-Schenck, N. (1985). *Educational audiology for the limited hearing infant and preschooler: An auditory-verbal program,* 2nd edition. Springfield, IL: Charles C. Thomas.

Power, D., Hyde, M., & Leigh, G. (2008). Learning English from signed English: An impossible task? *American Annals of the Deaf, 153*(1), 37–47.

Prinz, P. M., & Prinz, E. A. (1979). Simultaneous acquisition of ASL and spoken English (in a hearing child of a deaf mother and hearing father: Phase I: Early lexical development. *Sign Language Studies, 25,* 283–296.

Rall, E., & Brunner, E. (2006). Mentoring in audiology. *Seminars in Hearing, 27*(2), 92–97.

Ratner, N. B. (2006). Evidence-based practice: An examination of its ramifications for the practice of speech-language pathology. *Language Speech and Hearing Services in Schools, 37,* 257–267.

Reed, C. M., Rabinowitz, W. M., Durlach, N. I., Braida, L. D., Conway-Fithian, S., & Schultz, M. C. (1985). Research on the Tadoma method of speech communication. *Journal of the Acoustical Society of America, 77*(1), 247–257.

Reilly, J. S., McIntire, M., & Bellugi, U. (1990). Faces: The relationship between language and affect. In V. Volterra & C. J. Erting (Eds.), *From gesture to language in hearing and deaf children* (pp. 128–141). Berlin: Springer-Verlag.

Rodda, M., & Grove, C. (1987). *Language, cognition, and deafness.* Hillsdale, NJ: Lawrence Erlbaum.

Roush, J., & McWilliam, R. A. (1994). Family-centered early intervention: Historical, philosophical, and legislative issues. In J. Roush & N. D. Matkin (Eds.), *Infants and toddlers with hearing loss: Family centered assessment and intervention* (pp. 3–21). Baltimore: York Press, Inc.

Sander, E. (1972). When are speech sounds learned? *Journal of Speech and Hearing Research, 37,* 55–63.

Saracho, O. N., & Spodek, B. (1995). Children's play and early childhood education: Insights from history and theory. *Journal of Education, 177*(3), 129–148.

Satir, V., Stachowiak, J., & Taschman, H. (1975). *Helping families to change.* New York: Jason Aronson, Inc.

Schick, B. (2003). The development of American Sign Language and manually coded English systems. In M. Marschark & P. Spencer (Eds.), *Oxford handbook of deaf studies, language and education* (pp. 219–231). New York: Oxford University Press.

Schick, B., & Moeller, M. P. (1992). What is learnable in manually coded English sign systems? *Applied Psycholinguistics, 13,* 313–340.

Schick, B., Marschark, M., & Spencer, P. (Eds.). (2006). *Advances in the sign language development of deaf children.* New York: Oxford University Press.

Schildroth, A., & Hotto, S. (1993). Annual survey of hearing impaired children and youth: 1991–1992 school year. *American Annals of the Deaf, 138,* 163–168.

Schlesinger, H. S., & Meadow, K. P. (1972). *Sound and sign: Childhood deafness and mental health.* Berkeley, CA: University of California Press.

Schultz, M. C., Norton, S. J., Conway-Fithian, S., & Reed, C. M. (1984). A survey of the use of the Tadoma Method in the United States and Canada. *Volta Review, Oct/Nov,* 283–292.

Sedey, A. (2003). Communication approach used by children in Colorado. Unpublished raw data.

Sedey, A. L. (1996). *Speech intelligibility checklist.* Available from the Department of Speech, Language, Hearing Sciences, 2501 Kittredge Loop Road, Campus Box 409, Boulder, CO 80309.

Sheldon, M. L., & Rush, D. D. (2001). The ten myths about providing early intervention services in natural environments. *Infants and Young Children, 14*(1), 1–13.

Sherrick, C. E. (1985). Touch as a communicative sense: Introduction. *Journal of the Acoustic Society of America, 77*(1), 218–219.

Shriberg, L. D., Austin, D., Lewis, B. A., Sweeny, J. L., & Wilson, D. L. (1997). The percentage of consonants correct (PCC) metric: Extensions and reliability data. *Journal of Speech, Language, and Hearing Research, 40,* 708–722.

Shriberg, L. D., & Kwiatkowski, J. (1982). Phonological disorders III: A procedure for assessing severity of involvement. *Journal of Speech and Hearing Disorders, 47,* 256–270.

Sininger, Y. S., Doyle, K. J., & Moore, J. K. (1999). The case for early identification of hearing loss in children: Auditory system development. *The Pediatric Clinics of North America, 46*(1), 1–14.

Slobin, D. I. (1996). From "thought and language" to "thinking for speaking." In J. J. Gumperz & S. C. Levinson (Eds.), *Rethinking linguistic relativity* (pp. 70–86). Cambridge, UK: Cambridge University Press.

Snyder, L., & Yoshinaga-Itano, C. (1998). Specific play behaviors and the development of communication in children with hearing loss. *The Volta Review, 100*(3), 165–185.

Spencer, L. J., & Tomblin, J. B. (2006). Speech production and spoken language development of children using "total communication". In P. E. Spencer & M. Marschark (Eds.), *Advances in the spoken language development of deaf and* hard-of-hearing children (pp. 166–192). New York: Oxford University Press.

Spencer, P. E. (2000). Looking without listening: Is audition a prerequisite for normal development of visual attention during infancy? *Journal of Deaf Studies and Deaf Education, 5*(4), 291–302.

Spencer, P. E. (2004). Language at 12 and 18 months: Characteristics and accessibility of linguistic models. In K. Meadow-Orlans, P. Spencer, & L. Koester (Eds.), *The world of deaf infants: A longitudinal study* (pp. 147–167). New York: Oxford University Press.

Spencer, P. E., & Harris, M. (2006). Patterns and effects of language input to deaf infants and toddlers from deaf and hearing mothers. In B. Schick, M. Marschark, & P. E. Spencer (Eds.), *Advances in the sign language development of deaf children* (pp. 71–101). New York: Oxford University Press.

Stark, R. E. (1986). Prespeech segmental feature development. In P. Fletcher & M. Garman (Eds.), *Language acquisition*. Cambridge, UK: Cambridge University Press.

Stout, G. G., & Windle, J. V. E. (1992). *The developmental approach to successful listening*. Englewood, CO: Resource Point, Inc.

Stredler-Brown, A. (1998). Early intervention for infants and toddlers who are deaf and hard of hearing: New perspectives. *Journal of Educational Audiology, 6*, 45–49.

Stredler-Brown, A. (2004). Documenting functional benefit from FM technology. In D. Fabry & C. DeConde Johnson (Eds.), *ACCESS: Achieving clear communication employing sound solutions 2003*. London: Immediate Proceedings Limited.

Stredler-Brown, A. (2005). Family-Centered intervention: Proven strategies to assure positive outcomes. In R. Seewald & J. Bamford (Eds.), *A sound foundation through early amplification 2004: Proceedings of the third international conference* (pp. 185–195). London: Immediate Proceedings Limited.

Stredler-Brown, A. (2008). The importance of early intervention. In J. R. Madell & C. Flexer (Eds.), *Pediatric audiology: Birth through adolescence*. New York: Thieme Medical Publishers, Inc.

Stredler-Brown, A. (2009). Intervention, education, and therapy for children who are deaf or hard of hearing (pp. 934–954). In J. Katz, L. Medwetsky, R. Burkard, & L. Hood (Eds.), *Handbook of clinical audiology*. Baltimore, MD: Lippincott, Williams & Wilkins.

Stredler-Brown, A., & Arehart, K. (2000). Universal newborn hearing screening: Impact on early intervention services. In C. Yoshinaga-Itano & A. Sedey (Eds.), *The Volta Review, 100*(5), 85–117.

Stredler-Brown, A., Hulstrom, W. J., & Ringwalt, S. S. (2008). Early intervention. *Seminars in Hearing, 29*(2), 178–195.

Stredler-Brown, A., & Johnson, C. D. (2001). Functional auditory performance indicators: An integrated approach to auditory development. Retrieved November 23, 2009 from http://www.arlenestredlerbrown.com

Stredler-Brown, A., & Yoshinaga-Itano, C. (1994). The FAMILY Assessment: A multidisciplinary evaluation procedure. In J. Roush and N. D. Matkin (Eds.), *Infants and toddlers with hearing loss*. Baltimore: York Press.

Swisher, M. V. (1991). Conversational interaction between deaf children and their hearing mothers: The role of visual attention. In P. Siple & S. Fischer (Eds.), *Psychology: Volume 2: Theoretical issues in sign language research* (pp. 111–134). Chicago: University of Chicago Press.

Swisher, M. (1992). The role of parents in developing visual turn-taking in their young deaf children. *American Annals of the Deaf, 137*, 92–100.

Thayer, S. (1982). Social touching. In W. Schiff & E. Foulke (Eds.), *Tactual perception: A sourcebook*. Cambridge, UK: Cambridge University Press.

Tiberius, R. G. (2008). The renewal of mentoring. *Audiology Today, 20*(5), 19–28.

Tye-Murray, N. (1992). Articulatory organizational strategies and the roles of auditory information. *Volta Review, 94*, 243–260.

Tye-Murray, N. (1998). *Foundations of aural rehabilitation: Children, adults, and their family members*. San Diego: Singular Publishing Group, Inc.

Tyler, A. A. (2006). Commentary on treatment decisions for children with speech-sound disorders: Revisiting therapies in EBP. *Language, Speech, and Hearing Services in Schools, 37*, 280–283.

Valli, C., & Lucas, C. (1995). *Linguistics of American sign language*, 2nd edition. Washington, DC: Gallaudet University Press.

Volterra, V., Beronesi, S., & Massoni, P. (1994). How does gestural communication become language? In V. Volterra & C. Erting (Eds.), *From gesture to language in hearing and deaf children* (pp. 205–218). Washington, DC: Gallaudet University Press.

Vygotsky, L. (1962). *Thought and language*. Cambridge, MA: MIT Press.

Wallace, V., Menn, L., & Yoshinaga-Itano, C. (2000). Is babble the gateway to speech for all children? A longitudinal study of deaf and hard-of-hearing infants. *Volta Review, 100*(5), 121–148.

Watkins, S. (1993). *The SKI*HI resource manual*. Logan, UT: Hope, Inc.

Watkins, S., Taylor, D. J., & Pittman, P. (Eds.). (2004). *SKI-HI curriculum: Family-centered programming for infants and young children with hearing loss*. Logan, UT: HOPE, Inc.

Weichbold, V. (2006). Ten-year outcome of newborn hearing screening in Austria. *International Journal of Pediatric Otorhinolaryngology, 70*, 235–240.

White, K. R. (2003). The current status of EHDI programs in the United States. *Mental Retardation and Developmental Disabilities: Research Reviews, 9*, 79–88.

White, K. (2006). Early intervention for children with permanent hearing loss: Finishing the EHDI revolution [monograph]. *The Volta Review, 106*(3), 237–258.

Wilbur, R. (2000). The use of ASL to support the development of English and literacy. *Journal of Deaf Studies and Deaf Education, 5*, 81–104.

Woodward, J. C. (1972). Implications for sociolinguistic research among the deaf. *Sign Language Studies, 1*, 1–7, 72.

Yoshinaga-Itano, C. (2000). Development of audition and speech: Implications for early intervention with infants who are deaf or hard of hearing. In C. Yoshinaga-Itano & A. L. Sedey (Eds.), *Language, speech and social-emotional development of children who are deaf and hard-of-hearing: The early years*. *The Volta Review, 100*, 213–234.

Yoshinaga-Itano, C. (2003). From screening to early identification and intervention: Discovering predictors to successful outcomes for children with significant hearing loss. *Journal of Deaf Studies and Deaf Education, 8*, 11–30.

Yoshinaga-Itano C. (2004). Levels of evidence: Universal newborn hearing screening (UNHS) and early hearing detection and intervention systems (EHDI). *Journal of Communication Disorders, 37,* 451–465.

Yoshinaga-Itano, C. (2006). Early identification, communication modality, and the development of speech and spoken language skills: Patterns and considerations. In P. Spencer & M. Marschark (Eds.), *Advances in the spoken language development of deaf and hard-of-hearing children.* New York: Oxford University Press.

Yoshinaga-Itano C., Sedey, A., Coulter, D. K., & Mehl, A. L. (1998). The language of early- and later-identified children with hearing loss. *Pediatrics, 102*(5), 1161–1171.

Yoshinaga-Itano, C., Snyder, L., & Day, D. (1998). The relationship of language and symbolic play in deaf and hard-of-hearing children. *The Volta Review, 100*(3), 135–164.

Young, A., Carr, G., Hunt, R., McCracken, W., Skipp, A., & Tattersall, H. (2006). Informed choice and deaf children: Underpinning concepts and enduring challenges. *Journal of Deaf Studies and Deaf Education, 11*(3), 322–336.

Young, A., & Tattersall, H. (2007). Universal newborn hearing screening and early identification of deafness: Parents' responses to knowing early and their expectations of child communication development. *Journal of Deaf Studies and Deaf Education, 12*(2), 209–220.

Early Communication in Sign and Speech

Margaret Harris

Abstract

This chapter addresses two main issues. The first concerns the distinctive characteristics of successful communication strategies for young children with significant hearing losses, showing how these differ from successful communication strategies for young hearing children. Studies of parent–toddler communication are reviewed in order to identify features of good practice in the achievement of joint attention and the use of contingent language by the adult that serves to facilitate the young child's transition into language. The second part of the chapter considers the early use of language by deaf children who are acquiring a sign language—drawing on data from American Sign Language (ASL) and British Sign Language (BSL)—and those who are acquiring oral language. The rate of vocabulary development is considered, as well as the form and meaning of early signs and words. Evidence for the existence of specific language impairment in deaf children and its implications are also discussed. The chapter concludes by considering the impact of newborn hearing screening and early cochlear implantation on the development of early language and communication skills.

Keywords: deaf children, joint attention, vocabulary development parental signing, American Sign Language, British Sign Language

Children who have a severe-profound hearing loss at some point within the first months of life are often described as having "prelingual deafness," since they are unable to hear speech from the time that hearing children first begin to learn about language. At one level, however, the term "prelingual deafness" is misleading, since it disguises the fact that the early language experience of children with a congenital or early-acquired hearing loss is far from homogeneous. Most obviously, an important distinction must be drawn between the experience of the small minority of "prelingually deaf" children born to parents who are deaf and native users of a sign language and the experience of the great majority who are born to hearing parents. Other important variables affecting early experience are the age at which hearing loss is diagnosed and the kind of interventions that take place after diagnosis. These variations in early experience

give rise to a number of different questions about the early development of sign and speech.

Right from birth, deaf children of deaf parents are likely to have an early exposure to sign language that mirrors the spoken language exposure of hearing children born to hearing parents. If there are common pathways for the acquisition of sign and spoken languages, then we would expect that the acquisition of a sign language by born-deaf children whose parents are native signers would be very similar to the acquisition of spoken language by hearing children of hearing parents. We can therefore ask whether the first appearance of signs mirrors the first appearance of words both in terms of the age at which each can be understood and produced and also in terms of the content of early vocabulary.

The experience of the great majority of prelingually deaf children—those born to hearing parents—is likely to follow a rather different path, and it raises a different set of questions. Few hearing parents of deaf children can sign (or are even familiar with childhood deafness) when their child is born, although some choose to learn and some, although not usually achieving the fluency of a native signer, become very proficient. Other hearing parents choose to use spoken language with their deaf children, and this decision often goes hand-in-hand with considerations about the most appropriate form of amplification. In recent years, there have been considerable improvements in the technology of conventional hearing aids, and many children are now provided with digital aids. In addition, for the past 20 years, there has been a steady increase in the number of children who are considered candidates for a cochlear implant. With these children, we can ask how the provision of early amplification affects the development of spoken language.

This chapter is divided into four sections. It begins by considering the common origins of sign and speech in the development of social interaction between caretaker and child. The next two sections review recent evidence on the development of sign language and the development of spoken language. The final section considers some of the practical implications of the studies in all three areas of research.

Laying the Foundations for Language Development
Joint Attention and Early Language

To appreciate one of the most fundamental similarities between the acquisition of sign and spoken languages it is necessary to consider the social context in which young children learn to use language. The earliest communication between infants and their caretakers involves a great deal of mutual, face-to-face looking. This is an important component of dyadic (i.e., two-way) interaction (Tronick, Als, & Brazelton, 1980) that, over time, becomes increasingly complex as infants and caretakers begin to develop routines around frequent activities such as feeding, bath time, and games such as "peekaboo," in which one partner's face is briefly hidden from the sight of the other, only to reappear a few seconds later. Anyone who has interacted with a young child will know that familiar social routines like these are repeated many times over the course of a day, and this repetition allows the child to become an increasingly active partner in the routine, gradually learning to anticipate the next step in the sequence. For example, in the peekaboo game, children may anticipate

the reappearance stage by pulling off a cover placed over their head. Routines of this kind can be observed in both deaf and hearing infants; and parents who sign are likely to incorporate signs and gestures into the routines just as parents who use spoken language will incorporate words and gestures.

Young children's growing familiarity with games and routines plays an important part in early language development, as first highlighted by Bruner in a series of seminal papers (Bruner, 1975, 1983; Scaife & Bruner, 1975). Bruner argued that young children encounter language in a highly familiar social context because people communicate with them about familiar events and objects that form part of their daily routines. According to Bruner, this developing knowledge of the social repertoire allows babies to build up insights into the meaning of the language that, alongside gestures and facial expressions, adults use as part of these familiar routines.

Bruner does not give many specific examples of precisely how familiarity with the social context might help young children to understand what adults are saying to them but subsequent research has built up a detailed picture of the close relationship between early language and social routines for both deaf and hearing children. As part of a study of early vocabulary (Harris, Barlow-Brown, & Chasin, 1995), I kept a detailed record of the development of my own daughter, Francesca. One of the earliest indications she gave of beginning to understand language arose directly from her involvement in a routine that occurred several times a day, when her diaper was changed. Francesca always lay on a changing-table in her bedroom while this took place. From about 3 months of age, when Francesca had her new diaper on and her clothes refastened, I would take her by the hands, ask "Are you ready?" and then gently pull her up into a sitting position. When she was around 4 months old, I noticed that Francesca was starting to lift her head from the changing-table when I asked "Are you ready?" She did not try to lift her head as soon as I took hold of her hands but always waited for the crucial question. At first, Francesca would try to lift her head only when I asked the question in the specific context of diaper changing. However, 1 month later, her understanding had increased, so that she responded both when her father asked the question and also in other situations. Indeed, the whole routine had developed into a game in which Francesca lay on her back while one of us held her hands. She would look up at us intently and then attempt to pull herself up as soon as she heard "Are you ready?" This game was repeated many times in an increasing variety of situations.

Children's early understanding of words is often associated with specific routines that arise during dyadic—face-to-face—interaction and, as we see later in this chapter, many of the first words and signs that children understand and produce grow out of such routines. Around the middle of a child's first year, however, there is an important development in patterns of social interaction that provides a new opportunity for language development. Somewhere between 6 and 9 months, the amount of time spent in face-to-face interaction shows a marked decrease, as infants become increasingly interested in objects or events in the environment. This marks the beginning of triadic (i.e., three-way) interaction, involving caretaker, child, and the environment.

The development of triadic interaction affords an important opportunity for infant and caretaker to share joint attention to the external world. One easily identifiable sign of the emergence of triadic joint attention is the appearance of pointing. This provides a way for communicative partners to establish a joint frame of reference, which is a precondition for the acquisition and use of language (Butterworth, 2001). In other words, the fact that adult and infant are looking at and responding to the same objects and events in the environment paves the way for young children to learn about the language that is used by caretakers to describe these objects and events.

A nice illustration of the way that early language grows out of joint attention comes from a study of early signing (Clibbens & Harris, 1993). One of the first signs produced by a young child whose mother was a native signer of British Sign Language (BSL) was LIGHT. As for hearing children, whose early words are often simplified in comparison to the corresponding adult form, this early sign was simplified but, for present purposes, what was particularly interesting was that it was produced in the context of a very familiar and often-repeated routine. This involved the child pointing up at a light on the ceiling, which was invariably followed by the mother signing LIGHT, holding her hand in the air so that it was between the child and the light. As we see in the next section, the way that the mother was able to integrate her sign into this routine provided an ideal opportunity for the sign to be acquired.

Joint Attention in Deaf Children

Although both sign language and spoken language grow out of a common social context, a wealth of studies has highlighted some notable differences in the dynamics of joint attention for deaf and hearing children, and these have implications for early language development. An important point to make about these studies, which have been brought together in a recent review (Spencer & Harris, 2006), is that they have typically focused on deaf children who have had little or no benefit from early amplification. For these children, who have little or no access to speech in the early years, effective communication is predominantly visual. Thus, opportunities for language learning rely on the fact that both the object of joint attention and its verbal label are perceived through the visual modality, thereby creating a potential need for deaf children to divide attention in order to perceive "contingent naming."

Research into the signing strategies of mothers of young deaf children—and particularly those who are deaf themselves—suggests that many of the potential problems of divided attention can be resolved by adults adapting their signing (Spencer & Harris, 2006). For example, in order to make their signs visible to young infants, mothers may displace signs into a child's line of sight or onto the child's body or face (Harris, Clibbens, Chasin, & Tibbitts, 1989). With older infants, mothers may wait until the child looks up before they begin to sign. Strategies of this kind all help the child to make a link between ongoing events and the signs that accompany them but there are some important differences among the strategies. First, both the displacement of signs from normal location into the child's line of sight and the making of signs on the child's face and body are only possible when child and adult are in close proximity; and such strategies become increasingly difficult to use as children become more mobile and are no longer content to sit on their mother's lap or on the floor alongside her. Second, only some signs can easily be displaced and, even when this is possible, important information carried on the face of the signer is inevitably lost. Waiting to sign until a child pauses and looks up from an activity is potentially the most flexible strategy, but it will only be successful if the child turns to look at the mother and, in particular, the mother's face.

Because visual attention is so crucial for successful communication with deaf children, mothers who are deaf themselves—and thus very experienced at communicating with other people who are deaf—tend to be very proactive in gaining their young children's visual attention. They use a variety of strategies such as waving their hand in the child's line of sight, tapping the child on the arm, or even banging on the floor, so that vibrations carry across the room. They also use exaggerated facial expressions that help to sustain the children's attention and also provide them with important contextual information about ongoing events (Erting, Prezioso, & O'Grady-Hynes, 1990). Although there are large individual differences, hearing parents of deaf children tend to use such strategies rather less often. Indeed, hearing parents are often generally less sensitive to the visual needs of a deaf child and find it more difficult to coordinate their communication so that both the communication itself and the surrounding nonverbal context to which it relates are simultaneously visible to the child (Harris, 2001; Harris & Mohay, 1997).

A study of developing patterns of visual attention has shown that there is a fundamental difference in the dynamics of successful interaction between deaf and hearing infants and their mothers (Harris & Chasin, 2005). As already noted, deaf mothers with deaf children regularly elicit their attention through a variety of visual and tactile strategies, and this seems to be an essential aspect of successful communication with young deaf children (Spencer & Harris, 2006). In the Harris and Chasin study, as in earlier studies, deaf mothers of deaf children (Dd) showed most attempts to elicit their children's attention but there was also evidence of elicitation in both the deaf child–hearing mother dyads (Dh) and in dyads where the child was hearing but the mother was deaf (Hd). It was the dyads in which both partners were hearing that stood out because hearing mothers of hearing children almost never elicited attention. The reason for this became clear in looking at what attracted the children's attention.

For hearing children, sound played a very important role in attracting attention to the mother, and 70% of responsive looks (i.e., looks to the mother that were not the result of active elicitation) involved sound, either on its own or in conjunction with some action of the mother's (Figure 21.1). Much of this sound was, of course, speech, and the sound of the mother's voice had a powerful effect on the hearing children, very often resulting in rapid attention to the mother. The attention-grabbing effect of speech and sound on hearing children suggests why it is that hearing mothers of hearing children do not need to elicit attention since, as soon as they begin to talk or make a sound, their child will typically turn to look at their face.

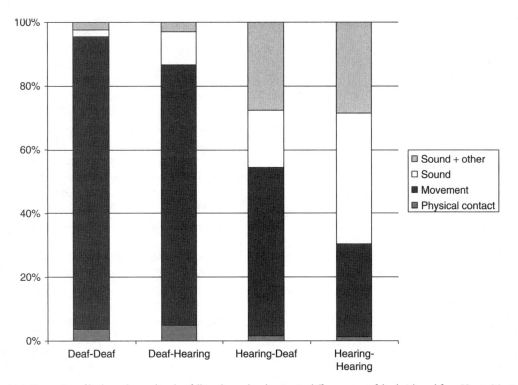

Fig. 21.1 Proportion of looks to the mother that followed sound and action in different types of dyad. Adapted from Harris, M., & Chasin, J. (2005). Attentional patterns in deaf and hearing infants: the role of auditory cues. *Journal of Child Psychology and Psychiatry, 46,* 1116–1123. With permission of the publisher.

As mothers of a deaf child cannot exploit the attention-directing properties of speech and sounds, they have to make use of something else and this is, most commonly, movement. However, a response to movement does not automatically bring attention to the face, as is the case with speech. Much of the mother's movements in the Harris and Chasin observations—except those that were attempting to redirect the child's attention—involved play objects. Mothers would often pick up a toy or book as they interacted with their child and this movement attracted the child's attention. Commonly, if children's attention was attracted in this way, their attention remained on the focus of the movement, that is, the play object. This did not present a problem for hearing children who could hear what their mother was saying while looking at the play object, and so be fully engaged in a triadic interaction. However, mothers of deaf children had to find alternative ways of getting children's attention onto their face so that they could communicate and, very often, they used physical strategies such as tapping, waving, or banging to redirect attention. The success of these strategies was evident in the fact that the total number of looks to the mother's face was similar for deaf children of deaf mothers and hearing children of hearing mothers, with the number of looks being significantly smaller in the other two groups.

The pattern that emerged in the Hd dyads (where children were hearing but mothers were deaf) is of particular interest because it shows the contribution that both partners make to the dynamics of successful communication. These hearing children of deaf parents responded more to movement than their peers whose parents were hearing and, not surprisingly, they also responded much more to sound than deaf children. Deaf mothers with hearing children often make use of sound to attract attention and may well speak to their children. At the same time, they also use the kind of strategies they would use with a deaf child. This pattern results in a unique style of interaction that paves the way for hearing children of deaf parents to become competent in both sign and spoken language.

One initially surprising finding to emerge from the Harris and Chasin study was that the children in the Dd and Hh groups (where mother and child had the same hearing status) turned to look at their mother *less often* than children in the two groups where the hearing status of the communicative partners differed. This is surprising because, as was noted earlier, the best-attuned interactions are likely to occur when mother and child have the same hearing status.

Almost certainly, the explanation for this apparent discrepancy lies in the fact that a more extended interaction was likely to follow on from a look to the mother in the Dd and Hh dyads because of the children's greater language ability. This explanation is consistent with Spencer's (2000) finding that episodes of joint visual attention to the mother were of longer duration when the hearing status of mother and child was the same, and a more sophisticated linguistic exchange was likely to ensue.

Looking to the mother's face presents a different opportunity for communicating with deaf and hearing children. Having established an opportunity for a communicative opening, a hearing child can turn away and communication can continue. For deaf children, however, sustained looking at the mother is necessary. This suggests that, as deaf children become more linguistically competent, they will show extended periods of looking that enable increasingly complex messages to be communicated. This expectation was borne out in a recent study that examined the development of looking behavior in deaf and hearing infants between the age of 9 and 18 months of age (Chasin & Harris, 2008). Two findings are of note. At each of the three age points that were examined, deaf children with deaf parents showed a higher proportion of looks to their mother's face than did deaf children of hearing parents. This supports the idea that the strategies that deaf mothers use to engage attention to the face are successful, so that their children become attuned to the communicative importance of the face at an earlier age than do deaf children of hearing mothers. The other notable finding was that deaf children of deaf mothers looked significantly longer at their mothers when they were 18 months old than did children of hearing mothers. This mirrors the earlier finding that the number of bouts of joint attention was similar for children of deaf and hearing children, but the bouts lasted longer for those with deaf parents (Meadow-Orlans & Spencer, 1996).

Early Sign Language Development

Given that children's early language and communication grow out of social exchanges with communicative partners, it might be expected that there would be many similarities between early signed and spoken languages. However, one hotly contested issue is whether the acquisition of sign language and spoken language follows a similar time course. A number of authors have argued for a "sign advantage." At it simplest, their argument goes something like this: Signs are easier for a baby to produce than spoken words because movements made with the hands are easier for babies than movements of the tongue and vocal tract. Some hearing parents have been so persuaded by this argument that they have introduced baby signs to their hearing children with the intention of promoting language development, following the advice set out in a best-selling book entitled *Baby Signs* (Acredolo, Goodwyn, & Abrams, 2002).

Superficially, this argument about the comparative ease of making signs and producing spoken words appears correct because the complex movements of the tongue and vocal tract required to produce all the phonemes in a language take a considerable time for children to master. However, it is often overlooked that there is also a very consistent developmental sequence in children's ability to produce complex hand movements (Butterworth, Verweij, & Hopkins, 1997), especially those involving two hands, and this has not been taken into account in considering children's ability to produce signs. Furthermore, as described later in the chapter, there are important issues concerning the use of gestures by deaf and hearing children and how these are interpreted by parents (Anderson, 2006; Anderson & Reilly, 2002).

The best way to determine whether there is a sign advantage is to examine the time course of early development of sign languages by deaf children. Before reviewing some of the evidence about sign development, it is important to begin with two caveats. First, language development is enormously variable, especially in the early stages that are the focus of this chapter. Most hearing infants begin to comprehend spoken words when they are around 7 or 8 months old. The first words to be understood are typically the child's own name and the names of other family members such as *mummy* and *daddy*, and the names of familiar objects such as *clock*, *drink*, and *teddy* (Harris, Yeeles, Chasin, & Oakley, 1995). However, from this fairly predictable starting point, children go on to build up their vocabulary and begin to combine words at very different rates. To give just one example, at the age of 16 months, girls understand just over 200 words on average and boys understand around 150. This difference between boys and girls is significant, although gender differences disappear as children get older (Fenson, Dale, Resnick, Bates, Thal, & Pethick, 1994). However, typically developing hearing children may understand anything from 100–300 words at 16 months and, importantly, this does not predict their later language development. This variability in typical language development means that we have to be very careful in evaluating data from studies of children

who are learning to sign, especially when studies involve only a small number of children.

The second caveat concerns home language. It is clear from studies of spoken language that the amount and type of language children hear at home can have a powerful effect on their language development, particularly in the early stages (Harris, 1992). Studies of spoken language development take it as given that normative data should come from studies of children who have at least one parent who is a fluent speaker of the language that is being acquired. It is also usual to consider only children who are acquiring a language as their main form of communication and so, for example, are not learning English as an additional language. It is important to apply the same stringent criteria to studies of sign language development and so to focus on deaf children whose parents are native signers and therefore fluent users of the target language. Since deaf children with deaf parents constitute less than 10% of the total population of children who can be regarded as prelingually deaf, it has taken some considerable time to accrue sufficiently large data sets. However, the good news is that a reliable picture of early sign development is now beginning to emerge.

Studies of early sign language acquisition have benefited considerably from the methodological advances that have been made in the study of spoken language acquisition. Much of the early evidence about the development of spoken language came from informal parental reports but, more recently, researchers have been able to gain standardized information from parents by asking them to complete a checklist of the gestures, words, and phrases that a young child might be expected to understand and produce. The Communicative Development Inventory (CDI) (Fenson et al., 1990) has been used extensively to gather data about early language development between 8 and 28 months. It has now been adapted for a number of different spoken languages and, more recently, it has been adapted to study the acquisition of sign languages. All the studies that I have included in this review have made use of adaptations of the CDI.

Acquisition of American Sign Language

The first sign language version of the CDI to be produced was for ASL. This was developed by Anderson and Reilly (2002). An initial issue raised by the authors of this pioneering study of sign acquisition was how accurate parents are in reporting their children's signs. Interestingly, precisely the same issue has been raised about parents' reports of their children's early words, and the conclusion has been that hearing parents are, on the whole, very accurate in their reports. However, it is noteworthy that parents are least reliable in reporting the very first words that are understood and produced, so it is important to ensure that these items, in particular, are accurately reported (Harris & Chasin, 1999).

The approach adopted by Anderson and Reilly was to videotape a subsample of children on or around the same day that parents completed the ASL version of the CDI. They then compared the children's level of signing on the videotape against parental reports. Fortunately, there was good agreement between the two measures, and this provided general support for the use of a parental checklist to find out about early sign language development. The specific issue of overreporting of early-acquired items was not directly addressed by the comparison of the signs on the video and those reported by parents using the checklist. However, this issue was addressed in the author's comparison of early signs and early gestures, which is discussed later in this section.

Another issue that Anderson and Reilly had to address was how to translate the items in the CDI so that they were appropriate for a sign language. Some items that feature prominently in early spoken vocabularies were removed from the ASL version. For example, there were a number of cases in which two distinct English words such as *eat* and *food* or *sit* and *chair* were expressed by very closely related forms of a single sign and other cases in which two words were expressed by the same sign (e.g., *horse* and *pony*). In each case, only one sign was included on the checklist. Other items, which have no correspondence to any item in the CDI, were introduced to reflect Deaf culture and experiences such TTY/TDD (typewriter and telecommunication devices used by deaf people). Two categories that appeared in the spoken English CDI were removed entirely. These were animal sounds, like *moo*, which commonly appear in early spoken vocabularies but are not used by young deaf children, and also body parts. The latter category highlights a significant difference between English and ASL and, indeed, between spoken and sign languages at a more general level. Spoken languages have labels for parts of the body, and the most frequent of these (e.g., *nose, mouth, and eyes*) are understood and produced early on in spoken vocabulary development. American Sign Language and BSL generally indicate parts of the body by pointing, and there is no specific sign.

Anderson and Reilly were able to recruit a total of 110 children and their parents to take part in the study. For the majority of children the ASL CDI checklist was completed on only one occasion—following the norming procedure for the original CDI—but 34 children were seen by the researchers several times. This latter group of children, who provided longitudinal data, was an important addition to the study because a real understanding of variation in early language development comes from studies that follow the same children over time.

The youngest age at which a child was reported as producing a sign was 8 months, when the parents reported the use of both MILK and BATH, and four other children were reported as having two or three signs by 10 months. One 11-month-old was reported as having 17 signs. Between the ages of 12 and 35 months, there was a considerable increase in the number of signs produced by the children as can be seen in Table 21.1.

There are a number of issues to highlight. First, as might be expected from previous studies of early spoken language development, there was very considerable variability in the number of signs that children were producing, as can be seen in the final column of Table 21.1, which shows the lowest and highest number of reported signs. The largest range occurred in children aged between 18 and 23 months, who produced between 39 and 348 signs. Since these findings come from the cross-sectional part of the study, it is not clear whether this high level of variability indicates that this particular age is one at which children are most likely to acquire language at different rates or that the children in the group were particularly heterogeneous. This is the kind of question that will only be answered by gathering more data on sign language acquisition.

Another question that Anderson and Reilly considered was whether the meaning of early signs is the same as that of early words. Given the earlier point about early language growing out of the social

Table 21.1 Growth of sign vocabulary as reported by Anderson and Reilly (2002)

Children's Age	Mean number of signs produced	Range of number of signs produced
8–11 months	8	2–17
12–17 months	61	7–107
18–23 months	149	39–348
24–29 months	252	102–417
30–35 months	380	249–518

interactions and routines that take place around young children, it might be expected that young children growing up in similar environments would tend to communicate about largely similar things. A comparison between the early-reported ASL signs and the early-reported English words in the CDI shows a remarkable overlap. For both deaf and hearing children, the names of people, animals, and things to eat were prominent, with signs and words that relate to actions being considerably less frequent. There were some relatively small differences. Early ASL vocabularies tended to have more animal names than early spoken English vocabularies. For example, the first 35 signs included not only CAT, DOG, and BIRD—all commonly used by young hearing children—but also RABBIT, COW, HORSE, and FISH. Anderson and Reilly suggest that this difference arises because of the greater use of animal sounds rather than names in conversation with hearing children. Comparisons of deaf and hearing mothers looking at books with their children confirm this suggestion because hearing mothers frequently talk about the sounds that animals make, whereas deaf mothers sign the name of the animal (Harris et al., 1989).

Another difference between early vocabularies in ASL and English was that the former contained more predicates. In this context, predicates are action words or social phrases such as SLEEP or CLAP that can be combined with naming words. Such items are generally infrequent in early vocabularies, in which the names of people and things predominate. Anderson and Reilly point out that the predicates, which feature in early sign vocabularies, usually have a strong iconic component. It is therefore difficult to distinguish early predicates from gestures. Both hearing and deaf children make use of gestures in their early communication. Typical early gestures include pointing, clapping, and waving goodbye— but whereas it is easy to distinguish between spoken words and gestures (since they make use of a different modality), it is by no means an easy task to do this for gestures and signs. Indeed, this difficulty can be seen as lying at the heart of determining whether there really is a sign advantage. The CDI data (Fenson et al., 1990) show that, on average, 8-month-old hearing children use around ten communicative gestures. Similar gestures, when produced by a deaf child who is learning to sign, might well be taken as signs (Anderson, 2006). It therefore seems reasonable to conclude that there is no real sign advantage, and that both deaf children learning to sign and hearing children learning to talk proceed at a very similar rate along a remarkably similar pathway.

Acquisition of British Sign Language

A recently completed study of deaf children's acquisition of BSL can provide further evidence about the development trajectories for sign languages (Woolfe, Herman, Roy, & Woll, in press). The study followed a cohort of 29 deaf children of deaf parents between the ages of 8 and 36 months. The educational levels of the mothers showed a wide range, with 11% having left school with no formal qualifications and 23% having a higher education degree. Fathers showed an essentially similar pattern.

One particularly innovative feature of the study was the use of a website that could be consulted by parents who wanted to know about the meaning of a particular item on the checklist. Since sign languages do not have a written form, parents may not be sure exactly which sign or signs corresponds to an item on the checklist. For example, the word "home" is represented by different signs according to whether it refers to a place (e.g., "my home") or to an action (e.g., goes/stays home). The content of the BSL version of the CDI was very similar to that of the ASL version from which it was adapted (Anderson & Reilly, 2002). In contrast to the Anderson and Reilly (2002) study, the signs for body parts were retained, since analysis revealed that their exclusion did not have a significant effect on the outcomes. A number of signs were added, including the addition of HOW-MUCH and HOW-MANY to the questions category, since these are single signs in BSL.

The educational levels of both mothers and fathers proved to have a significant effect on children's vocabulary size. Children of parents who had been educated to degree level or had a higher education certificate or diploma had significantly higher scores than did peers with parents of lower educational levels. This replicates the findings from many studies of spoken language development (Hoff, 2003), and it underlines the need to ensure that normative data on sign language acquisition are collected from samples with a wide range of parental education.

Receptive scores were consistently ahead of expressive scores, showing that, throughout this early period of language development, children tended to understand more signs than they could produce. Data on spoken language development would suggest that the discrepancy between what children can understand and what they can produce is usually greatest at the outset of language development, with the gap gradually closing over time (Harris, 2004). However, Woolfe et al. (in press) found an opposite pattern in that the difference between sign comprehension and production was *least* evident at the youngest ages. They suggest that this is a reflection of parents' difficulty in distinguishing signs from gestures. In other words, children who are learning to sign are producing gestures that are interpreted as signs by their parents. This interpretation echoes that of Anderson and Reilly (2002).

Averaged out across the sample, there was a smooth upward growth curve, but this masked some highly individual patterns of development. The pattern of individual variation was complicated by the fact that not all children were observed for the full duration of the study but, even so, it is striking that some children showed very slow progress while others showed a steep increase in the number of different signs they could produce. This pattern of highly variable rates of early vocabulary acquisition mirrors that for spoken English (Fenson et al., 1994).

Another question that is often asked about early vocabulary development in sign language is whether it shows a spurt—that is, a sudden increase in the rate at which new items are acquired. Such vocabulary spurts are found for many hearing children who are acquiring a spoken language—although by no means all. They are thought to be indicative of a change in the way that new vocabulary items are acquired, although there is some debate about the precise nature of the change that occurs (Harris, 2004). Anderson and Reilly (2002) did not observe growth spurts in ASL. However, Woolfe et al. (in press) found evidence of a spurt in vocabulary development for over half of the children in their sample for whom there were relevant data. (Some children were not recruited into the study until after the point at which a spurt might have been detected and other children did not have a sufficient number of observations.) Woolfe at al. suggest that the difference between their findings and those of Anderson and Reilly may have arisen because of a difference in the frequency of data collection. In Anderson and Reilly's study, the ASL data points were widely spaced, with an average of 6 months intervening between observations. In the BSL study, data were collected every 4 months. This difference of 2 months may have been enough to enable detection of changes in the rate of vocabulary learning, since such a change is something that typically occurs over a matter of weeks (Harris, 2004). It is therefore more likely to be detected when observations are frequent. However, as already indicated, not all children show a sudden upturn in the rate at which new items appear in their vocabulary. Furthermore, a vocabulary spurt appears to be common when children are acquiring a vocabulary with a preponderance of nouns, as is the case for spoken English. Children who are acquiring Korean, for example, do not show a vocabulary spurt, and this is thought to be because of the greater use of verbs in Korean both in speech to children and among adult users (Gopnik & Choi, 1995). More detailed and closely spaced observations will be required to provide a clear picture of the extent to which early sign language development is characterized by a vocabulary spurt, and we should not assume that the developmental trajectory will mirror that of spoken English, the language on which the original CDI (Fenson et al., 1990) was based.

Another intriguing aspect of the BSL findings was the lack of a gender difference. As noted earlier, the original CDI data for spoken American English (Fenson et al., 1990) showed that girls were ahead of boys in the early stage of vocabulary development. This gender difference for spoken English has been confirmed in other studies (Harris, 1995). The fact that boys and girls showed similar rates of vocabulary development for BSL may suggest that the early gender difference is limited to spoken languages. One possibility might be that girls show an early advantage in the processing of speech but not in the processing of a language that makes use of visual-spatial representations. However, given the large variability in early language development, it is important to collect more data before drawing firm conclusions about the presence or absence of gender differences.

One final aspect of the findings of the BSL CDI study is worthy of note. Woolfe et al. identified a small proportion of children whose language development was very slow. Two children (out of the total sample of 29) achieved scores below the 10th percentile. As the authors note, this proportion is very similar to that reported for specific language impairment among hearing children acquiring a spoken language. There are a number of practical issues arising from this finding that will be explored in the final part of the chapter. For the moment, I want to note the potential theoretical importance of this observation. If it turns out that specific language impairment transcends the modality of communication to affect both signed and spoken languages equally, this will suggest that the difficulties that some children experience with acquiring language must have their origin in some rather abstract properties of language or cognition.

The Development of Spoken Language

Since the first studies of language development in young deaf children were carried out, considerable advances have been made both in the diagnostic techniques and the range of interventions available for children who have a significant hearing loss. Many of these changes have had a significant impact on the development of spoken language.

Newborn Hearing Screening

One important step forward in some countries has been the introduction of hearing screening for all newborn babies (see Chapters 23 and 16, this volume). This is now carried out throughout the United Kingdom. and in a number of European countries, including Belgium and The Netherlands. It is also available in some parts of the United States and Canada, and throughout Australia. The advantage of universal newborn hearing screening (UNHS)—which uses an automated test that can be easily administered in the hospital or in the home—is that it allows identification of hearing loss within a few days of birth. Early identification can then provide the opportunity for parents to develop appropriate strategies for communicating with their children. It also allows the introduction of some form of hearing amplification at an early age, if this is appropriate.

Before the introduction of UNHS, the average age of diagnosis of a significant hearing loss was 15 months in Belgium (Deben, Janssens de Varebeke, Cox, & Van de Heyning, 2003) and 17 months in the United Kingdom (Davis, Bamford, Wilson, Ramkalawan, Forshaw, & Wright, 1997); and some children with a significant hearing loss were not identified until considerably later than this. The impact of UHNS on the age of diagnosis and subsequent intervention has been dramatic. A study of children on the Australian Hearing database (Ching, Oong, & Van Wanrooy, 2006) shows that children who were screened at birth were, on average, fitted with a hearing aid by the age of 3.7 months, whereas children who were not screened were not fitted with an aid until 17 months. A number of children in the database had passed the initial screening but were subsequently found to have a mild hearing loss. However, all children with severe to profound levels of loss had failed the initial screening, showing that UNHS provides a very reliable way of detecting severe to profound hearing loss at birth.

Because the roll-out of UNHS has occurred at the same time as advances in amplification, it is difficult, if not impossible, to disentangle the effects of early diagnosis from other factors when evaluating their impact on early communication. An extensive review of the effectiveness of UHNS in the United States (Thompson, McPhillips, Davis, Lieu, Homer, & Helfand, 2001) concluded that, although UHNS reliably decreased the age of diagnosis of hearing loss, evidence of long-term improvement in long-term speech and language skills was inconclusive (see Chapter 23, this volume). The authors of the review concluded by emphasizing the importance of carrying out longitudinal studies of the effectiveness of UHNS, while recognizing that such studies are difficult because of the many different variables that can affect language outcomes.

Recent studies, emanating from Canada (Durieux-Smith, Fitzpatrick, & Whittingham, 2008) and the United Kingdom (Kennedy, McCann, Campbell, Kimm, & Thornton, 2005), have confirmed that UHNS provides a reliable way of identifying hearing loss for children who are deaf or hard of hearing. However, the authors of the Canadian study conclude that "Improved speech and language development due to [UHNS and early intervention] is unlikely to be proved by acceptable scientific and ethical standards" (p. 9). What they mean by this is that randomized control trials to evaluate the wider benefits of early diagnosis, which are taken to be the gold standard for evaluating medical interventions, are unlikely to be carried out because it is already clear that UHNS is an effective way of identifying hearing loss. For this reason, it would be unethical to carry out a study in which one group of children was excluded from UHNS for comparison purposes. The authors of the UK study (Kennedy et al., 2005) were rather more optimistic in their conclusions, stating that "assessment of the effects of early intervention on the speech and language of the children … will be the subject to future reports" (p. 662). The first of these reports was published recently (Kennedy et al., 2006). It examined the language scores for a cohort of 120 children with a hearing loss of at least 40 dB, half of whom (61) were born after the introduction of UNHS to a number of centers in southern England. The other half of the cohort came from geographically adjacent centers where UNHS was not available at the time of the study. In all other respects, the two subgroups were equivalent and their levels of hearing loss were similar.

The assessment of the language ability of the children in the two groups was carried out during home visits by researchers who did not know when hearing loss had been identified. The age at which the language assessment was carried out varied, but the mean was 7.9 years. Data were collected both from parents and directly from an assessment of the children, using a variety of tests that covered vocabulary, grammar, and narrative understanding. Before describing the results, it is important to note that all children in the study had been offered audiological services following diagnosis, including high-quality commercial hearing aids. There have been significant advances in the choice of amplification systems that are available (Ackley & Decker, 2006) and, in the United Kingdom, these are provided by the state. All children were wearing their aids when the language assessments were carried out. A small number of children had cochlear implants in both the early-screened (five children) and nonscreened (11 children) groups.

Children who had benefited from UNHS had significantly higher receptive language scores than did those who were born in an area where this had not yet been adopted. This difference was equivalent to an increase of between 10 and 12 points in verbal IQ. There were, however, no differences in expressive language scores. The two aspects of language ability were assessed in rather different ways. Receptive language was assessed by standardized tests, whereas the measure of expressive language ability was derived from parental or professional report, which may have been less reliable. This difference in assessment reflects an asymmetry in clinical measures of language ability: There are many standardized tests of language comprehension but reliable measures of language production, beyond the level of early vocabulary, are derived from analysis of speech samples to produce measures of grammatical complexity. It is, however, important that stringent measures of language production are used in evaluating outcomes in order to derive a full picture of the benefits of UNHS.

Kennedy et al. (2006) note that their findings probably underestimate the benefits of neonatal hearing screening because, at the time their sample was recruited, the roll-out of the UNHS program was in its early stages in the United Kingdom. This meant that the confirmation of hearing impairment that follows on from a failure at the first stage of screening did not always occur on schedule, and there were sometime additional delays between the second stage and the provision of audiological services. Almost certainly these delays would have reduced the impact of early detection of hearing loss.

The Impact of Cochlear Implants

Increasing numbers of children in many centers across the developed world have benefited from the opportunity to receive a cochlear implant. Implants are not appropriate for all children with a significant hearing loss, and children will only be considered for a cochlear implant if they have a sensorineural hearing loss, an intact auditory nerve, and a cochlea that will enable the insertion of an electrode array. The decision to implant a young child is taken only after considerable discussion with the parents and a long series of assessments, which will include scanning of the cochlea to determine its suitability for implantation.

A study by Spencer (Spencer, 2004) of 13 prelingually deaf children who received their implants between 14 and 38 months found that a major factor in children's language development after implant was parental involvement. The children with the best language outcomes were those whose parents had engaged in a process of lengthy and in-depth discussions with health professionals before the implant operation took place. Spencer notes that such parents are likely to provide a high level of support for their children both before and after implantation (see Chapter 15, this volume).

Longitudinal studies of children from a number of implant centers are beginning to show just how much successful implantation can affect early spoken language development, particularly when implantation can take place in the first year or so of life, following the introduction of UNHS (Nicholas & Geers, 2006; Thoutenhoofd, Archbold, Gregory, Lutman, Nikolopoulos, & Sach, 2005). There is a strong correlation between language levels and age of implantation, with children who have been implanted at a younger age generally doing better than peers who have been implanted later. The amount of time that a child has been using an implant also predicts language level, leading to the conclusion that early implantation is most likely to result in age-appropriate language (Nicholas & Geers, 2008).

Given the strong evidence that earlier implantation has more powerful effects on language development, much recent discussion has revolved around the question of how early the optimal age of implantation should be. As the numbers of children who are implanted as infants or toddlers has increased, evidence that can address this question is beginning to emerge. One recent study charted the growth in spoken language development among a group of 29 children who had received an implant between the age of 10 and 40 months (Tomblin, Barker,

Spencer, Zhang, & Gantz, 2005). The children's language levels following implantation were assessed using two standardized measures of expressive language, one of which was a derived from direct observation of children's performance and the other based on parental report. On both measures, children implanted at an earlier age showed more rapid growth of language scores over time than those implanted later. Significantly, this finding held across the whole range of age at implant in the study, and children who received a cochlear implant at 12 months showed faster growth than those implanted at 15 months. However, in spite of the evidence that implanting a child at the age of 1 year might be most beneficial, the conclusion of the authors is suitably measured. Tomblin et al. stress the need to "continue to weigh the relative, expressive language benefit against the individual needs of each family, and the challenges associated with the clinical management of very young children" (p. 865).

There is also evidence that children who receive an implant rather later than the age of 12 months may still show considerable long-term benefits. Two recent studies have looked at the impact of cochlear implants on literacy (Archbold, Harris, O'Donoghue, Nikolopoulos, White, & Lloyd-Richmond, 2008; Vermeulen, van Bon, Schreuder, Knoors, & Snik, 2007). In the past, many deaf children have failed to achieve functional literacy, and even in recent studies, where the majority of children had not received a cochlear implant, literacy levels have remained low (Kyle & Harris, 2006). The study by Archbold et al. (2008) reported data on reading levels 5 and 7 years post implant. Children implanted before the age of 42 months had age-appropriate reading scores, whereas those who had received an implant after this age did not (see Chapter 9, this volume). This finding suggests that children may gain considerable benefits from a cochlear implant even if implanted in the second or third year of life.

Communication Choices for Parents

In light of the issues discussed in this chapter, it is pertinent to ask how the advent of newborn hearing screening and cochlear implants is affecting communication choices for young deaf children. Information that has been provided by parents and children who have been part of the extensive cochlear implant program in Nottingham (UK) shows that many parents—the great majority of whom are hearing—make use of signing once they know that their child is unable to hear spoken language. However, following successful implantation, there is a gradual transition to the use of more and more spoken language, with a corresponding decrease in the amount of signing (Watson, Archbold, & Nikolopolous, 2006; Watson, Hardie, Archbold, & Wheeler, 2008). Questioning of parents reveals that this gradual transition is driven by the changing communication needs of the child, and it shows that early use of sign language can be very important in supporting the development of spoken language after implantation.

The early use of sign in conjunction with spoken English is an aspect of language development among children with implants that is sometimes overlooked. For example, in the (Tomblin et al., 2005) study, the parents of 26 of 29 children were using both spoken and signed English at home. Furthermore, the language assessments carried out by the researchers made use of both modalities even though only spoken language abilities were reported. This is a further illustration of the way in which children and their parents make use of both sign and spoken language in the years immediately following implant.

Some Practical Implications

There are a number of practical implications of the research reviewed in this chapter. The first concerns effective communication with young deaf children. It is clear that the dynamics of effective communication—that is, communication that will enable children to develop proficient language skills—are different for deaf and hearing children. Effective communication with hearing children does not normally require mothers to use specific visual or manual means to elicit attention, since hearing children naturally turn to look at their mother when she begins to speak. On the whole, deaf mothers are better than hearing mothers at managing the complex visual needs of deaf children. However, some hearing mothers develop very effective communicative strategies with deaf children, and a number of recent intervention programs have shown that the most effective strategies—particularly the careful timing of utterances to coincide with the infant's visual attention—can be taught (Spencer & Harris, 2006). It is important to note that the management of visual attention is equally important for the early stages of spoken language and sign language development. Deaf children who are learning to talk gain important information about spoken language from watching the face of a communicative partner, and so the strategies that enable young children to learn early signs will also assist in the acquisition of early words.

Another underlying similarity in early signed and spoken communication to young deaf children is evident in the commonality of objects and events that are referred to by early signs and early words. Young deaf and hearing children use language to refer to remarkably similar things, reflecting the fact that early signs and early words are used to describe the objects and events that feature in the everyday lives of young children. During this early period, when children are building up their vocabulary, it is entirely possible for parents to sign and speak at the same time since most adult utterances to young children consist of one or two signs or words (Spencer & Harris, 2006). Many parents of young deaf children—even those who are part of a cochlear implant program—make use of both modalities in early communication. Over time, their use of sign and speech may change with the changing communicative needs of their child. This seems to occur quite naturally, reflecting the fact that parents are striving to communicate in the way that is most effective for their child. Choices about the best way to communicate should therefore be regarded as dynamic.

The second practical issue concerns the identification of specific language impairment in deaf children, a finding that suggests an important similarity between the acquisition of sign language and spoken language. The longitudinal study of BSL by Woolfe et al. (2010) identified a small number of children who, in spite of having deaf parents who were native signers, showed slow progress in learning to sign. These children might be thought of as having a form of specific language impairment. This conclusion echoes some of the most recent findings to emerge from analyses of language outcomes for children who have received an early cochlear implant. Such children might be expected to receive the most benefit from a cochlear implant. However, a recent study emanating from the Nottingham Implant Program describes a small number of children who, in spite of receiving a successful implant, show language difficulties that seem to be additional to those produced by their hearing losses (Hawker, Ramirez-Inscoe, Bishop, Twomeny, O'Donoghue, & Moore, 2008). Hawker et al. argue that these difficulties may have the same basis as the specific language impairment that is observed in hearing children, since it could not be explained as part of a general learning difficulty. This mirrors a finding of the Woolfe et al. study of BSL and, taken together, the two studies suggest that a small number of children who are prelingually deaf may have specific difficulties in acquiring language that transcend language modality.

Although the identification of specific language difficulties in children who are prelingually deaf is only just beginning, it is clearly an important area for future research and, equally importantly, the development of appropriate intervention strategies. An important first step is to ensure that deaf children's early linguistic and communicative development—whether signed or spoken—is monitored against appropriate norms, so that an atypical pattern of development can be detected as early as possible.

References

Ackley, R. S., & Decker, T. N. (2006). Audiological advancement in the acquisition of spoken language in deaf children. In P. E. Spencer & M. Marschark (Eds.), *Advances in the spoken language development of deaf and hard-of-hearing children* (pp. 64–84). New York: Oxford University Press.

Acredolo, L., Goodwyn, S., & Abrams, D. (2002). *Baby signs: How to talk with your baby before your baby can talk.* New York McGraw-Hill.

Anderson, D. (2006). Lexical development of deaf children acquiring signed languages. In B. Schick, M. Marschark & P. E. Spencer (Eds.), *Advances in the sign language development of deaf children* (pp. 135–160). New York: Oxford University Press.

Anderson, D., & Reilly, J. (2002). The MacArthur Communicative Development Inventory: The normative data from American Sign Language. *Journal of Deaf Studies and Deaf Education, 7*(2), 83–106.

Archbold, S., Harris, M., O'Donoghue, G., Nikolopoulos, T., White, A., & Lloyd Richmond, H. (2008). Reading abilities after cochlear implantation: the effect of age at implantation on outcomes at five and seven years after implantation. *International Journal of Pediatric Otorhinolaryngology, 72*(10), 1471–1478.

Bruner, J. S. (1975). The ontogenesis of speech acts. *Journal of Child Language, 2*(1), 1–19.

Bruner, J. S. (1983). The acquisition of pragmatic commitments. In R. M. Golinkoff (Ed.), *The transition from prelinguistic to linguistic communication* (pp. 27–42). Hillsdale, NJ: Erlbaum.

Butterworth, G. E. (2001). Joint visual attention in infancy. In G. Bremner & A. Fogel (Eds.), *Blackwell handbook of infant development* (pp. 213–240). Malden, MA: Blackwell.

Butterworth, G. E., Verweij, E., & Hopkins, B. (1997). The development of prehension in infants: Halverson revisited. *British Journal of Developmental Psychology, 15*, 223–236.

Chasin, J., & Harris, M. (2008). The development of visual attention in deaf children in relation to mother's hearing status. *Polish Psychological Bulletin, 39*(1), 1–8.

Ching, T. Y. C., Oong, R., & Van Wanrooy, E. V. (2006). The ages of intervention in regions with and without universal newborn hearing screening and prevalence of childhood hearing impairment in Australia. *The Australian and New Zealand Journal of Audiology, 28*(2), 137–150.

Clibbens, J., & Harris, M. (1993). The acquisition of formational parameters in British Sign Language: a case study. In D. Messer & G. Turner (Eds.), *Critical influences on child language acquisition and development* (pp. 197–208). London: Macmillan.

Davis, A., Bamford, J., Wilson, I., Ramkalawan, T., Forshaw, M., & Wright, S. (1997). A critical review of the role of neonatal hearing screening in the detection of congenital hearing impairment. *Health Technology Assessment, 1*(10), 1–176.

Deben, K., Janssens de Varebeke, S., Cox, T., & Van de Heyning, P. (2003). Epidemiology of hearing impairment at three Flemish institutes for deaf and speech defective children. *International Journal of Pediatric Otorhinolaryngology, 67*(9), 969–975.

Durieux-Smith, A., Fitzpatrick, E., & Whittingham, J. (2008). Universal newborn hearing screening: A question of evidence. *International Journal of Audiology, 47*(1), 1–10.

Erting, C. J., Prezioso, C., & O'Grady-Hynes, M. (1990). The interactional context of mother-infant communication. In V. Volterra & C. J. Erting (Eds.), *From gesture to language in hearing and deaf children* (pp. 97–106). Berlin: Springer-Verlag.

Fenson, L., Dale, P., Resnick, S., Bates, E., Thal, D., & Pethick, S. J. (1994). Variability in early communicative development. *Monographs of the Society for Research in Child Development, 59*(5), 1–73.

Fenson, L., Dale, P., Resnick, S., Bates, E., Thal, D., Reilly, J., et al. (1990). *MacArthur communicative development inventories: Technical manual.* San Diego: San Diego State University.

Gopnik, A., & Choi, S. (1995). Names, relational words, and cognitive development in English and Korean speakers: Nouns are not always learned before verbs. In M. Tomasello & W. E. Merriman (Eds.), *Beyond names for things: Young children's acquisition of verbs* (pp. 83–90). Hillsdale, NJ Erlbaum.

Harris, M. (1992). *Language experience and early language development: From input to uptake.* Hove: Lawrence Erlbaum Associates

Harris, M. (2001). It's all a matter of timing: Sign visibility and sign reference in deaf and hearing mothers of 18 month old children. *Journal of Deaf Studies and Deaf Education, 6,* 177–185.

Harris, M. (2004). First words. In J. Oates & A. Grayson (Eds.), *Cognitive and language development in children* (pp. 61–112). Oxford: The Open University/ Blackwell Publishing.

Harris, M., Barlow-Brown, F., & Chasin, J. (1995). The emergence of referential understanding: pointing and the comprehension of object names. *First Language, 15,* 19–34.

Harris, M., & Chasin, J. (1999). Developments in early lexical comprehension: a comparison of parental report and controlled testing. *Journal of Child Language, 26,* 453–460.

Harris, M., & Chasin, J. (2005). Attentional patterns in deaf and hearing infants: the role of auditory cues. *Journal of Child Psychology and Psychiatry, 46,* 1116–1123.

Harris, M., Clibbens, J., Chasin, J., & Tibbitts, R. (1989). The social context of early sign language development. *First Language, 9,* 81–97.

Harris, M., & Mohay, H. (1997). Learning to look in the right place: A comparison of attentional behavior in deaf children with deaf and hearing mothers. *Journal of Deaf Studies and Deaf Education, 2,* 95–103.

Harris, M., Yeeles, C., Chasin, J., & Oakley, Y. (1995). Symmetries and asymmetries in early lexical comprehension and production *Journal of Child Language, 22,* 1–18.

Hawker, K., Ramirez-Inscoe, J., Bishop, D. V., Twomey, T., O'Donoghue, G. M., & Moore, D. R. (2008). Disproportionate

language impairment in children using cochlear implants. *Ear and Hearing, 29*(3), 467–471.

Hoff, E. (2003). Causes and consequences of SES-related differences in parent-to-child speech. In M. H. Bornstein & R. H. Bradley (Eds.), *Socioeconomic status, parenting, and child development.* Mahwah, NJ: Lawrence Erlbaum Associates Publishers.

Kennedy, C. R., McCann, D., Campbell, M. J., Kimm, L., & Thornton, R. (2005). Universal newborn screening for permanent childhood hearing impairment: An 8-year follow-up of a controlled trial. *Lancet 366,* 660–662.

Kennedy, C. R., McCann, D. C., Campbell, M. J., Law, C. M., Mullee, M., Petrou, S., et al. (2006). Language ability after early detection of permanent childhood hearing impairment. *New England Journal of Medicine, 354*(20), 2131–2141.

Kyle, F. E., & Harris, M. (2006). Concurrent correlates and predictors of reading and spelling achievement in deaf and hearing school children. *Journal of Deaf Studies and Deaf Education, 11*(3), 273–288.

Meadow-Orlans, K., & Spencer, P. E. (1996). Maternal sensitivity and the visual attentiveness of children who are deaf. *Early Development and Parenting, 5,* 213–223.

Nicholas, J. G., & Geers, A. E. (2006). Effects of early auditory experience on the spoken language of deaf children at 3 years of age. *Ear and Hearing, 27*(3), 286–298.

Nicholas, J. G., & Geers, A. E. (2008). Expected test scores for preschoolers with a cochlear implant who use spoken language. *American Journal of Speech-Language Pathology, 17*(2), 121–138.

Scaife, M., & Bruner, J. S. (1975). The capacity for joint visual attention in the infant. *Nature 253,* 265–266.

Spencer, P. E. (2000). Looking without listening: Is audition a prerequisite for normal development of visual attention during infancy? *Journal of Deaf Studies and Deaf Education, 5,* 291–322.

Spencer, P. E. (2004). Individual differences in language performance after cochlear implantation at one to three years of age: child, family, and linguistic factors. *Journal of Deaf Studies and Deaf Education, 9*(4), 395–412.

Spencer, P. E., & Harris, M. (2006). Patterns and effects of language input to deaf infants and toddlers from deaf and hearing mothers. In M. Marschark & P. E. Spencer (Eds.), *Sign language development* (pp. 71–101). Oxford: Oxford University Press.

Thompson, D. C., McPhillips, H., Davis, R., Lieu, T. L., Homer, C. J., & Helfand, M. (2001). Universal newborn hearing screening: Summary of evidence. *Journal of the American Medical Association, 286,* 2000–2010.

Thoutenhoofd, E. D., Archbold, S. M., Gregory, S., Lutman, M. E., Nikolopoulos, T. P., & Sach, T. H. (2005). *Paediatric cochlear implantation: Evaluating outcomes.* London: Whurr.

Tomblin, J. B., Barker, B. A., Spencer, L. J., Zhang, X., & Gantz, B. J. (2005). The effect of age at cochlear implant initial stimulation on expressive language growth in toddlers. *Journal of Speech Language and Hearing Research, 48*(4), 853–867.

Tronick, E., Als, H., & Brazelton, T. B. (1980). Monadic phases: A structural descriptive analysis of infant-mother face to face interaction *Merrill-Palmer Quarterly, 26*(1), 3–24.

Vermeulen, A. M., van Bon, W., Schreuder, R., Knoors, H., & Snik, A. (2007). Reading comprehension of deaf children with cochlear implants. *Journal of Deaf Studies and Deaf Education, 12*(3), 283–302.

Watson, L. M., Archbold, S. M., & Nikolopolous, T. (2006). Children's communication code five years after cochlear implantation: Changes over time according to age at implant. *Cochlear Implants International, 7*(2), 77–91.

Watson, L. M., Hardie, T., Archbold, S. M., & Wheeler, A. (2008). Parents' views on changing communication mode after cochlear implantation. *Journal of Deaf Studies and Deaf Education, 13.*

Woolfe, T., Herman, R., Roy, P., & Woll, B. (2010). Early lexical development in native signers: A BSL adaptation of the CDI. *Journal of Child Psychology and Psychiatry, 51*(3), 322–331.

Language Acquisition and Critical Periods for Children Using Cochlear Implants

Shani Dettman *and* Richard Dowell

Abstract

The critical period hypothesis, as it relates to language acquisition, states that there is a limited window of opportunity for the infant to optimally process incoming acoustic input, learn to discriminate phonemes, and organize language into meaningful units. When auditory input is absent during the critical period, connections within the brain may tend to be organized in the absence of phonological discrimination. This may, in part, account for the long-term language processing difficulties that are often reported for children with significant hearing loss.

The advent of cochlear implants provided researchers with a unique opportunity to examine the impact of earlier versus later access to audition on emerging linguistic domains such as phonology, semantics, morphology, and syntax. The average language outcomes for profoundly hearing-impaired children over the past 20 years using either hearing aids or cochlear implants have been generally disappointing. In contrast, the most recent outcomes for profoundly deaf infants receiving cochlear implants before the age of 12 months show language development within the normal range. Technological advances in physiological studies and medical imaging, coupled with the results from the most recent formal language measures, appear to support the view that cochlear implants are now being applied early enough to maximize natural language development for infants and toddlers.

Keywords: cochlear implants, language development, critical periods

Language itself is not a unitary ability but consists of a number of skills that respond differently to different interventions.

—(*Musselman, Lindsay, & Wilson*, 1988, p. 87)

Language acquisition is complex, consisting of a number of domains such as phonology, semantics, morphology, and syntax. The presence of significant hearing loss in childhood can impair the acquisition of spoken language in each of these domains and can therefore impact all subsequent academic and vocational achievement. Over the past decade, the application of cochlear implants has provided important insights into language acquisition for children with significant hearing loss. In particular,

the differences in spoken language outcomes when cochlear implants are provided in infancy versus school age versus adolescence can assist our understanding of the critical periods for each language domain. The present chapter considers such issues in the domain of spoken languages; Chapter 19, this volume, addresses these issues from the perspective of signed languages.

The critical period theory suggests that there is a limited window of opportunity during which the infant can learn to process incoming acoustic information, establish neuronal connections, learn to discriminate phonemes, organize speech sounds into meaningful units, and learn his or her native language. If auditory input is absent or distorted during the critical language acquisition period, the brain will develop without making the auditory connections necessary for spoken language contrasts, and the child may demonstrate long-term language processing difficulties (Ruben, 1997).

The complexity of language—that is, phonological, semantic, morphological, and syntactic domains—complicates the adequate description of the critical period hypothesis (Singleton, 2005). A definition of phonology includes the sounds and sound combinations that afford meaning distinctions in a given language. For example, two sound contrasts, "lock" versus "rock" may create a meaning distinction; we recognize these as two separate nouns when using the phonological rules of English, whereas in Japanese this phonetic distinction has no linguistic significance. A native Japanese speaker may not even hear the difference between these words. When we produce "lock" with a rising, falling, or flat intonation, the word meaning is unchanged in English, thus intonation can have pragmatic weight (indicating mood) but not linguistic weight. In contrast, a rising versus falling pitch transition may afford a phonological distinction in a tonal language (such as Mandarin).

Understanding the importance of phonology for underpinning language acquisition is crucial for clinicians working with families of young children. An infant requires immersion in many thousands of hours of natural language in order to map out acoustic contrasts, determine what has phonological "weight," delimit word boundaries and determine linguistic meaning. This process scaffolds subsequent semantic, morphological, and syntactic constructions that are built by the child. A definition of semantics includes the meanings of words and relationships between words, and can be loosely equated with our use of vocabulary. A definition of morphology includes the use of inflections and morphemes to mark person, tense, and case (e.g., the plural "s" in English). Morphemes, which are the smallest unit of language, may be combined to form new words from existing words (e.g., happiness from happy). Morphological markers are determined by a set order of acquisition and are language specific. Syntax refers to the underlying grammatical rules that direct our ordered use of words.

A definition of language must also include its arbitrary and generative aspects. The words we use are fundamentally collections of phonemes that are arbitrarily ascribed to "label" shared objects, ideas, and concepts. Within a socialized society we have a shared agreement that a "book" is called a "book." Only onomatopoeic words "sound like" the thing they represent (e.g., hum, buzz, and crash). The agreed-upon meanings may be used to joke and pun. Adolescents like to break all the rules when adjectives such as "totally sick," "random," or "wicked" are positive affirmations.

The typically developing child has determined phonological weighting of his native language by age 1, is working on morphological rules from 2 to 4 years, and by age 5 has mastered an extensive receptive and expressive repertoire. At 5 years of age, he has completed acquisition of the rules governing the combination of words into phrases and sentences, can generate completely novel utterances, and make the necessary transformations to create negatives and questions. The language competence of the adult reader of this chapter differs from the 5-year-old in only two ways. The adult should demonstrate a larger vocabulary than the 5-year-old, and this receptive and expressive vocabulary continues to grow throughout adulthood. The adult should demonstrate more complex use of embedded and co-joined sentences (e.g., using "which," "who," "and," "if," "but," "so," and "because"). In all other respects, the language acquisition of the typically developing child is complete by the age of 5 years.

Our understanding of the impact of hearing loss for each language domain is still emerging. For example, the phonological critical period is thought to commence in the sixth month of fetal life, with a curtailing of abilities by 12 months chronological age. The advent of neonatal screening has led to earlier diagnosis and intervention, but few countries can claim the universal application of hearing aids for all children under 12 months (see Chapter 23, this volume). Hearing aids or cochlear implants that are applied after 12 months of age are already outside the critical period for phonological growth. Ruben (1997), describing language acquisition from a central nervous system developmental framework, suggested that the neural plasticity for syntactic development may still be present up to the fourth year of life, and plasticity for semantic development (and related vocabulary development) may remain up to and past puberty. Ruben concluded, however, that "insufficient early phonological input results in flawed semantic and syntactic capacities" (p. 204).

The concept of cumulative practice (Flexer, 2007) is important here too. The typically developing infant practices, stores, and builds a wealth of auditory and linguistic experiences prior to the emergence of his first spoken word. For the child with significant hearing loss, skills may be mastered on a delayed and extended time course (in fact, a later time course than the typical biological model). Not only is the child with significant hearing loss starting out later, he has a reduced total cumulative practice time in which to perfect his auditory skills.

Review of Critical Period Evidence

Historically, evidence for the critical period theory began with animal studies. Lorenz (1981) famously demonstrated the irreversible imprinting response for newly hatched goslings. Animals that were exposed to a maternal substitute during their critical period would apply their "following instinct" to the maternal impersonator. Studies of visual deprivation in kittens (Hubel & Wiesel, 1963, 1965) and humans (Sacks, 1993) also suggested that individuals deprived of visual stimuli at the critical developmental period remained visually impaired despite the restoration of sight.

The evidence for critical periods for *language* is derived from a wide range of sources including case descriptions of "feral" children, the universal perceptual theory, and examination of second-language learners. More recently, technological advances have enabled researchers to examine brain scans and recordings of brain activity during auditory and language processing tasks. In addition, the evidence regarding the importance of access to hearing at a young age for brain and language development is derived from animal studies and from research with young children using hearing aids.

In humans, the "Tarzan" myth proposed that the boy, recovered from the jungle after puberty, could learn language in adulthood. Our understanding of critical periods for language suggests that the truth is far more complex. Language deprivation studies such as the "Wild Boy of Aveyron" and "Genie" (Ward, 2007) suggested conflicting accounts as to whether semantic or grammatical aspects of language could be taught after puberty. There were also conflicting accounts of the rate at which acquisition could occur. Historically, these accounts of "feral," or deprived children tended to attract a range of interested scholars and those who exploited their stories, but rigorous meta-analysis that scientifically measured all variables (age at deprivation, degree of human socialization prior to deprivation, presence of additional cognitive or special needs, and presence of emotional and physical trauma) was not completed for these strange and special cases.

As mentioned previously, learning the specific phonetic and phonological constraints of our native language may be complete for normally hearing children by 12 months (Molfese, 1977; Ruben, 1997).

Infants are born with the sensory capacity to discriminate all possible phonetic contrasts across a wide range of native and non-native languages, and this ability is fine-tuned with experience in the first 6 months. For example, Spanish neonates may demonstrate the ability to discriminate phonemes "pa" and "ba" where Spanish adults cannot. At around 4–6 months, infants' vocalizations include a wide range of native and non-native phonemes as the child explores the motor productions for all possible speech sounds. Consider, as an example, the English speaking infant's use of "raspberries" and tongue clicks, even though these phonemes are not present in English words. From around 6–12 months of age, reorganization of perceptual responses to speech occurs. The child learns to say and understand sounds appropriate to his native language. It is a curious coincidence, not yet fully explored by the literature, that the child chooses to limit production to native phonemes at around the same stage that he shifts perceptual attention to his native phonological contrasts. To employ the Spanish example, by his first birthday, the infant stops babbling sounds that are not present in adult Spanish and has "lost" the ability to hear the difference between voiced and voiceless contrasts when these do not carry phonological weight in Spanish. Functional and structural changes in the brain appear around 10 months, which correspond with diminished discrimination abilities for non-native contrasts, and increased discrimination abilities for the sound contrasts that do carry meaning (phonotactic constraints) in the child's native language (Pisoni, Lively, & Logan, 1994; Werker & Tees, 1984).

Studies of language acquisition have shown that individuals who learn a second language later in life also demonstrate limitations in processing that relate to the characteristics of their first language. Subtle effects of the dominant language are also evident even in individuals who have simultaneous bilingual experience from birth and who appear equally fluent in both languages. These differences in processing ability are taken to demonstrate the critical period of early brain development for phonological distinctions. Stapp (1999) demonstrated that monolingual students could acquire native-like proficiency in discriminating non-native phonological contrasts but only after training.

Recent improvements in technology have enabled researchers to complete functional brain mapping via MRI (fMRI) and positron emission tomography (PET) studies to examine the degree of myelination and spatial representation in the cerebral cortex.

Myelination of the nerve fibers refers to the development of a sheath layer that starts during fetal development, but diminishes after childhood. Measurement of cortical activity using fluorodeoxyglucose PET studies suggested that adults with poor cochlear implant outcomes may be unable to access those auditory association cortices required for specialized speech processing (Green, Julyan, Hastings, & Ramsden, 2005). There are few fMRI and PET studies for pediatric users of cochlear implants, however.

Sharma, Dorman, and Spahr (2002) used P1 latencies to infer the maturational state of the auditory cortex in 104 congenitally deaf children who received cochlear implants between 1.3 and 17.5 years. The P1 latency derived from cortical auditory evoked potentials refers to the time delay from presentation of an auditory stimulus to the response in auditory thalamic and cortical regions. It varies with chronological age, becoming shorter as the normally hearing infant learns to respond to sound. Children who were implanted at younger than 3.5 years demonstrated greater plasticity than those implanted later. Even after prolonged duration of implant use, the cortical auditory evoked potentials of adolescent cochlear implant users contrasted with their normally hearing peers (Ponton & Eggermont, 2001). Atypical cortical waveforms suggesting persistent immaturity and/or abnormal organization of the auditory cortex were recorded for 23 experienced pediatric cochlear implant users who received implants around 12 years of age (Gordon, Tanaka, & Papsin, 2005).

In addition to brain lateralization and localization studies, which examine the brain at a gross structural level, physiological evidence for critical periods is emerging for both animals and humans. Cortical representations are constantly reorganized and optimized following meaningful practice in animals, which suggests that cortical plasticity is important for perceptual learning (Karni & Bertini, 1997; Katz & Shatz, 1996; Merzenich, Wright, Jenkins, Xerri, Byl, Miller, & Tallal, 1996). Deprivation studies in the animal model have demonstrated the effects of poor or absent auditory input on the developing auditory system (Hardie, Martsi-McClintock, Aitkin, & Shepherd, 1998; Shepherd & Hardie, 2001). Such research has also suggested that auditory stimulation via cochlear implants can help preserve the animal's auditory pathways and even reverse the effects of auditory deprivation (Matsushima, Shepherd, Seldon, Xu, & Clark, 1991; Shepherd, Hartmann, Heid, Hardie, & Klinke, 1997).

Evidence regarding the importance of access to hearing at a young age for language development is also derived from young children using hearing aids. A body of evidence has emerged demonstrating that, for hearing aid users, appropriate early intervention by 6 months of age was associated with improved receptive and expressive language outcomes (Yoshinaga-Itano, Sedey, Coulter, & Mehl, 1998). Children who were identified and aided in the first 2 months of life had significantly better language development than did children identified between 3 and 12 months of age (Apuzzo & Yoshinaga-Itano, 1995). Despite significant hearing loss and irrespective of sign/manual or auditory/oral approaches, these early-identified children were able to demonstrate language growth commensurate with normal hearing peers, albeit at the lower end of the normal range (Yoshinaga-Itano & Snyder, 1999; Yoshinaga-Itano, 2003).

Cochlear Implants in Children

The application of cochlear implants to pediatric populations provides a unique opportunity to examine the effects of "early" versus "late" auditory input on the developing brain. Extended periods of auditory deprivation have been found to be correlated with lower speech perception outcomes in studies of adults and adolescents using cochlear implants (Watson, Balko, Comer, Bishop, Reilley, & Backous, 2003). It has been suggested that once the auditorily deprived cortex has been reorganized, it may no longer respond to the auditory input provided by the cochlear implant (Doucet, Bergeron, Lassonde, Ferron, & Lepore, 2006). Elective cochlear implant nonuse following a lack of benefit is another measure of the importance of critical periods. The partial or nonuse rate is reported to be around 1%–10% and is higher for children who received implants at 9–12 years of age (Ray et al., 2006).

The first two children in the world to receive multichannel cochlear implants (in Melbourne, Australia) also provide evidence regarding critical periods for access to hearing for language acquisition. Both children demonstrated normal hearing in the first 3 years of life, but acquired profound to total hearing loss as a consequence of bacterial meningitis. In both cases, all auditory skills, phonological knowledge, and receptive and expressive language skills were quickly lost. Some vocabulary and grammatical skills were relearned using lip-reading and written materials. Hearing was partially restored when they received cochlear implants at 10 and 5 years of age, respectively (Clark et al., 1987), but this restoration of access to hearing for phonological and brain development was beyond the optimum critical period. In both cases, full-time implant use was rejected during adolescence, and they are part-time/nonusers of the technology today.

Many studies have demonstrated the substantial benefits available for speech perception and communication skills for profoundly deaf children using cochlear implants (Cheng & Niparko, 2000; Dowell, Dettman, Blamey, Barker, & Clark, 2002; Geers, Brenner, & Davidson, 2003; McConkey-Robbins, Koch, Osberger, Zimmerman-Phillips, & Kishon-Rabin, 2004; Pulsifer, Salorio, & Niparko 2003). Recent data indicate that, on average, young children using multichannel cochlear implants can understand 79% of phonemes in monosyllabic words and 53% of complete words in an open set assessment using the cochlear implant alone (Dowell et al., 2002). These results surpass the average scores for adults with acquired hearing loss using cochlear implants and are equivalent to scores achieved by children with moderate hearing losses using hearing aids (Leigh, Dettman, Sarant, Hollow, Dowell, & Briggs, 2008a).

Increasing numbers of children younger than 3 years of age are receiving cochlear implants due to the growing recognition of the efficacy of cochlear implants for young children, and the recent change in the United States Food and Drug Administration's cochlear implant age criteria to include infants with profound hearing loss. In addition, improvements in device technology and two decades of clinical experience with the cochlear implant in pediatric populations means that published research has now identified many of the variables leading to optimum speech perception and language outcomes. These include younger age at implantation (Dowell, Blamey, & Clark, 1995; Hammes, Novak, Rotz, Willis, Edmondson, & Thomas, 2002; McConkey-Robbins et al., 2004; Nikolopoulos, O'Donoghue, & Archbold, 1999; Zwolan, Ashbaugh, & Alarfaj, 2004), speech processor technology (Cowan et al., 1997; Moog & Geers, 2003), communication modes emphasizing an aural–oral approach (Geers, Brenner, & Davidson, 2000; Moog & Geers, 2003), absence of a developmental delay (Dettman, Fiket, Dowell, Charlton, Williams, Tomov, & Barker, 2004b; Dowell et al., 2002; Waltzman, Scalchunes, & Cohen, 2000), shorter duration of profound hearing loss (Miyamoto, Osberger, Todd, Robbins, Stoer, Zimmerman-Phillips, & Carney, 1994), greater preimplant residual hearing (Dettman, D'Costa, Dowell, Winton, Hill, & Williams, 2004a;

Eisenberg, Kirk, Martinez, Ying, & Miyamoto, 2004; Zwolan, Zimmerman-Phillips, Ashbaugh, Heiber, Kileny, & Teilan, 1997), and gender (Moog & Geers, 2003). Additional variables are known to impact language acquisition for children using hearing aids, such as family socioeconomic-status (Martineau, Lamarche, Marcoux, & Bernard, 2001), maternal education background (Musselman & Kircaali-Iftar, 1996), and optimum maternal input (Dettman, 2005), but these have only just begun to be considered for children using cochlear implants.

Despite our understanding of these variables, the literature concerned with children who have significant hearing loss and their language development is still complicated by inadequate research methodology. The number of confounding and interrelated variables requires a critical reader and careful review. In addition, it is possible that we have not yet seen enough children implanted within the critical periods for language—that is, under 12 months—to significantly override the outcome variability due to these other factors (see Chapter 9, this volume).

A literature review regarding the nature of language development for children with significant hearing loss should be based on a review of the best available research. Research may be graded according to its level, quality, relevance, and strength. The highest "level of evidence" refers to rigorous scientific methodologies such as systematic reviews of randomized controlled clinical trials (Level 1), or matched-pair designs (Level 2) (National Health and Medical Research Council, 1999). These levels of evidence, however, are often impractical in the study of communication development in young children and in children with hearing loss and, as a result, most published studies in the public health intervention field will be categorized as Level 3 studies. As such, the language development field is weighed down with author opinions, anecdotal reports, reports containing small numbers of subjects, and the inclusion of subjects with a wide range of confounding attributes. In mathematical terms, the power of any statistical test is reduced when subject numbers are low and the number of subjects needed to reach reliable conclusions also increases as the number of variables affecting the outcome increases. Researchers faced with small groups of children with multiple interacting variables can arrive at counterintuitive conclusions sometimes. Unfortunately, in reviewing the literature related to children with hearing loss, it is often necessary to include studies with their methodological flaws or have no studies to report at all.

The literature is also complicated by the interactions between variables intrinsic to the child, and variables that are extrinsic or environmental influences. For example, complex relationships have been found between the "age at access to hearing via a cochlear implant" variable and the "mode of communication" variable for speech perception (Bertram, Lenarz, Meyer, Battmer, & Hartrampf, 1995; Hellman, Chute, Kretschmer, Nevis, Parisier, & Thurston, 1991; Kirk, Miyamoto, Lento, Ying, O'Neill, & Fear, 2002), measures of consonant production, and tests of receptive and expressive language (Connor, Hieber, Arts, & Zwolan, 2000; Kirk et al., 2002).

Recent Studies on Language Outcomes for Children Using Cochlear Implants

In 2003, Geers and colleagues reported on data from 181 children, 8 to 10 years old, who received implants prior to 5 years of age from across the United States and Canada. This study represented the best attempt, to date, to direct careful attention to random sampling across the pediatric population; comprehensive measurement of outcomes for speech perception, speech production, language, and literacy; controls for known variables; and rigorous statistical analysis and interpretation of results. Once the variance from all measured variables was accounted for, Geers and colleagues arrived at two major conclusions. Firstly, that "data from this study indicate that higher expectations are appropriate for children with cochlear implants than were previously realistic for profoundly deaf children who wore hearing aids" (Moog & Geers, 2003, p. 124), and second that, "all performance outcome measures were significantly higher for children in educational environments emphasizing listening and speaking" (Moog & Geers, 2003, p. 124).

Published results for the Peabody Picture Vocabulary Test (PPVT; Dunn & Dunn, 1981, 1997) over time support this first point, that is, that higher expectations are warranted for children using cochlear implants. The PPVT is a measure of single-word receptive vocabulary. As a norm-referenced test, it allows comparison of an individual's performance with that of a well-defined reference group of American children with normal hearing and English as their primary language. The child's score on the PPVT is interpreted with reference to the typically developing child and expressed in terms of the child's equivalent language age. These results are frequently reported in terms of a language growth rate, where 1.0 is equal to normal development and indicates 1 year of equivalent language acquisition for each chronological year.

Use of the PPVT is widespread, and this facilitates comparisons from different data sets in various countries. In the past, language results for children using hearing aids have been reported at 0.43 and 0.33 (Boothroyd, Geers, & Moog, 1991; Geers & Moog, 1994). Those using cochlear implants fared only marginally better in the late 1990s and the decade commencing 2000, with language results of 0.58 (Geers & Moog, 1994), 0.63 (Blamey et al., 1998), 0.38 to 0.50 (Svirsky, 2000), 0.55 (Dettman, Dowell, Barker, Williams, Tomov, Latus, & Winton, 2001), 0.62 (Blamey et al., 2001), 0.71 (El-Hakim, Lavasseur, Papsin, Panesar, Mount, Stevens, & Harrison, 2001), and 0.56 (Webster, 2002).

In 2004, the PPVT data from 78 children with congenital/early onset of profound hearing loss ($n = 54$ aural–oral and $n = 22$ total communication) who received cochlear implants before 6 years of age (mean 3.50 years at confidence interval [CI], range 1.4–5.8 years, standard deviation [SD] 1.2 years) (Fig. 22.1) suggested that the average equivalent language age was only 0.56 of the chronological age (Dettman, Webster, & Dowell, 2004).

This group used a combination of signal processing strategies (59 = ACE/SPEAK, 17 = MSP/Multispeak) with full electrode insertion. Multiple regression analyses indicated that age at implant, mode of communication, speech processing strategy, and preoperative residual hearing were significantly associated with receptive vocabulary outcomes (Fig. 22.2).

By 2008, the PPVT data from 175 children using cochlear implants looked more positive (Dettman,

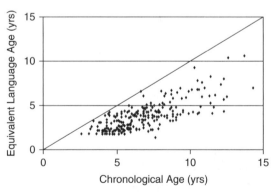

Fig. 22.1 Peabody Picture Vocabulary Test (PPVT) receptive vocabulary results for 78 children using cochlear implants. Average equivalent language age was 0.56 of chronological age. From Dettman, S. J., Webster, E., & Dowell, R. C. (May 2004). Long term language outcomes for children using cochlear implants. Paper presented at the VIII International Cochlear Implant Conference, Indianapolis. Used with permission.

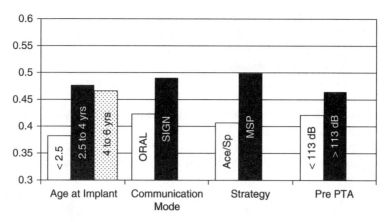

Fig. 22.2 Significant variables (age at implant, mode of communication, speech processing strategy, and preoperative residual hearing) against relative language delay (Peabody Picture Vocabulary Test) for 78 children using cochlear implants.

Hoenig, Dowell, & Leigh, 2008) (Fig. 22.3). An average rate of language acquisition of 0.85 was demonstrated. These children had congenital/early onset of profound loss (mean 0.34 years, range 0–5 years, SD 0.86), received implants at less than 6 years of age (mean 2.49 years at CI, range 0.53–5.82 years, SD 1.31years), used current signal coding schemes (SPEAK/ACE), used a range of communication approaches, and had a range of cognitive abilities. Three language tools were used (Rossetti Infant-Toddler Language Scale [RI-TLS], Rossetti 1990; PPVT, Dunn & Dunn, 1997, 1981; and Clinical Evaluation of Language Fundamentals [CELF-3 and 4], Semel, Wiig, & Secord, 1995, 2003).

Examining the language quotients—the ratio between a child's chronological and equivalent language age—provides only a snapshot of the child at one particular time. Svirsky, Teoh, and Neuburger

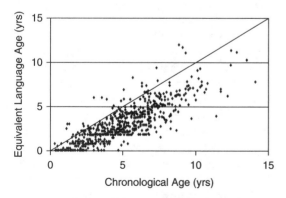

Fig. 22.3 Six hundred-fifty language quotients (RI-TLS, PPVT, CELF) from 175 children using cochlear implants over time. Average equivalent language age was 0.85 of chronological age.

(2004) demonstrated the need to examine child language acquisition over a number of time points. They analyzed the change in language development over time for three groups who differed on age at implant (N = 12 received cochlear implants under 12 months; N = 34 received cochlear implants between 12 and 24 months; and N = 29 received cochlear implants between 24 and 36 months). This developmental trajectory approach indicated significant speech perception and language advantages for children who received the implant before 2 years of age and a gradual decline in language acquisition as a function of age at onset of hearing using an implant.

Using this rate of change approach, data were analyzed for 23 children who had completed two or more language tests over time (Dettman et al., 2008). (Tests used included the RI-TLS, PPVT and CELF.) These children had stable bilateral profound hearing loss from birth (n = 19) or prelingual onset (due to meningitis, n = 4) (3 freq PTA 117.19 dB, range 100–125 dB, SD 8.52 dB). They received Nucleus cochlear implants at an average age of 1.90 years (range 1.05–4.55, SD 0.95), used current speech processors (programmed with SPEAK or ACE), had full electrode insertion, and used a range of communication approaches (n = 5 total communication, n = 18 aural–oral). It was hypothesized that more children would demonstrate a normal rate of language development if they received the implant in the first year of life. For children implanted after their first birthday, it was hypothesized that the "gap" between chronological age and "equivalent" language age would widen over time.

This study was unique in that it examined the children's progress using a checklist of preverbal communication behaviors (RI-TLS), then receptive vocabulary acquisition (PPVT), then receptive and expressive grammatical development (CELF). A significant relationship was found between language outcomes, age at implant, onset of loss, communication mode, and cognitive delay for these 23 children: those children who received their cochlear implant earlier, with a later onset of profound hearing loss, using a communication approach with aural–oral emphasis and no cognitive delay tended to demonstrate progress that was approaching that of their normally hearing peers.

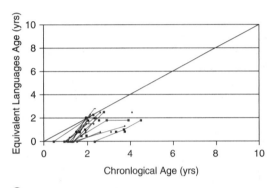

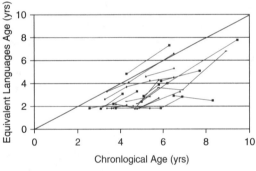

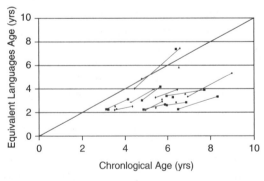

Fig. 22.4 a: Individual rates of language growth for 23 children using cochlear implants for the comprehension subscale of the RI-TLS. **b:** Individual rates of language growth for 23 children using cochlear implants for the Peabody Picture Vocabulary Test. **c:** Individual rates of language growth for 23 children using cochlear implants for the CELF-3 and CELF-4.

Flexer (2007) observed that the brain will tend to organize itself around what it receives, and emphasizes the importance of mastering skills as close as possible to the normal biological framework, thus optimizing developmental synchrony. It may be more important to gain early access to hearing, with all other choices regarding early intervention or mode of communication having secondary importance. Do we have enough evidence to suggest that the relative effects of other variables (for example, mode of communication) may be outweighed or, in fact, made redundant, when access to hearing is early enough to encompass critical periods of language acquisition? And do speech perception and linguistic benefits outweigh the surgical risks for infants younger than 12 months of age receiving implants?

Close inspection of the language outcomes literature reveals that very few children worldwide have received implants at less than 2 years of age, and fewer still at less than 12 months of age. Methodological difficulties, such as test selection and administration, and small sample sizes, are limitations faced by researchers investigating this population.

One of the earliest published articles evaluating the viability of providing cochlear implants to 11 children of less than 2 years of age was completed by Waltzman and Cohen (1998). In their data, methodological problems inherent in this population meant that it was not possible to directly compare speech perception outcomes for the children who received implants at less than 2 years of age with the children who were older at implantation. Typically, the older children had greater linguistic knowledge and could cooperate with test demands better than the younger children, and the study did not specifically examine language outcomes. Nikolopoulos et al. (1999) examined 126 children with congenital and prelingual onset of deafness who received cochlear implants between 22 and 82 months of age. Children who were older at implant initially performed tests better due to advanced cognitive skills, longer exposure to language, and greater familiarity with test conditions. Long-term data collection, however, indicated that the advantage diminished over time. By 3 and 4 years postimplant, children who were younger at implant overtook and outperformed the children who were older at implantation.

Difficulties demonstrating the "earlier is better" argument were also encountered by Hammes et al. (2002). They reported that speech perception and spoken language abilities were highest for the group who received the implant at the youngest age, but the group data for children implanted between 9 and 18 months only included three subjects who could perform the tests.

Lesinski-Schiedat, Illg, Heermann, Bertram, and Lenarz (2004) found that mean scores for 27 children who were implanted under 1 year of age were higher than mean scores obtained by 89 children implanted between 1 and 2 years of age. Both groups were tested at 2.5 years on closed-set and open-set speech perception tasks. The problem with reporting results in this way is that the younger group had, on average, 18–24 months' device experience, whereas the older group had, on average, less than 12 months' and in some cases only 6 months' device experience.

Lesinski-Schiedat et al. (2004) reported that at 3 months postimplant, voice control and oral competence was better for the older implanted group but this advantage diminished at all subsequent data collection intervals. There were no statistically significant differences between the younger or older groups for any of the outcome measures, and they attributed this to the small sample size of the younger group. The following studies report speech perception, production, and language results from children who received implants before their first birthdays. Taken together, the results indicate benefits from early access to hearing and no greater prevalence of surgical or medical complications. Svirsky, Teoh, and Neuberger (2004) examined 12 children implanted between under 12 months of age in comparison to 34 implanted between 12 and 24 months and 29 who were implanted between 24 and 36 months. The group who received implants at less than 12 months demonstrated normal language acquisition rates and entered school with normal language. Implantation before 12 months was associated with development of auditory perception for 18 children (Waltzman & Roland, 2005) and normalization of babbling in 10 infants (Colletti, Carner, Miorelli, Guida, Colletti, & Fiorino, 2005). Dettman, Pinder, Briggs, Dowell, and Leigh (2007) examined the language growth rates in addition to surgical and speech processor programming reports for 19 infants who received the implant at less than 12 months (mean age at implantation, 0.88 year; range, 0.61–1.07, SD 0.15) and compared these data with results from 87 toddlers (mean age at implantation, 1.60 year; range, 1.13–2.00, SD 0.24). No additional surgical or programming issues were found for the younger group. A subset of these children (11 infants and 36 toddlers) had completed

two or more language tests, enabling analysis of growth rates over time. Results for these 11 children implanted before 12 months of age indicated mean rates of receptive and expressive language growth that were comparable to normally hearing peers. In Figure 22.5, the mean rate of language development (1.12, solid line) for 11 children who received implant under 12 months was significantly greater ($p < 0.02$) than the mean rate (0.78, dashed line) achieved by 36 children who received implants as toddlers. More recent data for these children has revealed not only language benefits but speech perception and speech production benefits from earlier access to hearing (Leigh, Dettman, Holland, Dowell, & Briggs, 2008b).

Holt and Svirsky (2008) examined 96 children with congenital profound sensorineural hearing loss, all of whom were implanted prior to age 4, including six children implanted under 1 year of age. All developmental trajectories supported that earlier implantation was better than later implantation, but the difference for children receiving implants under 1 year compared to children receiving implants between 1 and 2 years of age was small, and related specifically to receptive language development.

Summary and Conclusions

The "simple argument for earlier cochlear implantation is to minimize or prevent a growing gap between a child's chronological age and his or her language age" (Rizer & Burkey, 1999, p. 1118). It is proposed that children receiving implants at an earlier age

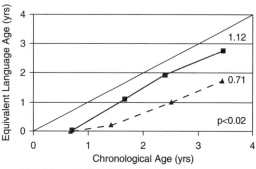

Fig. 22.5 Language comprehension rate (RI-TLS) for children receiving cochlear implants as infants (n = 11; solid line, mean age at confidence interval [CI] 0.90 years) and toddlers (n = 36, dashed line, mean age at CI 1.60 years). From Dettman, S. J., Pinder, D., Briggs, R. J. S., Dowell, R. C., & Leigh, J. R. (2007). Communication development in children who receive the cochlear implant younger than 12 months: Risks versus benefit. *Ear and Hearing, 28*, 11–18. With permission of the publisher.

would be closer to the critical period for language acquisition, and are at an optimum stage for a natural language immersion approach to language acquisition. The child is potentially still within the optimum stage for sorting out for himself the underlying phonological rules from which to build his lexicon and syntactic and semantic rules. In contrast, it is proposed that children who receive implants beyond the critical periods are more likely to experience a language teaching or didactic model of language acquisition, in which vocabulary and syntax are expressly taught.

The development of audiometric technology has now enabled the diagnosis of congenital hearing loss at birth, and modern hearing aids and cochlear implants are well established as safe and effective devices for infants and children. The demographic and developmental variables intrinsic to the child (onset, progression and degree of hearing loss, cognitive status, and gender) and environmental conditions (socioeconomic status, current speech processor, and communication approach with auditory–oral emphasis) that are associated with optimum spoken language outcomes are well known. Early interventionists strive to optimize the environment of the child, but the evidence suggests that the focus should shift to optimizing the most significant variable influencing outcomes; that is, age at access to adequate hearing across the speech frequency range.

The critical period hypothesis for language development has existed as an academic construct for many decades and is supported by recent results from the application of cochlear implants in infants. Children with congenital profound bilateral hearing loss can demonstrate normal language development following early cochlear implant surgery. To reach this potential, however, the fundamental phonological foundations of language need to develop very early in life. If a spoken language outcome is desired by the child and family, early and consistent access to the sounds of speech is essential.

References

Apuzzo, M., & Yoshinaga-Itano, C. (1995). Early identification of infants with significant hearing loss and the Minnesota Child Development Inventory. *Seminars in Hearing*, 16(2), 124–139.

Bertram, B., Lenarz, T., Meyer, V., Battmer, R. D., & Hartrampf, R. (1995). Performance comparisons in post-meningitic prelinguistic & congenitally deaf children. *Advances in Otorhinolaryngology*, 50, 134–138.

Blamey, P., Sarant, J., Serry, T., Wales, R., James, C., Barry, J. et al. (1998). Speech perception and spoken language in children with impaired hearing. *Proceedings of the Fifth International Conference on Spoken Language Processing*, Sydney, 6, 2615–2618.

Blamey, P. J., Sarant, J. Z., Paatsch, L. E., Barry, J. G., Bow, C. P., Wales, R. J. et al. (2001). Relationships among speech perception, production, language, hearing loss, and age in children with impaired hearing. *Journal of Speech, Language, and Hearing Research*, 44(2), 264–285.

Boothroyd, A., Geers, A. E., & Moog, J. S. (1991). Practical implications of cochlear implants in children. *Ear and Hearing*, 12, 81S-89S.

Cheng, A., & Niparko, J. K. (2000) Analyzing the effects of early implantation and results with different causes of deafness: meta-analysis of the pediatric cochlear implant literature. In J. K. Niparko, K. I. Kirk, A. M. Mellon, D. L. Tucci, & B. S. Wilson. (Eds.), *Cochlear implants: Principles & practices* (pp. 259–265). Philadelphia: Lippincott Williams & Wilkins.

Clark, G., M. Blamey, P. J., Busby, P. A., Dowell, R. C., Franz, B. K., Musgrave, G. N. et al. (1987). A multiple-electrode intracochlear implant for children. *Archives of Otolaryngology Head & Neck Surgery*, 113, 825.

Colletti, V., Carner, M., Miorelli, V., Guida, M., Colletti, L., & Fiorino, F. G. (2005). Cochlear implantation at under 12 months: Report on 10 patients. *Laryngoscope, 115*(3), 445–449.

Connor, C., Hieber, S., Arts, H., & Zwolan, T. A. (2000). Speech, vocabulary, and the education of children using cochlear implants: oral or total communication. *Journal of Speech, Language, and Hearing Research*, 43, 1185–1204.

Cowan, R. S. C., Barker, E. J., Pegg, P., Dettman, S. J., Rennie, M., Galvin, K. L. et al. (1997). Speech perception in children: effects of speech processing strategy and residual hearing. In G. M. Clark. (Ed.), *Cochlear implants*. XVI World Congress of Otorhinolaryngology - Head and Neck Surgery (pp. 49–54). Bologna: Monduzzi Editore.

Dettman, S. J. (2005). Primary caregiver input and communication development for children using the cochlear implant. Unpublished doctoral thesis, University of Melbourne, Australia.

Dettman, S. J., D'Costa, W. A., Dowell, R. C., Winton, E. J., Hill, K. L., & Williams, S. S. (2004a). Cochlear implants for children with significant residual hearing. *Archives of Otolaryngology Head & Neck Surgery*, 130, 612–618.

Dettman, S. J., Dowell, R. C., Barker, E. J., Williams, S. S., Tomov, A., Latus, K., & Winton, L. (2001, February). *Long term language outcomes for children using cochlear implants*. Poster session presented at the 8th Symposium on Cochlear implants in children, Los Angeles.

Dettman, S. J., Hoenig, N., Dowell, R. C., & Leigh, J. R. (2008, April). Long term language outcomes for children using cochlear implants: Are we still failing to close the gap? Paper presented at the 10th International conference on Cochlear Implants and other Implantable Auditory Technologies, San Diego, CA.

Dettman, S. J., Fiket, H., Dowell, R. C., Charlton, M., Williams, S. S., Tomov, A. M., & Barker, E. J. (2004b). Speech perception results for children using cochlear implants who have additional special needs. *The Volta Review, 104*(4), 361–392.

Dettman, S. J., Pinder, D., Briggs, R. J. S., Dowell, R. C., & Leigh, J. R. (2007). Communication development in children who receive the cochlear implant younger than 12 months: Risks versus benefit. *Ear and Hearing, 28*, 11–18.

Dettman, S. J., Webster, E., & Dowell, R. C. (May 2004). Long term language outcomes for children using cochlear implants. Paper presented at the VIII International Cochlear Implant Conference, Indianapolis.

Doucet, M. E., Bergeron, F., Lassonde, M., Ferron, P., & Lepore, F. (2006). Cross-modal reorganization and speech perception in cochlear implant users, *Brain*, *129*, 3376–3383.

Dowell, R. C., Blamey, P. J., & Clark, G. M. (1995). Potential and limitations of cochlear implants in children. *Annals of Otology Rhinology & Laryngology*, *166*, 324S–327S.

Dowell, R. C., Dettman, S. J., Blamey, P. J., Barker, E. J., & Clark, G. M. (2002). Speech perception outcomes in children using cochlear implants: Prediction of long-term outcomes. *Cochlear Implants International*, *3*, 1–18.

Dunn, L. M., & Dunn, L. M. (1997). Peabody Picture Vocabulary Test, 3rd edition. Circle Pines, MN: American Guidance Service.

Dunn, L. M., & Dunn, L. M. (1981). Peabody Picture Vocabulary Test, Revised. Circle Pines, MN: American Guidance Service.

Eisenberg, L. S., Kirk, K. I., Martinez, A. S. Ying, E. A., & Miyamoto, R. T. (2004). Communication abilities of children with aided residual hearing: comparison with cochlear implant users. *Archives of Otolaryngology – Head & Neck Surgery*, *130*(5), 563–569.

El-Hakim, H., Levasseur, J., Papsin, B., Panesar, J., Mount, R., Stevens, R., & Harrison, R. (2001). Assessment of vocabulary development in children after cochlear implantation. *Archives of Otolaryngology – Head & Neck Surgery*, *127*, 153–159.

Flexer, C. (March, 2007) Auditory brain development: A paradigm shift for children who are deaf or hard of hearing. Paper presented at the Australasian Conference on Listening and Spoken Language, Brisbane.

Geers, A. E., Brenner, C., & Davidson, L. S. (2003). Factors associated with development of speech perception skills in children implanted by age five. *Ear and Hearing*, *24*, 24S–35S.

Geers, A. E., & Moog, J. S. (1994). Spoken language results: Vocabulary, syntax, and communication. *The Volta Review*, *96*, 131–148.

Gordon, K. A., Tanaka, S., & Papsin, B. C. (2005) Atypical cortical responses underlie poor speech perception in children using cochlear implants. *Neuroreport*, *16*(18), 2041–2045.

Green, K. M. J., Julyan, P. J., Hastings, D. L., & Ramsden, R. T. (2005). Auditory cortical activation and speech perception in cochlear implant users Effects of implant experience and duration of deafness. *Hearing Research*, 2051–2052.

Hammes, D. M., Novak, M. A., Rotz, L. A., Willis, M., Edmondson, D. M., & Thomas, J. F. (2002). Early identification & cochlear implantation: Critical factors for spoken language development. *Annals of Otology, Rhinology & Laryngology*, *111*, 74–78.

Hardie, N. A., Martsi-McClintock, A., Aitkin, L., & Shepherd, R. K. (1998). Neonatal sensorineural hearing loss affects synaptic density in the auditory midbrain. *Neuroreport*, *9*, 2019–2022.

Hellman, S. A., Chute, P. M., Kretschmer, R. E., Nevins, M. E., Parisier, S. C., & Thurston, L. C. (1991). The development of a children's implant profile. *American Annals of the Deaf*, *136*, 77–81.

Holt, R. F., & Svirsky, M. A. (2008). An exploratory look at pediatric cochlear implantation: Is earliest always best? *Ear Hear*, *29*(4), 492–511.

Hubel, D. H., & Wiesel, T. N. (1963). Receptive fields of cells in striate cortex of very young, visually inexperienced kittens. *Journal of Neurophysiology*, *26*, 994–1002.

Hubel, D., & Wiesel, T. (1965). Binocular interaction in striate cortex of kittens reared with artificial squint. *Journal of Neurophysiology*, *28*, 1041–1059.

Karni, A., & Bertini, G. (1997). Learning perceptual skills: Behavioral probes into adult cortical plasticity. *Current Opinion in Neurobiology*, *7*, 530–535.

Katz, L. C., & Shatz, C. (1996). Synaptic activity and the construction of cortical circuits. *Science*, *274*, 1133–8.

Kirk, K. I., Miyamoto, R. T., Lento, C. L., Ying, E., O'Neill, T., & Fears, B. (2002). Effects of age at implantation in young children. *Annals of Otology, Rhinology & Laryngology*, *189*, 69–73.

Leigh, J. R., Dettman, S. J., Sarant, J., Hollow, R., Dowell, R. C., & Briggs, R. J. S. (2008a, April). Pushing the boundaries: changing selection criteria for paediatric cochlear implant recipients. Paper presented at the 10th International conference on Cochlear Implants and other Implantable Auditory Technologies, San Diego, CA.

Leigh, J., Dettman, S., Holland, J., Dowell, R., & Briggs, R. (2008b, May 25–29). Long-term language, speech production and speech perception outcomes for children who received a cochlear implant at or before 12 months of age. Paper presented at Reflecting Connections: A joint conference between New Zealand Speech-Language Therapists Association and Speech Pathology Australia, Auckland, New Zealand.

Lesinski-Schiedat, A., Illg, A., Heermann, R., Bertram, B., & Lenarz, T. (2004). Paediatric cochlear implantation in the first and in the second year of life: a comparative study. *Cochlear Implants International*, *5*(4), 146–159.

Lorenz, K. (1981). *The foundation of ethology*. New York: Springer-Verlag.

Martineau, G., Lamarche, P., Marcoux, S., & Bernard, P. (2001). The effect of early intervention on academic achievement of hearing-impaired children. *Early Education and Development*, *12*(2), 275–288.

Matsushima, J., Shepherd, R. K., Seldon., L., Xu, S. A, & Clark, G. M. (1991). Electrical stimulation of the auditory nerve in deaf kittens: Effects on cochlear nuclei. *Hearing Research*, *56*, 133–142.

Merzenich, M., Wright, B., Jenkins, W., Xerri, C., Byl, N., Miller, S., & Tallal, P. (1996). Cortical plasticity underlying perceptual, motor, and cognitive skill development: implications for neurorehabilitation. *Cold Spring Harbor Symposia on Quantitative Biology*, *61*, 1–8.

McConkey Robbins, A., Koch, D. B., Osberger, M. J., S. Zimmerman-Phillips, S., & Kishon-Rabin, L. (2004). Effect of age at cochlear implantation on auditory skill development in infants and toddlers. *Archives of Otolaryngology-Head & Neck Surgery*, *130*(5), 570–574.

Miyamoto, R. T., Osberger, M. J., Todd, S. L., Robbins, A., Stoer, B. S., Zimmerman-Phillips, S., & Carney, A. E. (1994). Variations affecting implant performance in children. *Laryngoscope*, *104*, 1120–1124.

Molfese, D. (1977). Infant cerebral asymmetry. In S. J. Segalowitz & F. A. Gruber (Eds.), *Language development and neurological theory* (pp. 22–37). New York: Academic Press.

Musselman, C., & Kircaali-Iftar, G. (1996). The development of spoken language in deaf children: Explaining the unexplained variance. *Journal of Deaf Studies and Deaf Education*, *1*(2), 108–121.

Musselman, C. R., Lindsay, P. H., & Wilson, A. K. (1988). An evaluation of recent trends in preschool programming for hearing-impaired children. *Journal of Speech and Hearing Disorders*, 53, 71–88.

Moog, J. S., & Geers, A. M. (2003). Epilogue: Major findings, conclusions and implications for deaf education. *Ear and Hearing*, 24, 121S-125S.

National Health and Medical Research Council. (1999). *A guide to the development, implementation and evaluation of clinical practiced guidelines*. Commonwealth of Australia.

Nikolopoulos, T. P., O'Donoghue, G. M., & Archbold, S. (1999). Age at Implantation: Its importance in paediatric cochlear implantation. *Laryngoscope*, 109, 595–99.

Pisoni, D. P., Lively, S. E., & Logan, J. S. (1994). Perceptual learning of nonnative speech contrast: Implication for theories of speech perception. In J. Goodman & H. C. Nusbaum (Eds.), *The development of speech perception: the transition from speech sounds to spoken words* (pp. 121–166). Chicago: MIT Press.

Ponton, C. W., & Eggermont, J. J. (2001) Of kittens and kids: Altered cortical maturation following profound deafness and cochlear implant use. *Audiology & Neuro-Otology*. 6(6), 363–380.

Pulsifer, M. B., Salorio, C. F., & Niparko, J. K. (2003). Developmental, audiological, and speech perception functioning in children after cochlear implant surgery. *Archives of Pediatrics & Adolescent Medicine*, 157(6), 552–558.

Ray, J., Wright, T., Fielden, C., Cooper, H., Donaldson, I., & Proops, D. (2006). Non-users and limited users of cochlear implants. *Cochlear Implants International*, 7(1), 49–58.

Rizer, F. M., & Burkey, J. M. (1999). Cochlear implants in the very young child. *Otolaryngology Clinics of North America*, 32, 1117–1125.

Rossetti, L. M. (1990). *The Rossetti Infant-Toddler Language Scale*. East Moline, IL: LinguiSystems.

Ruben, R. J. (1997). A time frame of critical/sensitive periods of language development *Acta Otolaryngologica*, 117, 202–205.

Sacks, O. (May 10, 1993). To see and not to see. *The New Yorker*, 59–73.

Semel, E., Wiig, E. H., & Secord, W. A. (1995) Clinical Evaluation of Language Fundamentals-Third Edition (CELF-3) San Antonio, TX: The Psychological Corporation.

Semel, E., Wiig, E. H., & Secord, W. A. (2003) Clinical Evaluation of Language Fundamentals-Third Edition (CELF-4) San Antonio, TX: The Psychological Corporation.

Sharma, A., Dorman, M. F., & Spahr, A. J. (2002). A sensitive period for the development of the central auditory system in children with cochlear implants: Implications for age of implantation. *Ear & Hearing*. 23(6), 532–539.

Shepherd, R. K., & Hardie, N. A. (2001). Deafness induced changes in the auditory pathway: Implications for cochlear implants. *Audiology and Neuro Otology*, 6, 305–318.

Shepherd, R. K., Hartmann, R., Heid, S., Hardie, N., & Klinke, R. (1997). The central auditory system and auditory deprivation: Experience with cochlear implants in the congenitally deaf. *Acta Otolaryngologica*, 532, 28S-33S.

Singleton, D. (2005). The critical period hypothesis: A coat of many colours. *International Review of Applied Linguistics in Language Teaching*, 43, 4, 269–285.

Stapp, Y. F. (1999). Neural plasticity and the issue of mimicry tasks in L2 pronunciation studies, *TESL-EJ: Teaching English as a Second or Foreign Language*, 3,(4), 1–24.

Svirsky, M. A. (2000). Language development in children with profound and prelingual hearing loss, without cochlear implants. *Annals of Otology, Rhinology, & Laryngology*, 109, 99S–100S.

Svirsky, M. A., Teoh, S-W., & Neuberger, H. (2004). Development of language and speech perception in congenitally, profoundly deaf children as a function of age at cochlear implantation. *Audiology and Neuro-otology*, 9, 224–233.

Waltzman, S. B., & Cohen, N. L. (1998). Cochlear implantation in children younger than 2 years old. *The American Journal of Otology*, 19, 158–162.

Waltzman, S. B. & Roland, J. T. (2005). Cochlear implantation in children younger than 12 months. *Pediatrics*, 116, 487–493.

Waltzman, S. B., Scalchunes, V., & Cohen, N. L. (2000). Performance of multiply handicapped children using cochlear implants. *The American Journal of Otology*, 21, 329–335.

Ward, A. (2007). Feral children. Retrieved May 12, 2007 from http://www.feralchildren.com/en/index.php

Watson, S. D., Balko, K. A., Comer, L. K., Bishop, R. D., Reilley, D., & Backous, D. D. (2003). Benefits of cochlear implantation in pre-lingual adult users: oral and manual communicators. *Cochlear Implants International*, 4, 75–76.

Webster, E. (2002). A retrospective study on the language outcomes in young children using cochlear implants. Unpublished master's thesis. University of Melbourne, Department of Otolaryngology, Australia.

Werker, J. F., & Tees, R. C. (1984). Cross language speech perception: Evidence for perceptual re-organisation during the first year of life. *Infant Behaviour and Development*, 7, 49–63.

Yoshinaga-Itano, C. (2003). From screening to early identification & intervention: Discovering predictors to successful outcomes for children with significant hearing loss. *Journal of Deaf Studies & Deaf Education*, 8(1), 11–30.

Yoshinaga-Itano, C., Sedey, A. L., Coulter, B. A., & Mehl, A. L. (1998). Language of early and later identified children with hearing loss. *Pediatrics*, 102, 1168–1171.

Yoshinaga-Itano, C., & Snyder, L. (1999). The relationship of language and symbolic play in deaf and hard-of-hearing children. *The Volta Review*, 100(3), 135–164.

Zwolan, T. A., Ashbaugh, C. M., Alarfaj, A. et al. (2004). Pediatric cochlear implant patient performance as a function of age at implantation. *Otology & Neurotology*, 25, 112–120.

Zwolan, T. A., Zimmerman-Phillips, S., Ashbaugh, C. J., Hieber, S. J., Kileny, P. R., & Teilan, S. A. (1997). Cochlear implantation of children with minimal open-set speech recognition skills. *Ear and Hearing*, 18, 240–251.Mousley, K. & Kelly, R. (1998). Problem-solving strategies for teaching mathematics to deaf students. *American Annals of the Deaf*, 143(4), 325–336.

PART 5

Hearing and Speech Perception

Newborn Screening and Earlier Intervention with Deaf Children: Issues for the Developing World

Greg Leigh, John P. Newall, *and* Anthony T. Newall

Abstract

The universal screening of newborn children for permanent hearing loss has become a standard health and educational service in many, if not most, developed countries. Developed nations, however, represent the minority of the world's population. Universal newborn hearing screening (UNHS) is far less frequently available in developing countries where hearing loss is often disproportionately prevalent. This chapter considers the issues associated with the development of newborn screening programs in developing countries, where the vast majority of the world's deaf children live. These issues include whether to screen all newborns or to employ a targeted approach of seeking only those children with known risk factors for hearing loss, the articulation of UNHS programs with appropriate support services for children and families, and the availability and quality of subsequent intervention in developing-country contexts. The question of economic affordability and the sustainability of expensive programs of screening in very poor countries is also considered, as are the ethical issues associated with providing (or not providing) access to such programs. It is concluded that successfully implemented UNHS programs stand to provide enormous benefits to deaf and hard-of-hearing (DHH) children and their families in developing countries. It is argued that such benefits will only accrue, however, if programs are well implemented and combined with adequate and effective follow-up.

Keywords: developing countries, health care, early intervention, universal newborn hearing screening, targeted newborn hearing screening

Internationally, newborn hearing screening (NHS) programs are now widespread, with an extensive literature base from which to draw conclusions about best practice. Similarly, there is extensive literature providing evidentiary support and multiple examples of best practice in regard to early intervention with deaf and hard-of-hearing (DHH) children. However, the specific issues associated with the provision of NHS and early intervention programs in developing countries have received much less attention. Examples of current practice and evidence for the effectiveness of those practices in developing countries are less available in the literature. This chapter explores current practice and seeks to identify those issues that must be addressed to secure earlier identification of hearing loss and early intervention in developing countries. In doing so, the case is made for much more to be done in these areas. In this regard, this chapter can be seen as a reminder of the current lack of international distributive justice in regard to services and opportunities for DHH children and the constant need to be alert to ways to redress that imbalance.

The Benefits of Earlier Intervention

Without specialized early intervention and subsequent education, DHH children will experience significant delay or disruption to the development of their language and communication abilities, their social and emotional development and, ultimately, their life options (Moeller, 2000; Yoshinaga-Itano, 2003). From a developed world perspective, the availability of the specialized interventions that are necessary to ameliorate those consequences is now the expected standard of care. Expectations continue to rise in regard to what the minimum standard of that care should be. In developed countries, the availability of effective strategies to identify children with hearing loss (of any degree) and of services to intervene in their development—audiologically, educationally, and, increasingly, medically—is unquestioned. Indeed, such services are most often provided as a public service initiative at no cost to the family.

The potential for effective intervention to provide positive linguistic and educational outcomes for DHH children is well understood. Also well understood is the idea that outcomes are greatly enhanced when hearing loss is identified and intervention is commenced at very early ages (Moeller, 2000; Yoshinaga-Itano, 2003; Yoshinaga-Itano, Sedey, Coulter, & Mehl, 1998; Yoshinaga-Itano, Coulter, & Thomson, 2001). The notion that children will develop their language and communication, cognitive, and social skills more effectively if intervention is commenced very early is grounded in the premise that there is an optimal period for the development of certain cognitive and linguistic abilities—particularly phonological perception and speech discrimination abilities (Ruben, 1997). In regard to the latter, it is argued that, because the plasticity of the nervous system is finite, a time-limited period is available for the development and organization of the auditory system (Kral & Tillein, 2006; Ruben & Rapin, 1980; Sharma, Dorman, & Spahr, 2002).

In this context, screening children's hearing at or soon after birth is considered to be the best possible strategy for ensuring effective intervention and subsequent development in children with hearing loss. Where NHS has been actively pursued, it is typically in one of two ways: (a) targeted hearing screening (THS) of children who are born with known risk factors for hearing loss or (b) universal newborn hearing screening (UNHS). This distinction, and the potential for either or both to be features of services delivered to children in developing countries, is discussed later in greater detail. It is sufficient to state at this point that UNHS is fast becoming the standard of care in the developed world (Grandori & Lutman, 1998; Joint Committee on Infant Hearing [JCIH], 2007).

In regions where NHS (particularly UNHS) has been effectively implemented, the average ages of both the identification of hearing loss and the

commencement of intervention strategies with DHH children have been significantly reduced (Durieux-Smith, Fitzpatrick, & Whittingham, 2008; Harrison, Roush, & Wallace, 2003). For example, Uus and Bamford (2007) reported a median age of first fitting with hearing aids of just 4 months for children identified with hearing loss through the UNHS program in England. In the Australian State of New South Wales, the average age of identification of congenital hearing loss fell from 18 months to just 1.6 months following the introduction of a UNHS program in late 2002 (New South Wales Health Department, 2006). Ching, Oong, and van Wanrooy (2006) reported that the median age at which children in New South Wales were first fitted with a hearing aid was 21.2 months for children born in 2001 but fell to just 3.4 months for children who were born in 2003, subsequent to the implementation of UNHS.

Much of the early evidence for the benefits of NHS came from the work of Yoshinaga-Itano and others, who conducted a range of studies following the introduction of screening in Colorado in the United States in the late 1990s. They compared the results of numerous developmental measures in DHH children for whom intervention was commenced either early (<6 months of age) or later (>6 months of age) (Yoshinaga-Itano, 2003; Yoshinaga-Itano et al., 2001; Yoshinaga-Itano et al., 1998). Those studies found that children who received early intervention had significantly higher scores on language, speech, and social-emotional measures. Similarly, Moeller (2000) found that children who began early intervention at a younger age had better outcomes than those starting at an older age.

Even though the benefits ascribed to the introduction of UNHS have become widely accepted, the evidence base for those benefits being sustained in the longer term has been questioned. Indeed, some systematic reviews (e.g., Puig, Municio, & Medà, 2005) have argued that there is insufficient evidence from well-controlled studies to confirm the long-term developmental benefits of UNHS. Recent studies examining language outcomes of early-identified DHH children at school age, however, have provided additional evidence of the benefits of UNHS. Kennedy et al. (2006) studied a group of 120 DHH children (mean age 7.9 years) in southern England, of whom 57 had their hearing loss confirmed by 9 months of age through UNHS. Receptive and expressive age-adjusted mean language scores were significantly higher for the early identified group than for the rest of the cohort.

Although the introduction of UNHS has been shown to be effective in lowering the age of intervention in developed countries, there has been relatively little attention to this issue in developing countries (Olusanya, Luxon, & Wirz, 2004, 2005), where the vast majority of the world's population resides.[1]

Incidence and Prevalence of Hearing Loss in the Developing World

In developing countries, there is a lack of adequate data to provide good estimates of the incidence of permanent congenital hearing loss in children. There are significant challenges in such countries to obtaining good epidemiological data. In the case of hearing loss in newborns, there is a particular conundrum, because data on the incidence of congenital hearing loss can only be reliable where effective NHS is in place. Indeed, prior to the advent of UNHS programs in developed countries, reliable estimates of the incidence of congenital hearing loss were also difficult to obtain. Although the likely range of incidence of significant permanent hearing loss in neonates has been held to be somewhere between 1 and 2 per 1,000 live births (Vohr, Carty, Moore, & Letourneau, 1998), subsequent studies that have addressed the influence of screening programs have suggested a figure at the lower end of that range. Indeed, Fortnum, Summerfield, Marshall, and Bamford (2001) suggested that "the yield from universal neonatal hearing screening will remain close to 1.06/1,000 live births" (p. 5).

Regardless of the prevalence of congenital hearing loss in the developed world, the prevalence of early childhood hearing loss (both congenital and acquired) in the developing world is likely to be higher—potentially much higher. This is partly because of the increased risk of preventable causes of infant hearing loss in developing countries such as meningitis, measles, mumps, and ototoxic drugs; and the impact of maternal infections such as rubella, cytomegalovirus (CMV), and syphilis. MacPherson and Swart (1997), as part of their review of childhood deafness in sub-Saharan Africa, concluded that there was a substantial likelihood of higher prevalence of hearing impairment in that region because of the presence of etiologies that are seldom found in developed countries—most notably, certain types of meningitis. Further, there is a likelihood of increased incidence of deafness associated with the poor maternal and child heath conditions that are linked to low socioeconomic status, the significant proportion of births occurring outside of hospitals,

and the lack of availability of effective postnatal care in many developing countries (Olusanya, Luxon, & Wirz, 2006b).

To the extent that prevalence has been reported in the literature, there are clear indications of higher rates of childhood deafness in the developing world. According to the India Human Development Report 1999 (cited by Kundu, 2000), the prevalence of hearing impairment in the West Bengal region of India is greater than 11 per 1,000 children aged between 0 and 4 years. Two other studies conducted in the subcontinent of Asia examined all levels and types of hearing loss in samples of school-age children. Jacob, Rupa, Job, and Joseph (1997) reported prevalence rates of 11.9% for hearing loss in a sample of children in India and the research team of Elahi, Elahi, Elahi, and Elahi (1998) found that 7.9% of Pakistani children in their study had some level of hearing loss. Bu (2004) estimated that in China, a country with a mixed profile in terms of economic and human development indices, the rate of significant permanent childhood hearing loss is likely to be as high as 3 per 1,000 children born. In a country with annual births in excess of 20 million, that represents 60,000 children with hearing loss being born each year.

Incidences such as these reported are clearly significantly greater than the rates typically reported in developed countries. Smith, Bale, and White (2005) argued that, when all permanent congenital and early-onset hearing loss is considered (i.e., not just congenital hearing loss), the expected prevalence in the developed world is likely to be as high as 2 to 4 per 1,000. Given the circumstances of the developing world, Olusanya and Newton (2007) have speculated that the incidence of permanent congenital and early-onset hearing impairment in those countries will be no less than 6 per 1,000 live births.

Whatever the actual rate of hearing loss in the developing world may be, the available evidence supports the conclusion that it will be substantially higher than that found in the developed world. Given this conclusion and the increasing evidence that earlier identification of hearing loss is associated with significantly improved developmental outcomes for DHH children, the question of whether there is a role for UNHS programs in developing countries is clearly a relevant one. However, as noted by Swanepoel (2005), the problems associated with effectively identifying and intervening in cases of hearing impairment in newborns and very young children in these countries at any stage—early or later—are likely to be exacerbated by the paucity of accessible health care, the lack of availability of specialized audiological services and, in many cases, the lack of capacity for treatment and educational systems to intervene in an effective manner. Nevertheless, the case for NHS and subsequent early intervention programs as important and potentially productive interventions warrants close examination and consideration.

Newborn Hearing Screening in Developing Countries: Issues and Potential Impediments

Economic and health care system barriers, combined with a range of cultural and other pragmatic issues (discussed later), are often cited as potential barriers to the implementation of NHS programs in developing countries (Olusanya, et al. 2004; Swanepoel, 2005). It has also been argued that, in countries where there are constant threats to infant health from factors such as famine or fatal disease, the focus should be on infant survival and not on broader aspects of well-being. Olusanya (2005) encapsulated this issue when she noted that "for governments and their donor partners already engrossed with prevailing fatal and communicable diseases, the persuasion is 'if it doesn't kill, it can wait'" (p. 737). Such arguments are perhaps understandable given the high rates of infant mortality in some developing countries (UNICEF, 2001). However, even in such circumstances, it may be argued that children require support to ensure their broader well-being and not just their survival. This argument is certainly not new.

The United Nations (UN) has long promoted the rights of all children to receive support for the advancement of their overall well-being and quality of life and not just their survival. Indeed, in 1959 the UN General Assembly expanded the Declaration of the Rights of the Child to define the rights of all children in all countries to include (a) opportunities and facilities to allow their physical, mental, moral, spiritual, and social development in a "healthy and normal manner" (Principle 2); (b) special care and protection for them and their mothers including "adequate prenatal and postnatal care" (Principle 4); and (c) such "special treatment, education, and care" as may be occasioned by disability (Principle 5) (United Nations General Assembly, 1959). In this context, the issues and the associated potential impediments pertaining to the implementation of UNHS and early intervention programs in developing countries warrant close consideration.

Targeted Versus Universal Newborn Hearing Screening

A primary issue in considering the case for NHS programs in developing countries is the question of whether any such program should aim to be universal—a more complex and potentially more expensive option—or follow a targeted screening approach based on the presence of risk factors in newborns. As a precursor to this discussion, it should be recognized that the success of any screening program in the developing world will depend upon, not only the ability to adequately screen the target population, but also the ability to provide efficient and effective follow-up diagnostic hearing assessments and subsequent intervention services for those infants who are referred from screening programs.

In regard to targeted screening, the risk factors for hearing loss in newborns are well documented and include, among others, family history of deafness; in utero infections such as CMV, rubella, syphilis, and toxoplasmosis; craniofacial abnormalities; physical characteristics associated with certain syndromes (e.g., the white forelock of Waardenburg syndrome); postnatal infections such as bacterial or viral meningitis; and head trauma (for a complete list see, for example, JCIH, 2007, p. 921). According to various reports from developed countries, 45%–50% of infants with significant hearing loss may be identified by testing only those infants for whom such risk factors are reported by parents, observed by health care personnel, or detected by specific procedures at or soon after birth (Davis, Bamford, Wilson, Ramkalawan, Forshaw, & Wright, 1997). Only a small percentage of all newborns have one or more of these recognized risk factors (for a list and review of the nongenetic causes of hearing loss see Roizen, 2003).

In contrast with UNHS programs, in which all newborns are screened, the number needed to be screened to identify a child with permanent congenital hearing loss through TNHS is substantially lower, as is the number of false-positive screening test results (Nelson, Bougatsos, & Nygren, 2008). In developed countries, it has been suggested that such an approach may result in a substantial reduction in cost (both overall and per baby identified with hearing loss) when compared with UNHS (Keren, Helfand, Homer, McPhillips, & Lieu, 2002). In developing countries, where children are more likely to have risk factors for deafness, however, the relative merits of UNHS versus TNHS cannot be assumed without further investigation.

Nevertheless, some developing countries have established TNHS programs, for example, Costa Rica (Madriz, 2000).

The most obvious shortcoming of a risk factor–based strategy is that more than half of infants with significant congenital hearing loss may not be identified early by such an approach (Project HIEDI, 2004; Thompson, McPhillips, Davis, Lieu, Homer, & Helfand, 2001). Many of the causes of hearing loss (particularly nonsyndromic genetic causes) simply do not have associated and easily identifiable risk factors. Further, in countries where the overall standard of health care is not high, there may be some difficulty in identifying the presence of risk factors because there may not be routine testing for neonatal conditions that are part of the set of risk factors for congenital hearing loss. In most developed countries many at-risk infants are captured in neonatal intensive care units (NICUs), in maternity wards where at-risk "registers" are in place, or at community health care check-ups where skilled child health professionals can check for the presence of a range of factors. These types of facilities are often not part of the health systems in developing countries. In fact, in developing countries, many babies will not be born in a hospital setting and consequently the opportunity for capturing this group may be lost (Olusanya, Luxon, & Wirz, 2005).

In developed countries, a consensus exists about the appropriateness and importance of universal screening. The consensus view is that *all* infants should be screened for hearing impairment at no later than 1 month of age (Centers for Disease Control and Prevention, 2008; Grandori & Lutman, 1998; JCIH, 2007). That standard remains to be achieved in many parts of the world where programs are still to be implemented or have yet to achieve full coverage because of staged development—as is the case in Australia for example (Leigh, 2006b). In some developed countries, UNHS programs were preceded by TNHS programs (e.g., as in parts of Australia and the United Kingdom). This type of staged approach may be a useful strategy for the introduction of screening in developing countries. Certainly, as noted earlier, targeted screening can be implemented at a much reduced cost. This must be balanced against the high proportion of children with hearing loss who will not be identified until a much older age. Clearly, the costs and benefits of the alternative approaches to screening need to be carefully evaluated in the context of any country considering these options.

Olusanya et al. (2004) suggested that, to raise awareness of the benefits of any type of NHS, the implementation of small non–government-funded TNHS programs may establish the evidence base to give governments an indication of the feasibility and benefits of broader programs in a particular country. Further, TNHS and/or pilot UNHS programs may allow a country's health system a chance to experiment with the many methodologies that can be used in a screening program. This was certainly the experience in Australia, where various state jurisdictions either implemented pilot programs or staged the introduction of programs en route to establishing universal programs (Leigh, 2006a).

Given the implementation costs associated with either form of NHS program in a developing country, other approaches to screening warrant some examination. Parent assessment, as recorded by questionnaires or interviews, is an example of a variation on the targeted screening model. This method of screening is relatively inexpensive and easy to implement. However, some previous research into the use of this approach (Watkin, Baldwin, & Laoide, 1990) found that, when deliberately questioned about their child's hearing, parents only correctly identified about 25% of infants with hearing impairment (although this figure rose to 50% for children with severe to profound hearing loss). Such an approach depends, in part, upon the base-level awareness of hearing loss and its sequelae among parents. Olusanya, Luxon, and Wirz (2006a) reported that Nigerian mothers had good overall levels of knowledge about causes of infant hearing loss and relatively high levels of awareness and acceptance of both early detection and early intervention. Given the potential for low-level literacy skills in many developing countries, however, difficulties with this approach may arise if questions are to be posed to parents in a written form, or if there is reliance on other written information being accessed by families.

Another possible variation to either approach to screening (UNHS or TNHS) includes the use of less sophisticated and less expensive screening test procedures. One such method is the use of noise-makers (often know as behavioral observation audiometry or distraction testing). This technique has a long history (Stewart-Brown & Haslum, 1987) and is still used in developed countries in clinical settings for some purposes (although mainly as an addendum to more precise methodologies). Traditionally, screening of a neonate's hearing using distraction testing was thought to be able to fairly reliably identify severe to profound hearing loss, but not perhaps mild or moderate hearing loss. Certainly it has been suggested that the sensitivity and specificity of such tests are insufficient for the detection of all levels of hearing impairment (Russ et al., 2005). This technique requires considerable skill and training to be used effectively. Nevertheless, this sort of testing can be performed relatively quickly and with only minor equipment costs, and warrants consideration in developing country contexts, even if only as an interim component in a staged development of a screening program.

Although strategies other than UNHS may be considered as interim approaches to detecting significant childhood hearing impairment in some developing countries, the longer-term goal of universal early detection remains an important consideration. If universal screening programs are to be implemented in a developing country, however, there remain other issues and potential impediments to be addressed.

Delivery Platform for Newborn Hearing Screening Programs

A core issue in the implementation of any program of UNHS is the attainment of universal coverage. To be considered successful, a UNHS program must capture all or a very large proportion of the newborns in a designated region. The Joint Committee on Infant Hearing (2007) suggested that, for a program to be considered universal, coverage of no less than 95% of a birth cohort should be achieved. Further, it is argued that this level should be achieved within 6 months of program initiation. In many cases in developed countries, programs have failed to reach this and/or other benchmarks for program implementation (Danahauer et al., 2006; Lin, Huang, Lin, Lin, & Wu, 2004; Mukari, Tan, & Abdullah, 2006). Indeed, the extent to which benchmarks are reached varies across countries and regions of countries that have UNHS programs. The practical hurdles to achieving these benchmarks are likely to be significantly higher in developing countries.

In most developed countries, a large percentage of births occur in hospital maternity wards. Hospitals, therefore, provide an excellent platform from which hearing screening programs can be implemented. Basing a UNHS program in maternity wards means that infants can be screened before discharge from hospital and there is, therefore, no need to persuade parents to bring a healthy baby back to a clinical setting for testing for an unobservable condition. Capture rates for "return to screening" type programs

are low in developed countries but, as noted by Olusanya et al. (2004), they are likely to be even lower in countries where it may be socially or culturally inappropriate to take children back to hospitals or clinics, which are seen as being exclusively for people who are sick.

In many regions of developed countries, a large percentage of newborns have routine and freely available contact with community health clinics very early in life. In many of these circumstances, community-based or joint hospital–community UNHS programs have been successfully established (e.g., as in the United Kingdom, Young & Andrews, 2001). In many developing countries, where neither hospital births nor community health clinic checks are the norm, alternative platforms from which a UNHS program can operate must be investigated.

Olusanya et al. (2004), among others, has suggested the use of preexisting health care delivery platforms, such as immunization clinics, for UNHS programs in developing countries. A South African study (Swanepoel, Hugo, & Louw, 2006) attempted just such a strategy. The researchers used a convenience sample of two representative clinics to implement screening for all children attending immunization. They were able to screen 93% of the children in those designated clinics. Other platforms for capturing a large percentage of newborns may be country-specific. Some regions may have to contend with newborn populations living in remote, difficult to reach areas. To obtain a good capture rate (and for obvious reasons of equity), a UNHS program must provide access to screening for all children. If equity of access to the program is to be achieved, screening must be provided without additional expense to these families and in a timely fashion. Some of these problems may be resolved if the local health care workers in remote regions can be involved in the UNHS program. However, the supply and support of such workers may be problematic. In developing regions where travelling for appointments may be physically or financially impractical, consideration should be given to including a provision for travel and accommodation assistance in the budget for the screening program, to increase the follow-up rate. Similarly, the provision of audiological services using remote access technologies (including via the cellular telecommunications network) may play a role in improving the potential for implementing UNHS programs in remote regions (Choi, Lee, Park, Oh, & Park, 2007; Givens, Blanavonich, Murphy, Simmons, Blach, & Elangovan, 2003; Krumm, Ribera, & Schmiedge, 2005).

Specificity of Screening: The Issue of False Positives

This chapter does not purport to address the myriad issues relating to the appropriate choice of test protocol or equipment for hearing screening programs in developing countries. However, as in developed countries, any UNHS program in the developing world must seek to ensure the lowest possible rate of false-positive screening results. This is imperative for two reasons: minimization of parental anxiety and reduction of overall costs. The first issue is not straightforward. Certainly, there is evidence that families of children who are incorrectly identified as having certain adverse conditions (other than hearing loss) through newborn screening may experience unnecessary anxiety (Marteau, 1989; Sorenson, Levy, Mangione & Sepe 1984; Chapter 16, this volume). Other researchers, however, have argued that any increase in maternal anxiety caused by a false-positive result on a hearing screening test is minimal (Clemens, Davis, & Bailey, 2000). Nevertheless, there are obvious ethical reasons for seeking to minimize the potential emotional impact on some parents of having to deal unnecessarily with the prospect of their child having a significant hearing loss. Further, it must be recognized that parental anxiety in both true- and false-positive cases may be increased if diagnostic testing and remediation are not available to families in a timely fashion. The potential for latency between referral from screening and the availability of full audiological assessment is significant in developing countries where infrastructure for testing is likely to be limited. The need for timely diagnosis is also important from a practical perspective. Diagnostic hearing assessment is difficult in infants between the ages of 3 and 6 months, and often requires sedation or anesthesia, facilities for which may be difficult to organize in developing countries. This potential must be considered in the development of any such programs.

The economic impetus for reducing the false-positive rate of a screening procedure (i.e., increasing the specificity of the screen) is also apparent. Because of the cost associated with conducting full audiological assessments, it is important that the number of needless assessments be kept to a minimum. Even with an acceptable specificity, the increased demand for full audiological assessments that is occasioned by a UNHS program is likely to draw heavily on both the economic and personnel resources of countries with already limited audiological infrastructure. In particular, there is likely to be a shortage of well-trained staff, particularly audiologists,

who are notably in short supply in developing countries (World Health Organization, 1998). In China, for example, where there are now UNHS programs in the majority of the provinces, the availability of full diagnostic assessment of hearing is limited by the lack of availability of qualified audiologists (Bu, 2004). According to Bu there are few, if any, audiologists in maternity and infant hospitals in China, even in the larger cities. Under such circumstances, the diagnostic assessment is typically left to other health care providers who may not be appropriately equipped or prepared to perform such tasks. Carried out effectively, full diagnostic assessment of hearing in infants requires highly skilled specialized staff and the availability of highly specialized equipment, such as diagnostic auditory brainstem response, otoacoustic emission, and tympanometric devices. These potential impediments to program success in many developing countries need to be addressed at the level of personnel training and development well before other aspects of program development can be considered.

Any discussion regarding the potential for false-positive results from a NHS program must consider the screening equipment and protocols that are likely to be employed in such a program. As noted by the Joint Committee on Infant Hearing (2007), the desirable standard for equipment is a physiological measure—either automated auditory brainstem response (AABR) or screening otoacoustic emission (OAE) testing. Each approach has benefits and limitations (for a more complete treatment of these issues of these alternatives see Leigh, Taljaard, & Poulakis, in press). Screening OAE tests are usually the cheaper of the two, and are also slightly quicker to administer. Otoacoustic emission (OAE) technology, however, offers a lower specificity and will not be sensitive to children with "neural" hearing losses such as auditory neuropathy/dyssynchrony (AN/AD) (Leigh et al., in press). This is a significant issue because, as suggested by Ngo, Tan, Balakrishnan, Lim, and Lazaroo (2006), such conditions may account for between 11% and 15% of the population of children with significant levels of hearing loss.

The use of OAEs is also negatively impacted by transient middle ear conditions such as otitis media, which may prevent a response being recorded. Notably, such conditions are likely to have higher prevalence in many developing countries. In comparison, AABR technology is relatively more expensive to acquire and has higher levels of expenditure associated with consumables. Also, as a screening procedure, AABR is slightly slower and, because a click stimulus is used, may miss children with certain audiometric configurations to their hearing loss. Automated auditory brainstem response does, however, have a higher specificity and will not report a false-negative result in the presence of AN/AD (Meier, Narabayashi, Probst, & Schmuziger, 2004; Oates & Stapells, 1998; Thompson et al., 2001).

Regardless of the equipment/approach chosen, most screening protocols call for a repeat screen when a positive indication of hearing loss is recorded on the first screen. This strategy leads to decreased rates of referral to follow-up audiological evaluation and the associated benefits in efficiency and cost-effectiveness (JCIH, 2007). This is particularly the case in regard to OAE technology. Spivak and Sokol (2004) demonstrated that employing a second OAE screen decreased the rate of referral from 22% to 2.9% for 726 children in a well-baby nursery. A variation on this multistage/single-technology protocol has been the use of a multistage protocol using both technologies. This approach was initially recommended by the National Institutes of Health (1993) and has been adopted by many screening programs internationally. In this scenario, OAE screening is typically conducted first, taking advantage of both the low cost as an inpatient procedure and the relative time efficiency (Spivak, 2007); AABR is then used as a repeat or "second-stage" screen.

Overall, there are compelling reasons to argue for the application of the more expensive technology of AABR in any situation, including in developing countries. The lower referral rate offered by AABR leads to fewer children being referred for diagnostic audiological assessment, which may reduce the overall cost of the program. The up-front screening costs from each approach need to be balanced against the costs associated with changes in referral rates. As already noted, in many developing country regions, it is difficult to provide full audiological assessments. In such contexts, minimizing referral to this process would seem to be imperative. Furthermore, in countries where there may be heightened culturally based anxiety associated with the identification of hearing loss, there is also the potential to alleviate parental concerns through lower rates of referral to follow-up audiology. For these reasons, consideration should be given to the use of a dual AABR protocol (AABR for screen and rescreen) to keep the false-positive results to a minimum (Clemens & Davis, 2001).

Loss to Follow-up

Obtaining a good coverage rate for screening and diagnostic assessment is of limited benefit in achieving the objectives of NHS (i.e., engagement of children with early intervention at the earliest possible stage) if there is significant loss to follow-up. Children can be lost to follow-up during the initial screening process, at the diagnostic assessment stage, or even post diagnosis but prior to remediation. Obviously, losses at any of these stages will lead to poorer outcomes for NHS programs. Danahauer et al. (2006) reviewed the data on NHS programs in the United States and reported that, although programs had very good rates of population coverage (>90%) for screening over the first 5 years of implementation, almost 45% of children who gained a positive (referral) result at screening were lost to follow-up before receiving their full diagnostic assessment. Over all jurisdictions in the United States, the follow-up rate has since improved but, on average, still does not meet JCIH benchmarks (Danahauer et al., 2006). Clearly, where children do not receive full audiological assessment to confirm and describe their hearing loss, they will likely not become engaged with the appropriate early intervention (audiological, medical, or educational).

Reducing loss to follow-up is a significant challenge to the effective implementation of NHS programs. As already discussed, the availability of infrastructure to provide audiological follow-up is a known issue of concern in many developing countries (see Bu, 2004, for example). This suggests that even greater difficulties are likely to be experienced in maintaining follow-up at acceptable levels in these contexts. A program conducted in Malaysia and described by Mukari et al. (2006), for example, showed target population coverage of 85%, but more than 43% of children who were referred to diagnostic audiology failed to return for follow-up. Clearly, such results undermine the effectiveness of screening programs. The case of a UNHS trial in South Africa offers another illustration of potential difficulties (Swanepoel et al., 2006). In this situation, a screening program was operated in the context of immunization centers using OAE screening equipment and tympanometry. Loss to follow-up proved to be a significant issue, with only 40% of children returning for a second screening, and only 11% for diagnostic assessment. Although these results must be interpreted with caution due to the small sample size, they serve to illustrate the problems facing hearing screening in developing regions.

Further analysis of the South African program sheds light on some other potential issues for developing countries. Swanepoel et al. (2006) reported that their program attained a reasonable coverage rate (>93%) but with a very high rate of positive (referral) results of 11%—a rate much higher than the JCIH benchmark of less than 4%. In this program, the target condition was unilateral or bilateral hearing loss. If the protocols employed had targeted only bilateral positive responses, then the referral rate would have dropped below the Joint Committee on Infant Hearing benchmark. This would have resulted in a greatly reduced cost of the screening program. For developing countries where resources (both economic and personnel) are scarce, targeting only bilateral hearing impairment may be a more efficient strategy. It should be noted, however, that a small but significant proportion of children referred for unilateral loss may be identified subsequently as having a bilateral hearing loss (Neault, 2005). These infants fall into two groups: (a) those with actual bilateral hearing loss at the time of screening, and (b) those with unilateral loss at the time of the screening but who subsequently develop a bilateral loss. The latter group may include children with a range of etiologies including hereditary, CMV, enlarged vestibular aqueduct, and other unknown factors (Neault, 2005). This issue requires further attention and a careful analysis of patterns of hearing loss progression in any programs that may be implemented on a bilateral referral basis only.

It is worth noting that, even with the level of public and private support available for UNHS programs in the United States, many are still far from attaining JCIH benchmarks for rate of follow-up to intervention (Danhauer et al., 2006). In developing countries, where fewer resources are available and known impediments exist to the provision of audiological follow-up, the achievement of these same benchmarks is likely to be even more difficult. Nevertheless, the aim for any program of NHS must be to attain levels of follow-up at least in accordance with the benchmarks set by the JCIH (2007) that 90% of children who are referred from screening should receive full audiological assessment by 3 months of age.

Cultural Beliefs and Stigma

In some developing countries, local customs and cultural beliefs may present another challenge to the establishment of NHS programs and/or the implementation of early intervention programs for children with hearing loss. The stigma attached to the presence of any disability, including hearing loss, may prevent parents from participating in the diagnostic process, attending follow-up intervention once they have been informed that their child has a

hearing loss, or accepting the use of hearing aids/cochlear implants (Olusanya et al., 2004). Such concerns may stem from a range of reasons, including the fact that, in some cultures (most notably some sub-Saharan African cultures), people may anthropomorphize the causes of conditions such as hearing loss with explanations being sought in the realm of the supernatural and relief from the condition being sought through alternative means such as traditional healers (de Andrade & Ross, 2005). Here again, however, the range of possible responses is considerable.

A survey conducted by Olusanya et al. (2006a) in Nigeria suggested that mothers had a predominantly positive view of neonatal hearing screening and of hearing aid use. They also found that efforts to promote the understanding of the benefits of early intervention may help alleviate some of the problems associated with stigma and alternative beliefs about causation and appropriate treatments. The most significant imperative to be drawn from consideration of these issues is the need to employ highly culturally sensitive practices in all developing countries, including, if necessary, collaboration between traditional health practitioners or religious leaders and professionals such as audiologists, teachers/therapists, and medical practitioners (de Andrade & Ross, 2005; MacPherson & Swart, 1997). These efforts may need to be directed not just at parents but also at local physicians and health care workers.

Availability and Quality of Subsequent Intervention

From a developed country perspective, the question of whether to introduce a program of NHS must be considered in the context of the availability of effective infrastructure for dealing with the consequences of the identification of permanent hearing loss. Indeed, ethical practice dictates that undertaking screening presupposes the availability of effective interventions to respond to the target condition once it is identified (Mant & Fowler, 1990; Wilson & Jungner, 1968). In the developed world, such interventions have been well established and available for a long time, albeit that prior to NHS programs they were typically designed for slightly older children (i.e., usually in the 2–5 year age range). Such interventions are typically multidisciplinary in nature, involving audiologists, speech and language pathologists, teachers of the deaf, other therapists and, increasingly, cochlear implant surgeons and associated medical personnel. Such personnel are highly trained and well remunerated. To varying extents, they operate in an environment in which there is an expectation of the availability of advanced technology for both assessment and intervention, including sophisticated medical technology, audiological test equipment, hearing aids, and cochlear implants. Depending on the country, the cost of provision of these interventions may be socialized or, at least, publicly subsidized. Most commonly, the educational component of intervention will be funded by the government.

In contrast, the context for the management of early childhood hearing impairment in the developing world is typically a very different one, although circumstances do vary greatly. To the extent that they exist at all, programs of intervention for children identified with hearing loss are often restricted to school-aged children (i.e., commencing at 5 or 6 years of age) and most commonly are delivered through traditional schools for the deaf. Early intervention programs, where they exist, are frequently of limited scope and without the breadth of multidisciplinary input identified earlier. Audiology, for example, is a relatively new profession in many developing countries, and audiologists are often not readily available in those contexts—particularly in parts of Asia (Bu, 2004, Mukari et al., 2006; Smith, 2003; World Health Organization, 1998). Similarly, there is frequently a lack of the audiological technology that characterizes programs in developed countries (Kumar, 2001). The World Health Organization (WHO) has estimated that, across the age range, approximately 30 million hearing aids are required in developing countries each year but that the current supply is less than 3% of that figure (Smith, 2003). The availability of hearing aids at an affordable cost is unquestionably a significant impediment to effective early intervention in many developing countries (Mukari, et al. 2006).

The WHO (2004) has taken initiatives in some developing countries to promote the development of audiological and associated support services and the provision of low-cost hearing aids. This has involved collaboration with hearing aid manufacturers to provide less sophisticated and more easily affordable devices that are easier to maintain. Increasingly, there is also support from the governments of some developing countries for the provision of hearing devices. Such socialized provision of audiological care and hearing devices is likely to increase in developing countries and/or to become part of public/private partnership arrangements that involve substantial input from charitable sources. In 2006, a private benefactor, Yungching Wang, the founder

and chairman of Taiwan's Formosa Plastics Corporation, donated 15,000 cochlear implant devices with associated financial support for the cost of the surgery for the benefit of deaf children in China (Zeng, 2007). Such charitable support arrangements may influence the pattern of provision of intervention services for children with hearing loss in other countries also.

As noted at the outset of this section, it is not ethically defensible to systematically seek to identify the presence of hearing loss through screening without ensuring that adequate services are available to provide intervention for children who are identified and their families. Equally, however, a case could be made that it is unethical to deny development of a screening program because of a lack of intervention/habilitation services. Clearly, the imperative for any country—developed or developing—should be to systematically develop *both* the availability of screening programs and the services required for follow-up intervention.

Economic Barriers

The issue of health care priority setting in developing countries is a major area of debate (Evans, Adam, Tan-Torres Edejer, Lim, Cassels, & Evans, 2005). As detailed earlier, the benefits of a successfully implemented NHS program are likely to far outweigh any negative outcomes associated with the program (e.g., false-positive results). However, given the limited health care resources available to developing countries, the benefits of any program should be considered in the context of those benefits that could be achieved if the resources were allocated to an alternative use (i.e., the benefits that are being foregone). To achieve the greatest benefit to society, the costs and benefits of alternative health care resource allocation need to be considered (McGuire, 2001). If this is not done, the health improvements achieved by funded programs may come at the cost of greater improvements foregone by those programs left unfunded (McGuire, 2001).

In developed countries, several cost-effectiveness analyses of UNHS have been conducted (Grein, Lemons, & Weiner, 2001; Kemper & Downs, 2000; Keren et al., 2002; Kezirian, White, Yueh, & Sullivan, 2001; Maxon, White, Behrens, & Vohr, 1995; Turner, 1991, 1992a, 1992b). Keren et al. (2002) concluded that, considering the long-term benefits of UNHS, such programs may be cost saving when compared to either targeted (high risk) or no-screen options. They found that the cost savings associated with UNHS programs came primarily from long-term outcomes, such as increased productivity. It does not necessarily follow, however, that these results can be generalized to developing countries (Drummond & Pang, 2001). For instance, the costs incurred and those avoided are likely to be substantially different for developing countries. In many low-income countries, it may be that competing health care priorities provide greater benefit to society at lower costs. To put this issue in context, Mencher and DeVoe (2001) noted that the cost of a single piece of equipment capable of both AABR and OAE screening (at that time approximately US$ 18,000) was less than half the Gross National Product (GNP) share of a single citizen of the United States. In contrast, the cost of such a piece of equipment was more than 20 times the GNP share of a single citizen in Nigeria. In that country, with approximately 6 million births per year, the costs associated with providing just the equipment for a viable UNHS program could be prohibitive. The additional recurrent costs of staffing and consumable materials, as well as the cost of follow-up audiology and earlier provision of rehabilitation/education services could make the introduction of NHS challenging. However, in middle-income countries, particularly those with existing health care infrastructure to allow appropriate follow-up, hearing screening is more likely to represent value for money.

In any country in which it is to be introduced, the impact of NHS—in terms of both costs and benefits—will need to be carefully considered. Some have argued that cost-effectiveness considerations may be ethically inappropriate when the alternative is not to screen (Olusanya et al., 2006b). However, this argument could be made for an almost inexhaustible number of health care interventions that would ideally be implemented in developing countries. When resources are limited, not all interventions can be funded. It would seem ethical to try to do the most "good" with whatever resources are available. Failure to at least consider both the costs and benefits of health spending alternatives is to abandon this aim.

Having noted the importance of cost-effectiveness considerations, such considerations should be just one part of the decision-making process and should be used in conjunction with all the available evidence. Nevertheless, the lack of cost-effectiveness information for developing countries in the existing literature is a major obstacle to effective decision making. Research initiated as part of the WHO Millennium Development Goals has begun to fill this gap, by developing standardized methods to evaluate the cost effectiveness of interventions for different regions (Adam, Lim, Mehta, Bhutta, Fogstad, & Mathai, 2005). This type of systematic approach, which can assess the interactions between interventions, can provide useful guidance to decision makers (Evans et al., 2005), but many interventions have yet to be considered. Given the burden of childhood hearing loss in the developing world (Olusanya & Newton, 2007), providing appropriate cost-effectiveness information on UHS programs in developing countries should be seen as a research priority.

The consideration of NHS programs is likely to involve a lengthy deliberative process in the case of each different developing country. Clearly, some economic realities and challenges must be recognized, both in advocating for NHS and in any attempt to introduce such programs on a large scale. The desirability of the early identification of hearing loss should not be abandoned; however, this aspiration needs to be considered in the broader context of trying to achieve the greatest reduction in childhood morbidity and mortality.

Summary and Conclusions

Without specialized intervention, DHH children will experience significant delay or disruption to the development of their language and communication abilities, their social and emotional development and, ultimately, their educational achievement and life options. Preeminent among the interventions that are known to ameliorate these effects are (a) the earliest possible identification of hearing loss through NHS, and (b) access to quality programs of early intervention aimed at ensuring early childhood development across a range of domains.

This chapter has identified a broad range of the issues that need to be addressed if earlier identification of hearing loss and early intervention for DHH children is to be secured as an outcome in developing countries. These issues include (a) the question of whether to screen all newborns or to employ a targeted approach of seeking only those children with known risk factors for hearing loss, (b) which delivery platform to use for screening programs (e.g., hospital-based versus community-based screening), (c) the need to ensure a low rate of false-positive screening results, (d) the requirement for appropriate audiological and educational follow-up after screening, (e) the need to accommodate or ameliorate the impacts of stigmatizing or action-limiting cultural beliefs and practices, (f) the need to ensure the subsequent provision of adequate services for early intervention and ongoing education, and

(g) the obvious question of economic affordability and sustainability of expensive screening programs in very poor countries.

One of the principal conclusions to be drawn from this review is that there is a long way to go to achieve a more just distribution of such services to children in developing countries. Given the potential for increased rates of hearing loss in developing countries, there has been some suggestion that the principal response should be to focus resources on the primary prevention of hearing loss in those situations (Smith, 2003). Primary prevention is clearly a worthy aim but, as noted by Olusanya et al. (2006b), "health care services in many of these countries are unlikely to develop rapidly to levels that will markedly curtail the incidence of congenital and early-onset hearing loss in the near future" (p. 590). The development and availability of secondary interventions, including NHS and early intervention programs, as described in this chapter, can therefore be seen as an important adjunct to primary prevention. The significant challenge remains how best to fund and manage the implementation of such initiatives.

Mechanisms for funding the introduction of services of the type and scale being discussed in this chapter in developing countries may include strategies such as (a) government funding and management, (b) private benefaction/charitable support, (c) private provision with user pays (i.e., nongovernment provision with user payment), and (d) funding and management by multinational nongovernment organizations (NGOs). Given the wide range of contexts that exist in the developing world, a case could be made for any or some combination of these mechanisms for funding of NHS initiatives. All are worthy of further examination (see Olusanya, 2007, for a more complete examination of some of these funding and management alternatives).

To conclude, it bears restatement that a successfully implemented NHS program stands to provide enormous benefit to DHH children and their families in developing countries. Such benefits will only accrue, however, if programs are well implemented and combined with adequate and effective follow-up. For the reasons noted, this will present a wide range of challenges, depending on particular national circumstances. The aspiration of providing NHS in developing counties must also be weighed carefully against the myriad other health care and human service priorities that developing countries face. As noted at the beginning of this chapter, the need for greater distributive justice in the provision of such services among the people of developing countries is clearly apparent—as is the need to find ways to fund and manage that provision.

[1] There is no single measure of what might be considered a "developing country." The International Monetary Fund's World Economic Outlook (IMF, 2008) divides the world into two major groups: 32 "Advanced Economies" and 152 "Emerging and Developing Economies." For the purposes of this discussion, this distinction is a useful one in that it groups countries according to their economic capacity to provide human services of the type being discussed here. Another indicator, the Human Development Index (HDI) combines measures of life expectancy, literacy level, educational attainment, and GDP per capita for countries worldwide. Using that index, the United Nations Development Program (UNDP) identifies countries as "Developed," "Developing," or "Underdeveloped." By either measure, the less-developed groupings (i.e., "Emerging and Developing Economies" or "Developing and Underdeveloped Countries") account for approximately 80% of the word's population and are the target of consideration in this chapter.

References

Adam, T., Lim, S. S., Mehta, S., Bhutta, Z. A., Fogstad, H., & Mathai, M. (2005). Achieving the millennium development goals for health: Cost effectiveness analysis of strategies for maternal and neonatal health in developing countries. *British Medical Journal, 331*, 1107–1110.

de Andrade, V., & Ross, E. (2005). Beliefs and practices of Black South African traditional healers regarding hearing impairment. *International Journal of Audiology, 44*(9), 489–499.

Bu, X. (2004, May). *Universal newborn hearing screening programs in China.* Paper presented at NHS 2004 International Conference on Newborn Screening, Diagnosis and Intervention, Milan, Italy.

Centers for Disease Control and Prevention. (2008). Early hearing detection &intervention (EHDI) program: Vision, mission, goals, program objectives and performance indicators. Retrieved August 25, 2008, from www.cdc.gov/ncbddd/ehdi/nationalgoals.htm

Ching, T. Y. C, Oong, R., & van Wanrooy, E. (2006). The ages of intervention in regions with and without universal newborn hearing screening and prevalence of childhood hearing impairment in Australia. *Australian and New Zealand Journal of Audiology, 28*(2), 137–150.

Choi, J. M., Lee, H. B., Park, C. S., Oh, S. H., & Park, K. S. (2007). PC based tele-audiometry. *Telemedicine and e-Health, 13*(5), 501–508.

Clemens, C. J., Davis, S. A., & Bailey, A. R. (2000). The false-positive in universal neonatal hearing screening. *Pediatrics, 106*(1): e7.

Clemens, C. J., & Davis, S. A. (2001). Minimizing false-positives in Universal Newborn Hearing Screening: A simple solution. *Pediatrics, 107*(3): e29.

Danahauer, J. L., Johnson, C. E., Finnegan, D., Lamb, M., Lopez, I. P., Meuel, C., et al. (2006). A national survey of pediatric otolaryngologists and early detection and intervention programs. *Journal of the American Academy of Audiology, 17*, 708–721.

Davis, A., Bamford, J., Wilson, I., Ramkalawan, T., Forshaw, M., & Wright, S. (1997). A critical review of the role of neonatal hearing screening in the detection of congenital hearing impairment. *Health Technology Assessment, 1*, 1–176.

Drummond, M. F., & Pang, F. (2001). Transferability of economic evaluation results. In M. F. Drummond & A. McGuire (Eds.), *Economic evaluation in health care: Merging theory with practice* (pp. 256–276). New York: Oxford University Press.

Durieux-Smith, A, Fitzpatrick, E, & Whittingham, J. (2008). Universal newborn hearing screening: A question of evidence. *International Journal of Audiology. 47*(1), 1–10.

Elahi, M. M., Elahi, F., Elahi, A., & Elahi, S. B. (1998). Paediatric hearing loss in rural Pakistan. *Journal of Otolaryngology, 27*(6), 348–353.

Evans, D. B., Adam, T., Tan-Torres Edejer, T., Lim, S. S., Cassels, A., & Evans, T. G. (2005). Achieving the millennium development goals for health: Time to reassess strategies for improving health in developing countries? *British Medical Journal, 331*, 1133–1136.

Fortnum, H. M., Summerfield, A. Q., Marshall, D. H., Davis, A. C., & Bamford, J. M. (2001). Prevalence of permanent childhood hearing impairment in the United Kingdom and implications for universal neonatal hearing screening: Questionnaire based ascertainment study. *British Medical Journal, 323*, 536–540.

Givens, G. D., Blanavonich, A., Murphy, T., Simmons, S., Blach, D., & Elangovan, S. (2003). Internet-based tele-audiometry study for the assessment of hearing: A pilot study. *Telemedicine and e-Health, 9*(4), 375–378.

Grandori, F., & Lutman, M. E. (1998). European consensus statement on neonatal hearing screening. *International Journal of Pediatric Otorhinolaryngology, 44*(3), 309–310.

Grein A. J., Lemons M., & Weiner G. M. (2001). What is the most cost effective strategy for implementing universal newborn hearing screening [abstr 1107]. *Pediatric Research, 49*, 195A.

Harrison, M., Roush, J., & Wallace, J. (2003). Trends in age of identification and intervention in infants with hearing loss. *Ear and Hearing, 24*(1), 89–95.

International Monetary Fund. (2008). World Economic and Financial Surveys: World Economic Outlook Database, April 2008 Edition. Retrieved September 1, 2008 http://www.imf.org/external/pubs/ft/weo/2008/01/weodata/groups.htm#oem

Jacob, A., Rupa, V., Job, A., & Joseph, A. (1997). Hearing impairment and otitis media in rural primary school in south India. *International Journal of Pediatric Otorhinolaryngology, 39*(2), 133–138.

Joint Committee on Infant Hearing. (2007). Year 2007 position statement: principles and guidelines for early hearing detection and intervention programs. *Pediatrics, 120*, 898–921.

Kemper, A. R., & Downs, S. M. (2000). A cost-effectiveness analysis of newborn hearing screening strategies. *Archives of Pediatric and Adolescent Medicine, 154*, 484–488.

Kennedy, C. R., McCann, D. C., Campbell, M. J., Law, C. M., Mullee, M., Petro, S., et al. (2006). Language ability after early detection of permanent childhood hearing impairment. *New England Journal of Medicine; 354*(20), 2131–2141.

Keren, R., Helfand, M., Homer, C., McPhillips, H., & Lieu, T. A. (2002). Projected cost-effectiveness of statewide universal newborn hearing screening. *Pediatrics, 110*, 855–864.

Kezirian, E. J., White, K. R., Yueh, B., & Sullivan, S.D. (2001). Cost and cost-effectiveness of universal screening for hearing loss in newborns. *Otolaryngology Head and Neck Surgery, 124*, 359–367.

Kral, A., & Tillein, J. (2006). Brain plasticity under cochlear implant stimulation. *Advances in Oto-Rhino-Laryngology. 64*, 89–108.

Krumm, M., Ribera, J., & Schmiedge, J. (2005). Using a telehealth medium for objective hearing testing: Implications for supporting rural universal newborn hearing screening programs. *Seminars in Hearing, 26*(1), 3–9.

Kumar, S. (2001) WHO tackles hearing disabilities in developing world, *Lancet, 358*, 219.

Kundu, C. L. (Ed.). (2000). *Status of disability in India – 2000.* New Delhi: Rehabilitation Council of India.

Leigh, G. (September 9, 2006a). *UNHS in Australia: We've come a long way!* Paper presented at 3rd Australasian Newborn Hearing Screening Conference, Melbourne, Australia.

Leigh, G. (2006b). UNHS in Australia: We've come a long way! *Audiology Now, 27*, 49–51.

Leigh, G., Taljaard, D., & Poulakis, Z. (in press). Newborn hearing screening. In C. Driscoll & B. McPherson (Eds.), *Newborn screening systems: The complete perspective.* San Diego: Plural Publishing.

Lin, C., Huang, C., Lin, C., Lin, Y., & Wu, J. (2004). Community-based newborn hearing screening program in Taiwan. *International Journal of Pediatric Otorhinolaryngology, 68*, 185–189.

MacPherson, B., & Swart, S. M. (1997). Childhood hearing loss in sub-Saharan Africa: A review and recommendations. *International Journal of Pediatric Otorhinolaryngology, 40*, 1–18.

McGuire, A. (2001). Theoretical concepts in the economic evaluation of health care. In M. F. Drummond & A. McGuire (Eds.), *Economic evaluation in health care: Merging theory with practice* (pp. 1–21). New York: Oxford University Press.

Madriz, J. (2000). Hearing impairment in Latin America: An inventory of limited options and resources. *Audiology, 39*, 212–220.

Mant, D., & Fowler, G. (1990). Mass screening: Theory and ethics. *British Medical Journal, 300*(6729), 916–8.

Marteau, T. M. (1989. Psychological costs of screening may sometimes be bad enough to undermine the benefits of screening. *British Medical Journal, 299*, 527.

Maxon, A. B., White, K. R., Behrens, T. R., & Vohr, B. R. (1995). Referral rates and cost efficiency in a universal newborn hearing screening program using transient evoked otoacoustic emissions. *Journal of the American Academy of Audiology, 6*, 271–277.

Meier, S., Narabayashi, O., Probst, R., & Schmuziger, N. (2004). Comparison of currently available devices designed for newborn hearing screening using automated auditory brainstem and/or otoacoustic emission measurements. *International Journal of Pediatric Otorhinolaryngology, 68*, 927–934.

Mencher, G. T, & De Voe, S. J. (2001). Universal newborn screening: A dream realized or nightmare in the making? *Scandinavian Audiology, 30*(Supplement 53), 15–21.

Moeller, M. P. (2000). Early intervention and language development in children who are deaf and hard of hearing. *Pediatrics, 106*, e43.

Mukari, S. Z., Tan, K. Y., & Abdullah, A. (2006). A pilot project on hospital–based universal hearing screening: Lessons learned. *International Journal of Pediatric Otorhinolaryngology, 70*, 843–851.

National Institutes of Health. (1993). Early identification of hearing impairment in infants and young children. *NIH Consensus Statement 1993 Mar 1–3, 11*(1), 1–24.

Neault, M. (2005) Progression from unilateral to bilateral loss. In Workshop proceedings: National workshop on mild and unilateral hearing loss. Retrieved November 20, 2008 from http://www.cdc.gov/ncbddd/ehdi/documents/unilateralhl/Mild_Uni_2005%20Workshop_Proceedings.pdf

Nelson, H. D., Bougatsos, C., & Nygren, P. (2008). Universal newborn hearing screening: Systematic review to update the 2001 US Preventive Services Task Force recommendation. *Pediatrics, 122* (1), e266–e276.

New South Wales Health Department. (2006). Ministerial standing committee on hearing annual report 2004–2005. Retrieved November 24, 2006 from http://www.health.nsw.gov.au/hearing/pdf/annual_report.pdf

Ngo, R. Y. S., Tan, H. K. K., Balakrishnan, A., Lim, S. B., & Lazaroo, D. T. (2006). Auditory neuropathy/auditory dys-synchrony detected by universal newborn hearing screening. *International Journal of Pediatric Otorhinolaryngology, 70,* 1299–1306.

Oates, P., & Stapells, D. R. (1998). Auditory brainstem response estimates of the pure tone audiogram: Current status. *Seminars in Hearing, 19*(1), 61-85.

Olusanya, B. O. (2001). Early detection of hearing impairment in a developing country: What options? *Audiology, 40,* 141–147.

Olusanya, B. O. (2005). Can the world's infants with hearing loss wait? *International Journal of Pediatric Otorhinolaryngology, 69,* 735–8.

Olusanya, B. O. (2007). Addressing the global neglect of childhood hearing impairment in developing countries. *PLoS Medicine, 4*(4), p. e74.

Olusanya, B. O., Luxon, L. M., & Wirz, S. L. (2004). Benefits and challenges of newborn hearing screening for developing countries. *International Journal of Pediatric Otorhinolaryngology, 68,* 287–305.

Olusanya, B. O., Luxon, L. M., and Wirz, S. L. (2005). Screening for early childhood hearing loss in Nigeria. *Journal of Medical Screening, 12,* 115–118.

Olusanya, B. O., Luxon, L. M., & Wirz, S. L. (2006a). Maternal views on infant hearing loss in a developing country. *International Journal of Pediatric Otorhinolaryngology, 70,* 619–623.

Olusanya, B. O., Luxon, L. M., & Wirz, S. L. (2006b). Ethical issues in screening for hearing impairment in newborns in developing countries. *British Medical Journal, 32,* 588–591.

Olusanya, B. O., & Newton, V. E. (2007). Global burden of childhood hearing impairment and disease control priorities. *The Lancet; 369,* 1314–1317.

Project HIEDI. (2004). *Improving outcomes for children with permanent congenital hearing impairment: The case for a national newborn hearing screening and early intervention programme for New Zealand.* Auckland: National Foundation for the Deaf.

Puig, T., Municio, A., Medà, C. (2005). Universal neonatal hearing screening versus selective screening as part of the management of childhood deafness. *Cochrane Database of Systematic Reviews 2005,* Issue 2. Art. No.: CD003731. DOI: 10.1002/14651858.CD003731.pub2.

Roizen, N. J. (2003). Non-genetic causes of hearing loss. *Mental Retardation and Developmental Disabilities Research Reviews, 9,* 120–127.

Ruben, R. J. (1997). A time frame of critical/sensitive periods of language development. *Acta Otolaryngologica, 117,* 202–205.

Ruben, R. J., & Rapin, I. (1980). Plasticity of the developing auditory system. *Annals of Otolaryngology, 89,* 303–311.

Russ, S. A., Poulakis, Z., Wake, M., Barker, M., Rickards, F., Jarman, F. C., et al. (2005). The distraction test: The last word? *Journal of Paediatrics and Child Health, 41,* 197–200.

Sharma, A., Dorman, M. F., & Spahr, A. J. (2002). A sensitive period for the development of the central auditory system in children with cochlear implants: Implications for age of implantation. *Ear and Hearing, 23,* 532–539.

Smith, A. (2003). Preventing deafness—an achievable challenge. The WHO perspective. *International Congress Series, 1240,* 183–91.

Smith, R.J., Bale, J. F., & White, K.R. (2005). Sensorineural hearing loss in children, *Lancet, 365,* 879–890.

Sorenson, J. R., Levy, H. L., Mangione, T. W., & Sepe, S. J. (1984). Parental response to repeat testing of infants with 'false-positive' results in a newborn screening program. *Pediatrics, 73*(2), 183–187.

Spivak, L. G. (2007). Neonatal hearing screening, follow up and diagnosis. In R. J. Roeser, M. Valente, & H. Hosford-Dunn (Eds.), *Audiology diagnosis,* 2nd edition (pp. 497–513). New York: Thieme.

Spivak, L. G., & Sokol, H. (May 2004). *Factors affecting effectiveness of newborn hearing screening protocols.* Paper presented at NHS 2004: International Conference on Newborn Screening, Diagnosis and Intervention, Milan, Italy.

Stewart-Brown, S., & Haslum, M. N. (1987). Screening for hearing loss in childhood: A study of national practice. *British Medical Journal, 294,* 1386–1388.

Swanepoel, D. C. D. (2005). Unpublished doctoral dissertation, University of Pretoria, South Africa.

Swanepoel, D., Hugo, R., & Louw, B. (2006). Infant hearing screening at immunization clinics in South Africa. *International Journal of Pediatric Otorhinolaryngology, 70,* 1241–1249.

Thompson, D. C., McPhillips, H., Davis, R. L., Lieu, T. A., Homer, C. J., & Helfand, M. (2001). Universal newborn hearing screening: Summary of evidence. *Journal of the American Medical Association, 286*(16), 2000–2010.

UNICEF. (2001). The state of the world's children: 2001. Retrieved September 30, 2008 from http://www.unicef.org/sowc01/toc.htm#

United Nations General Assembly. (1959). Declaration of the rights of the child: General Assembly Resolution 1386(XIV) of 20 November 1959. Retrieved September 15, 2008 from www.unhchr.ch/html/menu3/b/25.htmhttp://www.health.nsw.gov.au/hearing/pdf/annual_report.pdf

Uus, K., & Bamford, J. (2007). Effectiveness of population-based newborn hearing screening in England: Ages of intervention and profile of cases. *Pediatrics, 117*(5), e887–e893.

Turner, R. G. (1991). Modeling the cost and performance of early identification protocols. *Journal of the American Academy of Audiology, 2,* 195–205.

Turner, R. G. (1992a). Comparison of four hearing screening protocols. *Journal of the American Academy of Audiology, 3,* 200–207.

Turner, R. G. (1992b). Factors that determine the cost and performance of early identification protocols. *Journal of the American Academy of Audiology, 3,* 233–241.

Vohr, B. R., Carty, L. M., Moore, P. E., & Letourneau, K. (1998). The Rhode Island hearing assessment program: Experience with state-wide hearing screening (1993–1996). *The Journal of Pediatrics, 133,* 318–319.

Watkin, P. M., Baldwin, M., & Laoide, S. (1990). Parental suspicion & identification of hearing impairment. *Archives of Disorders in Childhood, 65,* 846–850.

Wilson, J. M. G., & Jungner, G. (1968). *Principles and practice of screening for disease: WHO Public Health Paper No. 3.* Geneva: World Health Organization.

World Health Organization. (1998). Report of the International Workshop on Primary Ear and Hearing Care, Co-sponsored by World Health Organization Africa Regional Office (AFRO), HQ and the University of Cape Town, South Africa (12–14 March 1998), WHO/PBD/PDH/00.10. Retrieved September 1, 2008 from http://whqlibdoc.who.int/HQ/2000/WHO_PBD_PDH_00.10.pdf

World Health Organization. (2004). *World Health Organization Prevention of Blindness and Deafness (PBD) guidelines for hearing aids and services for developing countries*, 2nd edition. Geneva: Author.

Yoshinaga-Itano, C. (2003). Early intervention after universal neonatal hearing screening: Impact on outcomes. *Mental Retardation and Developmental Disabilities Research Reviews*, 9, 252–266.

Yoshinaga-Itano, C., Sedey, A. L., Coulter, D. K., & Mehl, A. L. (1998). Language of early- and later-identified children with hearing loss. *Pediatrics, 102*, 1161–1171.

Yoshinaga-Itano, C., Coulter, D. K., & Thomson, V. (2001). Developmental outcomes of children with hearing loss born in Colorado hospitals with and without universal newborn hearing screening programs. *Seminars in Neonatology, 6*, 521–529.

Young, A., & Andrews, E. (2001). Parents' experience of universal neonatal hearing screening: A critical review of the literature and its implications for implementation of new UNHS programs. *Journal of Deaf Studies and Deaf Education, 6*, 149–160.

Zeng, F.-G. (2007). Cochlear implants: Why don't more people use them? *The Hearing Journal, 60* (3), 48–49.

Prelinguistic Vocalizations in Infants and Toddlers with Hearing Loss: Identifying and Stimulating Auditory-guided Speech Development

David J. Ertmer *and* Suneeti Nathani Iyer

Abstract

Many infants with hearing loss are identified during the first months of life through newborn hearing screening and follow-up diagnostics. These children are frequently fit with hearing aids before 3 months of age and those with severe-profound losses often receive cochlear implants soon after their first birthdays. To effectively serve this very young population, it is important to understand the prelinguistic phases of speech development and the effects of hearing loss and sensory aid use on this phenomenon. Prelinguistic vocal development is the process by which infants and toddlers produce utterances that are increasingly complex, phonetically diverse, and adult-like before saying words on a consistent basis. This chapter reviews research findings for typically developing infants and children with hearing loss, including those who receive cochlear implants at a young age. Differences between these two groups are examined to clarify the role of audition in facilitating vocal development. Vocalization types that provide evidence of advancement in vocal development and benefit from sensory aid use are identified. A clinically useful tool for evaluating the influence of hearing on speech development and a family-centered intervention strategy for stimulating vocal development are also presented.

Keywords: hearing loss, hearing impairment, speech development, infants, children, prelinguistic vocal development, cochlear implants

Families around the world are fascinated by the variety of sounds that infants and toddlers produce during the first 2 years of life. Granted, not all of these vocalizations are pleasant. Some, such as crying and fussing, cause adults to search out ways to soothe the child (and end the distressful clamor) as quickly as possible. Yet, many others evoke enjoyable interactions with caregivers. Oller (2000) describes these exchanges in his seminal account of the emergence of speech in infants:

> Babies cry and we react intuitively. Babies goo, and we smile, speaking in a special register that seems to be made precisely for talking to infants. Babies utter reduplicated babbling sounds, and we recognize those sounds as being nearly speech. The naturalness of these capabilities is comforting and fulfilling in ways that few aspects of life can be. (p. xvii)

As Oller's observations point out, prelinguistic vocalizations serve many important functions. Initially, they signal basic conditions such as hunger, discomfort, and contentment. Soon, however, vowel-like sounds and laughter begin to charm adults; promoting bonding, turn-taking, and joint attention—important building blocks for spoken language. And, as infants mature further, their vocalizations become increasingly similar to the speech patterns of the adults around them. These speech-like vocalizations are especially noteworthy because they demonstrate that children possess adequate hearing sensitivity and the auditory perceptual, cognitive, and speech–motor abilities necessary to become talkers.

The process by which children begin to produce increasingly complex, phonetically diverse, and speech-like utterances is known as "vocal development"

(Ertmer, Young, & Nathani, 2007). Researchers have characterized vocal development as a series of overlapping levels in which new kinds of vocalizations emerge and become more common over time (Koopmans-van Beinum & van der Stelt, 1986; Nathani, Ertmer, & Stark, 2006; Oller, 1980; Roug, Landberg, & Lundberg, 1989; Stark, 1980; see Vihman, 1996 for review). Advancements during this prelinguistic period provide a foundation for the development of meaningful speech (Vihman, Macken, Miller, Simmons, & Miller, 1985). Infants who have hearing loss, however, typically have deficits and delays during vocal development. These difficulties reflect an incomplete perception of the acoustic features of speech and place them at risk for not acquiring age-appropriate spoken language.

Newborn hearing screening has made it possible for children with moderate to profound hearing losses to be identified during the first month of life, fit with hearing aids soon after, and—if appropriate candidates—given cochlear implants between their first and second birthdays (or at even younger ages in some cases). As a result, many youngsters experience greatly improved access to speech models and auditory feedback at ages when basic spoken language skills are typically acquired. One of the first tasks that young sensory aid users face is to match the vocalizations that they produce to the speech models that they hear.

Early interventionists (EIs) such as teachers of children with hearing loss, audiologists, and speech-language pathologists, play a crucial role in providing auditory and speech stimulation for infants and toddlers who use hearing aids or cochlear implants. To be thorough, the initial phases of intervention must help infants and toddlers learn to detect, recognize, and comprehend environmental sounds and spoken language (Erber, 1982), *and* stimulate advancements in prelinguistic speech development (Ertmer, Young, Grohne, Mellon, Johnson, Corbett, & Saindon, 2002). This two-pronged focus ensures that children begin to associate speech sounds with the articulatory movements that produce them. Although auditory training has been a standard part of preprofessional education for many years, speech intervention for infants and toddlers has received much less attention, and has often promoted word production at the expense of earlier emerging, prelinguistic speech behaviors. Providing speech stimulation at the prelinguistic level requires knowledge of the typical patterns of vocal development, an understanding of the effects of hearing loss on vocalizations, and recognition of the kinds of utterances

that indicate that hearing has been used to modify speech. This chapter is intended to help EIs and others interested in the development of spoken language in children with hearing loss gain this knowledge and acquire new skills for assessing and stimulating early speech development.

Three main areas are addressed in the following sections. First, patterns of vocal development in children who have normal hearing are presented. This information provides an overview of the types of vocalizations that infants produce and the sequence in which they typically emerge. Next, the effects of moderate and severe-profound hearing losses on vocal development and the benefits of sensory aid use are considered. Based on recent research, this section highlights vocalization types that provide evidence of auditory-guided speech development. Finally, strategies for assessing and stimulating vocal development are described. Taken together, the information in this chapter can enable EIs to assist children in developing the vocalizations that are foundational for spoken language and captivating to caregivers around the world.

Typical Patterns of Vocal Development

At birth, babies cry. By 18 months of age, they say words and some, even sentences. How do children make so much progress in such a relatively short time? Researchers around the globe have arrived at remarkably similar conclusions regarding early speech development (Koopmans van Beinum & van der Stelt, 1986; Oller, 1980; Roug et al., 1989; Stark, 1980; Zlatin, 1975; see Vihman, 1996 for review). They have found that infants and toddlers appear to go through the same four to five developmental levels[1] before producing words and sentences. Each level is characterized by the acquisition of new developmental milestones. Following is a description of the various levels using the terminology and framework specified by the Stark Assessment of Early Vocal Development-Revised (SAEVD-R; Nathani et al., 2006). Readers are encouraged to visit www.vocaldevelopment.com to listen to audio examples of different vocalization types at each SAEVD-R level.

Levels of Vocal Development

According to the SAEVD-R, the first level of vocal development, *Reflexive[2] Vocalizations*, is evident in infants between birth and 2 months of age. Although most of the sounds produced at this level, such as crying and vegetative sounds (e.g., hiccups, coughs), are considered reflexive and not speech-like, one precursor of adult-like speech is commonly observed. *Quasi-resonant nuclei*[3] are primitive vowel-like sounds that are made with the vocal tract in an at-rest position. These sounds are typically characterized by acoustic energy in the lower frequencies, muffled resonance, nasality, and are perceived as brief "sighs" or "grunts." They may be produced singly or in a series. It should be noted that quasi-resonant nuclei may be punctuated by glottal stops or fricative-like sounds produced at the back of the throat.

The second level, *Control of Phonation*, emerges between 1 and 4 months of age, and is characterized by several speech-like sounds. More adult-like, but not fully mature vowel sounds, or *fully resonant nuclei*, emerge at this level. These vowel-like sounds are produced with a vocal tract that is postured (not at rest) and have acoustic energy across a wide range of frequencies; therefore, they sound much more adult-like than quasi-resonant nuclei (listen to audio examples at vocaldevelopment.com). They may have poor vocal quality (e.g., harshness), which makes them often difficult to recognize as specific adult vowels. Primitive consonant-like sounds and primitive consonant–vowel (C–V) combinations, especially consonants made at the back of the throat ("goos"; Oller, 1980, 2000), also emerge at this level. Examples of other consonant-like sounds produced at this level include raspberries, clicks, and trills. It should be noted that only supraglottal consonants (i.e., those articulated above the vocal folds) would be considered as "true" consonants; glottal sounds (e.g., /h/) would not be counted as consonants. Finally, families are often delighted as chuckling and laughter also emerge during this time.

The *Expansion* level emerges between 3 and 8 months of age. In this third level, vocalizations that are readily recognized as adult-like vowels are first produced. In addition, infants appear to explore the parameters of the vocal tract by producing high-pitched squeals. Squeals and vowel-like sounds may be produced with increased intensity and perceived as "shrieks" or "yells." This level is also characterized by the presence of *marginal babbling*. Marginal babbling refers to the production of a series of primitive consonant-like and vowel-like combinations. The formant transitions between the consonant-like and vowel-like sounds are considerably longer than in adult speech (often in excess of 120 ms), making the babble sound sloppy or slurred. These slow transitions distinguish marginal babbling from canonical babbling, which will be described in the next section.

The fourth SAEVD-R level, *Basic Canonical Syllables*, represents a major step in prelinguistic speech development. At this level, infants first produce adult-like syllables either singly or in groups. Canonical syllables are similar to marginal syllables in that they contain combinations of consonant-like and vowel-like elements (e.g., [ba], [di]). However, unlike marginal syllables, formant transitions between the consonant and vowel elements are rapid, leading to the perception of acceptably mature syllables. Canonical syllables typically emerge between 5 and 10 months of age. Oller et al. (Oller, Eilers, Basinger, Steffens, & Urbano, 1995) found that the age at the onset of *canonical babbling* is relatively consistent despite differences in gender, socioeconomic status, prematurity, and language background. Parents intuitively recognize the onset of these vocalizations and start responding to infants as if they were attempting to produce words. Some parents are even convinced that their children are actually saying words, such as "mama" (mommy) and "dada" (daddy), when they produce canonical syllables.

It should be noted that canonical syllable production can refer to both reduplicated babbling (e.g., [mamama]) in which the same consonants and vowels are repeated, and variegated babbling (e.g., [babida]) in which different consonants and vowels are produced). Although it was originally believed that reduplicated babbling emerged before variegated babbling (Oller, 1980; Stark, 1980), research by Mitchell and Kent (1990) and Smith, Brown-Sweeney, and Stoel-Gammon (1989) found an overlap in the onset of these types of babbling. Whispered vocalizations are also included under this level in the SAEVD-R; other researchers (e.g., Oller, 2000) include whispers in the earlier Expansion level.

The fifth level of the SAEVD-R, *Advanced Forms*, represents the highest level of prelinguistic vocal development. It is reached by infants sometime between 9 and 18 months of age and includes phonetically complex vocalizations, such as closed syllables (e.g., [din] for English-learning infants), diphthongs (e.g., [naI]), and canonical syllable strings produced with varied pitch and intonation (i.e., jargon). Whereas the first four levels are fairly universal, production characteristics of the fifth level may vary depending on the ambient language of the infant. Vihman (1993) observed that English-learning infants showed growth in the production of closed syllables as a function of age, but that infants learning French, Swedish, and Japanese did not show a similar pattern. This difference presumably occurred because closed syllables are relatively more common in English words than other languages. Similarly, whereas monosyllables (i.e., CV syllables) were predominant in early vocabularies of children learning English, German, and Dutch, disyllables (i.e., CVCV syllables) were prominent in children learning Spanish, Finnish, and Japanese. Bilingual children presented an even more complex picture depending on the languages being learned (Vihman & Croft, 2007). Thus, vocal development beyond the Basic Canonical Syllables level must be evaluated with reference to language spoken in the home.

Individual variability is also striking during the Advanced Forms level. This point was underscored in the classic investigation by Vihman et al. (1985). Although two girls in the study, Molly and Deborah, were matched for gender, socioeconomic status, and vocabulary size, Molly was clearly "systematic" (e.g., restricted consonantal repertoire) in her phonetic preferences, whereas Deborah was classified as "exploratory" (e.g., relatively large consonantal repertoire) in her productions. Therefore, individual differences also should be taken into account when evaluating the latter phases of vocal development.

Developmental Sequence of the Levels of Vocal Development

In addition to identifying the kinds of vocalizations that emerge at each level of vocal development, it is important to consider how children make progress toward becoming talkers. A recent cross-sectional study (Nathani et al., 2006) examined 30 typically developing infants, five each at 0–2, 3–5, 6–8, 9–12, 13–15, and 16–20 months of age. The findings indicated that infants younger than 9 months of age primarily produced vocalizations from Levels 1–3, whereas infants older than 9 months of age primarily produced vocalizations from Levels 3–5 (Figure 24.1). Level 1 vocalizations evidenced a sharp decrease to less than 10% of all vocalizations at 9 months of age and Level 2 vocalizations gradually decreased from 9 months onwards until they comprised less than 10% of all speech-like vocalizations by 20 months of age. Level 3 vocalizations were the most prominent form of vocalizations from 3–15 months of age. Level 4 vocalizations sharply increased at 9–12 months of age, and Level 5 vocalizations were produced in substantial quantities; that is, greater than 10% of all speech-like vocalizations, only by infants 16–20 months of age. Taken together, these data show trends toward the elimination of less speech-like vocalizations as increasingly adult-like and phonetically complex vocalizations become the dominant form of production.

In addition, Nathani et al. (2006) noted that the proportion of non–speech-like vocalizations (e.g., crying, vegetative sounds) to speech-like vocalizations (e.g., quasi-resonant nuclei, canonical syllables)

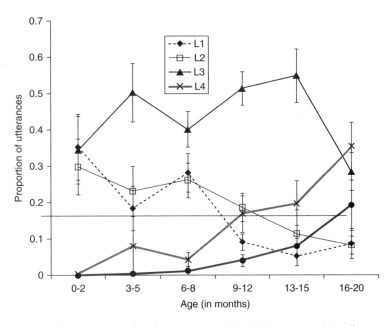

Fig. 24.1 Mean proportion (and standard error) of vocalizations across each level and age group. Originally appeared in Nathani, S., Ertmer, D. J., & Stark, R. E., Assessing vocal development in infants and toddlers, *Clinical Linguistics and Phonetics, 20*(5), 351–369, January 7, 2006, and reprinted by permission of the publisher (Taylor & Francis Ltd, http://www.tandf.co.uk/journals).

reduced substantially as children grew older (Figure 24.2). Whereas 33% of all vocalizations produced by 0 to 2–month-old infants were non–speech-like vocalizations, less than 10% of all vocalizations at 9 months of age were non–speech-like. Nathani et al. (2006) recommended that proportions of non–speech-like to speech-like vocalizations be used as a simple metric to evaluate progress in vocal production.

Amount of Vocalization or Volubility

Volubility, that is, the amount or rate of vocalization, has also received some attention in the literature on prelinguistic vocalizations. Rates of vocalization appear to increase with age for typically developing infants (Camp, Burgess, Morgan, & Zerbe, 1987; Nathani & Stark, 1996; Oller, Eilers, Steffens, Lynch, & Urbano, 1994; Oller et al., 1995). However, Oller et al. noted that this increase with age was seen only for infants from middle socioeconomic backgrounds; infants from low and very low socioeconomic groups did not evidence an increase in number of vocalizations with age. Thus, low socioeconomic status appears to be a risk factor for volubility. Other factors, such as prematurity or language background, did not affect this increase.

Volubility is typically measured in terms of *utterances* per minute. Published values across studies for typical volubility range from three to nine utterances per minute (Camp et al., 1987; Nathani & Stark, 1996; Oller et al., 1994, 1995; Vihman et al., 1985). One reason for the variation in reported values might be because the definition of an utterance has differed across investigations. Lynch, Oller, and Steffens (1989) and Stark (1980) defined an utterance as a "speech-like vocalization or group of vocalizations separated from all others by either audible ingressive breaths or by judges' intuitions about utterance boundaries, which are often indicated by a silence of one second or longer." On the other hand, in Nathani and Stark (1996), a 2-second pause was used as the primary criterion for segmenting utterances. Obviously, fewer utterances would be counted if the pause between vocalizations had to be at least 2 seconds than if the duration of the pause could vary based on judges' intuitions. Indeed, Nathani and Stark reported some of the lowest means for volubility for typically developing infants than other investigations. Vihman et al. (1985) also noted that individual differences can considerably influence prelinguistic volubility. Given this variation,

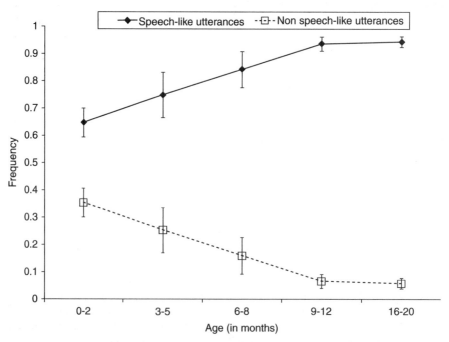

Fig. 24.2 Mean proportion (and standard error) of speech-like and non speech-like vocalizations across age. Originally appeared in Nathani, S., Ertmer, D. J., & Stark, R. E., Assessing vocal development in infants and toddlers, *Clinical Linguistics and Phonetics, 20*(5), 351–369, January 7, 2006, and reprinted by permission of the publisher (Taylor & Francis Ltd, http://www.tandf.co.uk/journals).

it is important that published data for rate of prelinguistic utterance production be used as a broad framework for comparison rather than as a single metric for assessment and intervention.

Vocal Development in Children with Hearing Loss

Research beginning in the 1980s has shown that there are similarities and differences between the prelinguistic vocalizations of typically developing children and those with bilateral, severe-profound hearing losses. It should be kept in mind that most of the children in these studies did not have the benefit of early identification through newborn hearing screening, they typically received analog hearing aids, and they were usually enrolled in intervention at older ages than is common today. Nonetheless, these early studies provided important information about the influence of hearing loss regarding the time course of vocal development and the characteristics of vocalizations that are most affected by the inability to hear conversational intensity speech well. The findings of these early studies and more recent findings for children who were identified through newborn hearing screening and were fitted with more modern technologies (e.g., cochlear implants) can help to identify the kinds of vocalizations that indicate that hearing is guiding prelinguistic vocal development. Armed with this information, EIs may be better-equipped to provide comprehensive and developmentally appropriate intervention to the very young children they serve.

Vocalization Similarities in Children With and Without Hearing Loss

Several aspects of vocal development appear to be relatively unaffected by hearing loss. For example, early reports speculated that volubility diminished after 6 months of age in the deaf infant (e.g., Lach, Ling, Ling, & Ship, 1950; Lenneberg, Rebelsky, & Nichols, 1965; Maskarinec, Cairns, Butterfield, & Weamer, 1981; Mavilya, 1972). Recent empirical investigations, however, have not supported this claim. Studies by Clement (2004), van den Dikkenberg-Pot, Koopmans-van Beinum, and Clement (1998), Moeller et al. (2007a), Nathani, Oller, and Neal (2007), and Iyer and Oller (2008b) have shown that infants with varying degrees of hearing loss vocalize to the same extent as their normally hearing peers, when matched for age or level of vocal development. Thus, sheer rate of vocalization appears to be relatively impervious to hearing loss.

Similarly, several kinds of *precanonical* vocalizations (i.e., those from SAEVD-R levels 1 – 3) do not appear to be affected by hearing loss. Squeals and raspberries are produced by infants both with and without hearing loss (Oller, Eilers, Bull, & Carney, 1985; Stoel-Gammon & Otomo, 1986). Iyer and Oller (2008a) also observed that quasi-resonant nuclei and marginal babbling were common to both infant groups. Furthermore, the production of quasi-resonant nuclei and marginal syllables diminished in both groups once canonical babbling began. Lynch, Oller, and Steffens (1989), however, observed that complete deafness did impact some of these precanonical vocalization types. They reported that the speech of a child with congenital absence of cochleas was dominated by quasi-resonant nuclei productions prior to the emergence of canonical babbling. Other precanonical sounds, such as fully resonant nuclei and marginal syllables, were rarely produced by this child. Taken together, these data suggest that unless there is complete loss of audition, a comparable variety of *precanonical* sounds are produced by infants and toddlers with normal hearing and those with hearing losses.

Vocalization Differences Between Children with and Without Hearing Loss
CANONICAL BABBLING

Oller and Eilers (1988; see Stark, 1983 also) were among the first to show that canonical babbling emerged at older than typical ages in children with hearing loss. The differences between the two groups of children were quite robust; causing the authors to recommend that infants who exhibited limited babbling(<20% of their spontaneous utterances) by 10 months of age should have a hearing test. These initial findings were replicated by Eilers and Oller (1994), Koopmans van Beinum, Clement, and van den Dikkenberg-Pot (2001), and Vinter (1994), confirming that children with severe-profound hearing losses who use hearing aids are delayed in the onset of babbling. Lynch et al. (1989) showed that canonical babbling could be eventually produced even by a child with total deafness due to a congenital lack of cochleas. Thus, the emergence of babbling does not, by itself, indicate that hearing has been used to guide speech development. However, the timely emergence of canonical babbling prior to 10 months of age appears to require auditory access to ambient speech models.

In addition to delayed onset of canonical babbling, children with hearing loss produce babbling less often than hearing peers. Infants with normal hearing begin to babble on a regular basis within 1 month after establishing these speech-like syllables (Lewedag, 1995; Oller, 2000). On the other hand, infants with severe to profound hearing loss are inconsistent in the production of babbling even 5–6 months after its onset (Eilers & Oller, 1994). Iyer and Oller (2008b) noted that growth in the proportion of canonical babbling was slower for children with severe to profound hearing loss than for those without hearing loss. The overall amount of canonical babbling produced by children with hearing loss has also been reported to be significantly less than that produced by children with normal hearing at comparable ages (Stoel-Gammon, 1988; Steffens, Eilers, Fishman, Oller, & Urbano, 1994; von Hapsburg & Davis, 2006). These studies highlight the importance of monitoring growth in the amount of canonical babbling (i.e., vocalizations from SAEVD-R levels 4 and 5) in addition to the onset of these speech-like utterances.

Further evidence of the role of audition in prelinguistic vocal development has been obtained from studies of children with moderate to severe hearing losses. Moeller et al. (2007a) compared the ages at which canonical babbling emerged in 12 children with early-identified hearing losses and 21 peers with normal hearing. They noted that two children with moderate hearing losses babbled on time, but that consistent production of babbled utterances was delayed—despite early identification of hearing loss. Nathani et al. (2007) examined the emergence of canonical babbling in four children with moderate to severe hearing loss and additional risk factors for developmental delay. They found that two children were delayed in their onset of babbling, and the two remaining children babbled within the typical age range. As in the Moeller study, however, fewer canonical syllables were produced by all infants with hearing loss than by typically developing controls. Relatedly, von Hapsburg and Davis (2006) noted that six children with mild to moderate-severe hearing losses produced canonical syllables in greater proportions than children with severe-to-profound hearing loss. Interestingly, four of these six children had similar proportions of canonical syllables as their peers with normal hearing. Moeller et al. (2007a) noted that children with moderate to severe hearing loss who produced a high percentage of precanonical vocalizations (e.g., 59%) during the first years of sensory aid use were found to have poorer word production skills during articulation testing at 3;0. In summary, it appears that moderate to severe hearing losses puts children at lower risk

for delays in starting to babble than for children with greater hearing losses, but that the amount of babbling both groups produce may be less than observed in children with normal hearing.

Studies of deaf children who receive cochlear implants also provide insight into the role of audition for the development of canonical vocalizations. In a study of seven children implanted by their third birthdays, Ertmer, Young, and Nathani (2007) found that three children had established (i.e., ≥20% of vocalizations within a 30-minute parent–child interaction) the Basic Canonical Syllables level *before* receiving their cochlear implants at 24, 30, and 36 months, respectively. Four other children had not established this level before they received implants. Three of these children (implanted at 28, 20, and 18 months) first established the Basic Canonical Syllables level relatively soon after implant activation: after 2, 6, and 2, months, respectively, of implant experience (recall that the range for typically developing children is 5–10 months of age). The remaining child in this study was implanted at 10 months and showed an atypical sequence of development by establishing the Advanced Forms level before the Basic Canonical Syllables level. However, when canonical utterances from both of these two levels were counted together, it was determined that the latter child required approximately 8 months of implant-aided hearing to establish well-formed canonical syllables. Thus, the four children who had not established the Basic Canonical Syllables level prior to receiving cochlear implants began to babble with comparable or fewer months of robust hearing (i.e., auditory access to conversational intensity speech) than observed for infants with normal hearing. Other researchers have also observed canonical babbling prior to implantation, and relatively rapid increases in babbling following cochlear implant activation in young children (e.g., Moeller et al., 2007a; Moore & Bass-Ringdahl, 2002; Schauwers, Gillis, Daemers, de Beuklaer, & Govaerts, 2004).

Taken together, these relatively small studies suggest that the rate at which canonical syllables are established following sensory aid fitting in non-babbling children can serve as an indication of auditory-guided speech development. Specifically, a near-typical rate of development can be inferred when canonical syllables constitute 20% or more of children's vocalizations within the first 5–10 months of cochlear implant or hearing aid use. If canonical babbling has already been established prior to sensory aid fitting, auditory benefit would be evidenced by increases in the frequency of well-formed canonical syllables until they form a majority of children's spontaneous utterances. These criteria should be considered preliminary until longitudinal studies with a larger number of young implant recipients can be completed.

SYLLABLE COMPLEXITY

In addition to delays in the onset of canonical babbling and reduced frequency of canonical utterances, the kinds of syllables produced also reflect the influence of hearing loss. Early studies by Stark (1983) and Stoel-Gammon and Otomo (1986) revealed that children with severe-profound hearing losses produced few complex syllable shapes (e.g., CVC, VC, CCV syllables, and jargon). More recently, Moeller et al. (2007a) confirmed this relationship by documenting a slower than typical increase in syllable shape complexity among children whose hearing losses were identified early in life. Slow acquisition of a variety of syllable shapes was also predictive of poor word production skills at 36 months for the children in this study. Similarly, Ertmer et al. (2007) found that no young cochlear implant users had established SAEVD-R level 5 prior to device activation. Delays in the emergence of complex and word-like syllable shapes are likely to interfere with the efficient acquisition of early phonological skills (Ertmer & Stark, 1995; Moeller, 2007a). The emergence and consistent use of complex syllable shapes and jargon appear to be important indicators of auditory-guided speech development and should be monitored to assess the benefit of hearing aids and cochlear implants in children who are learning English.

VOWEL AND CONSONANT INVENTORIES IN YOUNG CHILDREN WITH HEARING LOSS

Research has consistently shown that toddlers with severe-profound hearing losses have smaller vowel and consonant inventories than their age-matched peers with normal hearing (e.g., Kent, Osberger, Netshell, & Hustedde, 1987; Moeller, 2007a; Stoel-Gammon, 1988). Although some differences in outcomes are apparent across these investigations, tendencies to overproduce centralized vowels (e.g., / /), and delays in the emergence of consonants produced in less-visible places of articulation, as well as those with later-developing manners of production (e.g., fricative and affricates) are common. A few of the more revealing studies of prelinguistic speech development will be reviewed to look at these tendencies and the factors that may contribute to these difficulties.

Kent et al. (1987) provided possible explanations for the limited variety of vowels produced by children with hearing loss in a longitudinal study of identical twin boys. "Hal" was identified with a severe-profound, bilateral hearing loss at 3 months of age. His twin brother, "Ned" was found to have normal hearing. Recordings of both boys' vocalizations were made at 8, 12, 15, and 24 months of age. Acoustic analyses of vowel-like sounds showed that, by 15 months, Ned had refined the frequency range of the first and second formants to form an adult-like acoustic vowel space. At the same age, Hal's vowel space was much more restricted in formant frequency range than that of his twin brother. Based on this finding, it appeared that Hal produced fewer different vowel-like sounds because he did not vary his tongue postures as much as his brother. Monsen (1976) noted similar characteristics in older children with hearing loss. He attributed limited vowel diversity to three main factors: the incomplete auditory information that children receive, difficulty in seeing tongue positions as others produce vowels, and the limited orosensory feedback that children receive during vowel production. In short, children with severe-profound hearing losses have much difficulty using their senses to "discover" and replicate the distinct tongue postures needed to acquire a complete inventory of vowel types. Recent studies have shown that cochlear implants enable children to increase their vowel and diphthong inventories to normal or near-normal sizes (e.g., Ertmer, 2001; Ertmer et al., 2002; Moeller et al., 2007b; Serry & Blamey, 1999). Thus, increases in vowel and diphthong inventories after sensory aid fitting can provide another indication of auditory-guided speech development.

As with vowel inventories, delays in acquiring a variety of consonant types and features have been observed in young children with severe-profound hearing losses. Kent et al. (1987) found that Hal's spontaneous canonical vocalizations at 24 months contained mainly alveolar (77%) and bilabial (15%) consonants, whereas other places of articulation were seldom, if ever, observed. In contrast, Ned's speech contained consonants with a wide variety of places of articulation: bilabials (43%), dentals (13%), alveolars (22%), palatals (7%), velars (7%), and glottals (9%). Regarding consonant manner of production features, Hal produced stop consonants almost exclusively, whereas Ned produced stops, fricatives, glides, and trills. Although Hal increased his consonantal inventory between 8 and 24 months, Ned showed much larger increases. The authors concluded that auditory awareness of the "turbulence noise" (p. 73) associated with fricatives and affricates is a critical factor in learning to produce these sounds.

Stoel-Gammon (1988) compared the consonant inventories of 11 children with normal hearing (recorded between 4 and 18 months) and 14 children with hearing loss (12 with sensorineural hearing losses in the severe-profound range and two with conductive losses due to atresia). The latter children were divided into a younger group (recorded before 19 months of age) and an older group (recorded between 19 and 39 months of age). Transcription analysis revealed that the group with normal hearing showed an increase in the number of stable consonants produced (i.e., appearing two or three times per session depending on sample size). Their consonant inventories grew from an average of 4.5 types at 4–7 months to 8.7 consonant types at 15–18 months. The inventories of children in the younger hearing loss group were found to be comparable to the normally hearing group (4.3 consonant types, on average). However, children in the older hearing loss group actually had smaller inventories than those in the younger group (3.2 consonant types, on average). This surprising finding highlights the critical role that hearing acuity plays in acquiring consonants during the first 2 years of life.

Three conditions appear to account for the limited consonant variety noted by Kent et al. (1987) and Stoel-Gammon (1988). First, inadequate detection of speech features (voicing, manner of articulation, and place of articulation cues) and inadequate auditory feedback interfere with the perception and production of a full range of consonant types. Toddlers are not likely to develop a variety of consonants if they do not perceive the acoustic features that make phonemes distinctive. Second, the relatively greater visibility of some consonants (i.e., bilabials and labiodentals) provides an advantage in speech development over those that are not articulated in visible locations. To illustrate, Stoel-Gammon (1988) found that approximately 67% of the consonants in the inventories of children with severe-profound hearing losses were labials; only 2% were velars. Highly visible sounds such as /p/, /b/, /m/, and /w/ are also among the earliest emerging and most accurately produced consonants in the speech of deaf children studied by Smith (1977; for exception, see Kent et al., 1987). Finally, the manner in which consonants are produced may influence children's inventories. Both Stark (1983) and Stoel-Gammon (1988) found that toddlers with hearing loss produced a large number of prolongable or

"syllabic consonants" (Stark, 1983, p. 260) such as /m/ and /n/. Comparatively few stop or affricate consonants (e.g., /d/ or /t ʃ /) were produced. Based on this difference, Stoel-Gammon proposed that prolongable consonants provide "a different kind of tactile and kinesthetic feedback than stops and affricates" (p. 312). Because the former have long durations and relatively simple manners of production, they may be easier to say. In contrast, stops and affricates have short durations and require rapid and precise articulatory movements, making them more difficult to acquire without robust hearing.

Finally, Moeller et al. (2007b) concluded that consonant development in children with hearing loss was delayed but not qualitatively different from children with normal hearing. That is, consonants seem to be acquired in a typical order but are stabilized more slowly than that seen in children with normal hearing. Kent et al. (1987) and Moeller et al. (2007b) also noted that fricatives and affricates emerged more slowly in children with hearing loss than in children with normal hearing.

Although longitudinal studies of consonant inventories in infants and toddlers who use cochlear implants are scarce and usually involve a small number of participants, several investigations suggest that consonant inventories can be used to infer auditory-guided speech development. Three longitudinal case studies by Ertmer and colleagues found sizable increases in consonant inventories and increased diversity of consonant features during the first year of implant experience. Ertmer et al. (2002) found that "Michael" (implanted at 10 months) and "Diane" (implanted at 28 months) increased their consonant inventories from three to six and from two to seven consonants during the first 12 months of implant use. In addition, several new consonant features were observed: Diane began to produce glides (/w/ and /j/) and to produce less-visible alveolar (/n/ and /d/) and palatal (/j/) consonants; Michael added glides (/j/ and /w/) and fricatives /ʃ/ and expanded his places of articulation to include alveolar (/t/, /d/), palatal (/j/), and velar (/k/ and /g/) consonants. In an earlier study (Ertmer & Mellon, 2001), "Hannah" (implanted at 19 months) increased her inventory from two consonants (/m/ and /w/) after 4– months of cochlear implant experience to 10 consonants after 12 months of cochlear implant use. She also expanded the number of consonant features that she produced to include voiced and voiceless consonants (e.g., /k/ and /g/) and four new places of articulation: labiodentals (/v/), alveolars (/n/ and /d/), palatals (/ʃ/ and /j/), and velars (/g/).

Similarly, consonant manner features increased as she added stops (60% of consonants produced after 7 months of cochlear implant use), liquids (/l/), and fricatives (/f/ and /ʃ/.

Three advancements support the notion that the children in the Ertmer et al. studies (2001, 2002) used audition to guide speech development. First, the sizes of their consonant inventories after 1 year of cochlear implant use were well above the 3.2 consonant types found for children with hearing loss between 19 and 39 months old (Stoel-Gammon, 1988). Whereas this is encouraging, increased consonant inventory, by itself, might reflect maturation and intervention efforts as much as improved hearing. Stronger evidence of auditory-guided speech development can be seen in emergence of consonants with less-visible places of articulation and those with rarely reported manners of production (e.g., fricatives and affricates). These gains may be related to the ages at which children receive sensory aids.

Connor, Craig, Raudnebush, Heavner, and Zwolan (2006) found that children implanted before 30 months had an "early burst of growth" in consonant production accuracy (p. 628) not present in children implanted at older ages. Thus, children who acquire new consonants and vowels rapidly (within the first few months of sensory aid use) might also be showing the benefits of their improved hearing.

Finally, it is important to remember that many factors can affect children's speech development, including age at onset of hearing loss, age at identification, amount of residual hearing, and age at intervention (Geers, 2002; Moeller, 2000; Yoshinaga-Itano, Sedey, Coulter, & Mehl, 1998). Although common trends in speech development have been discussed, young children with severe-profound hearing losses may show considerable differences in their phonetic inventories. Some, such as Hal, may show a preference for alveolar stop consonants or less-visible consonants, whereas others may produce mainly easy-to-see labial sounds. Although variability in the composition of children's vowel and consonant inventories should be expected, in general, steady increases in the number of different vowels and consonants produced, increased production of consonants with less-visible places of articulation, and increased productions of fricatives and affricates appear to be signs of auditory-guided speech development.

OTHER ASPECTS OF PRELINGUISTIC VOCALIZATIONS

Little research has been conducted on prosodic aspects of prelinguistic vocalizations for both infants with and without hearing loss. Available data appear to indicate that infants with hearing loss might indeed differ from infants with normal hearing on prosodic characteristics (Clement, 2004; Iyer & Oller, 2008a; Kent et al., 1987; Nathani, Oller, & Cobo-Lewis, 2003; Stark, 1972). Infants with hearing loss have greater variability in their fundamental frequency values than infants with normal hearing (for exception, see Stark, 1972). In addition, the accumulated trends from several studies point to a higher mean fundamental frequency for infants with hearing loss, although statistically significant differences have not been obtained in any of these studies (Clement, 2004; Iyer & Oller, 2008a; Kent et al., 1987).

With respect to speech timing, infants with severe to profound hearing loss had longer durations of final syllables in utterances when compared to infants with normal hearing (Nathani et al., 2003). Lynch (1989) observed that in the case of the child with complete deafness, all syllables (i.e., final and nonfinal) were prolonged in duration when compared to infants with normal hearing. Taken together, this evidence indicates that prosodic aspects may need to be evaluated and targeted in addition to segmental and syllabic aspects in infants and toddlers with hearing loss. Observable changes toward closer to normal pitch, intonation, and speech timing may be noteworthy indicators of auditory-guided speech development. Further study is needed to explore this possibility.

Summary of Indicators of Auditory-guided Speech Development

The previously discussed studies have revealed much about the contributions of hearing to speech development. Young sensory aid users demonstrate the benefits of increased auditory perception when they overcome the limitations associated with hearing loss. Ever mindful that they can be expected to make some advancements as they mature, EIs can feel increasingly confident that hearing is guiding speech development as children's spontaneous vocalizations become more varied and adult-like. Signs of this progress include:

1. Increased production of canonical syllables (see SAEVD-R level 4) and the eventual dominance of adult-like syllables in the child's spontaneous utterances
2. Increased production of complex syllable shapes (see SAEVD-R level 5)
3. Increased vowel and diphthong diversity soon after sensory aid fitting

4. Increased diversity of consonants produced; especially those with less-visible places of articulation, such as /d/, /n/, /l/, /k/, and /g/, and later-emerging manners of articulation, such as fricatives and affricates (e.g., /f/, /v/, /s/, /z/, /ʃ/, /ʒ/, /dʒ/ and /tʃ/).

Clinical Implications for Early Interventionists
Assessing Progress in Auditory-guided Speech Development

This section describes two assessment tools for monitoring progress in vocal development. Procedures for these tools have been described in previous publications, so only a brief overview will be provided here. The first tool involves analyzing children's spontaneous utterances produced during play. The second is a short, game-like activity in which children are encouraged to imitate a variety of prelinguistic vocalizations. Results from each of these tools can be used to determine which levels of vocal development have been established and, through readministration, to monitor progress.

SPEECH SAMPLING

Ertmer and colleagues (Ertmer et al., 2002; see also Ertmer, 2005) consolidated the five levels of the SAEVD-R into a simpler, three-level system for classifying infant vocalizations. To use this system, EIs observe children during play with an adult and classify 50 of the child's spontaneous utterances as either "Precanonical Vocalizations" (SAEVD-R levels 1–3), "Basic Canonical Syllables," or "Advanced Forms." Table 24.1 provides descriptions and examples of the vocalizations found at each level. A detailed discussion of this assessment scheme can be found in Ertmer (2005). To assess progress, speech samples must be analyzed regularly (e.g., at 2-, 3-, or 4-month intervals) or whenever a shift in the kinds of vocalizations that the child produces is noticed. Table 24.2 provides guidelines for classifying children's utterances.

The following behaviors can serve as indicators of auditory-guided speech development when interpreting speech samples (Ertmer, 2005): (1) The production of utterances with Basic Canonical Syllables increases to 20% or more for at least two consecutive samples after sensory aid fitting, and the frequency

Table 24.1   Levels of vocal development

Precanonical vocalizations* Typical age of emergence: 0–6 months	Basic Canonical Syllables* Typical age of emergence: 6–10 months	Advanced Forms* Approximate age of establishment: 18 months
Definition Vocalizations *lacking* true vowels and true consonants in combination with a rapid transition between them.	Definition Vocalizations characterized by 1. Normal phonation 2. At least one consonant and one vowel in combination 3. Rapid transition between consonant and vowel (Oller & Lynch, 1992)	Definition Vocalizations that have the characteristics of Canonical Syllables but are more complex and later-emerging in typically developing children (Nathani, Ertmer, & Stark, 2002)
Examples: 1. Squeals, 2. Grunts, 3. Vowel-like sounds in isolation 4. Multiple vowel-like sounds in a series 5. Closants sounds such as clicks, lip smacks, or "raspberries" 6. Isolated consonants (e.g., /m/, /n/)	Examples: 1. CV syllables 2. CVCV syllables 3. Rhythmic production of reduplicated babbling (e.g., [bababababa]) 4. Rhythmic production of non-reduplicated babbling (e.g., [didapa]) 5. Whispered vocalizations	Examples: 1. Closed syllables (e.g., VC, CVC) 2. Consonant clusters (e.g., CCV) 3. Jargon (i.e., syllable strings with different vowels and consonants overlaid with rhythmic stress, intonation changes, or both)

*Audio examples of these types of vocalizations can be heard at www.vocaldevelopment.com (Ertmer & Galster, 2001).
Adapted from Ertmer, D. J. (2005). *The Source for Children with Cochlear Implants.* East Moline, IL: LinguiSystems, Inc., with permission from the publisher, LinguiSystems, Inc.

Table 24.2 Guidelines for classifying children's prelinguistic utterances

1.	An utterance is a vocalization or a group of vocalizations separated from other vocalizations by a pause of >1 second or an ingressive breath. Only one level is assigned to an entire utterance.
2.	Classify speech-related utterances only. Disregard coughs, crying, fussiness, laughs, snorts, burps, etc.
3.	Do not count /h/ as a consonant (C) when determining whether an utterance is from the Canonical Syllables or Advanced Forms level.
4.	Count glides (i.e., /j/ and /w/) as consonants only when they are combined with vowels (Vs) at rapid, adult-like rate (i.e., not produced slowly)
5.	Classify each utterance based on its most developmentally mature component. For example, if an utterance contains an isolated vowel, a CV syllable, and a CVC syllable, the entire utterance would be assigned to the Advanced Forms level because the CVC is the most advanced vocalization observed. Similarly, if an utterance contains a squeal, a grunt, and a CVCV vocalization, the entire utterance would be assigned to the Basic Canonical Syllables level because of the CVCV.

Adapted from Ertmer, D. J. (2005). *The Source for Children with Cochlear Implants.* East Moline, IL: LinguiSystems, Inc., with permission from the publisher, LinguiSystems, Inc.

of canonical syllables/babbling continues to increase with sensory aid experience; (2) a variety of consonants and vowels are produced in canonical syllables; (3) Advanced Forms comprise 20% or more of all utterances for two consecutive samples; and (4) utterances from the Precanonical level diminish and become less common than utterances from the Basic Canonical Syllable Level and those from the Advanced Forms level (e.g. Precanonical Vocalizations = 20%, Canonical Syllables = 50%, and Advanced Forms = 30% of a sample).

ANALYZING ELICITED SPEECH SAMPLES

A time-efficient alternative to analyzing spontaneous speech samples has also been recently developed. The Conditioned Assessment of Speech Production (CASP; Ertmer & Stoel-Gammon, 2008) was designed to monitor within-child progress in vocal development after sensory aid fitting. The CASP is based on three premises: (1) auditory access to conversational speech models and feedback through sensory aids will lead to noticeable advancements in vocal development; (2) sensory aid benefit is demonstrated when children imitate progressively more complex, phonetically varied, and speech-like vocalizations; and (3) toddlers can be conditioned to imitate developmentally appropriate speech stimuli that are modeled by familiar persons during a game-like activity.

The CASP consists of ten prelinguistic stimulus items (three precanonical, five basic canonical syllables, and two advanced forms) that are modeled by EIs and parents during an imitation activity. The CASP is given in the following way. The child observes as the EI models an item (e.g., [ma]) for the *parent* to imitate. The parent says the item and receives praise and a reward (i.e., a star from a Playskool Classical Stacker toy, a "ring and post" toy). The parent then turns to the child and repeats the stimulus item for the child to imitate. The parent praises and rewards the child with a star for responding. A second model is provided if the child doesn't vocalize or produces a phonetically dissimilar vocalization. The remaining items are elicited in the same way. Two EIs can administer the CASP if a parent is not available.

Child responses are scored using a graduated scale: Failure to response or a phonetically dissimilar response is assigned 0 points; partially acceptable responses are assigned 1 point; fully acceptable matches are assigned 2 points. A maximum score of 20 points can be achieved.

When administered regularly (i.e., at 2-, 3-, or 4-month intervals after sensory aid fitting) the CASP provides EIs with an objective, time-efficient way to monitor changes in vocal development and the emergence of auditory-guided speech development for a given child. A complete description of the development and field testing of the CASP, along with instructions and a scoring sheet, can be found in Ertmer and Stoel-Gammon (2008). A video demonstration can be accessed through the A.G. Bell Association for the Deaf web site at http://www.agbell.org/DesktopDefault.aspx?p=CASPDemo.

Stimulating Listening and Speech Development at the Prelinguistic Level

The special needs of infants and toddlers with hearing loss are typically addressed through a family-centered interventional approach that emphasizes a partnership between parents and EIs (Roush & Matkin, 1994). A key component of this approach is helping parents to provide listening, speech, and language stimulation during everyday interactions with their child. Information from analyzed speech samples and the CASP can be useful in selecting developmentally appropriate speech goals for these interactions. That is, either of these assessment tools can be used to determine whether Precanonical, Basic Canonical Syllables, and Advanced Forms levels have been established, are emerging, or are not within the child's repertoire. This knowledge can enable EIs to select targets (e.g., isolated vowels, CV syllables, CVC syllables, etc.) that are at or slightly above the child's current developmental level.

Short Periods of Prelinguistic Input (SPPI; Ertmer et al., 2008; Ertmer et al., 2002) is a research-based intervention approach that is intended for use by parents in everyday situations. The purpose of SPPI is to stimulate auditory perceptual development and advances in vocal development in a developmentally appropriate way. Using this approach, parents are encouraged to provide spoken models of vocalizations from the child's current level of development before introducing later-emerging and more complex vocalizations. These modeling periods are provided five times per day during 1-minute interactions between the child and a caregiver. During these short stimulation periods, parents repeat a speech target once every 5 seconds. This "say and pause" procedure provides multiple repetitions of the same target (i.e., concentrated modeling) while also giving the child opportunities to attend to and imitate the target between models.

Ertmer and Stoel-Gammon (2008) offer five reasons for using this approach. First, in children who are typically developing, simple vocalizations are produced before increasingly complex vocalizations (Nathani et al., 2006; Oller, 1980; Stark, 1980). Therefore, earlier emerging vocalization types (e.g., isolated vowels) are likely to be easier to imitate than more complex productions (e.g., CV, CVCV, and CVC syllables). Second, the acoustic characteristics of speech sounds are highlighted when they are said in isolation or in phonetically simple combinations. Repeated models of target vocalizations help children become aware of the unique acoustic characteristics of consonants and vowels. Third, targeting vocalizations that are at, or slightly above, children's current developmental level increases the likelihood of imitation and learning. Fourth, speech production practice may enhance auditory perception ability. Osberger (1983) demonstrated that the ability to say speech patterns actually preceded and facilitated auditory perception of the same patterns. Thus, concentrated modeling of prelinguistic vocalizations has the potential to stimulate growth in speech perception, as well as speech production ability.

Lastly, targeting nonmeaningful vocalizations during vocal play enables children to focus on speech and listening without the cognitive load associated with attaching meaning to speech sounds. Like infants who are typically developing, participants in SPPI are free to experiment with their own sound-making abilities and develop speech motor patterns before they are expected to say words. These short periods of prelinguistic stimulation are considered a supplement to the spoken language stimulation provided throughout the day.

It is important to note that the efficacy of SPPI has not been tested directly. However, it is supported by research showing the positive effects of concentrated modeling on infant speech (Kuhl & Meltzoff, 1996), by previously proposed models of intervention with toddlers who have communication disabilities (Stark, 1989), and by the use of concentrated modeling (focused stimulation), a well-accepted intervention technique in the field of communication disorders (Leonard, 1992). More information about SPPI can be found in Ertmer et al. (2002), Ertmer (2005), and Ertmer and Stoel-Gammon (2008). Video demonstrations of SPPI procedures can be accessed at www.vocaldevelopment.com (Ertmer & Galster, 2001).

Summary and Conclusions
Future Research Directions
This review has shown that hearing ability plays a major role in the process of vocal development, especially in the attainment of complex syllables and a broad array of consonants, vowels, diphthongs, and syllable shapes. The evidence cited also suggests that when infants and toddlers receive robust auditory access to conversational-intensity speech through their hearing aids or cochlear implants and intensive intervention, they are likely to make readily observable advancements toward mature speech patterns. Early interventionists who are familiar with the signs of auditory-guided speech development will recognize the attainment of these milestones and use them to monitor progress and to infer the effectiveness of sensory aid use in a difficult-to-assess population. When used in combination with parent reports and EI observations of listening and spoken language development, assessments of vocal development can provide a more comprehensive profile of children's abilities during the initial months of sensory aid use. This information can also be used to select developmentally appropriate speech goals for use in family-centered intervention.

Clearly, much knowledge about the nature of prelinguistic speech development has been gained over the last 40 years. Yet there is much more to be learned. In particular, little is known about the relationship between the vocalizations and their social functions; about prosodic aspects of vocalizations, about the time course for completing vocal development in children with moderate and severe-profound hearing loss, and about the effects of various amounts of auditory deprivation on prelinguistic speech development. Exploration of these areas can make important contributions to theories of language development (e.g., Locke, 1997) and holds considerable promise for improving clinical practices as well. Addressing these and other fertile research areas will require longitudinal studies with large numbers of children, and treatment studies to examine the efficacy of approaches to stimulating prelinguistic speech development. We look forward to the day when these efforts enable EIs to efficiently promote the delightful sounds of early childhood in youngsters with hearing loss.

Acknowledgments

The development of this chapter was supported by grants from the National Institute on Deafness and other Communication Disorders to the first (R01DC007863) and a subcontract to the second author (R01DC00484).

[1] Because the levels of vocal development often overlap in children's vocalizations, we will use the term "levels" in this chapter to characterize these advances rather than the older term "stages," which implies a more discrete progression and no overlap

[2] Different researchers have used varying terminology and somewhat different definitions to characterize these levels of vocal development based on somewhat different theoretical perspectives. For example, Oller (1980, 2000) refers to the first level as "Phonation," Stark (1980) refers to it as "Reflexive," and Koopmans-van Beinum et al. (1986) refer to it as "Uninterrupted Phonation." We have adopted the terminology and definitions used by Nathani et al. (2006) for the various levels because they represent an amalgam of previous models and include findings from contemporary research.

[3] Here and elsewhere, we use Oller's (1980, 2000) terminology in referring to infant speech sounds.

References

Camp, B. W., Burgess, D., Morgan, L. J., & Zerbe, G. (1987). A longitudinal study of infant vocalization in the first year. *Journal of Pediatric Psychology, 12*, 321–331.

Clement, C. J. (2004). *Development of vocalizations in deaf and normally hearing infants.* Unpublished doctoral dissertation, Netherlands Graduate School of Linguistics, Amsterdam.

Connor, C. M., Craig, H. K., Raudenbush, S. W., Heavner, K., & Zwolan, T. A. (2006). The age at which young deaf children receive cochlear implants and their vocabulary and speech-production growth: Is there added value for early implantation? *Ear & Hearing, 27*, 628–644.

Eilers, R. E., & Oller, D. K. (1994). Infant vocalizations and the early diagnosis of severe hearing impairment. *Journal of Pediatrics, 124*, 199–203.

Erber, N. (1982). *Auditory training.* Washington, DC: A.G. Bell Association for the Deaf.

Ertmer, D. J. (2005). *The Source for Children with Cochlear Implants.* East Moline, IL: LinguiSystems, Inc.

Ertmer, D. J. (2001). Emergence of a vowel system in a young cochlear implant recipient. *Journal of Speech, Language, and Hearing Research, 44*, 803–813.

Ertmer, D. J., & Galster, J. (2001). Vocal Development. Retrieved August 26, 2008 from www.vocaldevelopment.com

Ertmer, D. J., & Mellon, J. A. (2001). Beginning to talk at 20 months: Early vocal development in a young cochlear implant recipient. *Journal of Speech, Language, and Hearing Research, 44*, 192–206.

Ertmer, D. J., & Stark, R. E. (1995). Eliciting prespeech vocalizations in a young child with profound hearing impairment: Usefulness of real-time spectrographic displays. *American Journal of Speech-Language Pathology, 4*, 33–38.

Ertmer, D. J., & Stoel-Gammon, C. (2008). The Conditioned Assessment of Speech Production (CASP): A tool for evaluating auditory-guided speech development in young children with hearing loss. *The Volta Review, 108*, 59–80.

Ertmer, D. J., Young, N., Grohne, K., Mellon, J., Johnson, C., Corbett, K., & Saindon, K. (2002). Vocal development in young children with cochlear implants: Assessment and implications for intervention. *Language, Speech, and Hearing Services in the Schools, 33*, 185–196.

Ertmer, D. J., Young, N. M., & Nathani, S. (2007). Vocal development in young children with cochlear implants: A preliminary examination of sequence, time-course, and age-at-implantation. *Journal of Speech, Language, and Hearing Research, 50*, 393–407.

Geers, A. E. (2002). Factors affecting the development of speech, language, and literacy in children with early cochlear implantation. *Language, Speech and Hearing Services in the Schools, 33*, 172–183.

Iyer, S. N., & Oller, D. K. (2008a). Fundamental frequency development in typically developing infants and infants with severe to profound hearing loss. *Clinical Linguistics and Phonetics, 22*, 917–936.

Iyer, S. N., & Oller, D. K. (2008b). Prelinguistic vocal development in infants with typical hearing and infants with severe to profound hearing loss. *Volta Review, 108*, 115–138.

Kent, R. D., Osberger, M. J., Netsell, R., & Hustedde, L. C. G. (1987). Phonetic development in identical twins differing in auditory function. *Journal of Speech and Hearing Disorders, 52*, 64–75.

Koopmans-van Beinum, F. J., Clement, C. J., & van den Dikkenberg-Pot, I. (2001). Babbling and the lack of auditory speech perception: A matter of coordination? *Developmental Science, 4* (1), 61–70.

Koopmans-van Beinum, F. J., & van der Stelt, J. M. (1986). Early stages in the development of speech movements. In B. Lindblom & R. Zetterstrom (Eds.), *Precursors of early speech* (pp. 37–50). Basingstoke, Hampshire: Macmillan Press.

Kuhl, P. K., & Meltzoff, A. N. (1996). Infant vocalizations in response to speech: Vocal imitation and developmental change. *Journal of the Acoustic Society of America, 100*, 2425–2438.

Lach, R., Ling, D., Ling, A. H., & Ship, N. (1970). Early speech development in deaf infants. *American Annals of the Deaf, 115*, 522–526.

Lenneberg, E. H., Rebelsky, G. F., & Nichols, I. A. (1965). The vocalizations of infants born to deaf and hearing parents. *Vita Humana (Human Development), 8*, 23–37.

Leonard, J. S. (1992). Communication intervention for children at risk for specific communication disorders. *Seminars in Speech and Language, 12*, 223–235.

Lewedag, V. L. (1995). *Patterns of onset of canonical babbling among typically developing infants.* Unpublished doctoral dissertation, University of Miami, Coral Gables, FL.

Locke, J. (1997). A theory of neurolinguistic development. *Brain and Language, 58*, 265–326.

Lynch, M. P., Oller, D. K., & Steffens, M. (1989). Development of speech-like vocalizations in a child with congenital absence of cochleas: The case of total deafness. *Applied Psycholinguistics, 10*, 315–333.

Maskarinec, A. S., Cairns, G. F., Butterfield, E. C., & Weamer, D. K. (1981). Longitudinal observations of individual infants' vocalizations. *Journal of Speech and Hearing Disorders, 46*, 267–273.

Mavilya, M. P. (1972). Spontaneous vocalization and babbling in hearing-impaired infants. In G. Fant (Ed.), *International symposium on speech communication abilities and profound deafness* (pp. 163–171). Washington, DC: A.G. Bell Association for the Deaf.

Mitchell, P. R., & Kent, R. (1990). Phonetic variation in multisyllable babbling. *Journal of Child and Language, 17*, 247–265.

Moeller, M. P. (2000). Intervention and language development in children who are deaf and hard of hearing. *Pediatrics, 106*, E43.

Moeller, M. P., Hoover, B., Putman, C., Arbataitis, K., Bohnenkamp, G., Peterson, B., et al. (2007a). Vocalizations of infants with hearing loss compared with infants with normal hearing: Part I – Phonetic development. *Ear & Hearing, 28*, 605–627.

Moeller, M. P., Hoover, B., Putman, C., Arbataitis, K., Bohnenkamp, G., Peterson, B., et al. (2007b). Vocalizations of infants with hearing loss compared with infants with normal hearing: Part II – Transition to words. *Ear & Hearing, 28*, 628–642.

Monsen, R. (1976). Normal and reduced phonological space: The production of English vowels by deaf adolescents. *Journal of Phonetics, 4*, 189–198.

Moore, J. A., & Bass-Ringdahl, S. (2002). Infant vocal development in candidacy for and efficacy of cochlear implantation. *Annals of Otology, Rhinology, and Laryngology, 111*, 52–55.

Nathani, S., Ertmer, D. J., & Stark, R. E. (2006). Assessing vocal development in infants and toddlers. *Clinical Linguistics and Phonetics, 20*, 351–369.

Nathani, S., Oller, D. K., & Cobo-Lewis, A. B. (2003). Final syllable lengthening (FSL) in infant vocalizations. *Journal of Child Language, 30*, 3–25.

Nathani, S., Oller, D. K., & Neal, A. R. (2007). On the robustness of vocal development: an examination of infants with moderate-to-severe hearing loss and additional risk factors. *Journal of Speech, Language, and Hearing Research, 50*, 1425–44.

Nathani, S., & Stark, R. E. (1996). Can conditioning procedures yield representative infant vocalizations in the laboratory? *First Language, 16*(3), 365–368.

Oller, D. K. (1980). The emergence of the sounds of speech in infancy. In G. Yeni-Komshian, J. Kavanaugh, & C. Ferguson (Eds.), *Child phonology* (pp. 93–112). New York: Academic Press.

Oller, D. K. (2000). *The emergence of the speech capacity.* Mahwah, NJ: Lawrence Erlbaum Associates.

Oller, D. K., & Eilers, R. (1988). The role of audition in infant babbling. *Child Development, 59*, 441–449.

Oller, D. K., Eilers, R. E., Basinger, D., Steffens, M. L., & Urbano, R. (1995). Extreme poverty and the development of precursors to the speech capacity. *First Language, 15*, 167–188.

Oller, D. K., Eilers, R. E., Bull, D. H., & Carney, A. E. (1985). Pre-speech vocalizations of a deaf infant: A comparison with normal metaphonological development. *Journal of Speech and Hearing Research, 28*, 47–63.

Oller, D. K., Eilers, R. E., Steffens, M. L., Lynch, M. P., & Urbano, R. (1994). Speech-like vocalizations in infancy: an evaluation of potential risk factors. *Journal of Child Language, 21*, 33–58.

Oller, D. K., & Lynch, M. P. (1992). Infant vocalizations and innovations in infraphonology: Toward a broader theory of development and disorder. In C. A. Ferguson, L. Menn, & C. Stoel-Gammon (Eds.), *Phonological development* (pp. 509–536). Timonium, MD: York Press.

Osberger, M. J. (1983). Development and evaluation of some speech training procedures for hearing-impaired children: Toward a broader theory of development and disorder. In I. Hochberg, H. Levitt, & M. J. Osberger (Eds.), *Speech of the hearing-impaired: research, training, and personnel preparation* (pp. 333–348). Baltimore: University Park Press.

Roug, L. Landberg, I., and Lundberg, L. J. (1989). Phonetic development in early infancy: A study of four Swedish children during the first 18 months of life. *Journal of Child Language, 16*, 19–40.

Roush, J., & Matkin, N. D. (1994). *Infants and toddlers with hearing loss: family-centered assessment and intervention.* Baltimore, MD: York Press.

Schauwers, K., Gillis, B., Daemers, K., de Beukelaer, C., & Govaerts, P. J. (2004). Cochlear implantation between 5 and 20 months of age: The onset of babbling and the audiologic outcome. *Otology and Neurotology, 25*, 263–270.

Serry, T. A., & Blamey, P. J. (1999). A 4-year investigation into phonetic inventory development in young cochlear implant users. *Journal of Speech, Language, and Hearing Research, 42*, 141–154.

Smith, C. R. (1977). Residual hearing and speech production in deaf children. *Journal of Speech and Hearing Research, 18*, 795–811.

Smith, B. L., Brown-Sweeney, S., & Stoel-Gammon, C. (1989). A quantitative analysis of reduplicated and variegated babbling. *First Language, 9*, 175–189.

Stark, R. E. (1972). Some features of the vocalizations of young deaf children. In J. F. Bosma (Ed.), *Third symposium on oral sensation and perception: The mouth of the infant* (pp. 431–441). Springfield, IL: Charles C. Thomas.

Stark, R. E. (1980). Stages of speech development in the first year of life. In G. Yeni-Komshian, J. Kavanaugh, & C. Ferguson (Eds.), *Child phonology, Volume 1* (pp. 73–90). New York: Academic Press.

Stark, R. E. (1983). Phonatory development in young normally hearing and hearing-impaired children. In I. Hochberg, H. Levitt, & M. J. Osberger (Eds.), *Speech of the hearing-*

impaired: research, training, and personnel preparation. Baltimore: University Park.

Stark, R. E. (1989). Early intervention: When, why, how? *Infants and Young Children* (1), 44–53.

Steffens, M. L., Eilers, R. E., Fishman, L., Oller, D. K., & Urbano, R. C. (1994). Early vocal development in tactually aided children with severe-profound hearing loss. *Journal of Speech and Hearing Research, 37*, 700–711.

Stoel-Gammon, C. (1988). Prelinguistic vocalizations of hearing-impaired and normally hearing subjects: A comparison of consonantal inventories. *Journal of Speech & Hearing Disorders, 53*, 302–315.

Stoel-Gammon, C., & Otomo, K. (1986). Babbling development of hearing-impaired and normally hearing subjects. *Journal of Speech and Hearing Disorders, 51*, 33–41.

van den Dikkenberg-Pot, I., Koopmans-van Beinum, F. J., & Clement, C. J. (1998). Influence of lack of auditory speech perception on sound productions of deaf infants. *Institute of Phonetic Sciences: University of Amsterdam Proceedings, 22*, 47–60.

Vihman, M. M. (1993). Variable paths to early word production. *Journal of Phonetics, 21*, 61–82.

Vihman, M. M. (1996). *Phonological development: The origins of language in the child.* Cambridge, MA: Blackwell Publishers.

Vihman, M. M., Macken, M. A., Miller, R., Simmons, H., & Miller, J. (1985). From babbling to speech: A re-assessment of the continuity issue. *Language, 61*, 395–443.

Vihman, M., & Croft, W. (2007). Phonological development: Toward a "radical" templatic phonology. *Linguistics, 45* (4), 683–725.

Vinter, S. (1994). L'analyse du babillage: une contribution au diagnostic de surdité? (The analysis of babbling: A contribution to the diagnosis of deafness?) *Approche Neuropsychologique des Apprentissages chez l'Enfant, 6*, 232–238.

von Hapsburg, D., & Davis, B. L. (2006). Auditory sensitivity and the prelinguistic vocalizations of early-amplified infants. *Journal of Speech, Language, and Hearing Research, 49*, 809–822.

Yoshinaga-Itano, C. Sedey, A.L., Coulter, D. K., & Mehl, A. L. (1998). Language of early- and later-identified children with hearing loss. *Pediatrics, 102*, 1161–1171.

Zlatin, M. (1975). *Preliminary descriptive model of infant vocalization during the first 24 weeks: Primitive syllabification and phonetic exploratory behaviour* (Final Report, Project No 3–4014, NE-G-00–3–0077): National Institutes of Health Research Grants.

Children and Youth Who Are Hard of Hearing: Hearing Accessibility, Acoustical Context, and Development

Janet R. Jamieson

Abstract

Children and youth who are hard of hearing comprise a substantial proportion of the birth to young adult population with hearing loss, but in spite of this, researchers have paid scant attention to this group, in comparison to their peers who are deaf. However, there is currently a growing interest in the development of children whose hearing losses range from mild to severe. This focus has come about in part because of the widespread implementation of early hearing detection and intervention (EHDI), which is resulting in far earlier diagnosis and intervention—and improved outcomes across domains—than was evident in the past, and in part because of improved amplification technologies. Taken together, the overall impact of EHDI and improved amplification options is that there appears to be an increase in the population of children who are now able to develop functional communication skills more characteristic of hard-of-hearing children than of deaf children.

The aims of this chapter are to consider (1) the challenges inherent in interpreting research on individuals who are hard of hearing in the absence of a consistent definition, (2) outcomes in terms of speech and language development in children who are hard of hearing, (3) the vital role of acoustic ecology and hearing accessibility in the lives of children and youth who are hard of hearing, (4) the relationship between hearing accessibility and identity construction in hard-of-hearing adolescents, and (5) the actual and anticipated impact of newborn hearing screening and early intervention for this population.

Keywords: acoustic ecology, hearing accessibility, cochlear implants, early identification, hard-of-hearing children, speech development

Children and youth who are hard of hearing comprise a substantial proportion of the birth to young adult population with hearing loss (e.g., Gallaudet Research Institute, 2006-2007), but in spite of this, researchers have paid scant attention to this group in comparison to their peers who are deaf. In fact, children whose levels of hearing loss range from mild to severe have occasionally been labeled "forgotten" (Davis, 1990; Meadow-Orlans, Sass-Lehrer, Scott-Olson, & Mertens, 1998). Consistent with this, prior to the advent of universal newborn hearing screening (UNHS) programs, the gap between age of identification of hearing loss for children who

are deaf and those who are hard of hearing was noteworthy. For example, the Gallaudet National Parent Survey (Meadow-Orlans, Mertens, Sass-Lehrer, & Scott-Olson, 1997), conducted in 1996, was based on questionnaires completed by about 400 parents of children with hearing losses in 39 US states. Analysis indicated that the average age of identification for the children who were deaf was 14.5 months, whereas the average age for children who were hard of hearing was 28.6 months—more than a year later than their peers with more significant losses.

Within the past decade, UNHS programs and technological advances have contributed to a renewed theoretical and applied interest in children who are hard of hearing. The widespread implementation of early hearing detection and intervention (EHDI) programs is resulting in very early identification of hearing loss in infants and their subsequent enrollment in early invention, which is leading to more positive outcomes across domains, including speech, language, and listening, than has been evidenced in the past (e.g., Yoshinago-Itano, 2006). In addition to the early identification of infants who are hard of hearing, some factors have also been found to contribute to a blurring of the conventional distinction between "deaf" and "hard of hearing" among slightly older children, with the practical result that many children and youth who have more significant hearing losses actually function, at least part of the time, as though they are hard of hearing. For example, cochlear implants and other sensory devices often present a fascinating juxtaposition of a child who functions as both hard of hearing (when the device is functioning well and the child is progressing) and deaf (when the device is removed or malfunctioning).

For most children with hearing loss, functional listening ability (and subsequent communication skills) can develop and change over time, so that a child may be primarily a visual processor of information at one point in time, but primarily a visual-auditory processor later in development. Furthermore, the very nature of a hearing loss (such as progressive or fluctuating) may permit the child to function as a person who is hard of hearing (as defined by functional communication ability) at one point in development or in one setting and as a person who is deaf at another time or in a more noisy setting, respectively. In terms of contextual factors, the external variable of acoustical conditions may interfere with accessibility to the sound signal to the point at which a child who functions as hard of hearing (i.e., relies primarily on speech and listening for communication with others) in one setting may need to function as deaf (i.e., relies primarily on a visual approach to communication) in another.

Overall, then, the implications are that many children with significant hearing losses who would have functioned as deaf in the past now have additional opportunities to develop functional communication skills more typical of children who are hard of hearing, and children's functional communication skills may be viewed to some extent as dynamic and context-dependent. From this perspective, the population of children who function communicatively as hard of hearing, at least part of the time, appears to be both fluid and growing.

The first documented recognition of persons who are "partially hearing" dates back to the 19th century, when Jean Marc Gaspard Itard designed the first hearing aids for persons with impaired hearing (Itard, 1821). An interest in the psychological and social implications of being hard of hearing would wait for more than 150 years, however. A focus on the diverse experience of hearing loss and issues of the social identity of persons who are hard of hearing developed gradually in the 1990s, possibly in response to the recognition of Deaf culture (McKellin, 1994). It was around this time that researchers began to consider the social, rather than merely audiological, implications of being hard of hearing (e.g., Laszlo, 1994; McKellin, 1994) and aspects of the lived experience of persons who are hard of hearing (e.g., Dillon Edgett, 2002). As Ross (2008) stated, "A hearing loss in a child, of whatever degree, is not a benign condition. It has ramifications that can pervade every aspect of a child's life" (p. 1).

The aims of this chapter are to consider (1) the challenges inherent in interpreting research on individuals who are hard of hearing in the absence of a consistent definition, (2) outcomes in terms of speech and language development in children who are hard of hearing, (3) the vital role of acoustic ecology and hearing accessibility in the lives of children and youth who are hard of hearing, (4) the relationship between hearing accessibility and identity construction in adolescents who are hard of hearing, and (5) the actual and anticipated impact of newborn hearing screening and early intervention for this population. For a discussion of educational settings and support for mainstreamed students with hearing loss, see Chapter 6, this volume.

The Dilemma of Definition

Much of the research focused on children and youth with hearing losses describes the population somewhat generically as "hearing impaired" or "deaf or hard of hearing" or uses the term "deaf" to encapsulate the entire group. In these circumstances, it is impossible to say with assurance to what extent the findings reflect the performance or experiences of children who are hard of hearing. In other studies in which the term "hard of hearing" is defined, the parameters are often vague, ambiguous, or insufficiently specific as to limit generalizability to other populations. Overall, then, the confusion surrounding absent, inconsistent, or idiosyncratic definitions need to be discussed before considering the relevance of research findings to hard-of-hearing children and youth.

"Hard of Hearing": In the Absence of a Definition

It appears to be the case that the younger the subject population, the more likely researchers are to describe the participant group as a whole as "deaf and hard of hearing," "hearing impaired," or "with hearing losses." There are some very valid reasons for this choice of nomenclature. In the early stages of infancy, it seems reasonable to use such generic descriptors, given that, first, degree of hearing loss often cannot be determined with accuracy until later in development, and second, communication preference and most appropriate educational placement have not yet, of course, been determined. For example, Yoshinaga-Itano (2003) described the early-identified infants in her research as "children with hearing loss" and "children who are deaf and hard of hearing." Many researchers continue to use similar broad terms in studies of preschoolers with hearing loss (e.g., Antia & Ditillo, 1998; Nicholas & Geers, 2003), and again, this practice seems to be a reasonable and accurate reflection of the varying communication and educational paths the children might eventually follow. However, the use of such generic terms does not reliably differentiate subject populations by degree of hearing loss, and it may prove difficult to determine to what extent the findings may be consistent with other findings on children with hearing losses of similar age. On the other hand, later functional communication is determined by a range of factors, of which hearing level is only one. (By way of illustration, Nicholas and Geers [2003] described their subjects by levels of hearing loss, communication approach, and educational setting.) Overall, then, studies involving infants and preschoolers with hearing loss provide the most easily interpretable findings when the participants are described by relevant attributes in addition to—and including—hearing levels.

By the time they are school-aged, children with hearing loss may be distinguished by communication preference (e.g., sign or aural/oral) and/or educational setting (e.g., separate, specialized vs. integrated). The older the group under investigation (for example, adolescents vs. elementary school-aged), the more enduring the communication preference and type of educational setting are likely to be. Thus, many studies of children in the early elementary years may retain the use of "deaf and hard of hearing" (e.g., Antia, Sabers, & Stinson, 2006; Hyde & Power, 2003), whereas studies involving adolescents may distinguish the participants specifically as "hard of hearing" (e.g., Israelite, Ower, & Goldstein, 2002;

Punch & Hyde, 2005). In the latter circumstance, the basis for the distinction (e.g., hearing level, educational placement, communication preference, and/or self-identification) is clearly indicated. However, in some large-scale studies of mainstreamed adolescent students, the use of a more generic term of "hearing impaired" is used in recognition of the fact that the population may include both students who are deaf and those who are hard of hearing (e.g., Stinson, Whitmire, & Kluwin, 1996), whether determined by hearing level, communication preference, or self-identification.

The term "deaf" is sometimes used as an all-inclusive term meant to incorporate all the participants in a study with any degree of hearing loss. This practice is more common in studies of infants (e.g., Koester, Brooks, & Traci, 2000), preschoolers (e.g., Musselman, Lindsay, & Wilson, 1988), or occasionally among elementary school children (e.g., Figueras, Edwards, & Langdon, 2008; Nunes & Pretzlik, 2001). On the other hand, when the term "hard of hearing" is used, it seems to be accompanied by clear criteria for its definition (e.g., Israelite et al.; Brunnberg, 2005). In general, since the 1990s, when social and anthropological researchers began to distinguish between the experiences of persons who are deaf and those who are hard of hearing, the term "deaf and hard of hearing" has been used more conventionally than "deaf" in isolation as a generic descriptor.

It may be speculated that one final potential category referring to "hard of hearing" may exist. In studies in which the population under investigation is clearly and specifically described as "deaf" (for example, when identifying criteria include profound losses, Deaf cultural membership, and/or the use of sign language as a primary means of communication) (e.g., Kyle & Harris, 2006), it may be assumed that any children with hearing losses who do not meet those criteria are hard of hearing. In this case, the definition of "hard of hearing" would be one of exclusion.

"Hard of Hearing": When a Definition Is Provided

Increasingly, both as culturally Deaf persons have expressed the desire to be recognized as a distinct group and as the potentially significant impact of even mild or moderate hearing losses has been acknowledged, researchers and professionals have tended to describe more fully than previously—if not exactly *define*—their subjects. The nature of the description is very much affected by the perspective of the researcher (Tomblin & Hebbler, 2007).

Audiologists often avoid the terms "deaf" and "hard of hearing," preferring instead the more physical and precise categories of hearing loss. For example, Blamey (2003) suggested that from the perspective of spoken language development, children's hearing levels should be categorized as hearing (pure-tone averages, or PTA) up to 25 dB HL (hearing level), hard of hearing (PTA thresholds between 25 and 90 dB HL), and deaf (PTA thresholds in excess of 90 dB). By contrast, the Conference of Educational Administrators Serving the Deaf has long distinguished persons who are deaf from persons who are hard of hearing on the basis of functional communication abilities (Frisina, 1974). From this perspective, a person who is hard of hearing has developed speech and language skills primarily through the auditory mode and can understand speech through the ear alone, with or without an assistive listening device, whereas a deaf person has developed communication skills primarily through the visual channel and prefers a primarily visual means of communicating with others.

Many researchers whose interest concerns school performance describe children with hearing losses in terms of their educational placement. Although these researchers did not specifically identify the children as either "deaf" or "hard of hearing," the information about educational setting provides one additional important variable that helps the reader determine the possible generalizability of the findings to other children. For example, Antia et al. (2006) distinguished between children in regular classroom settings and those in specialized, separate placements. Other researchers, whose research focus may be primarily communication or social interaction, separate the groups of children in their research by communication approach (e.g., Punch & Hyde, 2005). From this perspective, those children who primarily use sign language as their preferred means of communication or who are educated in classrooms in which some form of sign is used would be considered "deaf," and children who use speech and who are integrated into regular classrooms could be described as "hard of hearing." However, many children are not so easily categorized: some children from Deaf families may have mild hearing losses and be fluent in both sign and speech, whereas some children with moderate hearing losses may benefit from consistent visual support in communication and be optimally placed in a setting in which some form of sign language is used.

Many researchers opt to describe their subject participants with a combination of descriptors. For example, Punch and Hyde (2005) described the youth in their research in terms of their hearing loss, educational placement, and absence of additional disabling conditions. The use of a combination of descriptors has the advantage of enabling the reader to make a more reasoned interpretation of the findings than might otherwise be possible. Finally, in recognition of the deep impact any degree of hearing may have on social aspects of an individual's life, some researchers have recently begun to ask their participants to self-identify as "hard of hearing" or "deaf" (e.g., Israelite et al.). This practice sidesteps the tricky issue of researcher-assigned categorization and is appropriate with research participants who are at least of secondary school age, when cultural affiliation is likely to have been considered.

Overall, then, a clear definition of "hard of hearing" that is consistent across development is far less important than a description of the relevant characteristics that pertain to the functional hearing level and communication skills, and, if applicable, the psychosocial adjustment, of the subject population. Throughout the remainder of this chapter, definitions of "deaf" and "hard of hearing" that relate to functional communication skills will be utilized.

Development of Communication Skills in Children Who Are Hard of Hearing

The social and academic problems that hard-of-hearing children may experience daily at school are masked by the fact that these children often do not stand out noticeably from their hearing peers, in marked contrast to children who are deaf. Nevertheless, the scant body of research that has examined the language, literacy, and speech abilities of infants and children who are hard of hearing underscores the considerable challenges even mild to severe hearing losses impose on development across these domains, although systematic studies of the communication development of children who are clearly identified as hard of hearing (i.e., who have hearing losses in the mild to severe range) are limited in number.

Development of Speech Skills

Prior to the advent of UNHS, very little was known about the vocal development of infants with mild to severe hearing losses. However, in two landmark studies, Moeller et al. (2007a, 2007b) investigated the phonetic development and transition to words of typically hearing infants and infants with early-identified hearing losses. The infants in the former group (*n* = 21) were enrolled in the study at 4 months of age and followed longitudinally until at least

36 months of age, while the infants with hearing losses ($n = 12$) were followed from 10 to 24 months of age. Nine of the 12 infants with hearing losses had unaided hearing levels at all or most frequencies in the mild to severe range, whereas the remaining three infants had received cochlear implants at least 12 months previously. The findings from the Moeller et al. (2007b) study suggest that early-identified hard-of-hearing infants continue to lag behind their typically hearing peers in aspects of phonetic and phonological development at 24 months of age, although it should be noted that the majority of skills developed in a manner similar to that found in the hearing peers. The researchers stressed that even early-identified infants have more restricted auditory experiences (due to factors such as background noise and consistency of hearing aid use) than hearing infants, and that early identification and early amplification alone are not necessarily sufficient to stimulate typical patterns of speech development in all children with hearing loss.

In the Moeller et al. (2007a) study, the infants with hearing loss appeared to make the transition from babble to words in a delayed but parallel manner to that of infants with normal hearing. These delays, in turn, appear to contribute to delays in expressive vocabulary development. Taken together, the findings from these two studies emphasize that although early identification, early intervention, and early access to amplification have been found to result in improved performance for infants in many broad aspects of language development (Apuzzo & Yoshinaga-Itano, 1995; Moeller, 2000; Yoshinaga-Itano, Sedey, Coulter, & Mehl, 1998), they do not eliminate all complexities that even a mild hearing loss may pose to the development of speech skills.

The finding that hard-of-hearing infants usually develop spoken language in a delayed but similar fashion to their peers has also been found among school-aged children. For example, Blamey, Paatsch, Bow, Sarant, and Wales (2002) evaluated the relationships between speech perception, spoken language, hearing level, and age-related measures of a group of 87 primary school children. All of the children had been fitted with either hearing aids or cochlear implants, and 15 of the children had aided hearing levels that were clearly in the hard-of-hearing range. For all children, there was improvement in both speech perception and spoken language over time after amplification (although the authors emphasized that a causal relationship one way or the other could not be implied). However, although age analyses revealed that the children showed strong receptive language growth, on average it was only at about two-thirds the rate one would expect for age-matched hearing peers. Consistent with Moeller et al. (2007a), Blamey et al. (2002) concluded that the complexities of developing spoken language are ameliorated, but not eliminated, by early amplification and specialized educational intervention.

During the past decade, with the widespread implementation of UNHS screening, many deaf children with profound or greater hearing losses have had improved early access to auditory–linguistic experiences than were previously available. This is in large part due to advances in amplification technology, particularly the cochlear implant. The improved auditory experience provided by cochlear implants, in comparison to that provided by hearing aids, has facilitated the acquisition of spoken language in many deaf children. Not surprisingly, there is a correlation between age at implantation and several aspects of communication development. For example, Geers (2004) followed 133 children with congenital hearing losses and 48 adventitiously deafened children, all of whom had received cochlear implants. She found an advantage for early implantation when speech and language outcomes were considered together in both groups. Similar findings concerning the benefits of early implantation are described by Nicholas and Geers (2006). Overall, then, over the past decade, the population of children who are functionally hard of hearing has been substantially augmented by the large numbers of deaf children who have received early access to auditory–linguistic experiences through successful early cochlear implantation.

Development of Language

In a review of the current state of knowledge of the language skills of children with mild to severe hearing losses, Moeller, Tomblin, Yoshinaga-Itano, Connor, and Jerger (2007c) noted, first, the paucity of research studies on the topic, and second, the fact that many of the studies reviewed involved children whose hearing losses were late-identified. Thus, their auditory–linguistic experiences differed in both quality and amplification from those of children identified through newborn hearing screening. In this review, Moeller et al. included studies of semantics, morphology, and syntax, and noted the pressing need for studies in areas such as pragmatics and narrative discourse that would shed additional light on the development of literacy and socialization skills.

Researchers have presented divergent findings, but overall it appears that mild to severe hearing losses result in delayed, although not deviant, language performance. For example, there have been divergent findings across the studies in terms of vocabulary and novel word learning skills in primarily school-aged children, with some researchers concluding that children with even mild hearing losses will show delayed but typical patterns of vocabulary development (e.g., Davis, Elfenbein, Schum, & Bentler, 1986; Davis, Shepard, Stelmachowicz, & Gorga, 1981) and word learning strategies (e.g., Lederberg, Prezbindowski, & Spencer, 2000), and other researchers reporting no significant differences between hard-of-hearing and age-matched peers with typical hearing (e.g., Gilbertson & Kamhi, 1995; Wolgemuth, Kamhi, & Lee, 1998). Consistent with the former reports, there is evidence from several studies that hearing loss in even the mild–moderate range can delay morphological development (e.g., McGuckian & Henry, 2007; Stelmachowicz, Pittman, Hoover, & Lewis, 2001).

Elfenbein, Hardin-Jones, and Davis (1994) conducted one of the few studies that examined syntactic development in the spoken language of children who were clearly identified as hard of hearing. They concluded that the frequency of grammatical errors was related to degree of hearing loss, and that the error rate of children with mild to moderate hearing losses did not approach the considerably higher error rate typically observed in students who are deaf. By contrast, in terms of receptive syntax abilities, Briscoe, Bishop, and Norbury (2001) and Nittrouer and Burton (2003) found that children who are hard of hearing perform comparably with age-matched peers with normal hearing, and Gilbertson and Kamhi (1995) found that a group of elementary school-aged children who were hard of hearing (Mean age = 9 years) performed comparably with a group of younger children with normal hearing (Mean age = 6; 5 years) on a test of understanding of grammar. Given these differences in research findings, Moeller et al. (2007c) called for an integrated approach to examining receptive and expressive syntactic development in children who are hard of hearing as a route to shedding light on how these children use grammatical devices to serve communicative purposes.

As Moeller et al. (2007c) pointed out, surprisingly little is known about the impact of a mild to moderate hearing loss on the development of literacy skills. Overall, it appears that children with mild to severe losses exhibit discrepant reading performance in comparison to their hearing peers (e.g., Davis, Elfenbein, Schum, & Bentler, 1986). However, Briscoe et al.

(2001) studied phonological processing skills and reading achievement of children aged 5–11 years with and without mild to severe hearing losses and found that the groups did not differ on any of the reading tasks. The children with hearing loss did exhibit poorer phonological processing skills than their typically hearing age-matched peers. Similar results were reported by Gibbs (2004). Moeller et al. suggested that the unexpected finding of comparable reading achievement accompanied by poorer phonological processing skills among the children who were hard of hearing may be at least partially due to the impact of advances in earlier identification, intervention, and technology.

Taking the research on language and literacy development together, Moeller et al. (2007c) called for a new generation of studies, focusing on children who have access to early identification, early intervention, and improved amplification, with an emphasis on prospective studies that will guide and inform effective intervention practices. At the same time, they stressed the importance of keeping in mind that mild hearing losses may be missed by early identification protocols, with the result that many children in this group may continue to have late access to typical auditory and linguistic experiences.

Acoustic Ecology and Hearing Accessibility

Taken together, all of the definitions of the term "hard of hearing" share at least two commonalities: first, the individual must have some degree of hearing loss, usually—but not always—in the mild to moderate or severe range; and second, the person who is hard of hearing relies *primarily* on speech and listening for functional communication. The implication of these two factors is that the challenge of seeking access to sound or living with inaccessibility or partial accessibility to sound—particularly the sounds of spoken language—is a central organizing factor in the lives of people who are hard of hearing. Thus, the concept of hearing accessibility, which refers to "the ways people use their hearing to achieve their goals in the varied situations of everyday life" (Laszlo & Pichora-Fuller, 2008, p. 1) is pivotal for understanding the experiences of children and youth who grow up in a world where the majority of the population has no hearing loss.

Recently, some researchers (e.g., McKellin, Shahin, Hodgson, Jamieson, & Pichora-Fuller, 2007) have emphasized the importance of "acoustic ecology," that is, the notion of how an individual's performance must be framed in the acoustic context of the activity, the participants, and the circumstances. In other words, "Our performance in understanding speech, listening to music, or doing work will depend not only on our ears, but also the environment in which we function" (Laszlo & Pichora-Fuller, 2008, p. 2). In the lives of children and youth who are hard of hearing, accessibility to sound is determined not only by the degree and nature of the hearing loss but also by the acoustic ecology, which varies in dramatic ways at different points in development across home and educational settings. For the most part, children who are hard of hearing find themselves in regular childcare and educational settings where they are integrated with their typically hearing peers. Because speaking and listening tend to be the primary modes of communication in teaching, learning, and conversational discourse in integrated placements, speech intelligibility is the major concern in the room acoustics of childcare and school settings (Picard & Bradley, 2001). In particular, reverberation times (which are affected by the shapes and surfaces in rooms) and background noise levels have been found to affect speech intelligibility in all settings. However, in spite of the crucial role of hearing *in*accessibility in the lives of children who are hard of hearing, there has been no interdisciplinary, systematic attempt from a developmental perspective to integrate what is known about the acoustic ecology of childcare and educational settings with the lived experiences of the children with hearing loss who inhabit them.

Hearing Accessibility in Early Childhood

Reliable and consistent access to sound is of fundamental importance to the development of early speech-based communication skills in infancy and early childhood. The home environment, which is typically characterized by quiet background noise levels (in comparison to group educational settings, such as classrooms) and favorable listening conditions, is an ideal context for the transmission and reception of speech signals. In addition, parents unwittingly tend to modify their one-to-one, infant-directed speech to increase the likelihood of the child receiving the message through their use of "motherese," that is, speech that is slower in pace, contains simple sentences with exaggerated intonation, and is marked by very clear pronunciation (Newport, Gleitman, & Gleitman, 1977). Thus, the combined acoustical characteristics of typical home settings and the communicative behavior of caregivers toward infants contribute to a very favorable acoustic ecology for the child's development of language and communication skills. Paradoxically, however, although home listening conditions and parent use of motherese would clearly optimize the potential for language uptake on the part of the infant who is hard of hearing, they may possibly also contribute to a late diagnosis by enhancing the child's opportunity to receive an accurate and clear signal and respond—at least intermittently—with a developmentally appropriate and expected response.

The very small body of research that has investigated noise levels in daycare and preschool settings indicates that infants, toddlers, and preschoolers who are placed in large group settings are exposed to much noisier environments than are found in home settings. For example, Truchon-Gagnon and Hétu (1988) found continuous sound levels in four daycare settings, averaged over 8 hours, varying between 72 and 80 dB. However, *average* noise levels mask the reality of noise in daycare settings; Truchon-Gagnon and Hétu found background noise to be characterized by occasional "spikes," or high instantaneous noise levels. In this connection, they found that everyday activities such as a door banging or child screaming were associated with noise levels in excess of 116 dB. Truchon-Gagnon and Hétu found several factors to be responsible for the high noise levels, the dominant ones being the number of individuals in a given setting and open versus closed plan settings. Most disturbing, perhaps, was the researchers' suggestion that "the responsiveness of caregivers to children is directly affected by noise" (p. 63). For infants and children with hearing losses, such noisy environments and occasional decreased caregiver responsiveness would interfere with access to an already impoverished or unclear speech signal. Some early interventionists who work with young children with hearing losses recommend home-based daycares as opposed to larger, institutionalized daycares precisely because of the smaller number of children and presumed lower noise levels in the home settings (e.g., S. Lane, personal communication, September 10, 2008).

Hodgson and Yang (2005) investigated the acoustical environment of a preschool for typically developing children and children with special needs, including children with hearing loss. The preschool accommodated about 65 children and 13 teachers and consisted of five classrooms and a gymnasium. The reverberation times and background noise measurements indicated that none of the classrooms met acceptable criteria as established by the American National Standard Institute (2002), specifically ANSI S12.60–2002. The researchers also administered a questionnaire to assess teachers' subjective responses to the acoustical and nonacoustical (such as lighting) environments in the classrooms. Teachers agreed that the nonacoustical environments were acceptable but that the acoustical environments were not.

Taken together, the rather limited research on the acoustic ecology of daycare and preschool settings suggests that optimal acoustical conditions are diminished with increasing numbers of persons in the room or adjoining rooms, as well as with classroom designs that were indicative of little apparent consideration of optimal acoustical conditions as specified by ANSI. Through subjective report, the responsive behavior of caregivers and teachers toward the children in their care was negatively affected by excessively high levels of background noise.

Elementary School Settings

Speech and language development occur with extraordinary rapidity in infancy and early childhood, but subtle aspects of communicative development continue throughout the elementary school years, in particular during the primary grades. Thus, it stands to reason that the younger the child (with or without a hearing loss), the greater the importance of optimal classroom acoustical conditions—and thereby optimal speech intelligibility—to developing speech, language, and listening skills. In most learning environments, the most important consideration for accurate speech perception is the signal-to-noise ratio (SNR), that is, the relationship between the intensity of the signal (e.g., the teacher's speech) and the intensity of the background noise at the child's ear (Crandell & Smaldino, 2000). Most researchers who have examined SNRs in elementary classrooms have found unfavorable SNRs that are not conducive to the development of speech and language—and, by extension, literacy—skills (Picard & Bradley, 2001). For example, Hétu, Truchon-Gagnon, and Bilodeau (1990) obtained acoustic measurements for 50 classrooms in six different elementary schools, and found that for the majority of classrooms, the level of background noise and reverberation time did not meet ANSI-established conditions for optimal speech intelligibility.

To complicate matters further, it has long been known that children with hearing losses need the SNR to be improved beyond that required by typically hearing students (Bess, Tharpe, & Gibler, 1986). This holds true even for children with mild degrees of hearing loss and unilateral losses (see Bess, 1985, and Crandell, Smaldino, & Flexer, 1995, for

a review of these investigations). For example, Finitzo-Hieber & Tillman (1978) found that children aged 8–12 years with mild to moderate degrees of sensorineural hearing loss performed significantly more poorly on speech perception tasks than did their peers with typical hearing across several listening conditions. In fact, in what would usually be considered an extremely good classroom listening environment, the children with hearing losses obtained speech perception scores of only 60%, as compared to 83% for their hearing peers. The urgency of equipping classrooms with optimal listening conditions for children with hearing losses was emphasized in a recent study in Poland, in which hearing screening was conducted on over 80,000 7-year-old school children. More than 20% of the children were found to have permanent or temporary hearing losses (Jarosz, 2008). Overall, then, the listening conditions in many elementary classrooms could accurately be described as frequently problematic for children with typical hearing (Shield & Dockrell, 2008) and hostile to children who are hard of hearing (Shield & Dockrell, 2003).

More recently, McKellin et al. (2007) uncovered the dramatic potential of noisy classrooms to alter the communication behavior of students. The conversational interaction of 36 typically hearing students (six students in each of a grade 1 3 split class, two grade 5 classes, and a grade 7 class) was examined. The student participants were grouped together and worked at their desks on the same activities as their fellow class members, who provided the naturally occurring background noise. Each chosen student wore a set of ear-level microphones, with one microphone in each ear, so that a stereo recording of the noise and conversation at the wearer's ear could be recorded. Analysis revealed that the pragmatics of conversational discourse were significantly altered as the level of background noise at ear level increased. In the midst of the noisy classroom activity, the children used strategies such as soliloquy and parallel talk, which reflected verbal and social isolation and which are often used by children who are hard of hearing. In fact, McKellin et al. devised the term "hearing impairing classrooms" in recognition of the power of the acoustic context to alter conversational discourse in such dramatic fashion.

Jamieson, Poon, Zaidman-Zait, and Hodgson (2009) investigated the peer interactions of 11 elementary students who are hard of hearing through classroom and playground observations and extensive interviews with their parents, classroom teachers, and teachers of the deaf and hard of hearing. Classroom acoustical measurements were also obtained. The absence or only partial availability of hearing accessibility in the classroom due to high levels of background noise led all of the children with hearing losses to rely heavily on visual cues, such as following the lead of other students during the transition from one activity to another. Such coping strategies—although effective as a means of supplementing or replacing missed teacher directives—came at a cost, however; from the earliest grades, the children ran the risk of systematically learning how to be followers far more than leaders.

Overall, in the Jamieson et al. (2009) study, the children's experiences of both hearing accessibility and inaccessibility in the classroom appeared to be impacted by the interaction of their hearing losses with a range of factors, including age, classroom activity, and teachers' understanding of the nature of hearing loss. Developmentally, the children in the early primary years (i.e., kindergarten through third grades) often experienced communication breakdowns in the classroom or on the playground with their peers, but because of their strong connection to and dependence on the teacher, the children usually relied on that adult to mediate. However, as the children entered the intermediate years (i.e., fourth through seventh grades), their affiliation with peers intensified (as was developmentally appropriate) and the informal peer–peer communication conveyed quietly in the noisy classroom environment became increasingly a pivotal part of the fabric of their social lives. The children with hearing losses frequently missed out on this interaction, often with severe social penalties:

> … A year or two ago, the children's conversation was less complicated and less rapid-fire, less witty, less all those things. It was easier for her to keep up. And I'd say the more she ages, the more she's unable to stay a part of the conversation. So I'd say more and more her strategy is that she's just leaving and just not bothering. (Mother of a girl in fourth grade)

As illustrated in this quote, some children who are hard of hearing have become social loners as early as the third or fourth grade.

The type of classroom activity has a direct bearing on the level of background noise and, hence, on children's hearing accessibility. Not surprisingly, group activities (such as cooperative learning activities) cause background noise levels to escalate; it is in such activities that children with hearing losses often become followers or even observers. However, even

relatively quiet activities such as weekly spelling tests can be problematic; as one mother stated, "A spelling test is not a spelling test for my daughter—it's a hearing test!" In connection with this, many parents reported that fatigue at the end of long days of focused attention was a chronic after-school complaint of their children.

The classroom teachers in the Jamieson et al. (2009) study seemed to understand hearing loss in a variety of ways. The most common perspective was from the viewpoint of the classroom as a whole. With increasing numbers of children with special needs integrated into regular classrooms, teachers' attention is often drawn to the most disruptive, such as children with behavior problems. In this environment, students with hearing losses who have become quiet followers appeared to attract little teacher attention. When teachers did express a concern about social isolates or poor academic performance, they tended overwhelmingly to attribute the difficulty to the child's personality or perceived academic potential, rather than the hearing loss or poor acoustical conditions.

The school playground—presenting perhaps the most acoustically inaccessible context of any school environment—is a primary social arena for children in elementary school, regardless of hearing status. Jamieson et al. (2009) found that children with hearing losses were differentially included or excluded from playground activities based in large part upon the interplay between hearing accessibility and age, gender, and choice of activity. For example, whereas the kindergarten children were content with solitary or physical play, as children entered the intermediate years the playground activities became increasingly social. Intermediate girls tended to form clusters and share verbal exchanges; the girls with hearing loss were usually unable to access these conversations and positioned themselves on the periphery of groups, in pairs with another marginalized student, or in solitary activities. Boys, on the other hand, experienced the most enduring social success and inclusion from the second grade onward when they became involved in sports activities, such as soccer, that required little verbalization. Consistent with the notion that the school playground presents daunting challenges in terms of social interaction for children who are hard of hearing, Brunnberg (2005) found that integrated children who were hard of hearing tended to play at the periphery of the playground, whereas their hearing peers played in the central interaction area. However, when the same hard-of-hearing children were placed in a separate school for children with hearing losses, they played in the central interaction area.

Overall, the classroom acoustic ecology for the elementary school-aged child who is hard of hearing is strongly and negatively impacted by poor classroom acoustics, high levels of background noise, reverberation, and teacher understanding of the nature of hearing loss. The hearing inaccessibility that characterizes school playgrounds appears to contribute powerfully to social exclusion at recess and other play times. A child's personal resilience, parental advocacy, active instruction, and monitoring by specialist teachers of the deaf and hard of hearing all appear to contribute to positive adaptive behavior and social and academic progress (Jamieson et al., 2009).

Secondary and Postsecondary Settings

There is almost no documented research on the acoustical conditions of secondary classrooms, but the findings that are available support the contention that listening conditions in high schools pose very serious noise problems to students (Hétu et al., 1990; Picard & Bradley, 2001). The additional hearing problem of tinnitus may pose further complexities for some students. Brunnberg, Lindén-Boström, and Berglund (2008) surveyed almost 3,000 15- and 16-year-olds in regular schools in one part of Sweden and found that 39% of students with and 6% of students without hearing loss reported tinnitus often or always during the preceding 3 months. The adolescents with both hearing loss and tinnitus reported considerably higher scores for mental health problems, substance abuse, and school problems than the other students in the study. It appears that for some students, acoustic ecology may be negatively impacted by both internal and external factors pertaining to their hearing accessibility.

Many of the acoustical barriers that existed for students with hearing losses in elementary and secondary school are present in postsecondary settings, although postsecondary classrooms often tend to be larger than public school classrooms and may be equipped with speech reinforcement systems that amplify the instructor's voice. The few studies that have investigated the acoustics of postsecondary classrooms suggest that many of the characteristics of postsecondary classrooms place students who are hard of hearing at a decided disadvantage. For example, Hodgson (1999) found that none of the 45 classrooms investigated at a Canadian postsecondary institution met the ANSI standard for classroom speech intelligibility, and some, in fact, were very poor. Consistent with this, Kennedy, Hodgson, Dillon Edgett, Lamb, and Rempel (2006) administered a questionnaire about perceived listening ease (PLE) to over 5700 students in 30 classrooms at the same university. They found that students with moderate to severe hearing losses reported low PLE in relation to their normally hearing peers. In fact, some students consider the acoustical context so crucial to their postsecondary experience that they give it high priority during course selection. In her study of the academic and social experiences of university students who are hard of hearing, Warick (2003) found that some students went so far as to select their courses based on the acoustical characteristics of the classrooms and the vocal abilities of the professor.

When the findings from research on classroom acoustics and psychosocial adaptation of children and youth who are hard of hearing are considered from an interdisciplinary perspective, it is clear that the acoustic ecology surrounding children and youth who are hard of hearing impacts the extent to which they experience hearing accessibility or inaccessibility. Speech and language development, social interaction, and academic performance are all affected.

Identity

Considerable evidence suggests that the experience of growing up as a child who is hard of hearing in a world where the majority of the population is typically hearing contributes heavily to the process of identity construction. Identity is composed of a broad range of components, such as gender, ethnicity, religion, and hearing status (Weisel, 1998). A child's hearing status is itself multifaceted: as is clear from the preceding discussion, functional communication ability and hearing accessibility vary in large part in relation to the changing features of the acoustic ecology of each situation. Optimal values of acoustical parameters may facilitate the effective use of a child's functional speech, language, and listening skills to the point at which the impact of the hearing loss may seem hidden or at least minimized. In noisy contexts, the same child may need to rely heavily on visual cues or even visual communication, and may effectively be functionally deaf in terms of communication approach. The critical point to underscore, perhaps, is not that these dramatic shifts in acoustic ecology occur in different situations, but, rather, that they are a recurrent, ongoing, everyday feature in the lives of children and youth who are hard of hearing.

Does the dynamic nature of the acoustical context, which so powerfully influences communication for children with hearing loss, impact the process of identity construction? Emerging evidence suggests that it does. Early in adolescence, when children experience strong peer affiliation and typically reject outward signs that set them apart from their peers, children who are hard of hearing have often been reported to shun obvious markers of hearing status such as hearing aids and FM systems (Jamieson et al., 2009; Jamieson, Zaidman-Zait, & Poon, 2008) or refuse to self-identify to their hearing peers as having a hearing disability (Kent, 2003). Research on slightly older students who publicly acknowledged their hearing loss indicates that most persons arrived at the designation of "hard of hearing" by comparing themselves to persons who are hearing and persons who are Deaf. For example, one secondary student remarked, "It's like you are surrounded by a variety of options—hearing, Deaf, and the HH [hard of hearing]—which makes it complicated to determine where one stands in life" (Israelite et al., 2002, p. 140). Consistent with the dominant social focus of adolescence, the hard-of-hearing students framed their identities as hard of hearing based in large part on social factors: "Life is easier because the two teachers helped me improve my communication skills so that in the future I would have better friends" (p. 143). In response to continuing uncertainty surrounding identity, some youth choose to affiliate with the Deaf community as a means of assessing the potential "goodness of fit" (Warick, 1994).

In contrast, the postsecondary students in Warick's (2003) research, who self-identified as hard of hearing, appeared to have resolved identity issues by a somewhat consistent comparison based on functional communication skills. They emphasized their similarity to hearing people in using spoken communication and their difference in terms of difficulties with hearing, and distinguished themselves from Deaf people in terms of communication and community affiliation. It appears that one's identity as "hard of hearing" is dynamic over the course of development and intertwined with a range of other variables. From this perspective, then, it may not be so much the case that persons who are hard of hearing are "between two worlds" (Harvey, 1998) as they are in different worlds at different points, in large part because of the variation in acoustic ecologies throughout their lives.

One consistent finding across research studies and developmental stage was the desire among children, youth, and adults who are hard of hearing to connect socially with other persons who share a similar hearing status (e.g., Jamieson et al., 2009; Warick, 2003). These findings support Hansen (2008), whose findings underscored the necessity of defining "hard of hearing" in terms of social consequences and adaptations, as well as audiological parameters, and Laszlo (1994), who acknowledged the broad diversity of persons who are hard of hearing but insisted that a hard of hearing identity exists nonetheless.

The Impact of Early Identification

The widespread implementation of UNHS and early intervention programs has the potential to impact the population of hard-of-hearing children and youth in at least three significant ways. First, as a result of early identification and intervention, many children who are hard of hearing will achieve higher levels of functional communication than has been previously documented, leading to more successful academic and social outcomes (see Chapters 16 and 23, this volume, for discussions of various aspects of newborn hearing screening). Second, many children with more significant hearing losses will benefit from early intervention and ultimately develop functional communication skills more characteristic of children with lesser degrees of loss. Indeed, this appears to be the case in jurisdictions where early identification programs have been in operation for some years (e.g., Yoshinaga-Itano, 2006). Finally, early identification of deafness allows for an earlier average age of cochlear implantation than was possible a decade ago, contributing to the potential for many deaf children to develop functional communication skills more typical of hearing or hard-of-hearing children than of deaf children (see Chapter 22, this volume, for a discussion of early cochlear implantation). Overall, then, it is expected that UNHS, early intervention programs, and improved opportunities for early auditory access will alter the population of children with hearing loss by increasing the proportion who may be identified as functionally hard of hearing, and, thereby, adding to the already considerable heterogeneity of the population of children and youth who are hard of hearing.

Summary and Conclusions

Research involving children who are hard of hearing has, for the most part, been difficult to interpret in terms of its generalizability because of a lack of clarity in definition. Broad terms such as "deaf and hard of hearing" lack the precision necessary to determine to what extent findings may be applicable specifically to children and youth who are hard of hearing. Increasingly, researchers have adopted the practice of defining the participants in their studies in terms of relevant characteristics, such as educational placement and communication approach. In general, in research on children with hearing loss, the category of "hard of hearing" refers to children with any degree of hearing loss who communicate primarily through speech and listening. The consistent provision of aided hearing levels would provide additional helpful information.

The notion of "acoustic ecology" and the integration of research from social scientists and physical acousticians provide a useful lens for investigating the experiences of children and youth who are hard of hearing and are encompassed within and affected by a multitude of acoustical contexts in their everyday lives. Given an emphasis on oral–aural communication, it is clear that acoustic ecology, which varies significantly across both individual situations and development more broadly (from home to school settings, for example) figures prominently in determining hearing accessibility for all children—but most especially for children who are hard of hearing. It is an ongoing challenge for a child who is hard of hearing to optimize hearing accessibility whenever possible and to develop adaptive coping strategies when it is not. Children are most centrally engaged in the development of speech and language skills in their youngest months and years, and so it stands to reason that this is when they would benefit most from environments with favorable acoustical conditions. Quite clearly, this is even more strongly the case for infants and children who are hard of hearing. Paradoxically, however, some settings in which many children are placed during the early stages of development, such as group daycares or elementary school classrooms, are characterized by excessively high levels of background noise and reverberation. Indeed, nonoptimal acoustical conditions appear to be typical of most classroom settings across secondary and postsecondary educational programs as well. The varying acoustic ecology surrounding children who are hard of hearing enables them to use their speech and listening skills to maximum benefit in favorable circumstances but renders them primarily reliant on visual cues in noisy situations.

The impact of living with a range of hearing accessibility (or, perhaps more to the point, hearing inaccessibility) on psychosocial development and identity construction may perhaps best be understood from a developmental perspective. For example, the effect of not overhearing the social conversation of peers is in large part dependent on the importance of peers at that point in development. As peer relationships assume increasing significance from a child's perspective over the course of the elementary school years, so, too, does the social impact of missing out on informal peer–peer discourse. Ultimately, this systematic process of social exclusion reported retrospectively by many—although not all—adults who are hard of hearing may contribute to a "hard of hearing identity," which is defined in large part by the desire for social affiliation with others of the same hearing status.

With the advent of early EHDI programs around the world and the dramatic technological improvements and innovations in assistive listening devices, the population of children and youth identifiable as hard of hearing will no doubt expand and diversify in the coming years. Studies on optimal acoustical conditions for daycares, preschools, and school and postsecondary settings are a research priority. In addition, it would be instructive to follow the progress of various groups of early-identified children, longitudinally at both the group level and through in-depth case studies, to investigate the academic and social strengths, needs, and outcomes of these children. The lives of young people who are hard of hearing are impacted by a broad range of factors, and in this connection an interdisciplinary approach—involving researchers who are themselves hard of hearing when possible and feasible—would help shed considerable light on the complex issues confronting these children.

Acknowledgments

Thanks to Drs. Murray Hodgson and Anat Zaidman-Zait for their helpful comments on an earlier version of this chapter.

References

American National Standard. (2002). *Acoustical performance criteria, design requirements, and guidelines for schools* (ANSI Publication S12. 60–2002). Melville, NY: Acoustical Society of America.

Antia, S. D., & Ditillo, D. A. (1998). A comparison of the peer social behavior of children who are Deaf/Hard of Hearing and Hearing. *Journal of Children's Communication Development, 19,* 1–10.

Antia, S. D., Sabers, D. L., & Stinson, M. S. (2006). Validity and reliability of the Classroom Participation Questionnaire with deaf and hard of hearing students in public schools. *Journal of Deaf Studies and Deaf Education, 12,* 158–171.

Apuzzo, M. L., & Yoshinaga-Itano, C. (1995). Early identification of infants with significant hearing loss and the Minnesota

Child Development Inventory. *Seminars in Hearing, 16,* 124–139.

Bess, F. (1985). The minimally hearing-impaired child. *Ear and Hearing, 6,* 43–47.

Bess, F., Tharpe, A., & Gibler, A. (1986). Auditory performance of children with unilateral sensorineural hearing loss. *Ear and Hearing, 7,* 3–13.

Blamey, P. J. (2003). Development of spoken language by deaf children. In M. Marschark & P. Spencer (Eds.), *Oxford handbook of Deaf studies, language, and education* (pp. 232–246). New York: Oxford University Press.

Blamey, P. J., Paatsch, L. E., Bow, C. P., Sarant, J. Z., & Wales, R. J. (2002). A critical level of hearing for speech perception in children. *Acoustics Research Letters Online, 3,* 18–23.

Briscoe, J., Bishop, D. V. M., & Norbury, C. F. (2001). Phonological processing, language, and literacy: A comparison of children with mild-to-moderate sensorineural hearing loss and those with specific language impairment. *Journal of Child Psychology and Psychiatry, and Allied Disciplines, 42,* 329–340.

Brunnberg, E. (2005). The school playground as a meeting place for hard of hearing children. *Scandinavian Journal of Disability Research, 7,* 73–90.

Brunnberg, E., Lindén-Boström, M., & Berglund, M. (2008). Tinnitus and hearing loss in 15–16-year-old students: Mental health symptoms, substance use, and exposure in school. *International Journal of Audiology, 47,* 688–694.

Crandell, C. C., & Smaldino, J. J. (2000). Classroom acoustics for children with normal hearing and with hearing impairment. *Language, Speech, and Hearing Services in Schools, 31,* 362–370.

Crandell, C., Smaldino, J., & Flexer, C. (1995). *Sound field FM amplification: Theory and practical applications.* San Diego, CA: Singular Press.

Davis, H. (1990). *Our forgotten children: Hard-of-Hearing pupils in the schools.* Bethesda, MD: SHHH Publications.

Davis, J. M., Elfenbein, J., Schum, R., & Bentler, R. A. (1986). Effects of mild and moderate hearing impairments on language, educational, and psychosocial behavior of children. *The Journal of Speech and Hearing Disorders, 51,* 53–62.

Davis, J. M., Shepard, N. T., Stelmachowicz, P. G., & Gorga, M. P. (1981) Characteristics of hearing-impaired children in the public schools. Part II: Psychoeducational data. *The Journal of Speech and Hearing Disorders, 46,* 130–137.

Dillon Edgett, L. M. (2002). *Help-seeking for advanced rehabilitation by adults with hearing loss: An ecological model.* Unpublished doctoral dissertation, University of British Columbia.

Elfenbein, J. L., Hardin-Jones, M. A., & Davis, J. M. (1994). Oral communication skills of children who are hard of hearing. *Journal of Speech and Hearing Research, 37,* 216–226.

Figueras, B., Edwards, L., & Langdon, D. (2008). Executive function and language in deaf children. *Journal of Deaf Studies and Deaf Education, 13,* 362–377.

Finitzo-Hieber, T., & Tillman, T. (1978). Room acoustics effects on monosyllabic word discrimination ability for normal and hearing-impaired children. *Journal of Speech and Hearing Research, 21,* 440–458.

Frisina, R. (1974). *Report of the committee to redefine deaf and hard of hearing for educational purposes.* Washington, DC: Conference of Educational Administrators of Schools and Programs for the Deaf.

Geers, A. (2004). Speech, language, and reading skills after early cochlear implantation. *Archives of Otolaryngology – Head and Neck Surgery, 130,* 634–638.

Gallaudet Research Institute. (2006–2007). *Annual Survey of Deaf and Hard of Hearing Children and Youth.* Washington, DC: Gallaudet University, Gallaudet Research Institute.

Gibbs, S. (2004). The skills in reading shown by young children with permanent and moderate hearing impairment. *Educational Research, 46,* 17–27.

Gilbertson, M., & Kamhi, A. G. (1995). Novel word learning in children with hearing impairment. *Journal of Speech and Hearing Research, 38,* 630–642.

Hansen, N. M. (July, 2008). *Putting numbers and words on the problems young people with hearing loss face in their everyday life.* Paper presented at the quintennial meeting of the International Federation of the Hard of Hearing, Vancouver, BC.

Harvey, M. A. (1998). *Odyssey of hearing loss: Tales of triumph.* San Diego, CA: Dawn Sign Press.

Hétu, R., Truchon-Gagnon, C., & Bilodeau, S. A. (1990). Problems of noise in school settings: A review of the literature and the results of an exploratory study. *Journal of Speech Language Pathology and Audiology, 14,* 31–39.

Hodgson, M. R. (1999). Experimental investigation of the acoustical characteristics of university classrooms. *Journal of the Acoustical Society of America, 106,* 1810–1819.

Hodgson, M., & Yang, W. (2005). Acoustical evaluation of preschool classrooms. *Noise Control Engineering Journal, 53,* 43–52.

Hyde, M., & Power, D. (2003). Characteristics of deaf and hard-of-hearing students in Australian regular schools: Hearing level comparisons. *Deafness and Education International, 5,* 133–143.

Israelite, N., Ower, J., & Goldstein, G. (2002). Hard-of-hearing adolescents and identity construction: Influences of school experiences, peers, and teachers. *Journal of Deaf Studies and Deaf Education, 7,* 134–148.

Itard, Jean Marc Gaspard. (1821). *Traité des maladies d'oreille et de l'audition.* Paris: Méquignon Marvis.

Jamieson, J. R., Poon, B. T., Zaidman-Zait, A., & Hodgson, M. (2009). *Peer interaction among children who are hard of hearing and their hearing peers in elementary school.* Manuscript submitted for publication.

Jamieson, J. R., Zaidman-Zait, A., & Poon, B. T. (July, 2008). *Hard of hearing children in the school years: Family needs for support and connection.* Paper presented at the quintennial meeting of the International Federation of the Hard of Hearing, Vancouver, BC.

Jarosz, M. (November, 2008). What can you hear, seven years old? *Ecophon Acoustic Bulletin, November, 2008.* Retrieved December 9, 2008, from http://www.acousticbulletin.com/EN/2008/11/what_you_can_hear_seven_years.html

Kennedy, S., Dillon Edgett, L., Hodgson, M., Lamb, N., & Rempel, R. (2006). Subjective assessment of listening environments in university classrooms: Perceptions of students. *Journal of the Acoustical Society of America, 119,* 299–309.

Kent, B. A. (2003). Identity issues for hard-of-hearing adolescents aged 11, 13, and 15 in mainstream settings. *Journal of Deaf Studies and Deaf Education, 8,* 315–324.

Koester, L. S., Brooks, L., & Traci, M. A. (2000). Tactile contact by deaf and hearing mothers during face-to-face interactions with their infants. *Journal of Deaf Studies and Deaf Education, 5,* 127–139.

Kyle, F. E., & Harris, M. (2006). Concurrent correlates and predictors of reading and spelling achievement in deaf and hearing school children. *Journal of Deaf Studies and Deaf Education, 11,* 273–288.

Laszlo, C. A. (1994). Is there a hard-of-hearing identity? *Journal of the Canadian Association of Speech-Language Pathologists and Audiologists, 18,* 248–252.

Lazslo, C., & Pichora-Fuller, K. (2008). *Moving toward the future: Creating a virtual institute for hearing accessibility research.* Retrieved August 21, 2008, from the Canadian Hard of Hearing-International Federation of the Hard of Hearing Congress 2008 web site: http://chha.ca/conference/2008/index2.php?content=workshop

Lederberg, A. R., Prezbindowski, A. K., & Spencer, P. E. (2000). Word-learning skills of deaf preschoolers: The development of novel mapping and rapid word-learning strategies. *Child Development, 71,* 1571–1585.

McGuckian, M., & Henry, A. (2007). The grammatical morpheme deficit in moderate hearing impairment. *International Journal of Language & Communication Disorders, 42*(S1), 17–36.

McKellin, W. H. (1994). Hearing and listening: Audiology, hearing, and hearing impairment in everyday life. *Journal of the Canadian Association of Speech-Language Pathologists and Audiologists, 18,* 212–219.

McKellin, W. H., Shahin, K., Hodgson, M., Jamieson, J., & Pichora-Fuller, K. (2007). Pragmatics of conversation and communication in noisy settings. *Journal of Pragmatics, 39,* 2159–2184.

Meadow-Orlans, K. P., Mertens, D. M., Sass-Lehrer, M. A., & Scott-Olson, K. (1997). Support services for parents and their children who are deaf or hard of hearing: A national survey. *American Annals of the Deaf, 142,* 278–293.

Meadow-Orlans, K. P., Sass-Lehrer, M. A., Scott-Olson, K., & Mertens, D. M. (1998). Children who are hard of hearing: Are they forgotten? *Perspectives in Education and Deafness. 16,* 6–8, 24.

Moeller, M. P. (2000). Early intervention and language development in children who are deaf and hard of hearing. *Pediatrics, 106,* 1–9.

Moeller, M. P., Hoover, B., Putman, C., Arbataitis, K., Bohnenkamp, G., Peterson, B., et al. (2007a). Vocalizations of infants with hearing loss compared with infants with normal hearing: Part II: Transition to words. *Ear and Hearing, 28,* 628–642.

Moeller, M. P., Hoover, B., Putman, C., Arbataitis, K., Bohnenkamp, G., Peterson, B., et al. (2007b). Vocalizations of infants with hearing loss compared with infants with normal hearing: Part I: Phonetic development. *Ear and Hearing, 28,* 605–627.

Moeller, M. P., Tomblin, J. B., Yoshinaga-Itano, C., Connor, C., & Jerger, S. (2007c). Current state of knowledge: Language and literacy of children with hearing impairment. *Ear and Hearing, 28,* 740–753.

Musselman, C., Lindsay, P., & Wilson, A. (1988). An evaluation of trends in preschool programming for hearing-impaired children. *Journal of Speech and Hearing Disorders, 53,* 71–88.

Newport, E. L., Gleitman, H., & Gleitman, L. R. (1977). Mother, I'd rather do it myself: Some effects and non-effects of maternal speech style. In C. A. Ferguson & C. E. Snow (Eds.), *Talking to children* (pp. 109–149). New York: Cambridge University Press.

Nicholas, J. G., & Geers, A. E. (2003). Personal, social, and family adjustment in school-aged children with a cochlear implant, *Ear and Hearing, 24* (Supplement), 46–58.

Nicholas, J. G., & Geers, A. E. (2006). The process and early outcomes of cochlear implantation by three years of age. In P. E. Spencer & M. Marschark (Eds.), *Advances in the spoken language development of deaf and hard-of-hearing children* (pp. 271–297). New York, NY: Oxford University Press.

Nittrouer, S., & Burton, L. T. (2003). The role of early language experience in the development of speech perception and language processing abilities in children with hearing loss. *The Volta Review, 103,* 5–38.

Nunes, T., & Pretzlik, U. (2001). Deaf children's social relationships in mainstream schools. *Deafness and Education International, 3,* 123–136.

Picard, M., & Bradley, J. S. (2001). Revisiting speech interference in classrooms. *Audiology, 40,* 221–244.

Punch, R., & Hyde, M. (2005). The social participation and career decision-making of hard-of-hearing adolescents in regular classes. *Deafness and Education International, 7,* 122–138.

Ross, M. (2008). *Definitions and Descriptions.* Pennsylvania SHHH: Dr. Mark Ross on Hearing Loss. Retrieved December 11, 2008, from http://www. pa-shhh.org/ross/ross.html

Shield, B. M., & Dockrell, J. E. (2003). The effects of noise on children at school: A review. *Building Acoustics, 10,* 97–116.

Shield, B. M., & Dockrell, J. E. (2008). The effects of environmental and classroom noise on the academic attainments of primary school children. *Journal of the Acoustical Society of America, 123,* 133–144.

Stelmachowicz, P. G., Pittman, A. L., Hoover, B. M., & Lewis, D. E. (2001). Effect of stimulus bandwidth on the perception of /s/ in normal and hearing-impaired children and adults. *The Journal of the Acoustical Society of America, 110,* 2183–2190.

Stinson, M., Whitmire, K., & Kluwin, T. (1996). Self-perceptions of social relationships in hearing-impaired adolescents. *Journal of Educational Psychology, 88,* 132–143.

Tomblin, B., & Hebbler, K. (2007). Current state of knowledge: Outcomes research in children with mild to severe hearing impairment – Approaches and methodological considerations. (2007). *Ear and Hearing, 28,* 715–128.

Truchon-Gagnon, C., & Hétu, R. (1988). Noise in day-care centers for children. *Noise Control Engineering Journal, 30,* 57–63.

Warick, R. (1994). A profile of Canadian hard-of-hearing youth. *Journal of Speech Language Pathology and Audiology, 18,* 253–259.

Warick, R. P. (2003). Voices unheard: The academic and social experiences of university students who are hard of hearing. Unpublished doctoral dissertation, University of British Columbia.

Weisel, A. (1998). An opening statement: Identity development and Deaf Education. In A. Weisel (Ed.), *Insights into Deaf Education: Theory and practice* (pp. 11–25). Tel Aviv, Israel: Academic Press of Tel Aviv University.

Wolgemuth, K. S., Kamhi, A. G., & Lee, R. F. (1998). Metaphor performance in children with hearing impairment. *Language, Speech, and Hearing Services in Schools, 29,* 216–231.

Yoshinaga-Itano, C. (2006). Early identification, communication modality, and the development of speech and spoken language skills: Patterns and consideration. In P. E. Spencer & M. Marschark (Eds.), *Advances in the spoken language development of deaf and hard-of-hearing children* (pp. 298–327). New York: Oxford University Press.

Yoshinaga-Itano, C. (2003). From screening to early identification and intervention: Discovering predictors to successful outcomes for children with significant hearing loss. *Journal of Deaf Studies and Deaf Education, 8,* 11–30.

Yoshinaga-Itano, C., Sedey, A. L., Coulter, B. A., & Mehl, A. L. (1998). Language of early- and later-identified children with hearing loss. *Pediatrics, 102,* 1168–1171.

Performance Outcomes for Adult Cochlear Implant Users

Camille C. Dunn, Ann Perreau, Kenneth Marciniak, Beth Macpherson, Richard S. Tyler, *and* Monika Kordus

Abstract

This chapter provides a summary of the history of cochlear implants, how a cochlear implant works, and the criteria for candidacy and how that has changed over the years. In addition, this chapter addresses critical issues related to whether profoundly deafened listeners should receive one or two cochlear implants. Speech recognition and localization performance of subjects who wear bilateral cochlear implants (simultaneous or sequentially implanted) will be discussed in comparison to subjects who wear only one cochlear implant or a cochlear implant and a hearing aid. In addition, this chapter will provide a review of the literature analyzing the effects of one versus two cochlear implants, as well as recommendations for who should receive bilateral cochlear implants. This chapter also briefly discusses shortcomings in testing methodology typically used to evaluate the performance of cochlear implants, and surveys future directions.

Keywords: cochlear implants, bilateral cochlear implants, unilateral cochlear implants, bilateral benefit

Cochlear implantation is a widely accepted medical intervention for restoring hearing sensations for persons with profound sensorineural deafness in both ears. A cochlear implant is a medical device surgically implanted into the cochlea that bypasses damage to the hair cells in the cochlea and directly stimulates the auditory or hearing nerve. In early stages of development, a cochlear implant served as an aid to lipreading for deaf and hard-of-hearing (DHH) individuals due to the very limited frequency or pitch information provided by the implant. However, cochlear implant technology has progressed over the last 20 years to such an extent that current cochlear implant users show remarkable improvements in their speech understanding and report an improved quality of life provided by the cochlear implant. Today, many cochlear implant users are able to talk on the telephone and hear well in a variety of communication situations. Some cochlear implant users do so well with their implant that

they elect to receive a second cochlear implant in the other ear.

History

Electrical stimulation of the cochlea dates back to the late 18th century, when Alessandro Volta first stimulated the auditory system by connecting a battery of 30 or 40 "couples" to two metal rods that were inserted into his ears. He reportedly perceived a sort of "a boom within the head," thereby leading the way for future investigations of electric stimulation in the auditory system. Immediately following Volta's experiment, however, there was a long period of uncertainty as to the usefulness of electrical stimulation for restoring hearing sensation, since many of the treatments at that time were too invasive for human use.

After years of continued research and attempts to stimulate the auditory nerve using various methodologies, the first commercially available cochlear implant, the House 3M single-electrode implant, was introduced to the market in 1972. The U.S. Food and Drug Administration (FDA) later approved the House 3M device for use in adults over 18 years of age with profound, bilateral sensorineural deafness. The House 3M single-electrode implant mostly provided listeners with sound awareness and very limited speech recognition abilities. During the 1970s, concurrent research by many individuals, including Graham Clark of the University of Melbourne, was undertaken on the development of a multichannel cochlear implant. With the availability of the multichannel device in 1984, speech recognition capabilities were far improved over that obtained with the single-channel device.

How a Cochlear Implant Works
Components
A cochlear implant consists of an external speech processor and transmitter coil (see Fig. 26.1A) and an internal receiver/stimulator (Fig. 26.1B). The speech processor picks up sounds via the microphone and converts the acoustic sound into a high-rate, electrical pulse that is amplitude-modulated by the envelope of the original signal and processed through several wide filter banks that code the pitch

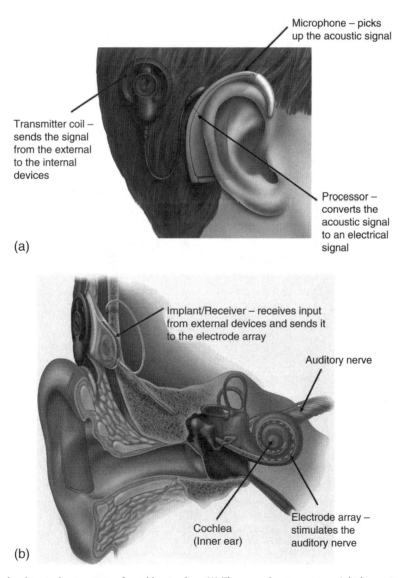

(a)

Microphone – picks up the acoustic signal

Transmitter coil – sends the signal from the external to the internal devices

Processor – converts the acoustic signal to an electrical signal

(b)

Implant/Receiver – receives input from external devices and sends it to the electrode array

Auditory nerve

Cochlea (Inner ear)

Electrode array – stimulates the auditory nerve

Fig. 26.1 External and internal components of a cochlear implant. (A) The external parts: processor (which contains the microphone) and the transmitter. (B) The internal parts: implant/receiver, and the electrode (array). Images courtesy of Cochlear Limited.

information of the sound. This signal is sent to the transmitter coil, which relays the signal across the skin using radio-frequency transmission until it reaches the internal receiver/stimulator. From the internal receiver/stimulator, the electrical signal is delivered to the electrodes in the cochlea along the electrode array, resulting in stimulation of different regions of auditory nerve fibers. Once the nerve fibers are stimulated, this information is processed by higher structures in the auditory system as it normally would be via acoustic stimulation. The frequency or pitch information of a sound provided by a cochlear implant is influenced by many factors, including the place in the cochlea that is being stimulated and the rate of stimulation provided by the pulse, as well as by other cochlear implant program settings.

Strategies

Over the years, numerous advancements have been made in cochlear implant technology, especially in how sound is processed through the implant. The way that a cochlear implant delivers stimulation to the auditory nerve is called a *processing strategy*. Initially, cochlear implant speech processing strategies provided only limited speech information, mostly coding the fundamental frequency of speech (e.g., F0, F1, F2). More modern cochlear implant processing strategies extract the envelope of the speech signal, stimulating the electrodes along the array in a sequential-like order (i.e., *continuous interleaved sampling* or CIS) or stimulating electrodes that match the highest peak of information (termed "maxima") in the signal (i.e., *advanced coding extracting*

or ACE). In general, most modern cochlear implant strategies code the temporal, or timing, cues of speech very well.

Once the cochlear implant processing strategy is chosen for each individual, the user is asked to rate the softness and loudness of the sound presented from each electrode to set the minimum and maximum current level that each electrode will stimulate. The audiologist can also make various adjustments and changes in settings to accommodate different listening environments for each user. These adjustments can then be saved as different programs and downloaded on the user's microprocessor. Generally, each cochlear implant microprocessor can be downloaded with three to four processing programs. An example of a program for a microprocessor is shown in Figure 26.2.

Who Gets a Cochlear Implant?

Following advancements in cochlear implant design and improvements in speech perception outcomes over time, the audiological criteria used to assess cochlear implant candidacy has also evolved. In general, the criteria have broadened to include a larger population of individuals with hearing loss. The changes in criteria can be grouped into three main areas: current age of cochlear implant candidate, age of onset of hearing loss, and degree of hearing loss. Other important factors influencing cochlear implant candidacy include an individual's medical status (e.g., healthy enough to undergo surgery, patent cochlea, no active middle ear infections), expectations prior to implantation, and ability to maintain and use the equipment or the

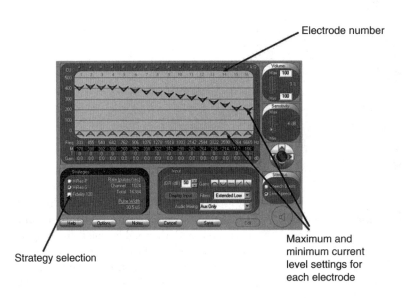

Electrode number

Strategy selection

Maximum and minimum current level settings for each electrode

Fig. 26.2 An example of an Advanced Bionics Cochlear Implant map.

availability of supportive individuals to help the person do so.

Adults

Originally, cochlear implantation in adults was limited to those over the age of 18 with postlinguistic onset of hearing loss and profound, bilateral sensorineural hearing loss. Cochlear implant candidacy has expanded now to include adults and young children with onset of hearing loss at any age. For adults, potential cochlear implant candidates are generally assessed based on the benefit they receive from hearing aids or traditional amplification on open-set sentence recognition. According to the FDA-approved guidelines for cochlear implantation, adults with limited aided benefit on sentence recognition tests (e.g., 50% or less in the ear to be implanted, 60% or less in best aided condition [Cochlear Limited, Physicians Packet Insert, 2006]) are considered for implantation. The most common cause of a bilateral sensorineural hearing loss in adults is the natural aging process. However, other likely causes might be noise exposure or heredity.

Children

Cochlear implantation in children has traditionally been reserved for children aged 2 through 18 years, but recent advancements have expanded this criterion to include implanting very young children. In fact, a number of cochlear implant centers have reported successful cochlear implantation in children as young as 7 months of age (Colletti, Carner, Miorelli, Guida, Colletti, & Fiorino, 2005; Dettman, Pinder, Briggs, Dowell, & Leigh, 2007; Waltzman & Roland, 2005). When implanting very young children, accurate audiological diagnosis of hearing loss is of utmost importance. The degree of hearing loss for young children is best determined using a comprehensive diagnostic test battery including auditory brainstem response (ABR) testing, otoacoustic emission (OAE) testing, steady-state evoked potential (SSEP) testing, and behavioral audiometry including unaided and aided audiometric thresholds. Behavioral audiometric thresholds for air and bone conduction are obtained using age-appropriate testing methods, such as conditioned play audiometric (CPA) techniques for children aged 24 months to 5 years, visual reinforcement audiometric (VRA) techniques for children aged 5 months to 30 months and/or behavioral observation (BOA) techniques for children aged 0 to 6 months.

Current cochlear implant candidacy includes children with: (a) severe-to-profound bilateral sensorineural deafness, (b) limited speech recognition abilities on developmentally appropriate sentence and word recognition tests, (c) high family/parental motivation and realistic expectations for the child's progress with an implant, and finally, (d) those who are healthy enough to undergo surgery. In addition, children should have a trial period of 3–6 months with appropriately fitted hearing aids to assess the benefits provided by amplification. For younger children, candidacy for cochlear implantation also includes lack of progress as determined by a plateau in auditory skill development. Unlike older children, young infants and toddlers cannot be assessed using traditional speech perception tests to evaluate the benefit from amplification and therefore require alternate methods to document performance. Lack of auditory progress for young children is often determined by subjective outcome measures given to parents and/or educators, such as the Infant-Toddler Meaningful Auditory Integration Scale (IT-MAIS) (Zimmerman-Phillips, Robbins, & Osberger, 2000) and the Meaningful Auditory Integration Scale (MAIS) (Robbins, Renshaw, & Berry, 1991), which consists of 10 questions regarding a young infant or toddler's auditory behavior. Tools such as the IT-MAIS and MAIS are most frequently used to assess the benefit of the child's personal amplification device(s); however, they can also be utilized after implantation to chart progress or improvements made by the child with his or her cochlear implant.

Cochlear implantation in children requires accurate audiologic diagnosis along with a thorough evaluation of the child's hearing and hearing aid history, communication mode, educational progress, and family support. In the remainder of this chapter, we will focus on outcomes for adults with one cochlear implant, two cochlear implants, or one cochlear implant and one hearing aid on opposite ears. We will also discuss the presumed benefits of binaural hearing and discuss examples of speech perception and localization and distance perception results as it relates to binaural hearing.

Speech Perception Performance
Unilateral Adult Cochlear Implant

Speech understanding is variable among cochlear implant recipients. Some individuals hear almost all that is said in a conversation, use the telephone with good success, and thoroughly enjoy listening to music, whereas others do not achieve these same abilities even after several years of implant use. Many factors influence the benefit provided by a cochlear implant. Some of the widely identified factors are age at implantation and duration of deafness (Cohen, Waltzman, & Fisher, 1993; Gantz, Woodworth, Knutson, Abbas, & Tyler, 1993; Rubinstein, Parkinson, Tyler, & Gantz, 1999; Tyler & Summerfield, 1996; van Dijk, van Olphen, Langereis, Mens, Brokx, & Smoorenburg, 1999). Specifically, people who are deaf and hard of hearing often achieve better performance with their cochlear implant when implanted at a younger age and/or who have a shorter duration of auditory deprivation (see Chapter 9, this volume).

Most adults receiving a cochlear implant have postlingual onset of deafness, meaning that the onset of profound hearing loss began after they acquired speech and language skills. Benefits from cochlear implantation for postlingually deafened adults are consistently reported in at least one dimension of listening (telephone use, one-on-one conversation, music perception, etc.). Recent studies have reported speech perception abilities of approximately 45%–60% on monosyllabic word recognition tests in quiet, and 75%–85% on sentence recognition test in quiet (Balkany et al., 2007; Helms et al., 1997; Koch, Osberger, Segel, & Kessler, 2004). These results show a remarkable improvement over preimplant scores (i.e., average monosyllabic word recognition is equal to approximately 3% and sentence recognition is equal to approximately 11%) (Balkany et al., 2007).

Additionally, successful telephone use with a landline or cell phone is achieved by many cochlear implant recipients. Anderson, Baumgartner, Boheim, Nahler, Arnoldner, & D'Haese (2006) conducted a self-report survey on telephone use for 196 cochlear implant users. Results revealed that 71% of listeners could use a landline phone with their cochlear implant with no reported problems, as compared to 40% of listeners who could use the phone prior to implantation. Additionally, 54% of listeners could effectively use a cell phone with their cochlear implant, although better speech understanding and greater confidence was reported when using a landline phone.

Despite these improvements in speech recognition, research has demonstrated that music perception for cochlear implant users is poorer than that of normal hearing individuals (Gfeller, Turner, Oleson, Zhang, Gantz, Froman, & Olszewski, 2007). Poorer music performance is likely due to the lack of accurate pitch perception by cochlear implants users and relatively poor transmission of frequency information by the implant. A study by Gfeller Oleson,

Knutson, Breheny, Driscoll, and Olszewski (2008) investigated whether music perception and appreciation could be predicted based on demographic and life experience variables and speech perception scores for 209 adult cochlear implant users. Results indicated that individual characteristics such as hearing history, age, and hearing aid use were associated with the accuracy and appraisal of music listening. Additionally, Gfeller et al. found that incidental music listening on its own does not lead to better music perception and enjoyment. Instead, formal music training was associated with greater accuracy and appraisal of music (Gfeller, 2008), indicating that cochlear implant users may benefit from music practice to increase their music perception abilities and appreciation.

Expectations and outcomes for adults with prelingual deafness receiving a cochlear implant are often different from those with postlingual deafness. For adults who are prelingually deafened, research has shown that they receive less improvement in open-set word recognition postoperatively as compared to adults who are postlingually deafened (Kaplan, Shipp, Chen, Ng, & Nedzelski, 2003; Skinner, Binzer, Fears, Holden, Jenison, & Nettles, 1992; Zwolan, Kileny, & Telian, 1996). However, many prelingually deafened adults show enhanced lipreading and hear environmental sounds with good success when using their cochlear implant. A study by Zwolan et al. (1996) documented cochlear implant use and satisfaction for 12 adult cochlear implant users who were prelingually deafened using self-report questionnaires and speech perception tests. Results of this study found that closed-set speech recognition abilities showed little to no improvement following implantation. However, for 8 of 12 listeners, they reported using their cochlear implant regularly as much as 10 hours per day and most individuals reportedly were satisfied with their speech understanding and understanding of environmental sounds provided by the implant. When asked what they liked most about their implant, comments such as "I can hear" and "easier for me to lipread" were noted. Therefore, when determining cochlear implant benefit for prelingually deafened adults, it is important that measures such as patient satisfaction and lipreading enhancement be considered.

Bilateral Cochlear Implant Users
Although the majority of cochlear implant recipients worldwide have only one cochlear implant, in more recent years, bilateral cochlear implantation

has been explored by many individuals who desire the benefits of binaural listening.

Bilateral cochlear implant users are divided into two groups: sequential or simultaneous. Sequential bilateral cochlear implant users are those who received their cochlear implants in two surgeries, separated by time. Simultaneous bilateral cochlear implant users, on the other hand, are those persons who received their cochlear implants during one surgical procedure. In this section, we will discuss some of the recognized benefits of listening with two ears, how those benefits are measured, and finally, performance results on simultaneously and sequentially implanted bilateral cochlear implant users.

PRESUMED BENEFITS OF LISTENING WITH TWO EARS

Being able to listen with two ears offers several benefits to the listener, including the effects of binaural summation, binaural squelch, the better-ear effect, and improved localization of sound.

The *binaural summation effect* occurs when a signal, such as speech information, originates from directly in front of the listener, presenting each ear with redundant timing, amplitude, and spectral information. When this redundant information is processed by the brain, the loudness of the sound is perceived to be doubled and can produce improvements in speech perception both in quiet and in noise.

To measure the binaural summation effect in a laboratory setting, speech is presented in quiet or in noise from the individuals 0-degree azimuth with the right and left ears tested individually and with both ears together. Scores with each ear tested individually are compared to the score when both ears are tested together. If there is an improvement in the speech perception score when both ears are used together over the individual ear scores, the listener was able to take advantage of the perceived doubling of the loudness of the sound.

When speech is presented to the front of the listener and noise is spatially separated from the speech, the two ears receive both similar and different timing, amplitude, and spectral cues. For example, in conversations, if the speaker is located in front of the listener and noise is off to the side, both of the ears will receive the same information from the front (speech), but different information for the noise off toward one side of the listener. As a result of the speech and noise being spatially separated, it is easier for the brain to separate the speech and the noise into separate auditory streams. The brain then combines the similar information and squelches the different information. This process is called the *binaural squelch effect* (Carhart, 1965; Middlebrooks & Green, 1991; Zurek, 1993). It results in an improvement of the signal-to-noise (S/N) ratio of about 5 dB for the normal hearing listener.

To test the binaural squelch effect in a laboratory setting, speech is presented in noise with speech emanating from the individuals' 0-degree azimuth and the noise either 90 degrees to the left or right of the individuals' 0-degree azimuth. Subjects are tested with the individual ear without the noise facing it (opposite the noise) and again with both ears together. The individual ear score is compared to the score when both ears are tested together. If there is an improvement in the speech perception score when both ears are used together over the individual ear score, the listener was able to separate the similar and dissimilar information, and therefore, squelch the unwanted information to focus specifically on the speech.

The *head shadow effect* is a physical effect that occurs when the head acts as a protective barrier to sound (Shaw, 1974). The head produces an "acoustic shadow" at the ear furthest from the sound source and, due to diffraction of sound around the head, the sound arriving at the ear farther from the source is attenuated relative to the sound arriving at the ear nearer the source (Dunn, Yost, Noble, Tyler, & Witt, 2006). Sound attenuation caused by the head shadow effect is produced when the wavelength of sound is shorter than the size of the object (e.g., the head) producing the shadow. Despite this being largely a physical effect, when listening with two ears, the brain must be able to attend to the ear with the better S/N ratio in order to be able to take advantage of this effect. The process of the brain attending to the ear with the better S/N ratio is called the *better-ear effect*.

To test this benefit in a laboratory setting, a speech signal is presented in noise with speech emanating from the individuals' 0-degree azimuth and the noise either 90 degrees to the left or right of the individuals' 0-degree azimuth. Subjects are tested with the individual ear with the noise facing it and again with both ears together. The individual ear score is compared to the binaural score. If there is an improvement in the speech perception score when both ears are used together over the individual ear score, the listener was able to take advantage of the ear with the better S/N ratio.

Finally, in our everyday listening environments, listeners are presented with sounds emanating from all directions. To be able to distinguish or *localize* which direction sound is coming from, two ears are necessary. Having two ears allows listeners to detect differences in timing and level differences between the two ears caused by the head shadow effect (Carhart, 1965; Dirks & Wilson, 1969; Durlach & Colburn, 1978; Yost & Dye, 1997). For example, if sound is coming from the left side of a listener, the sound will arrive at the left ear quicker than it will arrive at the right ear, and sound will be louder in the left ear than it will be in the right ear. When localizing with only one ear, the listener may be able to use spectral cues to determine sound directionality, however, this must be learned and is a very difficult task for these users.

SIMULTANEOUS BILATERAL IMPLANTATION

Studies evaluating the benefits of simultaneous bilateral cochlear implants often compare results of a single cochlear implant to that of two cochlear implants. Generally speaking, there are two different ways to make this comparison. One way is to compare the performance of a group of bilateral cochlear implant users to a group of unilateral cochlear implant users. This way is optimal because both of these groups will be tested in their most standard listening configuration. Very limited research is reported using this methodology, as a large number of users in each group are needed to overcome individual difference variability between the two groups. In a recent study by Dunn, Tyler, Oakley, Gantz, & Noble (2008), performance of 33 individuals with bilateral simultaneous cochlear implants and 33 with unilateral cochlear implants matched on age at implantation and duration of deafness were compared on word and sentence recognition. Average group results revealed a significant difference between the two groups, with the bilateral cochlear implant group scoring 19% higher for sentences and 24% higher for words. Additionally, Dunn et al compared performance on an eight-loudspeaker array localization testing paradigm on 12 individuals with bilateral simultaneous cochlear implants and 12 with unilateral cochlear implants, also matched by age at implantation and duration of deafness. Results showed that the bilaterally implanted group scored 25.4° (as measured by RMS-error) better than the unilaterally implanted group on localization ability. These results indicate that bilateral cochlear implant users achieve higher speech perception and localization scores than unilateral cochlear implant users with similar age and duration of deafness. It seems likely that the bilateral cochlear implant group is better able to combine the same information from both ears, therefore resulting in a better representation of the stimulus and more robust binaural summation effect.

A second way to compare the benefits of two cochlear implants is by having a bilateral cochlear implant user remove one of his cochlear implants and compare those results to performance when he is using both of his cochlear implants together. A disadvantage of this methodology is that by having him remove one cochlear implant, he is being tested in a listening condition that he is not used to (listening with one cochlear implant). However, the advantage of this methodology is that significantly smaller sample sizes are needed in the study, since the within-subjects design eliminates the need to control for subject variability. Thus, all comparisons are made within the same subject. This also provides a way to analyze individual data for the various effects of binaural hearing, such as the binaural squelch effect or better-ear effect.

Research on this most commonly used methodology reports that, in general, most users can take advantage of the better-ear effect, whereas fewer bilateral cochlear implant users show evidence of binaural squelch (Dunn, Tyler, Oakley, Gantz, & Noble, 2008; Laszig et al., 2004; Litovsky, Parkinson, Arcaroli, & Sammeth, 2006; Litovsky, Parkinson, Arcaroli, Peters, Lake, Johnstone, & Yu, 2004; Ricketts, Grantham, Ashmead, Haynes, & Labadie, 2006; Tyler, Dunn, Witt, & Preece, 2003). Additionally, subjective questionnaires administered to bilateral and unilateral cochlear implant users comparing emotional distress, hearing difficulty, and social restriction have indicated that the bilateral cochlear implant users observed significantly lower (less) handicap than did the unilateral cochlear implant users (Noble, Tyler, Dunn, & Bhullar, 2008).

We recently examined the performance of 20 simultaneous bilateral cochlear implant users from the University of Iowa who were tested on City University of New York (CUNY) sentences (Boothroyd, Hanin, & Hnath, 1985) in a bilateral listening condition and in a unilateral listening condition (removing one implant processor). The sentences were presented from the front and speech-noise babble was presented 90 degrees to the side directly facing the unilateral cochlear implant. This allowed analysis of each individual's ability to take advantage of the binaural squelch effect. All users had at least 12 months of cochlear implant experience (average = 30 months). Results showed that 13 of the 20 users benefited from the binaural squelch effect.

Four individuals showed no difference between their unilateral and bilateral score, and three showed a decrement in the bilateral listening mode. These results indicate that a large number of users from this cohort were able to take advantage of the binaural squelch effect.

Additionally, the same 20 simultaneous bilateral cochlear implant users were tested in a bilateral listening condition and in a unilateral listening condition (removing one implant processor), again using sentences presented from the front but with the speech-noise babble being presented 90 degrees to the side directly facing *away* from the unilateral cochlear implant. This allowed analysis of each user's ability to take advantage of the better-ear effect. Results indicated that all but three of the 20 users were able to attend to the ear with the better S/N ratio. Of the three users who did not benefit from the better-ear effect, two showed no difference between the unilateral and bilateral listening conditions and one individual showed a decrement in the bilateral listening condition over the unilateral condition. These results demonstrate that an even larger number of users from this cohort were able to take advantage of the better-ear effect in comparison to the binaural squelch effect. This is consistent with other research studying the presumed benefits of binaural hearing in bilateral cochlear implant users. In addition, when looking at the benefits received from both analysis with the 20 individuals, only three individuals were not able to take advantage of either the binaural squelch effect or the better-ear effect.

It thus appears that many listeners with bilateral cochlear implants can make use of binaural hearing, including summation, squelch, and selecting between one of two ears with a more favorable S/N ratio. For those listeners for whom we were not able to measure these effects, it is possible that they have asymmetrical limited nerve survival resulting in insufficient integration of the bilateral auditory information.

SEQUENTIAL BILATERAL IMPLANTATION

Because of the success from cochlear implants, many users of a single cochlear implant are considering receiving a second device. As sequential cochlear implantation becomes more popular in the cochlear implant community, it is important to consider how these two devices work together. Should audiologists attempt to match the processing in each ear as closely as possible, or will the brain just adapt to the independently fit ears? In addition, will the listener be able to integrate the sound between the two ears when they subsequently receive a second implant, even after years of acclimatization to the first cochlear implant? Specifically, for many individuals with sequential cochlear implants, a time lapse of several years may occur between the two implants, providing the listener with sound from different internal arrays along with differing number of channels, rate, and signal processing strategies between devices. Regardless, some studies have demonstrated that individuals can benefit from a second cochlear implant (Dorman & Dahlstrom 2004; Tyler, Noble, Dunn, & Witt, 2007). It is thought that several factors, including age at second implantation, length between implant surgeries, and age at first implant, can affect bilateral benefit. Two studies have shown that the length of time between cochlear implant surgeries affects potential bilateral benefit (Litovsky et al., 2006; Ramsden et al., 2005), whereas another study (Zeitler, Kessler, Terushkin, Roland, Svirsky, Lalwani, & Waltzman, 2008) suggests that duration between surgeries, length of deafness, and age at second implantation does not negate potential benefit.

We recently analyzed results for seven sequentially implanted bilateral users for a Consonant-Nucleus-Consonant (CNC) word recognition test. All but one individual had their second cochlear implant for 1 year or less; two individuals were prelingually deafened. For each of the seven individuals, scores with one implant prior to their second cochlear implant, scores with both cochlear implants, and the right and left implant individually were analyzed after receiving their second implant. The duration of time between the first and second cochlear implant ranged from 6;8 to 17 years. In addition, three individuals had two devices manufactured by different companies, and only two individuals had an equal number of frequency channels across ears. Results revealed that no individual showed a significant improvement or decrement when comparing their unilateral cochlear implant score before receiving their second cochlear implant to their bilateral score after receiving the second implant. However, at the time of this testing, only three individuals had their implants for 12 months or more, and two individuals were poorer performers overall. Results also showed that four individuals had large differences between their individual ears and, in all of these instances, the better ear was the ear that received the first implant.

Additionally, we studied performance for six of the seven cochlear implant users on CUNY sentences in noise facing the front. In contrast to the results in quiet on the CNC words, all of the participants showed a binaural summation effect when comparing their individual ear scores to their bilateral scores and all participants continued to demonstrate an ear preference toward the first ear to be implanted.

These results suggest that individuals receive some benefit from bilateral cochlear implants that are received in sequential surgeries. We highlight the possibility of obtaining binaural benefits when the two devices have a different number of electrodes, processing strategies, and numbers of frequency channels between the ears. These results also suggest that listeners who are implanted by as much as 17 years after the first implant can benefit from receiving a second cochlear implant on the opposite ear. It may be that binaural cochlear implant performance could be improved, however, with similar devices and signal processing across ears.

Cochlear Implant + Hearing Aid Users

Many cochlear implant users wear a hearing aid in the nonimplanted ear to complement use of the implant in the opposite ear. It is thought that providing a hearing aid in the nonimplanted ear combats auditory deprivation, thereby preserving the auditory pathways in that ear and enabling the listener to take advantage of possible binaural hearing benefits (Gelfand, Silman, & Ross, 1987). We have observed that many listeners who continue to wear a hearing aid on the opposite ear do so voluntarily, even though the hearing aided ear alone often provides little to no speech perception abilities. Listeners often report that the hearing aid "balances out their hearing" and "gives them spatial depth or color." In some cases, patients fitted with a hearing aid in the opposite ear for the first time after receiving their cochlear implant have demonstrated similar binaural hearing benefits as compared to listeners who have more hearing aid experience prior to receiving a cochlear implant (Ching, Incerti, & Hill, 2004).

Potential advantages for listeners with a hearing aid in one ear and a cochlear implant in the other ear include improved speech perception in spatially separate noise, improved localization of sound, and better appreciation of music over use of either a hearing aid or cochlear implant alone. Dunn, Tyler, and Witt (2005) studied binaural summation, binaural squelch, and localization in 12 adult listeners with a cochlear implant and hearing aid in opposite ears. Four of 12 participants demonstrated a binaural summation effect for CNC words presented in quiet and 7 of 11 participants showed a binaural summation effect for CUNY sentences presented in noise from the front. In addition, 6 of 10 participants showed a binaural squelch effect when using both the implant and hearing aid and 8 of 11 showed a binaural squelch effect when using either the implant or hearing aid when CUNY sentences were presented in spatially separate noise. Interestingly, some of the highest binaural advantages were recorded for the earliest implanted individuals (less than 3–6 months of implant use).

Sound localization in the horizontal plane was tested using an eight-loudspeaker array arranged in front of the subject. Results were separated by the pattern that emerged, either (1) accurate localization of the stimuli from all speakers (3 of 12 subjects), (2) dominant responses to the side of the cochlear implant (3 of 12 subjects), or (3) responses near the participant's midline (6 of 12 subjects). Dunn et al. (2005) reported that despite the patterns observed for localization performance among the subjects, large variability in localization errors occurred.

Results from Dunn et al. (2005) and other studies (Luntz, Shpak, & Weiss, 2005; Mok, Grayden, Dowell, & Lawrence, 2006; Tyler, Parkinson, Wilson, Witt, Preece, & Noble, 2002) have reported similar binaural advantages (e.g., binaural squelch, binaural summation, or localization) for many of the listeners with hearing aids and cochlear implants in opposite ears. It is likely that combining acoustic stimulation via a hearing aid with electric stimulation via a cochlear implant provides listeners with enhanced coding of voice fundamental frequency and improved pitch perception, with better representation of low-frequency sounds as compared to using electrical stimulation alone.

Music perception studies have shown that residual hearing in the nonimplanted ear provides better pitch discrimination and melody recognition over cochlear implant use alone. Kong, Stickney, & Zeng (2005) studied five individuals using a cochlear implant in one ear and a hearing aid in the other using a melody recognition test in which rhythmic information was removed from the melody and pitch was the only available cue to the user. Results indicated that melody recognition was variable across individuals when tested in all modes of listening, including with the cochlear implant, hearing aid, and cochlear implant plus hearing aid. However, performance on average with the hearing aid was 17% better than using the cochlear implant only and was similar to performance in the combined hearing aid and cochlear implant condition. These results demonstrate that residual hearing is beneficial for accurate music perception for listeners with a hearing aid in one ear and a cochlear implant in the other ear.

A possible disadvantage of utilizing a cochlear implant and a hearing aid in opposite ears is that the two ears may not be able to integrate the acoustic information from the hearing aid with the electrical information from the cochlear implant. In most cases, a listener's performance is significantly worse when using the hearing aid alone (without the cochlear implant) versus when using the cochlear implant alone. In fact, it is possible that for some listeners, their overall performance with the hearing aid alone may be at or near a floor effect (score <10% correct). Because of this, it is of interest whether the use of a hearing aid might actually cause a decrement to the listener's overall hearing ability when wearing the hearing aid in conjunction with the cochlear implant. We evaluated this on a group of 13 implant users using the CUNY sentence test presented from the front with noise either facing the hearing aid or facing the cochlear implant. The participants had used a cochlear implant and a hearing aid together for at least 3 months (the hearing aids were not specifically programmed or adjusted for this study). Participants were tested in the following listening conditions: hearing aid alone (HA), cochlear implant alone (CI), and the cochlear implant and the hearing aid together (CI+HA). Our results showed that when the hearing aid had the better S/N ratio, 7 of 12 subjects (58%) received a benefit from the hearing aid and 2 of 12 (17%) individuals showed a decrement in performance. The amount of benefit ranged from 47% to as little as 6%. When the hearing aid had the poorer S/N ratio, 6 of 13 subjects (46%) benefited from wearing the hearing aid, whereas only 1 of 13 subjects (8%) had a decrement. Even with a poorer signal to noise ratio, the hearing aid still benefited the listeners by as much as 27% to as little as 6%. These results help to explain why many listeners voluntarily continue to utilize a hearing aid following cochlear implantation in the opposite ear. For nearly half of the users tested in this study, although the hearing aid might not provide them with a significant amount of benefit when used solely, when used in conjunction to the cochlear implant it provides a benefit to nearly half or more of the users. In addition, these results suggest that the hearing aid causes a decrement to very few listeners.

Localization and Perception of Distance

Localizing sound (knowing where a sound comes from in space) is often reported by cochlear implant users as difficult and challenging, even for cochlear implant users with the highest speech perception scores. As mentioned previously, localization of sound is dependent on the ability to use differing timing and level information from the two ears. Most cochlear implant users have only one cochlear implant, and their ability to localize sound is limited. Listeners with one cochlear implant rely heavily on spectral cues and loudness differences to decide the location of a sound source in space. For example, if the sound is louder, then it could be assumed that the sound comes from their implanted side and, if the sound is softer, then the sound might originate from their nonimplanted ear. In comparison, listeners with two cochlear implants benefit from similar input to two ears, enabling them to use timing, level, and spectral cues to localize sound in space. Specifically, several studies have shown that localization performance for bilateral cochlear implant users is better than performance with one cochlear implant (Dunn et al., 2008; Gantz et al., 2002; Litovsky et al., 2004; Nopp, Schleich, & D'Haese, 2004; Schoen, Mueller, Helms, & Nopp, 2005; van Hoesel & Tyler, 2003).

To demonstrate performance differences in sound source localization, we studied data from seven listeners with normal hearing and 30 individuals with one and two cochlear implants (10 wore bilateral cochlear implants, 10 wore a unilateral cochlear implant, and 10 wore a unilateral cochlear implant and hearing aid contralaterally) that represent typical localization patterns that emerge for these listeners. Localization performance was assessed by presenting 16 different everyday sounds at a comfortable listening level (70dB[C]) through eight loudspeakers spanning a 108-degree horizontal arc in front of the listener (see Dunn et al., 2005 for more details). Localization errors (i.e., the sound originated from speaker 4, but the listener incorrectly responded with speaker 6) were represented by an average total root mean square (RMS) error, which is a single number taking into account variability and standard error in the responses by the listener. A lower RMS error score represents better performance. An RMS error of 0 degrees would indicate perfect localization.

Localization results for the seven normal hearing listeners proved to be excellent with RMS errors below 5 degrees. The bilateral cochlear implant users revealed responses with more variability in localization performance than was noted for normal hearing listeners. Localization RMS errors ranged between 11 and 20 degrees (mean = 15 degrees), which is worse than the 5 degrees of RMS error seen for normal hearing listeners. For the unilateral cochlear implant users, many listeners localized sound to the side of their cochlear implant, whereas other listeners' responses were isolated to the midline speakers. Overall performance for unilateral cochlear implant users resulted in significant localization errors with a range of 35–51 degrees RMS error (mean = 43 degrees). Localization results for listeners with a cochlear implant and hearing aid in opposite ears were extremely variable, with most of the responses concentrated to the midline speakers. RMS errors for listeners with a cochlear implant in one ear and a hearing aid in the other ranged from 28 to 51 (mean = 38 degrees), which is significantly worse than that seen for bilateral cochlear implant users and normally hearing listeners.

Overall, these results seem to indicate that cochlear implant users with two implants achieve good localization performance, but that, despite having input to two ears, performance does not reach levels achieved by normally hearing listeners. Listeners with one cochlear implant appear to be at a significant disadvantage compared to normally hearing listeners and bilateral cochlear implant users. For listeners with a single cochlear implant, significant localization errors were observed, with many listeners perceiving sound solely on the side of the implant. Finally, it appears that some listeners with a cochlear implant plus hearing aid are able to localize sound accurately and achieve good performance, overcoming any differences introduced by having two different devices in the ears. However, for some listeners with a hearing aid plus cochlear implant, their localization performance is poor, indicating that they are not able to adequately integrate information from the two ears.

Distance perception of a sound source is a critical aspect of localization that is also reportedly difficult for many listeners with hearing aids and cochlear implants. Although minimal research has examined the cues needed for distance perception, some studies have reported on certain aspects of distance perception that are of importance. According to Gardner and Gardner (1973), louder sounds are often judged closer to the listener than softer sounds. Therefore, if loudness is used by the listener as a cue for distance perception, then changes in distance could be predicted based on just-discriminable changes in the intensity of a sound (Middlebrooks & Green, 1991). Research also indicates that hearing with two ears is salient for judging the distance of sounds originating in the far field, or greater than 1 meter from the listener (Blauert, 1997). In comparison, when sounds are presented close to the listener (<1 meter away), performance is dominated by monaural cues related to the head shadow effect. Finally, research suggests that the nature of the acoustic environment influences distance perception. Namely, the ability to judge the distance of a sound source for listeners with hearing aids may be worse compared to normally hearing listeners when the primary cue to distance is based on the relationship of direct and reverberant sounds (Akeroyd, Gatehouse, & Blaschke, 2007).

We have developed a distance test that asks the listener to judge which of three loudspeakers produced the short, spoken phrase, "Hey, I am over here." The loudspeakers are arranged evenly over 10 meters from the listener, in a large enclosed space (about 9 × 6 × 2.7 meters). Using this test set-up, listeners were tested with the spoken phrase from the straight-ahead (0-degree) position with loudness level calibrated to 70 dB[C] at 0.5 meters from each loudspeaker. Additionally, the loudspeakers were at the midline, and sound was equal at both ears. The participants were asked to identify the speaker number from which the spoken phrase originated, and the overall percent correct and percent correct per loudspeaker was calculated for each condition. The order in which sounds were presented from the loudspeakers was randomized. Bilateral cochlear implant users were tested using their bilateral cochlear implants and with one unilateral cochlear implant only. Such data have not been published elsewhere in the literature.

Figure 26.3 shows preliminary results for two normally hearing listeners. Perfect performance is shown

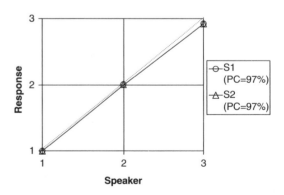

Fig. 26.3 Averaged responses on the three-speaker distance test for normal hearing listeners (*n* = 2). The horizontal axis represents the stimulus loudspeaker and the vertical axis represents the response by the listener. Average percent correct (PC) is shown for each listener in the legend.

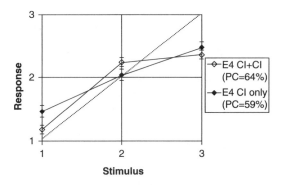

Fig. 26.4 Responses on the three-speaker distance test for subject E4. Results are shown with both cochlear implants (CI+CI) and with one cochlear implant removed (CI only). The legend shows the average percent correct (PC) for each listening condition.

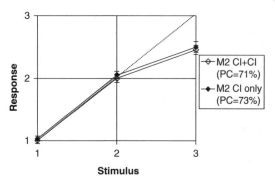

Fig. 26.6 Responses on the three-speaker distance test for subject M2 with both cochlear implants (CI+CI) and with one cochlear implant only (CI only). The legend shows the average percent correct (PC) for each listening condition.

on the graph by a diagonal line. The stimulus–response graph shows excellent performance for both normally hearing listeners by the diagonal line on the graph.

Figure 26.4–Figure 26.6 display the responses for three bilateral cochlear implant users on the three-speaker distance test. In Figure 26.4 (subject E4), performance using two cochlear implants resulted in fewer errors when the sound came from speakers 1 and 2, and poorer when the sound came from the farthest speaker. Using one cochlear implant only, results for subject E4 indicate good distance perception when sound was presented from speaker 2 and poorer distance perception when the sound came from the nearest and farthest speakers. Comparing the overall percentage for bilateral versus unilateral cochlear implant use for E4, performance was slightly better when bilateral cochlear implants were used (64%) versus when a unilateral

cochlear implant was used (59%). In Figure 26.5, results for subject R36b show good discrimination of the speaker closest to the listener (speaker 1) when using either one or two cochlear implants. However, for the farthest two speakers, performance with one cochlear implant resulted in fewer judgment errors as compared to listening with two implants for subject R36b. Figure 26.6 displays results for subject M2. For this individual, distance perception for speakers 1 and 2 was excellent and near that of normally hearing individuals. However, performance decreased for speaker 3, indicating that localization of distance was easier for subject M2 when sounds were closer.

Although data are presented here from a limited number of individuals, results indicate that distance perception is worse for cochlear implant users compared to normally hearing listeners. This is in agreement with previous findings showing that hearing aid users perform worse than normally hearing listeners on distance perception (Akeroyd et al., 2007). Furthermore, for the bilateral cochlear implant users, distance judgments were more accurate when the sounds were presented from the closest loudspeakers. For some individuals (R36b, M2), performance with two cochlear implants did not necessarily result in superior distance perception as compared to performance with a single cochlear implant. Future studies should continue to evaluate distance perception with more individuals using cochlear implants, hearing aids, or a combination of hearing aids plus cochlear implants.

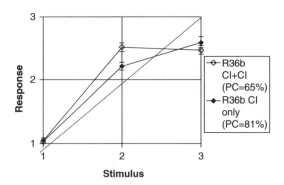

Fig. 26.5 Responses on the three-speaker distance test for subject R36b. Results with both cochlear implants (CI+CI) and with one cochlear implant only (CI only) are displayed. Average percent correct (PC) is shown in the legend for each listening condition.

Summary and Conclusions

Criteria for cochlear implantation have expanded over the last 20 years to include persons with pre- and postlinguistic hearing loss who are younger and have better hearing than previously considered. In fact, the number of individuals acquiring a cochlear implant has increased to more than 120,000 worldwide in recent years. As research and technology continues to better the design and function of cochlear implants, it is expected that cochlear implant devices will improve to provide listeners with even more benefit than currently reported.

We have shown that cochlear implantation results in numerous benefits, including improved speech perception abilities, better music appreciation and music perception, and better sound awareness. Additionally, performance outcomes for bilateral cochlear implant users through either sequential or simultaneous implantation show that listeners with two implants can take advantage of binaural hearing benefits, including the summation effect, the squelch effect, the better-ear effect, and improved localization. For listeners with a cochlear implant plus hearing aid, performance is often better with the hearing aid and cochlear implant over use of either device alone. Newly presented results on distance perception indicate that distance perception is worse for cochlear implant users compared to normally hearing listeners, and distance judgments for bilateral cochlear implant users were more accurate when the sounds were presented from the closest loudspeakers. Despite these positive outcomes in favor of bilateral cochlear implant use and hearing aid plus cochlear implant use, there are documented cases in which performance is not necessarily better. Further research efforts should focus on improvements in sound processing and fitting to maximize benefits for cochlear implant listeners.

Acknowledgment

This research was supported in part by research grant 2 P50 DC00242 from the National Institutes on Deafness and Other Communication Disorders, National Institutes of Health; grant RR00059 from the General Clinical Research Centers Program, Division of Research Resources, National Institutes of Health; the Lions Clubs International Foundation; and the Iowa Lions Foundation.

References

Akeroyd, M. A., Gatehouse, S., & Blaschke, J. (2007). The detection of differences in the cues to distance by elderly hearing-impaired listeners. *Journal of the Acoustic Society of America, 121*(2), 1077–1089.

Anderson, I., Baumgartner, W. D., Boheim, K., Nahler, A., Arnoldner, C., & D'Haese, P. (2006). Telephone use: what benefit do cochlear implant users receive? *International Journal of Audiology, 45*(8), 446-453.

Balkany, T., Hodges, A., Menapace, C., Hazard, L., Driscoll, C., Gantz, B., et al. (2007). Nucleus Freedom North American clinical trial. *Otolaryngology-Head & Neck Surgery, 136*(5), 757–762.

Blauert, J. (1997). *Spatial hearing: the psychophysics of human sound localization.* Cambridge: MIT Press.

Boothroyd, A., Hanin, L., & Hnath, T. (1985). A sentence test of speech perception: Reliability, set equivalence, and short term learning. Internal Report RCI 10, Speech and Hearing Sciences Research Center, City University of New York.

Carhart, R. (1965). Monaural and binaural discrimination against competing sentences. *International Audiology, 4*, 5–10.

Ching, T. Y., Incerti, P., & Hill, M. (2004). Binaural benefits for adults who use hearing aids and cochlear implants in opposite ears. *Ear & Hearing, 25*(1), 9–21.

Cochlear Limited. (2006). Introduction to cochlear implants candidacy criteria. Retrieved August 29, 2008 from http://www. cochlearamericas. com/Support/378.asp

Cohen, N. L., Waltzman, S. B., & Fisher, S. G. (1993). A prospective, randomized study of cochlear implants. The Department of Veterans Affairs Cochlear Implant Study Group. *New England Journal of Medicine, 328*(4), 233–237.

Colletti, V., Carner, M., Miorelli, V., Guida, M., Colletti, L., & Fiorino, F. G. (2005). Cochlear implantation at under 12 months: report on 10 patients. *Laryngoscope, 115*(3), 445–449.

Dettman, S. J., Pinder, D., Briggs, R. J., Dowell, R. C., & Leigh, J. R. (2007). Communication development in children who receive the cochlear implant younger than 12 months: risks versus benefits. *Ear & Hearing, 28*(2 Supplement), 11S–18S.

Dirks, D. D., & Wilson, R. H. (1969). The effect of spatially separated sound sources on speech intelligibility. *Journal of Speech and Hearing Research, 12*, 5–38.

Dorman, M. F., & Dahlstrom, L. (2004). Speech understanding by cochlear-implant patients with different left- and right-ear electrode arrays. *Ear & Hearing, 25*, 191–194.

Dunn, C. C., Tyler, R. S., & Witt, S. A. (2005). Benefit of wearing a hearing aid on the unimplanted ear in adult users of a cochlear implant. *Journal of Speech, Language & Hearing Research, 48*(3), 668–680.

Dunn, C. C., Tyler, R. S., Oakley, S., Gantz, B. J., & Noble, W. (2008). Comparison of speech recognition and localization performance in bilateral and unilateral cochlear implant users matched on duration of deafness and age at implantation. *Ear & Hearing, 29*(3), 352–359.

Dunn, C. C., Yost, W., Noble, W. Tyler, R. S., & Witt, S. (2006). Advantages of binaural hearing. In S. B. Waltzman & J. T. Roland Jr. (Eds.), *Cochlear implants* (pp. 205–213). New York: Thieme Medical Publishers.

Durlach, N. I., & Colburn, H. S. (1978). Binaural phenomena. In E. C. Carterette & M. P. Friedman (Eds.), *Handbook of perception* (Vol. IV, pp. 364–466). New York: Academic Press.

Gardner, M. B., & Gardner, R. S. (1973). Problem of localization in the median plane: effect of pinnae cavity occlusion. *The Journal of the Acoustical Society of America, 53*(2), 400–408.

Gantz, B. J., Tyler, R. S., Rubinstein, J. T., Wolaver, A., Lowder, M., Abbas, P., et al. (2002). Binaural cochlear implants placed during the same operation. *Otology & Neurotology, 23*, 169–180.

Gantz, B. J., Woodworth, G. G., Knutson, J. F., Abbas, P. J., & Tyler, R. S. (1993). Multivariate predictors of audiological success with multichannel cochlear implants. *Annals of Otology Rhinology Laryngology, 102*(12), 909–916.

Gelfand, S., Silman, S., & Ross, L. (1987). Long term effects of monaural, binaural and no amplification in subjects with bilateral hearing loss. *Scandinavian Audiology, 16*, 201–207.

Gfeller, K., Oleson, J., Knutson, J. F., Breheny, P., Driscoll, V., & Olszewski, C. (2008). Multivariate predictors of music perception and appraisal by adult cochlear implant users. *Journal of the American Academy of Audiology, 19*(2), 120–134.

Gfeller, K., Turner, C., Oleson, J., Zhang, X., Gantz, B., Froman, R., & Olszewski, C. (2007). Accuracy of cochlear implant recipients on pitch perception, melody recognition, and speech reception in noise. *Ear & Hearing, 28*(3), 412–423.

Helms, J., Mueller, J., Schoen, F., Moser, L., Arnold, W., Janssen, T., et al. (1997). Evaluation of performance with the COMBI40 cochlear implant in adults: a multicentric clinical study. *Journal for Otorhinolaryngology and Its Related Specialties, 59*(1), 23–35.

Kaplan, D. M., Shipp, D. B., Chen, J. M., Ng, A. H., & Nedzelski, J. M. (2003). Early-deafened adult cochlear implant users: assessment of outcomes. *Journal of Otolaryngology, 32*(4), 245–249.

Koch, D. B., Osberger, M. J., Segel, P., & Kessler, D. (2004). HiResolution and conventional sound processing in the HiResolution bionic ear: using appropriate outcome measures to assess speech recognition ability. *Audiology & Neurootology, 9*(4), 214–223.

Kong, Y., Stickney, G. S., & Zeng, F. (2005). Speech and melody recognition in binaurally combined acoustic and electric hearing. *Journal of the Acoustic Society of America, 117*(3), 1351–1361.

Laszig, R., Aschendorff, A., Stecker, M., Müller-Deile, J., Maune, S., Dillier, N., et al. (2004). Benefits of bilateral electrical stimulation with the Nucleus cochlear implant in adults: 6-month postoperative results. *Otology & Neurotology, 25*(6), 958–968.

Litovsky, R. Y., Parkinson, A., Arcaroli, J., Peters, R., Lake, J., Johnstone, P., & Yu, G. (2004). Bilateral cochlear implants in adults and children. *Archives of Otolaryngology-Head & Neck Surgery, 130*, 648–655.

Litovsky, R., Parkinson, A., Arcaroli, J., & Sammeth, C. (2006). Simultaneous bilateral cochlear implantation in adults: A multicenter clinical study. *Ear & Hearing, 27*(6), 714–731.

Luntz, M., Shpak, T., & Weiss, H. (2005). Binaural-bimodal hearing: Concomitant use of a unilateral cochlear implant and a contralateral hearing aid. *Acta Oto-Laryngologica, 125*(8), 863 – 869.

Middlebrooks, J. C., & Green, D. M. (1991). Sound localization by human listeners. *Annual Review of Psychology, 42*, 135–159.

Mok, M., Grayden, D., Dowell, R. C., & Lawrence, D. (2006). Speech perception for adults who use hearing aids in conjunction with cochlear implants in opposite ears. *Journal of Speech Language and Hearing Research, 49*(2), 338–351.

Noble, W., Tyler, R., Dunn, C. C., & Bhullar, N. (2008). Hearing handicap ratings among different profiles of adult cochlear implant users. *Ear & Hearing, 29*(1),112–120.

Nopp, P., Schleich, P., & D'Haese, P. (2004). Sound localization in bilateral users of MED-EL COMBI 40/40+ cochlear implants. *Ear & Hearing, 25*(3), 205–214.

Ramsden, R., Greenham, P., O'Driscoll, M., Mawman, D., Proops, D., et al. (2005). Evaluation of bilaterally implanted adult subjects with the Nucleus 24 cochlear implant system. *Otology & Neurology, 26*, 988–998.

Ricketts, T. A., Grantham, D. W., Ashmead, D. H., Haynes, D. S., & Labadie, R. F. (2006). Speech recognition for unilateral and bilateral cochlear implant modes in the presence of uncorrelated noise sources. *Ear & Hearing, 27*(6), 763–773.

Robbins, A. M., Renshaw, J. J., & Berry, S. W. (1991). Evaluating meaningful auditory integration in profoundly hearing-impaired children. *American Journal of Otology, 12*(Supplement), 144–150.

Rubinstein, J. T., Parkinson, W. S., Tyler, R. S., & Gantz, B. J. (1999). Residual speech recognition and cochlear implant performance: effects of implantation criteria. *American Journal of Otology, 20*(4), 445–452.

Schoen, F., Mueller, J., Helms, J., & Nopp, P. (2005). Sound localization and sensitivity to interaural cues in bilateral users of the Med-El Combi 40/40+cochlear implant system. *Otology & Neurotology, 26*(3), 429–437.

Shaw, E. A. (1974). Transformation of sound pressure level from the free field to the eardrum in the horizontal plane. *Journal of the Acoustical Society of America, 56*, 1848–1861.

Skinner, M. W., Binzer, S. M., Fears, B. T., Holden, T. A., Jenison, V. W., & Nettles, E. J. (1992). Study of the performance of four prelinguistically or perilinguistically deaf patients with a multi-electrode, intracochlear implant. *Laryngoscope, 102*(7), 797–806.

Tyler, R. S., Dunn, C. C., Witt, S. A., & Preece, J. P. (2003). Update on bilateral cochlear implantation. *Current Opinion in Otolaryngology-Head & Neck Surgery, 11*, 388–393.

Tyler, R. S., Noble, W., Dunn, C. C., & Witt, S. A. (2007). Speech perception and localization with adults with bilateral sequential cochlear implants. *Ear & Hearing, 28*(2 Supplement), 86S–90S.

Tyler, R. S., Parkinson, A. J., Wilson, B. S., Witt, S., Preece, J. P., & Noble, W. (2002). Patient utilizing a hearing aid and a cochlear implant: speech perception and localization. *Ear & Hearing, 23*(2), 98–105.

Tyler, R. S., & Summerfield, A. Q. (1996). Cochlear implantation: relationships with research on auditory deprivation and acclimatization. *Ear & Hearing, 17*(3 Supplement), 38S–50S.

van Dijk, J. E., van Olphen, A. F., Langereis, M. C., Mens, L. H., Brokx, J. P., & Smoorenburg, G. F. (1999). Predictors of cochlear implant performance. *Audiology, 38*(2), 109–116.

van Hoesel, R. J. M., & Tyler, R. S. (2003). Speech perception, localization, and lateralization with bilateral cochlear implants. *Journal of the Acoustic Society of America, 113*(3), 1617–1630.

Waltzman, S. B., & Roland, J. T., Jr. (2005). Cochlear implantation in children younger than 12 months. *Pediatrics, 116*(4), 487–493.

Yost, W. A., & Dye, R. H. (1997). Fundamentals of directional hearing. *Seminars in Hearing, 17*, 66S–77S.

Zeitler, D., Kessler, M., Terushkin, V., Roland, J., Svirsky, M., Lalwani, A., & Waltzman, S. (2008). Speech perception benefits of sequential bilateral cochlear implantation in children and adults: a retrospective analysis. *Otology & Neurotology, 29*(3), 314–25.

Zimmerman-Phillips, S., Robbins, A. M., & Osberger, M. J. (2000). Assessing cochlear implant benefit in very young children. *Annuals of Otology Rhinology & Laryngology, 185*(Supplement), 42–43.

Zurek, P. M. (1993). Binaural advantages and directional effects in speech intelligibility. In G. A. Studebaker & I. Hochberg (Eds.), *Acoustical factors affecting hearing aid performance*, 2nd edition. (pp. 255–276). Boston: Allyn & Bacon.

Zwolan, T. A., Kileny, P. R., & Telian, S. A. (1996). Self-report of cochlear implant use and satisfaction by prelingually deafened adults. *Ear & Hearing, 17*(3), 198–210.

PART 6

Cognitive Issues and Correlates of Deafness

Play and Theory of Mind: Indicators and Engines of Early Cognitive Growth

Patricia Elizabeth Spencer

Abstract

Play and Theory of Mind (ToM) result from a combination of maturation and experience. Play behaviors have often been used to index cognitive development in young deaf and hard-of-hearing (DHH) children, although relatively few reports are available on those under the age of 3 years. Available data indicate that the order of development of play behaviors in children with hearing loss parallels that of hearing children; however, delays occur at the symbolic level when language development and early communicative experiences are restricted. With the exception of a single report at 12 months, potentially explained by deaf mothers' accommodation of age-expected visual attention limitations, hearing status itself has not been shown to affect play development. Like play, behaviors indicating attainment of ToM have been found to correlate with language levels and differences in early opportunities to participate in conversational interactions. Differences in the development of ToM are more readily explained by common effects from hearing loss on experience than from hearing status or language modality alone. Like play, ToM abilities reflect cognitive attainments in taking and representing multiple perspectives, integrating information across time and contexts, and creating as well as retrieving from memory symbolic representations of objects and events. Activities in which play behaviors and ToM problem solving occur, therefore, provide highly conducive contexts for the development of more advanced cognitive concepts and abilities. Intervention to assure "on time" attainment of these two abilities thus may be critical for children's later abilities to acquire and synthesize information in typical learning environments.

Keywords: play, symbolic play, theory-of-mind, deaf, hard-of-hearing, cognition, infant, toddler

Macy looked through the basket of toys and pulled out a plastic telephone and a miniature wooden wagon. She carefully placed the phone's receiver across the upper edge of the bed of the wagon, looked up and smiled at her mother, then looked back down at the wagon and began to move her fingers as though typing out a message just below where the receiver was placed. Her mother tapped her on the shoulder and, when she looked up, signed "Try contacting Daddy." Macy turned the wagon and moved it closer to her mother. "You do it," she signed.

This play episode was observed during dyadic interaction between a deaf 28-month-old and her mother. It gives a few indications of the reasons why researchers and clinicians studying cognitive development have found the study of play to be of such interest. In this episode, Macy has remembered and replicated a series of actions that she has seen occur. This indicates that she has mentally or symbolically represented those actions and that they are embedded and retrieved as part of a functional "script." Macy receives and expresses communication during the episode, coordinates visual attention between her mother and the objects with which she is playing, and even shows understanding of her mother's physical and visual perspective by moving the pretended teletype display (TDD) so that she can reach and "see" it easily.

One goal of this chapter is to review studies of early play to identify influential factors and patterns in its development by DHH children. In addition, studies of the development of ToM, which refers to children's understanding that they and others have mental states—beliefs, desires, ideas, and so on—that are not always directly observable, are reviewed. Patterns of structural relationships between the two developmental phenomena, as well as shared influences in their development, are investigated. Attention is also paid to identifying early evidence given in play and ToM of patterns of cognitive skills that have been reported for older DHH students.

A number of researchers and educators have reported that DHH children have difficulties with varied components of cognitive and learning skills—at least after they reach formal schooling years. These difficulties include reduced memory for sequenced information (e.g., Cleary, Pisoni, & Geers, 2001; see also Chapter 29, this volume), decreased selective attention (Quittner, Smith, Osberger, Mitchell, & Katz, 1994; but cf. Chapter 30, this, volume), and problems making inferences and integrating varied experiences and concepts (Marschark & Hauser, 2008; see also Chapter 9, this volume). These difficulties have been noted despite the fact that there is little, if any, difference between average scores on tests of nonverbal cognitive abilities between children with and without hearing loss (Braden, 1994).

The difference in the profile of cognitive skills across DHH and hearing children has been suggested by some researchers (e.g., Quittner et al., 1994; Chapter 29, this volume) to stem from the presence or absence of hearing itself and the amount of experience children have in receiving and processing auditory signals. Others (e.g., Marschark & Hauser, 2008) have implicated the dual role that visual attention must play for children with hearing loss—receiving communication and language, as well as general information about the environment. Many have suggested that differences in early communicative and interactive experiences typical of most DHH children who have hearing parents, differences that undoubtedly contribute to language delays, also impact cognitive development. The rate of language development itself is generally assumed to affect children's readiness and ability to learn.

Researchers studying hearing infants have developed a number of procedures for assessing basic components of early cognition, including memory and the ability to coordinate information across modalities and over time (see e.g., Rochat, 2001; Woodward & Needham, 2009, for reviews). These approaches have apparently not been used in the study of infants with hearing loss, however. Instead, the focus of researchers investigating cognitive development of infants and toddlers with hearing loss has often been on their play behaviors, which are thought to provide a picture of emerging and maturing cognitive skills in DHH children (Spencer & Hafer, 1998), as well as in hearing children (Piaget, 1952, 1962).

Play can be conceived of as learning in action. Play progresses from simple undifferentiated actions on objects to actions specific to object characteristics and their use in daily life experiences to, at higher levels, substitution of objects for dissimilar ones in pretend activities and coordinating multiple objects in complex sequences. These activities and behaviors require increasingly efficient symbolic, sequential, memory, and retrieval abilities. In addition, instances of play in which a child causes a doll or similar toy to "act out" a behavior or in which the child herself adopts an imaginary role indicate the ability to recognize and "take on" the perspective of other persons, understanding to some extent what another person knows or how another person acts.

These abilities to take other perspectives and to understand what others know and are thinking are also critical components—but at a more complex level—of ToM abilities. Accordingly, researchers investigating cognitive development of somewhat older DHH children have increasingly focused their attention on ToM. A few researchers have pointed out the similarities in cognitive, as well as social, structures and experiences that underlie both of these domains (see, for example, Youngblade & Dunn, 1995, in regard to hearing children). Furthermore, investigations of the component cognitive abilities of both play and ToM, and their relation with early experiences and developing language skills, suggest that they may provide early indications of and indicate sources for the learning challenges just described for older DHH students.

Play and Early Cognitive Ability: Influences and Outcomes

One reason that play has provided an attractive means of assessing children's cognitive development is that it is usually so easily elicited in naturalistic or seminaturalistic situations. Most often, the researchers whose work is summarized in this chapter simply provided an interesting and age-appropriate selection of toys and asked mothers to sit and play with their children, as they do when they have time at home. Other researchers provided parents with checklists of typical child play behaviors that illustrate varied levels of sophistication and asked them to indicate what they have seen their children do.

Developmental levels of play that are typically attained during the infant and toddler period are usually described (e.g., McCune, 1995; McCune-Nicholich, 1983; Slade, 1987; Spencer & Hafer, 1998) as including the following progressively complex and cognitively sophisticated categories:

1. *Prerepresentational play (simple manipulation of objects; examining and manipulating more than one object in a coordinated fashion)*: Examples include visually examining and mouthing a toy or other object, banging two objects together, stacking objects or placing them into (and then usually out of) a container.

2. *Representational play (single pretend actions with realistic toys; sequenced, thematically related pretend actions with toys and, at an advanced level, combining those behaviors in canonical or specifically realistic orders)*: Examples include lifting a toy cup to mouth as though to drink but not evidencing surprise or dismay that it does not contain anything, using a toy hammer to beat on and thus "fix" multiple other toys or objects, engaging in realistic action sequences (such as pouring pretend tea into a cup, adding sugar and stirring, then pretending to drink).

3. *Symbolic play (pretend actions that give evidence, verbal or nonverbal, of having been planned; taking and playing the role of another—or having a doll or other toy do so; intentionally substituting one object for another in pretend play)*: Examples include engaging in an extended and apparently intentional search for a specific object (such as a specific toy tool) before pretending to use it to "fix" another toy, moving a small doll so that it appears to engage in a series of related and realistic actions, pretending to be another person or character (e.g., a little baby or an animal or another person) and engaging in actions that are usually performed by that other character (such as using a block to represent a car and moving it while making car-like noises), pretending to "feed" mother using movements but no objects at all to represent stirring in invisible pot or raising invisible spoon to her mouth.

All of the levels of play just described can and have been identified without any language being involved on the part of the child or an adult who is also engaging in the play (e.g., McCune, 1995). This lack of need to rely on language to identify the cognitive level of a play episode makes observations of play especially useful for the assessment of DHH children. However, despite the lack of need for expressive language evidence to identify play levels, strong associations have been found repeatedly between play and stages of language development that have been separately measured in investigations of hearing children. For example, representational play emerges along with production of spoken words at around 13 months of age (Bates, Bretherton, Snyder, Shore, & Volterra, 1980), and multiword utterances occur about the same time sequences of related symbolic play appear (e.g., McCune, 1995).

It is not clear whether these language–play associations indicate a causal relationship, and, if so, whether language influences play or vice versa (Bates, O'Connell, & Shore, 1984). Some researchers have pointed out that play experiences can have causal effects on language development by providing parents and others both the opportunity and the motivation to provide relevant language input (Spencer & Hafer, 1998). In addition, the ability to use and combine linguistic symbols may support memory for and retrieval of play actions (Spencer, 1996). It is probable that causal effects do occur between play and language, but that both the direction and the strength of such effects change over time and with development.

Social experiences also influence the development of play during the first years of life. Especially in dyadic situations, mothers' abilities to "scaffold" or to promote and extend play are critical, and young children typically demonstrate more advanced play behaviors during interactions with a supportive partner than when playing alone (e.g., Bornstein, Selmi, Haynes, Painter, & Marx, 1999). The existence of secure child–mother emotional attachment (Slade, 1987), as well as warm and responsive maternal behaviors and play suggestions (e.g., Fiese, 1990; Vibbert & Bornstein, 1989), are also associated with children's production of higher levels of play. Thus, the extent to which early interactions are characterized by mutual child–mother engagement and reciprocity relate to the play produced.

Early child–mother interactions that are characterized by a relative lack of reciprocity and ease of communication—which is often the case for children with hearing loss and hearing mothers (e.g., see Meadow-Orlans, Spencer, & Koester, 2004, and Spencer & Harris, 2006, for reviews)—may be less effective as contexts for the support of emerging cognitive skills. In addition, many DHH children continue even with the advent of early identification and intervention to experience delays in language development (Spencer & Harris). Both of these conditions might have effects on the development of early play and the efficacy of early dyadic play interactions to promote development across a number of domains, including cognition. It is possible, therefore, that the cognitive differences and difficulties noted for older deaf children and adolescents have roots that can be identified in early play.

Play of Young Deaf and Hard-of-Hearing Children

A number of researchers (e.g., Brown, Prescott, Rickards, & Patterson, 1997; Casby & McCormack, 1985; Darbyshire, 1977; Schirmer, 1989; Vygotsky, 1978) have documented deficiencies or delays in the play of DHH children over 3 years of age, even when there is no evidence of general cognitive delay. It has been reported that deaf children engaged in less "make believe" play, produced less sequenced play, were less likely to give evidence of preplanned play actions, and made fewer uses of object substitutions (pretending that one object was a different one) than hearing children of the same age. These studies included children whose diagnosis of hearing loss and subsequent intervention was provided at later ages than is common since the turn of the century, and they were typically characterized as having language delays more severe than might be expected with earlier intervention. However, the cognitive skills that were pointed out as being delayed, including reduced sequencing and planning, are reminiscent of current descriptions of older deaf learners' problematic cognitive processes (e.g., Marschark & Hauser, 2008).

Trends toward earlier identification of hearing loss have allowed studies of the play of younger DHH infants and toddlers. For example, Yoshinaga-Itano, Snyder, and Day (1998) used the Play Assessment Questionnaire (PAQ; Calhoun, 1987) to obtain parent report of play behaviors in cross-sectional groups of DHH children at 8–11 months, 14–17 months, 20–23 months, and 27–30 months. Approximately half of the 170 participants had hearing loss (ranging from mild to profound in degree) identified by 6 months of age, with the other half having a later diagnosis. No significant associations were found between play and mother educational level, family socioeconomic level, family ethnicity, child gender, child hearing level, age of identification, or the mode(s) of communication used. However, the developmental

hierarchy of play levels reported in studies of young children was confirmed with this sample of DHH children.

Scores on the PAQ increased with child age and were related to, but partially distinct from, scores on other measures of nonverbal cognitive development. Play–language relations were significant, however, and PAQ scores correlated with the development of symbolic gestures, the number of words and phrases understood, and the number of words produced. With language considered as an outcome measure, PAQ scores predicted 44% of the variance in vocabulary. In a separate analysis of apparently the same participants, Snyder and Yoshinaga-Itano (1998) again predicted language scores from play variables. By 20–23 months of age, they found that "auto-symbolic" play (simple or sequenced self-directed representational acts), as well as symbolic substitution play, predicted significant variance in total language scores. The researchers concluded that language and play skills are so closely associated in young deaf children that play observations can serve as a measure of general symbolic development.

Spencer (1996) conducted a more process-oriented study of deaf children between the age of 24 and 28 months, obtaining measures of language, an estimate of overall developmental levels, and detailed measures of behaviors during child–mother dyadic play. The study included ten children in each of three groups: deaf children with hearing parents (dH), deaf children with deaf parents (dD), and hearing children with hearing parents (hH). All of the deaf children had hearing loss identified by 18 months of age (late by current standards, but typical for the time in which the study occurred) and had participated in early intervention programming for at least 6 months. This study was notable in its inclusion of both groups of deaf children, dD and dH, in an attempt to differentiate effects of lack of auditory experience from effects of language delay. However, the small number of participants, along with the wide range of hearing loss (moderate to profound), suggests that conclusions from the study must be interpreted with caution.

General cognitive development was assessed by the Self-Help and Physical (motor development) subscales of the Developmental Profile II (Alpern, Boll, & Shearer, 1980), a parent-report screening instrument. All children's age-equivalent scores on these measures were within 3 months of their actual age, the range considered to be within normal limits on this instrument. The Communication subscale of the same instrument was used to obtain parent-report information that was then used to determine language levels. Levels were assigned after examination of the mothers' responses, with children classified by the number of words or signs reported to be in their expressive lexicon and the frequency of multiword/multisign utterances. Level 1 represented the production of fewer than 50 words or signs and rare multiword/multisign utterances; five dH children, two dD children, and two hH children were found to function at this level. Level 2 represented reported lexicons of more than 50 and fewer than 200 words/signs with occasional multiple word/sign productions; five dH children, six dD children, and three hH children functioned at this level. Level 3 represented lexicons of more than 200 words/signs and frequent multiword productions; two dD children and five hH children functioned at this level. Levels 2 and 3 are typical of hearing children at around 2 years of age, although wide variability is generally reported (Bates, Bretherton, & Snyder, 1988), and the majority of dD and hH children were reported to have expressive language skills consistent with these levels. In contrast, dH children were overrepresented in the L1 group, and none of them were in language group L3; however, half of the dH children were functioning at language level L2.

Extensive and detailed coding of play behaviors in the Spencer (1996) study was conducted using procedures developed by Slade (1987) and by McCune-Nicholich (1983; McCune, 1995) using videotapes of a 20 minute portion of a somewhat longer free play session between mother and child. When groups were compared based on child–mother hearing status, no significant difference was found in the *frequency* of children's play behaviors; however, both groups with deaf children were found to spend *longer times* in play than the hearing children. It therefore took longer for deaf children than for hearing children to engage in and produce the same amount of play behaviors. This interpretation is consistent with an earlier prediction by Wood (1989) that deaf children's need to divide visual attention between play and communication behaviors would result in their taking a longer time to acquire information (and, in this case, to act on their knowledge) than hearing children.

No other significant differences were found when the three hearing status groups of children were compared. That is, no differences other than the duration of time in play could be attributed to child hearing status or the combination of child and mother hearing status. When comparisons were made based on expressive language level groups, however,

other differences were found. Both time (duration) and frequency of sequences of play behaviors following a conventional or "canonical" order (e.g., "feed" bottle to baby doll, raise doll to shoulder to "burp the baby," then and only then put the baby to bed and cover her) were lower for the children in the lowest language group (L1) than for children in the other two language groups. In addition, although the frequency of pretend play activities that showed preplanning of actions was not systematically related to child hearing status, it was significantly higher for the group showing the most advanced expressive language (group L3) than for the two lower language groups.

The findings of Spencer's (1996) study suggested that different visual attention needs of deaf and hearing children have an effect, although not necessarily a deleterious one, on the timing of play behaviors produced as early as 2 years of age. More worrisome is the finding that children with delayed language showed less production of sequenced and of preplanned play, and the incidence of language delays was higher in the dH group, representing children who are generally most at risk for academic and learning difficulties.

Spencer and Meadow-Orlans (1996; Meadow-Orlans et al., 2004) followed-up Spencer's (1996) study by investigating play behaviors during the infancy period. Data were collected longitudinally, when children were 9, 12, and 18 months old, so that developmental trends might be identified. There were 15 dyads in the dH and hH groups; after two dyads dropped out of the study, there were 13 dyads in the group of deaf children with deaf parents. Play behaviors were coded in the same manner as in Spencer (1996), using the same coding rubric, but placing more emphasis on the earlier developmental levels. General development, again assessed on the Physical and Self-Help scales of the Developmental Profile II (Alpern, Boll, & Shearer, 1980), was within normal limits for all children.

Spencer and Meadow-Orlans (1996) obtained language measures for the children from transcription and coding of the actual communication produced in the 12- and 18-month play sessions. At 12 months, only two language levels were apparent: prelinguistic (no formal words or signs produced) and emerging lexicon (one or more single-word/sign utterances produced). By 18 months, three levels were observed: emerging lexicon, established single-word/sign utterances, and emerging multiword/multisign or syntactic utterances. At 12 months, more hearing and dD infants than dH infants were at the emerging lexicon level; at 18 months, the same pattern was evident, with almost all of the dH infants still at the emerging lexicon level. Spencer and Meadow-Orlans also related the children's play and their language skills to a global measure of the quality of mothers' interactive behaviors, defined as an average of ratings on flexibility, consistency, and sensitivity (Meadow-Orlans & Steinberg, 1993).

Analysis of these longitudinal data again showed that the progression of increasingly complex and symbolic play skills observed for young hearing children holds true for those who are deaf or hard of hearing, although the frequency and duration of different types of play varied across the groups at some ages. This was not the case at 9 months, when the hearing status groups were quite similar in the distribution of play behaviors, with only simple manipulation of single or multiple objects and a few simple representations of self-directed pretense observed. In fact, the emerging representational play noted at that age (e.g., child brings a toy bottle to her mouth but does not try to drink from it) may have indicated a recognition of objects and their functions rather than any real pretense.

At 12 months, however, there was a difference in the frequency and duration of sequences of representational play behaviors (e.g., performing several different actions using items from the tea set), with hearing children exceeding both dD and dH groups on this measure, as well as on duration of total representational play. This occurred despite similar language levels and maternal sensitivity ratings for the dD and the hearing group. That is, the difference between these two groups was limited to their production of the highest level of play evident at this age. It is probable that the play differences reflected deaf mothers' response to children's still immature visual attention skills—that is, due to their tendency to wait for their children to look up at them before communicating, deaf mothers tended to produce fewer language-based prompts that might have encouraged extended play sequences than did hearing mothers. Thus, although it was not specifically assessed, the researchers posited that dD children's play at this age was more independent and "solitary" than was the case for hearing children, whose mothers gave spoken guidance even while their children were not looking at them. The lag in sequenced representational play for dD children at 12 months had disappeared by 18 months, probably reflecting their increasingly flexible visual attention patterns and resulting changes in mothers' language behaviors.[1] Indeed, Spencer (1993a,b), in separate analyses of

these same videotapes, documented an increase in signed utterances by deaf mothers at 18-month compared to 12-month sessions. By 18 months of age, the amount of symbolic-level play that dD and hH children engaged in did not differ significantly.

Like dD children, dH also produced less sequenced representational play than hH children at 12 months; however, the dH children continued to lag behind the hH children at 18 months. They had increased their production of sequenced representation-level play, but produced less symbolic-level play (preplanned) than either other group at 18 months. By 18 months, rating of mother's sensitivity was the strongest predictor of child play, and child language level was also a significant predictor. Both of these measures were lowest for the dH group.

In summary, differences in the play skills of hearing and deaf children were seen as early as 12 months. This pattern at 12 months seemed, at least for group dD, to reflect demands on the visual attention characteristic of deaf as opposed to hearing children. The delay that appeared for deaf children at this age disappeared, however, for those with deaf mothers who seemed to intuitively meet their visual communication and attention needs. No effect from deafness itself was maintained at 18 months. However, the delay at 12 months for dH children continued at 18 months, suggesting an ongoing pattern of delayed attainment of more advanced play skills along with continuing language delays. To the extent that early dyadic play experiences provide the context, or as Spencer and Hafer (1998) called it, the "room" in which further development is supported, this group seemed to be in a situation in which remediating their delays might become more rather than less difficult. Not all researchers have found delays this early for deaf children, however. Bornstein et al. (1999) conducted a study of the representational abilities of deaf and hearing children, focusing on both play and language skills of children between the ages of 17 and 30 months. In contrast with the study by Spencer and Meadow-Orlans (1996), the study by Bornstein et al. was not longitudinal, and data were collected at a single point in time for each child (mean age = 23.1 months). The study included 20 dD, 22 dH, and 26 hH children.[2] Hearing losses ranged from severe to profound for children in the dD and dH groups. Age of diagnosis was, on average, less than 1 month for dD children and less than 10 months for dH children.

The children's language development was assessed using a variety of instruments, including the Early

Language Inventory (ELI; Bates, Benigni, Bretherton, Camaioni, & Volterra, 1979) and portions of the Reynell Developmental Language Scales-Second Revision (RDLS; Reynell & Huntley, 1985). Play was coded using a system highly similar to but less complex than that used by Spencer (1996), with codes similarly independent of child language (Bornstein et al., 1999). Play sessions included 10 minutes of solitary play (but in the presence of mother) and 10 minutes of dyadic child–mother play. Analyses considered the solitary and dyadic play separately.

Scores on all language measures showed a similar pattern among the three groups discussed here, with hearing children receiving the highest scores, followed by dD children and then dH children.[3] Despite these differences in language measures, significant differences among the three groups of children on the play measures were limited to the duration of child-initiated symbolic play (which was longer for hH than dH children). No significant group differences were found on the longest pretend play sequence during solitary play or the longest sequence during mother-initiated play in the dyadic situations. Similarly, no differences were found among the groups in substitutional play (which occurred rarely), nor in children's highest level of play in either solitary or dyadic contexts considered separately. Highest level of play initiated by mothers also failed to differ across groups. However, children in all groups engaged in more symbolic-level play when interacting with mothers than when in solitary play.

Both the ELI and RDLS related with measures of children's symbolic play within the dH group, but language and play measures were not significantly related in groups dD or hH, where mother and child hearing status was matched and language development correlated more closely with age. Despite the hH–dH difference on child-initiated symbolic play and the association between language and play for group dH, Bornstein's group concluded that "at least some core constituent of representational play reflects maturation or structural development…" and that "whatever group differences exist in the language domain … they appear not to spill over in any pervasive way to affect symbolic play" (p. 847).

Although the Bornstein group's (1999) proposal of an effect of general maturation on play would find wide agreement, their conclusion that language differences do not affect symbolic play not only disagrees with findings of other researchers but seems to contradict their findings for the dH group.

The language–play association for this group is consistent with much other research, and suggests that interactions between these two domains put dH children at risk for disruptions in cognitive development. In contrast with these researchers' conclusion that effects should dissipate with age, moreover, it seems reasonable to suspect that increasing delays in both domains may progressively affect the types of interactions and experiences afforded DHH children with delayed language.

Brown, Rickards, and Bortoli (2001) investigated the play of somewhat older deaf children ($n = 10$, average age around 30 months) who had quite significant language delays, comparing them with a matched group of hearing children. Brown et al.'s analyses focused on identifying similarities and differences in various cognitive components of play and comparing these components with a vocabulary measure. Observations of dyadic play at 28, 29, and 30 months, with play lasting about 10 minutes at each session, were combined for analysis. Participating dH children had profound hearing loss diagnosed between 5 and 18 months (mean = 11.3 months). The children were judged from screening tests or observations to be functioning cognitively in the low-average or higher range. At each of the sessions, mothers completed a short version of the MacArthur Communicative Development Inventory (Reznick & Goldsmith, 1989), providing a parent-report measure of expressive vocabulary. Unlike the children studied by Spencer (1996), Spencer and Meadow-Orlans (1996), or Bornstein et al. (1999), none of those in the Brown et al. study had deaf parents, and spoken language was the primary modality used by their mothers.

Striking differences were found between the mean levels of play behaviors of the two groups of children. Eight of the ten hearing children scored at the highest level possible, demonstrating "imaginary transformations"—that is, pretending about objects or persons that are not physically present. In contrast, only two of the deaf children reached as high as level 8, "agency attribution (adopts vocal or physical attributes of another)". Three of the deaf children showed combined action sequences, but none of them showed "ordered script-like sequences" equivalent to the canonically ordered sequences reported by Spencer and Meadow-Orlans (1996) to be associated with language skills at 18 months—nor did dH children demonstrate imaginary transformations.

When the cognitive components of the play measure were considered, group differences were again found. For example, hearing children scored higher than dH children for decontextualization—that is, they were more likely to engage in substitution play and to "invent" an imaginary object or substance. This is consistent with most earlier research on children from these two groups. Furthermore, hearing children showed higher levels of decentered play, being more likely than dH children to have a doll or a pretend entity produce play actions. Sequenced play was more common and generally more complex for hearing than deaf children, and hearing children were more likely to give evidence (verbal or nonverbal) of planning their play behaviors. Differences across all these cognitive components indicate that the play delays for the dH children in this study were pervasive and not merely limited to one subtype of play or another.

Brown et al. (2001) found that the vocabulary measure they used was significantly associated with the deaf children's production of decentered (involving another entity), sequenced, and planned play, but not with the degree of decontexualization of play, as in substitution of objects. It is possible that this is due to statistical limitations imposed by the limited amount of decontextualized play for the dH group. A somewhat different pattern was found for the hearing children, however, with decontextualized but not decentered play related to language. Brown et al. suggest that this difference may have been due to a ceiling effect for hearing children. The findings of this study indicate that strong effects on cognition, as seen in play behaviors, occur when language is significantly delayed. It would appear that these children's lack of accessible language models not only limited their language development but, in contrast with the suggestion of Bornstein et al., these effects spilled over into the cognitive domain. These effects may have been exacerbated to the extent that communication difficulties affected maternal contributions to play experiences, as Meadow-Orlans et al. suggest occurs (e.g., Meadow-Orlans et al., 2004; Spencer & Meadow-Orlans, 1996).

Behaviors of the same two groups studied by Brown et al. (2001) were further analyzed by Brown and Remine (2004) to identify relationships between maternal scaffolding behaviors and children's play. Although they found that mothers' participation in the play raised the highest level of play shown by hH children, this was not the case for their dyads of dH children. When mean levels of play were considered, both mothers' commentary (talking about the play) and active participation in the play were associated with higher levels of hearing children's play; only mothers' active participation, including modeling of pretend acts, was associated with mean levels of play in the dyads including deaf children.

The relative lack of impact from mothers' "commentary" in the dH group most probably resulted from the combination of the deaf children's substantial language delay, hearing loss limiting their understanding of their mothers' mostly spoken language, patterns of relatively noncontingent language from the mothers, and perhaps (although not addressed in the report) unmet needs related to visual integration of speechreading and attention to objects or the physical environment. Mothers of the deaf children seemed at least to be aware intuitively that active play and modeling were more effective supports than commentary in that they were more likely to produce the former than the latter types of behavior. Attention-getting behaviors were frequent, so it appears that the mothers were also aware that they needed to obtain their children's attention to modeled acts if they were to prompt successful engagement. Dyadic play episodes in the dH group were shorter, however, and tended to contain fewer play actions than in the group with hearing children. Overall, Brown and Remine (2004) painted a rather dismal picture, concluding that the mothers of the oral deaf children in their study had to "work hard to maintain a fluent, enjoyable experience for their child" (p. 148). It is not clear what all of the factors were that resulted in this picture; however, this situation suggests that there are increasing, not decreasing, effects on cognition when language remains severely delayed and when child–mother linguistic-level communication is difficult.

Summary

Because of the scarcity of longitudinal data on the play of deaf infants and toddlers (Spencer & Meadow-Orlans, 1996), developmental trends must be estimated by looking across the various studies available. Overall, DHH children develop and demonstrate play behaviors in the same order as that established for young hearing children. Differences have been noted, but only at the higher representational–symbolic levels. At the youngest ages evaluated (8–11 months by Yoshinaga-Itano et al., 1998, and 9 months by Spencer and Meadow-Orlans, 1996), no difference was suggested in the play of children with and without hearing loss. A difference was reported, however, by Spencer and Meadow-Orlans between deaf children (whether with deaf or hearing parents) and hearing children at 12 months. This difference has yet to be replicated or confirmed, but it suggests that, early in life, at the stage at which the ability to use symbols was emerging in both language and play, hearing status affected at least the demonstration of cognitively related behaviors. Although this difference resolved by 18 months, apparently due to adaptive mother communicative behaviors and children's maturing visual attention skills, it indicates that the paths of development can diverge temporarily and then rejoin at a later point. It also demonstrates that cognition, as seen through the "window" provided by observations of play (Spencer & Hafer, 1998), is the product of a highly integrated web of abilities and experiences—even during infant and toddler years.

Unfortunately, the developmental path (of components of cognition as well as language) for many of the dH children who participated in the studies reviewed here seems to have continued to diverge from that of the other children. The greatest differences were seen in acquisition and demonstration of higher levels of play—realistic and extended sequences of pretend play behaviors, changing of perspectives shown by engaging in role play or causing dolls or other objects to "act," and forming and holding in mind transformations of objects by substituting one for another in play acts. These differences can serve as markers for the need to institute or modify intervention efforts.

The need for intensified support in such cases is especially salient in that dyadic play experiences provide a major context for development—or, as Spencer and Hafer (1998) indicated, play can be envisioned as the "room" in which development is promoted. Lack of opportunities or abilities to engage in cognitively more advanced forms of play can limit or slow further growth. The effects of lessened experience in practicing the kinds of acts that occur in pretend or symbolic-level play (i.e., perspective taking, integration of thematic acts, and memory and retrieval of sequences of acts) can be expected to be seen in continued delays of analogous but linguistically and cognitively more advanced skills. Just such skills have been studied in investigations of what is referred to as "theory of mind" (ToM) abilities in somewhat older DHH children. These abilities involve understanding that other people have different knowledge, beliefs, and feelings based on their own perspectives and experiences (e.g., deVilliers, 2007; Leslie, 1994; Milligan, Astington, & Dack, 2007). Therefore, Youngblade and Dunn (1995) concluded from a study of hearing children that ToM abilities relate to and are promoted by earlier participation in pretend or symbolic play.

Theory of Mind

Beginning in the 1990s, researchers began to focus on the development of "theory of mind" in DHH children, a social-cognitive phenomenon that had already been studied for well over a decade in hearing children and that was of special interest to researchers interested in children with autism. Theory of mind abilities, which emerge in typically developing hearing children between 3 and 5 years of age, have been found to emerge much later in most deaf children. Studies indicating that deaf children acquire ToM abilities as late as 11 years—although reports of about 7 years are more frequent (e.g., Lundy, 2002)—suggest that delays in some aspects of cognition identified for at least a significant portion of the population in earlier studies of play continue into middle childhood.

The foundations of ToM are thought to reside in the same situations and be influenced by the same set of factors that influence the development of play—namely, interactive experiences and the richness of language models. More specifically, mothers' talk about mental states (e.g., Moeller & Schick, 2006; Peterson & Siegal, 1995, 2000), play with an older sibling (Youngblade & Dunn, 1995), joint or coordinated attention skills (Baron-Cohen, 1995; Charman, Baron-Cohen, Swettenham, Baird, Cox, & Drew, 2001), imitation of others' actions (Rogers & Pennington, 1991), and children's language skills (e.g., deVilliers & deVilliers, 2000; Peterson & Siegal, 2000) have variously and sometimes in concert been proposed to effect ToM development. As for play, both innate and experiential factors have been proposed to promote this growth (Baron-Cohen & Swettenham, 1996). Studies with DHH children have been focused primarily on assumed prerequisite language abilities, although some researchers (e.g., Peterson and Siegal, 1995) have suggested that the apparent influence of language delays actually stems not from some lack of abstract linguistic processing but instead from the lack of opportunities provided many deaf children to participate in conversations.

Theory of mind has been researched frequently through use of a "false belief" or "diverse belief" task (e.g., Remmel & Peters, 2008; Wellman & Liu, 2004). In one such task, sometimes referred to as the "Sally-Anne" task (the "change in location" task), a child sees a person (sometimes a puppet or doll) hide an object in one place and then leave the room. While the person is gone, someone else moves the hidden object to a new place. When the first person returns, the child is asked where this person thinks the object is—where he or she will look for it. A child with ToM will understand that the person did not see the object moved and will look for it in its original hiding place. This task clearly requires attention and memory skills, so control questions are usually asked by the examiner to assure that the child noticed and remembers where the object was first hidden.

In a similar task, sometimes called "appearance-reality" and sometimes "contents false belief" or "unexpected contents" (e.g., Courtin, 2000; Remmel & Peters, 2008; Wellman & Liu, 2004), the child is shown a familiar container that clearly indicates it contains a specific item. This could be, for example, a Band-Aid (adhesive bandage) container that, when opened, contains something different. The child is then asked what he or she originally thought was in the container. Ability to remember and to hold both types of objects in mind—the expected objects and the observed objects—is taken to indicate achievement of ToM. Sometimes the child is asked what a second person (or, again, a doll or puppet), who has not yet seen the container's actual contents, will think it holds.

Other related tasks tap into children's ability to appreciate the emotions or feelings of another person. One is called "diverse desires" and requires the ability to understand, for example, that a person whose food preference they have been told about will choose that food, instead of one that the child him- or herself prefers. Another tests the ability to understand that people can sometimes hide their true feelings by using facial expressions that are counter to those feelings—that is, to "fake" or hide true emotions. Fairly sophisticated language skills are clearly required simply to understand and respond to the questions that are most often asked during the administration of ToM tasks, but a number of researchers have created low-verbal or nonverbal tasks that appear to tap the same cognitive processes and understandings.

Selected Studies of Theory of Mind in Deaf Children

Courtin (2000) investigated both the effects of language skills and of early exposure to language in 155 deaf children between 5 and 8 years old, including orally trained deaf children with hearing parents (*n* = 45, average age 6 years, 11 months), signing deaf children of hearing parents (*n* = 54, average age 7 years, 4 months), and signing deaf children of deaf parents (*n* = 37, average age 6 years, 6 months). A group of 39 hearing children was also included,

but it is important to note that they were younger on average (with an average age of 5 years, 1 month) than any of the groups of deaf children. Courtin hypothesized that the fluent use of sign language and exposure to fluent signing from birth would accelerate development of ToM abilities due to experience with different visual perspectives and knowledge that another's view of a sign will differ from that of the signer. Courtin also expected that advanced play experiences and language acquisition resulting from early sign experience in the dD group would support faster ToM development.

The children were tested on false-belief (unexpected contents and unexpected change) tasks. As he expected, Courtin (2000) found no deficit or delay on these tasks for deaf children with deaf parents. In fact, by age 6 years, he found that the dD group was *more* likely to succeed on the tasks than the hearing children or than either group of dH children. The orally trained, but not the signing, dH children were less successful than the hearing children. Interpretation of Courtin's findings is complicated by the different mean ages across the groups of participants. In addition, Courtin pointed out the possibility that information from the tester's gaze, as well as other not-defined visual information, might have been available to assist the performance of the deaf children. To date, Courtin's finding of superior ToM performance from the dD group has not been convincingly replicated. However, his study clearly shows that the factor of deafness itself—that is, lack of access to sound and spoken language—does not impede ToM development.

Woolfe, Want, and Siegal (2002) supported the finding that dD children perform better on ToM tasks than dH children in their study of "native signing" deaf children (*n* = 20, mean age 5 years, 10 months) compared with "late signing" deaf children (*n* = 40, mean age 6 years, 8 months) and a comparison group of younger hearing children (*n* = 20 3-year-olds and 20 4-year-olds). In an attempt to decrease any effects from differences in rate of language development across the groups, Woolfe's group used a method for assessing ToM that decreased dependence on language to understand and to respond to the situations presented. Understanding of false belief was tested using cartoon drawings, in which the children were asked to select one of four pictured options that showed what a character in the cartoon was thinking. For example, one drawing was of a man fishing. The child was to open a flap that showed what was on the end of the man's line—either a fish or a shoe—while covering the picture of the man (thereby reinforcing the idea that the man could not see what was under the flap). The child was then asked to pick a picture that showed what the man thought was on his line. Even when the flap had covered a picture of the shoe, it was expected the child who had achieved ToM related to false beliefs would indicate a picture of a fish. In addition to the low-verbal ToM test, the deaf children's language skills were assessed using a test of receptive British Sign Language (BSL) syntax and morphology, and a general score for visually based cognition was obtained for each child on the Raven's Progressive Matrices (Raven, 1962). Native signers scored higher on the BSL test than did the late signers, but scores on the Raven's test did not differ significantly.

Although the native signing children in the Woolfe et al. (2002) study were significantly younger on average than the late signing children, the former group performed significantly higher than the latter on the ToM tasks. With all deaf children combined, standardized scores on the BSL test correlated significantly with scores on both the Raven's test and ToM tasks.

To determine whether language levels were the primary determiners of ToM performance, the researchers conducted a second analysis including only the dD and dH children (native signers and late signers, with a combined $n - 24$) whose receptive scores were within the average range on the BSL test (i.e., standardized scores ranged between 90 and 110). Even given this similarity in BSL scores, native signing children had significantly higher ToM scores than deaf children who had begun signing later. Because current proficiency in sign language syntax and morphology did not differ for these two subgroups taken from the initial dD and dH groups, the researchers concluded that differences in earlier communicative experiences and early opportunities to participate in and observe conversations must have influenced the development of ToM. In a further search for factors related to ToM, the deaf children (but not the hearing children) were assessed on a test of executive function. Executive function includes the ability to self-regulate behaviors, manage and sustain attention, and reflect on options long enough to allow effective problem solving (Hauser, Lukomski, & Hillman, 2008). Executive functioning was not found to relate to ToM abilities.

Peterson, Wellman, and Liu (2005) investigated patterns of performance on a variety of ToM tasks, looking for similarities or differences between dD (age range 6–13 years, $n = 11$), dH (ages 5.5–13 years, $n = 36$), hearing children with autism (6–14 years, $n = 36$), and typically developing hearing children (3.5–5.5 years, $n = 62$). The deaf children were classmates in educational programs using total communication (TC; sign plus speech). All children were tested on a set of five types of ToM tasks: recognizing diverse desires, understanding diverse beliefs, differences in knowledge access, false beliefs, and hidden emotions. When total scores on the ToM tests were compared, dD children scored significantly higher than later-signing dH children. Typically developing hearing children and those with autism had average scores between those of the two deaf groups, and these scores were not significantly different from each other or the deaf children. (Although the dD children who were native signers performed slightly better than the hearing children, the children in group dD were significantly older than the hearing children.)

The primary aim of the Peterson et al. (2005) study was to evaluate the order in which the various ToM tasks were achieved by the four groups of children, comparing it to the order that had been established by Wellman and Liu (2004) in a previous study of hearing children. In that study, the diverse-desires task had been found to be developmentally earliest, followed by (in order) understanding diverse beliefs, differences in knowledge access, false beliefs, and a task requiring recognition of hidden or "false" emotions. Peterson et al. (2005) found that this same developmental order held for the hearing children in their study and for both groups of deaf children. This indicates that even the late-signing dH children were developing ToM according to a typical pattern, despite a significant lag in age of accomplishment. In contrast, the children with autism showed a significantly different pattern of development, with hidden emotion problems passed before the false belief task. The researchers concluded that processing differences between children with autism and the other children resulted in their special difficulty with false-belief tasks.

In contrast with these studies, Al-Hilawani, Easterbrooks, and Marchant (2002) failed to find a difference in ToM performance between deaf and hearing children. Their cross-cultural study included third-graders in the United States and the United Arab Emirates (UAE) ($n = 22$ hearing children and 14 DHH children from each country). Their different pattern of findings, with both hearing and deaf children from the United States performing higher on the ToM task than hearing or deaf children from the UAE, might have been due to the different test procedures they used. However, Al-Hilawani et al.

suggested that the source of US/UAE difference might lie in discrepancies between the two countries in children's typical early communicative experiences. They noted that most children in the UAE have nannies during their early years, and these nannies often do not speak the children's native language. The researchers suggested that a lack of early exposure to vocabulary and to explanations of environmental events negatively influenced those children's development of ToM, a suggestion that supports the view that typical ToM delays for dH children result from the relative lack of such experiences.

Lundy (2002) more directly addressed potential effects of early language experiences on ToM in a study of 34 dH children, ranging in age from 5 to 10 years, who had hearing loss at or beyond 65 dB across the speech frequencies. Ten of the families in the study used only spoken language, and parents' sign language skills varied in the other families. Lundy was interested specifically in potential associations between ToM and parents' use of signs for terms related to mental or cognitive processes, proposing that meaningful exposure to such terms would prompt cognitive skills relating to achievement of ToM. The signing parents completed a checklist showing which of 25 terms they signed including, for example, "think," "forget," "know," "remember," "pretend," "believe," "make believe," and "notice." Children's language levels were measured using the Language Proficiency profile (LPP; Bebko & McKinnon, 1998), with ratings provided by children's teachers or language therapists.

The children were presented with four ToM tasks, including one focused on change of location, another on appearance–reality (in which, after being shown sponges that looked like rocks and being allowed to handle and reidentify them, the child was asked what a friend just entering the room would think the objects were), the unexpected-contents task, and a misleading picture task. This last task involved seeing a series of line drawings in which parts (e.g., dog's ears) were shown and the child was asked to guess what the drawing was a part of (a dog). A drawing of the full picture was then shown. After several of these pairs of pictures, a part–whole set was shown in which the first drawing was misleading, and the picture of the whole proved to be a surprise. The child was asked what a friend would think the second picture would be after seeing the first "part" picture. Two control questions were asked after the first ToM tasks to assure that the children understood what they were being asked and to check that they could remember the events

that they had been shown. Five of the children were unable to answer these questions, and their data were excluded from ToM analyses; these children also had low scores on the LPP, although it is not clear whether language or some other factors interfered with their being able to participate in the task.

Although similar tasks are typically passed by hearing children between 4 and 5 years of age, none of the deaf children under age 7 obtained scores high enough to earn a determination of an overall "pass" on the ToM tasks. They all passed the tests by the age of 9 years, however. Child age was found to be the dominant predictor of ToM scores, with the language measure adding little to the prediction. In contrast with earlier studies, therefore, Lundy (2002) found no overall cognitive–language level association. In addition, the number of cognitively related words parents reported they could sign did not relate significantly to ToM. This lack of significance may have resulted from the fact that the parents' sign abilities appeared to be quite low: only four parents reported knowing and using the signs for more than 16 of the 25 words. In addition, it is not clear whether the difference between tasks used in this and earlier studies led to different results.

The potential influence on ToM of mothers' use of terms for mental or cognitive processes was studied in more detail by Moeller and Schick (2006), who observed and transcribed mother and child language in a series of situations designed to encourage interactive language about mental states. Twenty-two dH children (age 4–10 years) and 26 hearing children (ages 4–6 years) with hearing mothers participated. Children's expressive syntax skills were measured by computing the Index of Productive Syntax (IPSyn; Scarborough, 1990) from 100 utterances. Mothers' number of different mental terms produced and the number of utterances that did not refer to mental states were counted. In addition, mothers' knowledge and production of signs for mental terms were tested using a flash card-based assessment. Questionnaires were used to obtain information about family signing practices and training. Children's ToM was tested using false-belief tasks, related to both unexpected-contents (in both traditional and low-verbal task variations) and change-of-location tasks.

Comparing the deaf and hearing groups, mothers of hearing children were found to use a greater diversity of mental state terms. Mothers' use of mental state terms was associated significantly with their knowledge of relevant signs, with children's expressive syntax scores, and with child ToM scores.

Interestingly, mothers' sign skills associated with the amount of specific sign instruction they had received and not the number of years they had been signing. Moeller and Schick suggested that this indicates the importance of hearing parents of deaf children participating in actual sign classes. Children who had siblings who signed also scored higher on ToM, although not higher than those with no siblings, suggesting an increased importance for whole-family sign skills in families with multiple children.

Further analyses showed that child age and language skills combined accounted for almost three-fourths of the variance in ToM scores. However, even after these two factors were considered, mothers' use of mental state terms still contributed significantly to the prediction of ToM. Additional analysis indicated that this result was not simply an effect of the amount of total maternal language, but was specific to language addressing mental states.

Mothers' use of mental state terms did not appear to relate to child hearing status itself, because there was no difference in their frequency or diversity when dyads of deaf children who obtained high scores on the ToM task (>75%) and of hearing children who scored equally high were compared. Lower rates of maternal use of mental state terms was found only for dyads of dH children who had low ToM scores. Given all of these results, Moeller and Schick (2006) concluded that ToM development was significantly related to mothers' use of mental state terms, but they pointed out probable bidirectional effects. That is, characteristics of mothers' sign skills and their use of abstract or mental state terms could be affected by indications of increased language skills and understanding on the part of their children.

Schick, deVilliers, deVilliers, and Hoffmeister (2007) looked closely at effects of both children's and mothers' language on ToM in a study that included four groups of children. In three of the groups, the children were deaf. This included a dD group in which families and children used American Sign Language (ASL) (n = 49), a group of dH children in which ASL was the primary language (n = 41), and another group of dH children in which only spoken language (n = 86) was used. Average child age in these groups ranged from 6 to almost 7 years, with an age range across the groups of 4–8 years. A group of hH children (n = 42) also participated, and these children's ages ranged from 4 to 6 years.

The researchers collected data in a variety of situations, some designed to greatly minimize language demands for presenting the problem and in children's responses. The situations presented included change in location; unexpected contents; a low-verbal hidden sticker game (Povinelli & DeBlois, 1992), in which the child needed to determine which of two adults actually knew the location of a sticker; and a pictorially based game, in which the child had to decide whether a character in a story would or would not be surprised at the outcome (P. deVilliers & Pyers, 2001, cited in Schick et al.).

Because an important research hypothesis was that use of language-minimal testing procedures would eliminate the difference between children with and without language delays, assessments of both vocabulary (receptive and expressive) and comprehension of syntax were conducted with the three groups of deaf children. A set of tests standardized on hearing children was administered to the oral dH children. In addition, a specific test of false-complement clauses (e.g., "She told the girl there was a bug in her hair"—when a picture showed it was a leaf not a bug) was conducted to follow up previous research findings (e.g., J. deVilliers & Pyers, 2002) that understanding of and memory for this syntactic structure directly influence ToM.

For the signing deaf children, analogous tests were developed in ASL, including a test of ASL sign vocabulary, a test of comprehension of ASL syntax (not including complement clauses), and a test of comprehension of false-complement clauses based on translation into ASL of the communication verbs used in the English-based test (p. 385). (Translations and test development were conducted by native signers, and pilot testing was conducted on all the newly created ASL assessments.) In addition, the general nonverbal cognitive skills of children in all deaf groups were assessed using the Differential Ability Scales (DAS; Elliott, 1990) and the Comprehensive Test of Nonverbal Intelligence-2 (Hammill, Pearson, & Wiederholt, 1996). The Knox Cube Test (Stone & Wright, 1979) was administered to assess nonverbal sequential memory.

There were no significant differences among the three deaf groups on the Knox Cube Test, despite its emphasis on sequencing, but signing dD children scored higher than oral dH children on the Pattern Construction subtest of the DAS. Deaf children with deaf parents also scored significantly higher than signing dH children on the measure of ASL vocabulary. But differences were not significant on the test of comprehension of ASL syntax and only approached significance on the test of understanding complement structures.

The 4- to 6-year-old hearing children and that portion of the dD group who were between those same ages performed similarly on the verbal ToM tasks, indicating neither advantage nor disadvantage associated with being deaf and using sign language. Moreover, both hH and dD groups did better than the two groups of deaf children with hearing parents. The same pattern of performance occurred on the low-language ToM tasks. These results held for the deaf groups even when scores on the DAS cognitive test were co-varied. Thus, delays in ToM sometimes associated with being deaf were better attributed to being deaf *and* having atypical early language experiences than to deafness alone.

Analyses of group differences at 7 years compared only the three groups of deaf children because no hearing children of that age participated in the study. At 7 years of age, signing dD children still performed significantly higher than the oral dH group on ToM tasks (low-verbal as well as verbal). However, the dH group in ASL programming appeared to be gaining on the dD group, and differences between those two groups were no longer significant.

Within-group analyses of both oral and signing dH children indicated that chronological age and the Knox measure of nonverbal memory for sequence were associated with ToM performance in the verbal as well as the reduced-language situations. This indicates a strong maturation component. In addition, language performance was associated with ToM scores for the dH children, signing or oral. With other factors controlled, vocabulary comprehension and understanding false-complement clauses (but not general syntax skills) predicted performance on the verbal ToM tasks for both groups of dH children. Processing of false-complement clauses was the only significant predictor among the language measures of dH children's performance on the low-verbal ToM tasks.

In summary, because dD and hH groups did not differ, Schick et al. (2007) concluded that neither child hearing status nor language modality explained functioning on either verbal or nonverbal ToM tasks. These findings are consistent with those of previous researchers. The level of language skills did associate with ToM, in that dH children were delayed in both language and ToM. The ToM delay extended to low-verbal as well as verbal testing contexts, so the researchers concluded that a combination of differences in communication experiences and language levels related to children's abilities to *reason* about mental states.

Schick et al.'s finding of a relationship between understanding false-complement linguistic structures and ToM tasks has not been supported by some

other researchers, including Cheung et al. (2004), who conducted a cross-cultural study comparing Cantonese- and English-speaking children's understanding of linguistic complement understanding and ToM. It is possible that the apparent relation between this specific syntactic concept and ToM in the Schick group's study results from its being one of the most complex and advanced syntactic structures used at the ages tested. Thus, as opposed to more general measures of syntax knowledge, tests assessing understanding of complements may focus on a child's highest level of language functioning and thereby differentiate more clearly among children.

To the extent that language skills and children's ability to access and learn from language addressed to them or occurring around them relates to ToM, it has been asked whether use of cochlear implants would result in promoting ToM development, especially of dH children. In many cases, use of cochlear implants provides significant access to spoken language (e.g., Geers, 2006) and, in addition, activation of a cochlear implant is typically followed by intense speech, language, and auditory therapy that provides support for vocabulary and syntactic development (Spencer, Marschark & Spencer, in press). Schick et al. (2007) included children with cochlear implants in their study, as did several of the other researchers whose work is discussed earlier in this chapter (e.g., Lundy, 2002; Moeller & Schick, 2006; however, the focus of their work was not on the effects of those children's cochlear implant use.

Macaulay and Ford (2006) specifically addressed whether age and length of cochlear implant use would, by increasing spoken language skills, also result in increased achievement of ToM. Participating children first used cochlear implants between 2 and almost 7 years (mean approximately 4 years). The children ranged in age between 4 and 11 years when data were collected. They were in programming using simultaneous sign plus spoken English (sign supported speech) but were apparently tested using spoken language only. Theory of mind tasks, including change of location and unexpected contents, were administered.

Children's scores on a measure of receptive vocabulary related significantly to their length of use of cochlear implants, but not to either chronological age or age of implantation (see Chapter 9, this volume). Macaulay and Ford (2006) found that, as in most of the studies summarized earlier, language levels correlated significantly with performance on ToM tasks. However, despite their cochlear implants—and a reported average gain of 12 months receptive language growth per year since implantation—the children still showed a significant delay overall in ToM development. The researchers estimated that there was generally a ToM 4-year delay, and that chronological age alone did not mediate those delays.

Another study of children using cochlear implants resulted in more positive findings. Remmel and Peters (2009) examined ToM, language, and the relation between the two abilities in 30 children using cochlear implants and in 30 hearing children. They examined the degree to which general language skills, complement syntax, age at implantation, and duration of use of implant were associated with performance on ToM tasks. Only three of the participating children with cochlear implants had some hearing at birth, and those children lost hearing by 12 months of age. The age range of the cochlear implant group was 3–12 years (average 7.5) when data were collected. Because of this wide age range, children with cochlear implants were divided into two age groups: younger (3–7.8 years) and older (8–12 years). The children with cochlear implants averaged 2.9 years of age when implants were first used, but the range of age at implantation was large—from 1.1 to 6.0 years. Although three of the CI children had previously been in TC environments, none was currently signing. All parents were hearing speakers of English. The children in the hearing group were between 4.5 and 6.5 years (mean = 5.2) of age.

Theory of mind was tested using the five-task scale developed by Wellman and Liu (2004), and control questions were asked to check for both comprehension and memory. In addition, nonverbal versions of false-belief tasks (Figueras-Costa & Harris, 2001) were administered, as was the false photograph test (Zaitchik, 1990) to test general representational abilities. Based on deVilliers and deVilliers (2000), a test of understanding complement syntax was administered, as was an activity requiring the child to explain a person's anomalous action. Finally, a test of auditory word perception (Phonetically Balanced Kindergarten Test; Haskins, 1949) and a variety of other standardized language scales were administered to children. Syntax production was measured by computing the IPSyn from language samples collected in response to wordless picture books.

Language scores obtained from the children with cochlear implants tended to be quite high, and this needs to be kept in mind during a discussion of results. For example, the children's performance on the memory for complement syntactic structures was near ceiling (although relatively few of the children actually produced this structure during expressive language samples), as were scores for understanding and producing spoken English. Almost half performed at or above norms for same-age hearing children. Scores on a cognitive task unrelated to ToM (reasoning about physical representations) were also high, and the presence of any cognitive disability had previously been ruled out for at least half of the CI children.

In this study, the children with cochlear implants did not differ from the group of hearing children on ToM, and the researchers concluded that the high language levels of children with cochlear implants, which they attribute to implant use, were responsible for this positive finding. For this cochlear implant group, chronological age and years using the implants were associated with ToM performance. Success on two of the ToM tasks associated significantly with total scores on expressive syntax; but, in contrast with the findings of Schick et al. (2007), no such correlation was found between ToM and the test of complement syntactic structures.

Unlike other studies involving deaf children, the children with cochlear implants in Remmel and Peters' (2008) study showed an order of difficulty on the ToM tasks that was similar to that of children with autism, rather than to typically developing hearing children: recognizing hidden or false emotions was easier than solving the false-contents task. The researchers suggested that, like children with autism, those using cochlear implants (often in school placements without other deaf children around) had more problematic interactions at school than is typical for signing deaf children (who are more often educated with other deaf children), and that this may have increased their sensitivity to hidden or falsified emotions shown through facial expressions.

Summary

Theory of mind appears to develop for deaf as it does for hearing children when: (a) the language of parents, siblings, and other persons is accessible to children from their earliest years; (b) this language is produced in supportive interactions; and, as a consequence, (c) the children acquire language skills at a typical rate that can both support and interact with other aspects of cognitive development.

Unfortunately, these conditions continue to be infrequent when the majority of deaf children—those with hearing parents—are considered. Even use of ASL as their first language does not seem to level the cognitive playing field for dH children, presumably because their early communicative interactions are limited due to parents' emerging sign skills and perhaps parents' lack of intuitive abilities to accommodate the attention patterns of DHH children. As with the development of play skills, however, development of ToM does not seem to be directly dependent upon either child hearing status or the language modality through which language is learned and used. It is, again, a web of interconnecting abilities and experiences that allows children to develop this cognition-related skill.

Because there is a pattern of dH children "catching up" and acquiring ToM skills later in childhood, it might seem that concerns about age of acquisition are excessive. However, as with play, the ability to use ToM concepts is important for the opportunities it provides for continued cognitive growth. If use of complement and other advanced syntactic structures are facilitative for developing ToM abilities, it may be because they allow children to talk about cause and effect as well as the truth (or at least the probability of truth) in communications and activities they have observed. The ability to step back, consider, and evaluate may be necessary foundations for the types of thinking required in academic settings.

Summary and Conclusions

Obviously, both play and ToM, while providing examples of cognition and learning during early months and years of life, are enmeshed in a tightly woven web of experience and development across multiple domains and contexts. Indeed, as Rogoff (1990, p. 9) stated, "The traditional distinction among cognitive, affective, and social processes becomes blurred once we focus on thinking as the attempt to determine intelligent means to reach goals [and]... problem-solving." As such, any differences between deaf and hearing children in aspects of cognitive development cannot be attributed to any single factor. This is undoubtedly the case for varied aspects of higher-level cognition, such as executive function, memory, and integration of information from diverse sources, as well as for the early-developing play and ToM abilities surveyed in this chapter.

Although the studies of early play and ToM reviewed in this chapter present some diverging findings, and many questions remain to be answered, some overall conclusions can be drawn. First, the preponderance of evidence suggests that hearing loss itself has no enduring effect on these early cognitive accomplishments when appropriate communication experiences (that include sensitivity to special demands for visual processing) are provided. Second, it is access to early communicative experiences, regardless of modality or use of any specific amplification device, that serve to prime the cognitive "engine." There is no evidence at this early stage that children with hearing loss must experience cognitive and learning difficulties later in life if they are given appropriate supports to early development.

Finally, an overview of available studies does not suggest that early delays in play or even in ToM abilities ameliorate with time. Instead, the longer such delays continue, the greater may be their effects on children's experiencing age-appropriate communicative and language-based interactions that typically support increasingly sophisticated concepts and learning skills. The key to preventing the learning and memory difficulties that have been reported for older deaf students may lie in increasing targeted supports for effective early interactions to facilitate cognitive growth during the first years of life.

Acknowledgments

The author would like to thank Dr. Ron Outen for helpful comments on earlier versions of this chapter.

[1] This pattern of an apparent but nonsustained delay at 12 months is evident in a parallel study of visual attention development that included most of the same participants (Spencer, 2000; Waxman & Spencer, 1997). In the attention study, it was concluded that differences in dD and hH mothers' behaviors at 12 months represent successful adaptations to the children's dominant modality for reception of communication and language—with attention behaviors of children in those groups being highly similar at 18 months (Spencer, 2000).

[2] In fact, Bornstein et al. (1999) included a fourth group of participants: hearing children with deaf mothers. They have not been discussed in this chapter, but data from a similar group is also available in the work of the Meadow-Orlans group (Meadow-Orlans et al., 2004), conducted at Gallaudet University's Center for Studies in Education and Human Development.

[3] Interestingly, Bornstein et al. (1999) found the group of hearing children with deaf mothers to have the highest scores of all the groups on a variety of measures, including language and sequenced symbolic play. These findings may indicate advantages of early access to communication in multiple modalities. (For example, Meadow-Orlans et al., 2004, indicated that deaf mothers were likely to use vocal language, as well as fluent signing, with their hearing children). Thus, hearing children with signing deaf parents may provide an interesting group in which to study the cognitive and linguistic effects of early multimodal communication experiences.

References

Al-Hilawani, Y., Easterbrooks, S., & Marchant, G. (2002). Metacognitive ability from a theory-of-mind perspective: A cross-cultural study of students with and without hearing loss. *American Annals of the Deaf, 147*, 38–47.

Alpern, G., Boll, T., & Shearer, M. (1980). *Manual: Developmental profile II (Revised)*. Aspen, CO: Psychological Development Publications.

Baron-Cohen, S. (1995). *Mindblindness: An essay on autism and theory of mind*. Cambridge, MA: MIT Press.

Baron-Cohen, S., & Swettenham, J. (1996). The relationship between SAM and TOMM: Two hypotheses. In P. Carruthers & P. Smith (Eds.), *Theories of theories of mind* (pp. 158–168). Cambridge: Cambridge University Press.

Bates, E., Benigni, L., Brethrton, I., Camaioni, L., & Volterra, V. (1979). *The emergence of symbols, cognition, and communication in infancy*. New York: Academic Press.

Bates, E., Bretherton, I., & Snyder, L. (1988). *From first words to grammar: Individual differences and dissociable mechanisms*. Cambridge: Cambridge University Press.

Bates, E., Bretherton, I., Snyder, L., Shore, C., & Volterra, V. (1980). Gestural and vocal symbols at 13 months. *Merrill-Palmer Quarterly, 26*, 407–423.

Bates, E., O'Connell, B., & Shore, C. (1984). Language and communication in infancy. In J. Osofsky (Ed.), *Handbook of infant development* (pp. 149–203). New York: Wiley.

Bebko, J., & McKinnon, E. (1998). Assessing pragmatic language skills in deaf children: The Language Proficiency Profile. In M. Marschark & M. Clark (Eds.), *Psychological perspectives on deafness*, Volume 2 (pp. 243–263). Mahwah, NJ: Lawrence Erlbaum Associates.

Bornstein, M., Selmi, A., Haynes, O., Painter, K., & Marx, E. (1999). Representational abilities and the hearing status of child/mother dyads. *Child Development, 70*, 833–852.

Braden, J. (1994). *Deafness, deprivation, and IQ*. New York: Plenum Press.

Brown, P. M., Prescott, S., Rickards, F., & Paterson, M. (1997). Communicating about pretend play: A comparison of the utterances of four year old normally hearing and hearing-impaired children in an integrated kindergarten. *Volta Review, 99*, 5–17.

Brown, P. M., & Remine, M. (2004). Building pretend play skills in toddlers with and without hearing loss: Maternal scaffolding styles. *Deafness and Education International, 6*, 129–153.

Brown, P. M., Rickards, F., & Bortoli, A. (2001). Structures underpinning pretend play and word production in young hearing children and children with hearing loss. *Journal of Deaf Studies and Deaf Education, 6*, 15–31.

Calhoun, D. (1987). *A comparison of two methods of evaluating play in toddlers*. Unpublished master's thesis. Colorado State University. Ft. Collins.

Casby, M., & McCormack, S. (1985). Symbolic play and early communication development in hearing-impaired children. *Journal of Communication Disorders, 18*, 67–78.

Charman, T., Baron-Cohen, S., Swettenham, J., Baird, G., Cox, A., & Drew, A. (2000). Testing joint attention, imitation, and play as infancy precursors to language and theory of mind. *Cognitive Development, 15*, 481–498.

Cheung, H., Hsuan-Chih, C., Creed, N., Ng, L., Wang, S., & Mo, L. (2004). Relative roles of general and complementation language in theory-of-mind development: Evidence from Cantonese and English. *Child Development, 75*, 1155–1170.

Cleary, M., Pisoni, D., & Geers, A. (2001). Some measures of verbal and spatial working memory in eight- and nine-year-old hearing-impaired children with cochlear implants. *Ear and Hearing, 22*, 395–411.

Courtin, C. (2000). The impact of sign language on the cognitive development of deaf children: The case of theories of mind. *Journal of Deaf Studies and Deaf Education, 5*, 266–276.

Darbyshire, J. (1977). Play patterns in young children with impaired hearing. *Volta Review, 79*, 19-26.

deVilliers, J. (2007). The interface of language and theory of mind. *Lingua, 117*, 1858–1878.

deVilliers, J., & deVilliers, P. (2000). Linguistic determinism and the understanding of false beliefs. In P. Mitchell & K. Riggs (Eds.), *Children's reasoning and the mind* (pp. 191–228). Hove, UK: Psychology Press.

deVilliers, J., & Pyers, J. (2002). Complements to cognition: A longitudinal study of the relationship between complex syntax and false-belief-understanding. *Cognitive Development, 17*, 1037–1060.

deVilliers, P., & Pyers, J. (2001). Complementation and false-belief representation. In M. Almgren, A. Barrena, M. Ezeizabarrena, I. Idiazabel, & B. MacWhinney (Eds.), *Research on child language acquisition: Proceedings of the 8th Conference of the International Association for the Study of Child Language* (pp. 984–1005). Somerville, MA: Cascadilla Press. [cited in Schick et al., 2007.].

Elliott, C. (1990). *Differential Ability Scales*. San Antonio TX: Psychological Corporation.

Fiese, B. (1990). Playful relationships: A contextual analysis of mother-toddler interaction and symbolic play. *Child Development, 61*, 1648–1656.

Figueras-Costa, B., & Harris, P. (2001). Theory of mind development in deaf children: A nonverbal test of false belief understanding. *Journal of Deaf Studies and Deaf Education, 6*, 92–102.

Geers, A. (2006). Spoken language in children with cochlear implants. In P. Spencer & M. Marschark (Eds.), *Advances in the spoken language development of deaf and hard-of-hearing children* (pp. 244–270). New York: Oxford University Press.

Hammill, D., Pearson, N., & Wiederholt, J. L. (1996). *Comprehensive Test of Non-Verbal Intelligence-2*. Los Angeles: Western Psychological Corporation.

Haskins, H. (1949). A phonetically balanced test of speech discrimination for children. Unpublished master's thesis. Northwestern University. Evanston, Illinois.

Hauser, P., Lukomski, J., & Hillman, T. (2008). Development of deaf and hard-of-hearing students' executive function. In M. Marschark & P. Hauser (Eds.), *Deaf cognition: Foundations and outcomes* (pp. 286–308), New York: Oxford University Press.

Leslie, A. (1994). *Pretending* and *believing*: Issues in the theory of ToMM. *Cognition, 50*, 211–238.

Lundy, J. (2002). Age and language skills of deaf children in relation to theory of mind development. *Journal of Deaf Studies and Deaf Education, 7*, 41–56.

Maculay, C., & Ford, R. (2006). Language and theory-of-mind development in prelingually deafened children with cochlear implants: A preliminary investigation. *Cochlear Implants International, 7*, 1–14.

Marschark, M. & Wauters, L. (2008). Language comprehension and learning by deaf students. In, M. Marschark & P. Hauser (Eds.), *Deaf cognition: Foundations and outcomes* (pp. 309–350). New York: Oxford University Press.

McCune, L. (1995). A normative study of representational play at the transition to language. *Developmental Psychology, 31*, 198–206.

McCune-Nicholich, L. (1983). *A manual for analyzing free play*. Unpublished manuscript.

Meadow-Orlans, K., Spencer, P., & Koester, L. (2004). *The world of the deaf infant*. New York: Oxford University Press.

Meadow-Orlans, K., & Steinberg, A. (1993). Effects of infant hearing loss and maternal support on mother-infant interactions at eighteen months *Journal of Applied Developmental Psychology*, *14*, 407–426.

Milligan, K., Astington, J., & Dack, L. (2007). Language and theory of mind: Meta-analysis of the relation between language ability and false-belief understanding. *Child Development*, *78*, 622–646.

Moeller, M. P., & Schick, B. (2006). Relations between maternal input and theory of mind understanding in deaf children. *Child Development*, *77*, 751–766.

Peterson, C., & Siegal, M. (1995). Deafness, conversation and theory of mind. *Journal of Child Psychology and Psychiatry*, *36*, 459–474.

Peterson, C., & Siegal, M. (2000). Insights into a theory of mind from deafness and autism. *Mind and Language*, *15*, 123–145.

Peterson, C., Wellman, H., & Liu, D. (2005). Steps in theory-of-mind development for children with deafness or autism. *Child Development*, *76*, 502–517.

Piaget, J. (1952). *The origins of intelligence in children*. New York: Norton.

Piaget, J. (1962). *Play, dreams, and imitation in childhood*. New York: Norton.

Povinelli, D., & DeBlois, S. (1992). Young children's (*Homo sapiens*) understanding of knowledge formation in themselves and others. *Journal of Comparative Psychology*, *106*, 228–238.

Quittner, A., Smith, L., Osberger, M., Mitchell, T., & Katz, D. (1994). The impact of audition on the development of visual attention. *Psychological Science*, *5*, 347–353.

Raven, J. (1962). *Coloured progressive matrices*. London: H. K. Lewis.

Remmel, E., & Peters, K. (2009). Theory of mind and language in children with cochlear implants. *Journal of Deaf Studies and Deaf Education*, *14*, 218–236.

Reynell, J., & Huntley, M. (1985). *Reynell developmental language scales*, 2nd edition, revised. Windsor, UK: NFER-Nelson.

Reznick, J., & Goldsmith, L. (1989). A multiple form word production checklist for assessing early language. *Journal of Child Language*, *16*, 91–100.

Rochat, P. (2001). *The infant's world*. Cambridge, MA: Harvard University Press.

Rogers, S., & Pennington, B. (1991). A theoretical approach to the deficits in infantile autism. *Development and Psychopathology*, *3*, 137–162.

Rogoff, B. (1990). *Apprenticeship in thinking: Cognitive development in social context*. New York: Oxford University Press.

Scarborough, H. (1990). Index of Productive Syntax. *Applied Psycholinguistics*, *11*, 1–22.

Schick, B., deVilliers, P., deVilliers, J., & Hoffmeister, R. (2007). Language and theory of mind: A study of deaf children. *Child Development*, *78*, 376–396.

Schirmer, B. (1989). Relationships between imaginative play and language development in hearing-impaired children. *American Annals of the Deaf*, *134*, 219–222.

Slade, A. (1987). Quality of attachment and early symbolic play. *Developmental Psychology*, *23*, 78–85.

Snyder, L., & Yoshinaga-Itano, C. (1998). Specific play behaviors and the development of communication in children with hearing loss. *Volta Review*, *100*, 165–186.

Spencer, P. (1993a). Communication behaviors of infants with hearing loss and their hearing mothers. *Journal of Speech and Hearing Research*, *36*, 311–321.

Spencer, P. (1933b). The expressive communication of hearing mothers and deaf infants. *American Annals of the Deaf*, *138*, 275–283.

Spencer, P. (1996). The association between language and symbolic play at two years: Evidence from deaf toddlers. *Child Development*, *67*, 867–876.

Spencer, P. (2000). Looking without listening: Is audition a prerequisite for normal development of visual attention during infancy? *Journal of Deaf Studies and Deaf Education*, *5*, 291–302.

Spencer, P. & Hafer, J. (1998). Play as "window" and "room": Assessing and supporting the cognitive and linguistic development of deaf infants and young children. In M. Marschark & D. Clark (Eds.), *Psychological perspectives on deafness*, Volume 2 (pp. 131–152). Hillsdale, NJ: Lawrence Erlbaum Associates.

Spencer, P., & Harris, M. (2006). Patterns and effects of language input to deaf infants and toddlers from deaf and hearing mothers. In B. Schick, M. Marschark, & P. Spencer (Eds.), *Advances in the sign language development of deaf children* (pp. 71–101). New York: Oxford University Press.

Spencer, P., & Meadow-Orlans, K. (1996). Play, language, and maternal responsiveness: A longitudinal study of deaf and hearing infants. *Child Development*, *67*, 3176–3191.

Spencer, P., Marschark, M., & Spencer, L. (in press). Cochlear implants: Advances, issues, and implications. To appear in M. Marschark & P. Spencer (Eds.), *Oxford handbook of deaf studies, language, and education*. Vol. 1, Revised. New York: Oxford University Press.

Stone, M., & Wright, B. (1979). *Knox's Cube Test*. Wood Dale, IL: Stoelting.

Vibbert, M., & Bornstein, M. (1989). Specific associations between domains of mother-child interaction and toddler referential language and pretense play. *Infant Behavior and Development*, *12*, 163–184.

Vygotsky, L. (1978). *Mind in society: The development of higher psychological processes*. Cambridge, MA: Harvard University Press.

Waxman, R., & Spencer, P. (1997). What mothers do to support infant visual attention: Sensitivities to age and hearing status. *Journal of Deaf Studies and Deaf Education*, *2*, 104–114.

Wellman, H., & Liu, D. (2004). Scaling of theory of mind tasks. *Child Development*, *75*, 523–541.

Wood, D. (1989). Social interaction as tutoring. In M. Bornstein & J. Bruner (Eds.), *Interaction in human development* (pp. 59–80). Hillsdale, NJ: Lawrence Erlbaum Associates.

Woodward, A., & Needham, A. (2009). *Learning and the infant mind*. New York: Oxford University Press.

Woolfe, T., Want, S., & Siegal, M. (2002). Signposts to development: Theory of mind in deaf children. *Child Development*, *73*, 768–778.

Yoshinaga-Itano, C., Snyder, L., & Day, D. (1998). The relationship of language and symbolic play in children with hearing loss. *Volta Review*, *100*, 135–165.

Youngblade, L., & Dunn, J. (1995). Individual differences in young children's pretend play with mother and sibling: Links to relationships and understanding of other people's feelings and beliefs. *Child Development*, *66*, 1472–1492.

Zaitchik, D. (1990). When representations conflict with reality: The preschooler's problem with false beliefs and "false" photographs. *Cognition*, *35*, 41–68.

Learning Disabilities in Deaf and Hard-of-Hearing Children

Lindsey Edwards

Abstract

This chapter starts with a brief historical overview of research on the cognitive abilities of deaf children, to provide a context for understanding learning disabilities in this group of children. Working definitions of learning disabilities will be presented, distinguishing between global disability and specific difficulties. Although much has been written about deaf children's cognitive abilities, good empirical evidence is patchy and findings are frequently contradictory. This makes it difficult to determine whether apparent specific difficulties are genuinely associated with hearing impairment, or the result of assessment methods or some other factor. However, some consistent findings have emerged and will be highlighted. Current research and views on established disorders such as dyslexia, dyspraxia, and auditory processing disorder (APD) in deaf children will be presented, as will the available knowledge base for other areas of cognitive functioning, for example executive function, memory, problem solving, and sequencing. Areas of overlap among the underlying cognitive processes will be emphasized. Despite a lengthy history of debate on the issue, assessment of learning disabilities in deaf children is in its infancy in terms of agreed methods, and the use of tests standardized on hearing children remains contentious. Issues relating to the use of neuropsychological and other tests are discussed, and a range of possible approaches are considered and appraised. Finally, suggestions for specific areas in need of further research spanning the whole field of learning disabilities in deaf children are outlined.

Keywords: learning disability, cognitive, dyslexia, auditory processing, assessment, response to intervention

Historical Context

Many aspects of our understanding of the consequences of deafness engender controversy and debate, and learning disabilities in deaf children is certainly one of them. From the earliest accounts by philosophers such as Aristotle, deafness has been associated with inferior intellectual ability. Research throughout much of the 20th century did little to alter this perception due to the use of inappropriate research paradigms, test materials, and administration procedures on heterogeneous groups of deaf children or adults. On this basis, all deaf people would have been considered to have learning disabilities. However, Vernon (1968/2005) reviewed 37 early studies of the intelligence of profoundly deaf children and concluded that the distribution of IQ scores is as great in deaf children as it is in hearing children. Overall, mean IQs were similar between the two groups. As he pointed out, this hides a large degree of variability linked to factors such as the etiology of deafness (e.g., prematurity, maternal rubella infection, or meningitis) and type of schooling (e.g., mainstream or school for the deaf), factors that may be linked to significantly lower IQs. Importantly, these associations cannot be considered causal, but rather arise as the result of the generalized learning disabilities and deafness having a shared etiology, and children with such disabilities being more likely to be educated in special schools for the deaf.

More recently, the cognitive abilities of deaf individuals have been described as being different—from those of their hearing peers, rather than inferior, as a result of differing approaches to learning, knowledge being organized in alternative ways, and varying levels of skills in different domains (Marschark, 2003). Many empirical studies have compared the cognitive skills of deaf and hearing children, with a variety of results, including some that suggest that deaf children cannot be distinguished from their hearing peers (see Marschark, 2003; Marschark, Lang, & Albertini, 2002; Mayberry 2002, for reviews). Although the position that deafness results in differences not deficiencies is a positive one in terms of the perception of deaf people, it also has the potential to do many deaf individuals a significant disservice: where genuine learning disabilities do exist, particularly of a subtle nature, these may be missed and appropriate intervention not provided, as the difficulties are seen as merely normal variations of deaf cognitive functioning.

Definitions of Learning Disabilities

Bearing this historical context in mind, for the remainder of this chapter the term "learning disabilities" will not be used to mean the global developmental delay or impairment of learning with which many deaf children undoubtedly have to contend. "Global" or "generalized learning disability" is diagnosed when a child's cognitive development is delayed in comparison with his or her equivalent-aged peers across all types of cognitive skills—reasoning, memory, attention, executive function, and so on. In contrast, "learning disability," often (confusingly) used interchangeably with "specific learning disability" is typically used to describe a learning problem that cannot be attributed to mental retardation, emotional disturbance, or to cultural, economic, or environmental disadvantage (Lyon, 1996). Included here are learning disabilities such as dyslexia, dyspraxia, APD, memory and executive function disorders, and specific language impairment.

An early, general definition of learning disabilities, provided by the (US) National Joint Committee on Learning Disabilities in 1981 states that:

> Learning disabilities is a generic term that refers to a heterogeneous group of disorders manifested by significant difficulties in the acquisition and use of listening, speaking, reading, writing, reasoning, or mathematical abilities. These disorders are intrinsic to the individual and presumed to be due to central nervous system dysfunction. Even though a learning disability may occur concomitantly with other handicapping conditions (e.g., sensory impairment, mental retardation, social and emotional disturbance) or environmental influences (e.g., cultural differences, insufficient/inappropriate instruction, psychogenic factors), it is not the direct result of those influences. (McLoughlin &Netick, 1983, pp. 21–22)

This clearly has relevance to the identification of learning disabilities in deaf children.

More specifically, in relation to deaf children, Laughton (1989, p. 74) proposed a working definition which states:

> Learning disabled, hearing impaired individuals have significant difficulty with the acquisition, integration, and use of language and/or non-linguistic abilities. These disorders are presumed to be caused by the coexisting conditions of central nervous system dysfunction and peripheral sensorineural hearing impairment and not by either condition exclusively. The condition can vary in its manifestations and degree of severity and can affect education, communication, self-esteem, socialization, and/or daily living activities throughout life.

Although these definitions are certainly not recent, and have been frequently cited, they have stood the test of time, and no newer, better definitions have been proposed. However, it should not be assumed that learning disabilities take exactly the same form, or have the same etiologies, presentations, or comorbidities in deaf as in hearing children. If such differences are the case, then the taxonomy and nosology of learning disabilities in this group would need to be reconsidered, as would their definitions, an area for future research.

Until relatively recently, despite the definitions given here, some professionals have maintained that learning disabilities cannot occur in conjunction with handicapping conditions such as deafness—any learning disabilities are assumed to be the result of the hearing loss, rather than an additional neurological dysfunction. Indeed, as recently as 2004, the Individuals with Disabilities Education Act Amendments (IDEA, 2004) included an exclusion clause that has been interpreted to mean exactly that. This seems to be an unhelpful position, which flies in the face of decades of the experience of educators of deaf children who are confident in asserting that they are able to identify a substantial subgroup of children for whom hearing loss is not the only obstacle to their academic progress, and is also increasingly inconsistent with the empirical evidence. For example, Samar (1999) reported that many teachers of deaf students claim that they are able to identify which students have atypical language development. In an early study, Elliot, Powers, and Funderburg (1988) surveyed teachers of deaf students and asked them what differentiated deaf children with learning disabilities from those without. In order of decreasing frequency, teachers cited memory problems, visual perception problems, attention problems, inconsistent performance, poor organizational skills, achievement/potential discrepancy, atypical language for hearing-impaired individuals, behavior problems, unusual learning styles, and a vague "other" category. Although many of these are not easily defined or operationalized, it is clear that the teachers had ideas about what constitutes a learning disability, even if a specific label or disorder was not articulated.

Recently, Soukup and Feinstein (2007) surveyed teachers of the deaf, 65% of whom reported that they used visual perception problems as a criterion to identify a learning disability, and 60% considered behavior problems indicative of learning disabilities. Only 46% cited an achievement/potential discrepancy as a criterion that they would employ.

Finally, before moving on from the issue of defining learning disabilities in deaf children, it is worth considering the philosophical context that informs such definitions. Learning disabilities only exist in those subjects (i.e., reading, writing, or mathematics) that are given importance by the society in which the individuals function, and as such reflect cultural values. This may be of particular relevance to deaf individuals with strong Deaf cultural identities, whose values may reflect different priorities.

Etiology and Prevalence

Learning disabilities may arise from a variety of factors affecting the neurobiological development of the brain, prenatally, perinatally, and during the child's development, particularly in the early years. They may be genetically determined, result from insult or injury to the brain, or be caused by environmental factors. In very many cases, the cause is unknown. However, certain etiologies of deafness are more frequently associated with learning disabilities, including meningitis, maternal rubella infection, cytomegalovirus infection, and prematurity. The causes of specific types of learning disability in hearing children are gradually becoming better understood, but remain something of an enigma in deaf children, largely as a result of little sound empirical

study in this group. It is important to remember that although learning disabilities may be associated with a number of conditions, not all children with these conditions will evidence a learning disability. Conversely, many deaf children who do have a learning disability will have no history of injury, infection, or genetic predisposition that could account for their difficulties. This does not make those difficulties any less real or significant.

Samar, Parasnis, and Berent (1998) discussed the etiologies of dyslexia, spatial cognition disorders, and memory disorders in deaf individuals along with the areas of the brain thought to be responsible for the observed deficits. Estimates of the prevalence (the total number of cases of a disorder in a population at a given time, or the total number of cases in a population, divided by the number of individuals in the population) of learning disabilities among the general population vary considerably as a function of the definition of learning disabilities, assessment protocols employed, sampling strategies, and diagnostic criteria. These issues become substantially more complex in deaf children, who comprise a group with enormous heterogeneity in terms of etiology of deafness, degree of hearing loss, age at diagnosis and aiding, access to language models, communication modes, cognitive ability, educational experience, and so on. Overall, around 40% of deaf people are considered to have a disability in addition to their deafness, which includes conditions such as deafblindness, global developmental delay, motor disorders, specific learning disabilities, and emotional or behavioral disorders (Gallaudet Research Institute, 2006). The majority of these are associated with syndromic causes of deafness, such as Usher syndrome and CHARGE association, or severe prematurity (see Chapter 12, this volume). In terms of specific learning disabilities, prevalence estimates vary greatly, from a little as 3% to as much as 60%, based on teacher surveys and reports of clinical judgements. The primary source of data comes from the annual Gallaudet Research Institute Survey of Deaf and Hard of Hearing Children and Youth, whose 2006–2007 survey indicated that nationally, 8% of the sample had specific learning disabilities. However, the definitions of specific learning disabilities used and diagnostic criteria employed are not reported. The particular subtypes of learning disabilities that are included in the category are not specified, although "speech or language impairment" is cited as a separate category with its own prevalence of nearly 25%. Also, the sample is likely to be somewhat skewed, as the survey probably does not include a significant number of children who are educated purely in mainstream settings. These children may have milder hearing losses and be the only hard-of-hearing children in their classes, but nonetheless have substantial learning disabilities.

Epidemiological research on specific diagnoses such as dyslexia, dyspraxia, or APD in deaf children or adults is almost nonexistent, with the exception of the Achievements of Deaf Pupils in Scotland project (ADPS, 2006), which provides figures for the period 2000–2004 for dyslexia, dyspraxia, autistic spectrum disorders, attention-deficit hyperactivity disorder, and social, emotional, and behavioral disorders. On the basis of the ADPS data, it is probably safe to assume that specific learning disabilities are at least as common as in the hearing population, where estimates are in the region of 3%–10% (see Edwards & Crocker, 2008).

Research

A decade ago, Samar et al. (1998, p. 200) commented that "theory and research on learning disabilities… in the deaf population have remained a mere backwater, burbling occasionally with statements of quandary and urgency by a few forward-looking commentators but largely bereft of strong conceptual or empirical currents." With a few exceptions, this is still largely true. The same authors made three important points to explain the paucity of research on learning disability in deaf children: (1) the complicated interaction of learning disability and deafness in mutually determining English-language learning and general academic achievement in the deaf population; (2) the ubiquitous and poorly understood role of cultural, cognitive, and linguistic diversity in determining normative learning patterns in the deaf population; and (3) the longstanding ill-preparedness of professionals in deaf education to deal with learning disabilities. These are in addition to the usual research problems of small sample size availability, poorly defined criteria for learning disabilities, and lack of valid evaluation instruments to operationalize the measurement of the relevant cognitive functions.

Dyslexia, Dyspraxia, and Auditory Processing Disorder

Edwards and Crocker (2008) provided working definitions and accounts of current research in the fields of dyslexia, dyspraxia, and APD, and discussed the implications for understanding these disorders in deaf children. There is a dearth of empirical study of these disorders in deaf children, in terms of etiology, diagnosis, and intervention, although the last of these has received some attention (e.g., Enns & Lafond, 2007; Gilbertson & Ferre, 2008). Dyslexia is characterized primarily by difficulties in acquiring reading and writing/spelling skills, and may be associated with more generalized language deficits. It is thought to be the result of a deficit in phonetic processing and has a very strong genetic basis (e.g., Cope et al. 2005; Francks et al. 2004). A child who has limited access to, or a distorted perception of, the sounds that comprise spoken words, is likely to be predisposed to experiencing difficulty developing phonemic awareness and in understanding the relationship between phonemes and graphemes, and therefore developing literacy skills.

Considerable research on the topic indicates that the association between hearing loss and phonological processing is not straightforward. For example, Trezek and Wang (2006) reported that acquisition of early reading skills is unrelated to degree of hearing loss. However, good phonological skills have also been associated with better reading skills in deaf children, as in their hearing peers (Dyer, McSweeney, Szczerbinski, Green, & Campbell, 2003; Perfetti & Sandak, 2000). Adams (1990) asserted that hearing the difference between phonemes is not essential for acquiring phonological knowledge, and this is supported by evidence from studies showing that deaf individuals with good reading skills do use phonological information (Hanson & Fowler 1987) and that phonological skills can be taught to deaf children (e.g., Trezek & Malmgren, 2005, Trezek & Wang, 2006; Trezek, Wang, Woods, Gampp, & Paul, 2007). This is reinforced by the findings of Trezek and Wang (2006) who demonstrated that severely to profoundly deaf 5- to 7-year-olds improved in their word reading, pseudoword decoding, and reading comprehension as a result of a phonics-based reading curriculum supplemented by Visual Phonics. Unfortunately, no control group was used, so that it is not possible to determine the extent to which improvements may have been over and above those of other teaching strategies. In contrast to such research findings, Harris and Moreno (2004), on the basis of findings from tests of short-term recall of pictures, orthographic awareness, and picture spelling, concluded that deaf children place little reliance on phonological coding, at least spontaneously.

The implications of the research findings on deaf children's phonological skills, in terms of understanding dyslexia in deaf children, are not clear. It is likely that deaf children with specific reading disabilities will demonstrate extremely poor phonological awareness at a level that is inconsistent with their access to auditory speech sounds, and when taking into account prior educational experience and teaching strategies for reading. As Samar et al. (1998) argued, lack of optimal auditory input of speech-based language is not sufficient to explain all the cases of deaf individuals who have poor phonological coding skills and therefore poor reading skills, not least because the disorder is known to have a strong genetic basis independent of deafness.

In addition to the typical problems of written letter-reversal, visually discriminating information, and poor short-term memory, the phonological development of individual deaf children should also be assessed in order to support a diagnosis of dyslexia. An empirical analysis of the phonological skills of deaf children identified as having specific reading disability (but not on the basis of their phonological skills to avoid circularity) would be helpful in clarifying the particular patterns of deficits associated with dyslexia in deaf children.

Research on the phonemic skills of deaf children, and insight into how they use knowledge of phonics to develop literacy skills, should inform the strategies used to promote their learning to read. Marlowe, Carney, McCormick, Rankin and Waddy-Smith (in press) emphasized the importance of direct, intensive, and systematic phonics instruction for deaf students to be fluent readers. However, they also argued that for such instruction to produce lasting benefits, students also need a rich language context to encourage fluency in a first language, such as sign language. Thus, deaf students generally, and by extension deaf students with a specific reading disability, would benefit from a "balanced literacy" strategy, combining bottom-up instruction in phonics and top-down instruction in which students derive meaning from rich language experiences, through a bilingual, bimodal approach.

Although there is a paucity of research into dyslexia in deaf children, research on dyspraxia and APD in this group is virtually nonexistent. Dyspraxia has a number of different forms, the two main ones being (1) impairment in the ability to plan, organize, and coordinate body movements, and (2) difficulty coordinating the movements required to produce speech (verbal dyspraxia). A handful of early studies sought to identity a profile of dyspraxic difficulties in deaf children involving fine finger movements, development of rhythm, memory for simultaneously presented visual information, and the movements of the speech musculature (e.g., Aplin, 1991; Van Uden, 1981, 1983). In the studies by Aplin and

Van Uden, a battery of neuropsychological tests was administered to deaf children, resulting in conflicting findings between the authors. Aplin was unable to replicate the results of Van Uden's work, which had supported a dyspraxic syndrome among deaf children. However, the characteristics of the deaf children differed significantly between the studies, particularly in terms of the age range, level of hearing loss, and nonverbal IQ. Thus, a valid and reliable test battery for identifying deaf children with dyspraxia was not established, as had been hoped. Only one subsequent research study has been reported that develops the issue further. Broesterhuizen (1997) extended Van Uden's eupraxia (the ability to quickly recall and skillfully automatize movements, especially of the hands and fingers)/dyspraxia model to younger deaf children aged 3.5–6 years. In that study, a variety of tests of fine motor skills and visual memory were used to predict speech skills, vocabulary, and reading ability, with Broesterhuizen concluding that such skills can explain individual differences in the normal language development of deaf children. No other empirical studies exploring dyspraxia in deaf children have been reported in the published literature. This is remarkable given how common the disorder is in the hearing population (estimates of around 10%; Dyspraxia Foundation, 2008), and the likelihood that it is at least, if not more prevalent among deaf individuals.

Auditory processing disorder is probably the most contentious specific learning disability diagnosis in deaf children. Auditory processing disorder has been defined by the American Speech-Hearing-Language Association (2005) as difficulties in the processing of auditory information in the central nervous system demonstrated by poor performance in one or more of sound localization and lateralization, auditory discrimination, auditory pattern recognition, temporal aspects of audition, auditory performance in competing acoustic signals, and auditory performance with degraded acoustic signals. Higher-order cognitive processes such as phonological processing, memory for auditory information, comprehension of auditory information, and language-related functions, although dependent on intact central auditory function, are not part of the definition of auditory processing in the sense intended here. This said, APD is considered an underlying cause of dyslexia in some cases. Supporting evidence for this comes from studies such as that of Baldeweg, Richardson, Watkins, Foale, and Gruzelier (1998), who showed that dyslexic subjects are impaired in auditory frequency discrimination; and Richardson,

Thomson, Scott, and Goswami (2004), who demonstrated that performance on auditory tasks relating to amplitude processing was associated with phonological awareness in dyslexic children. Sharma, Purdy, Newall, Wheldall, Beaman, & Dillon (2006) found significant associations between a number of measures of APD and reading fluency, accuracy, and nonword reading in children with reading disorders. However, not all children who have APD will be dyslexic, or vice versa.

In deaf children, the relationship between central auditory processing and the manifestation of learning disabilities is clearly going to be complex, both in terms of etiology and assessment. It is now generally accepted that APDs can coexist with peripheral auditory dysfunction (American Speech-Language-Hearing Association, 2005; Bellis, 2002 p. 215; Chermak, 2001). Inadequate or distorted access to sounds is likely to result in suboptimal development of the auditory pathways and centers of the brain, leading to some degree of APD, of some nature. The technical report of the American Speech-Language-Hearing Association (2005) discusses ways in which standard tests for APD may be applied to individuals with a peripheral hearing loss, but as is so common in psychophysiological and neuropsychological assessment of deaf individuals, the report advises caution in interpreting the results.

Memory, Executive Functioning, Problem Solving and Sequencing

Learning disabilities with regard to memory, executive functioning (EF), problem-solving, and sequencing do not constitute well-defined disorders or established diagnoses. Rather, they reflect areas of cognitive functioning in which deaf children have been found to have difficulty relative to their hearing peers. If these difficulties are severe, they will interfere with normal development and learning, and thus should be considered to constitute a specific learning disability. However, as will be seen, difficulties in these areas have strong links with the specific learning disabilities described in the previous section.

The study of memory functions in deaf children and adults has a history spanning almost a century, and findings from research in the last couple of decades only appears to be revealing greater complexities rather than resolving issues. Much research has focused on short-term and working memory, in which deaf children have consistently been found to show deficits in comparison with their hearing peers. However, this is a glaring overgeneralization,

as discussed in detail by Marschark and Mayer (1998). The important issue to consider when thinking about a memory deficit in the sense of a specific learning disability is that a number of factors will have contributed to the observed functioning, including the individual's primary mode of communication (sign or oral) and the nature of the materials to be remembered (verbal or nonverbal, linguistic or nonlinguistic, auditory or visual, simultaneous or sequential), and so on.

Although focusing on the details of how deaf children encode material is of importance in increasing theoretical understanding of memory processes in deaf children, of more pragmatic utility is furthering the understanding of the association between memory abilities, reading skills, and language development. In hearing children, working memory deficits differentiate dyslexic children from those with normal reading skills (e.g., de Jong, 1998; Helland & Asbjørnsen, 2004), and tests of auditory digit span are commonly used as a diagnostic test for dyslexia. Memory abilities of deaf children have similarly been found to be related to both reading and language fluency in deaf children (again see Marschark & Mayer, 1998, for a review). Harris and Moreno (2004) investigated deaf children's short-term memory span based on pictures that could be verbally encoded and found this predicted reading ability. Short-term memory span in the deaf children was comparable with hearing peers of the same reading age, but significantly lower than that of their chronological age peers.

It is not yet clear whether deaf children with a specific reading disability have working memory deficits comparable to their hearing dyslexic peers, or whether they can be assessed in a similar manner. However, Marlowe (1991) provided evidence that supports this contention. He tested four groups of children: deaf children showing atypical academic performance suspected of having learning disabilities, whose achievement scores were 2 years below the average of their deaf peers; deaf children without apparent learning disabilities; hearing, learning-disabled children; and hearing children without learning disabilities. Two nonlinguistic short-term sequential memory tasks were used, on which the learning-disabled deaf children performed significantly more poorly than their deaf peers. Marlowe concluded that a subset of deaf children who have average or better intellectual abilities and poor academic achievement can be accurately identified on the basis of a specific cognitive processing deficit. Also, learning-disabled children, regardless of hearing status, have significantly weaker short-term sequential memory ability than do nondisabled peers. Marlowe argued that in assessing for learning disabilities in deaf children, there is a need for both an ability/achievement discrepancy and an examination of underlying cognitive processes, for example in the areas of memory, attention, and visual-perceptual organization. Thus, overall, it seems that good working memory skills are of fundamental importance in supporting the normal development of reading in children, and may contribute to specific reading disabilities in both hearing and deaf populations.

Executive functions are organizational and self-regulatory cognitive abilities governed primarily by the prefrontal cortex; they encompass abilities such as planning, sequencing, problem solving, inhibition and impulse control, attentional processes, and working memory. The capacity theory of mind (ToM) is the ability to attribute mental states such as beliefs, intents, desires, pretending, and knowledge to oneself and others, and to understand that others have beliefs, desires, and intentions that are different from one's own. It is also sometimes considered a higher executive function. Theory of mind has received considerable attention in relation to deafness, as its development has been found to be significantly delayed in deaf children of hearing parents (see Edwards & Crocker, 2008, for an overview of research on this topic). As ToM could be classed a "metacognitive" function (awareness and use of the knowledge and experiences we have about our own cognitive processes) and not directly comparable with other executive functions, it will not be considered further here.

A number of studies have examined cognitive abilities that come under the executive function umbrella. Marschark (2003) reviewed evidence from research on problem solving and processing of relational versus individual-item information in deaf individuals, noting a number of differences in the information-processing strategies used by this group. More recently, Figueras, Edwards, and Langdon (2008) investigated the executive function of deaf 8- to 12-year-olds in comparison with their hearing peers, and concluded that the apparent deficits shown by the former were the result of their poorer language skills, rather than being an intrinsic consequence of deafness or true executive deficit per se. However, as they point out, regardless of the cause of differences in executive function, some deaf children do exhibit difficulties behaviorally, which has consequences for their learning and academic achievement. Unless these difficulties are more severe than typical of other deaf children though, they should not be considered suggestive of a learning disability.

Craig and Gordon (1991) argued that deaf children are deprived of a major portion of highly sequential and temporal information, which is normally conveyed auditorily, and that this will impact on academic achievement. They reported significant correlations between reading ability and performance on a number of "verbosequential" tasks in their sample of 35 deaf people, but the study did not include a hearing control group. The sample comprised individuals aged between 15 and 45 years, so it is difficult to draw inferences about the relevance for deaf children and learning disabilities. As part of a larger study, Khan, Edwards, and Langdon (2005) compared deaf and hearing children aged 2–6 years and found the former group performed significantly worse on two tests tapping problem solving involving visual sequential information (fluid reasoning)—working out the next items in repeating patterns of symbols, and the next in a sequence, such as increasing size of stimuli. The groups did not differ in their performance on tests of fundamental visualization (matching and picture context). This suggests that deaf children may have a specific difficulty in understanding and processing sequential information, even when it is presented visually (Marschark, 2003). Clinically, an association has been noted by the author between a particularly poor score on the fluid reasoning subtests of a standardized nonverbal test battery, along with a very significant discrepancy between fluid reasoning and fundamental visualization scores, and atypical language development following pediatric cochlear implantation.

Hauser, Lukomski, and Hillman (2008) highlighted the impulsivity characteristic of executive function in deaf children. They noted that the evidence for differences between deaf and hearing children is mixed, depending in part on the measure of impulsivity used, the etiology of deafness, and also on parental communication (i.e., deaf native signing parents versus hearing parents). On balance, it seems likely that apparent problems with impulse control are not the result of deafness per se, but rather a secondary consequence of the same factor that caused the deafness, particularly in deaf children of hearing parents.

At a behavioral level, assessed using the Behaviour Inventory of Executive Function (BRIEF; Gioia, Isquith, Guy, and Kneworthy, 2000), there is again some evidence that deaf children of hearing parents fare worse than deaf children of deaf parents

(Hauser, Lukomski, & Isquith, 2008; Oberg, 2007), although in the latter study none of the ratings were within the clinical range. Thus, overall, EF disorders are most likely to be present in deaf children whose hearing loss is caused by conditions such as meningitis, maternal rubella infection, or severe prematurity, and therefore occur alongside other specific or global cognitive or learning problems.

In the preceding discussion of cognitive processes in deaf children, the close relationship and interdependence of many of the functions can be seen. In particular, memory abilities appear as a recurrent theme, linked to a variety of learning disabilities. However, a number of etiologies of deafness involving trauma to the brain (e.g., meningitis, birth anoxia) may also result in focal brain damage, and it is therefore possible that specific memory deficits or problem-solving difficulties occur independently of other cognitive deficits or learning disorders. They may still have a significant but more general detrimental impact on learning and behavior, rather than resulting in specific reading or language disorders.

Assessment Issues

A number of possible strategies are available for assessing learning disabilities in deaf children, none of which can be considered ideal. All have their limitations, and so long as these are understood and acknowledged, the results of the assessments can be of value. However, great emphasis is typically placed on these assessments in terms of access to appropriate educational services, and therefore the findings need to be as valid and informative as possible. The results of any assessment must not be interpreted in isolation: children function and learn in context— including their family, educational setting, and cultural background. Their performance will also depend on their motivation, cooperation, and other temperamental and behavioral factors. Equally important is the proposal that learning disability assessments for deaf children should be multidisciplinary, involving appropriately qualified and experienced psychologists, speech and language specialists, teachers, audiologists, and physicians (e.g., Edwards & Crocker, 2008; Plapinger & Sikora, 1990; Roth 1991).

Morgan and Vernon (1994) discussed issues to be aware of when testing young deaf children for learning disabilities and provide a recommended battery of test. Although many of the specific tests cited have now been updated, the eight suggested categories of data remain valid: case history (primarily medical information), educational history, two measures of intellectual functioning (nonverbal), a measure of educational achievement, neuropsychological screening, assessment of adaptive behavior and functioning and/or classroom behavior, a current audiological evaluation and vision screening, and information on communication and language skills. In addition to these, information regarding any family history of specific learning disabilities is very informative, given the high rates of inheritance in the hearing population. Edwards and Crocker (2008) discussed the practicalities of assessing a young deaf child and provided suggestions for possible tests for dyslexia, dyspraxia, and APD. Plapinger and Sikora (1990) also provided recommendations for a range of assessment tools that they consider useful with deaf children, combining formal tests and curriculum-based evaluations. The Center for Academic Programs and Student Services provides guidelines for documenting a learning disability in Gallaudet University students, much of which is equally applicable to younger deaf children, particularly in terms of appropriate qualifications of the evaluator, writing the report, and making recommendations. The guidelines state that a comprehensive assessment battery and the resulting report should include a diagnostic interview, assessment of aptitude, academic achievement, information processing, and diagnosis. Areas of relevance to children in the interview include a description of the presenting problems, developmental, medical and psychosocial histories, and family history. The guidelines state that for tests of aptitude and achievement all subtests of assessment tests should be administered and the standard scores reported. Tests of specific areas of information processing should be administered, such as short- and long-term memory, sequential memory, audio and visual perception, processing speed, and motor ability. Nonstandard measures and informal assessment procedures and observations should be included as indicated clinically. The guidelines state that the resulting report should describe how the learning disability impacts on the individual's life and indicate the evidence for how the learning disability limits some "major life activity." The individual's profile of strengths and weaknesses must be shown to be related to functional limitations and thus lead to recommendations for accommodations in the educational environment.

Concordance of findings from different perspectives and professions lends validity and credibility to assessment conclusions. However, validity of conclusions is dependent on the validity and reliability of the individual tests, and the extent to which standard administration procedures need to be adapted to accommodate the child's hearing loss (see Maller, 2003, for a discussion of these issues).

When assessing deaf children for specific learning difficulties, the distinction made by Akamatsu, Mayer, and Hardy-Braz (2008) between language abilities and verbal thinking skills is important. The former comprises the language used for informal communication, whereas the latter is the language employed in less familiar contexts, including academic learning, and the ability to reason and solve problems verbally. The development of verbal thinking skills relies on complex interactions between a variety of more specific cognitive abilities such as fluid reasoning, auditory and visual processing, short-term memory, long-term retrieval, processing speed, and so on. Akamatsu et al. discussed the relationship between cognitive abilities and literacy skills, and argued that it is important to assess verbal thinking skills (or Verbal IQ) in deaf children to enable educators to accurately identify specific weaknesses and to plan effective teaching programs. They provided a useful discussion of the pros and cons of selecting appropriate subtests from large standardized tests in order to gain an accurate, broad picture of the child's cognitive abilities, considering this essential when identifying specific reading disabilities or predicting academic achievements within the deaf population.

Norm-referenced Testing/Achievement–Potential Discrepancy

Learning disabilities have traditionally been identified by comparing children's performance on norm-referenced IQ tests (often a nonverbal or "performance" test or these components of a test battery) with performance on norm-referenced achievement tests. A severe discrepancy between the two suggests that a child is not achieving to her cognitive potential, and therefore a learning disability is inferred. Nonverbal IQ is often used as the comparator since verbal IQ is more confounded by other factors; it does not just reflect innate language ability. Given that most deaf children attain low scores on achievement tests, this approach can be problematic. A number of factors may have contributed to the poor performance, aside from genuine learning disabilities: inadequate or inappropriate instruction or teaching practices, motivational issues, and prior language experience. Even when a deaf child has had access to good language models through sign language, and test materials are translated, this may alter test items, potentially making them more

difficult (see Gilbertson & Ferre, 2008 for a discussion of these issues). However, where the discrepancy is significantly in excess of that expected, taking into account the child's hearing loss and other relevant factors, it is possible that a genuine learning disability exists.

Support for the use of the achievement-discrepancy approach in deaf children comes from research indicating that deaf and hearing children may perform similarly on some standard psychometric tests. For example, Sikora and Plapinger (1994) reported effective detection of learning disabilities in deaf children using standard psychometric measures of IQ, general knowledge, expressive vocabulary, verbal and visual memory, visual-motor integration, and visual-perception skills. They found that deaf children with and without learning disabilities did not differ significantly in areas such as mathematics computational skills and experiential subjects such as science, but learning-disabled deaf children had substantially more difficulty in language-based areas such as reading, applied mathematics, social studies, and humanities.

A major drawback of this strategy is the need to use norms derived from hearing children for the majority of tests, as very few tests have been validated for use with deaf children or provide any data on their use in deaf children. The few exceptions to this include the TONI-2 (Mackinson, Leigh, Blennerhessett, & Anthony, 1997), Kaufman Assessment Battery for Children (Kaufman & Kaufman, 1983), Snidjers-Oomen Nonverbal Intelligence Test (Snijders, Tellegen, & Laros, 1989), NEPSY II (Korkman, Kirk, & Kemp, 2007), WIAT II (Wechsler, 2005), and Leiter-R (Roid & Miller, 1997). Unfortunately, most of these tests present data from very limited, heterogeneous samples of deaf children. Indeed, Maller (2003) argued that even deaf norms may not be representative or valid as the deaf population is so heterogeneous, and test items may have different meanings for deaf examinees. Also, using tests without deaf norms is contrary to the IDEA (1997), which states that any tests "must have been validated for the specific purpose for which they are used" (see Chapter 3, this volume). However, if followed to the letter, this is likely to lead to genuine specific learning disabilities of many deaf children remaining unidentified and therefore unremediated. In contrast with Maller's view, Plapinger and Sikora (1995) argued that tests of cognitive function and academic achievement using hearing norms can be used with confidence in deaf children with mild to moderate hearing loss. This is an issue that has yet to be adequately resolved, particularly in children with a severe or profound hearing loss.

Protocol-based Assessments Versus Individually Tailored Test Batteries

One strategy for identifying learning disabilities in deaf children is to use protocols comprising specific tests for specific suspected disabilities. For example, a protocol for assessing specific reading disability may include a test of general IQ, achievement tests of reading vocabulary and comprehension, a measure of working memory skills, and tests of phonemic awareness and processing such as rhyming, phoneme blending, and phoneme and syllable deletion. A test of pseudoword (nonsense word) decoding may also be included. An advantage of this approach is that if the same protocol is used consistently over a period of time, an invaluable database can be generated, thus increasing understanding of cognitive skills and information processing in deaf children. In the long term, the validity of the identification process will be improved. The disadvantage lies in the risk of looking for the "wrong" type of specific learning disability for that individual, finding no evidence to support the diagnosis, and thereby failing to identify a true disability of another sort. This is even more likely to happen if a referral has been made by a teacher or other professional asking for assessment for a particular learning disability, potentially undermining an open-minded, explorative approach.

The converse to this approach is to use an individualized battery of tests, based on a description of the difficulties the deaf child is experiencing in the classroom and at home. Such an assessment may look very similar to a protocol-based one and will include many of the same tests, particularly in terms of establishing the child's learning potential and academic achievements. Where it may differ is in the tailoring of the combination of tests or subtests chosen to assess a specific cognitive function, such as auditory memory or sequencing skills. Here it is important not to keep on testing until a deficit is found (if you look hard enough, it is almost inevitable that a child will perform poorly on some tests relative to others). To validate findings, it is essential that a number of tests assessing different aspects of the same cognitive function are used, and that a deficit is found on more than one related measure.

Response to Intervention

Given that the IQ–achievement discrepancy model described earlier has been severely criticized as a diagnostic approach in children (see Fuchs, Mock,

Morgan, & Young, 2003 for a discussion), there has been a need to provide a valid alternative for both researchers and practitioners. In the United States, this has recently taken the form of a Response to Intervention (RTI) process that involves monitoring a series of teaching interventions of increasing intensity to an individual child, until an effective intervention is identified. The number of tiers of intervention is typically three or four. The RTI assessment is used as an eligibility criterion for specific learning disability on the basis that a child who has a disability responds to a more intensive intervention than would a child who does not have a disability. Although it is still early, there is some evidence to support the use of this approach to identifying learning disabilities in hearing children (e.g., Marston, 2005; Vellutino, Scanlon, Small, & Fanule, 2006). Its supporters argue that it provides help more quickly to a greater number of students, it separates students with genuine learning disabilities from those who have had inadequate prior instruction, and does not exclude children with a learning disability on the basis of a low IQ.

Recently, the RTI model has been applied to deaf and hard-of-hearing children by Gilbertson and Ferre (2008), who suggested that it may be useful as it allows continuing evaluation of the effectiveness of the current curriculum and instruction for a particular child. Also, if all deaf students are monitored in this way, a profile of expected performance within the local circumstances can be developed that can inform judgments about an individual child's progress. Gilbertson and Ferre provided a detailed case example of how the model can be applied to a deaf child with positive results.

Although the RTI approach appears promising and has intuitive appeal, it has yet to been proven in terms of its reliability and validity, especially in deaf children. At present, it appears to have a number of drawbacks. First, there is no agreed-upon protocol for the implementation of the model, so that different numbers of tiers are used and interventions are delivered by a variety of professionals with varying levels of expertise. Second, it is also not always clear whether the criterion for diagnosing a learning disability is the RTI process itself, or the process as a precursor to more traditional evaluation. Third, the focus of the RTI approach has been on identifying and helping children with reading disabilities, which is an unfortunately narrow focus, given the high incidence of a broad range of learning disabilities in deaf children. In particular, for deaf children, there is a danger that this approach will either fail to identify, or take an unreasonably long time to identify, the nature of some subtle, very specific cognitive deficits that are undermining progress at school.

Future Research Directions

The possibilities are extensive for conducting research that will greatly inform the field of learning disabilities in deaf children. A range of issues needs to be addressed, from academic understanding of the causes of those disabilities, to developing reliable and valid assessment procedures, and devising and evaluating interventions. Greater emphasis could usefully be placed on processing disorders other than reading disorders, although this remains an area where there is considerable work to do. Perhaps one of the most pressing needs is to develop appropriate norms for deaf children for a broad range of tests, particularly those assessing specific cognitive functions and abilities, such as phonological awareness, sequential reasoning, auditory and visual memory, and visual–motor integration. This applies equally to tests of academic achievement and questionnaire measures of behavioral functioning. This is a daunting task if it is to be done adequately and include sufficient numbers of deaf children. A balance needs to be struck between choosing the most homogeneous group of deaf children possible (e.g., in terms of level of hearing loss, communication mode, schooling) in order to maximize interpretability, and including a more heterogenous group to improve the generalizability of the results.

Improved understanding of the etiologies of learning disabilities and their identification in deaf children may be achieved with the aid of neurophysiological procedures such as functional magnetic resonance imaging (fMRI) and mismatch negativity (MMN). Functional MRI has the potential to shed light on differences in neural organization between deaf children with and without learning disabilities and their hearing counterparts, thereby supporting diagnosis in the former group. Equally, MMN (an automatic brain response to changes in the frequency, duration, or intensity of a sound, or when one phoneme is replaced by another) allows the possibility of identifying children with an APD when a mild or moderate hearing loss is present.

If high-quality information on how deaf children perform on neuropsychological and achievement tests were to become available, it could be used to improve our understanding of the relationship between learning disabilities in deaf children and their hearing peers. Differences in etiology, presentation, and comorbidity may become apparent that could have implications for the definitions of the various learning disabilities. In the case of dyslexia, which is known to have a strong genetic basis in the hearing population, it would be informative to know whether the proportion of cases that could be accounted for genetically is similar in deaf children.

Although there is a growing literature on phonetic awareness and phonological processing in deaf children, the relevance of these to specific reading disabilities in deaf children should form the focus of future empirical study. Here, a developmental perspective is essential to determine normal patterns of the acquisition of phonological skills in deaf children, and then identify atypical ones. Early identification of deaf children at risk of reading disabilities is paramount, and it is likely that phonological skills will play an important role in this process. More generally, there is a need to develop valid and reliable assessment protocols for all types of learning disabilities. Whether these best take the form of psychometric assessment using the achievement–potential discrepancy model, or an RTI approach, or a combination of the two, needs to be empirically determined.

Moving on from epidemiological and assessment issues, perhaps the most important research area is that of remediation strategies and interventions. Despite the acknowledged need for research in this area, there remains little evidence-based guidance on what works for different disabilities and processing disorders.

Finally, no discussion of research in deaf children can close without reference to the burgeoning field of cochlear implant research. To date, much research in this area has focused on demonstrating the impact of implantation on the development of speech, language, and communication in deaf children. A more limited literature has addressed issues of cognitive ability and specific cognitive processes in implanted children (see Chapter 29, this volume). This could usefully be extended to explore cognitive predictors of unexpectedly poor progress in developing speech and language skills or academic attainments in implanted children, as well as improving the identification of information-processing deficits that may be hampering such progress.

Summary and Conclusions

There now seems little dispute that learning disabilities exist in deaf children, independent of the consequences of hearing loss for the development of language and other cognitive functions. A woefully small amount of research has focused on this area in the last decade, despite repeated calls for it from a variety of quarters, particularly when compared with the extensive literature that has emerged on cochlear implants. A few promising avenues are gradually being explored, for example in understanding phonological processing skills and the neurophysiological correlates of auditory processing difficulties.

Accurately identifying those children affected by a learning disability remains one of the most pressing and pertinent challenges facing both researchers and practitioners. The range of psychometric tests available for assessing neuropsychological functioning and achievement in hearing children has steadily increased in recent years, and many of these could be very informative if used appropriately in the assessment of deaf children's functioning. Although the debates over the correct approach to identifying learning disabilities rage on, there is a danger of "throwing out the baby with the bath water." Although the achievement–potential discrepancy model undoubtedly has its problems, it remains useful as a first indicator that a child is experiencing difficulties. It is also informative when there is evidence that a child is performing significantly more poorly on specific cognitive tests in comparison with their deaf peers. This said, the RTI approach is emerging as a promising strategy in deaf children, and merits further, systematic investigation.

References

Adams, M. (1990). *Beginning to read: Thinking and learning about print.* Cambridge, MA.: MIT Press.

ADPS. (2006). Retrieved November 23, 2009 from www. Education.ed.ac.uk/adps/survey/00-04

Akamatsu, C. T., Mayer, C. & Hardy-Braz, S. (2008). Why considerations of verbal aptitude are important in educating deaf and hard-of-hearing students. In: M. Marschark & P. C. Hauser (Eds.), *Deaf cognition: Foundations and outcomes* (pp. 131–169). New York: Oxford University Press.

American Speech-Language-Hearing Association. (2005). (Central) auditory processing disorders. Available at http://www.asha.org/members/deskref-journals/deskref/defauly

Aplin, D. Y. (1991). Identification of additional learning difficulties in hearing-impaired children. In D. S. Martin (Ed.), *Advances in cognition, education and deafness* (pp. 39–48). Washington, DC: Gallaudet University Press.

Baldeweg, T., Richardson, A., Watkins, S., Foale, C., & Gruzelier, J. (1999). Impaired auditory frequency discrimination in dyslexia detected with mismatch evoked potentials. *Annals of Neurology, 45,* 495–503.

Bellis, T. J. (2002). *When the brain can't hear: Unraveling the mystery of auditory processing disorder.* New York: Pocket Books.

Broesterhuizen, M. L. H. M. (1997). Psychological assessment of deaf children. *Scandinavian Audiology, 26,* Supplement 46, 43–49.

Chermak, G. (2001). Auditory processing disorder: An overview for the clinician. *The Hearing Journal, 54,* 10–25.

Cope, N., Harold, D., Hill, G., Moskvina, V., Stevenson, J., Holmans, P., et al. (2005). Strong evidence that KIAA0319 on chromosome 6p is a susceptibility gene for developmental dyslexia. *American Journal of Human Genetics, 76,* 581–91.

Craig, H. B., & Gordon, H. W. (1991). In D. S. Martin (Ed.) *Advances in cognition, education and deafness* (pp. 231–236). Washington, DC: Gallaudet University Press.

de Jong, P. F. (1998). Working memory deficits of reading disabled children. *Journal of Experimental Child Psychology, 70,* 75–96.

Dyer, A., McSweeney, M., Szczerbinski, M., Green, L., & Campbell, R. (2003). Predictors of reading delay in deaf adolescents: The relative contributions of rapid automatized naming speed and phonological awareness and decoding. *Journal of Deaf Studies and Deaf Education, 8,* 215–29.

Dyspraxia Foundation. (2008). Retrieved September 23, 2008 from www. Dyspraxiafoundation. org. uk

Edwards, L. C., & Crocker, S. (2008). Specific learning difficulties. In *Psychological processes in deaf children with complex needs: An evidence-based practical guide* (pp. 85–105). London: Jessica Kingsley Publishers.

Elliot, R. Jr., Powers, A., & Funderburg, R. (1988). Learning-disabled hearing-impaired students: Teacher survey. *The Volta Review, 90,* 277–286.

Enns, C., & Lafond, L. D. (2007). Reading against all odds: A pilot study of two deaf students with dyslexia. *American Annals of the Deaf, 152,* 63–72.

Figueras, B., Edwards, L., & Langdon, D. (2008). Executive function and language in deaf children. *Journal of Deaf Studies and Deaf Education, 13,* 362–377.

Francks, C., Paracchini, S., Smith, S. D., Richardson, A. J., Scerri, T. S., Cardon, L. R., et al. (2004). A 77-kilobase region of chromosome 6p22. 2 is associated with dyslexia in families from the United Kingdom and the United States. *American Journal of Human Genetics, 75,* 1046–1058.

Fuchs, D., Mock, D., Morgan, P. L., & Young, C. L. (2003). Responsiveness-to-treatment: Definitions, evidence, and implications for the learning disabilities construct. *Learning Disabilities Research and Practice, 18,* 157–171.

Gallaudet Research Institute. (2006). *Regional and national summary report of data from the 2006-2007 annual survey of deaf and hard of hearing children and youth.* Washington, DC: GRI. Gallaudet University.

Gilbertson, D., & Ferre, S. (2008). Considerations in the identification, assessment, and intervention process for deaf and hard of hearing students with reading difficulties. *Psychology in the Schools, 45,* 104–120.

Gioia, G. A., Isquith, P. K., Guy, S. C., & Kenworthy, L. (2000). *Behavior Rating Inventory of Executive Function.* Oxford: Pearson Assessment.

Hanson, V. L., & Fowler, C. A. (1987). Phonological coding in word reading: Evidence from hearing and deaf readers. *Memory and Cognition, 15,* 199–207.

Harris, M., & Moreno, C. (2004). Deaf children's use of phonological coding: Evidence from reading, spelling, and working memory. *Journal of Deaf Studies and Deaf Education, 9,* 253–268.

Hauser, P. C., Lukomski, J., & Hillman, T. (2008). Development of deaf and hard-of-hearing students' executive function. In M. Marschark & P. C. Hauser (Eds.), *Deaf cognition: Foundations and outcomes* (pp. 286–308). New York: Oxford University Press.

Helland, T., & Asbjørnsen, A. (2004). Digit span in dyslexia: Variations according to language comprehension and mathematics skills. *Journal of Clinical and Experimental Neuropsychology, 26*, 31–42.

Individuals with Disabilities Education Act Amendments of 2004, Pub. L. 108–446, 20 U. S. C. § 1401 *et. seq.*

Individuals with Disabilities Education Act of 1997, Pub. L. No. 105–17, § 1400 *et. seq.*

Kaufman, A. S., & Kaufman, N. L. (1983). *Kaufman Assessment Battery for Children.* Bloomington, MN: Pearson Assessments.

Khan, S., Edwards, L., & Langdon, D. (2005). The cognition and behaviour of children with cochlear implants, children with hearing aids, and their hearing peers: A comparison. *Audiology and Neurootology, 10*, 117–126.

Korkman, M., Kirk, U., & Kemp, S. (2007). *NEPSY II.* Oxford: Pearson Education Ltd.

Laughton, J. (1989). The learning disabled, hearing impaired student: Reality, myth, or overextension? *Topics in Language Disorders, 9*, 70–79.

Lyon, G. R. (1996). Learning disabilities. *The Future of children, 6*, 54–76.

Mackinson, J. A., Leigh, I. W., Blennerhassett, L., & Anthony, S. (1997). Validity of the TONI-2 with deaf and hard of hearing children. *American Annals of the Deaf, 142*, 294-299.

Maller, S. J. (2003). Intellectual assessment of deaf people: A critical review. In M. Marschark & P. Spencer (Eds.), *Oxford handbook of deaf studies, language, and education* (pp. 451–463). Oxford: Oxford University Press.

Marlowe, B. (1991). *Identifying learning disabilities in the deaf population.* Unpublished doctoral dissertation, Catholic University, Washington, DC.

Marlowe, B., Carney, M., McCormack, R., Rankin, E., & Waddy-Smith, B. (in press). Bringing research to the classroom: Promising practices in deaf reading education. *The California Reader.*

Marschark, M. (2003). Cognitive functioning in deaf adults and children. In M. Marschark & P. Spencer (Eds.), *Oxford handbook of deaf studies, language, and education* (pp. 464–477). Oxford: Oxford University Press.

Marschark, M., Lang, H. G., & Albertini, J. A. (2002). *Educating deaf students: From research to practice.* New York: Oxford University Press.

Marschark, M., & Mayer, T. S. (1998). Mental representation and memory in deaf adults and children. In M. Marschark & M. D. Clark (Eds.), *Psychological perspectives on deafness*, Vol. 2 (pp. 53–77). Mahwah, NJ: Lawrence Erlbaum Associates.

Marston, D. (2005). Tiers of intervention in responsiveness to intervention: Prevention outcomes and learning disabilities identification patterns. *Journal of Learning Disabilities, 38*, 539–544.

Mayberry, R. I. (2002). Cognitive development in deaf children: The interface of language and perception in neuropsychology. In S. J. Segalowitz & I. Rapin (Eds.), *Handbook of neuropsychology*, 2nd edition, Vol. 8, Part II (pp. 71–107). New York: Elsevier.

McLoughlin, J. A., & Netick, A. (1983). Defining learning disabilities: A new and cooperative direction. *Journal of Learning Disabilities, 16*, 21–23.

Morgan, A., & Vernon, M. (1994). A guide to the diagnosis of learning disabilities in deaf and hard-of-hearing children and adults. *American Annals of the Deaf, 139*, 358–370.

Oberg, J. (2007). *Assessing executive functioning in children with a hearing loss.* Unpublished masters thesis. Rochester Institute of Technology, Rochester, NY.

Perfetti, C. A., & Sandak, R. (2000). Reading optimally builds on spoken language: Implications for deaf readers. *Journal of Deaf Studies and Deaf Education, 5*, 32–50.

Plapinger, D. S., & Sikora, D. M. (1990). Diagnosing a learning disability in a hearing-impaired child. *American Annals of the Deaf, 135*, 285–292.

Plapinger, D. S., & Sikora, D. M. (1995). The use of standardized test batteries in assessing the skill development of children with mild-to-moderate sensorineural hearing loss. *Language, Speech, and Hearing Services in Schools, 26*, 39–44.

Richardson, U., Thomson, J. M., Scott, S. K., & Goswami, U. (2004). Auditory processing skills and phonological representation in dyslexic children. *Dyslexia, 10*, 215–233.

Roid, G. H., & Miller, L. J. (1997). *Examiners manual, Leiter International Performance Scale-Revised.* Dale, IL: Stoelting Company.

Roth, V. (1991). Students with learning disabilities and hearing impairment: Issues for the secondary and postsecondary teacher. *Topics in Language Disorders, 9*, 70–79.

Samar, V. J. (1999). Identifying learning disabilities in the deaf population: The leap from Gibraltar. *NTID Research Bulletin, 4*, 1–4.

Samar, V. J. Parasnis, I., & Berent, G. P. (1998). Learning disabilities, attention deficit disorders and deafness. In M. Marschark & M. D. Clark (Eds.), *Psychological perspectives on deafness*, Vol. 2 (pp. 199–242). Mahwah, NJ: Lawrence Erlbaum Associates.

Sharma, M., Purdy, S. C., Newall, P., Wheldall, K., Beaman, R., & Dillon, H. (2006). Electrophysiological and behavioural evidence of auditory processing deficits in children with reading disorder. *Clinical Neurophysiology, 117*, 1130–1144.

Sikora, D., & Plapinger, D. (1994). Using standard psychometric tests to identify learning disabilities in students with sensorineural hearing impairments. *Journal of Learning Disabilities, 27*, 352–359.

Soukup, M., & Feinstein, S. (2007). Identification, assessment, and intervention strategies for deaf and hard of hearing students with learning disabilities. *American Annals of the Deaf, 152*, 56–62.

Snijders, J. T., Tellegen, P. J., & Laros, J. A. (1989). *Snijders-Oomen Non-Verbal Intelligence Test: SON-R 5½-17. Manual and Research Report.* Groningen, Netherlands: Wolters-Noordhoff.

Trezek, B. J., & Malmgren, K. W. (2005). The efficacy of utilizing a phonics treatment package with middle school deaf and hard-of-hearing students. *Journal of Deaf Studies and Deaf Education, 10*, 256–271.

Trezek, B. J., & Wang, Y. (2006). Implications of utilizing a phonics-based reading curriculum with children who are deaf or hard of hearing. *Journal of Deaf Studies and Deaf Education, 11*, 202–213.

Trezek, B. J., Wang, Y., Woods, D. G., Gampp, T. L., & Paul, P. V. (2007). Using visual phonics to supplement beginning reading instruction for students who are deaf or hard of hearing. *Journal of Deaf Studies and Deaf Education, 12*, 373–384.

Van Uden, A. M. J. (1981). Early diagnosis of those multiple handicaps in prelingually profoundly deaf children which endanger an education according to the purely oral way. *Journal of the British Association of Teachers of the Deaf, 5*, 112–127.

Van Uden, A. M. J. (1983). *Diagnostic testing of deaf children: The syndrome of dyspraxia.* Lisse, The Netherlands: Swets and Zeitlinger.

Vellutino, F., Scanlon, D., Small, S., & Fanule, D. (2006). Response to intervention as a vehicle for distinguishing between children with and without reading disabilities: Evidence for the role of kindergarten and first-grade interventions. *Journal of Learning Disabilities, 39*, 157–169.

Vernon, M. (1968/2005). Fifty years of research on the intelligence of deaf and hard-of-hearing children: A review of literature and discussion of implications. Reprinted in *Journal of Deaf Studies and Deaf Education, 10*, 225–231.

Wechsler, D. (2005). *Wechsler Individual Achievement Test*, 2nd UK edition. Oxford: Pearson Education Ltd.

Executive Function, Cognitive Control, and Sequence Learning in Deaf Children with Cochlear Implants

David B. Pisoni, Christopher M. Conway, William Kronenberger, Shirley Henning, *and* Esperanza Anaya

Abstract

Clinical research on deaf children with cochlear implants has been intellectually isolated from the mainstream of current research and theory in neuroscience, cognitive psychology, and developmental neuropsychology. As a consequence, the major clinical research problems have been narrowly focused on studies of speech and language outcomes and the efficacy of cochlear implantation as a medical treatment for profound hearing loss. As noted in both of the National Institutes of Health (NIH) consensus statements on cochlear implants in 1988 and 1995 (NIDCD, 1988, 1995), little, if any, research has investigated the underlying psychological and neurocognitive factors that are responsible for the enormous individual differences and variability in the effectiveness of cochlear implants. In this chapter, we report some new research findings on executive function, sequence memory, and cognitive control in prelingually deaf children who have received cochlear implants. Our results demonstrate that several domain-general neurocognitive processes related to executive function and cognitive control processes, such as working memory capacity, fluency-speed, inhibition, and organization-integration sequencing skills, are strongly associated with traditional clinical speech and language outcome measures. These specific neurocognitive processes reflect the global coordination, integration, and functional connectivity of multiple underlying brain systems used in speech perception, production, and spoken language processing. We argue that these executive function and organization-integration processes contribute an additional unique source of variance to speech and language outcomes above and beyond the conventional demographic, medical, and educational factors. Understanding the neurocognitive processes responsible for variability in spoken language processing will help both clinicians and researchers explain and predict individual differences in speech and language outcomes following cochlear implantation. Moreover, our results also have direct application to improving the diagnosis, treatment, and early identification of young deaf children who may be at high risk for poor outcomes following cochlear implantation.

Keywords: cochlear implant, executive function, deaf, children, memory, speech perception, language

Our long-term goal is to understand and predict the enormous variability in speech and language outcomes in deaf children who have received cochlear implants as a treatment for profound deafness. As noted in both of the National Institute on Deafness and Other Communication Disorders (NIDCD) consensus statements on cochlear implants in 1988 and 1995, individual differences and variability in speech and language outcomes are significant clinical problems that have not been addressed adequately in the past. Little, if any, progress has been made in understanding the neurobiological mechanisms and neurocognitive processes that are responsible for the variability observed in speech and language outcomes following cochlear implantation.

Most of the past work on cochlear implants has been concerned primarily with documenting the "efficacy" of cochlear implantation as a medical treatment for profound deafness, focusing research efforts on demographic, medical, and educational variables as predictors of outcome and benefit. With the average age of implantation steadily decreasing because of the widespread use of universal newborn hearing screening, the ability to reliably predict the "effectiveness" of cochlear implants from behavioral measures obtained from infants and young children prior to implantation becomes critical to providing appropriate habilitation following implantation. Understanding sources of variability in speech and language outcomes after cochlear implantation is a complex and challenging problem requiring multidisciplinary research efforts from scientists with backgrounds in neuroscience, cognitive psychology, and developmental neuropsychology.

A Neurocognitive Approach to Individual Differences in Outcomes

To understand, explain, and predict variability in outcome and benefit, it is necessary to situate the problem of individual differences in a much broader theoretical framework that extends well beyond the narrow clinical fields of audiology and speech pathology and fully acknowledges variability in brain–behavior relations as a natural consequence of biological development of all living systems (Sporns, 1998). Development involves interactions over time between the biological state of the individual (genetics, biological structures, and characteristics) and specific environmental experiences (sensory input, external events that influence development such as toxic exposures). There is an increasing recognition that outcomes are not exclusively genetically or environmentally predetermined. Environmental experience allows complex biological systems to self-organize during the process of development (Thelen & Smith, 1994). Alteration in early auditory experience by electrical stimulation through a cochlear implant supports a process of neurobiological reorganization that draws on and influences multiple interacting neurocognitive processes and domains and is not isolated to only speech-language functioning.

The enormous variability observed in a wide range of speech and language outcome measures following cochlear implantation may not be unique to this particular clinical population at all but may reflect instead more general underlying sources of variability observed in speech and language in healthy typically developing normal-hearing children as well as adults (Cicchetti & Curtis, 2006). Moreover, because of the important contributions of learning and memory to the development of spoken language processing, it is very likely that the sources of the individual differences observed in speech and language outcomes in deaf children with cochlear implants also reflect variation in the development of domain-general neurocognitive processes, processes that are involved in linking and coordinating multiple brain systems together to form a functionally integrated information processing system (Ullman & Pierpont, 2005).

To investigate the sources of variability in performance and understand the neural and cognitive processes that underlie variation in outcome and benefits following implantation, it is necessary to substantially broaden the battery of outcome measures to assess a wider range of behaviors and information processing skills beyond simply the traditional clinical audiological speech and language assessment measures that have been routinely used in the past by researchers working on cochlear implants. Furthermore, it is also important to recognize that a child's failure to obtain optimal benefits and achieve age-appropriate speech and language milestones from his or her cochlear implant may not be due directly to the functioning of the cochlear implant itself but may reflect complex interactions among a number of contributing factors (Geers, Brenner, & Davidson, 2003).

In our research program, we adopt the general working assumption that many profoundly deaf children who receive cochlear implants, especially children who are performing poorly, may have other contributing neural, cognitive, and affective sequelae resulting from a period of deafness and auditory deprivation combined with a language delay before implantation. The enormous variability observed in speech and language outcomes may not be due to hearing per se or to processes involved in the early sensory encoding of speech at the auditory periphery (Hawker, Ramirez-Inscoe, Bishop, Twomey, O'Donoghue, & Moore, 2008). Evidence is now rapidly accumulating to suggest that other central cortical and subcortical neurobiological and neurocognitive processes contribute additional unique sources of variability to outcome and benefit that are not assessed by the traditional battery of speech and language measures.

Brain–Behavior Relations

Our approach to the problems of variability in outcome and benefit following cochlear implantation is motivated by several recent findings and new theoretical developments that suggest that deafness and hearing impairment in children cannot be viewed in isolation as a simple sensory impairment (see also Conrad, 1979; Luria, 1973; Myklebust, 1954, 1964; Myklebust & Brutten, 1953). The enormous variability in outcome and benefit reflects numerous complex neural and cognitive processes that depend heavily on functional connectivity of multiple brain areas working together as a complex integrated system (Luria, 1973). As Nauta (1964) pointed out more than 40 years ago, "no part of the brain functions on its own, but only through the other parts of the brain with which it is connected" (p. 125). As described in subsequent sections, we believe this is a promising new direction to pursue in clinical research on individual differences in profoundly deaf children who use cochlear implants.

Domain-general Cognitive Factors

Our recent work with preimplant visual–motor integration (VMI) tests that use only visual patterns and require reproduction and construction processes has found significant correlations with a range of conventional clinical speech and language outcome measures obtained from deaf children following implantation. Similarly, our recent findings on nonword repetition, talker discrimination, and implicit learning of probabilistic sequential patterns presented in the sections to follow suggest that an important additional source of variance in speech and language outcomes in deaf children with cochlear implants is associated with domain-general nonlinguistic executive-organizational-integrative (EOI) processes that involve executive function (EF), cognitive control (CC), and self-regulation (Blair & Razza-Peters, 2007; Figueras, Edwards, & Langdon, 2008; Hauser, Lukomski, & Hillman, 2008).

There is now good agreement among cognitive scientists that these so-called "control processes" rely critically on global systemwide executive attention processes that reflect organization-integration, coordination, functional connectivity, and close interactions of multiple neural circuits and subsystems that are widely distributed across many areas of the brain (Sporns, 2003). Although these EOI processes overlap partially with elements of the traditional construct of global intelligence, these two broad domains of cognitive functioning can be distinguished in several ways.

First, global intelligence includes functions and abilities, such as crystallized knowledge, reasoning, long-term memory, and concept formation, that are not generally thought to be a part of EOI processes (Kaufman & Lichtenberger, 2006; Lezak, Howieson,

Loring, & Hannay, 2004). Second, EOI processes are minimally dependent on the specific content of the information being processed; that is, they can be applied to almost any kind of neural or cognitive representation such as verbal, nonverbal, visual–spatial, sensory–motor (Hughes & Graham, 2002; Van der Sluis, deJong, & van derLeij, 2007). Global intelligence includes a component of content in the form of explicit declarative knowledge, accumulated experience, and acquired algorithms for problem solving. Third, recent neuroimaging studies have found differences in EOI processing ability and its relationship to brain function, even in groups of subjects that are matched on measures of global intellectual ability (e.g., Mathews, Kronenberger, Wang, Lurito, Lowe, & Dunn, 2005).

Executive-Organizational-Integrative Abilities in Cochlear Implant Outcomes

We hypothesize that EOI abilities are particularly important for speech-language development following cochlear implant because of strong reciprocal relations between the development of spoken language processing skills and the development of EOI abilities (Deary, Strand, Smith, & Fernandes, 2007; Hohm, Jennen-Steinmetz, Schmidt, & Laucht, 2007). Spoken language and verbal mediation processes provide the schemas and knowledge structures for symbolic representations that can be used for comprehension-integration (e.g., mental representation using language) and cognitive control, both of which are important EOI abilities (Bodrova & Leong, 2007; Diamond, Barnett, Thomas, & Munro, 2007; Lamm, Zelazo, & Lewis, 2006).

Additionally, early auditory experience promotes the ability to integrate temporal sequences into wholes (e.g., chunking auditory patterns into meaningful sounds and linguistic units) and to engage in fluent processing of temporal patterns. Executive-organizational-integrative processing also allows for the active control of selective attention, use of working memory, fluent speeded processing, and integration of multiple sources of information during spoken language processing. More efficient EOI processing therefore promotes better spoken language skills, whereas better language provides the key building blocks for the development of EOI abilities through verbal mediation and feedback processes (Bodrova & Leong, 2007). Because hearing loss, even mild hearing loss, interferes with critical early spoken-language experiences, we suggest that development of key EOI skills may be at risk in deaf children. A cochlear implant restores some of the components of auditory experience to a "fragile" EOI system, which in turn, becomes a fundamental influence on the ability to use spoken language to build speech and language processing skills that are key outcomes following cochlear implant.

Preliminary findings from our research, taken together with the theoretical approach articulated earlier, suggest that four key EOI areas may be involved in speech-language outcome following cochlear implant: working memory, fluency-efficiency-speed, concentration-vigilance-inhibition, and organization-integration. These abilities allow spoken language to be processed rapidly (fluency-efficiency-speed) into meaningful symbolic units (organization-integration), stored (working memory), and actively assigned meaning (organization-integration) while the individual maintains a focus on the relevant stimulus information (concentration-vigilance) and resists distracting impulses (inhibition). The need to process enormous amounts of novel auditory sensory input in the development of speech-language skills following cochlear implant therefore draws heavily on these domain-general EOI areas. A child's ability to effectively integrate, coordinate, and utilize these EOI abilities will impact on speech-language outcomes.

The hypothesis motivating our research program is that many deaf children who use cochlear implants may display delays or dysfunctions in several neurocognitive information processing domains in addition to their primary hearing loss and language delay. Some deaf children with cochlear implants may not show "age-appropriate" scores on a variety of conventional neuropsychological tests that, on the surface, appear to have little, if anything, directly to do with domain-specific sensory aspects of hearing or speech perception and spoken language processing, but reflect instead domain-general processes. Variability in these basic elementary information processing skills may ultimately be responsible for some of the individual differences observed in audiological, speech, and language outcome measures.

Nonword Repetition and Phonological Decomposition

To obtain additional knowledge about the underlying cognitive and linguistic processes that are responsible for the variation in speech and language outcomes following implantation and to broaden the information processing domains used in assessment, we carried out an unconventional nonword repetition study with a large group of deaf children to examine how they use sublexical phonological knowledge (Cleary, Dillon, & Pisoni, 2002; Dillon, Burkholder,

Cleary, & Pisoni, 2004). When we first proposed using this novel experimental procedure, the cochlear implant clinicians in our center argued that deaf children would not be able to do a task like this, because they did not know any of the nonwords and they could only do immediate repetition and reproduction tasks with words that they were familiar with and had in their mental lexicons. We explained that nonword repetition has been shown in numerous studies to be a valuable experimental methodology and research tool that could provide new fundamentally different information that was not available from any of the other standard clinical assessment instruments currently in use. Moreover, several studies have reported that nonword repetition scores were strongly correlated with vocabulary development and other language learning milestones in hearing children and other clinical populations (Gathercole & Baddeley, 1990; Gathercole, Hitch, Service, & Martin, 1997).

In our first nonword repetition study (Cleary, Dillon, & Pisoni, 2002), 88 pediatric cochlear implant users were asked to listen to recorded nonsense words that conformed to English phonology and phonotactics (e.g., "altupatory") and immediately repeat back what they heard over a loudspeaker to the examiner. Several measures of their performance on this task were obtained and then correlated with open-set word recognition scores from the Lexical Neighborhood Test (LNT), Forward Digit Span, Speech Intelligibility, Speaking Rate, Word Attack, and Rhyme Errors. The Word Attack and Rhyme Errors were obtained from an isolated single-word reading task that was collected as part of a larger research project carried out by Ann Geers and her colleagues (see Geers & Brenner, 2003).

As shown in Table 29.1, the transcription scores for both consonants and vowels, as well as the perceptual ratings of the nonwords obtained from a group of normal-hearing adults were all strongly correlated with the traditional clinical outcome measures we examined, suggesting that a common set of phonological representations and processing skills are used across a wide range of different language processing tasks, even single-word reading tasks.

Although nonword repetition appears at first glance to be a simple information processing task, it is actually a complex psycholinguistic process that requires the child to perform well on each of the individual component processes involving speech perception, phonological encoding and decomposition, verbal rehearsal and maintenance in working memory, retrieval and phonological reassembly,

Table 29.1 Nonword repetition scores

	Consonants (N = 76)	Vowels (N = 76)	Accuracy Ratings (N = 76)
LNT easy words	+.83***	+.78***	+.76***
LNT hard words	+.85***	+.71***	+.70***
MLNT	+.77***	+.74***	+.77***
Forward Digit Span	+.60**	+.62**	+.76***
Speech Intelligibility	+.91***	+.88***	+.87***
Speaking Rate	−.84***	−.81***	−.85***
Word Attack (Reading)	+.75***	+.72***	+.78***
Rhyme Errors (Reading)	−.63**	−.68**	−.54*

*$p<.05$, **$p<.01$, ***$p<.001$

Partial correlations between nonword repetition scores and several speech and language outcome measures (controlling for performance IQ, age at onset of deafness and communication mode) based on Cleary, Dillon, and Pisoni (2002); Carter, Dillon, and Pisoni (2002); Dillon, Cleary, Pisoni, and Carter (2004); and Dillon, Burkholder, Cleary, and Pisoni (2004).

phonetic implementation, and speech production. Moreover, the nonword repetition task, like other imitation or reproduction tests, requires additional organizational-integrative processes that link these individual component processes together to produce a unitary coordinated verbal response as output.

What unique and special properties does the nonword repetition task have that other conventional clinical speech and language tests lack? First, the stimuli used in nonword repetition tasks are novel sound patterns that children have not heard before. Thus, children must make use of robust adaptive behaviors and language processing strategies that draw on past linguistic experience in novel ways. Second, the nonword repetition task requires the child to consciously control and focus his or her attentional resources exclusively on the phonological sound properties of the stimulus patterns rather than the symbolic/linguistic attributes of the meanings of the words because there is no lexical entry in the mental lexicon for these particular stimulus patterns. Finally, the nonword repetition task, like other open-set spoken word recognition tests and reproduction tasks requires the subject to rapidly carry out phonological decomposition, reassembly of the structural description of the sound pattern, and verbal rehearsal of a novel and unfamiliar phonological representation in working memory, as well as implementation and reconstruction of a vocal articulatory–motor response linking perception and action. Given these specific processing activities

and the heavy demands on cognitive control and executive attention, it is not at all surprising that nonword repetition has proven to be very good at diagnosing a wide range of language disorders and delays that involve disturbances in rapid phonological processing of spoken language (Gathercole & Baddeley, 1990; Gathercole, Hitch, Service, & Martin, 1997).

Executive Function and Organizational-Integration Processes
Inhibition Processes in Speech Perception

Our interest in executive function and cognitive control processes began almost by accident with a small-scale pilot study carried out by Miranda Cleary that was originally designed to assess the talker recognition skills of deaf children with cochlear implants (Cleary & Pisoni, 2002). Using a same–different discrimination task, children heard two short meaningful English sentences in a row, one after the other, and were asked to determine if the sentences were produced by the same talker or different talkers. Half of the sentences in each set were produced by the same talker and half were produced by different talkers. Within each set, half of the sentences were linguistically identical and half were different. The results of this study are shown in Figure 29.1 for two groups of children, 8- and 9-year-old deaf children with cochlear implants, and a younger group of 3- to 5-year-old normal-hearing, typically developing children who served as a comparison group.

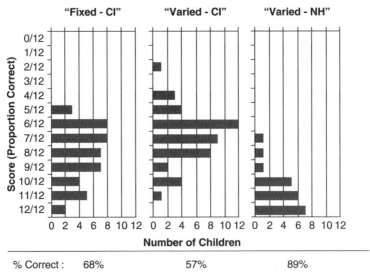

Fig. 29.1 Distribution of "same–different" sentence discrimination scores for cochlear implant users and normal-hearing controls in fixed- and varied-sentence conditions based on data reported by Cleary and Pisoni (2002).

Although the hearing 3- to 5-year-olds had little difficulty identifying whether two sentences were produced by different talkers in the varied-sentence condition as shown in the right-hand panel of Figure 29.1, the deaf children with cochlear implant had considerably more difficulty in carrying out this task. If the linguistic content of the two utterances was the same (left panel), children with cochlear implants performed the talker-discrimination task better than chance (67% correct). However, when the linguistic content of the two sentences differed in the varied sentence condition (middle panel), the performance of deaf children with cochlear implants did not differ from chance (58% correct) and was significantly worse than the group of younger normal-hearing children (89% correct).

The talker discrimination findings obtained by Cleary and Pisoni (2002) are theoretically significant because they suggest that pediatric cochlear implant users have considerable difficulty inhibiting irrelevant linguistic information in this sentence processing task. When both sentences are linguistically the same in the fixed-sentence conditions, the child can simply judge whether the voice is the same in both conditions because there is no competing semantic information to affect their discrimination response. In the varied-sentence condition, however, the child must be able to consciously control his or her attention and actively ignore and inhibit the differences in sentence meaning, the more dominant response mode, in order to selectively focus attention on the sound structure to make a decision about the speaker's voice.

An examination of the errors produced in the varied-sentence condition showed that the cochlear implant users displayed a significant response bias to incorrectly respond "different" more often than "same" for these pairs of sentences. In contrast, the normal-hearing children showed no evidence of any response bias in this condition. The differences observed in talker discrimination performance across these two sentence conditions suggest that basic sensory-auditory discriminative capacities are not the primary factor that controls performance in the same-different sentence discrimination task. Rather, discrimination performance is influenced by differences between the two groups in their ability to actively use cognitive control strategies to encode, maintain, monitor and manipulate representations of the talker's voice in working memory and selectively attend to a specific component perceptual dimension of the speech signal. These findings were even more remarkable because the control group of normal-hearing children was 3 years younger than the group of deaf children with cochlear implants. This initial study was followed up with a more extensive investigation of talker discrimination skills of deaf children with cochlear implants, which revealed strong correlations between talker discrimination and a wide range of speech and language outcome measures (see Cleary, Pisoni, & Kirk, 2005).

Neurocognitive Measures

To broaden the measures of outcome and benefit following implantation beyond the traditional endpoint speech and language assessments, we recently completed a new study that was designed to obtain additional neuropsychological measures of EF, CC, and EOI processes from a group of 5- to 10-year-old deaf children with cochlear implants. All but one of these children received their cochlear implants before 3 years of age. A group of chronologically age-matched typically developing, normal-hearing children was also recruited to serve as controls. Both groups received a battery of neuropsychological tests designed to assess selected aspects of EF and CC including verbal and spatial working memory capacity, inhibition, and processing speed, as well as fine motor control.

In addition to conventional performance measures of EF and CC obtained in the laboratory, we also obtained several additional measures using three parental report behavioral rating scales to assess EF and behavioral regulation, learning and executive attention, and attentional control and self-regulation in everyday real-world settings. More details of this study are reported by Conway et al. (in press-a). For now, however, we summarize a subset of the findings here for three of the neurocognitive performance tests, Fingertip Tapping (FTT), Design Copying (DC), and Stroop Color-word Naming (Stroop) that revealed differences in EOI functioning between the two groups of children (see also Figueras et al., 2008; Hauser et al., 2008, Pisoni et al., 2008). In the next section, we report the results of the three behavior rating scales.

NEPSY Fingertip Tapping (FTT) and Design Copying (DC)

Two of the performance measures from the NEPSY neuropsychological battery, the FTT and DC tests, revealed differences in performance between the cochlear implant and normal-hearing groups. The FTT subtest is part of the NEPSY sensory functions core domain and is designed to assess finger dexterity and motor speed. In the Repetitive Finger Tapping condition, the child is asked to make a circle with his or her thumb and index finger opening and closing it as fast as he or she can. In the Sequential Fingertip Tapping condition, the child taps the tips of his or her thumb to the index, middle, ring, and pinky making a circle with each finger. Both tests are carried out with the preferred and nonpreferred hands. The DC subtest of the NEPSY is part of the visuospatial processing domain that is used to assess a child's nonverbal visuospatial skills such as body movement and hand–eye coordination. DC measures the child's ability to reproduce and construct

visual patterns. The children were given 18 geometric designs and were asked to copy each design using paper and pencil. The DC is similar to the VMI that we used with younger children in our previous work, which was successful in uncovering preimplant behavioral predictors of outcome (Horn, Fagan, Dillon, Pisoni, & Miyamoto, 2007). The results for both the FTT and DC tests indicated that deaf children with cochlear implants performed more poorly than age-matched normal-hearing control children. Moreover, the mean scores for the cochlear implant group on the FTT were not only significantly lower than the normal-hearing children's scores, but they were also atypical relative to the published normative data. These results revealed weaknesses and delays in sensory-motor and visual-spatial domains that are consistent with our hypothesis that domain-general organizational-integrative processes are at risk in deaf children with cochlear implants.

Stroop Color Word Naming

Both groups of children were also administered the Stroop Color Word Test (SCWT), which consists of three subtests: a word reading subtest that requires reading a series of 100 alternating words (either red, green, or blue) aloud as quickly as possible, a color naming subtest that requires naming a series of 100 alternating colors (indicated by X's in the colors of red, green, or blue), and a color-word subtest that requires naming the color of ink used to print each of the words (red, green, or blue, when the word name and ink color are different). Because it is much easier to read words than name colors, the color-word subtest of the SCWT is considered to be an excellent measure of the ability to inhibit a more automatic dominant response (word reading) in favor of a more effortful color naming response. Automatic word reading interferes with color naming on the color-word subtest because the printed word and the color of the ink are different and compete with each other for attention and processing resources. Word reading causes interference with the more difficult controlled-processing task of color naming. However, this interference effect occurs only to the extent that word reading is more fluent and automatic than color naming.

Individuals with less fluent reading skills or delayed phonological processing skills often perform better on the color-word subtest because they experience less interference from the (normally automatic) word reading component of that subtest (Golden, Freshwater, & Golden, 2003). Increases in reading proficiency cause greater interference and, in turn, greater relative impairment in color-word subtest scores.

Results of the SCWT revealed similar performance speed on the color-word subtest for the two groups, although the cochlear implant group performed significantly more slowly on the word reading subtest. However, the two groups did not differ on the color naming subtest. The pattern of differences in word and color naming scores is consistent with less proficient phonological processing in the cochlear implant group and indicates that the word reading task was less automatized for the deaf children with cochlear implants. The cochlear implant group showed less interference from the word reading component of the color-word task and would have been expected to do better on the color-word task compared to the normal-hearing group, a pattern that is consistent with findings that less proficient readers do better than more proficient readers on the color-word task (assuming that other cognitive abilities are matched between the groups). The failure to find differences between groups on the color-word subtest may also reflect greater resistance to interference in the normal-hearing group than in the cochlear implant group. The pattern of Stroop word reading subtest results observed with the cochlear implant group further suggests less robust automatized lexical representations of color words in memory, as well as possible delays in verbal fluency and atypical attentional switching skills in reading isolated color words aloud.

BRIEF, LEAF, and CHAOS Rating Scales of Executive Function

To obtain measures of executive function as they are realized in everyday real-world environments like home, school, or preschool settings, outside the highly controlled conditions of the audiology clinic or research laboratory, we used a neuropsychological instrument called the Behavior Rating Inventory of Executive Function (BRIEF). Three different forms of the BRIEF are available commercially from PAR, with appropriate norms (Psychological Assessment Resources [PAR], Inc., 1996). One form was developed for preschool children (BRIEF-P: 2.0–5.11 years); another for school-aged children (BRIEF: 5–18 years), and finally one was also developed for adults (BRIEF-A: 18–90 years). The BRIEF family of products was designed to assess executive functioning in everyday environments (see Gioia, Isquith, Guy, & Kenworthy, 2000).

The BRIEF consists of a rating-scale behavior inventory that is filled out by parents, teachers, and/or daycare providers to assess a child's executive functions and self-regulation skills. It contains eight clinical scales that measure specific aspects of executive function related to inhibition, shifting of attention, emotional control, working memory, planning, and organization, among others. Scores from these subscales are then combined to construct two aggregate scales for the Behavioral Regulation Index (BRI) and the Metacognitive Index (MI). Each rating inventory also provides an overall Global Executive Composite (GEC) score.

The BRIEF has been shown in a number of recent studies to be useful in evaluating children with a wide spectrum of developmental and acquired neurocognitive conditions, although it has not been used with deaf children who use cochlear implants. From our preliminary work so far, we believe that this instrument may provide new additional converging measures of executive function and behavior regulation that are associated with conventional speech and language measures of outcome and benefit in this clinical population. Some of these measures can be obtained preimplant and therefore may be useful as behavioral predictors of outcome and benefit after implantation. Others are obtained after implantation and have turned out to have excellent clinical utility in the management and counseling of children with cochlear implants, especially poorer-performing children.

The BRIEF parent report rating inventory combined with clinical observations, parent interviews, and speech perception, and language and speech production assessments, has added an important new clinical component to our research and has generated numerous discussions with our colleagues in pediatric neuropsychology. Some parents of younger children often inquire whether their child's behaviors are similar to other children of the same age. Parents of older children have reported that their child is having more difficulty socially or academically, and can list concrete changes in behavior at home and performance in school. In both cases, parents are looking for normative benchmarks and specific suggestions because they either don't know if their child's behavior is typical for their age, or they want to know how to address manifested problems.

The information on executive function and cognitive control provided by the BRIEF clinical scales provides a quantifiable platform for broadening our discussions with parents to include possible underlying causes of particular behaviors and the effects of those behaviors on everyday real-world activities, as well as test performance. These discussions often lead to suggestions for intervention and aural rehabilitation. Discussions have included book recommendations, the role of parent training in effective behavior management, and referrals to child behavior specialists in our autism and attention-deficit hyperactivity disorder (ADHD) clinic. The BRIEF has also been used in our center to track changes in executive function and cognitive control over time and document improvements from one assessment interval to the next.

Our initial analysis of scores obtained on the BRIEF from 30 normal-hearing 5- to 8-year-old children and 19 hearing-impaired 5- to 10-year-old children with cochlear implants revealed elevated scores on several subscales. Figure 29.2a shows a summary of the BRIEF T-Scores for the GEC composite scale and the two aggregate scales, the MI and the BRI. The GEC, MI, and BRI scores were all significantly elevated for deaf children with cochlear implants than for normal-hearing children, although none of the means for the cochlear implant group fell within the clinically significant range.

Panels b and c in Figure 29.2 show the T-scores for the individual clinical scales of the BRIEF. Examination of the eight individual clinical subscales showed statistically significant differences in five of the BRIEF scales: initiation (INT), working memory (WM), planning and organization (PO), shifting (SH), and emotional control (EC). No differences were observed in organization of materials (OM), monitoring (MNTR), or inhibition (INH). The BRIEF scores provide additional converging evidence from measures of everyday real-world behaviors that multiple processing systems are linked together in development and that disturbances resulting from deafness and language delay are not domain-specific and only narrowly restricted to hearing, audition, and the processing auditory signals. The effects of deafness and language delay appear to be more widely distributed among many different neural systems and neurocognitive domains.

Two other parent- and teacher-report checklists have been developed at our ADHD clinic to evaluate executive functioning related to learning (Learning Executive and Attention Functioning scale [LEAF]) and behavior problems (Conduct-Hyperactive-Attention Problem-Oppositional Scale [CHAOS]) (Kronenberger & Dunn, 2008). Comparison of the CHAOS and LEAF scores between the cochlear implant and normal-hearing groups revealed elevated scores on most of the clinical subscales for the children with cochlear implants. In particular, as shown in Figure 29.3a and b, statistically significant differences were observed on the learning, memory, attention, speed of processing, sequential processing, complex information processing, and novel problem-solving subscales on the LEAF, and on the attention problems and hyperactivity scales on the CHAOS shown in Figure 29.3c. No differences were observed for organization and reading on the LEAF or for the oppositional problems and conduct disorder subscales on the CHAOS.

These new findings suggest that a period of profound deafness and associated language delay before cochlear implantation not only affects basic domain-specific speech and language processes but also affects self-regulation and emotional control, processes not typically considered to be comorbid with deafness and sensory deprivation. The scores on the BRIEF, LEAF, and CHAOS rating scales provide additional converging evidence and support for the general hypothesis that multiple processing systems are linked together in development, and that disturbances resulting from deafness and language delays are not domain-specific and restricted only to hearing, speech perception, and processing spoken language. The disturbances appear to be more broadly distributed among many different brain systems that are used in language processing, including other domains such as problem solving, writing, and numerical cognition, as well as emotional control, self-regulation, and control of action in novel situations requiring adaptive behaviors.

Implicit Learning of Sequential Patterns

Very little is currently known about how learning of complex sequential patterns contributes to language outcomes following cochlear implantation. At a fundamental level of analysis, all spoken language consists of sequences of linguistic units (phonemes, syllables, and words) built from a small inventory of elementary speech sounds organized in a linearly ordered temporal sequence (Lashley, 1951). These units of spoken language do not occur randomly, but are highly regular and tightly structured according to complex probabilistic relations that make human language predictable and learnable (Miller & Selfridge, 1950; Rubenstein, 1973). After acquiring knowledge about the probabilistic relations governing word order, an individual's knowledge of these sequential probabilities in language can enable a listener to reliably identify and predict the next word that will be spoken in a sentence (Elman, 1990; Kalikow, Stevens, & Elliott, 1977; Miller & Selfridge, 1950).

Several researchers have argued recently that language development reflects the operation of

Panel A: BRIEF Overall Summary

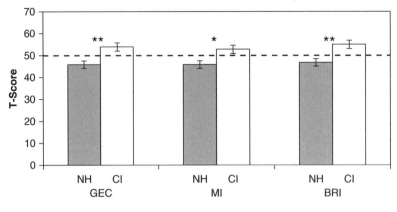

Panel B: BRIEF MI

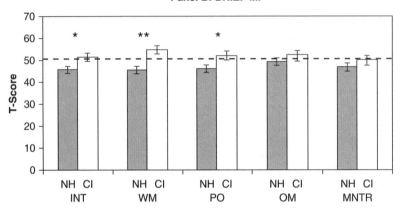

Panel C: BRIEF BRI

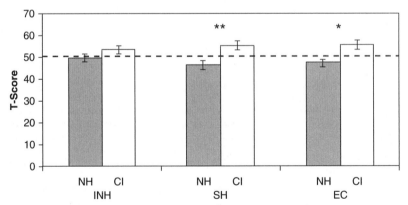

Fig. 29.2 Mean T-Scores for normal-hearing children and deaf children with cochlear implants obtained from the BRIEF parent-report behavioral rating inventory. Panel A shows the T-Scores for the Global Executive Composite (GEC), Meta Cognitive Index (MI) and the Behavior Regulation Index (BRI). Panel B shows the five individual MI clinical scales: Initiation (INT), Working Memory (WM), Planning and Organization (PO), Organization of Materials (OM) and Monitoring (MNTR). Panel C shows the three individual BRI clinical scales: Inhibition (INH), Shifting (SH) and Emotional Control (EC).

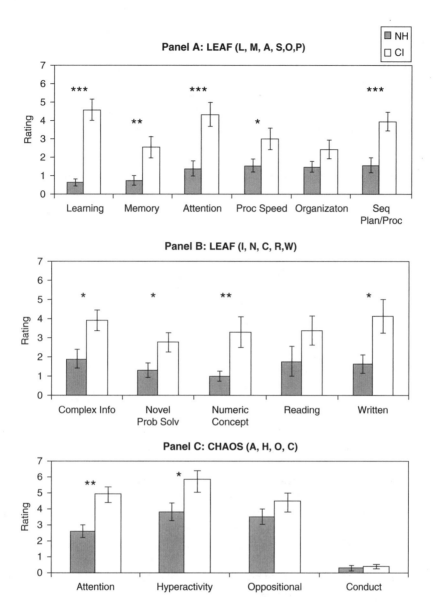

Fig. 29.3 Mean ratings for the normal-hearing children and deaf children with cochlear implants obtained from the LEAF parent-report behavioral rating inventory. Panel A shows the mean scores for: Learning, Memory, Attention, Processing Speed, Organization and Sequential Planning and Processing. Panel B shows the mean scores for: Complex Information Processing, Novel Problem Solving, Numerical Concepts, Reading and Writing. Panel C shows the mean ratings for the normal-hearing children and deaf children with cochlear implants obtained from the CHAOS parent-report behavioral rating inventory for: Attention, Hyperactivity, Oppositional and Conduct Disorders.

fundamental learning processes related to acquiring knowledge of complex probabilistic patterns. Implicit or "statistical learning" is currently thought to be one of the basic learning mechanisms used in language acquisition (Altmann, 2002; Cleeremans, Destrebecqz, & Boyer, 1998; Saffran, Senghas, & Trueswell, 2001; Ullman, 2004). There are many published examples of infants (Saffran, Aslin, & Newport, 1996), children (Meulemans & Van der Linden, 1998), adults (Conway & Christiansen, 2005), neural networks

(Elman, 1990), and even nonhumans (Hauser, Newport, & Aslin, 2000) demonstrating implicit learning capabilities.

These studies have demonstrated that humans, at least under typical (i.e., "normal") conditions of development, are equipped with the necessary raw learning capabilities to acquire the complex probabilistic structure found in language. Furthermore, recent findings from our research group have revealed a close empirical link between individual differences in implicit sequence learning and spoken language processing abilities (Conway, Baurenschmidt, Huang, & Pisoni, 2010; Conway, Karpicke, & Pisoni, 2007).

In our initial studies, young healthy adults carried out a visual implicit sequence learning task and a sentence perception task that required listeners to recognize words under degraded listening conditions. The test sentences were taken from the Speech Perception in Noise Test (SPIN) and varied on the predictability of the final word (Kalikow et al., 1977). Performance on the implicit sequence learning task was found to be significantly correlated with performance on the speech perception task—specifically, for the high predictability SPIN sentences that had a highly predictable final word. This result was observed even after controlling for common sources of variance associated with nonverbal intelligence, short-term memory, working memory, and attention inhibition (see Conway et al., 2010).

The findings obtained with adults suggest that general abilities related to implicit learning of sequential patterns are closely coupled with the ability to acquire and use information about the predictability of words occurring in the speech stream, knowledge that is critical for the successful acquisition of linguistic competence. The more knowledge that an individual acquires about the underlying sequential patterns of spoken language, the better one is able to use one's long-term knowledge of those patterns to perceive and understand novel spoken utterances, especially under highly degraded or challenging listening conditions. Although these initial studies provided evidence for an important empirical link between implicit learning and language processing in normal-hearing adults, in order to better understand the development of implicit learning it is necessary to investigate implicit sequence learning processes in both typically developing and atypically developing populations, specifically, profoundly deaf children who have been deprived of sound and the normal environmental conditions of development conducive to and appropriate for language learning.

In a recent study, we measured implicit sequence learning in a group of deaf children with cochlear implants and a chronologically age-matched control group of normal-hearing typically developing children to assess the effects that a period of auditory deprivation and delay in language may have on learning of complex visual sequential patterns (Conway et al., in press-b). Some evidence already exists that a period of auditory deprivation occurring early in development may have secondary cognitive and neural sequelae in addition to the obvious first-order hearing-related sensory effects (see Conrad, 1979; Luria, 1973; Myklebust & Brutten, 1953). Specifically, because sound is a physical signal distributed in time, lack of experience with sound may affect how well a child is able to encode, process, and learn sequential patterns and encode and store temporal information in memory (Fuster, 1995, 1997, 2001; Marschark, 2006; Rileigh & Odom, 1972; Todman & Seedhouse, 1994). Exposure to sound may also provide a kind of "auditory scaffolding" in which a child gains specific experiences and practice with learning and manipulating sequential patterns in the environment.

Based on our recent implicit visual sequence learning research with adults, we predicted that deaf children with cochlear implants would show disturbances in visual implicit sequence learning because of their lack of experience with auditory temporal patterns early on in development. We also predicted that sequence learning abilities would be associated with several different measures of language development in both groups of children.

Two groups of 5- to 10-year-old children participated in this study. One group consisted of 25 deaf children with cochlear implants; the second group consisted of 27 age-matched typically developing, normal-hearing children. All children carried out two behavioral tasks: an implicit visual sequence learning task and a sentence perception task. Several clinical measures of language outcome were available for the cochlear implant children from our larger longitudinal study. Scores on these tests were also obtained for the normal-hearing children. Our hypothesis was that if some aspects of language development draw on general learning abilities, then we should observe correlations between performance on the implicit visual sequence learning task and several different measures of spoken language processing. Measures of vocabulary knowledge and immediate memory span were also collected from all participants in this study, to rule out obvious mediating variables that might be responsible for any observed correlations. The presence of correlations between the two tasks even after partialing out the common sources of variance associated with these other measures would provide support for the hypothesis that implicit learning is *directly* associated with spoken language development, rather than being mediated by a third contributing factor.

Visual Implicit Sequence Learning Task

Two artificial grammars (Grammars A and B) were used to generate the colored sequences used in the implicit learning task. These grammars specified the probability of a particular color occurring given the preceding color in sequence. Sequence presentation consisted of colored squares appearing one at a time, in one of four possible positions in a 2×2 matrix on a computer touchscreen. The four elements (1–4) of each grammar were randomly mapped onto each of the four screen locations as well as four possible colors (red, blue, yellow, and green). The assignment of stimulus element to position/color was randomly determined for each subject; however, for each subject, the mapping remained consistent across all trials. Grammar A was used to generate 16 unique sequences for the learning phase and 12 sequences for the test phase. Grammar B was used to generate 12 novel sequences for the test phase.

For the implicit learning task, the children were told that they would see sequences of four colored squares displayed on the touch screen. The squares would flash on the screen in a pattern, and their job was to remember the pattern of colors on the screen and reproduce each pattern at the end of each trial. The procedures for both the learning and test phases were identical and, from the perspective of the subject, there was no indication of separate phases at all. The only difference between the two phases was which sequences were used. In the Learning Phase, the 16 learning sequences from Grammar A were presented first. After completing the reproduction task for all of the learning sequences, the experiment seamlessly transitioned to the Test Phase, which used the 12 novel sequences from Grammar A and 12 novel Grammar B test sequences.

The colored squares appeared one at a time, in one of four possible positions on the touchscreen. The four colors (red, blue, yellow, and green) of each grammar were randomly mapped onto each of the four screen location. The assignment of stimulus element to position/color was randomly determined for each subject; however, for each subject, the mapping remained consistent across all trials. The children were not told that there was an underlying grammar for any of the learning or test sequences or that there were two types of sequences in the Test Phase. The child simply observed the patterns and then reproduced the visual sequences.

Eisenberg Sentence Perception Task

For this task, we used a set of English lexically controlled sentences developed by Eisenberg, Martinez, Holowecky, and Pogorelsky (2002). The stimuli consisted of 20 lexically easy (i.e., high word frequency, low neighborhood density) and 20 lexically

hard (i.e., low word frequency, high neighborhood density) meaningful English sentences. The sentences were presented through a loudspeaker at 65 dB SPL. The children were instructed to listen closely to each sentence and then repeat back what they heard to the examiner, even if they were only able to perceive one word of the sentence. All of the test sentences were presented in random order to each child. Responses were recorded onto digital audio tape and were later scored off-line based on number of keywords correctly repeated for each sentence. The sentences were played in the quiet, without any degradation to the deaf children with cochlear implants. For the normal-hearing children, the original sentences were spectrally degraded to simulate a cochlear implant with a four-channel sine-wave vocoder (Shannon, Zeng, Kamath, Wygonski, & Ekelid, 1995; www.TigerSpeech.Com) to reduce their performance from ceiling levels.

In the implicit learning task, a sequence was scored correct if the participant reproduced each test sequence correctly in its entirety. Sequence span scores were then calculated using a weighted method in which the total number of correct test sequences at a given length was multiplied by the length, and then scores for all lengths were added together (see Cleary, Pisoni, & Geers, 2001). We calculated separate sequence span scores for Grammar A and Grammar B test sequences for each subject.

For each subject, we also calculated an implicit learning score (LRN), which was the difference in span scores between the learned grammar (Grammar A) and the novel grammar (Grammar B). The LRN score measures generalization indicating the extent that sequence memory spans improved for sequences that had been previously experienced during the initial Learning Phase. This score reflects how well memory spans improve for *novel* sequences that were constructed by the same grammar that subjects had previously experienced in the Learning Phase, relative to span scores for novel sequences created by the new grammar.

For the Eisenberg sentence perception task, percent keyword correct scores were calculated separately for easy and hard sentences. Each child received a forward and backward digit span score, reflecting the number of digit lists correctly repeated. Each child also received a standardized Peabody Picture Vocabulary Test (PPVT) score based on how many pictures were correctly identified and their chronological age.

Group Differences in Implicit Learning

Figure 29.4a shows the average implicit learning (LRN) scores for both groups of children. For the

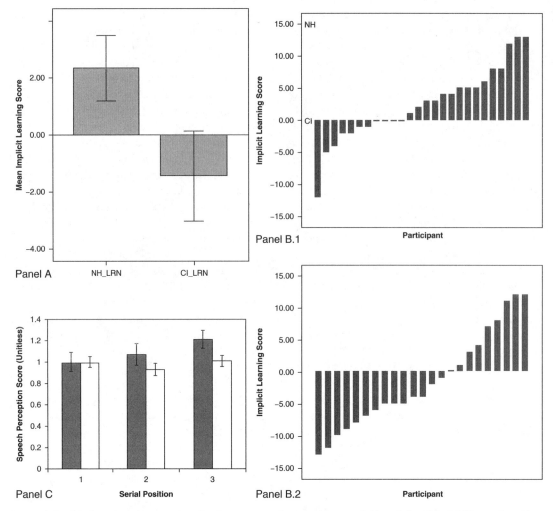

Fig. 29.4 Panel A shows the average visual implicit learning scores for normal-hearing children (*left*) and deaf children with cochlear implants (*right*). Panel B shows the implicit learning scores for individual children in the normal-hearing group (*Panel B.1*) and cochlear implant group (*Panel B.2*), ranked ordered from lowest to highest. Panel C shows the word recognition scores for normal-hearing (*gray*) and cochlear implant children (*white*) as a function of serial position within sentences for Word 1, Word 2, and Word 3. The ordinate shows a difference score that is computed by dividing the score at each word position by the score at Word 1, for the normal-hearing and cochlear implant groups separately.

normal-hearing children, the average implicit learning score (2.5) was significantly greater than 0, $t(25) = 2.24$, $p < .05$, demonstrating that, as a group, the normal-hearing children showed better learning of test sequences with the same statistical structure as the sequences from the Learning Phase. On the other hand, the average implicit learning score for the cochlear implant children was −1.43, a value that was not statistically different from 0, $t(22) = -.91$, $p = .372$. We also conducted a univariate ANOVA with the factor of group (normal-hearing, cochlear implant), which revealed a statistically significant effect of group on the implicit learning scores,

$F(1, 47) = 4.3$, $p < .05$. On average, the normal-hearing group showed greater implicit learning than the cochlear implant group, who in turn essentially showed no implicit learning on this task.

In addition to comparing group means, we also examined the distribution of individual scores for each of the two groups of children on the implicit learning task. Figure 29.4b shows the implicit learning scores for each individual participant in the normal-hearing group (top) and the cochlear implant group (bottom). Whereas 19 of 26 (73%) of the normal-hearing children showed an implicit learning score of 0 or higher, only 9 of 23 (39%) of the cochlear implant children showed a score above 0. Chi-square tests revealed that the proportion of learners to non-learners was significantly different for the normal-hearing children, $\chi^2(1) = 5.54$, $p < .05$, but not for the cochlear implant children, $\chi^2(1) = 1.08$, $p = 0.297$. That is, more than half of the normal-hearing children showed an implicit learning effect, whereas this was not the case with the cochlear implant children.

The present results demonstrate that deaf children with cochlear implants show atypical visual implicit sequence learning compared to age-matched normal-hearing children. This result is consistent with the hypothesis that a period of deafness and language delay may cause secondary disturbances and/or delays in the development of visual sequencing skills. In addition, for the cochlear implant children, we computed a partial correlation between their implicit learning score and age at implantation, with chronological age partialed out. Implicit learning was negatively correlated with the age at which the child received his or her implant and positively correlated with the duration of implant use. That is, the longer the child was deprived of auditory stimulation, the lower the visual implicit learning scores; correspondingly, the longer the child had experience with sound via his or her implant, the higher the implicit learning scores. These correlations suggest that exposure to sound (via a cochlear implant or otherwise) has secondary indirect effects on basic learning processes that are not directly associated with hearing, speech perception or language development per se; longer implant use appears to be associated with better ability to implicitly learn complex visual sequential patterns and acquire knowledge about the underlying abstract grammar that generated the patterns.

Implicit Learning and Sentence Perception

The observed individual differences in implicit learning were also correlated with performance on the Eisenberg sentence perception task, which measured how well a child can perceive words in meaningful sentences, a language processing task that involves the use of both bottom-up sensory perceptual processes as well as top-down conceptual knowledge of language. Based on our earlier work with adults, we hypothesized that implicit sequence learning would be directly related to the use of top-down knowledge in speech perception and, therefore, we predicted a significant association between these two tasks. To assess this prediction, we calculated partial correlations between the implicit learning score

and the two sentence perception scores (lexically easy sentences and lexically hard sentences), while controlling for the common variance associated with chronological age, forward digit span, backward digit span, and PPVT, and, for the cochlear implant children, age at implantation and articulation abilities as measured by scores obtained from the Goldman-Fristoe Test of Articulation (GFTA).

We found that implicit learning scores for deaf children with cochlear implants were associated with their ability to effectively use sentence context to guide speech perception, as reflected by the sentence perception difference score for combined lexically easy and hard sentences. Implicit learning was significantly correlated with the sentence perception difference scores, specifically, for the lexically hard sentences. These results suggest that better implicit learning abilities result in more robust knowledge of the sequential predictability of words in sentences, which leads in turn to better use of sentence context to aid speech perception, as reflected in the sentence perception difference score.

These results suggest that for the cochlear implant children, implicit learning is used to acquire information about word predictability in language, knowledge that can be brought to bear under conditions in which sentence context can be used to help perceive the next word in an utterance. If this is the case, then we would expect that the cochlear implant children, who scored worse as a group overall on implicit learning, will also be impaired on their ability to make use of the preceding context of a sentence to help them perceive the next word.

Figure 29.4c shows the performance of correctly identifying the three target words in the sentence perception task, as a function of the position in the sentence (first, second, or third), for the normal-hearing and cochlear implant children. Sentence context can do very little to aid perception of the first target word in the sentence; however, context is useful to help perceive the second and third target words, but only if the child has sufficient top-down knowledge of word order regularities. Indeed, the normal-hearing children showed an improvement in speech perception for the second and third target words. Their performance on the last word was statistically greater than performance on the first word, $t(25) = 4.2$, $p < .001$. In contrast, the cochlear implant children failed to show the same contextual facilitation. Their performance on the third word was no different than their performance on the first word in each sentence, $t(22) = .106$, $p = .92$. Unlike the normal-hearing children, the deaf children with cochlear implants do not appear to be using sentence context predictably to help them perceive the final word in the sentence. Thus, one way in which weak implicit learning abilities may reveal themselves are in situations in which word predictability and sentence context can be used together as a processing heuristic to guide spoken language perception.

Implicit Learning and Language Outcomes in Deaf Children with Cochlear Implants

We also found that implicit learning was positively and significantly correlated with three subtests of the Clinical Evaluation of Language Function-4 (CELF-4): Concepts and Following Directions, Formulated Sentences, and Recalling Sentences (Semel, Wiig, & Secord, 2003). These subtests involve understanding and/or producing sentences of varying complexity, tasks in which knowledge of word order predictability—that is, statistics of sequential probabilities in language—can be brought to bear to improve performance. Implicit learning was also positively and significantly correlated with receptive language on the Vineland Adaptive Behavior Scales (Sparrow, Balla, & Cicchetti, 1984).

The pattern of correlations obtained in our recent study suggests that implicit learning may be most strongly related to the ability to use knowledge of the sequential structure of language to better process, understand, and produce meaningful sentences, especially when sentence context can be brought to bear to aid processing. Importantly, this association does not appear to be mediated by chronological age, age of implantation, short-term or working memory, vocabulary knowledge, or the child's ability to produce speech. Moreover, these findings were modality-independent. The implicit sequence learning task used only visual patterns, whereas the sentence perception task relied on an auditory-only presentation of spoken sentences.

It is possible that experience with sound and auditory patterns via a cochlear implant, which generate complex, serially arrayed signals, provides a deaf child with critical experiences in perceiving and learning sequential patterns and establishing strong links between speech perception and production. A period of deafness early in development deprives a child of experience in dealing with complex sequential auditory input, which affects his ability to encode and process sequential patterns in other sense modalities as well (Myklebust & Brutten, 1953). Once electrical hearing is introduced via a cochlear implant, a profoundly deaf child begins for the first time to gain experience with auditory sequential input.

The positive correlation between length of cochlear implant use and implicit learning scores obtained even when chronological age was partialed out suggests that early experience and interactions with sound via a cochlear implant improves a deaf child's ability to learn complex nonauditory visual sequential patterns. Thus, it is possible that, given enough exposure and experiences with sound via a cochlear implant, a deaf child's implicit learning abilities will eventually improve to age-appropriate levels.

To explain these findings, we suggest that sound affects cognitive and linguistic development by providing a perceptual and cognitive "scaffolding" of time and serial order, upon which temporal sequencing functions are based (Conway, Pisoni, & Kronenberger, 2009). From a neurobiological standpoint, it is known that lack of auditory stimulation early in development results in a decrease of myelination and fewer projections out of auditory cortex (Emmorey, Allen, Bruss, Schenker, & Damasio, 2003)—which may also include connectivity to the frontal lobe. Neural circuits in the frontal lobe, specifically the prefrontal cortex, are believed to play a critical role in learning, planning, and executing sequences of thoughts and actions (Fuster, 1995, 1997, 2001; Goldman-Rakic, 1988; Miller & Cohen, 2001). It is therefore possible that the lack of auditory input and exposure to sound sequences early on in development, and the corresponding reduction of auditory-frontal connectivity, fundamentally alters the neural organization of the frontal lobe and the extensive connections it has with other brain circuits (Wolff & Thatcher, 1990), thus impacting the development of sequencing functions regardless of input modality (Miller & Cohen, 2001).

Theoretical and Clinical Implications

Many of the deaf children with cochlear implants tested in our studies also have comorbid disturbances and/or delays in several basic underlying neurocognitive processes that subserve information processing systems used in spoken language processing, and these disturbances appear to be, at least in part, secondary to their profound hearing loss and delay in language development (Conrad, 1979; Rourke, 1989, 1995). A period of profound deafness and auditory deprivation during critical developmental periods before implantation affects neurocognitive development in a variety of ways. Differences resulting from both deafness and subsequent neural reorganization and plasticity of multiple brain systems may be responsible for the enormous variability observed in speech and language outcome measures following implantation. Without knowing what specific underlying neurobiological and neurocognitive factors are responsible for the individual differences in speech and language outcomes, it is difficult to recommend and select an appropriate and efficacious approach to habilitation and speech-language therapy after a child receives a cochlear implant. More importantly, the deaf children who are performing poorly with their cochlear implants are not a homogeneous group, and may differ in numerous ways from one another, reflecting dysfunction of multiple brain systems associated with congenital deafness and profound hearing loss. From a clinical perspective, it seems very unlikely that an individual child will be able to achieve optimal speech and language benefits from his or her cochlear implant without knowing why the child is having speech and language problems and which particular neurocognitive domains underlie these problems.

Some profoundly deaf children with cochlear implants do extremely well on traditional audiological speech and language outcome measures, whereas other children have much more difficulty. The enormous variability in outcome and benefit following cochlear implantation is a significant clinical problem in the field, and it has not received adequate attention by research scientists in the past. Obtaining a better understanding of the neurocognitive basis of individual differences in outcomes will have direct implications for diagnosis, treatment, and early identification of deaf children who may be at high risk for poor outcomes after implantation. New knowledge about the sources of variability in speech and language outcomes will also play an important role in intervention following implantation in terms of selecting specific methods for habilitation and treatment that are appropriate for an individual child. We have now identified two potential areas of neurocognitive functioning that may underlie variability in speech and language outcomes: EOI processes and implicit sequence learning abilities.

The bulk of clinical research on cochlear implants has been intellectually isolated from the mainstream of current research and theory in neuroscience, cognitive psychology, and developmental neuropsychology. As a consequence, the major clinical research issues have been narrowly focused on speech and language outcomes and efficacy of cochlear implantation as a medical treatment for profound hearing loss. Little basic or clinical research in the past has investigated the underlying neurobiological and neurocognitive bases of the individual differences and variability in the effectiveness of cochlear implants.

Moreover, few studies have attempted to identify reliable early neurocognitive predictors of outcome and benefit or systematically assessed the effectiveness of specific intervention and habilitation strategies after implantation. We believe these are important new areas of clinical research on cochlear implants that draw heavily on basic research and theory representing the intersection of several closely related disciplines that deal with the relations between brain, behavior and development, memory and learning, attention, executive function, and cognitive control.

References

Altmann, G. T. M. (2002). Statistical learning in infants. *Proceedings of the National Academy of Sciences, 99*, 15250–15251.

Blair, C., & Razza-Peters, R. (2007). Relating effortful control, executive function, and false belief understanding to the emerging math and literacy ability in kindergarten. *Child Development, 78*, 647–663.

Bodrova, E., & Leong, D. J. (2007). *Tools of the mind.* Person-Merrill Prentice Hall: Columbus, OH.

Carter, A. K., Dillon, C. M., & Pisoni, D. B. (2002). Imitation of nonwords by hearing impaired children with cochlear implants: Suprasegmental analyses. *Clinical Linguistics & Phonetics, 16*, 619–638.

Cicchetti, D., & Curtis, W. J. (2006). The developing brain and neural plasticity: Implications for normality, psychopathology, and resilience. In D. Cicchetti & D. Cohen (Eds.), *Developmental psychopathology: Developmental neuroscience,* Vol. 2, 2nd edition. New York: Wiley

Cleary, M., Dillon, C. M., & Pisoni, D. B. (2002). Imitation of nonwords by deaf children after cochlear implantation: Preliminary findings. *Annals of Otology, Rhinology, & Laryngology Supplement-Proceedings of the 8th Symposium on Cochlear Implants in Children, 111*, 91–96.

Cleary, M., & Pisoni, D. B. (2002). Talker discrimination by prelingually-deaf children with cochlear implants: Preliminary results. *Annals of Otology, Rhinology, & Laryngology Supplement-Proceedings of the 8th Symposium on Cochlear Implants in Children, 111*, 113–118.

Cleary, M., Pisoni, D. B., & Geers, A. E. (2001). Some measures of verbal and spatial working memory in eight- and nine-year-old hearing-impaired children with cochlear implants. *Ear & Hearing, 22*, 395–411.

Cleary, M., Pisoni, D. B., & Kirk, K. I. (2005). Influence of voice similarity on talker discrimination in normal-hearing children and hearing-impaired children with cochlear implants. *Journal of Speech, Language, and Hearing Research, 48*, 204–223.

Cleeremans, A., Destrebecqz, A., & Boyer, M. (1998). Implicit learning: News from the front. *Trends in Cognitive Sciences, 2*, 406–416.

Conrad, R. (1979). *The deaf schoolchild.* London: Harper & Row, Ltd.

Conway, C. M., Bauernschmidt, A., Huang, S. S., & Pisoni, D. B. (2010). Implicit statistical learning in language processing: Word predictability in the key. *Cognition.*

Conway, C. M., & Christiansen, M. H. (2005). Modality-constrained statistical learning of tactile, visual, and auditory sequences. *Journal of Experimental Psychology: Learning, Memory & Cognition, 31*, 24–39.

Conway, C. M., Karpicke, J., & Pisoni, D. B. (2007). Contribution of implicit sequence learning to spoken language processing: Some preliminary findings with normal-hearing adults. *Journal of Deaf Studies and Deaf Education, 12*, 317–334.

Conway, C. M., Karpicke, J., Anaya, E. M., Henning, S. C., Kronenberger, W. G., & Pisoni, D. B. (in press-a). Nonverbal cognition in deaf children following cochlear implantation: Motor sequencing disturbances mediate language delays. *Developmental Neuropsychology*.

Conway, C. M., Pisoni, D. B., Anaya, E. M., Karpicke, J., & Henning, S. C. (in press-b). Implicit sequence learning in deaf children with cochlear implants. *Developmental Science*.

Conway, C. M., Pisoni, D. B., & Kronenberger, W. G. (2009). The importance of sound for cognitive sequencing abilities: The auditory scaffolding hypothesis. *Current Directions in Psychological Science*.

Deary, I. J., Strand, S., Smith, P., & Fernandes, C. (2007). Intelligence and educational achievement. *Intelligence, 35*, 13–21.

Diamond, A., Barnett, W. S., Thomas, J., & Munro, S. (2007). Preschool program improves cognitive control. *Science, 318*, 1387–1388.

Dillon, C. M., Burkholder, R. A., Cleary, M., & Pisoni, D. B. (2004). Nonword repetition by children with cochlear implants: Accuracy ratings from normal-hearing listeners. *Journal of Speech, Language and Hearing Research, 47*, 1103–1116.

Dillon, C. M., Cleary, M., Pisoni, D. B., & Carter, A. K. (2004). Imitation of nonwords by hearing-impaired children with cochlear implants: Segmental analyses. *Clinical Linguistics and Phonetics, 18*, 39–55.

Eisenberg, L. S., Martinez, A. S., Holowecky, S. R., & Pogorelsky, S. (2002). Recognition of lexically controlled words and sentences by children with normal-hearing and children with cochlear implants. *Ear & Hearing, 23*, 450–462.

Elman, J. L. (1990). Finding structure in time. *Cognitive Science, 14*, 179–211.

Emmorey, K., Allen, J. S., Bruss, J., Schenker, N., & Damasio, H. (2003). A morphometric analysis of auditory brain regions in congenitally deaf adults. *Proceedings of the National Academy of Sciences, 100*, 10049–10054.

Figueras, B., Edwards, L., & Langdon, D. (2008). Executive function and language in deaf children. *Journal of Deaf Studies and Deaf Education, 13*, 362–377.

Fuster, J. (2001). The prefrontal cortex—an update: Time is of the essence. *Neuron, 30*, 319–333.

Fuster, J. (1997). *The prefrontal cortex*. Philadelphia: Lippincott-Raven.

Fuster, J. (1995). Temporal processing. In J. Grafman, K. J. Holyoak, & F. Boller (Eds.), *Structure and functions of the human prefrontal cortex* (pp. 173–181). New York: New York Academy of Sciences.

Gathercole, S., & Baddeley, A. (1990). Phonological memory deficits in language disordered children: Is there a causal connection? *Journal of Memory and Language, 29*, 336–360.

Gathercole, S. E., Hitch, G. J., Service, E., & Martin, A. J. (1997). Phonological short-term memory and new word learning in children. *Developmental Psychology, 33*, 966–979.

Geers, A., & Brenner, C. (2003). Background and educational characteristics of prelingually deaf children implanted for five years of age. *Ear & Hearing, 24*, 2S–14S.

Geers, A., Brenner, C., & Davidson, L. (2003). Factors associated with development of speech perception skills in children implanted by age five. *Ear & Hearing, 24*, 24S–35S.

Gioia, G. A., Isquith, P. K., Guy, S. C., & Kenworthy, L. (2000). *BRIEF™: Behavior Rating Inventory of Executive Function Psychological Assessment Resources*, Inc. (PAR): Lutz, Florida.

Golden, C. J., Freshwater, S. M., Golden, Z. (2003). *Stroop Color and Word Test Children's Version for Ages 5-14*. Stoelting Company: Wood Dale, IL.

Goldman-Rakic, P. S. (1988). Topography of cognition: Parallel distributed networks in primate association cortex. *Annual Reviews of Neuroscience, 11*, 137–156.

Hauser, M. D., Newport, E. L., & Aslin, R. N. (2000). Segmentation of the speech stream in a non-human primate: Statistical learning in cotton-top tamarins, *Cognition, 75*, 1–12.

Hauser, P. C., Lukomski, J., & Hillman, T. (2008). Development of deaf and hard-of-hearing students' executive function. In M. Marschark & P. C. Hauser (Eds.), *Deaf cognition: Foundations and outcomes* (pp. 268–308). New York: Oxford University Press.

Hawker, K., Ramirez-Inscoe, J., Bishop, D. V. M., Twomey, T., O'Donoghue, G. M., & Moore, D. R. (2008). Disproportionate language impairment in children using cochlear implants. *Ear & Hearing, 29*, 467–471.

Hohm, E., Jennen-Steinmetz, C. Schmidt, M. H., & Laucht, M. (2007). Language development at ten months. *European Child & Adolescent Psychiatry, 16*, 149–156.

Horn, D. L., Fagan, M. K., Dillon, C. M., Pisoni, D. B., & Miyamoto, R. T. (2007). Visual-motor integration skills of prelingually deaf children: Implications for pediatric cochlear implantation. *The Laryngoscope, 11*, 2017–2025.

Hughes, C., & Graham, A. (2002). Measuring executive functions in childhood: Problems and solution? *Child and Adolescent Mental Health, 7*, 131–142.

Kalikow, D. N., Stevens, K. N., & Elliott, L. L. (1977). Development of a test of speech intelligibility in noise using sentence materials with controlled word predictability. *Journal of the Acoustical Society of America, 61*, 1337–1351.

Kaufman, A. S., Lichtenberger, E. O. (2006). *Assessing adolescent and adult intelligence*, 3rd edition. New York: Wiley.

Kronenberger, W. G., & Dunn, D. W. (2008). *Development of a very brief, user-friendly measure of ADHD for busy clinical practices: The CHAOS Scale*. Poster presented at the 2008 National Conference on Child Health Psychology. Miami Beach, FL, April 11, 2008.

Lamm, C., Zelazo, P. D., & Lewis, M. D. (2006). Neural correlates of cognitive control in childhood and adolescence: Disentangling the contributions of age and executive function. *Neuropsychologia, 44*, 2139–2148.

Lashley, K. S. (1951). The problem of serial order in behavior. In L. A. Jeffress (Ed.), *Cerebral mechanisms in behavior* (pp. 112–146). New York: Wiley.

Lezak, M. D., Howieson, D. B., Loring, D. W., & Hannay, H. J. (2004). *Neurological assessment*. New York: Oxford University Press.

Luria, A. R. (1973). *The working brain*. New York: Basic Books.

Marschark, M. (2006). Intellectual functioning of deaf adults and children: Answers and questions. *European Journal of Cognitive Psychology, 18*, 70–89.

Mathews, V. P., Kronenberger, W. G., Wang, Y., Lurito, J. T., Lowe, M. J., & Dunn, D. W. (2005). Media violence exposure and frontal lobe activation measured by fMRI in aggressive and non-aggressive adolescents. *Journal of Computer Assisted Tomography, 29*, 287–292.

Meulemans, T., & Van der Linden, M. (1998). Implicit sequence learning in children. *Journal of Experimental Child Psychology, 69*, 199–221.

Miller, E. K., & Cohen, J. D. (2001). An integrative theory of prefrontal cortex function. *Annual Reviews in Neuroscience, 24*, 167–202.

Miller, G. A., & Selfridge, J. A. (1950). Verbal context and the recall of meaningful material. *American Journal of Psychology, 63*, 176–185.

Myklebust, H. R. (1964). *The psychology of deafness.* New York: Grune & Stratton.

Myklebust, H. R. (1954). *Auditory disorders in children.* New York: Grune & Stratton.

Myklebust, H. R., & Brutten, M. (1953). A study of visual perception of deaf children. *Acta Otolaryngology, 105*(Supplement), 126.

Nauta, W. J. H. (1964). Discussion of 'Retardation and facilitation in learning by stimulation of frontal cortex in monkeys.' In J. M. Warren & K. Akert (Eds.), *The frontal granular cortex and behavior* (pp. 125–135). New York: McGraw-Hill.

NIDCD. (1988). *Cochlear implants.* NIH Consensus Statement, May 4, Vol. 7.

NIDCD. (1995). *Cochlear implants in adults and children.* NIH Consensus Statement, May 15–17, 13, 1–30.

Pisoni, D. B., Conway, C. M., Kronenberger, W. G., Horn, D. L., Karpicke, J., & Henning, S. (2008). Efficacy and effectiveness of cochlear implants in deaf children.' In Marschark & P. Hauser (Eds.), *Deaf cognition: Foundations and outcomes* (pp. 52–101). New York: Oxford University Press.

Rileigh, K. K., & Odom, P. B. (1972). Perception of rhythm by subjects with normal and deficient hearing. *Developmental Psychology, 7*, 54–61.

Rourke, B. P. (1989). *Nonverbal learning disabilities.* New York: The Guilford Press.

Rourke, B. P. (1995). *Syndrome of nonverbal learning disabilities.* New York: The Guilford Press.

Rubenstein, H. (1973). Language and probability. In G. A. Miller (Ed.), *Communication, language, and meaning: Psychological perspectives* (pp. 185–195). New York: Basic Books, Inc.

Saffran, J. R., Aslin, R. N., & Newport, E. L. (1996). Statistical learning by 8-month-old infants. *Science, 274*, 1926–1928.

Saffran, J. R., Senghas, A., & Trueswell, J. C. (2001). The acquisition of language by children. *Proceedings of the National Academy of Sciences, 98*, 12874–12875.

Semel, E., Wiig, E. H., & Secord, W. A. (2003). *Clinical evaluation of language fundamentals, fourth edition (CELF-4).* Toronto, Canada: The Psychological Corporation/A Harcourt Assessment Company.

Shannon, R. V., Zeng, F. -G., Kamath, V., Wygonski, J., & Ekelid, M. (1995). Speech recognition with primarily temporal cues. *Science, 270*, 303–304.

Sparrow, S. Balla, D., & Cicchetti, D. (1984). *Vineland Adaptive Behavioral Scales.* Circle Pines, MN: American Guidance Service.

Sporns, O. (1998). Biological variability and brain function. In J. Cornwell (Ed.), *Consciousness and human identity* (pp. 38–56). Oxford: Oxford University Press.

Sporns, O. (2003). Network analysis, complexity, and brain function. *Complexity, 8*, 56–60.

Thelen, E., & Smith, L. B. (1994). *A dynamic systems approach to the development of cognition and action.* Cambridge: The MIT Press.

Todman, J., & Seedhouse, E. (1994). Visual-action code processing by deaf and hearing children. *Language & Cognitive Processes, 9*, 129–141.

Ullman, M. T. (2004). Contributions of memory circuits to language: The declarative/procedural model. *Cognition, 92*, 231–270.

Ullman, M. T., & Pierpont, E. I. (2005). Specific language impairment is not specific to language: The procedural deficit hypothesis. *Cortex, 41*, 399–433.

Van der Sluis, S., de Jong, P. F., & van der Leij, A. (2007). Executive functioning in children, and its relations with reasoning, reading, and arithmetic. *Intelligence, 35*, 427–449.

Wolff, A. B., & Thatcher, R. W. (1990). Cortical reorganization in deaf children. *Journal of Clinical and Experimental Neuropsychology, 12*, 209–221.

Working Memory, Deafness, and Sign Language

Matthew L. Hall *and* Daphne Bavelier

Abstract

Working memory (WM) refers to the human capacity to encode, store, manipulate, and recall information. A proper understanding of WM therefore provides essential insights into human cognition. This chapter reviews available research concerning the impact of deafness and sign language use on WM, much of which comes from the study of a single subcomponent of WM termed short-term memory (STM). We argue that excessive focus on STM (the ability to encode, store, and retrieve a sequence of unrelated words *in serial order*) to the exclusion of other WM subprocesses has caused an extreme interest in phonological coding at the expense of other known codes used in WM, in particular visual but also episodic codes. Deafness and use of a sign language may result in greater reliance on not only visual but also episodic coding, as compared to what is typically observed in hearing nonsigners. This multiple coding hypothesis calls into question whether the robust phonological bias described in hearing individuals should be taken by researchers, clinicians, and educators as the gold standard for deaf populations.

Keywords: working memory, deafness, sign language, short-term memory, digit span, phonological store, multiple coding hypothesis, episodic buffer

A review of the studies that compare short-term memory (STM) in deaf and hearing populations highlights an advantage for speech in STM tasks using digit or letter span, but not in those using visuospatial stimuli. The findings have remained relatively consistent over time, but their interpretation has been less clear. Some have argued that those working memory (WM) components that process visuospatial information also process sign language, whereas others have suggested that the differences can be explained by factors like articulatory duration or simple auditory deprivation (for a discussion see Wilson, Bettger, Niculae, & Klima, 1997). Still others have proposed that signers are impaired when it comes to retaining information about temporal order but advantaged for remembering spatial locations (for a discussion see Bavelier, Newport, Hall, Supalla, & Boutla, 2008).

We posit that the data are best captured by recognizing that signers and speakers share the same WM architecture, but preferentially rely on different WM subprocesses. Speakers depend on the phonological loop to a much greater extent than signers, who in turn rely on distributed coding across phonological, visuospatial, and also episodic processes. According to this view, the speech-sign differences in memory tasks are not indicative of fundamental differences in WM capacity between deaf and hearing people, but rather reflect different processing biases in WM as a function of auditory deprivation and language exposure. We therefore urge educators and clinicians to be cautious when interpreting the results of standardized tests, and call on researchers to give due attention to the less-investigated aspects of WM in both signers and speakers.

Working Memory and Short-term Memory

Working memory is the set of cognitive functions that allow individuals to actively maintain and manipulate information in the service of cognition, as when performing mental arithmetic. For example, when mentally computing 27 times 5, the outcome of one mental operation (e.g., 5 times 7) needs to be kept in mind while computing a second mental operation (e.g., 5 times 2). It is widely accepted that WM is not a unitary construct but rather can be subdivided into different component processes, including separate buffers for the temporary maintenance of phonological, visuospatial, and episodic information, as well as a "central executive" system that coordinates and prioritizes information as needed by the task (Baddeley, 1986; Miyake & Shah, 1999; Norman & Shallice, 1980).

Much of WM research has focused on the STM subset of WM. The term *short-term memory* currently is used primarily to refer to the ability to keep information in mind in the exact serial order in which it was presented. A common example is that of being told a phone number and remembering the numbers while looking for a piece of paper and a pencil to jot them down. This task requires maintaining both the identity of the to-be-remembered items and the order in which they were presented. Crucially, however, no other kind of mental computation is required. For the purpose of this chapter, we will restrict our use of the term "short-term memory" to the maintenance-only aspect of WM.

Holding on to a phone number for a few minutes is a standard example of linguistic STM, as the memory representations being held in active memory are language-based. Since the seminal work of Baddeley and collaborators (Baddeley & Hitch, 1974), much research has documented the inner workings of linguistic STM, at least in hearing speakers. The to-be-remembered numbers are encoded in the phonological buffer and refreshed through an active rehearsal process (also known as the articulatory loop), ensuring active maintenance of their memory traces over time. Short-term memory capacity is claimed to be time-limited, such that the number of units that can be retained in STM is a function of how many units can be subvocally articulated in about 2 seconds (Baddeley & Lewis, 1984). Together, the phonological buffer and the articulatory loop are commonly referred to as the *phonological loop*.

Working memory is far from a unitary construct (Fig. 30.1), and the phonological loop is not its only subcomponent. For example, when recalling how to go from school to home, visuospatial WM is typically recruited (Kosslyn, 1980). In that case, the memory representations are akin to mental maps of

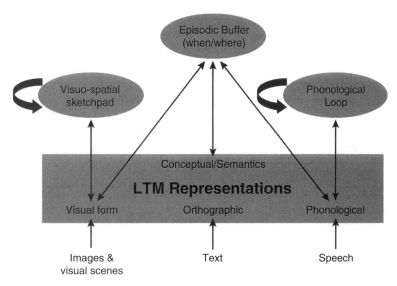

Fig. 30.1 The multicomponent working memory (WM) architecture (adapted from Baddeley, 2000, Figure 1, pp. 421). Multiple representations in long-term memory (LTM) are activated upon presentation of a stimulus. Working memory relies on the active maintenance of these representations during the short retention interval. Although different forms of information preferentially engage different buffers (speech for the phonological loop, visual images for the visuospatial sketchpad), WM relies on these multiple codes and their proper binding into a unified memory trace—the episodic trace—so as to capture the specifics of the episode to be remembered. In contrast, performance on serial short-term memory (STM) tasks, at least in speakers, is predominantly under the control of the phonological loop, with names stored in the phonological buffer and refreshed through the articulatory loop.

the path being taken. Rehearsal in that system may occur through eye movements or movements of attention (Awh & Jonides, 2001; Postle et al., 2006). Although less studied, tactile, and olfactory buffers are also likely candidates for remembering either touch or odors for short periods.

A third important construct in WM is the episodic buffer. The concept of episodic traces in memory was initially championed by Tulving (1983); here, we will focus on episodic memories that support WM, in contrast to long-term episodic memories that enable the remembering of past experience (Tulving, 2002). Representations in the episodic buffer are defined by the time and place of occurrence of the event to be remembered, as well as any information concerning that event. Episodic traces encode what happened, when it happened, and where it happened. Thus, a patient with an impaired phonological loop may be able to read a rather long text and report on the content of what was just read thanks to the episodic buffer (Baddeley, 2003a; Baddeley, 2000; Rudner & Ronnberg, 2008). Likewise, visual information can be dynamically updated across time through episodic representations, allowing a driver to brake to avoid a pedestrian, even if that pedestrian is temporarily occluded from view (Pylyshyn, 1989).

A key function of WM is to prioritize information. As new information is being retrieved, new computations are being performed and old information either becomes obsolete or needs to be maintained for further computations. This dynamic aspect of memory is often referred to as the *central executive* (Baddeley, 2003b). This construct can be conceived of as the "orchestra director" that controls the different memory buffers and their interactions, by either focusing attention on one of them, dividing resources among several of them, or switching attention from one buffer to another. Although sometimes caricatured as a homunculus, the central executive may act automatically by changing the availability of the various memory representations either at the level of the three buffers discussed earlier or in long-term memory (Cowan, 2008).

We will see that deaf individuals and hearing individuals share the same set of components in their WM architecture. Yet, each population exhibits different biases in the extent to which they engage these memory buffers, leading to differences in behavioral outcomes across groups.

Common Working Memory Architecture Across Deaf and Hearing

The WM architecture just proposed was developed on the basis of evidence from hearing individuals only. However, because the prevailing view is that these WM systems are a part of the human genetic endowment and not a consequence of auditory experience, there is no reason to suspect that deaf individuals differ substantially in their basic WM architecture. Although this claim has been uncontroversial with respect to WM components such as the visuospatial sketchpad, episodic buffer, and central executive, it has been necessary to verify the existence of a sign-based phonological loop through empirical research. Ultimately, behavioral and brain imaging studies have confirmed the existence of the same WM components in deaf and hearing populations.

As with speech, the earliest explorations of the phonological loop in American Sign Language (ASL) relied on sign-based errors. Bellugi, Klima, and Siple (1974–1975) discovered that when deaf signers made mistakes on a memory task, their incorrect responses often shared sublexical structure with target items, such as handshape, location, or movement. (This is what is meant by "phonology" as applied to ASL.) They took this finding to imply that signers relied on memory representations that were based on the linguistic structure of ASL. The existence of a phonological loop in deaf signers is further evidenced by reports of effects considered in the literature to be diagnostic of the phonological loop in speakers. For example, linguistic STM in signers is affected by signed phonological similarity (Conrad, 1970, 1972; Wilson & Emmorey, 1997), sign length (Wilson & Emmorey, 1998), manual articulatory suppression (Losiewicz, 2000; MacSweeney, Campbell, & Donlan, 1996; Wilson & Emmorey, 1997), and irrelevant signed input (Wilson & Emmorey, 2003). These results indicate that, like speakers, native ASL signers rely on sign-based phonological encoding and a subarticulatory mechanism to rehearse signs in linguistic STM (for a review see Wilson & Emmorey, 2000).

Brain imaging studies further support this view, indicating a high degree of similarity across deaf signers and hearing speakers during STM tasks (Bavelier, Newman, Mukherjee, Hauser, Kemeny, Braun, & Boutla, 2008; Buchsbaum, Pickell, Love, Hatrak, Bellugi, & Hickok, 2005; Rönnberg, Rudner, & Ingvar, 2004). Neuroimaging studies of the neural systems underlying STM performance in hearing speakers during each of the three main stages of STM—encoding, maintenance, and recall—reveal distinct patterns across stages within an overlapping frontoparietal network (Chein & Fiez, 2001; Henson, Burgess, & Frith, 2000; Manoach, Greve,

Lindgren, & Dale, 2003; Rypma & D'Esposito, 1999). Whereas brain activation during encoding reflects in large part the sensory characteristics of the information to be laid down in STM, and recall reflects the motor requirements of executing the response, all three processing stages have been found to rely on the integrity of a wide frontoparietal circuit (for a meta-analysis see Wager & Smith, 2003). Similarly, brain imaging studies of deaf signers performing a STM task reveal greater participation of brain structures related to visual processing during the initial encoding of the information and of the hand motor areas during final recall of information, as expected. More importantly, the same frontoparietal network described to mediate STM in speakers was also observed in deaf signers, with its recruitment appearing independent of the modality of the language (Bavelier, Newman et al., 2008; Buchsbaum et al., 2005).

This finding supports the view that signed and spoken STM rely on a similar architecture. These effects are not restricted to deaf signers; their appearance in studies of hearing native signers as well (Ronnberg et al., 2004) demonstrates that they result from sign language use. Signers and speakers do not differ in terms of the overall network of areas engaged during a STM task; rather, the only noticeable difference is in the degree to which these memory systems contribute to each stage of STM. In particular, deaf signers were observed to rely to a greater extent than hearing speakers on passive memory storage areas during encoding and maintenance, but on executive process areas during recall (Bavelier, Newman et al., 2008). This work is in line with the present proposal of a common WM architecture in deaf signers and hearing speakers, with differences in the way each population engages various components of this architecture for a given memory task.

Differences in Linguistic Short-term Memory Span

Despite the architectural similarity of WM between deaf signers and hearing speakers, differences have been documented in STM span, especially when using linguistic stimuli. Span measures are traditionally derived from serial recall tasks in which participants are required to recall the words or items presented in their exact order of presentation. As such, they necessarily test STM. A common task used to measure the capacity of linguistic STM is the digit span task, in which participants are required to recall sequences of digits in the same order as presented (i.e., serial recall). The maximal number of

items recalled in the correct order is considered the capacity limit of memory. The exact size of this capacity limit varies across individuals and interestingly, individuals with higher capacity limits have been argued to be more efficient (as measured in terms of speed and accuracy) in a wide range of language processing tasks, and in particular during the acquisition of reading skills (Engle, Kane, & Tuholski, 1999). It is therefore understood that, for hearing individuals, characterizing the cognitive mechanisms underlying the development and specialization of linguistic STM capacity will shed light on the development of literacy. Do the same relationships apply to the deaf population?

This is a central question in WM research and deafness, as a host of studies report shorter spans in deaf than in hearing individuals. The first such report dates back to Pintner and Patterson (1917), who used visually presented digits and established a shorter span in deaf than in hearing children and adults. The seminal work of Conrad in the 1970s further established this effect (Conrad, 1970). Since then, much work has been done showing that this effect is not due to the use of printed materials that deaf participants are unlikely to be familiar with or the requirement to write down the response. Indeed, the effect remains when participants are tested using their native language, sign language, at input and output (Bellugi et al., 1974–1975; Bellugi & Siple, 1974; Boutla, Supalla, Newport, & Bavelier, 2004; Geraci, Gozzi, Papagno, & Cecchetto, 2008; Marschark, 1996).

Articulation Rate and Differences in Linguistic Short-term Memory Span

A common explanation in the field is that signs take longer to articulate than speech (Marschark, 2005; Wilson & Emmorey, 1997). This concern is motivated by the fact that, among speakers, digit span varies cross-linguistically as a function of how long it takes to articulate a series of digits in a given language. In languages like Chinese, where digit names are quick to articulate, digit span is high (Elliott, 1992). In languages like Welsh, where digit names take longer to produce, digit span is low (Ellis & Hennelly, 1980). Might a cross-linguistic difference in articulation rate explain the STM span discrepancy between ASL and English?

It is certainly true that lexical signs in ASL typically take longer to articulate than words in English (Bellugi & Fisher, 1972). However, most STM span tasks are conducted using letters or numbers, which are considerably simpler than lexical signs. If the smaller STM span in ASL were due to articulatory duration, we would expect the items tested in these span tasks to take longer to articulate than their English equivalents. Boutla et al. (2004) tested this prediction and found that, despite a significant difference in STM span between English and ASL, articulation rate for the items tested did not differ. To avoid phonological similarity within the stimulus set, Boutla et al. (2004) tested letters in ASL, but digits in English. This stimulus choice has been criticized as a potential confound (Wilson & Emmorey, 2006a, 2006b). However, more recent evidence indicates that the STM span discrepancy remains even when comparing items of the same stimulus class. First, Bavelier et al. (2006, 2008) replicated the effect comparing first fingerspelled and English letters and then ASL and English digits. Second, Geraci et al. (2008) replicated the discrepancy and extended it to the use of words in Italian Sign Language (LIS) as compared to spoken Italian words that were matched on articulatory duration.

Finally, a meta-analysis of studies conducted in our laboratory over the past several years reveals a striking pattern of results. The filled symbols in Figure 30.2A show the mean digit and/or letter span from 14 groups of native English speakers (*n* = 199; 318 observations) as a function of their articulation rate. Over 70% of the variance in span (range: 5.65–8.06) is predicted by articulation rate alone. Equally striking is that the spoken STM span of oral deaf and hard-of-hearing participants (Fig. 30.2A, *open circles*) is predicted by this same line. This suggests that for speech, the amount of time it takes to articulate items is the primary determinant of STM span, and that this relationship holds even when fluency varies. There is also no evidence that digits have a special status over letters in memory; the fact that digit span is typically higher than letter span in English speakers can be satisfactorily explained by differences in articulation rate. In contrast, the filled symbols in Figure 30.2B show the mean ASL digit and/or letter span of 13 groups of native ASL signers (*n* = 170; 229 observations) as a function of their mean articulation rate for those same materials. Although ASL STM span ranges from 4.17 to 6.58, this variation is not predicted by articulation rate, either across all participants (r^2 = .0008) or for native signers only (r^2 = .0029).

Clearly, the robust relationship between articulation duration and span seen in speakers across wide variations in language fluency does not apply to signers. Together, the reviewed findings show that differences in STM capacity between signers and speakers cannot simply be explained by differences in articulation rate across languages.

Auditory Deprivation and Differences in Linguistic Short-term Memory Span
Effects observed in deaf signers may reflect the impact of auditory deprivation or/and that of use of a visuo-manual language. In the case of STM spans, there is clear evidence that signing alone can induce the effect.

A difference in serial STM span using linguistic stimuli has been observed not only between deaf signers and hearing speakers, but also *within bilingual*

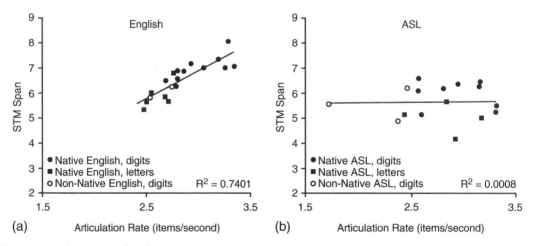

Fig. 30.2 Articulation rate predicts short-term memory (STM) in English (panel A) but not signers (panel B). Filled symbols represent native speakers (English: all hearing subjects; ASL: deaf, hearing, and hard-of-hearing subjects with deaf parents). Open symbols represent non-native speakers (English: hard-of-hearing, oral deaf; ASL: Non-CODA interpreters, non-CODA non-interpreters, oral deaf). Regressions are calculated over all data points displayed.

individuals, depending on whether they were tested in a signed or in a spoken language (Boutla et al., 2004; Ronnberg et al., 2004). Although this phenomenon is also observed in bilinguals whose two spoken languages differ in articulation rate, such as Welsh and English (Ellis & Hennelly, 1980), as we just discussed, this standard explanation in terms of a difference in articulation rate across the language tested does not hold for English-ASL bilinguals (Boutla et al., 2004, Figure 2). Rather, this apparent discrepancy within individual ASL-English bilinguals can be further localized to specific stages of the STM process. American Sign Language-English bilinguals who were presented with ASL stimuli showed a longer span if asked to recode the stimuli in a speech-based memory code rather than keeping to a sign-based memory code (Hall & Bavelier, submitted). This finding is all the more surprising given that recoding into a different language is typically viewed as taxing to the WM system and thus expected to decrease span, compared to keeping information in the same language. Together, these findings point to the initial encoding and maintenance of information in a sign-based code as resulting in a shorter STM span. Importantly, the reviewed research in bilinguals indicates that a shorter STM span should be expected when testing in sign language, independently of auditory deprivation.

On the basis of the evidence reviewed so far, it might seem reasonable to conclude that sign language may be a poor choice when it comes to developing WM skills. It is not the case, however, that signing always leads to lesser WM performance. First, Hall and Bavelier (ibid) presented ASL-English bilinguals with digit sequences in either ASL or English and factorially manipulated the code used during recoding (sign vs. speech) and recall (sign vs. speech). Although the presentation and recoding stages favored speech-based representations, using sign during the recall phase led to *longer* spans than recalling in speech (all other parameters being equal). Clearly, sign use is not always an impediment to span size. Second, it is important to stress that not all memory spans are shorter in signers. Visuospatial spans are equivalent or larger in signers, as detailed later. Finally, as we discuss in the next paragraph, the studies that have compared signers to speakers in linguistic memory tasks document equivalent recall performance whether speech or sign is used, as long as the task does not require maintenance of the serial order.

Free recall, or the capacity to report a supra-span list in any order, is equivalent in adults deaf ASL signers and hearing English speakers (Hanson, 1982, 1990). Hanson's results from between-subjects studies have been replicated in within-subject studies. Bavelier et al. (2008) administered a free recall task to native ASL-English hearing bilinguals and found that, although subjects were more likely to spontaneously retain order information in the English condition, they recalled just as many items in the ASL condition. Boutla et al. (2004) found equivalent speaking span in deaf native signers and hearing native speakers using an ASL adaptation of Daneman and Carpenter's (1980) speaking span task, which does not require subjects to encode serial order. In this task, deaf subjects were presented with a list of signs. Rather than recalling the list in order, their task was to generate a separate ASL sentence for each word in the list. The fact that deaf signers and hearing speakers performed equivalently suggests that the factors responsible for the differences in STM span were not central to this task, which is arguably closer to the demands of natural language use than a tasks-like digit span.

Unfortunately, much less evidence is available from children concerning WM tasks. A study by Liben (1979) documents similar performance between deaf and hearing children when presented with a set of 16 line drawings to recall. (Although the abstract mentions lesser recall in the deaf children, the careful reader will see that deaf and hearing recall is equivalent in 17 of the 18 comparisons made. A very anomalous data point in deaf third graders entirely drives the population difference—see Table 1, p. 111.). Unlike the typical free recall paradigm used in adults, the items were presented at once rather than serially, thus making a direct comparison difficult. Interestingly, deaf and hearing children were similarly able to use semantic information to organize recall. In light of the difference in outcome when comparing deaf and hearing adults on STM serial span tasks versus WM tasks, further investigations of WM in deaf children would seem highly valuable.

In summary, the speech-based advantage documented by STM studies is restricted to linguistic serial span tasks. In other words, it only applies to tasks that use stimuli that can be named and that require items to be recalled in the correct temporal order. It happens that such serial span tasks have been the focus of much study in speakers, probably due to the prevalence of speech-based coding strategies in speakers (Cowan, Saults, & Brown, 2004). However, recall of ordered lists of nameable items is not by any means a general feature of linguistic

WM. On all other aspects of linguistic WM, signers and speakers appear comparable.

Consequences of Differences in Linguistic Short-term Memory Span

The research we just reviewed indicates that the serial STM span for linguistic stimuli is greater in individuals who rely on a speech-based code than in those who do not rely on such a code, either because of the language they use (signed language) or because of a lack of experience with speech-based representations, as in the case of profoundly deaf individuals. What, if any, are the theoretical and practical consequences of this difference?

First, as STM serial span tasks remain prevalent in the clinical and educational settings (Pisoni, 2001), it will be crucial to not compare the scores of deaf individuals to the established norms for hearing individuals. Indeed, clinical and educational evaluation of WM capacities in deaf individuals often rely on span measures such as those just discussed (see for example the digit span in the Wechsler Scale of Intelligence). A span of 4 in a deaf individual should not be compared to the benchmark of 7+/−2 derived from studies of speakers, but rather to the 5+/−1 observed in deaf signers. Just as one would compare Welsh speakers to one another rather than to English speakers (see Ellis & Hennelly, 1980), one should compare deaf individuals to their appropriate benchmark. In the absence of such a reevaluation, patients or students who rely on a sign-based code are at risk of being misdiagnosed and misjudged.

Second, the ability to repeat a meaningless sequence is only interesting to the extent that it predicts other cognitive skills, such as reading or the ability to perform mental arithmetic. This link has been established when testing hearing children in a spoken language; however, whether such a relationship holds for deaf children remains largely unexplored. Combined with the fact that recent advances in the field of WM cast doubts on the usefulness of STM span tasks as predictive of executive skills and cognition in general (Cowan, Elliott, Saults, Morey, Mattox, Hismjatullina, & Conway, 2005), this work highlights the importance of going beyond STM span measures and developing WM measures that more directly predict cognitive capacities.

Third, under the assumption that a bigger STM span is better for cognition, it might be tempting to think that if we could simply teach deaf individuals to rely on speech-based representations in memory, their STM span would increase, and that in turn might increase cognitive skills across the board. However, to embrace such an interpretation would be to miss a major point. We do not dispute that if deaf individuals were to rely on speech-based representations in STM tasks, their span scores would likely increase (cf. Chapter 29, this volume). It is the second step, the leap from increased STM serial span performance to general cognitive improvement, on which we strongly urge caution. The work on hearing bilinguals illustrates the potential pitfall of this argument. It is true that the STM span of bilinguals can be increased by switching from a sign-based to a speech-based code. Yet, most will agree that this increase does not reflect a general change in the cognitive abilities of the individual tested. This calls for caution when considering the proposal of increasing the STM span of deaf individuals to achieve greater parity with their hearing peers. If the increase in span is mediated through a switch from a sign-based to a speech-based code, as is the case in bilinguals, its consequences for cognitive abilities are likely to be limited to tasks that rely heavily on memory mechanisms involving speech-based representations, such as rehearsal, but may be of lesser consequence otherwise.

Differences in Visuospatial Short-term Memory Span
Enhanced Visuospatial Short-term Memory in Deaf Signers

In contrast to the lower performance observed in linguistic STM tasks, deaf signers perform as well as, and sometimes better than, hearing individuals in serial STM tasks that do not use linguistic stimuli, such as the Corsi block task. This task is a visuospatial equivalent of the digit span task. Typically, participants are presented with a board on which there are nine cubes. The experimenter touches a sequence of cubes one after the other. The participant is asked to reproduce the sequence executed by the experimenter. The test starts with short sequences (one or two cubes). Sequence length increases as in the digit span, and testing typically stops when participants make two errors at a given list length. Most studies focusing on deaf native signers, children or adults, report a longer visuospatial span than in hearing nonsigners (Hirshorn, Fernandez & Bavelier, submitted; Geraci et al., 2008; Wilson et al., 1997). Two studies of deaf participants with more diverse backgrounds revealed a similar visuospatial span to hearing participants (Alamargot, Lambert, Thebault, & Dansac, 2007; Logan, Mayberry, & Fletcher, 1996; note that these two studies use a two-dimensional computer adaptation of the Corsi block task whereas the others use physical blocks).

Exposure to sign during development may be an important factor for exhibiting a visuospatial STM advantage, as exemplified by a study in which three groups of hearing children were studied. The first group enrolled in a sign language class, the second group enrolled in a spoken second-language class, and the third group received no such instruction (Capirci, Cattani, Rossini, & Volterra, 1998). Children who received sign instruction exhibited significantly increased visuospatial span at the end of their year of training, whereas the other groups did not. Exposure to sign early in life may be crucial, as hearing individuals who acquired British Sign Language (BSL) as adults showed the same Corsi span performance as hearing controls unfamiliar with sign language (Keehner & Gathercole, 2007). The available literature therefore indicates an advantage in the Corsi block task for deaf native signers, with a possible effect due to early exposure to sign. The relative contribution of auditory deprivation versus sign exposure to this enhancement remains, however, to be more fully elucidated.

The view that deaf signers have enhanced visuospatial skills finds further support in the literature (Emmorey, Kosslyn, & Bellugi, 1993). Tests of mental rotation (Emmorey & McCullough, 1998; McKee, 1988), memory for number in spatial arrays (Zarfaty, Nunes, & Bryant, 2004), and face recognition (Bellugi & Hickok, 1993) all reveal significant advantages for deaf signers. In addition, a strong preference in deaf children for spatial coding in memory has been reported. When deaf and hearing children are asked to recall the "middle" digit from a group of three sequentially presented digits, but with a temporal order incongruent with the left-to-right spatial order, deaf children choose the spatially middle digit whereas hearing children choose the temporally middle one (Hermelin & O'Connor, 1975; O'Connor & Hermelin, 1973). Additional evidence, albeit indirect, comes from a Concentration/Memory game study in which subjects had to remember the spatial locations of cards of faces or shoes and then find their matches in a matrix of cards (Arnold & Mills, 2001). The use of a within-category set (all shoes or all faces) prevented efficient verbal tagging of the objects. Under these circumstances, deaf signers needed fewer attempts to find the matches than did hearing nonsigners. Together, these results are suggestive of a visuospatial advantage in deaf signers. The relative contributions of deafness and signing in those effects is not always known. Some aspects of visuospatial processing, such as mental rotation or face processing, can clearly be modified through signing alone; yet for other visuospatial tasks the evidence is less clear (see Emmorey, 1998; Keehner & Gathercole, 2007 for evidence that hearing signers outperform hearing nonsigners on these tasks).

Temporal Order, Deafness, and the Visual Modality

The shorter span observed in deaf signers when using linguistic serial span tasks has led some to argue that there may be qualitative differences in the processing of temporal order information between deaf and hearing individuals (Bavelier et al., 2008; Bonvillain, AlthausRea, Orlansky, & Slade, 1987; O'Connor & Hermelin, 1973; Wilson, 2001). The argument is generally based on the idea that the visual modality is specialized for processing information presented simultaneously across space, whereas the auditory modality is specialized for processing information presented sequentially across time. In addition to being an oversimplification of the visual and auditory systems, this view predicts that deaf individuals should be disadvantaged on most tasks requiring temporal processing. Indeed, under the assumption that audition is typically the dominant sensory modality for time processing, lack of audition may be expected to lead to deficits in temporal processing (Heming & Brown, 2005; Kowalska & Szelag, 2006; Sterritt, Camp, & Lipman, 1966). As we reviewed earlier with the Corsi block span, deaf signers are in fact advantaged on some tasks involving temporal order, provided that these tasks fall outside the linguistic domain. In addition, deaf and hearing individuals have also been found to perform similarly on tasks that require matching or copying temporal patterns in the motor domain (Anooshian & Bryan, 1979; Blair, 1957), as well as on fine temporal order judgment in the visual modality (Mills, 1985; Nava, Bottari, Zampini, & Pavani, 2008; Poizner & Tallal, 1987).

Thus, performance differences in temporal order processing are not seen in the visuospatial or motor domains, but rather appear to be restricted to memory tasks that rely on the use of lists of unrelated nameable items. Therefore, the sign disadvantage noted on linguistic serial STM tasks is not due to a generalized problem in encoding temporal order per se. Rather, we propose below that this discrepancy emerges from the greater tendency of hearing individuals to rely on chunking temporally adjacent units and on rote rehearsal of speech-based representations in the phonological loop. These two strategies naturally preserve the type of serial information required in linguistic serial recall tasks.

American Sign Language and the Visuospatial Loop

Enhanced memory for spatial locations in deaf signers could be viewed as the signature that WM in deaf signers is mediated through the visuospatial sketchpad. After all, even linguistic information in ASL contains visuospatial information, and the observed STM span for linguistic stimuli falls precisely in the range that Cowan (2001) has argued to be characteristic of information that is not processed by the phonological loop. However, recent developments in the field make this view unlikely.

There is now good evidence that signed languages are full-fledged natural languages, and that they embody all the levels of representations, including phonology, morphology, and syntax, found in natural languages. As such, memory in deaf signers exhibits all of the effects diagnostic of the phonological loop described in speakers (see earlier review). Deaf signers, therefore, rely on sign-based phonological encoding and a subarticulatory mechanism to maintain signs in linguistic STM (for a review see Wilson & Emmorey, 2000), dispelling the view that hearing speakers rely on the phonological loop but deaf signers rely on the visuospatial sketchpad for linguistic memory. This is not to say that the modality of the language does not affect memory processes (Wilson et al., 1997). We argue here that signers and speakers are comparable in their reliance on phonological encoding, but differ in their use of rehearsal, with speakers displaying an overwhelming reliance on rehearsal. The view that memory for linguistic material involves two distinct phonological processes is not new. Studies using articulatory suppression have identified, on the one hand, phonological information in long-term memory that is not subject to suppression and, on the other hand, phonological information in the rehearsal loop that may be actively suppressed (Besner, 1987; Besner & Davelaar, 1982).

The view that memory for linguistic material is mediated through the phonological loop and memory for visual images is mediated through the visuospatial sketchpad is, at best, a gross approximation. Recent work on visual memory identifies two rather different paths to memory for visual images: one for locations, and another for objects. First, memory for spatial locations appears to be truly based on a visuospatial buffer and on a prospective motor code for simulation or rehearsal (Awh & Jonides, 2001; Postle et al., 2006) in a manner much akin to the phonological buffer and the articulatory

loop for spoken information. For example, STM for locations can be mediated by preparing for a motor plan toward the to-be-remembered location (saccade or grasp) and retaining that motor plan as a prospective memory (Curtis, Rao, & D'Esposito, 2004). In some cases, allocating covert attention to the to-be-remembered locations has been hypothesized to be enough to refresh memory for locations (Awh & Jonides, 2001). Whether such movements of attention can be dissociated from an intention to move the eyes remains a topic of debate, but together this work points to visuospatial coding and prospective motor planning as key components of that memory system. Short-term memory for ASL may rely in part on such processes (Wilson, 2001); more work is needed, however, to confirm this view. Second, memory for visual objects relies on a different set of mechanisms. Memory for visual objects relies on object feature coding, as well as on the phonological codes that the object and its features evoke (e.g., coming up with the sound form "red truck" upon seeing the picture of a red truck). Much of the research on STM for objects documents that, upon viewing an object, its name is retrieved and used to mediate STM performance (Della Sala, Gray, Baddeley, Allamano, & Wilson, 1999; Postle, D'Esposito, & Corkin, 2005; Postle & Hamidi, 2007; Smith, Jonides, Koepe, Awh, Schumacher, & Minoshima, 1995). Accordingly, and unlike memory for positions, memory for objects engages similar brain regions in the left hemisphere as memory for linguistic stimuli (Smith et al., 1995). In speakers, the contribution of the phonological loop in STM tasks for visual objects is so prevalent that it has hindered, if not prevented, the study of the other buffer systems that may contribute to memory (Brandimonte, Hitch, & Bishop, 1992). Some studies have tried to disable this phonological route by using concurrent articulatory suppression or by presenting participants with entirely novel shapes. Interpretation of the former is difficult, as it changes the nature of the test to a dual task and thus introduces new confounds; even in the latter case, when novel shapes are used, participants are found to give names to the novel objects or scenes so as to better perform the memory task, thus defeating the purpose of using novel shapes (for discussion of this issue see Cowan et al., 2005; Postle & Hamidi, 2007). This work illustrates that memory processes may be best understood as multiple components working in parallel, rather than specialized components for different types of information.

The earlier sections outlined the properties of WM as they relate to deafness and sign language. The next sections turn to the practical and theoretical consequences of this work.

Caveats in Using a Linguistic Short-term Memory Span as a Predictor of Working Memory

On the basis of the highly specific difference in linguistic STM span, it may be tempting to conclude that sign language use compromises WM capacity for language functions and that speech is therefore preferable. This view, rooted in the use of linguistic serial span tasks to measure memory capacity, is ill-conceived. As argued by Cowan et al. (2005), linguistic serial STM span tasks may be far from optimal for measuring general WM capacity. Indeed, by heavily weighing on rote rehearsal and temporal grouping processes (e.g., chunking), these tasks reveal the characteristics of these processes but fail to uncover the more fundamental aspects of WM, such as flexible retrieval and manipulation of information in the service of cognition. The rather automatic chaining of words that supports rote rehearsal is a far cry from the complex set of interactive routines that allow humans to retrieve information and perform computation on line. In accordance with this view, the recent literature on WM suggests that STM serial span tasks are poor predictors of other cognitive skills. An exhaustive review by Cowan et al. (2005) argues that STM span tasks capture only a small portion of inter-individual differences on cognitive and psychometric measures. This is in accord with an earlier meta-analysis (Mukunda & Hall, 1992). These authors tested within-age correlations between various WM tasks and aptitude tests in adults and children. The digit span task captured only a small amount of the variance ($R = .22$). In contrast, a WM task such as the reading span was a more robust predictor ($R = .43$). The reading span was developed by Daneman and Carpenter (1980) to better capture WM during language processing. The reading span requires subjects to read several sentences aloud and then report the last word of each read sentence. Order of recall is irrelevant. As with most WM tasks, rote rehearsal and chunking are not effective strategies, due to the need to continually process new information. Note that on a sign-adapted equivalent of Daneman and Carpenter's speaking span task, deaf signers and hearing speakers did not differ (Boutla et al., 2004).

It is important to recognize that the ability to maintain temporal order information is a key component of cognition. It is necessary during language parsing or for core cognitive skills such as understanding causes and effects (McElree, Foraker, & Dyer, 2003; Sperber, Premack, & Premack, 1995). The crucial issue concerns how one should test for this ability. We suggest that by relying so heavily on rote rehearsal and grouping over time, STM span tasks highlight capacities that are specialized for ordered recall of word lists in speakers, but do not capture the essence of the temporal processing that supports language or cognitive skills in general. Recent research that goes beyond STM for lists of unrelated items provides support for this point. First, it has been argued that for materials that provide a conceptual frame, such as scenes or sentences, STM performance is based on the episodic buffer and not on ordered phonological representations like those mediating rote rehearsal (Potter, 1999; Potter & Lombardi, 1990).

Second, much of the work on sentence processing and WM documents that the type of order information necessary during sentence processing differs from that which mediates recall of unrelated words (Lewis, Vasishth, & Van Dyke, 2006; McElree et al., 2003). Temporal processing as indexed by STM serial span tasks is slow and rather inflexible, as items are chained one after the other through rehearsal. In contrast, the type of temporal order processing required in most cognitive tasks is fast and quite flexible, allowing a recombination of components. This latter temporal information is hypothesized to be available at the level of the episodic buffer. This view holds that, although many linguistic processes include elements that are serially ordered on the surface (e.g., the order of phonemes in a spoken word, or lexical items in a signed sentence), this is not the level of representation that is recruited for WM or cognition at large. For example, when reading a sentence, each word is encountered in serial order. However, when comprehending a sentence, one does not simply store an ordered list of lexical items; instead, temporal order is combined with the derived syntactic and semantic information to support understanding. The episodic buffer becomes the key element, as it directly links semantic information already associated with the to-be-remembered item, to the context in which the item occurred, including temporal information. It is by this mechanism that even patients with significant phonological loop problems can understand and recall paragraphs of prose. Thus, the weakness of the serial span task as a predictor of cognition is that it does not engage the same type of temporal order processing or the same type of memory representations as those involved in language comprehension and production, and cognitive manipulation in general. Attempts to link differences in literacy to deficits in linguistic STM span (Alamargot et al., 2007) should, therefore, be considered with caution.

New Advances in Working Memory Research and Predictions: The Multiple Coding Hypothesis

A reemerging view in the field of WM is that of the multiple-coding hypothesis (Bavelier, 1999; Postle & Hamidi 2007; Wickens, Nield, Tuber, & Wickens, 1973), which holds that memory is best served by recoding the information into as many mental codes as possible. Such multiple-coding renders the trace more resistant to specific interference, and naturally allows the various dimensions associated with an event to become integrated into one memory trace. There is much evidence for the availability of multiple memory codes upon presentation of a stimulus. For example, upon hearing the speech sound corresponding to dog, a phonological code (e.g., /d/ /ɔ/ share/g/) is quickly derived, which then contacts with its corresponding semantic code (conceptual information about dogs). As activation spreads through long-term memory, orthographic codes and further lexical information become available (Harm & Seidenberg, 1999). Similarly, upon viewing a visual scene, semantic information is quickly retrieved, thus allowing further phonological and lexical information to be activated (Intraub, 1981; Potter, 1975a, 1983; Rousselet, Fabre-Thorpe, & Thorpe, 2002). As captured by the proposal of Baddeley and collaborators, each of these codes has a role to play in the STM maintenance of incoming information. On these grounds, the observed patterns of similarities and differences between deaf signers and hearing speakers may reflect differences in the degree to which these populations preferentially rely on one versus another of these multiple codes. All populations are assumed to access these memory codes, but hearing speakers exhibit a strong tendency to rely on speech-based codes and the articulatory loop across a variety of tasks, not only for tasks using linguistic stimuli, but also when asked to remember pictures or simple visual shapes. On the other hand, deaf signers viewing sign stimuli would engage sign-based phonological representations, memory for spatial locations, and memory

for semantic information in a more balanced fashion. Such multiple recoding may be relatively automatic for signers, as spatial and semantic information is known to be readily afforded by visual presentation (Potter, 1975b; Thorpe, Fize, & Marlot, 1996).

The multiple coding hypothesis not only holds that information gets recoded in as many memory codes as the stimulus affords, but also highlights the central role of episodic coding in the establishment and maintenance of short-term memories. Encoding in the episodic buffer allows for a unique representation in memory of an event in the world, by appropriately tagging each event with respect to its location of appearance, its time of appearance, and the context in which it appeared. This level of encoding is a cornerstone of cognition, and has been hypothesized to provide the elementary functions necessary to develop skills as varied as the ability to track several objects over time (Pylyshyn, 2007), the ability to enumerate quantities (Carey & Xu, 2000; Feigen, Dehaene, & Spelke, 2004), and to bootstrap linguistic distinctions like that between mass and count nouns (Huntley-Fenner, Carey, & Solimando, 2002), to cite a few. A level of processing so central to cognition would benefit from further characterization. In part, this level has been difficult to study in speakers, because they readily default to the phonological loop whenever possible. To avoid such bias, recent tasks have mostly increased in complexity, requiring subjects to multitask on several memory codes at once. Such complexity introduces unwanted complications (see Cowan et al., 2005, for a discussion of these complications). Deaf signers may provide a more direct route to studying episodic coding, as the phonological loop bias that typically overshadows other types of coding in hearing individuals is not as dominant (for a similar point see Rudner & Rönnberg, 2008).

Caveats About the Deaf Population Studied

Most of the data reviewed here were collected from deaf native signers, who make up only a small percentage of the Deaf community (<8%). The focus on deaf signers has been scientifically motivated by the desire to study the impact of auditory deprivation on cognitive processes in the absence of other potentially confounding factors, such as delayed first-language acquisition, neurological sequelae associated with late-onset deafness, or atypical socialization patterns, to cite a few. Yet, understanding the fundamentals of WM in deaf native signers provides only a starting point for exploring how WM might differ in deaf populations with different characteristics (e.g., children and adults with cochlear implants, deaf individuals who do not sign, etc.). It will be crucial in future work to be more inclusive and characterize how deaf populations with different backgrounds vary in their WM processes.

Summary and Conclusions

Working memory is clearly fundamental to all areas of cognition. The evidence reviewed here demonstrates that deaf and hearing individuals have access to the same subsystems for WM. Accordingly, deaf and hearing populations exhibit similar WM capacity and overlapping brain systems for WM. This basic equivalence has been obscured by excessive focus on STM serial span tasks, which highlight the efficiency of articulatory rehearsal in speakers rather than serve as a reliable predictor of WM (Cowan et al., 2005).

The observation that speakers generally outperform signers in linguistic serial span tasks has led to the notion that speech-based skills must therefore be preferred over other skills in the service of cognition, particularly in reading (e.g. Wang, Trezek, Luckner, & Paul, 2008). However, the evidence reviewed suggests that such an assumption may be misguided. Most cognitive activities involve much more than simply retaining strings of items in serial order, a task at which the phonological loop excels. When faced with complex and naturalistic tasks, both deaf and hearing individuals have a full complement of WM systems at their command. Although signers and speakers may differ in the extent to which they call upon any given subsystem, the available evidence indicates that their ultimate attainment is equal.

Acknowledgments

We are indebted to M.C. Potter, E.L. Newport, and T. Supalla for the many insightful discussions over the years that have led to this work. We thank N. Fernandez and B. McDonald for their helpful comments on the manuscript, and B. Hubert-Wallander for help with figures and manuscript preparation. This work was supported by the National Institutes of Health (DC04418) and the Charles A. Dana Foundation.

References

Alamargot, D., Lambert, E., Thebault, C., & Dansac, C. (2007). Text composition by deaf and hearing middle-school students: The role of working memory. *Reading and Writing*, 20(4), 333–360.

Anooshian, L., & Bryan, J. (1979). The effects of early auditory deprivation on temporal perceptions: A comparison of hearing and hearing impaired children on temporal pattern matching tasks. *Journal of Speech and Hearing Research*, 22, 731–746.

Arnold, P., & Mills, M. (2001). Memory for faces, shoes and objects by deaf and hearing signers and hearing nonsigners. *Journal of Psycholinguistic Research*, 30(2), 185–195.

Awh, E., & Jonides, J. (2001). Overlapping mechanisms of attention and spatial working memory. *Trends in Cognitive Sciences*, 5(3), 119–126.

Baddeley, A. (1986). *Working memory*. Oxford: Clarendon Press.

Baddeley, A. (2003a). Working memory and language: An overview. *Journal of Communication Disorders*, 36, 189–208.

Baddeley, A. (2003b). Working memory: Looking back and looking forward. *Nature Reviews Neuroscience*, 4, 829–839.

Baddeley, A., & Hitch, G. J. (1974). Working memory. In G. H. Bower (Ed.), *The psychology of learning and motivation* (Vol. 8, pp. 742–775). London: Academic Press.

Baddeley, A., & Lewis, V. (1984). When does rapid presentation enhance digit span? *Bulletin of the Psychonomic Society*, 22(5), 403–405.

Baddeley, A. D. (2000). The episodic buffer: a new component of working memory? *Trends in Cognitive Sciences*, 4(11), 417–423.

Bavelier, D. (1999). Role and nature of object representations in perceiving and acting. In V. Coltheart (Ed.), *Fleeting memories* (pp. 151–180). Cambridge, MA: MIT Press.

Bavelier, D., Newman, A., Mukherjee, M., Hauser, P., Kemeny, S., Braun, A. R., & Boutla, M. (2008). Neural correlates of short-term memory span in deaf native signers. *Cerebral Cortex*, 18(10), 2263–2274.

Bavelier, D., Newport, E. L., Hall, M. L., Supalla, T., & Boutla, M. (2006). Persistent difference in short-term memory span between sign and speech: Implications for cross-linguistic comparisons. *Psychological Science*, 17(12), 1090–1092.

Bavelier, D., Newport, E. L., Hall, M. L., Supalla, T., & Boutla, M. (2008). Ordered short-term memory differs in signers and speakers: Implications for models of short-term memory. *Cognition*, 107(2), 433–459.

Bellugi, U., & Fisher, S. (1972). A Comparison of sign language and spoken language. *Cognition*, 1, 173–200.

Bellugi, U., & Hickok, G. (1993). Clues to the neurobiology of language. In R. Broadwell (Ed.), *Decade of the brain* (Vol. 1).

Bellugi, U., Klima, E., & Siple, P. (1974-1975). Remembering in signs. *Cognition*, 3(2), 93–125.

Bellugi, U., & Siple, P. (1974). Remembering with and without words. In F. Bresson (Ed.), *Current problems in psycholinguistics* (pp. 215–236). Paris: Centre National de la Recherche Scientifique.

Besner, D. (1987). Phonology, lexical access in reading, and articulatory suppression: A critical review. *Quarterly Journal of Experimental Psychology*, 39A, 467–478.

Besner, D., & Davelaar, E. (1982). Basic processes in reading: Two phonological codes. *Canadian Journal of Psychology*, 36, 701–711.

Blair, F. X. (1957). A study of the visual memory of deaf and hearing children. *American Annals of the Deaf*, 102, 254–263.

Bonvillain, J. D., AlthausRea, C., Orlansky, M. D., & Slade, L. A. (1987). The effect of sign language rehearsal on deaf subjects' immediate and delayed recall of English word lists. *Applied Psycholinguistics*, *8*, 33–54.

Boutla, M., Supalla, T., Newport, L., & Bavelier, D. (2004). Short-term memory span: insights from sign language. *Nature Neuroscience*, *7*, 997–1002.

Brandimonte, M. A., Hitch, G. J., & Bishop, D. V. M. (1992). Influences of short-term memory codes on visual image processing: Evidence from image transformation task. *Journal of Experimental Psychology: Learning, Memory, and Cognition*, *18*, 157–165.

Buchsbaum, B., Pickell, B., Love, T., Hatrack, M., Bellugi, U., & Hickok, G. (2005). Neural substrates for verbal working memory in deaf signers: fMRI study and lesion case report. *Brain and Language*, *95*(2), 265–272.

Capirci, O., Cattani, A., Rossini, P., & Volterra, V. (1998). Teaching sign language to hearing children as a possible factor in cognitive enhancement. *Journal of Deaf Studies and Deaf Education*, *3*, 135–142.

Carey, S., & Xu, F. (2000). Infants' knowledge of objects: beyond object files and object tracking. *Cognition*, *80*(1–2), 179–213.

Chein, J. M., & Fiez, J. A. (2001). Dissociation of verbal working memory system components using a delayed serial recall task. *Cerebral Cortex*, *11*, 1003–1014.

Conrad, R. (1970). Short-term memory processes in the deaf. *British Journal of Psychology*, *61*(2), 179–195.

Conrad, R. (1972). Short-term memory in the deaf: A test for speech coding. *British Journal of Psychology*, *63*(2), 173–180.

Cowan, N. (2001). The magical number 4 in short-term memory: A reconsideration of mental storage capacity. *Behavioral and Brain Sciences*, *24*, 87–185.

Cowan, N. (2008). What are the differences between long-term, short-term and working memory? *Progress in Brain Research*, *169*, 323–338.

Cowan, N., Elliott, E. M., Saults, J. S., Morey, C. C., Mattox, S., Hismjatullina, A., & Conway, A. R. A. (2005). On the capacity of attention: Its estimation and its role in working memory and cognitive aptitudes. *Cognitive Psychology*, *51*, 42–100.

Cowan, N., Saults, J. S., & Brown, G. D. (2004). On the auditory modality superiority effect in serial recall: Separating input and output factors. *Journal of Experimental Psychology: Learning, Memory, and Cognition*, *30*(3), 639–644.

Curtis, C. E., Rao, V. Y., & D'Esposito, D. (2004). Maintenance of spatial and motor codes during oculomotor delayed response tasks. *Journal of Neuroscience*, *24*(16), 3944–3952.

Daneman, M., & Carpenter, P. A. (1980). Individual differences in working memory and reading. *Journal of Verbal Learning and Verbal Behavior*, *19*, 450–466.

Della Sala, S., Gray, C., Baddeley, A., Allamano, N., & Wilson, L. (1999). Pattern span: A tool for unwelding visuospatial memory. *Neuropsychologia*, *37*, 1189–1199.

Elliott, J. M. (1992). Forward digit span and articulation speed for Malay, English and two Chinese dialects. *Perceptual and Motor Skills*, *74*, 291–295.

Ellis, N. C., & Hennelly, R. A. (1980). A bilingual word-length effect: Implications for intelligence testing and the relative ease of mental calculation in Welsh and English. *British Journal of Psychology*, *71*, 43–51.

Emmorey, K. (1998). The impact of sign language use on visuospatial cognition. In M. Marschark & M. D. Clark (Eds.), *Psychological perspectives on deafness* (Vol. 2, pp. 19–52). Mahwah, NJ: Lawrence Erlbaum Associates, Inc.

Emmorey, K., & McCullough, S. (1998). Mental rotation within linguistic and non-linguistic domains in users of American sign language. *Cognition*, *68*(3), 221–246.

Emmorey, K. D., Kosslyn, S. M., & Bellugi, U. (1993). Visual imagery and visual-spatial language: Enhanced imagery abilities in deaf and hearing ASL signers. *Cognition*, *46*, 139–181.

Engle, R. W., Kane, M. J., & Tuholski, S. W. (1999). Individual differences in working memory capacity and what they tell us about controlled attention, general fluid intelligence, and functions of the Prefrontal Cortex. In A. Miyake & P. Shah (Eds.), *Models of working memory: mechanisms of active maintenance and executive control* (pp. 102–134). New York: Cambridge University Press.

Feigen, L., Dehaene, S., & Spelke, E. (2004). Core systems of number. *Trends in Cognitive Science*, *8*(7), 307–314.

Geraci, C., Gozzi, M., Papagno, C., & Cecchetto, C. (2008). How grammar can cope with limited short-term memory: Simultaneity and seriality in sign languages. *Cognition*, *106*(2), 780–804.

Hall, M., & Bavelier, D. (submitted). Short-term memory in sign vs speech: The source of the serial span discrepancy.

Hanson, V. L. (1982). Short-term recall by deaf signers of American Sign Language: Implications of encoding strategy for order recall. *Journal of Experimental Psychology: Learning, Memory, and Cognition*, *8*(6), 572–583.

Hanson, V. L. (1990). Recall of order information by deaf signers: Phonetic coding in temporal order recall. *Memory and Cognition*, *18*(6), 604–610.

Harm, M., & Seidenberg, M. (1999). Phonology, reading acquisition, and dyslexia: Insights from connectionist models. *Psychological Review*, *106*(3), 491–528.

Heming, J. E., & Brown, L. N. (2005). Sensory temporal processing in adults with early hearing loss. *Brain and Cognition*, *59*(2), 173–182.

Henson, R. N. A., Burgess, N., & Frith, C. D. (2000). Recoding, storage, rehearsal and grouping in verbal short-term memory: an fMRI study. *Neuropsychologia*, *38*, 426–440.

Hermelin, B., & O'Connor, N. (1975). The recall of digits by normal, deaf and autistic children. *British Journal of Psychology*, *66*(2), 203–209.

Hirshorn, Fernandez, N., & Bavelier, D. (submitted). Routes to short-term memory indexing in deaf native users of American Sign Language.

Huntley-Fenner, G., Carey, S., & Solimando, S. (2002). Objects are individuals but stuff doesn't count: Perceived rigidity and cohesiveness influence infants' representations of small groups of discrete entities. *Cognition*, *8*, 203–221.

Intraub, H. (1981). Rapid conceptual identification of sequentially presented pictures. *Journal of Experimental Psychology: Human Perception and Performance*, *7*(3), 604–610.

Keehner, M., & Gathercole, S. E. (2007). Cognitive adaptations arising from non-native experience of sign language in hearing adults. *Memory and Cognition*, *35*(4), 752–761.

Kosslyn, S. M. (1980). *Image and mind*. Cambridge, MA: Harvard University Press.

Kowalska, J., & Szelag, E. (2006). The effect of congenital deafness on duration judgement. *Journal of Child Psychology & Psychiatry*, *47*, 946–953.

Lewis, R. L., Vasishth, S., & Van Dyke, J. A. (2006). Computational principles of working memory in sentence comprehension. *Trends in Cognitive Sciences*, *10*(10), 447–454.

Liben, L. S. (1979). Free recall by deaf and hearing children: Semantic clustering and recall in trained and untrained groups. *Journal of Experimental Child Psychology*, *27*(1), 105–119.

Logan, K., Mayberry, M., & Fletcher, J. (1996). The short-term memory of profoundly Deaf people for words, signs, and abstract spatial stimuli. *Applied Cognitive Psychology*, *10*, 105–119.

Losiewicz, B. L. (2000). A specialized language system in working memory: Evidence from American Sign Language. *Southwest Journal of Linguistics*, *19*(1), 63–75.

MacSweeney, M., Campbell, R., & Donlan, C. (1996). Varieties of short-term memory coding in deaf teenagers. *Journal of Deaf Studies and Deaf Education*, *1*(4), 249–262.

Manoach, D. S., Greve, D. N., Lindgren, K. A., & Dale, A. M. (2003). Identifying regional activity associated with temporally separated components of working memory using event-related functional MRI. *Neuroimage*, *20*, 1670–1684.

Marschark, M. (1996). *Influences of signed and spoken language on memory span*. Paper presented at the Annual Meetings of the Psychonomic Society, Chicago, IL.

Marschark, M. (2005). Cognitive functioning in deaf adults and children. In M. Marschark & P. E. Spencer (Eds.), *Oxford handbook of deaf studies, language and education* (pp. 464–474). Oxford: Oxford University Press.

McElree, B., Foraker, S., & Dyer, L. (2003). Memory structures that subserve sentence comprehension. *Journal of Memory and Language*, *48*(1), 67–91.

McKee, D. (1988). An analysis of specialized cognitive functions in deaf and hearing signers. *Dissertation Abstracts International*, *49*:768.

Mills, C. (1985). Perception of visual temporal patterns by deaf and hearing adults. *Bulletin of the Psychonomic Society*, *23*, 483–486.

Miyake, A., & Shah, P. (1999). Toward unified theories of working memory: Emerging general consensus, unresolved theoretical issues, and future research directions. In A. Miyake & P. Shah (Eds.), *Models of working memory: Mechanisms of active maintenance and executive control*. New York: Cambridge University Press.

Mukunda, K. V., & Hall, V. C. (1992). Does performance on memory for order correlate with performance on standardized measures of ability? A meta-analysis. *Intelligence*, *16*(1), 81–97.

Nava, E., Bottari, D., Zampini, M., & Pavani, F. (2008). Visual temporal order judgment in profoundly deaf individuals. *Experimental Brain Research*, *190*, 170–188.

Norman, D., & Shallice, T. (1980). *Attention to action: Willed and automatic control of behaviour*. San Diego, CA: University of California.

O'Connor, N., & Hermelin, B. M. (1973). The spatial or temporal organization of short-term memory. *Quarterly Journal of Experimental Psychology*, *25*, 335–343.

Pintner, R., & Patterson, D. G. (1917). A comparison of deaf and hearing children in visual memory for digits. *Journal of Experimental Psychology*, *2*, 76–88.

Pisoni, D. B. (2001). Cognitive factors and cochlear implants: Some thoughts on perception, learning and memory in speech perception. *Ear and Hearing*, *21*(1), 70–78.

Poizner, H., & Tallal, P. (1987). Temporal processing in deaf signers. *Brain and Language*, *30*, 52–62.

Postle, B. R., D'Esposito, M., & Corkin, S. (2005). Effects of verbal and nonverbal interference on spatial and object visual working memory. *Memory and Cognition*, *33*(2), 203–212.

Postle, B. R., & Hamidi, M. (2007). Nonvisual codes and nonvisual brain areas support visual working memory. *Cerebral Cortex*, *17*(9), 2151–2162.

Postle, B. R., Idzikowski, C., Sala, S. D., Logie, R. H., & Baddeley, A. D. (2006). The selective disruption of spatial working memory by eye movements. *Quarterly Journal of Experimental Psychology*, *59*(1), 100–120.

Potter, M. C. (1975a). Meaning in visual search. *Science*, *187*(965–966).

Potter, M. C. (1975b). Time to understand pictures and words. *Nature*, *253*(5491), 437–438.

Potter, M. C. (1983). Representational buffers: The eye-mind hypothesis in picture perception, reading, and visual search. In K. Rayner (Ed.), *Eye movements in reading: Perceptual and language processes*. New York: Academic Press.

Potter, M. C. (1999). Understanding sentences and scenes: The role of conceptual short-term memory. In V. Coltheart (Ed.), *Fleeting memories*. Cambridge: MIT Press.

Potter, M. C., & Lombardi, L. (1990). regeneration in the short-term recall of sentences. *Journal of Memory and Language*, *29*, 633–653.

Pylyshyn, Z. W. (1989). The role of location indexes in spatial perception: A sketch of the FINST spatial-index model. *Cognition*, *32*, 65–97.

Pylyshyn, Z. W. (2007). *Things and place*. Cambridge: MIT Press.

Rönnberg, J., Rudner, M., & Ingvar, M. (2004). Neural correlates of working memory for sign language. *Brain Research; Cognitive Brain Research*, *20*(2), 165–182.

Rousselet, G. A., Fabre-Thorpe, M., & Thorpe, S. J. (2002). Parallel processing in high-level categorization of natural images. *Nature Neuroscience*, *5*, 629–630.

Rudner, M., & Rönnberg, J. (2008). The role of the episodic buffer in working memory for language processing. *Cognitive Processing*, *9*(1), 19–28.

Rypma, B., & D'Esposito, M. (1999). The roles of prefrontal brain regions in components of working memory: Effect of memory load and individual differences. *Proceedings of the National Academy of Sciences, United States of America*, *96*, 6558–6563.

Smith, E. E., Jonides, J., Koeppe, R. A., Awh, E., Schumacher, E. H., & Minoshima, S. (1995). Spatial versus object working memory: PET investigations. *Journal of Cognitive Neuroscience*, *7*(3), 357–375.

Sperber, D., Premack, D., & Premack, A. J. (Eds.). (1995). *Causal cognition: A multidisciplinary debate*. New York: Oxford University Press.

Sterritt, G. M., Camp, W., & Lipman, B. S. (1966). Effects of early auditory deprivation upon auditory and visual information processing. *Perceptual and Motor Skills*, *23*, 123–130.

Thorpe, S., Fize, D., & Marlot, C. (1996). Speed of processing in the human visual system. *Nature*, *381*(6 June), 520–522.

Tulving, E. (1983). *Elements of episodic memory*. Oxford: Clarendon Press.

Tulving, E. (2002). Episodic memory: from mind to brain. *Annual Review of Psychology*, *53*, 1–25.

Wager, T. D., & Smith, E. E. (2003). Neuroimaging studies of working memory: A meta-analysis. *Cognitive, Affective, & Behavioral Neuroscience*, *3*(4), 255–274.

Wang, Y., Trezek, B. J., Luckner, J. L., & Paul, P. V. (2008). The role of phonology and phonologically related skills in reading instruction for students who are deaf or hard of hearing. *American Annals of the Deaf*, *153*(4), 396–407.

Wickens, D. D., Nield, A. F., Tuber, D. S., & Wickens, C. D. (1973). Stimulus selection as a function of CS1-CS2 interval in compound classical conditioning of cats. *Journal of Comparative Physiological Psychology*, *85*(2), 295–303.

Wilson, M. (2001). The case for sensorimotor coding in working memory. *Psychonomic Bulletin and Review, 8*(1), 44–57.

Wilson, M., Bettger, J. G., Niculae, I., & Klima, E. S. (1997). Modality of language shapes working memory: Evidence from digit span and spatial span in ASL signers. *Journal of Deaf Studies and Deaf Education, 2*(3), 150–160.

Wilson, M., & Emmorey, K. (1997). A visuospatial "phonological loop" in working memory: Evidence from American Sign Language. *Memory & Cognition, 25*(3), 313–320.

Wilson, M., & Emmorey, K. (1998). A "word length effect" for sign language: Further evidence for the role of language in structuring working memory. *Memory & Cognition, 26*(3), 584–590.

Wilson, M., & Emmorey, K. (2000). When does modality matter? Evidence from ASL on the nature of working memory.

In K. Emmorey & H. Lane (Eds.), *The signs of language revisited. An anthology to honor Ursula Bellugi and Edward Klima.* (pp. 135–142). Mahwah, NJ: Lawrence Erlbaum Associates.

Wilson, M., & Emmorey, K. (2006a). Comparing sign language and speech reveals a universal limit on short-term memory capacity. *Psychological Science, 17,* 682–683.

Wilson, M., & Emmorey, K. (2006b). No difference in short-term memory span between sign and speech. *Psychological Science, 17*(12), 1093.

Wilson, M., & Emmorey, K. D. (2003). The effect of irrelevant visual input on working memory for sign language. *Journal of Deaf Studies and Deaf Education, 8*(2), 97–103.

Zarfaty, Y., Nunes, T., & Bryant, P. (2004). The performance of young deaf children in spatial and temporal number tasks. *Journal of Deaf Studies and Deaf Education, 9*(3), 139–181.

Paradigm Shifts, Difficult Truths, and an Increasing Knowledge Base in Deaf Education

Patricia Elizabeth Spencer *and* Marc Marschark

Abstract

Three major paradigm shifts or advances in knowledge have occurred in education and services for deaf and hard-of-hearing persons over the 20th and early 21st centuries: (1) sign languages have been recognized as complete and viable natural languages, leading to more appreciation for use in educational settings, as well as among deaf people; (2) technological advances, including more sophisticated hearing aids and cochlear implants, have increased access to sound and to spoken language; and (3) the identification of hearing loss in infancy and accompanying early intervention services have raised the rate and level of children's developmental progress. Despite advances, significant problems remain to be addressed. These include a lack of information about the development and needs of hard-of-hearing persons—despite the fact that they compose the largest proportion of the population with hearing loss, and with persons using cochlear implants functionally increasing that proportion. In addition, persons with multiple disabilities and those living in nonindustrialized countries have been insufficiently studied, and appear not to be benefiting from the aforementioned advances. Information is also lacking on causes of and effective responses to specific cognitive profiles identified for students with hearing loss, on effects of specific educational intervention approaches, and on patterns of social-emotional development and their interaction with other developmental areas. Increased focus is needed on the development and evaluation of interventions designed to assure that the advances made are shared across the population and impact varied aspects of development and achievement.

Keywords: deaf, hard-of-hearing, advances, knowledge base, research needs

Editors Note: As with the first Oxford Handbook of Deaf Studies, Language, and Education, *the two editors initially wrote the first and last chapters of this volume independently (note order of authorship on each). The first chapter was intended to provide an overview of the state-of-the-art of the field, with a particular emphasis on our reasons for pursuing a second volume: the desire to provide an up-to-date perspective on where the field is and where it is going, to own up to our own shortcomings in bridging the research–practice divide, and the need to bring together diverse kinds and sources of information relevant to deaf studies, language, and education into a (somewhat) coherent, synergistic whole. The final chapter was planned as an epilogue, outlining ways in which the chapters of this volume have moved us ahead and identifying "holes" that we have not been able to fill in either volume. It was with considerable surprise that, when we exchanged drafts, we found that the two chapters had almost the same foci, even if they came from somewhat different perspectives. After debating whether one or the other chapter should be eliminated or changed, we arrived at the unanimous conclusion that such convergence was telling us something—something about the field, those who work in it, and those for whom the work is done. So be it.*

Writing the final chapter of a volume like this one is a bit like cleaning up after a family reunion. First thoughts concern who got along and who didn't, who brought what, and who was missing.

The last of these invariably leads to discussion of how things have changed—and some ways in which they haven't. With fond memories (and some regrets) everyone then comes back to the present and looks to the future. "There is no way we would do this again!" But, then, someone has to.

Despite the remaining unfulfilled promises (see Chapter 1, this volume), the field of education for and research involving deaf and hard-of-hearing (DHH) persons has shown great advances recently. The chapters in this volume document those advances and put them into context(s). Of course, not all the questions have been answered, and there are others begging to be asked. There is much to be learned about the foundations of language, learning, culture, and social-emotional processes in deaf adults and children, just as there is still a substantial gap in translating many lines of research into effective practice. But we have not been standing still. Since the middle of the last century, for example, three paradigm shifts have occurred in the field of research and practice with deaf children and adults. We remember clearly how our lives and our work were affected by all three, even if some of the changes may have preceded the professional careers of many readers.

The first of these revolutionary changes was the scientific recognition of natural sign languages as viable and complete members of the family of languages (Stokoe, 1960/2005). (Many deaf people knew this all along, of course—but it apparently came as a surprise to some of them, as well as to the primarily hearing world of linguistics and psychology.) This led to a return to promoting the use of signs, although often not fully expressed sign languages, in the education of deaf children and to increased research interest in the communities of Deaf persons around the world (Woll & Ladd, 2003). It also enlarged the scope of what was thought of as "normal," and it without doubt enhanced the visibility and the stature of deaf persons in many, if not most, industrialized countries. This stature was confirmed, and the revolution was clearly underway, when fast-food and other entrepreneurial ventures began airing television advertisements with deaf, signing actors.

In addition to social advances, the shift to recognition and appreciation of natural sign languages and Deaf communities also changed the direction of scientific research and led inexorably to greater numbers of researchers and greater diversity in their backgrounds. Linguists, neuroscientists, sociologists, and anthropologists, both deaf and hearing, joined those educators and psychologists whose interests had already directed them toward research on deaf-related issues. Researchers already working in the field found their efforts subtly refocused. Overall, there was a sense of change, a sense of increasingly positive expectations, and a heightened appreciation by professionals working in "deafness" for the contributions of professionals from varied and diverse disciplines—and, as well, for the contributions of deaf scientists and members of the Deaf community to research and practice. There can be no denying that this shift resulted in faster and often less-biased accrual of research data and in improvements in the life experiences of many children and adults with hearing loss.

Then, although there was some temporal overlap, came the second shift. Technological advances promised that at least some people who were deaf could begin to receive and process auditory (or, some would say, "auditory-like") information (see Harkins & Bakke, 2003). Cochlear implants, at first designed for older persons who lost hearing fairly late in life, proved to be effective for many if not most children who had never heard or had heard only briefly before becoming deaf. At first, this seemed to be a direct challenge to the recognition that had by the late 20th century been accorded the Deaf community and the role of signing, if not sign language, in the lives of deaf people. Signing once again became a "straw person" against which those devoted to the development of spoken language skills could target their research and their practice. However, the very fact of the technical advance again widened the perspectives of professionals (not to mention parents) involved with deaf children and adults—and as any good teacher or cognitive scientist will tell you, encountering different views tends to result in a more complex and sophisticated zeitgeist. This, in turn, tends to lead to more advanced understandings and conceptual approaches to problem solving. Despite some initial discomfort in situations in which, for example, a neuroscientist, an engineer, a teacher, and a sociologist might enter into a discussion about research methods and results, original standpoints are often altered, and new and more cognitively sophisticated concepts can be generated. With luck and rational discussion, that may prove to be the outcome of this technological revolution (especially if we can get beyond the digging in of heels and gritting of teeth that has been commonplace in this field).

But wait, there's more. About the same time as the emergence of advanced educational (see Chapter 7, this volume) and audiological (see Chapter 26, this volume) approaches, new cost-effective technologies were emerging that made the identification of hearing loss during early infancy more widespread. It soon became apparent that early identification followed by quality early intervention programming could significantly enhance both the rate and the sophistication of DHH children's language development. These improvements quickly were recognized as influencing development in other domains as well (see Chapters 20 and 21, this volume). Invigorated by this progress, the field began to include professionals focused on early child development (yes, even infancy), cognitive as well as linguistic issues, family functioning and support (see Chapters 3 and 16, this volume) and, just as importantly, professionals in related medical and technological fields. Having facilitated meetings of hearing and deaf professionals from as many as 12 disciplines, as well as parents (themselves also often professionals in one field or another) of the children involved in such studies, we can state with confidence that the resulting discussions are lively. At the same time, although respect is shown and changes occur in individual's knowledge and beliefs, "agreement" cannot be said to characterize many of these meetings. Differences in opinion still occur—some based on evidence, some on experience, and some on philosophy. Perhaps not surprisingly, then, the virtual meeting represented by the chapters in this volume can be similarly characterized. But as Jean Piaget noted, it is in disequilibrium that cognitive advances are made.

The mix of topics represented in these chapters, as well as the backgrounds of the contributors, exemplify the diversity of investigations occurring and of information becoming available about DHH persons, their experiences, their learning styles, and their accomplishments, as well as about the approaches being taken to answer questions and overcome challenges that still remain. Researchers and service providers, as well as parents of children with hearing loss and DHH persons themselves, should be excited to see that professionals can address issues—from basic cognitive science to educational practice to culture and identity—from the variety of perspectives that are represented in this volume. We hope and believe that these chapters are indicative of a new openness between and among disciplines and will help to move some of the emotionally charged beliefs in the field to a more evidence-based level of discussion.

Indeed, this is a time of hope and change. The old expectations about the potential for children and adults with hearing loss have undergone rapid change. We can both remember the electrifying moment in 1988 when I. King Jordan told the world that "deaf people can do anything except hear." We suspect that Dr. Jordan would not at all mind the following, more recent comment from the father of a fluently signing child with an early-identified, profound hearing loss, now using a cochlear implant, who had just read aloud a passage from a textbook in clearly articulated speech: "Oh, yeah," the father said. "She's still deaf, but now she can hear." But in some ways, such advances only make the problems, gaps in knowledge, and as-yet-unfulfilled promises that much more evident and therefore increasingly difficult to ignore. So, let us touch on a few difficult, or at least uncomfortable, truths.

First, an alert reader may have noticed use of the term "deaf" in many statements above instead of the term "deaf and/or hard-of-hearing" frequently used in research and practice literature. This is because it is the group that is deaf about whom we know the most. As the Jamieson, Antia et al., and Marschark et al. chapters of this volume all point out, we still lack much information about the developmental influences and outcomes for students who are hard of hearing. This is a critical shortcoming, given that children with mild to severe hearing losses comprise a larger group than those who are profoundly deaf, and many, if not most, children who use cochlear implants function as if they are hard-of-hearing children. The argument for increased focus on this group of children (and perhaps adults as well) has been effectively made by Moeller, Tomblin, Yoshinaga-Itano, Connor, and Jerger (2007), and is implicit in many reports of research on the functioning of audiologically deaf children using cochlear implants. Increasing attention by researchers to the needs of children (as well as older persons) who are hard of hearing leads us to hope that more resources and more research will be directed toward methods to assure that their full potentials are achieved. However, it is a "difficult truth" that this large, diverse part of the population has been largely ignored. Perhaps their very diversity—in hearing abilities, as well as in many other areas of development—has deterred researchers, who need to be able to control "extraneous" variables. Perhaps research with hard-of-hearing youth and adults simply has not been considered as exciting as that with young deaf children.[1] Either way, the needs of hard-of-hearing persons can no longer be ignored.

Second, it should be noted that much of the research demonstrating positive results both for early intervention and for use of cochlear implants has highlighted children with average or above-average cognitive functioning (e.g., James, Rajput, Brinton, & Goswami, 2008; Stacey, Fortnum, Barton, & Summerfield, 2006). The presence of social, cognitive, or motor disabilities has been shown to limit benefits from cochlear implantation, and, in fact, many studies of outcomes from cochlear implant use have specifically excluded children with multiple disabilities (see Beadle, McKinley, Nikolopoulos, Brough, O'Donoghue, & Archbold, 2005). Thus, despite advances in our knowledge about causes and responses to multiple disabilities (Chapters 12 and 28, this volume), individuals with such challenges often have not benefited from the advances described earlier. Further, the degree to which they benefit—as well as the conditions under which benefits are best promoted—are little understood and rarely investigated. Given repeated indications that this is a large and growing segment of the population of individuals who are deaf or hard-of-hearing, additional efforts in research and the evaluation of programming efforts are an absolute necessity. Like many early studies of deaf children without additional disabilities, studies of this more complex portion of the population could profit from qualitative, process-oriented research designs or single-subject studies assessing the effects of particular interventions. Practices of either ignoring the relatively high frequency of disabilities among DHH persons or of considering these diverse individuals as one amorphous group simply will not move understanding and services ahead.

A third difficult and regrettable truth is that, as Leigh et al. (Chapter 23, this volume) point out, the advantages and advances of early identification of and intervention for hearing loss remain unavailable to the majority of the world's population of DHH children. Developing nations are estimated to have much higher rates of child hearing loss than more developed, industrialized countries, largely the result of differences in health-related conditions and the availability of medical services. Meanwhile, services in even some of the more developed countries remain far behind what is possible, and many questions remain about best, or at least most efficient methods of both identification and intervention for hearing loss in vast areas of the world. These questions need to be addressed systematically and energetically. Advances implemented in the most affluent and developed areas of the world should not allow us to forget that such advances need to be extended in ways that are appropriate for cultures and realities that differ from those in which they were initially developed.

Fourth, identification of differences in subcomponents of cognition (see Chapters 9, 29, and 30, this volume) between students with and without hearing loss lead to two associated questions: What is their source? What kind of interventions can best support learning by either taking advantage of or by remediating these differences? Answers proposed for the first question include the presence or absence of hearing experience and associated effects on neural development (Nicholas & Geers, 2007), secondary effects of levels of language use and ages at which they are attained (Hauser, Lukomski, & Hillman, 2008), and differences in interactive experiences during the early years (Marschark & Wauters, 2008).

It is probable that the primary source(s) will be found to differ depending upon the specific cognitive skill or ability being addressed—but to our minds, satisfactory answers are not available about causal factors for the learning differences that have been identified. That does not mean that answers to the second question need wait until investigation of causes is further along. It is time to begin systematically applying evidence-based intervention and remediation approaches that are aimed at matching the profiles of cognitive abilities as they are identified, not just for large groups of DHH students but for individuals. Such interventions could make use of a response-to-intervention (RTI) approach, an educational and assessment practice that is similar in structure to single-subject research designs in which an individual serves as his or her own control (and is also similar to the "diagnostic-teaching" model that was prevalent in some deaf education settings in the 1970s and 1980s). Systematically designed and evaluated interventions focused on individuals can provide a first step toward acting on rather than simply discussing learning and cognitive patterns of students with hearing loss. Specific approaches toward promoting both literacy and mathematics achievement of DHH students (Chapters 8, 10, and 11, this volume) that are already being implemented might be enriched by specifically targeting interventions to cognitive profiles (Akamatsu, Mayer, & Hardy-Braz, 2008).

Finally, although there has been considerable research and theoretical conceptualizing about identity formation in deaf as well as hard-of-hearing persons (Chapters 13 and 14, this volume), a stronger database is needed on social-emotional strengths and needs, as well as on patterns of development in children with hearing loss. In what way might psychosocial aspects of development reflect or potentially influence patterns of cognition and learning abilities? What long-term psychosocial effects will result from the technological advances and the changes in (or at least the increased options for) educational placements and communication being experienced (see Chapters 6, 15 and 17, this volume)? How does culture mediate development in various developmental domains?

Work on aspects of social-emotional development also needs to proceed with recognition that teachers and others who are directly engaged with DHH students continue to comment about an apparently high prevalence of behavioral and related difficulties. This situation continues in spite of all of the other advances that have been noted here and in other publications. Yes, prevalence and origins of social-emotional and behavioral difficulties must be systematically investigated to a greater extent. But identifying sources for such difficulties in patterns of parent–child interaction, language delays, peer experiences, or even alleged but not always clearly diagnosed organically based disabilities (e.g., autism and attention-deficit disorders) may not be sufficient. At best, such determinations would be only half the job. As with all the other areas we have discussed, systematic implementation of alternative interventions and nonbiased evaluation of results are required. Recognizing and validating the difficult truth of social-emotional and behavioral problems in the population of DHH children and adolescents is needed. To do otherwise benefits no one.

Despite these difficult, uncomfortable truths about gaps in knowledge and practice, the chapters of this volume remind us of all that has been learned and all that we are in the process of learning. Formerly contentious issues (e.g., effectiveness of intervention during infancy, benefits of cochlear implants, and effectiveness of sign languages to support development) can now be discussed with reference to burgeoning databases—and in most company, the discussion can be amicable. Much more is known now about language development across modalities and over time (see, for example, Chapters 18, 19, 21, 22, and 24 in this volume). Although it remains an area in need of intense research, significant amounts of data are available about educational approaches and outcomes (e.g., Chapters 11, 15, and 18 this volume), and researchers focused on basic cognitive processes have begun generating

testable hypotheses that have the potential to affect educational interventions (e.g., Chapters 9, 29, and 30, this volume).

The information presented in this volume is only a sampling of that being generated in the field. If our current pace can be maintained, it is almost impossible to envision the outcome of research and practice over the rest of this new century. Even given this rate of progress, however, we are confident that more than a few questions will remain. We are, however, equally confident that the diligent work of researchers, educators, and DHH persons themselves will have resulted in resolving most of the difficult issues and truths we have outlined here. It is our hope that this volume and the efforts of all the authors whose work is included will prove to contribute significantly to such a resolution … and to the raising of new questions that must be answered.

Note

[1] In the late 1980s, for example, a proposal by Spencer to present data on interactive behaviors of hard-of-hearing infants was rejected by a committee of a national research and practice organization, which stated that "This is just not a very interesting population."

References

Akamatsu, C. T., Mayer, C., & Hardy-Braz, S. (2008). Why considerations of verbal aptitude are important in educating deaf and hard-of-hearing students. In M. Marschark & P. C. Hauser (Eds.), *Deaf cognition: Foundations and outcomes* (pp. 131–169). New York: Oxford University Press.

Beadle, E. A. R., McKinley, D. J., Nikolopoulos, T. P., Brough, J., O'Donoghue, G. M., & Archbold, S. M. (2005). Long-term functional outcomes and academic-occupational status in implanted children after 10 to 14 years of cochlear implant use. *Otology & Neurotology, 26,* 1152–1160.

Harkins, J. E., & Bakke, M. (2003). Technologies for communication: Status and trends. In M. Marschark & P. E. Spencer (Eds.), *Oxford handbook of deaf studies, language, and education* (pp. 406–419). New York: Oxford University Press.

James, D., Rajput, K., Brinton, J., & Goswami, U. (2008). Phonological awareness, vocabulary, and word reading in children who use cochlear implants: Does age of implantation explain individual variability in performance outcomes and growth? *Journal of Deaf Studies and Deaf Education, 13,* 117–137.

Marschark, M., & Wauters, L. (2008). Language comprehension and learning by deaf students. In M. Marschark & P. C. Hauser (Eds.), *Deaf cognition: Foundations and outcomes* (pp. 309–350). New York: Oxford University Press.

Moeller, M. P., Tomblin, J. B., Yoshinaga-Itano, C., Connor, C. M., & Jerger, S. (2007). Current state of knowledge: Language and literacy of children with hearing impairment. *Ear & Hearing, 28,* 740–753.

Nicholas, J. G., & Geers, A. E. (2007). Will they catch up? The role of age of cochlear implantation in the spoken language development of children with severe to profound hearing loss. *Journal of Speech, Language, and Hearing Research, 50,* 1048–1062.

Stacey, P. C., Fortnum, H.M., Barton, G.R., & Summerfield, A.Q. (2006). Hearing-impaired children in the United Kingdom, I: Auditory performance, communication skills, educational achievements, quality of life, and cochlear implantation. *Ear & Hearing. 27,* 161–186.

Stokoe, W. (1960/2005). Sign language structure: An outline of the visual communication system of the American deaf. *Studies in Linguistics, Occasional Papers 8.* Buffalo, New York: University of Buffalo, Department of Anthropology and Linguistics. (Reprinted in *Journal of Deaf Studies and Deaf Education, 10,* 3–37).

Woll, B., & Ladd, P. (2003). Deaf communities. In M. Marschark & P.E. Spencer (Eds.), *Oxford handbook of deaf studies, language, and education* (pp. 151–163). New York: Oxford University Press.

AUTHOR INDEX

A

Aan den Toorn, W., 175
Abbas, P. J., 394
Abdullah, A., 350
Abrams, D., 321
Ackley, R. S., 326
Acredolo, L., 321
Adam, T., 354, 355
Adams, L., 50
Adams, M., 428
Adams, M. J., 114, 428
Adelstein, A., 287
Admiraal, R., 178
Aghababian, V., 114
Ahlberg, A., 158, 162, 163
Ahlström, M., 204, 237
Ahmad, W., 201, 202
Aitkin, L., 334
Akamatsu, C., 102, 103
Akamatsu, C. T., 45, 46, 63, 102, 103,
    129, 151, 203, 214, 433, 476
Akamatsu, T., 19, 294
Akamatsu, T., 19
Akeroyd, M. A., 400, 401
Alamargot, D., 147, 464
Alant, E., 112, 120
Alarfaj, A., 335
Albertini, J., 64, 112, 145, 151, 204
Albertini, J. A., 34, 64, 76, 112, 145, 147,
    148, 151, 160, 204, 294, 426
Alegria, J., 7, 21, 136, 147
Algozzine, B., 87
Al-Hilawani, Y., 417
Allamano, N., 466
Allen, J. S., 454
Allen, S., 219
Allen, T. E., 7, 47, 48, 76, 111, 156, 157,
    161, 164, 198
Allen, T. E., 47, 48
Alpern, G., 410, 411
Als, H., 317
AlthausRea, C., 465
Altmann, G. T. M., 449
Altuna, D., 233
Al-Yagon, M., 252, 256
Amitay Ben-Ami, N., 257
Anagnostou, F., 229
Anastasopoulos, L., 289
Anaya, E. M., 132, 133, 450
Andersen, J., 230
Andersen, K., 75

Anderson, D., 283, 287, 304, 305,
    321, 322, 323, 324
Anderson, G., 201, 202
Anderson, H., 66
Anderson, I., 394
Anderson, K., 232
Anderson, K. L., 232, 252
Anderson, M., 148
Andrews, C. E., 147
Andrews, E., 244, 350
Andrews, J., 128, 201, 202, 294
Andrews, J. F., 50, 93, 100, 128, 201,
    202, 294
Angus, D., 243
Anooshian, L., 465
Ansell, E., 9, 65, 158, 159, 162, 163,
    164, 165
Anthony, J. L., 113
Anthony, S., 433
Antia, S., 8, 64, 258
Antia, S. D., 8, 64, 73, 74, 75, 76, 77,
    78, 79, 82, 83, 84, 85, 88, 89, 130,
    254, 255, 258, 378, 379
Antonovsky, A., 255
Aplin, D. Y., 429
Appadurai, A., 220
Apuzzo, M., 47
Apuzzo, M. L., 47, 242, 380
Aram, D., 112, 120
Arbataitis, K., 292, 365, 366
Arcaroli, J., 396
Archbold, S., 204, 227, 228, 229, 230,
    231, 232, 233, 234, 327, 335
Archbold, S. M., 5, 128, 132, 133,
    134, 140, 204, 227, 228, 229, 230,
    231, 232, 233, 234, 236, 326, 327,
    335, 476
Arehart, K., 32, 300, 301, 303
Arehart, K. H., 303
Arends, J., 275
Arfe, B., 146, 150
Arhya, I. N., 270
Arijon, D., 218
Armstrong, D., 216
Árnason, L. A., 133
Arnold, P., 199, 203, 465
Arnold, R., 222
Arnoldner, C., 394
Arnos, K., 214
Aronoff, M., 216, 270, 272, 275,
    276, 277
Arts, A., 233

Arts, H., 336
Arts, H. A., 233, 336
Asbjørnsen, A., 430
Asch, A., 205
Asch, S. E., 252
Aschendorff, A., 398
Ashbaugh, C. J., 335
Ashbaugh, C. M., 335
Asher, J. H., 270
Asher, S. R., 255
Ashmead, D. H., 396
Aslin, R. N., 449
Astington, J., 412
Atkin, K., 201, 202
Austin, D., 308
Avraham, K. B., 214
Awh, E., 460, 466
Axelrod, C., 186
Aylesworth, S., 95

B

Babb, I. G., 101
Babu, M., 179
Backous, D. D., 334
Baddeley, A. D., 9, 442, 443, 459,
    460, 466
Baddeley, A. D., 459, 460
Baer, R., 50
Bahan, B., 196, 200, 211, 217,
    218, 227, 236, 294
Bailey, A. R., 351
Bailey, D., 300
Bailey, J., 151
Bailly, D., 176
Bain, L., 228, 254, 260, 299
Baird, G., 415
Baker, C., 203, 300
Baker, R., 94
Baker, S., 115
Bakke, M., 93, 474
Balakrishnan, A., 351
Baldeweg, T., 429
Baldwin, M., 244, 245, 349
Bale, J. F., 347
Balkany, T., 234, 394
Balko, K. A., 334
Balla, D., 454
Bambara, L. M., 182
Bamford, J., 241, 302, 325, 346, 348
Bandura, A., 77, 258
Banks, J., 121, 133, 146
Barbaranelli, C., 77

479

Barham, J., 160
Baringer, D. G., 244, 245
Barker, B. A., 152, 326
Barker, E. J., 335, 336
Barker, M. J., 251
Barkmeier, L., 120
Barlow-Brown, F., 317
Barman, C. R., 99
Barneavdelinge, S. H., 302
Barnett, W. S., 441
Baron-Cohen, S., 415
Barrett, P., 103, 203
Barry, J., 136
Barton, C., 98
Barton, G., 176, 231
Barton, G. R., 130, 176, 230, 231, 476
Barton, L. E., 147
Bashir, A. S., 144, 146, 149, 150, 151
Basile, M., 64
Basinger, D., 362
Bass-Ringdahl, S., 366
Bat-Chava, Y., 81, 82, 89, 197, 198,
    237, 254, 260, 261
Bates, E., 287, 289, 304, 321, 409,
    411, 413
Batshaw, M., 173
Battmer, R. D., 336
Bauer, L., 273
Bauernschmidt, A., 450
Bauman, H., 18
Bauman, H. -D., 18, 196, 212, 218,
    219, 221
Baumgartner, W. D., 394
Bavelier, D., 9, 133, 217, 458, 460, 461,
    462, 463, 464, 465, 468
Baynton, D., 203
Baynton, D. C., 203, 212
Beadle, E. A. R., 132, 230, 476
Beaman, R., 430
Beaton, C., 98
Beattie, R., 21, 22
Beatty, J., 183
Beazley, S., 245
Bebian, A., 218
Bebko, J., 10, 409
Bebko, J. M., 9, 10, 140, 409
Becker, S., 299
Beckman, A., 244, 245
Behrens, T., 3
Behrens, T. R., 3, 354
Belfield, C., 41
Bell, A. G., 5, 26, 212
Bell, D., 1
Bell, L., 295, 300
Bellis, T. J., 430
Bellman, S., 228
Bellugi, U., 9, 217, 281, 283, 284,
    302, 305, 460, 461, 465
Bench, R. J., 252
Bender, R., 24, 26
Benedict, H., 304
Benigni, L., 413
Benson, P. V., 115

Bentler, R., 252
Bentler, R. A., 252, 381
Berberian, A., 20
Bereiter, C., 145
Berent, G. P., 146, 427
Bergeron, F., 334
Bergeron, J., 112
Bergeson, T., 227
Berglund, M., 385
Berke, J., 173
Berla, N., 46
Bernard, P., 335
Berninger, V. W., 145
Bernstein, P., 203
Beronesi, S., 304
Berry, J., 198, 201
Berry, J. W., 198, 201
Berry, S. W., 393
Bertini, G., 333
Bertram, B., 336, 339
Bertrando, R., 87
Besner, D., 466
Bess, F. H., 3, 45, 300, 383
Bess, F. H., 45
Bettger, J. G., 10, 217, 458
Bhullar, N., 396
Bhutta, Z. A., 355
Bialystok, E., 283
Bibby, M., 19, 45
Biemiller, A., 43
Biesold, H., 27, 213
Billingsley, B. S., 42
Bilodeau, S. A., 383
Binyamini, K., 257
Binzer, S. M., 394
Birch, J., 28
Birch, J. W., 6, 28
Birdsong, D., 283
Bird, R., 161
Bishop, A., 160
Bishop, D. V., 328
Bishop, D. V. M., 328, 381, 440, 466
Bishop, J., 227
Bishop, R. D., 334
Blach, D., 350
Black, J. E., 282
Blackorby, J., 43, 44
Blackwell, P. M., 148
Blaha, K., 185
Blaha, R., 185
Blair, C., 441
Blair, F. X., 465
Blair, H., 8
Blair, J. C., 74, 75
Blake, K. D., 178, 179
Blamey, P., 121, 136, 308, 336
Blamey, P. J., 121, 136, 251, 308, 335,
    336, 367, 379, 380
Blanavonich, A., 350
Blanchfield, B., 43
Blaschke, J., 400
Blatto-Vallee, G., 9, 160
Blauert, J., 400

Blennerhassett, L., 433
Blitzer, T., 204
Block, J., 180
Blondeau, R., 146
Bodner-Johnson, B., 4, 47, 161, 248, 299
Bodrova, E., 441
Boheim, K., 394
Bohnenkamp, G., 292, 365, 366
Boll, T., 410, 411
Bolster, L., 86
Bonder, F., 61
Bonds, B. G., 50
Bonet, J., 20, 22
Bonvillain, J. D., 465
Bonvillian, J., 176
Bonvillian, J. D., 176, 302, 304, 305
Booij, N., 60
Boothroyd, A., 129, 131, 252, 336, 396
Boothroyd-Turner, D., 129, 131
Borden, G. J., 252
Boren, N., 148
Borja, R. R., 98
Bornstein, H., 295
Bornstein, M., 409, 412, 413, 422
Bornstein, M. H., 303
Borovsky, A., 137, 287
Bortoli, A., 413
Bos, H., 175
Boscolo, P., 146, 150
Bosker, R., 68
Bosker, R. J., 58, 65, 68
Bottari, D., 465
Bougatsos, B. S., 242
Bougatsos, C., 348
Bourgeois, J., 96
Boutla, M., 458, 460, 461, 462, 463, 467
Bova, M., 205
Bow, C., 121, 136
Bowe, F., 201
Bowen, M., 44
Bowen, S., 48, 50, 294
Boyer, M., 449
Bracewell, R., 144
Brackenbury, T., 121
Brackett, D., 76
Braden, J., 408
Bradley, J. S., 382, 383, 385
Bradley, L., 114
Brady, S. A., 113, 114
Braeges, J., 77, 88
Braida, L. D., 293
Brainsky, L., 228
Brandimonte, M. A., 466
Brashears, M. E., 221
Braun, A. R., 460
Braverman, B. B., 94
Brazelton, T. B., 317
Breheny, P., 394
Breivik, J., 203
Breivik, J. K., 203, 220
Brenner, C., 6, 231, 232, 233,
    335, 440, 442
Bretherton, I., 409, 411

Brethrton, I., 413
Brewer, D. J., 42
Brewer, D. M., 87
Briars, D., 159
Brigance, A. H., 48
Briggs, L. C., 270
Briggs, R., 339
Briggs, R. J., 227, 393
Briggs, R. J. S., 227, 335, 339, 393
Brill, H. J., 307
Brinton, J., 112, 130, 476
Briscoe, J., 381
Broesterhuizen, M. L. H. M., 429
Brokx, J. P., 394
Brokz, J., 235
Bromley, K., 50
Brookhouser, P. E., 308
Brooks, L., 378
Brough, J., 132, 230, 476
Browder, D., 87
Brown, A., 181
Brown, A. S., 181, 303
Brown, D., 178
Brown, F., 187
Brown, G. D., 463
Brown, L. N., 465
Brown, P., 254
Brown, P. M., 254, 410, 413, 414
Brown, R., 305
Brown-Sweeney, S., 362
Brownell, C., 80
Brownstein, Z., 214
Bruce, S. M., 184, 185, 186
Brueggemann, B. J., 199, 200, 203,
    204, 205
Bruer, J., 300
Bruininks, R. H., 78
Bruner, J., 121
Bruner, J. S., 121, 317
Brunnberg, E., 378, 384, 385
Brunner, E., 309
Bruss, J., 454
Brutten, M., 441, 450, 454
Bryan, A., 215
Bryan, J., 465
Bryant, J., 162, 163
Bryant, P., 1, 114, 160, 465
Bryden, M. P., 287
Bu, X., 347, 351, 352, 354
Buchsbaum, B., 460, 461
Bull, B., 47
Bull, D. H., 365
Bull, R., 160
Bullard, C., 46, 82, 83, 85
Bullis, M. B., 47
Burch, S., 201, 213
Burchett, R., 50
Burdick, S., 203
Burger, T., 228
Burgess, D., 364
Burgess, N., 460
Burgess, S. R., 113, 114
Burke, T. B., 205, 213, 215

Burkey, J. M., 339
Burkhauser, R. V., 258
Burkholder, R. A., 132, 442, 443
Burman, D., 1
Burnet, J., 26
Burnham, D., 94
Burns, M. S., 121
Burton, L. T., 381
Burton, M. J., 101
Bush, G. W., 37
Bush, R., 180
Butterfield, E. C., 365
Butterworth, G. E., 318, 321
Byl, N., 334
Byrnes, B., 121

C
Cairns, G. F., 365
Calderon, L., 243
Calderon, R., 2, 4, 6, 46, 77, 115, 227
Caleffe-Schenck, N., 306
Calfee, R. C., 147, 151
Calhoun, D., 304, 410
Calvert, D. R., 113, 121
Camaioni, L., 413
Camarata, S., 60, 139
Cambra, C., 148
Cambron-McCabe, N., 42
Camp, B. W., 364
Camp, W., 465
Campbell, D., 164
Campbell, K. U., 114
Campbell, M. J., 325
Campbell, R., 150, 428, 460
Caniglia, J., 148
Cannon, J., 118
Capirci, O., 465
Cappelli, M., 79
Caprara, G., 77
Carbin, C. F., 271
Carey, A., 3, 241, 304
Carey, S., 468
Carey-Sargeant, C., 242
Carhart, R., 395, 396
Carmi, R., 269
Carner, M., 339, 393
Carney, A. E., 111, 335, 365
Carney, M., 429
Carnine, D., 44
Carpenter, P. A., 463, 467
Carpenter, T. P., 158, 159
Carr, G., 248, 297
Carter, A. K., 443
Carter, K., 43, 47, 50
Carter, R., 200
Carty, B., 214, 215
Carty, L. M., 347
Caruso, R., 180
Casby, M., 410
Cash, P., 164
Cass, H., 183
Cassels, A., 354
Cassirer, E., 184

Casterline, D. C., 281, 283
Cattani, A., 465
Caudle, S., 229
Cavender, A., 103
Cavicchiolo, S., 235
Cawthon, S., 64
Cecchetto, C., 461
Ceriani, N., 235
Cessna, K. K., 50
Chamberlain, C., 6, 10, 112, 120, 288, 289
Chapman, S. R., 144
Charleson, E., 161
Charlesworth, A., 118, 119
Charlesworth, R., 118, 119
Charlton, M., 335
Charman, T., 415
Chase, E. H., 147
Chasin, J., 317, 318, 319, 320,
    321, 322
Chastel, M., 102
Chatterji, M., 120
Chaves, T., 22
Chein, J. M., 460
Chen, D., 185
Chen, J. -K., 288
Chen, J. M., 394
Cheng, A., 335
Chermak, G., 430
Cherney, J. L., 204
Chess, S., 176, 181
Cheung, H., 420
Chien, S., 158
Ching, T., 3
Ching, T. Y., 398
Ching, T. Y. C., 3, 305, 306, 325, 346, 398
Cho Lieu, J. E., 300
Choi, J. M., 350
Choi, S., 324
Chomsky, N., 279
Chorost, M., 213, 215
Chou, C., 98, 164
Christensen, K., 202
Christenson, S. L., 46
Christiansen, J. B., 204, 237
Christiansen, M. H., 449
Christoff, D., 44
Chrosniak, P. N., 115
Chudowsky, N., 37
Chudowsky, V., 37
Chute, P. M., 231, 232, 336
Cicchetti, D., 440, 454
Cinamon, R. G., 258, 259, 260
Clark, E. V., 287
Clark, G., 334
Clark, G. M., 334, 335
Clark, J. F., 227, 230
Clarke, J., 122
Clay, M. M., 64, 118, 119
Cleary, M., 128, 408, 442, 443, 444, 451
Cleeremans, A., 449
Clemens, C. J., 351, 352
Clement, C. J., 365, 369
Clibbens, J., 318

Clymer, E. W., 93
Cobo-Lewis, A. B., 369
Cohen, J. D., 454
Cohen, J. M., 47
Cohen, N., 235
Cohen, N. L., 235, 335, 338, 394
Cohen, O. P., 47
Cohen, P., 181
Cohen, S., 146
Cohn, J., 219
Colburn, H. S., 396
Cole, E. B., 306
Cole, K., 112
Coleman, H., 180, 198
Colin, S., 113
Collazo, J., 201
Colletti, L., 339, 393
Colletti, V., 339, 393
Collins, A. M., 145
Collins, R., 199
Collins, S., 201
Collura, K., 98
Comer, L. K., 334
Commerson, R., 222
Compton, M. V., 47
Condon, M., 298
Coninx, S., 307
Conlin, K., 186
Conner, K. N., 63
Connor, C., 112, 128, 132, 233,
    336, 380
Connor, C. M., 112, 113, 128, 132,
    133, 152, 233, 336, 369, 380
Conrad, R., 441, 450, 454, 460
Conte, M. P., 146
Conti-D'Antonio, M., 87
Convertino, C. M., 9, 10, 48, 62, 65, 77,
    86, 115, 137
Convertino, C. M., 6, 8, 48, 128,
    137, 139
Convertiono, C., 247
Conway, A. R. A., 464
Conway, C. M., 132, 133, 445, 449,
    450, 454
Conway, D., 148
Conway-Fithian, S., 293
Cook, E. T., 120
Cook, L. G., 144
Cook, P., 219
Cooney, J., 9, 112
Cooper, E. B., 255
Cooper, R., 146
Cope, N., 428
Coppola, M., 271, 275, 277
Coranzza, S., 175
Corballis, M., 217
Corbett, C., 200, 201
Corbett, E., 20
Corbett, K., 361
Corina, D., 217, 283
Corina, D. P., 9, 217, 283
Corker, M., 196, 200, 201
Corkin, S., 466

Cornett, O., 21, 296
Cornett, R. O., 21, 296
Cornoldi, C., 122, 133
Coryell, J., 255
Coscas, G., 178
Costello, E., 148
Coulter, B. A., 334, 380
Coulter, D. K., 3, 73, 241, 242
Coulter, D. K., 302, 346, 369
Courtin, C., 416
Covell, J., 202
Cowan, N., 460, 463, 464, 466, 467,
    468, 469
Cowan, R. S. C., 335
Cox, A., 415
Cox, T., 325
Coyle, D., 243
Coyne, G., 96
Cozad, R. L., 308
Cradler, J., 50
Craft, A., 164
Craig, H. B., 431
Craig, H. K., 369
Craig, W., 27
Crandell, C., 383
Crandell, C. C., 383
Creed, P., 199
Creed, P. A., 199, 259
Creemers, B. P. M., 58, 59
Cremers, C., 180
Cripps, J., 214
Crocker, S., 229, 428, 431, 432
Croft, W., 363
Croneberg, C. G., 281, 283
Crooke, P., 89, 255
Crosson, J., 135
Crouch, B. A., 211, 212, 281
Crouch, R., 204
Croucher, S., 195
Crowe, K., 3
Crystal, D., 216
Cue, K., 82, 83, 85
Culbertson, D. S., 305
Culpepper, B., 3
Curtis, C. E., 466
Curtis, W. J., 440
Curtiss, S., 282, 287
Cymerman, E., 113

D

Dack, L., 415
Daemers, K., 366
Dahlstrom, L., 397
Daisey, M. E., 296
Dale, A. M., 460
Dale, N., 183
Dale, P., 321
Dale, P. S., 304, 321
Damasio, H., 454
Damen, G., 180, 228, 230
Damen, G. W., 231
Damen, G. W. J. A., 180, 228, 230, 231
Damen, S., 181

Danahauer, J. L., 350, 352
Daneman, M., 463, 467
Danhauer, J. L., 301
Daniele, V. A., 99
Daniels, T., 79
Danneker, J. E., 87
Dansac, C., 147, 464
Darbyshire, J., 410
Darling-Hammond, L., 41, 42, 45, 53
Davelaar, E., 466
Davenport, S., 180
Davey, B., 113
Davidson, A., 202
Davidson, L., 440
Davidson, L. S., 335, 440
Davidson, M., 219
Davila, J., 201
Davis, A., 241, 302, 325, 348
Davis, B. L., 366
Davis, C., 95
Davis, H., 376
Davis, J., 304
Davis, J. M., 76, 304, 308, 381
Davis, L., 211, 212
Davis, L. J., 203, 205, 211, 212
Davis, M. R., 97
Davis, R., 325
Davis, R. L., 242, 325, 349
Davis, S., 161, 162
Davis, S. A., 161, 162, 351, 352
Day, D., 3, 304, 410
Day, J., 3
D'Costa, W. A., 335
de Andrade, V., 353
Deary, I. J., 410
Deben, K., 325
De Beni, R., 122, 133
de Beukelaer, C., 366
DeBlois, S., 419
DeCaro, J. J., 259
De Chouly de Lenclave, M., 176
Decker, T. N., 326
DeConde-Johnson, C., 115
Deen, L., 177
Degener, S., 151
de Groot, V., 94
Dehaene, S., 468
Deignan, E., 81, 254, 260, 261
de Jong, P. F., 430, 441
De Jong, R. A., 60
De Kort, A., 178
DeLana, M., 128, 294
Deland, F., 22
Delgado, G., 202
Delgado, R. E., 308
Della Sala, S., 466
Dellon, J., 101
Denkers, I., 177
Deno, S., 114
Denteneer-van der Pasch, W., 176
Derrida, J., 221
Derry, H., 203
DesGeorges, J., 244

Deshler, D., 41
Deshler, D. D., 41, 121
DesJardin, J., 4
D'Esposito, D., 466
D'Esposito, M., 461, 466
Destrebecqz, A., 449
Detterman, D. K., 2, 60
Dettman, S., 339
Dettman, S. J., 227, 335, 336, 337, 339, 393
de Uzcategui, C. A., 243
de Villiers, J., 284
deVilliers, J., 161, 415, 419, 421
de Villiers, P., 284
deVilliers, P. A., 146, 161, 415, 419, 421
deVilliers, P. A., 146
Devine, D., 201
Devine, O., 302
De Voe, S. J., 355
D'Haese, P., 307, 394, 399
Diamond, A., 441
Diaz, J. A., 43, 47
Dickensen, D. K., 289
Dietz, C., 164
Dietz, C. H., 156, 164, 165
DiGello, E., 148
Dillier, N., 398
Dillon Edgett, L., 385
Dillon Edgett, L. M., 377
Dillon, C., 204
Dillon, C. M., 152, 204, 442, 443, 445
Dillon, H., 3, 430
Dillon Edgett, L. M., 377, 385
DImaggio, G., 195
Dirks, D. D., 396
Ditillo, D. A., 378
Dittillo, D. A., 78
Dively, V., 201
Dobosh, P., 198
Dockrell, J. E., 383
Dodd-Murphy, J., 300
Doney, A., 228
Donlan, C., 460
Donne, V., 66
Dorman, M. F., 334, 346, 397
Dostie, D., 216
Doucet, M. E., 334
Dowaliby, F., 259
Dowaliby, F. J., 66, 99, 259
Dowell, R., 236, 339
Dowell, R. C., 227, 335, 336, 337, 339, 393, 398
Downey, D. M., 146
Downing, J., 187
Downs, M., 297
Downs, S. M., 354
Doyle, K. J., 305
Dozier, T., 41
Drew, A., 415
Driscoll, V., 394
Drummond, M. F., 348
Drye, C., 89, 255
Dryer, M. S., 275

Dublmeier, J., 164
Dudley, P., 164
Dunbar, J., 43
Duncan, J. F., 308
Dunlap, G., 182
Dunn, C., 201
Dunn, C. C., 201, 395, 396, 397, 398, 399
Dunn, D. W., 441, 447
Dunn, J., 408
Dunn, L. M., 336, 337
Dunst, C. J., 299
Durieux-Smith, A., 79, 243, 325
Durlach, N. I., 293, 396
Durunoglu, A. Y., 114
Dutton, J., 42
Duyk, G. M., 269
Dwyer, F., 217
Dye, G. A., 50
Dye, P., 9, 10, 15
Dye, R. H., 396
Dyer, A., 428
Dyer, L., 467

E

Easterbrooks, S. R., 44, 58, 65, 112, 113, 114, 115, 117, 118, 122, 165, 417
Easterbrooks, S. R., 44, 58, 65
Easton, D., 96
Ecalle, J., 113
Eccarius, M., 304
Edmondson, D. M., 335
Edwards, J. A., 97
Edwards, L. C., 228, 229, 378, 431, 441
Edwards, L. C., 428, 431, 432, 441
Edwards, S., 120
Edyburn, D., 93
Efrati, M., 255
Efron, C., 257
Egbert, V., 89, 255
Egelston-Dodd, J., 102
Eggermont, J. J., 334
Eichen, E. B., 284, 285
Eichwald, J., 3
Eilers, R., 365
Eilers, R. E., 307, 362, 364, 365, 366
Eisenberg, L., 246
Eisenberg, L. S., 246, 251, 335, 451
Eisenberg, S., 95
Eisenberger, J., 86, 87
Eisler, M., 252
Ekelid, M., 451
Ekman, E., 252
Elahi, A., 347
Elahi, F., 347
Elahi, M. M., 347
Elahi, S. B., 347
Elangovan, S., 350
Elbedour, K., 269
Eldredge, N., 89, 200, 201, 254
Eleweke, C. J., 299
Elfenbein, J., 381
Elfenbein, J. L., 308, 381

El-Hakim, H., 133, 336
Elliot, L., 95, 96, 98
Elliot, R., Jr., 427
Elliott, C., 419
Elliott, E. M., 464
Elliott, J. M., 461
Elliott, L. L., 447
Elliott, M., 198
Elliott, S., 78, 89
Elliott, S. N., 75, 78, 79, 89
Ellis, N. C., 461, 463, 464
Elman, J., 137, 287
Elman, J. L., 137, 287, 447, 449
Elton, F., 271
Elvers, G. C., 97
Emerton, G., 199
Emmorey, K. D., 10, 217, 283, 284, 454, 460, 461, 462, 465, 466
Emmorey, K. D., 460, 465
Enerstvedt, R. T., 183
Engen, E., 148
Engle, R. W., 461
English, K., 87, 227, 230
Enns, C., 428
Epstein, K., 160
Erber, N., 361
Erber, N. P., 305, 306, 361
Ericsson, K. A., 150
Eriks-Brophy, A., 6
Erikson, E., 195, 196, 258
Erkam, U., 228
Erting, C. J., 211, 295, 296, 319
Ertmer, D. J., 361, 366, 367, 368, 369, 370, 371, 372
Esler, A. N., 46
Espin, C., 114
Estabrooks, W., 6, 293, 294, 306
Eubank, L., 283
Evans, A., 216
Evans, C. J., 305
Evans, D., 1
Evans, D. B., 1, 354, 355
Evans, I. M., 187
Evans, J., 161
Evans, T. G., 354
Even, P., 98
Evenhuis, H., 177
Everhart, V., 96, 157, 159
Everhart, V. S., 96, 128, 130, 137, 139, 157, 159
Ewing, K., 165
Ewing, K. M., 43, 47, 49
Ewoldt, C., 148

F

Fabbretti, D., 146
Fabich, M., 6, 112, 129, 141, 152, 160, 231
Fabre-Thorpe, M., 468
Fadiga, L., 183
Fagan, M., 204
Fagan, M. K., 137, 138, 152, 204, 445
Falick, T. G., 146

Fanule, D., 434
Farrelly, S., 102, 103, 203
Fears, B., 336
Fears, B. T., 336, 394
Feigen, L., 468
Feinstein, S., 427
Feldman, J., 43
Fennema, E., 165
Fenson, L., 304, 321, 323, 324
Fernandes, C., 441
Fernandez, N., 464
Fernandez, P., 176, 181
Ferre, S., 428, 433, 434
Ferreira-Brito, L., 272
Ferrini-Mundy, J., 42
Ferron, P., 334
Feuerstein, R., 121
Fewell, R., 304
Fewell, R. R., 304
Fiedler, C. R., 87
Fields, B., 164
Fiese, B., 409
Fiez, J. A., 460
Figueras, B., 137, 378, 431,
    441, 445
Figueras-Costa, B., 421
Fiket, H., 335
Findley, L., 219
Finitzo-Hieber, T., 383
Fiorino, F. G., 339, 393
Fischer, L. C., 198
Fischer, R., 211
Fischer, S., 202
Fischer, S. D., 202, 284
Fischgrund, J., 201
Fischgrund, J. E., 148, 201
Fisher, L., 251
Fisher, S., 461
Fisher, S. G., 394, 461
Fishman, L., 366
Fitch, W. T., 279
Fitzgerald, E., 27
Fitzgerald, S. M., 151
Fitzgibbon, C. T., 255
Fitzpatrick, E., 243, 245, 325
Fize, D., 468
Flavell, J. H., 77
Fleck, M. B., 186
Flege, J. E., 283
Fletcher, J., 464
Flexer, C., 293, 306, 332, 338, 383
Flexer, R. W., 50
Floden, R. E., 42
Florian, V. A., 147
Flower, L., 145
Foale, C., 429
Fogassi, L., 183
Fogstad, H., 355
Folven, R. J., 302, 304, 305
Fonzi, J., 9
Foorman, B. R., 112
Foraker, S., 467
Ford, R., 420

Formby, C., 308
Forshaw, M., 241, 302, 325, 348
Fortnum, H., 176, 231
Fortnum, H. M., 130, 176, 231, 476
Foster, S. B., 82, 83, 85, 100, 202,
    254, 256
Foster, S. B., 100
Foster, W. A., 113
Foucault, M., 213
Fowler, C. A., 428
Fowler, C. H., 87
Fowler, G., 353
Fox, L., 173, 187
Fox, M., 220, 221
Francis, H. W., 231, 232
Francis, P., 95, 96, 98
Francks, C., 428
Frank, A. L., 255
Frank, K. A., 258
Frank, Y., 251
Franke, M., 165
Franklin, A. J., 200
Franklin, S. V., 147, 150
Frederickson, C., 144
Frederickson, J. D., 144
Fredrick, L., 118
Freeman, M., 50
French, M., 271
French, M. M., 271, 305
Freshwater, S. M., 445
Fridriksson, T., 164
Friederici, A. D., 284
Friedman, T. B., 270
Frisina, D., 28
Frisina, R., 379
Frith, C. D., 460
Frith, U., 289
Fritschmann, N. S., 121
Froman, R., 394
Frostad, P., 158, 159, 162, 163
Fuchs, D., 434
Fuchs, L., 114
Fullmer, K., 180
Funderburg, R., 427
Furman, N., 212
Furth, H. G., 8, 303
Fuson, K., 163
Fuster, J., 450, 454
Fyfe, R., 121, 133, 146

G
Gabbard, S. A., 303
Gabbert, G., 233
Gaffney, M., 302
Gage, J., 97
Gallaudet, E., 26
Gallaudet, T., 25
Galster, J., 370, 372
Galvin, K. L., 335
Gamino, J. F., 144
Gampp, T. L., 428
Gantz, B., 394
Gantz, B. J., 231, 326, 394, 396, 399

Garcia, J., 295
Gardner, H., 217
Gardner, M. B., 400
Gardner, R. S., 400
Garmon, L., 282
Garnett, C., 22
Garrison, W., 88
Gatehouse, S., 400
Gates, A. I., 147
Gathercole, S., 442, 443
Gathercole, S. E., 442, 443, 465
Gatlin, S., 42
Gauna, K., 216
Gaustad, M., 9, 162
Gaustad, M. G., 9, 76, 85, 162
Gearhart, M., 161
Geenens, D., 186
Geers, A. E., 6, 73, 112, 113, 128, 129,
    130, 131, 132, 133, 134, 135, 136,
    137, 138, 140, 152, 204, 230, 231,
    232, 234, 380, 408, 420, 440, 442
Geers, A. E., 129, 130, 132, 133, 136,
    230, 233, 234, 252, 293, 297, 326,
    335, 336, 369, 378, 380, 408, 420,
    440, 442, 451, 476
Geers, A. M., 335, 336
Geeslin, J. D., 112, 120
Geffner, D., 308
Gehring, I., 235
Geiger, L., 251
Gelfand, S., 398
Gentner, D., 145
Gentry, M. A., 128, 294
George, L., 78
George, L. B., 78, 257
Geraci, C., 461, 462, 464
Gerner de Garcia, B. A., 112
Gerrits, E., 235
Gersten, R., 93
Gerton, J., 198
Getty, L., 203
Gfeller, K., 394
Ghani, H., 231
Gibbs, S., 381
Gibler, A., 383
Gifford-Smith, M., 80
Gilbertson, D., 428, 433, 434
Gilbertson, M., 131, 381
Gillis, B., 366
Gioia, G. A., 446
Givens, G. D., 350
Glazenwski, B., 186
Gleitman, H., 382
Gleitman, L. R., 382
Glickman, N., 197, 198
Godber, Y., 46
Goffman, E., 199
Gokhale, S., 174
Gold, T., 307
Goldberg, D., 212
Goldberg, D. M., 212, 306
Goldberg, L. R., 129, 130
Golden, C. J., 445

Golden, Z., 445
Goldfield, B. A., 304
Goldhaber, D. D., 42
Goldin-Meadow, S., 268, 273, 287
Goldman-Rakic, P. S., 454
Goldsmith, L., 413
Goldstein, G., 199, 200, 378
Goldstein, H., 252
Goldstein, M. H., 293
Gombert, J. E., 120
Gonsoulin, T., 197
Goodman, J. C., 287
Goodman, K. W., 234
Goodwyn, S., 321
Gopnik, A., 324
Gordon, A. G., 176
Gordon, H. W., 431
Gordon, J., 24
Gordon, K. A., 334
Gorenflo, D., 203
Gorga, M. P., 76, 381
Goswami, U., 112, 130, 429, 476
Goswami, U. C., 112, 128, 130, 131,
    133, 136, 137, 140, 429, 476
Gottardo, A., 114
Gourgey, A. F., 77
Govaerts, P. J., 366
Gozzi, M., 461
Grace, C., 200, 201, 202
Grafman, J., 160
Graham, A., 441
Graham, I. D., 243
Graham, J., 229
Graham, P. A., 41
Grandori, F., 3, 346, 349
Grant, N., 200, 202
Grantham, D. W., 396
Graves, D., 148
Graves, P., 95
Gray, C., 121, 133, 146, 466
Gray, R., 215
Gray, T., 102
Grayden, D., 398
Green, D. M., 395, 400
Green, D. R., 302
Green, K. M. J., 334
Green, L., 428
Greenberg, M. T., 2, 4, 6, 115, 243
Greenberg, M. T., 77, 115, 120, 227, 243
Greenberg, S. F., 42
Greeno, J., 159
Greenough, W. T., 282
Greenspan, I. S., 186, 187
Greenwald, S., 181
Greenwood, G. S., 255
Gregg, K. R., 283
Gregory, S., 3, 204, 227, 228, 229,
    233, 234, 236, 237, 243, 326
Grein, A. J., 354
Gresham, F. M., 75, 79, 89
Greve, D. N., 460
Grialou, T. L., 178
Griffin, H. C., 183

Griffin, P., 121
Griffiths, A. J., 66
Griggs, M., 242, 247
Grimshaw, G. M., 287
Groce, N., 19, 221
Groce, N. E., 19, 221, 269, 274
Grohne, K., 361
Groht, M., 148
Grosse, S. D., 302
Grove, C., 303
Grushkin, D. A., 199, 200, 294
Grushkin, D. A., 149
Gruzelier, J., 429
Guarinello, A., 20
Guberman, S., 161
Guede, N. L., 270
Guida, M., 339, 393
Gunther, K., 22, 23, 27
Gustason, G., 28, 295
Gustason, J., 28
Gutfreund, M., 161
Guy, S. C., 446

H
Hadjikakou, K., 196
Hafer, J., 408, 409, 412, 415
Hage, C., 296
Hakuta, K., 283
Halas, M., 146, 147
Haley, J., 298
Hall, B., 178
Hall, M., 463
Hall, M. L., 458, 463
Hall, S., 211
Hall, T., 121
Hall, V. C., 467
Hallau, M., 46
Hallett, D., 1
Halliday, M. A. K., 145
Hamidi, M., 466
Hamilton, L., 295
Hamilton, L. B., 295
Hamlin, L., 95
Hammes, D. M., 335, 338
Hammill, D., 419
Hammill, D. D., 151, 419
Hancin-Bhatt, B. J., 114
Handley, M., 117
Haney, M., 185
Hanin, L., 396
Hanks, J. A., 42
Hannay, H. J., 441
Hannay, J., 229
Hansen, N. M., 386
Hanson, A., 293
Hanson, V. L., 428, 463
Hardie, N., 334
Hardie, N. A., 334
Hardie, T., 230, 236, 327
Hardin-Jones, M. A., 308, 381
Hardy-Braz, S., 46, 151, 433, 476
Harkins, J. E., 93, 474
Harlan, D., 95

Harm, M., 468
Harmon, D., 216
Harney, J., 82
Harris, D. P., 147
Harris, K. S., 252
Harris, M., 43, 113, 120, 128, 231, 300,
    317, 318, 319, 320, 321, 322, 323,
    327, 328, 378, 409, 428, 430
Harris, P., 421
Harrison, D. R., 148
Harrison, M., 346
Harrison, R., 336
Hart, B., 115, 161
Harter, S., 195
Hartman, M., 164
Hartmann, R., 334
Hartrampf, R., 336
Hartshorne, N., 178
Hartshorne, T., 178
Hartshorne, T. S., 178
Hartung, J. P., 304
Harvey, M., 199
Harvey, M. A., 199, 243, 386
Harvey, S., 47
Hasenstab, S., 234
Hasenstab, S. M., 234, 306
Haskins, H., 421
Hastings, D. L., 334
Hatrack, M., 460
Haualand, H., 213, 220
Haude, R. H., 10
Hauser, M. D., 279, 445
Hauser, P. C., 9, 47, 48, 115, 121, 122,
    128, 151, 417, 460
Hauser, P. C., 47, 48, 128, 431,
    441, 445, 460
Hawker, K., 328, 440
Hawkins, L., 47
Hay, J., 273
Hayes, J. R., 145
Haynes, D. S., 396
Haynes, O., 409
Haynes, O. M., 303, 409
Heafner, T., 50
Heavner, K., 369
Hebbler, K., 378
Heefner, D. L., 151
Heenan, R. A., 118, 119
Heermann, R., 339
Hefland, M., 242
Heid, S., 334
Heider, F., 146
Heider, G. M., 146
Helfand, M., 325, 348, 349
Helig, J. V., 42
Helland, T., 430
Heller, J., 159
Hellman, S. A., 336
Helmke, A., 59
Helms, J., 201, 394, 399
Heming, J. E., 465
Hendershot, G., 203
Hendershott, A., 243

Henderson D., 243
Henderson, A. T., 46
Henderson, J., 95
Henderson, S., 205
Hendriks, M. A., 68
Hennelly, R. A., 461, 463, 464
Hennies, J., 22
Henning, S., 133
Henning, S. C., 132, 133, 450
Henry, A., 138, 381
Henson, R. N. A., 460
Hergils, L., 245
Herman, R., 323
Hermans, H., 195
Hermelin, B., 465
Hermelin, B. M., 465
Hermsen, L. M., 147, 150
Hernández, M., 201
Herrmann, D., 182
Hertzog, M., 94
Hess, U., 252
Hétu, R., 203, 382, 383
Hickok, G., 217, 460, 465
Hiddinga, A., 219
Hieber, S., 233, 336
Hieber, S. J., 233, 335, 336
Hildebrand, M. S., 214
Hill, K. L., 335
Hill, M., 398
Hillegeist, E., 160
Hillman, T., 115, 128, 417, 431, 441
Hind, S., 302
Hiner, J., 98
Hinman, A., 181
Hinnant, J. T., 270
Hintermair, M., 22, 196, 198, 199, 204, 229, 299
Hismjatullina, A., 464
Hitch, G. J., 9, 442, 443, 459, 466
Hnath, T., 396
Hodges, A. V., 234
Hodgson, M. R., 381, 382, 383, 385
Hodgson, M. R., 385
Hoefsloot, L., 180
Hoemann, H. W., 147
Hoemann, S. A., 147
Hoenig, N., 337
Hoffmeister, R., 284
Hoff, D. J., 37
Hoff, E., 307, 323
Hoffman, K., 195
Hoffman, M., 121
Hoffmeister, R., 161, 196, 200, 211, 294, 419
Hogan, A., 5
Hoggart, R., 211
Hohm, E., 441
Holcomb, R., 20
Holcomb, T., 21
Holcomb, T. K., 21, 255
Holden, T. A., 394
Holden-Pitt, L., 43, 47
Holland, J., 339

Hollow, R., 335
Holowecky, S. R., 451
Holt, J., 7, 73, 112
Holt, R. F., 339
Holtzman, D., 42
Homer, C., 348
Homer, C. J., 242, 325, 348, 349
Honeycutt, R. L., 150
Hong, Y., 102, 103
Hoover, B., 292, 365, 366
Hoover, B. M., 292, 365, 366, 381
Hopkins, B., 321
Horn, C., 95
Horn, D., 204
Horn, D. L., 133, 152, 445
Horn, P., 284
Horsley, I. A., 255
Horstmanshof, L., 103, 203
Horten, L., 164
Hotto, S., 112, 303
Houston, D. M., 227
Houtenville, A. J., 258
Houtveen, A. A. M., 60
Howard, W., 148
Howarth, C. I., 66
Howarth, S. P., 66
Howell, J., 46
Howell, J. J., 46, 47, 294
Howell, M., 114
Howieson, D. B., 441
Huang, C., 350
Huang, S. S., 450
Hubel, D., 333
Hubel, D. H., 333
Hudgins, C. V., 308
Hughes, C., 441
Hughes, E. K., 242
Hugo, R., 350
Hulstrom, W. J., 293
Humes, L. E., 45
Humphries, T., 196, 199, 201, 204, 211
Hunt, R., 243, 248, 297
Huntley, M., 413
Huntley-Fenner, G., 468
Hurford, J. R., 267
Hurting, R., 252
Hustedde, L. C. G., 367
Huston, S., 114, 115
Huttenlocher, J., 113
Hutton, C., 217
Huttonlocher, J., 304
Huygen, P., 178
Hyde, M., 46, 72, 73, 74, 75, 82, 83, 158, 161, 199, 204, 214, 228, 234, 252, 259, 295, 378, 379
Hymel, S., 255

I

Ibertsson, T., 133, 140
Ilicak, S., 228
Illg, A., 339
Incerti, P., 398
Inceselu, A., 228

Ingvar, M., 460
Innes, J., 164
Innes, J. J., 47, 164
Intraub, H., 468
Iran-Nejad, A., 120
Irwin-De Vitis, L., 50
Isquith, P., 431
Isquith, P. K., 431, 446
Israelite, N., 199, 200, 378, 386
Itard, J. M. G., 281, 377
Iwasaki, S., 302
Iyer, S. N., 365, 366, 369

J

Jackson, C. W., 299
Jackson, D. W., 94
Jackson, L., 97, 98
Jackson, R. A., 255
Jacob, A., 347
Jacobs, P., 200
Jacobson, E., 151
Jakobson, R., 274
Jambor, E., 198
James, D., 112, 120, 130, 131, 132, 137, 476
Jamieson, J. R., 19, 45, 161, 381
Jamieson, J. R., 383, 384, 385, 386
Jankowski, K., 201
Jansen, C., 182
Janssen, C., 177
Janssen, M., 182, 186
Janssen, M. J., 182, 184, 186
Janssens de Varebeke, S., 325
Jarosz, M., 383
Jatho, J., 201
Jenison, V. W., 394
Jenkins, J., 114
Jenkins, W., 334
Jennen-Steinmetz, C., 441
Jensema, C., 73, 94
Jensema, C. J., 73, 94, 147
Jensen, J. H., 230
Jerger, S., 113, 380
Jimenez-Sanchez, C., 76
Job, A., 347
Johannsen, K., 214
Johansson, M., 178
Johns, J., 114
Johnson, B., 47
Johnson, C., 8, 73, 146, 361
Johnson, C. A., 128, 130, 131, 133, 136, 137, 140
Johnson, C. D., 301, 302, 306, 307
Johnson, D., 304
Johnson, H., 34
Johnson, H. A., 34, 45, 47, 147
Johnson, H. D., 81
Johnson, J., 283
Johnson, L., 87
Johnson, R., 221
Johnson, R. C., 211, 221
Johnson, R. E., 295, 296
Johnston, T., 203, 205

Johnstone, P., 396
Jones, E. A., 298
Jones, G., 119
Jones, J. K., 43, 47, 49
Jones, L., 201, 202
Jones, P., 8, 73
Jones, T., 165
Jones, T. W., 43, 47, 49, 165
Jongmans, M. C. J., 178
Jonides, J., 460, 466
Jonsson, M. H., 230
Joosten, T., 178
Jordan, D. L., 100
Jordan, I., 28
Joseph, A., 347
Josvassen, J. L., 230
Joyeux, D., 176
Julyan, P. J., 334
Jungner, G., 353
Juré, R., 176
Jusczyk, P. W., 304

K

Kaderavek, J., 112, 120
Kalikow, D. N., 447, 450
Kalmanson, B., 186
Kam, D., 98
Kamath, V., 451
Kame'enui, E., 114
Kamhi, A. G., 131, 300, 301, 381
Kampfe, C. M., 243
Kane, M. J., 461
Kaplan, B., 182
Kaplan, D. M., 394
Kappas, A., 252
Karchmer, M., 57, 73, 76, 161, 196, 202
Karchmer, M. A., 47, 48, 57, 72, 73, 76,
    161, 196, 202, 227, 252
Karni, A., 333
Karpicke, J., 132, 133, 450
Karvonen, M., 87
Kastetter, S. K., 234
Katz, D., 408
Katz, L. C., 334
Katz-Kaseff, M., 164
Kaufman, A. S., 433, 441
Kaufman, N. L., 433
Kavanagh, F., 64
Kazmi, H., 42, 286, 287
Keehner, M., 465
Kegl, J., 271
Kelly, A. B., 148
Kelly, L., 113
Kelly, L. P., 113, 147
Kelly, R., 1, 9, 65, 95, 96, 100, 101, 104,
    158, 159, 161, 162, 164, 165
Kelly, R. R., 1, 65, 95, 100, 101, 104
Kemeny, S., 460
Kemme, H., 177
Kemp, S., 433
Kemp, V., 158
Kemper, A. R., 354
Kennedy, C. R., 242, 325, 326, 346

Kennedy, P., 78
Kennedy, S., 385
Kennewell, S., 97
Kenney, P., 151
Kent, B. A., 199, 203, 235, 237
Kent, B. A., 386
Kent, R., 362
Kent, R. D., 362, 367, 368
Kenworthy, L., 446
Keren, R., 348, 354
Kessler, D., 394
Kessler, M., 397
Kettel, J., 252
Kezirian, E. J., 354
Khan, S., 138, 431
Kidd, D., 161
Kiese-Himmel, C., 300
Kileny, P. R., 335, 394
Killoran, J., 177, 178, 179, 182
Kilsby, M., 180
Kimberling, W., 179
Kimm, L., 325
King, C., 120, 146
King, C. M., 101, 120, 146
Kingma, J., 181
Kinuthia, W., 202
Kinzie, S., 203
Kircaali-Iftar, G., 335
Kirk, K. I., 233, 251, 335, 336, 444
Kirk, U., 433
Kisch, S., 204, 270
Kishon-Rabin, L., 335
Klawe, M., 97
Kleean Alter, J., 146
Klein, B., 89, 255
Klein, D., 288
Klein, M., 185
Kleiner, A., 42
Klima, E., 460
Klima, E. S., 281, 283, 458, 460
Klima, S. L., 217
Klimacka, L., 252
Klinke, R., 334
Kluwin, T. N., 5, 7, 47, 57, 58, 148, 165,
    197, 378
Kluwin, T. N., 51, 53, 57, 58, 73, 74,
    75, 76, 78, 81, 148, 165, 197, 228,
    229, 378
Knapp, H., 283
Knight, C., 267
Knokey, A. M., 43, 44
Knoors, H., 60, 66, 79, 80, 81, 82, 152,
    172, 184, 231, 327
Knopik, S. N., 152
Knutsen, J., 204
Knutson, J. F., 231, 237, 394
Kober, N., 37
Koch, D. B., 335, 394
Koch, M., 297
Koch, M. E., 231, 297
Kochhar, A., 214
Kochkin, S., 203
Koeppe, R. A., 466

Koester, L., 409
Koester, L. S., 378
Koh, S., 28, 378, 409
Koh, S. D., 6, 28
Kong, Y., 398
Koopmans-van Beinum, F. J., 361,
    365, 373
Koppers, E., 176
Korkman, M., 433
Korn, S. J., 176, 181
Korvorst, M., 160
Kosslyn, S., 10, 217
Kosslyn, S. M., 10, 217, 459, 465
Kowalska, J., 465
Kozleski, E., 41
Kozulin, A., 121
Krabbe, P., 228
Krabbe, P. F. M., 180, 228
Kraiger, K., 59
Kral, A., 346
Kreimeyer, K., 8, 255, 258
Kreimeyer, K. H., 8, 73, 76, 88, 89, 254,
    255, 258
Krentz, C., 219
Kress, G., 145
Kretschmer, L. W., 146
Kretschmer, R. E., 336
Kretschmer, R. R., 146
Kritchevsky, M., 9
Kritzer, K., 157, 160, 161, 164, 165
Krohn, E., 148
Kronenberger, W., 133
Kronenberger, W. G., 133, 441,
    447, 454
Krull, K., 229
Krumm, M., 350
Kuhl, P. K., 300, 372
Kühn-Inacker, H., 307
Kumar, A., 179
Kumar, S., 354
Kundu, C. L., 347
Kuntze, M., 217
Kupermintz, H., 34, 62
Kurtzer-White, E., 243, 244
Kusche, C. A., 120
Kuschel, R., 273
Kushalnagar, P., 229
Kusters, A., 220
Kwan, Y., 163
Kwiatkowski, J., 308
Kyle, F., 113, 120
Kyle, F. E., 113, 120, 327, 378
Kyriakides, L., 58, 59

L

Laakso, M., 213
Labadie, R. F., 396
LaBerge, D., 115
Lach, R., 365
Ladd, P., 2, 5, 196, 201, 202, 204,
    220, 268, 474
Lafond, L. D., 428
LaFromboise, T., 198

Lagati, S., 177
Lahtinen, R., 179
Lake, J., 396
Lalande, N., 203
Lalwani, A., 397
Lamarche, P., 335
Lamb, C., 161
Lamb, N., 385
Lambert, E., 147, 464
Lamm, C., 441
Lancon, C., 114
Landberg, I., 361
Lane, H. B., 5, 8, 114, 196, 200, 201, 202, 203, 204, 211, 227, 236, 271, 273, 281, 289, 294
Lane, H. B., 114
Lane, S., 295, 300
Lang, H., 59, 64, 100, 101, 112, 145, 161, 162, 165
Lang, H. G., 34, 59, 63, 64, 65, 66, 76, 99, 100, 101, 104, 112, 145, 160, 161, 162, 165, 227, 294, 426
Langdon, D., 378, 431, 441
Langereis, M. C., 231, 394
Laoide, S., 349
Larkin, J. H., 159
Larock, D., 115
LaRock, D., 65, 247
Laros, J. A., 433
Larsen, S. C., 151
Larson, J., 95
LaSasso, C., 113, 114, 119, 202
Lashley, K. S., 447
Lassonde, M., 334
Laszig, R., 398
Laszlo, C., 199, 200
Laszlo, C. A., 377, 386
Latus, K., 336
Laucht, M., 441
Laudanna, A., 175
Laughton, J., 306, 426
Lauwerier, L., 176
Lawrence, D., 398
Lawson, D., 9
Lazaroo, D. T., 351
Lazslo, C., 381, 382
Le Blanc, R., 19
Leahy, M. J., 258
Leary, M., 195
Leblanc, R., 45
Lechart, J., 21
Lechat, J., 7, 136
Lederberg, A., 112
Lederberg, A. R., 51, 112, 304, 381
Lederberg, R., 174
Lee, C., 89
Lee, H. B., 350
Lee, R. F., 381
Leet, H., 299
Leigh, G., 45, 46, 295, 349, 351
Leigh, I. W., 93, 196, 198, 199, 200, 202, 204, 237, 433
Leigh, J., 339

Leigh, J. R., 227, 335, 337, 339, 393
Lem, P., 68
Lemons M., 354
Lenarz, T., 336, 339
Lenneberg, E. H., 283, 365
Lento, C. L., 112, 336
Lentz, E., 219
Leonard, J. S., 372
Leonard, L. B., 112
Leong, D. J., 441
Lepore, F., 334
Lepoutre, D., 139
Lesinski-Schiedat, A., 339
Leslie, A., 415
Letourneau, K., 347
Levasseur, J., 336
Levin, H., 41
Levine, L. M., 78
Levine, S., 113
Levitt, H., 95, 308
Lewedag, V. L., 366
Lewis, A., 60
Lewis, B. A., 308
Lewis, D. E., 381
Lewis, M. D., 441
Lewis, M. S. J., 94
Lewis, R. L., 467
Lewis, V., 459
Leybaert, J., 7, 113, 120, 128, 136, 147, 157, 162, 296
Lezak, M. D., 441
Li, Y., 228, 229, 299
Liang, Y., 270
Liben, L. S., 9, 463
Lichtenberger, E. O., 441
Lichtman, J., 300
Liddell, S. K., 295, 296
Lieu, T. A., 348, 349
Lieu, T. L., 242, 325
Liles, M., 97
Lillio-Martin, D., 217
Lillo-Martin, D., 144, 305
Lim, S. B., 351
Lim, S. S., 354, 355
Limbrick, E. A., 64, 66
Lin, C., 350
Lin, F., 230
Lin, F. R., 230
Lin, Y., 350
Lindén-Boström, M., 385
Linder, T. W., 186, 187
Lindgren, K. A., 460
Lindholm-Leary, K., 59
Lindsay, P., 378
Lindsay, P. H., 331, 378
Ling, A. H., 365
Ling, D., 18, 293, 365
Ling, L., 231
Lipman, B. S., 465
Liss, M. B., 94
Litovsky, R. Y., 396, 399
Liu, B., 98, 164
Liu, C., 98, 102, 103, 164

Liu, D., 415, 416, 417
Liu, G., 217
Liu, S., 283
Liu, Y., 64, 77, 88, 95, 96
Lively, S. E., 333
Livingston, S., 147, 148
Lloyd Richmond, H., 231, 327
Lloyd, H., 230
Lloyd, K., 214
Lock, E., 130, 285, 286, 287
Locke, E., 42
Locke, J., 373
Locke, J. L., 300, 373
Loeterman, M., 94
Loew, R., 201
Logan, J. S., 333
Logan, K., 464
Logiodice, C., 148
Lohle, E., 228
Lombardi, L., 467
Loncke, F., 60, 139
Long, G., 77, 88
Long, G. I., 121
Long, G. L., 59, 77, 88, 100, 121
Long, J., 120
Lonigan, C. J., 113, 114
Lopez, L., 295
Lorenz, K., 282, 333
Loring, D. W., 441
Losiewicz, B. L., 460
Louw, B., 350
Love, T., 460
Lovett, H., 49
Lowe, M. J., 441
Lucas, C., 294
Lucas, T., 42
Luckasson, R., 174
Luckner, H., 8
Luckner, J., 37, 73, 82, 83, 112, 117, 159
Luckner, J. L., 9, 37, 41, 42, 43, 44, 45, 46, 47, 48, 49, 50, 73, 76, 77, 82, 83, 85, 87, 112, 117, 159, 469
Luetke-Stahlman, B., 295
Luft, P., 50
Luiken, H., 174
Lukomski, J., 115, 128, 236, 417, 431, 441
Lumley, J., 161
Lund, N. J., 308
Lundberg, L. J., 361
Lundy, J., 415, 418, 420
Luntz, M., 398
Luria, A. R., 441, 450
Lurito, J. T., 441
Lusin, N., 212
Luterman, D., 227, 228, 230, 243, 244
Lutman, M., 3, 228, 229, 232
Lutman, M. E., 3, 227, 228, 229, 232, 233, 326, 346, 349
Luxford, W., 203
Luxon, L. M., 347, 349, 353, 355
Lynch, M. P., 307, 364, 365, 369, 370
Lyon, G. R., 426
Lyxell, B., 133

M

Ma, L., 165
Macaulay, C., 420
MacFarland, S., 176, 182, 183
MacGregor, L., 121
Macias, G., 77
Mackall, P., 97
MacKay, S., 78
Macken, M. A., 361
MacKenzie, I., 199, 203
MacKinnon, G. E., 287
Mackinson, J. A., 433
MacLean, M., 114
MacLeod-Gallinger, J., 121
Macleod-Gallinger, J., 47
MacPherson, B., 347, 353
MacSweeney, M., 460
Madriz, J., 349
Madsen, A., 161
Maffi, L., 216
Magnan, A., 113
Magnuson, M., 245
Magondwa, L., 23
Mahoney, G., 67
Mahoney, T., 3
Mainzer, R., 41
Malecki, C., 78
Malinger, G., 173
Maller, S. J., 433
Mallory, J., 59, 100
Malmgren, K. W., 114, 428
Malone, M. N., 112
Malzkuhn, M., 219
Mandel, D. R., 304
Mandke, K., 259
Mann, V. A., 113
Mann, W., 305
Manoach, D. S., 460
Mant, D., 353
Mar, H., 186, 187
Marchant, G., 417
Marchark, M., 294
Marcoux, S., 335
Marcus, A., 198
Marentette, P. F., 302
Marge, D. K., 32, 299
Marge, M., 32, 299
Markel, N., 252
Markides, A., 254, 255
Marlot, C., 468
Marlowe, B., 429, 430
Marr, M., 88
Marsaja, I. G., 221, 270, 274, 275, 277
Marschark, M., 4, 6, 7, 8, 9, 10, 34, 42,
    43, 47, 48, 51, 62, 63, 64, 65, 66,
    69, 76, 77, 86, 96, 112, 115, 121,
    122, 128, 129, 130, 133, 135, 137,
    139, 141, 145, 146, 151, 157, 159,
    160, 161, 164, 165, 204, 217, 226,
    227, 231, 233, 238, 243, 247, 251,
    255, 292, 294, 296, 408, 410, 420,
    426, 430, 431, 450, 461, 476

Marston, D., 434
Martin, A. J., 442, 443
Martin, D. S., 17, 64, 81, 82, 89,
    164, 165
Martin, D. S., 64, 302
Martin, T., 201, 202
Martineau, G., 335
Martinez, A. S., 335, 451
Martins de Oliveira, J., 183
Martsi-McClintock, A., 334
Marx, E., 409
Marx, E. S., 303, 409
Marzano, R., 59, 60
Maskarinec, A. S., 365
Mason, C. Y., 87
Mason, M., 158, 162, 163
Mason, P., 203
Massi, G., 20
Massoni, P., 304
Masteller, A., 9, 137
Mastropieri, M. A., 42
Mathai, M., 355
Mather, N., 48
Mather, S., 63
Mathews, V. P., 441
Matkin, N. D., 371
Matsushima, J., 334
Matthews, T. J., 64
Mattox, S., 464
Mauk, G., 3
Mauk, G. W., 3, 244, 245
Maune, S., 398
Maurique, M., 176
Mavilya, M. P., 365
Maxon, A. B., 76, 354
Maxwell, M., 148
Maxwell, M. M., 146, 148
Maxwell-McCaw, D., 198, 237
Mayberry, M., 464
Mayberry, R., 112, 120, 146, 161,
    164, 302
Mayberry, R. I., 6, 10, 42, 112, 120, 130,
    146, 161, 164, 283, 284, 285, 286,
    287, 288, 289, 302, 426
Mayer, C., 19, 45, 46, 63, 102, 103,
    114, 129, 145, 147, 148, 151, 203,
    294, 433, 476
Mayer, R. E., 102
Mayer, T. S., 430
Mayne, A., 3
Mayne, A. M., 3, 241, 304
McAdams, D., 202, 205
McAnally, P., 115, 119, 120
McAnally, P. L., 115, 119, 120, 148
McArdle, B. M., 228
McCabe, A., 289
McCann, D., 325
McCann, R., 94
McCauley, R. W., 78
McClure, W., 22
McConkey Robbins, A., 296, 297, 335
McCormack, R., 429
McCormack, S., 410

McCracken, W., 242, 248, 297
McCroskey, R., 27
McCullough, S., 465
McCullough, S. H., 217, 465
McCune, L., 186, 409, 411
McCune-Nicholich, L., 409, 411
McCune-Nicholich, L. A., 303, 409, 411
McDonnell, A., 184
McDougle, C., 173
McElree, B., 467
McEvoy, C., 9, 137
McGahee-Kovac, M., 87
McGarr, N. S., 252, 308
McGough, S., 118
McGough, S. M., 44, 118
McGrath, P. J., 79
McGrew, K., 48, 152
McGuckian, M., 381
McGuire, A., 354
McIntire, M., 302
McKee, B., 95, 96
McKee, B. G., 63, 95, 96, 121, 139
McKee, D., 465
McKee, R., 202
McKellin, W. H., 377, 381, 383
McKinley, D. J., 132, 230, 476
McKinnon, E., 418
McKinnon, E. E., 9, 418
McKnight, T. K., 120
McLoughlin, J. A., 426
McMahon, R. K., 50
McNabb, M., 50
McNaughton, S., 64
McNeill, D., 268
McNeill, J., 159
McPherson, M., 221
McPhillips, H., 242, 325, 348, 349
McSweeney, M., 428
McWhirter, J. J., 198
McWhorter, J., 268
McWilliam, R. A., 299
Meador, H., 203
Meadow, K., 6, 28
Meadow, K. P., 6, 28, 303, 304
Meadow-Orlans, K. P., 3, 4, 9, 300,
    303, 320, 376, 409, 411, 412,
    413, 414, 422
Meadow-Orlans, K. P., 376
Meath-Lang, B., 147, 148
Medà, C., 346
Mehl, A., 31, 73
Mehl, A. L., 31, 73, 302, 334, 346,
    369, 380
Mehta, P., 229
Mehta, S., 355
Meier, R., 294, 302, 305
Meier, R. P., 294, 302, 304, 305
Meier, S., 352
Meir, I., 216, 270, 271, 272, 275,
    276, 277
Meisels, S., 186, 187
Mellon, J., 361
Mellon, J. A., 361, 368

Meltzoff, A. N., 300, 372
Mencher, G. T., 355
Menn, L., 308
Mens, L. H., 394
Mercer, C. D., 114
Mercer, K. D., 114
Mertens, D., 165, 300
Mertens, D. M., 165, 300, 376
Merzenich, M., 334
Mesibov, G., 176
Messenheimer, T., 121
Metcalfe-Haggert, A., 140
Metzger, M., 114
Meulemans, T., 449
Mewborn, D., 165
Meyer, A., 51
Meyer, T. A., 251
Meyer, V., 336
Michael, R., 229
Middlebrooks, J. C., 395, 400
Middleton, A., 205
Mikulincer, M., 256
Miles, B., 184, 185
Miller, E., 112
Miller, E. K., 112, 454
Miller, G. A., 447
Miller, J., 361
Miller, K., 46
Miller, K. J., 46, 82, 83, 85
Miller, L., 95
Miller, L. J., 95, 433
Miller, M., 20, 113
Miller, M. D., 20, 113, 114
Miller, R., 121, 361
Miller, S., 334
Milligan, K., 412
Mills, C., 465
Mills, M., 465
Mindess, A., 221
Minoshima, S., 466
Miorelli, V., 339, 393
Mirenda, P., 174
Mischel, W., 195
Mishler, E., 205
Mitchell, D. R., 61
Mitchell, P. R., 362
Mitchell, R., 57, 161, 196, 199, 202, 204
Mitchell, R. E., 57, 72, 73, 76, 161, 196, 199, 202, 204, 227, 252
Mitchell, T., 408
Mitchell, T. V., 217, 408
Miyake, A., 459
Miyamoto, R. T., 227, 251, 335, 336, 445
Mobley, R., 119
Mock, D., 434
Modlo, M., 50
Moeljopawiro, S., 270
Moeller, M. P., 3, 5, 37, 45, 46, 47, 111, 112, 113, 129, 130, 131, 139, 242, 292, 295, 298, 302, 303, 304, 308, 346, 365, 366, 367, 368., 369, 379, 380, 381, 415, 418, 419, 420
Mohay, H., 319

Mok, M., 398
Molfese, D., 333
Molis, M., 283
Möller, C., 179
Monaghan, L., 220
Monikowski, C. M., 77
Monsen, R., 367
Monsen, R. B., 251, 252, 308, 367
Montgomery, G., 204
Montgomery, L., 1
Montoya, M., 228
Moody, A., 44
Moog, J., 6, 113, 231, 234
Moog, J. S., 6, 113, 132, 231, 234, 252, 297, 335, 336
Moore, D., 217
Moore, D. R., 217, 328, 440
Moore, J. A., 366
Moore, J. K., 305
Moore, M., 243
Moore, P. E., 347
Moores, D. F., 7, 17, 19, 20, 21, 24, 25, 26, 27, 52, 73, 74, 76, 77, 145, 160, 161, 165, 196
Moores, D. F., 52, 201, 302
Mootilal, A., 78
Morales Angulo, C., 302
Moreno, C., 9, 10, 157, 159, 160, 162, 163, 164, 428, 430
Morey, C. C., 464
Morf, C., 195
Morford, J., 287, 302
Morford, J. P., 268, 287, 302
Morgan, A., 97, 432, 434
Morgan, D., 148
Morgan, D. D., 63, 148
Morgan, L. J., 364
Morgan, P. L., 434
Morkovin, B., 27
Morningstar, M. E., 50
Morozova, N., 27
Mortensen, L., 3
Morton, C. C., 214
Moser, J., 158
Moskowitz, G., 195
Moss, K., 185
Most, T., 8, 72, 74, 75, 112, 130, 136, 204, 229, 251, 253, 255, 256, 257, 258
Mount, R., 336
Mouradian, V., 146, 147
Mousley, K., 158, 159, 161, 162
Mudgett-DeCaro, P. A., 259
Mueller, J., 399
Muenning, P., 41
Muir, S. G., 9, 37, 76, 77, 87, 112
Muir, S. G., 9, 294
Mukari, S., 231, 232
Mukari, S. Z., 231, 232, 350, 352, 354
Mukherjee, M., 460
Mukunda, K. V., 467
Müller-Deile, J., 398
Mundy, L., 205, 215

Municio, A., 346
Munro, J., 121
Munro, S., 441
Munroe, S., 181
Murphy, T., 350
Murray, D., 305
Murray, J., 203, 212, 213, 220
Musselman, C. R., 78, 79, 81, 82, 146, 214, 331, 335, 378
Musselman, C. R., 331
Muysken, P., 275
Myklebust, H. R., 146, 441, 450, 454
Mylanus, E., 180, 228
Mylanus, E. A., 231
Mylanus, E. A. M., 180, 228, 231

N
Nafstad, A., 183, 184, 186
Nagy, W. E., 114
Nahler, A., 394
Naidu, S., 4
Nakamura, K., 199, 220
Nance, W. E., 214
Narabayashi, O., 352
Narbona, J., 176
Natale, F., 175
Nathani, S., 307, 361, 363, 364, 365, 366, 369, 370, 373
Nauta, W. J. H., 441
Nava, E., 465
Nazir, T. A., 114
Neal, A. R., 307, 365
Neault, M., 353
Nedzelski, J. M., 394
Needham, A., 408
Needham, E., 118, 119
Neill, J., 164
Nelson, C., 178, 184, 186, 187
Nelson, D. L., 137
Nelson, H., 242, 245, 246
Nelson, H. D., 242, 245, 246, 348
Nelson, J., 219
Nelson, K., 176, 294, 304
Nelson, K. E., 60
Nespor, M., 276
Netick, A., 426
Netsell, R., 367
Nettles, E. J., 394
Neuberger, H., 337, 339
Neuroth-Gimbrone, C., 148
Neuss, D., 79
Neville, H. J., 9, 217
Nevins, M. E., 232, 336
Newall, P., 430
Newman, A., 460, 461
Newman, R. S., 114
Newport, E., 275, 277, 294, 302, 305
Newport, E. L., 275, 277, 283, 284, 294, 302, 304, 305, 382, 445, 449, 458
Newport, L., 461
Newton, V. E., 347, 355
Ng, A. H., 394
Ngo, R. Y. S., 351

Nicholas, J. G., 73, 129, 130, 132, 133, 136, 230, 233, 293, 326, 378, 380, 476
Nichols, I. A., 365
Niculae, I., 458
Nield, A. F., 468
Niemeyer, J. A., 47
Nijssen, F., 68
Nikelski, E. J., 216
Nikolaraizi, M., 196
Nikolopolous, T., 327
Nikolopoulos, T., 136, 227, 230, 232, 327
Nikolopoulos, T. M., 227
Nikolopoulos, T. P., 128, 132, 227, 228, 230, 231, 232, 233, 326, 335, 339, 476
Niparko, J., 230
Niparko, J. K., 230, 231, 246, 335
Nittrouer, S., 381
Noble, T., 215
Noble, W., 395, 396, 397, 398
Nonaka, A. M., 270, 274
Nopp, P., 399
Norbury, C. F., 381
Norman, D., 459
Normand, C., 232
Norris, C., 102
Northern, J., 203
Norton, S., 246
Norton, S. J., 246, 293
Norwich, B., 60
Nougaret, A. A., 42
Novack, L. L., 305
Novak, M. A., 335
Nover, S. M., 50
Nuerk, H., 160
Numbers, F. C., 308
Nunen, T., 181
Nunes, T., 1, 9, 10, 79, 80, 82, 157, 159, 160, 162, 163, 164, 228, 378, 465
Nussbaum, D., 297
Nygern, P., 242
Nygren, P., 348
Nyst, V., 270, 276
Nystrand, M., 144, 145, 150

O

Oakley, S., 396
Oakley, Y., 321
Oates, P., 352
Obenchain, P., 308
Oberg, J., 431
Oberman, L. M., 183
O'Brien, J., 49
O'Connell, B., 409
O'Connor, N., 465
Oddy, A., 157
Odom, P. B., 450
O'Donnell, N., 181
O'Donoghue, G., 231, 232, 327
O'Donoghue, G. M., 128, 132, 227, 230, 231, 232, 233, 327, 328, 335, 440, 476

Oghalai, J., 229
O'Grady, L., 217, 305
O'Grady Hynes, M., 217
O'Grady-Hynes, M., 319
Oh, S. H., 350
Ohlwein, S., 300
Ohna, S. E., 237
Olds, H., 307
O'Leary, S., 236
Oleson, J., 394
Oller, D. K., 307, 308, 361, 362, 364, 365, 366, 369, 370, 372, 373
Olson, D., 145
Olszewski, C., 394
Olusanya, B. O., 347, 348, 349, 353, 355, 356
O'Neill, C., 228, 229, 232
O'Neill, T., 336
Oong, R., 325, 346
Orlansky, M. D., 305, 465
Ormrod, J. E., 51
O'Rourke, T., 21
Ortony, A., 120
Osberger, M., 408
Osberger, M. J., 251, 304, 335, 367, 372, 393, 394, 408
Osbourne, T., 7
Osugi, Y., 269, 271, 273
Otomo, K., 365, 367
Ottem, E., 9, 133
Otterstedt, L., 213
Owen, V., 187
Ower, J., 199, 200, 378

P

Paatsch, L., 121, 136
Padak, N. D., 147
Padden, C. A., 6, 63, 112, 128, 147, 196, 199, 201, 204, 211, 216, 270
Padden, C. A., 6, 147, 272, 275, 276, 277
Pagliaro, C. M., 9, 65, 158, 159, 162, 163, 164, 165
Pagliaro, C. M., 65, 164, 165
Paige, R., 35
Painter, K., 409
Painter, K. M., 303, 409
Paivio, A., 122
Pakulski, L., 112, 120
Panesar, J., 336
Pang, F., 348
Pans, D., 235
Papagno, C., 461
Papsin, B., 336
Papsin, B. C., 334, 336
Paradise, J., 3
Parasnis, I., 9, 202, 259, 427
Paris, D., 201
Parisier, S. C., 336
Park, C. S., 350
Park, K., 185
Park, K. S., 185, 350
Parker, K. R., 178
Parker, R., 300

Parkin, I., 23
Parkinson, A., 396
Parkinson, A. J., 396, 398
Parkinson, W. S., 394
Parks, E., 101
Parson-Tylka, T., 295, 300
Pastorelli, C., 77
Paterson, M., 410
Patterson, A., 252
Patterson, D. G., 461
Patterson, R., 252
Paul, P., 94, 113, 146
Paul, P. V., 94, 113, 146, 428, 469
Pavani, F., 465
Payne, J., 119
Pearson, N., 419
Peet, H., 22, 25
Pegg, P., 335
Peisner-Feinberg, E. S., 289
Peled, M., 130, 136
Pelz, J., 10, 48
Penfield, W., 282, 283
Peng, S. C., 251
Pennings, R., 180
Pennington, B., 415
Penuel, W. R., 102
Percy, S., 230
Peretsky, D., 112
Perfetti, C. A., 112, 428
Perold, J. L., 229
Perrett, D. I., 184
Peters, D., 47
Peters, K., 10, 415, 416, 421
Peters, R., 396
Peterson, B., 292, 365, 366
Peterson, C., 415, 417
Peterson, K., 98
Peterson, M., 8
Peterson, M. E., 8, 42, 74
Pethick, S. J., 304, 321
Petitto, L., 294, 304
Petitto, L. A., 216, 294, 302, 304, 305
Pfau, R., 175
Phillips, W., 27
Piaget, J., 303, 408
Pianta, R. C., 59
Picard, M., 382, 383, 385
Pichora-Fuller, K., 381, 382
Pickell, B., 460
Pickering, D., 60
Piercy, S., 44
Pierpont, E. I., 440
Pillard, R. C., 271
Pilling, D., 103, 203
Pimentel, J., 255
Pinder, R., 227, 339, 393
Pineda, J. A., 183
Pintner, R., 461
Pipp-Siegel, S., 3, 241
Pisoni, D., 128, 133, 138, 204, 251, 408
Pisoni, D. B., 128, 132, 133, 138, 152, 204, 251, 304, 333, 408, 442, 443, 444, 445, 450, 451, 454, 464

Pisoni, D. P., 333
Pittman, A. L., 381
Pittman, P., 242, 295, 307
Pizzuto, E., 305
Plapinger, D., 433
Plapinger, D. S., 432, 433
Poe, D. M., 289
Pogorelsky, S., 451
Poizner, H., 283, 465
Polat, F., 235
Polazzo, M. G., 122, 133
Pollack, D., 22
Pollock, D., 293, 306
Pollock, J. E., 60
Pontecorvo, C., 146
Ponton, C. W., 334
Poon, B. T., 383, 386
Poor, G. S., 101
Porter, J., 9
Porter, J. E., 9, 93
Posey, D., 173
Postle, B. R., 460, 466, 468
Potter, M. C., 467, 468
Poulakis, Z., 242, 351
Povinelli, D., 419
Power, D. J., 21, 23, 28, 46, 72, 73, 74,
    75, 82, 83, 103, 158, 203, 204, 214,
    228, 234, 252, 295, 378
Power, D. J., 214
Power, M., 203
Power, M. R., 103, 203
Powers, A., 427
Powers, A. R., 146, 427
Powers, S., 7, 8, 46, 76
Prasad, C., 178
Preece, J. P., 396, 398
Preisler, G., 20, 21, 28, 204, 237
Premack, A. J., 467
Premack, D., 467
Preminger, J. E., 95
Prescott, S., 410
Presseisen, B. Z., 121
Pressley, M., 86, 87
Pretzlik, S., 228
Pretzlik, U., 79, 80, 82, 378
Prezbindowski, A. K., 381
Prezioso, C., 319
Price, D., 94
Prickett, H., 120
Prinz, E. A., 304
Prinz, P., 148
Prinz, P. M., 148, 304, 305
Prior, P., 145
Pritchard, R. J., 150
Probst, R., 352
Proctor, A., 293
Proksch, J., 133
Puig, T., 346
Pulsifer, M. B., 335
Punch, R., 199, 259, 378, 379
Purcell-Gates, V., 151
Purdy, S. C., 430
Putman, C., 292, 365, 366

Putnam, R., 221
Pyers, J., 419
Pylyshyn, Z. W., 460, 468
Pyman, B., 138

Q

Quamma, J. P., 120
Quartararo, A., 19
Quartz, S., 185
Quigley, S., 28, 115, 146
Quigley, S. P., 128, 115, 119, 120,
    146, 148
Quittner, A., 408
Quittner, A. L., 138, 408

R

Raban, B., 118, 119
Rabinowitz, W. M., 293
Radutzky, E., 175
Rajput, K., 112, 130, 476
Rall, E., 309
Ramachandran, V. S., 183, 184
Ramirez-Inscoe, J., 328, 440
Ramkalawan, T., 241, 302, 325, 348
Rampelli, L. P., 146
Ramsden, R., 397
Ramsden, R. T., 334, 397
Ramsey, C. L., 6, 61, 63, 112, 128
Ramsey, C. L., 61, 63
Ramsey, S., 94
Rankin, E., 429
Rao, V. Y., 466
Raphael, L. J., 252
Rapin, I., 176, 346
Rappold, R. P., 59, 100
Rappolt, G., 51
Rasinski, T. V., 115
Ratner, N. B., 300, 301
Raudenbush, S. W., 369
Raven, J., 417
Ray, B. B., 102
Ray, J., 334
Rayner, K., 112
Razza-Peters, R., 441
Read, B. K., 258
Readence, J. E., 87
Rebelsky, G. F., 365
Reed, C. M., 293
Reed, S., 8, 46, 73, 76, 77, 86, 87, 294
Reese, W., 252
Reeves, D. B., 42
Regenbogen, L., 178
Rehling, B., 103, 203
Reich, C. F., 64
Reilley, D., 334
Reilly, J. S., 283, 287, 302, 304, 305,
    321, 322, 323, 324
Reilly, J. S., 302, 304, 305
Remine, M., 414
Remmel, E., 10, 415, 416, 421
Rempel, R., 385
Renard, M., 222
Rennie, M., 335

Renshaw, J. J., 393
Renshaw, P. D., 255
Renting, B., 66
Resnick, S., 321
Reynell, J., 413
Reznick, J., 413
Reznick, J. S., 304, 413
Rhoades, E., 6
Rhoten, C., 6, 112, 129, 141, 152, 231
Rhyne, J., 176
Ribera, J., 350
Rich, J. S., 304
Richardson, A., 97, 429
Richardson, J., 121
Richardson, J. T. E., 100, 121
Richardson, U., 429
Richburg, C. M., 129, 130
Richmond, H. L., 128
Richter, B., 228
Rickards, E. P., 89
Rickards, F. W., 118, 119, 121, 242,
    410, 413
Rickards, F. W., 242
Ricketts, T. A., 396
Riggio, M., 185
Riksen-Walraven, J. M. A., 182, 186
Rileigh, K. K., 450
Riley, M., 159
Ringwalt, S. S., 293
Risely, T., 161
Risley, T. R., 115
Rittenhouse, R., 120
Riverin, L., 203
Rivers, J. C., 41
Rivers, R., 148
Rizer, F. M., 339
Rizolatti, G., 183
Rizzoltti, G., 183
Robbins, A., 335
Robbins, A. M., 233, 304, 335, 393
Roberson, J. L., 66
Roberts, L., 282, 283
Robey, R., 115, 116
Robinson, K., 234
Robinson, M., 164
Rocha do Amaral, J., 183
Rochat, P., 408
Rødbroe, I., 183, 184, 186
Rodda, M., 299, 303
Roelofs, E., 68
Rogers, S., 415
Rogoff, B., 422
Roid, G. H., 433
Roizen, N. J., 348
Roland, J., 397
Roland, J. T., 339, 397
Roland, J. T., Jr., 393
Ronen, T., 257
Ronnberg, J., 460, 461, 463, 468
Roper, T., 157
Roschelle, J., 102
Rose, D. H., 51
Rose, H., 219

Rose, S., 115, 119, 120, 148
Rosen, R., 28
Ross, E., 353
Ross, L., 398
Ross, M., 76, 199, 227, 230, 377
Rossetti, L. M., 337
Rossini, P., 465
Roth, V., 432
Rotz, L. A., 335
Roug, L., 361
Rourke, B. P., 454
Rouse, C., 41
Roush, J., 299, 346, 371
Rousselet, G. A., 468
Rowland, C., 185
Roy, P., 323
Rozier, E., 235
Ruben, R. J., 332, 333, 346
Rubenstein, H., 447
Rubinstein, J. T., 394
Rudmin, F., 201
Rudner, M., 460, 468
Rudolph, S. M., 41
Rupa, V., 347
Rush, D. D., 301
Russ, S. A., 245, 350
Ryan, T., 121
Rypma, B., 461

S
Sabers, D., 48, 77
Sabers, D. L., 48, 77, 378
Sach, T., 228, 229, 230, 231, 232,
     233, 234
Sach, T. H., 230, 326
Sach, T. M., 227
Sacks, O., 218, 333
Saffran, J. R., 449
Sahlén, B., 133
Saindon, K., 361
Sall, N., 187
Salmi, E., 213
Salorio, C. F., 335
Sam, D., 198, 201
Sam, D. L., 198, 201
Samar, C. F., 230
Samar, V., 202
Samar, V. J., 9, 202, 259, 427, 428, 429
Samuels, S. J., 115
Sandak, R., 428
Sandel, M., 205, 222
Sander, E., 308
Sanders, W. L., 41
Sandler, W., 216, 221, 268, 270, 271,
     272, 275, 276, 277
Santana, A., 20
Sapere, P., 6, 48, 62, 77, 86, 128
Saracho, O. N., 304
Sarant, J., 121, 136, 335
Sarchet, T., 6, 128
Sass-Lehrer, M. A., 4, 32, 47, 248, 300
Sass-Lehrer, M. A., 376
Satir, V., 298

Saulnier, K., 295
Saulnier, K. L., 295
Saults, J. S., 463, 464
Saunders, E., 203
Saunders, J. L., 258
Saxe, G., 161
Scaife, M., 317
Scalchunes, V., 335
Scanlon, D., 434
Scarborough, H., 418
Scarborough, H. S., 113, 114, 418
Scardamalia, M., 145
Schalock, R., 174
Schauwers, K., 366
Scheerens, J., 58
Scheetz, N. A., 64
Schenker, N., 454
Scherer, M., 255
Schick, B., 34, 47, 62, 63, 86, 161, 164,
     284, 294, 295, 302, 305, 415, 418,
     419, 420, 421
Schildroth, A., 303
Schilperoord, J., 94
Schimmel, C., 120
Schirmer, B., 118, 151, 410
Schirmer, B. R., 44, 118, 151, 187, 410
Schleich, P., 399
Schleper, D., 147
Schlesinger, H. S., 304
Schley, S., 151
Schlumberger, E., 176
Schmaling, C., 220
Schmidt, M. H., 441
Schmidledge, J., 350
Schmitendorf, K., 299
Schmitz, K. L., 151
Schmuziger, N., 352
Schoen, F., 399
Schoenmaker, A., 181
Schopler, E., 176
Schrader, F. -W., 59
Schreuder, R., 152, 231, 327
Schuch, A., 119
Schuengel, C., 182
Schultz, M. C., 293
Schum, R., 381
Schumacher, E. H., 466
Schumaker, J. B., 121
Schwartz, I. S., 182
Schweigert, P., 185
Scott, D. A., 269
Scott, S., 254, 260, 297
Scott, S. K., 254, 260, 297, 429
Scott-Olson, K., 376
Scruggs, T. E., 42
Seal, B. C., 88
Seaton, J. B., 115
Seaver, L., 248
Sebald, A., 112
Sebald, A. M., 9, 112
Secada, W., 158, 162
Secord, W. A., 337, 454
Sedey, A., 3, 73, 302, 308

Sedey, A. L., 3, 73, 233, 241, 302, 304,
     308, 334, 346, 369, 380
Seedhouse, E., 450
Seewagen, R., 62, 77, 86
Segel, P., 394
Seidenberg, M., 468
Seidenberg, M. S., 112, 282, 468
Sejnowski, T. J., 185
Seldon, L., 334
Selfridge, J. A., 447
Selmi, A., 409
Selmi, A. M., 303, 409
Semel, E., 337, 454
Senge, P., 42
Senghas, A., 221, 271, 272, 273, 275,
     276, 277, 449
Serrano Pau, C., 158, 159
Serry, T. A., 367
Service, E., 442, 443
Serwatka, T. S., 66
Shah, P., 459
Shahin, K., 381
Shallice, T., 459
Shannon, R. V., 451
Shapiro, B., 173
Sharma, A., 334, 346
Sharma, M., 430
Shatz, C., 334
Shaver, J. P., 254
Shaw, E. A., 395
Shaw, P. C., 151
Shea, V., 176
Shearer, M., 410, 411
Sheffield, V. C., 269
Sheldon, L., 227
Sheldon, M. L., 301
Sheng, Z., 164
Shepard, N. T., 76, 381
Shepherd, R. K., 334
Sherer, K. R., 252
Sherrick, C. E., 293
Shield, B. M., 383
Ship, N., 365
Shipp, D. B., 394
Shore, C., 409
Shores, A., 230
Shpak, T., 398
Shriberg, L. D., 308
Shriver, E. K., 173
Shroyer, E., 47
Shulman, L., 165
Siegal, M., 415, 416
Siegel, L. S., 114
Siegel, S., 243
Sieving, P., 180
Sikora, D., 433
Sikora, D. M., 432, 433
Silberman, R. K., 186, 187
Silbert, J., 114
Sillari, J., 186
Silman, S., 398
Simmons, H., 361
Simmons, S., 350

Simms, L., 8
Simon, A., 112
Simon, H. A., 150
Simpson, P. A., 148
Singer, B. D., 144, 146, 149, 150, 151
Singleton, D., 332
Singleton, J. L., 63, 148, 268
Sininger, Y. S., 305
Siperstein, G. N., 89
Siple, P., 460, 461
Sirvage, R., 221
Sitzmann, T., 59
Skelton, T., 205
Skinner, M. W., 394
Skipp, A., 204, 234, 297
Skutnabb-Kangas, T., 216
Slade, A., 409, 411
Slade, L. A., 465
Slavin, R. E., 88
Slobin, D. I., 303
Slofstra-Bremer, C., 61
Smaldino, J., 383
Smaldino, J. J., 383
Small, A., 214
Small, S., 434
Smiler, K., 202
Smiley, P., 304
Smith, A., 354, 356
Smith, B., 42
Smith, B. L., 42, 362
Smith, C. R., 368
Smith, D. H., 63
Smith, D. L., 211, 271
Smith, E. E., 461, 466
Smith, L., 408
Smith, L. B., 408, 440
Smith, M. D., 82, 83
Smith, N., 275
Smith, P., 441
Smith, R. J., 214, 347
Smith, S., 199, 203, 235, 237
Smith, T., 186
Smith-Lovin, L., 221
Smoorenburg, G. F., 394
Snider, B. C., 211
Snieders, J., 174
Snijders, J. T., 433
Snik, A. F., 180, 231, 327
Snik, A. F., 231
Snoddon, K., 213, 214
Snow, C. E., 121
Snyder, B., 86, 87
Snyder, L. S., 3, 146, 303, 304, 334,
    409, 410, 411
Snyder, L. S., 146
Sokol, H., 352
Solar, J., 22, 50
Solimando, S., 468
Soloway, E., 102
Solvang, P., 220
Sonksen, P., 183
Sorkin, D., 199
Sorkin, D. L., 199, 232, 233

Soukup, M., 427
Souriau, J., 184
Spahn, C., 228, 229
Spahr, A. J., 334, 346
Spandel, V., 151
Sparrow, S., 454
Speel, M., 235
Spelke, E., 468
Spencer, L., 420
Spencer, L. J., 6, 135, 152, 231, 292,
    326, 420
Spencer, P., 129, 152, 161, 204, 226,
    227, 233, 238, 251, 255, 294, 408,
    409, 410, 411, 412, 413, 414, 415,
    420, 422
Spencer, P. E., 6, 7, 8, 46, 51, 129, 130,
    133, 138, 139, 152, 161, 204, 226,
    227, 231, 233, 238, 251, 255, 292,
    294, 300, 301, 304, 318, 319, 320,
    326, 327, 328, 381, 408, 409, 410,
    411, 412, 413, 414, 415, 420, 422
Sperber, D., 467
Spivak, L. G., 352
Spodek, B., 304
Sporns, O., 440, 441
Squires, B., 283
Stacey, P., 176, 231
Stacey, P. C., 130, 132, 136, 137,
    138, 176, 231, 476
Stachowiak, J., 298
Stallings, L. M., 112
Stanovich, K. E., 113
Stanwick, R., 157
Stapells, D. R., 352
Stapp, Y. F., 333
Stark, R. E., 307, 361, 362, 364, 365,
    367, 368, 369, 370, 372, 373
Stauffer, R. G., 117
St-Cyr, C., 203
Stecker, M., 398
Stedt, J., 19
Steely, D., 59, 99, 104
Steffens, M., 364, 365
Steffens, M. L., 362, 364, 365, 366
Stein, M. S., 95
Steinberg, A., 201, 228, 303, 412
Steinberg, A. G., 201, 228, 254, 260,
    299, 303, 412
Steinfield, A., 95
Stelmachowicz, P. G., 76, 381
Stephenson, B., 44, 58, 65, 117, 165
Sterkenburg, P., 182
Sterritt, G. M., 465
Sterritt, M., 197
Stevens, K. N., 447
Stevens, R., 336
Stevenson, H. W., 114
Stewart, D., 47, 59, 164
Stewart, D. A., 47, 51, 53, 59, 63, 89,
    164, 228, 229
Stickney, G. S., 398
Stiggins, R. J., 151
Stillman, R., 187

Stinson, M., 5, 7, 64, 95, 96, 98, 197, 378
Stinson, M. S., 5, 7, 47, 48, 57, 58, 64,
    73, 74, 75, 77, 78, 79, 80, 81, 82,
    85, 88, 89, 95, 96, 98, 197, 254,
    256, 260, 378
Stinson, S., 95, 96
Stobbart, C., 112, 120
Stockton, J. D., 99
Stoel-Gammon, C., 362, 365, 366, 367,
    368, 369, 371, 372
Stoep, J., 174
Stoer, B. S., 335
Stokes, J., 5
Stokoe, W., 216, 217, 222
Stokoe, W. C., 2, 216, 217, 222,
    281, 283
Stone, C. A., 145
Stone, E. M., 269
Stone, M., 419
Stoner, M., 122
Storbeck, C., 23
Stout, G. G., 306
Strand, S., 441
Strangman, N., 51
Strassman, B., 9, 77, 86, 120
Stredler-Brown, A., 32, 242, 247, 293,
    294, 298, 299, 300, 301, 306,
    307, 308
Streng, A. H., 148
Strong, C. J., 254
Strong, M., 148, 161
Stronge, J. H., 41
Stuart, A., 148
Stuckless, E., 28, 95
Stuckless, E. R., 6, 28, 95
Stuckless, R., 95
Studdert-Kennedy, M., 267
Suarez, M., 89
Suddendorf, T., 184
Sullivan, S. D., 354
Summerfield, A., 176, 231
Summerfield, A. Q., 130, 176 231,
    394, 476
Supalla, T., 220, 269, 275, 277,
    458, 461
Susser, E., 181
Sutherland, H., 242, 247
Sutton, V., 218, 219
Sutton-Spence, R., 271
Svartholm, K., 147, 148
Svirsky, M., 233, 397
Svirsky, M. A., 112, 233, 251, 336,
    337, 339, 397
Swanepoel, D., 350, 352
Swanepoel, D. C. D., 347, 348,
    350, 352
Swanson, H. L., 114, 145
Swart, S. M., 347, 353
Sweeny, J. L., 308
Sweeten, T., 173
Swettenham, J., 415
Swisher, M., 300
Swisher, M. V., 10, 300

Symons, F., 300
Szanto, G., 146
Szczerbinski, M., 428
Szelag, E., 465

T

Taeschner, T., 146
Tait, M., 233
Tait, M. E., 228, 233
Tajfel, H., 197
Talbot, K. F., 10
Taljaard, D., 351
Tallal, P., 334, 465
Tallerman, M., 267
Tan, H. K. K., 351
Tan, K. Y., 350
Tanaka, S., 334
Tangney, J., 195
Tan-Torres Edejer, T., 354
Tao, W., 180
Tardy, M., 114
Tarver, S., 114
Taschman, H., 298
Tatar, D. G., 102
Tattersall, H., 3, 242, 243, 244, 245,
    246, 247, 248, 297
Tatum, B., 195, 196
Taub, S., 218, 219
Taylor, D. J., 295, 307
Taylor, L., 219
Tees, R. C., 282, 333
Teilan, S. A., 335
Telian, S. A., 394
Tellefson, M., 185
Tellegen, P. J., 433
Teller, H., 82
Tellings, A., 24, 201
Templin, M., 147
Teoh, S. -W., 337, 339
Terushkin, V., 397
Tervoort, B., 26
Test, D. W., 87
Thagard, E., 120
Thai, D., 304
Thal, D., 246, 321
Thal, D. J., 246, 304, 321
Tharpe, A., 138, 383
Tharpe, A. M., 138, 203, 383
Thatcher, R. W., 454
Thayer, S., 293
Thebault, C., 147, 464
Thelen, E., 440
Thelin, J., 178
Theunissen, M., 177
Thomas, J., 441
Thomas, J. F., 335, 441
Thomas, S., 121
Thompson, D. C., 242, 325, 349
Thompson, K., 184
Thompson, L. A., 2, 60
Thompson, V., 3
Thomson, D., 180
Thomson, J. M., 429

Thomson, V., 31, 241, 242, 303, 346
Thornton, R., 325
Thorpe, S., 468
Thorpe, S. J., 468
Thorsen, C., 52
Thoutenhoofd, E. D., 6, 133, 227, 228,
    231, 232
Thoutenhoofd, E. D., 326
Thumann, H., 8
Thurston, L. C., 336
Tibbitts, R., 318
Tiberius, R. G., 309
Tierney, R. J., 87
Tijsseling, C., 24
Tijssling, C., 24
Tillein, J., 346
Tillman, T., 383
Ting, S., 102
Titterington, J., 138
Titus, J., 157
Tobey, E., 6, 128, 231
Tobey, E. A., 6, 128, 231, 233
Todd, S. L., 335
Todini, L., 235, 236
Todman, J., 450
Tolar, T., 174
Tomann, A., 217
Tomasello, M., 174
Tomblin, B., 378
Tomblin, J. B., 113, 152, 251, 292, 326,
    327, 378, 380
Tomov, A., 336
Tomov, A. M., 335, 336
Toner, J. G., 138
Torres, S., 136
Toscano, R. M., 139
Traci, M. A., 378
Transler, C., 120
Traxler, C., 111
Traxler, C. B., 8, 111, 138, 156, 157, 161
Trezek, B. J., 114, 428, 469
Trimble, J., 200
Trivette, C. M., 299
Troia, G., 145
Tronick, E., 317
Truax, R., 148
Truchon-Gagnon, C., 382, 383
Trueswell, J. C., 449
Tsiakpini, L., 307
Tuber, D. S., 468
Tuchman, R. R., 176
Tucker, B., 204
Tucker, P. D., 41
Tuholski, S. W., 461
Tulving, E., 460
Turner, C., 394
Turner, C. W., 251, 394
Turner, G. H., 220
Turner, J., 197
Turner, R. G., 354
Tvingstedt, A., 81, 204
Tvingstedt, A. L., 81, 204, 237
Twomey, T., 328, 440

Tye-Murray, N., 294, 306, 307
Tyler, A. A., 301
Tyler, R., 396
Tyler, R. S., 394, 395, 396, 397,
    398, 399
Tyszkiewicz, E., 5

U

Ugazio, G., 235
Ullman, M. T., 440, 449
Urbano, R., 362, 364
Urbano, R. C., 362, 364, 366
Uus, K., 241, 346

V

Valentine, G., 205
Valli, C., 294
Van, B. W., 231
Van Ambt, C. M., 58
Van Balkom, H., 61, 174
van Bon, W., 152, 327
Van Cleve, J. V., 211, 212, 281
Van Cutsem, M., 157, 162
Van de Grift, W. J. C. M., 60
Van de Heyning, P., 325
Vandell, D. L., 78, 257
Van den Broek, E., 177
van den Broek, P., 114
van den Dikkenberg-Pot, I., 365
Van den Tillaart, B., 186
VanderArk, W. D., 234
van der Leij, A., 441
Van der Linden, M., 449
Van der Schuit, M., 174
Van der Sluis, S., 441
van der Stelt, J. M., 361
Van Dijk, J., 176, 178, 179, 180, 181,
    182, 183, 184, 185, 186, 187
van Dijk, J. E., 394
Van Dijk, R., 175, 184
Van Dyke, J. A., 467
Van Helvoort, M., 175
van Hoek, K., 305
Van Hoek, K., 217
van Hoesel, R. J. M., 399
Van Leeuwen, A. M., 241
van Olphen, A. F., 394
Van Ramshorst, T., 177
van Son, N., 94
Van Splunder, J., 177
Van Uden, A. M. J., 429
van Wanrooy, E., 346
Van Wanrooy, E. V., 325, 346
Van Weerdenburg, M., 61
Vasilyeva, M., 113
Vasishth, S., 467
Vass, M., 133
Vath, R., 102
Veenman, S., 68
Velásquez, J., 201, 202
Vellutino, F., 434
Venkatesh, C., 179
Verbeck, A., 26

Vermeulen, A., 134, 152
Vermeulen, A. M., 134, 152, 231, 327
Vermeulen, L., 180
Vernon, M., 6, 28, 425, 432, 434
Verpoorten, R., 176
Verschuure, H., 177
Vervloed, M., 172, 184
Verweij, E., 321
Vesel, J., 101
Vesey, K., 199, 200
Vibbert, M., 409
Viehweg, S., 8
Viehweg, S. H., 8, 74
Vignare, K., 59, 100
Vihman, M., 363
Vihman, M. M., 361, 362, 363, 364
Vinter, S., 365
Virnig, S., 120
VL2, 217
Vohr, B., 246
Vohr, B. R., 246, 347, 354
Volterra, V., 146, 175, 304, 409,
    413, 465
von Hapsburg, D., 366
Vural, M., 228
Vygotsky, L., 303, 410
Vygotsky, L. S., 121, 303, 410

W

Waddy-Smith, B., 297, 429
Wade-Woolley, L., 114
Wager, T. D., 461
Wagner, R. K., 114
Wake, M., 242
Walberg, H. J., 58
Wald, R., 204
Wald, R. L., 204, 237
Walden, B., 242
Wales, R., 136
Walker, L., 121
Walkerdine, V., 161
Wallace, J., 346
Wallace, V., 308
Wallvik, B., 213
Waltzman, S., 397
Waltzman, S. B., 335, 338, 339,
    393, 394, 397
Walworth, M., 21
Wang, Y., 94, 428, 441, 469
Want, S., 416
Ward, A., 333
Ward, P., 94
Warick, R., 199, 200, 386
Warick, R. P., 199, 200, 385, 386
Washabaugh, W., 269, 274, 275,
    277, 279
Washburn, A., 28
Waterman, A., 195
Watkin, P. M., 244, 245, 349
Watkins, S., 242, 295, 297, 306, 307, 429
Watkins, T., 148
Watson, D. R., 138
Watson, L., 136

Watson, L. M., 136, 230, 233, 234,
    236, 327
Watson, S. D., 334
Wauters, L., 42, 51, 63, 79, 80, 81,
    82, 121, 130, 133, 135, 139, 408,
    410, 476
Waxman, R., 422
Wayne, A. J., 41
Weamer, D. K., 365
Webb, R., 220, 269
Webster, A., 146, 147
Webster, E., 336
Wechsler, D., 433
Wedell-Monnig, J., 161
Weed, K. A., 187
Wehmeyer, M., 174
Wei, B., 236
Weichbold, V., 302, 307
Weinberg, N., 197
Weiner G. M., 354
Weiner, M. T., 93
Weinert, F., 59
Weisel A., 258, 259
Weisel, A., 229, 254, 257, 258, 385
Weiss, A., 146
Weiss, H., 398
Welles, E. B., 211
Wellman, H., 415, 416, 417
Werker, J., 282
Werker, J. F., 282, 333
Werner, H., 22, 182
Westling, D. L., 173, 187
Wheeden, C. A., 67
Wheeler, A., 204, 230, 233, 234, 235,
    236, 237, 327
Wheeler, L., 183
Wheldall, K., 430
White, A., 128, 231, 327
White, C., 5
White, K., 3, 300
White, K. R., 3, 300, 302, 347, 354
Whitehurst, G. J., 113
Whiten, A., 184
Whitmire, K., 77, 78, 79, 80, 81, 378
Whittingham, J., 325
Whynes, D., 228, 230, 231, 232, 233, 234
Wickens, C. D., 468
Wickens, D. D., 468
Widen, J. E., 246
Wiederholt, J. L., 419
Wiesel, A., 204
Wiesel, T., 333
Wiesel, T. N., 282, 333
Wigus, S., 146
Wiig, E. H., 337, 454
Wilbur, R., 294
Wilbur, R. B., 146, 148
Wilcox, P., 219
Wilcox, S., 216
Wiles, J., 148
Wiley, E., 283
Willard, T., 219
Willerman, R., 302

Williams, C., 113
Williams, C. L., 113, 148
Williams, J. H. G., 184
Williams, K. T., 34, 47, 62, 86
Williams, K. T., 47
Williams, R., 211
Williams, S. S., 335, 336
Willis, M., 335
Willmes, K., 160
Wilson, A., 202, 378
Wilson, A. K., 202, 331, 378
Wilson, B., 199, 200
Wilson, B. S., 199, 200, 398
Wilson, D. L., 308
Wilson, I., 241, 302, 325, 348
Wilson, J. M. G., 353
Wilson, K. M., 147, 151
Wilson, L., 164, 466
Wilson, M., 458, 460, 461, 462, 464,
    465, 466
Wilson, R. H., 396
Wilson, S. M., 42
Winata, S., 270, 273
Windle, J. V. E., 306
Winn, S., 45
Winton, E. J., 335
Winton, L., 336
Wirsching, M., 228
Wirz, S. L., 347, 349, 353, 355
Wisher, R., 59
Witcher, P., 288
Witt, S., 395, 398
Witt, S. A., 395, 396, 397, 398
Wittrock, M. C., 102
Wolbers, K. A., 151
Wolff, A. B., 454
Wolgemuth, K. S., 381
Wolk, S., 112
Woll, B., 268, 271, 323, 474
Wood, D., 411
Wood, D. J., 66, 411
Wood, E. J., 230
Wood, H. A., 66
Wood, W. M., 87
Woodcock, R., 48
Woods, D. G., 428
Woodward, A., 408
Woodward, J., 271
Woodward, J. C., 271, 294
Woodworth, G. G., 394
Woolfe, T., 323, 324, 328, 416, 417
Woolgar, A., 5
Wray, A., 267
Wright, B., 334, 419
Wright, B. A., 252, 334, 419
Wright, M., 136
Wright, S., 241, 302, 325
Writer, J., 183
Wu, C., 200, 202
Wu, J., 350
Wu, Y. H., 252
Wyatt, J. R., 231
Wygonski, J., 451

X

Xerri, C., 334
Xu, F., 468
Xu, S. A., 334

Y

Yan, B., 114
Yang, J., 98, 164
Yang, W., 382
Yarger, C. C., 46, 82, 83, 294
Yeakle, M. K., 255
Yeeles, C., 321
Yeni-Komshian, G. H., 283
Ying, E., 112, 336
Ying, E. A., 112, 335, 336
Yoshinaga-Itano, C., 3, 4, 5, 112, 113, 135, 137, 139, 146, 241, 242, 243, 246, 299, 302, 303, 304, 307, 308, 334, 346, 369, 378, 380, 386, 410
Yoshinago-Itano, C., 45, 47
Yost, W., 395
Yost, W. A., 395, 396
Young, A., 3, 297, 350

Young, A. M., 3, 242, 243, 244, 245, 246, 247, 248, 297, 350
Young, C. L., 434
Young, J., 112
Young, N., 361
Young, N. M., 361, 366
Young III, J., 9
Youngblade, L., 408
Youngs, P., 41
Yu, G., 396
Yueh, B., 354
Yuker, H. E., 252

Z

Zaghis, A., 235
Zaidman-Zait, A., 383, 386
Zaitchik, D., 421
Zamel, V., 148
Zampini, M., 465
Zandberg, S., 252
Zarcadoolas, C., 148
Zarfaty, Y., 160, 465
Zatorre, R., 216
Zawolkow, E., 295

Zazove, P., 203
Zea, M. C., 198
Zeitler, D., 397
Zelazo, P. D., 441
Zeng, F., 398
Zeng, F. -G., 354, 398, 451
Zerbe, G., 364
Zeshan, U., 281
Zevenbergen, R., 158
Zevin, J. D., 282
Zhang, X., 326, 394
Zigmond, N., 66
Zimbardo, P., 77
Zimerman-Phillips, S., 251
Zimmer, K., 305
Zimmerman-Phillips, S., 335, 393
Zlatin, M., 361
Zupan, M., 6, 128
Zurek, P. M., 395
Zweibel, A., 214
Zwolan, T., 133, 233
Zwolan, T. A., 112, 133, 152, 232, 233, 335, 336, 369, 394
Zwolen, T. A., 233

SUBJECT INDEX

A

AAEE. *See* American Association for Employment in Education (AAEE)

AAIDD. *See* American Association of Intellectual and Developmental Disabilities (AAIDD)

ABSL. *See* Al-Sayyid Bedouin Sign Language (ABSL)

Academic discourse, deaf-gain and, 217–18

Achievements of Deaf Pupils in Scotland project (ADPS), 428

Acoupedics, 22

Acoustic ecology, 381–85

ADA. *See* Americans with Disabilities Act (ADA)

Adaptive instruction, 60

Adequate Yearly Progress (AYP), ESEA/NCLB and, 35

ADHD clinic. *See* Attention-deficit hyperactivity disorder (ADHD) clinic

ADPS. *See* Achievements of Deaf Pupils in Scotland project (ADPS)

Advanced bionics cochlear implant map, 392*f*

Advanced Forms level, SAEVD-R, 362

Age of acquisition
    effects on outcome of sign language, 283–88
        experimental studies of, 284–86
        L1 exposure is delayed until adolescence, 286–88
        variation in age of acquisition, 283–84
    effects on outcome of spoken language, 282–83

Al-Sayyid Bedouin Sign Language (ABSL), 269–70. *See also* American Sign Language (ASL)
    age of, 273
    word order in, 275

Alternative and augmentative communication (AAC) aids, 174

American Annals of the Deaf, 25

American Association for Employment in Education (AAEE), 44

American Association of Intellectual and Developmental Disabilities (AAIDD), 174

American Sign Language (ASL), 2, 19. *See also* Al-Sayyid Bedouin Sign Language (ABSL)
    acquisition of, 321–23
    in children with hearing loss, 294
    deaf studies and, 211–12
    media for development of proficiency in, 101–2
    proficiency level of deaf adults grouped by, 288*f*
    and visuospatial loop, 466–67

Americans with Disabilities Act (ADA), 38

ASD. *See* Autism spectrum disorders (ASD)

ASL. *See* American Sign Language (ASL)

Attention-deficit hyperactivity disorder (ADHD) clinic, 447

Auditory communication, in children with hearing loss, 293–94

Auditory deprivation, and differences in STM, 462–64

Auditory-guided speech development
    assessing progress in, 370–71
    indicators of, 369–70

Auditory neuropathy/dyssynchrony (AN/AD), 351, 352

Auditory processing disorder (APD), 429–30

Auditory verbal instruction, 21–22

Auditory–verbal therapy (AVT), 5, 22

Auditory–vocal spoken language, 18

Auditory–oral approach, in children with hearing loss, 294

Auditory–verbal approach, in children with hearing loss, 294

Autism spectrum disorders (ASD), 172
    deaf students with, 176

Automated auditory brainstem response (AABR), 351

Automatic speech recognition, 95

AVT. *See* Auditory–verbal therapy (AVT)

B

Backward planning, 50

Basic canonical syllables, SAEVD-R, 362

Behavior Rating Inventory of Executive Function (BRIEF), 446–47

Belgian French Sign Language (BFSL), 162

Better-ear effect, 395

BFSL. *See* Belgian French Sign Language (BFSL)

Bilateral cochlear implant users, 394–98
    presumed benefits of listening with ears, 395–96
    sequential bilateral implantation, 397–98
    simultaneous bilateral implantation, 396–97

Bilingual–bicultural (Bi-Bi) education, 21

Bilingual communication, in children with hearing loss, 294

Binaural summation effect, 395

Bowling Alone: The Collapse and Revival of American Community, 221

Brain–behavior relations, 440–41

BRIEF. *See* Behavior Rating Inventory of Executive Function (BRIEF)

Brigance Comprehensive Inventory of Basic Skills-Revised, 48

British Sign Language (BSL), 19
    acquisition of, 323–24

BSL. *See* British Sign Language (BSL)

C

CAEBER program. *See* Center for ASL/English Bilingual Education and Research (CAEBER) program

Canadian Working Group on Childhood Hearing (CWGCH), 245

Canonical babbling
    SAEVD-R and, 362
    vocalization differences in children with and without hearing loss, 365–67

Captioning, 93–96
    classroom, 95–96
    television, 93–94
    Web media and videos, 94–95

CASE. *See* Conceptually Accurate Signed English (CASE)

CASP. *See* Conditioned Assessment of Speech Production (CASP)

Catell-Horn-Carroll (CHC) theory, 151–52

CDI. *See* Communicative Development Inventory (CDI)

Center for ASL/English Bilingual Education and Research (CAEBER) program, 8

Central executive, working memory
  and, 460
CHAOS. *See* Conduct-Hyperactive-
  Attention Problem-
  Oppositional Scale (CHAOS)
CHARGE syndrome, 173, 178–79
  CHD 7hd gene in, 178
  diagnosis of, 179
CHD 7hd gene, 178
*Child-Guided Strategies for Assessing
  Children Who Are Deafblind or
  Have Multiple Disabilities*, 187
CHIP. *See* Colorado Home Intervention
  Program (CHIP)
Classroom captioning, 95–96
Classroom curriculum design, 60
Classroom instruction, for deaf students,
  61–68
  adapted to learning style and cognitive
    profile, 65
  classroom participation, 64
  language of instruction, 63–64
  opportunity to learn, 66
  in regular and special education,
    comparison, 66–68
  strategies, 64–65
  teacher–student relationship and
    hearing status, 65–66
Classroom participation
  academic outcomes and, 77
  classroom instruction for deaf
    students, 64
  of DHH children/students, 88
Classroom Participation Questionnaire
  (CPQ), 48, 88
Clerc's system of instruction, 25
Co-enrollment classroom,
  instruction in, 67
Coalition of Organizations for Accessible
  Technology (COAT), 95
COAT. *See* Coalition of Organizations for
  Accessible Technology (COAT)
Cochlear implants/implantation, 227–29
  in adults, 393
  age of implantation affect reading
    ability, 133–34
  in children, 393
    and language acquisition, 334–36
  and choice of communication mode,
    233–34
  components of, 391–92, 391*f*
  criteria to assess candidacy for,
    392–93
  in deaf children, 6–7
  and deaf students, 129–30
  educational attainment and, 231–32
  educational management and, 232–33
  history of, 390–91
  identity and, 203–4
  impact on spoken language
    development, 326–27
  implicit learning and language outcomes
    in deaf children with, 454

individual rates of language growth for
    children using, 338*f*
  language, cognition, and reading of
    children functionally hard of
    hearing, 130–33
  and localization and perception of
    distance, 399–401
  outcomes of, 229–34
    educational implications, 230–34
    and EOI abilities, 441–42
    parental concerns, 234
  overview, 226–27
  parental perspectives in, 227–29
    decision-making process, 228–29
    process of implantation, 229
  recent studies on language outcomes
    for children using, 336–39
  relations of cognition and reading in
    children with, 137–38
  relations of language and reading in
    children with, 134–37
  and speech perception performance,
    393–99
    bilateral cochlear implant users,
      394–98
    and hearing aid users, 398–99
    unilateral adult cochlear implant,
      393–94
  for Usher syndrome, 180
  views of young people with, 234–37
  working of, 391–92
Cognitive ability
  play and early, 408–14
  play of young DHH children/
    students, 410–14
Cognitive development, EBP and
  measurement of, 303–4
Cognitive diversity, and deaf-gain, 216–18
  redefining nature of language, 216–17
  sign languages and academic
    discourse, 217–18
  visual language/visual learning, 217
Colorado Home Intervention Program
  (CHIP), 3
Communication adaptations, 45
Communication approaches, of children
  with hearing loss, 293
  auditory communication, 293–94
  combining visual and auditory
    modalities, 295–96
  comparative description of, 296–97
  early efforts to use objective and
    prescriptive procedures to
    select, 297–301
    current efforts to provide unbiased
      representation, 298–99
    monitoring efficacy of selection,
      299–300
    providing access to complete
      language model, 300–301
  visual communication, 294–95
Communication mode, cochelear
    implants and choice, 233–34

Communication skills, in children who
    are hard-of-hearing, 379–81
  development of language skills, 380–81
  development of speech skills, 379–80
Communicative Development Inventory
  (CDI), 321
Conceptually Accurate Signed English
  (CASE), 294–95
Conditioned Assessment of Speech
  Production (CASP), 371
Conduct-Hyperactive-Attention
  Problem-Oppositional Scale
  (CHAOS), 447
Congenital rubella syndrome (CRS), 181
Consonant inventories, in young children
  with hearing loss, 367–69
Content instruction, 99–100
Convention on the Rights of Persons with
  Disabilities (CRPD), 38–39
Council of Europe Disability
  Action Plan, 39
CPQ. *See* Classroom Participation
  Questionnaire (CPQ)
Creative diversity, and deaf-gain, 218–19
Creoles, 268
Critical period for language, 281
  evidence for, 333–34
  implications of, 289
Critical period learning, 282
CRPD. *See* Convention on the Rights of
  Persons with Disabilities
  (CRPD)
CRS. *See* Congenital rubella syndrome
  (CRS)
Cued speech, 7
  in children with hearing loss, 294
  defined, 21
Cultural beliefs, and NHS programs in
  developing world, 353
Cultural diversity, and deaf-gain, 219–21
  deaf collectivist culture and future of
    community, 221
  international sign and signed
    languages, 220–21
  transnational deaf community,
    219–20
Cultural stigma, and NHS programs in
  developing world, 353

D

Deaf Acculturation Scale (DAS), 198
Deaf and hard-of-hearing (DHH)
    children/students, 2. *See also*
    Hard-of-hearing children
  benefits of earlier intervention, 345–47
  classroom participation, 88
  communication and literacy for
    success of, 86
  effective education for, 58
  effective instruction in general
    education settings, 59–60
  EHDI and, 31–32
  general education classrooms

academic outcomes, 73–77
characteristics in, 73
social outcomes, 77–82
support needed to succeed in, 84–89
handheld technologies, 102–4
for communication, 102–3
for educational interventions with, 103–4
IDEA and, 34
interactive whiteboard for instructing, 97
learning strategies for, 86–87
mathematics instruction and learning of
achievement and performance, 157–60
factors in mathematics performance, 160–64
instruction, 160–65
overview, 156–57
play of young, 410–14
receiving specific services from itinerant teachers, 84t
responsibilities of itinerant teachers of, 82–84
self-advocacy, 87–88
social supports, 88–89
speech intelligibility of
educational implications and future research, 260–61
effects on attitude, 253–55
effects on social and emotional aspects, 255–58
relation with occupational competence, 258–60
tablet PC, 98–99
teacher preparation program, 42–45
Deaf children/students
cochlear implants for, 6–7, 129–30
educational placements for, 7–8
language development and joint attention in, 318–20
selected studies of ToM in, 416–21
sign language for, 6
spoken language for, 5–6
Deaf collectivist culture, 221
Deaf community sign language, 270–72
linguistic origins of, 271
new, 271–72
social characteristics, 270–71
Deaf education
during 1900 to 1960, 27
from 1960 to present, 27–28
advancement in, 2
18th century, 23
basic research in, 8–10
Bi–Bi instruction and, 21
early identification and intervention in, 2–5
historical complexities in, 18–19
history of methods for, 21–22
issue of language modality in, 5

levels of effort to develop evidence base in, 117–18, 117t
manual communication in, 63
paradigm shifts in, 473–77
person-centered planning in, 50
promise of, 7–8
promise of language in, 5–7
response to intervention (RTI), 48
in 19th century Europe, 23–25
deaf teachers, 25
Germany, 23–24
International Convention of Milan, 24–25
Netherlands, 24
in United States, 25–27
deaf teachers, 26–27
growth of oral education, 26
Deaf-gain, 215–16
cognitive diversity and, 216–18
redefining nature of language, 216–17
sign languages and academic discourse, 217–18
visual language/visual learning, 217
creative diversity and, 218–19
cultural diversity and, 219–21
deaf collectivist culture and future of community, 221
international sign and signed languages, 220–21
transnational deaf community, 219–20
Deaf Identity Development Scale (DIDS), 198
Deaf space, 218–19
Deaf Studies
defined, 210–11
in late 20th century, 211–12
in 21st century, 212–15
existential threats, 213–15
lessons from history of normalization, 212–13
threat to deaf bodies, 214–15
Deaf Studies Digital Journal, 218
Deaf teachers
in 19th century Europe, 25
in United States, 26–27
Deaf walk, 221
Deaf writers
focussing on, 149–50
focussing on pedagogical context, 150–52
language-learning disabilities and, 149
product and process, 146–48
theoretical perspective, 145–46
Deafblindness, 177
assessment of students with congenital, 186–87
and intellectual disability, 177
intervention and educational curriculum for children with, 182–86
syndromic, 178–81

CHARGE syndrome, 178–79
congenital rubella syndrome, 181
Usher syndrome, 179–81
Deafness. See also Hearing loss
ASD and, 176
early identification, 241–48
impact on parents, 242–44
influence of, 246–48
overview, 241–42
timing of, 244–46
envisioning childhood, 246–48
etiology of, 173
intervention, communication, and sign development in persons with, 174–76
students with intellectual disabilities and, 173–76
visuospatial short-term memory span and, 165
Decision-making, in cochlear implants/ implantation, 228–29
DEIP. See Diagnostic Early Intervention Program (DEIP)
Design Copying (DC), 445
DHH children/students. See Deaf and hard-of-hearing (DHH) children/students
Diagnostic and Statistical Manual of Mental Disorders, 176
Diagnostic Early Intervention Program (DEIP), 298
DIDS. See Deaf Identity Development Scale (DIDS)
Disability
ADA definition of, 38
international progress to protect people with, 38–39
Dyslexia, 428–30
Dyspraxia, 428–30

E
EAHCA. See Education for All Handicapped Children Act (EAHCA)
Early hearing detection and intervention (EHDI), 242
Early hearing detection and intervention (EHDI) programs, 31–32
Early sign language development, 320–24
acquisition of ASL, 321–23
acquisition of BSL, 323–24
EBP. See Evidence-based practices (EBP)
Economic barriers, and NHS programs in developing world, 354–55
Edmark Reading Program, 120
Education for All Handicapped Children Act (EAHCA), 30
Educational attainment, and cochlear implants/implantation, 231–32
Educational curriculum, for children with deafblindness, 182–86

Educational management, and cochlear implants/implantation, 232–33
Effective education, for DHH children/students, 58
EHDI. *See* Early hearing detection and intervention (EHDI) programs
Eisenberg sentence perception task, 451
Elementary and Secondary Education Act/No Child Left Behind Act (ESEA/NCLB), 35–37
  differentiated accountability program, 36–37
Elementary school settings, hard-of-hearing children and, 383–85
Emerging sign language
  deaf community sign language, 270–72
    new, 271–72
    social characteristics, 270–71
  functions of, 274–75
  language interference from spoken language, 275
  linguistic complexity in, 277
  overview, 267–69
  relation of characteristics of community with features of, 277–78
  theoretical significance of, 276–78
  use of space in, 275–76
  variables in, 272–76
    characteristics of sign language communities, 272–74
    properties of language, 274–76
  village sign language, 269–70
  word order in, 275
Emotional stability, and Usher syndrome, 180–81
EOI abilities. *See* Executive-organizational-integrative (EOI) abilities
ESEA/NCLB. *See* Elementary and Secondary Education Act/No Child Left Behind Act (ESEA/NCLB)
Ethnic identity, 200–203
Evidence-based practices (EBP), 44, 301–2
  document developmental outcomes, 302–8
    development of functional auditory skills, 305–7
    measuring cognitive development, 303–4
    semantic development, 304–5
    speech development, 307–8
    syntax development, 305
  setting high expectations, 301–2
Executive function, 443–44
  BRIEF, LEAF, and CHAOS rating scales of, 446–47
Executive functioning, 430–32
Executive-organizational-integrative (EOI) abilities
  in cochlear implant outcomes, 441–42

Expansion level, SAEVD-R, 362
Expressive language modes, description of, 297*f*

F
FAPE. *See* Free Appropriate Public Education (FAPE)
Fingertip Tapping (FTT), 445
Free Appropriate Public Education (FAPE), 33
French Sign Language (LSF), 271
Friendship, DHH children/students and, 80–81
FTT. *See* Fingertip Tapping (FTT)
Fully resonant nuclei, SAEVD-R, 362
Functional Assessment of Students Who Are Deaf or Hard of Hearing, 48
Functional Auditory Performance Indicators (FAPI), 307
  hierarchy of auditory skills in, 306*t*
Functional auditory skills development, EBP and, 305–7
  collecting evidence, 306–7
  impact of hearing loss, 306
  listening conditions affects, 307*t*

G
Gallaudet Research Institute (GRI), 72
Gallaudet sign dialect, 26
Gallaudet University program, 8
General education classrooms, for DHH children/students
  academic outcomes, 73–77
    Academic Competence score for, 75
    factors contributing to, 76–77
  characteristics in, 73
  social outcomes, 77–82
    factors contributing to, 81–82
    friendship among peers, 80–81
    social acceptance, 79–80
    social interaction and social competence, 78–79
  teachers support in, 82–89
    responsibilities of itinerant teachers, 82–84
    support needed to succeed, 84–89
Genetics, and identity, 204–5
GRI. *See* Gallaudet Research Institute (GRI)

H
Handheld technologies, for DHH children/students, 102–4
  for communication, 102–3
  for educational interventions with, 103–4
Hard-of-hearing children. *See also* Deaf and hard-of-hearing (DHH) children/students
  in absence of definition, 378
  acoustic ecology and hearing accessibility, 381–85
  in early childhood, 382–83

elementary school settings, 383–85
  secondary and postsecondary settings, 385
  communication skills of, 379–81
    development of language skills, 380–81
    development of speech skills, 379–80
  identity of, 385–86
  impact of early identification, 386
  when definition provided, 378–79
Head shadow effect, 395
Health Related Quality of Life (HRQL) instruments, 230
Hearing accessibility, 381–85
  in early childhood, 382–83
  elementary school settings, 383–85
  secondary and postsecondary settings, 385
Hearing aid users, cochlear implants and, 398–99
Hearing aids, identity and, 203
Hearing loss. *See also* Deafness
  children with and without vocalization differences in, 365–69
    vocalization similarities in, 365
  impact on speech development, 307–8
  impact on functional auditory skills development, 306
  incidence and prevalence in developing world, 347–48
  semantic development and impact of, 304
  syntax development and impact of, 305
Hearing test, child, 2–3
Home sign, 268, 287
HRQL instruments. *See* Health Related Quality of Life (HRQL) instruments

I
Iconicity, 174
IDEA. *See* Individuals with Disabilities Education Act (IDEA)
Identity
  defined, 195
  ethnic dimension, 200–203
  of hard-of-hearing children, 199–200, 385–86
  importance of, 195–96
  technology, science and, 203–5
    cochlear implant, 203–4
    genetics, 204–5
    hearing aids, 203
  theoretical conceptualization of, 197–99
IEP. *See* Individualized Education Program (IEP)
IFSP. *See* Individualized Family Service Plan (IFSP)
Implicit learning
  group differences in, 451–53

and language outcomes in deaf children with cochlear implants, 454
and sentence perception, 453–54
of sequential patterns, 447–54
Individualized Education Program (IEP)
backward planning and, 50
ESEA/NCLB and, 36
IDEA and, 33–34
Individualized Family Service Plan (IFSP), 31
Individually tailored test batteries *vs.* protocol-based assessment, 434
Individuals with Disabilities Education Act (IDEA), 32–35
ADA and, 38
aids and services to children, 34
children placement in, 34–35
evaluation of children and, 33
Infant and Toddler Program of, 33
measurable goals for children, 33–34
Section 504 of the Rehabilitation Act and, 37–38
Infant and Toddler Program, of IDEA, 33
Infant-Toddler Meaningful Auditory Integration Scale (IT-MAIS), 393
Inhibition processes, in speech perception, 443–44
Instruction
adaptive, 60
correlates of good reading, 120–22
to DHH students by interactive whiteboard, 97
effective
general education settings and, 59–60
orientation and, 59
and mathematics performance of DHH children/students, 164–65
in special education, 60–61
strategies for, 60
Instructional practice
approach to problem, 117–18
levels of evidence and relation to reading in, 115–17
reading curriculum, 118–20
with evidence for hearing and DHH children/students, 118–19
with growing evidence for DHH children/students, 119–20
Intellectual disability
deaf students with, 173–76
deafblindness and, 177
intervention, communication, and sign development in persons with, 174–76
Interactive whiteboards, 96–97
International Convention of Milan, 24–25
International Sign (IS), 220–21
Israeli Sign Language, 271–72

IT-MAIS. *See* Infant-Toddler Meaningful Auditory Integration Scale (IT-MAIS)
Itinerant teachers
competencies needed by, 83*t*
percentage of DHH children/students receiving specific services from, 84*t*
responsibilities of, 82–84
teacher preparation program and, 46*t*

J
JCIH. *See* Joint Committee on Infant Hearing (JCIH)
Joint attention
and early language, 317–18
in deaf children/students, 318–20
timing of identification of deafness and, 245–46

K
Knoors principles, in special education, 60–61

L
La Langue des Signes de Quebecois (LSQ), 19
Language acquisition, 331–33
of ASL, 321–23
of BSL, 323–24
cochlear implants in children and, 334–36
Language development
early sign, 320–24
acquisition of ASL, 321–23
acquisition of BSL, 323–24
laying foundations for, 317–20
joint attention and early language, 317–18
joint attention in deaf children, 318–20
Language development in, deaf children, 318*f*–20
Language Learning, effects of early experience on later, 286*f*
Language mixing principle, 61
Language proficiency, DHH children/students, 86
LEAF. *See* Learning Executive and Attention Functioning scale (LEAF)
Learning disabilities
achievement-potential discrepancy in, 433–34
assessment issues in, 432–33
definitions of, 426–27
dyslexia, dyspraxia, and APD, 428–30
etiology and prevalence of, 427–28
future research directions for, 435
historical context, 425–26
memory, executive functioning, problem-solving, and sequencing, 430–32
norm-referenced IQ tests for, 433–34

protocol-based assessments *vs.* individually tailored test batteries, 434
research in, 428
response to intervention, 434–35
Learning Executive and Attention Functioning scale (LEAF), 447
Least Restrictive Environment (LRE), 33
Linguistic complexity, in emerging sign language, 277
Linguistic short-term memory span differences in, 461–64
articulation rate and differences in, 461–62, 462*f*
auditory deprivation and differences in, 462–64
consequences of differences in, 464
predictor of working memory, 467–68
Loneliness and Social Dissatisfaction Questionnaire, 255
LRE. *See* Least Restrictive Environment (LRE)
LSQ. *See* La Langue des Signes de Quebecois (LSQ)

M
MAIS. *See* Meaningful Auditory Integration Scale (MAIS)
Manual alphabets, defined, 20
Manual communication, in deaf education, 63
Manually Coded English (MCE), 295
MAP. *See* Measures of Academic Progress (MAP)
Marginal babbling, 362
Mathematics instruction and learning, of DHH children/students
achievement and performance, 157–60
problem solving, 158–60
factors in mathematics performance, 160–65
instruction, 164–65
language, 161–64
number knowledge and processing, 160–61
overview, 156–57
teacher preparation and, 165
Mathematics performance, of DHH children/students, 160–65
instruction and, 164–65
language and, 161–64
number knowledge and processing and, 160–61
Meaningful Auditory Integration Scale (MAIS), 393
Measures of Academic Progress (MAP), 120
Media, for development of proficiency in sign language, 101–2
Memory, 430–32
MHI. *See* Minimal hearing impairment (MHI)
Mills vs. Board of Education, 32

Minimal hearing impairment (MHI), 130
Minnesota Child Development
        Inventory, 246
More knowledgeable other (MKO), 121
Multiple disabilities, etiology of, 173

N

NAPMERD. *See* National Action Plan for
        Mathematics Education
        Reform for the Deaf
        (NAPMERD)
National Action Plan for Mathematics
        Education Reform for the
        Deaf (NAPMERD), 156, 157
National Council of Teachers of
        Mathematics (NCTM), 156
National Cued Speech Association, 7
National Institute of Child Health and
        Human Development, 173
National Institute on Deafness and Other
        Communication Disorders
        (NIDCD), 439
National Technical Institute for the Deaf
        (NTID), 62
NCTM. *See* National Council of Teachers
        of Mathematics (NCTM)
Neo-oralism, 27
NEPSY. *See* Neuropsychological battery
        (NEPSY)
Neurocognitive approach, to individual
        differences in outcomes
    brain-behavior relations, 440–41
    domain-general cognitive factors, 441
    EOI abilities in cochlear implant
        outcomes, 441–42
    theoretical and clinical implications,
        454–55
Neurocognitive measures, 444–47
    BRIEF, LEAF, and CHAOS rating
        scales of executive function,
        446–47
    Design Copying, 445
    NEPSY Fingertip Tapping, 445
    Stroop Color Word Test, 445–46
Neuropsychological battery (NEPSY), 445
New York Institution for the Instruction
        of the Deaf and Dumb, 25
Newborn hearing screening program
        (NHSP), 242
    in developing world, 348–55
        availability and quality of
            subsequent intervention,
            353–54
        cultural beliefs and stigma, 353
        delivery platform, 350
        economic barriers, 354–55
        loss to follow-up, 352–53
        specificity of screening, 351–52
        targeted *vs.* UNHS program,
            348–50
NHSP. *See* Newborn hearing screening
        program (NHSP)
Nicaraguan Sign Language, 271

NIDCD. *See* National Institute on Deafness
        and Other Communication
        Disorders (NIDCD)
Nonword repetition, 442–43
    scores, 443*t*
Norm-referenced IQ test, for learning
        disabilities, 433–34
NTID. *See* National Technical Institute
        for the Deaf (NTID)

O

Occupational competence, speech
        intelligibility and, 258–60
OMIM. *See* Online Mendelian
        Inheritance in Man (OMIM)
Online Mendelian Inheritance in Man
        (OMIM), 178
Oral education, growth in
        United States, 26
Oral–aural instruction, 21
Organizational-integration processes,
        443–44
Orientation, effective instruction and, 59
Otoacoustic emission (OAE), 351–52
Out-of-class learning, 100–101

P

PAR. *See* Psychological Assessment
        Resources (PAR)
Parent's Evaluation of Aural/Oral
        Performance of Children
        (PEACH), 305
Paris National Institute for the Deaf, 25
PATHS curriculum. *See* Promoting
        Alternative Thinking Strategies
        (PATHS) curriculum
Peabody Individual Achievement Test, 131
Peabody Picture Vocabulary Test (PPVT),
        336, 336*f*, 451
PEACH. *See* Parent's Evaluation of
        Aural/Oral Performance of
        Children (PEACH)
Pedagogical shifts, writing and, 148–49
Pendred syndrome, 173
*Pennsylvania Association for Retarded
        Children (PARC) vs.
        Commonwealth of
        Pennsylvania*, 32
Person-centered planning, 50
Phonation, SAEVD-R and control of, 362
Phonological awareness, 113–14
Phonological decomposition, 442–43
Phonological loop, working memory
        and, 459
Pidgin Signed English (PSE), 294
Pidgins, 268
PLAI. *See* Promoting Learning through
        Active Integration curriculum
        (PLAI)
Play
    and early cognitive ability, 408–14
    of young DHH children/students,
        410–14

Play Assessment Questionnaire (PAQ), 410
PPVT. *See* Peabody Picture Vocabulary
        Test (PPVT)
Precanonical vocalization, 365
Prelinguistic utterances, guidelines for
        classifying children, 371*t*
Prelinguistic vocalizations, prosodic
        aspects of, 369
Problem solving, 430–32
    mathematics performance of DHH
        children/students and,
        158–60
    relative difficulty, 158–59
    solution strategies, 159–60
Processing strategy, cochlear implants and,
        391–92
Promoting Alternative Thinking Strategies
        (PATHS) curriculum, 120
Promoting Learning through Active
        Integration curriculum
        (PLAI), 185
Protocol-based assessments *vs.* individually
        tailored test batteries, 434
Psychological Assessment Resources
        (PAR), 446

Q

Quality of life, and cochlear implants/
        implantation, 230
Quasi-resonant nuclei, SAEVD-R, 362

R

RDLS. *See* Reynell Developmental
        Language Scales-Second
        Revision (RDLS)
Reading curriculum, and instructional
        practice, 118–20
    with evidence for hearing and DHH
        children/students, 118–19
    with growing evidence for DHH
        children/students, 119–20
Reading development
    challenges in school years, 111–13
    segments of populations with
        different needs, 112–13
    early skills and relation to later,
        113–15
Real-time speech-to-text service, 95
Receptive language modes, description
        of, 296*f*
Reciprocal teaching, 61
Reflexive vocalizations, SAEVD-R,
        361–62
Response to intervention (RTI), 48
Reynell Developmental Language
        Scales-Second Revision
        (RDLS), 413
RIT. *See* Rochester Institute of
        Technology (RIT)
Rochester Institute of Technology
        (RIT), 62
Rochester Method, 28
RTI. *See* Response to intervention (RTI)

S

SAEVD-R. *See* Stark Assessment of Early Vocal Development-Revised (SAEVD-R)
Screening Instrument for Targeting Educational Risk Teacher Rating (SIFTER), 75, 232
SCWT. *See* Stroop Color Word Test (SCWT)
Section 504 of the Rehabilitation Act, 37–38
SEE I. *See* Seeing Essential English (SEE I)
SEE II. *See* Signing Exact English (SEE II)
Seeing Essential English (*SEE* I), 28
Self-advocacy, in DHH children/students, 87–88
Semantic development, EBP and, 304–5
    collecting evidence, 304–5
    impact of hearing loss, 304
Sense of Coherence Scale, 255
Sequencing, 430–32
Sequential bilateral implantation, 397–98
Short Periods of Prelinguistic Input (SPPI) approach, 372
Short-term memory (STM), 458
    working memory and, 459–60
SIFTER. *See* Screening Instrument for Targeting Educational Risk (SIFTER); Screening Instrument for Targeting Educational Risk Teacher Rating (SIFTER)
Sign language. *See also* Spoken language
    age of acquisition effects on outcome of, 283–88
        experimental studies of, 284–86
        L1 exposure is delayed until adolescence, 286–88
        variation in age of acquisition, 283–84
    for deaf children, 6
    deaf-gain and, 217–18, 220–21
    Deaf Studies and threat to, 213–14
    defined, 19
    emerging. *See* Emerging sign language and mathematics, 162–264
    media for development of proficiency in, 101–2
    skill and reading development, 288–89
Sign language communities, characteristics of, 271
    age of language, 273
    distribution of deaf people in community, 273–74
    exposure to other sign languages, 274
    size of community, 272–73
    social status of deaf people, 274
Sign language literature, 219
Sign Language of the Netherlands (SLN), 174–75
Sign-supported speech (SSS), 295
Sign systems, defined, 20

Signing Exact English (*SEE* II), 28
Signing Naturally, 101
Signing Science dictionary, 101
Silent Reading Fluency Test (SRFT), 120
Sim Com. *See* Simultaneous communication
Simultaneous bilateral implantation, 396–97
Simultaneous communication, 295–96
    defined, 20
SLN. *See* Sign Language of the Netherlands (SLN)
SMART Board, 97
SNARC. *See* Spatial numerical association of response codes (SNARC)
SOAR-High Distance Learning Program, 99
Social acceptance, of DHH children/students, 79–80
Social competence, academic outcomes of DHH children/students and, 78–79
Social-emotional functioning, speech intelligibility and, 255–58
Social interaction, academic outcomes of DHH children/students and, 78–79
Social Skills Rating System (SSRS), 75
SOV order. *See* Subject-object-verb (SOV) order
Spatial numerical association of response codes (SNARC), 160
Special education
    instruction in, 60–61
        Knoors principles in, 60–61
        lack of output thinking in, 58
        spread effect and, 252–53
Specific language impairment, 131
Speech development, at prelinguistic level, 371–72
Speech development, EBP and, 307–8
    collecting evidence, 308
    impact of hearing loss, 307–8
Speech in Noise Test (SPIN), 450
Speech intelligibility, of DHH children/students
    educational implications and future research, 260–61
    effects on attitude, 253–55
        perceived personal qualities, 254–55
    effects on social and emotional aspects, 255–58
    relation with occupational competence, 258–60
Speech perception, inhibition processes in, 443–44
Speech perception performance, cochlear implant and, 393–99
    bilateral cochlear implant users, 394–98
        presumed benefits of listening with ears, 395–96

sequential bilateral implantation, 397–98
simultaneous bilateral implantation, 396–97
and hearing aid users, 398–99
unilateral adult cochlear implant, 393–94
Speech sampling, 370–71
    analyzing elicited speech samples, 371
SPIN. *See* Speech in Noise Test (SPIN)
Spoken language. *See also* Sign language
    age of acquisition effects on outcome of, 282–83
    for deaf children, 5–6
    development of, 325–28
        communication choices for parents, 327–28
        impact of cochlear implants, 326–27
        newborn hearing screening, 325–26
    language interference from, 275
SPPI. *See* Short Periods of Prelinguistic Input (SPPI)
Spread effect, 252
    listener's experience and, 252
    regular and special education and, 252–53
SRFT. *See* Silent Reading Fluency Test (SRFT)
SSRS. *See* Social Skills Rating System (SSRS)
Stanford Achievement Test Series, 48
Stark Assessment of Early Vocal Development-Revised (SAEVD-R), 361
    level of vocal development and, 361–63
Stimulating listening, at prelinguistic level, 371–72
STM. *See* Short-term memory (STM)
Stroop Color Word Test (SCWT), 445–46
Student production of captions, 102
Subject-object-verb (SOV) order, 275
Syllabic consonants, 368
Syllable complexity, in children with and without hearing loss, 365–67
Syndromic deafblindness, 178–81
    CHARGE syndrome, 178–79
    diagnosis of, 179
    congenital rubella syndrome, 181
    Usher syndrome, 179–81
        emotional stability and, 180–81
        medical considerations and therapies for, 180
Syntax development, EBP and, 305

T

Tablet PC, 97–99
TEACCH. *See* Treatment and Education of Autistic and Related Communication Handicapped Children (TEACCH)

Teacher preparation, 42
    adult-to-adult relationships and,
        46–47
    common practices of effective
        teachers, 42
    communication adaptations in, 45
    coursework and experiences to prepare
        future itinerant teachers, 46t
    for DHH children/students, 42–45
    evidence-based practices (EBP), 44
    framework for determining individual
        needs and curriculum
        focus, 51f
    issues affecting, 42–46
        cultural identity and, 44
        educational difficulties, 43
        lack of programs, 45
        process of licensing teachers, 43
        shortage of teachers, 44–45
    and mathematics instruction and
        learning, 165
    recommendations for, 45–52
        positions offered to graduates after
            preparation program, 46–47
        reconceptualization of deaf
            education, 45
        reconceptualize service delivery
            options, 47–50
        using, integrating, and sharing
            technology, 50–52
Technical signs, media support acquisition
    of, 101–2
Television captioning, 93–94
TEMA-3. See Test of Early Mathematics
    Ability (TEMA-3)
Test of Early Mathematics Ability
    (TEMA-3), 157
Test of Written Language (TOWL-3), 151
The Case Against Perfection, 222
*The first steps of a deafblind child towards
    language*, 182
Theory of mind (ToM), 415–16
    in deaf children, selected studies,
        416–21
    false/diverse belief, 415–16
    foundations of, 415
ToM. See Theory of mind (ToM)
Total Communication, 296
    defined, 19–20
TOWL-3. See Test of Written Language
    (TOWL-3)
Transnational deaf community,
    219–20
Treatment and Education of Autistic and
    Related Communication

Handicapped Children
    (TEACCH), 176
Twinschool program, 67

U
UDL. See Universal Design for Learning
    (UDL)
UNHS. See Universal newborn hearing
    screening (UNHS)
Unilateral adult cochlear implant, 393–94
United Kingdom's Human Fertilisation
    and Embryology Act
    (HFEA), 215
Universal Design for Learning (UDL),
    51–52
Universal newborn hedaring screening
    (UNHS), 2, 241
    timing of identification of deafness
        and, 244–46
    vs. targeted, in developing world,
        348–50
Usher syndrome, 173, 179–81
    emotional stability and, 180–81
    medical considerations and therapies
        for, 180

V
*van Dijk Approach to Assessing Children
    Who Are Deafblind or Have
    Multiple Disabilities*, 187
van Dijk curriculum, 182–86
    building blocks of, 183–85
        calendar system, 185
        co-active movement, 183–84
        imitation, 184
        objects of reference, 185
        resonance, 183
        symbols, 184–85
    principles of, 182–83
    validity of, 185–86
Video captioning, 94–95
Village sign languages, 269–70
    language interference from spoken
        language, 275
    vocabulary comparison in, 270
Visual communication, in children with
    hearing loss, 294–95
Visual implicit sequence learning task,
    450–51
Visual language, 217
Visual learning, 217
Visual-motor sign language, 18
Visuospatial short-term memory span,
    differences in, 464–67
    ASL and visuospatial loop, 466–67

deaf signers and enhanced, 464–65
    temporal order, deafness, and visual
        modality, 465
Vocal development
    in children with hearing loss, 365–70
    levels of, 361–63, 370t
        developmental sequence of,
            363–64
        typical patterns of, 361–65
Vocalization
    amount of, 364–65
    differences in children with and
        without hearing loss, 365–69
    similarities in children with and
        without hearing loss, 365
Volta Review, 26
Volubility, 364–65
Vowel inventories, in young children with
    hearing loss, 367–69

W
Web-based instruction, 99–101
    content instruction, 99–100
    participation in out-of-class learning,
        100–101
    for student research, 101
Web media captioning, 94–95
WebQuests, 52
Wechsler Intelligence Scale for Children
    (WISCIII), 131
What Works Clearinghouse (WWC), 118
Wolf-Hirschhorn syndrome, 173
Woodcock-Johnson III Test of Achievement,
    48
Word order, in emerging sign language,
    275
Working memory (WM), 458
    architecture across deaf and hearing,
        460–61
    architecture of multicomponent, 459f
    and caveats about deaf population
        studied, 468–69
    central executive and, 460
    linguistic short-term memory span as
        predictor of, 467–68
    new advances in research and
        predictions of, 468
    phonological loop and, 460
    and short-term memory, 459–60
Written language, 144–45
WWC. See What Works Clearinghouse
    (WWC)

Z
Zone of proximal development (ZPD), 121